THE ELIZABETHAN WORLD

This comprehensive and beautifully illustrated collection of essays conveys a vivid picture of a fascinating and hugely significant period in history. Featuring contributions from thirty-eight international scholars, the book takes a thematic approach to a period that saw the defeat of the Spanish Armada, the explorations of Francis Drake and Walter Ralegh, the establishment of the Protestant Church, the flourishing of commercial theatre and the works of Edmund Spencer, Philip Sidney and William Shakespeare.

Encompassing social, political, cultural, religious and economic history, and crossing several disciplines, *The Elizabethan World* depicts a time of transformation and a world order in transition. Topics covered include central and local government; political ideas; censorship and propaganda; parliament; the Protestant Church; the Catholic community; social hierarchies; women; the family and household; popular culture, commerce and consumption; urban and rural economies; theatre; art; architecture; intellectual developments; exploration and imperialism; Ireland; and the Elizabethan wars. The volume conveys a vivid picture of how politics, religion, popular culture, the world of work and social practices fit together in an exciting world of change and will be invaluable reading for all students and scholars of the Elizabethan period.

Susan Doran is Senior Research Fellow in History at Jesus College, Oxford. Her publications include numerous essays, articles and books on Elizabeth I and the Tudors, including *Monarchy and Matrimony: The Courtships of Elizabeth I* (1996) and *The Tudor Chronicles* (2008). Her latest book, co-edited with Paulina Kewes, is *Doubtful and Dangerous: The Question of Succession in Late Elizabethan England* (to be published in 2014).

Norman Jones is Professor and Chair of History at Utah State University. His many publications include *The Birth of the Elizabethan Age: England in the 1560s* (1992) and *The English Reformation: Religion and Cultural Adaptation* (2002). He is also co-editor of *A Companion to Tudor Britain* (2004).

THE ROUTLEDGE WORLDS

THE REFORMATION WORLD
Edited by Andrew Pettegree

THE MEDIEVAL WORLD
Edited by Peter Linehan and Janet L. Nelson

THE BYZANTINE WORLD
Edited by Paul Stephenson

THE VIKING WORLD
Edited by Stefan Brink in collaboration with Neil Price

THE BABYLONIAN WORLD
Edited by Gwendolyn Leick

THE EGYPTIAN WORLD
Edited by Toby Wilkinson

THE ISLAMIC WORLD
Edited by Andrew Rippin

THE WORLD OF POMPEII
Edited by John J. Dobbins and Pedar W. Foss

THE RENAISSANCE WORLD
Edited by John Jeffries Martin

THE EARLY CHRISTIAN WORLD
Edited by Philip F. Esler

THE GREEK WORLD
Edited by Anton Powell

THE ROMAN WORLD
Edited by John Wacher

THE HINDU WORLD
Edited by Sushil Mittal and Gene Thursby

THE WORLD OF THE AMERICAN WEST
Edited by Gordon Morris Bakken

THE OTTOMAN WORLD
Edited by Christine Woodhead

THE VICTORIAN WORLD
Edited by Martin Hewitt

THE ORTHODOX CHRISTIAN WORLD
Edited by Augustine Casiday

THE SUMERIAN WORLD
Edited by Harriet Crawford

THE ETRUSCAN WORLD
Edited by Jean MacIntosh Turfa

Forthcoming:

THE FIN-DE-SIÈCLE WORLD
Edited by Michael Saler

THE MORMON WORLD
Edited by Carl Mosser and Richard Sherlock

THE ATLANTIC WORLD
Edited by William O'Reilly

THE ELIZABETHAN WORLD

Edited by

Susan Doran
and Norman Jones

LONDON AND NEW YORK

First published in paperback 2014

First published 2011
by Routledge
2 Park Square, Milton Park, Abingdon, Oxon OX14 4RN

Simultaneously published in the USA and Canada
by Routledge
711 Third Avenue, New York, NY 10017

Routledge is an imprint of the Taylor & Francis Group, an informa business

British Library Cataloguing in Publication Data
A catalogue record for this book is available from the British Library

Library of Congress Cataloging in Publication Data
The Elizabethan world / edited by Susan Doran and Norman Jones.
— 1st ed.
p. cm. — (The Routledge worlds)
Includes bibliographical references and index.
1. Great Britain—History—Elizabeth, 1558–1603.
2. Great Britain—Social life and customs—16th century.
3. England—Civilization—16th century. I. Doran, Susan.
II. Jones, Norman L. (Norman Leslie), 1951–
DA355.E624 2010
942.05′5—dc22 2010004243

ISBN13: 978-0-415-40959-9 (hbk)
ISBN13: 978-0-415-71297-2 (pbk)

Typeset in Sabon by
Florence Production Ltd, Stoodleigh, Devon, UK

Printed and bound in the United States of America by Publishers Graphics, LLC on sustainably sourced paper.

CONTENTS

ILLUSTRATIONS

FIGURES

TABLES

CONTRIBUTORS

Susan Amussen is Professor of History at the University of California, Merced. She is the author of *An Ordered Society: Gender and Class in Early Modern England* (1988) and *Caribbean Exchanges: Slavery and the Transformation of English Society* (2007), as well as numerous articles on society and culture in early modern England.

Ian Archer has been Fellow, Tutor and University Lecturer in History at Keble College, Oxford since 1991. He is the author of various studies on the social and political history of early modern London, a Literary Director of the Royal Historical Society, Academic Editor of *The Bibliography of British and Irish History*, and a Co-Director of the Oxford Holinshed Project.

Cyndia Susan Clegg is Distinguished Professor of English in Seaver College, Pepperdine University. She has published widely on both early modern print culture and English Renaissance literature. Her recent books include: *Press Censorship in Caroline England* (Cambridge University Press, 2008), *The Peaceable and Prosperous Regiment of Blessed Queene Elisabeth: A facsimile from Holinshed's Chronicles* (Huntington Library Press, 2005), *Press Censorship in Jacobean England* (2002), and *Press Censorship in Elizabeth England* (1997). Her scholarly articles have appeared in *Renaissance Quarterly, Shakespeare Quarterly*, the *Ben Jonson Journal, Huntington Library Quarterly*, Blackwell Shakespeare companion volumes, and essay collections published by Routledge, Palsgrave, and Oxford and Cambridge University Presses.

J. P. D. Cooper teaches History at the University of York. He is author of *The Queen's Agent: Francis Walsingham at the Court of Elizabeth I* (2011) and *Propaganda and the Tudor State* (2003), and co-editor of *Henry VIII: Arms and the Man* (2009). He is currently working on two projects: a book on Elizabethan Ireland, and a study of St Stephen's Chapel in the Palace of Westminster.

John Craig is Professor of History at Simon Fraser University and author of *Reformation, Politics and Polemics: The Growth of Protestantism in East Anglian Market Towns, 1500–1610* (2001). He co-edited with Patrick

Collinson, *The Reformation in English Towns, 1500–1640* (1998) and with Patrick Collinson and Brett Usher, *Conferences and Combination Lectures in the Elizabethan Church: Dedham and Bury St Edmunds, 1582–1590* (2003).

Freyja Cox Jensen is Lecturer in History at the University of Exeter, and was previously a Junior Research Fellow at Christ Church, Oxford. She works on classical reception and the history of the book, and her monograph, *Reading the Roman Republic in Early Modern England*, was published in 2012.

David Dean is Professor of History and Co-Director of the Centre for Public History at Carleton University, Ottawa. The author of *Law-Making and Society in Late Elizabethan England* (1996, 2002), he has co-edited three collections of essays and published numerous articles on early modern English history and on topics such as controversies in national museums and re-staging the past. A Fellow of the Royal Historical Society and a Life Member of Clare Hall, Cambridge, David has been Company Historian to Canada's National Art Centre's English Theatre Company since 2008.

Janet Dickinson researches and writes on the political and cultural history of sixteenth-century England. She has held posts at a number of institutions and currently teaches for the University of Reading, the Open University, and the University of Oxford. She is a committee member and Conference Secretary of the Society for Court Studies. Her first book, *Court Politics and the Earl of Essex, 1589–1601* was published by Pickering and Chatto in December 2011 and she is now working on the Elizabethan nobility and on the final years of Elizabeth I's life.

Matthew Dimmock is Senior Lecturer in English Literature and Co-Director of the Centre for Early Modern Studies at the University of Sussex. He is interested in the writing of cultural encounter and is the author of *New Turkes: Dramatizing Islam and the Ottomans in Early Modern England* (2005), editor of *William Percy's Mahomet and His Heaven: A Critical Edition* (2007) and co-editor (with Andrew Hadfield) of *The Religions of the Book: Christian Perceptions, 1400–1660* (2008). He is currently completing a monograph, provisionally titled *Fabricating Muhammad: English Imaginings, 1400–1750*.

Susan Doran is Senior Research Fellow in History at Jesus College, Oxford. Her publications include numerous essays, articles and books on Elizabeth I and the Tudors, including *Monarchy and Matrimony: The Courtships of Elizabeth I* (1996) and *The Tudor Chronicles* (2008). Her latest book, co-edited with Paulina Kewes, is *Doubtful and Dangerous: The Question of Succession in Late Elizabethan England* (to be published by MUP in 2014).

David Edwards is Senior Lecturer in the School of History at University College Cork and a Director of the Irish Manuscripts Commission. He has published extensively on the history of sixteenth- and early seventeenth-century Ireland and Britain. His previous books include *The Ormond Lordship in County Kilkenny, 1515–1642: The Rise and Fall of Butler Feudal Power* (2003), *Age of Atrocity: Violence and Political Conflict in Early Modern Ireland* (2007) and *Gaelic Ireland, c.1250–c.1650: Land, Lordship and Settlement* (2001).

Henry French is Professor of Social History in the Department of History at the University of Exeter. He has published a number of studies of parish government and its contribution to the identity of the 'middle sort of people' in early modern England, including *The Middle Sort of People in Provincial England, 1600–1750* (2007) and collaborated with Professor Richard Hoyle on the study of landholding and society in the Essex village of Earls Colne, published as *The Character of English Rural Society: Earls Colne 1550–1750* (2007).

Paul Griffiths is Professor or Early Modern British Cultural and Social History at Iowa State University. He is author of *Lost Londons: Change, Crime, and Control in the Capital City, 1550–1660* (2008) and *Youth and Authority: Formative Experiences in England 1560–1640* (1996). His next book will be on information cultures in sixteenth- and seventeenth-century England.

Tara Hamling is a RCUK Research Fellow in the Department of History, University of Birmingham. Her research focuses on the visual and material culture of post-Reformation Britain. She is author of *Decorating the Godly Household: Religious Art in Post-Reformation Britain* (2010) and co-editor of two books; *Art Re-formed: Re-assessing the Impact of the Reformation on the Visual Arts* (with Richard L. Williams, 2007) and *Everyday Objects: Medieval and Early Modern Material Culture and its Meanings* (with Catherine Richardson, 2010).

Paul E. J. Hammer is Professor of History at the University of Colorado at Boulder. His publications include *The polarisation of Elizabethan politics: the political career of Robert Devereux, 2nd earl of Essex, 1585–1597* (Cambridge, 1999), *Elizabeth's wars: society, government and society in Tudor England, 1544–1604* (Palgrave, 2003), *Warfare in early modern Europe* (ed., Ashgate, 2007) and many articles on Elizabethan politics and political culture. He is currently completing a book on Essex Rising and the end of Elizabethan politics.

Steve Hindle is Director of Research at the Huntington Library in San Marino, California. He is the author of *The State and Social Change in Early Modern England, 1550–1640* (2000) and *On the Parish? The Micropolitics of Poor Relief in Rural England, c.1550–1750* (2004), and has published a series of articles on social relations in English rural communities. He is currently working on a study of the Warwickshire parish of Chilvers Coton, provisionally entitled *The Social Topography of a Rural Community*.

R. W. Hoyle is Professor of Rural History at the University of Reading. He has written extensively on the public finance, rural history and popular politics of the sixteenth century, including *The Pilgrimage of Grace and the Politics of the 1530s* (2001) and *The Character of English Rural Society: Earls Colne, 1550–1750* (with Professor Henry French). He also, when the time allows, writes on the history of northern England and the rural history of more recent times.

Martin Ingram is an Emeritus Fellow, Tutor and University Lecturer in History at Brasenose College, Oxford. His publications include *Church Courts, Sex and Marriage in England, 1570–1640* (1987), and numerous articles on crime and the law, sex and marriage, religion and popular customs. Currently his principal project is on regulating sex in England before, during and after the Reformation. He has also published on the history of climate.

Norman Jones is Professor and Chair of History at Utah State University. His monographs include *Faith by Statute, Parliament and the Settlement of Religion 1559* (1982); *God and the Money Lenders. Usury and Law in Early Modern England* (1989); *The Birth of the Elizabethan Age: England in the 1560s* (1992); *The English Reformation: Religion and Cultural Adaptation* (2002). He co-edited, the Robert Tittler, *A Companion to Tudor Britain* (2004); and, with Daniel Woolf, *Local Identities in Late Medieval and Early Modern England* (2007). He was a Senior Visiting Research Fellow at Jesus College, Oxford in 2008–2009, when much of the editing of this volume was done.

Peter Iver Kaufman holds the George Matthews and Virginia Brinkley Modlin Chair at the University of Richmond and is Professor Emeritus at the University of North Carolina, Chapel Hill. He is the author of, among other books, *Thinking of the Laity in Late Tudor England* (2004), *Incorrectly Political* (2007) and *Religion Around Shakespeare* (2013).

Krista Kesselring is Associate Professor of History and Gender and Women's Studies at Dalhousie University, Halifax, Nova Scotia. Her publications include *Mercy and Authority in the Tudor State* (2003) and *The Northern Rebellion of 1569: Faith, Politics and Protest in Elizabethan England* (2007). She has most recently co-edited, with Tim Stretton, a collection of essays entitled *Married Women and the Law: Coverture in England and the Common Law World* (2013).

Muriel McClendon is Associate Professor of History at the University of California, Los Angeles. She is the author of *The Quiet Reformation: Norwich Magistrates and the Emergence of Protestantism in Tudor Norwich* (1999). She co-edited *Protestant Identities Religion, Society, and Self-Fashioning in Post-Reformation England* (1999). She has published articles on urban culture and religion in early modern England and is currently engaged in research on gender and Reformation in Norwich.

Anne McLaren is a Senior Lecturer in the School of History, University of Liverpool. Her publications include *Political Culture in the Reign of Elizabeth I: Queen and Commonwealth 1558–1585* (2nd edn, 2006), 'Contesting the Monarchical Republic: Jacobean Conceptions of Kingship', in John McDiarmid (ed.), *The Monarchical Republic of Early Modern England: Essays in Response to Patrick Collinson* (2007),'Rethinking Republicanism: *Vindiciae, contra tyrannos* in Context', *Historical Journal* (2006), and 'Gender, Religion, and Early Modern Nationalism: Elizabeth I, Mary Queen of Scots, and the Genesis of English Anti-Catholicism', *American Historical Review* (2002). Her forthcoming book, *Embodied Kingship: Regicide and Republicanism in England, 1570–1650*, investigates the relationship between king-killing and early modern state formation.

Ken MacMillan is Professor of History at the University of Calgary. He is editor of *John Dee: The Limits of the British Empire* (2004) and author of *Sovereignty and Possession in the English New World: The Legal Foundations of Empire*

(2006) and *The Atlantic Imperial Constitution: Centre and Periphery in the English Atlantic World* (2011).

Steven W. May is the author of *Sir Walter Ralegh* in Twayne's English Authors Series (1989), *The Elizabethan Courtier Poets* (University of Missouri Press, 1991), *Queen Elizabeth I: Selected Works* (Washington Square Press, 2004), and *Elizabethan Poetry: A Bibliography and First-Line Index of English Verse, 1559–1603* (Continuum Publishing, 2004). His on-going research interests include English manuscript culture, the late Renaissance court, and editing early modern texts. He retired from full-time teaching in 2004 and is now affiliated with Emory University and the University of Sheffield.

Natalie Mears is a Senior Lecturer in Early Modern British History at the University of Durham. She has published *Queenship and Political Discourse in the Elizabethan Realms* (2005), as well as a number of articles on Elizabeth's reign, on court politics and on the 'public sphere'. She was also co-editor, with Alec Ryrie, of *Worship and the Parish Church in Early Modern Britain* (2012). She is co-investigator, with Philip Williamson and Stephen Taylor (both Durham), on the AHRC-funded project, 'British state prayers, fasts and thanksgivings, 1540s to 1940s', and is lead editor of the first of a three-volume edition, *National Prayers: Special Worship since the Reformation*, arising from the project, to be published in 2013.

Darren Oldridge teaches History at the University of Worcester. He has written on early modern systems of belief, witchcraft and the Devil. His books include *Strange Histories* (2005) and, as editor, *The Witchcraft Reader* (2nd edn, 2008). Presently he is writing *The Devil: A Very Short Introduction.*

David Potter was brought up in Birmingham and studied at Durham and Cambridge. He is at present Reader in French History at the University of Kent, Canterbury, where he now lives. His interests cover the history of France and the sixteenth century and Anglo-French relations. His books include: *War and Government in the French Provinces: Picardy 1470–1560* (1993); *A History of France, 1460–1560: the Emergence of a Nation State* (1995); *The French Wars of Religion: Selected Documents* (1998); *Un homme de guerre au temps de la Renaissance: la vie et les lettres d'Oudart du Biez, maréchal de France et gouverneur de Picardie et de Boulogne (vers 1475–1553)* (2001); *The Short Oxford History of France: France in the Later Middle Ages (c.1200–1500)* (2003); *Foreign Intelligence and Information Gathering in Elizabethan England: Two English Treatises on the State of France, 1579–84* (2005); *Renaissance France at War* (2008). He has just completed *Henry VIII and Francis I, the Final Conflict: the Anglo-French Struggle, 1540–47* and is working on an edition of the letters of Antoine de Bournon, king of Navarre.

Joad Raymond is Professor of Renaissance Studies at Queen Mary, University of London. He is the author of *The Invention of the Newspaper: English Newsbooks, 1641–1649* (1996), *Pamphlets and Pamphleteering in Early Modern Britain* (2003) and *Milton's Angels: The Early Modern Imagination* (2010), editor of *The Oxford History of Popular Print Culture*, vol. 1: *Cheap*

Print in Britain and Ireland to 1660 (2011), and editor of several books on early modern news. He is presently editing Milton's Latin Defences for the Oxford Complete Works and directing an international collaborative project on early modern European news networks.

David Harris Sacks is the Richard F. Scholz Profesor of History and Humanities at Reed College, where he has taught since 1986. He holds his BA in History from Brooklyn College (1963) and his Ph.D. in History from Harvard University (1977). He has been the recipient of fellowships from the John Simon Guggenheim Foundation, the American Council of Learned Societies, the National Endowment for the Humanities (twice), the John Carter Brown Library, the Folger Shakespeare Library, and the Woodrow Wilson International Center for Scholars. Along with publishing a number of articles, essays, review articles, and reviews on aspects of early modern British social, economic, political and intellectual and cultural history, he is the author of *Trade, Society and Politics in Bristol, 1500–1640* (1985) and of *The Widening Gate: Bristol and the Atlantic Economy, 1450–1700* (1991), editor of an edition of Ralph Robynson's sixteenth-century translation into English of Thomas More's *Utopia* (1999), and, with Donald R. Kelley, of a collection of essays entitled *The Historical Imagination in Early Modern Britain: History, Rhetoric, and Fiction, 1500–1700* (1997).

Bill Sheils is Professor of History and Head of Department at the University of York. He has worked on post Reformation religion in England across denominational boundaries for most of his professional life, writing on both puritans and Catholics with special focus on relations at the local level. In 2008–9 he was President of the Ecclesiastical History Society and the volume for his Presidency, 'God's Bounty? The Church and the Natural World' was published in the series Studies in Church History earlier this year.

Alexandra Shepard is Reader in Early Modern History at the University of Glasgow. Besides several essays on gender and social relations in early modern England, she is the author of *Meanings of Manhood in Early Modern England* (2003) and co-editor, with Phil Withington, of *Communities in Early Modern England* (2000). She is currently preparing a book on worth, status and self-description in England between 1550 and 1700.

Tim Stretton is Professor of History at Saint Mary's University in Halifax, Nova Scotia. He recently co-edited, with Krista Kesselring, *Married Women and the Law: Coverture in England and the Common Law World* (2013) and is the author of *Women Waging Law in Elizabethan England* (1998) and a number of essays concerning women's legal rights in pre-modern England.

William J. Tighe is Associate Professor of History at Muhlenberg College in Pennsylvania. His Ph.D. work focused on the Gentlemen Pensioners at the court of Queen Elizabeth I and over the past decade he has embarked on a wide-ranging study of the most intimate servants of that queen, known collectively as the Privy Chamber. Among his publications are 'A Nottinghamshire Gentleman in Court and in Country: the Career of Thomas Markham of

Ollerton (1530–1607)', *Transactions of the Thoroton Society of Nottinghamshire* (1986); 'The Gentlemen Pensioners, the Duke of Northumberland and the Attempted Coup of July 1553', *Albion* (1987); 'Courtiers and Politics in Elizabethan Herefordshire: Sir James Croft, His Friends and His Foes', *Historical Journal* (1989); '"To Run with the Time": Archbishop Whitgift, the Lambeth Articles and the Politics of Theological Ambiguity in late Elizabeth England', *Sixteenth Century Journal* (1992); and 'Country into Court, Court into Country: John Scudamore of Holme Lacy and his Circles' in *Tudor Political Culture*, ed. D. E. Hoak (Cambridge, 1995).

Brett Usher is Visiting Research Fellow in History at the University of Reading, and Research Associate of *The Oxford Dictionary of National Biography*, to which he contributed more than fifty entries on Tudor and Jacobean clergymen and their patrons. With Patrick Collinson and John Craig, he edited *Conferences and Combination Lectures in the Elizabethan Church, 1582–1590* (2003). He is currently working on the sequel to his *William Cecil and Episcopacy, 1559–1577* (2003).

Joseph P. Ward is Associate Professor and Chair of History at the University of Mississippi. He is the author of *Metropolitan Identities: Trade Guilds, Identity, and Change in Early Modern London* and editor of, most recently, *Violence, Politics, and Gender in Early Modern England.*

Richard Williams is an Associate Lecturer in the History of Art at Birkbeck College, University of London. Since completing his doctorate at the Courtauld Institute followed by a research fellowship granted by the Paul Mellon Centre (Yale University), he has specialised in the cultural impact of the Reformation in England. His numerous publications have focused on Protestant and Catholic religious imagery in Elizabethan England.

EDITOR'S NOTE

Our convention with footnotes is only to reference quotations. The secondary sources used by contributors appear in the Further Reading.

ABBREVIATIONS

BHC	Bridewell House of Correction
BL	British Library
CSP For.	*Calendar of State Papers Foreign, Elizabeth*. Joseph Stevenson, A.J. Crosbly, A.J. Butler, S.C. Lomas, A.B. Hinds, R.B. Wernham, eds. London, 1863–1950. 23 vols.
CSP Scot.	*Calendar of State Papers, Scotland*. Jos Bain, et al. eds. Edinburgh and Glasgow, 1989–1952. 13 vols.
Cal. Sp. Irel.	*Calendar of State Papers, Ireland*. H.C. Hamilton, ed. London, 1912. 12 vols.
CSP Span.	*Calendar of State Papers, Spanish, Elizabeth*. M.A.S. Hume, ed. London, 1892–9. 4 vols.
CSP Ven.	*Calendar of State Papers Relating to English Affairs in the Archives of Venice*. Rawdon Brown, Cavendish Bentinck, and Horatio Brown, eds. London, 1864–98. 9 vols.
CUL	Cambridge University Library
GL	Guildhall Library, London
HMC	Historical Manuscript Commission
LMA	London Metropolitan Archives
NLI	National Library of Ireland
NRO	Norwich Record Office
RO	Record Office
TCD	Trinity College Dublin
TNA	The National Archives of the United Kingdom

CHAPTER ONE

INTRODUCTION

Susan Doran and Norman Jones

The idea of a book on the 'Elizabethan World' may seem to give an undue importance to England in the second half of the sixteenth century. Certainly, other volumes in this series have a better claim to use the all-encompassing term 'world'. Even Andrew Pettegree's *The Reformation World* or Beat Kümin's *The European World, 1500–1800* incorporate an entire continent, not to mention its overseas empires. England from 1558 until 1603, however, was just a kingdom, within a relatively small archipelago off Continental Europe; it had no permanent colonies, was limited in its military manpower and consequently exercised far less power and influence on the Continent than either Valois France or Habsburg Spain. So why the 'Elizabethan World'?

Elizabethan England occupies an unusual and important historical space in the world. In all of the 'Anglo zone' – those global places where English is spoken and written – Elizabethan history and culture have long enjoyed a mythic status. The 'Golden Age of English Literature' is securely, if not entirely accurately, located in the Elizabethan period, as it was a time when the commercial theatre flourished, Edmund Spenser and Philip Sidney produced their poetic masterpieces and William Shakespeare was in full creative bloom. The Church of England traces its roots back to the 1559 Elizabethan Settlement of the Church, reveres John Jewel and Richard Hooker as its founders, and sees the Elizabethan 'middle way' as a crucial element in the Anglican identity. The Elizabethan period also marks the foundation of the early British Empire owing to Francis Drake's circumnavigation of the globe and Walter Ralegh's sponsorship of the early colonisation of Roanoke (renamed Virginia in Elizabeth's honour). The events and people of the time are some of the most colourful and best known in British history; the defeat of the Spanish Armada in 1588 provides one of its most famous victories and seems to mark England's emergence as a naval power; Elizabeth I is perhaps the best known of its monarchs; and who hasn't heard of William Shakespeare? While Hollywood has obviously contributed to the period's fame in the twentieth and early twenty-first centuries, the people and events in Elizabeth's reign appeared much earlier as subjects of novels by Sir Walter Scott, a play by Friedrich Schiller, operas by Rossini and Donizetti and a significant number of Victorian paintings and children's books.

In this volume, we have decided to deal with the issue of the 'world' in three ways. First, we have invited historians to recapture aspects of the 'worldview' of Elizabethans by looking at such matters as political ideas, popular culture, economic preoccupations and the nature of local communities. Second, we have asked some of our contributors to consider how Elizabethans interacted with the outside world and understood England's place in it. Third, we have commissioned essays that confront, and sometimes challenge, the myths relating to the importance of the Elizabethan period in the history of the English-speaking world. Given that the book is built around the reign of Elizabeth I, we have also included essays on the Queen herself, the political environment within which she worked and the nature of governance during her period of rule.

Histories of the Elizabethan era written before the late twentieth century tended to focus on the Queen herself, high politics, political institutions, foreign policy and religion. Scholars of the 1920s, 1930s and mid-century decades, tempered in the fights with Fascism and Communism, sought to understand the creation of the political institutions that shaped the freedoms being defended against modern 'isms'. Sir John Neale's histories of parliament, for example, teased out the origins of the modern parliamentary system dominated by the House of Commons, though in doing so ignored the power and importance of the Elizabethan aristocracy and clergy. Important political biographies included Neale's popular 1934 biography of the Queen, which portrayed her as a master politician, and Conyers Read's volumes on Sir Francis Walsingham and William Cecil, Lord Burghley, all of which remain unsurpassed in their archival mastery. By the third quarter of the twentieth century, however, the historiography began to move away from biographies, towards studies that contextualised high politics within state and local institutions. Wallace MacCaffrey wrote beautifully detailed books on the Elizabethan regime and the Queen herself. Penry Williams studied the structures of government, having earlier breathed life into the Council of Wales. Sir Geoffrey Elton concentrated on the actual functioning of state institutions, writing on Elizabethan parliaments and challenging the earlier interpretations of Sir John Neale. R. B. Wernham investigated the making of Elizabethan foreign policy, using the Armada crisis as the fixed star around which his work turned. However, approaches to the politics of Elizabeth's reign have changed greatly in more recent decades. For one thing, historians are as much (if not more) interested in political ideas and culture as in political events and institutions. They have also extended their interests to embrace, far more than did their predecessors, the cultural ideas and values about the economy and society in general. This trend will be evident in many of the essays here.

As far as Elizabethan religious history was concerned, debates over recusancy, puritanism and the birth and nature of the Anglican tradition of worship were raging in the nineteenth century as emancipated Catholics, High Church, Low Church and Dissenting scholars fought to establish the legitimacy of their denominational positions. Despite doing us the service of publishing great source collections, these men used history to defend their own denominational identities and theological propriety. They consequently constructed religious pigeonholes which led, as Christopher Haigh once remarked, to debates among historians about how many puritans can fit into a minibus. These denominationally biased histories practically ignored the broad middle ground of opinion and practice – all those men and women who conformed quietly to the law and became Elizabethan Protestants of some sort. 'Prayer Book Protestants' had to wait until the late twentieth century to find scholars who would represent them.

The denominational pigeonholes began to fall apart after 1980 as scholars such as Patrick Collinson, Christopher Haigh and Judith Maltby started to ask new sorts of questions about how religion was lived rather than attempting to count pious noses. The realisation that the English Reformation should be seen as 'Reformations', rather than a linear progression towards triumphant Protestantism, also opened up new questions about Elizabethan religion, emphasising the process of reform and its cultural results rather than religion per se. As Peter Kaufman points out in this volume, there were many fashions of godliness, many of them lumped together as 'puritanism', but varying widely in their sentiments, their ecclesiology, and their social impact. Strikingly, a search in the Royal Historical Society's bibliography for works published after 2000 that include the word 'puritan' in their titles produces only four hits. A search for titles including the terms 'religion' and 'culture' produces hundreds of hits. And once culture was introduced, the great majority of people who simply conformed became a legitimate subject of study. Prayer-book worship is now seen as a major new cultural form. Simultaneously as the interest in puritans, those putative heralds of the Civil War and American values, declined, the religious culture of Elizabethan Catholics has become a very active field of research.

The social history of the era was, until the later twentieth century, more about Dogberry and his funny fellows than about serious social scientific understanding. F. W. Emmison, for instance, edited record collections that gave us anecdotal materials for social history, without providing thorough contextual analyses. The quality of the prose written by A. L. Rowse has kept his social/cultural history of Elizabeth's reign in print, but, once again, it is anecdotal rather than analytical. The revolution in social history set off by scholars such as Keith Wrightson, David Levine and Margaret Spufford, as well as the Cambridge Population Group, has changed the foci of research to local communities and the building of large data sets that allowed patterns to be seen across *la longue durée.*

Overall then, a number of new questions and methods has widened the study of the Elizabethan world. Broadly expressed, our understanding of it is now firmly located in cultural history rather than in the history of events. Recently, scholars have been much more interested in the ways that events can be situated in value systems than in detailing the actual events themselves. Indeed, only now is it appropriate to talk of an Elizabethan 'world' as only now is an understanding of the worldview of Elizabethans high up the agenda of scholars. These kinds of approaches, as can be seen in this volume, borrow from anthropology, sociology, literary theory, gender studies, political theory, religious studies and other fields for insights into the sources. For instance, feminist questions about Elizabeth's place as a female monarch in a patriarchal culture have led to fruitful explorations that have resulted in new readings of the evidence. Placing religion into political culture has led to the discovery of the 'monarchical republic' of Elizabethan England, a world run by men whose reading of Roman history encouraged a new understanding of the English state. This interest in cultural expression has refreshed the study of Elizabethan popular culture and social history. Both areas are now being studied in their own right but also are now tied to more elite culture.

The elite culture of Tudor England is also benefiting from a fresh look. For a long time, the Latinate, pan-European education and outlook of educated Elizabethans were overshadowed by scholarly interest in vernacular culture. However, as the cultural turn has taken hold, it has become more and more difficult to ignore the fact that educated Elizabethans were reading the classics and the Latin works of their Continental colleagues. It came as a revelation to us, as editors, to see that it was necessary to reach into the rising generation of scholars to find a person, Freyja Cox Jensen, who could understand this Latinate culture. Perhaps the universities and the neo-Latin authors are now to receive the attention they deserve.

The trend in political history therefore is away from the study of governmental structures and toward the exercise of government. The debates over monarchical republicanism were stimulated in part by the study of local units of administration. However, these same local studies are bumping up against the historical neglect of the administrative activities of the Crown. In the post-Eltonian world, major institutions of the central government have been neglected. A full study of the Elizabethan Privy Council is in progress, but still a long way from completion. Studies of the court have tended to be cultural, rather than administrative. The governmental role of the aristocracy is in need of further work. If the mid-twentieth century ignored them because of its Marxist/liberal assumptions about the uselessness of nobles, the current age likes their culture but neglects their power. So, although the study of the Elizabethan age is vibrant, there is still much to do. Furthermore, many issues are contested. In this volume, for example, David Dean disagrees with Natalie Mears about the ways in which parliament was used by privy councillors, and there are also disagreements over the ways in which gender influenced behaviour in Elizabethan court and culture, with Natalie Mears and Susan Doran finding gender less important in understanding Elizabethan politics than does Anne McLaren.

Debates over the role of gender and counsel return us to the person whose name denotes all we are talking about, Elizabeth. Because we recognise that readers need to have some background and framework for the remaining chapters in the volume, the rest of this introduction provides a short biography of the Queen and a broad outline of the key political events of her reign. Historians have traditionally divided the reign into roughly three periods: 1558–69, 1569–85 and 1585–1603. Although these are artificial and far from satisfactory, the compartments prove useful for providing a guide to the nature and composition of the government and the political preoccupations of the Privy Council and social elite during a long reign.

ELIZABETH'S EARLY LIFE

Elizabeth was born on 7 September 1533, the daughter of Henry VIII and his second wife Anne Boleyn. During the first two and a half years of her life, she was heir presumptive to the throne, taking precedence over her half-sister Mary, who had been excluded from the succession in 1533 when Henry's marriage to Katherine of Aragon was pronounced invalid. However, after Anne was executed in 1536,

Elizabeth too was bastardised by the Church and debarred from the succession by Act of Parliament. For the remainder of her father's life, she lived in one or other of the minor royal palaces situated in the county of Hertfordshire, and on the whole her visits to court were rare and brief. The one important exception was in June 1544 when Elizabeth, together with Mary and their younger half-brother Edward (born in 1537) joined the household of Katherine Parr, Henry's sixth and last wife, while the King was fighting in France. By this time, Elizabeth's royal status was acknowledged, for the parliament of 1543–4 had restored her to the succession, third in line behind Edward and Mary if both died without issue, even though the taint of her bastardy was not removed.

Elizabeth's early education seems to have been in French and Italian carried out by members of her household, notably Katherine Champernowne (subsequently Astley). Once she was restored to the succession, new tutors were appointed: William Grindal, a classical scholar, who was part of the evangelical, humanist circle based at Saint John's College, Cambridge, and Jean Belmaine, who taught her handwriting as well as French. It is probable that Elizabeth's famed studies in Latin and Greek began at this time when she was ten or eleven years old. Over the next few years, Elizabeth produced three works of translation that have survived: an English version of Marguerite d'Angoulême's, *Le Miroir de l'âme pécheresse* entitled 'Glasse of the synnefull soule'; a French translation of Erasmus' *Dialogus Fidei;* and a French, Italian and Latin translation of Katherine Parr's 'Prayers and Meditations'. All these works show that in her adolescent years Elizabeth was exposed to the Christian humanist spiritual writings favoured by the religious evangelicals in Katherine Parr's household.

On Henry VIII's death, Elizabeth and her half-sister became major landowners, each inheriting manors that were worth about £3,000 a year. Mary (now in her thirties) at once set up her own independent household, but the thirteen-year-old Elizabeth was based until May 1548 in the household of her stepmother and Lord Thomas Seymour, Katherine's new husband. Then, in early 1549, Elizabeth was suddenly placed under house arrest. Seymour (by then a widower) had attempted a coup, and the subsequent investigations revealed his plan to marry Elizabeth without first securing the consent of Edward VI's Privy Council, a plot that amounted to treason. Under interrogation, the fifteen-year-old Elizabeth remained remarkably self-possessed, with the result that she was cleared of involvement in Seymour's marital ambitions. Nonetheless, her reputation was tarnished by her servants' revelations that she and Seymour had engaged in inappropriate flirtatious behaviour while they both lived in the same house and he was still married to Katherine. Elizabeth had to work hard on her image to repair the damage.

It was during Edward's reign that Elizabeth became drawn into the Protestant faith, perhaps under the influence of her chaplain Edmund Allen, the evangelical catechist, who also introduced Johannes Spithovius, a pupil of Melanchthon's, to Elizabeth's schoolroom. Her classical education also developed under the guiding hand of Roger Ascham who became her tutor after the death of Grindal in 1548.

With the accession of Mary in July 1553, Elizabeth's position became more difficult and very dangerous, for she was openly out of sympathy with the religion of the new regime. She absented herself from the requiem mass that Mary had ordered for their dead half-brother, and initially excused herself from services in the royal chapel. When she attended mass for the first time on 8 September 1553, she made a public display of her reluctance to go, complaining loudly 'all the way to church that her stomach ached, wearing a suffering air'. It was no wonder that an observer commented: 'everyone believes she is acting rather from fear of danger and peril than from real devotion.' By November 1553, Mary confided to her minister, Lord William Paget, and the imperial ambassador that she would like to exclude her sister from the succession because she was a heretic and a bastard; and to make her feelings clear, Mary denied Elizabeth the precedence she was due as heir presumptive and allowed her to leave court.

During Wyatt's rebellion of January 1554, the government obtained evidence that Elizabeth had prior knowledge about the conspiracy to depose Mary and place her on the throne. Consequently, on 11 February, Elizabeth was arrested. Over the next few weeks she remained in virtual isolation in Whitehall Palace while Sir Thomas Wyatt and other conspirators were interrogated in an effort to incriminate her further. Under questioning, Elizabeth denied involvement and gave nothing away, but on 18 March she was conveyed to the Tower, where she remained for two months, no doubt terrified that she would be executed just like the totally innocent Lady Jane Grey and her husband. Periodically questioned, Elizabeth stalwartly defended herself, while Sir Thomas Wyatt from the scaffold asserted her innocence. The government consequently could prove nothing against her; but in order to prevent further plots forming around her Elizabeth was dispatched in May 1554 to the royal hunting lodge at Woodstock in Oxfordshire. There she was confined under close guard for nearly a year. Once queen, it served Elizabeth to present this period of her life as a time of great danger; it also suited Protestants such as the martyrologist John Foxe to write of Elizabeth's miraculous preservation from execution or murder, for it cast her as a providential princess protected by God from the cruel Catholics.

The period of house arrest ended in April 1555. However, after Elizabeth's return to Hatfield, several members of her household became embroiled in fresh conspiracies against Mary and were arrested. This time Elizabeth was treated leniently. The council installed Sir Thomas Pope in her household for four months to keep an eye on the princess, but he was instructed to treat her honourably. Few people in 1556 believed that Mary would produce an heir, and consequently her English councillors and Spanish husband wanted Elizabeth kept alive and at liberty to prevent the accession of Mary, Queen of Scots, the granddaughter of Henry VIII's elder sister, who was betrothed to the son of the king of France. To keep Elizabeth pro-Habsburg and tie her into the Catholic fold, Philip tried to arrange a marriage between the princess and one of his allies, but Elizabeth and Mary for their own different reasons were uncooperative.

As Mary's health deteriorated during 1558, Elizabeth made preparations for her accession, developing connections with Marian councillors, building up a political following and trying to raise troops in the event of a challenge to the throne. While the political manoeuvring was helpful, military preparations proved unnecessary since Mary's own supporters – both her widower, Philip II, and ex-councillors – made sure that Elizabeth would succeed peacefully. Philip II sent his envoy (Count of Feria) to Hatfield while Mary was still alive to assure her of his support. Mary's councillors kept quiet the news of the Queen's death which took place early on 17 November until the Lord Chancellor, Archbishop Nicholas Heath of York, announced it along with Elizabeth's accession in parliament – a most unusual procedure since precedent dictated that parliament should be immediately dissolved on a monarch's death. However, the parliamentary endorsement of Elizabeth's accession was intended to pre-empt any challenge to her title to be queen, especially from Mary, Queen of Scots, who was by then married to the dauphin of France. It succeeded in its purpose.

THE FIRST PHASE OF THE REIGN: 1558–69

Elizabeth's inheritance in November 1558 was far from ideal, and the problems she faced required immediate decisions. England was officially still at war against France, though hostilities had effectively ceased after François Duc de Guise had captured Calais the previous January. Elizabeth's first task on her accession, therefore, was to negotiate a peace that would not involve the humiliating surrender of territory. With few cards to play, she was largely unsuccessful. Despite a face-saving clause, the Treaty of Cateau-Cambrésis signed in April 1559 left Calais in French hands. Unwilling to accept the permanent loss of England's last outpost on the Continent, Elizabeth agreed in 1562 to send troops to help the Huguenots in their war against the French Catholics in return for the recovery of the town. But, as is explained in Chapter 36, the English expedition to France failed, exposing the inadequacies of England's military and strategic position.

Relations with France were also troubled at this time because of the close dynastic relationship between Mary, Queen of Scots, and the French crown, until the death of the Dauphin in December 1560, and the powerful Guise family thereafter. Since Mary was the Catholic claimant for the throne of England, many Elizabethans feared that she would receive French backing in an attempt to oust Elizabeth. Francophobia therefore dominated the first decade of the reign, and it only began to subside in 1570 when the Guises were temporarily less influential at the French court. Negotiations could then be opened for a marriage alliance between Elizabeth and Henri, Duc d'Anjou, the brother of Charles IX of France. When these talks failed, an Anglo-French defensive treaty was signed at Blois (April 1572).

The Catholic and dynastic threat from Mary, Queen of Scots, was at the forefront of the government's consciousness during the 1560s, and it affected Elizabeth's relationship with Scotland as well as France. In late 1559, Elizabeth was persuaded to give support to the Protestant lords in Scotland, who had taken up arms against the regent, Mary of Guise, in order to stop the northern kingdom from operating as a base for the invasion of England on behalf of Mary, Queen of Scots. Although the actual military operation was disappointing in its effectiveness, as Paul Hammer later explains, England's intervention nonetheless proved to be a political success. French troops left Scotland, and Protestants took control of the government. Even Mary's return to Scotland in 1561 did not immediately end England's good relationship with the Scottish government. Certainly, Elizabeth's refusal to acknowledge Mary formally as her heir caused diplomatic tension between the two regimes, but the presence of the anglophile Earl of Moray and Lord Maitland of Lethington in Mary's government eased interactions. However, Mary's marriage to her cousin Henry Lord Darnley in 1565 changed matters, creating near panic amongst some of Elizabeth's privy councillors who detected, in Mary's choice of husband, a sinister plot to challenge their mistress's title to the throne. They consequently greeted Mary's deposition in 1567 and subsequent flight into England with delight in the hope that she would be kept securely imprisoned for the rest of her days.

Alongside these international problems lay domestic ones. The state of the economy and royal finances badly needed attention at Elizabeth's accession, since the Crown had built up a sizeable debt during the French war while the realm was racked by high prices (aggravated by a debased coinage), harvest failures, a slump in the cloth trade and a major demographic crisis caused by outbreaks of influenza, sweating sickness and plague. Chapters 24 to 26 throw much light on the nature of the economic problems and the ways in which Elizabethans tackled them during the reign.

Perhaps most problematic of all for the Queen in November 1558 were the religious and dynastic questions that needed to be quickly settled: what form of Christianity should England follow? Whom should the Queen marry to settle an uncertain succession? The religious question was dealt with in Elizabeth's first parliament when the Acts of Supremacy and Uniformity were passed, notwithstanding strong opposition in the House of Lords. In 1563, after a new bench of bishops had been appointed, convocation (the Church's governing body) approved the Thirty-Nine Articles of Religion. The nature of the formal religious changes, the structure of the Elizabethan Church and the communal relations between different confessional groups are the subject of Part II of this book and need not be discussed further here. However, it is important to emphasise at this juncture that the religious settlement disappointed many, if not most, Protestants, who wanted to see a greater degree of reformation than the Queen had offered. Disillusionment began to set in amongst them when Elizabeth refused to allow the discussion of Bills relating to religion in the Parliaments of 1566 and 1571. Tensions also arose between Elizabeth and Protestant ministers who strongly objected to parts of the 1559 Prayer Book and 1559 royal injunctions after the Queen ordered Matthew Parker, her Archbishop of Canterbury, to impose conformity to the religious settlement in 1564.

As for the marriage issue, Elizabeth of course remained a virgin queen, rejecting many suitors during the first decade of the reign, including Philip II of Spain, King Eric of Sweden and the Archduke Charles of Austria. However, no one then knew that Elizabeth would remain single, and the question of the Queen's marriage was a live issue during the 1560s. It was also a politically divisive one, as some Elizabethans favoured a foreign candidate while others preferred an Englishman, principally Robert Dudley. Yet as long as the Queen remained unmarried, demands arose that the succession question be resolved and, as Anne McLaren later makes clear, the succession issue was even more difficult and divisive than the marriage one.

Even with these contentious issues, there was a surprising degree of political stability during this decade. The discarded Marian councillors, courtiers and deprived bishops left political life quietly and did not become embroiled in plots or conspiracies against the Queen. Privy councillors learned to work together despite personal rivalries and disagreements over details of policy. Apart from close kinship networks, those who attended regularly were united in their personal loyalty to the Queen and their commitment to Protestantism. The Catholic threat at home seems to have been a background noise, an irritant, but not overly intrusive; it therefore did not result in widespread purges of Catholics from local government or a heavy-handed implementation of the Act of Uniformity that might stir up active resistance.

THE SECOND PHASE: 1569–85

This second phase of Elizabeth's reign began and ended with a crisis. Both crises were in fact a series of events that, taken altogether, revealed England's vulnerability abroad and at home. The first one commenced in December 1568 when Anglo-Spanish relations suddenly and dramatically deteriorated. This was largely the result of a diplomatic misunderstanding, which led the Spanish government in the Netherlands to seize English goods and impose an embargo on English commerce. Elizabeth naturally retaliated in kind, and trade officially ceased between England and the Spanish empire until 1574. During this standstill, English privateers preyed on Spanish shipping in the Channel, Atlantic and Caribbean, further antagonising the government of Philip II. Outraged by these provocations and irritated by Elizabeth's protection of religious refugees from the Netherlands, the Spanish ambassador, Guerau de Spes, fomented conspiracies against the Queen, while Philip II promised support for Catholics risings within her realm.

Elizabeth faced two major risings in 1569. In Ireland, a 'shadowy convention' of lords offered the crown of Ireland to Philip II in the spring, and in June, Sir Edmund Butler and Sir James Fitzmaurice orchestrated risings in the province of Munster.[1] Although Butler did not make religion his cause, Fitzmaurice issued a proclamation upholding the Catholic Church, and the English government consequently perceived the Irish rebellion to be religious in origin and inspiration. The second rising was in northern England where the Earls of Northumberland and Westmorland came out in open revolt in November 1569. As K. J. Kesselring and Janet Dickinson both explain, this too was a rising largely inspired by religion. By December 1569 both revolts were effectively over, although another short-lived rebellion, led by Lord Dacre, erupted in the north in February 1570. However, the rebels slipped over the border into Scotland where they joined forces with the adherents of Mary, Queen of Scots, and were calling on the French to supply them with aid in a civil war against the regency government of Mary's son, the infant James VI.

Despite fairly easy victories over the English and Irish rebels, the Catholic challenge to the Protestant Elizabethan regime continued to look acute. In February 1570, Pope Pius V issued the bull *Regnans in excelsis* excommunicating the Queen and releasing English subjects from obedience to her. The following year, the English government learned of a plot engineered by a Florentine banker Roberto Ridolfi for a Spanish invasion of England backed by the Pope and involving Mary, Queen of Scots, and the Duke of Norfolk. These events seemed like a wake-up call to many Protestants. They now demanded the execution of the Scottish queen, who was living under house arrest in England, and heavier penalties for English Catholics. Elizabeth was able to save Mary from the axe, but not Norfolk.

Once the immediate crisis of 1569–71 had blown over, England remained relatively secure and stable for several years. Certainly, anxieties beset the government about the Catholic threat, but it seemed on the whole to be contained at home and abroad. Despite the bull of excommunication, most English Catholics remained loyal or silent. The danger from Mary, Queen of Scots, was lessened when the pro-Marian Scottish lords were defeated by the forces of the Earl of Morton, who then went on to act as an effective regent for James VI. After the failure of the Ridolfi Plot, Philip II was keen to restore commercial and diplomatic relations with England, not least so that he could concentrate his attention on defeating the rebels in the Netherlands. Elizabeth was equally keen to end the embargo and to avoid further confrontation with Philip. With this end in view, she avoided giving direct military aid to the King's Protestant rebels and instead tried to broker a diplomatic solution that would safeguard her co-religionists and remove the Spanish military presence from northern Europe. She also avoided direct intervention in the French religious wars. The Treaty of Blois with France held firm, in spite of the French government's collusion in the Saint Bartholomew's massacre of French Protestants and Elizabeth's covert assistance to the Huguenots.

During the same period, domestic politics were generally less contentious than they had been earlier. Elizabeth's marriage ceased to be a live issue until late 1578, when Elizabeth's negotiations to marry François, Duc d'Anjou, briefly stirred up a political storm that absorbed much of the political nation. The political debates surrounding the succession issue subsided after the Treasons Act of 1571 banned public discussion of the succession. Elizabeth's religious policy, however, brought her into conflict with many of her Protestant subjects, especially when she suspended Archbishop Edmund Grindal of Canterbury from his duties in June 1577. Grindal's offence was his refusal to implement Elizabeth's order to ban 'prophesyings' (meetings in which the gospel was propounded and discussed before a lay and clerical audience). A number of councillors and many clerics approved Grindal's stance, although they wished he had used more moderate language when challenging the Queen's authority. Even more of them were dismayed that Elizabeth seemed to be paying more attention to silencing Protestants than taking strong action against Catholics. However, these disagreements were contained, and the regime pulled together in maintaining a united rhetorical stance against both recusants and subversives.

After 1578, a series of events occurred on the Continent and in Britain that reignited a sense of crisis not seen since 1571. Most important of all, it became increasingly clear that Philip II was likely to accomplish his mission to restore order and to extirpate heresy in the Netherlands, for his new governor-general, Alexander Farnese, Prince of Parma, was proving remarkably successful in returning the southern provinces to Spanish rule. During Parma's campaigns of the early 1580s, city after city in Flanders capitulated. Then, in July 1584, William of Orange was assassinated, leaving the northern provinces leaderless and demoralised. At the end of the year, Parma began a blockade of Antwerp, and the Protestant rebels in the Netherlands seemed on the brink of defeat, leaving England to stand alone to defend the Protestant cause and to face the might of Spain. That 'might' seemed even more imposing given Philip II's recent successful military campaign in Portugal in 1580 and his acquisition of the Portuguese throne, empire and imposing navy. By this stage, no one in England was in any doubt of Philip's hostile intentions towards Elizabeth and Protestant England. In 1579, the King had sponsored a small army, led by James Fitzmaurice, that had landed in Ireland and called for a Catholic rebellion against the Queen. In 1583, it was revealed that the Spanish ambassador had been plotting with a Catholic gentleman, Francis Throckmorton, and the Guise family to replace Elizabeth with Mary. In early 1585, news leaked into England of Philip's secret Treaty of Joinville (1584) with the Duc de Guise, the leader of the Catholic League, and it was all too easy to believe (falsely in fact) that they had declared a commitment to destroy heresy in the whole of Europe, including England. In May 1585, Philip's seizure of English shipping in Spanish ports convinced Elizabeth's council that he intended to use the vessels in an armada against England.

Within England itself, the English government was preoccupied with the spectre of Catholic plots to assassinate the Queen, liberate Mary and raise Catholics in rebellion. The arrival of a tiny Jesuit mission in 1580, the discovery of the Throckmorton Plot in 1583 and the various testimonies given by spies and informers convinced privy councillors and members of parliament that an international Catholic conspiracy was afoot. To deal with it there were calls for even tougher legislation against English Catholics and for the death of Mary, or at the very least her exclusion from the succession. As a result, stringent legislation was passed in parliament against Catholic recusants and Jesuit priests. However, Elizabeth refused to allow discussion of the succession and put off the trial and execution of Mary for as long as she could: Mary was tried for treason in 1586 and executed in 1587. Nonetheless, in 1584, many people in England signed a Bond of Association promising to murder anyone (meaning Mary) who made an attempt on Elizabeth's life.

England seemed in the early 1580s to have few, if any, useful allies other than the Protestant rebels in the Netherlands. The French Huguenots were on the defensive against the Catholic League. The entente with Scotland was ruptured after the thirteen-year-old James VI threw off the tutelage of the Earl of Morton in 1579 and fell under the spell of Esmé Stewart, seigneur d'Aubigny, a French cousin who was believed to be attached to the Guise party in France. Although James was soon detached from his cousin, Scottish politics became unstable and unpredictable, as different Scottish lords – not to mention the Kirk – tried to obtain control of the King's person and to exercise power. In 1585, Elizabeth could not even be certain that James would not ally with Spain. No wonder then that Elizabeth and her government decided that they could not afford to see Antwerp fall to Parma or to allow a total Spanish victory in the Netherlands.

THE FINAL PHASE: 1585–1603

The final phase of Elizabeth's reign was dominated by war. For over fifteen years English armies were committed to fighting against Spain on a variety of fronts: the Netherlands, France and Portugal. At the same time, English navies, comprising royal and private shipping, were engaged in patrolling the Channel and undertaking privateering ventures that helped fund the expeditions on land. In the mid-1590s, ever-increasing numbers of soldiers were sent to repress rebellion in Ireland.

Of course, the English victory over the Spanish Armada is the best-known event of the war, and for centuries afterwards it assumed a mythic place in England's national history. Only towards the end of the twentieth century did historians begin to question the extent of the English victory under the command of Lord Admiral Howard of Effingham. It is now generally accepted that the English navy was unable to inflict serious damage on the Armada, while it sailed up the Channel and failed to destroy it in the all-day battle of Gravelines. The role of the Dutch in blockading Bruges and preventing Parma's troops from liaising with the Armada is also fully recognised today. Nonetheless, it is still true that England was saved from invasion in 1588 and that its navy played an important part in this success. English fire ships successful broke up the Armada formation, and afterwards the fighting power of the English fleet forced the battered Armada to sail northwards around Scotland and Ireland on a return journey that resulted in horrific losses of men and ships.

At the same time, historians now appreciate that the English victory was no major turning point in European history. As Paul Hammer shows in a later chapter, the English victory in 1588 was not followed up with other significant victories either on land or sea. Furthermore, Philip II soon rebuilt his navy, turning it into 'the largest battle fleet which had existed in Europe up to then', while the English navy remained 'too small to achieve supremacy outside home waters'.[2] Spain continued as the supreme military power in Europe for decades to come, until challenged in the seventeenth century by France; England stayed a second- or third-rate power until the eighteenth century.

The cost of warfare was enormous and could not be funded by the Queen's ordinary income or the spoils from privateering. The Continental war was expensive enough but once the Nine Years' War in Ireland broke out in 1594 the drain on the Crown's resources was colossal. Consequently the Queen had to resort to financial expedients such as selling lands, incurring debts, exploiting purveyance and requesting further subsidies from parliament. To avoid distributing land or annuities as part of her patronage, she extended the use of customs privileges and issued monopolies as political rewards. By this means, claims Simon Adams, she 'shifted the burden' of rewarding her servants 'from the crown to the commonwealth'.[3] The commonwealth was also expected to bear the burden of warfare by paying more dues and billeting troops, all this at a time when economic conditions severely deteriorated. As will be seen in a variety of later chapters, bad harvests, high prices, unemployment and new bouts of disease (plague and influenza) resulted in considerable social distress and turmoil after 1585.

Until recently, historians saw the 1590s as a time of political, as well as social, tensions, where 'factionalism' reared its head at court and in the council, bringing to an end the consensus politics of the 1570s and 1580s. Both Simon Adams and Wallace T. MacCaffrey, for example, detected an Essex faction and 'an anti-Cecil coalition' emerging in the early 1590s and engaging in a bitter struggle for power that culminated in an attempted 'coup' by Robert Devereux, 2nd Earl of Essex in 1601.[4] However, while recognising that political rivalries and disputes over policy often arose between the Cecils (Burghley and his son, Robert) and Robert Devereux, 2nd Earl of Essex, Natalie Mears questions in her chapter the existence of 'factionalism' before 1596. Up to that point, she writes, their rivalry 'did not constitute factionalism because there was no attempt by either Essex or Cecil to create a group of followers who owed exclusive loyalty to them in opposition to the other'. This is true. Furthermore, it should not be forgotten that, even though Essex and Robert Cecil sometimes disagreed over policy, they often collaborated until at least 1597.

During this period, the Cecils do not seem to have been engaged in a bitter power struggle with the Earl. When the men competed over patronage, the Cecils cannot be found working in an underhand way to prevent the promotion of Essex's friends. The Earl's lack of success in securing the offices of secretary for William Davison, of lord warden of the Cinque Ports for Robert Sidney, and attorney general for Francis Bacon was not because of Cecilian machinations but because the Queen thought, with good reason, that these men were unsuitable for the posts they wanted.

However, even if politics at the centre were no more 'factional' in the 1590s than they had been in the 1570s, they did seem to be more bad-tempered and less collegial. Essex's frustration at his failure to persuade Elizabeth to pursue a more aggressive military strategy on the Continent or to promote his friends made him an often disaffected presence on the council and at court. Overly sensitive and often paranoid, he seemed only too ready to believe that his failures were all Robert Cecil's fault; and he was encouraged in this delusion by his inner circle. Essex's extraordinary expressions of contempt for his sovereign when he could not get his own way, his explosion of anger in her presence and disobedience of her commands were new. Norfolk, Burghley, Leicester and Hatton would not have dreamt of behaving in so disrespectful a fashion; that Essex did reflected and contributed to a decline in the Queen's personal authority.

Elizabeth's last years saw a radicalisation of religion in the realm. Just as politics became more divisive, so religious lines hardened. Richard Hooker's defence of – you could almost say creation of – the Anglican position was provoked by his disputes with godly theologians such as William Travers in the 1580s. Archbishop Whitgift turned the mechanism of the Ecclesiastical High Commission against ministers who refused to swear to articles that bound them to his version of orthodoxy, forcing on them further radicalisation. In addition, Whitgift's attention to theological orthodoxy encouraged the emergence of a Calvinist orthodoxy in Cambridge and Oxford, which, in turn, spun into nasty disputes over how and when grace was procured, and if it could be lost. Although the Calvinists of Elizabeth's Church were at daggers drawn over such doctrines, they were all agreed in their distrust of their more moderate brethren, who held that a person could, by his actions, influence his salvation.

As the establishment became more insistent upon orthodoxy, more separatist groups appeared. These, as Peter Kaufman points out, claimed their right to lay participation and to separate into congregations of believers who could voluntarily follow the Gospel. No wonder they deeply irritated and alarmed the clerical establishment!

In the Catholic community, which was facing more and fiercer persecution, there were splits over leadership and ecclesiology. Some sided with the Jesuits, and others rejected them, struggling over whether there should be a secular archpriest to oversee England and whether Jesuits had to obey anyone other than their own order, or if secular priests would have to obey a Jesuit. These disputes incorporated battles over how to resist Elizabeth's Church. By late in the reign many Catholics were arguing that it was possible to get along with the State Church and were supporting moves towards toleration. But not all of them: those who insisted on resistance eventually produced the Gunpowder Plot of 1605.

CONCLUSION

It is evident from this introduction that political, religious, social and economic historians today do not view the Elizabethan period as a golden age. Most of the chapters that follow reinforce this interpretation, showing Elizabeth's reign to be marked by dynastic uncertainty, religious divisions, social tensions, economic difficulties and a cultural fear of disorder. To deal with these problems, the government was both repressive and authoritarian, interfering in the economic, social and cultural lives of the nation in a manner that today's society would call tyrannical. Nonetheless, as K. J. Kesselring acutely observes, 'much depends on one's vantage point'. Compared to France, Scotland and the Netherlands, England was a haven of religious peace and political order; and even Spain, which was less troubled by religious unrest, experienced two major revolts. The economic and social problems that accompanied population growth and long periods of warfare were not unique to England. Likewise, plague and harvest failures were endemic in early modern societies. The Elizabethan government – both central and local – tackled these problems with the same kinds of remedies that were attempted by governments elsewhere in Europe but apparently with a greater degree of success, for England was not rocked by the widespread urban and rural risings provoked by economic distress that took place in many other countries.

On the cultural side, though, it could be claimed that Elizabethan England did enjoy something of a golden age. Our contributors show that despite the decay or disappearance of some traditional rituals and celebrations (such as religious play cycles and church ales) England's cultural life was rich and dynamic during this period. An increasing number of professional playwrights produced dramas of ever-greater sophistication for London and provincial audiences. While literacy was by no means universal, it rose dramatically during the Elizabethan period and was increasingly expected of not just gentlemen but also men among the middling sort. The growth of a print culture encouraged the dissemination of ballads and songs for popular enjoyment, devotional works for edification and the exchange of ideas and information. Poetry permeated everyday life, and the better poets experimented with a much wider range of genres, and (as Steven May explains) they successfully used form and rhetoric to enhance meaning and the aesthetic experience. The innovative musical madrigals and airs of composers such as John Dowland, Thomas Morley and Thomas Weelkes also enjoyed great popularity. William Byrd, sometimes described as the Shakespeare of English music, wrote in a variety of genres, including sacred music, motets, verse anthems, songs, instrumental consorts and keyboard music. His influence on later generations of both English and Continental composers was immense. As far as art and architecture are concerned, the Elizabethan period saw an expansion in the production of secular paintings and buildings. Although the style has often been criticised by admirers of the Italian Renaissance, painters and builders developed a unique style that was innovative and readily identifiable. In all fields of culture, England built on its own vernacular traditions but was far from impervious to developments on the Continent, whether Netherlandish ornamentation, Italianate poetry or the general Renaissance emphasis on classical forms and texts.

William Camden, Elizabeth's first biographer, created a nostalgic Elizabethan world in the early seventeenth century. Within a decade of the old Queen's death, English people were looking at her age as a special time in the history of their nation. As our authors demonstrate, her reign was clearly a transitional time that saw the emergence of a stronger nation-state, of the national religion, and of economic and social changes that were formative for the nation of England, the United Kingdom and all the cultures of the Anglo zone. Elizabethan England may have been a small world, but it certainly earned a place in the history of the world.

FURTHER READING

Bonfield, L., Smith, R. and Wrightson, K. (eds), *The World We Have Gained: Histories of Population and Social Structure* (Oxford: Basil Blackwell, 1986).

Collinson, Patrick, *The Elizabethan Puritan Movement* (London, 1967).

—— *Godly People: Essays in English Puritanism and Protestantism* (London, 1984).

—— 'The Elizabethan Church and the New Religion', in Christopher Haigh (ed.), *The Reign of Elizabeth I* (Basingstoke, 1984), pp. 169–94.

—— *Elizabethan Essays* (London, 1994).

—— 'The Politics of Religion and the Religion of Politics in Elizabethan England', *Historical Research*, 82 (215) (2009): 74–92.

Elton, G. R., *The Parliament of England, 1559–1581* (Cambridge, 1986).

Haigh, Christopher, 'The Church of England, the Catholics and the People', in Christopher Haigh (ed.), *The Reign of Elizabeth I* (Basingstoke, 1984), pp. 195–220.

—— *English Reformations: Religion, Politics and Society under the Tudors* (Oxford, 1993).

—— 'The Taming of Reformation: Preachers, Pastors and Parishioners in Elizabethan and Early Stuart England', *History*, 85 (280) (2000): 572–88.

—— '"A Matter of Much Contention in the Realm": Parish Controversies over Communion Bread in Post-Reformation England', *History*, 88 (291) (2003): 393–404.

—— *The Plain Man's Pathways to Heaven: Kinds of Christianity in Post-Reformation England, 1570–1640* (Oxford, 2007).

Levine, G. and Wrightson, K., *The Making of an Industrial Society: Whickham 1560–1765* (Oxford: Oxford University Press, 1991).

MacCaffrey, Wallace T., *The Shaping of the Elizabethan Regime* (Princeton, NJ, 1968).

—— *Queen Elizabeth and the Making of Policy, 1572–1588* (Princeton, NJ, 1981).

—— *Elizabeth I: War and Politics, 1588–1603* (Princeton, NJ, 1992).

—— *Elizabeth I* (London, 1993).

Maltby, Judith D., *Prayer Book and People in Elizabethan and Early Stuart England* (Cambridge, 1998).

Neale, J. E., *Queen Elizabeth* (London, 1934).

—— *Elizabeth I and Her Parliaments*, 2 vols. (London, 1953–7).

Read, Conyers, *Mr. Secretary Walsingham and the Policy of Queen Elizabeth*, 3 vols. (Oxford, 1925).

—— *Mr. Secretary Cecil and Queen Elizabeth* (London, 1955).

—— *Lord Burghley and Queen Elizabeth* (London and New York, 1960).

Spufford, M., *Contrasting Communities: English Villagers in the Sixteenth and Seventeenth Centuries* (Cambridge: Cambridge University Press, 1974).

Wernham, R. B., *Before the Armada: The Growth of English Foreign Policy, 1485–1588* (London, 1966).

—— *The Making of Elizabethan Foreign Policy, 1558–1603* (Berkeley, Calif., 1980).

—— *After the Armada: Elizabethan England and the Struggle for Western Europe, 1588–1595* (Oxford, 1984).

—— *The Return of the Armadas: The Last Years of the Elizabethan War against Spain, 1595–1603* (Oxford, 1994).

Williams, Penry, *The Council in the Marches of Wales under Elizabeth I* (Cardiff, 1958).

—— *The Tudor Regime* (Oxford, 1979).

Wrightson, K. and Levine, D., *Poverty and Piety in an English Village: Terling, 1525–1700* (Oxford, Oxford University Press, 1995).

Wrigley, E. A. and Schofield, R. S., *The Population History of England, 1541–1871: A Reconstruction* (Cambridge: Cambridge University Press, 1989).

NOTES

1 Steven G. Ellis with Christopher Maginn, *The Making of the British Isles: The State of Britain and Ireland, 1450–1660* (Harlow, 2007), p. 234.

2 Jan Glete, *Warfare at Sea, 1500–1650: Maritime Conflicts and the Transformation of Europe* (London, 2002), pp. 161, 164.

3 Simon Adams, 'The Patronage of the Crown in English Politics', in John Guy (ed.), *The Reign of Elizabeth I: Court and Culture in the Last Decade* (Cambridge, 1995), pp. 20–45; p. 40.

4 Simon Adams, 'Eliza Enthroned? The Court and Its Politics', in Christopher Haigh (ed.), *The Reign of Elizabeth* (Basingstoke, 1984), pp. 55–77; p. 68.

PART I

GOVERNANCE AND POLITICS

CHAPTER TWO

GOVERNING ELIZABETHAN ENGLAND

Norman Jones

England's national government had a simple mandate: to keep the peace and defend the realm against external and internal enemies. Historically, the English people had, time after time, seen that peace broken by over-mighty subjects, and the Tudor monarchs worked hard to force them into obedience, but they walked a fine line since they had so little direct control over local governments. Those were in the hands of local aristocrats, oligarchs and landed gentlemen. They had to be encouraged to co-operate with the monarchy to enforce the law, keep the peace, collect the taxes and defend the realm.

The governance of Elizabethan England was about structures and hierarchies, but it was also about a world of personal connection, honour and expertise. Loosely formal, it depended heavily on the will, knowledge and motivation of a few hundred gentlemen and nobles for its effectiveness. It was guided by law and custom, but the understanding of these by the ruling classes determined what could actually be accomplished. Consequently, any discussion of Elizabethan government requires that a description of the formal points of contact be matched with a discussion of the way government was actually carried out through overlapping formal and informal grids of power. Other authors in the collection take up diverse parts of this system, but in this chapter we shall look from the top down.

Recent work on the state in early modern England has emphasised the role played by semi-independent local authorities and local people who used the state as a tool to solve particular local issues. Steve Hindle has argued that law was a lever in the hands of people who sought protection, increasing the power of the state from the grass roots up. As he says, early modern English governance was not arcane or remote. It was a process in which subjects were intimately involved and one which they learned to manipulate and even change in their own interest.

Michael Braddick and John Walters have argued in a similar fashion. They downplay the central institutions of the state, stressing instead the importance of the network of local officeholders who were instrumental in creating and evolving the ways in which the Crown's agencies worked. These agencies were set in a hierarchy and might appear to be distinct, but they were experienced as part of an organic local order. Together they created the basis for the early modern 'power grid'. Individuals' placing on this three-dimensional grid was determined by the number of hierarchies in which they participated and the degree to which their ranking within those separate hierarchies was mutually reinforcing.

This emphasis on the importance of the local negotiation and consumption of government has taken the focus off of the central state. Although Geoffrey Elton showed Thomas Cromwell and other proto-bureaucrats improving the agencies of central government as part of the 'Tudor Revolution in government', and Joel Hurstfield argued for a Tudor despotism, the new historiography now pays little attention to them. Moreover, Simon Adams's dismissal of faction as a political force in Elizabethan politics has taken the focus away from great ministers such as Burghley and Leicester. Patrick Collinson famously talked about the 'republic' of Swallowfield, and Phil Withington has explored the semi-autonomous powers of public deliberation and implementation practised by the oligarchies that governed the chartered boroughs. All of these scholars make the Crown's role look strangely passive within the state. And yet the Queen and her council did run what state there was, legitimatising the context within which negotiations of power took place. It is clear that the Queen and her ministers understood this negotiation. This chapter explores how government from the top orchestrated the co-operation given and necessarily relied on local authorities to enforce its bidding. It explores structures, the political culture of the nation and the managerial skill of its leadership.

THE MACHINERY OF GOVERNMENT

National government began with the Queen. All its functions were carried out in her name, and her favour empowered or disempowered those who governed. She was the essential fount of authority. The royal will was directed through the Privy Council, the group of powerful nobles and administrative experts who oversaw the Queen's government. Contrary to the practice of Queen Mary, Elizabeth's council was a small group of between eighteen and thirteen. It tended to shrink over time, too, concentrating power in fewer hands. These men served by royal appointment and drew much of their real power from association with the Queen, though they also had their own networks based upon their wealth and status. As Sir Robert Naunton, a younger Elizabethan with much experience of royal courts at home and abroad, observed:

> Her Ministers and Instruments of State, such as were *participes* and bare a great part of the burthen, were many, and those memorable, but they were onely Favorites, not Mimions [sic]; such as acted more by her own Princely rules and judgements, then by their own wills and appetites, which she observed to the last.[1]

The Privy Council was a remarkably stable group, dominated by Sir William Cecil, Principal Secretary of the Privy Council from 1558 until 1571, and then Lord Treasurer Burghley until his death in 1598. He was also master of the Court of Wards from 1561, giving him great influence over powerful families. Also important was Robert Dudley, Earl of Leicester, Elizabeth's personal favourite and, in the early 1560s, a leading candidate to be her husband. He became a member of the Privy Council in 1562, formal recognition of his already influential position. Dudley died in 1588, and there were others who rose to share in the power, such as Sir Christopher Hatton, supposedly a favourite because of his skill at dancing and flirting. Hatton became a privy councillor in 1577 and Lord Chancellor in 1587, despite his lack of legal experience. Sir Francis Walsingham replaced Burghley as Principal Secretary to the Privy Council in 1573. Referred to by Elizabeth as her 'Moor', Walsingham became an administrative linchpin until his death in 1590.

In the 1590s many of her old team died, and Burghley, increasingly decrepit, began transferring business to his son, Sir Robert Cecil. Robert would become Elizabeth's Principal Secretary in 1596. He and his father were accused by enemies of setting up a *regnum cecilianum,* making England their family business. When his father died in 1598, Robert also became Master of the Court of Wards. However, the Cecils had a great rival in young Robert Devereux, Earl of Essex. Before his revolt and execution in 1601, he used his place as favourite to install his adherents in positions of influence, creating factions in a court weakened by the old age of the Queen and Lord Burghley and jostled by a rising younger generation of hungry courtiers.

One of Elizabeth's important tasks was to rein in favourites and councillors who became over-mighty in the use of her name, for not all of them, as Naunton remarked, were to be found in the catalogue of saints. This she could do with exquisite verbal violence and the threat of removing their access to her royal person. These men, used to rule, had to be reminded that they were only tenants at will in her favour, which was only purchased by their good behaviour.

The Privy Council officially extended its authority through a stream of letters sent to local rulers. They were omnicompetent, mirroring the absolute authority of the Queen. They could meddle in anything, frequently inserting themselves into local affairs when either equity or prejudice demanded it. Through them passed the warrants, the Bills under the Great Seal, and other instruments that dealt with the Queen's property and expressed her influence at the local level. In any meeting they might create an ad-hoc commission to investigate anything, anywhere, approve a string of appointments to ecclesiastical benefices, grant licences to the keepers of alms houses to raise money, order a murder investigation, grant a licence to sell wine, pardon felons, forgive merchants who had forfeited their rights by marrying foreigners, or ensure the defence of the realm.

The business of the Privy Council was organised by its secretaries. Occasionally there were two of them, but for large parts of Elizabeth's reign there was only one. These secretaries were, in effect, the chief executive officers of the Crown in domestic and foreign affairs. As Sir Robert Cecil wrote, the secretary 'out of confidence and singular election has liberty to negotiate at discretion at home and abroad with friends and enemies, in all matters of speech and intelligence'. However, he remained at the mercy of the Queen, for 'The place of a secretary is dreadful if he serve not a constant prince, for he that liveth by trust, but to serve truly; so, he that liveth at mercy had need be careful in choice of his masters.'[2]

The secretaries served as the go-betweens for the Queen and the Privy Council, working with both at once in what was often a two-way balancing act. The Privy

Council functioned as a cabinet, but with ill-defined powers, and, ultimately, the Queen had to ratify its choices. It could recommend policy, but it was not free to act on its own. It was in the Council that many of those who were responsible for governing came together in a complex set of overlapping roles and duties. Many were powerful in their own right, with vast lands and extensive networks of patronage. Sir Nicholas Bacon is a good example. Lord Keeper from the accession until his death in 1579, he was the son of a sheep reeve who brought to the Council ties with several important circles. These included the connections created by extensive family properties in East Anglia, as well as links wrought by marriage and kinship networks – he was brother-in-law to Sir William Cecil, to Sir Thomas Gresham, the Crown's leading financial adviser, and to Francis Russell, 2nd Earl of Bedford. His brothers were powerful members of London livery companies. A religious reformer, he and Matthew Parker, Elizabeth's first Archbishop of Canterbury, had been student friends at Corpus Christi College in Cambridge. He was educated at Gray's Inn, and he had extensive legal connections through his work as a lawyer in the courts of augmentations and wards. As his wealth increased, so did his power in East Anglia.

Everyone on the council had multiple roles at multiple levels in local, regional and national government. That was one of the secrets of its effectiveness. It added influence and connection to the weight of its orders issued in the Queen's name. Moreover, it meant that their local knowledge could be brought to bear on locales through their supervision of special commissions. Generally including a few council members, these commissions required the local gentlemen to conduct investigations, such as those ordered in 1564 in every shire to look for tax evaders by noting whose wives wore satin-lined hoods. This required local observation, and it was a handy tool to discover who had enough money to support a horseman for the militia.

Another example of the Council's reach is that, joined by the chief justices of the courts of Queen's Bench and Common Pleas, it could function as the court of Star Chamber. Star Chamber was a popular court, as it was able to cross jurisdictional lines and to resolve disputes with simple procedures. It could not take life or property, so it mostly dealt with breaches of public order (especially violations of royal proclamations), enforcement of the law and the abuse of justice. Members of the council sitting in the Star Chamber heard more than 30,000 cases in Elizabeth's reign, giving the councillors an important perspective on the nation. There, their duties as managers and judges blended.

The Star Chamber sometimes functioned as a court of appeal, and the presence of the chief justices of Queen's Bench and Common Pleas underscores this. These justices presided over the common-law system used by Queen's Bench against felons and the equity system used in Common Pleas, which heard civil cases. Their courts joined with the court of Chancery, which had both common-law and equity aspects, to form the courts of record for the kingdom. All of these courts used cumbersome procedures, poached on one another's jurisdictions and required specialised lawyers, who could, in the case of common law, speak and write the arcane Law French of the Inns of Court. Equity courts functioned in Latin and English, but the central record was in Latin.

Chancery was an especially large and important court. Charged with seeing to it that right was done to subjects, it could apply principles of equity to cases in which common law applied a blind, rigid obsession with form over matter. Chancery also wrote, sealed with the Great Seal and recorded all the documents that authenticated royal grants, as well as the writs that began legal actions in other courts. As Elizabeth's reign went on, it became more and more bogged down, unable to keep up with the demand for enrolments.

The justices from all of these courts were used to working together. They often met together in the court of Exchequer chamber for formal consultation. Sometimes it was to advise the Queen on legal issues, and sometimes it was to work out reasonable solutions to problems of law. Of course, justices also sat as advisory members in the House of Lords, under writs of assistance, and they worked together on the assize circuits. Because royal justices went on assize, they travelled the nation and met its local leaders in ways that must have been useful to their colleagues. Many were also related by marriage – Lord Burghley and Lord Keeper Bacon were brothers-in-law as well as judges and members of the Privy Council. All of this encouraged more unity in action than is apparent in the organisation chart.

Complicating the legal system were the Councils of the Marches and the North, the government of the Duchy of Lancaster and the Stannary courts in Cornwall. John Cooper explores these bodies elsewhere in this volume, but it should be pointed out that their semi-independent status meant that they were tied to the Crown's government as much through the men appointed to run them as by reporting lines.

The Lord Treasurer of England sat in the Privy Council, which gave it an overlap with the processes of taxation and expenditure. He oversaw the machinery of tax collection as well as sitting in the court of the Exchequer, which had jurisdiction over revenues, such as customs duties and criminal fines, owed to the Crown. William Paulet, Marquess of Winchester, was Treasurer when Elizabeth came to the throne, holding the office until his death in 1572, when he was succeeded by Burghley, who held it until his death in 1598. It then passed to Thomas Sackville, Lord Buckhurst. All of them presided over a creaking system of finance.

On the revenue side, the bulk of the Crown's income was expected to come from rents on the Queen's properties, feudal dues, the 'profits of justice' and the clerical tax of first fruits and tenths. Theoretically, parliament only provided extra money through taxation in times of national emergency. However, the rapid inflation and increasing costs of defence meant that taxes and clerical subsidies were requested at almost all Elizabeth's parliaments and that there was never enough money. The situation was especially bad in the last decades of the reign when the continuous warfare – explored by Paul Hammer elsewhere in this volume – created fiscal crises.

Compounding the problems facing Elizabeth was the poor system of tax assessment and collection. The tax of fifteenths and tenths, levied on moveable property, and the subsidy, levied on income, were widely evaded and, even when paid, were badly under-assessed because of inflation. Deepening the problem was a primitive system of accounting. However, although the Council certainly understood the issues, it shied away from reassessment. It appears that councillors were unwilling to antagonise the gentlemen and aldermen who both collected and paid the taxes. Neither Winchester nor Burghley ever increased their personal assessments, and they did not seem inclined to increase others' valuations. Burghley seemed content to sell patents and monopolies to ensure the Crown's revenues without requiring greater administrative effort. These tax farms, and the system of informers that reported infractions in return for a share of the fines, essentially privatised collection of duties and enforcement of laws. Naturally, the farmers sought to maximise their revenue, creating intense public resentment that boiled over in the attack on monopolies in the Parliament of 1601.

The Church was a source of revenue, too, and the Crown had a complicated relationship with the bishops. The Acts of Supremacy and Uniformity passed in 1559 had restored the Crown's control of the Church by making Elizabeth its supreme governor in England and enforcing the use of the Book of Common Prayer in all churches. Statute law also gave the Queen the right to exchange property with bishops when their sees were vacant, providing a disincentive for appointing bishops. The tax of first fruits and tenths meant that clerical offices provided a regular income to the Crown. These, too, tended to be commuted to fixed annual payments to ensure easier accounting.

The Act of Supremacy granted the Queen the power to appoint commissioners to enforce the religious settlement. She did so in July of 1559, appointing the two archbishops and fifteen non-ecclesiastics to the commission. Given broad authority over religious matters, they dealt with 'abuses, offences, contempts and enormities, spiritual and ecclesiastical'.[3] By the 1580s, this commission had evolved into the court of High Commission which functioned as a regular court. The ecclesiastical commission had the advantage, for the Queen as well as for plaintiffs, that it covered the entire nation, reaching beyond particular dioceses. In Archbishop Whitgift's battles with dissenters, separatists and recusants this was distinctly useful, as was its procedure that required people to swear to tell the truth before being informed of charges against them.

The existence of this court underscores the fact that the bishops of the Church of England were now royal appointees, dependent in ways the secular magistrates were not on the goodwill of the Queen. They would fight a running battle with her to save their lands and authority, often losing. Nonetheless, bishops in their dioceses were great men, with great authority and responsibility, as well as their own official staffs who, in co-operation with the churchwardens of every parish, governed the spiritual lives of the people through the church courts.

Besides the bishops, sheriffs, justices riding assize circuits and lords lieutenant were the primary connectors between local governors in their 'countries' and the Queen's government. Sheriffs were charged with collecting money owed to the Crown, executing judicial writs, empanelling juries, arresting accused felons and traitors and keeping the county gaol. Appointed annually, being a sheriff was burdensome and expensive. It usually only came once in a gentleman's life, which meant that there were few highly practised sheriffs and that there were always a number of former sheriffs in the neighbourhood.

One Tudor innovation in local government was the office of lord lieutenant. Growing out of the need to muster troops efficiently in times of crisis, the appointments of the lords lieutenant began to be regularised in the 1550s. By later in Elizabeth's reign there were regular districts for them, not always corresponding with shire boundaries. Each lord lieutenant was expected to levy, muster, arm and command the militia in his district. He also had the unpleasant job of levying men for the wars and seeing to it that they were paid 'coat and conduct' money. Informally, the office became an important connection between the court and the localities, since the lords lieutenant served longer and could be expected to undertake other royal commissions as needed. The office was often held by aristocrats who already had great power in their localities, such as the Earl of Arundel in Sussex. But no matter what their title and authority, they still had to work with their gentry colleagues to achieve results, using all of the formal and cultural tools at their disposal.

Naturally, they nominated deputy lieutenants, who had to be local gentlemen approved by the council, to carry out the work. They often had to interpret the Privy Council's orders to suit local conditions. In 1586, the deputy lieutenants of Hertfordshire wrote to the council a belated response to articles and instructions their lord lieutenant, the Earl of Leicester, had forgotten to give them. Once they had the document, they were confused, because the orders talked about guarding the coast, and, as they truthfully reported, Hertfordshire has no coast. They apologised for not mustering the militia because harvest time and bad weather made it inconvenient. Although each of the justices of the peace (JPs) on the quorum was ordered by the council to provide a horseman armed with heavy pistols, the deputies were sure the council was mistaken, since the JPs were already paying for units of lances and light horse and could not afford to support more troopers. Therefore, the deputies sought clarification from the council. Told to keep careful watch on papists, they responded, 'God be thanked for it', that there were no wilful recusants in the shire.[4]

The deputy lieutenants and the captains that reported to them were, by late in the reign, organising 'trained bands' who were replacing the feudal levies. Although every man was still expected to own arms, and to practise regularly with the longbow, select companies were armed with more modern weapons and taught how to use them. About a tenth of the militia was in these bands so that, in 1588, the nation had an army of about 26,000 men with some level of training. Chosen from the respectable classes, they were not deployed overseas. Soldiers for Ireland and the Netherlands were pressed among vagabonds and prisoners.

All of these governing groups came together at the assize sessions. At these sessions prisoners accused of felonies and remanded to gaol by the quarter sessions, quarterly meetings of the JPs, were tried before the royal judges and local juries of twelve men. At the same time, a grand jury might be set up and instructed to make inquiries into particular issues, from which indictments could grow. At quarter sessions and assizes sermons were preached to the assembled crowd. These judicial sessions were a time when the Crown could communicate to the local justices what it wanted them to do, and the local men could communicate to the justices concerns to be carried back to London. The sessions were important expressions of the shared nature and responsibility of rule in the English state.

Lord Keeper Nicholas Bacon regularly addressed the justices about to depart on the circuit, giving them instructions to impart to the JPs. The messages he delivered were often about new laws, or concerns about poor enforcement of existing laws, but these lectures also contained reflections on the problem of getting JPs to act appropriately. Bacon told the justices in Hilary Term 1565:

> [I]t is to be feared that if out of the whole nomber of justices that nomber were taken out whiche do daylie their diligence more to serve the private affection of them selves and friendes as in over throwinge an enemye or mayneteyninge a frinde a servaunte or a covanante then to mayneteyne the comon good of their countrey respecting more the persons then the matters. And againe a seconde number deduced from the totall also conteyninge all such persons as keepe the name and place of a justice more for reputacion sake then for any care they have to parforme their office. . . . doubtless the remainder would be very small.

Bacon went on to invite the justices to join him in counselling the Queen to send letters to the JPs demanding that they certify how many people they had arrested for breaking the law, so that the 'drones' could be known from the bees, and the slackers could be punished 'to their ignominy'.[5] Ignominy may seem a strange punishment, but it affected a gentleman's honour to be criticised by the ruling community, making it an effective tool of government.

Tudor magistrates were expected to enforce the laws on the books, and some of the more conscientious bought Fitzherbert's *Justice of the Peace* or Lambard's *Eirenarchia* as handbooks to their duties and the relevant statutes. They were primarily reactive, however, just as the Crown was reactive. What did not threaten the peace was not their immediate concern, and they were generally reluctant to act when it would disturb the fabric of their community, since some statutes were intrusive and required a great deal of work to enforce.

The meaning of the law was often unclear, but, when it came to statute law, every man who was expected to enforce it was presumed to have been involved in making it. They, or their representatives, sat in parliament and accepted the principle that what they approved they should enforce. To an extent, it was also through parliament that communication was maintained with the magistracy, although its haphazard meetings were unpredictable. It did, however, give the ruling class a sense of participation in government that could be used to satisfy their fears and needs, just as they were expected to agree to things such as taxation through it. As David Dean notes in his chapter, parliament was the ultimate expression of the political theatre binding the ruling elite together. The Queen in parliament co-opted the ruling classes to obey and enforce the laws they made together as representatives of their brethren from Saint Michael's Mount to Berwick.

POLITICAL CULTURE

The magistrates' self-interests and political self-conceptions were played out within the constraints of law, custom, honour and community. At the heart of the secular political system were *ius* and *lex*, custom and law, which were venerated like revealed truth. The values and methods taught by the legal system bound the rulers' behaviour. For men of the magisterial classes, honour was essential to maintain and a guiding force in issues of government. Born into late-medieval conceptions of community and duty, Elizabethans were dealing with an increasingly self-aware and centralising state by adapting their inherited tools of governance.

Those tools had been shaped by the customs of feudal monarchy, which emphasised that governance was a duty of the man that held property and social rank, secular or ecclesiastic. Hierarchical, it rested on the Great Chain of Being, in theory, but one's place in the chain was affected by one's duties and one's wealth. Sir Thomas Smith, writing in the 1560s, justified hierarchy in a way that tied it directly to a person's role in the community. The upper classes, he said, ruled in the commonwealth

> as vertue of auncient race is easier to be obtained, for the example of the progenitors, for the abilitie to give to their race better education and bringing up for the enraced love of tenants and neybors to such noblemen and gentlemen, of whom they holde and by whom they doe dwell.[6]

It was a corollary, however, that men who had recognised skills or new wealth deserved to be moved up the hierarchy, giving Tudor England an 'open' elite connecting duty with position, so men of talent or power-giving riches moved into governance and from governance up the social ladder.

The basic qualification to be a JP was to hold property worth 40 shillings per annum. These were the same people eligible to sit in parliament, but appointment to the justices' bench and election to parliament were about station rather than party or policy; local authority remained in the hands of the leading families, often for generation after generation as they fulfilled their appointed role. This was so much the case that 'election' to parliament is better characterised as 'selection', since knights of the shires were, when the system was working properly, chosen by the leading county families. There were no campaigns, no platforms, and only a rudimentary shouting match served as an election. The result was that many of the men who served in parliament also sat on the county bench. They enforced the laws they made, and they made the laws based on their experiences.

If the county was governed by landed gentry who served out of place and duty, the towns were managed by oligarchs were played similar roles. Most aldermen and burgesses were chosen by the guilds and companies of their towns, and they oversaw justice, enforced the laws and selected members of parliament without reference to any constituency but their fellow freemen of the city.

Lower on the governmental scale were the truly local units of parishes and manors. As Henry French discusses elsewhere in this volume, their jurisdictions were evolving in Elizabeth's reign, with the parish becoming more useful as an arm of the Crown than was the manorial leet court, which had less flexibility. In all cases, however, these administrative units were run by the local elites. At this level, they were bound much more by custom, and they depended upon the local knowledge of the men who ran them. Elizabethan statutes expected the parish churchwardens to administer poor relief precisely because they were in a position to know who was deserving of help and who was not.

The key to this sort of self-governance was obedience arising from honour. The local magistracy had to be obedient to its betters, and, in theory, ultimately to the Queen. Since it was a voluntary system, willingness to obey had to be maintained. Concepts of honour and self-interest mixed into this obedience, since it was about one's place in society and one's duty: *noblesse oblige*.

The glue that bound the magistracy to their mistress was the deference due to a woman of high degree, destined by birth and divine providence to a reign ratified by parliament. All of this tied into the conceptions of personal honour that went along with a hierarchical society. Although the society was certainly patriarchal, obedience and deference were essential parts of its social psychology. Elizabeth, as she often reminded people, was a 'prince', and her father's daughter. As such, she commanded deference and expected obedience. Balancing the deference, however, was aristocratic honour. The gentlemen who were expected to run local government were very aware that lineage and service made one gentle, and it was this sensibility that created the interface of government. Service was expected as a duty, but honour had to be maintained.

Listen to the way in which William Parr, Marquess of Northampton, a member of the Privy Council, and Lord Lieutenant of Cambridgeshire and Buckinghamshire, tried to negotiate obedience to an order for a general muster. Writing to his deputies, he gently reprimanded them for their failure to hold proper musters, sending in old certificates of musters instead. Wondering if they were being legalistic or just forgetful, he expatiated on how he knew their loyalty to the Queen and their country; he explained how their disobedience 'toucheth me in estimation', and he urged them to consider how appreciative the Queen would be of their good service. If they did not do good service, however, he would rather hide their behaviour from Her Majesty than have her know of their dishonour. Pleading and shaming, he tried to get the command carried out.[7]

Mervyn James stressed the importance of concepts of lineage and honour to governance in the north, but William Palmer argues that this was a two-way street. The magistracy was in a Neoplatonic universe in which honour and duty flowed both towards and away from the centre. They may have had duties to their betters and their queen, but they also had duties to their families and localities that made their responses much more a matter of self-interest than is sometimes admitted. Concepts of honour, obedience, lineage and service certainly motivated people, but honours, and slight, were in the eyes of the beholder, just as when to serve and how enthusiastically was a calculation that related to values that were more localised than general. As Palmer says, ultimately it was about survival. Honour was a 'discourse tool' that could be used to justify behaviour.

Honour, of course, could prompt people to act outside or beyond the law. An offence might demand a response, as Lord Scrope reminded Francis Walsingham when he wrote of the situation on the northern border in 1583:

> That it wil be hard or rather impossible to stay her Majesties subjects from taking revenge – which yf yt should fall owt before the Borders be strengthened, yt is to bee looked for that the Scottes in requitall of anie such revenge taken, will attempt somewhat that may not in honour bee putt up, and so consequently breed such a breach of the amitie as will not easely be solved.[8]

In short, honour might require the local gentry to make war on the Scots, no matter what the Queen desired.

The Crown operated within this world of touchy honour, hierarchical and patriarchal conceptions, and amateur legalism, all of which structured issues of marriage, lineage, economic well-being and self-respect. This made governing an art requiring deft understanding of how to use these values to encourage co-operation among the governing classes and to prevent the sorts of disaffection that were so possible under the circumstances.

The Queen had an important role to play in this, since her favour was sought by all, and a slight from her could cause ill feelings to fester into resentment. Moreover, she was the *fons et origo* of patronage, and she took giving it seriously. Famously reluctant to spend money or give out titles, she, nonetheless, could if she was pleased. The hope of her pleasure kept men trying for her patronage, or for the patronage of her confidants, which might lead to her patronage. Performance in hopes of uncertain reward sums up the dance. Of course, patronage could be given by any person or corporation that had a source of revenue to allocate, and men on the make needed to attach themselves to someone who could help them. Was there a direct quid pro quo, in governance terms? Not usually, but when you took someone's gift, you owed service in return – and when you performed service, you hoped for tangible reward.

Having performed good service, you were in a position to petition for favour. Rewards included the use of a piece of property, the income of an office (generally held for life, no matter how one performed in it), the goods of forfeited felons, pensions, monopolies, patents and other instruments that brought with them revenues that were not directly paid by the Crown. These gifts were especially popular with Elizabeth because they cost nothing out of pocket and could be very lucrative to the recipient. For instance, the Earl of Leicester's 'farm' on the import of sweet wines was a nice reward for his service. He had to pay the Crown £6,000 per annum for the right to collect the customs on sweet wine, but it yielded a great deal more. His patent was valuable enough that he could mortgage it, to raise money for other purposes. After Leicester died, it passed to the Earl of Essex and then to Lord Treasurer Buckhurst, still farmed for £6,000, despite decades of inflation.

Francis Alford exemplifies the ways in which patronage and politics worked together, while demonstrating the uncertainty of reward that went along with a patron and client system. Alford was a civil lawyer trained in Oxford. A cousin of Lord Buckhurst, Francis's brother Roger was a trusted servant of William Cecil, and Francis knew some bishops from his days in Oxford, so he had friends in high places. He served in parliament nine times, too. Like all men of ambition, he was constantly seeking promotion through his powerful friends. He was suspected of being a Catholic – his wife was one – and his parliamentary speeches on Mary, Queen of Scots, showed undesirable moderation. Perhaps he was irritating, too, so his suits almost always failed, but he kept trying. In one letter to Burghley he neatly catches the misery of a client seeking patronage. Rejected in his suit to create an alms house out of a former chantry, he wrote 'that being refused by your Lordship in a very trifle I am greatly troubled, not for the importaunce or gaine of the thinge but that I hoped I stood in that good opinion and favor with your Lordship that in a reasonable sute I might have found favorable regard.'[9]

Alford may have been lucky to escape the burden of office. It was often worse to receive one, since you were expected to carry out its duties with money from your own pocket. The Queen might get around to repaying your expenses, but there was no guarantee that investment made in her service would be competently rewarded. People performed and hoped for preferment, but some ran up large debts on the Queen's behalf. Therefore, it was essential that the gentlemen 'pricked' for service had sufficient wealth to afford their duties. They were expected to spend it in service. In towns this sometimes resulted in men refusing office, since it was so ruinously expensive to pay for the expected feasts and festivities, as well as the increased running costs to their households as mayors and aldermen. But for those seeking honour and status, an appointment was confirmation of both. So was the ability to advance their families.

The interlocking layers of governance pressured magistrates to do their duty, but everyone understood that their enthusiasm for obedience could be sharpened or blunted by local and personal concerns. Dynastic and patronage issues were especially important in leveraging their co-operation.

Burghley knew this instinctively. His deep enthusiasm for genealogy made him a natural for the lucrative office of master of the Court of Wards and Liveries, which he held from 1561 until 1598. As master, he was charged with the welfare of minor sons and daughters of men who owed knight service to the Crown. The Court of Wards allocated guardianships, which meant that the children and their lands were leased for a fee, to the enrichment of the person who bought the wardship. The guardian also had the right to arrange the children's marriages. Becoming a guardian could be wildly lucrative, sometimes with returns in the thousands of per cent on the purchase, although the costs of getting one could also be high. Using this peculiar feudal court, Burghley could indirectly reward service and loyalty while influencing the families who either aspired to good marriages for their children or who were under the thumb of the court. As a way of rewarding service, it could grant a wardship without directly costing the Treasury a penny. This was clearly understood by Burghley, and he expressed it in writing when the Archbishop of Canterbury sought control of one of the Earl of Oxford's manors during his minority. The Earl was, at the time, Cecil's ward, but the Master of the Wards saw the politics of the case clearly. He concluded that although the case was legally odd, Oxford's inheritance could be used to please Parker. Doing so was of great importance, and it would cost the Crown nothing. He allowed Parker a third of the rent during the Earl's minority.[10]

Wardships were a form of patronage that was only loosely connected to the Queen, but which, stretching over the entire nation, gave Burghley influence, knowledge and money everywhere. It let him assert his influence on the future of lineages, helping families rise or fall in status. Burghley profited directly from this, as can be seen from his guardianship of the Earl of Oxford. Oxford was twelve when his father died in 1562, so Cecil had the use of his estates until he reached majority in 1571; in December of that year, Anne Cecil, at the Earl's request, married him. The marriage was a disaster, but it placed Burghley within the circle of the greatest aristocrats in the land, links that both confirmed his real power and gave him formal standing in society.

The importance of family connection in this small political world is suggested by random artefacts. For example, in 1592, Burghley took three pages of his little pocket diary to work out the genealogy of Richard Egerton, the father of Thomas Egerton. At that moment, Thomas, an illegitimate son, a reformed recusant and a very good lawyer, was a candidate for lord chancellor of England. Burghley, as was his custom, was doing his homework on the candidate, pondering his connections to other families, such as the Caves and the Champernowns. In the end, Egerton had to settle for the position of attorney general. We cannot know if his poor family connections were held against him, but it is obvious that Burghley cared.

That family was important as a political consideration we can see if we look at the complex ties between men who sat in Elizabeth's parliaments. Their biographies have all been written, allowing us to see their networks and their roles in local politics. What they tell us is that genealogical and geographical affinity was often more potent in encouraging action than religious affiliation. Added to this was sometimes membership of the small societies of Cambridge and Oxford colleges and the various inns of court. The leaders of Elizabeth's government in the first half of the reign were bound together by their 'Cambridge connection'. They had known one another at Cambridge and even had the same tutors. These sorts of ties meant that the men who governed existed within a tight web of connection that frequently gave them shared values – such as the Protestantism of the Cambridge men of the 1530s and 1540s – and shared interests. They married one another's sisters, invested together, served together in local government and frequently mustered together. Using them within their informal networks was a skill that Burghley had, being a beneficiary of the network himself.

The importance of informal networks that knit the court and the country together can be seen in the life of John Scudamore of Holme Lacey, the grandson of a John who had been *custos rotulorum* of Herefordshire and one of the people accused of recusancy by Bishop Scory of Hereford. Born into a good county family, he married well, with the support of Leicester, and, in his second marriage became a kinsman of the Queen. Made a JP for the county in 1569, he became a gentleman pensioner to the Queen in 1571, with an active role at court.

The reward for his activity at court came in his home country. Chosen as steward of Hereford, in opposition to a candidate proposed by the Earl of Essex, he was appointed to the Council of the Marches of Wales. As Bill Tighe has observed of him, his career illustrates the reciprocal relationship between courtiership and country status. He was exactly the sort of person whose loyalty, knowledge and connection could be use to promote royal government in the localities. He was a conduit for information and influence flowing between his two worlds.

One of the results of this informal networking is a lack of records. These men did not need to write down what they understood instinctively. At the same time, the system had the drawback that these networks were unlikely to push the interest of the central government before that of their 'country' and their families. They would have seen the task of the Crown as securing their property and interest.

EFFECTIVENESS OF GOVERNMENT

If the task of governing was expected to protect property and interest and to provide security and justice, did it succeed? Michael Pulman, in one of the only thorough attempts to understand the Privy Council's role, concluded that when it came to enforcing its own orders, the Privy Council 'found it extremely difficult to get things

– anything – done'.[11] Their orders often fell on deaf ears, and, since exhortation was seldom followed with other actions, it was hard to get local magistrates to listen. As far as he can discover, their scolding letters often ignored the real situation on the ground. A string of admonitions and threats to embarrass and dishonour the recipients often had little effect. If councillors wanted to frighten people into obedience, they did have the power to command attendance at the council, forcing a costly and indeterminate stay in London on the person summoned.

Of course, the failure to comply was often the fault of the council itself, since its orders were not always clear. In 1569, in the tense days before the Northern Rebellion, the council ordered all JPs to swear the Oath of Supremacy. However, they failed to explain what ought to be done with justices who refused to swear. In Hertfordshire, John Scudamore of Kenchurche would not take the Oath. He had made this clear in a letter to his fellow justices, but he was on the bench when oaths were being taken. 'For as much as your honours did not express your meaning unto us to deal with such recusants, we are much perplexed', wrote his fellow justices before, at Scudamore's own suggestion, placing him in the custody of the sheriff. He was not, at that time, removed from the bench.[12]

However, the system worked, almost because of the latitude growing from confusion. The Crown operated within the constraints and expectations of a system which had many informal aspects and which had limited aims. It succeeded because it was responsive to the needs and prejudices of the men of property and yet was accessible to people needing justice. It was responsive to crises, and it was incapable of being too intrusive. As Penry Williams observed, ad-hoc commissions and the manipulation of landowning influences were harnessed to energetic rule in the centre.

Elizabeth, Burghley and his colleagues on the Privy Council managed by using their knowledge of people and places, tools of honour and lineage, applications of the law, parliamentary persuasion, patronage and, sometimes, fear and love. The political culture taught them that connection and self-interest, in combination with law, duty and godly responsibility, worked together to keep the peace.

Within the hierarchical world of Elizabethan politics, the Queen and her ministers had to accept their place and allow all the other magistrates their own. In recognising their reciprocal duties they created a polity that worked, within its limited objectives, well enough to satisfy most of them, most of the time.

FURTHER READING

Bernard, G. W., *Power and Politics in Tudor England* (Aldershot, 2000).

Braddick, Michael J., *State Formation in Early Modern England, c. 1550–1700* (Cambridge, 2000).

Cromartie, Alan, *The Constitutionalist Revolution: An Essay on the History of England, 1450–1642* (Cambridge, 2006).

Cust, Richard, 'Honour and Politics in Early Stuart England: The Case of Beaumont V. Hastings', *Past and Present*, 149 (1) (1995): 57–94.

Elton, G. R., *The Tudor Constitution* (Cambridge, 1960).

Goldie, Mark, 'The Unacknowledged Republic: Officeholding in Early Modern England', in Tim Harris (ed.), *The Politics of the Excluded, c. 1500–1850* (Basingstoke, 2001), pp. 153–94.

Greir Evans, Florence M., *The Principal Secretary of State: A Survey of the Office from 1558 to 1680* (Manchester, 1923).
Heal, Felicity, 'Food Gifts, the Household and the Politics of Exchange in Early Modern England', *Past and Present,* 199 (1) (2008): 41–70.
Hindle, Steve, *The State and Social Change in Early Modern England, c. 1550–1640* (New York, 2000).
Hoak, Dale (ed.), *Tudor Political Culture* (Cambridge, 1995).
Hurstfield, Joel, *The Queen's Wards: Wardship and Marriage under Elizabeth I* (London, 1958).
—— *Freedom, Corruption and Government in Elizabethan England* (London, 1973).
James, Mervyn, *English Politics and the Concept of Honour, 1485–164.* Past and Present Supplements, 3 (Oxford, 1978).
Kishlansky, Mark A., *Parliamentary Selection: Social and Political Choice in Early Modern England* (Cambridge, 1986).
MacCaffrey, Wallace, *The Shaping of the Elizabethan Regime* (London, 1969).
McDiarmid, John F. (ed.), *The Monarchical Republic of Early Modern England: Essays in Response to Patrick Collinson* (Aldershot, 2007).
Pearson, Daphne, *Edmund De Vere (1550–1604): The Crisis and Consequences of Wardship* (Aldershot, 2005).
Pulman, Michael B., *The Elizabethan Privy Council in the Fifteen-Seventies* (Berkeley, Calif., 1971).
—— 'An Interjection of the Royal Prerogative into the Legal and Ecclesiastical Affairs of Cheshire in the Fifteen Seventies', *Albion,* 5 (3) (1973): 226–36.
Questier, Michael C., *Catholicism and Community in Early Modern England: Politics, Aristocratic Patronage and Religion, c. 1550–1640* (Cambridge, 2006).
Smith, Alan G. R., *The Government of Elizabethan England* (London, 1967).
Tighe, William, 'Country into Court, Court into Country: John Scudamore of Holme Lacy (c. 1542–1623) and His Circles', in Dale Hoak (ed.) *Tudor Political Culture* (Cambridge, 1995), pp. 157–78.
Wall, Alison, '"The Greatest Disgrace": The Making and Unmaking of JPs in Elizabethan and Jacobean England', *English Historical Review,* 119 (481) (2004), pp. 312–32.
Williams, Penry, *The Council in the Marches of Wales under Elizabeth* I (Cardiff, 1958).
—— *The Tudor Regime* (Oxford, 1979).
Withington, Phil, *The Politics of Commonwealth: Citizens and Freemen in Early Modern England* (Cambridge, 2005).
Wrightson, Keith, 'Two Concepts of Order: Justices, Constables and Jurymen in Seventeenth-Century England', in John Brewer and John Styles (eds.), *An Ungovernable People the English and Their Law in the Seventeenth and Eighteenth Centuries* (London, 1980), pp. 21–46.

NOTES

1 Robert Naunton, *Fragmenta Regalia; or, Observations on the Late Queen Elizabeth, Her Times and Favorits* (London, 1641), p. 6.
2 'The State and Dignity of a Secretary of State's Place', in *The Harleian Miscellany* (London, 1744–6), vol. II, p. 265.
3 1 Eliz. I, C. 1.
4 TNA SP 12/86, fols. 148–9.
5 San Marino, Henry E. Huntington Library, HM 1340, fols. 29–30.
6 Thomas Smith, *De republica anglorum: The Maner of Governement or Policie of the Realme of Englande* (1583), Chapter 20, ll. 9–20.

7 *Manuscripts of Lord Montague of Beaulieu*, Historical Manuscripts Commission (1900), pp. 9–11.

8 'Defence of the English Border (September 1583)', *Calendar of Border Papers*, vol. I: 1560–95 (1894), pp. 108–11, item 175. Available online at www.british-history.ac.uk/report.aspx?compid = 45747&strquery = honour (accessed 21 October 2008).

9 BL Lansdowne 55, fol. 196.

10 TNA Ward 9/129, fol. 145; cited in Daphne Pearson, *Edmund De Vere (1550–1604): The Crisis and Consequences of Wardship* (Aldershot, 2005), p. 35.

11 Michael Pulman, *The Elizabethan Privy Council in the Fifteen-Seventies* (Berkeley, Calif., 1971), p. 202.

12 TNA, SP 12/60/ fol. 6.

CHAPTER THREE

THE QUEEN

Susan Doran

Writing about Elizabeth I is not easy. This statement may seem absurd given the seemingly never-ending production of biographies of the Queen and studies of her reign. Nonetheless, it is true that any attempt to get behind royal decisions and to uncover the beliefs, attitudes, character and influence of Elizabeth encounters serious problems, not least because of the nature of the source materials. Unlike William Cecil, Lord Burghley, Elizabeth did not leave behind a wealth of memoranda that can reveal her thinking about the political issues of the day. Compared to her father, Henry VIII, her annotations on documents were few and sparse, so again it is difficult to separate her own views from those of her counsellors. Drafts of her letters were often in another person's hand, and we cannot know how far they represent her own or her secretary's work. Similarly, when amendments were made to drafts, and a final letter emerged in a different form, it is impossible to tell whether her wording or that of an adviser had prevailed. Elizabeth's letters were clearly a collaborative venture, but the process of co-production eludes, and sometimes divides, historians.

When it comes to Elizabeth's own literary productions – her poems, prayers and translated prose and verse – questions also have to be asked about authorship. Of the poems ascribed to Elizabeth, only two survive in her handwriting. Consequently, some scholars do not accept the remainder as her compositions and understandably dismiss them as unsafe indicators of her inner mind or literary talents. Attempts to uncover the nature of the Queen's religious belief and form of piety by studying the prayers she is thought to have composed have been subjected to similar criticisms. Because very few of the manuscript copies are definitely in her hand, many scholars consider it unwise to assume that the residue were royal compositions. Even those prayers in French, Italian, Greek, Latin and English that were copied out and contained in a tiny girdle book of devotions are not incontestably in the Queen's own hand and so are not incontrovertibly her own compositions. As a result, some scholars, such as Steven May and Henry Woudhuysen, question whether the prayers can indeed be treated as 'a glimpse, not otherwise readily available, into the inner life of Elizabeth' as W. P. Haugaard claimed some twenty-five years ago.[1] The status of the various devotional books that were printed under the Queen's

Figure 3.1 Frontispiece showing Queen Elizabeth I at prayer, from John Day's *Christian Prayers and Meditations*, 1569. Image © Lambeth Palace Library, London, UK/The Bridgeman Art Library.

name or using her authorial persona is equally problematic. Take the 1569 *Christian Prayers and Meditations.* Although the frontispiece depicts Elizabeth as its author by showing her in private prayer kneeling before a prie-dieu with her crown resting above an open prayer book (see Figure 3.1), she did not compose many (possibly any) of the prayers in the collection. Some were drawn from the 1559 liturgy while most were taken from Henry Bull's 1568 version of John Bradford's *Private Prayers and Meditations,* which in turn translated Juan Luis Vives' *Preces et meditationes diurnae.*

Although Elizabeth's speeches are some of the best known of her writings, they too require careful scrutiny and interpretation. As Leah Marcus has pointed out, there are several different extant versions of them, some of which may have been drafts for set speeches, that Elizabeth then delivered extemporaneously or from notes; others appear to have been written by auditors; still others were revised after their delivery, possibly by Elizabeth herself, for a particular audience in mind before they were printed or circulated. A couple of the most quoted passages – her 1559 assertion that she would want her epitaph to read 'A virgin pure untill her death' and the 1588 oration delivered before her troops at Tilbury – have reached historians from seventeenth-century printed adaptations and differ (in some places significantly) from contemporary manuscript versions. Once again, we cannot be certain about what exactly Elizabeth brought to the process of composition or what her listeners actually heard.

Moving from what Elizabeth wrote herself to what her contemporaries wrote about her creates another set of problems. So much of the contemporaneous literature is either sycophantic, self-seeking, propagandist or epideictic that it is often difficult to judge how much if any of its content is reliable: should we question, for example, the essence of Roger Ascham's seemingly overblown description of Elizabeth's linguistic talents – 'they be fewe in nomber in both the universities or els where in England, that be tonges comparable with her Majestie'?[2] His praise has usually been accepted uncritically, but, as modern scholars observe, Elizabeth's juvenile Latin shows 'she was an enthusiastic but hurried grammarian', while her mature writings in French, Italian, Latin and Greek 'are recurrently patterned on the form and word order of English'.[3]

Similarly, how are we to interpret descriptions of Elizabeth's conduct? After all, not only was she was always performing 'upon a stage for all the world to behould', as she herself admitted, but, even more problematically, her performance was written up and framed by writers with their own particular outlook and agenda.[4] What are we to make, for example, of Elizabeth's behaviour during the pre-coronation procession of 14 January 1559, as described in the pamphlet that was printed nine days afterwards by Richard Tothill and is thought to have been written by Richard Mulcaster? Some scholars (including John Neale and more recently Kevin Sharpe) treat the text as an accurate account of the pageants, the Queen's conduct and her reception by the crowd, while others (notably William Leahy) dismiss it as an utterly unreliable text because of its 'ideological positioning' as a work of governmental propaganda.

In part because of a growing awareness of these kinds of difficulties with the sources, scholars have recently tended to focus on the 'Elizabethan regime' rather than the Queen herself, concentrating on its structure, politics and personnel. As Patrick Collinson recently noted, 'the essence of this new approach . . . is to be less Queen fixated'.[5] The writers of the other chapters in this section of the book do just this and examine the personnel and institutions of government, but this essay is unfashionably and unashamedly 'queen fixated'. I try to locate Elizabeth's views on some key matters of state, in particular those on which she had views clearly distinct from many within her government. I then go on to discuss issues related to the question of her image, as projected by herself and her subjects. Because space is short, I have chosen to assume rather than demonstrate that Elizabeth retained the prerogatives of royal power and that her views and actions were essential to the policy-making process.

RELIGION

Despite the problems outlined above, Elizabeth's statements and actions are sufficiently consistent to allow us to say something meaningful about her religious beliefs, policy and style of piety. All historians now recognise that she was a committed Protestant. Of course, as the daughter of Henry VIII and Anne Boleyn, she had a vested interest in denying papal authority, but as a young princess she had also seemed comfortable in the atmosphere of evangelical piety at Edward VI's court, where she presented herself as a devout Protestant princess, dressing modestly, translating psalms and reading the vernacular Bible. Edmund Allen, the evangelical catechist, was her chaplain, and Johannes Spithovius, a pupil of Melanchthon's, became a member of her household during this period. Like many other high-profile Protestants, Elizabeth attended mass under Mary, but she conformed with public bad grace and turned a blind eye to her servants' non-attendance. Furthermore, while under house arrest at Woodstock, Elizabeth demanded an English bible, even though such devotion to 'the Word of God' at that time was associated with heresy. Consequently, Protestants at home and on the Continent were elated when Elizabeth succeeded to the throne, believing that she would bring the 'days of darkness' under her predecessor to an end. During the period of the Marian persecutions, 'we wisht for our Elizabeth', Thomas Brice repeated some seventy-two times in his verse register of the Marian martyrs printed in 1559 (once at the end of each stanza), until eventually 'God sent us our Elizabeth'.[6]

Despite these expectations, during her first few weeks on the throne, Elizabeth revealed little about her future intentions concerning a church settlement. In the proclamation announcing her accession, for example, she ordered her subjects 'not to attempt upon any pretense the breach, alteration, or change of any order or usage, presently established within this our realm'.[7] Consequently, Catholic masses continued to be celebrated in England's churches, while a requiem mass was held for the departed Mary at Westminster Abbey on 13 December. The Catholic bishops who had survived the epidemics of 1558 were left undisturbed in their sees, while some eleven ex-Marian councillors, including Archbishop Nicholas Heath of York, were reappointed to Elizabeth's Privy Council. So, although the heresy trials had ceased and accused heretics were released from prison, there was no immediate public sign that Elizabeth would re-establish a Protestant church in England.

Yet, a closer look at the composition of her Privy Council indicates that Elizabeth favoured religious change from the outset. Of the ex-Marian councillors reappointed, nine had served for a time under Edward VI and were therefore thought not to be Catholic ideologues; of the remaining two, the Catholic Earl of Derby was unlikely to attend meetings regularly but too powerful to ignore, while Heath was thought (albeit mistakenly) to be a moderate who would conform to the royal will. The nine new council members were all Protestants, and most of them had previously sat on Edward VI's council. Two (Francis Earl of Bedford and Sir Francis Knollys) had gone into exile under Mary while two others (Sir Edward Rogers and William Parr, now restored to his title of Marquess of Northampton) had spent time in prison during the Marian years.

Towards the end of December, Elizabeth signalled her intention to introduce a new reformation. Probably, by that time, she felt more confident that no rival

Catholic claimant to the throne would materialise. Furthermore, there was good reason to expect that the Habsburgs would not abandon their alliance with England, provided that she did not move her church in too radical a direction. After all, the Holy Roman Emperor had recently agreed to a political settlement (the 1555 Peace of Augsburg) that recognised the right of the German princes to organise their own churches along Lutheran lines, so why should the Habsburgs not accept her right to do the same?

Elizabeth's earliest public action came on Christmas Day 1558 when she famously 'rose and departed' from the chapel royal straight after the reading of the Gospel and before the adoration of the sacrament, because the officiant refused to follow her instructions not to elevate the host.[8] Two days later, Elizabeth issued a proclamation which not only ordered that the Litany, Lord's Prayer and Creed should henceforth be recited in English, but more importantly intimated that a parliament would soon be held to discuss and introduce changes in 'matters and ceremonies of religion'.[9] Then, at her coronation on 15 January 1559, the eucharist service was taken by the new dean of the chapel royal (George Carew) who almost certainly consecrated the host in English and did not elevate it for adoration. Elizabeth's coronation oath, moreover, closely followed the novel one devised by Archbishop Cranmer for Edward VI, and, if Dale Hoak is correct in his analysis, Cecil inserted an extra line in the oath whereby the Queen swore to act 'according to the Laws of God, [and] the true profession of the Gospel established in this Kingdom'. This new form of words had a distinct Protestant flavour.[10] Meanwhile, the previous day's coronation pageants – arranged by the citizens of London but approved by the Queen and council – were full of Protestant imagery and conveyed a clear message to the audience about the government's future plans; as one observer (the Mantuan Il Schifanoya) explained, the pageant held at Conduit purported to show 'that hitherto religion had been misunderstood and misdirected, and that now it will proceed on a better footing'.[11] According to Mulcaster's pamphlet, the other pageants were equally Protestant in their message. Whether or not his text was totally accurate does not matter greatly; what is important is that a semi-official account of the procession printed in January 1559 presented Elizabeth as a Protestant queen and signalled that her government intended religious change.

But what kind of change would Elizabeth introduce? Here historians are uncertain. Today, few, if any, accept Neale's interpretation that Elizabeth wanted to establish a Henrician rather than an Edwardian church in 1559. As already shown, Elizabeth gave every indication that she intended more substantial change and that her personal religion was not simply reformist or evangelical. Unlike her father, she clearly accepted justification by faith alone and rejected transubstantiation. However, it is less apparent whether Elizabeth wanted a religious settlement based on Edward VI's 1549 Prayer Book, which was Lutheran in tone, or one based on the 1552 Prayer Book, which reflected the doctrines and liturgy of the Swiss Reformed churches. In 1982, Norman Jones argued that she always intended to have the second Prayer Book. However, more recently, Roger Bowers claimed that she originally wanted the restoration of the 1549 liturgy but had to change direction sometime in late March 1559 when she realised that she could not command the political support for a more Lutheran settlement. The evidence to support Bowers' interpretation is now pretty much discredited, and historians think it improbable that the settlement that emerged in April 1559 was any different from that proposed to parliament the previous February. Nevertheless, it does seem likely that Elizabeth favoured the ceremonial of the 1549 liturgy and the theology of the corporeal presence that informed its communion service. Furthermore, Elizabeth was aware of the obvious political advantages in associating her church with the Lutheran Confession which was internationally the more acceptable face of Protestantism. At any rate, early in 1559, the German Lutheran Margrave Albert of Brandenburg believed that Elizabeth intended 'to profess the Confession of Augsburg', while the Lutheran reformer, Paulus Vergerius, informed Duke Christopher of Wurtemburg that she 'is minded to institute and restore religion *iuxta Confessionem Augustanam*'.[12] At various times during the early years of her reign, Elizabeth hinted that she liked the Augsburg Confession (the confession of faith of the Lutheran church) and accepted its understanding of the corporeal presence in the eucharist.

Elizabeth's conduct during her coronation procession also indicated that she was more moderate in her Protestantism than some of her more zealous subjects would have wished. Although Mulcaster pointed to 'two principal signes' of the new queen's godliness, they hardly indicated that she intended a radical reformation during her reign. Take the first sign, that is, the prayer she uttered at the Tower of London in which she compared herself to the prophet Daniel delivered by God out of the lion's den. While this point of comparison may have been partially inspired by the presence of lions in the zoo at the Tower, her decision to define herself as the essentially passive Daniel rather than as one of the more assertive Old Testament enemies of idolatry (such as Kings David or Josiah or the judge Deborah) was surely deliberate and significant. The prayer, moreover, noticeably concentrated on how God had treated her so 'wonderfully and mercifully' but said nothing about her duty to God. The second sign, namely Elizabeth's enthusiastic reception of the English bible at the Little Conduit in Cheapside, certainly signified a love of *verbum dei,* but many Protestants might have been even better pleased had she displayed a similar fervour at the pageant that represented her as a new Deborah. According to Mulcaster's account, at the fifth and last pageant, which depicted 'Deborah with her Estates Consulting for the Good Government of Israel', a young boy spoke out to explain that Israel's sole female judge was a 'worthy precedent' for the Queen, since God had chosen both women to rule in order to carry out his purpose of removing idolatry from the land. The child's verse then went on to imply that if Elizabeth followed Deborah's example – ruled justly and put her Canaanite foes (i.e. Catholics) to flight – then she too would enjoy a long and happy period of rule. But Mulcaster made no mention of Elizabeth's reaction to *this* speech; we have to assume therefore that she simply swallowed hard and moved on.

Consequently, discerning readers of the Mulcaster pamphlet should have been unsurprised that the Elizabethan religious settlement of 1559 did not in fact cleanse the realm of idolatry or introduce a style of worship similar to that found in the best Reformed churches on the Continent. Although the 1559 Act of Uniformity swept away the Latin mass and reintroduced the Edwardian Prayer Book of 1552 with only minor modifications, the changes in the communion service harked back to 1549 in three important respects: the new words recited by the minister on delivering the bread and wine allowed the possibility of belief in a corporeal presence; the omission of the 'black rubric' removed the disclaimer that kneeling at communion implied adoration; and ministers were expected to wear copes. It would be perverse not to accept that these changes were the result of Elizabeth's direct influence, especially as the royal injunctions of July 1559 reinforced the conservative features and retained other practices present in the 1549 liturgy that were evidently dear to her heart. In the injunctions, the corporeal presence was implied in the reference to 'the communion of the very Body and Blood' and in the order that wafers rather than ordinary bread be used in the service. The injunction on images moved away from the total ban of the late Edwardian years and only prohibited those that encouraged 'all superstition and hypocrisy'; as a result, Elizabeth could continue to have a silver crucifix in her chapel during the 1560s, to the dismay of many Protestants.[13] There is some evidence that the Queen also wanted to retain altars but, if so, she had to give way on this point. She proved better able to protect liturgical music in the injunction that made provision for choirs in collegiate churches and cathedrals. Her conservatism on all these matters did not mean that she was either sympathetic to Catholicism or seeking to persuade Catholics that she was. Again, we can see her in tune with the Lutheran Confession. For Luther, altars, images, music and ornaments were adiaphora (non-essential matters of faith) and were consequently retained in many Lutheran churches of Scandinavia and North Germany.

Elizabeth was confident and outspoken about her Protestant credentials. She justified her church to Catholics abroad on the grounds that its doctrine and liturgy were based on the Scriptures, while she portrayed herself to her subjects as the enemy of ignorance and superstition (code for Catholicism). For example, the royal preface to the first Book of Homilies issued in 1559 explained that the sermons should be read to drive away 'erroneous and poysoned doctrines tending to superstition and Idolatry'.[14] Similarly, in the preface to the 1559 royal injunctions, she spelled out that the orders were intended for 'the advancement of the true honor of Almighty God, the suppression of superstition . . . and to plant true religion'.[15] However, that particular statement displayed, and accurately revealed, a set of priorities that distinguished her from her later Protestant critics, for it mentioned the honour of God both separately from, and positioned before, the removal of superstitions. Elizabeth was thus able to defend practices that other Protestants deemed superstitious, such as kneeling at times of supplication, bowing at the name of Jesus and using wafers at communion – all on the grounds that 'Almighty God is at all times to be honoured with all manner of reverence that may be devised.'[16]

The importance of showing reverence before God was a common theme for Elizabeth and seems to have been a deeply felt dimension to her personal piety. She enjoined it in special sets of prayers authorised for use in times of emergency, and it was probably through her influence that 'reverence' to God was strongly emphasised in the revised Book of Homilies produced in 1563. While the reformers in convocation overruled her objections and included a condemnation of all images as idolatrous in the third homily, the Queen apparently left her mark on the book with the introduction of the first and second homilies which dealt with 'the right use of the Church or Temple of God and of the reverence due unto the same'. Irreverence in church, as defined in the second homily, was not just unseemly chatter during the service but included a parishioner's failure or refusal to participate in communal worship properly; reverence to God, it explained, required silent and diligent attention to the minister reading from the Book of Common Prayer, 'which cannot be when every man and woman . . . prayeth privately, one askyng, another gevyng thankes, another readyng doctrine'. Reverence also involved taking communion appropriately and not as if one was eating and drinking at home; in other words, according to the Queen, it should be taken kneeling rather than sitting or standing.[17]

In addition to the emphasis on reverence, Elizabeth's own brand of Protestantism, as expressed in her writings, tended to repeat certain themes: her belief in justification by faith alone, but suspicion of predestinarianism; a preference for the reading of set prayers or passages from scripture over preaching; her providential right to rule and her subjects' obligation to obey; her wish to sustain peace, charity and harmony within her realm and her corresponding dislike of division and disunity; and an unwillingness to open up debate over matters of doctrine that 'some thinks a thing, some other, whose judgment is best God knows'.[18] While there is no reason to doubt Elizabeth's spiritual commitment to these principles, they unquestionably had a political dimension too, sitting easily with the royal supremacy, the divine right of kings and a culture of obedience, including conformity to the Book of Common Prayer. No wonder Elizabeth found herself at odds with the 'godly' and that she was prepared to tolerate Catholics, provided that they externally conformed and displayed loyalty to the Crown.

MARRIAGE AND SUCCESSION

Scholars remain divided over whether or not Elizabeth deliberately chose to remain single. Relying largely on some of her own statements, many biographers are convinced that the Queen resolved from the outset of her reign (and possibly even earlier) that she would never marry, either as the result of a psychological reaction to childhood traumas or because she believed that marriage for a female ruler was incompatible with power. However, other scholars, including myself, judge Elizabeth's position to have been more flexible, and we interpret her statements as far more provisional in their tone. In her famous 1559 speech to parliament, where she asserted that she was well contented with her unmarried state and declared that she would be content for her tombstone to say that she 'lived and dyed a virgin', she nonetheless admitted the possibility that 'it may please God to enclyne my harte to an other kynd of life'. After this, it took another twenty-seven years before Elizabeth again referred to herself as a virgin in a public setting. By that time, the question of her marriage was no longer a live political issue, and in the speech she was simply voicing her concerns about ordering the execution of Mary Stuart: 'What will theie not now say, when it shall be spread, that for the safetie of her life, a maiden Quene could be content to spill the blood even of her owne kinswoman?' she asked her parliament on 24 November 1586.[19]

Otherwise, Elizabeth announced that she was prepared to marry in order to satisfy her subjects and to safeguard the succession. On 10 April 1563, in her draft speech to parliament, she wrote:

> And by the way, if any here dowte that I am, as it wer, by vowe or determination bent never to trade that life, pute oute that heresie; your belefe is awry, for as I think it best for a privat woman, so do I strive with my selfe to thinke it not mete for a prince, and if I can bend my wyl to your need, I wyl not resist suche a mynde.[20]

Similarly, in November 1566, she announced:

> I saye ageyn, I wyll marrye assone as I can convenyentlye, yf God take not hym awaye with whom I mynde to marrye, or my self, or els sum othere great lette happen. I can saye no more exept the partie were presente. And I hope to have chylderne, otherwyse I wolde never marrie.[21]

In addition to expressing her willingness to marry for the good of the realm, Elizabeth convinced observers at court that she *wanted* to marry on at least two occasions: the first was between late 1560 and early 1561, when the favoured suitor was Lord Robert Dudley; the second was between 1578 and 1581, when a dynastic marriage alliance with François, Duc d'Anjou, was discussed. Elizabeth was obviously attracted to Dudley and hoped that marriage to him would produce a Protestant heir. However, the harm that this marriage would do to her reputation finally scuppered the match, since not only was Dudley's lineage undistinguished, but, more importantly, scandalous rumours circulated that he had murdered his wife so that he could marry the Queen. As for the Anjou match, although the need for an heir was raised by its supporters, the succession issue did not motivate the Queen. She initially wanted the marriage to sort out an intractable set of international problems arising from the revolt of the Netherlands against Spain; and then in 1581 she resumed the match in order to forge an alliance with France against Spain. In fact, the prospect of Elizabeth becoming pregnant was a serious drawback to the match, as the danger of a woman over forty-five dying in childbirth was considerable.

Elizabeth pushed hard for the Anjou marriage; in addition to its perceived political advantages, she liked Anjou when they met and probably believed that she could control the much younger man. However, strong opposition in the Privy Council, the court and the country at large eventually convinced her that marriage to a French Catholic who insisted upon access to a private mass would erode her popularity and endanger her security. Although Elizabeth always asserted that her choice of husband was her own private decision, she ultimately could not ignore her subjects' feelings on the matter. Wyatt's rebellion of 1554 and the deposition of Mary, Queen of Scots, in 1567 had supplied recent and alarming lessons about the dangers of making an unpopular marriage.

Throughout the royal matrimonial negotiations during her reign, Elizabeth's behaviour was remarkably consistent. She quickly dismissed those candidates in whom she had no interest: the Duke of Savoy, Philip II, the Duke of Holstein,

Prince Eric of Sweden, the Earl of Arran and more besides. Those candidates whom she considered more suitable were told that she needed to see them in person, and, while this demand may have been a delaying tactic, it is just as likely that Elizabeth was determined to avoid a disastrous and humiliating marriage such as her father's brief union with Anne of Cleves. Once negotiations for a marriage proceeded, the discussions centred on the terms of Mary I's matrimonial treaty with Philip of Spain, and Elizabeth would not budge from the 1553 articles that totally excluded the royal consort from political power and made him responsible for the payment of his household. On the question of religion, Elizabeth was adamant that her husband should attend Protestant services and be denied the mass in England; only in the case of François d'Anjou was she prepared to waive the latter condition. All the negotiations with foreign Catholic princes, however, foundered on the rock of religion.

Elizabeth considered the topic of her marriage to be an *arcana imperii* (a mystery of state) that was consequently outside the competence of parliament or public debate. As a result, she was incensed when John Stubbs published his pamphlet *The Discoverie of a Gaping Gulf* against the Anjou match in 1579. Apart from railing against its content, she condemned the book as a popular libel that gave ordinary subjects 'authority to argue and determine in every blind corner at their several wills of the affairs of public estate, a thing most pernicious in any state'.[22] The punishment Elizabeth meted out to Stubbs and his associates was draconian; each lost a hand. By contrast, she took no action against Philip Sidney, even though his manuscript 'Letter to Queen Elizabeth' against the Anjou marriage was equally unwelcome. Her forbearance towards Sidney was because his 'Letter' was deferential in tone, limited in circulation and dressed up as a courtier's private counsel to the Queen.

Like the marriage issue, Elizabeth considered the succession to be a matter for the royal prerogative and outside the arena of public debate. She consequently reacted angrily when a pamphlet on the succession was published in 1563 and even considered indicting its author, John Hales, for initiating a debate on the issue. On the grounds that 'yt ys monstruous that the ffeete sholde dyrecte the hed', she forbade parliament to discuss the succession on its own initiative, petition her to name an heir or attempt to exclude certain candidates. If there was ever a good time to tackle the succession, she told the 1566 Parliament, 'I wyll deale therein for your saftye and offer it unto yow as your prynce and hed withowt request'.[23] Nonetheless, Elizabeth could not deny that parliament had the right to authorise the line of succession; after all, her own title to the throne was so dependent upon parliamentary authority. For this reason she assented to the 1571 Treasons Act that made it high treason during Elizabeth's lifetime, and a lesser offence once she was dead, to refute the right of the Queen in parliament to decide upon the succession.

But Elizabeth would not settle the succession. She consistently gave the same reasons for her refusal, sometimes to parliament and, on two occasions in 1561, to the Scottish ambassador. In the first place, she contended, nominating a successor would encourage political instability: 'it is to be feared that if they [my subjects] knew a certain successor of our crown they would have recourse thither'. Drawing on her own experience during her half-sister's reign, she feared that an heir presumptive might become the focus of plots or the centre of an alternative court while she was still alive. Second, 'there be so manye competytors' that it would not be easy to decide between them. Disputes would arise and errors might be made – as indeed, she pointed out scathingly, they had been in 1553 when doctors of divinity had 'openly preached and sette forthe that my systere and I were bastardes'. Third, 'princes cannot like their own children, those that should succeed unto them'. This fact would make life very difficult for any heir who was Elizabeth's own subject and would trouble her relationships with a foreign ruler, such as Mary, Queen of Scots, or her son James. Then, because it 'is hard to bind princes by any security where hope is offered of a kingdom', these two Scottish monarchs might well carry out independent policies that were against England's interests or provide assistance to Elizabeth's enemies in the hope of obtaining the throne before her death. Finally, there was no assurance at all that Elizabeth's nomination would resolve the succession issue. Henry VIII had tried and failed to end debate about it in the 1544 statute and his will, while Edward VI's attempt to exclude his sisters had fallen through. Ultimately, 'when I am dead, they shall succeed that has most right,' Elizabeth stated confidently, presumably (she thought) through the agency of a divine providence that had secured her own position on the throne.[24]

Nonetheless, although Elizabeth refused to name her heir, she did endeavour to ease the way for a Stuart succession. Indeed, her strong objections to parliament discussing the issue during the 1560s arose in part because of the Commons' hostility to Mary, Queen of Scots. Unlike her Protestant subjects, Elizabeth believed that Mary had the best claim to the throne; as she confessed to the Scottish ambassador in 1561, 'I here protest to you in the presence of God I (for my part) know none better, nor that myself would prefer to her.'[25] Elizabeth accordingly did her utmost to protect the Stuart claim. Apart from refusing to listen to parliamentary petitions that she exclude Mary from the succession, Elizabeth put obstacles in the way of rival claims. In 1561, she sent Katherine Grey, Mary's main competitor, to the Tower after she was found to be pregnant, and later Elizabeth exerted her influence so that an ecclesiastical commission would judge Katherine's clandestine marriage invalid and declare her two sons bastards. In 1564, Elizabeth tried to make Mary's eventual succession more acceptable in England by proposing (albeit unrealistically) that she marry Robert Dudley, newly raised to the earldom of Leicester. While Mary was imprisoned in Lochleven Castle on July 1567, Elizabeth even thought of adopting her infant son and having him educated in England where he would learn about his future kingdom. Admittedly, this plan was a desperate device to prevent James from being conveyed to France, but it again demonstrated Elizabeth's recognition of the strength of the Stuart claim by right of primogeniture. After James remained in Scotland and took on Mary's kingship, Elizabeth would have no talk of the succession; excluding Mary, as her parliament and most of her ministers wanted, threatened the principle of the divine right of kings.

Once Mary had been executed, Elizabeth could have named James VI her heir without inciting serious protest at home; as a Protestant male, James was an acceptable future king to many in England despite his nationality and upbringing. However, Elizabeth thought it better to keep everyone in suspense for she trusted neither James nor her subjects. The latter might be attracted to the rising sun, while the former displayed too independent a mind for her to feel safe. So Elizabeth dangled the prospects of the succession before James to encourage his good behaviour towards her and the realm but refused to name him heir notwithstanding his repeated requests. Besides the political dangers involved, such a volte-face would not be easy for a monarch who so highly prized the virtue of constancy and whose personal motto was *semper eadem* (always the same).

IMAGE

Today's scholars generally doubt the existence of a 'cult of Elizabeth' and dismiss E. C. Wilson's view (as developed in his influential 1939 publication, *England's Eliza*) that the many flattering portraits and lavish poetical praise of the Queen amounted to spontaneous expressions of adoration. We are now only too aware that a narrow elite commissioned these works and usually for self-interested ends. Furthermore, they do not tell the whole story, for criticisms of the Queen were voiced by many of her subjects whether courtiers, preachers or members of the commons that were often dressed up and disguised as praise.

Scholars today also question Roy Strong's argument that the Queen and her government developed a personality cult around Elizabeth as part of its propaganda 'to buttress public order' and to ensure her subjects' loyalty and obedience in the absence of a standing army and police force.[26] We now recognise that multiple and sometimes contradictory images of the Queen existed rather than a uniform 'cult' stimulated or fashioned by the regime. The royal image was created by people with different purposes and audiences in mind. The creative process, moreover, was often a collaborative exercise; for example, the manuscript and printed texts of courtly entertainments had input from patrons, actors, musicians, the Queen and the court, not to mention the individuals who wrote up the spectacles which they observed. The different, and sometimes divergent, personal and political purposes of these individuals all influenced the image of the Queen that finally emerged.

Since the 1980s, most discussions about Elizabeth's image have highlighted issues relating to her gender; there is a huge body of work on this subject, some of it produced by historians but much by scholars of Renaissance literature. Their central concern is how gender construction and expectations influenced both Elizabeth's self-representation and the image of the Queen projected by her subjects. In the words of Louis Montrose, the representations of the Queen and her power 'not merely were consequences of the ruler's gender but were themselves particular constructions of it' because the Queen embodied an anomaly in a patriarchal society, 'a challenge to the homology between the hierarchies of rule and gender'.[27] A number of literary scholars such as Leah Marcus and Lisa Hopkins have suggested that this contemporary anxiety about female rule resulted in the imaginative association of Elizabeth with troubling female characters such as Joan La Pucelle in Shakespeare's *1 Henry VI* or Titania in *A Midsummer Night's Dream*. Other scholars, meanwhile, have focused on the strategies that Elizabeth herself employed to bolster a monarchical authority potentially weakened by the Queen's gender. Carole Levin is but one who focused on her self-fashioning as the Virgin Queen and mother of her people, while Mary Beth Rose argued that Elizabeth created a 'heroic persona by monopolizing all gendered positions' in her speeches.[28]

None of these interpretations is uncontested, however. Some historians remain deeply sceptical about the validity of such gender analyses of Elizabeth's image, not least because they are often based on theory and sometimes expressed in impenetrable language. While these historians (including myself) accept that Elizabeth's gender was obviously relevant to her image, they question how far representations of the Queen reflected or were designed to combat gender anxiety about female rule in a patriarchal society. Equally, although they acknowledge that her representation was clearly affected by her gender, they point out that it also mirrored that of contemporary European kings and her male Tudor forebears. So, like her Continental counterparts, Elizabeth was often represented as a classical deity, but in her case it was usually Venus, Diana or Pallas Athene rather than Hercules, Apollo or Mars; and, like previous English monarchs, Elizabeth continued to perform the sacred royal Maundy Thursday ceremony of washing the feet of poor people, but in her case she was surrounded by women not men. To explore this issue further, I shall examine Elizabeth's representation as a providential monarch, virgin queen, 'political hermaphrodite' and a mother of her people.

Elizabeth's representation as a providential ruler certainly arose in part as a response to her gender. John Aylmer, for example, played the providential card in his 1559 *An Harborowe for Faithfull and Trewe Subiectes* to puncture the arguments of John Knox, whose *The First Blast of the Trumpet against the Monstrous Regiment of Women* had appeared the previous year. Arguing that God sometimes elevated women to leadership roles for his own mysterious reasons, Aylmer claimed that God placed Elizabeth on the throne to cut off the Roman headship of the English church and to uproot idolatry from the land. In this providential role, he explained, the Queen followed the precedent of Old Testament heroes, including Deborah, who had been called upon to judge, and Judith and Esther, who had been used to save God's chosen people from idolatrous enemies. Knox took on board this argument when, after Elizabeth's accession, he tried to wriggle out of his earlier blanket condemnation of female rule; he wrote a letter to the new queen explaining that divine providence allowed her the exceptional right to rule provided that she did so as God's instrument.

Nonetheless, the representation of Elizabeth as a providential monarch was not always gendered nor simply or primarily used as a device to justify the rule of a woman. For one thing, Elizabeth was as often associated with Old Testament male figures as female ones. The dedicatory epistle in the Geneva Bible of 1560, for example, called her a Zerubabbel 'for the erecting our spiritual Temple in planting and maintaining his holy word' and a Josiah for destroying idolatry. Preachers compared her to Moses for delivering the English people from slavery under the Pope, to David for defeating the enemies of true religion, to Solomon for bringing prosperity to the realm, and to Josiah for cleansing it of idolatry and restoring God's word. A ballad of 1585 likened her deliverance from the Throckmorton Plot to the preservation of Shadrach, Meshach and Abednigo from the fiery furnace kindled by Nebuchadnezzar.

Furthermore, Elizabeth's providential status had at least two other purposes. First, it was often employed to parry the challenge of those Catholics who denied Elizabeth's right to rule on the grounds of her illegitimate birth and false religion.

James Pilkington took on the Catholics in this way in a sermon preached in 1561, printed with additions in 1563. Like Aylmer, Pilkington maintained that God had chosen to work through Elizabeth – a weak vessel – in order to demonstrate his power. Preaching a few years into Elizabeth's reign, Pilkington could also argue that the prosperity of England under her rule was further testimony of her right to the throne and the legitimacy of her religious policies. Second, fashioning Elizabeth as a providential ruler allowed Protestants to dispense advice and to deliver warnings to their queen. To take one of many examples, in a book of psalms, printed in Geneva in 1559 and dedicated to Elizabeth, the anonymous translator and editor likened the Queen to the providential ruler David. Elizabeth had been saved miraculously, he wrote, 'from the furie of suche as soght your blood', while David had endured 'perils and persecutions' before 'he came to the royal dignitie'. So now Elizabeth had to follow the model of David and carry out God's purpose. Like David in the Psalms, she had to put her faith in God 'so to be zealous of his glorie, obedient to his wil, careful and diligent to suppress all papistrie, vice & heresie, and to cause the light of God's holy worde spedely to shine throughout all your dominions'. If Elizabeth did this, God 'will honour you and make your kingdome stable, he wil blesse you with a godlie prosperitie and mainteine you in perfect peace and quietnes' just as he had preserved David from his enemies once king and enlarged his dominions.[29]

Elizabeth herself was uneasy about this form of representation, because it had the potential to undermine her absolute right to rule by 'Inheritaunce, statutes, and law of the realme'. Her objections are laid out in marginal notes written on a copy of the letter from John Knox that had grudgingly accepted Elizabeth's position as providential ruler. They included: 'God hath made her our prince by due title of birth and law and not by extraordinarie miracle without former right'; 'if you take from her God's meane of of lawfull descent, ye abuse providence, and do wrong to her and her issue'; and the emphasis on divine providence was 'Perilous to a well settled state' as it meant that subjects could remove their allegiance to their monarch at will as well as select whomsoever they chose to succeed her.[30] Despite these understandable reservations, Elizabeth used the providential image whenever it suited her and on her own terms. Early in her reign, she acknowledged that she had God to thank for delivering her safely from her enemies during her sister's reign and allowing her to take the throne. Later on, she attributed the successes of her reign to divine providence, so when justifying her policies to parliament in 1576, she said in one version of her closing speech:

> And as for those rare and speciall bennefitte's which have manie years followed and accompanied my happie raine, I attribute to God aloane the prince of rule and count my self no better then his hand maide . . . Thease 17 yeares God hath both prospered and protected you with good success under my direction, and I dought not but the same maintaining hand will guide you still.[31]

Presenting herself as God's instrument was for Elizabeth not so much an answer to those who challenged a woman's right to rule as a defence against criticisms of her actions, or non-actions.

The image of Elizabeth as an Old Testament figure and providential ruler endured throughout the reign in pageants, plays, prayers, sermons and devotional works. However, during the second half of the reign, Elizabeth was also portrayed as a Virgin Queen. But was she lauded as a second Virgin Mary? A number of art historians and literary scholars have argued that the imagery traditionally used to describe the Virgin Mary – including virgin mother, bride, *ancilla* (or handmaid), merciful intercessor, a walled garden and a thornless rose – were applied to Elizabeth in literature, drama and the visual arts. A few have also suggested that the adulation of the Queen expressed in the Accession Day celebrations resembled the earlier cult of the Virgin Mary; indeed, this was a criticism levelled at the 17 November celebrations by contemporary Catholics seeking to make a polemical point. However, there are dissenting voices, including my own. We point out that the symbols associated with the Virgin Mary had other meanings: the rose, for example, was connected to the Tudor dynasty; the pearl to virginity in general, as well as to uniqueness (based partly on the pun of perles with peerless); hence, a ballad of 1584 could refer the Queen as 'the peerles pearle of princes all' whose like on earth was never seen.[32] If anything, as Helen Hackett explains, Elizabeth was portrayed as the polar opposite to the Virgin Mary: while the Queen represented the true church and nurtured it with the spiritual food of the Bible, the Madonna represented the 'false' one, administering poison. This polarity was brought home in an incident that occurred during the Queen's stay at Euston Hall, the home of the Catholic Edward Rookwood in 1578. According to Richard Topcliffe, an 'idol' of the false virgin was found and burned by the order of the Virgin Queen.

It was in 1578 that the language and iconography of perpetual and powerful virginity made their first appearances in representations of the Queen. Before that year, Elizabeth was depicted in paintings as a chaste and marriageable queen; after it, portraits represented her virginity as both a source and expression of her power.

The series of Sieve Portraits, produced between 1579 and 1582, were amongst the first paintings to link Elizabeth's virginity to England's imperial power; in each of them, a globe was positioned in a spatial relationship with a circular sieve – a symbol of virginity because of the well-known story of the Vestal Virgin, Tuccia, who carried water in a sieve to prove her virginity. During the same period, Elizabeth also came to be lauded as a virgin queen in poetry, masques and entertainments. At Norwich in the summer of 1578, she was addressed as an 'Unspoused Pallas' and 'a Virgine pure, which is and ever was' in one of the masques performed before her. Edmund Spenser's *April Eclogue* licensed in December 1579 represented Elizabeth as the Venus Virgo of Virgil's poetry. I have argued elsewhere that the emergence of the iconography of the Virgin Queen at this time was part of the weaponry employed by opponents of the Anjou matrimonial negotiations. Thereafter, it caught on and gained currency as a courtly fashion with an intent both to flatter and also, in many cases (including that of Edmund Spenser's *Faerie Queene*), to criticise the Queen. Courtiers and poets were the main creators of the image, though certainly Elizabeth helped to foster it in her entertainments at court (such as the 'Four Foster Children of Desire') and in the miniatures she commissioned, where she was portrayed as the goddess Diana or Cynthia. Whenever Elizabeth was depicted or addressed as the Virgin Queen, it is very rare indeed to see any unambiguous allusions to the Virgin Mary. Far more common were the direct iconographic or poetic references to the classical goddesses Diana, Cynthia and Astraea or to Petrarch's chaste maidens, Laura and Tuccia.

It was Christopher Haigh who first called Elizabeth a 'political hermaphrodite'. By this he meant that Elizabeth adopted a rhetoric that presented her in traditional male and female roles and with masculine and feminine attributes and characteristics; in the 'Golden Speech' to parliament in 1601, for example, Elizabeth referred to herself as king, prince and queen, sliding easily from one gender to another. Linked to this hermaphrodite rhetoric was Elizabeth's exploitation of the legal theory of the king's two bodies, namely that a monarch has both a natural body, which reflects its gender, age and eventual mortality, and a political body, which is untouched by biology, and that these two bodies are united through the sacred ritual of anointing at the coronation. As Carole Levin explained, Elizabeth presented herself as 'both woman and man in one, both king and queen together, a male body politic in concept while a female body natural in practice'.[33] In her first recorded speech, Elizabeth alluded to this idea when she told her lords: 'I am but one body naturally considered, though by His permission a body politic to govern.' In several speeches delivered in the 1560s, she developed it by portraying herself as 'feminine' in her natural body but with a male authority and 'masculine' virtues that she had acquired as a result of her divine kingship and royal inheritance from her father. In one well-known example, she told a parliamentary delegation that was urging her to marry:

> thowghe I be a woman yet I have as good a corage awnswerable to mye place as evere my fathere hade. I am your anoynted Queene. I wyll never be by vyolence constreyned to doo anye thinge. I thanke God I am in deed indued with suche qualytyes that yf I were turned owte of the realme in my pettycote I were hable to lyve in anye place of Chrystendom.

The reference to a 'weak woman's body' and to the 'heart and stomach of a queen' in the Queen's celebrated Tilbury speech was therefore a long-held and central part of Elizabeth's self-representation.[34]

The notion of the Queen's two bodies also pervaded her subjects' representations of Elizabeth. The doubled body trope could offer reassurance not only that a queen had the valour to lead her nation successfully against foreign foes but also that her very success would not subvert existing gender hierarchies. So, after the defeat of the Spanish Armada, James Aske could triumphantly proclaim:

> Although she be by *Nature* weake,
> Because her sex no otherwise can be:
> Yet wants she not the courage of her Sire,
> Whose valour wanne this *Island* great renowne.[35]

Nonetheless, the rhetorical device of the king's two bodies had purposes that went beyond addressing issues specific to her gender. During the last two decades of the reign, the difficult subject of the Queen's mortality and an uncertain succession could equally well be tackled through reference to the Queen's two bodies.

Figure 3.2 Queen Elizabeth I (the Siena 'sieve' portrait, c. 1580–3). Pinacoteca Nazionale, Siena, Italy/Alinari/The Bridgeman Art Library.

Figure 3.3 Queen Elizabeth I (the 'Ermine' portrait, *c.* 1585).
Image from Hatfield House, reproduced courtesy of the Marquess of Salisbury.

As Helen Hackett has shown, poets of the 1590s used a range of imaginative metaphors to express the idea that the monarchy and body politic would survive intact, despite the death of Elizabeth's natural body and the lack of a biological or named heir. In her later portraits, her age was dealt with by the 'masque of beauty' whereby the Queen ceased to be painted as a relatively naturalistic woman and instead became simply a representation of monarchical power. Surrounded by symbols of monarchy, she was projected first and foremost as an expression of the body politic.

In the 'Ermine' portrait, for example (see Figure 3.3), her natural body virtually disappears, as her clothes merge into the background and her face is untouched by age. Most prominent in the painting are emblems reflecting her descent (the jewel hanging from her collar known as the Three Brothers, once the possession of the Duke of Burgundy, that was acquired by her father); her sovereignty (the sword of state); her virginity (the ermine); and her preferred policy of peace (the olive branch). Elizabeth here is an icon not a person. When Isaac Oliver attempted to paint her natural body, with her face marked by time, the miniature was left uncompleted and the artist received no further commissions from the Queen or her government (see Figure 3.4).

Elizabeth's double body also came to be identified with the land of England. This sometimes had a gendered aspect such as when metaphors in the courtly entertainments held in the summers of the 1560s and 1570s linked the potential fertility of her body with that of the English countryside which was then in flower. Similarly, after 1585, Elizabeth's virginal body was allowed to stand imaginatively for the realm with its territorial borders intact despite the aggression of its male foes. However, at other times, the association of Elizabeth with the land is recognisably just a device to assert the Queen's sovereignty over her territory. Christopher Saxton's 1579 atlas of England does just this by stamping the royal coat of arms prominently on the maps of each of England's counties and by providing an engraving of the Queen on the book's frontispiece. In full royal regalia and flanked by the figures of cosmography and geography, Elizabeth is represented as the sovereign ruler of all the land she surveys.

Elizabeth's summer progresses also enacted her sovereignty over the realm. Unlike her father and siblings she made a point of travelling in great state through the southern half of her kingdom, taking over her hosts' homes as royal palaces and entering cities in ceremonial. The 'Ditchley' portrait – probably commissioned by Sir Henry Lee to commemorate Elizabeth's visit his manor of Ditchley in Oxfordshire in August 1592 – expressed her possession of the land symbolically, with her body towering over the realm and her feet placed on the parts of England where she went on progress, leaving in shadow the north, the area she never visited (see Figure 8.1, p. 143).

Figure 3.4 Queen Elizabeth I, miniature portrait by Isaac Oliver, *c.* 1590–2. Victoria & Albert Museum, London, UK/The Bridgeman Art Library.

Progresses were important to Elizabeth. For much of the reign, she insisted on going on them despite the expense and the burdens they imposed on the organisers and her hosts. As seen, they had a value in asserting her sovereignty; equally, travelling through the realm – like royal entries into cities – provided her with opportunities to display, and reinforce, the bonds of mutual love between herself and her subjects that was another fundamental facet of her self-representation. So, while she maintained a distance during the proceedings to enhance the sense of mystery in her presence, she also introduced a note of intimacy into her contacts with her subjects. In this behaviour she was very different from her Continental counterparts, though not dissimilar to that of her father, who could also combine majesty with familiarity. The Spanish ambassador commented with some disapproval how in the summer of 1568 she 'ordered her carriage sometimes to be taken where the crowd was thickest and stood up and thanked the people'.[36] On other occasions she reassured nervous speakers, gave profuse thanks to her hosts and entered into dialogue with performers of the entertainments. Through these interactions, Elizabeth aimed to project a caring and loving relationship with her subjects.

Elizabeth as a loving princess, the mother of her people, was a topos that permeated much of the panegyric surrounding her. Whatever their motives, in this respect all the manufacturers of Elizabeth's positive image told the same story. Mulcaster's account of the coronation procession maintained:

> she did not only shew her most gracious loue toward the people in generall, but also priuately if the baser personages had either offred her grace any flowres or such like, as a signification of their good wyll, or moued to her any sute, she most gently, to the common reioysing of all the lookers on, & priuate comfort of the partie, staid her chariot, and heard theyr requestes.

Twenty-five years later, a ballad of 1584 described how Elizabeth on her entry into London greeted spectators graciously:

> And bowing down on every side,
> most lovingly unto them all:
> A poore man at the length she spied
> which down before her grace did fall
> And curteously she then did stay
> To heer what he had then to say.[37]

Not all her subjects accepted this image. Many Protestants criticised Elizabeth for not taking the Reformation further, not securing a Protestant succession nor pursuing a more aggressive Protestant foreign policy. Yet, even these detractors projected the image of Elizabeth as a caring prince with the best interests of her people at heart; it lay at the heart of the genre of epideictic literature that used praise as a mask for criticism.

Elizabeth had multiple images, far more than have been discussed here or than was usual for English monarchs before her reign. The malleability of her image owed much to her gender and her status as an unmarried woman, but it was also the outcome of a Renaissance culture that adored emblems and conceits and embraced chivalry and classicism. The image was widely transmitted in a range of media from portraits to poetry, from sermons to civic entries, from miniatures to medals, some of which were confined to court although much was disseminated in the public domain. Without the development of a print culture during her reign, most of the representations would be lost to historians.

CONCLUSION

Many historians – and notably John Neale – were unable to separate parts of the image from the reality, and they uncritically portrayed Elizabeth as a heroic figure, the caring mother of her people and the embodiment of the English nation. Some twenty years ago, the Neale panegyric came under attack as scholars attempted to strip away the image from what they saw as the reality of a queen who put her own personal and political interests before those of her subjects and who was far less successful than her admirers and own propaganda asserted. One amongst the new generation of critics is Christopher Haigh, whose cold, hard and unsentimental look at the Queen has rightly won many admirers. 'Elizabeth had deliberately chosen the role of a loving queen', he wrote, 'and she played it throughout her reign – but it was only a role.' Nonetheless, there is good reason to believe that Elizabeth believed she was projecting a political truth. As far as she was concerned, she devoted herself to wearisome public affairs, was forced to make personal sacrifices (including rejecting marriage and executing a kinswoman) and had been subjected to assassination threats and threatened with deposition, all for the sake of her realm and religion. Mistakes had been made – and she was the first to admit that she was not infallible – but the mutual love between herself and her subjects seems to have been one of her enduring convictions – if not, she was a consummate actress!

So, despite the difficulties in writing about Elizabeth, there is a great deal to say, far more than can be done in a mere 9,000 words. As will be evident from other essays in this section, the Queen was at the centre of England's political and cultural life. Other essays will also discuss her influence in the debates about foreign policy and war. Here, the emphasis has been on those aspects of the Queen's policies that fell within the royal prerogative and on the subject of her representation, all issues that have absorbed historians' attention whenever they have been 'queen fixated'.

FURTHER READING

Archer, Jayne E., Goldring Elizabeth and Knight, Sarah (eds.), *The Progresses, Pageants and Entertainments of Queen Elizabeth I* (Oxford, 2007).

Barrett Graves, Debra, Eldridge Carney, Jo and Levin, Carole (eds.), *Elizabeth I: Always Her Own Free Woman* (Burlington, Vt., 2003).

Beal, Peter and Ioppolo, Grace (eds.), *Elizabeth I and the Culture of Writing* (London, 2007).

Bowers, Roger, 'The Chapel Royal, the First Edwardian Prayer Book, and Elizabeth's Settlement of Religion, 1559', *Historical Journal*, 43 (2) (2000): 317–44.

Collinson, Patrick, 'Windows in a Woman's Soul: Questions about the Religion of Queen *Elizabeth* I', in Patrick Collinson (ed.), *Elizabethan Essays* (London, 1994), pp. 87–118.

—— *Elizabeth I* (Oxford, 2007).

Doran, Susan, *Monarchy and Matrimony: The Courtships of Elizabeth I* (London, 1996).
—— 'Elizabeth I's Religion: The Evidence of Her Letters', *Journal of Ecclesiastical History*, 51 (4) (2000): 699–720.
Doran, Susan and Freeman, Thomas S. (eds.), *The Myth of Elizabeth* (Basingstoke, 2003).
Hackett, Helen, *Virgin Mother, Maiden Queen: Elizabeth I and the Cult of the Virgin Mary* (Basingstoke, 1995).
Haigh, Christopher, *Elizabeth I* (Harlow, 1988).
Haugaard, William P., 'Elizabeth Tudor's Book of Devotions: A Neglected Clue to the Queen's Life and Character', *The Sixteenth Century Journal*, 12 (2) (1981): 79–106.
Hoak, Dale, 'The Coronations of Edward VI, Mary I, and Elizabeth I, and the Transformation of the Tudor Monarchy', in C. S. Knighton and Richard Mortimer (eds.), *Westminster Abbey Reformed, 1540–1640* (Aldershot, 2003), pp. 114–51.
Jones, Norman, *Faith by Statute: Parliament and the Settlement of Religion, 1559* (London, 1982).
Kewes, Paulina, 'Two Queens, One Inventory: The Lives of Mary and Elizabeth Tudor', in Kevin Sharpe and Steven N. Zwicker (eds.), *Writing Lives: Biography and Textuality, Identity and Representation in Early Modern England* (Oxford, 2008), pp. 187–207.
King, John N., 'Queen Elizabeth I: Representations of the Virgin Queen', *Renaissance Quarterly*, 43 (1) (1990): 30–75.
Leahy, William, 'Propaganda of a Record of Events? Richard Mulcaster's *The Passage of Our Most Drad Soveraigne Lady Quene Elizabeth*', *Early Modern Literary Studies*, 9 (1) (2003): 1–20.
Levin, Carole, *The Heart and Stomach of a Queen* (Philadelphia, Pa., 1994).
Levine, Mortimer, The Early Elizabethan Succession Question, 1558–1568 (Palo Alto, Calif., 1966).
Loades, David, *Elizabeth I: A Life* (London, 2006).
Marcus, Leah, *Puzzling Shakespeare: Local Reading and Its Discontents* (Pittsburgh, Pa., 1988).
Marcus, Leah S., Mueller, Janel and Rose, Mary Beth (eds.), *Elizabeth I: Collected Works* (Chicago, Ill., 2000).
May, Steven W., 'Queen Elizabeth Prays for the Living and the Dead', in Peter Beal and Grace Ioppolo (eds.), *Elizabeth I and the Culture of Writing* (London, 2007), pp. 201–11.
Montrose, Louis, *The Subject of Elizabeth: Authority, Gender and Representation* (Chicago, Ill., 2006).
Neale, John, *Elizabeth I and Her Parliaments*, 2 vols. (London, 1953–7).
Richards, Judith M., 'Love and a Female Monarch: The Case of Elizabeth Tudor', *Journal of British Studies*, 38 (2) (1999): 133–60.
Rose, Mary Beth, *Gender and Heroism in Early Modern English Literature* (Chicago, Ill., 2002).
Starkey, David, *Elizabeth* (London, 2000).
Strong, Roy, *Gloriana: The Portraits of Queen Elizabeth I* (London, 2002).
Walker, Julia M. (ed.), *Dissing Elizabeth* (Durham, NC, 1998).
Whitelock, Anna and Hunt, Alice (eds.), *Tudor Queenship: The Reigns of Mary and Elizabeth* (Basingstoke, 2010).
Woodhuysen, H. R., 'The Queen's Own Hand: A Preliminary Account', in Peter Beal and Grace Ioppolo (eds.), *Elizabeth I and the Culture of Writing* (London, 2007), pp. 1–27.

NOTES

1 William P. Haugaard, 'Elizabeth Tudor's Book of Devotions: A Neglected Clue to the Queen's Life and Character', *Sixteenth Century Journal*, 12 (2) (1981): 79–106.

2 Revd Dr Giles, *The Whole Works of Roger Ascham* (1865), sig. H.

3 Aysha Pollnitz, 'Christian Women or Sovereign Queens? Representing the Schooling of Mary I and Elizabeth I', in Anna Whitelock and Alice Hunt (eds.), *Tudor Queenship: The Reigns of Mary and Elizabeth* (Basingstoke, 2010); Janel Mueller and Leah Marcus (eds.), *Elizabeth I: Autograph Compositions and Foreign Language Originals* (Chicago, Ill., 2003), p. xxvi.

4 T. E. Hartley, *Proceedings in the Parliaments of Elizabeth I*, 3 vols (Leicester, 1981), vol. II, pp. 44–5.

5 Patrick Collinson, 'Pulling the Strings: Religion and Politics in the Progress of 1578', in Jayne E. Archer, Elizabeth Goldring and Sarah Knight (eds.), *The Progresses, Pageants and Entertainments of Queen Elizabeth I* (Oxford, 2007), p. 124.

6 Thomas Brice, *A Compendiou[s Regi]ster in Metre Contei[ning the] Names, and Pacient Suffry[ngs of the] Membres of Iesus Christ . . .* (London, 1559).

7 Paul L. Hughes and James F. Larkin (eds.), *Tudor Royal Proclamations: Volume II the Later Tudors* (New Haven, Conn., 1969), pp. 99–100.

8 *Calendar State Papers Venetian, 1558–1580*, p. 2 (hereafter *CSP Ven.*); *Calendar State Papers Spanish, 1558–67* (hereafter *CSP Span.*), p. 17.

9 Hughes and Larkin, *Tudor Royal Proclamations*, pp. 102–3.

10 Dale Hoak, 'The Coronations of Edward VI, Mary I, and Elizabeth I, and the Transformation of the Tudor Monarchy', in C. S. Knighton and Richard Mortimer (eds.), *Westminster Abbey Reformed, 1540–1640* (Aldershot, 2003), pp. 114–51.

11 *CSP Ven.*, pp. 11–19. Anon, *The Passage of Our Most Drad Soveraigne Lady Queen Elizabeth through the Citie of London to Westminster the Daye before Her Coronacion* (London, 1559). William Leahy, 'Propaganda of a Record of Events? Richard Mulcaster's *The Passage of Our Most Drad Soveraigne Lady Quene Elizabeth*', *Early Modern Literary Studies*, 9 (1) (2003): 1–20.

12 *CSP For., 1558–9*, pp. 109, 221.

13 Hughes and Larkin, *Tudor Royal Proclamations*, pp. 117–32; especially Injunctions 20 (communion) and 2, 23 and 35 (images).

14 *Certayne Sermons Appoynted by the Quenes Maiestie . . . Newly Imprinted in Partes Accordynge as Is Mencioned in the Booke of Commune Prayers* (London, 1559).

15 Hughes and Larkin, *Tudor Royal Proclamations*, II, p. 165.

16 For example, *A Fourme of Common Prayer to Be Vsed, and So Commanded by Auctoritie of the Queenes Maiestie, and Necessarie for the Present Tyme and State 1572, 27. Octob.* (London, [1572]) sig. Aii. Hughes and Larkin, *Tudor Royal Proclamations*, pp. 117–18, 129, 131.

17 Kenneth Fincham and Nicholas Tyacke, *Altars Restored: The Changing Face of English Religious Worship, 1547–c. 1700* (Oxford, 2007), pp. 42–3; *The Seconde Tome of Homelyes . . .* (London, 1563), especially sig. B(B) iii.

18 Leah S. Marcus, Janel Mueller and Mary Beth Rose (eds.), *Elizabeth I: Collected Works* (Chicago, Ill., 2000), p. 62.

19 Hartley, *Proceedings in the Parliaments of Elizabeth I*, vol. I, pp. 44–5; vol. II, p. 267.

20 Marcus et al., *Elizabeth I*, pp. 36–8, 78; British Library Lansdowne MS 94 fol. 30r.

21 Hartley, *Proceedings in the Parliaments of Elizabeth I*, vol. I, p. 147.

22 Hughes and Larkin, *Tudor Royal Proclamations*, II, p. 449.

23 Hartley, *Proceedings in the Parliaments of Elizabeth I*, vol. I, p. 148.

24 Marcus et al., *Elizabeth I*, pp. 58–70, 96–7.

25 Marcus et al., *Elizabeth I*, p. 63.

26 Roy Strong, *Cult of Elizabeth* (London, 1977), p. 16.

27 Louis Montrose, *The Subject of Elizabeth: Authority, Gender and Representation* (Chicago, Ill., 2006), p. 1.

28 Christopher Haigh, *Elizabeth I* (Harlow, 1988), p. 25; Mary Beth Rose, *Gender and Heroism in Early Modern English Literature* (Chicago, Ill., 2002), p. 27.

29 *The Boke of Psalmes . . . Tra[n]slated Faithfully According to the Ebrewe; with Brief and Apt Annotations in the Margent . . .* (Geneva, 1559), sigs. 2ii–*Iiii.

30 British Library, Additional MS. 32091, fols. 168 R and V.

31 Hartley, *Proceedings in the Parliaments of Elizabeth I*, vol. I, p. 472.
32 Richard Harrington, *A Famous Dittie of the Ioyful Receauing of the Queens Moste Excellent Maiestie, by the Worthy Citizens of London the xii Day of Nouember, 1584. at Her Graces Comming to Saint Iames* (London, 1584).
33 Haigh, *Elizabeth I*, p. 22; Carole Levin, *The Heart and Stomach of a King: Elizabeth I and the Politics of Sex and Power* (Philadelphia, Pa., 1994), p. 121.
34 Marcus et al., *Elizabeth I*, pp. 52, 326; Hartley, *Proceedings in the Parliaments of Elizabeth I*, vol. I, p. 148.
35 James Aske, *Elizabetha Triumphans* . . . (London, 1588), p. 2.
36 *CSP Span.*, pp. 50–1.
37 Harrington, *A Famous Dittie.*

CHAPTER FOUR

THE COUNCIL

Natalie Mears

In May 1598, a tense and fractious debate occurred in the Privy Council between those, led by William Cecil, Lord Burghley, who favoured peace with Spain, and others, led by the Earl of Essex, who favoured war. According to William Camden, Burghley told the Earl that 'he breathed forth nothing but War, Slaughter, and Bloud.' After further 'hot Dispute', Burghley 'drew forth a Psalm-book, and, saying nothing pointed him to this verse, "*men of Bloud shall not live out half their days*".'[1] Burghley's actions were prophetic – Essex was executed less than three years later – but the incident illuminates some aspects of the Elizabethan Privy Council's duties whilst raising questions about others.

The Privy Council had its origins in the Council Attendant, one of three large, fluid and overlapping councils that developed under Henry VII from the King's or Great Council, the other two being the Council in Star Chamber and the Council Learned-in-the-Law. It emerged through a series of reforms by Cardinal Wolsey and Thomas Cromwell, along with impetus from Henry VIII himself and criticisms of 'bad counsellors' during the Pilgrimage of Grace (1536). By 1540, its membership was defined, and it had its own clerk and registers, though the council's title remained vague: it was variously called the Council Attendant on His Person, the Secret Council, the Privy Council, the Council in His Majesty's Household, the Privy Council Attendant on His Person until contemporaries settled on 'Privy Council'. By the reign of Elizabeth, it was an integral part of the fabric of government.

Though most of the council's meetings were dominated by administrative issues – implementing and supervising policy; dealing with problems and issues raised by individuals, towns, boroughs and counties – as the incident in 1598 demonstrated, its central duty was to advise the monarch and to support him or her in the process of policy-making. Moreover, it is this aspect that has most fascinated and intrigued historians and one where there is little consensus on key issues. For this reason, this chapter will focus primarily on the question of the council's advisory role and the nature of Elizabeth's queenship.

To understand the debate about the council's advisory role, we have to go back in the historiography nearly a century, to Sir John Neale and Conyers Read.

Working independently, they both argued that Elizabethan governance was based on social and personal relationships that Elizabeth developed with courtiers and councillors, such as Burghley and Leicester. They argued that the council had a crucial role in counselling but was divided by factionalism based on either ideological conflict over war (Read) or personal rivalries (Neale). Neale's and Read's arguments were challenged in the mid-twentieth century by Sir Geoffrey Elton who, though working principally on the Henrician period, influenced historians' understanding of Tudor governance as a whole. Elton argued that the sixteenth century saw the emergence of a 'national, bureaucratic' government under the aegis of Thomas Cromwell. Central to this was the development of the Privy Council in the 1530s and its establishment as the main advisory and policy-making body by Elizabeth's reign.

Though Elton's arguments were highly influential, a number of leading historians remained dissatisfied with his emphasis on institutions. They believed that personal relationships between monarchs and their advisers remained important and felt that the role of ideology had been ignored, particularly in explaining tensions between advisers. Simon Adams, Wallace MacCaffrey and Penry Williams, to name only those who worked on Elizabeth's reign, re-emphasised and explored, in varying degrees, the importance of social connections and clienteles; Adams also mounted an effective and persuasive critique of the extent to which the Elizabethan Privy Council was divided by faction. This was developed further in the 1990s by historians such as John Guy and Stephen Alford who explored the relationship between the institutions that Elton had argued were central to governance, the people who staffed them and the ideas and assumptions that those people held, derived from their background, education and religion. Of particular interest were contemporary theories and practice of counselling and how they shaped each other, all of which elucidated further the role of the Elizabethan Privy Council.

As a result, the importance of social and personal relationships and of ideology in shaping politics regained pre-eminence. But, though revisionist historians identified the court as the main political forum, the council continued to be seen as the principal advisory body. For example, Adams argued that policy-making was conducted by an inner ring of privy councillors whose position was secured as much, if not more, through prior membership of the council than one's personal relationship with Elizabeth. Rarely was counsel seen as emanating from outside the council, although Christopher Haigh noted isolated examples, which he explained as instances when Elizabeth deliberately sought to circumvent the council because they disagreed with her.

Despite Adams's critique of factionalism, there is an ongoing debate on the extent of political consensus on the council. Christopher Haigh and Susan Doran have both argued that the council was divided at key moments, for example, during Elizabeth's marriage negotiations. Others have suggested that the council was united but at odds with the Queen herself. Feminist historians, such as Mary Thomas Crane, Mary Hill Cole and Anne McLaren, have argued this was because of Elizabeth's gender: Elizabeth needed to challenge patriarchal values that disputed women's ability to rule and to impose her authority on her male advisers. Conversely, John Guy, Patrick Collinson, Stephen Alford and others have argued that disagreements arose because of fundamental differences over political beliefs (specifically the role of counsel) and religion (that Elizabeth was too conservative). Elizabeth stifled consultation on key issues that would maintain and preserve Protestantism – her marriage, the succession, Mary, Queen of Scots, church reform, intervention in Scotland and the Netherlands – and refused to implement councillors' policies.

This chapter re-examines and questions the role of the Privy Council as the principal advisory body by looking at the relationship between the council, its members, the Queen, other courtiers and the ideas people held about how governance should work. It will look at the changes that took place over the last fifteen years of the reign and situate Elizabethan practices in a European context. It will also address briefly the council's relationship with the court and parliament. Throughout, a distinction will be made between 'councillors' (those offering Elizabeth advice through the Privy Council) and 'advisers' (those, including privy councillors, offering advice more informally either individually or as a group).

COUNSELLING AND POLICY-MAKING

We have no direct evidence of the council's role in counselling Elizabeth because the council's registers do not record the substance of debates on policy, only the dates of meeting, who attended and summaries of the letters that were written in reply to local problems raised by individuals, towns and boroughs. We only get some sense of discussions from memoranda that individuals, particularly Burghley, drew up examining key issues.

Alford has used these memoranda to highlight how the council worked and to argue that the council was the principal advisory body in government. He claims that the council's debate in December 1559 about whether England should intervene in Scotland on behalf of the Protestant Lords of the Congregation 'established a pattern of action by Council throughout the decade'.[2] Councillors met without Elizabeth to discuss policy; to preserve confidentiality, the council's clerks had to leave the meeting, and a record of the discussion was made by Burghley. This explains why the discussions do not appear in the council's registers. Once settled on a course of action, it advised the Queen, and she was expected to make a decision. Burghley was the central figure: he not only acted as a channel of communication between the Queen and the council but also seems to have directed and led the meetings, shaped the agenda, circulated memoranda for discussion and, where appropriate, prepared final drafts of documents for signature. Michael Pulman points to similar practices taking place in the 1570s and argues that they arose partly because Elizabeth preferred to decide whether or not to implement a particular course of action rather than to choose between numbers of different options.

However, when we try to map the memoranda produced by Burghley and others for many key meetings onto the Privy Council registers we see that they usually do not fit. There are seventeen meetings or series of related meetings on major issues for which we have memoranda. Ten of these cannot be mapped onto meetings as recorded in the registers: four on the Darnley marriage in 1565; one on the cessation of arms in Scotland in 1571; one each in 1576 and 1578 on the Dutch revolt; a series of meetings in 1579 on Elizabeth's proposed marriage to the Duc d'Anjou and two meetings in 1580 on the Dutch Revolt and Scotland respectively. These meetings were either held on different days or in different locations to those recorded in the registers or, if they occurred on the same day, different councillors were present. Though the council's registers do not survive for the other seven occasions, there are a number of indications in the memoranda to suggest they also occurred on different dates or were attended by different councillors.

This would suggest that the meetings were held separately from those of the Privy Council, a conclusion that is reinforced by three pieces of evidence. First, Elizabeth was present and an active participant in the meeting of 1576, an unprecedented situation for a formal Privy Council meeting in her reign as far as the registers attest. Second, in 1579, Elizabeth made an explicit distinction between the group of advisers who were to discuss her proposed marriage to François, Duc d'Anjou, and the Privy Council who were deputed to examine the marriage treaty, should the Queen agree to the French proposal. Third, the council's own clerks were not used as secretaries during these more informal meetings. We know that the clerks could be asked to leave the council chamber when sensitive or confidential issues were discussed: this happened to William Paget in 1541 when councillors met with the chief justices and 'other of the King's learned counsel', to discuss Lord Dacre's case.[3] However, the clerks' absence reinforces other evidence that suggests these meetings were different in kind to those of the Privy Council.

If these meetings did operate separately from the Privy Council, it suggests that the Privy Council was not the primary advisory body under Elizabeth; indeed, it may have had only a limited role in discussing major political issues. Instead, Elizabeth selected advisers to meet separately from the council to discuss issues and to advise her. These advisers were all privy councillors, with Burghley, Leicester, Sussex, Walsingham (after his appointment as secretary in 1573) and, to a lesser extent, Dr Thomas Wilson, Walsingham's fellow principal secretary, as the most regular appointees. However, they do not seem to have operated as an 'inner ring' of councillors as Adams has argued, because Elizabeth appears to have selected them because of her personal relationship with them, not their conciliar status. Her close relationships with Leicester and Burghley, though very different, are well known. Experience in Ireland (Sussex) or diplomacy (Walsingham and Wilson) may have recommended these men to her service initially, but greater bonds of trust appear to have developed with them than with other councillors, such as Sir Walter Mildmay. In Walsingham and Wilson's case, this may have been reinforced by their roles as principal secretaries and hence a key channel of communication to and from the Queen, though this seems not to have fostered a close relationship between Elizabeth and Sir Thomas Smith. For example, Elizabeth called Walsingham her 'Moor', and, even in times of tension, such as during his embassy to France in 1581, he felt able to respond to her criticisms with humour: 'the lawes of Ethiopia my native soyle are verie severe against those that condemne a person unheard … I should then be worthie to receave the most sharpe punishment that either the Ethiopian severitie or Dracus lawes can yeilde.'[4] As has been suggested, perhaps she admired his sardonic humour – not least because it was like her own. The importance of personal relationships over conciliar status is highlighted by Elizabeth's inclusion of Lord Hunsdon in the marriage debates in spring 1579. Never politically prominent, he was her cousin and had been able to assume unofficially an ad-hoc role as an adviser prior to his formal appointment to the council in 1577.

Before examining why Elizabeth chose to select advisers to meet separately from the Privy Council to discuss political issues, it is important to note that she also sought advice from individuals on an ad-hoc basis. For instance, she sought advice informally from Leicester on both the marriage proposals of Charles IX in June 1565 and of Archduke Charles of Austria in 1569. On hearing the news of the death of the Regent of Scotland in November 1572, Elizabeth talked 'to and fro' with Leicester about the need to support the anglophile Scots.[5] Convinced by his arguments that a speedy response was imperative, she immediately sought Burghley's opinion on what support would be most effective, rather than convening the Privy Council.

Those she sought advice from individually were often those men whom Elizabeth selected to discuss issues collectively; this is unsurprising, as they represented her most experienced and trusted advisers. But she also asked the advice of men who were not members of the council, including Sir Nicholas Throckmorton (ambassador to France and to Mary Stuart in the 1560s) and, two decades prior to his appointment to the council, Sir Thomas Heneage (treasurer of the chamber).

Elizabeth also listened carefully to advice from her ambassadors and agents, to make use of the inside knowledge they acquired and of the connections they developed with foreign monarchs and courtiers. Thomas Randolph and Henry Killigrew (Scotland), John Somers (France and the Netherlands) and Edward Stafford (France) are good examples. For instance, in 1581, Elizabeth was persuaded by Randolph's advice that it would be better to use diplomatic means to secure the release from prison of the former regent of Scotland, the Earl of Morton, even though this conflicted with the advice from her specially selected advisers.

Although Elizabeth tended to seek the advice of men, there is evidence that she also had a group of female intimates. She did not discuss political issues with them, but they did act as 'barometers' of her moods and channels of communication between her and even her most trusted advisers. Guzman de Silva, a Spanish ambassador early in Elizabeth's reign, was advised to cultivate Elizabeth Brooke, Marchioness of Northampton, who was regarded as 'in high favour with the queen [and] has served His Majesty [Philip II] when opportunity has occurred'.[6] Frances Newton, Lady Cobham, was an important contact for Burghley, especially when Elizabeth refused to speak to him after the execution of Mary Stuart. There is also some evidence that Elizabeth used female companions as go-betweens, as when she used Mary Sidney to sound out the Spanish ambassador, Alvaro de la Quadra, about the proposed marriage to Archduke Charles in 1559.

The active role that Elizabeth played in organising political discussion and counselling was characteristic of other stages of policy-making. She received information directly and indirectly through letters that she read herself or asked others to summarise for her. On 9 August 1581, for example, she read Walsingham's letters to both her and Burghley before listening to the latter's advice.[7]

THE ROLE OF GENDER

Why did the Privy Council play a less prominent role in counselling than is usually perceived? Feminist historians have argued that Elizabeth's relationship with the Council was governed by her gender. Contemporary texts such as John Knox's

The First Blast of the Trumpet against the Monstruous Regiment of Women (1558) questioned the legitimacy of regnant queens, whilst others, notably John Aylmer's *An Harborowe for Faithfull and Trewe Subiectes* (1559), defended female monarchy principally because an English queen would rule with the advice of (male) councillors and parliament. In this climate, it is argued, Elizabeth found herself at loggerheads with her councillors and could only assert her authority either by subverting or bypassing the council (as argued by Mary Thomas Crane and Mary Hill Cole) or by accepting the need for advice from godly, male advisers (Anne McLaren).

There is little evidence that Elizabeth tried to manipulate or subvert humanist conventions of counselling – specifically, appointing old men, the archetypal 'good counsellor' – to assert her authority, as Crane argues. She was well aware of humanist ideas of counselling because, like a number of her advisers, including Burghley, Thomas Smith, Thomas Wilson and Nicholas Bacon, she had received a fashionable humanist education in the 1540s. However, though the majority of her privy councillors and other advisers were older than her in the first thirty years of her reign, this was because she tended to appoint men who had been members of her household as a princess, were her relations, had had Henrician, Edwardian or Marian experience or, in the case of Derby, Pembroke and Shrewsbury, were leading magnates who could represent the Crown in the localities and provide military support. Inevitably, they were older than the Queen; their age was not the prime factor in her selection, but trust and experience.

Similarly, though councillors complained about the hiatus her royal progresses caused in counselling and policy-making – delaying communication, discussion and decision-making – it is difficult to sustain Cole's arguments that progresses were deliberate attempts to subvert the council. They occurred irregularly and took up a smaller proportion of time than the court's usual residence at the royal palaces in and around London. They were also organised for practical reasons, notably to escape hot summers in the capital or to display or impose royal authority in the provinces.

Likewise, though Elizabeth referred to herself as 'God's creature, ordained to obey his appointment' and, at times, represented herself as a 'providential monarch', she did not believe that she had to rely on male advisers, as McLaren argues. Though in her speech in November 1558 she stated she would 'direct all my actions by good advise and counsel', she made it clear that she ruled and her councillors were her assistants: so that 'I with my Ruling and you with your service may make a good account to Almighty God.'[8] She agreed that she would listen to advice, but only when she thought it fit, 'And for Counsel and advise I shall accept you of my Nobility and such others of you the Rest as in consultation I shall think meet.'[9] This was reiterated in a sharp rebuke she offered to Mary, Queen of Scots, in 1582 for writing to the Privy Council instead of herself:

> [Elizabeth] does find it strange that she [Mary] should direct her letters unto her Council, as unto her principal members of this Crown . . . whereof her Majesty cannot otherwise conceive but that she [Mary] does not repute her to be so absolute as that without the assent of such whom she [Mary] terms "principal members of the Crown" she [Elizabeth] cannot direct her policy . . . For although her Highness does carry as great regard unto her Council as

> any of her progenitors have done and has just cause so to do in respect of their wisdom and fidelity, yet she [Mary] is to be let understand that they are Councillors by choice, and not by birth, whose services are no longer to be used in that public function then it shall please her Majesty to dispose of the same.[10]

In fact, Elizabeth was more likely to dismiss gender conventions than to manipulate or defer to them. In her speech to the Commons on 28 January 1563, she acknowledged that her marriage was politically important, but she denied that, 'being a woman wanting both wit and memory', she needed to be counselled more thoroughly than a king. '[Y]et the princely seat and kingly throne wherein God (though unworthy) hath constituted me, makes these two causes to seem little in mine eyes, though grievous perhaps to your ears.'[11] She saw herself as both 'imitator' and 'heir' to her father, Henry VIII, 'a king whom philosophers regard as god on earth'.[12]

Neither does it appear that Elizabeth used informal groups of personally selected counsellors or sought advice from individuals to sideline the council and maintain control of policy-making. First, many of those with whom she regularly consulted were privy councillors. Second, informal consultations offered flexibility and privacy and were more practical means of discussing policy, especially on sensitive issues such as her marriage, the succession, Mary Stuart and war. As Walsingham and others noted, they allowed issues to be discussed 'off the record', policies examined discreetly, options explored, particularly with other monarchs, without losing face or being openly committed.

In fact, contemporary political treatises, such as Elyot's *The Boke Named the Gouernour* (1531), expected policy-making to work in these ways. Counselling was 'a necessarily collegial enterprise'.[13] Advisers were the king's *amici principis,* literally the 'king's friends', whose duty was to ensure that the monarch ruled for the benefit of the common weal. Counsel was defined as a dialogue or a consultation in which issues were 'passed with much and long deliberation to be revolved and tossed in the mind', enabling them to be thoroughly examined and the prince and his advisers assured that the best course had been adopted.[14] Advisers were supposed to tell the monarch hard truths, but they had to offer their advice at the right time, place and in a soothing manner, something that the *amici principis,* as the monarch's friends, were more likely to achieve.

Elizabeth's informal groups of selected advisers and her political discussion with individuals fitted this bill. She seems to have been present at the meetings in April 1570 and January 1576 when Mary, Queen of Scots, and the Dutch Revolt respectively were discussed. In meetings called to discuss a league with France in August 1581, Elizabeth actively engaged in debates with Burghley, Leicester, Sussex and Hatton. Advisers sought to ensure that she was genuinely convinced about a course of action. In June 1578, Wilson reported with satisfaction that Elizabeth was 'inwardly moved to do good' and 'satisfied in conscience, how to deal' with the Dutch rebels.[15]

Of course, things did not always go smoothly. Councillors could become angry when Elizabeth appeared neither to listen nor to accept their advice. In 1578, Sir Francis Knollys barked at Wilson, 'if her Majesty does not suppress and subject her own will and her own affections unto sound advice of open counsel, in matters touching the preventing of her danger, then her Majesty will be utterly overthrown.'[16] They also sometimes doctored information the Queen received. In 1586, Hatton and Walsingham, 'blott[ed] out some things' in a letter they showed to Elizabeth from Leicester in the Netherlands, 'which they thought would be offensive, and mending some other parts as they thought best'.[17]

These tensions did reflect differences of opinion between the Queen and her advisers about their respective political roles. These included Ciceronian ideas about citizenship (specifically that citizens had a role in counselling the monarch) and concerns that women were less able to govern than men. They also reflected divergences in opinion over religion – with some, like Burghley, Walsingham and Leicester, feeling Elizabeth was too conservative – and other key political issues, including the marriage and succession, Mary Stuart, Catholic conspiracy and the Dutch Revolt.

However, it is important not to push these tensions too far. First, gendered criticisms of the Queen were relatively rare. Knollys drew on negative stereotypes of women to criticise Elizabeth's actions in January 1569 (over Mary and the Northern Rising) and January 1578, but other crucial debates did not provoke the same censures. Second, councillors recognised that Elizabeth had to be convinced and, on personal issues like her marriage, had to make the final decision herself. In 1579, for example, Sussex argued, 'her heart is to be guided by God's direction and her own because no man can know the inward direction of her heart . . . [neither] can any man give counsel therein.'[18] Even Knollys sought to moderate his harsh tone, 'Her Majesty knows that I am loath to offend her . . . And indeed my speech has no grace worthy of her Majesty's ears, God has denied it me, [Therefore] I do utter my unworthy speech unto her Majesty.'[19] Ultimately, as Burghley told Sir Ralph Sadler, they knew that 'our part is to counsel, and after to obey the commander.'[20]

Third, councillors were willing to offer counsel outside formal Privy Council meetings. Burghley suggested that Elizabeth select a group of advisers to discuss her proposed marriage with Henri d'Anjou, in 1571. Walsingham did the same for Anglo-Scottish relations in 1583. Councillors also took the initiative to advise Elizabeth informally. In April 1586, Burghley and Walsingham 'this morning at sermon time . . . came to her Majesty' to persuade her not to order Leicester to resign the governor-generalship of the Netherlands.[21]

Elizabeth did not deliberately sideline the Privy Council in order to impose her authority. Though there were tensions between her and her councillors, these derived more from differences about their respective political roles and about religion than from the Queen's gender. Rather, her use of informal groups and her practice of seeking advice from individuals stemmed from the practical advantages these methods had and were underlined by common assumptions about how counselling should work – assumptions that were shared by her privy councillors.

THE EUROPEAN PERSPECTIVE

Elizabeth's use of informal groups of counsellors and ad-hoc counselling instead of the Privy Council had clear parallels with Mary I's practice. Mary also used a small group of individuals whom she personally selected to discuss policy, comprising the Earls of Arundel and Pembroke; Stephen Gardiner, Bishop of Winchester; Bishop Thirlby of Ely; Sir Robert Rochester; Sir William Paget; Sir William Petre and Cardinal Pole. Like Elizabeth's groups, it was an informal group that functioned separately from the Privy Council: Pole, Mary's closest adviser and the most important member of the group, was not a member of the council.

Elizabeth's and Mary's practice was similar to that of male monarchs in England and France. Between the fall of Wolsey and the emergence of the fully fledged Privy Council, Henry VIII was advised on major issues by an informal group of counsellors attendant on him, including the Dukes of Norfolk and Suffolk, the Earls of Wiltshire and Sussex, the Marquess of Exeter, Stephen Gardiner, William, Lord Sandys, Sir William Fitzwilliam and (after 1530) Thomas Cromwell. This continued in the late 1530s and in early 1540 when policy was discussed as often by the King and Cromwell alone as by the council. As with its Elizabethan successors, these informal discussions enabled Henry to discuss discreetly sensitive ideas and policies, such as the divorce. Reports from the Venetian ambassadors to France indicate that a *conseil des affaires* – a small group of intimate advisers who discussed political issues with the king at his *lever* – emerged under Francis I prior to 1526 and assumed a dominant position in counselling on Francis's return from captivity. This practice, rooted in the reigns of Charles VII, Charles VIII and Louis XII, was continued by Henri II, Charles IX and Henri III. Henri IV tended to use more ad-hoc meetings of ministers and magnates to sound out opinions, but their consultative function was the same.

Informal groups of advisers were also established as standard practices in contemporary political literature. We have already noted the similarities between Elizabeth's practice and Elyot's important treatise; they were also discussed in Elyot's other important treatises, *Pasquil the Playne* (1533), *Of that Knowlage, Whiche Maketh a Wise Man* (1533) and *The Image of Gouernance* (1541). Elyot argued that the leading *amici principis* – those held in particular favour by the king – formed the *consilium amicorum* (council of friends). In France, one of the leading sixteenth-century political treatises, Claude de Seyssel's *La Grant Monarchie de France* (written 1515; printed 1519) outlined a similar arrangement. Seyssel's treatise underlines the likelihood that Elizabeth adopted these practices because they were practical and useful rather than as ways of sidelining the council to assert her own control. Seyssel argued that the importance of the *conseil secret* (comparable to Elyot's *consilium amicorum*) was that it allowed the king to discuss important matters among a few well-chosen counsellors prior to wider debate. This was not only more effective, because decisions could be reached more quickly and more easily, but, more crucially, it preserved confidentiality for important or sensitive issues.

THE 1590s

So far, nothing has been said of the final fifteen years of Elizabeth's reign, and all the evidence has been drawn from the 1560s, 1570s and 1580s. John Guy has argued that Elizabeth's reign saw a decisive break in the mid-1580s, with major changes in the political agenda and political beliefs. The central political issues prior to Mary Stuart's execution – Elizabeth's marriage, the succession and Catholic conspiracy – now faded as Mary was replaced by the (Protestant) James VI as Elizabeth's heir presumptive. New to the agenda was the war with Spain, with the attendant issue of taxation as well as dearth, vagrancy and crime. In political beliefs, Guy argues the first thirty years of the reign were dominated by ideas of the 'mixed polity' – that the monarch governed in conjunction with the Privy Council and parliament – and republicanism. In Elizabeth's final years, Guy argues, the regime became more authoritarian, republican ideas were unwelcome, and greater emphasis was placed on the royal prerogative by councillors, even though this was precisely the time when Elizabeth's grip on politics weakened and policies were more likely to be taken out of her hands (with her tacit consent). Though some historians have questioned the extent to which the political agenda changed – in particular, that the succession and Catholic conspiracy continued to be matters of debate – Guy's emphasis on the distinctive quality of Elizabeth's final years is important and is particularly appropriate to an analysis of the role of the Privy Council.

The final fifteen years of the reign saw a major change in the composition of the Privy Council. Many key figures died, including Leicester (in 1588), Walsingham (in 1590), Sir James Croft (in 1590), Hatton (in 1591), Hunsdon (in 1596) as well as magnates such as Shrewsbury (in 1590) and Derby (in 1593). Burghley did not die until 1598, and, though he remained active until the last, he turned more and more responsibility over to his second son and political heir, Sir Robert Cecil. Cecil was just one of two younger men who were appointed to the council: in August 1591, aged twenty-eight. The other, in 1593, was Robert Devereux, 2nd Earl of Essex and Leicester's stepson; he was Elizabeth's last favourite and four years Cecil's junior. Whilst Cecil's appointment was startling in the context of complaints, contemporary and modern, of Elizabeth's reluctance to promote the younger generation (he had no political experience), it was also unusual as Elizabeth was loath to replace old friends and servants.

This reluctance has led historians to emphasise that the size of the council shrank considerably during the Queen's final years: from twenty-one in 1558 to ten by 1598. However, these numbers belie a more complex situation, as Elizabeth's early Privy Council included a number of members, particularly magnates, who did not attend council meetings regularly, if at all. By the 1590s, many of these had died and were not replaced, leaving the council smaller but with a higher proportion of active members. It is true, however, that there was a huge generational divide: in 1591, Robert Cecil was the only member to have been born after 1540.

The current orthodoxy suggests that the Council's business also grew and that it met more regularly – averaging a meeting every four days between 1597 and 1598 – though this may change when David Crankshaw publishes a detailed study of the Elizabethan Council. If the council's business did increase, then this owed much to the war with Spain and growing disorder in Ireland: they had to disburse money, convey instructions to military commanders, order local musters; mobilise soldiers and organise equipment and supplies. The burden of enforcement lay with local officials and commanders, but they did lodge complaints with the council if they met resistance which they expected councillors to address.

At the same time, the Council still had to fulfil its usual functions of overseeing local governance and officials, through which most domestic issues (law and order, welfare and the maintenance of infrastructure) were addressed. It was not helped by harvest failures in the 1590s, particularly those in 1596 and 1597, which led to problems of dearth, vagrancy and crime. Emergency measures restricting grain movement had to be implemented whilst the failure of the poor law to provide adequate assistance had to be tackled: with rising agricultural prices and plummeting wages, approximately two-fifths of the population fell below the margin of subsistence in these years. In addition, the council retained a quasi-judicial role to resolve suits that could not or had not been settled elsewhere, and, despite the development of the roles of the Star Chamber, the court of Requests and the Chancery, it saw a rising tide of petitions from suitors arrive in its chamber. Indeed, so many petitions were received that the council complained in 1589 and 1591 that it could not fulfil its other responsibilities and attempted, with only partial success, to refer as many cases as possible to other courts.

Councillors worked hard to meet all these demands, and many, such as Burghley, Cecil, Essex, Buckhurst, Hatton and Lord Admiral Howard, were assiduous attendees. It also helped that many had local followings, often reflected in their appointments as lord lieutenants in the counties, which facilitated the communication and enforcement of orders in the localities. But the fact remained that they were a small body with limited support staff; royal finances had been improved but remained inadequate even for peacetime, and, unlike their Continental counterparts, their country had no standing trained army. Few councillors had any (recent) military experience. As the theatre of war moved from England's doorstep, with the Armada in 1588 and Ireland, to the Netherlands, Spain and the Spanish fleets from the New World, logistics became more difficult, the council more stretched and its limitations clearer. Faced with these challenges, the council coped remarkably well.

Whether the regime became more authoritarian, as Guy argues, however, is debatable. The council punished political and religious nonconformity harshly. Two men were tortured and hanged for their participation in the Oxfordshire Rising of 1596, in which only a handful of rebels had turned up, while Archbishop Whitgift pursued a campaign for conformity against the 'puritans'. The council's defence of private property and property-owners in the face of growing dearth and crime was replicated in the localities by assize judges, justices of the peace and other officials as they closed ranks against the poor, servants, the unemployed and vagrants. Cawdrey's Case, heard in the court of Queen's Bench in 1591, upheld the Queen's 'imperial' authority against ideas of the 'mixed polity' and Presbyterianism. On the council itself, there were fewer debates, and Burghley, in his position of Lord Treasurer, regularly signed warrants for payment on the council's behalf without consulting them.

Whitgift's campaign against the puritans was in line with Elizabeth's own religious views, but the council's reaction to the Oxfordshire Rising was provoked as much, if not more, by the regime's fear of unrest during times of war and dearth than its authoritarianism. Ideas of the 'mixed polity' and republicanism, though increasingly associated with Catholic polemics on the succession, continued to be articulated in political treatises, notably about Irish reform. As we have seen for the meeting in May 1598, debate was not wholly absent from the council; indeed, it tended to occur when Burghley deliberately absented himself from meetings because he foresaw a clash with Whitgift on specific issues. The tension between them suggests that, even if Burghley was more conservative in the 1590s, there remained differences of opinion amongst councillors on religion as well as foreign policy.

Until Crankshaw publishes his study of the council, we will have little idea of exactly how counselling and policy-making worked in the final years of the reign. Historians such as Wallace MacCaffrey and Paul Hammer have argued the council took a lead role, though much of their evidence is drawn from administration rather than counselling, particularly in terms of the management of the wars. It is quite possible that the council did assume a greater advisory role in the 1590s than before and that the discussion of policy, evident during the fracas between Burghley and Essex in May 1598, was not unusual. As noted above, many of Elizabeth's most trusted advisers had died by 1591, and she did not forge such close relationships with newer appointees; they also lacked experience. Equally, however, her most trusted adviser, Burghley, survived and was active until 1598; Hunsdon died only in 1596; and Cobham, who had earlier been on the periphery of her trusted advisers, died in 1597. It seems unlikely that Elizabeth would have wholly given up earlier practices even if the pool of people on whom she could call had shrunk dramatically. It is unfortunate that most of the papers of Lord Buckhurst have been lost, as they could shed light on both this otherwise shadowy, long-standing privy councillor and royal cousin and on late-Elizabethan politics more generally.

Historians have instead focused on the impact of Cecil's and Essex's arrival on the political scene and the extent to which Elizabeth's final years saw the revival of factionalism on the council. In the early 1590s, relations between the two men were characterised by rivalry and competition as both sought to establish their political credentials and position. Tensions erupted periodically: over the appointment of the attorney-generalship and solicitor-generalship in 1593 and the investigation of charges against Elizabeth's doctor, Rodrigo Lopez, of plotting to poison the Queen in 1594. When Cecil suggested that Essex's favoured candidate for the attorney-generalship, the inexperienced and out-of-favour Sir Francis Bacon, should settle for the post of solicitor, Essex retorted, 'Digest me no digestions; for the attorneyship for Francis is that I must have.'[22] These tensions were exacerbated by different interests and approaches. Essex was committed to the defence of international Protestantism through military intervention; he also saw himself as a representative of the French code of *noblesse d'épée,* which privileged aristocratic status and martial law and honour over all hierarchies as well as civil and common law. By contrast, Cecil adopted a more cautious outlook, favoured peace and represented the French *noblesse de robe:* a meritocracy based on education and skill rather than blood that championed royal service and upheld the royal prerogative.

However, this rivalry did not constitute factionalism because there was no attempt by either Essex or Cecil to create a group of followers who owed exclusive loyalty to one in opposition to the other. The situation only changed in 1596 when Cecil was made principal secretary, an appointment Elizabeth probably made in revenge for Essex ignoring her orders by taking Cadiz (temporarily) and popularising his achievements with printed ballads and pamphlets. The Earl had long sought to reinstate William Davison (first appointed in 1586), who had been suspended after delivering Mary Stuart's sealed execution warrant to a group of privy councillors in 1587 who then dispatched it to Fotheringhay under their own warrant; Elizabeth later argued that she had not meant him to reveal to fellow councillors that the warrant had been sealed. The Earl saw this failure as a personal and political slight, and, though there were attempts to maintain a modus vivendi, rivalry turned quickly into factionalism. Essex became increasingly paranoid and isolated. He stormed at appointments, promotions and policy decisions, as demonstrated by the council meeting in May 1598. He also demanded exclusive support from courtiers: in July 1598, Lord Grey complained to Lord Cobham that Essex, 'has forced me to declare myself either his own or friend to Mr Secretary [i.e. Cecil], and his enemy: protesting that there could be no neutrality'.[23]

But, even at this point, it was a curious, lop-sided factionalism. Unlike Essex, Cecil did not gather a band of loyal supporters, preferring to maintain good relations with all, both long-established friends such as Buckhurst as well as those, like Nottingham, who were closely, though not exclusively, identified with Essex. Essex's isolation was reinforced by his increasingly erratic behaviour, which encouraged councillors to rally to the defence of the establishment, entrenching Cecil further into their ranks. The peace the Earl negotiated with the Earl of Tyrone when he was sent to quell revolt in Ireland, his bursting in on Elizabeth on his return when she was in a state of *déshabillé* and his ill-conceived rebellion in February 1601 sealed his fate, not the factional plotting he alleged.

THE COUNCIL AND THE COURT

Elton argued that because the Privy Council became the main advisory and policy-making body from the 1530s it superseded the royal household and the court as the main political forum in Tudor politics. This has reinforced a perceived antithesis between the 'court' and the 'council'. However, Elizabeth's use of individual counsellors and informal groups questions these assumptions. Her practice suggests that the court, rather than the Council, was the main political forum; it also elides the alleged differences between 'council' and 'court'. Advisers were selected for their personal relationship with the Queen rather than any official post they held on the council. Those that were privy councillors also usually held posts in the chamber or Privy Chamber in the royal household blurring the lines between the council and the court. Most crucially, political consultation did not take place in the council but in informal meetings and ad-hoc dialogue.

This would question Simon Adams's argument that court politics was subsumed into conciliar politics. In fact, it seems to be the other way round. Indeed, it is important to recognise that the boundaries between the council and the rest of the court were fluid. Though Elizabeth may have used informal groups of advisers to discuss sensitive political issues discreetly, she could never wholly restrict debate, and counsellors traded information and discussed political issues with their colleagues, family and friends. For instance, Sir Walter Mildmay, a privy councillor but not amongst Elizabeth's trusted inner circle, seems to have obtained a copy of Sussex's memoranda on the Anjou marriage in 1579, as he addressed many of the Earl's points in a meeting on 6 October, before the Earl himself spoke. Political debate was not restricted to men: women took a prominent part. Lady Burghley talked about the Archduke Charles match with both Guzman de Silva and the French ambassador, Paul de Foix, in 1565.

THE COUNCIL, PARLIAMENT AND THE OUTSIDE WORLD

A final issue to explore is the Privy Council's relationship with parliament and political debate in print. Geoffrey Elton, Michael Graves and Patrick Collinson have argued that the council employed 'men of business' to stage debates, in parliament or in printed pamphlets, on crucial issues to force Elizabeth's hand and to 'bounce' her into decisions. These included on the succession in the parliamentary sessions of 1563 and 1566, the 'alphabet bills' on religious reform in 1566 and 1571 and John Stubbs's pamphlet, *The Discoverie of a Gaping Gvlf* (1579), that attacked the Queen's proposed marriage to François, Duc d'Anjou, in 1579. Elton, Graves and Collinson also argued these 'men of business' were used to manage the House of Commons, to examine key problems and to prepare printed propaganda. They were secondary political figures at court, men such as Robert Beale, one of the clerks of the Privy Council, or other functionaries, including Thomas Norton (Remembrancer to the Lord Mayor of London), William Fleetwood (Recorder of London), and a number of the Speakers of the House of Commons.

However, research on key episodes has questioned the extent to which these men were council puppets. For example, Alford has shown that there was no explicit attempt by Cecil or other councillors to 'plant' speeches in the Commons in 1563 or 1566 to encourage Elizabeth to settle the succession. Rather, parliament shared councillors' concerns and worked closely, of its own volition, to try and force Elizabeth to settle the succession. Similarly, it has been impossible to forge convincing connections between John Stubbs and Leicester and Walsingham, who are argued to have sponsored the production of the *Gaping Gvlf*. Stubbs does seem to have obtained some conciliar memoranda through his friends, Baptist Hickes and Vincent Skinner, who were Burghley's secretaries. But evidence suggests that he acted independently, believing he had a responsibility to counsel the Queen and because he was anxious about the ramifications of the marriage for the preservation of Protestantism. With Skinner and Hickes, he had earlier attacked Archbishop Parker in print for his role in the Vestiarian Controversy.

CONCLUSION

It is perhaps perverse to spend much of a chapter on the Elizabethan Privy Council denying its importance and downgrading its role in one of the key tasks: counselling. The Council was not an insignificant body in Elizabethan governance. In a diverse and, by modern standards, decentralised realm with a relatively poor sense of delegation and limited resources, it played a pivotal role in disseminating royal commands, managing policy, channelling communication between the centre and localities, maintaining law and order and addressing domestic defence. Considering its resources, it fulfilled these growing demands remarkably well, perhaps largely thanks to the diligence of many of its leading members.

However, the enormous influence that Elton's work has had on our understanding of Tudor politics may have exaggerated the Privy Council's importance, as an institutional body, in counselling and policy-making. Evidence suggests that, for at least the first thirty years of the reign, these responsibilities were fulfilled by councillors and others working informally at the behest of the Queen. They were able to assume these roles because of their close relationship with Elizabeth, which, in turn, was recognised by appointment to the Privy Council. This was not to say that some, such as Burghley, believed that a Privy Council, as an institutional body, should not play a central role in counselling, but they also had to take account of the views and actions of Elizabeth.

As noted above, there were clear similarities between Elizabeth's methods of counselling and those in contemporary France. How typical of Continental Europe was the council's role and significance? In comparison to its nearest neighbours and rivals, France and Spain, the English conciliar system was smaller and less sophisticated. For instance, whereas England had just the Privy Council, supplemented by the Councils of the North, the Marches of Wales and the Privy Council of Ireland, Spain had seven main councils (Castile, Aragon, Portugal, Flanders, Inquisition, Orders and Crusade) and seven further supplementary councils that reported either to the Consejo Real (the Council of Castile) or of Aragon. There was also a strict demarcation of duties and a complex system to manage incoming business. Though there were closer similarities with France's conciliar system, the career structure in the latter was more rigid and ministerial responsibilities and specialisms more developed than in England. These differences were partly because, unlike the Valois and Habsburg regimes, the Tudors had not been involved in large-scale, protracted warfare for much of the century. But territorial size was crucial: Spain's proliferation of councils was accelerated by territorial expansion in the New World.

Though MacCaffrey has seen the Spanish system as the antithesis of the English and 'the exemplar of maturity', it was not without its problems.[24] Arising from the immense size of the Spanish Empire, procedures were Byzantine, the workload was immense, the councillors were seen as corrupt and were quick to undermine their colleagues, and the secretaries wielded much influence because they were the channels of communication between the councils and the King. The councils had no policy-making role, and the system continued to rely on the active participation of the monarch, something that Philip accentuated by his desire 'to read almost anything that came across his desk'.[25] By comparison, the smaller, more collegial English Privy Council, even if it did not assume as large a role in policy-making as Elton suggested, seems to have been as, if not more, effective; a sign that, perhaps, less was more.

FURTHER READING

Adams, Simon, 'Faction, Clientage and Party: English Politics, 1550–1603', *History Today*, 32 (12) (1982): 33–9.

—— 'Eliza Enthroned? The Court and Its Politics', in Christopher Haigh (ed.), *The Reign of Elizabeth I* (Basingstoke and London, 1984), pp. 55–77.

Alford, Stephen, *The Early Elizabethan Polity: William Cecil and the British Succession Crisis, 1558–1569* (Cambridge, 1998).

Cole, Mary Hill, *The Portable Queen: Elizabeth I and the Politics of Ceremony* (Amherst, Mass., 1999).

Collinson, Patrick, 'The Monarchical Republic of Queen Elizabeth I', *Bulletin of the John Rylands University Library of Manchester*, 69 (2) (1987): 394–424.

—— 'Puritans, Men of Business and Elizabethan Parliaments', *Parliamentary History*, 7 (2) (1988): 187–211; reprinted in Patrick Collinson (ed.), *Elizabethan Essays* (London, 1994), pp. 59–86.

—— 'The Elizabethan Exclusion Crisis and the Elizabethan Polity', *Proceedings of the British Academy*, 84 (1994): 51–92.

Crane, Mary Thomas, 'Video and Taceo: Elizabeth I and the Rhetoric of Counsel', *Studies in English Literature, 1500–1900*, 28 (1) (1988): 1–15.

Doran, Susan, *Monarchy and Matrimony: The Courtships of Elizabeth I* (London, 1996).

Elton, G. R., 'Tudor Government: The Points of Contact. II: The Council', *Transactions of the Royal Historical Society*, 5th Series, 25 (1975): 195–211.

Graves, M. A. R., 'The Management of the Elizabethan House of Commons: The Council's "Men-of-Business"', *Parliamentary History*, 2 (1) (1983): 11–38.

—— 'Elizabethan Men of Business Reconsidered', *Parergon*, 14 (1) (1996): 111–27.

Guy, John, 'The French King's Council, 1483–1526', in Ralph A. Griffiths and James Sherborne (eds.), *Kings and Nobles in the Later Middle Ages: A Tribute to Charles Ross* (Gloucester and New York, 1986), pp. 274–94.

—— 'The Privy Council: Revolution or Evolution?' in Christopher Coleman and David Starkey (eds.), *Revolution Reassessed: Revisions in the History of Tudor Government and Administration* (Cambridge, 1986), pp. 59–85.

—— (ed.), *The Reign of Elizabeth I: Court and Culture in the Last Decade* (Cambridge, 1995).

McLaren, A. N., *Political Culture in the Reign of Elizabeth I: Queen and Commonwealth, 1558–1585* (Cambridge, 1999).

Mears, Natalie, 'Counsel, Public Debate, and Queenship: John Stubbs's *The Discoverie of Gaping Gulf*, 1579', *Historical Journal*, 44 (3) (2001): 629–50.

—— 'Politics in the Elizabethan Privy Chamber: Lady Mary Sidney and Kat Ashley', in James Daybell (ed.), *Women and Politics in Early Modern England, 1450–1700* (Basingstoke, 2004), pp. 67–82.

—— *Queenship and Political Discourse in the Elizabethan Realms* (Cambridge, 2005).

Neale, J. E., 'The Elizabethan Political Scene', *Proceedings of the British Academy*, 34 (1948): 97–117; reprinted in J. E. Neale, *Essays in Elizabethan History* (London, 1958), pp. 59–84.

Pulman, Michael Barraclough, *The Elizabethan Privy Council in the Fifteen-Seventies* (Berkeley, Calif., 1971).

Read, Conyers, *Mr Secretary Walsingham and the Policy of Queen Elizabeth*, 3 vols. (Oxford, 1925).

—— *Mr Secretary Cecil and Queen Elizabeth* (London, 1955).

—— *Lord Burghley and Queen Elizabeth* (London, 1960).

Wright, Pam, 'A Change in Direction: The Ramifications of a Female Household, 1558–1603', in David Starkey, D. A. L. Morgan, John Murphy, Pam Wright, Neil Cuddy and Kevin M. Sharpe (eds.), *The English Court: From the Wars of the Roses to the Civil War* (London, 1987), pp. 147–72.

Younger, Neil, 'If the Armada Had Landed: A Reappraisal of England's Defences in 1588', *History*, 93 (311) (2008): 328–54.

NOTES

1 William Camden, *The History of the Most Renowned and Victorious Princess Elizabeth, Late Queen of England,* 3rd edn (London, 1675), p. 555.
2 Stephen Alford, *The Early Elizabethan Polity: William Cecil and the British Succession Crisis, 1558–1569* (Cambridge, 1998), p. 69.
3 William Paget to Sir Thomas Wriothesley, 27 June 1541, *Letters and Papers, Foreign and Domestic, Henry VIII,* ed. J. S. Brewer et al., 22 vols. (London, 1864–1932), vol. XVI, p. 450.
4 BL, Harleian MS 6265, fols. 71v–72r.
5 The Earl of Leicester to Lord Burghley, 4 November 1572, Hatfield House, Hertfordshire, Cecil MSS 7, fol. 57.
6 Memorandum of the Count of Feria, 1559, *Letters and State Papers Relating to English Affairs, Preserved Principally in the Archives of Simancas* (hereafter *CSP Span.*), ed. M. A. S. Hume, 4 vols. (London, 1892–9), vol. I, p. 36.
7 Burghley to Walsingham, 10 August 1581, BL, Harleian 6265, fols. 52r–52v.
8 *Wordes Spoken by Her Maiestie to Mr Cicille* (20 November 1558), TNA, SP12/1/6A, fol. 12.
9 TNA, SP12/1/6A, fol. 12.
10 Sir Francis Walsingham to the Earl of Shrewsbury, 30 July 1582, in Edmund Lodge, *Illustrations of British History, Biography and Manners,* 3 vols. (London, 1791), vol. II, pp. 276–7.
11 Queen's Answer to the Commons' Petition, 28 January 1563, TNA, SP12/27/36, fol. 143.
12 Maria Perry, *The Word of a Prince: A Life from Contemporary Documents* (London, 1990), pp. 37–8.
13 F. W. Conrad, 'The Problem of Counsel Reconsidered: The Case of Sir Thomas Elyot', in Paul A. Fideler and T. F. Mayer (eds.), *Political Thought and the Tudor Commonwealth: Deep Structure, Discourse and Disguise* (London, 1992), p. 89.
14 Sir Thomas Elyot, *The Boke Named the Gouernour* (London, 1531), fols. 252v–53r.
15 Thomas Wilson to William Davison, 5 June 1578, TNA, SP83/7/5.
16 Sir Francis Knollys to Thomas Wilson, 9 January 1578, BL Harleian MS 6992, fol. 89.
17 Thomas Dudley to Leicester, 11 February 1585, BL Cotton MS Galba C. 9, fol. 79v.
18 *Obyectyons to Be Made against the Marryage, Mar. 1579,* Hatfield House, Hertfordshire, Cecil MSS 148, fol. 12.
19 BL Harleian MS 6992, fol. 89.
20 William Cecil to Sir Ralph Sadler, 14 January 1569, BL Additional MS 33593, fol. 129.
21 Burghley to Leicester, 1 April 1586, BL Cotton MS Galba C. IX, fol. 167.
22 Sir Anthony Standen to Anthony Bacon, 3 February 1594, in Thomas Birch (ed.), *Memoirs of the Reign of Queen Elizabeth,* 2 vols. (London, 1754), vol. I, pp. 152–3.
23 Lord Grey to Lord Cobham, 21 July 1598, Hatfield House, Hertfordshire, Cecil MSS 54, fol. 75.
24 Wallace T. MacCaffrey, *Elizabeth I: War and Politics, 1588–1603* (Princeton, NJ, 1992), p. 20.
25 Geoffrey Parker, *The Grand Strategy of Philip II* (New Haven, Conn., 1998), p. 27.

CHAPTER FIVE

FAMILIA REGINAE
The Privy Court

William Tighe

This essay deals with those men and women, numbering about thirty-five at any given time, and totalling upwards of seventy-five (at least) in the course of the reign – so far as accurate numbers can be ascertained – who held offices in the Privy Chamber, plus the Esquires of the Body, who superintended the Chamber (or 'Household above Stairs') at night, as well as, if to a lesser extent, the nature and functions of the offices which they held. The Privy Chamber was a court department with a clear institutional identity; by contrast, to select the Esquires for the Body, with no more than a glance at two or three other positions, on the one hand, and to pass over the Band of Gentlemen Pensioners, a guard corps of fifty men (and five officers), of whom twenty-five were on duty at any given time, stationed in the Presence Chamber, on the other, may appear arbitrary, but it reflects my own judgement that positions in the 'outer' Chamber could confer significant and frequent access to the Privy Chamber personnel, and possibly to the monarch herself. In addition, I have had to set aside the Maids of Honour, who numbered five or six at any given moment, plus the Mother of the Maids, who have hitherto been tangential to my research. These courtiers who form the focus of the essay would have been individuals whose duties in all cases could, and in most cases would, bring them into close personal proximity with the Queen, and with whom, as the following incident, among others related in this essay, illustrates, she would have dealt on a personal level rather than merely on an official one. They were, in other words, the closest approximation that she was to have to a family as queen. (Indeed, I would prefer to use that word, 'family', given its original Latin sense as denoting those who dwell together in a house, rather than more 'distancing' terms such as 'attendants' or 'entourage' or 'servants' or even 'companions', accurate as each of these is in its own way, as it gets us closer to the Rankean ideal, so desirable if unattainable, of seeing 'how things actually were'.)

On Monday, 1 February 1585, Frances Howard, a daughter of William, 1st Lord Howard of Effingham (d. 1572) and a sister of Charles (d. 1624), the 2nd Lord and the future Earl of Nottingham and commander of the English fleet assembled to withstand the 1588 Spanish Armada, and herself a Gentlewoman of the Queen's Privy Chamber since November 1568, wrote a two-and-one-half-page letter to Edward Seymour, Earl of Hertford (d. 1621). Although she was not to marry Hertford for well over a year, already she signed the latter as the Earl's 'moste faythfull louvyng obedient w.(ife) durynge lyfe'.[1] The letter, in fact, concerned the latest episode in the attempt which had already stretched out for nearly a decade to win the Queen's consent for the match between the couple. For Frances Howard, the marriage, when it came, was to be her first and only one, and childless, but for the Earl it was to be the second of three. His clandestine marriage to Lady Katherine Grey in 1560, the mother of his two sons, had prompted the Queen's confinement of the couple in the Tower and then their forcible separation, extending down to the hapless Lady Katherine's death in 1567. Understandably enough, in these circumstances the couple did not care to risk marrying quietly and presenting the Queen with a *fait accompli* in the manner of other courtiers, such as John Scudamore and Mary Shelton, another Privy Chamber lady and the Queen's cousin, who had married in that fashion in very late 1573 or very early 1574 and who – or at least Shelton – had to endure both 'bloes and yevell wordes' from her mistress as well as some months of banishment from the court before being restored to favour, but rather sought to win her agreement beforehand.[2] To that end, her brother Charles had spoken to the Queen to request her to give her consent. As Frances Howard reported, the Queen seemed 'some thynge moved' at his words but then asked if Hertford had asked him to speak for the match. Effingham replied no but had been compelled to speak because it had been only the fear of offending her that had delayed its conclusion and that he was certain of Hertford's honourable intentions. This evidently hit a sore spot in the Queen's mind, and the exchange took an alarming turn, one which requires an extended quotation from the letter. 'Her maiestie repleyed agayne' – evidently a thought she had voiced on previous occasions:

> that che was suer you mente it not but that you wolde be contented to geve her a pensyon, to the wyche my brother made aunswar that he wold never lyke of it nor never acounte me for hys syster if I wolde consent to it and that it touched her maiestie in honor to have any gentellwoman aboute her to take a pensyon of any man in suche a maner. Her maiestie rose up and lafte with these wordes, that he had done the part of a good brother and as he ought to doe, but stell che saed che thought it was no parte of your desier.

The next day, the Queen asked her when Hertford would next be at court and then went on to ask her whether she really wanted to marry the Earl, and why. She replied that it was a matter of long-continued affection and that she would count herself the 'hapyes woman in the worlde' if the Queen would permit the marriage. Then, as she continued in her letter,

> Many perswasons che used against maryge and the inconvenyense thereof and how lettell you wolde care for me, telyng me how well I was here and hoe muche che cared for me. I humble thanked her maiestie and did acknowleg as muche. Many kynde speeches passed betwyne us but in the end che resoned with me that att your coming if it were your contentment and lykynge che wolde not be against my desier and good fourtune.

She went on to mention the Queen's continued 'good wordes' on many occasions since their conversation and concluded, 'swet lorde the worste is paste and I warrant you che will nevar speke one angery worde to you.'[3] The couple, wed at last in December 1585, enjoyed a decade or more of marriage, until the Countess died on 14 May 1598, according to her monument in Westminster Abbey, aged forty-four and childless. Incidents such as this demonstrate the close and 'jealous' interest that the Queen took in her 'familiar' servants and companions, as well as her desire to retain their presence around her regardless of their matrimonial status.

The Tudor court, and indeed the courts of individual Tudor and Stuart monarchs, have received a great deal of attention from historians in recent decades, but as yet there has been no comprehensive study of the Elizabethan Privy Chamber and its personnel. In this essay, rather than rehash or reassess these institutional or political studies, I propose to assume them and instead to work from the centre outwards: to examine the positions, and the individuals who held them, beginning with the Privy Chamber and its staff and extending outwards into the Chamber, the 'above stairs' department of the court, the *Domus Regis Magnificencie* under the Lord Chamberlain, and for the most part ignoring the Household properly speaking, the 'below stairs' *Domus Regis Providencie* under the Lord Steward, when there was one, or the Treasurer of the Household and his under-officers when there was none. My aim is more at providing a prosopological survey of the more important offices and officeholders at the Elizabethan Court, reckoning 'important' in this context as meaning serving in positions that gave one frequent personal access to the Queen, or at least the possibility of such access, since it was this access that made such service desirable and such positions important to their holders. I assume as well that the Queen would have recognised by sight and name most if not all of the individuals who served in such positions, although I do not think that this assumption is susceptible of proof. Finally, and to a degree arbitrarily, this essay will not for the most part attend to individuals holding great offices of state, even when such offices remained officially situated in the 'outer' Chamber, as did the secretaryship and its occupant or occupants, and had not gone out to become effectively heads of independent departments, as had the Master of the Horse or the Master of the Great Wardrobe.

The prehistory, institutionalisation and development of the Privy Chamber under the first three Tudors have been treated in detail elsewhere, but the advent of a female monarch necessitated adjustments. Mary Tudor, as queen, had a full complement of men and women serving in her Privy Chamber: 'Ladies of the Privy Chamber', often the wives of prominent officials, who seem to have been supernumeraries whose presence might be required on formal occasions; 'Gentlemen of the Privy Chamber' and 'Gentlewomen of the Privy Chamber'; 'Grooms of the Privy Chamber' and their female counterparts, 'Chamberers'. When Elizabeth I succeeded her sister, she maintained most aspects of the Marian Privy Chamber but with a smaller number of working personnel, and, in particular, a great reduction in the number of male members.

The household list drawn up for the purpose of provision of apparel for the Queen's coronation on 15 January 1559 breaks up the Privy Chamber into the following categories and numbers: the Bedchamber (four women), Chamberers (three women), the Privy Chamber without wages (seven women), Maids of the

Privy Chamber (six women), Gentleman of the Privy Chamber and Master of the Jewel House (one man), Gentleman Usher of the Privy Chamber (one man), Maids of Honour (six women, plus the 'Mother of the Maids'), Extraordinaries of the Privy Chamber when summoned by the Queen (eleven women) and (included in the list between the Privy Chamber personnel and those of the 'outer' Chamber) a group entitled 'Ladies and Gentlemen of the Household' which consisted of eighteen women only – no men's names appeared on it.[4] It appears that those included in the last two categories were supernumeraries, where I have been able to identify them, the wives or daughters of courtiers (such as the wife of James Marvin, one of the Esquires for the Body) or government officials (such as the wives of Sir Thomas Benger, Sir William Cecil and Sir Nicholas Throckmorton) or worthy widows, such as the widow of Sir John Cheke or, for a more obscure example, Elizabeth Snowe (d. 1587), widow of Richard Snowe (d. 1554), whose identity with the 'extraordinary' of 1559 is assured only by the passing mention in her will of a cup received from the Queen as a New Year's gift; one, at least, of the Privy Chamber extraordinaries, Mistress Edmondes, later became a Gentlewoman of the Privy Chamber; and another, Lady Cheke, had been a member of Elizabeth's household since the early 1540s and was to remain an 'unfeed' member of the Queen's 'family' for the entirety of the reign. It appears that the differentiation between women of the Bedchamber and those of the Privy Chamber was an innovation of Elizabeth's reign – it does not appear on any lists of the personnel of the Marian Privy Chamber – and that this differentiation was a matter of status and access rather than of departmental division, although it anticipates James I's creation in 1603 of a Bedchamber department and staff distinct from the Privy Chamber. Moreover, the categories of the 'Privy Chamber without wages' and 'Maids of the Privy Chamber' were to prove ephemeral, as on later lists (most of them fee lists) those without wages disappear, and the rest, together with the 'Maids' reappear as 'Gentlewomen of the Privy Chamber' receiving the same wages as those of the Bedchamber.[5]

Who were these familiars who attended upon the Queen? Many of them, if not most of them, had been in Elizabeth's household by the time of Henry VIII's death, if not earlier. A list drawn up sometime, probably early, in Elizabeth's first year as queen, and partly illegible, lists as the Bedchamber gentlewomen Katherine Astley, Katherine Knollys, Blanche Parry and Elizabeth Norwich. Save for Lady Knollys, wife of Sir Francis Knollys and the daughter of Mary Boleyn, the Queen's aunt, possibly by her husband Sir William Carey but just as possibly by Henry VIII (like her brother Henry, Lord Hunsdon), and who was to remain in her Bedchamber position until her death in 1569, all of them had been in Elizabeth's service by 1547. Astley (previously Katherine Champernown) and Parry had been among those appointed no later than when Elizabeth's household had been established at some point in or after 1537. Astley (d. 1565) was the wife of John Astley, who was to serve as Master of the Jewel House until his death in 1596 and was also one of only two men to hold the position of Gentleman of the Privy Chamber under Elizabeth; Blanche Parry (d. 1590) had been Elizabeth's nurse in her infancy; and Elizabeth Norwich (d. c. 1594), about whose career scant information survives, was later to marry Sir Gawain Carew (d. 1585).

Next in the 1559 list come seven Privy Chamber gentlewomen: Elizabeth Cliffe (or Clyve), Brigit Skipwith, Elizabeth Markham, Anne Wingfield, Elizabeth Saintlowe (or Saint Loe), Margaret Willoughby and Lettice Knollys. Cliffe (who disappears after Elizabeth's first year on the throne) has so far eluded identification, while Wingfield (who continues in her position until 1571), may have been a half-sister of Elizabeth Saintlowe. Skipwith, whose birth in February 1521 is recorded in her family's Book of Hours, later married Brian Cave and remained in the Privy Chamber until 1588. Markham, who subsequently married John Harington (and became the mother of the Queen's godson of the same name, the witty author of *The Metamorphosis of Ajax*) and remained in the Queen's service until her death in 1579 and Willoughby, who by her marriage a year later to Matthew Arundell of Wardour Castle became the perhaps unwitting ancestress of a long line of recusants and who continued in her position to her death in 1584, were more prominent. Saintlowe, the famous Bess of Hardwick – an identity that has been questioned but which appears to be clinched by her later correspondence with some of her former female Privy Chamber fellows now at the Folger Library – had been one of Elizabeth's gentlewomen in the latter years of Henry VIII's reign, and her third husband, Sir William Saint Loe (d. 1565), served as Captain of the Guard from the beginning of the reign until his death. However, she was suspended from her position in 1561 after meddling in the matrimonial intrigues of the early years of the reign, and although she appears to have been paid, irregularly, by the Keeper of the Privy Purse, the wages due her in her office in 1563, she had left the Privy Chamber by the time of her marriage to the Earl of Shrewsbury in 1568. She was to outlive the Queen, with whom her subsequent relations were frequently uneasy and occasionally fraught, dying in 1608. Lettice Knollys, a daughter of Sir Francis and Lady Katherine, for whom the Queen came to have a settled dislike, if not detestation, after her clandestine 1578 marriage to the Earl of Leicester – even the son of her first marriage, Robert Devereux, the 2nd Earl of Essex, was unable to reconcile the Queen to his mother – left the Queen's service after only a year. All of these women of the Bedchamber and Privy Chamber received annual wages of £33 6s. 8d. Strangely absent from this list, although clearly appointed to the Privy Chamber at the same time, as the accounts of the Cofferer of the Household demonstrate, was Katherine Carey, a daughter of Lord Hunsdon, who some seven years later married the future Earl of Nottingham and whose death on 25 February 1603 added to the Queen's melancholy listlessness at the onset of her fatal illness.

The three Chamberers of 1559 were Elizabeth Marbury, Dorothy Broadbelt and Frances Newton. Marbury, who served until 1570, has likewise eluded identification, as has Broadbelt, who served Elizabeth from 1543 until 1577 and in the mid-1560s married John Abington of the Counting House, who became Cofferer of the Household in the year preceding his death in 1581. Frances Newton subsequently married William, Lord Cobham, and remained a Chamberer until her death in 1592. The Chamberers, the female equivalents of the Grooms, and as such technically the holders of menial offices who dressed in livery outfits, received £20 in annual wages.

The male staff of the Privy Chamber was smaller in numbers. John Astley was the only Gentleman, serving from the beginning of the reign to his death in 1596;

his only companion in that position was to be Christopher Hatton, from 1572 to his death in 1591. Three men served as Gentleman Usher of the Privy Chamber – an office which generally had two simultaneous incumbents under the later Tudors – in the course of the reign. John Norris, the religiously conservative elder brother of the Henry Norris of Henry VIII's Privy Chamber who had been executed in 1536 as one of Anne Boleyn's supposed paramours and whose son, another Henry, was to be ennobled in 1572, had served as a Gentleman Usher in the Chamber of Henry VIII and Edward VI and then under Queen Mary became both a Gentleman Usher of the Privy Chamber and Black Rod (Usher of the Order of the Garter and of the House of Parliament). Initially he seemed destined to be relegated back to the 'outer' Chamber (where he is listed as the first of the quarter waiters on the list drawn up for Elizabeth's coronation in January 1559), but on 31 January of that year he had a warrant for his wages as one of the Privy Chamber, and he held the position until his death in January 1577. Dru Drury's warrant as Gentleman Usher was dated 3 January 1559, the date of the official appointment of almost all of the 'feed' staff of the Privy Chamber, and he held the position until his death in extreme old age in April 1617. However, he was to be removed – or perhaps suspended would be a better term – between 1560 and 1577. He evidently offended the Queen in the course of the first year of her reign by expressing disapproval of Lord Robert Dudley's familiarity with her – according to one report even threatening to kill him – and as a result had been committed to the Fleet prison in September 1559, from which he wrote, seemingly to the Privy Council, on 15 January 1561, to ask their aid in seeking the Queen's forgiveness and for clemency. Drury's replacement, Sir George Howard, a brother of Henry VIII's fifth queen and Master of the Armoury from the beginning of the reign, was appointed in August 1572 although he had exercised the office for over a year previously and held it until his death in 1580. Drury's return followed the death of John Norris in 1577; two years later, he was knighted, and after Howard's death in 1580 he remained as sole Gentleman Usher of the Privy Chamber for the rest of the reign, serving also as Lieutenant of the Tower in 1595–6. The Gentlemen each received £33 6s. 8d. in annual wages; the Gentlemen Ushers each £30.

There were generally four Grooms of the Privy Chamber at any one time under Mary and Elizabeth. Elizabeth's first four were to have been Thomas Astley, Henry Seckford (or Sackford), John Baptist Castellion (Castiglione) and Thomas Commaunder, but the last of these made his deathbed will and died on 2 January 1559, and in his place came John Tamworth, who also served as Keeper of the Privy Purse until his death in April 1569. Astley, who served until his death in August 1595, was a brother of John Astley of the Jewel House. Castellion, who first appears in an English context (along with several other Italians) among the English force besieging Boulogne in 1544, was in Elizabeth's household by the time of Henry VIII's funeral in February 1547, is said to have been her Italian teacher and served until his death in February 1598. Seckford, a nephew of Sir Thomas Seckford (d. 1587), a Master of Requests and Surveyor of the Court of Wards from the beginning of Elizabeth's reign, served in the Privy Chamber all through it, after 1569 also as Keeper of the Privy Purse, and subsequently down to his death in October 1610; under James he also held the office of Master of the Tents, Halls and Pavilions.

Ten further men served as Grooms of the Privy Chamber in the course of the reign. First came Thomas Litchfield, a lutenist and perhaps lute teacher to the Queen, in March 1559, until his death in 1586. Then, in 1562, came Edward Carey (d. 1618), a cousin of Henry Carey, Lord Hunsdon, and grandfather of Lucius Carey, Viscount Falkland, host of the Great Tew circle in the 1630s, who served out the remainder of the reign and succeeded John Astley in 1596 as Master of the Jewel House. In 1569, Henry Middlemore replaced John Tamworth after the latter's death, but there is a puzzle here. Sir Nicholas Throckmorton had written to the Queen on 18 November 1558 to solicit one of these groomships of the Privy Chamber for 'my cosyne harry mydylmore', and at last in 1569 he got it, holding it until his death in 1592.[6] The puzzle is that while the records of livery clothing granted to the Privy Chamber grooms in the Lord Chamberlain's department of the royal household demonstrate that he held the position during these years, the fact that his name never appears among those of his fellow grooms in the Cofferer's accounts, where the payment of their wages was recorded, seems to indicate that his status remained that of an 'extraordinary' and 'unfeed' groom rather than an 'ordinary' and 'feed' one. If, as is likely, he was the otherwise unidentified Mr Middlemore who wrote to the Queen in 1588 about the losses that he had incurred by serving her 'in this place' for twenty years without compensation, this demonstrates the reality of the puzzle without explaining it.

Thomas Knyvett (d. 1622), a son of a Gentleman of the Privy Chamber to Henry VIII, held the position in 1570 until his ennoblement in 1603 by James I, and he also obtained from the Queen the position of warden of the Mint. Thomas Gorges was appointed in 1571. What connections brought him to this position are not easy to discover, despite his having an older brother, William, who had been one of the band of Gentlemen Pensioners since early in Mary Tudor's reign, but his initially risky marriage to the young widowed Marchioness of Northampton, one of the Privy Chamber ladies, cemented his position there, and he was to serve as one of its gentlemen ushers under James I, until his death in March 1610. William Killigrew, who began to receive livery garments as a Groom of the Privy Chamber in 1574 but received a warrant for his fee only in 1578, was a younger brother of the Cornish Protestant, Marian exile and Elizabethan diplomat Sir Henry Killigrew, an associate if not a client of the Earl of Leicester; he served there until the end of Elizabeth's reign and under James I became Chamberlain of the Exchequer until his death in 1622. Ferdinando Richardson, alias Heyborne, who entered the Privy Chamber in 1587, appears to have replaced the deceased Thomas Litchfield as its 'musician in residence'. Heyborne, unlike the lutenist whom he succeeded, was a virginal player and minor composer and had been a student in his youth of Thomas Tallis. He retained his position under James I until 1611 and died in 1618. Edward Darcy, a grandson of Thomas, Lord Darcy of Templehurst, who had been one of the leaders of the Pilgrimage of Grace and was executed in its aftermath, and son of an Edwardian Lieutenant of the Tower who had died early in Elizabeth's reign, probably owed his entrée to another Groom of the Privy Chamber, his father-in-law Thomas Astley. Darcy's name appears in the livery lists beginning in 1581, but his fee warrant came only in 1595, the year of Astley's death. He left his position at the beginning of James I's reign and died in 1618. Edward Denny, who received livery garb as a Groom of the Privy Chamber from 1582 until his death in 1600, but who, like John Tamworth and Henry Middlemore earlier in the reign, never received a fee warrant, was a son of the Sir Anthony Denny (d. 1549) who had been Groom of the Stool to Henry VIII at the end of his reign. He had been born in 1547 and spent much of the period from the late 1570s into the 1590s in military activities, on the seas against Spain and especially in Ireland, where he received extensive grants of Desmond lands in Kerry and where his descendants later resided. Michael Stanhope, finally, the youngest of the five sons of Sir Michael Stanhope, a follower of the Duke of Somerset who had been executed along with the Duke in February 1552, was a brother of Sir John Stanhope whose court career culminated with his becoming Treasurer of the Chamber in 1596, an office he held until 1616. He began to serve in the Privy Chamber in 1586 but did not receive a 'feed' appointment until 1598. He left his position as groom at the beginning of James I's reign, although if the claim on his tomb inscription in the parish church of Sudborne, Suffolk, that he served King James 'in the same place' for the rest of his days (he died in 1621) is accurate, he may well have become a Gentleman of the Privy Chamber subsequently.

Returning to the Privy Chamber women, we have to face the difficulty that a number of the women who held a position there of 'gentle' status received neither wages nor livery garments, and whose names are accordingly included on none of the lists recording grants of wages or of such garments, or of the payment of subsidy assessments as members of the royal household. There are name lists generated for Elizabeth's coronation in January 1559 and for her funeral in April 1603, which provide otherwise unrecorded ones, but beyond these one has to rely on allusions in correspondence, grants and other documents. These women certainly included two who, alongside the previously mentioned Katherine (Champernown) Astley and Blanche Parry, had been appointed as 'handmaids' to the Lady Elizabeth by 1543. The first of these was Elizabeth Fitzgerald (or simply 'Garret'), a daughter of Gerald Fitzgerald, Earl of Kildare, who had died in the Tower of London in December 1534. She and her two brothers – Gerald (d. 1585), who had been spirited away to Italy and returned to England at the close of Edward VI's reign and was restored to the family earldom by Mary Tudor, and Edward, who was raised in England at Henry VIII's expense, became a Gentleman Pensioner in 1549 and served as lieutenant of that corps from early in Mary's reign until his death in 1590 – were the only offspring of the family who survived the executions in 1537 of their five uncles and half-brother 'Silken Thomas' after the suppression of the latter's rebellion of 1534–5. Entitled 'the fair Geraldine' by the poet Earl of Surrey, she married Sir Anthony Browne, the King's Master of the Horse, late in Henry VIII's reign, and some years after Browne's death in 1548, Edward, Lord Clinton, whom Queen Elizabeth created Earl of Lincoln and who served her in the last decade of his life as Lord Admiral, and continued to be one of the Queen's intimate companions until her death in March 1590. The second 'handmaid' was Mary Hill, a daughter of a sergeant of the cellar to Henry VIII, Richard Hill. She married, first, in 1547 or 1548, Sir John Cheke, the humanist and Greek scholar, and after his death in 1557, in 1559 or 1560, Henry Mackwilliam (1532–86), who soon thereafter became a Gentleman Pensioner. 'Lady Cheeke' (as she was always termed) remained a fixture at court for the rest of the reign, dying in 1616, and was almost certainly the last survivor of Elizabeth's household of 1543. Other such 'unfeed' Privy Chamber women included Elizabeth Brooke Cobham (d. 1565), second wife of William Parr, Marquess of Northampton; Lady Mary Sidney (d. 1586), daughter of John Dudley, Duke of Northumberland and wife of Sir Henry and mother of Sir Philip Sidney; Margery Williams Norris (d. 1599), daughter of Lord Williams of Thame and wife of Henry, Lord Norris of Rycote (the Queen's 'Crow'); and Anne Russell Dudley (d. 1604), daughter of Francis Russell, Earl of Bedford, and wife of Ambrose Dudley, Earl of Warwick. Perhaps the most exotic of these women, though, was Helena, Marchioness of Northampton.

Born Elin Ulfsdotter Snackenborg, the daughter of a Swedish nobleman and high councillor of Sweden, Helena had come to England as a teenaged attendant upon the Swedish royal princess Cecilia, Margravine of Baden, in 1565. The recently widowed Marquess of Northampton (William Parr), about thirty-five years her senior, was smitten by her and wooed her. She proved willing enough to be wooed by the decrepit nobleman and remained behind in England when Princess Cecilia and her entourage departed the realm in 1566, but the Queen refused to allow them to marry because of the existence of Parr's first wife, from whom Archbishop Cranmer had granted him a divorce in 1548 but the validity of whose marriage to him had been upheld in church courts during Mary's reign. It was only after that first wife died early in 1571 that the marriage could go ahead, and the Marquess died barely five months after it. Some few years later, she married Thomas Gorges, one of the Grooms of the Privy Chamber, evidently without awaiting the Queen's permission, and so had to endure a spell of banishment from the court and her husband one of incarceration. The couple went on to have at least eight children, and both were quickly back in favour. The Marchioness served as chief mourner at the Queen's funeral, outlived her husband by twenty-five years and died aged eighty-six in April 1635.

In addition to the fifteen women who comprised the 'feed' personnel of the Privy Chamber as constituted in January 1559, fourteen more were appointed to positions there in the years between 1560 and 1602. Judging by the fees which were allocated to them, nine of them were Chamberers and five of them Gentlewomen. The Gentlewomen were Dorothy, daughter of Henry, Lord Stafford (himself son and heir of the Duke of Buckingham executed for treason in 1521) and widow of her distant cousin Sir William Stafford, who served from 1562 to 1603, and died in 1604; Elizabeth, daughter of Sir Francis Knollys and his wife, Lady Katherine, one of the Bedchamber women, who later married Sir Thomas Leighton and served the reign through, dying in 1619 or 1620; Frances, daughter of William, Lord Howard of Effingham, appointed in 1568, who subsequently, in difficult circumstances and after years of waiting, as we have seen above, married Edward, Earl of Hertford, and served until her death in 1598; Dorothy, daughter of Christopher Lytcott of Swallowfield, Berkshire, a former servant of Anne Boleyn, and wife of Christopher Edmondes, who served from 1570 until the end of the reign, and died in 1614 or 1615; and Mary Ratcliff, only daughter of Sir Humfrey Ratcliff of Elstow, Bedfordshire, a younger son of the 1st Ratcliff Earl of Sussex, who had been a Gentleman Pensioner from the corps' creation in 1539. She had come to court as a Maid of Honour around Michaelmas 1566, remained there as such for a decade or more (she never married) and in 1589 received a warrant (backdated to 1587) for her fee as a Gentlewoman. She held the position until the end of the reign, dying in 1617 or 1618.

The ten Chamberers included Elizabeth, daughter of Anthony Sandes of Throwley, Kent, who served from 1560 to her death in 1585 and who married Sir Maurice Berkeley; Nazareth (d. 1583), daughter of Sir John Newton and sister to another Chamberer, mentioned previously; Frances, Lady Cobham, who served from 1564 to 1572 and left at the time of her ultimately calamitous marriage to Thomas, Lord Paget; Elizabeth, daughter of the Lady Dorothy Stafford mentioned in the previous paragraph, who served from 1568 to her death in 1599 and who married successively Sir William Drury and Sir John Scott; Mary, daughter of Sir John Shelton of Shelton, Norfolk and a second cousin of the Queen on the Boleyn side, who served from 1571 to the end of the reign (which she outlived by barely four months) and who married the Gentleman Pensioner John Scudamore (who had obtained his court position in 1571 through his father-in-law Sir James Croft) in late 1573 or early 1574; and Katherine (d. 1615), a daughter of Sir Thomas Paston (d. 1550), who had been a Gentleman of the Privy Chamber to both Henry VIII and Edward VI, who served from 1577 until the end of the reign and who about the time of her appointment married Henry Newton, with the result that she was sister-in-law to two other Privy Chamber ladies. A more obscure Chamberer was Jane Brussels (alias Hawkes), who served from 1577 to her death in 1599, and who married William Heneage some four years before her death. She appears to have been the daughter of two Flemings, Francis Haec, a Gentleman Pensioner from 1544 into the 1560s, and Barbara Haec, a Gentlewoman of Mary Tudor's Privy Chamber who continued to serve at court in some unknown capacity as late as 1587; if this identification is correct, it is the sole clear case of a continuity of sorts in personnel between the Privy Chamber of Mary's reign and that of Elizabeth. Margaret, daughter of Charles Vaughan of Hergest Court, Herefordshire, became a Chamberer in 1589 and married Sir John Hawkins little more than a year before the latter's death in 1595. She served until the end of the reign and died in 1619 or 1620. The careers of the final two Chamberers remain largely unknown, despite all efforts. Lucy Hyde, who served from 1593 to the end of the reign, appears to have been a daughter of William Hyde of Throcking, Hertfordshire, who had been an associate of the Dudleys for many years before his death in 1580. Towards the end of the reign, or perhaps just after, she married Sir Robert Osborne of Northamptonshire, but her life remains otherwise obscure. Even more obscure is the identity of the Anne Vavasour who became a Chamberer in June 1602. It is difficult to believe that she could be the same Anne Vavasour who, as a Maid of Honour, had given birth in 1581 to an illegitimate son of the Earl of Oxford or who lived without marriage with Sir Henry Lee for nearly twenty years before his death in 1611 and, after a subsequent marriage, was prosecuted for bigamy and who in many accounts is described as a Bedchamber woman to the Queen. (That Anne Vavasour was one of the subjects of the mock epitaph that began, 'Here lies that good knight, old Sir Harry / with her he loved but ne'er would marry.') More likely, she was another Anne Vavasour, subsequently the wife of Sir Richard Warburton of London.

Personal relationships – kinship with the Queen and, just as important if not more, with the group of women and men who had formed her original 'household family' as far back as its constitution in 1537, and later their spouses and progeny – were thus the fundamental determinant in the choice not only of the personnel of the Privy Chamber in 1559 but throughout the ensuing decades of the reign. Fully to trace the kinship and marital ties among the staff would no doubt demonstrate them to be an even more closely knit group of individuals than is evident already from the foregoing account – and this, in turn, was probably at least as much a factor as the ageing of the Queen and her increasing aversion to gratifying or refusing suitors in accounting for her well-remarked difficulty of access, especially to 'outsiders' and 'new men' in the last decade or more of the reign. Thus, to pick the Lady Stanhope who appears as one of the ladies of the Privy Chamber on the household list for Queen Elizabeth's funeral on 28 April 1603, if she is, as is likely, the wife of Sir John Stanhope, by that date both Vice-Chamberlain and Treasurer of the Chamber, she proves to be also Margaret, a daughter of Lady Cheke of the Privy Chamber by her late husband Henry Mackwilliam, a Gentleman Pensioner.

Outside of the Privy Chamber in the 'outer' Chamber, there were a number of court offices which would have been positions of influence according their degree of regular contact with the Queen, which could vary both by the significance of the office and the length of service of an individual officeholder. That they might have had occasional or even frequent opportunities to influence the Queen can be seen in the struggle over the succession to the office of Groom Porter of the Household, on the face of it a menial position of no great significance, concerned as it was with the provision of tables, chairs and fires, as needed, for the royal lodgings but also with providing playing cards and dice for gaming there, as well as supervising the gaming. Thomas Cornwallis, a Gentleman Pensioner from Mary's reign in the 1550s, had held the office from 1568; his father and uncle had held it earlier, the one under Edward VI, the other in the first decade of Elizabeth's reign. Towards the end of his life, in 1597, he sought to have his office granted in reversion to another Thomas Cornwallis, a cousin, and to that end joined with yet another cousin to them both, Sir William Cornwallis, the conformable elder son of the recusant Sir Thomas Cornwallis who under Mary Tudor had successively held the offices of Treasurer of Calais and Comptroller of the Household, who had served for the past sixteen years as his deputy, to frustrate Lord Buckhurst's attempt to gain the office for his kinsman, the Gentleman Pensioner John Parker. In a letter to Sir Robert Cecil, designed to advance the suit, Sir William mentioned his title as Groom Porter 'to bring a payre of cards in to the prevy chamber at x of the clocke at night'.[7] This oblique reference to nocturnal gaming witnesses to how the holder of such an office in the 'outer' Chamber could use his position to have privileged access, if not to the Queen herself – for he did not specify the identity of those with whom he played cards – then at least to those serving in the innermost Bedchamber circle of the Privy Chamber. In these offices, too, kinship ties counted for a great deal – but here the kinship ties were not so closely bound up with personal relationships with the Queen or other members of the Queen's 'family' as in the Privy Chamber. This might be a factor – old Thomas Cornwallis's uncle Francis, his predecessor as Groom Porter, had been a member of Elizabeth's household by 1547 – but the ties might just as well be with past holders of the same, or similar, offices under previous monarchs, or, as in the case of those few offices which appear to have been prestigious positions with few, rare or uncertain duties, such as those of Carver, Cupbearer, Sewer (*scutellarius*; the person responsible for seeing to the tableware and its setting) and the amorphous group of Gentlemen Waiters, with members of favoured noble or gentle families.

Of these offices in the 'outer' Chamber, some were positions of importance and patronage, such as those of the Vice-Chamberlain, the Treasurer of the Chamber and the Captain of the Gentlemen Pensioners and the Captain of the Guard. Often in the course of Elizabeth's reign, a single individual held more than one of these significant offices simultaneously, and in some cases there were vacancies of some duration between one holder's leaving the office and the appointment of a replacement. Thus, Sir Francis Knollys was Vice-Chamberlain from 1559 to 1570 and Captain of the Guard from 1565 to about 1572, as well as Treasurer of the Chamber from 1566 to 1570 (he gave up two of these to become Treasurer of the Household, a more purely administrative office, in 1570), Sir Christopher Hatton, Captain of the Guard from about 1572 to his death in 1591 and Vice-Chamberlain from 1577 to 1587 (when he became Lord Chancellor), Sir Thomas Heneage Treasurer of the Chamber from 1570 to his death in 1595 and Vice-Chamberlain from 1587 onwards, and Sir John Stanhope, Treasurer of the Chamber from 1596 to 1618 and Vice-Chamberlain from 1601 to 1616. Thomas Radcliffe, Earl of Sussex, was Captain of the Gentlemen Pensioners from about 1554 to his death in 1583 and Lord Chamberlain from 1572 onwards. Henry, Lord Hunsdon, immediately succeeded Sussex as Captain and two years later succeeded Lord Howard of Effingham as Lord Chamberlain, holding both offices until his death in 1596. When Hunsdon died, his son and heir George succeeded his father as Captain immediately and a year later succeeded William, Lord Cobham, as Lord Chamberlain, holding both offices until shortly after the succession of James I when, mortally ill, he quitted them all.

If, however, we seek positions which might have offered access and influence comparable to a degree with those within the Privy Chamber, the only possible candidate is that of Esquire for the Body. Before the creation of the Privy Chamber in 1519, this had been a very important position, and one whose holders served in various capacities, by night and by day, in close proximity to the monarch. Afterwards, their importance declined, but under the Tudors, and even beyond – the office was abolished in 1702 – their office remained more than a sinecure. It was they, or one of them, who accompanied the monarch when he pleased to walk in the privy garden or elsewhere, carrying a cloak for his use if needed (perhaps in case of rain or foul weather?); it was they who supervised the making of the royal bed at night; and, above all, it was they who exercised at night-time the authority of royal officials over the whole Household, both above and below stairs, save for the Privy Chamber. If the monarch or others of the Privy Chamber required food or drink at night, it was the Esquires for the Body who fetched it from the cupboard – or to it, assisted by the Groom Porter, if it was lacking the requisite victuals. If urgent matters required that the monarch be awakened during the night, it was they who went to the Bedchamber and instructed the Privy Chamber staff on 'night duty' (a gentlewoman and a chamberer) to do so.[8]

In Elizabeth's reign, as previously, there were four Esquires for the Body at any time. Information about the group is very hard to come by. Other than incidental references to individual esquires in grants and correspondence, the only sources which enable them to be identified are the household establishment lists of various sorts. These produce ten names but no doubt there were others whom the relative paucity of these lists overlooks, as well as extraordinaries and supernumeraries – Sir Walter Ralegh, for instance, may have begun his court career around 1581 as an Esquire for the Body – and the surviving Elizabethan docquet book recording grants under the signet from January 1585 to March 1597 records the names of three more: William Carr, Everard Digby (described in the grant as an 'extraordinary') and Sir Horatio Pallavicino, not mentioned as such elsewhere. And of these ten, although most of their family names are familiar to those acquainted with the Elizabethan aristocracy and gentry, their careers, and in some cases their identities, are obscure. The best known, thanks to his voluminous and detailed correspondence with successive Earls of Rutland now in the Manners family archives, was Roger Manners of Uffington, Lincolnshire, a son of the 1st Earl, who served as Esquire for the Body from early in Mary Tudor's reign until his death in 1607 (although from 1583 onwards he was in semi-retirement). By contrast, Sir James Marvin of Founthill, Wiltshire, who served from 1559 to 1603 and died in 1611, a very wealthy man, has left almost no record of his court career. Nor has Henry Fortescue (d. 1576) of Falkbourne, Essex, or Nicholas Poyntz (d. 1585) of Iron Acton, Gloucestershire, who served for the better part of the first decade of the reign. It is hard to identify the Oliver Saint John who served in the late 1560s and early 1570s, or the John Saint John of the late 1570s and the 1580s, or the George Bourchier (d. 1605) who served in the 1590s. Contrarywise, Henry Knollys, who served for some fifteen years before his death in 1583, and Robert Knollys (d. 1618), who succeeded him and held the position until 1603, were both sons of Sir Francis Knollys, and Edmund Carey (d. 1637) of Culham, Oxfordshire, who served for a few years, perhaps a decade, until 1603, when he became a Gentleman of the Privy Chamber to James I (as his tomb inscription records), one of the many sons of Henry, Lord Hunsdon. It may be that these esquireships served as honourable positions conferring status on their holders but demanded little of them in the way of onerous duties, and that men could pass easily out of them, whether moving 'upwards' or 'sideways', to more significant positions, save in the case of the genial and seemingly unambitious Manners and the surprisingly shadowy Marvin. As in the case of the offices of Cupbearer (about three at any time), Carver (one at any time) or Sewer (three or four at any time), the names of the holders of an esquireship demonstrate that, with rare exceptions among the esquires, they went to the sons of families such as the Careys, Howards, Knollys, Norrises, Russells, Sidneys and Willoughbies which had already held offices at the court or were favoured among the nobility.

The long-standing notion that the Queen excluded the women around her from meddling in affairs of moment, confining them to matters of minor patronage, has been comprehensively called into question by Charlotte Merton, who provides detailed evidence of the involvement of some of these women in matters of what may be termed 'high patronage', although much less for their involvement in policy-making – a view echoed more recently in a study of Blanche Parry, which cites the characterisation by Parry's great-nephew Rowland Vaughan as 'a Trinity of Ladies, able to work miracles' of his kinswoman Parry, the Countess of Warwick and Mary Scudamore.[9] This may well be true, despite the lack of much evidence for their influence outside of patronage matters for which there is indeed hard evidence of their connections and ability to influence the Queen. The 'statistical evidence', such as it is, is ambiguous. The signet office docquet book already referred to in this essay records the name of the individual who procured the Queen's signature for grants to individual recipients. Between January 1585 and March 1597, twenty-six such grants were procured by members of the female staff of the Privy Chamber, seven by Lady Stafford, six by Lady Scudamore, six by Lady Warwick and one each by seven other ladies. On the other hand, forty-one such grants were procured by the male staff, all of them grooms, nineteen of them by William Killegrew and the rest by others. Qualitative evidence, where it exists, is more vivid, but difficult to generalise from. It is, in any case, too considerable a matter to discuss within the confines of this essay, but let us end with two vignettes concerning Lady Scudamore. Both bear on the issue of the influence that one of her 'familiars' could bring to bear on the Queen, one in a concrete and particular instance, the other on how the personal 'style' of a person in such a position could assist or (as in this case) be thought to hinder suits in which she involved herself.

In March 1597, Sir Robert Sidney, eager to be relieved of his position as governor of Flushing and to return to England, was seeking the position of Warden of the Cinque Ports, made vacant by the death of William, Lord Cobham. Sidney's agent in London, Rowland Whyte, presented the letter to Penelope, Lady Rich (a daughter of Lettice Knollys and her first husband, Walter Devereux, Earl of Essex, and wife of Robert, Lord Rich) to be presented to the Queen; in the event, however, it was Lady Scudamore who presented it to her. When the Queen took it, his account continues, she asked Lady Scudamore:

> how yt came to her hands; she answered, that my Lady Sidney desired her to deliver yt to her Majestie from her Husband. Doe you not know the Contents of yt, sayd the Queen; no Madam says she. Then her Majesty said, here is much adoe about the Cinq Portes. I demanded of my Lady Skudmore what she observed in her Majestie, while she was a reading of yt; who sayd, that she read yt all over, with two or 3 Pughs.[10]

Since the burden of the letter was the unsuitability for the position of the man to whom the Queen soon granted it, Cobham's heir, Henry, Lord Cobham, the 'pughs' probably represent sceptical or derisive snorts as the Queen read the letter.

Some years earlier, on 21 December 1593, Lady Scudamore's own effectiveness as a patron had been disparaged in a letter from George Boleyn, Dean of Lichfield, to Gilbert Talbot, Earl of Shrewsbury. As Boleyn, possibly an illegitimate son of Anne Boleyn's brother, Viscount Rochford, referred to Lady Scudamore as 'my good frende and cosen whome I love well' and as both the Earl and Countess were on terms of close friendship with Sir John Scudamore and his wife, the letter is significant and trustworthy – and also clearly meant to be private and confidential. Shrewsbury and Boleyn were trying to delay the confirmation of a lease that the

Dean and Chapter had made to Sir Thomas Stanhope, Shrewsbury's enemy, seemingly with the support of the Queen. Shrewsbury was seeking to make the Queen aware, through Lady Scudamore, of the injury that the lease would do to his interests and how much it would also injure that of the diocese but had heard nothing from the court by the time that he wrote to the Dean. Boleyn, in his comprehensive reply, characterised his cousin as 'one that is wonte to delaye more than needes and looseth many a tide for the takynge, thowge she must watche for her tyde if she will speede her businesse'. After discussing the details of the lease, he returned to the matter of getting his letter and that of the chapter to the Queen:

> ffor my1. Chambrelayne certainly will not deliver it: and as for my cosen Skydmore or Scudamour there is no full confidence in her. Experto crede Roberto is an old proverb. But as her speeche is fayre & as smothe [struck through] smoothe as a reede: so do I beseche your honor to take this as a watche worde spoken under benedicite, because I feare a writt called ne noceat. ffor women be waspish and will do a man more harme whan they be angred then good whan they be quiet. And therefore the Countesse I trust shall not knowe of this leaste one woman tell an other, as Graeculus graeculo gaudet.[11]

Once again we have fleeting glimpses of the ways in which those closest to the Queen could, and no doubt very often, even constantly, did turn their positions to their own advantage and deploy their influence to benefit friends and clients and to disadvantage those who were neither. Further research is required into some of the subjects sketched out in this essay with respect to the Elizabethan court, as well as into comparisons with the structural, functional and personnel patterns of other European princely courts in the sixteenth century – comparisons which should not be confined to those with France and Scotland which have become customary over the past two decades but which should attempt to draw in the two Scandinavian royal courts, Portugal before 1580 and Spain – but those are subjects for other essays and books.

FURTHER READING

Arnold, Janet (ed.), *Lost from Her Majesties Back* (London, 1980).

Chambers, E. K., *The Elizabethan Stage* (Oxford, 1923).

Loades, David, *The Tudor Court* (London, 1986).

MacCaffrey, W. T., 'Talbot and Stanhope: An Episode in Elizabethan Politics', *Historical Research*, 33 (1960): 73–85.

Marlow, Richard, 'Sir Ferdinando Heyborne Alias Richardson', *The Musical Times*, 115 (1974): 736–9.

Maxwell, Susan, 'Henry Seckford: Sixteenth-Century Merchant, Courtier and Privateer', *The Mariner's Mirror*, 82 (1996): 387–97.

Mears, Natalie, *Queenship and Political Discourse in the Elizabethan Realms* (Cambridge, 2005).

Merton, Charlotte, 'The Women Who Served Queen Mary and Queen Elizabeth: Ladies, Gentlewomen and Maids of the Privy Chamber, 1553–1603', Ph.D. thesis, Cambridge University, 1992.

Richardson, Ruth Elizabeth, *Mistress Blanche, Queen Elizabeth I's Confidante* (Little Logaston, 2007).

Starkey, David (ed.), *The English Court: From the Wars of the Roses to the Civil War* (London and New York, 1987).
Wyatt, Michael, *The Italian Encounter with Tudor England* (Cambridge, 2005).

NOTES

1 *Longleat Seymour Papers*, vol. V, fols. 164–5; calendared in HMC, *Report on the Manuscripts of the Most Honourable the Marquess of Bath Preserved at Longleat*, vol. IV, *Seymour Papers, 1532–1686* (London, 1968), p. 158.
2 Belvoir Castle, *Letters and Papers*, vol. V, fol. 210. I quote from a photocopy, of the obverse side only, supplied to me in 1991 by the Belvoir Castle Estate of an undated letter from Eleanor Bridges to the Earl of Rutland. It is calendared in *HMC, Twelfth Report, Appendix, Part IV, The Manuscripts of His Grace the Duke of Rutland, G. C. B., Preserved at Belvoir Castle* (London, 1888), vol. I, p. 107.
3 *Belvoir Castle, Letters and Papers*, vol. V, fol. 210.
4 TNA, LC 2/4/3, pp. 104–5.
5 TNA, PROB 11/70, fols. 139v–140f (Will of Elizabeth Snowe, Widow, of Chicksands, Beds. The Elizabethan lists of 'feed' Privy Chamber personnel date from 1559 (BL, Lansdowne MS 3, fols. 191–2), 1580 (BL, Lansdowne MS 29, fols. 161–2), 1582 (BL, Lansdowne MS 34, fols. 76–7) and 1589 (BL, Lansdowne MS 59, fols. 43–4). These lists indicate that the differentiation between those women of the Bedchamber and those of the Privy Chamber cannot be determined on the basis of lists which merely indicate the date of appointment and wages of particular individuals: e.g., Lady Cobham, who appears in the 1559 list as one of the Chamberers of the Privy Chamber with that position's annual wages of £20, appears on the others as one of the Bedchamber women, but with the same £20 as her annual wages.
6 TNA, SP 12/1/4; SP 12/228/1 is the petition of 'Mr Middlemore' from around 1588.
7 TNA, SP 12/263/75.
8 It is difficult to find information about these esquires in modern historiography, so much so that one has to have recourse to Samuel Pegge, *Curialia; or, An Historical Account of Some Branches of the Royal Household ... Part I* (London, 1782), the first section of which is devoted to the 'obsolete office' of the Esquires for the Body.
9 Ruth Elizabeth Richardson, *Mistress Blanche, Queen Elizabeth I's Confidante* (Little Logaston, 2007).
10 Arthur Collins (ed.), *Letters and Memorials of State* (London, 1746), vol. II, p. 97.
11 Lambeth Palace Library, Shrewsbury MS 707, fols. 221–2.

CHAPTER SIX

POLITICAL IDEAS
Two concepts of the State

Anne McLaren

Early modern political ideas drew on conceptions of the body with an immediacy and specificity that we find difficult to recapture. English men and women regarded themselves as living in a 'body politic', and organological metaphors featured prominently in political debate. The MP who announced in 1566 that 'the prince and commonwealth ioyned together make a perfect man consisting of head, bodie and members' affirmed what was, for contemporaries, a truism that was both profound and compelling.[1] The 'perfect man' was, of course, Christ. Thus, the body politic denoted a quasi-spiritual union of king and subjects, joined together by bonds of faith and allegiance in the service of God. This understanding of political and what we would call national identity focused enormous attention on the physical body of the king, who represented (in Paul Friedland's terms 're-presented') the realm and its inhabitants in his person. We see it expressed in striking visual form in the famous title page of Thomas Hobbes's 1651 work, *Leviathan* (Figure 6.1), where many small male bodies compose the figure of the king. 'The life of a king containes a thousand thousand liues,' wrote one contemporary, articulating another truism. Those monsters of nature who were prepared to commit or countenance regicide were 'no lesse then *Regnicides*' – that is, killers of kingdoms.[2]

'Power . . .; sustaining strength; likeness to the sun as a source of light and fertility; wholeness: these are the attributes of kingship, and all masculine in their associations', as Jean Wilson reminds us; they came vividly to life in the person of Louis XIV of France, the Sun King, who reigned from 1638 to 1715 (see Figure 6.2).[3] The king's virility and virtue preserved and protected his people and order itself. Once married, those traits also enabled the king to produce heirs of his line and loins to succeed him, thereby securing the perpetuity of what we would call the state. The strength of this conviction, and the danger perceived to attend the hiatus that occurred at the king's demise, are apparent in the popular acclamation that announced a monarch's death, well established by the sixteenth century. 'The king is dead, long live the king' reveals two key beliefs: first, that kingship was a masculine prerogative, and second that only dynastic succession, by transferring the essence of kingship immediately from the body of one true king to another, securely maintained the body politic in continuous existence.

Figure 6.1 Thomas Hobbes, *Leviathan* (London: Andrew Crooke, 1651). Holmes Collection, Library of Congress, Rare Book and Special Collections Division. Image courtesy of the Rare Book Division of the Library of Congress.

Figure 6.2 Louis XIV as Apollo in *Le Ballet de la nuit* (1653). Louis celebrated his military victories over the series of popular rebellions known as the 'Fronde' (1648–53), and hence the consolidation of his absolute power, by dancing the role of the Sun King Apollo in this court ballet. Image courtesy Bibliothèque Nationale de France.

Over the sixteenth century, as religious reformation divided Europe into warring camps of Protestants and Catholics, the body of the monarch acquired heightened significance. In a 'king-saturated mental world' – one that regarded confessional plurality as, at best, a necessary evil – it was axiomatic that the one religion binding subjects in allegiance to their king and to God would be the king's, and that it would be the one true religion.[4] That conviction made the king responsible in new ways for the spiritual as well as the temporal well-being of his subjects. It also made him newly vulnerable to allegations of tyranny should he fail in his duty to God and his subjects; and tyrants, by breaking faith in this way, could be legitimately deposed, even (some argued) killed if necessary, in order to preserve the confessional integrity of the body politic.

During the forty-four years of Elizabeth's reign, the person charged with ensuring the survival of the English body politic, and the maintenance of its Protestant identity, was a virgin queen who was the last of her line. Further, for the first thirty years of the reign (until her execution in 1587), her heir presumptive was her Catholic cousin Mary Stuart, better known to history as Mary, Queen of Scots. For contemporaries, unless alternative arrangements were put in place, the death of the last Tudor would lead to one of two outcomes. Either the English crown and nation would fall to the Scottish queen, or it would descend into the 'unspeake-able miseries of civill warres' – all too vividly remembered from the Wars of the Roses of the fifteenth century – as men battled for the succession.[5]

Because the succession was so vitally important, news of this impasse at the political centre quickly percolated into the public sphere. We see evidence of the political passions that it aroused in the parliamentary debate of 1566, when a cluster of MPs accused Elizabeth of dereliction of duty. Their attack threatened her political legitimacy, while the terms in which it was couched convey the perceived connection between female rule and tyranny. Only 'cowards, and such as are hated of their owne people, and timorous women' refused to provide a known successor, one MP announced. Her inaction threatened to reveal her not as a natural parent to her subject children but rather as 'a step-mother, nay . . . a parricide of her Country': an unnatural ruler who 'had rather that England which now breathed with her breath, should together with her expire, than survive her'.[6]

The succession crisis thus conflated issues of monarchical authority, gender and confessional conviction, and it shaped political ideas of the age. In this chapter I want to investigate those ideas by focusing on the debate over the unsettled succession that occurred early in the reign. This one was concentrated around Elizabeth's second Parliament, which met initially in 1563 and then again, after a three-year prorogation, in 1566. The first session met after the Queen's near-death from smallpox the previous year, the second after Mary, Queen of Scots, had married and given birth to a son. Because the stakes were so high, it involved a wide and, by the standards of the time, socially diverse audience. We have evidence of its widespread dissemination in Parliament and 'out of doors': in manuscript and print, in letters, tracts, pamphlets and books. Recapturing how contemporaries understood what was at issue and the terms of the debate reveals what J. G. A. Pocock has called 'the present of practical necessity' as Elizabethans confronted it.[7] From there we can appreciate how they manoeuvred within existing socio-cultural paradigms to respond to that necessity, and how those manoeuvres changed the parameters of political thought. I will begin by explaining why the succession was controversial and considering the claims of the main claimants, Mary, Queen of Scots, and Lady Katherine Grey. The next section analyses two key 1565 pamphlets, to show how and with what consequences writers manipulated legal principles to muster support for each and to disallow the claims of the other. The conclusion explores how this debate promoted the articulation of contrasting constitutional theories of parliamentary sovereignty and absolutism that continued to be debated, in increasingly oppositional terms, through to the English Civil Wars of the seventeenth century.

THE SUCCESSION ISSUE

Disquiet concerning female rule continued to reverberate throughout the reign. 'It is certain that the English [will] never again submit to the rule of a woman,' the French ambassador de Maisse confidently, if erroneously, asserted in 1597, six years before Elizabeth's death.[8] In the early years of the reign, however, the related issue of the succession was brought to fever pitch by the generally shared conviction that only Elizabeth's 'weak and feeble' body preserved the life of the realm and, for many, the Protestantism with which the English nation was increasingly identified. We see evidence of the resulting anxieties in the spate of prophecies predicting that Elizabeth would reign for only a short time or die within a year, and in the formal appeals for the Queen to marry that were delivered in 1559, 1563, 1566 and 1576. But Elizabeth did not marry. Moreover, she steadfastly refused to pronounce on the matter of the succession herself or to allow it to be officially aired, either by her Privy Councillors or in Parliament. Attention thus shifted to the question of who should gain the crown should she die without legitimate issue, and debate moved out of doors.

The immediate problem was the lack of established principles, or 'laws', as contemporaries used the term, to determine monarchical succession. This was a strongly hierarchical lineage society. Generally shared convictions about due order decreed that, unless there were impediments, the nearest legitimate heir in blood should succeed, with males succeeding before females and elder children before younger. In England, however, Henry VIII's attempts to secure a male heir had complicated matters. Over the reign, three Succession Acts introduced unprecedented, and controversial, innovations. First, by announcing that only one of the King's children, his son Edward, had been conceived and born in a legitimate marriage, Henry bastardised his two daughters, Mary and Elizabeth. Next, in an attempt to shore up the succession by making his illegitimate son, the Duke of Richmond, eligible to inherit, an Act was passed in 1536 that empowered Henry to nominate a successor from beyond the ranks of legitimate successors should he and any legitimate heir die without issue. Presumably this was intended as a safety net lest Henry's third wife, Jane Seymour, prove no more successful than her predecessors in producing sons. By 1544, that eventuality appeared increasingly likely. Richmond's unexpected death in 1536 left Henry with only one surviving son, Edward: aged seven in 1544, and reputedly sickly. In these unpropitious circumstances, Henry VIII acted once again. A third Succession Act restored Mary and Elizabeth to the succession – not, however, as legitimate children of the King but rather by paternal nomination. Finally, within sight of death in 1546, Henry used his will to attempt one final breach with tradition. Should he and his direct heirs (including Mary and Elizabeth) die without issue, he stipulated that the crown would pass in the first instance to the children of his younger sister's second marriage, the Grey family. The elder collateral line, now vested in the two-year-old Mary, Queen of Scots, figured only among the 'next Ryghtful Heires' referred to in an auxiliary clause.[9] Thus, Elizabeth was the last of Henry VIII's direct heirs, but her legitimacy was disputable. By the time she inherited the throne, the two collateral branches were firmly associated with Catholicism and Protestantism, respectively, and confessional conviction had become attached to succession politics.

If there were no explicit laws governing monarchical succession, there were, by contrast, strongly held views about who had the right to be king. When Henry VIII substituted bastards for his legitimate collateral heirs in the 1544 Succession Act he was, in Eric Ives's words, 'driving a coach and horses' through one of the most powerful: that a bastard should not wield sovereign power.[10] To early modern men and women, bastards were unclean in the eyes of God, and bastard blood was tainted blood. In part, the prejudice arose because bastardy was not regarded as a social construct whose definition depended on societally determined marriage laws. Instead, contemporaries regarded it as a 'natural' trait that, like gender, strongly influenced, if it did not determine, character. '[O]ne, emong a thousande is good, yet most are . . . giuen to wickednesse, and persecution,' noted one writer in 1569. '[T]here is more abomination in one bastard, then in. lxix. lawfull sonnes.'[11] This mentality had European currency. It informed civil and canon law and, in England, the common law, all of which penalised bastards in various ways. But common law was the most draconian, both because of its narrow definition of what constituted a valid marriage and because it stigmatised the bastard issue as well as his or her erring parents.

The strength of English people's commitment to legitimacy in blood was demonstrated when Mary Tudor swept to power in 1553, her Catholicism notwithstanding. In this light it is revealing that the inaugural act of Mary's reign – the one that announced her right to the throne to her people – focused on 'declaring the Quenes Hyghnes to have bene borne in a most just and lawfull Matrimonie'.[12] This statute did specifically mention, and repeal, Henry's succession legislation (in so far as it applied to Mary; it pointedly exempted Elizabeth), but this was a secondary order of business. In contrast, the analogous legislation that greeted Elizabeth's accession, the 1558 Act of Recognition, invoked the 1544 Succession Act as the primary ground of her entitlement and contained no reference to her parents' marriage. Instead, it circumvented the issue of her legitimacy by referring vaguely to her lawful descent from the 'Bloodd royall of this Realme of Englande'.[13] Rehearsing these matters in the early seventeenth century, the historian William Camden puzzled over the failure to rescind the legislation that had bastardised Elizabeth, recognising that it opened the door to challenges to her right to rule that punctuated her reign. He concluded that the careful wording of the Act represented a wise determination not to 'new-gall the sore which was with age over-skinned' by using statute law to pronounce yet again on the legitimacy of Henry's marriages.[14] Inevitably this would lead to debate on the perceived merits and demerits of Henry's bedfellows' characters, and, in view of contemporary views of blood-relatedness, those of their children. By reflecting on Henry himself, it might also undermine the authority of the Church of England.

This complicated background sheds light on Elizabeth's rooted aversion to any and all discussion of the linked matters of marriage and succession, and it informed the succession debate that began after her near-death from smallpox in 1562. At that time, the two main contenders for the succession were Henry VIII's collateral heirs through his elder and younger sisters: Mary, Queen of Scots, and Lady Katherine Grey, respectively. From the Elizabethan point of view, both candidates' claims were problematical, and not only because they were women. As we have seen, in his final will Henry VIII attempted to divert the succession from the elder branch of his extended family to the younger. This contravention of established norms of inheritance and descent was controversial, however. So too was the status of the will itself. Throughout our period it was widely debated whether the will, and specifically this provision, reflected Henry VIII's wishes or those of a cabal of Privy Councillors who, as the King lay dying, took advantage of their access to the King's signature stamp to mould their preferred political settlement.

Leaving aside the will – which disappeared early in Elizabeth's reign – Mary, Queen of Scots, was undoubtedly the stronger candidate. Not only was she nearest in birth to the Tudor progenitor, Henry VII, but she was also the only living descendant whose legitimacy in blood could not be challenged with a charge of bastardy arising from doubtful marriages. By 1566, she had strengthened her hand, in dynastic terms, by marrying an Englishman, her and Elizabeth's cousin, Henry Stuart, Lord Darnley, who himself had strong blood claims to the English throne. That union had produced a male child. On the other hand, she was female, the daughter of England's ancient enemies, the Scots, she was Catholic, and, as a result, there was 'continuing, implacable hostility towards [her] among influential and articulate sections of the community'.[15]

Until her death in 1568, the most plausible alternative claimant was Lady Katherine Grey. True, she was female, and descended from Henry VIII's younger sister, but she was English, Protestant and demonstrably fertile. By 1563, she had borne two sons, fathered by an English Protestant peer, Edward Seymour, Earl of Hertford. However, even if the validity of Henry VIII's will was accepted, as well as his personal right to determine regal succession, Grey's claim was weakened by doubts about her legitimacy in blood. Her father and her elder sister, Lady Jane Grey, the Nine Day Queen, had been executed for treason less than ten years earlier for participating in the unsuccessful attempt to divert the succession from the blood-right heir, Mary Tudor, to a Protestant line. In common law, treason 'corrupted' the blood. Like bastardy, it severed the bloodline that otherwise guaranteed the transmission of property and status. '[The traitor's] Children become base and ignoble, and his blood so stained and corrupted that they cannot inherit to him or any other [ancestor],' one legal commentator explained.'[16] Again, it is revealing that, despite Privy Councillors' unwillingness to 'new-gall the sore' produced by Henry VIII's chequered marital career, very soon after Elizabeth's accession Parliament passed an Act that restored her in blood to another convicted 'traitor', her mother Anne Boleyn. The statute (I Eliz. c. 23) was a back-door way of quietly securing Elizabeth's status as noble and heritable, without directly challenging Henry VIII's legislative pronouncements. In Katherine's case, no analogous stratagem was on offer. Far from recognising her potential entitlement in any way – for which there was considerable popular, and conciliar, support – Elizabeth kept her imprisoned from 1561, when word of her relationship with Hertford leaked out, until her death in 1568.

Doubtful marriages compounded Katherine's equivocal status, from two directions. First, the validity of her Tudor grandmother's second marriage, to Charles Brandon, Duke of Suffolk, was questionable. Since it had been contracted when Brandon's first wife was still alive, on one view of the matter it was bigamous. Yet this was the marriage that had transmitted Tudor royal blood to the Grey line in the first place. If it were deemed to be invalid, then the Grey children, and their children's children, would be illegitimate.

But there was more. The status of Grey's own marriage to the Earl of Hertford, and thus the legitimacy of their children, was also contentious, in two ways. In 1553, in order to set the seal on one of the key political alliances that brought Lady Jane Grey to the throne, Katherine had been married to the Earl of Pembroke's eldest son, Henry Herbert. When political circumstances changed after Mary I's accession, Pembroke alleged that the marriage had not been consummated and arranged for it to be dissolved. But by 1560, with Katherine once again a desirable commodity, Pembroke switched tack and tried to re-establish the marriage. These manoeuvres raised doubt about whether Katherine was a married woman rather than a virgin. And if the 1553 marriage had been consummated, then, according to contemporary beliefs about marriage, she remained Herbert's wife, despite the notional dissolution and the parties' complete lack of subsequent contact.

At the same time, and possibly in response to Pembroke's initiative, Katherine married Hertford in a clandestine ceremony at Hertford's house, with only Hertford's sister and an unidentified clergyman in attendance. That marriage was consummated immediately afterwards, and in the spring of 1561 Katherine gave birth to Edward Seymour, the future Viscount Beauchamp, the first of her two sons. Very soon thereafter, in 1562, an ecclesiastical high commission was convoked to pronounce on the validity of this marriage and the legitimacy of its fruit. By then there were no witnesses. Hertford's sister had died in the interim, and the clergyman had disappeared. Under pressure from the Queen, the commission duly declared that there had been no marriage, with the implication being that Katherine must be viewed as the adulterous mother of bastard offspring – and hence personally unfit to rule.

Perhaps the general recognition of the political significance of Katherine's marital status explains why, throughout Elizabeth's reign, many continued to regard her, and after her death her sons, as having a valid claim to the throne, the commission's determination notwithstanding. A contemporary journal conveys this perception very clearly and also gives evidence of the widespread public discussion of these matters of state. The journal writer reports that because Grey and Hertford's marriage 'coulde not be disproved' when the commissioners began their investigation, 'it was thought by the people that . . . they would attempte to prove the L. Fraunces her mother a bastard and so to dysheritt her of the tytell to the crowne.' The next entry turns to the rumour that the 'queen myndeth to establyshe the succession of the crowne'. Evidently 'the people' greeted this announcement with a certain amount of scepticism: 'she will not do yt', some said, 'because she is persuaded that if there were any heire apparante knowne the people would be more affectionate to *him* than to her' (note the pronoun). Later, during the trial but before the commission reached its verdict, he recounted the 'comen brute' that Katherine and Hertford would be separated in terms that would make impossible any future attempt at a 'legitimate' marriage and disallow Katherine and her son's claims, possibly by statute: 'Some thincke he shalbe divorced, some that she shalbe restored to the earle of Pembrock his sonn, some that the childe shalbe made a bastard, some that she shalbe dyshabled of the inheritance of the crowne, for that the L. Fraunces was not legitimate.'[17]

Retrospectively surveying the terrain, William Camden summarised the state of play as follows:

> the hot Protestants thought that the Queene of Scots, though her Title were most undoubted, yet because she was of another Religion, was to be rejected upon very high and subtill points of Law; and of the Papists some, and the greatest part of all indifferent men, thought she was to be admitted, as being the true and undoubted heire by Lawe.[18]

'Lawe' versus 'Law'. If 'hot protestants' who wanted to prevent Mary's accession at all costs were to stand any chance of success, they would have to make a convincing case *in law* that disabled her candidacy, and it would have to carry weight across the religio-political spectrum. The case they began to articulate identified Mary's alien status as an insuperable legal impediment. To us it may appear axiomatic that foreign birth would constitute a significant impediment to wielding sovereign power, and one that could readily translate into a legal requirement that inheritors to kingdoms be native born. But this was not the case in early modern dynastic monarchies, when, certainly at the level of the Crown, blood right trumped what we would call national identity. Indeed, as Keechang Kim has brilliantly demonstrated, in the sixteenth century the concept of systematic legal discrimination against the foreign born of whatever status as 'aliens' was a 'radically new idea' which this succession crisis did much to naturalise.[19]

Thus, ideologically engaged Protestants lighted on this strategy not because Elizabethans found the idea intuitively plausible but rather because, in view of Mary's commanding claims, they had little alternative. Support in law for the proposition could be adduced from a common-law ruling that denied aliens the right to inherit property in England. With ingenuity and determination it might be possible to argue that that ruling also applied to monarchical succession. As we shall see, Protestant polemicists were quick to follow this line. A measure of their success appears in a debate over the succession held at Lincoln's Inn in 1566. The law students concluded that, because she had been born in Scotland, 'by all the laws and customs of England', Mary was ineligible to succeed, 'even if she were the nearest in birth and the ablest'.[20] Still, the applicability of common-law rulings to the inheritance of a crown – a very different kind of property – was by no mean generally accepted or unproblematic.

Interjections in the succession debate were ideologically charged and violently partisan, as succession politics in personal monarchies always are. But the need to persuade the widest possible audience, and the risk of incurring the Queen's wrath, meant that writers generally introduced the subject in disinterested terms. Writers on both sides declared that they sought only to determine whether the impediments of bastardy or alien status effectually invalidated either woman's claim. However, they quickly moved on to adduce as substantiating evidence for the case *in law* the two women's alleged characters. The resulting debate thus fused the personal attributes of the nearest competitors (including confessional conviction) with the legitimacy of their claims to the throne. Did Mary Stuart's blood inheritance entitle her to an English crown? Or was she irredeemably 'alien': Scottish (and Catholic), and as such both foreign and an enemy to England? Was Katherine Grey the bastard product of an adulterous liaison, and herself the progenitor of bastards? And could bastards inherit the throne? Those who sought to disbar Mary, Queen of Scots as an alien had first to make the case for the absolute primacy of common law over other legal systems. Their eventual success over the 1560s and 1570s fuelled what J. G. A. Pocock identifies as the 'great hardening and consolidation of common-law thought' in the second half of the sixteenth century, and this was one undoubtedly one of the key political developments of the reign, in the realm of ideas as much as practical politics.[21] Yet, as we shall see, because its strictures against bastardy glanced so directly at the Queen, common law remained a double-edged sword.

TWO KEY SUCCESSION PAMPHLETS

Two key pamphlets that appeared in print in 1565 give us a sense of the cut and thrust of the debate. They are *Allegations against the Surmised Title of the Quine of Scotts and the Favorers of the Same* (hereafter *Allegations Against*) and, in response, *Allegations in Behalf of the High and Mighty Princess the Lady Mary, Now Queen of Scots, against the Opinions and Books Set Forth in the Part and Favour of the Lady Katherine, and the Rest of the Issues of the French Queen, Touching the Succession of the Crown* (hereafter *Allegations in Behalf*).[22] 'Allegation' meant the action of making a charge before a legal tribunal. The titles suggest that the anonymous authors regarded themselves as addressing the body politic conceived of as a kind of public legal tribunal, and, unsurprisingly, they reflect Mary, Queen of Scots's commanding status as heir presumptive.

The author of *Allegations Against* piously denied any desire to see Mary, Queen of Scots, excluded from the succession should she be called to the crown 'according to the Laws of the Land'. Ostensibly he has written the tract merely to clarify the legal position. On his reading, Mary's Scottish blood disallows her claim. In support he adduces the common-law maxim that aliens cannot inherit property in England. Some will question the applicability of common law to a case concerning the crown. Such men he dismisses as little better than aliens themselves: 'In [this] opinion they shew themselves great strangers in their own country, and very strangely affected and little to understand, or else slenderly to regard under what law they be born as subjects.' Most parts of Christendom are governed almost exclusively by Roman civil law and canon law, and their indigenous or 'municipal' law applies only in regard to some few, insignificant matters. In England, this is not the case, for England is an empire: 'in this our realm it is certain: that generally we know, nor are bound to acknowledge, no other law, than our own.' We are, he reiterates, 'bound to our own imperial and natural laws of this realm of England, and to no other'.[23]

Yet the form of the pamphlet suggests that he is far from certain that this argument will hold, let alone carry the day. Thus, the rhetorical centre of the tract is devoted to exploiting the ambiguous meaning of 'alien' in ways that convict Mary of possessing bad blood, defined in several senses. In common law, 'alien' simply described a person who was born out of the king's allegiance. John Rastell's enduringly popular *Exposicions of the Termes of the Laws* defines 'Alyon' as 'he of whom the father is born, and he himself also born out of the legeance of our lord the king, but if an alyon come and dwells in Eng, *which is not of the king's enemies,* and here hath issue, this issue is no alyon but English' (my italics).[24] In its opening pages, the *Allegations Against* draws on English hatred of the Scots to convict Mary and her tribe of being incorrigibly 'of the king's enemies' and thus irredeemable enemies to England. He also denies the possibility of naturalisation for her or for her successors. If Mary were not by law the rightful heir – and the title makes it clear that in his view she is not – then it would be 'plain folly, yea a great madness; for us by our consent, to suffer either her or any that should be born of her body to come unto the government'. What would her accession mean, except that England would become 'bond and subject unto a foreign nation'? 'And with what mind can we suffer these things of the Scots', he demands indignantly; 'a people by custom and almost nature our enemies, thirsty of our blood poor and miserable by their country and envious of our welfare'? Moreover, should Mary gain the crown, Englishmen's subordinate status will continue not only during her lifetime but forever after, 'in the days of her children and the rest of her succession'. The example of William the Conqueror proves that foreigners who take possession of a land through conquest remain forever essentially alienated from the subjected realm. William's descendants and creations, from that day to this, 'although that they were born in England, had yet always minds rather to be compted normans than English'.[25]

If the legal case is as indisputable as the author claims, and the consequences of a Marian succession so disastrous, why then does her candidacy muster support? As explanation, in his peroration he draws on the reformed Protestant definition of 'alien' as those excluded from God's grace. The *locus classicus* for this definition was Ephesians 2:11–13, widely quoted throughout the period (here in the Geneva Bible translation):

> Wherefore remember that ye [were] in time past Gentiles in the flesh . . . That ye were, I say, at that time without Christ, and were aliantes from the common wealth of Israel, and were strangers from the couenants of promise, and had no hope, and were without God in the world. But nowe in Christ Iesus, ye which once were farre off, are made neere by the blood of Christ.

The invocation allows him to conflate Mary, Queen of Scots' prospective regime with that of Elizabeth's now demonised predecessor, the Catholic Mary Tudor. Mary, Queen of Scots, and her supporters have embraced 'corrupt religion'. They are 'aliens' because, having turned against God, they have become insensible to the claims of commonwealth and country. They await only the opportunity to return to 'their accustomed idolatry and wonted cruelty, [and] to wash their hands in the blood of the faithful'.[26]

Thus, in order to see off Mary's commanding blood claim, the author of the *Allegations Against* buttressed his appeal to common law with a potent and innovative blend of arguments, drawing on anti-Scottish xenophobia, advanced Protestant theology and an interpretation of the legacy of William the Conqueror that anticipated the 'Norman yoke' myth that was to flourish during the Civil War period. It was answered by an author who, in the *Allegations in Behalf*, adopted a strategy that was similarly inventive to foreground the issue of bastardy. Commandeering language associated with evangelical Protestantism and supporters of Katherine Grey, he invoked common law in support of Mary, Queen of Scots, on the basis of her purity of blood. This was a clever tactic. His appeal to Scripture and common law positioned him as a 'true Englishmen', not one of the 'strangers' of 'corrupt religion' excoriated by the author of the *Allegations Against*. By raising the issue of Elizabeth's own legitimacy, the tract powerfully supported the view, then being canvassed, that Elizabeth should publicly acknowledge Mary's status as her heir on the basis of blood right. By 1565, this was regarded as a plausible way out of the succession impasse, even among some committed Protestants. Increasingly, radical Protestant attacks on Mary, in Scotland and in England, came to appear dangerously threatening, not simply to any given monarch's right to rule but more broadly to monarchical authority itself. The author makes the case implicitly – Mary's name is mentioned only once, in the title, and Elizabeth is not mentioned at all – but, as we shall see, powerful evidence exists for reading 'between the lines' of the tract in this way.

The rhetorical centre of this piece is bastardy in blood and its alienating effects. The author's starting point 'in law' is the invalid marriage contracted between the Duke of Suffolk and Mary Tudor – void, he argues, because it occurred during the lifetime of Suffolk's first wife. That the children of the union and their descendants – down through and including Lady Katherine Grey – were bastardised as a result is acknowledged 'both according to Divine, Canon, and Civil Lawe, and . . . according to the Lawe of Nature and Reason'. But pre-eminently that sanction is resoundingly declared in English common law: 'And that one borne of a second Wyfe (the first still lyvinge . . .) shuld be taken or compted for legitimate or inheritable, is not auctorized by our Lawe', and this is 'th'absolute Judgment of our Lawe'.[27] Moreover, the strictest construction of bastardy applies, because the matter must be judged 'according to the Law of the Realm', which is, of course, common law, and common law does not allow for the legitimation of bastard children. At this point he introduces the relative laxity of civil and canon law in regard to legitimation to reinforce the absolute sanction against bastard claims to the throne across all legal systems. Legitimation, when it is allowed, does no more than remove some civil disabilities; it has no bearing on succession to a crown. Even a papal bull, had one been obtained before England threw off the Pope's authority to become a people of God, would not have sufficed. 'And the reason is, that whosoever is born bastard, though he be after made legitimate, is ever reputed, notwithstanding, as infamous.' Universally, in England, as throughout Christendom, bastards cannot pretend to 'a *Royal Dignity, in the which the whole state of the Common Wealth has interest*'.[28]

The legal case established, the author settles back to dilate on bastardy's irremediable, and hereditary, taint. He uses the disputable legitimacy of the marriage between Lady Katherine and the Earl of Hertford – or, as he puts it, their 'carnal company' – to depict her and her issue, present and future, as incapable of the crown on the grounds of moral infamy:

> And how can she be countyd worthy to come to a Kingdome . . .? Surely, yf she were the next Heire of the Bloud Royal [which she is not], her Fault is much the greater so fowlie to have spottyd the same: For as by this Whoredome she hath deservyd grevous Punishment, in *disparaging and disablinge the Blodd;* so hath she, by vyolatinge Maryage, cut off all hope of havinge lawfull Issue by her to succeede and possesse the Crown heereafter. For by the Law that God gyveth, Deut. 23. A Bastard, and unlawfull borne Person, may not beare rule in the Church or Common-Weale: He is counted a *Stranger,* as the Hebrewe word importith; and to the perpetuall detestation of Whoredome was this Lawe made, to punishe the Parentes Faultes justly in their Children.[29]

Having thus turned the tables on his adversaries by attaching alien status to bastardy, the author concludes by impugning as un-English and ungodly those who would advance the claims of the Suffolk line:

> [W]hose English Harte wold it not grieve, even to every parte of it, to fynde any such Bookes countenanced, or accompt made of such Bastardie [*sic*] slippes . . . to enherite so noble a Realme, our most deere and natural Countrey? . . . What is he that esteemith or tendrith the prosperyte of the Countrie in the favour of God, or the good fame or fortune of the Worlde, that wold seeke to exalt vnto the Government therof such *infamous and spottyd titles,* with which is lynked always such wrathe of God . . . before the vnstainyd true and perfect Inheritors apoynted by him, and by his Lawes, to set forth his glory . . .?[30]

Compelling evidence for this reading of the tract comes by way of a contemporary manuscript 'Letter'. Fairly fuming with rage, the writer of the 'Letter' charges that 'the author [of the *Allegations in Behalf*] goeth falsely about to prove that not only the French Queen's issue but all the whole issue of King Henry VII's children now alive and born within the realm are illegitimate.'[31] The resulting swath would include Elizabeth herself, as well as all the nearest blood competitors – leaving standing, albeit in Edinburgh, only one rightful heir, the pure-bred Mary, Queen of Scots. He rails against what he regards as the author's cynical manipulation of law, intended, he believes, not only to forward Mary's candidacy but to do so by challenging Elizabeth's status as rightful inheritor. To this end, '[h]e patcheth a piece of the common law' to the prohibition against bastards holding office in Deuteronomy 23:2. The 'patching' makes very clear 'whom he would men should note and take for a bastard: for . . . the ground of all his discourse, [is] to prove that the child of the second wife, the first being alive, is a bastard and cannot inherit by the common law of this realm'.[32] This, of course, was exactly Elizabeth's position, when, after a divorce of dubious legality, Henry VIII married Anne Boleyn during Katherine of Aragon's lifetime. In his succession acts, Henry VIII attempted to fix each new arrangement by enacting that any who challenged the new status quo, together with 'their aiders, counsellors, maintainers, and abettors', would be guilty of high treason. The writer of the 'Letter' himself refers to this legislative history – in order to warn compatriots not to divert from their primary duty of allegiance to the Queen, regardless of her legitimacy. They must 'honor and serve as true obedient subjects our own kings' children, of whom we know none alive at this day but our most lawful Sovereign Lady, Queen Elizabeth'. The succession case advanced in the *Allegations in Behalf* 'reacheth farther than the French Queen's children and may by law reach you too if you be either a counsellor or an abettor of this author', he tells them.[33]

TWO CONCEPTS OF THE STATE

The early Elizabethan succession crisis focused attention on a dilemma that was endemic to personal monarchy: the disparity between the 'weak and feeble body' of the monarch, any monarch, and the god-like role that he assumed at his coronation. What human being could claim the right to be king? In England, the Henrician Reformation raised this quandary to a peak of intensity for reasons both theological and, as we have seen, genealogical. In Elizabeth's reign it would be possible to conclude that there were no legitimate successors to Henry VIII (except, possibly, the Queen herself), and that damning impediments attached to representatives of both collateral lines. Without a settled succession, at the Queen's death the realm would die a spectacular death by collapsing into anarchy. This was viscerally and universally understood as a return to the succession wars of the fifteenth century, the Wars of the Roses. That prospect in turn suggested that any subsequent inheritor, foreign or domestic, would fight his way to the throne with the sword, either directly or with an army raised on his or her behalf. Nor was it possible to think of alternatives to monarchy. For the great majority of Elizabethan men and women, monarchy was the only God-ordained form of government. If these intractable local difficulties did not dislodge that conviction, they might, however, cast doubt on the principle of dynastic succession. Certainly in the English case it seemed peculiarly incapable of ensuring the accession to the throne of godly adult male warriors who, if they were not altogether godlike, might at least possess personal attributes that – as in the case of Shakespeare's Henry V – would mystify the disparity between the ideal king and his human personification.

Confronting these intractable dilemmas forced conceptual innovation in the realm of political ideas. Among other outcomes, theorists sought to envisage kingship in terms that would compensate for the inevitable personal incapacities of individual monarchs and to give those terms of reference commanding legal standing. They did so by exploring the political possibilities of the corporate body politic in order to conjure up an 'artificial man' who could effectively embody the State – as Thomas Hobbes was to do, in a later, related project, in the pages of *Leviathan* (Figure 6.1). In conclusion, I want to consider as contributions to the succession debate two such 'physiological fictions': Sir Thomas Smith's theorisation of parliamentary sovereignty and the concept of the king's two bodies which promoted an absolutist ideology. In England the latter was codified and influentially disseminated by the legal expert and law reporter Edmund Plowden. Read in this context, we can appreciate the partisan dimension to their work, the Protestant Smith writing to disallow Mary, Queen of Scots's claims, the Catholic Plowden to support them.

In 1565, during his posting as ambassador to France, Smith wrote a famous description of the English polity, *De republica anglorum.* Despite the title, Smith wrote in English, and (as historians have begun to appreciate) the text is in significant ways normative rather than narrowly descriptive. The work circulated widely in manuscript, although it was not published until 1583. Nowhere is its normative character more apparent than in his description of the role and status of parliament. In Elizabeth's reign, as in those of her predecessors, the permanent continuous government consisted of the Queen, her privy councillors, judges and other officials. In Sir John Seeley's words, 'in Queen Elizabeth's reign it would not have been natural . . . in describing the government of England to mention parliament at all. Not exactly that parliament was subservient, but that, in general parliament was not there.'[34] Parliament was one among many of the king's courts. It was, in effect, a consultative assembly with limited powers which the reigning monarch summoned from time to time, for specific purposes, and it sat infrequently.

What a contrast with Smith's description! He begins his chapter on parliament by announcing that 'The most high and absolute power of the realme of Englande, is in the Parliament.' Parliament, as body politic, contains 'the power of the whole realme both the head and the bodie' because it represents (re-presents) 'everie Englishman . . . from the Prince (be he King or Queene) to the lowest person of Englande'. In view of the prevailing understanding of kingship with which we began, what is striking is Smith's insistence that this super body carries political clout because of its inclusivity and because of the relative equality of all its members; in this context the Queen figures as an 'honorary male'. Each act done there is 'the Princes and whole realmes deede', he tells us, and he draws on warrior culture to clarify his meaning. Just 'as in warre where the king himselfe in person, the nobilitie, the rest of the gentilitie, and the yeomanrie is, there is the force and power of Englande', so in peacetime this same plenitude of power attaches to Parliament, whether or not it is actively in session. And this virility, and perpetuity, makes of Parliament the 'highest court', or what we might call the final court of appeal: the 'deeds' done in Parliament are 'firme, stable, and *sanctum,* and [are] taken for lawe'. How revealing that among Parliament's law-making powers the staunchly Protestant Smith includes as well as 'giv[ing] forms of succession to the crowne', the right to legitimate bastards and, by absolving them of crimes committed against temporal laws, to restore them absolutely 'in bloud and name'![35] These were prerogatives that, in canon law, belonged either to the prince or the pope.

Smith's conception of parliament's legislative omnicompetence, and the suggestion that the monarch functioned within its corporate body as one member only, were both explored in radicalising terms as the reign progressed. A dramatic, but logical, extension occurred in a House of Commons debate when, following the execution of Mary, Queen of Scots, in 1587, the succession crisis reappeared in the altogether more extreme form that was to dominate political debate in the last decade of Elizabeth's reign. One MP announced that, in matters of religion and succession, Parliament was empowered to act to preserve the nation for God, if need be in opposition to the Queen. The 'three estates' that he referred to, conventionally identified as king, lords and commons, or 'king-in-parliament', did not include the Queen as a separate 'estate'. Rather, he viewed parliament, which he glossed as the House of Commons specifically, as being capable of acting on behalf of the Queen and the realm in matters that were fundamental to the survival of the body politic – and as having done so by effecting Mary's execution. Referring to the 1571 Treason Act, this MP demanded of the House the answer to 'one question':

> Under the warrant of God's law, what may not this House do? I mean the three estates of the land. To deny the power of this House you know is treason: therefore to say that this House is not able to cut off ten such serpents' heads as [Mary, Queen of Scots'] is, not able to reform religion and establish succession, it is treason; for why? To deny the power of this House is treason.[36]

We know that Parliament proved to have the capacity as an institution to become a co-ordinate branch of government. Famously, during the civil wars of the seventeenth century, the House of Commons itself claimed sovereign power, claiming that it alone – certainly not the king, and no longer the House of Lords – truly represented the nation. But during Elizabeth's reign that understanding of the English constitution would have been inconceivable. Instead, it was the theory of the king's two bodies, midwifed by the Catholic lawyer Edmund Plowden, that gained general acceptance among Elizabethans and approval from their queen.

The theory of the king's two bodies had a long history and retained European currency until well into the eighteenth century. It evolved in part as a means explaining how it was that, because 'the king never dies', the body politic remained in continuous existence. To explain, the king was envisaged as having two capacities, figured as bodies. Unlike other men,

> he has two Bodies, the one whereof is a Body natural, consisting of the natural Members as every other Man has, and in this he is subject to Passions and Death as other Men are; the other is a Body politic, and the Members thereof are his Subjects, . . . and he is incorporated with them, and they with him, and he is the Head, and they are the Members, and he has the sole Government of them; and this Body is not subject to Passions as the other is, nor to Death, for as to this Body the King never dies.

The body politic, which contains the 'Office, Government and Majesty royal', is 'more ample and large than the Body natural'. It is this amplitude that allows the body natural of the king to exercise 'sole Government', once their union has been effected. Again, as in Smith, we see the connection between (metaphorical) bodily *vis* and political potency. There is also a mystical dimension, analogous to the purging power of the sacraments. The conjunction of the two bodies 'wipes away every Imperfection' of the natural body: 'His Body politic, which is annexed to his Body natural . . . draws the Body natural, which is the lesser, and all the effects thereof to itself, which is the greater.' In this transaction, the body politic literally transforms the body natural. It makes the king of 'another Degree than [his body natural] should be if it were alone by itself'.

It is clear that in England over the 1550s and 1560s this physiological fiction was increasingly widely discussed and disseminated within the legal community, as the realm confronted the challenges of minor, female and Catholic incumbents of the imperial crown. It helped to explain not only why the king never dies but also why, once joined to his body politic, he (or she) was never subject to 'the Imbecility of Infancy or old Age, [or] to the like Defects that happen to the natural Bodies of other People'. Far-sightedly, in view of Henry VIII's succession manoeuvres, in the 1540s Plowden began keeping a record of relevant cases that drew on this theory. In 1571 he published them as *Les Commentaries, ou, Les Reportes . . . de divers cases . . . en les temps des raignes le Roy Ed. le size, le Roigne Mary, le Roy & Roigne Philip & Mary, & le Roigne Elizabeth,* more commonly referred to as *Plowden's Reports,* and subsequently reissued many times through the eighteenth century. But prior to the publication of the *Reports,* in 1566, Plowden wrote a treatise which Marie Axton rightly identifies as the 'locus classicus' of the theory in England in which he in effect glossed those legal cases.[37] *A Treatise of the Two Bodies of the King, Vis. Natural and Politic . . . the Whole Intending to Prove the Title of Mary Quene of Scotts to the Succession of the Crown of England* put the theory of the king's two bodies into wider and more general circulation and pointed its specific applicability to the succession debate.

In his Prologue, Plowden announced that he was provoked to write in response to the common-law case against Mary, Queen of Scots, that he had encountered in several books, including the *Allegations Against.* He was not persuaded by the 'high and subtill points of Law' that these authors advanced, although he feared that others might be:

> When I had read [these books] I could not but marvel at the audacity of their authors who seemed to be very insufficient in learning of the laws of this realm to treat of that matter . . . And albeit to the learned their ignorance is well perceived, yet to the unlearned (to whose hands also the said books come) it is not so.[38]

Again we see how the succession debate encouraged the widespread dissemination of political ideas and evidence of the ways in which participants in that debate addressed and reached opinion out of doors. In the *Treatise,* Plowden argued the case for blood-right succession and the purging power of the crown. First he poured scorn on the idea that Mary was an 'alien'. 'The Scots are not out of the allegiance of England,' he states, because earlier Scottish kings have acknowledged the overlordship of English kings. But even if she were regarded as an 'alien', and even if the common-law ruling against alien inheritance were regarded as being applicable to monarchical succession, she could not be disabled from inheriting the crown on the basis of blood right. Moreover, those putative incapacities would not survive her accession. At that moment her incorporation in the 'body politic of King' would purge her of that, or any other, perceived bodily defects.

In the 1560s, Plowden's explication of the theory of the king's two bodies provided a powerful rationale for accepting Mary, Queen of Scots's status as heir presumptive. But, significantly, then and later it also served to confirm the legitimacy of Elizabeth's queenship. The theory worked to Elizabeth's advantage for several reasons, at this time, and again during the succession crisis that dominated her 'last decade'.[39] First, it postulated that her possession of the crown – not 'law', lawyers, or parliament – removed any possible taint that attached to her natural body. Second, because it asserted the independent power of the crown, it provided her with support in her continuing battle to legitimate her status as a fully empowered, autonomous ruler. Third, by reinforcing the legitimist case for blood-right succession, it also de-emphasised, at least, the necessity for her to produce an heir of her own body. In her old age, after the execution of Mary, Queen of Scots, in 1587, it buttressed her authority by enhancing the unofficial status as heir presumptive of Mary's son, James VI of Scotland, who, in 1603, gained the throne as the first of the Stuart kings of England. Finally, Plowden's theory made succession to the crown a special case of inheritance which, as it were, transcended but did not contradict common law. Thus it did not, immediately, challenge what was coming to be the primacy of English common law, or the status of the House of Commons in particular as its interpreter. Those challenges lay in the future, later in Elizabeth's reign, and more obviously in the seventeenth century, in the reigns of her Stuart successors.

In a conversation with the Scottish ambassador at this time, which Elizabeth knew would be widely reported, she announced that she was married to the realm. She referred to succession in exactly the terms that we have encountered in this chapter. Surely we are right to read this statement as her own contribution to that debate, as she invokes the theory of the king's two bodies on behalf of her indisputable right to the throne and to the exercise of untrammelled monarchical authority:

> The Disceptation [dispute] concerning the Right of the Kingdom, I have always mightily avoided; for the Controversy hath been already so much canvass'd in the Mouths of many, concerning a just and lawful Marriage, and what Children were Bastards, and what Legitimate, according as every one is addicted to this or that Party, that by reason of these Disputes, I have hitherto been more backward in marrying. Once, when I took the Crown publicly upon me, I married myself to the Kingdom, and I wear the Ring, I then put on my Finger, as a Badg thereof; however, my Resolution stands, *I will be Queen of Englande, as long as I live.*[40]

The theory of the king's two bodies became newly relevant in the seventeenth century once James VI of Scotland claimed the English crown in 1603. In 1608, a famous legal case, the case of the *Post-Nati,* sought to define the extent of the new king's power over the now-conjoined realms of England and Scotland. In his brief, the king's spokesman, Francis Bacon, theorised Stuart absolutism by drawing on and extending Plowden's conceptualisation of the omnicompetent royal body. Taking as a given that the king's body politic 'worketh so upon his natural person, as it makes it differ from all other the natural persons of his subjects', he then declared that a converse operation applies. Having been transformed through its incorporation into the body politic of the realm, the now supranatural body of the king thereafter 'hath an operation and influence into his body politic'. This 'operation and influence' reconfigured the formerly independent kingdoms of England and Scotland as a united kingdom (or British empire) that, uniquely engendered by the Stuart race of kings, became uniquely their property.[41] Thus, in Bacon's formulation, the king's power is absolute because from the moment of his accession he shapes the state in his own image. Or, as King James explained to his subjects, at his coronation the king becomes 'a naturall Father' to all his children-subjects, English and Scottish alike, and similarly endowed with power of life and death over them all.[42]

Of course, Elizabethan political ideas were not exclusive to the England of Elizabeth. Over the sixteenth and seventeenth centuries, as religious reformation challenged old orthodoxies throughout western Europe, people grappled in new ways with the problem of how to define, preserve and protect the body politic. In personal monarchies, the resulting tensions raised questions that became, and remained, hotly contested. Did the king himself, in his person and as God's vicar, embody the nation? '*L'état, c'est moi*', the French King Louis XIV is alleged to have said, in a sentence that has come to encapsulate the theoretical underpinning of the French *ancien régime* (see Figure 6.2). Or was that feat of representation a collective and collaborative enterprise in which other agents and institutional organs played a vital role? And if the king embodied the nation, then what, if any, limitations might apply to his absolute power, and how might they be applied? What if he became tyrannical? Arguably the terms in which Englishmen asked, debated and finally answered those questions derived very immediately from the history that I have outlined here. We have seen how that history sowed the seeds for Stuart absolutism. It also allowed for the articulation of a view of Parliament as an assembly that was immediately responsible to God and that also represented the nation. Thus, if God punished his people by sending a tyrannical ruler in place of a true king, it could, in theory at least and as a last resort, embody and enact the state; even, if necessary, fight the king to preserve the body politic. To many that point seemed to have arrived by 1642, when the political nation divided into warring camps that contemporaries identified as Royalists – and 'Parliamentarians'.

FURTHER READING

Arnold, Oliver, *The Third Citizen: Shakespeare's Theater and the Early Modern House of Commons* (Baltimore, Md., 2007).

Axton, Marie, 'The Influence of Edmund Plowden's Succession Treatise', *Huntington Library Quarterly*, 37 (3) (1974): 209–26.

Barkan, Leonard, *Nature's Work of Art: The Human Body as Image of the World* (New Haven, Conn., 1975).

Boehrer, Bruce Thomas, *Monarchy and Incest in Renaissance England: Literature, Culture, Kinship and Kingship* (Philadelphia, Pa., 1992).

Cromartie, Alan, *The Constitutionalist Revolution: An Essay on the History of England, 1450–1642* (Cambridge, 2006).

Elton, G. R., 'The Divine Right of Kings', *Studies in Tudor and Stuart Politics and Government*, 4 vols. (Cambridge, 1974), vol. II, pp. 193–214.

Friedland, Paul, *Political Actors: Representative Bodies and Theatricality in the Age of the French Revolution* (Ithaca, NY, 2003).

Giesey, Ralph E., 'The Juristic Basis of Dynastic Right to the French Throne', *Transactions of the American Philosophical Society*, New Series, 51 (5) (1961): 3–47.

Hale, David George, *The Body Politic: A Political Metaphor in Renaissance English Literature* (The Hague, 1971).

Helmholz, R. H., *Canon Law and the Law of England* (London, 1987).

Ives, Eric, 'Tudor Dynastic Problems Revisited', *Historical Research*, 81 (212) (2008): 255–79.

Kantorowicz, Ernst H., *The King's Two Bodies: A Study in Mediaeval Political Theology* (Princeton, NJ, 1997). First published 1957.

Kelly, Henry Ansgar, *The Matrimonial Trials of Henry VIII* (Palo Alto, Calif., 1976).

Kim, Keechang, *Aliens in Medieval Law: The Origins of Modern Citizenship* (Cambridge, 2000).

Levine, Mortimer, 'A "Letter" on the Elizabethan Succession Question, 1566', *The Huntington Library Quarterly*, 19 (1) (1955): 13–38, p. 37a.

—— *The Early Elizabethan Succession Question, 1558–1568* (Palo Alto, Calif., 1966).

McCoy, Richard C., *Alterations of State: Sacred Kingship in the English Reformation* (Columbia, NY, 2002).

McLaren, Anne, 'Reading Sir Thomas Smith's *De republica anglorum* as Protestant Apologetic', *Historical Journal*, 42 (4) (1999): 911–39.

—— 'Gender, Religion, and Early Modern Nationalism: Elizabeth I, Mary, Queen of Scots, and the Genesis of English Anti-Catholicism', *The American Historical Review*, 107 (3) (2002): 739–67.

Neale, J. E., 'Parliament and the Succession Question in 1562/3 and 1566', *The English Historical Review*, 36 (144) (1921): 497–520.

Phillips, James Emerson, *Images of a Queen: Mary Stuart in Sixteenth Century Literature* (Berkeley, Calif., 1964).

Pocock, J. G. A., *The Ancient Constitution and the Feudal Law: A Study of English Historical Thought in the Seventeenth Century – a Reissue with Retrospect* (Cambridge, 1987).

Sharpe, Kevin, *Remapping Early Modern England: The Culture of Seventeenth Century Politics* (Cambridge, 2000).

Starkey, David, 'Representation through Intimacy: A Study in the Symbolism of Monarchy and Court Office in Early Modern England', in John Guy (ed.), *The Tudor Monarchy* (London, 1997), pp. 42–77.

Wilson, Jean, *Entertainments for Elizabeth I* (Woodbridge, 1980).

NOTES

1 T. E. Hartley (ed.), *Proceedings in the Parliaments of Elizabeth I*, 3 vols. (Leicester, 1981–95), vol. I, pp. 130–1.

2 Thomas Adams, *Englands Sicknes, Comparatively Conferred with Israels Diuided into Two Sermons, by Tho. Adams* (London, 1615), p. 46.

3 Jean Wilson, *Entertainments for Elizabeth I* (Woodbridge, 1980), p. 3.

4 Lincoln Kirstein, *Four Centuries of Ballet: Fifty Masterworks* (New York, 1984), pp. 74–7.

5 Alan Cromartie, *The Constitutionalist Revolution: An Essay on the History of England, 1450–1642* (Cambridge, 2006), p. 90.

6 Hartley, *Proceedings in the Parliaments of Elizabeth I*, vol. I, p. 91.

7 William Camden, *Annales rerum gestarum angliae et hiberniae regnante Elizabetha* (1615 and 1625) with the annotations of Sir Francis Bacon. Available online at www.philological.bham.ac.uk/camden/1565e.html#1566.

8 J. G. A. Pocock, *Virtue, Commerce and History: Essays on Political Thought and History, Chiefly on the Eighteenth Century* (Cambridge, 1985), p. 13.

9 André Hurault, Sieur de Maisse, *A Journal of All That Was Accomplished by Monsieur De Maisse, Ambassador in England from King Henry IV to Queen Elizabeth Anno Domini 1597*, trans. and ed. G. B. Harrison and R. A. Jones (London, 1931), pp. 11–12.
10 Thomas Rymer, *Foedera, conventiones, litterae, et cujuscunque generis acta publica, inter reges angliae et alios quosvis imperatores, reges, pontifices principes, vel, communitates habita aut tractata* (*Treaties, Agreements, Letters and Public Acts Whatsoever Made or Agreed between the Kings of England and Other Emperors, Kings, Popes, Princes or Communities*) (London, 1712), V. 14, pp. 110–17; quote on p. 114.
11 Eric Ives, *Henry VIII* (Oxford, 2007), p. 88.
12 Lemeke Avale, *A Commemoration or Dirige of Bastarde Edmonde Boner, Alias Savage, Usurped Bisshope of London* (London, 1569), fol. Av. V.
13 *Statutes of the Realm,* I Mary St. 2. C. 1.
14 *Statutes of the Realm,* I Eliz. C. 3.
15 Camden, *Annales.*
16 James Emerson Phillips, *Images of a Queen: Mary Stuart in Sixteenth Century Literature* (Berkeley, Calif., 1964), p. 112.
17 [Thomas Forster], *The Lay-Mans Lawyer; or, The Second Part of the Practice of Law* (London, 1654), p. 2.
18 *A 'Journal' of Matters of State Happned from Time to Time as Well Within and Without the Realme from and Before the Death of King Edw. the 6th Untill the Yere 1562*, in Ian W. Archer, Simon Adams, G. W. Bernard, Paul E. J. Hammer, Mark Greengrass and Fiona Kisbey (eds.), *Religion, Politics, and Society in Sixteenth-Century England* (Cambridge, 2003), pp. 52–122q; pp. 96–8.
19 Camden, *Annales.*
20 Keechang Kim, *Aliens in Medieval Law: The Origins of Modern Citizenship* (Cambridge, 2000).
21 Phillips, *Images of a Queen,* p. 112.
22 J. G. A. Pocock, *The Ancient Constitution and the Feudal Law: A Study of English Historical Thought in the Seventeenth Century* (Cambridge, 1987), pp. 31–2.
23 Anon., *Allegations against the Surmised Title of the Qvine of Scotts and the Fauorers of the Same* (London, 1565), attributed to John Hales.
24 Anon., *Allegations against the Surmised Title,* pp. 3, 10.
25 John Rastell, *Exposicions of the Termes of the Laws* (London, 1567), fol. 17.
26 Anon., *Allegations against the Surmised Title,* pp. 4–5.
27 Anon., *Allegations against the Surmised Title,* p. 26.
28 *Allegations in Behalf,* pp. 8, and again on P. 10.
29 *Allegations in Behalf,* p. 12; author's italics.
30 *Allegations in Behalf,* p. 13.
31 *Allegations in Behalf,* p. 18.
32 Mortimer Levine, 'A "Letter" on the Elizabethan Succession Question, 1566', *The Huntington Library Quarterly,* 19 (1955): 13–38, fol. 37a.
33 Levine, 'A "Letter" on the Elizabethan Succession Question', fol. 38a.
34 28 HVIII, C. 7; *Statutes of the Realm,* III, 655–62; 'The Letter', fol. 38b.
35 Sir John Seeley, *Introduction to Political Science: Two Series of Lectures* (London, 1886), p. 256.
36 Sir Thomas Smith, *De republica anglorum* (London, 1583), Book II, Chapter 1, 'Of the Parliament and the Authoritie thereof', p. 78, available online at www.constitution.org/eng/repang.htm.
37 Hartley, *Proceedings in the Parliaments of Elizabeth I,* vol. II, p. 232.
38 Marie Axton, 'The Influence of Edmund Plowden's Succession Treatise', *Huntington Library Quarterly,* 37 (3) (1974): 209–26; p. 209.
39 Quoted in Mortimer Levine, *The Early Elizabethan Succession Question, 1558–1568* (Palo Alto, Calif., 1966), p. 93.
40 John Guy (ed.), *The Reign of Elizabeth I: Court and Culture in the Last Decade* (Cambridge, 1995).

41 George Buchanan, *The History of Scotland Written in Latin by George Buchanan; Faithfully Rendered into English* (London, 1690), Book 17, p. 157.

42 Francis Bacon, 'The Case of the Post-Nati of Scotland', *The Works of Francis Bacon,* ed. James Spedding, Robert Ellie and Douglas Heath, 14 vols. (Stuttgart, 1961–3), vol. VII, pp. 665, 667, 641–79.

CHAPTER SEVEN

PARLIAMENT

David Dean

In 1584, the much-travelled Pomeranian aristocrat Lupold von Wedel sailed from Flushing (Vlissingen) to England. Arriving in London on 17 August, he travelled throughout England and Scotland until the following April. One of the highlights of his visit was his witnessing of the opening of Parliament on 23 November 1584. Wedel watched as the streets near Westminster were prepared for an impressive royal procession from the Palace of Whitehall to the Palace of Westminster where both houses of parliament would meet with the monarch. He saw row upon row of sumptuously dressed knights, lords, royal officials and guards, heralds, trumpeters and servants. Elizabeth wore a crown and her long red velvet parliament robes trimmed with ermine; she rode in a half-canopied litter upholstered with gold and silver cloth. Before her was carried the royal regalia, beside her were the royal bodyguard in tabards of red cloth trimmed with gold, and behind her rode twenty-four gorgeously attired women. Wedel was also present at the opening ceremony in the Parliament Chamber within Westminster. The room was dominated by a dais on which stood the royal throne with its canopy and embroideries of gold, silver and pearls. At the centre of the chamber were four woolsacks, covered in red cloth, on which the lord chancellor, judges, secretaries and clerks sat. On the benches covered in red satin that surrounded the woolsacks were the bishops and noblemen of the realm. 'In this manner', Wedel tells us, 'did this present Parliament commence. They sat every day till Christmas, but not the Queen who . . . is present only on the first and last days'.[1]

Wedel's account reminds us of the importance of display in the political culture of Elizabethan England. The procession to the opening of Parliament was then, as now, one of the most impressive state rituals anyone might see in their lifetime. The opening ceremony itself, a semi-public occasion to which Wedel secured privileged access, was also an opportunity to display the full authority of the realm, for here the majesty of the three essential components of Parliament – Crown, Lords and Commons – were assembled. However, Wedel is able to tell us nothing about what happened in the many weeks between the opening and closing ceremonies for these proceedings were closed to him. Only Members of Parliament (MPs), the noblemen and bishops summoned to sit in the House of Lords or those selected to sit in the House of Commons through elections, as well as the judges and officials such as the clerks were entitled to attend. What the members of the two houses did during that time is known to us from the official journals kept by the clerks, from private diaries kept by members and by the evidence of many Acts, Bills, committee papers and proposals for legislation that have survived. How important these activities were for the political life of the nation has been a matter of considerable debate among historians over the past fifty years.

Wedel was fortunate to have timed his visit so well because Parliament was not a regular event. Elizabeth ruled for forty-four years. During that time she summoned only ten parliaments which met in thirteen parliamentary sessions. The average duration of these sessions was under ten weeks. To put it another way, over a forty-four year reign, Parliament was in session for only 140 weeks. There were often gaps of three or four years between parliaments, particularly in the first half of the reign. Parliament, then, was not a regular form of government in the modern sense of the word. It had very specific functions, and vitally important ones for the governing of the nation, but it had no role in the day-to-day business of ruling the country. The government's need for revenue was the primary reason for the summoning of a parliament, but because parliamentary statutes had the greatest force in law, parliaments were also called when new laws were required.

One of the Parliament's most important functions was to authorise taxation or to offer 'supply' to the Crown. It was customary for the first parliament of each reign to grant tonnage and poundage, a tax on imports and exports, to a new monarch for their lifetime. Thereafter, monarchs were expected to ask for parliamentary approval of two types of taxes. The fifteenth and tenth was a tax on moveable goods in rural and urban communities, but because the amounts had been fixed for generations it brought in less and less money. The lay subsidy, a tax on the incomes of lay persons, yielded more revenue than fifteenths and tenths but was dependent on assessments which were outdated or inaccurate. Many of the leading gentry and noblemen, even members of the government, deliberately under-assessed themselves, and in 1593, the Chancellor of the Exchequer, Sir John Fortescue, claimed that inflation, under-assessment and avoidance meant that the subsidy brought in less than half of what it had done in Henry VIII's day. Parliament also ratified the clerical subsidy, based on more recent and accurate assessments, but, because it taxed only the clergy, it brought in less than the lay subsidy. The clerical subsidy was voted by the convocations of Canterbury and York, composed of lower houses of clerical representatives and upper houses of bishops, whose meetings coincided with those of Parliament.

Taxation was not the only reason why parliaments were summoned. Although Parliament did not put laws into practice and therefore played no part in law enforcement, it was the most important law-making body in the kingdom. Monarchs could issue orders and regulations through royal proclamations, but these lacked the legal authority of an Act of Parliament whose Acts comprised statute law. It was a sign of the importance of statute law that books of statutes began to be published as collections of 'statutes at large' in Elizabeth's reign. An Act or statute was made law by an enacting clause that literally stated it had the authority of the Queen, Lords and Commons of England. The thirteen sessions of Elizabeth's ten parliaments passed 433 Acts. All began life in one of the two houses as a Bill, were approved by the members of the other house and received the royal assent. Over 900 other legislative proposals in the form of Bills failed. Most did not emerge from the house in which they had been initiated; others passed one house but not the other; a few passed both but changes made by the second house were unacceptable by the first. Time was also a major factor in preventing Bills from becoming law, but so too was opposition to a measure. Seventy-two Bills passed both houses only to be vetoed by the Queen, usually a sign that she or her Privy Council, or both, disapproved of the measure.

The law-making and tax-granting functions of Parliament led contemporaries to conclude that although it was called only occasionally, it was the supreme legal authority in the country. As the diplomat and Principal Secretary Sir Thomas Smith put it in 1565, the 'most high and absolute power of the realme of England is in the Parliament'.[2] Towards the end of the reign, the great theologian Richard Hooker wrote that Parliament, alongside convocation, 'is that whereupon the very essence of all government within this kingdom doth depend'. Both men argued that Parliament was an assembly that represented everyone. Hooker put it this way: 'It is even the body of the whole Realm, it consisteth of the *King* and of all that within the *Land* are subject unto him for they all are there present either in person, or by such as they voluntarily have derived their very personal right unto.'[3]

Smith, writing his treatise in France, was anxious to show that Elizabeth, both a Protestant and a woman, ruled as completely as had her male predecessors and Catholic half-sister. Hooker, writing his *Laws of Ecclesiastical Polity* to celebrate the Elizabethan compromise (Calvinist in theology yet retaining many structural elements of Catholicism), insisted on the right of Parliament to legislate on religious affairs. Smith follows his explanation of the representative nature of Parliament with a long list of what Parliament can do; Hooker offers an extensive discussion disproving the idea that the English parliament was merely a temporal court 'as if it might meddle with nothing but only leather and wool'.[4]

What Smith and Hooker were articulating was a notion of representation in which Lords and Commons represented the full range of interests in the realm but were not accountable to anyone but themselves. This was certainly true of the temporal peers or nobility (dukes, marquises, earls and barons, the latter styled simply as 'Lord'), and it may also have been true of the spiritual peers (the bishops), although they may have had a duty to represent the views of convocation. MPs in the Commons were elected (or more often selected, as there were few truly contested elections) to represent counties (as knights of the shire), cities (as citizens) or boroughs (as burgesses), but there was no obligation for them to report back, or be accountable, to those who elected them. In practice, some members, particularly those of urban communities, did report on the progress and fate of legislation they had been instructed to promote, but this in itself does not mean they were accountable to the public in the modern sense or even compared to other contemporary representative assemblies such as the *Sejm* in Poland.

Those sitting in Parliament saw themselves as collectively embodying the whole realm and considered it their duty to prepare Bills to remedy a myriad of problems and to give counsel to the monarch and her government. They helped to shape governance in a wider sense too, for here were assembled men who were part of the governing elite. For the duration of a parliament they sat in the Lords as peers or in the Commons as MPs, but outside of Parliament, for the many years in which there were no parliaments, these men were lord or deputy lieutenants, sheriffs and justices of the peace; they were members of guilds and local councils; they were lawyers or clergymen, leading merchants or scholars; they were leaders of their county communities and of their parishes; they were landowners and heads of households. In 1601, almost half the MPs were university men, 16 per cent had one or more parents who were of noble status, and 80 per cent had fathers who were knights, esquires or country gentlemen.

When this elite group of men was summoned to Parliament, they knew that one of the major reasons for their gathering was the Crown's need for money. While monarchs had other sources of revenue, customs duties and rents for example, parliamentary taxation was essential especially at times of crisis, such as wartime, but increasingly also in peacetime. Convincing Parliament to offer supply required a good deal of management by the government because the lay subsidy (an Act which included the fifteenth and tenth) was always initiated in and by the Commons. At the opening of each session, the lord keeper or lord chancellor delivered a sometimes lengthy account of foreign affairs that was aimed to justify the request for a subsidy. These points were reiterated by the Speaker of the Commons, always a government nominee, by those Privy Councillors who sat in the house and by a selected few eloquent, industrious and influential men who lobbied for the official view.

The first two parliaments, 1559 and 1563, were held when England was at war with France; some resistance was encountered when a subsidy was requested in the second session of the second Parliament (1566–7) because the war was over. However, by now, most parliament men recognised the Crown's need for more financial aid, and subsidies were granted readily in the third Parliament of 1571 and in the last two sessions of the fourth Parliament in 1576 and 1581. By the time Wedel witnessed the opening of the fifth Parliament, the international situation had worsened: Philip II of Spain had become King of Portugal, and the Protestant Dutch rebellion against Spanish rule was in need of support, particularly after the assassination of its leader, William the Silent, a few months earlier. With the English expedition to support the Dutch and the subsequent war with Spain, which lasted into the next century, and the Earl of Tyrone's rebellion in Ireland in the 1590s, it is not surprising to see frequent parliaments, all of which required subsidies. Parliaments met from late November 1584 to late March 1585, again from late October 1586 to late March 1587 (the sixth of the reign) and once more from early February to late March 1589. This seventh Parliament deviated from tradition by offering not one subsidy, but two, and in each of the next three parliaments (1593, 1597–8 and 1601) multiple grants were offered – three in the first two and four in the last. By the end of the reign the English were being taxed at unprecedented levels with the approval of Parliament.

The Crown's dependence on parliamentary subsidies made it vulnerable to criticism and made it likely MPs would give vent to their concerns. In making his request in 1559, for example, Lord Keeper Sir Nicholas Bacon opened the way for discussion on the matter of the Queen's marriage and the question of the succession in the absence of any heir. The Commons sent a large delegation to urge the Queen to marry, and she responded a few days later saying that she would be content to die a virgin but was willing to marry and even make provision for an heir if circumstances changed. Their petition was accepted because it refrained from telling her whom to marry, and when.

While the Commons did not explicitly demand a quid pro quo for granting a subsidy, there was one gesture of gratitude which was expected and offered: the general pardon. This Act released subjects from penalties imposed for crimes committed, except for a large number of serious offences such as arson, treason and witchcraft. There was also an expectation that the Queen and her councillors would listen to good counsel. As the levels of taxation rose, MPs warned of the effects on the poor. In 1593, the Commons thought to offer two subsidies, but the government, through an intervention by the Lords, made it clear that three were needed. This caused concern on procedural grounds but also, as George Strode, MP for Wareham, noted in his recently rediscovered diary, because members were worried that the burden on the poor would cause unrest 'and many other reasons were aleaged by manye worthye persons who pleaded for their Countryes'.[5] Indeed, the economic crisis and dearth that came soon after this parliament ended was one of the worst in the century. In 1597–8, more concern about the poor was voiced, and MPs considered the possibility of novel taxes such as parish levies. More advice was given in the final parliament of the reign in 1601 which produced a poor law that became one of the most enduring statutes of any Elizabethan parliament.

The range of Acts and Bills initiated in these ten parliaments was very large and covered almost all topics imaginable. If we take one day's business in the two houses on Monday, 19 May 1572, we find the Lords ordered their legal assistants to take a Bill they had approved providing for the punishment of rogues and vagabonds and the relief of the poor to the Commons. So too was the Bill on counterfeiting foreign coin after it received its third and final reading. A first reading was given to a Bill punishing rebels and then the house adjourned. In the lower house on the same day, the clerk's journal duly reveals that the two Lords' Bills (on vagabonds and coin) arrived. The Commons immediately gave a first reading to the Lords' Bill on counterfeiting coin and first readings to Bills initiated in their own house concerning Worcester, Middlesex freeholders and timber. They also gave a first reading to a 'nova' bill (so described when a Bill was so heavily revised and altered, usually by a committee appointed on its second reading, that it came back and began a new process) dealing with fraudulent land grants and sales. Promoted by a particular MP, the person who defrauded him was supposed to appear that day, but this was postponed. The Commons gave second readings to Bills repealing a former Act concerning Shrewsbury, clarifying an Act of Henry VIII's reign concerning recoveries (restorations of former rights) and on presentations (lay ownership of church positions), rites and ceremonies in the Church, corrupt clerical tax collectors and defendants' rights in jury selections. The second reading was an important stage in the process of law-making, for sometimes the House voted for the Bill to be passed on to a committee for further discussion, revision and amendment, which is what happened in the case of the Bills on recoveries, presentations and another Bill on Middlesex jurors. If at the second reading the Bill was considered to need no further discussion or revision, then it was ordered to be 'ingrossed' or written on parchment, and this is what happened in the case of the Bills on Shrewsbury, rites and ceremonies, tax collectors and juries.

Yet this is not all the Commons did on that day. Arthur Hall, an MP in this parliament for Grantham who had made an unpopular speech expressing sympathy for Mary, Queen of Scots, and Thomas Howard, Duke of Norfolk, seven days earlier, was brought to the bar charged with seven offences. Hall apologised and was sent off with a lecture from the Speaker. Hall's actions were at odds with the mood of both houses, for the Queen's safety, which had been threatened by the Duke's plot (aka the Ridolfi Plot) to free and marry Mary, was the most important reason for the calling of this parliament. Many position papers were prepared, some by or for the government, others by individual members, urging the Queen to execute both plotters. As one member, Paul Wentworth, put it crudely but succinctly, their choice was between 'an axe or an acte'.[6] To the bitter disappointment of most, the Bill against the Scottish queen was denied royal approval. Uniquely, this parliament was not called for financial reasons (a subsidy had been granted at the previous parliament a year earlier) and it also met, unusually, in May.

Politics, or high affairs of state, could thus become a preoccupation of Parliament even though it had no role to play in the day-to-day business of government. On several occasions during Elizabeth's reign, her Privy Councillors, or some of them, saw Parliament as a way to pressure the Queen to do something which she had been refusing to do; encouraging the drafting of Bills and petitions on particular issues might work where their pleas from the council table or their lobbying at court had failed. The case of Mary, Queen of Scots, in 1572 was a case in point, for much of the debate in both houses had been shaped and guided by members of the government and those willing to promote the cause on their behalf. While the Queen's refusal to approve the Bill prohibiting Mary's succession was frustrating for the Paul Wentworths of the house, it was no less so for the Queen's leading adviser, Lord Burghley, who wrote of his frustration to another Privy Councillor, the Secretary, Sir Francis Walsingham. Perhaps their efforts did ensure that the Duke, who had been condemned to death for treason in January, met his fate in June.

Historians have debated the political importance of Parliament in this instance and in general. Sir John Neale argued in the 1950s that the Parliament of 1572 was an example of the key role Parliament played in the political life of the nation. For him, the failure of the Act against Mary was a sign that this was 'an unproductive session'. By contrast, for Sir Geoffrey Elton, writing in the 1980s, 1572 showed that Parliament played a very minor role in politics; it 'need never have got involved in the first place' and only did so because Privy Councillors, such as Burghley, saw an opportunity to put pressure on the Queen by using Parliament 'as an instrument of propaganda'.[7] For Elton, the session was productive; for example, it approved a new poor law, a statute that Neale chose not to mention. More recently historians have sought to recognise the role of Parliament in the politics of the nation while also acknowledging the importance of its legislative record. There is little doubt, for example, that discussions of the intervention in the Netherlands in the Parliament of 1586–7, a parliament whose opening the Queen refused to attend because she knew its main business would be the fate of Mary, Queen of Scots, in light of the Babington Plot, reveals an important role for Parliament as a forum in which those representing the realm could engage with the key issues of the day. The anger expressed in the Commons over monopolies (licences granted by the Crown to control manufactures, sold at a premium to the highest bidder) was a major political issue which Elizabeth and her ministers had to manage in 1597–8 and especially 1601.

The largest area of disagreement between Neale and Elton's interpretation of Parliament came over religion. The Rites and Ceremonies Bill of 1572, designed to remove all remaining Catholic elements in the church service, was, for Neale, the product of a well-organised puritan opposition to the Queen and her government's desire to reform the Church slowly. Elton and others have argued that the puritans were a vocal but insignificant group. They played virtually no role in the making of the Elizabethan settlement of 1559, and while Parliament was certainly a forum for puritan agitation and criticism, for example by promoting the 1572 *An Admonition to Parliament* urging radical reform, including the abolition of bishops, they failed to achieve much in terms of legislation. However, there is no doubt that later in the reign puritan-inclined MPs succeeded in drawing attention to Archbishop Whitgift's attack on radical ministers which removed them from their church livings by forcing them to subscribe to restrictive articles and using the ecclesiastical courts against them. Attempts at radical reform such as Anthony Cope's 'bill and book' campaigns to secure a learned ministry, better church attendance and attacks on the ecclesiastical courts and oaths were successful in their own terms, for raising debate in Parliament, where members from all regions of England were gathered, and would assist in furthering reform in local communities; achieving an Act was not necessarily the only measure of importance or success.

Experiencing Parliament was not always conducive to the government's needs or supportive of its perspective. In his 1593 diary, Strode reveals much camaraderie with those opposed to Archbishop Whitgift's attempts to root out puritan dissidents. He describes James Morice's speech launching the attack as 'very wise, grave, eloquent and learned'. While an unknown diarist notes that James Dalton of Lincoln's Inn 'spake with much earnestnes' against Morice, Strode calls it 'a raylinge speech'. In contrast to the anonymous diarist, who notes briefly what Dalton said before moving on to the next speaker, Strode comments that the speech 'did much dislike the house that they were fayne to hemme and putt him out'. His hostility towards those who opposed Morice is clear when he writes that Dr Lewen 'pleaded for the prelates' (a pejorative term for bishops).[8]

When the Queen responded to Morice's speech by prohibiting any further discussion of religious matters, summoning him to court and placing him under house arrest, Strode tells us that many MPs openly complained that what had been said and done in the Commons had been reported to her. Secretary Robert Cecil, 'supposing himselfe to be touched with this', argued that since the business of Parliament was 'as common in polles [Saint Paul's cathedral and churchyard, the latter being a popular gathering place dominated by bookstalls] and in taverns' and so well known to strangers, then the Queen 'might as well knowe' it too. Strode noted this down and decided to set out his own reasons why he thought Cecil was wrong. First, because strangers could do neither good nor harm 'to the cause', it was safe for them to know the business of the house; the Queen, on the other hand, could cause harm, as, indeed, she had done by preventing Morice's proposals from being considered. Second, Strode thought that since the Queen had the power to veto a Bill 'it is not fitt that she should be acquainted with it at the first'. This led him to reflect on the role of the Commons in representing the realm:

> bycause the Commons are better acquainted with the grievance of the countrye then she is and therefore yt is good reason that they should prefer billes accordingly and not to be thus stopped . . . it would greeve any good Christian to com so far out of his country and to lye at greate charge to any parlament herafter.[9]

His experience in Parliament, witnessing its procedures and debates, participating in its business, had a profound enough effect to cause him to not only note down what he had experienced but also to engage with arguments he had heard, *in extensio,* on paper, for his own edification and enlightenment. Other Elizabethans, such as Thomas Cromwell and Hayward Townshend, kept even more detailed diaries of their experience in Parliament, although they lack the self-reflection that is so striking in Strode's account.

Strode was also angry when the Privy Council proved willing to allow puritans (or, as Strode put it, 'the best Christians') as well as Catholics to be caught up in a Bill punishing those refusing to attend divine services. He vilifies a speech in the Bill's favour by 'yonge Sandes [Edwin Sandys] the bishopps sonne' (who spoke for an hour, taking up so much time that Strode was unable to speak himself) and commends those by Henry Finch, Nicholas Fuller and Edward Lewknor who wanted radical Protestants excluded. Strode was a stroppy backbencher: he opposed the Privy Councillor Sir Thomas Heneage on one issue and corrected Speaker Coke on matters of procedure. Strode tells us that his criticism of a proviso to the Bill during the committee's deliberations made Cecil 'verye angrye with me and said that I had spoken above twentye tymes alreadye'.[10] Strode and his friends 'were overruled', and the Bill eventually passed. For Strode, his parliamentary experience reinforced his sense of 'us' and 'them', with lines drawn in this case over how to treat radical Protestants.

Contemporaries recognised that there was political conflict in Parliament, with opposing sides facing off against each other, and these could be over subsidies, religion or more mundane matters, even Hooker's 'leather and wool'. Townshend, who kept a very detailed diary of the 1601 Parliament, noted that Devon's MPs joined forces to oppose a Bill on fustian cloths, revealing that the Bill had its supporters and detractors. In 1593, when the Lords urged the Commons to increase their offer from two to three subsidies, Robert Beale protested and cited precedents that convinced Speaker Coke but not, an unknown diarist tells us, the Privy Councillors or the courtiers. On the next day of business Beale stood up and said that he had been mistaken, but Strode tells us that Beale was made to recant and implies that he was prohibited from attending Parliament thereafter. Two other MPs who spoke against the government line, Francis Bacon and Henry Unton, suffered royal disapproval once the Parliament was over, proof that what you said during a session could have profound effects on your political life thereafter, even if only in the short term.

The political role of Parliament and the politics of law-making were shaped by particular events and circumstances. Because there were thirteen sessions over forty-four years, the political, religious, economic, social and cultural contexts of each meeting were different from the last and from the next. The Parliaments of the 1560s met in the first decade of a new reign, when most expected their queen to marry and settle the succession through the birth of a legitimate heir, and these hopes continued into the 1570s and 1580s. The restoration of Protestantism dominated the first parliament of the reign, and the limitations of that settlement led some who saw it as a beginning rather than an end as only the first step towards a truly godly Protestant Church, to seek further religious reforms in each Parliament until the end of the reign, but especially in those of the 1570s. With the outbreak of war in Spain, foreign policy matters were discussed in the parliaments of the second half of the reign to a greater degree than earlier, and the tensions caused by war preparations, such as the exercise of royal purveyance to supply the troops, were not simply matters of economics but of politics too. With the severe economic crisis in the middle years of the last decade of Elizabeth's reign, Parliaments spent more time than before debating and drafting laws on enclosure, depopulation and poor relief.

While the clerks only noted the titles of Bills and their proceedings, the survival of all of the Acts and many of the Bills which were promoted allows a rich picture of the sheer immensity and diversity of the law-making process to be recovered. Their preambles, which justify each measure, are worthy of careful study in revealing how contemporaries conceptualised the problems they identified in their world. However, it is in the survival of private members' diaries and journals that the dynamics of Parliament can be seen and more may yet be discovered. Historians are only now fully utilising these diaries and accounts, not simply for information about procedures, the contents of Bills and the day-to-day business of Parliament, but for what they tell us about Parliament as a public institution, as a forum for debate, as a place in which knowledge and ideas could be transferred. Parliament was, in Geoffrey Elton's oft-cited phrase, a valuable 'point of contact' between the Crown and the governing elites, between the centre and the locality, but it was also an opportunity for men from across the country to meet and exchange ideas, to find common ground and to shape a dynamic political culture. As was suggested earlier, this was not only an opportunity, but a duty, because such men assumed their role was to offer counsel to their monarch, and to her councillors sitting in the Commons. Individual MPs seized upon the chance to become better governors, learning from their parliamentary experience. Strode recorded 'Certaine breife thinges w[hi]ch I observed' in the 1593 Parliament, including the number of parishes in England and Wales, the number of alehouses, the number of strangers (foreigners) in London, all of which were mentioned during debates on various Bills. He also made notes on parliamentary procedures and events such as collecting money to pay for a clock, all recorded as if he were keeping a commonplace book.[11]

The way Parliament functioned was shaped and framed by the spaces which it occupied. It is curious that an institution that played such an important part in the constitutional development of the nation occupied borrowed buildings, for although a seventeenth-century artist might label the Common's meeting place as 'Parlament

Figure 7.1 Anthonis van den Wyngaerde's panorama of the Palace of Westminster. Image © Ashmolean Museum, University of Oxford, UK/The Bridgeman Art Library.

House', it was, in fact no such thing.[12] On the opening day of an Elizabethan parliament, the Queen, Lords and Commons assembled in the White Chamber in the royal palace of Westminster. They reassembled there on the closing day of Parliament. In the intervening period, the Lords stayed in the White Chamber for their deliberations while the Commons removed themselves to Saint Stephen's Chapel.

Anthonis van den Wyngaerde's panorama of the Palace of Westminster (Figure 7.1) eleven years after the Commons began sitting in Saint Stephen's Chapel shows clearly the relationship between Abbey, Westminster Hall, the White Chamber and the chapel itself. It also reveals its height (100 feet with its clerestory) but the floor space was quite small (26 feet wide and 90 feet long). When the chapel had been converted into a college chapel, the five bays were interrupted by a screen between the second and third bays, thus dividing the chapel into two distinct spaces: a chapel proper with choir stalls and an ante-chapel. The screen, which was wide enough to have stairs leading to a gallery above, gave access from the ante-chapel to the chapel through a double door at its centre. The move, at the beginning of Edward VI's reign, from the chapter house of Westminster Abbey to this smaller collegiate chapel (only 54 feet long) had important effects on the business, proceedings and political culture of the Elizabethan Commons.

One was overcrowding. In the first parliament of the reign there were 400 members, a number which grew to 462 in the last parliament of the reign. Despite the addition of benches and cross-benches, space was tight, and complaints were made about jostling and rulings made prohibiting spurs and swords. Cramped space might be an obvious explanation for the high degree of absenteeism. Another effect was the physical manifestation of hierarchy. The former altar space allowed for a raised Speaker's chair, and to his right sat the Privy Councillors sitting in the

Commons and the citizens of London, perhaps occupying the space where originally the monarchs had sat in the chapel.

The chapel's height allowed for an institutional development in the history of the Commons: the construction of a record room to keep the journals, Bills and position papers, as well as rooms for the clerk and the sergeant, a privy and a committee room. Procedurally, the double door leading from the chapel to the ante-chapel served as a convenient means to divide the house into ayes and nays on the occasion where a division was needed to determine a vote. Especially important for the culture of Parliament, was the ante-chapel itself for it provided a place for those not able to attend proceedings to jostle for the attention of members as they entered and departed the chamber. The ante-chamber, or what it now became, a lobby, became a very important and dynamic space for politicking and influencing the business of the house, providing a degree of access from the busy public spaces in and around Westminster Hall, offices and yards of the palace and ensuring that the private world of the Commons sat within a larger public political space.

Within the private world of the Commons chamber – although on occasion 'strangers' were able to sit and watch proceedings illicitly – the move into Saint Stephen's Chapel created an intimate if crowded debating chamber. John Hooker, chamberlain of the city of Exeter and its MP in 1571 and 1586, wrote that the lower house, longer than it was wide, was 'made like a Theater, having foure rowes of seates one aboove an other round about the same'.[13] Strode was reminded of the seating in London's infamous cockpits. In the abbey's chapter house, members would have sat in a long arc facing the Speaker. Now, except for those on the cross-benches, MPs faced each other. Thus a more dynamic and, to borrow Hooker's metaphor, theatrical space was created for speech, laughter, coughing, spluttering, gestures and silence.

The journals kept by contemporaries offer occasional glimpses of this, as do attempts to regulate behaviour. Smith asserted that in debates there was 'marvelous good order used in the lower house' with 'the greatest modestie and temperance of speech'.[14] Rules formulated to govern how men should speak betray a different story. MPs were to avoid 'nipping or unreverent speech', deliver their speeches facing the Speaker and not another member, no member should be named but only described and no one was to speak until another has finished.[15] Decorum was not always followed, as in 1584–5 when the Solicitor complained that during a reading of a Lords' Bill many members had 'cryd away with it', accusing them of 'levity and rashnes', or as we saw in 1593 when Strode notes that men made noises during Dalton's unpopular speech.[16]

The Lords sat in the White Chamber in the Palace of Westminster. It was 27 feet wide by 70 feet long and so not much different from Saint Stephen's, but with some seventy members rather than over 400, it was much less crowded. The chamber was decorated in crimson and had tapestries on the walls, a fireplace provided warmth, and there was a large lancet window on the north end where, marking the limits of the debating chamber, there was a railing covered in crimson. Below this was space for petitioners and MPs attending the Lords. Although the most frequently reproduced picture we have of Elizabeth in Parliament is that showing the Queen presiding over the Lords with the Speaker being presented to her engraved to illustrate Sir Simonds D'Ewes's *Journals of all the Parliaments of Queen Elizabeth*

Figure 7.2 *Queen Elizabeth in Parliament*, Renold Elstrack (1570–1630?). Engraving in Robert Glover, *Nobilitas politica vel ciuilis*. London: William Jaggard, 1608, frontispiece. By permission of the Folger Shakespeare Library.

published in 1682, the closest contemporary picture comes from the herald Robert Glover's posthumous publication, *Nobilitas politica vel civilis* (1608) which was engraved by Renold Elstrack (Figure 7.2). It depicts an open windowed hall, but in its essentials the image is similar to, and quite possibly derived from, the drawings prepared by the heralds for the opening of Parliament.

If the layout of the Commons reminded contemporaries of a cockpit or a theatre, Elstrack's depiction of the Lords shows the royal dais and carpet projecting into the chamber like an Elizabethan thrust stage. Debates in the Lords and the Commons can also be helpfully described as political theatre, and the many texts thrown up by the activities of Parliament offer a promising new approach to political culture in the period. The performance was framed by the rituals of the opening and closing days. At the opening, in the presence of the Queen, the lord keeper (or lord chancellor) declared the reasons for the summons before the assembled Lords and the Commons with their speaker crowded at the bar of the chamber. On the closing day, again in the Lords' chamber with the Commons and their speaker standing at the bar, the Queen received the speaker's oration, which prefaced their offer of a subsidy and the lord keeper (or lord chancellor) replied on behalf of the Queen. On many occasions in these parliaments Elizabeth herself spoke before the Bills which had been approved by the two houses were presented to her, with the titles read out by the clerk of the Crown in chancery and their fate declared by the clerk of the parliament in French, emphasising Parliament's Anglo-Norman traditions. In the days framed by these ceremonies, the Lords and Commons met

Figure 7.3 Elizabeth in parliament, frontispiece of Sir Simonds D'Ewes, *A Compleat Journal of the Votes, Speeches and Debates, Both of the House of Lords and House of Commons Throughout the Whole Reign of Queen Elizabeth, of Glorious Memory* published by Paul Bowes in 1693 (the first edition was printed by John Starkey in 1692). © The British Library Board. 806.i.4, frontispiece.

separately but their deliberations also were punctuated by rituals that had all the hallmarks of a theatrical event, such as the disabling and enabling speeches surrounding the nomination of a Speaker, receiving delegations from the other house or the drama of a division.

Yet it was in the daily business of debate that Parliament as theatre is revealed most vigorously. What evidence we have suggests that some speeches were lively, entertaining and inspiring; others were pedantic and long-winded. In the middle of the monopolies debate one member caused laughter when he asked if bread was not among the list of manufactures affected by such abusive grants; on another occasion we learn from a diarist that a speech was long, tedious and off-topic. In writing and delivering their speeches, Parliament men drew on their life experience, on their knowledge of particular trades and activities, on what they had read and what they had heard, and they betray skills derived from their school training in rhetoric. Some speeches were clearly written to flatter and ingratiate the member with those in authority; others were doggedly critical of the regime.

Speeches were influential enough for some City companies to try and bribe their way into the chamber of certain members to get a look at a speech before it was delivered, or to wine, dine and even offer financial gifts to members to speak on their behalf. Position papers and sheets of arguments were copied in numbers. Ideas circulated on paper, in manuscript; some may have been printed but in such small numbers and because they were so ephemeral few Elizabethan examples have survived. Case studies of local disputes that ended up in Parliament indicate the importance of the circulation of texts and their place in the business of Parliament. When Yarmouth and Lowestoft turned to Parliament for a solution to their dispute over herring, they circulated papers asserting the merits of their case and the faults of their opponents. These ranged from technical discussions of the fishing industry to summaries of legal jurisdictions and brief accounts of the history of the dispute. These papers reveal the rhetorical strategies that their authors thought would work. Yarmouth sought support from other incorporated towns by suggesting that if their 'libertyes' could be dispensed with, so could others. They employed the rhetoric of the commonweal: if Yarmouth's economy suffered, so would the fishing and maritime industries of 'the whole Commonwealth'. They appealed to a sense of nationalism and to national security, for a strong Yarmouth would be a bulwark against Spanish invaders and piracy. They drew in other discourses too, including the Calvinist emphasis on industry and hard work and the threat of disorder. Dividing a paper into two convenient headings, 'Lowestoft Complaynentt', 'Yarmouth Defendant', is a clear indication that such papers were meant to be used in the house, in the committee appointed to meet in the nearby Exchequer Chamber and by those working the lobby and the yards and public spaces around Saint Stephen's Chapel.[17]

The financial accounts of London's companies give colour to the importance of lobbying in Parliament and the strategies adopted. In 1593, the Brewers' Company campaigned against one Bill promoted by the City regulating beer prices and another which the Coopers' Company wanted to prevent brewers from making barrels. The two companies found themselves shelling out considerable sums in the hope of either securing a favourable Act or defeating an unfavourable Bill. They paid out money for the writing out of Bills and proposals, to obtain copies of rival measures, for lists of committee members and for legal advice, sometimes from parliamentary officials. Both companies paid fees to door-keepers and other officials and sometimes payments for additional services. The Brewers paid money 'to Mr Seriante Harris for his councell in this bill and to speake againste the same', to a Privy Councillor's chamber-keeper 'for helpinge us to his honors speach' and 'to the Clarke of the parliaments man to give us notice if any bill should come againste us'. Entries in the Coopers' records show payments of a similar nature and sometimes to the same people.[18]

Some speeches, particularly those of the Queen, were copied, edited and printed for wider dissemination. Although the extensive use of print in parliamentary contexts was to come after Elizabeth's reign, parliamentary statutes were another obvious use of print culture to reveal the business of Parliament to the wider nation. Almost all statutes contained a preamble that explained the purpose of the provisions and enactments that followed. Many were printed in folio, but a few, such as the 1598 Act against rogues and vagabonds, were printed as broadsides to encourage their posting for public display. Proclamations sometimes presented extracts and abridgements of statutes. If recent work on sermons and pamphlet literature are anything to go by, future historians of Elizabeth's parliaments will have much to say about the shape, style and content of parliamentary speeches and the nature of debate, about ideology and ideas, the dissemination of information and especially about parliament's role in shaping a public.

Elizabethan audiences were used to parliaments as an irregular, but necessary, indeed essential, part of the political landscape. In a rare stage direction, William Shakespeare notes that a group of lords are to 'Enter, as to the Parliament' (*Richard II,* Act IV, Scene 1). No groundling would have been surprised to hear Henry VI declare, in meeting the challenge of Richard, Duke of York, that he would not 'make a shambles of the parliament house' (*3 Henry VI,* Act I, Scene 1). To Elizabethans, good monarchs worked well with parliaments and would never hesitate to summon them at time of need. As Shakespeare's hero, Henry V, declares on learning of his father's death: 'Now call we our high court of parliament; And let us choose such limbs of noble counsel, That the great body of our state may go In equal rank with the best govern'd nation' (*2 Henry IV,* Act V, Scene 2). Parliament appears frequently in the history plays as an arena in which the politics of the Wars of the Roses are played out, and this had great meaning for Elizabethan audiences who well knew that Acts of Parliament settled succession matters. They would also take Mistress Page's proposal to punish Falstaff in a parliamentary way – 'Why, I'll exhibit a bill in the parliament for the putting down of men' (*Merry Wives of Windsor,* Act II, Scene 1) – for wishful thinking, although they certainly knew that Parliament had the authority to pass laws on any matter and perhaps, even, that in some parliaments the value of the entertainment they were enjoying had been called into question.

Parliament was many things: a ritual process, political theatre, a law-making institution, a tax-approving body, a public assembly of subjects where the issues of the day could be debated, proposals aired and solutions reached, where counsel might be sought, or given, where consensus might be reached or oppositions revealed. Parliament was an essential part of state formation in early modern England, and its nature was mirrored in councils, wards and parishes across the country, in juries empanelled before justices, in the stannary courts and parliaments of Devon and Cornish tin miners and even in the group of inhabitants in Swallowfield, Wiltshire, who, faced with the horrors of the crisis of the mid-1590s, met and drew up a set of articles 'to the end we may the better & more quietly lyve together in good love & Amyte to the praise of God, and for the better servynge of her Ma[jes]tie when wee meete together', words which might serve as a description of an ideal parliamentary session.[19] For many Elizabethans, parliament had deep historical roots in the consultative assemblies of their Anglo-Saxon forebears, the occasions of its meeting under the Norman, Plantagenet, Lancastrian, Yorkist and Tudor monarchs yielding a rich treasure of precedents.

Yet perhaps the strongest indication of the importance of parliament in Elizabethan England comes from a man who first as the Queen's secretary and then as her lord treasurer influenced its proceedings in every session from the beginning of her reign until his own death in 1598. Fearing for his sovereign's life, William Cecil, Lord Burghley, dared contemplate what might happen should she be assassinated. How would the country be governed? Who, in the absence of a clear successor, would choose who should succeed her? Clearly, Burghley thought, the council would have to meet in emergency session, and as many of the elite as it were possible to get together, but ultimately he thought a parliament would have to be summoned for it was there and only there that the safety of the realm could be assured.

FURTHER READING

Alford, Stephen, *The Early Elizabethan Polity: William Cecil and the British Succession Crisis, 1558–1569* (Cambridge, 1998).

Braddick, M. J., *The Nerves of State: Taxation and the Financing of the English State, 1558–1714* (Manchester, 1996).

Collinson, Patrick, *Elizabethan Essays* (London, 1994).

Dean, David, *Law-Making and Society in Late Elizabethan England: The Parliament of England, 1584–1601* (Cambridge, 1996, 2002).

Dean, D. M. and Jones, N. L. (eds.), *The Parliaments of Elizabethan England* (Oxford, 1990).

Elton, G. R., *The Parliament of England, 1559–1581* (Cambridge, 1986).

Graves, Michael A. R., *The Tudor Parliaments: Crown, Lords and Commons, 1485–1603* (Harlow, 1985).

—— *Elizabethan Parliaments, 1559–1601*, 2nd edn (Harlow, 1996).

—— *The Parliaments of Early Modern Europe* (Harlow, 2001).

Guy, John (ed.), *The Tudor Monarchy* (Oxford, 1988).

—— *Politics, Law and Counsel in Tudor and Early Stuart England* (Aldershot, 2000).

Hartley, T. E., *Elizabeth's Parliaments: Queen, Lords and Commons, 1559–1601* (1992).

—— (ed.), *Proceedings in the Parliaments of Elizabeth I*, 3 vols. (Leicester, 1981, 1995).

Hasler, P. W., *The History of Parliament: The House of Commons, 1558–1603*, 3 vols. (London, 1981).

Hoak, Dale (ed.), *Tudor Political Culture* (Cambridge, 1995).

Jones, Clyve and Kelsey, Sean (eds.), *Housing Parliament: Dublin, Edinburgh and Westminster*, Special Issue of *Parliamentary History*, 21 (2002).

Jones, Norman and Dean, David (eds.), *Interest Groups and Legislation in Elizabethan Parliaments*, Special Issue of *Parliamentary History*, 8 (1989).

Kishlansky, M., *Parliamentary Selection: Social and Political Choice in Early Modern England* (Cambridge, 1986).
Kyle, Chris R., 'Parliament and the theater of state: the construction of texts', *Shakespeare Studies* 30(2002): 31–5.
Kyle, Chris R. and Peacey, J. (eds.), *Parliament at Work: Parliamentary Committees, Political Power and Public Access in Early Modern England* (Woodbridge, 2002).
Loades, David, *Power in Tudor England* (Basingstoke, 1997).
—— *Tudor Government: Structures of Authority in the Sixteenth Century* (Oxford, 1997).
McLaren, A. N., *Political Culture in the Reign of Elizabeth I: Queen and Commonwealth, 1558–1585* (Cambridge, 1999, 2006).
Mears, Natalie, *Queenship and Political Discourse in the Elizabethan Realms* (Cambridge, 2005).
Neale, J. E., *Elizabeth I and Her Parliaments,* 2 vols. (London, 1953, 1955).
Peacey, Jason (ed.), *The Print Culture of Parliament,* Special Issue of *Parliamentary History,* 26 (2007).
Smith, D. L., *The Stuart Parliaments, 1603–1698* (London, 1999).

NOTES

1 Victor Von Klarwill, *Queen Elizabeth and Some Foreigners* (London, 1928), pp. 332–5.
2 Sir Thomas Smith, *De republica anglorum,* ed. Mary Dewar (Cambridge, 1982), p. 78.
3 Arthur Stephen McGrade (ed.), *Richard Hooker, of the Laws of Ecclesiastical Polity* (Cambridge, 1989), p. 192.
4 McGrade, *Richard Hooker,* p. 192.
5 Bodleian Library, Dep. E. 468, fol. 19v.
6 T. E. Hartley (ed.), *Proceedings in the Parliaments of Elizabeth I,* 3 vols. (Leicester, 1981–1995), vol. I, p. 376.
7 G. R. Elton, *The Parliament of England, 1559–1581* (Cambridge, 1986), pp. 376, 377.
8 Bodleian Library, Dep. 3. 468, fols. 8v and following; Hartley, *Proceedings in the Parliaments of Elizabeth I,* vol. III, pp. 76–80.
9 Bodleian Library Dep. E. 468, fols. 11v–12v.
10 Bodleian Library, Dep. E. 468, fols. 12v–19.
11 Bodleian Library, Dep. E. 468, fols. 28v–29.
12 Wenceslaus Hollar's *View of Westminster, c.* 1647; reproduced in Howard Colvin, 'Views of the Old Palace of Westminger', *Architectural History,* 9 (1966), Fig. 5.
13 Vernon F. Snow, *Parliament in Elizabethan England: John Hooker's Order and Usage* (New Haven, Conn., 1977), p. 163.
14 Smith, *De republica anglorum,* p. 82.
15 Paul L. Ward, *William Lambarde's Notes on the Procedures and Privileges of the House of Commons (1584)* (London, 1977), pp. 63–4.
16 Hartley, *Proceedings in the Parliaments of Elizabeth I,* vol. II, p. 117.
17 David Dean, 'Parliament, Privy Council, and Local Politics in Elizabethan England: The Yarmouth-Lowestoft Fishing Dispute', *Albion,* 22 (1) (1990): 53–6.
18 David Dean, 'London Lobbies and Parliament: The Case of the Brewers and Coopers in the Parliament of 1593', in Norman Jones and David Dean (eds.), *Interest Groups and Legislation in Elizabethan Parliaments: Essays Presented to Sir Geoffrey Elton,* Special Issue of *Parliamentary History,* 8 (1989): 353–61.
19 Steve Hindle, 'Hierarchy and Community in the Elizabethan Parish: The Swallowfield Articles of 1596', *Historical Journal,* 42 (2) (1999): 835–51.

CHAPTER EIGHT

CENTRE AND LOCALITIES

J. P. D. Cooper

For the historian aspiring to write on Tudor government, the starting point still has to be Geoffrey Elton. Published in 1960, *The Tudor Constitution* presents 450 pages of documents and commentary describing Crown and council, seals and secretaries, church and parliament, before turning at last to the agencies of local government, which it dispatches in only twenty. Elton's respect for his adopted England, and the structures that had sustained its liberty, led him naturally to focus on the central institutions of the Tudor state. But Elton was also hindered, as he pointed out, by the absence of research on the localities: 'Attempts to understand how the Government's orders were transmitted and executed, how the localities ran their affairs, or how these things developed in time, meet unsolved problems at every turn.'[1]

What has changed in the half-century since Elton sounded this rare note of defeat? A milestone was Penry Williams's *The Tudor Regime,* which assessed the officials who administered England and Wales, the imprint of monarchical rule on the life of the nation and the responses of ordinary subjects from compliance to resistance – government as it actually functioned. Local studies have progressively shed their antiquarian associations. The Elizabethan county has emerged as something more than an effective administrative unit; it was also a source of identity, the subject of surveys and scholarly investigation and, perhaps, a focus of political allegiance. Reformation scholarship, meanwhile, has expanded beyond its traditional territory of theology and high politics to consider questions of reception and policing in the parishes. This depth of analysis was nigh impossible before the establishment of county record offices, whose archives provide the means to test traditional assumptions about the strength of the Tudor state.

Provincial England was no passive observer of the politics and personalities orbiting the Tudor monarchy. If policy was determined in the palaces of Westminster and Whitehall, its enforcement turned on the co-operation of local elites and subjects. The Crown nurtured the allegiance of the localities through ceremonial, print and the pulpit. When this dialogue broke down, the results could be disastrous, as a litany of Tudor rebellions had demonstrated: Yorkshire, Kent and Cornwall all had traditions of popular protest. By comparison with the reigns of her predecessors, however, Queen Elizabeth's was relatively quiet. The revolt of the northern earls in 1569 was far smaller than the Pilgrimage of Grace, and lacked the patriotic appeal of Thomas Wyatt's uprising against Queen Mary. Riot was uncommon and violence exceptional, even during the dearth of the 1590s. This was due in large part to the local governors who mediated statutes and royal proclamations, guided by a sense of responsibility to their communities as well as to the Crown. Schemes of poor relief, trialled by individual towns before being adopted as a national campaign, also helped to hold subjects in obedience to the higher powers.

The theme of centre and localities assumes a deeper significance when set in a British context. From Henry VIII's reign onwards, English monarchs asserted their claim to be kings of Ireland, while Wales was effectively absorbed into the kingdom of England. Elizabeth and her ministers perceived Ireland and Wales not as separate dominions but as one body politic with England, fused together in the person of the Queen. In the eyes of the Crown, the various Tudor territories could present common problems of governance. Similar solutions, however, might produce dramatically different results, as when English attempts to carry the Protestant Reformation to Ireland were violently resisted. Scotland was a separate nation, but its land border with England and its proximity to Ulster, coupled with the growing possibility of a Stuart succession to a united throne, made it subject to repeated English intervention during Elizabeth's reign. The study of Tudor state-building demands an integrated approach, with the English regions set alongside the other components of a polity that was increasingly being conceptualised as 'Britain'.

Viewed from a European perspective, Elizabethan England was both remarkably unified and closely governed. There was no English equivalent of the French provincial estates, or the devolved power structures of Philip II's Spain. Elizabeth lacked the reserves of money and manpower enjoyed by her brother monarchs in Europe, but within her own realm she was unquestionably sovereign. Her English subjects spoke one language, varying in accent and dialect but intelligible throughout the kingdom and fast becoming standardised by print. Antiquaries such as William Camden knew that England was an ancient landscape. Its monarchy had a lineage dating to Anglo-Saxon times, and some of its towns and roads were even older, built by the Roman civilisation that the Elizabethans so admired. More recent history had seen a campaign of centralisation accompany the break with Rome. In 1533, the year of Elizabeth's birth, parliament had confirmed England's status as an 'empire', united under one crown. Sanctuaries and a scattering of medieval franchises had been abolished to ensure that the royal writ ran everywhere. When she inherited the throne in 1558, Elizabeth became queen of all England.

That said, her realm was also a diverse place, and government was not everywhere the same. The Council of the North dispensed justice and investigated Catholic recusants from its base at York. Royal authority in the north, the Midlands and the south-west was filtered through the palatinates and great estates of the Crown, the Duchies of Lancaster and Cornwall and the Earldom of Chester. Wales had a council of its own, whose remit included several adjoining English counties. The language, custom and culture of Elizabethan Wales were overwhelmingly Welsh. The Cornish language was weaker than its cousin, a casualty of the Tudor reformations of religion, but it clung stubbornly to the western parts of Cornwall. Beyond the mainland lay the Channel Islands, French-speaking and ruled under the

Crown by bailiffs and jurats, and the Isle of Man, with a language close to Gaelic and laws that were Norse in origin. The diversity of the Queen's dominions found expression in the heraldry of her funeral cortège in 1603, in which England, Wales, Ireland, Cornwall and Chester were represented by separate processional banners.

How did the relationship between centre and localities develop during the reign of Elizabeth, and what were the dynamics of change? The existence of an English nation-state was several degrees closer by 1603 than it had been in 1558. London and the royal court played an increasingly dominant role in political and intellectual culture. The extension of the parliamentary franchise to new boroughs accelerated the traffic between the shires and the centre. Print, both sacred and secular, had a unifying potential all of its own. The survival of the Elizabethan regime in face of Catholic conspiracies and foreign invasion meant that English identity became progressively bound up with Protestantism, with weighty implications for the future of the British Isles. The sinews of the state also strengthened in more tangible ways. The commitment of English troops to the Netherlands in 1585 moved the government towards a permanent war footing, prompting the regularisation of the lieutenancy system and the refortification of the exposed south coast.

But for some Elizabethans, state-building came at a price. Catholics and puritans had at best an uneasy place within the new national compact, and at worst were left out altogether. Wales was accepted into England on less than equal terms, and whatever survived of native Cornish culture was rapidly withering on the vine. Most significant of all, perhaps, was the social polarisation that followed on this shifting balance between region and nation. As the shire gentry were drawn towards the bright lights of the capital and the royal court, so they compromised their traditional place within local society. In October 1596, the Earl of Bath warned that gentlemen ought to return to their estates in case the 'inferior multitude' should mobilise in protest against hunger and poverty.[2] The Oxfordshire rising of the following month was abortive, but its intentions had been chilling: landlords guilty of enclosure and exploitation were to be slaughtered in their beds, with the London apprentices rising in sympathy. In previous Tudor reigns, the gentry had often led popular protest; in Oxfordshire, at least, they had become its principal target.

OFFICERS AND GENTLEMEN

In the early 1560s, Sir Thomas Smith, a classicist and civil lawyer who was serving as Elizabeth's envoy in France, was inspired by a sense of 'yearning for our commonwealth' to write a treatise on the government of England. *De republica anglorum* was finally published in 1583, intended for a foreign audience as well as shire administrators, and it celebrated the superior institutions of Smith's native land. Assessing the power of the English monarchy, he observed:

> Although in times past there were certaine countie Palatines, as Chester, Durham, Elie, which were *hault* justicers, and writtes went in their name and also some Lorde marchers of Wales, which claymed like priviledge. All these are nowe worne away. The supreme justice is done in the kinges name, and by his authoritie onely.[3]

The sovereignty of the Crown over the localities was the bedrock of the Elizabethan state. All legal jurisdiction stemmed from the monarch, whether the common-law courts of King's Bench, Common Pleas and Exchequer, or the equity practised by the court of Chancery. Star Chamber, essentially the Privy Council sitting as a court of law, investigated cases of riot and enforced royal proclamations. The disintegration of traditional feudalism meant that tenants now looked to the Crown, rather than the manorial courts, for redress of their grievances over enclosure and encroachments on the commons. Royal justice came in different forms: thus the Council of the North was armed with a commission of oyer and terminer to investigate cases of felony, murder and sedition, and courts of Great Sessions in Wales took the place of King's Bench and Common Pleas in the English system. The Duchy of Lancaster, held by the Crown since 1399, had its own court of Duchy Chamber in Westminster Hall, and tin-mining in the west of England was regulated by ancient customary law under the aegis of the Duchy of Cornwall. But in all her dominions, Elizabeth enjoyed a legal supremacy that the kings of France might have envied.

Twice a year, the Crown as law-giver travelled the counties in the form of the justices of assize, who communed with local governors and filed reports on the state of the peace in addition to holding court. The assizes were occasions of ceremonial as well as business, an affirmation of the power vested by God in Queen Elizabeth to judge her subjects. Day to day, however, law and government in the localities depended on an unpaid royal official. Thomas Smith described the justice of the peace (JP), or magistrate (the latter was increasingly common, in conscious imitation of Roman precedent), as a gentleman in whom 'for the repressing of robbers, theeves, and vagabunds, of privie complots and conspiracies, of riotes and violences, and all other misdemeanors in the common wealth, the prince putteth his special trust'.[4] Quarter sessions, when JPs came together to investigate crimes ranging from murder, rape and theft to witchcraft and unlawful games, were solemn gatherings attended by sheriff, gaoler and coroner as well as the jurors representing the county. A few lines from the hand of a magistrate were enough to imprison an offender. To this medieval criminal jurisdiction the Elizabethan regime added a weight of initiatives aimed at social regulation. Excess of wages and excess of apparel, recusants and Gypsies, taverns and the grain supply, all came under the magistrate's remit. Where once there had been four or eight JPs in every shire there were now thirty or forty, thought Smith, 'either by increase of riches, learning, or activitie in policie and governement'; Norfolk saw its magistrates' bench almost double to sixty-one over the course of Elizabeth's reign. But if the growing burdens of the office are clear, then so is the prestige that it brought. Pressure to expand the peace commission came more from the gentry than the Crown, and books advising JPs on their duties were eagerly consumed. William Lambarde's *Eirenarcha,* printed in 1581, went through eight further editions before the end of the reign.

Even if Elizabeth had possessed the resources to create a paid bureaucracy in the localities (and she assuredly did not), it is difficult to imagine that the realm would have been much better administered, and a system dependent on salaries would probably have been open to corruption. As it was, local elites competed for the honour of serving queen and commonwealth. There were some problems, however, that demanded a more unified solution than could be provided by a bench of fifty or sixty JPs. Henry VIII had appointed lieutenants in the northern and western parts of his kingdom to review their security during the 1530s and 1540s, and the experiment was greatly extended by the Duke of Northumberland in Edward VI's reign. Elizabeth initially adopted her sister's more cautious approach to the lieutenancy, alert to the dangers of creating a new sort of regional magnate. But when Philip II began preparing for his enterprise of England, the creation of a chain of a command that could respond swiftly to invasion became an urgent priority.

Penry Williams describes the lieutenancy as 'by far the most important development in county administration during the sixteenth century'.[5] If the justices of assize represented the legal dignity of the Crown in the localities, then the lord lieutenants exercised its military function. From 1585, commissions of lieutenancy were regularly issued to peers and privy councillors to galvanise the English provinces against the expected onslaught from Spain. Lieutenants and their deputies, the latter drawn from the resident shire gentry, were expected to supervise the local musters and trained bands and to maintain the county armouries, assisted by professional muster-masters and provost-marshals. They collected the forced loans that funded the coastal defences ordered by the Crown and raised levies of men for offensives in the Netherlands and northern France. They also undertook to ensure good order in the shires, whether by monitoring the grain supply or by keeping Catholic recusants under surveillance in case they should make common cause with Spain. Constant communication was maintained with the Privy Council.

The lieutenancy system certainly looks impressive, and there is no doubt that it kept the government better informed about the state of the peace in the shires than it would otherwise have been. As personal representatives of the Queen, the lieutenants forged new and permanent links between the Crown and the localities; they are appointed by the monarch to this day. How the Elizabethan lieutenants would have fared as military commanders if Spanish troops had landed, as they nearly did in 1588 and threatened to do on several further occasions, is another question. There is also the possibility that by challenging the legal processes and prestige of quarter sessions, the lieutenancy accentuated divisions between a 'county' interest among the gentry, represented by JPs, and the royal court. Hassell Smith's study of Norfolk claims that deputy lieutenants had become 'overlords' by the early 1590s, reducing JPs 'to little more than assistants' and regulating local affairs from the observance of Lent to the planting of mulberry trees.[6] There was also disquiet about the appointment of provost-marshals from 1589, who executed martial law upon vagabonds and the vagrant poor as well as demobilised soldiers, and reported directly to the lord lieutenants. William Lambarde protested to the grand jury of Kent in 1591 that provost-marshals, 'this new invention' brought in by queen and council, constituted a threat to English common law and liberty, 'to our no less shame than charge'.[7]

Can Elizabethan England be described as a network of 'county communities'? The case is put by Hassell Smith:

> in late Tudor and early Stuart England most people who could think politically regarded themselves as members of a county community which had its own

> economic, social, and political character, and which stood apart from, sometimes even in opposition to, the greater but remoter community of the nation, of which . . . they were none the less also conscious.[8]

The gentry of later sixteenth-century Norfolk can thus be divided into 'court' and 'county' justices, defined both by their politics and their religion; the two were linked, as when puritan magistrates spearheaded opposition to ship money and other impositions of central government in the 1590s. A similar case has been made for Kent, that quarter sessions became a political expression of the county community. Elsewhere, the model works less well. In Suffolk and Dorset, for instance, the campaign against ship money was led by the deputy lieutenants, fulfilling their role as mediators between the localities and the Crown. The idea of the county community also raises more fundamental problems. The political and religious culture of a shire could vary with its topography and land use. Devon was divided between lowland and upland, coastal plain and moor; the conflicts of the 1640s revealed contrasting patterns of allegiance to Parliament and Crown that had been long in the making. The current generation of historians would also broaden the definition of 'people who could think politically' to include the groups that Sir Thomas Smith termed 'the fourth sort of men which doe not rule'.[9]

Notions of 'county community' and 'country opposition' clearly invite searching questions, but they are too important simply to discard. If a principled resistance to aspects of Crown policy had emerged in certain English shires in the 1580s and 1590s then it provides a context, and perhaps a partial explanation, for the growing antagonism between court and country under the first two Stuarts. When the Elizabethan gentry spoke of their 'country', they generally meant their county rather than the nation. Their sense of affinity was confirmed when they came together at assizes and quarter sessions, to witness hangings or to deliver royal proclamations. The gentry of a shire were linked by ties of kinship and marriage, by education or military service, by mutual interests in hunting or antiquarianism. Whether this adds up to a 'county community' depends on the shire, and the precise period, under investigation. Penry Williams concludes that 'most men of worth and importance belonged to several communities: to parish, hundred, county and nation'.[10] Catholics and the godly, for instance, had debts of allegiance to their co-religionists, but these mostly coexisted with their loyalties to their fellow gentlemen, to the monarchy, and to England. For those who could afford it, the year could be split between London, the royal court and periods in the country, a custom maintained by the English aristocracy into the twentieth century.

BORDERLANDS AND MIDDLE SHIRES

Like those other great controversies once favoured by historians of early modern England, namely the rise of the gentry and the causes of the British civil wars, the long debate about the Tudor 'revolution in government' has now largely run its course. Geoffrey Elton's forensic examination of the sixteenth-century state, and the career of Thomas Cromwell in particular, has been qualified, modified and challenged by generations of his own research students and others without any single model emerging to rival the clarity and consistency of the old. Although the battle has focused on the 1530s and 1540s, the implications for the reign of Elizabeth are nonetheless profound. If we agree that there was a permanent Tudor 'achievement', then how should we assess the contribution of Elizabeth and her regime? Was the later sixteenth century a time of growth and innovation in the royal administration, or essentially a holding operation – maybe even a falling away from the stability and efficiency of Cromwellian government?

The theme of centre and localities provides an opportunity to frame specific answers to these questions. Elton's interest in the Privy Council led him also to consider the regional councils that exercised administrative and judicial power in the north, the West Country and Wales. Cromwell's Council of the West had disappeared again by the end of Henry VIII's reign, replaced by the lieutenancy of the Russell Earls of Bedford and, from 1585, by Sir Walter Ralegh as Lord Warden of the Stannaries. The equivalent councils in Wales and the North, however, continued to play an active role in governing and policing their respective regions in Elizabeth's reign. The work of Steven Ellis, meanwhile, has prompted us to reconsider the whole question of centre and periphery within the Tudor territories. As Ellis points out, the 'borderlands' of the English state – Wales, Ireland, the far north of England and the Channel Islands – 'actually comprised over half the geographical area of the Tudor state', encouraging a reassessment of their place within the Tudor polity and the words we use to describe them.[11]

Studies of individual communities have demonstrated the danger in assuming that distance from London equated to a lukewarm or hostile attitude towards the Crown. Difference from the norm of lowland English government did not have to mean disloyalty; indeed, the reverse could be the case. Cheshire, for instance, had a long history as a palatinate, with ancient privileges and a symbolic link to the Crown through the earldom of Chester, proudly catalogued by William Smith in his *Vale-royall of England* of about 1588. Tim Thornton has explained how local political culture accommodated itself to the changing shape of Tudor government, allowing Cheshire 'to take a new place within the territories of the English Crown, at once closer and at the same time with its identity secured'.[12] A parallel can be drawn with the Elizabethan south-west, where gentry families, such as the Godolphins, were able to profit from the offices of the Duchy of Cornwall, and tenants benefited from generally stable rents and entry fines. The creation of six new parliamentary boroughs in Cornwall under Elizabeth, four of them Duchy-owned or influenced, probably reflects the petitioning of the local political nation rather than a Crown campaign to pack the House of Commons. Its forty-four MPs left Cornwall grossly over-represented until the Reform Acts of the nineteenth century.

Notwithstanding the claims of some historians, the Duchy of Cornwall was not a type of devolved local government but a royal estate, effectively subsumed within the Crown during Elizabeth's reign in the absence of a male heir. Its political influence was not limited to the gentry, since it was also responsible for overseeing the lucrative tin industry in Cornwall and Devon. Printed descriptions of the tinminers of the west of England, together with their own statements as litigants or jurors, reveal a long-standing belief that they were under the direct protection of the Crown. Sir John Doddridge's *History of the Ancient and Moderne Estate* of Wales, Cornwall and Chester, published in 1630, observed that 'kings of this land in former times . . . have endowed the Tynners with sundry priviledges for their good governement'; this was reflected in the material culture of the stannaries, such as the ducal or royal arms stamped on tin ingots and the weights that measured them.[13] The loyalty of both Cornish and Devon tinners to Charles I in the 1640s was visceral and had been centuries in the making. In similar vein, Andy Wood's study of the lead-miners of the Derbyshire Peak has explained how a fierce sense of local identity and occupational solidarity could be compatible with an expressed allegiance to the monarch as Duke of Lancaster. In complaints to Privy Council or parliament they represented themselves as the 'king's miners' working in the 'king's field', and in their moot hall at Wirksworth a standard measure known as the 'king's dish', donated by Henry VIII, was kept on permanent show. Wood describes the moothall as a 'memory palace' for the Derbyshire miners, a perpetual reminder of the antiquity and royal sanction of their rights.[14]

Loyalism was not the rule everywhere, however. In the north of England the Elizabethan regime continued to face significant challenges to its secular and spiritual authority. The Reformation had bitten deeply in a region where faith had traditionally been defined by monastic houses and sacred drama, leaving a residual Catholicism that could be reawakened by the relatively few seminary priests who elected to conduct their mission there. The magnate power of the Earls of Northumberland and Westmorland was depleted rather than destroyed, as demonstrated by their 1569 uprising against the Protestant settlement of religion, when mass was celebrated once more in Durham cathedral. The exiled presence of Mary, Queen of Scots, defiantly Catholic and increasingly eager to conspire against the English establishment that had imprisoned her, was a constant source of agitation for Lord Burghley and Sir Francis Walsingham; Elizabeth's horror of regicide kept Mary safe from execution until the Babington plot settled the issue. Alarming tales filtered through from Walsingham's agents in the Catholic community, of high mass sung in York Castle prison and country houses fitted out with priest-holes.

Further north still, in Tynedale and Redesdale, law and order remained an unresolved problem. The borders with Scotland continued to witness cattle-raiding or reiving between the English 'surnames' and their Scots equivalents; the records of quarter sessions and gaol delivery for Northumberland detail 108 incidents of livestock theft between 1601 and 1603, and these were only the cases that made it to court.[15] Since English border law was customary rather than codified, the wardens of the marches were free to apply it as they saw fit. Parliament was compelled to legislate in 1601 against the borderers who were kidnapping and ransoming people from Cumberland, Northumberland and Westmorland, 'whereof many of the inhabitants thereabouts are much impoverished, and the service of those borders and frontiers much weakened and decayed, and divers towns thereabouts much dispeopled and laid waste'.[16] The northern marches remained more a borderland than a middle shire until the early seventeenth century.

Judged by the standards of the English lowlands, government in the north depended on an untidy array of commissions and personalities. The borders were divided for military purposes into the east, middle and west marches, each with its own warden. Durham retained the form if not the substance of a palatinate under its bishop, and the county returned no members to the House of Commons until the late seventeenth century. One of the grievances of the Earl of Westmorland in 1569 was that the Protestant Bishop of Durham had usurped his traditional right to muster the men of the bishopric. Lancashire was both a county palatine and a royal duchy, each boasting its own seal, and lay outside the jurisdiction of the Council of the North except in ecclesiastical affairs. The lands of the Duchy of Lancaster extended far beyond the confines of the county, with important implications for the stewardship of dissolved monastic estates.

By recruiting its membership from the local aristocracy, the Council of the North sought to co-opt their affinities and influence for the benefit of the Crown. As a strategy it had the advantage of economy, as well as providing a means for the northern political nation to compete for royal favour. Its risks, however, were exposed by the crisis of 1569: the Earls of Northumberland and Westmorland were both members of the council. In Elton's opinion, it was the defeat of their revolt that gave Elizabeth and Cecil the chance to complete the work that Henry VIII and Cromwell had begun in the wake of the Pilgrimage of Grace. In 1572, Henry Hastings, Earl of Huntingdon, assumed the presidency of the council and hence the responsibility for enforcing royal policy and adjudicating disputes between private parties in the northern parts of the realm. His twenty-three years as effective viceroy, albeit in close collaboration with the Privy Council, did much to ensure peace and the provision of justice in the north, and his uncompromising attitude towards Catholics forced waverers and church papists to choose between the Church of England and outright recusancy. Writing to Walsingham from Newcastle in March 1581, Huntingdon could report that 'for the common people thorrowe thys hole Northe in which I doo serve, I do assure you, in no parte of England is queene Elysabeth owre gracyous soverayne more reverencyd than she ys heare'; and if trouble did threaten, he knew he could call on 'the ayde of the good subiectes in Yorkeshyre'.[17] By the time of Huntingdon's death in 1595, the prospect (albeit unspoken, in deference to Elizabeth herself) of an Anglo-Scots union under a Protestant king was reducing tension in a region that had suffered centuries of cross-border skirmishing and warfare.

Like the Council of the North, the Council in the Principality and Marches of Wales owed its origins to the Yorkist administration of the late fifteenth century and its reconstruction to Thomas Cromwell. In addition to the twelve shires of Wales, it exercised authority over the English counties of Monmouth, Gloucester, Hereford, Worcester and Shropshire; Cheshire was excluded from its jurisdiction in 1569. The Elizabethan council was instructed to repress 'all manner of murders, felons, burglaries, rapes, riots, routes, unlawful assemblies, unlawful retainers, regrators, forestallers, extortioners, conspiracies, maintenances, perjuries, of what kind soever they be'.[18] It acted as its own Star Chamber and Chancery, and a commission of oyer and terminer allowed it to try cases of treason. In theory it had the power to hang murderers and felons, although there is no evidence that it did so during the reign of Elizabeth, in sharp contrast to the presidency of Bishop Rowland Lee during the 1530s. Minor offenders could be whipped, pilloried or imprisoned in Ludlow Castle. The council was also charged with investigating enclosure and the decay of agriculture, enforcing the recusancy laws, and hearing cases of *cymorth* or the illegal exaction of gifts in money or kind, and it could determine a variety of civil cases.

It has often been remarked that Wales, resembling Ireland in its topography, religious culture, language and custom, should differ so markedly from its western neighbour in its response to English imperial expansion. No doubt the Council in the Marches played its part in establishing peace and relative conformity in Elizabethan Wales. So far as he can be, given the patchiness of the evidence, Penry Williams is positive in his assessment of the council: 'in checking violence, punishing forcible entries, establishing the possession of land, it could and probably did do a great deal.'[19] The records which do survive suggest vigorous administrative and legal activity; the council made periodic assaults on recusancy and was not afraid to use torture to extract intelligence from Catholic missionary priests and lay folk; and its military role expanded to match the new threat from Spain. The analysis of institutions, however, can only take us so far in explaining the contrast between Wales and Ireland, not least because Sir Henry Sidney combined his presidency of the Welsh council with postings as Lord Deputy of Ireland.

Two additional factors came into play in Wales, neither of them applicable to Ireland. First, the Elizabethan regime was willing to compromise over the use of the Welsh language in church, whereas the campaign to plant English civility in Ireland meant that Gaelic was viewed with the deepest suspicion. An Act of 1563 authorised parish churches to display Welsh versions of the Scriptures side by side with the English. A prayer book and New Testament duly appeared in 1567, with the whole Bible following in 1588, and in 1595 a Welsh rendering of John Jewel's *Apologia ecclesiae anglicanae*. Although the hope was that Welsh speakers 'may, by conferring both tongues together, the sooner attain to the knowledge of the English', the effect was to legitimate Welsh culture within a devotional setting. Richard Davies was able to argue in his preface to the Welsh New Testament that the Christian message was carried to Britain by Joseph of Arimathea five centuries before the Roman mission of 597; Protestantism, and not the *ffydd Saeson* or 'faith of the Saxons', was thus the true religion of the Britons.[20] The second factor influencing the integration of Wales into England was the attitude of the Welsh gentry. The Acts of Union of 1536–43 had brought them the chance to sit in Parliament, to become magistrates and to seek service at court. English common law gave greater protection to their landed estates, which could now be passed down intact by primogeniture and not split through partible inheritance. The founding of Jesus College, Oxford, by a group of Welsh scholars in 1571 provided new opportunities for the sons of the gentry, and many also studied at the Inns of Court in London. In the preface to his Welsh grammar of 1567, the Catholic exile Gruffydd Robert satirised the Welsh gentlemen who abandoned their native tongue on seeing the steeples of Shrewsbury and the River Severn and chose to speak bad English.

MAPPING ENGLISH IDENTITY

The relationship between the centre and the localities of the Elizabethan state has become much clearer since Geoffrey Elton wrote *The Tudor Constitution*. National and provincial archives have both contributed to a new sort of local history, alert to the complex interactions between the Crown and the counties. Churchwardens' and borough accounts, lists of the JPs in attendance at quarter sessions, the records of Star Chamber and the common-law courts and gentry correspondence have all been used to recover the history of the kingdom beyond the council, court and Parliament. The regional impact of the Reformation is much better understood now than it was in Elton's day, and popular religion has become a subject in its own right. Rebellion and riot have been documented in detail, the pioneering work of Anthony Fletcher and C. S. L. Davies in the later 1960s carried forward by John Walter, Andy Wood and David Underdown. Comparisons with Wales and Ireland have encouraged a subtler reading of England's own internal dynamics. The process of reassessment is ongoing. It is perhaps too early to gauge the impact of *The Oxford Dictionary of National Biography,* with its hundreds of Elizabethan parliamentarians and priests, lawyers and courtiers, rebels against the Crown and agents in its service. Suffice to say that *The Oxford Dictionary of National Biography* allows as never before for a narrative of Elizabeth's reign from the perspective of its local elites, from the grandees who ran the lieutenancy to the lesser gentry families who supplied the magistrates' bench and responded to the many petty dictates of Tudor rule.

As the basic administrative unit of provincial England, the county deserves the scholarly attention that it has received. Justice, taxation and the muster system were all organised on a county basis. The knights of the shire elected to Elizabethan parliaments were deemed socially superior to the members returned by the towns. Parliament itself has been reassessed as a point of contact between the centre and the localities, not least by Elton in his later career. The Elizabethan volumes published by the History of Parliament Trust have allowed the careers of knights and burgesses to be understood within their county contexts. Provincial politics did not become redundant once members had reached Westminster. Historians have preferred to focus on the controversies over religion, succession and foreign policy that seem to reveal Elizabethan MPs in conflict with the royal prerogative, but this should not obscure parliament's role as the broker of local affairs. Maintaining a man in the Commons was costly, and towns expected a return on their investment; the relief of unemployed cloth workers, or the repair of a harbour wall, could be every bit as pressing as matters of state. Where county society was more overtly politicised, as Hassell Smith argues for Norfolk, issues which had already been debated at a local level were submitted to parliament 'for final resolution'.[21]

At their polemical height, the parliaments of Elizabeth's reign gave voice to a sense of national identity that echoed the Reformation statutes of the 1530s. When Privy Council, peers and commons gathered to denounce the seditious activities of Jesuit priests, or to bay for the execution of Mary, Queen of Scots, or to plan for an emergency administration in the event of Elizabeth's violent death, they spoke a language that increasingly conflated the national interest with the Protestant faith. News of their deliberations was broadcast to the shires by pamphlet literature and sermons as well as the MPs themselves. This anti-Catholic rhetoric was one aspect of an emerging definition of Englishness to which the artistic 'cult' of Elizabeth, the defeat of the Armada and the war in Ireland all made their own contributions. National and Protestant identities found public expression in the provincial bonfires, feasting and bell-ringing that had come to mark Elizabeth's accession day by the 1570s. On the London stage, the English history plays of Marlowe and Shakespeare dealt with related themes of monarchy and patriotism, although whether dramatic exploration extended to endorsement on the playwrights' part is a moot point.

At the same time, Elizabethans were interested as never before in the make-up of provincial England: its age-old division into rapes and lathes and wapentakes, its diverse customs and occupations, its natural and human history. The intellectual and literary 'discovery' of England, in some ways a continuation of the labours of John Leland in Henry VIII's reign, was another part of this search for a Protestant national identity. William Lambarde's *Perambulation of Kent,* published in 1576 and the earliest example of an English county history, was duly suspicious of records that had been penned by monks and looked back with derision upon the medieval devotional cults of Thomas Becket and the rood of Boxley. Something of the same tone can be found in the writings of another gentleman antiquary, Richard Carew, whose *Survey of Cornwall* appeared in the last year of Elizabeth's reign. Carew scorned the 'idle-headed seekers' who in popish times had cast palm crosses into a holy well in hope of predicting the future, and he proudly recalled the year of 1588, 'when the Spanish floting Babel pretended the conquest of our Iland'. At the same time, however, Carew could praise his Catholic recusant neighbour Nicholas Roscarrock 'for his industrious delight in matters of history and antiquity'.[22] For Carew, at least, the bonds of class and scholarship could prove stronger than the fractures caused by religion.

The life of Richard Carew illustrates some of the many ways in which centre and localities were connected in Elizabeth's reign. Following an education at Christ Church, Oxford, and the Middle Temple, Carew was content to settle on his Cornish estate, absorbed in his books and his beehives when not serving the Queen as magistrate, sheriff or deputy lieutenant. His *Survey* is an eclectic document, covering every aspect of his native shire from its flora and fauna, climate and agriculture to its traditions, sports and language (if his mistakes imply that he didn't himself speak Cornish, Carew was intrigued by its apparent similarity to Greek). His description of Cornwall is thoroughly researched, as in his detailed explanation of the tin-mining industry, but also affectionate and sometimes light-hearted – a celebration of local society rather than a work of Protestant propaganda. Carew addressed the Society of Antiquaries on 'the antiquity, variety, and etimology of measuring land in Cornwayl', and signalled his connections with the wider Renaissance by translating an Italian poem about the first crusade and a medical treatise in Spanish.[23] A coin in Carew's possession, dating from the reign of Domitian and found in a tin-working, reminded him of the connections between his own world and that of ancient Rome. In the words of Alexandra Walsham, the antiquarianism that Carew represented 'played a part in promoting, rather than intrinsically undercutting, the power of central government and in facilitating the growth of a national as well as a regional consciousness'.[24] *The Survey of Cornwall* speaks of a loyalty to the shire as an imagined community that was a novel feature of Elizabeth's reign. But Carew's identity as a Cornishman was in no way antagonistic to the other imagined communities that he inhabited: a corresponding amateur scholar, a patriotic Englishman and always a gentleman.

Carew hoped that a second edition of his book would be accompanied by the map of Cornwall produced by John Norden, although this was not achieved in his lifetime. By 1603, England was not only more intensely governed than ever before; it was also much better known, thanks to the labours of surveyors and map-makers such as Norden and chorographers such as Lambarde and Carew. The Tudor period has been characterised as a time of 'cartographic revolution', with activity peaking during the latter half of Elizabeth's reign.[25] In 1579, the Yorkshireman Christopher Saxton produced what was in effect the first national atlas of England and Wales, consisting of thirty-four county maps plus one of all 'Anglia', based on surveys of his own. Although not a servant of the Crown, Saxton did benefit from considerable royal patronage, including grants of land as well as the exclusive right to profit from his printed maps. Burghley was swift to recognise the governmental implications of Saxton's enterprise and acquired the proofs of his county maps. These became the core of a personal collection that included surveys of royal estates, maps of Ireland and plats dating from the 1530s and 1540s that Burghley plundered from Henry VIII's library at Whitehall. Annotations reveal the various uses to which he put his maps: military (the parts of the Dorset coast where invaders might land), administrative (noting the composition of the peace commission for each county) and religious (identifying the recusant families of Lancashire or Sussex). In a visual affirmation of the reach of Elizabethan government and hence of Burghley's own power, the gallery of his house at Theobalds was decorated with a map 'of the Kingdom, with all its cities, towns and villages mountains and rivers', together with the arms of all the landed families of England.[26]

Another cartographer to feature in Burghley's collection was John Norden, who went on to serve James I as surveyor of the Duchy of Cornwall. Norden set out in the 1580s to compile a series of county surveys known collectively as the *Speculum britanniae*. If John Norden the surveyor may be identified with the Protestant controversialist of the same name, then religion was presumably an additional motivation. Norden coupled his newly surveyed maps with descriptions of the history, economy and society of communities from Cornwall to Northamptonshire, including Jersey, Guernsey and the Isle of Wight. Of all Norden's efforts, only Middlesex and Hertfordshire were published in his lifetime, although his maps met with greater success and several were reprinted in the 1607 edition of Camden's *Britannia*. Norden set new standards by marking roads on his maps and experimented with symbols and a grid-reference system. Between them, Saxton and Norden compassed and conceptualised the English landscape with a skill that would not be challenged until the one-inch maps of the Ordnance Survey appeared in 1801.

One of the most celebrated images of Elizabeth I, the 'Ditchley' portrait by Marcus Gheeraerts the Younger, depicts the Queen as a latter-day Colossus atop a massive map of England, her feet resting on Oxfordshire (see Figure 8.1). Counties, watercourses, towns and Hampton Court palace are set in a stylised landscape that suggests familiarity with the printed maps of Saxton and Norden. The portrait was commissioned by Sir Henry Lee, presumably for the festivities marking the Queen's 1592 visit to his seat at Ditchley, when Elizabeth symbolically wakened a slumbering knight in a pavilion bedecked with allegorical paintings. The progresses of Elizabeth occasioned controversy in their own time, as they have among the historians and literary critics who seek to explain them. To some they represent a theatrical coming of the court to the country, loaded with displays of allegiance and the rituals of gift exchange. Felicity Heal has observed how Elizabeth elected to emphasise the 'public and performative' qualities of her progresses rather than the hunting favoured by Henry VIII and James I.[27] For Mary Hill Cole, the progresses were not only a portable public stage from which Elizabeth could interact with her

Figure 8.1 Queen Elizabeth I (The 'Ditchley' portrait, *c.* 1592) by Marcus Gheeraerts the Younger. Image © National Portrait Gallery, London.

subjects but also a deliberate dislocation of the royal household, creating 'a productive confusion that enabled the Queen to avoid decisions, delay meetings, and retreat from unwanted visitors'.[28] Other interpretations are less enthusiastic, taking their cue from Elizabeth's own ministers. Walsingham resented the time wasted on progress when 'we are altogether given to banquettinge', and Burghley fretted about their prodigious and ever-rising expense.[29]

Elizabeth made twenty-three progresses to the provinces and was entertained by some 400 hosts: peers and privy councillors, the shire gentry, town corporations and the two universities, to say nothing of the humbler sort who must have watched the festivals and royal entries put on for her entertainment. For practical or security reasons she chose not to travel to the remoter, more Catholic or less obviously English parts of her realm. Whereas her grandfather and father both journeyed to York, for instance, Elizabeth preferred to stay within fifty miles' ride of London, where the majority of the active political nation was concentrated. This places a limit on readings of Elizabeth's progresses as a 'performance of royal chorography', or a ritual dance expressive of 'the mystical relationship between her "Virgin" body and the fertile matter of England'.[30] But the fact that her hosts (mostly) welcomed a royal visit, and the amount of capital that the Queen herself invested in them, imply that the progresses were a significant tool of Elizabethan statecraft: an opportunity for sovereign and subjects to meet and to some extent to do business, against a backdrop of magnificence and splendour.

Elizabeth's preference for pageantry over policy, combined with the simple fact of her longevity, worked to stabilise the relationship between the centre and the localities of her realm. The England that she inherited in 1558 had lived through a generation of religious and administrative upheaval, which had placed an unprecedented strain on the principle of absolute allegiance to the Crown. By redefining doctrine and liturgy, by creating the crime of treason by words, and in Mary's reign by an intense persecution of Protestant heresy, the state had come to intervene in the lives of provincial subjects as never before. War with France and the garrisoning of Ireland had meant the mobilisation of soldiers and mariners, and the resources to pay for them. The authority of the Crown had been challenged by regional rebellion in 1536–7, 1549 and 1554. Northumberland's attempted coup of July 1553 had seen the throne itself contested, with rival proclamations sent out by Queen Jane in London and Queen Mary in East Anglia.

By emphasising the value of conformity and common prayer, the Elizabethan religious settlement damped down at least some of the fires that had been threatening the ties of community and returned the English parish church to a predictable rhythm. The avoidance of war until the mid-1580s reduced the need for the subsidies and forced loans that Elizabeth's predecessors had been forced to levy. Crown and Parliament had time to revive the commonwealth ideas piloted by Cromwell and the Duke of Somerset but lost amidst the many other demands of government in the 1530s and 1540s. As the House of Commons grew in numbers and the size and competence of the peace commission steadily expanded, more of the gentry of England and Wales were drawn into the service of monarchy and nation. Village greens and town squares hosted popular celebrations of Elizabeth's accession day each 17 November, while churches rang their bells, purchased prayers for the Queen and displayed the royal arms in carved wood or stained glass. Although social and political tensions were rising again in the last decade of the reign, the characteristic Tudor partnership between Crown and gentry was firmer than ever. Among the crowds cheering the accession of James I in 1603, few could have predicted the coming breakdown in communication between court and country, let alone its tragic consequences.

FURTHER READING

Barber, Peter, 'Monarchs, Ministers, and Maps, 1550–1625', in David Buisseret (ed.), *Monarchs, Ministers and Maps* (Chicago, Ill., 1992).

Braddick, Michael J., *State Formation in Early Modern England, c. 1550–1700* (Cambridge, 2000).

Carew, Richard, *The Survey of Cornwall*, ed. John Chynoweth, Nicholas Orme and Alexandra Walsham (Exeter, 2004).

Cole, Mary Hill, *The Portable Queen: Elizabeth I and the Politics of Ceremony* (Amherst, Mass., 1999).

Cooper, J. P. D., *Propaganda and the Tudor State: Political Culture in the Westcountry* (Oxford, 2003).

Elton, G. R., *The Tudor Constitution* (Cambridge, 1960).

Hassell Smith, A., *County and Court: Government and Politics in Norfolk, 1558–1603* (Oxford, 1974).

Loades, David, *Tudor Government: Structures of Authority in the Sixteenth Century* (Oxford, 1997).

ODNB 'John Norden', 'Christopher Saxton'.

Smith, Alan G. R., *The Government of Elizabethan England* (London, 1967).

Williams, Penry, *The Council in the Marches of Wales under Elizabeth I* (Cardiff, 1958).

—— *The Tudor Regime* (Oxford, 1979).

—— 'The Crown and the Counties', in Christopher Haigh (ed.), *The Reign of Elizabeth I* (Basingstoke, 1984), pp. 125–46.

Younger, Neil, *War and Politics in the Elizabethan Counties* (Manchester, 2012).

NOTES

1 G. R. Elton, *The Tudor Constitution* (Cambridge, 1960), p. 451.

2 John Walter, 'A "Rising of the People"? The Oxfordshire Rising of 1596', *Past and Present*, 107 (1) (1985): 90–143; p. 91.

3 Thomas Smith, *De republica anglorum*, ed. Mary Dewar (Cambridge, 1982), pp. 1, 87.

4 Smith, *De republica anglorum*, p. 104.

5 Penry Williams, 'The Crown and the Counties', in Christopher Haigh (ed.), *The Reign of Elizabeth I* (Basingstoke, 1984), pp. 125–46; p. 126.

6 A. Hassell Smith, *County and Court: Government and Politics in Norfolk, 1558–1603* (Oxford, 1974), pp. 129–30.

7 Hassell Smith, *County and Court*, p. 132.

8 Hassell Smith, *County and Court*, p. 108.

9 Smith, *De republica anglorum*, p. 76.

10 Williams, 'The Crown and the Counties', p. 137.

11 Steven G. Ellis, 'Tudor State Formation and the Shaping of the British Isles', in Steven G. Ellis and Sarah Barber (eds.), *Conquest and Union: Fashioning a British State* (London, 1995), p. 42.

12 Tim Thornton, *Cheshire and the Tudor State, 1480–1560* (Woodbridge, 2000), p. 62.

13 J. P. D. Cooper, *Propaganda and the Tudor State: Political Culture in the Westcountry* (Oxford, 2003), p. 191.
14 Andy Wood, *The Politics of Social Conflict: The Peak Country, 1520–1770* (Cambridge, 1999), p. 170.
15 S. J. Watts, *From Border to Middle Shire: Northumberland, 1586–1625* (Leicester, 1975), p. 249.
16 Elton, *Tudor Constitution*, p. 210.
17 San Merino, CA., Henry E. Huntington Library, Hastings Correspondence, HA 5356.
18 Penry Williams, *The Council in the Marches of Wales under Elizabeth I* (Cardiff, 1958), p. 48.
19 Williams, *Council in the Marches*, p. 324.
20 J. Gwynfor Jones, *Early Modern Wales, c. 1525–1640* (London, 1994), pp. 150, 154.
21 Hassell Smith, *County and Court*, p. 335.
22 Richard Carew, *The Survey of Cornwall*, ed. John Chynoweth, Nicholas Orme and Alexandra Walsham (Exeter, 2004), fols. 84r, 127v, 144r–v.
23 Carew, *Survey of Cornwall*, p. 21.
24 Carew, *Survey of Cornwall*, p. 25.
25 P. D. A. Harvey, *Maps in Tudor England* (London, 1993), p. 7.
26 Peter Barber, 'Monarchs, Ministers, and Maps, 1550–1625', in David Buisseret (ed.), *Monarchs, Ministers and Maps* (Chicago, Ill., 1992), pp. 57–98; p. 76.
27 Felicity Heal, 'Giving and Receiving on Royal Progress', in Jayne Elisabeth Archer, Elizabeth Goldring and Sarah Knight (eds.), *The Progresses, Pageants, and Entertainments of Queen Elizabeth I* (Oxford, 2007), pp. 46–61; p. 50.
28 Mary Hill Cole, 'Monarchy in Motion: An Overview of Elizabethan Progresses', in Jayne Elisabeth Archer, Elizabeth Goldring and Sarah Knight (eds.), *The Progresses, Pageants, and Entertainments of Queen Elizabeth I* (Oxford, 2007), pp. 27–45; p. 27.
29 Cole, 'Monarchy in Motion', p. 33.
30 Jayne Elisabeth Archer and Sarah Knight, 'Elizabetha Triumphans', in Jayne Elisabeth Archer, Elizabeth Goldring and Sarah Knight (eds.), *The Progresses, Pageants, and Entertainments of Queen Elizabeth I* (Oxford, 2007), pp. 1–23; pp. 1, 5.

CHAPTER NINE

PARISH GOVERNMENT

H. R. French

> English rural society was neither in a state of Hobbesian 'warre' nor a geographical scattering of small, introspective corporate republics waiting to be integrated into a larger body politic by the outward-orientated 'middling sorts'.[1]

> The parish, no less than the county commission of the peace, was subject to the growing pretensions of the Elizabethan state . . . By the early seventeenth century, therefore, the relatively autonomous medieval parish had become incorporated within a national system of provincial government.[2]

In many respects, the reign of Elizabeth marks an interpretative crossroads in the history of the parish, and its government, between the fourteenth and the nineteenth centuries. It is in the later sixteenth century that four contrasting historiographical themes intersect and bear on the nature, purposes and significance of parochial government. Two tell the stories of decline. The first of these is the 'Reformation' narrative epitomised by Eamon Duffy's *Voices of Morebath,* in which the vitality of late-medieval parochial piety (and organisation) is extinguished by Reformation edicts. The second is the parallel (but unrelated) interpretation in which the jurisdiction of the manor is superseded by that of the parish in Elizabeth's reign, a process charted in most depth by Marjory McIntosh. The other two depictions of the Elizabethan parish are stories of growth and development. The first is the most familiar of all these accounts – the story of the eventual creation of what have become known as the Elizabethan poor laws, brought into being in 1597 and 1601, whose longevity projects the historical significance of Elizabeth's reign on into the early nineteenth century at least, which has been charted in most depth by Paul Slack and Steve Hindle. The second is built upon this development and interprets the implementation of the parochial poor-law system as a pivotal moment in the projection of the power of the 'state' into the life of the parish and the integration of the life of the parish into the concerns of that 'state'. This interpretation has been advanced most eloquently by Hindle and Michael Braddick. Some dimensions of these debates stretch beyond the concerns of this chapter, but all emphasise the continuing historical significance of apparently obscure issues about the nature of parochial government, and its personnel, in Elizabeth's reign.

The discussion in this chapter will concentrate on several aspects of this history, and these debates. First, it attempts the difficult task of trying to characterise the state of parish government at the beginning of Elizabeth's reign and to assess its significance in relation to other sources of authority within the parish. Second, it considers the impact of change on parish government, particularly the effects of the gradual evolution of a parish-based poor-law system through the later sixteenth century. Third, it discusses the social identity of these governors and, in particular, says something about the nature and bases of their position in the parish. Fourth, it assesses *how* these parochial rulers attempted to govern their parishes and whether the religious or economic impacts of Elizabeth's reign hardened their attitudes to 'disorder'. Finally, the chapter considers the significance of the parish in relation to some of the interpretations outlined above, notably whether by 1603 the civil parish, and its rulers, had emerged as an arm of the 'state'.

The two decades preceding the start of Elizabeth's reign were obviously highly disturbing for the governors of many English parishes. In addition to the dramatic changes to the liturgy and fabric of the parish church, parishes had also to accustom themselves to ongoing processes of administrative change. The destruction of approximately 30,000 parochial chantries in 1548 had involved not only the appropriation by the Edwardian government of relatively large amounts of endowed parish property, but also (with it) the ending of an unspecified amount of charitable spending and the winding up of the confraternities that governed such organisations. There were also losses among an unspecified number of the 20,000 or more parochial chapels, many of whose foundations were connected to saints' cults and were therefore dissolved after 1540. The Reformation era also inflicted damage on parish almshouses and hospitals. Perhaps half the 500 or so almshouses in pre-Reformation England were closed, though thousands of other parochial endowments remained. Administrative sleight of hand was also sometimes required to prevent the secular elements of purgatorial endowments being lost as the chantries were dissolved, as happened at Cratfield, Suffolk. While it is likely that not every parish possessed a confraternity, a saint's chapel or an almshouse, and that considerable overlap existed between the main trustees of these institutions and the rulers of the parish, this change may have narrowed the opportunities for involvement in office holding or in organising festivals, processions or ales for many of the parish's inhabitants. The main casualties of such changes may have been women deprived of formal guild and informal organisational roles, and poorer male householders, deemed insufficiently 'worthy and discreet' to compete effectively for the fewer posts available.

Yet the Reformation era had also imposed new responsibilities on the parish and had begun to reshape its institutions. While some parish charities had long carried with them obligations to maintain bridges or sluices, from 1555 all parishes were required to appoint a surveyor of the highways, who was allowed to levy rates (usually in lieu of labour services by householders) to repair them. Two years later, parishes gained responsibility for providing and maintaining weapons under the militia statute. At the same time, the constable – originally a manorial officer

– continued his slow, but steady absorption into the government of the parish (and the kingdom). Tudor legislation transformed constables incrementally from executive legal officers of the manorial lord to local administrators for the Justices of the Peace (JPs), responsible for the apprehension and punishment of vagrants, the gathering of national and county taxation, and parochial militia organisation, among many other duties. Elizabeth's reign also saw the foundation of many new endowed parochial charities, particularly in London, primarily to assist (and, in the process, helping to define) the 'deserving' or 'impotent poor' – those that were 'good and godly living, and had most need of relief', as Sir John Cheyney's will put it in 1585.[3] These trusts required trustees, some of whom were often gentry, but others of whom were drawn from the upper echelons of the parish, such as 'six of the most substantial men' called upon to administer a dole at Ivinghoe, Buckinghamshire, in 1576.[4]

So, although the 'magisterial' Reformation had pruned back many aspects of parochial organisation and participation, it had also created some new opportunities for office holding. As will be discussed more fully below, there has been considerable discussion among historians about the net effects of these changes on social relations and about whether they entrenched power in the parish more securely in the hands of a propertied oligarchy than had previously been the case. Of course, it should be remembered that the government of the parish was by no means confined *to* the parish, and its offices, in Elizabeth's reign. In many parts of England, manorial courts leet were still highly active, prosecuting large numbers of criminal misdemeanours, regulating commodities and retailing, supervising the collective regulation of commons, wastes and boundaries, and determining by-laws and customs. However, McIntosh suggests that there were quite marked regional trends. By 1600, manorial courts leet were least active in East Anglia, the south-east and the south-central Midlands, having seen their business transfer to the sessions of the peace or the church courts. In the west and south-west, courts leet continued to deal 'vigorously with a wide range of public issues' to the end of Elizabeth's reign.[5] Even so, this level of activity remained lower than the manorial jurisdictions of Cumberland, Westmorland, Lancashire, Yorkshire, Durham and Northumberland, where the volume of business was sometimes higher in 1600 than a century before. McIntosh observes that 'increasing attention to misconduct in local courts of the West, Southwest, and North more than offset the growing lassitude of those located in the Midlands, East Anglia, and Southeast'.[6] As a consequence, it appears that in many parts of the country the interpretative orthodoxy of the death of the manor court and the rise of the parish, derived primarily from studies of the poor law, may be (at best) only part of the story.

Why was this? To some extent it reflected the broader jurisdictional inheritance of these regions. In the north-east and north-west, in particular, the separate palatinate jurisdictions of Chester and Durham, as well as the distinct (civil) legal system of the Duchy of Lancaster, and arrangements of border land tenure (known as 'tenant-right') may have preserved local courts as the obvious first port of call, rather than distant and somewhat alien royal courts.[7] In addition, topography and the distance from Westminster ensured that local justice remained considerably more accessible and cheaper than the royal alternative. As will be shown more fully below, the parish structure was hardly suited to superseding the administrative systems of the manor. While many northern manors were much larger than some of their south-eastern counterparts, at perhaps 5,000 acres compared to 1,000–2,000 acres, they were dwarfed by some northern parishes. The parish of Prestbury, Cheshire, totalled 63,000 acres, with twenty-eight settlements and ten chapelries, while the parish of Whalley, Lancashire, contained 106,395 acres and fifty townships. It was impossible to govern these ecclesiastical units with the forms of administrative machinery, such as a single set of parish officers allied to an annual gathering of ratepayers, employed in the nucleated lowland parishes, where church, settlement and parochial boundaries were often co-extensive. Either parish administration had to be devolved to the level of the sub-township (hamlet or chapelry), or, as was often the case, other, far smaller, administrative units continued to be preferred, such as the manor. In the west of England (outside Cornwall), jurisdictions and topography were less obstructive, but regionally distinctive systems of manorial land tenure, and the presence in some counties (such as Dorset) of large ecclesiastical or institutional estates, may have ensured the vitality of manorial administration until the mid-seventeenth century. Only in the (more populous) south Midlands, East Anglia and south-east England had manors finally become too weak to resist the rise in the powers of the JP, his sessions of the peace, the expanding secular role of the parish and the increased use of the church courts to police parish morals at the end of Elizabeth's reign.

As Richard Smith pointed out in 1984, the gradual shift from manor to parish did not necessarily represent the integration of 'introspective corporate republics . . . into a larger body politic by the outward-orientated "middling sorts"'.[8] Although early modern historians, such as Steve Hindle, have favoured this interpretation and seen the Elizabethan poor law as the mechanism responsible, Smith suggested that while the parish was a new location for this process, the process itself had a medieval ancestry. In particular, he suggests that in the era after the Black Death, manorial enforcement of legislation such as the 1351 Statute of Labourers required co-ordination with JPs and made constables and manorial jurors agents of Parliament, as well as local representatives of 'the employer category of tenant farmers'.[9] As Smith and other studies of late-medieval manorial government have shown, these tenant farmers were in a similar relative social position to their late-sixteenth-century counterparts in parish government and had similarly oligarchic tendencies. In these respects, Hindle's distinction between the 'ascending' source of power for manorial government (that is, authority derived from the locality) and the 'descending' authority of the parish (enforcement using authority drawn from the top of the governmental system) may still be slightly too sharp in the sixteenth century.[10] Manors were no longer purely private instruments of landlord power or communal self-government, while parish office also derived part of its authority from its capacity to represent local interests and powerbases.

Given these apparent equivalences, why was most of the new empowering legislation over poor relief, moral, justice and militia administration given to the parish and not the manor in Elizabeth's reign? This is very difficult to answer. As suggested below, the urban origins and concerns of much poor-law legislation may have shifted the focus away from the manor as the 'natural' unit of administration, because most large corporate towns were (among other things) parochial but non-manorial. The fact that much of the administrative concern about rising poverty, underemployment and vagrancy came from justices and MPs in the areas of weak manorial government and compact, largely nucleated parishes (the south Midlands, East Anglia and the south-east) might also have been significant. In addition, McIntosh had observed that in legal terms manors were not the most appropriate entities to enforce such legislation because, although they possessed stewards and officers who served for annual terms, manorial juries and bodies were 'events' rather than 'institutions', with no formal corporate existence outside the court meeting. Similarly, while manorial lords and tenants might hold property individually and collectively, manorial institutions did not – unlike parishes and their charitable endowments – nor could they raise taxes. McIntosh suggests that the powers of leet courts were too inflexible and oriented too much towards regulation and punishment, not relief. 'When a punitive policy was no longer appropriate within a given community, the customary authority of the Leets over social and economic issues was taken up by other local agencies.'[11]

For these reasons, the parish emerged gradually as the pre-eminent local institution for the administration of poor relief, even if it shared the task of government, social regulation and charity with leets, archdeaconry courts, petty sessions, charities, almshouses and school foundations – as well as its personnel. As Slack, Hindle and McIntosh have all noted, throughout the sixteenth century, legislation about poverty increasingly enjoined a twin-pronged approach. This required parish governors first to identify and distinguish the 'deserving' from the 'undeserving' poor, by identifying their needs, examining their circumstances and judging their personal disposition against an increasingly well-defined set of stereotypes and criteria. Second, constables were required to punish or exclude those who were deemed 'undeserving' – vagrants and the 'idle' or able-bodied poor – while churchwardens or others in the parish had to organise forms of relief (food, clothing, housing, work or monetary doles) to the 'deserving'. The problem for legislators was to devise mechanisms that would ensure enforcement of these provisions in the parish. The 1572 statute entrusted JPs with the enforcement of these voluntary *parochial* poor rates thereby including officials who were otherwise sometimes removed from the day-to-day government of the parish. In effect, this meant that while administration of the relief system occurred at the level of the parish, scrutiny and enforcement remained with the justice (and depended on his diligence or simply his proximity to the parish concerned). In 1598, responsibility for the compulsory rating, collection and policing of payment and disbursements was vested in the newly created overseers of the poor. Magisterial oversight remained, but enforcement was now devolved to the parish, the base unit of administration within the system.

As Slack and Fideler observed, much of the initiative for this legislation, and many of the examples on which it was based, came from the parishes of the larger corporate cities and towns, such as London, Norwich, Ipswich, York, Exeter, Cambridge or Chester, where compulsory rates and institutional 'bridewells' began in the 1540s and 1550s. It was in these centres of production and consumption that the concurrent pressures of in-migration, trade depression and the dissolution of many existing charitable institutions had their first and greatest effects. The size of these burdens explains the precocity of the efforts towards *compulsory* provision in these towns, but they were sometimes matched by initiatives in rural parishes, particularly in populous villages or small towns under the influence of preaching clergy in southern and eastern England. Hindle noted that the alternative method of raising parochial funds, the church ale, had disappeared from East Anglia, Kent and Sussex by the 1570s, partly because of the use of funds from parish endowments, but (presumably) also because of the increased frequency of compulsory rating, as in many Essex, Suffolk, Bedford and Kent parishes before the 1590s. Like manorial jurisdictions, voluntary poor boxes, ales and wakes survived well into the seventeenth century as fund-raising activities in the south-west and north of England, despite sporadic magisterial and clerical opposition, although Hindle has cautioned that in many southern and Midland counties compulsory rating and parochial administration did begin fairly swiftly after 1601, even if surviving evidence of it is patchy until the mid-seventeenth century.

So, by 1603, it appears that many parishes in the south and Midlands were equipped with the full panoply of parish officers – two churchwardens and their assistants (sometimes called sidesmen), two surveyors of the highways, two constables and as many as four of the new overseers of the poor. Some made do with fewer, often only one churchwarden (sometimes the same person for several years), no sidesmen, a single constable and perhaps two overseers. In many other cases, these statutory officers were merely part of an already dense parochial foliage that had sprouted offshoots such as auditors of the parish accounts, assessors of rates, not to mention residual manorial posts, such as the ales-taster or street scourers. In towns, these patterns were complicated by the intersecting hierarchies of the borough, with its burgesses or freemen, chief burgesses and aldermen, the officers of trade guilds, jurors in borough courts, ward constables and the trustees of parochial or borough charities and institutions (almshouses and schools). In the countryside, the trustees of charitable endowments exerted considerable influence over the running of the parish because, in the absence of rates, they had often supplied a proportion of its income or controlled assets (such as houses or land) that had a measurable impact on relief.

Perhaps inevitably, trustees such as these, and diligent holders of parish office, tended to coalesce into ruling cliques or core groups around which a wider circle of the less committed, less prosperous or less domineering inhabitants of the parish rotated. Again, this trend can be seen in the late-medieval parish. Beat Kümin noted that 'the local elite who worshipped in the most prestigious parts of the church – groups like the "masters", the "feoffees" or the "auditors" gradually assumed a disproportionate role in parochial affairs.'[12] Such oligarchies were most likely to appear in corporate towns, where they derived their power and administrative experience from their extra-parochial responsibilities, for example as aldermen, but they also emerged before 1560 in smaller townships such as Hadleigh (Suffolk), Morebath (Somerset), Stanford-in-the-Vale (Berkshire) and Prescot (Lancashire). Kümin stresses that at this time, at least, these parochial supervisors seem to have been chosen by the wider body of householders. However, Gervase Rosser has observed that among the parochial guilds of late-medieval England (particularly in towns) 'social respectability' was often a criterion of membership, and something that was policed by the guild ordinances, in ways that bear 'close comparison with the social credit accruing to the member of a sect after the Reformation', or to positions of authority within the parish.[13]

By the end of the sixteenth century, though, less representative but more formally constituted groups of rulers were beginning to emerge in some parishes. The diversity of forms of parish meetings and systems of government means that generalisations are difficult to sustain. However, in most parishes at least one meeting was held each year, usually immediately after Easter, at which the parish officers presented their accounts and the next year's officers were chosen. Again, these followed on from pre-Reformation practice, with some London parishes in the 1630s being able to cite written evidence for such meetings dating back to the mid-fifteenth century. Where there were no formal restrictions on attendance, it is likely that a portion at least of the householders in the settlement turned up to hear how their money had been spent, and (possibly) to choose the next incumbents – the problem is to determine the size of this portion. As parish populations expanded through the later sixteenth century, there was a diminishing possibility that such a selection really *was* made by all the parishioners. We might suspect that the parish followed the manor, where rights were restricted increasingly to those who held land directly from the lord (his 'tenants'), to the exclusion of sub-tenants, who leased property from these tenants, or build hovels on the waste, such as at Hoddesdon, Hertfordshire, where by 1594 landlords had allegedly created fifty-eight cottages 'out of Barnes, Stables, Kytchynes', with another eighteen cottages constructed on manorial waste lands that were 'fit onlie for beggars'.[14] In the parish, too, by the early seventeenth century, it seems that however few the formal restrictions on attendance at the parish meeting, increasingly 'parishioner' was equated with 'householder' (that is, owner or primary tenant of a property, *and* head of its household), rather than with every 'resident', whatever their status. Sometimes these 'more deserving' parishioners were referred to as the 'auntientes of our parish', those best qualified by longest residence, most extensive service and largest property there.[15] The effect was that by the early seventeenth century perhaps only one-third to a half of those eligible to serve in parish office actually did so.

The most drastic administrative response to these effects of population growth and poverty was to engineer a more formal closure of the parish meeting, by instituting a 'close' or 'select vestry' – that is, by restricting membership of the parish's deliberative body to a self-selecting group of parishioners, usually no more than twelve or twenty-four in number. As with most other aspects of parish government, these moves had been anticipated in the fifteenth and early sixteenth centuries. In 1635, for example, the parishioners of Saint Leonard's, Shoreditch, stated that they had possessed rights to a select vestry by use and prescription since 1523. In Essex, the very restrictive Braintree 'Company of Four-and-Twenty' may have been meeting since at least 1565, forty-six years before it obtained a bishop's faculty order to support its existence. Such bodies had a very different character and intensity to the usual 'open' parish vestry. Where the latter might often amount only to one general public meeting plus perhaps half-a-dozen ad-hoc gatherings of officers each year, the former might assemble monthly, even weekly, involve a tightly knit group of participants, exert strong influence over the parish officers and take decisions in secret.

Although such bodies could emerge in any location, Hindle observed that they were 'especially common in the counties of Northumberland and Durham during the late sixteenth century', while by 1638 as many as fifty-nine of London's 109 parishes had 'select' vestries.[16] To some extent, this metropolitan and northern distribution of restrictive parochial government reflects an administrative response to two distinct local problems. In London, advocates of such bodies claimed that restrictive parish government was necessary to preserve order among the populous, mobile and often turbulent metropolitan congregations. So, Thomas Lane remarked of Saint Mildred-in-the-Poultry in 1594 'every one of the parrishe be he never so Base or quarrelling a man being by some termed the maior parte hathe had equall voice and hearing and borne lyke swaye as the chiefest man of the parrishe'.[17] The fear of men such as Lane was that the rapidly increasing 'maior parte' of the parishioners would out-shout and out-vote the 'chiefest' men, with adverse consequences both to social authority, and to the burden of the poor rates. In such circumstances, the exclusive 'select vestry' may have appeared to the capital's ecclesiastical and secular authorities to be a bulwark to 'good order', ensuring government by socially trustworthy individuals.

Why was this body also popular in the sparsely populated upland parishes of Northumberland, Durham and some parts of Lancashire? As was suggested above, the problem here was one of geographic, rather than demographic, size. The difficulty in the huge northern parishes, with their multiple townships and chapelries, was to co-ordinate government, particularly the levying and distribution of rates, over such a wide area. Here, 'select' vestries came to function more as 'federal' assemblies of the officers from each township or parochial 'division', than as the means to police overflowing, unruly urban congregations. So, even in 1555, Prescot, Lancashire, possessed a committee of eight for purposes of audit and appointment in a parish that encompassed fifteen townships and 37,221 acres. Elsewhere, particularly in the populous south and east, Hindle concludes that there was an increasing tendency towards formal exclusivity through the adoption of 'select' vestries through the later sixteenth and seventeenth centuries. In many other parishes, population increase, economic polarisation and the consequent subtly changing assumptions about residence and property qualifications may also have ensured that nominally 'open' vestries no longer actually embodied 'the holl consent of the holl parish', that the clerk of Bethersden, Kent noted confidently in the 1560s.[18]

When we multiply the variation in the forms of vestries and the details of their operation by the diversity of agriculture, industry, land ownership and wealth accumulation in Elizabethan England, the complexity of the results should make us wary of generalising about the wealth and status of parish rulers. The social complexity of parishes could vary considerably. Settlements such as Highley, an unenclosed village in south Shropshire, contained four social strata. At the top were six large farmers, assessed at £7–8 in the Henrician subsidy of 1543, who controlled perhaps half the farm land in the settlement. Below them was a much larger group of smaller farmers, perhaps one-third of the families in the village, who enjoyed real, if relatively modest prosperity from their 20- to 40-acre holdings. At their bottom edge, this group shaded into a group of craftsmen and cottage-dwellers, perhaps a quarter of the families in the village, most of whom were still prosperous enough in terms of goods or wages to be included in the Henrician subsidies.

Below this group were a growing number of day-labourers and farm and domestic servants, who comprised the remaining quarter of the population in the Elizabethan period.

While the population of Highley was divided in terms of wealth, authority was still relatively widely distributed. The manorial jury continued to draw on a range of tenants, including cottage-dwellers and craftsmen. In the parish, although records are patchy, for the office of churchwarden 'it is apparent that low financial status was no bar', with the office being held by one servant, two cottage-dwellers, as well as the more prosperous husbandmen and yeomen.[19] The post seems to have been tied to properties, rather than people, so that a wide selection of the village's inhabitants served, sometimes as replacements for women or the wealthy. So, while the population of this village was certainly quite clearly stratified in terms of wealth (but with a relatively wide 'middle' layer), access to office remained relatively open.

In urban parishes, the social hierarchy was often more extended, and polarised. In the small parish of Saint Michael's, in Elizabethan Chester, the social order was manifested within the seating plan of the church, but only roughly. Freemen, who dwelt in the prestigious houses along one of the town's main thoroughfares, were given precedence in the location of their private pews over ordinary, non-free householders, while the poor cellar-dwellers were placed at the back of the church on the 'common seats'. This reflected wealth, because pew rents varied from as much as £1, down to 1s. per annum. However, *within* these divisions, age was also used to determine precedence, with more venerable freemen being placed ahead of their juniors. Alldridge suggests that although the Reformation first cut back the opportunities for lay involvement in the government of Chester's parishes, the developing machinery of local administration soon provided new roles. By 1630, Saint Mary's had acquired two churchwardens, assisted by two sidesmen, two surveyors of the highways, four 'collectors for the poor' and ten 'sessors for the poor', as well as oversight of eight charitable endowments.[20] This opened up opportunities to a relatively wide swathe of the parish's residents, because twenty new recruits were required to fill these posts each year. While Chester's borough government was restricted to those enjoying rights of freedom, parish government was slightly more open, but not much. While a few of the lower status officers (such as sidesmen) were drawn from the non-free householders, the positions of parish rate assessors and auditors were concentrated firmly in the hands of the wealthy urban elite. 'Office holding, like seating in church, was hierarchically conceived.'[21] It was also like parish seating in that it reflected age. In Saint Mary's, 'swornmen were typically in their 20s, churchwardens in their 30s and auditors and sessors in their 40s.'[22] While this system certainly reserved considerable authority to the older, more prosperous inhabitants, Alldridge suggests that it avoided the narrow oligarchic tendencies of the 'select' vestry, because auditors had to 'work through annually accountable officers' drawn from the ranks of the younger, less wealthy householders.[23] So, in the more stratified social hierarchy of Chester, social divisions were deeper than in many smaller villages, and more entrenched, but the existence of a multi-layered and overlapping system of parish and borough government allowed a swathe of residents to have access to authority, albeit on quite unequal terms.

In London, these trends were magnified. On the one hand, opportunities for the exercise of authority were greater than in other English towns, as responsibility at the level of the street was overlain by that in the parish, the livery company, the ward and finally the city council. On the other, though, the social order of the capital resembled a very tall, sharply tapering pyramid, with an exceptionally wide base. Most of those who scaled the first or second levels never got anywhere near the top. Ian Archer suggested that in the small, wealthy parishes inside the city walls, office holders were drawn from the top 50 per cent of the residents. In the large, populous, poor parishes immediately outside the walls, the proportion who became office holders may have been only 25 per cent. Selection reflected status, which depended heavily on wealth. In Elizabethan London, wealth seems to have been associated strongly with payment of the subsidy, that is, royal taxation, as much as with local taxation (unlike in rural parishes where parish taxes were important because there were often comparatively few subsidy payers). In Cornhill, Archer found that in the 1580s while three-quarters of street scavengers and petty ward jurymen were assessed at less than £8 per annum in the subsidy (with 14 per cent exempt from the tax), over one-third of constables and half the churchwardens were assessed at this rate. By contrast, two-thirds of the parish 'auditors' were liable for more than £8 per annum, while all the ward's six common councillors crossed this threshold. As a consequence, the auditors were sometimes described as the 'worshipful' or 'elders of the parish'.[24]

In the tightly packed intra-mural and populous extra-mural parishes, it seems that the choice of officers for the parish *and* the ward was usually confined to the vestry (whether 'select' or, nominally, 'open'), or to a similarly restrictive assembly of parishioners. So, for example, although the records of Saint Bartholomew Exchange and Saint Margaret Lothbury state that the vestry was attended by 'the most of the parisheoners', these rarely amounted to more than a quarter of the household heads.[25] However, the marked difference in the sizes of city and suburban parishes meant that these tight governing groups could represent very different proportions of their inhabitants. In particular, Archer notes the situation in Saint Olave's Southwark in 1589. Here, subsidy payers comprised only 27 per cent of the parish, but the vestry was even more exclusive than this, consisting only of those who paid at least £10 per annum. Their influence spread across a range of other institutions, through the governorship of the parish school and the commissions for sewers. They were also related by ties of business, marriage and a shared commitment to the 'hotter sort of Protestantism'. While these strengthened the exclusivity of the group, to some extent it also indicated how embedded they were within the parish, and how their power (like that of the parochial elites of Highley or Chester) depended on their remaining points of social continuity in the midst of constant geographical mobility.

If the rulers in most parishes were often (and perhaps increasingly) wealthier than the bulk of their neighbours, how did they relate to those in whose name they governed? This question has provoked considerable debate among historians, with Elizabeth's reign being regarded by some as the period in which deep social and cultural splits emerged between rulers and ruled in the parish. Initially, the debate focused on the impact of 'puritan' ideas within the parish. In particular, Keith Wrightson and David Levine's study of the Essex village of Terling suggested that divisions about moral reform amplified economic and social tensions created by rapid population growth, increasing under-employment and competition for resources. The prosperous prospered in late Elizabethan Terling, as grain and commodity prices rose, while the poor found their position eroded by dearth and sharp falls in the value of real wages. Among the parish rulers, concerns about poor relief led to increased scrutiny of the behaviour of the poor (as revealed by the number of alehouses and illegitimate births). This campaign was given a sharp ideological edge by three successive 'puritan' clergymen, from the end of Elizabeth's reign until the 1630s. However, as Martin Ingram later showed, such processes of social and moral regulation were evident in many parishes, whether or not they were under the auspices of 'puritan' activists among the parish authorities. Much of this regulation was a fairly functional parochial 'belt-tightening' exercise, of trying to limit the amount of expenditure by keeping an eye on the types of behaviour that were seen as responsible for it. However, the controversial element of the 'Terling thesis' was that the 'godly' message 'was disproportionately successful among the upper and middling ranks of parish society', who then sought to implement it by reforming the lives of the poor.[26] The main opponent of this view was Margaret Spufford, who in 1985 attempted to show that these campaigns for moral reform were cyclical between the fourteenth and seventeenth centuries, reflecting the changing relationship between population and resources, rather than the socially and chronologically specific attractions of 'puritanism' to parochial elites in the late sixteenth century.

Since the mid-1980s, this debate has progressed in two slightly different directions, neither of which has engaged directly with this central proposition. McIntosh's work on the lesser courts of England between the fourteenth and late sixteenth centuries has spanned the positions outlined by Wrightson and Spufford. On the one hand, McIntosh identified rising concern with 'disorder' (unruly alehouses, sexual misconduct and general personal 'ill-rule') from the 1460s and 1470s, generally in large, populous parishes, with relatively wide wealth disparities that might have been the first to experience the cyclical problems of migration and population growth. By the 1520s, such 'disorderly' behaviour was being reported more widely, among different types of settlement, even in 'arable, nucleated villages with open fields'.[27] By the 1580s these offences were no longer being reported very frequently to the lesser courts. On the other hand, though, McIntosh suggested that religious change added a distinct ideological element to such efforts to impose control. Although these efforts would have been likely anyway, because of the cyclical upturn in population (and downturn in real wages) 'by 1600 some communities with an activist puritan presence were operating on a rather different basis . . . even if such reform undercut the social goals that had previously justified attempts to limit wrongdoing'.[28] However, apart from noting the (often short-lived) personal impact of a charismatic preaching clergy, McIntosh did not find enough evidence to explore the larger question of what motivated the parish rulers in certain settlements to adopt such reforming ideas.

Other studies have located the reasons behind such imperatives less in terms of the social specificity of immediate religious innovations and more in the larger processes of 'state formation' and economic development. Steve Hindle has sought to demonstrate how the parish became 'a local extension of state authority', as 'the interests of local oligarchies intersected with the centralized policies of Church and State', particularly through administration of the poor law.[29] However, although he has detected a range of religious impulses at work in his detailed and very wide-ranging analysis of parochial efforts to relieve, employ the 'deserving' poor, and to reform or exclude the 'undeserving' poor, he has not suggested that these can be attributed primarily to the actions of 'middling' puritans. Andy Wood has depicted the same identity of interests between an expanding Tudor 'state' and parochial rulers, but has suggested that its ultimate cause lay in governmental initiatives to bolster local administration and poor relief after the 1549 rebellions. By this means, parish governors were peeled away from the populace as 'the relationship between local office-holding and state power was deepened over the course of the sixteenth century'.[30] Their control of the machinery of the parish relief helped them to divide and rule the poor, so that by 1600 'the "better sort of people" now stood for a very different set of principles from the "honest men" who, between 1381 and 1549, had formed the public leadership of popular insurrections.'[31]

As historians such Dyer, Rosser and McIntosh have noted, late-medieval English parishes were also highly stratified in terms of wealth and authority, and in terms of manorial and parochial government. They were never pristine representatives of a largely egalitarian, 'communal' way of life. The rapid population growth of the first three decades of Elizabeth's reign intensified existing social divisions, so that a smaller proportion of the inhabitants were brought into the ambit of office holding, and the parish ratepayers gained stronger, and increasingly unavoidable, financial incentives to regulate the behaviour of recipients. At the same time, some puritan clergy targeted their message consciously at the 'chief men' of their parishes, in an attempt to co-opt 'the magistrate' and his parochial representatives to instil a new, 'godly' order.[32] On occasion, they may even have welded them together into unofficial presbyteries of 'lay elders' through the vehicle of the 'select vestry', as in the Essex townships of Finchingfield and Braintree. Where this occurred a really intense, ideological trench warfare might erupt between two conflicting notions of 'community': one that put the maintenance of neighbourly 'charity' and harmony above immediate behavioural conformity and one that sought to recast the notion of the harmonious community *through* ideological and behavioural conformity. The effects on those who experienced this conflict were often profound, such as in the Dorset village of Mapperton, where parishioners complained that the new 'puritan' clergyman had stirred up so much ill-feeling that 'we live a most tormentable and miserable and ungodly life . . . for before these came to dwell amongst us we lived in love and charity.'[33] The administration of the parish and of its institutions and resources provided the field on which much of this conflict was conducted. It also tended to produce the archetypical 'Terling thesis' evidence base, in which a 'godly' parish elite are detected regulating their unruly neighbours through the church courts and administration of the poor law. However, this material reveals much less about the 'conformable' poor, who converted, but who do not show up in these types of prosecutions, only appearing instead in the (rarer) instances of citations for liturgical nonconformity and 'gadding' to sermons outside the parish. It also downplays the other fundamental hierarchy at work in these communities: age. Many of the offences that parochial administrators sought to reform in the 1580s and 1590s were 'young people's' offences – alehouse-haunting, sexual impropriety and real or perceived disobedience to their elders – committed by the kingdom's 1 million additional inhabitants born since the start of the reign. As Von Friedeburg noted in the Essex village of Earls Colne, 'offenders, no matter what their offences, were primarily young. Few were above thirty when presented for the first time.'[34] These young, single labourers and servants rarely committed a second offence in the village, often because they had moved on in an attempt to 'shift' for themselves somewhere else.

It is evident, therefore, that the history of parochial government in this period was often marked by the efforts of a relatively elevated, unrepresentative elite to regulate the lives and behaviour of their poorer, more marginal neighbours, often under the influence of novel religious imperatives. However, it is equally clear that this was not always the whole story. The social problems, and some of the responses adopted, were prefigured during the population crises of the early fourteenth century and foreshadowed by the upsurge in village regulation after 1460. The initiatives taken by the governors of sixteenth-century parishes may therefore have had earlier precedents, but as Wrightson has observed, they occurred in changed economic and ideological circumstances. These were sometimes epitomised by the characteristic crackdowns by groups of fervently reforming 'middling' parish notables on the behaviour of the 'poorer sort'. Yet, although these incidents exemplified stark differences in the distribution of status and power *between* social groups in the village, they might also conceal equally pervasive conflicts between the old and the young, the settled and the mobile *within* these groupings. This evidence can also obscure those ordinary individuals who conformed to, or were actually enthusiastic about, a reformed religion that was sometimes dramatic, exciting and novel, or seemed to offer compelling answers to personal and societal dilemmas.

Did Elizabeth's reign see the creation of an entity described over 200 years later by the poet John Clare as 'the parish state'?[35] Clare had in mind a double-edged jurisdiction, in which the puffed-up 'governors' of these petty, tyrannical kingdoms lorded it over their unfortunate 'subjects', while at the same time deriving their authority from their role as cogs in a larger, very powerful but also unforgiving administrative machine, designed to grind the faces of the poor. Formally, Elizabeth's reign *did* see the enactment and extension of legislation and (in many areas) the development of the processes that eventually defined Clare's traumatic adult life. By 1603, the mechanisms for a national system of poor-relief collection, distribution and oversight had been established. These not only embodied the will of the Elizabethan Privy Council and parliaments but also depended upon the accumulated powers of Tudor government to be put into effect. In this sense, we might see the forms of parish government inspired by the Elizabethan poor law as a projection of the powers of 'the State' into the lowest tier of administration. We might also see it as a process in which the officers of this administrative tier were incorporated into, and aligned with, the interests and purposes of that 'state'.

However, much of this was form rather than substance, principle rather than practice, and built on earlier legislative initiatives. Elizabeth's regime may have increased its demands on parochial authorities, but it lacked the administrative machinery for the minute enforcement of common responses within strict deadlines. Forms of local administration continued to reflect variations in lordship, the historical development of land tenure, the effects of topography and the geographical size of administrative units, as well as the stratification and population density of particular settlements. The civil parish – administering poor relief provision, coercing the 'able-bodied poor', maintaining the highway, keeping the Queen's peace and mustering its militia men – had to fit into the existing administrative 'ecology' of the settlement during Elizabeth's reign, even if it eventually came to dominate it in most cases. As has been suggested, though, even in 1603 the manor was not moribund as an instrument of local regulation in many northern and western parts of England. This was, in part, because in these regions the parish was a much larger and less wieldy administrative instrument than it was in the nucleated settlements of Midland England or the tightly packed countryside of the southern counties.

As a result, in many parts of England (particularly the north and west), a comprehensive system of compulsory parochial rating and pension payments only evolved thirty or forty years after the end of Elizabeth's reign. Church ales, wakes and revels continued, much to the disgust of the religiously more 'precise' inhabitants. In some places, the poor continued to be relieved in kind, rather than in money, by licensed forms of begging or by gifts of food organised in rotation by 'house-row'. As Hindle and McIntosh have illustrated in such convincing detail, even where compulsory rating systems were established, they usually existed alongside a plethora of private endowments, doles, almshouses and bread or clothing charities. For the recipient, ratepayer or overseer, these local accretions must surely have overwritten the national system, emphasising the importance, and the politics, of 'belonging' to *a* specific parish, rather than to *the* parish, in general. The national system that did emerge by 1603 also built in a fundamental structural tension between every unit of administration from which it was constructed, by tying poor relief eligibility to legal settlement and then allowing parishes to sue each other about these settlement rights. This entrenched a 'parish-mindedness' among these authorities and may have encouraged a culture of 'local xenophobia' against outsiders and limited the extent of common purpose among parish elites as arms of 'the State'.[36] In some respects, it was these local variations in provision, and the potentially arbitrary authority wielded by some parochial governors (despite oversight by JPs) against which Clare eventually expressed such bitter resentment.

These developments occurred at a time of rapid population growth, which inflicted an ever-increasing burden on all the systems of government, administration, law enforcement and relief provision, and reached crisis proportions in the dearth years between 1594 and 1597. In most parishes, this demographic rise was seen as a rapid rise in the most marginal inhabitants – young, single, rootless, property-less, job-seeking men and women, either native or incomers. They tested most aspects of the evolving systems of parish administration, posing a threat to household and social authority and moral order, extra competition in an already overcrowded labour market, and a further drain on communal resources. The presence of such indigent young people obviously further exacerbated the growing divide between the self-sufficient or prospering households and those exposed to varying degrees of poverty. As numerous parish studies have suggested, these increasingly entrenched positions could spur the creation of oligarchic groupings of parish officers and vestrymen, drawn from the wealthier ratepayers, farmers or tradesmen. Again, there was considerable geographic variation, with the most populous, most stratified urban parishes, and the largest, most scattered rural parishes being the most likely to constitute formally closed 'select' vestries. These demographic pressures also accentuated the growing divide between the legally settled, and the 'strangers', at *all* social levels. In many other parishes where the formal composition of the office-holding group did not change, the meaning of social terminology sometimes shifted, so that decisions on behalf of the 'inhabitants' or 'parishioners' often referred to just the ratepayers or settled household heads, not all the settlement's residents. Although historians of the later Middle Ages would not regard these divisions as new, or unprecedented, they were certainly more acute by the end of Elizabeth's reign than they had been in many areas for over 250 years.

These complications may explain why the Elizabethan parish does not fit easily into interpretative templates that depict it either as an extension of late-medieval lordship or as an early step in the formation of a more modern military-fiscal-welfare state. It remained highly variegated because it had to fit the contours of the existing, very uneven administrative terrain. It accommodated huge local and regional variations in the types of jurisdictions and the forms of bodies created to govern them. It tolerated the growth of diverse, and unique, parish 'cultures' of government and relief, because it lacked the machinery to be prescriptive. While it may have incorporated local administrators into the wider aims of the State (notably the aversion of large-scale disorder through the provision of the most basic levels of subsistence), it left the running of this 'state' very much in their hands. Ultimately, then, the longevity of the Elizabethan 'system' of parish government was due, in large measure, to the fact that it operated so unsystematically.

FURTHER READING

Alldridge, Nicholas, 'Loyalty and Identity in Chester Parishes, 1540–1640', in S. J. Wright (ed.), *Parish, Church and People: Local Studies in Lay Religion, 1350–1750* (London, 1988), pp. 85–124.

Archer, Ian W., *The Pursuit of Stability: Social Relations in Elizabethan London* (Cambridge, 1991).

Bettey, Joseph H., 'Land Tenure and Manorial Custom in Dorset, 1570–1670', *Southern History*, 4 (1982): 33–54.

Braddick, Michael J., *State Formation in Early Modern England, c. 1550–1700* (Cambridge, 2000).

Cunich, Peter, 'The Dissolution of the Chantries', in P. Collinson and J. Craig (eds.), *The Reformation in English Towns, 1500–1640* (Basingstoke, 1998), pp. 159–74.

Duffy, Eamon, 'The Godly and the Multitude in Stuart England', *The Seventeenth Century*, 1 (1) (1986): 31–55.

—— *The Voices of Morebath: Reformation and Rebellion in an English Village* (New Haven, Conn., 2001).

Dyer, Christopher, 'The English Medieval Village Community and Its Decline', *Journal of British Studies*, 33 (4) (1994): 407–29.

Emmison, Frederic G., *Early Essex Town Meetings: Braintree, 1619–36; Finchingfield, 1626–34* (London and Chichester, 1970).

Farnhill, Ken, 'Religious Policy and Parish "Conformity": Cratfield's Lands in the Sixteenth Century', in K. L French, G. Gibbs and B. Kümin (eds.), *The Parish in English Life, 1400–1600* (Manchester, 1997), pp. 217–29.

Fideler, Paul A., *Social Welfare in Pre-Industrial England* (Basingstoke, 1976).

French, Henry R., *The Middle Sort of People in Provincial England* (Oxford, 2007).
Griffiths, Paul, 'Secrecy and Authority in Late Sixteenth and Early Seventeenth Century London', *Historical Journal,* 40 (4) (1997): 925–51.
Haigh, Christopher, 'The Character of an Antipuritan', *Sixteenth-Century Journal,* 35 (3) (2004): 671–88.
Hanawalt, Barbara, '"Good Governance" in the Medieval and Early Modern Context', *Journal of British Studies,* 37 (3) (1998): 246–57.
Hindle, Steve, *The State and Social Change in Early Modern England, 1550–1640* (Basingstoke, 2000).
—— 'The Political Culture of the Middling Sort in English Rural Communities, *c.* 1550–1700', in T. Harris (ed.), *The Politics of the Excluded, c. 1550–1850* (Basingstoke, 2001), pp. 125–52.
—— *On the Parish? The Micro-Politics of Poor Relief in Rural England, c. 1550–1750* (Oxford, 2004).
Hoyle, Richard W., '"An Ancient and Laudable Custom"? The Development and Definition of Tenant Right in the North-West in the Sixteenth Century', *Past and Present,* 116 (August) (1987): 24–55.
Hunt, William, *The Puritan Moment: The Coming of Revolution in an English County* (Cambridge, Mass., 1983).
Ingram, Martin, *Church Courts, Sex and Marriage in England, 1570–1640* (Cambridge, 1987).
Kent, Joan, *The English Village Constable, 1580–1642: A Social and Administrative Study* (Oxford, 1986).
Kümin, Beat, 'The Secular Legacy of the Late Medieval Parish', in C. Burgess and E. Duffy (eds.), *The Parish in Late Medieval England: Proceedings of the 2002 Harlaxton Symposium* (Donington, 2006), pp. 95–111.
McCampbell, Alice E., 'The London Parish and the London Precinct', *Guildhall Studies in London History,* 2 (1976): 107–124.
McIntosh, Marjory K., 'Social Change and the Tudor Manorial Leets', in J. A. Guy and H. G. Beale (eds.), *Law and Social Change in British History* (London and New Jersey, 1984), pp. 73–85.
—— *Controlling Misbehaviour in England, 1370–1600* (Cambridge, 1998).
—— *Poor Relief in England 1350–1600* (Cambridge, 2012).
—— *Poor Relief and Community in Hadleigh, Suffolk 1547–1600*, Studies in Local and Regional History, vol. 12 (Hatfield, 2013).
Nair, Gwyneth, *Highley: The Development of a Community, 1550–1880* (Oxford, 1988).
Orme, Nicholas, 'The Other Parish Churches: Chapels in Late Medieval England', in C. Burgess and E. Duffy (eds.), *The Parish in Late Medieval England: Proceedings of the 2002 Harlaxton Symposium* (Donington, 2006), pp. 78–94.
Rosser, Gervaise, 'Communities of Parish and Guild in the Late Middle Ages', in S. J. Wright (ed.), *Parish, Church and People: Local Studies in Lay Religion, 1350–1750* (London, 1988), pp. 29–55.
Rushton, Peter, 'The Poor Law, the Parish and the Community in North-East England, 1600–1800', *Northern History,* 25 (1989): 135–52.
Scarisbrick, J. J., *The Reformation and the English People* (Oxford, 1984).
Slack, Paul, 'Poverty and Social Regulation in Elizabethan England', in C. Haigh (ed.), *The Reign of Elizabeth I* (Basingstoke, 1984), pp. 221–42.
—— *Poverty and Policy in Tudor and Stuart England* (London, 1988).
Smith, Richard M., '"Modernization" and the Medieval Village Community in England: Some Sceptical Reflections', in A. R. H. Baker and D. Gregory (eds.), *Explorations in Historical Geography: Interpretative Essays* (Cambridge, 1984), pp. 140–79.

Snell, Keith D. M., 'The Culture of Local Xenophobia', *Social History*, 28 (1) (2003): 1–30.
—— *The Parish and Belonging: Community, Identity and Welfare in England and Wales, 1700–1950* (Cambridge, 2006).
Spufford, Margaret, 'Puritanism and Social Control?' in A. Fletcher and J. Stevenson (eds.), *Order and Disorder in Early Modern England* (Cambridge, 1985), pp. 41–57.
Thomas, Keith, 'Age and Authority in Early Modern England', *Proceedings of the British Academy*, 62 (1976): 205–48.
Von Friedeburg, Robert, 'The Reformation of Manners and the Social Composition of Offenders in an East Anglian Cloth Village: Earls Colne, Essex, 1531–1642', *Journal of British Studies*, 29 (4) (1990): 347–85.
Webster, Tom, 'Stephen Marshall and Finchingfield', *Studies in Essex History* 6 (Chelmsford, 1994).
Wood, Andy, *The 1549 Rebellions and the Making of Early Modern England* (Cambridge, 2007).
Wrightson, Keith and Levine, David, *Poverty and Piety in an English Village Terling, 1525–1700*, 2nd edn (Oxford, 1995).

NOTES

1 Richard M. Smith, '"Modernization" and the Medieval Village Community in England: Some Sceptical Reflections', in A. R. H. Baker and D. Gregory (eds.), *Explorations in Historical Geography: Interpretative Essays* (Cambridge, 1984), pp. 140–79; p. 178.
2 Steve Hindle, 'The Political Culture of the Middling Sort in English Rural Communities, *c.* 1550–1700', in Tim Harris (ed.), *The Politics of the Excluded, c. 1550–1850* (Basingstoke, 2001), pp. 125–152; pp. 136–7.
3 Steve Hindle, *On the Parish? The Micro-Politics of Poor Relief in Rural England 1550–1750* (Oxford, 2009), p. 147.
4 Hindle, *On the Parish?* p. 125.
5 Marjorie Keniston McIntosh, *Controlling Misbehaviour in England, 1370–1600* (Cambridge, 1998), p. 44.
6 McIntosh, *Controlling Misbehaviour in England,* p. 45.
7 R. W. Hoyle, '"An Ancient and Laudable Custom"? The Development and Definition of Tenant Right in the North-West in the Sixteenth Century', *Past and Present,* 116 (August) (1987): 24–55.
8 Smith, 'Modernization', p. 178.
9 Smith, 'Modernization', p. 175.
10 Hindle, 'The Political Culture of the Middling Sort', p. 128.
11 Marjorie Keniston McIntosh, 'Social Change and the Tudor Manorial Leet', in J. A. Guy and H. G. Beale (eds.), *Law and Social Change in British History* (London and New Jersey, 1984), p. 76.
12 Beat Kümin, 'The Secular Legacy of the Late Medieval Parish', in C. Burgess and E. Duffy (eds.), *The Parish in Late Medieval England* (Harlaxton Medieval Studies, 14, Donnington, 2006), pp. 95–111; p. 109.
13 Gervase Rosser, 'Communities of Parish and Guild in the Late Middle Ages', in S. J. Wright (ed.), *Parish, Church and People: Local Studies in Lay Religion, 1350–1750* (London, 1988), pp. 29–35; pp. 36–7.
14 Hindle, *On the Parish?* p. 325.
15 Ian W. Archer, *The Pursuit of Stability: Social Relations in Elizabethan London* (Cambridge, 1991), p. 69.
16 Steve Hindle, *The State and Social Change in Early Modern England, 1550–1640* (Basingstoke, 2000), p. 210. A. E. McCampbell, 'The London Parish and the London Precinct', *Guildhall Studies in London History,* 11 (2) (1976): 107–124; p. 109.
17 Archer, *Pursuit of Stability,* p. 71.

18 Hindle, *State and Social Change*, p. 209.
19 G. Nair, *Highley: The Development of a Community, 1550–1880* (Oxford, 1988), pp. 128–9.
20 N. Alldridge, 'Loyalty and Identity in Chester Parishes, 1540–1640', in S. J. Wright (ed.), *Parish, Church and People: Local Studies in Lay Religion, 1350–1750* (London, 1988), pp. 85–124; p. 104.
21 Alldridge, 'Loyalty and Identity', p. 106.
22 Alldridge, 'Loyalty and Identity', p. 107.
23 Alldridge, 'Loyalty and Identity', p. 112.
24 Archer, *Pursuit of Stability*, p. 67.
25 Archer, *Pursuit of Stability*, pp. 70–1.
26 Keith Wrightson, 'Postscript: Terling Revisited', in Keith Wrightson and David Levine (eds.), *Poverty and Piety in an English Village: Terling, 1525–1700*, 2nd edn (Oxford, 1995), pp. 186–220; p. 207.
27 McIntosh, *Controlling Misbehaviour*, p. 180.
28 McIntosh, *Controlling Misbehaviour*, p. 208.
29 Hindle, *State and Social Change*, pp. 128, 147.
30 Andy Wood, *The 1549 Rebellions and the Making of Early Modern England* (Cambridge, 2007), p. 198.
31 Wood, *The 1549 Rebellions*, p. 207.
32 William Hunt, *The Puritan Moment: The Coming of Revolution in an English County* (Cambridge, Mass., 1983), pp. 130–55.
33 Christopher Haigh, 'The Character of an Antipuritan', *Sixteenth-Century Journal*, 35 (3) (2004): 671–88; p. 688.
34 Robert Von Friedeburg, 'The Reformation of Manners and the Social Composition of Offenders in an East Anglian Cloth Village: Earls Colne, Essex, 1531–1642', *Journal of British Studies*, 29 (4) (1990): 347–85; p. 373.
35 J. Clare, *The Parish*, ed. E. Robinson (Harmondsworth, 1985), p. 63.
36 K. D. M. Snell, 'The Culture of Local Xenophobia', *Social History*, 28 (1) (2003): 1–30; Hindle, *On the Parish?* pp. 327–37.

CHAPTER TEN

CENSORSHIP AND PROPAGANDA

Cyndia Susan Clegg

The premise that Tudor monarchs effectively deployed propaganda as a prominent political strategy has become a commonplace in studies of Tudor England, although to what end shifts with the interpretive winds. In mid-twentieth-century accounts heralding Tudor monarchs' political effectiveness, Edward Hall's *Chronicle* – reputedly 'the most ambitious of the inspired works of propaganda in the first half of the sixteenth century' – was thought to have taught 'one imperative' political lesson: since rebellion and civil dissention would lead to the kingdom's destruction, hierarchy and order were requisite.[1] A few decades later, images of monarchical power and authority present in court spectacle and art sought the subjects' good will and devotion, especially during the reign of Elizabeth I, whose 'cult', according to Roy Strong, was a triumph of propaganda. By the end of the twentieth century, the Tudors had become authoritarian despots who employed propaganda (and censorship) to disguise their failures. For the most part, because we have imposed an Enlightenment value system, we have misunderstood the role of both propaganda and censorship in Tudor England. During the reign of Elizabeth, propaganda and censorship rarely sought the same ends. Sometimes, however, they did, and these are the circumstances that reveal both the distinctive character of Elizabethan printed propaganda and the roles propaganda and censorship played in government administration.

Some scholars envision Elizabethan propaganda as compensatory for the regime's inadequacies. According to John Cooper, even though Tudor monarchy insisted upon its authority, 'its ability to impose its will on the kingdom was governed by its limited administrative and military resources. In such circumstances, propaganda and persuasion became a vital tool of politics.'[2] Vital though it may have been, propaganda, according to Christopher Haigh, masked the truth of Elizabeth's incompetence. 'The monarchy of Elizabeth I was founded upon illusion. She ruled by propagandistic images which captivated her courtiers and seduced her subjects – images which have misled historians for four centuries.'[3]

Envisioning Tudor rule as dependent upon propaganda also has its detractors – not the least being Geoffrey Elton, who cautioned that 'reveries on accession tilts and symbolism' and 'gallants and galliards' detracted from the real work of

Elizabethan historiography, getting 'to the roots of political life'.[4] While Elton saw little historical relevance in the 'cult of Elizabeth', Sydney Anglo questioned whether Tudor court spectacle actually constituted propaganda. To him, discussions of royal imagery 'assume the very things that ought to be proved: government planning in the creation and propagation of political symbolism on the one hand; and the existence of a sophisticated and informed public response on the other'. Anglo reminds us that propaganda's business is 'by definition, to propagate and persuade'. However persuasive they may have been, Elizabethan progresses, portraits and Accession Day tilts were not widely propagated, and only a 'tiny minority of people' actually saw the Queen on progress. 'Cartloads of emblematic flowers, an energetic reworking of all the threadbare conventions of courtly love, adaptations of classical myth, and ingenious manipulation of Christian imagery' existed, but their purpose was the 'ceaseless adulation of Elizabeth', not public persuasion: 'The whole panoply of panegyric was aimed upward to please the monarch, not downward to persuade doubting courtiers of the rectitude of the regime.'[5]

While Anglo focuses on royal image and ritual, he does consider, albeit briefly, the medium commonly associated with propaganda: printing.

> The potential power of the press, both in terms of providing sophisticated visual propaganda and disseminating it, seems so obvious to us that we readily assume that it was consistently and effectively used in Tudor England to enhance people's perception of the dynasty. Certainly, control of printing by licensing, censorship and prosecution, was vigorously if fitfully maintained from the time of Thomas Cromwell; writers were commissioned to advance arguments favourable to royal policies, and other authors offered apologetics spontaneously and without official encouragement.[6]

Anglo's remarks are helpful in two ways, one intended, the other inadvertent. He reminds us how readily we assign to another era's propaganda characteristics more appropriate to our own experience. For us, printed texts, persuasive and widely propagated, provide an effective propaganda medium, so we assume Tudor monarchs employed print similarly. At the same time he eschews an anachronistic view of Tudor propaganda, he embraces a version of Tudor censorship that has contributed to the very perspective on propaganda he repudiates. If 'certainly' government licensers allowed only books favourable to the government or acceptable to official tastes to be printed, and if unapproved books were censored and their authors and printers prosecuted, then necessarily printed texts – texts containing official positions that were widely propagated – were indeed propaganda. This premise of the first clause of Anglo's sentence beginning with 'Certainly' is, however, distinct from and unrelated to the act of propagandising envisioned in the second clause – commissioning writers 'to advance arguments favourable to royal policies'.

Ironically, the link Anglo envisions between censorship and propaganda betrays precisely the kind of anachronistic interpretation he repudiates. We have come to regard propaganda and censorship not as separate practices but as two sides of a coin – a counterfeit coin at that – largely because we associate them with practices of twentieth-century totalitarian regimes. One of the most influential studies of early modern press censorship, Fredrick Siebert's *Freedom of the Press in England,*

1476–1776 (1952), likened Tudor government to the Communist government of Soviet Russia, which controlled all the communication media in order to suppress anything that might undermine the Soviet system.[7] From the 'free world's' perspective, such manipulative Soviet practices were necessarily dishonest and false. Indeed, even today, most scholars concur with Deborah Shuger's assessment that 'a discourse that sacrifices truth to present the issues as a clear contest between good and evil is usually considered propaganda: it is, in fact, a standard definition of propaganda.'[8] The certain link between censorship, lies and propaganda colours the otherwise solid work of Tudor historians such as Haigh and Cooper. Bad governments employ propaganda; good governments tell the truth. Imposing modern value judgements derived from a conceptual model of totalitarian government may distort our understanding of how propaganda and censorship actually operated during Elizabeth's reign – something we can correct by recontextualising the intersections of Elizabethan censorship and propaganda.

HOLINSHED'S *CHRONICLES:* A PARADIGM FOR PROPAGANDA AND CENSORSHIP

One particular instance when censorship and propaganda met exposes the political role that propaganda, licensing, censorship and sanctions played during Elizabeth's reign. In February 1587, the Privy Council called for the censorship of the second edition of Holinshed's *Chronicles,* a massive history often disparaged as propaganda. Its colophon imprint, '*cum privilegio*', has been misunderstood to signify government approbation. Before the London Company of Stationers obtained their printing monopoly in 1557, individual printers and publishers sought and received grants under the Privy Seal (a privilege) which assured them the exclusive proprietary right to a title. Occasionally such privileges reflected royal patronage – Richard Grafton's Great Bible, for example. Similarly, books that issued from the King's Printer, a position created by royal patent, often bore the *cum privilegio* imprint even when they were not commissioned by the monarch. Elizabeth bestowed printing privileges on whole classes of books: primers, ABCs, catechisms, Latin books, schoolbooks and (important for our purpose) chronicles and histories. In 1580, the Earl of Leicester and Sir Christopher Hatton secured the privilege to print 'all Dictionaries in all tongues, all Chronicles and histories whatsoever' for London Stationer Henry Bynneman, who had printed Polybius' *Historiae* (1568), Thomas Walsingham's *Historia brevis* (1574), John Stow's *Summarie of English Chronicles* (1574) and the first edition of Holinshed's *Chronicles.*[9] When Bynneman died in 1583, his agents, Henry Denham and Ralph Newberry, obtained his privilege to print histories, and on 30 December 1584 Henry Denham and Ralph Newberry entered in the Stationers' Registers their 'license and allowance' 'by the Queene maiesties graunte' to print a list of eight titles, headed by Holinshed's *Chronicle* in folio.[10] This printing privilege accounts for the 1587 edition's colophon imprint '*cum privilegio*'. Since Denham and Newberry's privilege in Holinshed was second-hand, it seems unlikely that Queen Elizabeth took much interest in the book's propagandistic potential.[11]

It has also been widely assumed that any book printed '*cum privilegio*' would have received an official licenser's approval. The matter of 'licensing', however, is as vexed as the question of privilege. During the reign of Elizabeth, the word 'licence' actually referred to an early version of 'copyright' (a propriety right) held not by a book's author but by its publisher. The London Stationers' Company's master and wardens granted licences to company members, who then, for a fee, could have their licence entered in the Stationers' register book. The licence was distinct from 'allowance' or 'authorisation', an official censor's grant of approval. Most authorisers were clergymen in the vicinity of Saint Paul's Cathedral yard, home to printing houses and booksellers' shops. The master and wardens often made the Stationers' licence contingent on 'allowance', but not always. Generally they required allowance only for religious texts, works in translation and political writing. Considerable latitude existed in the practice of official allowance. Certainly (here the word is appropriate), all Stationers recognised that their monopoly (and thus their livelihood) depended on preventing books opposing Elizabeth or her religion from being printed, but it is a mistake to interpret Elizabethan licensing and authorisation as a system of wholesale ideological control.

The licensing of both editions of Holinshed's *Chronicles* exhibits the system's latitude. The Stationers' Register's entry for the first edition, made the year following the book's printing, fails to indicate that the book was seen and allowed. The entries in the Stationers' Register relevant to the second edition reflect jockeying among the Stationers for rights to title, since some of the original partners in the venture had died and their rights had been assigned (as Bynneman's patent had). Indeed, had it not been for the complicated partnership patterns, the second edition would not have appeared in the registers at all. According to Stationers' Company custom, a licence was issued only once for all editions. Subsequent editions were neither re-licensed nor reauthorised. Hence, for example, the 1590 licence granted for Edmund Spenser's *Faerie Queene* applied not only to the first three books that comprised the 1590 text but also to the additional three that constituted the 1596 edition. Even with such substantial additions, the title was neither re-entered in the Stationers' Register nor reauthorised. Similarly, even though the 1587 edition contained new material for 1577 through 1586, no new licence was requisite. Neither Holinshed's nor Spenser's publishers were engaging in anything other than regular practices in the trade.

Elizabeth's government may have been uninterested in patronising or authorising Holinshed's *Chronicles*; both editions, however, aroused the government's interest after publication. In December of 1577, concerned that a few passages in Richard Stanyhurst's Irish history negatively portrayed a political faction allied with the Tudors, the Privy Council ordered the Bishop of London to stay the *Chronicles*' sales until the book could be 'reformed'. On 13 January 1578, having received notice from the Lord Treasurer that Stanyhurst had corrected the text, the Council ordered the Bishop to release the stay. The 1587 *Chronicles*' censorship was more extensive.

On 1 February 1587, the Privy Council wrote to the Archbishop of Canterbury asking him to stay the sale of a 'newe book', of Holinshed's *Chronicles,* until the 'augmentation' which contained 'reporte of matters of later yeeres that concern the State, and are not therfore meete to be published in such sorte as they are delivered' could be 'reformyd'.[12] The letter assigned the task of reformation to three men: Thomas Randolph, a diplomat who had recently negotiated a treaty between Elizabeth and James VI; Henry Killigrew, another diplomat practised in both Dutch and Scottish affairs; and John Hammond, a civil lawyer and High Commission member, who examined Edmund Campion, the Jesuit tried for treason in 1581. These men's scrutiny of the *Chronicles*' new additions produced cuts in the Scottish history that might have jeopardised Randolph's recent treaty agreement. In the continuation of the 'History of England' they proposed changes that enhanced the Earl of Leicester's stature (significant because he was currently leading English forces in the Netherlands), distanced England from the Duc d'Alençon (who had recently offended the Dutch) and insisted that the English judicial system conducted trials and executions only according to due process of law. Although the censors dictated the changes, Abraham Fleming, Denham's 'corrector', performed them with unusual care. He replaced entire gatherings with cancels written to connect logically with preceding and subsequent text. The censorship and revision was performed within a month of the Privy Council's order, but, before the 'reformed' book went on sale, new political developments required further censorship: Mary, Queen of Scots' execution and a foreign-policy shift in the Netherlands from a military to a diplomatic approach. At this stage, revisions introduced a briefer and less congratulatory account of Leicester's military campaign and moderated Fleming's fiercely anti-Catholic and luridly violent account of the Babington conspiracy and its punishment. The report of Mary's trial and sentencing remained untouched.

The 1587 Holinshed example offers an extraordinary glimpse of censorship and propaganda working together. It provides a government rationale for censorship – the book's 'reporte of matters of later yeeres that concern the State, and are not therfore meete to be published in such sorte as they are delivered'. We know the expertise of those called upon to review the text, and we have textual variants that record changes. While the 1587 uncensored version does not reflect the government's interest in an official version of history, the censored version does. The changes the censors made in the text shows that that they were concerned less about the *Chronicles*' effect on Elizabeth's loyal subjects than on an international audience. Here censorship and propaganda seek to project an image of English government designed to calm diplomatic waters and quiet international Catholic critics. This is pointedly clear in the passages related to the Jesuit Edmund Campion's execution.

Both the censored and uncensored versions fully report Campion's treason trial, conviction and execution. The censors, however, suppressed this account of Catholic outrage:

> No sooner had justice given the blow of execution, and cut off the foresaid offendors from the earth; but certeine enimies of the state politike and ecclesiastike, greatlie favouring them, and their cause, which they falslie gave out to be religion, dispersed abroad their libels of most impudent devise, tending to the justifieng of the malefactors innocencie, to the heinous and unrecompensable defamation of the course of justice and judgement against them commensed and finished: in so much that speaking of the daie whereon they died, they blushed not to intitle them martyrs.[13]

The censored text contained a Latin poem illustrative of 'things not publishable' – that Campion was brought to trial not for a crime but for his religion – and then adds the comment: 'Thus slanderouslie against the administration of justice scattered these vipers brood their lieng reports, therein to the skies advancing the children of iniquitie as spotlesse; yea forging most monstrous fables.'[14] Campion's trial and execution provoked a propaganda war about Catholic persecution and English justice that included Cardinal William Allen's *A Briefe Historie of the Glorious Martyrdom of XII Reverend Priests* (1582); Lord Burghley's defence of English policy, *The Execution of Justice in England* (1583); and Allen's reply to Burghley, *A True Sincere and Modest Defence of English Catholiques That Suffer for Their Faith Both at Home and Abrode* (1584). The Catholic side maintained that English Catholics, particularly Jesuits and priests executed for treason, were religious martyrs who died for their faith. Elizabeth's government asserted that the English justice system duly prosecuted and punished Jesuits and priests who served as the Pope's agents: 'the pope having with other princes practised the death and deprivation of our most gratious princesse, and utter subversion of hir seat & kingdome, to advance his most abominable religion'.[15]

The Campion material censored from Holinshed draws attention to a central link between censorship and propaganda during the reign of Elizabeth. Although not always working together, both oppose what Elizabeth and her ministers regarded as Catholic political action. Before considering the wider aspects of this effort, another facet of the Holinshed censorship and revision, that relating to Mary, Queen of Scots, and the Babington conspiracy, tells us more about the audience the censors envisioned. On 8 February 1587, one week after the initial censorship order, Mary, Queen of Scots, was secretly executed at Fotheringay. By 17 February, clearly seeking damage control, Burghley prepared a memo for immediate distribution justifying state action. On 18 February, the Earl of Arundel approached the Spanish ambassador in Paris to inform him officially of Mary's execution. On 27 February, a licence for a ballad entitled 'An Excellent Dyttye Made As a Generall Rejoycinge for the Cutting of the Scottishe Queene' was entered in the Stationers' Register, suggesting that it took from eighteen to twenty days for Mary's death to become common knowledge in London. These events contributed to the second effort to censor and revise the *Chronicles*. Prior to all this, in wrestling with the advisability of Mary's execution, Burghley's strongest argument against it was 'the offence that hir friends will conceive shall provoque them'.[16] The cancels that appeared following this final stage of censorship, while they do not rescind any material relating to Mary's trial, render far less provocative the account of her co-conspirators' experience of English justice.

Although the facts of the Babington conspiracy and the conspirators' trial and execution survived censorship, the account's style is radically altered – as the fairly objective passage from the cancel shows.

> [O]rder was taken for a verie strict inquirie and search universallie to be made for their apprehension, which was accordinglie executed, in so much that the conspirators distressed and succorless were put to verie hard shifts by this inquisition and pursute, and in tine apprehended, to the great rejoicing of the citizens of London.[17]

This replaces a two-column folio page recounting every step in the public officers' relentless pursuit of the conspirators.[18] Similarly, the cancel characterises the conspirators' encounter with the law as an orderly process and executions as merely 'judgement':

> After due examination had, & no rigor used either by torture or torment, the wicked wretches guiltie consciences driving them to voluntarie confession . . . Seven of them appeared at Westminster on the thirteenth daie of September, who all pleaded giltie, and therefore had no jurie, but were condemned, and had judgement on the next morrow.[19]

The original text implied that the confessions resulted from torture ('some rigor used') and described the executions in shocking detail: 'Now when these venemous vipers were thus hewne in peeces, their tigers hearts burned in the fire, and the sentence of law satisfied: their heads and quarters were conveied awaie in baskets, to be fixed upon poles and set over the gates of London.'[20] The uncensored report, which vilifies the conspirators and shows public support to be squarely behind the government's actions, employs strategies more like what might be expected of government propaganda than that in the cancels. Indeed, in their initial review of the text, the government's appointed censors had made no objections. What had been acceptable before Mary's execution became objectionable afterwards, but to whom?

Since Fleming's Protestant enthusiasm and anti-Catholic rhetoric were the objects of censorship, concern for England's Protestant population seem unlikely. Instead, Burghley's apprehension about executing Mary points to government fear not simply that her execution might offend her friends, but that they might 'conceive' of the offence as some sort of provocation. The Catholic question for Elizabeth's ministers was never simply a matter of religious belief or resistance to the Elizabethan religious settlement, nor was it just the shadow the Northern Rebellion cast; it involved instead foreign threats and foreign alliances: Spain, France, even Scotland. As loath as Elizabeth may have been to have her people regard their system of justice as unfair, coercive or even, as Fleming's narrative had suggested, doggedly ruthless in its pursuit of offenders, the risk of rebellion an account like Fleming's might provoke paled next to the risk inherent in provoking Mary's powerful Catholic 'friends'.

The censorship and revision of Holinshed's *Chronicles,* although a singular event (I know of no other text similarly censored and revised), reveal that Elizabethan censorship and propaganda was far less concerned with disobedience and disorder than has been thought. Indeed, the censors ignored tales of rebellion and usurpation rife in the *Chronicles.* The *Chronicles*' censorship and revision occurred in a particularly fraught historical moment when the government, instead of simply suppressing the book, instigated changes that it hoped would calm international diplomatic waters. Whether it did so by outright falsehood is another question. The answer lies in a particularly vexed area of historical assessment. Deciding whether, indeed, Catholic priests (or Mary, Queen of Scots) died as martyrs for their faith or were justly prosecuted under the ancient law of England lies beyond this study. For the purpose of understanding Elizabethan censorship and propaganda, recognising that the Catholic question seriously exercised Elizabethan government suffices. Exorcising the demon of Catholic political action served as censorship's predominant end and propaganda's central focus.

INSTRUMENTS OF CONTROL AND PROPAGATION

The law courts represented the principal venue for rooting out genuinely offensive texts. On some occasions, the writing that incited prosecution also elicited a government effort to counteract it – usually through a royal proclamation. Two grounds existed for prosecuting cases involving the written word: treason and seditious libel. The law of treason was statutory and included writing, printing or publishing (disseminating) anything that denied the monarch's authority or supremacy (jurisdiction over the ecclesiastical state). Such prosecutions, although infrequent, did occur. John Copping and Elias Thacker, followers of the Separatist Robert Browne were tried and executed in 1583 for denying the Queen's supremacy in matters of religion. Since, according to papal bull, Elizabeth was a heretic who had no rightful claim to authority over the Church, authors and printers of Catholic texts that charged the Queen with heresy also could be prosecuted under the treason statutes. One such case occurred in 1584 when William Carter was tried, convicted and executed for treason for printing Gregory Martin's *A Treatise of Schism,* a book that openly charged the English Church with heresy and covertly suggested that if Catholic women followed Judith's example, 'they might destroye Holofernes, the master heritike . . . and never defile their religion.'[21]

Prosecutions for seditious libel were more complicated. Slander and libel came within the jurisdiction of both canon and common law. When either offence was directed at a person of importance, be it lord, bishop or judge, the offence came within the statutory definition of *scandalum magnatum,* which, although it did not criminalise spreading rumours about the nobility, stressed the danger false rumour posed to the government by dividing the king from his people or from powerful landholders. Tudor treason statutes, extending this principle to crimes against the English crown (including, in the case of Mary, to the Queen's husband), established that libelling or slandering the monarch was an act of seditious libel because it alienated the monarch from his or her people. In 1579, John Stubbs was prosecuted in the court of Queen's Bench under the Marian treason statute for writing *The Discovery of a Gaping Gulf,* a book that libelled the Queen's suitor (the Duc d'Anjou) and his family. In 1582, Stephen Vallenger was tried in the court of Star Chamber for seditious libel. The authorities had found in his possession a copy of *A True Report of the Death and Martyrdome of M. Campion Jesuite and Priest.* While the recusant Thomas Alfield wrote the pamphlet, at the trial Vallenger admitted to authoring one of the libellous poems the book included – the poem referred to in the passage censored from Holinshed's *Chronicles* that celebrated Campion as a martyr. The government responded to Stubbs's *The Discovery of a Gaping Gulf,* to Robert Browne's books, and to the proliferation of texts celebrating Campion's martyrdom and criticising Elizabeth's government by issuing royal proclamations stating the government's objections to the books' contents and calling upon the Queen's 'loving subjects' to deliver the books to the authorities. Issuing proclamations for matters prosecuted in the courts underscores the usefulness of proclamations as propaganda tools.

As administrative tools, royal proclamations were only as effective as their own provisions made them. In the matter of censorship, declaring a book's dangers and calling for subjects to surrender their copies to authorities rarely removed books from circulation, especially when they were printed abroad and circulated surreptitiously. We know, for example, that *Leicester's Commonwealth* was widely read and even though suppressed by proclamation, was still readily available a year later. According to Paul L. Hughes and James F. Larkin, Tudor proclamations adopted rhetorical strategies to persuade their audiences to assent to the proclamation's specific demands. This assessment, however astute, really does not apply to Elizabeth's proclamations that perform the routine acts of cancelling law-court terms, setting wages, regulating imports and exports, prescribing appropriate apparel or requiring abstinence from meat. While these may construct appropriate images of the Queen for the task at hand – well advised on economic issues, considerate of the customs of the Church, worried about extravagant dress – they are rarely 'gauged' to the audience's particular psychology. Proclamations, however, that concern extraordinary events employed a variety of persuasive devices to sway their audiences. Sometimes they contained carefully reasoned argument and measured language; other times, they employed highly polarised language to recount only one perspective. With only a few exceptions, the extraordinary events that elicit the propagandistic proclamations involve some aspect of Catholic political action. Among these are several proclamations that censor Catholic writing.

Elizabeth issued eleven censorship proclamations: six directed at Catholic texts, four at radical Protestant publications, and one at a political libel (*The Discovery of a Gaping Gulf*). Proclamations against publications related to the Family of Love, along with those noted above against the Brownists, eschew flagrantly propagandistic rhetoric, although they readily condemned the sects. The same may be said of the proclamation against *An Admonition to Parliament* (1572), which censors it, and another book, defending the action only as an afterthought to expressing 'her highness' indignations' at those who do not conduct religious services according to the Book of Common Prayer.[22] The proclamation against the Marprelate tracts exercises far less restraint. Even so, its attack on puritanism, implicit in its characterisation of the tracts' aim to 'persuade and bring in a monstrous and apparent dangerous innovation within her [the Queen's] dominions and countries in all manner ecclesiastical government' is remarkably moderate. It appeals to the continuity of the religious settlement 'established by law and so quietly of long time continued'. Marprelate's 'rash and malicious purpose . . . to dissolve the estate of the prelacy' and his effort to 'make a dangerous change in the form and doctrine and the use of divine service' are characterised as 'lewd and seditious practices' tending 'to the manifest willful breach of a great number of good laws and statutes of this realm, inconveniences nothing regarded by such innovations'.[23] By framing puritan innovations as unmindful of the 'inconveniences' and by emphasising the laws and statutes, the proclamation distances itself from Marprelate's polarising rhetoric. Such a tactic betrays the proclamation's real end: consolidating the middle ground of public opinion. This proclamation, of course, represented only a fraction of the Bishop of London's propaganda effort against Marprelate that employed professional writers such as Thomas Nashe, John Lyly and Anthony Munday to write anti-Martinist pamphlets and plays.

The six proclamations against Catholic texts exercise far less rhetorical restraint. Except for the 1569 proclamation calling upon Elizabeth's subjects to 'forbear utterly from the use and dealing' in Catholic books written in response to Bishop

Jewel's challenge, these respond to Catholic political propaganda. None of the proclamations named specific titles, although they all characterised the authors as 'obstinate and irrepentant traitors' and described the texts as nothing less than 'calumniations' against the Queen, her ministers and her government, seeking her overthrow so that the Catholic religion could return. In short, all of these proclamations make the same case that Burghley made in *The Execution of Justice,* that the Pope and his agents caused all unrest and rebellion in England, and that their actions, while pretending only to restore Catholic religion, sought to do so by overthrowing Elizabeth's government. Unlike the proclamations addressing separatist or puritan books, the proclamations against Catholic texts employ language that purposefully seeks to polarise. On one side stands England, a place of 'loving subjects' universally constant and obedient 'within the bond of common peace', content in their happy government and blessed by God. On the other stand her enemies: 'despisers of God's true religion', both 'disloyal, rebellious, and traitorous subjects of this realm' and 'Jesuits and seminary priests' sent by the Pope – 'by whom and their adherents sundry false, slanderous, and seditious rumors and reports tending wholly to move the people's hearts to discontentment and offense have been commonly bruited and given out'.[24] Like the Catholic books they opposed, these proclamations relied upon a construction of deviant otherness by which England's normative and idealised self could be defined.

While Catholic books provided occasions when proclamations employed polarisation as a means of persuasion, other proclamations still related to the Catholic question introduced other techniques. Leah Marcus has noted Elizabeth's use of epithets in proclamations' formulaic openings to construct for herself a second male identity as a prince rather than a princess. Such a strategy, I have found, appears primarily in proclamations that envision an international as well as a domestic audience. For example, a 1597 proclamation ordering that peace be kept on Scottish borders refers to a similar order published 'by our good brother the King of Scots' and extols the proceedings 'between us, the two princes'.[25] The proclamation's purpose, while calling upon the English to keep the peace, appears more interested in cementing English–Scottish relations. A 1591 proclamation prohibiting trade with Spain does so by similar royal authority 'as in a princely providence we are bound to do'.[26] A 1597 proclamation that essentially authorises English piracy against ships carrying munitions or victuals to Spain refers to 'the Queen's majesty being amongst other princes'. The proclamation justifies seizing Spanish goods on the grounds that 'it is lawful for her being a monarch and prince sovereign' and that it is a recourse such 'as other kings have always in like cases used'.[27] Except for the one that, for all practical purposes, legalised piracy against Spain, these proclamations employed the rare device of having the proclamation speak in the first person, rendering the proclamations' demands both immediate and authoritative.

The effectiveness of the royal first person as a propaganda device may be seen in a 1591 proclamation prohibiting trade with Spain. Written three years after the Spanish Armada, this proclamation fully exploits the English victory as a sign of God's persistent favour: 'Forasmuch as it is manifestly seen to all the world how it hath pleased Almighty God of his most singular favor to have taken this our realm into his special protection these many years.'[28] Elizabeth's God-given responsibility rests in protecting her subjects 'in the profession of his holy gospel' and defending her 'realms and dominions' against the open wars of her Catholic enemies. Furthermore, God having called upon her diligently to assure by 'all good, politic, and lawful means', she has assured that her enemies were not strengthened by the aid of food and other provisions for war. She has been so effective in this that only one enemy remains, Spain, with whom she has sought a diplomatic solution, but the King of Spain has refused. England, thus, must be in constant readiness, although – 'blessed by God's singular favor with the plenty of corn and all other victual, and with furniture of sundry kinds of munition meet for the sustentation and defense of our own people' – such readiness is not a problem. Spain, however, lacking 'of such kind of victual, specially of corn and munition for the war', must resort to trade. In light of that, the proclamation prohibits anyone residing in Elizabeth's realms from trading with Spain. The proclamation's language and aims are inordinately elevated for simply restricting trade. Other proclamations related to trade with foreign states other than Spain made straightforward demands on English subjects. In the 1591 proclamation, burnishing England's image takes precedence to declaring the Spanish trade embargo.

Only a month after introducing the embargo, another propagandistic proclamation appeared, again employing the royal first person. This one established a commission against seminary priests and Jesuits and took full advantage of the occasion to extend the work done in the trade embargo proclamation by declaiming further against Spain. It begins:

> Although we have had probably cause to have thought that now towards the end of 33 years, being the time wherein Almighty God hath continually preserved us in a peaceable possession of our kingdoms, the former violence and rigor of the malice of our enemies, specially of the King of Spain, would, after his continuance in seeking to trouble our state without any just cause so many years, have waxed faint and decayed in him and all others depending on him.[29]

The current problems are, first, that Spain has begun 'a most unjust and dangerous war for all Christendom against the present French King'; second, that the king of Spain has 'procured . . . a vassal of his own, to be exalted into the papacy', a man who will make war against France; third, that Spain is preparing a force against England and fostering treason in young men bringing papal bulls 'pretending to promise heaven to such as will yield, and some of cursings threatening damnation and hell to such as shall not yield to their persuasions'. The proclamation says England has previously known such practices and those perpetrators were 'impeached by direct execution of laws against traitors for mere treasons, and not for any points of religion as their fautors would color falsely their actions'. After forcefully reiterating that 'none do suffer death for matter of religion', the proclamation turns to the subject at hand. Jesuits and seminarians are boasting to the Spanish king that if next year he were to invade England, he would find 'many thousands . . . of able people that will be ready to assist such power as he shall set on land'. To counter all these threats, the proclamation announces England's course of action: requiring the ecclesiastical state's diligence to 'retain our people steadfastly in the profession of the gospel', asking all people 'with their hands, purses, and advices', as well as their prayers, to defend their country against 'ravening strangers, willful destroyers of their native country, and monstrous traitors', and establishing commissions 'in every shire, city, and port towns' to discover anyone persuading obedience to the Pope or King of Spain. Since these 'venomous vipers' are 'by common experience' known to come in disguise, not only should anyone who has arrived within the last year be interrogated, but a general investigation for strangers should be made.[30] Dated the same day, a second proclamation specifies the questions that should be asked of suspects.

The argument of these anti-Spanish, anti-Jesuit, anti-seminary-priest proclamations differs little from the five proclamations that censor Catholic books: the Pope and his agents by sundry means treasonously threaten England's peace, and although God's favour and goodness and the Queen's just rule have preserved the nation, English law justifies acting against the traitors to preserve the State. These proclamations invoke God to justify the government's actions and blatantly vilify the enemy; in short, they engage in the kind of polarising discourse that properly (or improperly) belongs to propaganda. These are also the proclamations rendering the Queen's voice most immediate and envisioning her princely power most clearly.

MARY, QUEEN OF SCOTS: SHIFTING THE STRATEGY

One proclamation addressing the Catholic question which is uniquely moderate is that on 4 December 1586 declaring Mary, Queen of Scots' treason sentence. Like other proclamations concerning Catholic political practices, this one is very long and employs multiple explanatory clauses before coming to its purpose. Also, like many of those, Queen Elizabeth's voice is immediate. The proclamation blames the conspiracy on 'divers . . . wicked persons' – but not Mary. With regard to her, it expresses chagrin:

> in very truth we were greatly and deeply grieved in our mind to think or imagine that any such unnatural and monstrous acts should be either devised or willingly assented unto against us by her, being a princess born, and of our sex and blood, and one also whose life and honor we had many times before saved and preserved.[31]

Despite convincing evidence, confessions, a commission's findings and 'great deliberation', Elizabeth resisted declaring the sentence determined by parliament that Mary 'had compassed and imagined . . . divers things tending to the hurt, death, and destruction of our royal person, contrary to the form of the said statute'. She now assents, she maintains, only because she is finally persuaded that 'without the publication and due execution of the said sentence' no means exist to protect 'the surety of our royal person' and to preserve parliament and the realm.[32] In its verbal restraint, its precise invocation of law and procedure, and its personification of Elizabeth, this represents a masterpiece of persuasion.

The proclamation was only one of many efforts to influence opinion on Mary's sentence. We have already seen how censorship and revision brought greater gravity and decorum to Holinshed's *Chronicles*' account of the Babington conspiracy.

In addition, in 1586, the Queen's printer issued *The Copie of a Letter to the Right Honourable the Earle of Leycester,* imprinted with the Queen's arms, which begins with a letter to Leicester, a little over two pages long, explaining that the author has finally found the proper occasion to 'testifie' his 'duetifull reverence' by reporting speeches delivered to Elizabeth 'in a late weightie cause dealt in this Parliament'. The letter, written by Robert Cecil, is signed 'R.C.' Neither the letter nor the title page indicates that the weighty cause is Mary, Queen of Scots, but the publication contains a brief of the Lord Chancellor's speech upon delivering Parliament's petition asking Elizabeth to publish Mary's sentence; an extract of the Speaker of the House's speech to Parliament 'containing divers apparent and imminent dangers, that may grow to her Maiesties most Royal person, and to her Realme from the Scottish Queene and her Adherent'; a report of Elizabeth's answer to Parliament deferring her answer; the report of a second meeting between Elizabeth and the Lord Chancellor where he describes Parliament's unsuccessful effort to find a way both to save Mary's life and to preserve Elizabeth and her realm; an extract of the Speaker's speech on the second occasion; and Elizabeth's second answer, or as she deemed it, her 'answere without answere'.

This pamphlet testifies to the great deliberation referred to in the sentencing proclamation between Parliament and Elizabeth. Parliament saw Mary's death as necessary because 'she is the foundation whereon all the evill disposed do build, she is the roote from whence all rebellions and treacheries to spring.' Elizabeth experienced conflict between her 'great griefe . . . that such a one of State and kin, should neede so open a declaration' and Parliament's 'so provident and careful' counsels for the safety of her life. In his letter, Cecil betrayed the publication's purpose: it would allow Leicester (and all the pamphlet's readers) to 'admire the rare perfections' of the Queen's 'mind and approved Judgement . . . worthie of eternal monument and everlasting memorie'. Like the proclamation, this pamphlet immortalises both Elizabeth's grief at having to condemn Mary and her judicious rule over a realm governed by law.[33]

Unlike other examples of Elizabethan propaganda, we have some measure of how effective the propaganda portraying Elizabeth's reluctance to judge Mary was. In *The Faerie Queen's* thinly veiled allegory, Edmund Spenser re-enacts Mary's trial. At the trial's conclusion, Mercilla's (Elizabeth's) actions virtually dramatise the pamphlet and proclamation.

> Though plaine she saw by all, that she did heare,
> That she of death was guiltie found by right.
> Yet would not let iust vengeance on her light
> But rather let instead thereof to fall
> Few perling draps from her faire lampes of light;
> The which she couering with the purple pall
> Would haue the passion hid, and vp arose withall.[34]

Mercilla's role here is not to judge but to uphold the rule of law, despite considerable personal pain – precisely the proclamation's point. That Elizabeth's role in Mary's condemnation and execution still elicits historical controversy further witnesses the propaganda's effectiveness.

PROPAGANDA AND RULE

Like many other occasions when propaganda and censorship coincided, the government sought more to influence international opinion on Mary's condemnation than to elicit a response from English subjects. (The one exception to this was the Marprelate affair.) At stake was the world's judgement on whether actions Elizabeth took to protect England – from censoring books to allowing piracy to publishing sentence against a foreign national – were legitimate responses to what Elizabeth's ministers regarded as Catholic treason – the efforts of the Pope, the King of Spain, priests, Jesuits and controversialists to re-establish Catholicism in England by overthrowing Queen Elizabeth. Sometimes, however, censorship and propaganda did not coincide. No government effort was made to counter John Hayward's *The First Part of the Life and Raigne of King Henrie IIII* or to explain why it was suppressed or why the Bishop of London banned several satires in 1599. Propaganda unrelated to censored texts also existed, but much of this was unofficial and, indeed, may not have been 'official' propaganda at all. Writers such as Thomas Churchyard, Anthony Munday, Edward Hake and James Aske praised Elizabeth and her chief ministers (including the Earls of Leicester and Essex), recounted English brilliance in war and foreign affairs and, consistent with official propaganda, berated traitors and criminals. These, however, were not really propaganda, since, like Anglo's 'Cartloads of emblematic flowers' they participated in the 'panoply of panegyric . . . aimed upward to please the monarch'. The 'real' Elizabethan propaganda effort – one widely propagated and committed to persuading – was not directed 'downward' from monarch to subjects. Instead, it was propagated outward across international borders. Furthermore, it did not necessarily sacrifice truth to present one side of an issue. Instead, it usually entered into a conversation, real or imagined, with an opponent and marshalled evidence, often historical, it deemed authentic. Effectively assessing Elizabethan propaganda, then, requires discerning the presence of the opposite side's argument and how the propaganda responds to it.

One of the earliest full-fledged propaganda efforts is particularly instructive on this account – that which appeared from the pen of Thomas Norton, MP, in 1569 and 1570, and probably initiated what would become the war between Catholic and English propagandists. The earliest of these, *To the Queenes Maiesties Poore Deceiued Subiectes of the Northe Contreye* (1569), characterised the Northern Rebellion as serving 'the turne of our forrein enemies' who have 'traitorously corrupted' the English 'misleaders'.[35] In 1570, *A Bull Graunted by the Pope to Doctor Harding* prints a papal bull offering reconciliation to English Catholics, along with a form of absolution in Latin and English. Norton explained that, rather than reconciliation, the bull's true intention was to foster rebellion. The bull, according to Norton, declared that English Catholics must perform 'perfect penance' and 'for amendes they must enter into actuall rebellion, and that is the naturall Satisfaction to the sea of Rome, wherby the Queene and realme are encombred'.[36] That the bull had circulated three years earlier evidences, Norton alleges, its responsibility for the Northern Rebellion. While Norton did not write these pamphlets in reply to censored texts, their rhetorical strategies establish a precedent for later propaganda that did. Like books of religious controversy, Norton's pamphlets repeat in their entirety the positions taken by the opposition – in the first case, rebel leaders' claims against the English government; in the second, the bull and form of absolution – and reply to them. Norton's propaganda thus participates in a two-way conversation just as later propaganda that responded to censored texts would. Censorship, although intended to suppress unacceptable texts, rarely removed them from circulation. Propaganda sought to remedy this by providing the alternative and official perspective on whatever objectionable positions the censored texts voiced. One-sided, intent on persuading, and widely published, these official responses seem to possess the attributes we commonly associate with totalitarian regimes, but instead they participated in a two-sided conversation in which each side was heavily invested in the truth of their position.

This returns us to the question of whether or not Elizabethan propaganda, like modern propaganda, persuaded by lying and appealing to people's fears and prejudices. If the people of Elizabethan England feared political disorder and war, the Queen's death, or Protestantism's destruction, then the answer to the latter part of the question is, indeed, yes. The matter of lies is vastly more complicated. Neither Elizabeth's regime's censorship nor its propaganda would credit as true the claim Catholics relentlessly advanced: that they were prosecuted for their religion and not for crimes against the State. As for the matter of Elizabeth's regime 'ruling' through the propagandistic 'cult of Elizabeth', that much of what constitutes this cult is directed upwards to the Queen rather than downwards to subjects seriously challenges this. Furthermore, remarkably little printed propaganda was directed at Elizabeth's subjects. Proclamations and pamphlets exist that offered rationales for government action, but they possess few of the strategies commonly associated with propaganda. Indeed, propagandistic proclamations account for less than 5 per cent of the whole. With the exception of the government's response to Martin Marprelate, the significant propaganda efforts – those often associated with censorship – address an international audience and seek to shore up Elizabeth's relationship with other European powers. In high politics such as these, 'ruling' by propaganda (and censorship) would have been impossible, but propaganda and censorship could fashion Elizabeth as a fellow prince whose authority, embodied in her ambassadors and their diplomatic missions, could not be slighted.

FURTHER READING

Anglo, Sydney, *Images of Tudor Kingship* (London, 1992).

Clegg, Cyndia Susan, *Press Censorship in Elizabethan England* (Cambridge, 1997).

Cooper, John P. D., *Propaganda and the Tudor State* (Oxford, 2003).

Grave, Michael A. R., *William Cecil, Lord Burghley* (London and New York, 1998).

Haigh, Christopher, *Elizabeth I* (London and New York, 1988).

Hamilton, Donna B., *Anthony Munday and the Catholics, 1560–1637* (Aldershot, 2005).

Lander, Jesse M., *Inventing Polemic: Religion, Print, and Literary Culture in Early Modern England* (Cambridge, 2006).

MacCaffrey, Wallace, *Queen Elizabeth and the Making of Policy, 1572–1588* (Princeton, NJ, 1968).

Marcus, Leah, *Puzzling Shakespeare: Local Reading and Its Discontents* (Berkeley, Calif., 1988).

Mears, Natalie, *Queenship and Political Discourse in the Elizabethan Realm* (Cambridge, 2005).

Milward, Peter, *Religious Controversies of the Elizabethan Age* (London, 1977).
Sharpe, Kevin, *Selling the Tudor Monarchy: Authority and Image in Sixteenth-Century England* (New Haven, Conn., 2009).
Shuger, Debora, *Censorship and Cultural Sensibility* (Philadelphia, Pa., 2007).
Strong, Roy, *The Cult of Elizabeth* (Berkeley, Calif., 1977).
Whitehead, Bertrand, *Brags and Boasts: Propaganda in the Year of the Armada* (Stroud, 1994).
Wilson, E. C., *England's Eliza* (Cambridge, Mass., 1939).
Yates, Frances, *Astraea: The Imperial Theme in the Sixteenth Century* (London and Boston, Mass., 1975).

NOTES

1 Gordon Zeeveld, 'Richard Morison, Official Apologist for Henry VIII', *Publications of the Modern Language Association of America,* 55 (2) (1940): 406–25; p. 43. Lily B. Campbell, *Shakespeare's 'Histories': Mirrors of Elizabethan Policy* (San Marino, Calif., 1947), p. 67.
2 John P. D. Cooper, *Propaganda and the Tudor State* (Oxford, 2003), p. 210.
3 Christopher Haigh, *Elizabeth I* (London and New York, 1988), p. 7.
4 G. R. Elton, 'Tudor Government: The Points of Contact – The Court', *Transactions of the Royal Historical Society,* Series 5 (26) (1975): 211–19; p. 219.
5 Sydney Anglo, *Images of Tudor Kingship* (London, 1992), pp. 3, 46, 107, 125–8.
6 Anglo, *Images of Tudor Kingship,* p. 120.
7 Fredrick Siebert, *Freedom of the Press in England, 1476–1776* (Urbana, Ill., 1952), p. 13.
8 Deborah Shuger, *Censorship and Cultural Sensibility* (Philadelphia, Pa., 2006), p. 29.
9 The royal printing patent for all dictionaries and chronicles was granted to Bynneman on 28 April 1580: *Calendar of the Patent Rolls Preserved in the Public Record Office, Elizabeth I* (London: HM Stationery Office, 1929), vol. 8, no. 1594.
10 *Calendar of the Patent Rolls, Elizabeth,* vol. II, pp. 331–2.
11 For a fuller discussion of the conditions of publication as well as the censorship of Holinshed's *Chronicles,* see Cyndia Susan Clegg (ed.), *The Peaceable and Prosperous Regiment of Blessed Queene Elisabeth* (San Marino, Calif., 2005), Introduction.
12 *Acts of the Privy Council,* vol. XIV, p. 311.
13 Holinshed, 1587, p. 1329, sigs. A32–43; uncensored.
14 Holinshed, 1587, p. 1329, sigs. A55–9; uncensored.
15 Holinshed, 1587, p. 1322.
16 *HMC Salisbury,* vol. 3, No. 435.
17 'Tine' probably means 'time'. I depend here on the cancel in the Huntington Library's Bridgewater copy.
18 Holinshed (1587), p. 1553, sigs. A73–B6; (cancelled text). Huntington Library's Bridgewater copy.
19 Holinshed (1587), p. 1563, sigs. B27–1565 B45 (uncensored). Huntington Library, Book Club of California fragment.
20 Holinshed (1587), p. 1555, sig. A61 (cancelled text). Huntington Library's Bridgewater copy.
21 Holinshed (1587), p. 1574, sigs. A22–6 (uncensored). Huntington Library, Book Club of California fragment.
22 Gregory Martin, *A Treatise of Schisme* (London, 1978), D2r. I consider this fully in *Press Censorship in Elizabethan England* (Cambridge, 1997), pp. 93–5.
23 Paul L. Hughes and James F. Larkin, *Tudor Royal Proclamations* (New Haven, Conn., 1969), vol. II, pp. 375–6.
24 Hughes and Larkin, *Tudor Royal Proclamations,* vol. III, pp. 34–5.
25 Hughes and Larkin, *Tudor Royal Proclamations,* vol. III, p. 14.

26 Hughes and Larkin, *Tudor Royal Proclamations*, vol. III, p. 181.
27 Hughes and Larkin, *Tudor Royal Proclamations*, vol. III, p. 84.
28 Hughes and Larkin, *Tudor Royal Proclamations*, vol. III, p. 185.
29 Hughes and Larkin, *Tudor Royal Proclamations*, vol. III, p. 83.
30 Hughes and Larkin, *Tudor Royal Proclamations*, vol. III, p. 86.
31 Hughes and Larkin, *Tudor Royal Proclamations*, vol. III, pp. 89, 91–1.
32 Hughes and Larkin, *Tudor Royal Proclamations*, vol. II, p. 528.
33 Hughes and Larkin, *Tudor Royal Proclamations*, vol. II, pp. 530–2.
34 R[obert] C[ecil], *The Copie of a Letter to the Right Honourable the Earle of Leycester* ... (London, 1586), sigs. Aiiiv; Eiii; Eiiv, Aiiiv.
35 Edmund Spenser, *The Faerie Queene*, ed. A. C. Hamilton (London and New York: Longmans, 1977), Book 5, Canto 9, Stanza 50, lines 3–9.
36 Thomas Norton, *To the Queenes Maiesties Poore Deceiued Subiectes of the Northe Contreye, Drawne into Rebellion by the Earles of Northumberland and Westmerland* (London, 1569), sig. A4v.
37 Thomas Norton, *A Bull Graunted by the Pope to Doctor Harding & Others* (London, 1570), sig. B2.

CHAPTER ELEVEN

IRELAND
Security and conquest

David Edwards

When Elizabeth I succeeded her half-sister Mary as Queen of England in November 1558, she inherited a number of problems that would seriously test her ability to govern. War abroad, with France and Scotland, and economic recession at home are usually recognised as her main challenges. Not the least of her difficulties, however, was the mounting unrest and bloodshed afflicting her other kingdom, Ireland, and the spiralling cost of trying to control it. The trouble was that Ireland was quite unlike England. A kingdom more in name than reality, even in 1558 it retained many of the characteristics of a barely incorporated colony, with the majority of the population speaking Irish, not English, and following their own laws and customs under the rule of autonomous dynastic lords.

Since the middle of her father's reign, essentially to negate papal rights over Irish sovereignty, the Crown had been energetically pursuing a more direct form of rule there than it had previously enjoyed. Towards this end, in 1541, the parliament in Dublin (the English colonial capital) had passed 'The Act for Kingly Title'. Highly aspirational, this had declared all the inhabitants of Ireland – the Gaelic population, as well as those of English origin, the 'Anglo-Irish' – to be a single community of subjects under the Crown of England, governed by English law and institutions. At first, efforts to give actuality to this new Tudor kingdom had proceeded through political persuasion, treaty-making and a commitment to anglicise the country by extending a fully English legal framework across it. But progress had been slow. Crown officials had soon grown impatient, and policy had become markedly more coercive. The small permanent army first introduced in 1534 had quadrupled in size by the 1550s, averaging approximately 2,000 troops per annum across the decade. Moved as much by what it perceived as the recalcitrance of many Irish lords as by the prospect of Franco-Scottish interference, by the time of Elizabeth's accession the government was committed to conquering large parts of its kingdom in order not only to impose anglicisation, or 'English civility', but also to uphold the monarchy and to make kingship rest on subjection instead of rhetoric.

AN INHERITED WAR

Even as Elizabeth waited at Hatfield for news of Mary's death, the royal army had just returned to Dublin from its second amphibious invasion of east Ulster in less than a month – and this barely four months after it had been employed in a major expedition westwards, traversing bogland and forest, into the midlands, north Munster and across the river Shannon into Connacht.[1] Significantly, the approach of winter saw a scaling down, but not an end, of military operations. Probably the first letter that Elizabeth received from Ireland as monarch came from a combat zone in another part of the country, south Leinster, written in the provincial stronghold of Leighlin Castle by the English Viceroy, the Earl of Sussex, as he staged a demonstration of royal might designed to intimidate the Gaelic chieftains of the area and to dissuade them from commencing a new rebellion. The letter (addressed not to Elizabeth but to her predecessor, having been dashed off in the last days of Mary's life) is full of soldierly concerns such as the difficulties of terrain and the unfitness of the troops, but for the new queen its most striking feature would have been its confident anticipation of further campaigns to come.[2] Evidently, for all the Viceroy's charging about, his declared intention of accelerating the acceptance of royal authority and English customs through a programme of regional conquest was some way short of 'mission accomplished'.

Indeed, the situation was rapidly deteriorating. According to other reports, central and eastern Ulster, the midlands and the borders of the English Pale were devastated. Thousands were dead, and dearth and famine was widespread, a direct consequence of the scorched-earth tactics employed by both government and insurgent forces. Sussex tried to mask the strength of the resistance he was encountering, but the Irish way of fighting – guerrilla warfare – was proving embarrassingly effective. Even as he boasted of the success of an attack on Scots-Gaelic elements in faraway Antrim, he had to report the loss of an important border castle close to Dublin, in Westmeath, 'partly by treason and partly by the negligence of them that had the charge'.[3] Conditions were similarly less than secure along Ireland's western Atlantic seaboard, as the government's principal Gaelic ally, Connor, Earl of Thomond, was only a puppet ruler with a powerful enemy and limited local support. Most dangerous of all, however, was Shane O'Neill. Once a friend of the Crown, he was now its principal enemy, having been mishandled (and underestimated) by successive administrations. Already Shane had outwitted two major expeditions led against him, at huge expense, by Sussex. The need to reduce him was growing urgent. Besides threatening to destroy the government's hard-won influence in Ulster, his existence as a bulwark of Gaelic defiance and aristocratic autonomy was daring others to imitate him, and it seemed only a matter of time before France and the French party in Scotland would seek to utilise him in a second front in the war with England. (Such fears were well founded, for about this time a senior French minister advised François II of the potential helpfulness of 'le Grand O Neal le premier dudit royaume'.)[4]

And so it was that from the very onset of Elizabeth's reign Ireland appeared much as it would seem for the rest of her rule: partly beyond government control, its lords, if provoked, able to mount annoyingly effective resistance that tested England's financial and military strength and discomfited the regime internationally.

This is not to say that Ireland in 1558 constituted an entirely negative inheritance. Sizeable parts of it were actually easy to govern. The 'English Pale' covered an area stretching along the eastern coastline from Carlingford Lough southwards to Bray Head, and inland from Athboy, County Meath, to Athy, County Kildare. The most prosperous and densely settled region of the country, the bulk of its people were descended from medieval English colonists and, despite strong and growing ties with Gaelic society, remained largely anglophile in their political and cultural orientation. Ever since the dissolution of the monasteries (1536–42), from which they had derived great benefit, the Pale nobility and gentry had readily acquiesced in the reimposition of direct rule from Whitehall, and their willingness to provide military support in the form of a 'general hosting' or 'rising out' had been a major factor in encouraging the Crown to pursue its goals more forcefully. In truth, the renascence of royal power had excited many Palesmen. Besides the prospect of gaining territory beyond their borders by participating in the government's advance, they also hoped – nay, expected – to play a leading role in the management of the extended royal polity, and to do so as *equal partners* with English-born officials who were arriving in the country in growing numbers. Other areas were equally dependable. In the south-east, the inhabitants of Counties Wexford, Waterford, Kilkenny and part of Tipperary were particularly supportive of the monarchy, forming a 'Second Pale'. Similarly well inclined were the southern and western coastal towns of Cork, Kinsale, Limerick and Galway and the communities of their hinterlands, not to mention a number of biddable Gaelic dynasties scattered around the country whose leaders figured friendship with the Crown might strengthen their regional standing. For all these advantages, however, in November 1558 the prevailing mood in government remained one of caution and uncertainty.

DETERMINING POLICY

To forsake or maintain the policy of conquest: that was one key question confronting Elizabeth. To replace or reappoint Sussex as viceroy: that was another. For well over a year, criticism of Sussex's conduct had been spreading through Whitehall. The premier lord in the Pale, the recently restored Earl of Kildare, had been alienated by Sussex's refusal to grant a full restoration of his earldom; via the efforts of Kildare's English countess, rumours of bias, high-handedness and general misrule in Ireland were soon in circulation at the royal court. The Crown's leading representative in the south-west, the old Earl of Desmond, added his voice, challenging the efficacy of Sussex's soldiering; so too the Archbishop of Armagh, George Dowdall, who laid particular stress on the cruel and unruly behaviour of the Viceroy's officers and the misery suffered by loyal subjects as a result of his poor leadership.[5] Yet, crucially, though they railed at the gaucheness of its implementation, each of these critics supported conquest as an appropriate policy for Ireland. As Dowdall sanctimoniously put it when addressing the English Privy Council, the conquest and colonisation of selected Gaelic territories was 'Truly . . . the most godly way of reformation, and most profitable and commodious to [the Crown] and that poor realm'.[6] All that was needed, it seemed, was better management.

Sussex was perhaps fortunate that in the weeks immediately preceding Elizabeth's accession Desmond and Primate Dowdall both died. Had they lived, his journey to court to defend his record would have been more difficult. The alleged excesses of the army, accused of committing widespread theft, oppression and murder, might have proven especially troublesome to him, as a few years later the Queen was moved to ask questions over quite similar charges made by far less influential persons. As it was, however, the young monarch did require changes which were broadly sympathetic to the wishes of the Earl's critics. Thus, although she decided to retain Sussex as governor, and even to promote him (from Lord Deputy to Lord Lieutenant, with a significantly higher salary), with characteristic equivocation she also partly undermined him by encouraging Kildare to act as a counterweight.

But it was primarily considerations of economy that influenced Elizabeth's initial articulation of Irish policy. Desperate to cut the cost of the wars being fought by the Crown, she ordered Sussex to immediately reduce the royal army by more than a fifth (from 2,400 men in 1558 to 1,900 in 1559) and to seek peace with Shane O'Neill and the Ulster Scots. The Queen's intentions have confused historians, with some contending she was disinclined to conquest, but on balance it seems that instead she was merely hoping to pursue it more gradually, and less expensively. Hence her prioritising the completion of the Laois–Offaly plantation and the conquest of the Gaelic midlands, because it seemed both practicable and comparatively cheap; so too her attitude to Ulster, which she wanted to see colonised and brought under greater English influence, but not until success was more certain. Acknowledging the need to maintain the goodwill of the Anglo-Irish community, besides her support of Kildare she augmented their role on the Irish Privy Council, announcing several new appointments, the most important of which was the naming of Kildare's dynastic rival, the 'Black' Earl of Ormond, as Lord Treasurer and, as such, the most senior member of the council after the Viceroy and Lord Chancellor (Kildare was suitably aggrieved).

Her chief concern in Irish affairs, however, was revealed by her insistence – just as a reform of the coinage was getting under way in England – that Sussex and the Council continue to pay the army with low-grade coin. Given that the burden of devalued money would fall mainly on the recession-affected populations of the Pale and Second Pale, her commitment to cheaper government was hardly consistent with rewarding Anglo-Irish loyalty; on the contrary, it smacked strongly of taking it for granted.

The Queen's support of a limited conquest was bolstered a year later, when (the new coin having been minted) she allowed troop numbers to rise once more, and Sussex was able to resume the assault on central and east Ulster. Hitherto, her ruminations on Irish affairs had given only brief consideration to the security question, but the Viceroy, reinstated, pressed the case powerfully. Despite detesting Ireland, 'which I have often wished to be sunk in the sea', Sussex was convinced that it was necessary to seize military control lest the French or some other 'foreign power' 'set foot therein' and use it as a springboard to bring 'ruin to England' with the help of malevolent local lords; the power of O'Neill and the MacDonnells must needs be eradicated. His views chimed well with other royal advisers. Even when, after 1560, France began sliding into religious civil war, English policy-makers remained wary of foreign interference. Elizabeth's re-establishment of Protestantism as the state religion left England isolated as the main Protestant power in western Europe and seemed to increase the possibility that Ireland, the least Protestant and

Figure 11.1 The Irish loyalist: portrait of Thomas Butler, 10th Earl of Ormonde, 1532–1614. Attributed to Stephen van der Meulen. Photo © National Gallery of Ireland.

least obedient part of her inheritance, would be targeted by external Catholic regimes looking to expose the Queen's tenuous grip on power as a young unmarried female.

Although Sussex proved unable to deliver the sort of security that he had promised, and was eventually replaced in 1565 by Sir Henry Sidney, by prioritising the subjugation of Ulster he had already committed the Crown to a major challenge that would require constant attention for many years. Moreover, his analysis that Ireland was best approached as a security problem, requiring a strong hand and a stronger army, proved highly durable – especially when, following her 1570 excommunication by Pope Pius V, Elizabeth brought Sussex into the inner ring of her ministers at Whitehall and so made it possible for him to influence the framing of Irish policy until his death in 1583. As an increasingly prominent member of the English Privy Council, he was able to reach common ground with fellow councillors, such as Lord Burghley, the Earl of Leicester, Sir Francis Walsingham and Sir James Croft, that Ireland was important enough to England's interests to merit closer, more concentrated attention. All shared a pronounced interest in security issues, and when between them they placed the council's occasional committee on Irish affairs on a semi-permanent basis it was hardly surprising that the government continued to lay especial emphasis on military and security matters in the years ahead.

By and large, therefore, the Irish viceroyalty remained what it had been since the mid-1540s, a military-cum-security position. Each of Sussex's successors was required to act the part of soldier-governor, responsible for the vigorous expansion of the Crown's interests by martial as well as civil means. Some of those that Elizabeth chose for the post, such as the veteran Sir William Drury (Viceroy, 1578–9) or the nobleman Lord Grey de Wilton (1580–2) were soldiers first, administrators second, but even Sir William Fitzwilliam (Acting Governor, 1560, 1561–2, 1568–9; Viceroy, 1571–5, 1588–94), while far happier behind his desk, had extensive military experience and would not have been considered otherwise.

SLOWER CONQUEST, SOARING COST

It will not have gone unnoticed that the pursuit of greater security under soldier-governors diverged from Elizabeth's abiding desire for cheaper government. Invariably equivocal, she never quite settled this contradiction, and instead attempted to reconcile force with economy by condemning those she charged with extending her Irish kingdom to an often torturous struggle with her for sufficient resources to do the job. No viceroy before the 2nd Earl of Essex (1599) and Lord Mountjoy (1600–3) ever had the army he felt he needed, a circumstance which, to some degree, explains why the conquest of hostile outlying areas took as long as it did, with some remaining unconquered and unincorporated even at the Queen's passing in 1603.

And yet, thanks to the security imperative that underpinned Elizabethan Irish policy, the fact remains that the army was maintained at a sufficiently high level to combat native guerrilla resistance and *gradually* to advance a conquest. Even before 1580, when a Continental Catholic invasion seemed imminent, this was the case. Time and again, Elizabeth's efforts to reduce the army were undone, with local uprisings and rumours of foreign interest requiring that fresh levies be raised

Figure 11.2 Garrison government: Carrickfergus Castle.
Image courtesy Northern Ireland Environment Agency.

almost as soon as she had announced her intended trimmings. On average, between 1559 and 1575, nearly 2,200 men served in the royal garrison every year in Ireland – barely 200 fewer than the Earl of Sussex had commanded in 1558–9 when the army was engaged in widespread, multi-theatre operations. A similar force was employed during the 1580s and early 1590s, once a major rebellion in Munster had been defeated and the province (theoretically) secured by plantation. Although ultimately conquest was assured only with a much larger force (the army leaped to 20,000 troops by the battle of Kinsale, Christmas 1601–2), this was due entirely to the growing emergency of Elizabeth's final years and the scale of the Spanish threat. For most of the rest of the reign, a force that was an eighth or a tenth of this size was usually adequate to defend royal power and slowly to extend it, piecemeal.

The cost of even this smaller force was prohibitive. Figures compiled from the surviving Treasurer-at-War accounts reveal most (but not all) of the Queen's outlay on Ireland. They show that, decade by decade, the cost of securing the country rose from an average of more than £20,000 per annum during the 1560s, to nearly £30,000 in the 1570s, before climbing to more than £40,000 in the 1580s and almost £60,000 in the 1590s. Elizabeth shouted and argued, incredulous that the 1560s levels could not be maintained. Yet this hardly compared to the explosion in expenditure after 1594 (and especially after 1598). The Nine Years' War, or 'Tyrone's Rebellion', as it is sometimes called, cost the Crown a staggering £1,925,000 between mid-1594 and March 1603 – that is, more than £210,000 per annum. By then, of course, the Queen's hand had been forced. In order to prevent Ireland providing the stepping stone for a Spanish invasion of England, she had had to relinquish her preferred policy of gradual expansion and piecemeal conquest for an all-out war of survival.

It might be argued that the fact that the Crown sustained such an enormous jump in expenditure after 1594 is proof of the restraint that it had shown beforehand

– that, in effect, Elizabethan military policy in Ireland for much of the reign was very limited indeed and barely signified a real commitment to conquest. But this is shaky ground. No English monarch was prepared to raise taxes in England and Wales to the sort of levels Elizabeth had to during the 1590s in order merely to overawe the whole of Ireland: higher taxation was invariably unpopular, a precipitous step; Ireland was already at least partly under royal control; and, frankly, the Crown usually had more important demands on its revenues elsewhere. It was only when England itself was threatened that the size of operations undertaken after 1594 seemed justified. Just because the scale of what happened then was much greater than what had occurred earlier should not detract from the seriousness of earlier developments. The best way to approach Elizabethan Irish military policy is to ask how it was that limited conquest, consistently pursued for most of the reign, had eventually to yield to something much more drastic. Why was it that the army's endeavours, instead of gradually reducing resistance to the royal government and the threat of foreign interference, had ultimately been confronted by a rebel–invader combination so dangerous that the Queen had virtually to mortgage the monarchy to pay for its suppression? Could the post-1594 crisis have been averted if previous royal policy had been less militarised, or if the military had behaved less abrasively? The aggressive character of English rule between 1558 and 1594 was unmistakeable for those who were on the receiving end. The fact that the Crown's enforcers were sustained on a relatively tight budget hardly made their actions more tolerable; quite the opposite, as we shall see.

THE CHARACTER OF CROWN GOVERNMENT

Of course, the purpose of Elizabethan rule in Ireland was *not* solely its military subjection. As Lord Burghley stated in a private memorandum, the ideal approach to Irish affairs was to pursue the 'reformation' of the country 'by order of justice' 'as well [as] by force'.[7] Hand in hand with military expansion, the Queen's viceroys gave much thought to developing stronger institutions of civil governance, which they generally viewed as elemental to the Crown's ultimate goal – making the kingdom a functioning reality. Accordingly, mindful of government arrangements in the north of England and in Wales, Viceroy Sussex urged the establishment of provincial presidencies and councils in Munster, Connacht and Ulster to better integrate the regional nobility into government structures and to serve as a vanguard for the expansion of English common law. The Ulster presidency scheme stalled (Sussex wanted it for himself), but the Earl's successor, Sir Henry Sidney, succeeded in introducing presidencies in Munster and Connacht by 1569. As a prerequisite for the spread of English-style shire administration beyond its late medieval base, eight new counties were created in 1570, four each in Connacht and Ulster, and, in Munster, County Waterford and parts of Counties Tipperary, Limerick and Cork were reshired. There was also innovation in the state capital. To free the Irish council of a growing judicial burden, Sussex sought the creation of a new prerogative court called Castle Chamber (modelled on the English court of Star Chamber). It appears to have commenced work in 1563 and, having overcome some teething difficulties, was permanently established in 1571, after which its members met twice a week to oversee the correction of infringements of public order and to deal with petitions.

These reforms notwithstanding, however, the extent to which the Irish administration was militarised, with the army captains and their followers far outnumbering other agents of the Crown, gave the government a disproportionately martial aspect that tended more to set Ireland apart from conditions in England than to draw it closer. By the middle of the Queen's reign, professional English soldiers who had made their careers in the country had begun to penetrate the Irish Privy Council, the main executive body of the government, from where royal policy was interpreted and put into effect. Besides the viceroy and the marshal of the army, the promotion to council membership of leading military officers such as Sir Edward Fitton (first appointed a councillor in 1569), Sir Henry Cowley (1574), Sir Nicholas Malby (1575) and Sir Thomas Le Strange (1583), served to ensure that martial and security causes were paramount in discussions at the council table. By itself this need not have been terribly significant, had it not been accompanied by a growing blurring of the distinction between the civil and military members of the council. Because martial office was a rich source of revenue for the holder, several Irish councillors whose function was supposedly entirely civil, such as the Lord Chancellor and Keeper of the Seal, the Vice-Treasurer, the Secretary-of-State, the Master of the Rolls and the Chief Baron of the Exchequer, sought and attained military positions for themselves, securing commissions, command of companies and the custody of certain royal forts. That to acquire such perquisites they had to depend on the generosity of the Viceroy, whose power in theory they were meant to check, proved no obstacle. To quote Sir William Gerrard, one of the few independent councillors of the period, whatever decision the Viceroy made, invariably 'all the Council like sheep to the water' supported it.[8] Manifestly, the civil side of the administration did not have as strong a voice as it might. The privileging of military concerns went largely unquestioned.

This state of affairs directly affected the plight of English law and institutions. During the five years he spent as Chancellor (1576–81), Gerrard was increasingly irked by what he perceived as the barefaced insincerity of the pronouncements of the Viceroy and council about their promotion of the common law. Having journeyed to different parts of the country he found not only that no new counties had been erected since 1570 but also that where new shires had been announced proper court sessions had, often, yet to begin. Worse, even in the English Pale there was no regular assize circuit, with some of the chief justices unwilling to travel beyond Dublin, and the sheriffs and commissioners of the peace appointed by the government seemed sometimes to be highly ignorant of English legal practices.[9] Thanks to the eruption of the Munster rebellion in 1579 it was several years before Gerrard's desire for the regularisation of assizes and the creation of more counties was realised.

When finally it happened, it proved to be too little too late. By the mid-1580s, rather than evolve into a normal kingdom governed by the rule of law, Ireland had developed into a fully fledged security state dominated by soldiers and the military interest. While Governors Sidney and Fitzwilliam, for instance, might have reassured the Queen that they were eagerly directing their efforts towards the promotion of common law and 'English civility', in truth they had made the common law play second fiddle to martial law as they constructed an alternative, coercive, regime based on emergency powers and arbitrary severity. Although historians long ago dismissed the notion of a 'Tudor despotism' existing in England and Wales, it is not so easy to reject it as an applicable model for Elizabethan Ireland.

As in so much else, the government's growing reliance on martial law and its attendant powers of summary execution can be traced back to Sussex. In the late 1550s, looking to increase the authoritarian options that were available to him, the Earl had adapted martial law as it was usually used in England, for use against rebels *during* their rebellion, to enable it to be used in Ireland against suspected rebels *prior* to their rebellion. Accordingly, those he rewarded with commissions of martial law were able to kill almost anyone they wished, rebel or not (peers and major landowners excepted). Ironically, the growing aggression that this cultivated was greatly furthered by Elizabeth's desire to curb military expenditure. For the magical thing about martial law was that it was self-financing. As a reward for their services, martial-law commissioners were entitled to danger money in the form of a one-third share of the goods and possessions of anyone they killed. By granting martial-law commissions to his army officers, Sussex had, first, succeeded in controlling their demands for better pay by providing an additional source of income. Second, by granting commissions to others not in the army (gentlemen clients, native loyalists) he had offset the Queen's troop reductions by financing ancillary paramilitary activity. Third, by dismissing the need to keep accounts of martial-law revenues, he had enabled commissioners to maximise the profits that were to be had from killing. And fourth, by refraining from trying by court martial those who were accused of exceeding their authority (instead offering them pardons, through his vice-regal prerogative) he had guaranteed that martial law could operate with absolute abandon throughout the country, for terror's sake.

On succeeding him, first Sidney and then Fitzwilliam had enthusiastically followed his lead. Before 1565, martial law had largely been confined to the eastern half of the island; thereafter it went nationwide. During his first viceroyalty (1565–71), Sidney issued at least ninety commissions, more than one every three weeks, a rate which Fitzwilliam (1571–5) maintained. When Sidney returned to head his second administration (1575–8), far from easing off, he had even greater recourse to martial law, appointing new commissioners at the rate of one a fortnight. The effect was extraordinary. In the first twenty years of Elizabeth's rule, Ireland was increasingly in the grip of military and security agents of the Crown authorised to carry out killings and punishments with impunity and to seek enrichment in the process.

It is not that the viceroys intended wholesale slaughter. Martial law was supposed to underpin more normal constructive contact between the Crown and its subjects in border areas. But as the energy behind civil reform dissipated and the captains and other military men became the main face of royal power in the localities, this was soon forgotten. Granting commissions, moreover, was a great source of vice-regal patronage, with army officers and others clamouring for favour, offering personal loyalty (and who knows what else) in return. Why bother to make a fuss over how the commissions, once granted, were applied? Did their use not serve to assert government power over 'wild Irish' lineages, whose leaders were mulish, unwilling to offer obedience unless forced to? The fact that there was an entrepreneurial dimension to how the commissioners behaved, treating their jurisdictions as franchises where the subject populations could be exploited alive (through protection rackets) or dead (through the collection of 'traitor's goods') was of little consequence compared to the aggrandisement of royal authority that it facilitated. And all too often, when native lords and chieftains reacted adversely to such provocation, striking back against their tormenters, their 'rebellions' seemed merely to justify the necessity of pre-emptive martial authority. The harsh and callous logic of military security has rarely been more circular – or counter-productive.

Eventually, in 1585, Elizabeth ordered a reduction of the government's reliance on martial law, and in 1591 announced its abolition, but by then the damage was done. Across Gaelic Ireland, as might be expected, the antagonistic antics of military officials hardly endeared the Queen to the people. As well as being commonly spoken of derogatorily, as a *cailleach,* or wicked hag, she was increasingly seen as a tyrant. But the inhabitants of Anglo-Irish districts were no less angered. As one anxious observer stated in 1581, 'the Ancient English subject is driven often times to forsake his living', compelled 'for more assurance' to leave the Pale for the Gaelic north because of the peril posed by martial-law commissioners determined to kill or evict 'whom they list'. The Anglo-Irish also found the burden of maintaining the army unbearable. Though Elizabeth had years earlier required the reform of military taxation in Ireland, replacing the hugely unpopular 'cess' (a system of free quarter) with a negotiated levy known as composition, her orders went largely unheeded, the cess was still in use, and in settled areas at night-time the Crown's troops roved about, living off the 'good subjects' at sword point.[10]

The fact that increasingly from the 1570s many of the English soldiers and officials were Protestants did not help. This, of course, was essentially a matter of demography: prior to that time the majority of the people of England and Wales were Catholic, having been born and grown up before Protestantism took hold in their country. However, as soon as committed Protestants began appearing in royal service, a new dimension was added to the already volatile situation in Ireland, where the population was monolithically Catholic. Henceforth, such military operations as involved encounters with Catholic clergy, churches and monasteries would be far more likely to be accompanied by religiously motivated hatred and violence than previously. However, it was the fusion of mounting religious intolerance with the harsh arbitrary nature of the military and security policy that became potentially the most dangerous development of all. Responding to a variety of Catholic threats, from rebels at home, to events in France, Rome and the Netherlands abroad, in the course of the 1570s the Queen's advisers determined that Catholics should not be appointed to Crown office, being generally untrustworthy – 'Romish caterpillars' – and prone to foreign manipulation. It was a decision that made a harsh kind of sense in England, where conversions to Protestantism were proceeding steadily, with a supply of Protestant ministers available to preach. But it was wholly inappropriate for Ireland, where Crown security was hardly well served by further antagonising its native supporters because of their faith. If hereafter the government's course was to be that of minority Protestant rule, and enforced by unscrupulous methods, how would the loyalists react? Would they remain loyal?

THE NATIVE LOYALIST EXPERIENCE

To a large extent, the government was fortunate, as many loyalists stayed loyal. Take the great climax of the reign, Christmas Eve 1601, and the battle of Kinsale, when Elizabeth's last viceroy, Lord Mountjoy, needed all the assistance he could muster to prevent the northern rebel armies of Tyrone and O'Donnell linking up with the Spanish invaders. That day, the second-largest section of the English army was commanded by a leading Gaelic-Irish nobleman, Donough O'Brien, 4th Earl of Thomond. In the thick of the battle, when Mountjoy despatched his cavalry against Tyrone, galloping into the fray was the Anglo-Irish magnate Richard Burke, Lord Dunkellin (future Earl of Clanricarde), who threw himself upon the enemy and was later knighted for his bravery. And then there was Sir Christopher St Lawrence, son and heir of the Baron of Howth. He played a crucial role in the immediate aftermath of the battle, ensuring that the crown victory became a rout when he set upon Tyrone's retreating forces and butchered them.

Kinsale was momentous, as everyone knows, but it was not the only important action in which native loyalists were to the fore. Indeed, had they not performed similarly earlier, the war might conceivably have turned out very differently. Of particular note, the 'Black' Earl of Ormond, Thomas Butler, had served as Acting Commander-in-Chief of the Queen's forces for a year and a half before Essex's arrival in 1599. When in August 1598 the English marshal, Sir Henry Bagenal, had led 4,000 royal soldiers straight into the jaws of Tyrone's waiting gunners at the Yellow Ford, the way to Dublin – and total rebel victory – was left wide open. Arriving from his Kilkenny base, Ormond had slammed the door shut, strengthening the Pale with a force partly raised from his own lands and had then sent an expedition into southern Ulster in the hope of discouraging Tyrone; he succeeded. Then, weeks later, in October 1598, Ormond had had to prevent a major new uprising in Munster from spreading; had he responded less quickly, the province and its strategic Atlantic coastline would have been much harder to retrieve. If in the end it was Mountjoy who sealed English victory in the war, during and after Kinsale, the ageing Ormond could be said to have been nearly as important, having done most to avert English defeat.

The full extent of the Crown's reliance on native military assistance has long caused confusion, with scholars tending to assume that the English army in Elizabethan Ireland was precisely that – an army of Englishmen – and that the Irish element of the army was for the most part supplementary. This had probably been the case early in Elizabeth's reign, under Sussex, and it certainly was the case at the very end, when Essex and Mountjoy took command of a huge royal force composed mostly of raw recruits from England and Wales. At the beginning of the Nine Years' War, however, it seems that at rank-and-file level, among the ordinary troops, the army had become far more Irish than English. This was partly a matter of cost. Because Irish troops were cheaper to maintain than English ones, entrepreneurial English captains greatly preferred them, and in Dublin and London senior officials turned a blind eye to the practice in order to comply with the Queen's insistence on economy. But it also made military sense. English conscripts were often reluctant soldiers, prone to desertion; the Irish, in contrast, viewed soldiering as a good livelihood and usually only went missing if they were not paid. Table

Figure 11.3 Charles Blount, Lord Mountjoy, later Earl of Devonshire by unknown engraver, published by Henry Balam, line engraving (*c.* 1600–25). Image © National Portrait Gallery, London.

11.1 shows that the army used by Ormond to confront Tyrone and his confederates when the Nine Years' War entered its most critical phase during 1598 was more than two-thirds composed of Irish-born troops, with the Anglo-Irish dominating the cavalry while the largest element of the foot soldiers were men of Gaelic ethnic origin. If they had not been willing to fill the ranks, the war might have turned out differently.

Nevertheless, even if many natives had stayed loyal and provided crucial military service, they and their leaders were not necessarily entirely reconciled to developments in Crown government. From their perspective, the most striking thing about their situation was the fact that, notwithstanding their growing military importance,

Table 11.1 Ethnic composition of the royal army in Ireland, March 1598

	Horse	*Foot*
English-born	100 (20%)	2,220 (37%)
Palesmen/Anglo-Irish	290 (55%)	1,500 (25%)
'Mere' Irish/Gaelic	130 (25%)	2,350 (38%)

Source: NLI, Ms 2559: Ormond Papers/Army lists, item 1.

their overall role in the State was actually declining. On the Irish Privy Council native representation had slumped. Prior to Elizabeth's accession almost half the council was Anglo-Irish (none were Gaelic-Irish); though increasing their numbers early in her reign, by 1594 – on the eve of the Nine Years' War – just two of the fourteen members were Anglo-Irish (again, there were no Gaels). Other areas of government were much the same. In the army, by the time of Kinsale – the Earl of Ormond having retired due to the onset of blindness – the only Irish lord to hold an established senior position was Thomond.

What made this especially unpalatable by 1601 was the fact that things had been much the same for over twenty years. During the southern war of 1579–83, just one senior army position had been occupied by a native nobleman, the lord generalship of Munster, held by Ormond. Although the Earl had triumphed, and had been greatly aided by local lords and allies such as the Muskerry MacCarthys, Castleconnell Burkes and Decies Fitzgeralds, the anticipated rewards for loyalty had not materialised. When the plantation of Munster followed fast on the heels of Ormond's victory, no native supporter of the Crown – not even Ormond – was assigned a share of the colony. Eventually, after a parliamentary petition by Anglo-Irish MPs in his favour in 1585 (and the Earl's own careful lobbying of the Queen at court), Ormond was granted a share, but the exclusion of other deserving loyalists left a bitter taste. Even a minimal reward, such as the appointment to military office, seemed out of reach. In the far-flung network of royal forts that had sprung up around the country there were almost no Irish-born constables. The Irish could serve and die as soldiers, but they could not share power.

Religion, it is clear, was one of the main reasons for the loyalists' growing exclusion. In 1580, the 11th Earl of Kildare had been forced out of government office and placed under arrest because of his Catholicism and the suspicion that he was involved in a conspiracy. More and more such fears agitated the Queen's leading advisers. Even at Kinsale, Mountjoy – a supposed moderate – had been unsure of Saint Lawrence, and his heavy reliance on Thomond was due mainly to his knowledge that the Gaelic earl was a Protestant. But deep-lying cultural suspicions also played a part. The strangeness of Irish conditions disturbed English observers. Not only were loyalist lords of English descent (the Anglo-Irish) openly Catholic, but they seemed not fully English either. Many of them spoke Gaelic, had Gaelic servants, wives and concubines and had adopted many Gaelic practices. Far from maintaining themselves apart, some of them had become practically indistinguishable from the 'wild Irish', and almost all of them, even the most anglicised, such as Ormond, were linked by strong ties of kinship to rebels, or else to the brothers and cousins of rebels. For most of the Anglo-Irish (especially those beyond Dublin) local concerns were paramount, the situation in England too distant to get excited over. Increasingly, in the latter part of the reign, while the loyalists continued to see themselves as indispensable, to the New English security class they seemed unreliable.

In the end it is likely that many loyalists avoided open disloyalty – revolt – because, for all their difficulties, alternative forms of opposition were available. The extent to which Irish lords and gentry were attached to some of the great figures at the Elizabethan court is a topic deserving much closer attention than it has hitherto received. Elizabeth's main advisers (Burghley, Leicester, Walsingham, Sussex, Croft and later Robert Cecil and Essex) all had Irish clients and exercised their influence to see favours passed or grievances mollified. The Earl of Ormond, moreover, ultimately owed his great prominence and material success in royal service to his own personal standing at Whitehall as the Queen's only Irish favourite. Although this insured the animosity of successive English viceroys bothered by his power, it also enabled him to provide patronage and protection to many Irish, confident (most of the time) that Elizabeth would honour the promises he made on her behalf. Regarding the growing sectarianism of government policy, it seems most native loyalists were prepared to ignore it, in the quite rational expectation that it was but a temporary aberration, and that Elizabeth would soon revert to the less strident religious approach that her government had followed earlier. Besides, failing that, Elizabeth would soon die, and be replaced on the throne by James Stuart. As the son of the Catholic royal martyr Mary, Queen of Scots, he was bound, it was thought, to protect Catholicism.

AVOIDABLE REBELLIONS

In the final analysis, however, the growing antagonism between English officialdom and the loyalist community was of crucial importance in the history of Elizabethan Ireland, for the simple fact that many of the principal rebellions of the period were led by members of the native nobility who earlier in their careers had been willing to co-operate with the Crown – Shane O'Neill (in revolt 1557–9, 1560–1, 1562–7), Sir Edmund Butler (1569–70), the Earl of Thomond (1570), Rory Oge O'More (1571–2, 1573–5, 1577–8), the Earl of Desmond (1579–83), Viscount Baltinglass (1580–2) and the Earl of Tyrone (1594–1603).

This was most clearly the case with the rebels of Anglo-Irish origin. As noted above, long before going out into revolt Garret Fitzgerald, 15th Earl of Desmond, had been appointed to the Irish Privy Council and had served on a number of crown expeditions. James Eustace, 3rd Viscount Baltinglass, had been raised in a staunchly anglophile household and had followed his father – also a member of the Council – into the crown service. The leader of the Butler Rebellion of 1569, the Earl of Ormond's brother Sir Edmund Butler, had first come to prominence as a fairly typical Butler loyalist in the late 1550s and had seen active royal service in all four provinces before eventually turning 'traitor'.

Though a culture of loyalism was generally absent from the Gaelic-Irish territories (it became a feature of Gaelic identity only after 1603, following the Stuart succession), several of the main Gaelic rebels of the mid- and later sixteenth century had been happy to seek friendship with the Crown prior to their insurrections. This is why the revolt in 1570 of Connor O'Brien, 3rd Earl of Thomond, was such a shock to Elizabeth and her ministers. He owed his installation as earl to English assistance, had usually been careful to maintain contact with Dublin and London and was even attached to the Duke of Norfolk's grouping at Whitehall. The rebellion of Rory Oge O'More in April 1571 was rather less surprising, yet on closer inspection it emerges that a year before rising up he had submitted to Sidney and the council and had actually entered into Crown service in Laois as a follower of the English seneschal Francis Cosby, prepared to fight for the Crown against local rebels in return for a grant of part of his family's former estates. Shane O'Neill, too, had attempted closer links with the government the better to secure his future, initially in the mid-1550s but most famously in 1562, when he had presented himself at court accompanied by a guard of galloglasses; indeed, he had even agreed to accept the introduction of an English presidential jurisdiction in Ulster. But by far the best example of a major Gaelic warlord who turned from loyalty and collaboration to defiance and insurrection was, of course, the most dangerous rebel of all, Hugh O'Neill, 2nd Earl of Tyrone. Long before entering the field against the Crown, Tyrone had been raised in the Pale with an English settler family. He had given military assistance to the 1st Earl of Essex's colonising efforts in Clandeboy in 1573–5, to Viceroy Grey de Wilton's campaigns against Desmond in Munster in 1580, and in 1588, when survivors of the Spanish Armada had put ashore on the Donegal coast, his forces had put 300 of them to death in cold blood.

At one time, it was thought that most of these were always rebels, steadfastly opposed to English power throughout their lives, but detailed historical investigation has gradually succeeded in exploding such myths. Far from being opposed in principle to Crown government, it was particular aspects of policy, or the antics of individual Crown officers, that drove these men and their followers to revolt; in other words, each of their rebellions might have been avoided, and English power advanced without their opposition, had the Crown been willing to modify certain policies or required its officials to act less provocatively. Shane O'Neill had sought recognition of his right to succeed his father to the earldom of Tyrone. In 1559, and again in 1562, he had been led to believe that the Crown would yield to his request, only for his enemy, Viceroy Sussex, to have the government retract its assurances and adopt a much tougher stance. Shane was left feeling deceived and in no little danger. A sense of betrayal and personal peril likewise animated Rory O'More, who had his promises of land thrown back in his face by Sidney and feared assassination by Seneschal Cosby. Not forgetting Desmond: he felt unable to come in to the government in 1579 after Sir Nicholas Malby had pre-emptively (using martial law) attacked his tenants, destroyed his property and seemed determined to harm him and his family. Even Hugh O'Neill, Earl of Tyrone, might have stepped back from revolt had he not become convinced that a clique of high-ranking officials were committed to removing him from the scene, by almost any method, because he had grown too powerful.

More generally, a growing sense of dread about the severity of royal power animated many who rebelled. Shane O'Neill presented a number of complaints to Elizabeth in the early 1560s, alleging that Sussex was orchestrating a government murder programme against the provincial nobility and supplied her with examples of treacherous captures and assassinations, kangaroo-court executions and massacres. The subsequent escalation of martial law and the perpetration of atrocities such as the massacre of O'Neills and O'Mores who were invited to attend parleys at Belfast (1574) and Mullaghmast (1577) confirmed the growing notoriety of the administration. Mistrust ruled.

Had Elizabeth been prepared to take more seriously the reports of such occurrences and ordered proper investigations – as she eventually did, too late, by the early 1590s – how much trouble might have been avoided, and how much bloodshed? One of the most telling commentaries on the failure of her government in Ireland is the fact that rebellions became less easy to contain once they had broken out, as a common anxiety over royal 'security' policy drove disparate groups closer together. Religion is known to have been one of the main causes of the two Fitzmaurice revolts, in 1569 and 1579, but it was a shared hatred of the greed for land and money of the Crown's captains and military policemen that drove first Sir Edmund Butler and later Sir John of Desmond to support Fitzmaurice. Fitzmaurice had precious little in common with these men otherwise, and usually they would have viewed him with hostility, and he them. The Baltinglass revolt of 1580 was similar, attracting the sympathy and support of both the Wicklow chieftain Feagh McHugh O'Byrne and of many hitherto loyal Wexford gentry, because of the provocative behaviour of Sir Thomas Masterson, the Crown's martial enforcer in Ferns Castle. When Tyrone, desperate for Anglo-Irish allies, had succeeded in attracting the support of Walter Nugent in 1601, this followed the burning of Multyfarnham friary, a Franciscan community under Nugent family protection, by Crown forces, and the cold treatment of the head of the lineage, Christopher, Lord Delvin, a leading Catholic loyalist, on account of his religion.

Much if not all of this had been avoidable. On arriving in London from Edinburgh, James I had to contend with the financial cost; the Irish had to count the dead. Just as when Elizabeth had succeeded in 1558 the country was ravaged by war and famine. But whereas earlier the damage was confined to central and east Ulster, and to the borders of the Pale, in 1603 the entire country was affected. The body count was appalling.

FURTHER READING

Brady, Ciaran, *The Chief Governors: The Rise and Fall of Reform Government in Tudor Ireland, 1536–88* (Cambridge, 1994).

—— 'The Captain's Games: Army and Society in Elizabethan Ireland', in Thomas Bartlett and Keith Jeffery (ed.), *A Military History of Ireland* (Cambridge, 1996), pp. 136–59.

—— *Shane O'Neill* (Dundalk, 1996).

Canny, Nicholas, *The Elizabethan Conquest of Ireland: A Pattern Established, 1565–1576* (Hassocks, 1976).

—— *Making Ireland British, 1580–1650* (Oxford, 2001).

Connolly, S. J., *Contested Island: Ireland 1460–1630* (Oxford, 2007).

Carey, Vincent, 'The End of the Gaelic Political Order: The O'More Lordship of Laois, 1536–1603', in P. Lane and W. Nolan (ed.), *Laois: History and Society* (Dublin, 1999), pp. 213–56.

—— *Surviving the Tudors: The 'Wizard' Earl of Kildare and English Rule in Ireland, 1537–1586* (Dublin, 2002).

Crawford, Jon G., *Anglicizing the Government of Ireland: The Irish Privy Council and the Expansion of Tudor Rule, 1556–1578* (Dublin, 1993).

—— *A Star Chamber Court in Ireland: The Court of Castle Chamber, 1571–1641* (Dublin, 2005).

Donovan, Brian, 'Tudor Rule in Gaelic Leinster and the Rise of Feagh McHugh O'Byrne', in Conor O'Brien (ed.), *Feagh McHugh O'Byrne: The Wicklow Firebrand* (Rathdrum, 1998), pp. 118–49.

Edwards, David, 'The Butler Revolt of 1569', *Irish Historical Studies*, 28 (111) (1993): 228–55.

—— 'Ideology and Experience: Spenser's *View* and Martial Law in Elizabethan Ireland', in H. Morgan (ed.), *Political Ideology in Ireland, 1541–1641* (Dublin, 1999), pp. 127–57.

—— 'The MacGiollapadraigs (Fitzpatricks) of Upper Ossory, 1532–1641' in P. Lane and W. Nolan (eds.), *Laois: History and Society* (Dublin, 1999), pp. 327–76.

—— *The Ormond Lordship in County Kilkenny, 1515–1642: The Rise and Fall of Butler Feudal Power* (Dublin, 2003).

—— 'The Escalation of Violence in Sixteenth-Century Ireland', in David Edwards, Padraig Lenihan and Clodagh Tait (eds.), *Age of Atrocity: Violence and Political Conflict in Early Modern Ireland* (Dublin, 2007), pp. 34–78.

Edwards, David, Lenihan, Padraig and Tait, Clodagh (eds.), *Age of Atrocity: Violence and Political Conflict in Early Modern Ireland* (Dublin, 2007).

Fissel, Marle Charles, *English Warfare 1511–1642* (London 2001).

Hammer, Paul E. J., *Elizabeth's Wars: War, Government and Society in Tudor England, 1544–1604* (Basingstoke 2003).

Highley, Christopher, 'The Royal Image in Elizabethan Ireland', in Julia Walker (ed.), *Dissing Elizabeth* (London, 1998), pp. 60–76.

Lennon, Colm, *Sixteenth-Century Ireland: The Incomplete Conquest*, 2nd edn (Dublin, 2005).

Maginn, Christopher, *'Civilizing' Gaelic Leinster: The Extension of Tudor Rule in the O'Byrne and O'Toole Lordships* (Dublin, 2005).

McCormack, Anthony, *The Earldom of Desmond, 1463–1583: The Decline and Crisis of a Feudal Lordship* (Dublin, 2005).

McGowan-Doyle, Valerie, '*The Book of Howth:* The Old English and the Elizabethan Conquest of Ireland', unpublished Ph.D. thesis, University College, Cork, 2005.

McGurk, John, *The Elizabethan Conquest of Ireland: The Burdens of the 1590s Crisis* (Manchester, 1997).

Morgan, Hiram, *Tyrone's Rebellion: The Outbreak of the Nine Years' War in Tudor Ireland* (Dublin, 1993).

—— (ed.), *The Battle of Kinsale* (Bray, 2004).

—— '"Never Any Realm Worse Governed": Queen Elizabeth and Ireland', *Transactions of the Royal Historical Society*, 14 (2004): 295–308.

—— '"Slán dé fút go hoíche": Hugh O'Neill's Murders', in David Edwards, Padraig Lenihan and Clodagh Tait (eds.), *Age of Atrocity: Violence and Political Conflict in Early Modern Ireland* (Dublin, 2007), pp. 95–118.

Palmer, Patricia, *Language and Conquest in Early Modern Ireland: English Renaissance Literature and Elizabethan Imperial Expansion* (Cambridge, 2001).

Palmer, William, *The Problem of Ireland in Tudor Foreign Policy, 1485–1603* (Woodbridge, 1994).

Quinn, D. B., *The Elizabethans and the Irish* (Ithaca, NY, 1966).

Sheehan, Anthony J., 'Irish Revenues and English Subventions, 1559–1622', *Royal Irish Academy Proceedings*, 90C (1990): 35–65.

Silke, John J., *Kinsale: Spanish Intervention in Ireland at the End of the Elizabethan Wars* (Liverpool, 1971).

NOTES

1 The first expedition into Ulster had lasted six weeks, from 10 August until 21 September (TCD, MS 581, fols. 86r–89v). The second was apparently much shorter, lasting about a week, early in October (TNA, SP 62/2/71, 75). The midlands, Munster and Connacht outing also lasted six weeks, from 14 June to 25 July (Lambeth Palace Library, MS 621, fols. 20v–23r).
2 TNA, SP 62/2/75.
3 TNA, SP 62/2/75.
4 Mary Ann Lyons, *Franco-Irish Relations, 1500–1610: Politics, Migration and Trade* (Woodbridge 2003), pp. 116–19; p. 118.
5 TNA, SP 62/2/44–5.
6 BL, Harleian MS 35, No. 4.
7 *Cal. SP Ire., 1571–5,* No. 1280.
8 Crawford, *Anglicizing the Government,* pp. 35–7; p. 35.
9 Charles McNeill (ed.), 'Lord Chancellor Gerrard's "Notes of His Report on Ireland"', *Analecta Hibernica,* 2 (1931): 124, 185–7.
10 TNA, SP 63/90/69.

PART II
RELIGION

CHAPTER TWELVE

NEW WINE INTO OLD BOTTLES

The doctrine and structure of the Elizabethan church

Brett Usher

Elizabeth I inherited an island kingdom on the scattered western outskirts of Christendom which for little short of 1,000 years – indeed, almost until the moment of her birth in 1533 – had remained in thrall to the dominating influence of the church of Rome.

When her grandfather, Henry VII, took the throne by conquest in 1485, the structure and official doctrine of *Ecclesia anglicana,* although challenged by the 'Lollard' followers of the English reformer John Wycliffe earlier in the century, remained precariously intact. Yet Lollards still skulked in corners, and it had become clear that wholesale reform of the church could not be far off. The new king's mother, Margaret Beaufort, Countess of Richmond, herself encouraged 'humanist' scholars who were attempting to remedy perceived abuses within the church and to purge it of superstition and obscurantism. Desiderius Erasmus, for example, spent three years at Cambridge (1511–14) working on his Greek New Testament.

Elizabeth's father, Henry VIII, and his chief minister, Cardinal Thomas Wolsey, showed sympathy to the 'New Learning' but none at all to Martin Luther's full-frontal attack in 1517 on traditional Catholic doctrine and upon papal pretensions and corruptions. Indeed, Henry's *Assertio septem sacramentorum* (1521), condemning Luther's theological position, earned him Pope Leo X's gratitude and the title 'Defender of the Faith' – ironically, one used by English monarchs to this day and enshrined in the abbreviation 'FD' (*Fidei Defensor*) on both British and Commonwealth coinage. Henry's break with the papacy a decade later had nothing to with doctrine and worship and everything to do with his overmastering desire to annul his first marriage to Katherine of Aragon and to provide England with a male heir. Pope Clement VII, under the thumb of Katherine's nephew the Emperor Charles V, could not or would not grant Henry an annulment on the grounds of affinity in canon law. After 1529, parliamentary legislation little by little loosened England's ancient ties with the papacy, even as the hapless Pope Clement sanctioned the appointment as Archbishop of Canterbury of Henry's chosen candidate, Thomas Cranmer, a reformer waiting in the wings.

Much was to flow from Henry's pragmatic discarding of Clement VII. Clearly the original 'Reformation', which he and his advisers forced through successive parliamentary sessions after 1529, was in the first place an act of state: England was declared to be an 'empire', subject to no superior earthly authority, and Henry himself *always to have been* 'Supreme Head of the Church of England', a title usurped by the Bishop of Rome time out of mind. Harnessing the widespread disaffection with Roman hegemony which was the groundswell of the European Reformation, Henry unwittingly paved the way for the gradual introduction of increasingly advanced reformist doctrines. Since he himself was little disposed to embrace any of them, the 1530s and 1540s saw a bewildering number of sea changes in the theological position of the English church. Despite all alarms and excursions and the adoption of an English bible and litany, Henry was to die in 1547 as an essentially Catholic monarch, who, in the name of his newly recovered supremacy, simply denied the authority of the pope.

Thereafter, Archbishop Cranmer and the reforming party, largely muzzled during Henry's last years, finally came into their own. Evangelical advances under the boy-king Edward VI culminated in 1552 in the adoption of a fully Protestant prayer book. Had not Edward died in July 1553 there would undoubtedly have been further ecclesiastical reform according to the latest Continental models. The accession, however, of the Roman Catholic Mary I meant that the realm was returned to papal obedience for five and a half increasingly violent years. Many Protestants departed into exile in Europe or else lived fugitive lives within England. Five Edwardian bishops, including Cranmer, were burnt at the stake, as were several hundred hapless men and women throughout the English shires who refused to renounce their Protestant beliefs. Widespread revulsion at this policy of repression was coupled with mounting fears that, after Mary's marriage to Philip of Spain in 1554, England would fall under the domination of the Habsburg Empire should she give birth to an heir. None materialised, and, after the loss of Calais in January 1558, a body blow to English pride, Mary was to measure out her last ten months of life as a bitterly disappointed woman. Amidst scenes of universal rejoicing within the ranks of England's anti-Catholic survivors, Elizabeth was unreservedly accepted as Mary's successor. Philip, automatically stripped of his empty title 'King Consort', had been long absent from England and made no attempt to encourage English Catholics to resist the inevitable.

DOCTRINE AND WORSHIP TO 1603

As Anne Boleyn's daughter, Elizabeth was the living symbol of her father's break with Rome, and, with congratulations pouring in from every evangelical quarter, she can have been under no illusion that much was expected of her. Although by temperament and upbringing undoubtedly a convinced Protestant, she never displayed that sense of zeal which had propelled her half-sister into wrecking the Edwardian Settlement of religion and returning her realm to papal obedience. Whilst hers, like Edward's, was to be a 'reformed' church, it was to be neither doctrinaire nor dogmatic. In the first place, therefore, it must be emphasised that the Elizabethan Settlement did not create 'Anglicanism' as that term is now used. No contemporary churchman would have understood the word, and it cannot be meaningfully applied until, in the early nineteenth century, the English Protestant tradition began to spread throughout an increasingly English-speaking world. In 1559, the new leaders of the church began their pastoral work, if not with a blank sheet, at least with very considerable latitude of interpretation in doctrinal matters:

> The genius of the Elizabethan Settlement was its vagueness. Emphasizing the community of Christians, it remained carefully indistinct about the specific theological models that undergirded its liturgy, and which might have divided Christians from one another. This allowed the English to agree on justification by faith alone without defining how grace worked.[1]

The theological background that informs this 'vagueness' has come increasingly under the microscope, and Henry VIII's break with Rome has been recently described as part of a widespread movement to create a 'third way' in religion 'that was neither in thrall to Luther nor the pope'.[2] This concept may or may not prove useful in the long term, but certainly there was to be no shortage of alternatives to Luther's stridently pessimistic polemic, harping constantly on man's inability to fend for himself and his consequent need to rely on God in all things. Huldrych Zwingli of Zurich (d. 1531) was equally clear about the paramountcy of the Bible, the legality of clerical marriage, the parasitic invasion of the Church by monasticism and the idolatrous use of images as an aid to worship. Yet he insisted that man had a right to exercise his God-given reason in worldly matters. Zwingli's son-in-law, Heinrich Bullinger, had, through his reception of English exiles during Mary's reign, and then through his writings, a more lasting, 'rational' effect on Elizabethan churchmanship than Luther.

Other traditions had sprung up. Archbishop Cranmer covertly forged links with numerous evangelicals abroad whose views on images, eucharistic doctrine and a raft of other issues nudged Henry's secular Reformation in the direction of a very individual relationship with the burgeoning community of Europe's reformed churches. Given his head by Edward VI's government, Cranmer went head-hunting on the Continent and scored a notable string of successes. Martin Bucer of Strasbourg and the Italian reformer Peter Martyr Vermigli accepted professorships at Oxford and Cambridge. Other visitors included Bernadino Ochino of Siena and John à Lasco (Jan Laski) of Poland, who was permitted to create a 'stranger church' in London for fugitive Protestants from abroad. This experiment was to provide a useful blueprint and model for beleaguered *English* Protestants, who, during Mary's reign, managed to maintain a clandestine congregation there under the government's very nose. Bucer died in 1551; Martyr, Ochino and Laski survived the reign, departing hastily at Mary's accession. Despite the hopes expressed by Elizabeth's leading ecclesiastics at the beginning of the new regime, the Queen never invited Martyr back to England – a distinct disappointment to his English disciples, in particular John Jewel, who returned from exile to become Bishop of Salisbury and to write his *Apologia ecclesiae anglicanae* (1562).

Until the appearance of Richard Hooker's *Ecclesiastical Polity* (1593–1604), this short Latin treatise became the mainstay of the English 'third way' for two generations. Despite the tremendous importance attached to it by contemporaries and by later commentators, Jewel had little to say about recent theological developments abroad, insisting only that a True Church should be based on what could be gleaned from Scripture and the writings of the ancient fathers. He eschews the nice distinctions which increasingly divided Lutherans from the new orthodoxies of Zurich, Strasbourg and, above all, Geneva.

Although the subterranean influence of Bullinger, Bucer, Martyr and Ochino on the first generation of Elizabethan divines remains incalculable, it was the teachings of John Calvin of Geneva that, during the 1550s, came to dominate Protestant belief and practice in the Netherlands and Switzerland, as well as parts of France and Germany. The Geneva Bible (largely the work of English exiles living there during the Marian years) as well as Calvin's own writings (most notably *The Institutes of a Christian Man*) combined to enjoy an influence unequalled by any other theological tradition which had moved beyond that of Luther. Elizabeth herself deeply distrusted the Genevan ascendancy for she could never forget that it had spawned John Knox's *The First Blast of the Trumpet against the Monstrous Regiment of Women* (1559), inveighing against female rulers, and she correctly discerned that its theocentric tenets were at the core of 'puritan' opposition to her Erastian Settlement. It is, however, current wisdom that by 1590 the English and Welsh clergy, along with their (largely Presbyterian) Scottish brethren, were yoked together in a 'Calvinist consensus'. Who precisely coined that phrase remains hotly disputed.

Calvin accepted the proposition enunciated by Luther that the justification of ever-sinful man was to be measured by faith *alone*. The grim consequence of his glossing of Luther was the notion of 'predestination': all men and women had been marked out in the mind of God before their birth for 'election' or damnation. From that followed the even more chilling hypothesis that Christ had died *only* for 'the elect'. Even before Elizabeth's death such doctrines came under threat from a new generation of theologians, variously described as 'anti-Calvinist', 'anti-predestinarian' or, to simplify more complex issues, 'Arminian' (the Dutch Calvinist Jakobus Arminius having come to doubt that Christ can have died only for 'the elect'). Thus, despite its towering influence for more than a century, Calvinism was never the official creed of the Church of England but rather the most strident of several competing traditions of reformed theology available to committed Protestants.

In any case, the first generation of 'Elizabethan' clerics necessarily embraced a very mixed bunch of men, most of them ordained under the Roman rite. If many who had contrived to survive from the reign of Henry VIII were convinced 'Romanists' at heart, concerned above all to retain their benefices through thick and thin, they were not necessarily cynical time-servers. What could they do except soldier on in the face of yet another U-turn in governmental policy? If the new 'godly' derided them as 'old mass priests' they were not deterred from their conscientious duty to minister to their congregations according to the new rules.

Evangelicals who had first learnt their Protestantism under Henry or Edward might cast a backward glance towards the original tenets of Luther or Zwingli. There were also those who knew something of the teachings of Bucer and Peter Martyr under the boy-king or, at least, had been ordained according to the first English Ordinal between 1550 and July 1553. A significant and influential band of brothers had sniffed the exciting air of Zurich, Strasbourg and Geneva during exile in Mary's reign; an unquantifiable number had engaged in clandestine resistance to her regime throughout the British Isles during the same period. Leavening the lump was a substantial body of men who had taken advantage of the Edwardian government's endorsement of clerical marriage, had been deprived of their benefices under Mary as a result and, in 1559, were entitled to reclaim them. If marriage was not precisely the badge of an evangelical churchman – many clergy had taken the opportunity to legitimise a liaison with their 'housekeepers' – it is a reasonable assumption that the majority of married clergy broadly welcomed the Elizabethan Settlement.

The latter was based wholly on parliamentary legislation, hinging upon acceptance of the Oath of Supremacy and the Act of Uniformity. Any ordained man who refused to acknowledge that Elizabeth, rather than the Pope, was 'Supreme Governor' of the Church of England – upon advice she accepted that, for a woman, the title was more appropriate than 'Supreme Head' – was suspended from all ecclesiastical functions and deprived of his preferments. Minor Catholic orders, from the tonsure to subdeacon, ceased to be valid. The Roman Missal was once again set aside, and after midsummer 1559 public worship was conducted in the vernacular by means of the new Book of Common Prayer and the Bible in English translation.

Give or take a handful of doctrinal nuances, these measures returned the Church of England to the point on the Protestant map which it had occupied from 1552 until Edward VI's death one year later. The new Prayer Book was perhaps as much as could have been expected from a queen who, it was to prove, would always proceed with caution in religious matters. Yet clearly it required some amplification if parliamentary principles were to be translated into parochial practice. In the first place, therefore, Elizabeth authorised a royal visitation of the English and Welsh parishes, conducted in late 1559. It was modelled on that carried out a decade earlier by the government of Edward VI, when visitors traversed the country distributing copies of Cranmer's *First Book of Homilies* (1547), Erasmus' *Paraphrases upon the Gospels in English* (1548) and a set of injunctions. In 1559, fifty-six brief articles of enquiry were drawn up, as well as a more amply worded set of fifty-three injunctions. They were intended to establish the Supremacy and the new prayer book as the basis of a revived Protestant regime which, although not disdaining their influence, held aloof from Continental models.

The Royal Supremacy, ordered to be proclaimed from the pulpit, was paramount. 'Superstitious' and 'idolatrous' practices, heresies and sorcery were all comprehensively condemned and orders made for their extirpation. The preaching of the gospel was emphasised: a quarterly sermon was to be delivered by the incumbent or else by a qualified preacher at his appointment. Additional sermons by (duly licensed) visiting preachers were approved and encouraged. Failing all else, incumbents were ordered to read from the pulpit one of Cranmer's homilies. If there were to be no sermon, the Lord's Prayer, the creed and the Ten Commandments should be recited so that parishioners might gradually learn them by heart. Within three months of the visitation the parish was to acquire an English Bible 'of the largest volume in English' and, within twelve months, Erasmus' *Paraphrases*, both to be available for study in the church outside the time of divine service. The royal injunctions were to be read out at least once a quarter, and all clergy were ordered to obtain a New Testament both in Latin and English and a personal copy of the *Paraphrases* for 'conferring the one with the other': thus they could be examined 'how they have profited in the study of Holy Scripture'. There followed numerous injunctions concerning the regulation of parish life (see below).[3]

The royal visitation set the tone for England's 'third way' in doctrine and worship for the rest of the reign. The new bench of bishops used the injunctions as a blueprint for the subsequent oversight of their dioceses and, apparently with Elizabeth's tacit consent, proceeded to draw up a list of 'considerations' and 'interpretations' in order to fine-tune them for practical purposes.[4] It was to prove the only time that the Queen sanctioned any modification of the 1559 legislation. The primary result of the bishops' deliberations was that the Prayer Book's 'ornaments rubric', enjoining the use of the ancient canonical vestments, was effectively abandoned: Elizabethan controversies concerning clerical dress would focus only on the use of the surplice during divine service and the wearing of the tippet, square cap and long gown in public.

Iron was pumped into the blood of this fledgling Church with the appearance of Jewel's *Apology* in 1562 and then in 1563 of a more extensive catechism, written by Alexander Nowell, Dean of Saint Paul's, and a *Second Book of Homilies*, masterminded by Jewel. Early in 1563, convocation – the Church's governing body, which sat conterminously with Parliament – thrashed out a definitive set of regulations, known today as the Thirty-Nine Articles, 'for the Avoiding of Diversities of Opinions, and for the Establishing of Consent touching True Religion'. They reiterated the implicit assumptions of the injunctions of 1559 regarding received Protestant notions of salvation and good works, condemning 'Romish' doctrines of 'Purgatory, Pardons, Worshipping and Adoration . . . Images . . . Reliques, and also invocation of Saints' as 'fond thing[s] vainly invented'. Only two of the seven sacraments sanctioned by Rome (as defended by Henry VIII in 1521) remained valid: those of baptism and the Lord's Supper, which was to be received 'in both kinds', whereas, under Roman obedience, the laity had received bread only and not wine. 'Those five commonly called Sacraments . . ., Confirmation, Penance, Orders, Matrimony and extreme Unction, are not to be counted for Sacraments of the Gospel'.[5] The remaining articles emphasised the 'Erastian' nature of the Church – that is, its dependence on the temporal power – as well as such matters as clerical marriage, the regular use of the homilies and the consecration and ordination of bishops and clergy.

Elizabeth ratified the Thirty-Nine Articles by statute following the Parliament of 1571. Yet they were merely the skin and bones of what would develop into an English Protestant tradition. How to bind the hearts and minds of Elizabeth's subjects to this halfway house of a 'reformed' Church – fully Romanist in structure and discipline and yet vehemently anti-Romanist in sentiment and in its theological stance? John Foxe (d. 1587) was determined to show that there was a common bond between the survivors of the Marian regime: the inspiring example of the Protestant martyrs. That many of the humbler men and women whose deaths he chronicled would have been hard put to it to define their beliefs beyond a detestation of the pope and the mass was beside the point. *Actes and Monuments*, a comparatively slim volume on its appearance in 1563, was revised and expanded thereafter, reaching a fourth edition of massive breadth under Foxe's supervision in 1583. It became the most influential gloss ever published on the history of English religion, spawning myriad abbreviated versions for over 300 years. Where families could afford it, the 'Book of Martyrs' became a household treasure, piously bequeathed – often to daughters, in order that they should read it to their children, thus firmly implanting Protestant values in the minds of succeeding generations.

Foxe's work exerted a unique impact on his contemporaries and thus in creating a 'national' church. Otherwise, the evidence of books bequeathed by Elizabethan clergy – a useful index of what was being taught to the average parishioner – presents an eclectic round-up of all the reforming traditions which had sprung up since Luther nailed his theses to the door of Wittenberg Cathedral in 1517. If the works of Calvin and Bullinger's *Decades* loom largest, Erasmus' *Paraphrases* had, as we have seen, become required reading in clerical households, and many clergy also owned a copy of the Lutheran Wolfgang Musculus' *Commonplaces*. The most frequently reprinted guides to godliness under Elizabeth included the works of the early English evangelist Thomas Becon and two volumes by celebrated Marian martyrs: John Bradford's *Godlie Meditations upon the Lordes Prayer* and Hugh Latimer's collected sermons. The Genevan tradition yields treatises by Calvin's successor, Theodore Beza, and the sermons of Edward Dering, whose outspokenness before Elizabeth ruined his career. Henry Bull's *Christian Prayers* (1568) and James Cancellar's *The Alphabet of Prayers* (1564) proved two of the most successful home-grown guides to lay piety. Later there sprang up a 'sociological' tradition of popular theology, often written in the form of dialogue for the 'better instruction' of the 'unlearned'. This was spearheaded by two Essex clergymen, George Gifford and Arthur Dent. Dent's *A Sermon of Repentance* (1582) was reprinted thirty-nine times up to 1642, and his other best-seller, *The Plaine Mans Path-way to Heaven* (1601), a major influence on John Bunyan, achieved twenty-seven editions by 1682.

A judicious mingling of reforming doctrines – humanist, Lutheran, Zwinglian, Bucerian and Calvinist (the latter at first imbibed wholesale but finally likewise consigned to the melting pot) – was to shape the course of a practical, pragmatic theological tradition that gradually eschewed fanatical extremes. Elizabeth herself may well have approved of such a cautious mode of doctrinal 'pick and mix', tempered as it necessarily was by the retention of a modified 'Romanist' conception of hierarchy (bishops, priests and deacons). What she cannot have foreseen was that the tensions precariously held in check within her very personal vision of *Ecclesia Anglicana* would burst forth in the socio-political cataclysm of the Civil Wars of the 1640s. Charles II's restoration to his father's throne in 1660 proved the most significant watershed between the Elizabethan settlement and the ecclesiastical reforms effected under Victoria. Charles's settlement of religion bade farewell to 'puritanism' by consigning its most intransigent adherents to a more-or-less-tolerated 'Free Church' substratum of British society. This was the springboard from which the 'Anglican' tradition of the last 200 years would finally emerge.

THE STRUCTURE OF THE CHURCH: (1) THE DIOCESES

What above all marked out Elizabeth's settlement from the majority of reformed churches abroad was its strong sense of identity with the (idealised) early church that existed before the days of Romish corruptions. Thus it would continue to be governed by bishops – men, often from the humblest of backgrounds, who at the stroke of her pen ceased to be private citizens and became instead members of the House of Lords, possessors for life of landed estates and active leaders – moral, judicial, financial and military – of provincial society.

Under papal hegemony, western Christendom had evolved a complex hierarchical structure. 'Provinces' – modelled on those of the Roman Republic – were placed under the supervision of an archbishop directly responsible to Rome. These in turn were divided into smaller units ('dioceses') governed by a bishop responsible to his archbishop. The bishop presided over the local communities within his diocese, the parishes.

Since the seventh century, England had been divided into two provinces: Canterbury and York. Rivalry between the two incumbent archbishops, theoretically equals under Roman obedience, had long been resolved by the sixteenth century, and it was accepted that the Archbishop of Canterbury took precedence, with the additional title 'Primate of All England'. The Archbishop of York had to remain content with the lesser designation 'Primate of England'. Nor, if Canterbury was vacant, was he entitled to exercise jurisdiction in the south. As 'dean' of the southern province, it was the Bishop of London who exercised de-facto 'metropolitan' rights and, at the heart of Elizabeth's reign, this was to have profound consequences. In 1577, the Queen suspended Edmund Grindal, her second Archbishop of Canterbury, for refusing to suppress clerical meetings known as 'prophesyings'. Thereafter, John Aylmer, Bishop of London, was saddled with the burden of discharging Grindal's duties as archbishop and metropolitan until the latter's death in 1583 and the appointment of John Whitgift as his successor.

When Henry VIII succeeded his father in 1509, the diocesan structure and ecclesiastical landscape of England and Wales had remained virtually unaltered for nearly 300 years. Things were to change dramatically during Elizabeth's childhood. Having reclaimed his usurped Supreme Headship, Henry and his advisers – most notably Thomas Cromwell, appointed 'vicegerent in spirituals' – headed off in several directions, which proved more secular than doctrinal. The dissolution of the monasteries (1536–40) wrought the most drastic revolution in the social life of the English people since the Norman Conquest: approximately one-third of all landed estates in England and Wales were transferred from direct obedience to Rome to the economic control of the Crown. Given this vast accumulation of wealth, Henry was in a position to lay one of the ghosts that haunted him: the potentially fatal re-emergence of a still powerful feudal aristocracy, which, with various degrees of reluctance, had accepted his father's assumption of the Crown fifty years earlier. His 'new men' – royal servants – or else local gentry with a vested interest in backing the Tudor status quo were rewarded with landed estates out of this massive windfall, either by royal grant or by purchase at advantageous prices. Not a few were granted peerages as a result of their enhanced economic status. Such scions of the ancient nobility as Henry felt he could trust were likewise granted substantial pickings, and henceforth the Tudor regime was largely assured of loyal support in the provinces.

Along with the pacification of what remained of the ancient aristocracy (after a string of judicial murders) went the curbing of the economic power of the realm's prince-bishops. Measures – often underhand and punitive – were put in place to ensure that, while still enjoying landed estates during their tenure, they remained for the future subordinate to the Crown as ecclesiastical civil servants in lawn sleeves, rather than as independent operators with access to the Roman Curia. The cult of Archbishop Thomas Becket, the 'saint' who had defied Henry II in the name of the pope and whose shrine was the objective of generations of 'Canterbury pilgrims', was ruthlessly destroyed.

At the same time, it was recognised that many dioceses, whose contours had remained unaltered since the creation of the Welsh sees and those of Ely and Carlisle in the twelfth century, were too large to be administered efficiently even by the most conscientious of bishops. The plan was therefore conceived of creating a number of new sees and converting some of the abandoned abbey churches into cathedrals to serve as their ecclesiastical centres. Only six such dioceses – all in the event poorly endowed and henceforth permanently underfunded – finally came into being: Bristol, Chester, Gloucester, Oxford, Peterborough and Westminster (suppressed in 1550). The most ambitious ecclesiastical project of Edward VI's reign, the division of Durham by the creation of a diocese of Newcastle, fell to the ground with Edward's death, and thereafter episcopal boundaries remained undisturbed until the reign of Victoria.

At Elizabeth's accession, therefore, the Church of England and Wales consisted of twenty-seven dioceses on the mainland, plus the curious island jurisdiction of Sodor and Man, which had remained a small, independent outpost of Christendom until incorporated by Act of Parliament (1542) within the province of York. Otherwise, the northern province consisted only of York itself along with Durham, Carlisle and Chester (after 1541). The remaining dioceses, including all four in Wales, fell to the jurisdiction of the Archbishop of Canterbury.

With two exceptions, and despite a vast disparity in income between them, the twenty-eight dioceses were equal in the eyes of the English law. Those exceptions were Sodor and Man, whose bishop (effectively appointed at the nomination of its feudal overlord, the Earl of Derby) was not entitled to a seat in the House of Lords and of whose financial affairs the Exchequer never seems to have taken cognizance; and the palatine see of Durham, still known as 'the land of the prince-bishops'. The County Palatine jealously preserved a range of ancient privileges which it had gradually amassed from the Crown as a 'buffer state' between England and Scotland. When, at the beginning of Elizabeth's reign, the government attempted to 'detain' some of the demesnes of Durham and Winchester by annexing them to the Crown, it discovered to its cost that it was riding roughshod over legal rights, the existence of which it could not ignore. Compromise was effected: the estates in question were finally restored to their bishops in return for a 'pension' to the Crown, equivalent to the income they would have yielded had they been 'detained'.

A bishop's ancient duty was to oversee his 'flock', his pastoral staff symbolising his role as good shepherd. One of the most potent weapons in the armoury of the early reformers was a general perception that this ideal had been virtually lost to sight. Throughout Christendom, bishops were widely regarded as no more than 'great lords' or 'lordly prelates'. Thus, the vital difference between Elizabeth's bishops and their Roman Catholic predecessors was that they were expected to be fully resident chief pastors whose primary function was to direct the spiritual life of their dioceses. Gone were the days when bishoprics would be bestowed on absentees – senior government officials or career diplomats – as a convenient way of providing them with an income. Mary I's two lord chancellors – Stephen Gardiner, Bishop of Winchester, and Nicholas Heath, Archbishop of York – were the last of the line. No member of Elizabeth's episcopal bench was ever appointed to high political office, and only one – John Whitgift, her third and last Archbishop of Canterbury – was admitted to the Privy Council. The business of central government became the preserve of laymen. Only on their sporadic visits to London to attend parliament were Elizabethan bishops invited to play any positive role in it, and even then their influence was marginal. Their principal function was to preside over the upper house of convocation and to consider motions from the elected lower house (usually concerning taxation and leases or else petitions for liturgical reform) and, if appropriate, to pass them on to the House of Commons. Since, as Supreme Governor, Elizabeth consistently parried all parliamentary attempts to introduce measures which would in any way modify the 1559 Settlement, little came of their deliberations beyond their acquiescing in grants to the Crown of clerical 'subsidies' (monies over and above direct taxation).

An Elizabethan bishop's first duty on appointment, therefore, was not to wade into the political fray but rather to face reality by settling with the court of Exchequer for his tax liability to the Crown during his tenure of office. His principal burden was to discharge his 'first fruits' – one year's income from his estates, payable by six-monthly instalments. He 'compounded' with the remembrancer of first fruits and tenths, when dates were set for such payments and, with sureties to guarantee his 'bonds', was expected to meet his deadlines on pain of distraint for default. In practice no Elizabethan bishop was ever suspended because of debts owing to the Crown, and, as the reign wore on, the valuable concession of paying by yearly, rather than half-yearly, instalments became the norm. After 1560, few bishops were required to produce sureties, compounding on their own recognisances, while some privileged recruits to the bench were excused their first fruits entirely. 'Tenths' – 10 per cent of the taxable value of the see – became payable as annual income tax from the date of the last instalment for first fruits.

THE STRUCTURE OF THE CHURCH: (2) THE PARISHES

Within the English and Welsh parochial system, beneficed clergy were technically described as either 'rector' or 'vicar'. A rector – colloquially known as 'parson' – enjoyed for life the freehold of the benefice, financed principally by his parishioners in the shape of 'great', 'small' and 'mixed' tithes – that is, one tenth of all yearly profits from agricultural land, produce and livestock. Where the great tithes were legally 'appropriate' to some other ecclesiastical authority (such as a cathedral chapter), or 'impropriate' to a layman who had acquired them by grant or purchase, the parish was served by a vicar (never referred to as 'parson'), who received a guaranteed stipend from the small and mixed tithes.

The dissolution of the monasteries added a third category to the roll-call of incumbent clergy. Many parishes had been part and parcel of the freehold of monastic foundations, who were therefore entitled to collect their tithes and, in exchange, appointed a monk or some other cleric to 'serve the cure'. When at the dissolution such 'cures' passed into the hands of laymen the latter were obliged, like their monastic predecessors, to make provision for a resident pastor. Such clerics came to be known as 'perpetual' or 'donative' curates, receiving a stipend – usually minimal – from the new freeholder. Having no legal claim on the tithes, they were regarded as non-taxable wage-earners. Rectors and vicars were by contrast obliged like their bishops to pay tax by compounding for the discharge of their first fruits at six-monthly intervals over two years. Benefices deemed to be virtually impoverished – vicarages rated for tithes in the *Valor ecclesiasticus* (1535) at under £10 per annum and rectories at under 10 marks (£6 13s. 4d.) – were, however, exempt.

The day-to-day running of the parishes fell to (usually two) laymen, known as churchwardens, who were elected annually. The office of churchwarden was not one to be envied and many qualified to hold it did their best to avoid the responsibility. It was necessarily the preserve of the local elite – yeoman farmers, established tradesmen, members of gentry families – since it required competence in the 'three Rs': reading, writing and arithmetic. It also involved two heavy responsibilities. Incoming churchwardens could look forward between them to the compilation, over twelve months, of a minute inventory of parish disbursements (6d. to Smith for clearing the churchyard, 3d. to Mother White for washing the church linen, etc.) as well as the tricky business of reporting regularly to the ecclesiastical authorities on the activities of their clergy, schoolmasters, friends and neighbours (see below).

THE BISHOP IN HIS DIOCESE

With one exception (Anthony Kitchin, Bishop of Llandaff), the bishops who had served Mary refused the Oath of Supremacy and were accordingly deprived. Thus committed Protestants were swept into the highest echelons of power. And yet, by authorising no reshaping of the administrative structure of the Church, Elizabeth was effectively asking them to pour new wine into old bottles. They were expected to graft revived Protestant doctrines onto an irrational agglomeration of episcopal, decanal and 'peculiar' jurisdictions owing allegiance to a bewildering and sometimes competing network of church courts which had straggled into being over the previous 500 years. The officials appointed to run them were by and large laymen trained in civil law, administering as best they could such portions of the ancient Roman canon law as remained valid in the wake of Henry's break with the papacy.

A new diocesan was in the first place confronted by his dean and chapter, the permanent staff of his cathedral church. It was they who had formally invited him to accept his new office, if by a convenient fiction. Once the Crown had decided to appoint, a licence (*congé d'élire*) was issued to the chapter, authorising a free and unprejudiced election to its vacant see. By the same post there arrived a separate letter naming the Crown's official candidate. Following royal assent to the unsurprising denouement, the dean and chapter formally welcomed the bishop to his *cathedra* (cathedral chair) by solemn enthronement.

Cathedral chapters had rights and privileges which might conflict with the best interests of the see as a whole or with the personal agenda of their bishop: there are many examples of chapters defending their corner on principles which sometimes added up to no more than bloody-mindedness. Contention could be particularly acrimonious when bishops claimed the right to 'visit' their chapters and correct perceived abuses within them.

Such disputes stemmed in part from the question of what was meant by the exercise of 'ordinary jurisdiction'. In all sees this fell principally to the bishop, who thus had full powers to regulate the spiritual, moral and (in so far as it involved church property) the economic and legal life of the bulk of parishes within the diocese. If a benefice was in his personal gift as 'ordinary', he 'collated' a new incumbent to its 'spiritualities', directing the appropriate subordinate – an archdeacon or commissary – to 'induct' to the 'temporalities' (the freehold rights). If the right to present to the benefice (the 'advowson') lay elsewhere, he was obliged instead to 'institute' the candidate presented to him by the 'true patron' (*verus patronus*) – the legal owner of the advowson or else temporary possessor of it 'for that turn' (*pro hac vice*) by grant or purchase from the owner. Patronage disputes – who in truth *was* true patron 'for that turn'? – were frequent and could lead to months of hearings in the church courts before a new incumbent was finally installed. Even then, appeal to a higher authority might overturn the institution of a man whose patron's title to the benefice was subsequently challenged. The Crown itself was not exempt from such procedures and is often found submitting to the decisions of its own courts in the matter of *ius patronatus*.

The process could be further complicated by the ancient law of 'lapse'. If a lay patron failed to present a satisfactory candidate within six months from its voidance a benefice 'lapsed' to the *collation* of the bishop. If the bishop failed to collate within six months the right of collation fell to his archbishop. If the archbishop similarly failed to collate, then the right to *present* was deemed to 'lapse' to the Crown.

Within the geographical confines of his diocese, moreover, a new bishop was to discover that ordinary jurisdiction in certain parishes was exercised by some other ecclesiastical authority. Such 'peculiars' were most commonly in the hands of his dean and chapter, a fellow bishop or a collegiate foundation such as Westminster Abbey. All appointed 'commissaries' to oversee such parishes on their behalf. Those of the Archbishop of Canterbury were dignified by the title of dean. The commissary responsible for his peculiars in Essex and Suffolk, for example, was known as dean of Bocking; that for his peculiars in London as dean of the Arches.

Thus, historians who confront a diocese and attempt to interpret what was happening within it, at any given period, face many problems of interpretation. In a very real sense there is actually no such thing as a diocese at all: within its geographical boundaries lay a network of competing jurisdictions, and the bishop himself was essentially *primus inter pares,* first among equals. His diocese, moreover, was for administrative purposes subdivided into smaller geographical units called archdeaconries. An archdeacon was known to the lawyers, if not necessarily to laymen, as *oculus episcopi* – the 'little eye of the bishop'. (He had once been responsible for the oversight of 'rural deaneries' – even smaller local units – but by 1558 no rural deans had been appointed within living memory.) Between them, the dioceses were subdivided into nearly sixty archdeaconries. The vast see of Lincoln embraced no fewer than seven; London, Norwich and York five each. The Bishop of London also appointed two personal commissaries with full jurisdiction over certain parishes and probate jurisdiction in others which otherwise fell to the archdeacon.

The vital legal difference between archdeacons and commissaries was that the former were collated to a cathedral stall for life or until resignation, whereas the latter, as the title implies, were appointed by revocable commission. This nice distinction mattered little to Elizabethan parishioners. Their local archdeacon or commissary was the most familiar figure in the ecclesiastical hierarchy who ever swam into their ken, and he had a regular impact on their lives. He and his officials travelled the countryside, annually or bi-annually, as a roving court, his 'apparitor' – a special messenger – having visited every parish in order to summon its clergy, schoolmaster(s) and churchwardens to the church where the court would sit. His powers of coercion and correction were identical to those of the bishop in many respects but strictly subordinate to the bishop's own disciplinary and administrative directions.

The bread-and-butter work of all church courts – and their principal source of income – was the regular granting of probate or else of letters of administration for the estate of those dying intestate. The probate jurisdiction of archdeacons and commissaries was restricted to the wills of testators who left estate *only* within parishes under their control: all others had to be proved 'in consistory' or, if there was estate in more than one diocese, in the 'prerogative' courts of Canterbury or York.

THE CONSISTORY COURT

The bishop's consistory court, which met regularly in the cathedral city during the established legal terms (Michaelmas, Hilary, Easter and Trinity) was the fount of episcopal authority. The bishop himself might choose to preside, particularly if an important case was to be heard, but routine business was generally left to his chancellor – commonly known as 'vicar general' – and to the court's permanent officials, acting in concert with the bishop's examining chaplains in clerical matters.

The act books of the church courts have been comprehensively ransacked for evidence concerning religious developments during the reign, from Roman Catholic recusancy to the most extreme forms of Protestant nonconformity. To examine them *in toto,* however, is to discover that their daily work was rarely contentious in a doctrinal sense. 'Office' business (prosecution under canon law for moral or religious offences) pales into comparative insignificance when compared to the courts' other legal responsibilities. 'Instance' cases (the settling of party versus party disputes under civil law) loom larger in the records, the bulk of them concerned with tithe disputes and testamentary matters. And from such ostensibly routine hearings much might flow. A will could be challenged on technical grounds while those named as executors or overseers might formally renounce their obligations. Matrimonial causes, from breach of contract through to the extremity of divorce *a mensa et toro* – judicial separation in the modern sense of the phrase, rather than freedom to remarry – were another constant strand in the courts' activities.

Judicial orders and *licences,* therefore, in every conceivable form, were the most frequent concern of the consistory court. From cradle to grave Elizabeth's subjects were inexorably tethered to ecclesiastical rules and regulations. Although, because of its urgency, baptism always remained a parish affair, midwives required a licence to practise: midwifery thus became the first official occupation open to women. Their licences conferred the right to baptise *in extremis* – a contentious issue in Protestant theology. Parish schoolmasters likewise received a licence to teach only after due examination. Whilst most men and women were married in the bride's parish after 'banns' had been duly proclaimed three times from the pulpit, the consistory court books contain swathes of special licences for the wedding to take place elsewhere.

A clergyman jealously guarded his letters of orders, issued by the bishop(s) who had ordained him, and had to exhibit them on demand when he went before any ecclesiastical court. Trusted incumbents might be allowed to preach within their own cures but as the educational qualifications of the clergy improved dramatically throughout the reign (by 1603, few beneficed men, at least in the home counties, did not possess an Oxbridge degree) it became de rigueur for a man to hold a licence to preach elsewhere, either from his diocesan, his archbishop or his university.

In many parishes the incumbent was an absentee. Although it was one of the bedrocks of the Protestant ethic that every community should have a resident pastor, wholly committed to his flock, 'pluralism' – the holding of more than one preferment – remained endemic in the Elizabethan church and was officially condoned, by letters of plurality, if a man's two parishes were within reasonable distance of each other, provided that he appointed a 'stipendiary curate' to serve the parish in which he did not regularly reside. Such curates received a quarterly payment out of the incumbent's emoluments as their stipend. They required a licence to serve, granted only after due examination of their credentials by the bishop's officials.

During the vacancy of any rectory or vicarage letters of sequestration were issued – usually to the churchwardens – so that the parish's income should be legally overseen until a new incumbent was installed. The sequestrators were then obliged to account to him for their stewardship since the voidance. Similarly, letters of sequestration would automatically be issued by his ordinary, following a communication from the exchequer, if an incumbent failed to compound for his first fruits. A resident curate or some other local clergyman was ordered to serve the cure during a vacancy or period of suspension. Thus variations on the theme of regularising parish life – as much secular and practical as spiritual – were legion.

VISITATIONS

The consistory court was most active during the weeks following the bishop's visitation of his diocese, his principal means of pastoral oversight and also an extra source of income, deriving from fees payable by the clergy. In canon law he was obliged to carry out a primary visitation within eighteen months of appointment and to conduct visitations every three years thereafter, except within York (every four years) and Norwich (every seven years). Conscientious diocesans undertook such visitations personally, health and circumstances permitting, but subordinates might be delegated to visit in their name. The process began with the issuing of visitation articles to every parish in which the bishop exercised ordinary jurisdiction, delivered to the churchwardens by apparitors. There followed a strenuous series of journeys by the bishop and/or his officials as they convened in recognised ecclesiastical centres throughout the shires within his jurisdiction.

It has been emphasised that all Elizabethan episcopal visitation articles derived ultimately from those of the royal visitation of 1559 which, emphasising the ground rules of Protestant worship above all, thereafter imposed a stream of directives concerning the duties of the clergy and the proper use of ecclesiastical resources. A fortieth part of parochial revenues should be assigned to the poor while every clergyman with an income of £100 a year was expected to provide an 'exhibition' (yearly stipend) worth £3 6s. 8d. so that a poor scholar might attend university. All extraneous revenues were likewise to be diverted to the use of the poor and a church 'poor box' set up to encourage charitable giving by the better-off. Such outdoor relief was more pleasing to God than the bestowing of money on 'pardons, pilgrimages, trentals, decking of images, offering of candles, giving to friars, and upon other like blind devotions'.

The parish register of baptisms, marriages and burials was to be regularly written up and kept in a parish chest with two sets of keys, one for the incumbent and one for the churchwardens. The yearly practice of 'beating the bounds' in order to proclaim a parish's geographical identity was to be maintained (all other 'superstitious' processions to cease) as well as due observation of rogationtide (the reading in church during Ascensiontide of the litany of saints acceptable within Protestant worship).

As to the clergy, some had formerly embraced 'fond phantasies rather than God's truth' but all were to be treated with respect. They were to wear 'such seemly habits, garments, and such square caps, as were most commonly and orderly received in the latter year of King Edward VI'. Their right to marry was recognised but the frequenting of alehouses was not. Rather, they should engage in 'honest exercises' because they 'ought to excel all other in purity of life' as an example to their flocks 'to live well as Christianly'. They were to admit none to communion who were not in love and charity with their neighbours; to preach against any violation of the 'laudable ceremonies of the Church'; and to instruct the young for half an hour before evening prayer, encouraging them to learn the catechism. Public prayers were to be conducted on Wednesdays and Fridays and parishioners should be exhorted to kneel reverently and bow their head at the name of Jesus. All readers should peruse their texts beforehand so that they might read 'leisurely, plainly, and distinctly'. Except in certain collegiate foundations and cathedrals there was to be no choral singing but rather 'modest and distinct song' so that the words might be plainly understood.

As to parishioners, church attendance was obligatory, and all should attend their own parish church and no other. They were to receive communion three times a year (Easter, Whitsuntide and Christmas). Their tithes were to be paid to the incumbent according to custom. No alehouses were to remain open during the time of divine service, nor should anyone disturb the preacher or dispute 'rashly and contentiously' about Holy Scripture. All were duty-bound to report any manifestations of Roman Catholic recusancy, and 'three or four discreet men' were to be appointed to 'denounce' all who proved 'slack or negligent in resorting to the church'. Schoolmasters should teach only from authorised texts and instil in their pupils a sense of true religion. It was with all these directives in mind that the bishop drew up his articles.

He and his visitors arrived in the church where the visitation was to be conducted with a pre-prepared 'call book'. For every parish this listed the clergy and schoolmasters who were believed to be in place. Incumbents and their churchwardens were then summoned in due order, along with any resident curate and schoolmaster(s), according to the rural deanery into which their parish fell. Clergy then exhibited their letters of orders and any licences for preaching and plurality; stipendiary curates and schoolmasters their licences to serve. Should any previously unrecorded curate or schoolmaster present himself his name was duly entered in the call book with a marginal note that his credentials for serving in the parish be examined and a licence issued to him.

Clergy and churchwardens were then questioned on oath on the basis of the latter's 'presentment' – their written answers to the bishop's articles. What was the condition of the church fabric (the patron was responsible for the upkeep of the chancel), the state of the churchyard and of the 'parsonage house'? Did the parish have everything necessary for the proper conduct of holy communion – a chalice, a patten for the wafer-bread, a 'fair linen cloth' for the communion table? Was the parish register properly kept in the parish chest along with the chalice and patten? Was there, as directed in the royal injunctions of 1559, an English bible, the two books of Homilies and the *Paraphrases* of Erasmus?

So much for the bricks and mortar of parish life. What of its actual conduct? Most crucially, was the incumbent resident, and, if not, did he provide an adequate curate to serve in his stead? Were the prescribed quarterly sermons duly preached and, conversely, had any unauthorised preacher occupied the pulpit?

Beyond these routine but vital enquiries, the bishop's articles were partly dictated by his own proclivities and preoccupations. He might be concerned to know whether the youth of the parish were not only catechised but prepared for confirmation (though in truth we know little about confirmation at this period). Visitation articles pinpoint infinite variations on local concerns which by turns were religious, social and moral.

As the reign wore on, much more emphasis came to be laid upon strict observance of the Book of Common Prayer in all points. By the time of John Whitgift's appointment to Canterbury in 1583, the charge of 'ritual nonconformity' could ensnare any clergymen who had reservations about its doctrinal or liturgical provisions. Bishops of Whitgift's stamp were concerned above all to know whether they used the cross when baptising, insisted on the ring at marriage ceremonies and wore the surplice during divine service. Not all diocesans, however, were so prescriptive and might frame their articles with a 'get out' clause: did the incumbent *usually* use the surplice etc.? Thus, many puritan clergy were able to salve their consciences with promises of 'partial conformity'.

Once clergy matters had been dispatched, the court examined cases concerning the laity, and it was here that parish tensions could most easily show themselves. Churchwardens' presentments might be suspect on two fronts: a natural reluctance to incriminate friends and relations on the one hand; on the other, a chance to settle old scores and isolate those whom the parish elite considered to be undesirable members of the community. Absence from church and, more particularly, from communion aroused suspicions of recusancy which in the last analysis might result in criminal prosecution. Disturbances in church or churchyard before, during or after divine service also attracted the court's attention, as well as seating arrangements within the nave and 'superstitious' ringing of bells. More serious were charges of holding or attending 'conventicles' – irregular religious meetings conducted either by laymen or else by unauthorised ministers. These raised the spectre of 'separatism', the ultimate threat to the Elizabethan religious establishment, which could tolerate a certain strain of 'moderate puritanism' but not the outright rejection of all directives concerning religious observance.

The churchwardens were finally expected to report any known sexual irregularities within their parish. Since many presentments were based merely upon rumour or 'common fame', the ecclesiastical courts came to be widely resented and dubbed 'bawdy courts'. Bridal pregnancy, adultery and 'whoredom' were the most commonly reported offences, homosexuality and incest appearing only rarely in the records. The former was virtually undetectable if the parties were discreet while incest seems not to have excited the horror and disgust which later generations increasingly exhibited towards it. (Indeed, the extent to which it has been tolerated or simply ignored within the 'nuclear family' was not properly understood until the 1970s.) Contemporaries were by contrast more aware than might have been anticipated of the dangers of venereal disease: even within marriage a man or woman might be accused of 'burning' his or her partner. Predictably, however, many of the churchwardens' concerns were as much practical as moral. Prostitution and the harbouring of unmarried mothers could lead to a burden on the poor rate. Spouses who lived apart might foment social discord within the parish.

THE AFTERMATH OF VISITATION

Once the bishop's officials had finished their work throughout the diocese the 'call book' was closed and an 'act book of office' created to take further cognizance of its scribbled memoranda. Thereafter, all parties involved in cases which the visitors elected to pursue were personally examined in the consistory court. The records of such proceedings are of great value to historians since they often preserve statements and depositions taken down verbatim: the closest we can ever get to an Elizabethan 'tape recording' and the rhythms of common speech. Many cases dragged on interminably, constantly prorogued or delayed by the non-appearance of the parties summoned. Others simply petered out for reasons unknown. The judge's canonical duty of reconciliation out of court probably accounts for many party-versus-party disputes; referral to a higher authority for some of those concerning the clergy.

Thus we finally reach the ecclesiastical courts' Achilles' heel: they possessed few powers of punishment and coercion, having no right to arrest or imprison. They might impose penance in church, before the whole congregation, particularly in the case of sexual misdemeanours. They could and did excommunicate for all offences, including failure to answer a summons, but such knee-jerk response to routine matters triggered widespread resentment as an unacceptable misuse of what was meant to be a solemn ritual. Judges were often thrown back on the ancient procedure known as 'compurgation', the bringing before them of 'honest' friends and neighbours who duly swore on oath to the innocence of the accused. Obviously the process was open to flagrant abuse. Neither is it clear what further steps the judge was entitled to take if such abuse was suspected or effectively proven.

In such circumstances it is hardly surprising that, from the 1570s, there evolved a more draconian method of dealing with serious misdemeanours. The royal commissioners for ecclesiastical causes, appointed by letters patent, began sitting as a regular court, with rights of arrest and imprisonment in cases of recusancy and defiant nonconformity. 'High Commission' proved a deeply divisive innovation since it was in effect a kangaroo court, using the oath *ex officio mero,* by which the accused was expected to swear to tell the truth before he knew what charges were to be brought and was thus pledged to incriminate himself. This tactic was fiercely opposed by common lawyers, flying as it did in the face of the cherished English legal principle that a man was innocent until pronounced guilty by a jury. The High Commission was abolished by parliament in 1649 and – a disaster for historians – its records ordered to be destroyed. Like the outmoded, medieval tomfoolery of compurgation, its dubious legal procedures were not revived at the restoration of Charles II.

FURTHER READING

Birt, H. N., *The Elizabethan Settlement of Religion* (London, 1908).
Brigden, Susan, *London and the Reformation* (Oxford, 1989).
Collinson, Patrick, *The Elizabethan Puritan Movement* (London, 1967).
—— *Archbishop Grindal, 1519–1583: The Struggle for a Reformed Church* (London, 1979).
—— *The Religion of Protestants: The Church in English Society, 1559–1625* (Oxford, 1982).
—— *Godly People* (London, 1983).
—— *Elizabethans* (London, 2003).
Emmison, F. G., *Elizabethan Life: Morals and the Church Courts* (Chelmsford, 1973).
Fincham, Kenneth, *Prelate as Pastor: The Episcopate of James I* (Oxford, 1990).
Frere, W. H., and Kennedy, W. M. P. (eds.), *Visitation Articles and Injunctions of the Period of the Reformation,* 3 vols. (London, 1910).
Garrett, C. H., *The Marian Exiles* (Cambridge, 1938).
Gee, Henry, *The Elizabethan Clergy and the Settlement of Religion, 1558–1564* (Oxford, 1898).
Grindal, E., *The Remains of Edmund Grindal,* ed. W. Nicholson (Cambridge, 1843).
Haigh, Christopher, *Elizabeth I* (London, 1988).
Haugaard, W, P., *Elizabeth and the English Reformation* (Cambridge, 1968).
Heal, Felicity, *Of Prelates and Princes* (Cambridge, 1980).
Heal, Felicity, and O'Day, Rosemary (eds.), *Church and Society in England: Henry VIII to James I* (London, 1977).
Humphery-Smith, Cecil R. (ed.), *The Phillimore Atlas and Index of Parish Registers* (Chichester, 1984).
Jones, Norman L., *Faith by Statute: Parliament and the Settlement of Religion, 1559* (London, 1982).
Lake, Peter, *Moderate Puritans and the Elizabethan Church* (Cambridge, 1982).
—— *Anglicans and Puritans?* (London, 1988).
MacCulloch, Diarmaid, *Reformation: Europe's House Divided, 1490–1700* (London, 2003).
Marshall, Peter and Ryrie, Alec (eds.), *The Beginnings of English Protestantism* (Cambridge, 2002).

O'Day, Rosemary, *The English Clergy: The Emergence and Consolidation of a Profession* (Leicester, 1979).
Parker, M., *The Correspondence of Matthew Parker,* ed. J. Bruce and T. Perowne (Cambridge, 1853).
Paule, George, *The Life of John Whitgift . . . Archbishop of Canterbury,* 2nd edn (London, 1698).
Payne, Ernest A., *The Free Church Tradition in the Life of England* (London, 1944).
Porter, H. C., *Reformation and Reaction in Tudor Cambridge* (Cambridge, 1958).
Usher, Brett, 'Durham and Winchester Episcopal Estates and the Elizabethan Settlement: A Reappraisal', *The Journal of Ecclesiastical History,* 49 (3) (1998): 393–406.
—— *William Cecil and Episcopacy* (Aldershot, 2003).
—— 'Queen Elizabeth and Mrs Bishop', in Susan Doran and Thomas S. Freeman (eds.), *The Myth of Elizabeth* (Basingstoke, 2003).
Usher, R. G., *The Rise and Fall of the High Commission* (Oxford, 1913).
Wabuda, Susan and Litzenberger, Caroline (eds.), *Belief and Practice in Reformation England* (Aldershot, 1998).
White, F. O., *Lives of the Elizabethan Bishops of the Anglican Church* (London, 1898).
Williams, Glanmor, *Wales and the Reformation* (Cardiff, 1997).

NOTES

1 Norman Jones, 'Introduction: Known for Their Works – Living and Writing Early Modern English Religious History', in Susan Wabuda and Caroline Litzenberger (eds.), *Belief and Practice in Reformation England* (Aldershot, 1998), pp. 1–19; p. 13.
2 Diarmaid MacCulloch, 'The Latitude of the Church of England', in K. Fincham and P. Lake (eds.), *Religious Politics in Post-Reformation England* (Woodbridge, 2006), pp. 41–59; p. 42.
3 W. P. M. Kennedy, *The 'Interpretations' of the Bishops and Their Influence on Elizabethan Episcopal Policy* (London, 1908).

CHAPTER THIRTEEN

PARISH RELIGION

John Craig

THE WORLD OF THE PARISH

That compact expression, 'self-government at the king's command', frequently applied to Tudor governance, might, by April 1559, equally be applied to parish religion for the Elizabethan Act of Supremacy brought the Church once again under the authority of the Crown, yet the practice of religion at the level of the parish was deeply informed by local customs, identities, boundaries and office-holders. The parish was, of course, the smallest and most basic unit of governance within the English church. The term itself seems not to have developed until the thirteenth century in England although related terms such as 'priest shire' and 'shrift shire' date back to the eleventh or late tenth century, but an Old English equivalent for *parochia* cannot be found. Once received, however, the term proved remarkably fertile, spawning a variety of combinations. In early modern England there were more than 9,000 parishes spread across the country with their parish churches, parish priests or ministers, parish clerks, parish bounds, parish constables, parish wardens, parishioners, parish ales, parish poor, parish meetings, parish rates and other parish coinages. Parish lands were lands owned by the parish; the moon might be referred to as a parish lantern, and if something was done on the cheap it was parish-rigged. In its broadest sense, however, the parish referred to a unit of governance that embraced both the sacred and secular, the ecclesiastical and the civil, although the growth of civil responsibilities placed upon the parish was one of the major developments of the sixteenth century, enshrined most clearly in the passage of the Elizabethan poor laws. Yet, where parish rates or a parish clerk can be clearly defined, the limits of parish religion are ambiguous and complicated still further by the variety of parishes found within England.

The overlap with civil administration and local government often owed much to the fact that parishes tended to be coterminous with townships, but this was more true of southern England than it was of the north, where parish boundaries often sprawled over a number of townships. The huge parish of Prescot in Lancashire encompassed sixteen separate townships. Historians and historical geographers often speak of open and closed parishes, referring to those parishes which were large in size, heavily populated with dispersed settlements and loose governing arrangements located in areas of extensive commons, fens, forests or uplands. Closed parishes were commonly lowland parishes with concentrated landholding, small in size and population, possessing nucleated settlements and restricted parish oligarchies. The typology, as Keith Wrightson has confessed, is crude, but one that contains much truth. By 1500, there were, moreover, enormous differences to be found between the experiences of urban parishioners in London, Bristol or Norwich and those of parishioners in parts of rural Lancashire or Cumbria. Further complicating these structural differences was the fact that by the time Elizabeth came to the throne two generations of religious change and a range of fiercely contested opinion and belief might be found within local communities. And the worship of the parish church was something quite distinct from the worship of the chapel royal, the great cathedrals or collegiate churches or what one might have found in Oxbridge colleges or the chapels of the Inns of Court.

In spite of all these variations, there can be little doubt that throughout the reign of Elizabeth I the parish, with its focus in the parish church, was of central importance to the lives of most men and women. The church was often the most substantial and permanent building in most villages and the centre of much activity. It acted as school, storehouse, arsenal, fire station and perhaps even library. Parish services were not only occasions for communal worship but also an important forum for news and information. Announcements about strayed animals might follow the proclaiming of wedding banns. Manor court orders were published in the church, documents were kept in the parish chest, rents were sometimes paid in the parish porch, and the church was the venue for meetings of vestrymen, churchwardens, overseers of the poor, petty sessions, the archdeacon's court which perambulated and sometimes meetings of quarter sessions. It remained the venue for elections to office, audit meetings, business transactions and a range of festive and communal celebrations, although these became rarer in some centres and regions as the years passed. The legislative zeal of the Tudors placed an increasingly heavy burden of secular legislation on the shoulders of the parish. The thin end of the wedge came with the passing of statutes concerning the repair of roads and bridges and the extermination of vermin, such as moles and hedgehogs. The wedge itself came in 1598 with the passing of the first comprehensive poor-law requirements that laid the responsibility for poor relief and for the punishment of vagabonds squarely in the hands of the parish and its officers. In spite of these challenges, the parish endured. Although the ancient claim to comprehensiveness – that everyone was a parishioner and that the parish embraced all – had, by 1700, been irreversibly destroyed, many of the elements of the Elizabethan parish would live on well into the nineteenth century.

While much of this world has been lost, a great deal of information can be gathered about the lives of parishioners, especially from the records produced by the higher officers and courts of the Church. Consistory court material, the records of the archdeacon's court, popularly known as the bawdy court due to the preponderance of allegations concerning sexual offences, and the records of visitations, all cast much light on the lives of both parsons and parishioners. The volume edited by J. S. Purvis entitled *Tudor Parish Documents of the Diocese of York* (1948) relied almost entirely on such material. Yet the recorded descriptions of the parish church (the chancel is not whited nor paved in such decent sort as it ought to be), behaviour of parishioners (squabbling and fighting over pews) and clerical standards (their curate does not celebrate and read the divine service plainly and distinctly), unsurprisingly reflected the life of the parish seen primarily from the perspective of those in authority. The parish itself produced two main records: parish registers and churchwardens' accounts. Parish registers, records of the christenings, burials and marriages in the parish, ordered to be kept from 1538 onwards, survive for many parishes from the latter part of Elizabeth's reign. Only about one-eighth of all English parishes have registers that date back to 1538, and most of these are later copies. The value of parish registers cannot be overstated, and it is from such sources that the population history of England and Wales, with all the attendant questions concerning fertility rates, illegitimacy, social mobility and family structure, has been carefully reconstructed. The other body of material is churchwardens' accounts. These are the records of parochial income and expenditure, a seemingly tedious subject but one which historians have been increasingly exploiting in their search for evidence about parish life.

HISTORIOGRAPHY AND THE PROBLEM OF CONFORMITY

Over the past fifty years, a growing body of scholarship has appeared that, in a variety of ways, often more obliquely than directly, bears upon the experience of English parishioners from the opening years of the sixteenth century to the close of the seventeenth. For too long parish life was treated as something quaint and of antiquarian interest, an approach found in the limited study by Tindal Hart, *The Man in the Pew, 1558–1660* (1966). With the explosion of interest in social history, the parish attracted the attention of social and economic historians asking questions about social relations and the plight of the poor. It has been brought under scrutiny by historians interested in state formation and popular protest. In a famous, if debated, construction, Christopher Hill argued that during the sixteenth and seventeenth centuries, the early modern English parish was secularised, and parish religion was the essential context for Keith Thomas's and Alan MacFarlane's quite different treatments of allegations of witchcraft and the evidence of popular belief. For a variety of reasons and with a multiplicity of approaches and questions, the separate strands of historical inquiry found a locus in the parish and its sources. Chief among these approaches was an interest in religious change at the level of local communities, if not initiated by A. G. Dickens, then certainly propelled by him, as his call for an account of the Reformation that sought to address the concerns of ordinary men and women was taken up by a generation of researchers who combed through wills, probate inventories, parish registers, church court cases and parish accounts. Although much of this work was initially organised around the concept of county communities, an important collection of essays edited by Susan Wright marked a shift towards a closer engagement with parish religion. Parishioners and parish activities loom large in works as diverse as Eamon Duffy's important study of late-medieval religious culture, *The Stripping of the Altars* (1992); Patrick Collinson's depiction of *The Religion of Protestants* (1982); Beat Kümin's analysis of *The Shaping of a Community: The Rise and Reformation of the English Parish, c. 1400–1560* (1996); Judith Maltby's *Prayer Book and People in Elizabethan and Early Stuart England* (1998); Christopher Haigh's *The Plain Man's Pathways to Heaven* (2007) and the work done by Christopher Marsh on church seating, Steve Hindle on Rogationtide processions and Jeremy Boulton on parish participation in communion services, to name but a few. An attempt to think more systematically about how these varied approaches might complement and inform each other can be seen in the way in which historians as distinct as Steve Hindle, Beat Kümin and Peter Marshall – all based at Warwick University – have collaborated to host an important annual conference on the parish and parish material, insisting upon the importance of comparative history and interdisciplinary approaches.

It is more than a little ironic, therefore, that *Elizabethan* parish religion, as distinct from popular religion or early modern mentalities, has struggled to find a place in this flourishing field. There is no modern study of the activities and experiences of Elizabethan parishioners as a subject in its own right. There are at least two reasons for this. The first is that some of the best work on the early modern parish is not much interested in the particular problems of the Elizabethan church. Eschewing older historiographical approaches and chronologies, the tendency is to think more broadly about questions of social and cultural change in ways that are no longer bound to the particular problems of Elizabethan ecclesiastical and political history. Keith Wrightson's seminal essay on the politics of the parish, which responded in part to Patrick Collinson's call to examine the 'social depth of politics' in local communities, is a particularly notable example of this trend. The second reason is bound up with what might be called the problem of conformity. Revisionism and the effect of the local turn in Reformation scholarship have stressed the conservative character of much of English society. While the weight of historical opinion currently favours the notion that England's parishes did not become Protestant until twenty or so years into the reign of Elizabeth I, paradoxically, some of the most interesting recent work on local responses to reformation statutes focuses on the earlier reigns of Edward VI and Mary I. The effect of this is to reinforce the marginalisation of Elizabethan parochial life. It is striking that Eamon Duffy's treatment of the Devonshire parish of Morebath has very little to say about the Elizabethan experiences of its conforming priest, Sir Christopher Trychay. The central narratives for the Elizabethan decades are still dominated by terms of establishment and opposition – the creation of an 'Elizabethan settlement' and the emergence of Catholic recusants and zealous puritans, dissenting movements at opposite ends of a religious spectrum that shared a common opposition to Elizabeth's *via media*. Not least among the difficulties of this powerful myth is the way that it either dismisses or sidelines the experiences of most parishioners who quietly and dutifully conformed to the terms of Elizabethan religion.

The problem of conformity has always had a confessional and polemical edge. Debates about Elizabethan parish life began in the sixteenth century and centred on the problem of reformation. For Catholic polemicists such as John Rastell, services in the vernacular had divided congregations of the 'simple folk' into two; there were those of 'the old making' who understood 'the sentences but by halfes' bearing 'very litle away' and those of 'the new making' who listened only 'to mainteine talke there upon, or to appose the priest, or to judge the priest, or condemne the church of God'.[1] Twenty years later, godly preachers such as George

Gifford and Arthur Dent castigated what they believed was widespread ignorance of basic Christian doctrine. As far as true repentance was concerned, George Gifford wrote that 'the greatest multitude of men' were 'as blind as beetles in this point', but these were necessary and polemical positions in their campaign to establish support for a preaching ministry and not descriptions of parish life.[2] An earlier generation of reformers, men such as Edward Dering, were convinced that the central obstacles to effective reform were greedy impropriators and patrons, careless ministers, magistrates and even the Queen herself. Conforming parishioners were used as the proverbial nose of wax, twisted to suit a variety of positions. Early in the twentieth century, the subject was still deeply coloured by confessional positions. In 1914, W. P. M. Kennedy published a small work entitled *Parish Life under Queen Elizabeth: An Introductory Study*. Kennedy was an Irish Catholic, an expert in ecclesiastical and constitutional history and friend and collaborator of W. H. Frere, who had published his own survey of Elizabethan and Jacobean church history in 1904. Both works were full-blooded confessional histories, Catholic ripostes to the work of Mandell Creighton. Apart from a grudging sympathy for Matthew Parker, Kennedy struggled to find anything good to say about his subject. The royal supremacy had reduced parochial life to a 'dreary round of inquiry and inquisition'. Elizabethan bishops were men on the make; the clergy were 'as colourless, as factious and as incompetent as their bishops'. Parish worship 'may be summed up as disintegrated and drastic – the cause of serious parochial friction'. Fundamentally, the mass of ordinary people were bewildered, having lost their moral compass:

> a generation brought up in an atmosphere of religious movements and dragooned from one religious camp to another was hardly likely to know what to do, or say or believe. There was no security that their acceptance of a new state of affairs today would be pleasing to the government tomorrow. This instability and lack of certainty produced a wide spirit of moral weakness which is too often forgotten in studying Elizabethan England.

And in a sentence that foreshadowed a great deal of historical inquiry over the coming century, Kennedy argued that 'the strong men in reality were the conscientious puritans and Catholics who had the courage to refuse a position which gradually made itself secure'.[3] In all this, Kennedy was echoing the judgement of his colleague, W. H. Frere, whose account of the English church in the reigns of Elizabeth and James found the subject of parish life painful in the extreme: 'genuine religion was so uncommon as to be almost negligible. Whatever may be said of Elizabethan England in its relation to nationality, foreign affairs and literature, it must be confessed that the state of parish life was deplorable.'[4]

Although few today would endorse the views either of Frere or Kennedy, once the more overtly confessional statements are removed, their highly coloured account of parish life is not a world removed from the assumptions of more recent historians. Whether depicted by Christopher Haigh as the 'intractable and unteachable' parishioners allegedly unmoved by the ministry of pious Richard Greenham in the Cambridgeshire parish of Dry Drayton or the resistant, agnostic, heterodox sceptics drawn by Keith Thomas, conforming parishioners remain in the historiographical wilderness where Kennedy and Frere parked them a century ago. This is not to overlook the valiant efforts of historians as different as A. L. Rowse, Patrick Collinson, Margaret Spufford and Judith Maltby in persuading us otherwise, but a powerful set of assumptions drawn from the rhetoric of Elizabethan polemicists, both Catholic and puritan, and supported by the arguments of social historians such as Keith Thomas and revisionists such as Christopher Haigh still holds sway. Despite this, there can be no doubt that over the course of Elizabeth's reign, England became both a Protestant nation and a nation of Protestants and the experience of parish conformists was at the heart of this process.

ELIZABETHAN PROTESTANTISM

Parish religion in Elizabethan England was a return to the reformed religion first enacted during the reign of Edward VI. At one level, Elizabethan Protestantism was established with the formulation, enactment and implementation of the crucial Acts of Uniformity and Supremacy, approved in late April 1559, that served as the twin pillars of the 'Elizabethan Settlement' of that same year. As already discussed, the Act of Uniformity authorised the use of the 1552 prayer book with certain revisions and was followed by the promulgation of the Thirty-Nine Articles of Faith by convocation in 1563 and given statutory authority in 1571. Royal and episcopal visitation articles and injunctions spelled out in greater detail the implications of the twin Acts of Supremacy and Uniformity and arguably had the more immediate and continuing presence in defining and shaping parish religion. The royal injunctions of 1559 were ordered to be read aloud to parishioners once each year, and, although it is rare to come across evidence that this was followed, we know that the parishioners of the London parish of Saint Botolph's Aldgate who came to morning prayer on Boxing Day, 1586, heard the minister 'reade a part of the Queen's Majesties Injunctions' as well as part of the homily concerning the nativity of Christ.[5]

It was the duty of each bishop and archdeacon to conduct regular visitations that tested the degree to which parishes conformed to the Act of Uniformity. Articles were drawn up by the ecclesiastical authorities seeking information from and about parish clergy and churchwardens concerning a variety of issues. The royal articles and injunctions of 1559, albeit addressed primarily towards the clergy, included a series of instructions for all parishioners. Three months after the visitation of 1559, each parish was ordered to provide 'a Bible of the largest volume in English' and, within a year's time, Erasmus' *Paraphrases* on the Gospels. Registers were to be kept diligently, tithes paid, a pulpit erected, the weekly services attended, all images, shrines, candlesticks and paintings to be 'utterly extinct', a poor box and parish chest maintained and all 'notorious offenders' or those who disturbed services reported to the ecclesiastical courts. Visitation articles borrowed heavily from previous sets, but there was always room for variation, reflecting the concerns of a particular diocese or bishop. Archbishop Grindal's articles of 1577 for the province of Canterbury were typical of the sorts of questions that were posed in the second decade of Elizabeth's reign. Within the course of sixty-five detailed inquiries, Grindal wanted to know whether the parish church was equipped with 'all thinges necessarie and requisite for common prayer, and administration of the Sacraments'. These included the Book of Common Prayer, a Psalter, the English Bible, the two tomes of Homilies, the *Paraphrases* of Erasmus, a table of the Ten Commandments, a pulpit, a table for Holy Communion with a 'fayre lynnen cloth' and 'some covering of Silke, Buckram, or other such like', a Communion cup, a surplice, a parish chest for the register book and a poor box. Grindal also asked if all altars and rood lofts had been removed, whether the nave and chancel were in good repair and if all books 'which served for the superstitious Latine service, be utterly defaced, rent, and abolished'. He enquired after any 'that useth to praye in English, or in Latine upon Beades or other such like thing' and asked whether churchwardens and sworn men had concealed any crime or disorder. He wanted the names of those who resorted to popish priests, those who prayed using rosaries, all 'notorious evil lyvers', blasphemers, adulterers, fornicators, incestuous persons, bawds, those that used sorcery or witchcraft and all that absented themselves from the services on Sundays or holy days or that behaved in an irreverent manner in church. In theory, there were few areas of the life of the parish that escaped the probing of ecclesiastical authority, and the articles and injunctions passed down to the dioceses, cathedrals and colleges bear ample testimony to the vigorous effort made on the part of the Church to implement their policy of reformation.[6]

The thrust of such evidence suggests that obedience and order were the touchstones of Elizabethan religious policy. Even if the words were not hers, Elizabeth was famously uninterested in opening 'windows into men's souls'. Obedience was all; men's consciences were not to be meddled with. Men and women were deemed to be 'well ordered in religion', or 'loyal in religion', 'conformable' or 'unconformable'. In a variety of ways, parishioners were reminded that royal authority and ecclesiastical authority were one and the same thing. Paintings of the royal arms were set up in many parish churches, prayers were offered each Sunday for the Queen, and, following the revolt of the northern earls in 1569, a new homily condemning rebellion was issued. Church attendance was from the outset deemed a mark of loyalty to the Crown.

Yet it would be wrong to see the official attitude solely in terms of obedience. There was a creative tension at work. Parishioners, defined by authority, were not only spoken of in terms of ordered obedience, in terms of their relationship with ecclesiastical lordship and the Crown. The language used in divine service, the language of the Homilies, Prayer Book and Bible spoke, at least potentially, of a quite different set of allegiances, a relationship with Almighty God. The Crown was not unaware of the radical message that could be drawn from the Scriptures, and, while it urged parishioners to read the Bible as the 'very word of God and the special food for man's soul', it took pains to warn against presumption. The Bible was to be read 'with great humility and reverence'. But the homily on the 'reading and knowledge of holy scripture' unashamedly exhorted parishioners to 'diligently search for the well of life in the books of the Old and New Testament' and to 'hear, read and know these holy rules, injunctions and statutes of our Christian religion' to 'lay up in the chest of our hearts these necessary and fruitful lessons'. This was more than reformist rhetoric preparing the intellectual ground upon which notions of order and deference were inculcated, but a central tenet of reformed Protestantism with its appeal to the authority of the Word. Yet the message was utterly mixed; social concerns mingled with spiritual lessons and how such messages were interpreted and understood by parishioners is far from clear.[7]

Elizabethan clergy played a vital part in conveying that message, and it would be hard to overestimate the central role they played in the lives of Elizabethan parishioners. They officiated at the baptism of infants, the churching of thankful mothers, the catechising of children, the celebration of the Eucharist, the proclamation of wedding banns, the exchanging of marriage vows and services for the dead. It is important to remind ourselves of how much clerical life touched the people of the parish for there has been a tendency, seen primarily in the celebratory accounts of particular clergymen, to focus on one function alone, that of preaching, an emphasis which clearly owed much to contemporary discussion of clerical roles and was reflected in the hundreds of sermons printed in this period. Yet many ministers possessed no licence to preach, and there was much more to clerical life than sermons. There was a living to be made, and given the slender stipends that prevailed in the early modern period it comes as no surprise to find clergymen actively engaged in forms of by-employment that made the difference between abject poverty and relative wealth. Some, such as John Favour, vicar of Halifax, spent time in the practice of physic and exercising justice in the commonwealth. Others zealously worked their glebe (land attached to a benefice), collected, or perhaps sued for, their tithes, peddled their literacy, reconciled neighbours and, in a variety of ways, were brought face to face with their neighbours and parishioners, friends and enemies. The transformation of the office from that of celibate confessor presiding over the mysteries of the sacrament in Latin to that of married, bearded minister of the Word in English was one of the most striking transformations of the sixteenth century.

If part of the effect of the changes at the Reformation, the stripping away of church wealth, its subjection to the State, the introduction of the vernacular and the new theology, served to rob the clergy of its mystery, of its sacramental power, and to diminish the differences between the clergy and the laity, the new emphasis upon a preaching ministry, upon literacy, learning and godliness produced its own form of authority, seen in the contemporary reputations of celebrated preachers such as Richard Greenham or John More, the 'apostle of Norwich'. Just how these products of the universities related to the majority of their parishioners is a good question, not least when spiritual concerns overlapped with financial ones. The Elizabethan preacher Edward Dering believed that most parishes were marked by 'sutes and controversies . . . the Parson against the Vicar, the Vicar against the Parson, the Parish against both, and one against another, and al for the belly'. Those parishes with true ministers, 'by whom the parish is stirred up to all love, to God first, and then mutually one to another' were 'scarce one parish of an hundred', or 'scarce two or three in a sheere', but statements like these were part of the rhetorical repertoire of the godly preacher.[8]

In spite of the powerful position of the clergy, it is impossible to conceive of Elizabethan parish religion without the selfless or self-interested co-operation of thousands of men and women throughout the realm. From churchwardens to dogwhippers, the parish communities of Elizabethan England were utterly dependent upon the willing co-operation of thousands of middle-income householders, yeomen and husbandmen, tradesmen and artisans, who served as parish wardens, parish clerks, sidesmen, sextons and bell-ringers. Churchwardens, in particular, were vital officers in the administration of parish life. Sir Thomas Smith, in a famous passage from *De republica anglorum,* placed churchwardens within the 'fourth sort of men which doe not rule', described them as having 'no voice nor authoritie in our common wealth', and argued that the office was not at first 'imployed uppon such lowe and base persons'. This seems hard to credit, and throughout Elizabeth's reign, the office was largely filled by men of middle wealth. They were brokers, vital points of contact as representatives of their parish, gathering, selecting and presenting information under oath for and to their ecclesiastical superiors. In larger parishes, they were assisted by sworn men or sidesmen who served as their additional ears, eyes and hands. Parish clerks served a similar function to ministers, and closer attention to this neglected office would reveal much about the workaday life of Elizabethan parishes. The absence of a parish clerk was keenly felt. At the end of Elizabeth's reign, Anthony Rugg, vicar of Yetminster in Dorset, bitterly resented the lack of assistance when he took services at the nearby chapel of Chetnole. The surplice at Chetnole was 'rent and torne' and they lacked 'a sufficient bible', for the bible at Chetnole 'is of a very small printe so that in darke weather, a man that can see well, can scarcely reade in it', but it was the absence of a parish clerk that most irritated Rugg, 'by meanes whereof the minister (in seeking from house to house for the Chappell doore keye, in ringing, cheeming, tolling, bringing the bookes in place and putting on his surplesse by himself alone) is made as it were a slave to the great reproche of his callynge and slander of the gospel'.[9]

PARISH WORSHIP

In 1577, when William Harrison, vicar of the Essex parish of Radwinter, came to give an account of parish worship, the confident note struck was palpable. There was 'nothing read in our churches but the canonical Scriptures'. The Psalter was read through every thirty days, the New Testament four times a year and the Old Testament once a year. A generation or more of using the English Bible and Book of Common Prayer had done its work. He described the 'good and godly exercises' that occupied the Sabbath day and boasted that all was done 'in our vulgar tongue, that each one present may hear and understand the same'. The work of Reformation had improved clerical standards and stimulated greater literacy with the result that 'the ignorant' had learnt 'divers of the Psalms and usual prayers by heart' and 'such as can read' prayed with their minister 'so that the whole congregation at one instant pour out their petitions unto the living God for the whole estate of His church in most earnest and fervent manner'.[10]

Historians such as Horton Davies, Keith Thomas and Christopher Haigh beg to differ. In terms that perhaps say more about their own attendance at compulsory services, far from fervency, Elizabethan services were mind-numbingly boring occasions. Davies argued that because Elizabethan services 'were set off by so little ceremony and symbolism, church attendance must have been excessively dull'. Many were in church 'by compulsion, not by choice' and that 'the services were long and routine and . . . most churches were crowded. In such circumstances it is not surprising that many should find the worship boring, or that misbehaviour and shouting, not to mention scuffling, were frequent interruptions of the service'.[11] Keith Thomas argued that the tone of many Elizabethan congregations 'seems to have been that of a tiresome class of schoolboys'.[12] Even sermons, which might have held parishioners' attention, were, according to Christopher Haigh, met with 'sheer uncomprehending boredom'.[13] There is no need to discount the evidence that some parishioners slept through sermons or squabbled over seating. But this evidence is routinely either exaggerated or misapplied. It matters that the main reason we know of such behaviour is because snoring in sermons or fighting over seats was condemned by dominant groups of householders and accepted by the overwhelming majority of parishioners as lapses from the expected and accepted norms.

Parish services were vital occasions in the creation of Protestant England. Law, custom and zeal worked together to ensure that few households persisted in absenting themselves from weekly services. In form and structure, they were deliberately repetitive occasions. Repetition was the mainstay of much lay participation in the weekly service and lay at the heart of catechetical instruction, formal education and the more specialised practice of retaining and rehearsing the main points of sermons preached. As Patrick Collinson has argued, 'it would be foolish to deny to either the Homilies or the Book of Common Prayer the capacity to distil and drop into the mind, almost by an osmotic process, familiar forms of words which may have done more than anything else to form a Protestant consciousness.'[14] The services ensured that over the course of a year a substantial portion of the Bible was read aloud and the Book of Psalms was given pride of place. The official Homilies were an amalgamation of Protestant exhortation and social instruction, but it is revealing that the authorities revised these addresses to ensure that the language used was clear and accessible. Historians have little access to osmosis, but the combined effect on the populace of the constant use of the Book of Common Prayer, Homilies, sacraments, Scripture and catechisms must have had an effect. Richmond Noble devoted a whole book to the subject of Shakespeare's familiarity with the Bible and Book of Common Prayer.[15] In 1600, William Fayrecliff, a clothier of Bury Saint Edmunds, wrote in his will of his belief in the resurrection 'accordinge to the Articles of my faythe'.[16] When Robert Smith, servant to the Northamptonshire gentleman and MP George Carleton, wrote his will, he began with the following invocation: 'Blessed be God in all his giftes and holy in all his workes, oure help is in the name of the Lorde whoe hath made bothe heaven and earthe, blessed be the name of the Lord from thys tyme forth and forevermore', words taken from the 'grace after supper' contained in the 1559 printed Litany used in the Queen's chapel.[17] Catechising young people took place at the evening service, and, by 1593, even the acerbic Philip Stubbes was prepared to claim that Protestant children were able to discern Catholic errors:

> since the word of God came abroade, and that it was lawful for every one to reade it in their mother tongue, the least child that is (almost) can spye out theyr knavery, theyr shuffling, and jugling: that both they, and their pestilent religion is out of conceipt with most men.[18]

Even the evidence of popular irreverence, such as the mocking words spoken by a tailor in Wisbech that demonstrated familiarity with the communion service, provides further proof of the power of osmosis.

Parish services were also crucial occasions for communication and news, and this not only in those parishes which had no licensed preacher. There was of course a layer of essential local news in the announcing of wedding banns, the tolling of funeral knells and the performance of christenings, churchings and marriage ceremonies, but within the framework set by the Book of Common Prayer, services were actually more varied than has been realised. There is some evidence that in a number of parishes, texts such as the English translation of Erasmus's *Paraphrases,* or perhaps by the 1580s, the translation of Heinrich Bullinger's *Decades,* Thomas Cooper's *Exposition of the Old Testament,* or Thomas Becon's *A New Postil* were being used in place of the *Homilies,* and many parishes were also willing purchasers of a steady stream of occasional services of prayer and thanksgiving. These told parishioners of events such as the siege and deliverance of Malta in 1565, the earthquake of 1580, the discovery of the Babington plot, the naval expeditions of 1596 and 1597 along with celebrating the Queen's Accession Day and the victory over the Spanish Armada. Official briefs informed parishioners of tragedies both personal and corporate and appealed to ideals of charity and neighbourliness. On 31 January 1591, in the London parish of Saint Botolph's Aldgate, a collection for John Bennet raised 3s. 4d., but before the members of the congregation took any coins out of their purses, they heard that Bennet was a Devonshire man and a sailor 'who had both his legges shott off in a ship withe Sir Martin Frobusher' and was awaiting surgery in the house of Thomas Hall, a local tippler.[19] There were weekly collections in this parish for distressed individuals, many of them sailors, but similar appeals for aid, most especially following the catastrophe of destructive urban fires, circulated throughout England.

By 1580, the interiors of Elizabethan parish churches had been renovated in a way that emphasised the centrality of listening to sermons and participating in a vernacular service. Anything that was deemed a distraction from the centrality of the word preached was removed or minimised. Rood screens separating the nave from the chancel were dismantled, pulpits erected and a range of varied types of seating – forms, benches and pews – were set up in the nave. The walls of parish churches were whitewashed and sentences from Scripture painted on the whitened surface. Copies of the English Bible and the *Paraphrases* were chained to lecterns in the nave. Parish church interiors became lighter as plain clear glass replaced the stained glass in windows. If these changes represented a view of the interior space of reformed worship cleansed of the peril of idolatry (itself the subject of the longest of the Homilies) as prescribed by Elizabethan bishops, part of the success of the Elizabethan church lay with an essentially flexible accommodation of local customs, liturgical variety and lay initiatives. Bishops insisted on order, reverence and decorum in worship but it was local communities that found a solution to the problem of misbehaving dogs by paying for a dogwhipper. Parishioners were not to unquiet or grieve their ministers with noise, but allowance was given for audible engagement with sermons as well as for the sighs and groans of heartfelt prayer. One of the most remarkable and significant developments in the Elizabethan church was the incorporation of metrical psalmody, a lay and devotional practice that spread from private homes into parish churches, rather than the other way round. The practice of metrical psalm singing was perhaps the most powerful of the persuasive weapons in the armoury of English Protestantism. The royal injunctions of 1559 gave only grudging permission for congregational singing in parish worship, and the authorities did not require the purchase of books of metrical psalms as they did the Bible, Book of Common Prayer or Homilies. Despite this, as both Ian Green and Hannibal Hamlin have shown, popular demand for the metrical psalter exploded in a way matched by no other text during the reign of Elizabeth, and congregational psalm singing spread like wildfire, eventually all but eliminating the choirs of men and boys singing polyphony from parish churches. The inclusion of female voices in the singing of metrical psalms must have been a crucial factor in the popularity of the psalms, a feature often commented on as novel. As early as September 1559, the diarist Henry Machyn recorded hearing the singing at 'Sant Antholyns in Budge Row, after Geneve fassyon' with the comment 'men and women all do syng and boys.'[20] It was not long before the authorities dropped any opposition they might have had to the practice, and many of the services of occasional prayer and thanksgiving incorporated the singing of specific psalms. When some parishes, in order to maximise participation, adopted the even more novel practice of 'lining out', that is for a parish clerk to sing each line and have the congregation repeat it, no Elizabethan bishop objected.

THE PRACTICE OF PARISH RELIGION

But how did all this work in practice? In keeping with the tenets of revisionism, historians have sought their answer in the nostalgic account written by Roger Martyn, a parishioner of Long Melford in Suffolk, lamenting the disappearance of the world he had known as a child or in the detailed recreation of the parish accounts controlled by the enigmatic priest of Morebath, Sir Christopher Trychay. The note is the same: loss and decline. But not all parishioners thought like Roger Martyn, and many Englishmen and women lived in places other than Morebath. The detailed records of income and expenditure from the bustling, raucous, suburban parish of Saint Botolph's Aldgate in London, home to perhaps more 3,000 communicants by 1580, provides another perspective on religious change. This was not a wealthy parish: the bulk of parish income came from burial fees, the hiring of various burial cloths and tolling the bells. The parish was run by a powerful vestry who kept themselves warm at their meetings with coal fires. They were the ones that ensured that the wages of the clock-keeper were paid, that oil and grease were bought for the clock and bells, that bell ropes were spliced and that benches, forms and pews were repaired. They purchased bread and wine for communion services and responded to the articles that came from the archdeacon of London. At the end of the fiscal year, they had their accounts audited. The accounts attest to the regular and unobtrusive maintenance of the fabric of the church. This is not the stuff of stories to make the pulse race, and it is easy for the historian to turn aside, convinced that Elizabethan conformity is not a story worth telling. Forty years earlier, the situation was quite different. Turning to the accounts that begin in 1547 is to confront a tale of stark division between a group of evangelicals and conservatives vying for control of the parish church and services. It is rare to witness such conflict on the pages of parish accounts, but the contest can be tracked in folio after folio. To give but a flavour: the accounts record (and one would want to know more about the scribe recording such matters) that on 17 July 1547 the parish purchased six books of the Psalms in English 'to have the service of the Church there upon them sung, to the end that the people should understand to praise God better. William Rofford, curate, resisted and would not sing or say.' Rofford, the curate, was eventually dismissed but not before the conflict went before the Lord Mayor of London and Protector Somerset. With the evangelicals in control, the scribe writing these accounts would refer positively to the 'faithful' of the parish and dismissively to a chantry priest as a 'dead soule prest'. When the parish sold 'four old Latin service books', they were further described as books 'which the people did not understand'.[21] The addition of this unusual layer of editorial comment allows us to explore something of the motivations behind the actions of both evangelicals and conservatives in the course of the Reformation commencing in the reign of Edward VI, the return to Catholic ways under Mary I and the restoration of Protestantism under Elizabeth. The drama of the earlier accounts, however, serves to reinforce the prejudice that the settled years of Elizabeth's reign reveal only dutiful obedience.

What makes the choice of Saint Botolph's Aldgate particularly compelling is the survival of a set of memoranda books kept by the parish clerk in the 1580s and 1590s. These volumes are the closest we have to what might be termed a parish diary kept by a remarkable parish clerk, Thomas Harridance, who was scrupulous in his recording of parish events. Every sermon preached, every homily read, every communion service with numbers of communicants and the amounts of bread and wine, every public penance performed, every notice proclaimed – all these, and much more besides, were written down, creating a layer of 'thick description' for close to twenty years, against which the formal parish accounts can be laid and which together open up the character of Elizabethan Protestantism. The amount of recorded detail is formidable. For the single month of January 1591 (chosen at random), there are 117 separate entries providing the details of seventeen christenings, nineteen churchings, fourteen weddings, thirteen burials and wedding banns being announced thirty-seven times. Not a single day passed without some incident or activity involving the parish church. Given London's mortality rates, this was a parish in which the rituals of life and death were tightly interwoven. On the same day, 1 January 1591, George Rowland, a cook dwelling in Ball Alley in the liberty of East Smithfield, brought a living son and dead daughter to the parish church; his infant son Garth was christened and the body of his two-year-old daughter Katherine was buried. In 1583, the chief parishioners organised a voluntary subscription to employ a preacher, and from that date the parishioners had sermons both morning and evening on Sundays and lectures on Thursdays. If this smacked of puritanism, it was a puritanism that embraced the services prescribed by the Book of Common Prayer. Churchings were routinely performed as were private communions. On 7 March 1587, Robert Heaz, the minister of the parish with two churchwardens and two sidesmen went to the house of Mr Alexander Harding in order to speak with Mrs Harding 'concerning her absence from the church'. They discovered that gout had prevented her from attending parish services but 'as concerning religion, she said she trusted to be saved only by the death and merits of Jesus and by no other means' and that she hoped to take part in a communion service very soon.[22] A later entry records that the sacrament was brought to her home. Suspicious solicitude for the spiritual comfort of a gouty parishioner went hand in hand with the triumphant pealing of bells four weeks earlier, on 9 February, 'and was for Joye that the Queene of Skottes that Ennemye to ower most noble

Queenes Majestie and ower countrie was beheaded. For the which the Lorde God be praysed and I wold to God that all her conffederates weare knowne and cutt of By the lyke meanes.'.[23] When the English fleet went out in August 1596, 'a prayer of thankesgiving & for continewance of good successe to hir Majesties forces was read in the parish church' and 'at nyght there weare Bonefyers made Thoroghout all the Cittie'.[24] This was a deeply hierarchical and patriarchal community that provided some modest relief to the poor. There were weekly collections each Sunday for those with grim tales of suffering. The poor box in the church was opened regularly, as on 6 January 1591, by Mr Heaz and two churchwardens. They found 20s. 6d., 'which money was by them incontinently distributed to the poore of this parishe where as most neede requyred', and parishioners too poor to pay the fees for weddings, churchings or burials were not charged. These entries disclose the central features of Elizabethan parish religion in action, stimulated by preaching, aggressively Protestant, profoundly patriarchal and all scrupulously recorded. For Thomas Harridance, the parish clerk, his work, as he said on more than one occasion, was 'I trust to god his glorie & all our comforts.'[25]

FURTHER READING

Booty, John (ed.), *The Book of Common Prayer 1559* (Charlottesville, Va., 1976).

Boulton, J. P., 'The Limits of Formal Religion: The Administration of Holy Communion in Late Elizabethan and Early Stuart London', *The London Journal*, 10 (2) (1984): 135–54.

Clay, W. K., *Liturgies and Occasional Forms of Prayer Set Forth in the Reign of Queen Elizabeth* (Cambridge, 1847).

Collinson, Patrick, *The Religion of Protestants* (Oxford, 1982).

Craig, John, *Reformation, Politics and Polemics: The Growth of Protestantism in East Anglian Market Towns* (Aldershot, 2001).

—— 'Psalms, Groans and Dog-Whippers: The Soundscape of Sacred Space in the English Parish Church, 1547–1642', in Will Coster and Andrew Spicer (eds.), *Sacred Space in Early Modern Europe* (Cambridge, 2005), pp. 104–23.

Cressy, David, *Bonfires and Bells: National Memory and the Protestant Calendar in Elizabethan and Stuart England* (Berkeley, Calif., 1989).

—— *Birth, Marriage and Death: Ritual, Religion, and the Life-Cycle in Tudor and Stuart England* (Oxford, 1997).

Duffy, Eamon, *The Stripping of the Altars: Traditional Religion in England, c. 1400–c. 1580* (New Haven, Conn., 1992).

—— *Voices of Morebath: Reformation and Rebellion in an English Village* (New Haven, Conn., 2001).

French, K. L., Gibbs, Gary, and Kümin, Beat (eds.), *The Parish in English Life, 1400–1600* (Manchester, 1997).

Griffiths, J. G. (ed.), *The Two Books of Homilies Appointed to Be Read in Churches* (Oxford, 1859).

Haigh, Christopher (ed.), *The Reign of Elizabeth I* (Basingstoke, 1984).

—— *The Plain Man's Pathways to Heaven: Kinds of Christianity in Post-Reformation England, 1570–1640* (Oxford, 2007).

Hindle, Steve, 'Beating the Bounds of the Parish: Order, Memory, and Identity in the English Local Community, *c.* 1500–1700', in M. Halvorson and K. Spierling (eds.), *Defining Community in Early Modern Europe* (Aldershot, 2008), pp. 205–28.

Hunt, Arnold, 'The Lord's Supper in Early Modern England', *Past and Present*, 161 (1998): 39–83.

Ingram, Martin, *Church Courts, Sex and Marriage in England, 1570–1640* (Cambridge, 1987).

Kümin, Beat, *The Shaping of a Community: The Rise and Reformation of the English Parish, c. 1400–1560* (Aldershot, 1996).

Maltby, Judith, *Prayer Book and People in Elizabethan and Early Stuart England* (Cambridge, 1998).

Marsh, Christopher, 'Common Prayer in England, 1560–1640: The View from the Pew', *Past and Present*, 171 (2001): 66–94.

Spufford, Margaret, *Contrasting Communities: English Villagers in the 16th and 17th Centuries* (Cambridge, 1974).

—— 'Can We Count the "Godly" and the "Conformable" in the Seventeenth Century?' *Journal of Ecclesiastical History*, 36 (1985): 428–38.

—— 'The Importance of Religion in the Sixteenth and Seventeenth Centuries', in Margaret Spufford (ed.), *The World of Rural Dissenters, 1520–1725* (Cambridge, 1995), pp. 1–102.

Tate, W. E., *The Parish Chest: A Study of the Records of Parochial Administration in England* (Cambridge, 1946).

Ware, S. L., *The Elizabethan Parish in Its Ecclesiastical and Financial Aspects* (Baltimore, Md., 1908).

Wright, S. J. (ed.), *Parish, Church and People: Local Studies in Lay Religion, 1350–1750* (London, 1988).

Wrightson, Keith, 'The Politics of the Parish in Early Modern England', in P. Griffiths, A. Fox and S. Hindle (eds.), *The Experience of Authority in Early Modern England* (Basingstoke, 1996).

Wrightson, Keith, and Levine, David, *Poverty and Piety in an English Village, Terling, 1525–1700.* (Oxford, 1995).

NOTES

1 John Rastell, *A Confutation of a Sermon* (Antwerp, 1564), sig. Hiiiiv.

2 George Gifford, *Foure Sermons upon the Seven Chiefe Vertues* (London, 1582), sig. B5r.

3 W. P. M. Kennedy, *Parish Life under Queen Elizabeth: An Introductory Study* (London, 1914), pp. vii–viii, 21, 31, 73.

4 W. H. Frere, *A History of the English Church in the Reigns of Elizabeth and James I* (London, 1904), p. 158.

5 Guildhall Library (GL), London, MS 9234/3, fol. 9v.

6 *Articles to Be Enquired of, Within the Province of Canterburie* (London, 1577).

7 J. G. Griffiths (ed.), *The Two Books of Homilies* (Oxford, 1859). The language is taken from the homily on the reading and knowledge of Holy Scripture.

8 Edward Dering, *A Briefe & Necessary Instruction* (London, 1572), sigs. Aviiv–Aviiir.

9 Wiltshire County Record Office, D5/28/9/13.

10 Georges Edelen (ed.), *The Description of England by William Harrison* (Ithaca, NY, 1968), pp. 33–5.

11 Horton Davies, *Worship and Theology in England, from Cranmer to Hooker, 1534–1603* (Princeton, NJ, 1970), pp. 213–14.

12 Keith Thomas, *Religion and the Decline of Magic* (London, 1971), p. 162.

13 Christopher Haigh, 'The Church of England, the Catholics and the People', in Christopher Haigh (ed.), *The Reign of Elizabeth I* (Basingstoke, 1984), p. 208.

14 Patrick Collinson, 'The Elizabethan Church and the New Religion' in Christopher Haigh (ed.), *The Reign of Elizabeth I* (Basingstoke, 1984), p. 179.

15 Richmond Noble, *Shakespeare's Biblical Knowledge and Use of the Book of Common Prayer* (London, 1935).

16 West Suffolk Record Office, Bury Saint Edmunds, IC 500/1/59/85.
17 TNA, London, PCC, PROB 11/56, fol. 23.
18 Philip Stubbes, *A Motive to Good Workes* (London, 1593), p. 152.
19 GL MS 9234/3, fol. 23r.
20 J. G. Nichols (ed.), *The Diary of Henry Machyn* (London, 1848), p. 212.
21 GL London MS 9235/1, fols. 2r–30r.
22 GL London, MS 9234/1, fol. 46r.
23 GL London, MS 9234/1, fol. 31v.
24 GL London, MS 9234/4, fol. 21v.
25 GL London, MS 9234/3, fols. 12v–23v.

CHAPTER FOURTEEN

THE GODLY, GODLIER AND GODLIEST IN ELIZABETHAN ENGLAND

Peter Iver Kaufman

John Craig's essay in this volume reports from the parishes that custom, law and zeal brought most Elizabethans to church. Hence, the laity learned about the Bible and the Book of Common Prayer, despite preachers' complaints that parishioners slept through sermons. But not all late Tudor Christians were satisfied with what they learned. Catholics who came to avoid the fines assessed on absentees were no doubt diffident. Historians refer to them now as 'church papists' to distinguish them from Catholics who stayed away. And along with the drowsy and dutifully yet grudgingly present, there were others – in the pulpits as well as the pews – who were discontented with the religious settlement. They argued that more ought to be done to bring the English church – its liturgy and discipline – into line with churches on the Continent that they considered to be more competently and completely reformed. Percival Wiburn, who had visited several of those churches in the 1560s, shortly after having been suspended from his ministry for refusing to wear prescribed vestments, was among this last set of malcontents for a spell. And when the government pressed bishops in 1576 to suppress the public preaching called prophesyings, which he outspokenly advocated in Northamptonshire, Wiburn was further aggrieved. Nonetheless, in 1581, he professed that he was happy he lived and preached in a 'gospelling state'.[1]

Wiburn was then divinity lecturer at the cathedral in Rochester, writing to answer Catholics who protested the laws that required attendance at reformed worship, in his view 'wholesome laws here established for the abrogating of poperie, superstition, [and] treason ... and the good establishing of Christ's true religion, godlinesse, and honestie'. Wiburn was sure the Catholic apologists for absence could cleverly plump for a 'hotchpotche of all wickednesse' while pretending to defend conscientious objections and conscience itself from coercive Calvinists. At their best, the Catholic plaintiffs were crafty philosophers, Wiburn averred, contrasting their craft, cunning, cruelty, superstition and political mischief with 'gospelling' and godliness in reformed circles. And that contrast, he said, reflected the differences between biblical theology and what passed for wisdom in Catholic thinking. Roman Catholics looked to Aristotle, a formidable 'orator', he granted, when they were not genuflecting before Aquinas, who was 'halfe a philosopher and halfe a divine'.

The reformed Christian, however, 'must fetch from God and his will and approbation that that is good and trie it by the touch of his word and lawe, which is our only rule to know good and bad by'. The wisest philosophers, Wiburn went on, had 'confesse[d] and professe[d] the uncertaintie and weakenes of man's mind and understanding'. Nonetheless, Catholics who cited them and 'screetched' in the Queen's ears their justifications for avoiding the Established Church's services arrogantly paraded their contrived certainties. Avoiding reformed services and sermons, they also avoided 'the touch of [God's] word' and, if only implicitly, claimed superiority for their liturgy, philosophy and hierarchy.

Wiburn crossed the Established Church's authorities and was suspended from preaching a few years after publishing his defence of (and satisfaction with) 'the wholesome laws here established' and 'the good establishing of Christ's true religion'. But he gave historians one place to start looking for the godly, because his equation of godliness and a 'gospelling state' provides a minimum standard. Anyone who passionately opposed Catholics' philosophy and casuistry, cited biblical passages and precedents against Catholics' appeals to conscience, dreaded the fall-out in England should those appeals prevail and alluded to the connections between 'poperie' and treachery could qualify. 'The less godly', Christopher Haigh suggests, 'regarded papists as quirky individuals . . . with a few odd ideas, but essentially harmless.'[2]

But we begin with Wiburn because he also set the bar higher. In 1581, he seemed exhilarated, altogether pleased with the 'laws here established . . . for the good establishing of . . . religion'. Years before and after, however, he defied archbishops, bishops and their ecclesiastical commissioners who were empowered to protect the Established Church from implacable contrarians. So his insolence put him among those reformers, whose signatures alongside his on at least one petition that their church 'rather goe forward to perfection than backward' ensured them all a place among those reformers branded as puritans. They seem not to have objected strenuously to being called more forward and more precise than their critics, but they called themselves 'godly', robustly contending that there was more to godliness than serving up a scalding appraisal of Roman – and old English – Catholicism.

AGGREGATING THE GODLY, GODLIER AND GODLIEST

So keeping the godly together was tricky. From what Wiburn wrote, we know to include among them persons who signalled their intention to abandon Catholic liturgy, philosophy and hierarchy for the Queen's religious settlement. Yet we now know that many among them resented what they took to be the residual Catholicism of reformed religion's prayer book, the ostensibly Catholic vestments which reformed priests were required to wear and the power given to diocesan executives. The resentful – the disaffected pastors and the commoners attentive to them as well as those pastors' influential lay patrons – occasionally referred to themselves as godly. The most uninhibited insinuated that they were godlier than others in their 'gospelling state'.

But Thomas Lever was somewhat more discreet. Before Elizabeth's turn at the crown, while her half-brother, King Edward VI, counselled by Thomas Cranmer, seemed to speed the reform along, Lever's sermons extolled its advantages for England's commoners. In 1553, when Mary I succeeded her half-brother, Lever left the realm, worshipping in exiles' churches on the Continent where, by necessity, the parishioners had a large part in parish government. He returned at Elizabeth's accession to become archdeacon of Coventry and hatched a plan 'for some reformacyon of the ministrye'. He feared that the progress of religious reform might stall, if some customs held. Specifically, he mentioned that continued deference to lay proprietors (that is, people who owned church livings as private property and were patrons of livings) allowed irresponsible, if not also incompetent, candidates to take too many of the realm's pulpits. In other words, lay proprietors tended to nominate favourites, and the bishops were too often ready to acquiesce in the choices of leading lay benefactors. This pattern of patronage, at best, secured unremarkable incumbents, Lever argued, recommending that godly parishioners have the right to endorse candidates and, by implication, veto their candidacies after thorough reviews.[3] Probationary periods were later suggested, and the general thrust of Lever's plan seems to have been discussed at length during the 1560s, because resistance to it intensified. Critics insisted that lay and local control was never tried or seriously considered at the earliest Christians' councils or conferences. True, the apostles called commoners together, but neither Paul nor his associates welcomed lay participation. Christian commoners congregated in the first and second centuries to hear what authorities were saying, yet not to have their say. Some deliberations were public, conducted *coram omnibus* (before all), but conformist critics inferred from biblical references to public assemblies that no deliberations were held *ab omnibus* (by all). Conferences were staged for the people yet not *with* the people in any meaningful way.[4]

In Elizabethan England, the reformed laity was a work in progress. Indeed, as this contribution – and the sixteenth century – concludes, we shall find godlier preachers assiduously grooming parishioners, endeavouring to inspire self-discipline. Yet clerical impatience with, and mistrust of, the commoners was not often or easily overcome. Few Lever-like initiatives to have the godly laity assemble to deliberate critical parish decisions were discussed. During the 1580s, as increasing numbers of expatriate English Catholics returned to the realm as missionaries from seminaries on the Continent, some leading puritans feared that reformed parishioners might not be sufficiently reformed and informed to resist the Catholic resurgence. Sermon after sermon redrew the line that divided godliness from superstition and idolatry. When told that a pope's authority was infallible, the godly should be ready to reply that the pope was 'merely a priest in Italy [who] hath exalted himself above all that is God'. George Gifford, a puritan preacher in Essex, took pains to explain how that upgrade or promotion happened, yet he was also concerned that parishioners' curiosity could get out of hand. Questions about doctrine 'make strife and debate', he has a protagonist say in a study of 'countrie divinitie', which expresses regret that some of the godly-yet-not-fully-regenerate (the reformed parishioners who do not 'feele that God . . . reneweth [them] by repentaunce') figured that they could do without sermons and get all the edification they needed by reading Scripture.[5]

Gifford is something of a pivot. He enables us to turn from our first two aggregates of godly Elizabethans – conformists who identified godliness with reformed religion and with the 'wholesome laws here established for the abrogating of poperie' and puritans who stayed within the Established Church yet thought those laws insufficient to complete its reform – to a third. Reformers such as Gifford, Wiburn and Lever bitterly criticised 'papist practices' and pretensions. They rated their queen and regime highly for having devised disincentives to Catholic worship and thought their 'gospelling state' was godly, to a point. But they ran afoul of officials when they reached that point. Gifford found too much objectionable in the authorised prayer book to swear, as required, that it was 'a godly and vertuouse book, agreable, or at least not repugnant to the Word of God'.[6] He refused to subscribe and swear, and thereby put his ministry at risk. Early in 1585, he was deprived of his place at the communion table. But parish puritans backed him and appointed him lecturer. He lost his role as minister yet, as lecturer, shared the pulpit. Dissident, he was not wholly disaffected. Indeed, he turned on – and allows us to turn to – Christians whose disillusionment with the established churches was more comprehensive than his. Robert Browne, for one, was unhappy with the pace of reform and with the ministry of the established churches. He left Cambridge to drum up support elsewhere in East Anglia, where his unlicensed sermons attracted the troop that, Gifford tells us, called itself 'the persecuted remnant, the pure afflicted' as it followed Browne into exile in the Netherlands.[7]

The irony is that Gifford, who mocked the defiance of 'our Brownists', was a notorious nonconformist. Archbishop Whitgift called him 'a ringleader of the rest'.[8] Yet Gifford distinguished himself from the separatists. His defiance, that is, his refusal to say that the Prayer Book was 'godly and veruouse', was well reasoned, he maintained, and based on perceived incongruities between what that book prescribed or countenanced and what Christians' sacred texts described and commended. Browne was imperceptive, Gifford claimed, and those he led into schism were 'blinded by their stubborn pride'. They 'proclaimed all the ministers of our churches' – conformists and conscientious, biblically learned nonconformists alike – 'to be . . . sonnes of the pope'. Gifford granted that, to avoid 'inconvenience', reformed clergy often deferred to their godly 'prince', permitting Elizabeth's government to legislate some uniformity and to prohibit worship by whim. The more ardent reformers might not be completely content with the place reserved in the liturgy for what looked to them to be residual Catholic practices, but they agreed, Gifford said, that, 'all the foulest things being abolished and the substaunce of trueth brought in', English churches were rightly 'reputed godlie churches'. It was 'mad furie' to argue otherwise 'under the appearance of fervent zeal and rigorous severitie against all sinne'.[9]

'Mad furie', that is, to claim to be godlier than the godlier. Rather than collaborate with moderate puritans, whom conformist critics considered too fervent, overheated or overly zealous, the separatists lumped those critics together with moderates and exhibited a fervency bordering on 'furie'. Timothy Scott McGinnis judiciously sifts Gifford's anti-separatist treatises and discovers that they not-so-subtly adjusted a 'rhetorical tack employed by defenders of the established church'. Those 'defenders', apologists for conformity, identified 'two forces' that opposed their efforts. One was Catholic: English expatriates-turned-Jesuit-missionaries, obstinate resident recusants, and England's enemies abroad, particularly Guiscard and Habsburg papists. The second 'force' was puritan: contentious persons styling themselves 'godly', indefatigably expressing dissatisfaction with the Established Church and 'gospelling state', experimenting with Presbyterian polity and denying the Queen her right to oversee the government of her church. McGinnis has Gifford shift puritans into the centre; 'non-conforming and well-intentioned' dissidents join conformists there in a coalition against the extremes of Catholicism and subversive separatism – the godly and godlier become partners in an effort to protect the realm from the ungodly and the godliest.[10]

Gifford did not stride into this controversy unaccompanied. Nonconformists of various stripes took pains to distance themselves from the likes of Browne and his accomplice William Harrison in the 1580s and from a trio of radicals executed in 1593 for having disputed the 'good establishing' of their realm's religion: Henry Barrow, John Greenwood and John Penry. Those radicals seemed misguided to the moderates, yet, in theory, all nonconformity and godliness required a modicum of self-segregation that could be construed as the early stages of separatism. Alexandra Walsham suggests that separation from 'the carnal multitude' was 'a perennial theme'; statements advocating separation can be drawn from puritans' correspondence, tributes to colleagues and confessional autobiographies. The 'dissociation' from godly yet uncomplaining conformists amounted to a 'self-imposed apartheid'. And, Walsham continues, 'many puritans deliberately courted and cultivated their own unpopularity'.[11]

The late-Elizabethan separatists had a titanic talent for precisely that. They outspokenly made a virtue of separation; authorities usually made it something of a necessity. From 1593, laws were passed against 'conventicles', unauthorised assemblies of the godly. Many had become 'more starkly divisive' when the Queen and regime increasingly suppressed dissidents' preaching, as Patrick Collinson explains, observing nonetheless that a 'semi-separatism or merely social separatism' had been around for some time. Late-medieval Lollards met for impromptu exegesis and mutual encouragement. In the sixteenth century, subparochial sets met to discuss sermons. They 'always had the potential to become, or give birth to, a separated and gathered church', and historians would be remiss, Collinson proposes, were they to leave unnoted the 'rudderless drift of many a conventicle into separatism'. Still, the current seems not to have been as strong as his proposal implies. Many Reformed Christians who gathered in supplemental assemblies, perhaps unselfconsciously attesting that they were godlier than their conformist colleagues appear, with few exceptions, to have accepted – with a wink, perhaps – what Wiburn called 'the good establishing of Christ's true religion' in late-Tudor England.[12]

The hundred or so who gathered to worship at Plumbers' Hall in London by the mid-1560s was one of those exceptions. Collinson's influential article on Jacobethan conventicles neglects them, yet he wrote them into his splendid biography of Edmund Grindal, the bishop whose suspension of some local ministers prompted the Plumbers' Hall secession. Grindal summoned the lay participants to answer for their action in 1567. He likely had already heard their reasons for worshipping independently: kneeling and crossing prescribed by the established Church's Prayer Book offended them; the 'idolatrous gear' (also prescribed) made their pastors look like Catholic priests; timid church officials, resisting radical change and 'defend[ing] idolatry and papistry', 'brought the gospel and sacraments into bondage'.[13]

Familiar complaints in the 1560s, yet the Lord Mayor of London joined Grindal and his deputies to hear them. Authorities, no doubt, repeated in the closed-door session what they maintained publicly, that the realm was blessed with a godly queen who would surely prevent her religious settlement from slipping towards superstition. Prescribed vestments were hardly 'idolatrous'; the 'gear' simply served to distinguish shepherds from their sheep, much as long scarves distinguished aldermen from ordinary citizens. Kneeling and crossing showed respect, not idolatrous adoration. Grindal referred to a letter from Swiss reformers who apparently cautioned their godly English colleagues against separating from the Established Church to protest against gestures or garments that were neither 'impious' nor 'wicked' but 'indifferent' and inconsequential. With extreme displeasure, Grindal referred to dissidents' readiness to test drive innovations, abandoning all that seemed Catholic, except the church buildings. Yet the godly assembled at Plumbers' Hall, of course, had left those churches as well, because certain preachers of whom they approved had been silenced by the very officials who, they charged, were letting papists preach all around London. Their 'godly prince' and gratitude for the reformation notwithstanding, secessionists who had been summoned, 'severing [them]selves from the society of other Christians . . . condemn not only us but also the whole state of the church'; so said Grindal, stressing lay adversaries' arrogance rather than the absurdity of their objections.[14]

AGGRAVATING THE GODLY, GODLIER AND GODLIEST

Grindal and Gifford were cut from the same cloth. They concurred that the reformed should be preaching the process of reform into a higher gear and accelerating certain changes yet were intolerant of other, radical changes that the secessionists insolently proposed. But Gifford was a pastor, whom we shall revisit in the last section of this chapter. Grindal became Bishop of London on his return from exile. In 1563, at the convocation of clergy, he joined former exiles and their 'forward' friends to press for further liturgical reforms. He let refugees from the Continent set up broadly participatory regimes in London churches. Yet when dissidents at Plumbers' Hall, de facto, assembled for extra-parochial services, he interrogated, berated and eventually reintegrated them. (We can only infer the last of these, namely reintegration, because there is no record of their persistence or punishment.) He left London for York, staying but briefly as archbishop there before returning south to succeed Matthew Parker as Archbishop of Canterbury in 1576, just as Elizabeth decided to suppress prophesying, which featured consecutive, weekday public sermons. Grindal tried to get the government to relent. He collected precedents for public preaching and for lay participation in the prophecies, circulated the collection to build support among suffragans, lectured the Queen on the separation of church and state and – for his troubles – was sequestered, humiliated and marginalised for the remainder of his period of office.

Grindal's death in 1583 brought John Whitgift to Canterbury and Lambeth Palace. The latter had appalled the master of his college at Cambridge, Peterhouse, by expressing support for the dons of nearby Saint John's who were protesting prescribed vestments in the 1560s. But Whitgift gave up his opposition to the 'idolatrous gear' and became reconciled with his master, Andrew Perne. The two defended conformists' reservations in the early 1570s, when William Fulke, who had led the godly faction at Saint John's during the earlier protest, pressed for greater lay participation in parish government. Whitgift distinguished himself simultaneously when answering Thomas Cartwright's criticisms of 'wholesome laws here established' for their churches and 'gospelling state'. When called to Worcester, then Bishop Whitgift expressed regret for his belligerence against puritan Cartwright, perhaps to appease influential and godlier lay patrons in his diocese. Nonetheless, and not surprisingly, Whitgift's remarks continued to crystallise conformist opposition to the puritans. Their disdain for the Prayer Book's rubrics, he said, signalled their antipathy toward 'the whole order, state, and government of this churche of England'; 'In effect [they] undermine it all.'[15]

Save for that spell in the early 1560s, the godlier greatly aggravated Whitgift, and he returned the disfavour. His inaugural sermon as Archbishop of Canterbury set the tone not only for his twenty-year period in office but also for the anti-puritan polemic that persisted long afterward. He compared England's puritans with anabaptists on the Continent. Both sets of self-righteous reformers, he noticed, treated reformed magistrates as though they were persecutors, the sixteenth-century equivalents of ungodly Roman officials who had hounded Christ and the apostles. Moreover, on the puritans' reading of recent history, it was they who were the apostles' heirs; what Whitgift and conformists thereafter contended, though, was that these 'sectaries', much as the anabaptists, became adept at 'construing things in the worst part' and at finding 'old popish trash' where there was none, in the churches they hoped to subvert, calling their subversion reform. Whitgift's sermon mercilessly assailed those English anabaptists, also known as puritans; they were headstrong, irascible, irrational and unapostolic. They 'break the peace of the church' for 'slight causes'.[16]

Dudley Fenner responded. During Grindal's tenure at Canterbury, he had returned to the realm from self-imposed exile only to leave again soon after the start of Whitgift's appointment. Fenner asserted that godly Christians had a duty 'to complayne of the evilles fallen out in the church', notably, 'superioritie' in the ministry – that is, episcopacy. Bishops had no place in the first Christians' organisational strategy, Fenner insisted, suggesting, in effect, that they were part of that 'old popish trash' that needed dumping.[17] He all but called highly placed prelates predators, and, in some circles, they appeared to be living down to that characterisation. For Whitgift, his suffragans and their ecclesiastical commissioners were trawling for chronic complainers whom the Archbishop described as 'meanly qualify'd' for the ministry. When those nonconformists' patrons suggested that the trawling recalled the terrorist tactics of the Spanish Inquisition, Whitgift fired back that his accusers had exaggerated his cruelty and underestimated how seductive and subversive England's 'contentious' and 'audacious' complainers were.[18]

Whitgift was clearly affronted by the accusations which originated with Robert Beale, Clerk of the Queen's council, and Francis Knollys – and which Lord Burghley repeated. Still, Whitgift retained his sovereign's support. From 1586, he served on her council and, that year, witnessed the last puritan campaign to push reform through a Tudor Parliament. After that, many of the godlier agitators would adapt the tactics of their moderate colleagues, 'keeping their heads down' as Patrick Collinson notes and awaiting the death of 'their deeply unsympathetic queen'.[19] William Perkins at Cambridge, often stabled with those moderates, lamented that Whitgift continued to hound nonconformist preachers. Compelling them to leave the ministry, Perkins suggested, amounted to ecclesiasticide; too few parishes; 'one of a thousand', he exaggerated, had been left with competent and conscientious incumbents.[20]

Of course, some conformists were glad to have Whitgift, as the Established Church's sentinel (*excubitor*), toss out and keep out preachers who had used their pulpits to turn parishioners against their realm's religious settlement.[21] The Archbishop expected that the laity who had been misled by nonconformists would come to see that much maligned bishops were not 'such men as [the critics] wold make us'. The critics were inveterate and venomous complainers, Whitgift suggested; envy, not piety, motivated them. They 'coloured their doings' as godliness and painted bishops as tyrants, but they were clueless about the challenges that the church authorities faced.[22]

A few of the godly declined to accept those challenges at the start of Elizabeth's reign. The eviction of nearly all the Marian bishops left plenty of vacancies. Eminent exiles Thomas Sampson, Miles Coverdale and Anthony Gilby, however, found other employment more to their liking. Gilby accepted a lectureship in Leicestershire. Sampson accepted a prebend at Durham and, soon after, assumed responsibilities at Christ Church, Oxford. Coverdale had been Bishop of Exeter in happier times, before Queen Mary's accession, but was disinclined to resume high office. He was granted a living in London by Grindal, who, along with several other returning exiles, was willing to become a bishop. The signatures of several on a 'declaration' supporting greater lay and local say in parish government led one to infer that exiles-turned-bishops thought their new queen's accession and their nominations marked an important departure and promised swift and sweeping changes.[23] If so, they were disappointed. And dissidents, including Sampson and Gilby, blamed them. By mid-decade, episcopacy became the enemy, and subsequent bishops who harassed their critics thereafter, in effect, also smudged the reputations of the mitred Marian exiles John Jewel, Robert Horne, Richard Cox, John Scory, James Pilkington, John Parkhurst, even Grindal. The very existence of an ecclesiastical hierarchy in their religiously reformed realm aggravated the radical puritans whose efforts to disseminate arguments against episcopacy aggravated prelates in the hierarchy's upper tiers. What distinguished the godly in high office from their purportedly godlier, aggravated and aggravating critics was the sense that episcopacy was salvageable and serviceable, if not also scriptural.

George Downham's report of his experiences is instructive. Although a bishop's son, he was drawn to the critics of episcopacy while he studied in Cambridge during the early 1580s. Justifications for episcopal jurisdiction struck him as unsound. The critics' emphasis on preaching appealed to him. Downham went so far as to sign a petition favouring greater tolerance for separatists. The godliest as well as the godlier, that is, came close to 'turning' this bishop's son, if we may trust his short memoir, tellingly deposited in a sermon delivered twenty years later at the consecration of the Bishop of Bath and Wells. The occasion must have appeared to be the perfect time to recount his previous wavering and its finale. Downham disclosed that his postgraduate encounters in the ministry spurred him to appreciate the value of ecclesiastical administration, specifically, diocesan centralisation. He learned how useful it was to have bishops and their deputies on call to resolve 'parishionall' problems. And he found that, without diocesan discipline, radical and unruly clerical colleagues tended to innovate and to disturb parishioners with odd liturgical gestures and strange doctrines. Bishops were necessary, he said, for what Wiburn called 'the good establishing of Christ's true religion [and] godliness'. But Downham's ostensible pragmatism, on this count, did not dispel all his earlier doubts about bishops' legitimacy, until he remembered the advice of Richard Greenham, preacher at Dry Drayton, near Cambridge, and mentor to many godly reformers – Gifford and Browne among them. Greenham often counselled the younger set to test preferences for episcopacy or for alternatives against evidence left by the apostles, according to Downham, who promptly did so. His sermon reported the results, which put the bishops' position in a positive frame. For episcopacy proved to be biblically correct as well as managerially prudent, and that proved to Downham that its critics suffered from selective amnesia, because they mistook what was 'generally and perpetually used in all Christian churches in the first three hundred yeares after Christ' for medieval Catholic aberrations. Downham was sure that anyone who meticulously combed the Bible for passages related to church government would conclude that little was done in Christian antiquity 'without controlment', without the authorisation of early modern bishops' ancestors.[24]

Downham's friendship with Richard Bancroft, whose sermon at Paul's Cross in early 1589 garrisoned arguments for the Established Church's diocesan government with biblical precedents, may have prompted the former's embrace of *iure divino* episcopacy. We hear more of and from Bancroft in short order, but first we revisit claims that nearly netted Downham for the opposition. In Cambridge and London, the godlier insistently attributed a 'falling away in religion' to episcopal mis-management and set the abolition of episcopacy as a precondition for the revival of 'personal zeal in every parish'.[25] They hoped to replace the diocesan organisation with some version of the consistory-cum-synod system variously adapted by Swiss reformers and in parts of France. An apologist for bishops' regimes replied that, if zeal was what the godlier were after, they need look no further than England's Marian martyr-bishops. 'Clerolaicall consistoriens' across the Channel, he said, could not rival the likes of Thomas Cranmer, Nicholas Ridley and Hugh Latimer.[26] Yet hauling heroes into the rancorous debate, according to bishops' critics, missed the point, which may have impressed Downham at first, the point being that high office too often doused enthusiasm for reform. Critics conceded that many bishops displayed godliness but before their 'little fyre[s]' could grow into a bonfire of the vanities they were distracted by those vanities. They became known for finery rather than fervour, for 'popish lordlynes' rather than for piety.[27]

And the godlier or puritan critics scoffed at the conceit that bishops were biblical. They were 'usurpers', John Penry charged, amplifying what Dudley Fenner and other radical nonconformists said during the 1570s and 1580s. Fenner, for one, sometimes seemed resigned to having the realm's bishops as figureheads because

Elizabeth was committed to her highly placed prelates. But Fenner's alternative to strong diocesan organisation was local polling. He would not have commoners 'beare the whole sway without the government and direction of elders', he explained, yet, if elders or presbyters botch the job and local elections become unpleasant, if not also 'unlawfull', he would have the Queen intervene to 'disanull' the results. What is most striking, though, is not just Fenner's naivety about his sovereign's interests but the invisibility of the bishops he sidelined. Their participation had historically limited the 'liberty of Christians', so they had no place between congregational caucuses and their godly prince.[28]

An anonymously published conversation about 'the strife in our church' incorporates what was increasingly the establishment's rejoinder to its critics during the 1580s and 1590s. After an interlocutor echoed the complaints that bishops were unbiblical, uncaring, and 'unthrift[y]', he finished by savouring the irony that puritan critics who thought themselves far godlier than their godly diocesans nonetheless were 'full of hatred and malice'. Richard Bancroft added 'envy and evil surmising' and excoriated the critics for twisting sacred texts to serve their purposes. They were not unlearned, he allowed, so they could see that the Bible encouraged 'superioritie' in ministry. They simply wanted to stage a coup to seize the said superiority from their bishops. They were the usurpers or, to be precise, would-be usurpers. Their bishops were the apostles' heirs. 'The government of . . . our bishops is lawful and godlie.' [29]

Downham preached about Greenham's part in his change of mind, yet, as noted, Bancroft's sermon may have bestirred him as well as many godly others to concede the plausibility of *iure divino* episcopacy. Thomas Bilson fortified that position with two hefty treatises on church government that retrofitted the role of bishop into the experience of the earliest Christians. The jurisdiction of bishops was as old as Christianity, Bancroft and Bilson – then Downham – professed; everything in the parishes had been arranged with the first bishops' 'liking and assent'. On occasion, they shared power with local leaders to peel off support from other locals, less to their 'liking', Bilson went on, but bishops soon saw that a more expeditious way to check 'the rashness and rudeness of many that are [more] often ledde with affection than with discretion' was to exercise authority directly. Thus, congregations in Christian antiquity were 'forced' to affiliate with 'the church of some city by whose bishop their presbyters, living, were governed and, dying', were replaced.[30]

Whitgift, Bancroft and Bilson, as Bishop of Worcester for barely four months before becoming Bishop of Winchester, presumed to exercise that authority over their clergy, save that they and fellow bishops replaced dissident pastors before they died. Bishops' godlier critics continued to protest, much as they had at Plumbers' Hall in the 1560s, in Parliament during the 1570s and 1580s, before the bishops themselves and in petitions to the Queen and her council. The protests – some spare, others loaded with data – declared that pruning nonconformist preachers deprived the realm of effective evangelists. To the problem so posed, conformists replied that sermons of the disaffected merely spread disaffection. They reassured the government that bishops had plenty of replacements, men who might not meet puritans' soaring standards – 'who have not the gifte of utterance and audacitie to preach' yet who were good guides nonetheless, 'well hable to catechize and privately to exhort'.[31]

One could argue that agitation against such claims had pretty much played out by the end of Elizabeth's reign. Many of the godlier lost their pulpits; some lost heart. In 1604, their new king let it be known at a conference at Hampton Court, to which several puritans were summoned, that bishops and their jurisdiction were 'agreeable'. Also in 1604, Archbishop Whitgift was succeeded by Bancroft, who, as noted, had confirmed that 'the government of . . . our bishops is *lawful* and *godlie*'. The godliest – in our aggregation, puritan separatists – objected to both italicised claims. Other puritans, who pulled up shy of separation, disputed the second term and grudgingly accepted the first, and are, in this account, the godlier who referred to themselves as 'godly'. But, as Bancroft's declaration makes clear, conformists were not ready to cede that term to their critics.

GROOMING THE GODLIER

Bancroft, Bilson, Whitgift and their conformist colleagues kept their godlier critics from refashioning the Established Church. Many critics, therefore, increasingly applied themselves to restructuring the laity's desires. That had been one objective of reformed sermons from the time Elizabeth pushed reform through parliament, though she was not a consistent partisan of reformed preaching. She expected her bishops to suppress the prophesyings and to cork the expression of dissent during public sermons. The godlier, however, tirelessly pressed for more preaching: Catholics needed convincing, and too many Protestants' faith seemed too tepid. Converting the ungodly and grooming the godlier required preachers, aided by the authors of devotional literature, to inspire something of a makeover of the late Tudor religious personality.

Yet the realm's commoners were adept at evasive manoeuvres. Were it not for puritans' complaints, their dodges and excuses might have left no textual trace. In George Gifford's *Countrie Divinity*, for example, one character enquires of a zealous comrade whether frequently 'gadding to' sermons and more than a nodding acquaintance with Scripture were all that indispensable. 'Is it not enough for plaine countrie men . . . to have their ten commaundmentes, the Lord's Prayer', and the distillation of reformed doctrine that could be found in short creedal statements? 'I think those may suffice us.' As for sermons, Gifford's rustic enquires, 'Are none indued with God's Spirite but such as runne to heare preaching?'[32]

The addiction to sermons and lectures, which propelled a number of the godlier beyond the precincts of their home parishes ('gadding', that is), was probably, as Christopher Haigh surmises, 'a minority taste', although it does attest the importance that the godlier attached to pulpit oratory that helped the laity 'lay up' God's Word. They trusted such 'laying up' would stir repentance and change lives.[33] Sermons saved souls made humble and contrite by what they heard and made more pleasing to God by what they did. Yet the evasive were resourceful; they said that they were 'afraid to be brought to the knowledge and feeling of their sinnes, for feare . . . they shoulde be driven unto dispaire'. They were not yet lost, Gifford calculated, but they were 'farre off', whereas 'those [who] are pricked and wounded with their sinnes . . . are in the way of repentaunce'.[34]

Would a merciful God demand such 'pricking' and 'wounding'? Evasive manoeuvres included creditable questions of this sort as well as cranky ones.

Scrupulous Gifford inscribed and answered an assortment of them in his *Divinity*. But, in effect, the entire treatise, others like it and many a godlier sermon struggled to explain the nature and extent of God's mercy and its vexing connection with the requirement of repentance. Gifford insisted that mercy and pardon were not earned by repentance; nonetheless, they could not be had without it. Repentance – particularly 'the feeling of their sinnes' along with a remorse that tempts the faithful to despair – signalled that God had chosen the repentant without any regard for their merits. David Como suggests that this explanation for 'pricking' and 'wounding' was the puritans' way to cope with 'the messy realities of pastoral practice'. Puritan pietists seemed to straddle the fence between early modern sola-fideism and the late-medieval *facere quod in se est.* (Faith alone saved – but only accompanied by strenuous efforts to personalise precisely that assurance of one's election.) And Como concludes that 'there is good reason to believe that the system proved effective for the vast majority of the godly.'[35]

The preachers took their straddling seriously. Gifford referred to reconciling the gift of faith, supposedly unmerited, with the necessity for repentance as 'a deepe peece of divinity'. Yet he also scolded the evasive for being deliberately 'doltish', for failing to plumb the depths. The protagonist Zelotes, in *Countrie Divinity*, is 'greeved to see [his rustic interlocutor's] gross and palpable blindness'. Zealots of his stripe, in life and in literature, apparently earned their names and reputations for being 'over holy', for meddling and for spreading gloom with the gospel. 'Doe yee not see', Zelotes asks, knowing too well the answer, 'that those [who] doe shew ye the daunger of damnation doe it for your profit?'[36] But in conformists' circles, a commoner's 'palpable blindness' was less worrisome than the fanatical zeal with which the godlier tried to cure it. Too many meddled too clamourously; 'every ... prentice [and] artificer', forgetting his station, presumed to pronounce on the reformation of church and character.[37]

Richard Cosin, a close associate of Whitgift, Bancroft and Bilson, wrote at length about one instance of such forgetfulness. In London, during the summer of 1591, William Hacket and two cronies 'seditiously filled our streets with their ... hypocriticall outcries of "Repent"'. Cosin linked that episode with disturbances that brought down the ecclesiastical and secular regimes in Münster in 1534, mining the vein Whitgift opened when he paired anabaptists with puritan extremists. Did Cosin wince or wink when he recalled that both Hacket and the Münster prophets, notably Jan of Leiden, 'pretended' to be 'ravished by the spirit', indulged in melodramatic displays of self-degradation, and claimed to have the ability, as a result, to discern and damn others' personal sins and political shortcomings? Hardly any of the godlier warmed to Hacket's blend of sorcery and spiritual enthusiasm, yet Cosin made certain that conformists remained deaf to puritans who tried to distance themselves from the abrasive company that collected around the eccentric prophet. Cosin, that is, cast the godlier as Hacket's 'disciplinarian schoolemasters' and contended that their pupil's excesses were precisely what grooming the godly could come to.[38]

To the historian Theodore Dwight Bozeman, the godlier were 'passionate disciplinarians'. His superb study of their thinking begins with an acknowledgement that the godly's pervasive mistrust of Catholicism – unreformed and ungodly, to their mind – stirred their faith in faith, the robust fideism of reformed religion in England. The Elizabethan godly trusted that God's pardon was given in and with faith without 'antecedent conditions'. Yet Bozeman appreciates that the godly conceived of 'saving faith' as 'an intriguingly dual affair'. Christian redemption was 'a complex of pardon plus moral remodeling'. The latter began with a 'knowledge and feeling' of one's sins, as Gifford's zealot explained, then passed through repentance, led to an assurance of election, evolved into guilt for the arrogance or complacency that developed from assurance and returned the faithful to the knowledge and feeling of those new but all-too-familiar sins.[39] Yet the cycle appeared to Richard Greenham, that much admired pastor who seems to have pointed Downham and Browne in opposite directions, as a 'changeable course'. Lively faith in their election periodically reacquainted the faithful with their sinfulness and led them to 'complaine of [their] lumpish, earthly, and dead spirits'.[40]

Baldly put, the fact that frequent cascades of doubt did not douse faith was a sign that the godlier, who persisted through the deluges to love and seek to please God, were already saved. They were groomed to persist and to see the soteriological meaning of their persistence. They were cajoled and consoled, alternatively. Cambridge's most distinguished teacher of godly preachers, William Perkins, assigned the faithful 'spiritual exercises' and encouraged pastors to oversee their completion. What most merits our attention at the moment is the direction that complacent Christians probe for 'some little feeling of [their] wants'. Finding that 'little feeling' was the breakthrough. For Perkins, it was the start of the 'pricking and wounding' that preceded 'godly sorrow' and repentance. The godlier would have to groom themselves, however, to ensure that the 'exercises' were completed advantageously. They should catalogue their 'wants' or shortcomings and show in and by their prayers that they had come to 'see and feele [their] spiritual povertie [and] be displeased with' themselves.[41]

John Phillips deposited similar advice in a sermon he preached while still a Cambridge student. He first warned of God's indignation. Elizabethan sinners were compared with the 'subtill scribes, the proud pharisies, and the deceitfull saducees' for having excused rather than purified themselves. Then Phillips urged 'repentaunce . . . and heartie sorrowe' by which sinners were transformed into prodigals. Literary historians have been known to indict puritan preachers for promoting such sorrow and despair, for decentring and destabilising late Tudor (and early modern) personality, yet Phillips summoned and Perkins urged prodigals to fashion from their anguish a godlier – grateful and gratified – identity.[42]

If sermons and devotional literature did the job that Perkins and others set for them, the godly laity would come to see that despairing of God's pardon was a symptom of desiring it and that desires for God's grace and pardon, as Thomas Wilcox explained, were signs that the first was present and the second, promised. Nature was numb to the 'pricking' and 'wounding'. So only grace could penetrate nature's defences and get the faithful to 'feel' their sins and to feel remorse for having offended God.[43] But sermons and devotional literature ought to be supplemented by the examples of, and conferences with, other pious Christians. The faithful 'must use good company', puritan preacher and diarist Richard Rogers mandated; 'they must bee much mooved and drawen by the reports of other godly.'

Mutual aid and what puritans' critics – including Gifford's rustic in *Countrie Divinity* – called 'meddling', ensured that grooming issued in discipline that could be enforced in congregations and in smaller aggregations of the godly.[44]

What most aggravated the godlier were failures on that front: indiscipline. According to Patrick Collinson, 'no blemish of the Elizabethan church was more prominent or more wounding to the puritan conscience.' Godly conformists were less wounded and more confident that bishops, archdeacons and church courts would 'provide credible checks on the moral and religious conduct of an emancipated laity'. The godly, then, were satisfied with the settlement of religion in late-Tudor England, and their satisfaction aggravated their godlier colleagues, whose expressions of dissatisfaction aggravated the godly establishment. The expressions varied, and some of the godlier, we may assume, lay low and muttered their protests in select company. Others, however, aired their grievances and saw indiscipline as a 'flaw' 'incidental to the usurpation by the bishops and archdeacons and their officials of powers of correction which were properly congregational'.[45] And the godliest among the godlier were not just outspoken: they were impatient to start afresh and did so, earning their superlative, in our terms, not necessarily by their righteousness but by their impatience.

FURTHER READING

Bozeman, Theodore Dwight, *The Precisianist Strain: Disciplinary Religion and Antinomian Backlash in Puritanism to 1638* (Chapel Hill, NC, 2004).

Brachlow, Stephen, *The Communion of Saints: Radical Puritanism and Separatist Ecclesiology, 1570–1625* (Oxford, 1988).

Coffey, John and Lim, Paul C. H. (eds.), *The Cambridge Companion to Puritanism* (Cambridge, 2008).

Collinson, Patrick, *The Elizabethan Puritan Movement* (London, 1967).

—— 'Ecclesiastical Vitriol: Religious Satire in the 1590s and the Invention of Puritanism', in John Guy (ed.), *The Reign of Elizabeth I: Court and Culture in the Last Decade* (Cambridge, 1995).

—— *From Cranmer to Sancroft* (London, 2006).

Haigh, Christopher, *The Plain Man's Pathways to Heaven: Kinds of Christianity in Post-Reformation England, 1570–1640* (Oxford, 2007).

Kaufman, Peter Iver, *Thinking of the Laity in Late Tudor England* (Notre Dame, Ind., 2004).

Lake, Peter, *Moderate Puritans in the Elizabethan Church* (Cambridge, 1982).

—— *Anglicans and Puritans? Presbyterianism and English Conformist Thought from Whitgift to Hooker* (London, 1988).

Lake, Peter, and Questier, Michael, *The Antichrist's Lewd Hat: Protestants, Papists, and Players in Post-Reformation England* (New Haven, Conn., 2002).

McGinnis, Timothy Scott, *George Gifford and the Reformation of the Common Sort: Puritan Priorities in Elizabethan Religious Life* (Kirkland, Mo., 2004).

Spufford, Margaret, 'Puritanism and Social Control?' in A. J. Fletcher and J. Stevenson (eds.), *Order and Disorder in Early Modern England* (Cambridge, 1985).

Wallace, Dewey D., *Puritans and Predestination: Grace in English Protestant Theology* (Chapel Hill, NC, 1982).

Walsham, Alexandra, 'Frantick Hacket: Prophecy, Sorcery, Insanity, and the Elizabethan Puritan Movement', *Historical Journal*, 41 (1998): 27–66.

Watt, Tessa, *Cheap Print and Popular Piety, 1550–1640* (Cambridge, 1991).

NOTES

1 Percival Wiburn, *A Checke or Reproof of Mr. Howlet's Untimely Shreeching in Her Majesty's Eares* (London, 1581), fol. 73v and, for what follows, fols. 72v–77v.
2 Christopher Haigh, *The Plain Man's Pathways to Heaven: Kinds of Christianity in Post-Reformation England, 1570–1640* (Oxford, 2007), p. 198.
3 London, Inner Temple Library, Petyt MS 538/38, fol. 71r.
4 Oxford, Bodleian Library, Selden Supra MS 44, fols. 67v–70v.
5 Compare George Gifford, *A Briefe Discourse of Certaine Pointes of the Religion which Is Among the Common Sort of Christians which May Bee Termed the Countrie Divinitie* (London, 1583), fols. 61v–63v with Gifford's *A Dialogue between a Papist and a Protestant* (London, 1583), fols. 89r–91v, 103v–104v.
6 BL, Additional MS 48064, fol. 44v.
7 George Gifford, *A Plaine Declaration that Our Brownists Be Full Donatists* (London, 1590).
8 BL, Lansdowne MS 42, fol. 105r.
9 Gifford, *Plaine Declaration,* p. 8.
10 T. Scott McGinnis, *George Gifford and the Reformation of the Common Sort: Puritan Priorities in Elizabethan Religious Life* (Kirksville, Mo., 2004), pp. 84–109.
11 Alexandra Walsham, 'The Godly and Popular Culture', in John Coffey and Paul C. H. Lim (eds.), *The Cambridge Companion to Puritanism* (Cambridge, 2008), pp. 291–3.
12 Patrick Collinson, *From Cranmer to Sancroft* (London, 2006), pp. 148, 160–1, 166–8.
13 *The Remains of Archbishop Grindal,* ed. William Nicholson (Cambridge, 1843), p. 209.
14 *Remains of Archbishop Grindal,* p. 202.
15 BL, Lansdowne MS 42, fol. 185.
16 John Strype, *The Life and Acts of John Whitgift* (Oxford, 1822), vol. III, pp. 70–81; Oliver Ormerod, *The Picture of a Puritane* (London, 1605), K1r–K2r.
17 Dudley Fenner, *A Defence of the Godlie Ministers against the Slaunders of D[r] Bridges* (Middelburg, 1587), B1v–B2r.
18 BL, Additional MS 22473, fols. 8v–11r and 19v–20r; Additional MS 15891, fol. 127r.
19 Patrick Collinson, 'The Religious Factor', in Jean-Christophe Mayer (ed.), *The Struggle for Succession in Late Elizabethan England: Politics, Polemics, and Cultural Representations* (Montpellier, 2005), pp. 246–7 and 254–7.
20 William Perkins, *Of the Calling of the Ministrie* (London, 1605), A8v–B3v and C8v–D1r.
21 CUL, MS Mm 1. 43, pp. 452–5.
22 BL, Lansdowne MS 61, fol. 5r.
23 Cambridge, Corpus Christi College, Parker Library, MS 121, fols. 152–3.
24 George Downham, *Two Sermons* (London, 1608), pp. 25–8, 51–2, 58, 73–4.
25 BL, Lansdowne MS 97, fol. 106.
26 William Barlow, *The Sermon Preached at Paul's Crosse* (London, 1606), fol. 3v.
27 BL, Additional MS 27632, fol. 48r.
28 Dudley Fenner, *A Counter-Poyson Modestly Written* (London, 1584), fols. 28–34; and John Penry, *A Briefe Discovery of the Untruthes and Slaunders against the True Governement of the Church of Christ* (Edinburgh, 1590), fol. A4r.
29 Richard Bancroft, *A Sermon Preached at Paul's Crosse* (London, 1588), pp. 4–6, 69, 76–7, 89; Anon., *A Dialogue Concerning the Strife in Our Church* (London 1584), pp. 126–7.
30 Thomas Bilson, *The Perpetual Governement of Christ's Church* (London, 1593), pp. 327, 359–60.
31 BL, Harleian MS 280, fol. 157v.
32 George Gifford, *Countrie Divinitie,* fols. 28r–29r.
33 Haigh, *The Plain Man's Pathways to Heaven,* p. 40.
34 Gifford, *A Briefe Discourse of Certaine Pointes,* fol. 36r.
35 David Como, *Blown by the Spirit: Puritanism and the Emergence of an Antinomian Underground in Pre-Civil-War England* (Palo Alto, Calif., 2004), p. 132.
36 Gifford, *A Briefe Discourse of Certaine Pointes,* fols. 30v–34v.

37 London, Dr Williams's Library, Morrice MS B2, fols. 18r and MS C, p. 228.
38 Richard Cosin, *Conspiracie for Pretended Reformation* (London, 1592), pp. 88–97.
39 Timothy Dwight Bozeman, *The Precisianist Strain: Disciplinary Religion and Antinomian Backlash in Puritanism to 1638* (Chapel Hill, NC, 2004), pp. 32–4, 136–44, 173–7.
40 See Richard Greenham's Sermon, 'Quench Not Thy Spirit', in *The Workes of the Reverend and Faithfull Servant of Jesus Christ, M[r] Richard Greenham* (London, 1605), pp. 243–4.
41 William Perkins, *A Graine of Mustard Seed or the Least Measure of Grace that Is or Can Be Effectuall to Salvation*, appended to *Two Treatises* (London, 1597), pp. 43–7.
42 John Phillips, *A Sommon to Repentance* (London, 1584), sigs. D1r–D4r.
43 Thomas Wilcox, *A Discourse Touching the Doctrine of Doubting* (London, 1598), p. 273.
44 Richard Rogers, *A Garden of Spirituall Flowers* (London, 1609), sigs. A5v–A7r.
45 Patrick Collinson, *The Elizabethan Puritan Movement* (London, 1967), p. 346.

CHAPTER FIFTEEN

THE CATHOLIC COMMUNITY

William J. Sheils

At her accession, Elizabeth I inherited a divided nation, but one in which those attached to traditional religious practice were almost certainly in the majority. The strength of that attachment, and the precise theological understanding of those who held to it remain matters for debate, but the reign of her sister Mary had witnessed a return to Rome and revival in the institutions and administration of the Church under the direction of Cardinal Pole. English Catholicism was not the insular, backward-looking religion of traditional historiography but one led by able bishops who commanded a scholarly following at the universities and the support of important sections of the political nation, at court and in the provinces. The legacy of the reign of Elizabeth's brother, the young Edward VI, meant, however, that Protestants could also claim these characteristics, though many of them had been in exile under Mary, where they had been exposed to the reformed ecclesiology of the lower Rhineland. This was not the Protestantism of the young queen. As the daughter of Anne Boleyn and educated in the household of Katherine Parr, Elizabeth's religion was undoubtedly Protestant but was essentially an evangelical, Christocentric religion that retained an attachment to Lutheran sacramental theology and a devotion to the symbol of the cross. She had conformed outwardly to the Marian Church and sought as advisers fellow evangelicals who did likewise. Uncertainty therefore characterised the hopes of both Catholics and Protestants in November 1558.

The Parliament of 1559 removed that uncertainty in one important respect: the Royal Supremacy was restored and a Protestant prayer book, based on that of 1552, introduced. This required careful management in parliament, and a majority in the House of Lords was only secured by the exclusion of two bishops and an abbot; even then the Act of Uniformity was only passed by three votes, with all bishops present opposed and, perhaps more importantly in the long run, two of Mary's privy councillors and seven peers also voting against. The Marian bishops, except for Kitchin of Llandaff, all resigned, and their example was followed by a number of cathedral clergy and about 200 parish priests. Most of the parish priests remained in England, where many embarked on roving ministries, saying mass to congregations in their neighbourhoods or, as in Lancashire, sustained by a network of sympathetic gentry, but a significant number of cathedral clergy and some scholars from the universities went into exile in the early 1560s, based chiefly in Louvain. From there they embarked on a scholarly printed challenge to the nascent Protestant Church at home.[1]

In the early 1560s, both theological and political positions and alliances remained fluid and ambiguous so that for many of the laity there was no real demand to stand up and be counted, and the conservative nature of the Queen's Protestantism provided a salve to the less tender consciences. Many conservative parochial clergy, therefore, continued to serve in the new Church, the most celebrated example being that of Christopher Trychay of Morebath in Devon, who had been trained in an essentially pre-Reformation model of priesthood and who combined his commitment to the Supremacy with a traditional sacramental understanding of his ministry. Such men could be found in many parishes throughout England, but not all led their congregations into the new Church as did Trychay. In the north, former monks and Marian priests served parishes which later became centres of recusancy, and most spectacularly the vicar of Bonnington in Lincolnshire continued to provide all seven sacraments, including auricular confession, as late as 1576. In such places, continuity rather than change was the distinctive feature of the Church, but by the later 1560s such equivocations were becoming more difficult. In England, the convocation of 1563 formalised the Thirty-Nine Articles in a distinctly reformed direction theologically whilst retaining the Church's conservative liturgical and ecclesiological structure; in Europe, the ending of the Council of Trent in 1564 and the Helvetic Confession of Faith of 1566 sharpened confessional identities on both sides. Attendance at Protestant services was condemned by the Pope, and, whilst diplomatic negotiations between crown and papacy continued throughout the 1560s, these were effectively brought to an end by the papal bull of 1570 excommunicating Elizabeth as a heretic and absolving her subjects from the duty of obedience to her.

By that date, English Catholic scholars abroad had already engaged in literary polemic with the leaders of the Elizabethan Church, of which the theological dispute between Bishop John Jewel and the exiled Marian Oxford Professor of Hebrew, Thomas Harding, is the most famous. Other former Oxford scholars such as Thomas Stapleton entered the debate by contesting the Protestant view of the English past, and the exiles at Louvain also collaborated on an edition of the Latin works of Sir Thomas More to complement the volume of his *English Works* published under Mary. By the end of the 1560s it was clear that however much Catholics at home might accommodate their practice to the new circumstances the intellectual and political boundaries between the Elizabethan Church and post-Tridentine Catholicism in Europe were clearly marked. Thus, 1570 marked a watershed in the history of relations between English Catholics and the Tudor state, a point emphasised by the most significant modern historian of English Catholicism, John Bossy, who chose that date as the starting point of his magisterial study *The English Catholic Community, 1570–1850*.

That year was enclosed by two attempts to destabilise the new regime. The Rising of the Northern Earls in 1569 under the banner of restoring Catholicism led to the execution of its leaders and the flight of several prominent participants, including members of the Percy and Clifford families, into exile, thereby adding a group of lay political exiles to the existing scholarly and clerical Catholics abroad. These lay men and women migrated to Paris, where Scottish Catholic supporters of Mary, Queen of Scots, were also present. By this time Mary had fled Scotland to seek the protection of her English cousin, but her presence in England quickly became a focus for disaffected Catholics. The discovery of the Ridolfi Plot in 1571, which sought to place her on the throne, led the regime to further distrust the loyalty of their Catholic subjects, and the principal Catholic layman in the country, the Duke of Norfolk, was executed for his part in the plot. It is from this date that specifically anti-Catholic legislation, as opposed to that simply seeking to enforce uniformity, can be traced.

In framing that legislation, both parliament and the Privy Council were more vigorous than the Queen. The Parliament of 1571–2 brought in some anti-papal measures, but the Queen resisted further legislation against her Catholic subjects. In domestic terms, crown policy seemed to be predicated on a slow decline of traditional Catholicism as the generation of conservative Marian clergy, both within and outside the Established Church, died out, but this was reckoned without the energy and initiative of the early exiles. From the mid-1570s, English priests trained at Douai, the seminary founded by Cardinal William Allen in 1568, for the English Mission, as it was called, began to arrive to serve surviving Catholic families and to proselytise. Cuthbert Mayne, who pursued a roving ministry on the Tregian family estates in Cornwall, was the first of these to be executed in November 1577, under ancient treason legislation, but the steady inflow of priests and, especially, the arrival of the Jesuits in 1580, and the open challenge to the legitimacy of the Elizabethan Church set out by Edmund Campion and Robert Persons, made further legislation desirable. Accordingly, in 1581, Parliament made it treasonable to reconcile anyone to the Catholic Church and increased the financial penalties for absenting oneself from church to the potentially crippling level of £20 a month. The opening of the English College in Rome in 1580 epitomised a revival in papal self-confidence which, combined with fear of Spanish aggression, made the regime uneasy about the international situation, whilst the continuing arrival of priests, the destabilising presence of Mary, Queen of Scots, and a hardening of attitude among some Catholic gentry who were increasingly excluded from what they considered to be their rightful role in national and local government increased mistrust at home. The Parliament of 1585 ordered all priests trained abroad to leave the country within forty days on pain of death, whilst any lay men or women found to be harbouring priests were also guilty of treason. The immediate consequence of this legislative process was to produce what Peter Lake and Michael Questier have termed a 'puritan moment' within English Catholicism, marked in print by an increasingly provocative political stance expressed by the publication in 1584 of William Allen's *Trewe Relation* and *Leycester's Commonwealth*, produced by Persons and his circle, and made manifest in practice by the Babington and Throckmorton plots of 1583 and 1585–6, the execution of Mary, Queen of Scots, in 1587, and the failure of the Spanish Armada the following year.[2] In drawing the legislative boundaries between the State and its Catholic subjects so fiercely the regime not only sought to isolate Catholics from their Protestant neighbours but also to expose divisions within the Catholic community which had been present from the beginning of the reign. In the early years of the reign, when the future seemed uncertain, the issue of loyalism or defiance, co-operation or recusancy, could be shelved, but as the regime became established and acquired a sense of permanence, those dilemmas could no longer be ignored.

SURVIVAL AND REVIVAL

Despite the terms of the 1559 settlement, the English Church of the 1560s continued to retain many features of traditional religion, not least perhaps in its liturgical forms, if not in their theological definition. This conservatism was marked at the very top, with the royal chapel retaining its crucifix and candles, and despite determined episcopal leadership, matters in the parishes were even less clear-cut. Rood screens and lofts were retained in dioceses as disparate as Exeter, Norwich and York. The tolling of bells for the dead continued in parishes throughout the country, and extra liturgical celebrations, such as the cycle of Mystery Plays performed at Corpus Christi, continued to be performed, albeit fitfully, in cities such as York. If England was Protestant, for many of the laity the character of its Protestantism remained to be defined, and in several parishes, as at Morebath in Devon or Masham in Yorkshire, liturgical implements and vestments were retained by individuals, with the knowledge of their clergy, in anticipation of a return to more traditional devotions. In such circumstances, it is difficult to assess the impact of the Reformation on the people and, therefore, also on popular piety, but it is clear from the work of Eamon Duffy and others that many of the conforming church-going laity of early Elizabethan England retained a strong attachment to aspects of the devotional life of the late-medieval Church whilst accepting the ministrations and hearing the sermons of their ministers. Among the clergy there were many whose formation and early career had been within the Catholic Church, and the new demands of ministry were not always speedily introduced. This was most obvious in the case of preaching, on which the shortcomings of many parochial clergy were recognised by both the bishops and their radical opponents.

It is important to keep in mind this background of uncertainty in considering the later history of Catholicism, for it was in the context of that uncertainty that the Marian priests who left the Elizabethan Church operated. They provided an alternative, and by virtue of their ordination in the English Church, a legitimate priestly ministry to those Catholics unwilling to attend the parish church or who did so uneasily. They often had recourse to gentry support, and they occasionally used the concealed liturgical instruments which had formerly belonged to their parishes. In the words of the committed reformer and former exile Edwin Sandys, reporting on his diocese of Worcester in 1564, they were 'Popish and perverse priests which misliking religion have forsaken the ministry and yet still live in corners, are kept in gentlemen's houses and have great estimation with the people'. Men such as John Coppinge, a founding fellow of Manchester College in 1533 but removed from office in 1559, who carried on a roving ministry in Lancashire and Cheshire into the 1570s, were the physical manifestation of continuity and survival, terms which were contested at the time and have remained so in historiography to this day.

At a time when novelty and change were considered to be signs of instability and falsehood, claims to continuity had powerful rhetorical force. Thus, when the recusant Lady Cecilia Stonor declared in 1584 that she 'was born in such a time when the holy mass was in great reverence, and brought up in the same faith ... I hold me still to that wherein I was born and bred', she was not merely making a statement of fact as she saw it but was also challenging the legitimacy of the reformers' claims. Continuity had rhetorical force in political terms too: *Leycester's Commonwealth,* a tract produced by English Catholics in France, also in 1584, blamed the current difficulties of the realm on the factious puritan councillors of the Queen, who had replaced those whom the exiles considered the natural loyal governors of the realm, the Catholic nobility and gentry. The presence of Marian priests, over 130 of whom were imprisoned at some stage, and the example of imprisoned bishops such as Thomas Watson of Lincoln, who survived into the 1580s, gave support to Lady Stonor's claim, whilst the execution of the Duke of Norfolk and the exile of the Earl of Westmorland in the early 1570s reflected the views of the radicals. Continuity was also expressed by the continued Catholicism of prominent gentry families scattered throughout the realm; the Stonors in Oxfordshire, the Bedingfields in East Anglia, the Treshams in Northamptonshire stand as examples which could be found in any English county. In some areas, especially in Lancashire but also in other northern and western counties, such families were sufficiently numerous for the government to feel the need to bypass local officials and to supervise regional administration through especially appointed councils. Even in parts of the country not especially identified with Catholicism the Catholic gentry impeded the progress of reform and thwarted the ambitions of the first generation of Elizabethan bishops such as Curteys at Chichester or Parkhurst at Norwich. There were regional and geographical continuities as well; Lancashire, the North Riding of Yorkshire and Monmouthshire remained continuing strongholds of Catholicism through to the eighteenth century, as did parts of Worcestershire and West Sussex. Thus, social and geographical continuity were added to contemporary rhetoric to make the case for Elizabethan Catholicism as an example of survivalism, and there is no doubt that the former Marian clergy played a crucial role in sustaining a sacramental life which was nurtured and protected by prominent gentry families scattered throughout the realm. The characteristic of this Church was, however, one of decline, 'from monopoly to minority' in the words of Christopher Haigh.[3] Haigh was responding to John Bossy's analysis, following that of the eighteenth-century bishop Richard Challenor, which saw Elizabethan Catholicism as an essentially new creation of the seminary priests and Jesuits, who, from the mid-1570s, brought the Catholic Reformation from the Continent to England, reinvigorating and transforming a devotional community on the verge of dissolution. For Bossy, the central figures in the story were not the laity but the clergy, who inherited a leaderless church unsure of its direction. Bossy's church was the creation of the exile community of the early 1560s, which provided the intellectual challenge to the Elizabethan settlement and, in the person of William Allen, the administrative and political skills to create an institution at Douai which would provide a training for young Englishmen, many it must be said the sons of old gentry households, willing to serve as priests on what they called, perhaps significantly, 'the English Mission'.[4] Douai was a classic foundation of the Catholic Reformation, a seminary, where the curriculum reflected the revised Thomism of the Tridentine Church. To this seminary, which remained in numbers at least the most significant source of priestly ministry in England, was added in 1580 the

English College at Rome, and behind that, the resources of the Society of Jesus, and in particular the political and organising energy of Robert Persons.

At the heart of the debate over continuity or revival are a number of questions about what Bossy called, in an earlier article, 'the character of Elizabethan Catholicism'.[5] What did it owe to traditional piety? How much had the revival of clerical institutions under Mary produced a vigorous priesthood in the early years of Elizabeth? Were the gentry or the clergy the dominant influence within the Catholicism? And how did Catholics organise their relations with the regime and the Established Church? It is undoubtedly the case that there was much affection for what Eamon Duffy has called 'traditional religion' in the early years of Elizabeth's reign, and it is equally clear that the Marian clergy played an important part in sustaining the faith of English Catholics during the early decades of Elizabeth's reign. But, as Duffy has shown, the rapid collapse of traditional piety from the mid-1580s suggests that a community based on these two pillars would have been in great difficulty without the influx of the seminary priests. The question to address, therefore, is, did the mid-1570s represent a break with the past or not?

As a sacramental religion, the priestly function lay at the centre of Catholicism, and so the clergy were essential to its continuity, but priests needed funds both for training abroad and for protection and support whilst ministering in England. For this the support of the gentry was essential. Many of these gentry families boasted a long-held loyalty to their religion and were soon to experience a history of suffering, social and financial if not physical and fatal, which became a central feature of their self-identity and that of their community. They saw themselves as an excluded minority forced into the byways of public life. Such a man was the Northamptonshire squire Sir Thomas Tresham. His family had long played a major role in county politics, and under Mary in national politics through her Privy Council, and Thomas was sheriff of the county in 1575 despite his conservative views. Perhaps a 'church papist', his children were baptised in the parish church, but a meeting with Robert Persons in 1580 hardened his conservative sympathies into recusancy and he was excluded from local office thereafter. His personal loyalty to the regime was not in doubt, though he experienced periods of imprisonment at times of heightened political crisis and gave shelter to priests in his house at Rushton near Oundle. He and his tenants were often in dispute with his Protestant neighbours, but he regularly paid his recusancy fines to the State, mortgaging his own property to do so, and embarked on a building programme incorporating the Triangular Lodge at Rushton, which expressed his devotion to the Trinity, and an unfinished lodge at Lyveden, which he emblazoned with images of the Passion, a strongly traditional devotional motif but one which also linked the contemporary suffering of his community to that of Christ. Like Cecily Stonor, Tresham saw himself as part of an enduring church whose present fate it was to patiently bear the sufferings of the time. Similar loyalty to the State could be found elsewhere: among the Bedingfields at Oxburgh in Norfolk, whose tombs continued to dominate the interior of their parish church despite their Catholicism, or the Meynells at North Kilvington in Yorkshire who, living in a part of the country less exposed to Protestant evangelisation, maintained a modest place in local government.

Both the Bedingfields and Meynells sent their children to the Continent to be educated, and some became priests or nuns, and Douai and the English College each included children of these families or their tenantry among their early recruits. Continuity is also suggested by the geographical distribution of the seminarians, with large numbers coming from traditional centres such as Lancashire and parts of south Wales, where popular attachment to Catholicism remained strong. Indeed, in Haigh's analysis, it was the failure of these priests to capitalise on this popular attachment on their return and, instead, to minister in the households of the southern and Midland gentry which contributed to what he saw as the 'failure' of the mission. For Bossy, however, the experience of the seminary and the circumstances in which they found themselves ministering transformed the returning priests' understanding of the mission. Their avowed purpose was to minister to an existing community, thereby acknowledging continuity, and to ensure that it had the spiritual and social resources sufficient to equip it to survive in a hostile environment. This required fresh strategies: in spiritual terms, a reflective devotional life based on post-Tridentine spirituality functioning within an essentially domestic context, an approach that implied a strong emphasis on the gentry household at the expense of popular public ritual. This was best expressed in Robert Persons' *The First Book of Christian Exercise* (later *The Christian Directory*), a pastoral work of Christian formation first published in 1582, which was to have enormous influence on both Catholic and Protestant pastoral theology. This was, indeed, a break with the past. The sacraments remained at the heart of the faith but they would be of little avail if 'we chuse them not well by depe consideration, nor doe not digest them well in our hartes, by the heate of meditation: they helpe us little to good lyfe, no more than a preservative put in a mans pocket can helpe his healthe'.[6]

If this privileged the spirituality of the gentry household as the model for English Catholics it was also a strategy that made sense in social and political terms. As leaders of the community, the gentry financed the mission, supported their neighbouring co-religionists and sustained the sacramental life of the Church by protecting its priests and making their houses, in the country and also in London, available as mass centres. Further, the clergy were keen, publicly at least, to ensure that the laity did not collude with the Elizabethan Church, and, as confessional lines hardened, they inveighed against those earlier compromises by which Catholics attended the minimum of public worship needed to avoid the penalties of the law. The argument had already been set out in another book by Persons, *Reasons of Refusal* (1580), in which he viewed the practice of attending public worship as dangerous to the integrity of the Church and likely to lead to apostasy by the individual. For many gentry, however, full recusancy came at a considerable cost, both financially and politically, and a variety of compromises had been devised to enable such families to function within the State. Most famously, the arrangement whereby the male head of the household would attend church while his wife remained recusant was so widespread that Bossy has called Elizabeth's reign the 'matriarchal' period in Catholic history, and the importance of gentry women in passing on the faith to their children is attested by the responses of intending priests to questions about their family background on their entry to the seminary at Douai. In these circumstances, compromise did much to sustain the faith, and this was acknowledged in the pastoral advice given to priests on the mission through the casuistical writings provided for them, but the public rhetoric, whereby recusancy was the only legitimate position to hold, remained uncompromising. It is such recusants, who remained separate from the Established Church and with 'more or less frequent contact with the clergy', who made up Bossy's *Catholic Community*, whose numbers he estimated at about 40,000, or 1 per cent of the population, by 1603. There were many others whom contemporaries would have recognised as 'Catholic' but who are not included in this definition; some knowledgeable observers suggested that for every recusant there were three or four other 'Catholics at heart' who attended Established Church services to varying degrees. These 'church papists' covered a wide spectrum of activity and engagement, and, whilst some such families, such as the Brudenells of Deene, would eventually return to the Established Church during the seventeenth century, others, as we have seen, continued to provide priests for the mission. Whatever multiplier one might apply, and statistics are notoriously difficult to pin down, it seems clear that, under Elizabeth, recusants comprised a minority of those who described themselves as Catholics or were so described by their contemporaries. They were the 'hotter sort' of Catholics, who adhered to a revived and transformed post-Reformation religiosity, but they existed within a larger and more disparate communion, many of whose members saw themselves as part of a continuing devotional tradition.

CATHOLICS AND THE REGIME

One issue that divided members of the community was political: how to conduct relations with the regime. The religious uncertainty of the early years of the reign was matched by political ambiguity, at least until the papal bull of 1570, and the rebellion and plots associated with it. Thereafter, matters became more polarised, but the failures of those attempts to subvert the regime suggested to many English Catholics that loyalism and quiet withdrawal from public affairs was the best guarantee of the survival of both themselves and their faith. International affairs, however, made this position difficult; especially after the violent events in Paris on Saint Bartholomew's Day in 1572 in which thousands of French Protestants were murdered, and in the face of Spanish ambitions, both against the regime itself and during the Dutch revolt in the 1580s. However much the clergy might claim that they were in England simply to minister to their co-religionists, or however fulsomely the gentry expressed loyalty to the Queen, events in Europe indicated that peaceful accommodation was not likely to offer a way forward. The regime recognised this, and from the 1570s Parliament embarked on specifically anti-Catholic legislation which gathered momentum in the 1580s. This policy not only sharpened divisions between the regime and its Catholic subjects but also antagonised divisions within the Catholic community itself. Faced with the executions of missionary priests and also of some lay men and women who sheltered them, the Catholic community was destabilised. Some were radicalised and worked to overthrow the regime, by force if necessary, hoping to place Mary Stuart on the throne, whilst others sought to be allowed to practise their religion peaceably and argued for accommodation with the government. These positions cut right through the community, with laity and clergy being found on both sides. They came to a head in the 1590s, following the execution of Mary, Queen of Scots, and the defeat of the Spanish Armada, in what have come to be known as 'the Wisbech stirs' in which an apparently trivial dispute over precedence among the Catholic priests held prisoner there revealed deep divisions among the clergy on how they viewed the Church in England. The secular clergy sought to curtail the increasing influence, as they saw it, of the Jesuits and especially of Robert Persons, who was by then rector of the English College in Rome, over policy. The secular clergy viewed the mission as a continuation of the medieval Church and sought the establishment of normal ecclesiastical discipline, with bishops at its head, whilst the Jesuits opted for a more fluid structure reflecting a missionary enterprise, and, influenced by them, Pope Clement VIII appointed an archpriest, George Blackwell, to oversee the clergy. Blackwell's canonical status was uncertain, and the seculars, suspecting the influence of Persons and Henry Garnet, the senior Jesuit on the mission, on Blackwell's appointment, rejected his authority and appealed to Rome. The final years of Elizabeth's reign saw the mission disrupted by a clerical dispute over ecclesiastical authority between the Jesuits and the Appellants, as this group of seculars came to be known. The matter was closed, if not resolved, in 1602 when the Pope acceded to many of the Appellant arguments, reduced the influence of the Jesuits over the archpriest and required him to bring seculars onto his council. The dispute was mired in ecclesiastical politics but also had its roots in a fundamental difference over the nature of the post-Reformation Catholic Church in England: was it a continuation of the traditional church or a missionary endeavour that required new instruments? As we have seen, that difference has been reflected in the subsequent historiography, but in 1602 it seemed like a victory for the traditionalist and quietist faction among the clergy over their missionary and activist colleagues. How was this reflected in the wider community?

The career of Anthony Browne, Viscount Montague, can be taken as an example of the moderate tendency within English Catholicism. Browne's actions, and those of his household, in the febrile years of the 1580s have recently been examined by Michael Questier. Browne never explicitly endorsed Catholic activism, was untouched by the Throckmorton and Babington conspiracies, in which some of his Sussex neighbours and relatives were embroiled, and he consistently supported those who argued for some conformity to the Established Church rather than outright recusancy, remaining a 'church papist' himself throughout his life. Despite his acknowledged Catholicism, Montague continued to play a part in local government throughout the 1580s and even in national affairs, being enlisted as one of the opponents of his activist co-religionists as a commissioner at the trial of Mary, Queen of Scots. For Browne, there was no conflict between his religion and loyalty to the regime, and, in August 1591, his household at Cowdray was honoured by a visit from Elizabeth during her summer progress. Browne's case is interesting not just as an example of moderate Catholicism but also in demonstrating that such moderation did not necessarily involve withdrawal into an introspective household piety (and Browne's household was a pious one) but was also compatible with continued political activity and ambition. This continued after Browne's death in 1592 when the household was run by his widow Lady Magdalen. She built a chapel with choir and pulpit in which sermons were preached nearly every week and mass was celebrated on solemn feast days to a congregation of about 120, half of whom received the sacrament. The religious life of the Browne household transcended the 'domestic household piety' which has dominated much of the historiography of gentry Catholicism in this period, and it acted as a focus of Catholic devotion for co-religionists across the region. As the century drew to a close, its devotional tenor became more recusant, and it became increasingly suspect in the eyes of its Protestant neighbours, one of them noting in 1597 that 'since the Lady Montagues coming to dwel at Battle religion in that countrey, and especially in that towne, is greatly decayed.'[7]

That more intransigent stance was also adopted by the 2nd Viscount, Anthony Maria, whose previously conformist position moved to one of separation from the Established Church, a position he defended in a manuscript tract written for his daughter in 1597. Although he came under increasing scrutiny by the regime, was kept under house arrest for a time and was on the fringes of the Essex circle, he tried to keep his religious views from political entanglements, emerging by the end of the reign as a supporter of the Apellants and an acknowledged leader among the English Catholic laity by the Pope who, in a *breve* of 1603 offered a plenary indulgence to those faithful who visited his chapel on appointed feast days. The careers of both viscounts, grandfather and grandson, demonstrate that accommodation with the regime could coexist with continuing political engagement, a rigorous devotional life centred on the rosary and a leadership role within the Catholic community which carried far beyond the household.

This was not a model favoured by radicals, and especially the Jesuits, who viewed the history of English Catholicism within a wider European struggle. Here we turn to Robert Persons. Operating from Rome, Persons acquired a status among the Elizabethan regime similar to that which neo-cons in the USA currently attribute to Osama bin Laden. He stood for everything which was subversive of English interests, and his hidden hand was discerned behind every plot and assault on the regime, both internal and external. After a successful academic career at Oxford, where he was forced to resign from his fellowship at Balliol in 1574, Persons entered the Jesuit order in July 1575, and was ordained priest in 1578. He and his fellow Jesuit Edmund Campion, another ex-Oxford scholar, arrived on a mission to England in the spring of 1580, with instructions to stay out of political discussion. Having convened a synod of Catholic clergy in London, in which he spoke out against church papistry, Persons set out on a tour of the Midlands and the West Country, establishing a printing press at Stonor Park. The mission was undermined by the publication of Campion's combative challenge to his Protestant opponents at Oxford, the *Decem rationes,* which led to its author's subsequent arrest and execution for treason in 1581. Persons fled abroad, from where he worked tirelessly, in print and through action, to advance his view of the Catholic cause in England. We have already noted the important pastoral contribution Persons made through *The Christian Directory* of 1582, but this was only one aspect of his work. In 1582 he was in the Iberian peninsula trying to secure Philip II's support for an ultimately abortive invasion of Scotland, and the following year he was in Paris and Rome trying unsuccessfully to enlist support for an invasion of England, later working among English exiles fighting for the Spanish in the Netherlands to further this. Persons never gave up on Philip II, actively producing materials for distribution in England in anticipation of a successful outcome to the Armada and devising plans for a Catholic restoration. He continued to place misguided hopes in Philip's intentions towards England into the 1590s, but by this time he was also actively laying the foundations for more long-term projects. He founded English seminaries at Valladolid and Seville, a school at Saint-Omer in 1593 and a hospice at Sanluar. He was an active rector of the English College at Rome and continued his writing career, involving himself in the debate over the succession, published in 1595, and circulating a manuscript tract, a 'Memorial for the Reformation of England', setting out his plans for a Catholic restoration in which the Jesuits would play a key role. Persons' writing in defence of the faith involved him in acrimonious disputes with leading Protestants, but neither was it universally welcome among his co-religionists. His intransigence on matters of recusancy and on accommodation with the regime divided the community, especially during the Appellant disputes at the end of the reign, when internecine polemical divisions among Catholics were exploited by the regime.

By that time, Persons was also engaged in writing an alternative history of English religion to challenge that in Foxe's *Actes and Monuments*. Published just after Elizabeth's death as *A Treatise of Three Conversions,* Person's history restored to English Catholics a sense of their own past, linking them to the early 'conversions' of England by Joseph of Arimathea (first century CE), under Pope Eleutherius (third century CE) and by the followers of Saint Augustine (sixth century CE). This turning away from recent history to the Roman roots of English religion was followed by an analysis of Foxe's martyrs. Persons concluded that these martyrs were pseudo-martyrs, who in fact rejected the faith for which the early true martyrs of the Church had died.

By entering the debate on martyrdom Persons was trespassing on heavily contested ground, between Catholics and Protestants and among Catholics themselves who, by this time, had seen many priests and some lay men and women executed for treason. Though some of these had been actively involved in political activity, many priests, such as John Boste who was executed at Durham in 1594 after a ministry of thirteen years in the northern marches, had had no contact with political dissidents; their priesthood itself was construed as treason. Boste had been executed alongside another priest and a gentleman supporter, but perhaps the most famous lay victim of the regime was the York butcher's wife, Margaret Clitherow, pressed to death in 1585 for refusing to plead after being convicted of harbouring priests. Clitherow's death reminds us of the urban and non-gentry support for Catholicism, not just in the north but also in London, where the prisons provided access to the sacraments and the support of fellow Catholics, albeit in a rather different context to that of the country house. Clitherow's execution became a cause célèbre, images of her death were deployed by Catholics pamphleteers abroad, such as Richard Verstegan, to undermine the regime, and a manuscript account of her life and death circulated among Catholics at home, stressing the importance of remaining true to the faith and not compromising with the regime. As the account of recent martyrs published by Thomas Worthington, President of Douai, and the frescoes in the chapel of the English College at Rome declaimed to the young students at both places, martyrdom was a fate which many of them might be called upon to embrace and through which they would also be linked to the saints of the Church, such as their English predecessor Thomas Becket.

COMMUNITY AND CULTURE

Suffering and, if need be, martyrdom became for English Catholics a signifier of the truth for which they stood and an intrinsic part of their identity, but, as we have seen, it was only one element in an identity that incorporated a wide range of experiences, geographic, social and political, as well as devotional. If the Montagues and Robert Persons can be taken as illustrative of the two main political options available to Catholics, it must be noted that there was a wide range of alternatives within those positions and that individuals moved between them over time, either through conviction or prudence, and that, as the Queen's reign drew to its close, the prospect of James, the son of the executed Mary Stuart, acceding to the throne altered the political arithmetic for all parties. Within that political experience English Catholics were not hermetically sealed from events on the Continent, and relations with the regime were just as likely to be affected by suspicion of Spanish intentions or news of atrocities in the French wars of religion as by internal politics. Even more so, events in that other Elizabethan realm, Ireland, where there was a Catholic majority and where the Reformation made slow progress in the face of an often rebellious people, were likely to colour the regime's attitude to its Catholic subjects in England. The history of that island is the subject of another chapter, but it is important to recognise the significance of events in Ireland, or rather how contemporaries understood those events, for the political context of English Catholicism.

The geographical distribution of Catholics has already been noted, and, notwithstanding concentrations in the north and west, their presence was ubiquitous, especially in areas such as West Sussex or the Warwickshire–Worcestershire border which were distant from effective ecclesiastical supervision. The discussion has also suggested that this was a largely rural phenomenon based round the country house, but this was not always the case. In rural upland regions, such as the North York moors behind Whitby, the scattered nature of settlement required a roving ministry among the minor landholders and farmers of the region, and Catholics could be found in towns and cities too. In fact, the town of Whitby provided the landfall and point of departure for those priests working in the northern countryside, and the case of Margaret Clitherow demonstrates the foothold that Catholicism had secured among some of the prosperous artisans and professionals in York. Similar concentrations could be found at Newcastle upon Tyne and Worcester, but by far the largest concentration of urban Catholics was to found in the capital. Here, however, they did not penetrate the civic elites but were found among the artisan communities in the sprawling suburbs, around the embassy chapels and in the environs of the Inns of Court, and in particular the Middle Temple, which was thought of as a den of popery because of the suspect gentry who passed through its doors. The London lodgings of these gentry, and the households of Catholic nobility, such as that of Viscount Montague in Southwark, provided shelter for the many priests working in the metropolis, men such as John Gerard, who was able to move clandestinely around the busy city. Even when captured, some priests were able to carry on ministering to their incarcerated co-religionists, and, in the 1590s, prison congregations have been identified in both London and York in much the same way as Protestant congregations had survived in Mary's reign.

It is apparent from the discussion so far that the gentry was a crucial element in Catholic survival, and much of the evidence we have for non-gentry Catholicism relates to tenants or other clients of gentry households, but it would be wrong to suggest that 'the people' were simply a passive element in the story. Christopher Haigh has written about Lancashire, where travelling priests commanded widespread popular devotion, and a raft of parishes spread along the northern boundary of the Yorkshire Moors contained significant numbers of Catholics among the farming and peasant community. In these regions it was they, and not the gentry, who influenced the character of the mission, and in the final decade of Elizabeth's reign the recruits admitted to the seminaries in Europe were divided more or less equally between gentry and commoners. Such commoners were dominant in the towns, and the example of the most famous commoner Margaret Clitherow also raises the question of gender. As adherents of a religion banned by law it was often prudent for the male head of the household to conceal his religion through occasional conformity whilst his wife remained recusant, and there are many examples of such arrangements. In a fugitive Church, worship had to be contained within protected spaces, usually the household, and this again placed significant responsibility on the role of women, both in arranging for sacramental worship and the visits of priests and for the organisation of the devotional life of the community. The lives of both the dowager Viscountess Montague and the butcher's wife Margaret Clitherow testify to the key role played by women of both aristocratic and commoner status in sustaining household religion in very different social contexts.

The mass and the sacraments were at the heart of the Catholic community, but for many Catholics they were not readily available; thus, a devotional life which preserved one's faith in the absence of these conduits of grace was essential. A distinctive element in Catholic devotion focused on the rosary, a prayer cycle which organised the ministry of Christ around the figure of the Virgin. Catholics were encouraged to place themselves and the nation under Mary's guidance and protection by regular recital of the prayers, both privately and communally, and sodalities of the rosary were encouraged by the clergy, especially by the Jesuit Henry Garnet. Rosary beads were often taken by convicted priests to the scaffold, making this prayer an active feature in the struggle with Protestantism as well as a pious aid to personal faith. Nor was it the only aid available to Catholics. A search for suspect objects in Lewes, Sussex, in 1582 uncovered catechisms, bibles, books of controversy, nineteen large pictures and twenty-seven small ones, 'a little green box containing whiter cake broken with Agnus dei', a small collection of crucifixes, brooches, several pairs of rosary beads and three relics; clothing of Saint Cedwall and pieces of bone from Saint William and Saint Mary Magdalene. Elsewhere, in the absence of such specific devotional artefacts Robert Southwell encouraged Catholics to conceptualise their households as sacred space by turning each room into a 'chapel' by dedicating it or its furnishings to a saint and indeed recommended that this be taken beyond the house itself, so as to make 'walks as it were short pilgrimages'.[8] In the 1590s, Southwell also produced meditative verse and prose that focused on the redemption of the individual through penance and which was to have significance influence across confessional boundaries, as indeed had Persons' *The Christian Directory*. The same can be said for the greatest cultural achievement of the exile community, the publication of the Douai–Rheims translation of the Bible, which was to have a great influence on the language of the Authorised Version of 1611. More generally, the playwright Ben Jonson used drama in the Catholic cause during his flirtation with Rome at the turn of the century, and the religion of Shakespeare, and its significance for interpreting his works, remains a matter for debate among literary scholars. Thus, while maintaining a distinctive devotional life, Elizabethan Catholics produced cultural artefacts which were to have a profound influence on English literary and artistic culture.

English Catholics were separated from their Protestant neighbours by their religious loyalty, a separation which was forcefully maintained by their priests, in public at least, and was reflected in the way they organised their devotional lives. Beyond that, however, they held a wide range of views on other aspects of life, how to negotiate with the regime, whether to attend church, how to deal with one's neighbours and whom to marry, and in all these cases separation was neither the best nor the most available option. There were indeed recusant households, but all kinship networks included close relations across the confessional divide, most dramatically illustrated by the experience of the Throckmortons of Coughton in Warwickshire during the 1580s when a son, Francis, was executed for the plot that bears his name whilst a cousin, Job, was a radical puritan opponent of the Established Church and a leading parliamentary opponent of Mary Stuart. Lower down the social scale, survival depended on good neighbourly relations between Catholic and Protestant as existed in the moorland farming community of Egton in Yorkshire. Individual lives too could cross and recross the confessional boundary, and there were several examples of former priests, such as Thomas Bell, turning their pen against their former colleagues. Others, such as the former puritan John Gennings, marched in the opposite direction, whilst a few, such as Leonard Rountree, went back and forth several times. Such men were not numerous, but their lives remind us that not only was there a wide range of opinions and positions available within the Catholic community but that in religious, political, social and cultural contexts, the boundaries between English Catholics and their Protestant neighbours were far more porous than contemporary polemic might suggest. Catholics in the reign of Elizabeth were a distinctive element in society but one without the cohesion implied by the term 'community', and they played a more central part in the life of the nation than either they, or their opponents, thought at the time, or indeed, than many historians have thought subsequently.

FURTHER READING

Anstruther, G., *The Seminary Priests, 1558–1603* (Ware and Durham, 1968).

Aveling, Hugh, *Northern Catholics, the Catholic Recusants of the North Riding, 1558–1791* (London, 1966).

Bossy, John, *The English Catholic Community, 1570–1850* (London, 1975).

Dillon, Anne, *The Construction of Martyrdom in the English Catholic Community, 1535–1603* (Aldershot, 2002).

Duffy, Eamon, *The Stripping of the Altars: Traditional Religion in England, c. 1300–c. 1600* (New Haven, Conn., 1992).

Haigh, Christopher (ed.), *The English Reformation Revised* (Cambridge, 1981).

Houliston, Victor, *Catholic Resistance in Elizabethan England: Robert Persons' Jesuit Polemic* (Aldershot and Rome, 2007).
Lake, Peter and Questier, Michael, *The Antichrist's Lewd Hat* (New Haven, Conn., 2002).
McClain, Lisa, *Lest We Be Damned: Practical Innovation and Lived Experience among Catholics in Protestant England, 1559–1642* (London, 2004).
McCoog, Thomas, *English and Welsh Jesuits, 1550–1650* (1994).
McGrath, Patrick, *Papists and Puritans under Elizabeth I* (London, 1967).
Milward, Peter, *Religious Controversies of the Elizabethan Age* (London, 1977).
Mullett, Michael, *Catholics in Britain and Ireland, 1558–1829* (London, 1998).
Questier, Michael, *Conversion, Politics and Religion in England, 1580–1625* (Cambridge, 1996).
—— *Catholicism and Community in Early Modern England: Politics, Aristocratic Patronage and Religion c. 1550–1640* (Oxford, 2006).
Rowlands, Marie (ed.), *Catholics of Parish and Town, 1558–1778* (1999).
Shagan, Ethan (ed.), *Catholics and the Protestant Nation; Religious Politics and Identity in Early Modern England* (Manchester, 2005).
Walsham, Alexandra, *Church Papists: Catholicism, Conformity and Confessional Polemic in Early Modern England* (Woodbridge, 1993).

NOTES

1 Patrick McGrath, *Papists and Puritans under Elizabeth I* (London, 1967), pp. 58–64.
2 Peter Lake and Michael Questier, *The Antichrist's Lewd Hat* (New Haven, Conn., 2002), p. 285.
3 Christopher Haigh, 'From Monopoly to Minority: Catholicism in Early Modern England', *Transactions of the Royal Historical Society*, 5th Series, 31 (1981): 229–47, and his more recent overview of the debate, 'Catholicism in Early Modern England, Bossy and Beyond', *Historical Journal*, 45 (2) (2002): 481–94.
4 John Bossy, *The English Catholic Community, 1570–1850* (London, 1975), pp. 11–76.
5 John Bossy, 'The Character of Elizabethan Catholicism', *Past and Present*, 21 (1962): 39–59.
6 Robert Persons, *The First Booke of the Christian Exercise Appertaining to Resolution* (1582), Part 1, Chapter 2, p. 16.
7 Michael Questier, *Catholicism and Community in Early Modern England: Politics, Aristocratic Patronage, and Religion, c. 1550–1640* (Cambridge, 2006), p. 218.
8 Henry Garnet, *The Societie of the Rosary* (1596/7); Lisa McClain, *Lest We Be Damned: Practical Innovation and Lived Experience among Catholics in Protestant England, 1559–1642* (New York, 2004), pp. 56–9, 81–108.

PART III
SOCIETY

CHAPTER SIXTEEN

SOCIAL HIERARCHIES

Susan D. Amussen

> Almighty God hath created and appointed all things in heaven, earth, and waters, in a most excellent and perfect order.[1]
>
> The heavens themselves, the planets, and this centre
> Observe degree, priority and place. . . .
> Take but degree away, untune that string,
> And hark! What discord follows.[2]

Everyone in Elizabethan England agreed on the importance of hierarchy; at the same time, many – like Shakespeare's Ulysses – were alarmed about the ways in which people failed to respect the established order. While everyone agreed on the importance of social order, not all agreed on exactly what it was, nor did everyone agree on who fit where in it. The social hierarchy was described as one of status, where position depended on birth and role; in practice, it was beginning to include aspects of class, where wealth and property were more important than birth. Because of the growing wealth of some farmers and merchants, the social order was not as neat in practice as in theory. Furthermore, the expectation that the social hierarchy was equivalent to the moral one created many tensions. Finally, the boundaries between levels of the social order were not always clear. The fluidity of social hierarchy contributed not only to the development of the English economy and state but also to tensions within it: what the social hierarchy meant for individuals was frequently negotiated and contested. Different hierarchies – of gender, age and marital status – governed behaviour in different contexts. Social hierarchy was a theory but it was also performed and contested. Each of these dimensions is important to an understanding of social order in Elizabethan England.

IMAGINING ORDER

The social order was, in theory, simple. In the various descriptions of the social order from the Elizabethan period, there is a clear consensus. According to the Homily on Good Order and Obedience, 'In earth [God] hath assigned and appointed kings, princes, with other governors under them, in all good and necessary order.'

> Every degree of people in their vocation, calling, and office, hath appointed to them their duty and order: some are in high degree, some in low; some kings and princes, some inferiors and subjects; priests and laymen, masters and servants, fathers and children, husbands and wives, rich and poor; and every one have need of other: so that in all things is to be lauded and praised the goodly order of God.[3]

The Homily's vision identifies several different hierarchies, political, religious, social, economic and familial. It also assumed that these hierarchies were parallel and mutually reinforcing. Such an assumption was commonplace. John Fit John's *A Diamond Most Precious* had a citizen explain to a boy that 'obedience is a lowly and harty submissyon of ourselves to God, and afterwardes to our Parentes, to the Majestrates, to our superyours, and to al those to whom GOD hath committed the rule and governaunce of his flocke'.[4] However, it is not difficult to see that those who were superior in some relationships – masters, for instance – were inferiors in others, as subjects or laypeople, for example. Women appear explicitly only as wives, where they are subordinate to men, but as mistresses and even more as widows they might have authority over male servants. While my focus in this essay is on hierarchies outside the household, we must remember that Elizabethans would not always have found this a useful distinction.

The two most complete descriptions of the English social order are Sir Thomas Smith's *De republica anglorum: A Discourse on the Commonwealth of England,* written in the early 1560s and circulated widely in manuscript before it was published in 1583, and William Harrison's *Description of England,* which first appeared as part of *Holinshed's Chronicles* in 1587. Each of these works placed the social order in a larger framework. Smith, as a former diplomat and courtier, was interested in government and political order; Harrison, a Protestant clergyman, linked the social hierarchy to social and economic life. Both, however, provide largely similar discussions of the social hierarchy. In Harrison's words, 'we in England divide our people commonly into four sorts, as gentlemen, citizens or burgesses, yeomen, and artificers or laborers.' Smith's discussion of labourers is, typically, called 'Of the Fourth Sort of Men which Doe Not Rule.'[5]

Both Smith and Harrison wrote in most detail about their first group, the gentry and aristocracy. These people, the 'top' of the English social order, were themselves divided in two, the 'greater sort' and 'they that are simply called gentlemen'.[6] The 'greater sort' were the 'princes, dukes, marquises, earls, viscounts and barons', that is, 'lords and noblemen'; below them are 'knights, esquires, and last of all, they that are simply called gentlemen'.[7] For each of the types of lords and noblemen, Harrison provides a definition and a lengthy discussion of the origin of the title; he also discusses bishops, whose rank in England was equivalent to that of nobles. The higher nobility (other than princes, a title restricted to sons of the king) were either given their titles by the king, or were the eldest son of a nobleman. On the other hand, knight was a title that could only be earned and was not inherited; as Harrison pointed out, the title had initially been a military one. Harrison briefly refers to the Knights of the Bath, who have a role at a coronation, and then provides a lengthy discussion of the Order of the Garter – the most distinguished order of knighthood in England: membership was an individual achievement, not inherited, and the number strictly limited to twenty-six. In his discussion of the nobility, Harrison makes repeated references to the Latin or French etymology of titles, to chivalric orders in Spain and France, and to Roman custom. These references suggest that this hierarchy reflects a universal pattern and is natural. Smith spends little time on the upper nobility – whose status corresponds to that of Roman senators – but provides an extensive discussion of how knights are made. Again, frequent classical comparisons underline the natural, and therefore fixed, nature of the hierarchy.

After their detailed discussion of the nobility, both Harrison and Smith turn to the 'gentlemen'. This group was particularly troubling to the Elizabethans. For Harrison, 'Gentlemen be those whom their race and blood, or at the least their virtues, do make noble and known.' In addition, Sir Thomas Smith wrote,

> Whosoever studieth the lawes of the realm, who studyeth in the universities, who professeth liberall sciences, and to be shorte, who can live idly and without manual labor, and will bear the port, charge, and countenance of a gentleman, he shall be called master, for that is the title which men give to esquires and other gentlemen.[8]

The last qualification is the crucial one. Having begun with race and blood, Smith ends with wealth. 'Gentleman' was a permeable category, shaped by how people lived rather than who they were. One way in which gentle status was confirmed was by the possession of a coat of arms, which was officially only granted by the College of Heralds to those who could prove three generations of gentle status. The business of coats of arms was open to manipulation, however; Smith alleges that arms could be bought for money. William Shakespeare's father John applied for a coat of arms based on his civic office in 1568; the coat of arms was finally issued – probably paid for by his son – in 1596. Not everyone cared about formal gentry status. Thus, the Somerset antiquarian Thomas Gerard wrote of the men of Martock,

> wealthy and substantial men though none of them the best bred, which is the cause their neighbours about them are apt enough to slander them with the title of clowns; but they care not much for that, knowing they have money in their purses to make them gentlemen when they are fit for the degree.[9]

The lack of a fixed boundary for gentle status facilitated social mobility, but it also created uncertainty and conflict over what kind of respect was owed to whom.

Below the gentlemen were the 'citizens and burgesses'. By this both Smith and Harrison meant those who had the 'freedom' of their town or city and were liable to hold office. Those cities and towns that were 'corporate boroughs' sent members to Parliament. Otherwise, according to Smith (revealing his political preoccupations), 'they be of none accompt.'[10] Among the 'citizens and burgesses', Harrison was most interested in the merchants, 'although they often change estate with gentlemen, as gentlemen do with them, by a mutual conversion of the one into the other.'[11] Harrison thought that the merchants were responsible for the rising cost of goods and for shortages of domestic goods. While Harrison admired the expanding geographical range of English trade, he did not admire the rising prices which were the result of sixteenth-century inflation.

The next social group of interest to Smith and Harrison were yeomen. The definition initially offered was the formal, legal one: yeomen held land as freehold and had an annual income of 40 s.: this was the qualification for voting in elections for knights of the shire. Yet both Harrison and Smith noted that it was not just income that mattered; yeomen were (according to Harrison) 'settled or staid . . . being married and of some years', unlike those who were unmarried, who were 'likely to be still fleeting, how hither, now thither, which argueth want of stability'. They were not gentlemen, and, according to Smith, gave 'the honour to al which be or take upon them to be gentlemen, and yet they have a certain preheminence and more estimation than laborers and artificers, and comonly live welthilie, keep good houses, and do their businesse, and travaile to acquire riches'. They were thrifty and hard-working and thus often able to buy land from 'unthrifty gentlemen', 'and often, setting their sons to the schools, to the universities, and to the Inns of the Court, or otherwise leaving them sufficient lands whereupon they may live without labor, do make them by those means to become gentlemen'. Yeomen were accorded the honorific of 'Goodman'. It was, both Smith and Harrison reminded their readers, the *yeomen* archers of England who did such damage to the French in battle.[12] And yeomen played an important role in the government of their communities.

The final group of people was called by Smith 'those who do not rule'. This group, numerically the largest of all, was quickly dismissed. It included 'day laborers, poor husbandmen, and some retailers (which have no free land), copyholders, and all artificers, as tailors, shoemakers, carpenters, brickmakers, masons, etc.'. They have 'neither voice nor authority in the commonwealth, but are to be ruled and not to rule over'. Harrison added to this group 'our great swarms of idle serving-men'.[13] Both these descriptions, then, are morally weighted. Rather than describing the largest group in society in most detail, they focus on the more important groups, dismissing the vast majority of the population because of their insignificance in the political and social order.

The hierarchical framework of society was echoed in numerous household manuals of the Elizabethan period. While these focused on the household, they always placed the household in a larger framework. Just as Fit John's *Diamond Most Precious* linked submission to God, parents and rulers, so did many other writers. Fifty years after Fit John wrote, William Gouge's popular *Of Domesticall Duties* offered a similar sentiment: 'Necessary it is that good order be first set in families: for as they were before other polities, so they are somewhat the more necessary: and good members of a family are like to make good members of a Church and Commonwealth.'[14]

As society was imagined in Elizabethan England, it was always hierarchical. Different hierarchies were expected to fit inside each other like a set of Russian matryoshka dolls. Everyone knew their place and deferred to those above them. But, as the fuzzy boundary between yeomen and gentlemen demonstrates, even the theory was never that neat. Embodying the theory was always more difficult, not only because people did not always believe or behave as they were supposed to but because the different hierarchies of family, church and nation were occasionally at odds with each other.

EMBODYING ORDER

Hierarchies were made visible on a daily basis. It did not have to be a major occasion for the social order to be visible. The practice of 'hat honor', when men doffed their hats to other men was one. Other courtesies – including the depth of a bow or curtsey – also signalled differences in rank. So did forms of address. Titles of honor, from 'Prince' or 'Duke' to 'Sir' are obvious signs of rank. But even below the ranks of the titled, address told a story. 'Master' and 'Mistress' were terms of respect, for the minor gentry; 'Goodman' and 'Goodwife' were also terms of respect, given to prosperous farmers and their wives. Clergy were often accorded the honorific of 'Sir', as a mark of their status and education.

Most people saw the social order represented on ritual occasions. The coronation of a monarch, or the ceremonial opening of parliament, provided a view of the political order. In towns and cities, civic processions provided a visible representation of local hierarchy. Each Sunday in church, parishioners sat in seats assigned on the basis of their house or their place in society. In more informal contexts, there were differences in property and dress between those at different levels of society. All of these embodied social hierarchies in concrete ways.

The social order was most elaborately visible at court, where the various rituals served to distinguish the Queen from ordinary mortals. Thomas Platter recorded with some astonishment watching the Queen in her Presence Chamber at Nonsuch Palace that 'I am told that they even play cards with the Queen in kneeling posture.'[15] Any time the Queen went anywhere,

> the Lord Chamberlain walks first, being followed by all the nobility who are in court, and the Knights of the Order that are present walk after, near the Queen's person, such as the Earl of Essex, the admiral, and others. After come the six heralds who bear maces before the Queen. After her march the fifty gentlemen of the Guard, each carrying a halberd, and sumptuously attired, and after that the Maids and Ladies who accompany them, very well attired.[16]

The procession, in other words, placed the Queen's most trusted servants closest to her, and, through the elaborate structure of the procession, reminded everyone who saw it of her importance.

Ceremonial processions, such as those of the court, also represented the social order. Such processions might celebrate civic holidays, such as the 17 November celebrations of the Accession of Queen Elizabeth. In towns with royal charters, there was often a civic procession on the day the new town officers were installed. The most famous and elaborate of these was the Lord Mayor's procession in London. While explicitly a celebration of the political order of London, political power in the city belonged to its most prosperous citizens. On the day the new mayor was to be installed, he was led through the city by the aldermen and sheriffs in scarlet livery. The procession then transferred to barges on the Thames, led by the barge belonging to the new mayor's company; the rest of the London companies followed in order of rank. At Westminster, the mayor was inducted by the Barons of the Exchequer, the procession re-formed and returned to the Guildhall for a feast. Over the course of Elizabeth's reign, the Lord Mayor's procession was accompanied by increasingly elaborate pageants. Often these were allegorical representation of the new mayor's company, its history and its loyalty to the Queen. The pageant in 1590 was put on by the Fishmongers' Company, to which John Allott, the new mayor, belonged. The pageant emphasised the City's loyalty to the Queen, saying:

> Faithfull and loyall are hir subjects seene
> Concord unites them still in loyall bands
> Their tender hearts is linked to our Queenes
> And concord craves no other at their hands
> Thus loyaltie and concord doth agree
> That London still therein shall famous bee.[17]

The pageant included both allegorical characters such as Fame and God's Truth, but also historical ones, such as Richard II, who had granted the original charter to the Fishmongers, and Sir William Walworth, a fishmonger and Lord Mayor in 1375 and 1381, who had won acclaim by killing the rebel Wat Tyler in 1381. The inclusion of Walworth emphasised the Fishmongers' loyalty to the Crown.

Such elaborate processions depended on the wealth of London, but even in smaller towns and cities civic ritual provided occasions to display the social order. In York, midsummer was celebrated with a procession of civic dignitaries and armed citizens. Elizabethan Bristol recognised eleven feast days on which the mayor and aldermen dressed in their ceremonial scarlet robes: those of the mayor and former mayors included cloaks with fur and felt trim, while the aldermen wore only gowns. They processed from the Guildhall to the cathedral to hear a sermon. In the early seventeenth century, a special gallery was added to the cathedral by the pulpit for the council; special seats underneath were reserved for the many noblemen, or the king, as well as the wives of the council and clergy. The procession, and its destination, emphasised the harmony between the civic and religious hierarchies. While smaller towns might have less frequent processions, Bristol was not alone in having seats in church dedicated to the town or city council.

Civic displays of hierarchy were not always so solemn. In Liverpool in 1576, the Mayor ordered a large bonfire in the market square and ordered all householders to light fires outside their houses. Then the Mayor and the rest of the town council had a banquet, and the Mayor served sack, white wine and sugar at his door to all who came, 'lauding and praising God for the most prosperous reign of our … most gracious sovereign'.[18] A similarly hospitable display of civic hierarchy was ordered in Marlborough, Wiltshire, in 1590; the aldermen decided that each of them should host the householders of his ward in his home to 'drink together as neighbours and friends'. Then all the townspeople would go to the Mayor's house and celebrate together.[19]

These civic occasions were elaborate and formal events. More usually, people saw the social order visibly represented in church every Sunday. In many parishes seats were assigned to houses, suggesting a conception of social order that was static. While custom might rule, when conflicts emerged higher authorities got involved. In 1633, Dr Clement Corbett, the Vicar-General of the diocese of Norwich, found that men and women of the parish of West Walton sat together 'whereby there is no decencie and order', and instructed the churchwardens to assign men and women to different aisles, so that there would be 'decent and good order in the church'. In addition to separating men and women, the churchwardens were to attend to 'the degrees and qualities of the persons by you to be removed, displaced, and placed'.[20] Churchwardens drew up seating plans that took account of varied criteria – from 'degree and ability', 'ranke and order', 'qualities and worth', 'callings', 'merits', 'conditions' and 'means'.[21] In the parish of Saint Ebbe's, in Oxford, seats were assigned not by houses but by 'qualities, estates and degrees'. It should be obvious that these were not always the same: one might be a person of great merit but lesser means. A seating plan based on houses did not reflect either moral virtue or (necessarily) wealth. Because there were different bases for different hierarchies – whether of family, age, marital status or wealth – church seating often reflected complex decisions about where people should sit. Thus, in Sutton in the Isle of Ely, Richard Upchurch, a gentleman, was seated in the last of the men's seats: he was a habitual drunkard who 'goeth rayleing up and down the streate in the night'; William Bond, a 'common drunckard, swearer, and blasphemer' was given no seat at all.[22] Such decisions remind us that a place – particularly a higher place – in the social hierarchy came with expectations. Those who did not fulfil their obligations might lose status.

As the case of Sutton suggests, in most parishes, men and women were seated separately. A witness in Saint Ebbe's, who had lived in Essex, Hertfordshire and Gloucestershire as well as Oxford, averred that 'the custom in all the said churches was always for men to sit there in seats by themselves apart from women and women likewise by themselves'. Women might be ranked differently from their husbands: in Sutton, the wife of William Bond was given a seat close to the front of the women, in spite of her husband's behaviour. Frequently there were separate seats for servants; and unmarried women and men were seated separately from those who were married. In some parishes, older people were allowed to move closer to the front so they could better hear the sermon. In Tarrant Crawford in Dorset, when the seats in the church were reassigned in 1637, not only were the men separated from the women, but the first seat on the women's side was assigned to the midwife at christenings and churchings.[23]

If the seating plans of churches made the hierarchy – or at least one version of it – visible, hierarchy was also supposed to be visible in dress. A series of medieval statutes, reaffirmed and revised under Henry VIII and Philip and Mary, regulated who could wear what clothing, and particularly access to luxury clothing. The statute of 24 Henry VIII was explicit about the connection of fabric to rank. Cloth of gold, silver or tinsel and cloth mixed with gold or silver, as well as sables were only to be worn by earls or above, though viscounts and barons could wear them in doublets and sleeveless coats. Woollen cloth made outside England, as well as crimson, scarlet or blue velvet, and furs were the province of dukes, marquises, earls (as well as their children) and barons and Knights of the Garter. Velvet, leopard fur, embroidery and 'picking or printing' with gold silver and silk were more widely available – to anyone with an income of over £200 a year, as well as barons' sons and knights. Finally, silk, satin, taffeta, satin and damask, as well as a variety of furs, and velvet in any garments other than jackets and doublets, were restricted to those whose income exceeded £100 a year. The statute passed in 1554 limited the wearing of silk in various accessories (hats, bonnets, girdles, etc.) to particular groups: the son and heir of a knight, those with income from lands of £20 a year, or goods worth £200. Additionally, the penalties of the Act were not to apply to 'any person being above a knightes son or doughter, or being wife to any of them' as well as those who had served as officers of any corporate borough or town, and royal servants wearing royal livery. The penalties were heavy: three months' imprisonment and a fine of £10 for each day the offending silk was worn. Furthermore, if a master had a servant who offended against the Act and did not put him out of service, he was fined £100. A final clause noted that 'Women maye wear in their Cappes Hattes, Gyrdells and Hoodes as they or any of them might use and weare lawfully, before the making of this act.'[24] The complexity of the Act of Philip and Mary – starting with a strong assertion but quickly limiting it with exceptions – is itself a mark of how difficult it was to draw boundaries of acceptable behaviour. In theory, you needed to be of a certain rank to wear silk in your hat. But income could provide the equivalent of rank, as could holding civic office: wealth and political role complicated a theoretically fixed system. Gender created a whole other set of issues, as in effect the statute did not apply to women. Within a year of her accession, Elizabeth issued a proclamation notifying her subjects of her intent to enforce those statutes. Similar proclamations were issued in 1562, 1566, 1574, 1577, 1580, 1588 and 1597. The proclamations usually summarise the relevant statutes, though the repetition suggests that they were singularly ineffective. By 1597, the proclamation – which provided extensive detail on precisely which garments might have what kind of fabric or ornamentation – was immediately followed by another, 'Dispensing Certain Persons from Statutes of Apparel'. This, like the exceptions in the statutes, mentioned servants and officers of the royal household, various government officials, including the Lord Chancellor and Lord Treasurer; those who had taken degrees at Oxford or Cambridge; and for the doublets of servants of noblemen and gentlemen. Finally, heralds, henchmen and pursuivants at tournaments or jousts were also exempt. Once again, politics and service provided alternative routes to the display of status.

The purpose of sumptuary legislation was to make status visible. As in the descriptions of the social order, the boundaries around the top tiers are considered particularly important. Yet, especially with exemptions for servants wearing a master's livery, and for income, it was evident that it would never be possible to fully enforce such visual demarcations. These complications provide the basis for a wide range of contests about social hierarchies visible in English society.

CONTESTING HIERARCHIES

The prescriptive discussions of hierarchy make it all seem so simple. Once hierarchy starts being embodied, as in cases around church seats, it becomes more complicated. While there is no doubt that most of the time most people did not contest the social hierarchy, the times and places they do so help us better understand how hierarchy worked. On the simplest level, the rules about dress were widely ignored. For all the legislation, people wore clothes they should not have. Some were alleged to spend all their money on dress. Thomas Platter reported that women who 'wear velvet for the street [are] quite common with them – who cannot afford a crust of dry bread at home'.[25] The embodiment of the local hierarchy in church seats was a regular source of local conflict. Finally, on occasion, men made claims of equality with those ostensibly their betters. These contests over the hierarchy help us see the points of tension in society and the varied ways in which the hierarchy was defined and used.

Many of the conflicts over church seats reflected the different possible criteria for assigning places in church. An unusually well-documented dispute erupted in Fressingfield, Suffolk, in 1634, and it suggests the complexity of church seating arrangements. The central problem was how to accommodate the wealthiest inhabitants of the village. The Baker family, as lay impropriators of the rectory, sat in the chancel, the most prestigious seats. Until about 1624, the Sancroft family, which had lived in the parish for some 300 years, had also been allowed to sit in the chancel. Meanwhile, some time around 1585, John Lawrence, a preacher and gentleman who had purchased a large house, Fressingfield Hall, had been allowed to build a pew for his household at the front of the church on the north side. His stature is suggested by the fact that a seat – really just a bench – for his servants was placed behind his seat. When the Sancrofts were removed from the chancel in 1624, they persuaded Mrs Kempe, who now owned the Lawrence house, to allow them to make a partition halfway along the maid's seat. Alas, in 1634, William Grudgfeild, Mrs Kempe's son, reneged on the agreement because he needed more seats for his servants.

The testimony raised many issues. First, many witnesses suggested that the Sancrofts' longevity in the parish meant that they deserved a seat of some distinction, while Grudgfeild was a newcomer. That is, though in theory people might think a seat belonged to a house, parishioners took account of who lived in that house. Second, villagers were unwilling to allow too great a symbolic distance between the newcomers, the Grudgfeilds, and the Sancrofts with their long history in the parish. Finally, the problem was exacerbated because of the lack of space in the church: the church could seat 300, but there were 600 inhabitants in the parish and 400 communicants. The demographic pressures of the period, and the increasing wealth of some parishioners, made it more likely that there would be conflicts over status. Where it would be easy to find a place for two major families, when there were four or five it became more complicated. The placement of people in church often reflected an attempt to balance past and present.

It was not only the wealthy who disputed church seats; such disputes appeared at many levels of the social hierarchy, though mostly among householders. In the parish of Saint Ebbes, in Oxford, a suit began when a woman began to sit in the men's seats, apparently claiming a seat she believed marked her status. In Saint Ebbes, as we have seen, seats were assigned not by houses, but by 'qualities, estates and degrees'.[26] In the parish of Saint Giles, Norwich, William Balliston sued John Fayerman, who had been placed in his seat in the church. Balliston was, according to his witnesses, a 'grave, substantiall man well descended and one of the better sorte of credit and esteeme', while Fayerman was 'a meane poore man', who worked as a twisterer and kept an inn – 'in his substance and every other way' inferior to Balliston.[27] In 1596, William Balding was placed in the seat in the chancel of Burston church in which Mr Oldman, a gentleman, used to sit, but Oldman came into the pew and tried to push Balding out, telling him that 'there was no seat for a butcher'; in this case, the parson and the churchwardens disagreed: in spite of Oldman's status, he had not taken communion for several years and had not sent the young people of his household to be catechised. Butchers were often prosperous, and evidently local opinion placed Balding in the upper ranks of local society.[28] More often, all we know is that there was a conflict in the church, and the underlying arguments are unclear. Over and over, however, those who lost visible status resented the power of churchwardens to remove them from their seats. On some occasions the competing criteria for status are clear. In 1609, in the parish of Bawdeswell, Norfolk, Robert Skener's wife objected when the churchwardens sought to move her from her usual seat to some newly built seats near the clock 'where the poore and such as took almes did sytt'. Since her husband contributed to poor relief, she thought this was wrong. However, in testimony, some neighbours agreed with the churchwardens, because the Skeners were living as 'inmates' (lodgers) in another house, and it was not appropriate for her to sit with 'others much her betters'.[29]

Conflicts over church seats were usually not conflicts over the nature of the social order but over where people fit in it. That is, they were contests over how people were related to each other in a particular local hierarchy and who determined their place. Other social conflicts bore more directly on the notion of the hierarchy altogether. Such challenges took two forms. Most often, people simply refused the deference that was thought to be due to those who were their superiors. One thing we know about early modern society is that people were very sensitive to slights to their reputation. In a cash-poor society, reputation – or 'credit' in the language of the time – had economic as well as social consequences. Such sensitivity is abundantly clear in the defamation cases that filled the church courts. These cases often reveal an additional level of offence when local elites were insulted by those who were supposed to be inferior to them. Thus the offence when Thomas Copping called Thomas Spooner, Gent., a 'common drunckard' was magnified because of the disrespect to a gentleman.[30] In 1590, Edward Crispe of Bireham Newton was presented to the archdeacon for calling the minister a 'skurvye knave, loggerheaded knave, doltish knave'.[31] Another clergyman, Richard Huxley of Ashill, sued Humphrey Wilson for calling him 'a shitten priest, a shagge ragged knave and a base slave'.[32] In such cases, the status of the person offended was as significant as the insults themselves.

Absolute claims of equality were more serious than insults. William Byrde of West Lynn, Norfolk, refused to pay a rate because of the idleness of the Justice of the Peace, Humphrey Guybon, Esq. When refusing, Byrde not only complained about Guybon's idleness (insulting enough) but said that 'he [Byrde] was as good a man as he.' The combined refusal to do his civic duty and his claim of equality brought him before Guybon to explain himself.[33] A similar line was taken by Peter Hunt in speaking to Mr Samuel Oates. Hunt called Oates a 'rascally knave' and then said 'that he was as good a man as he the said Mr. Oates'.[34] Such claims of equality provide a reminder that not everyone accepted the full implications of the social order of early modern England.

A significant number of defamation suits around issues of status involve clergy, either as the person insulting or the person insulted. Their presence reflects their ambiguous social position. As clergy, they were entitled to respect as if they were gentlemen. However, they often derived their income by collecting tithes (one-tenth of a harvest) from their parishioners, making them dependent on those they were supposed to teach. As gentlemen, they were expected to live without manual labour, but they might not have the money to do so. Both clergy and parishioners found themselves unhappy with this situation. Sometimes this was expressed with simple disrespect: 'a furred mitten would conteyne as much good doctrine as Mr. Hooke had, and hee would prove himself an honester man than Mr. Hooke'; 'Mr Nuttall was a proper parson to make a Bishopp in hell . . . a turde in his teeth'; 'Mr Robinson would speake beyond his book and playe the knave & tell a lye as soon as another man.'[35] On other occasions, clergymen expressed their own frustration with the ambiguity of their social position, and particularly their struggle to collect tithes. In 1605, the rector of Tuttington, Norfolk, got angry with one parishioner while reckoning for tithes and pulled him 'by the beard and said hang up all such knaves as have £30 a year by land and have but the tythe of one cow for the pore parson'.[36] In a similar context, Mr Hodgson, the rector of Stradsett, Norfolk, told Francis Piggott, Gent., that 'I am as good a man as you and an honester man than you and that you have cosened me of ten pounds.' The testimony in this case indicates that Piggott was the local gentleman, on whom Hodgson may well have been dependent for his living. Having to collect tithes and balance the tensions of spiritual and social status were clearly difficult; at least one witness claims that Piggott had told Hodgson that his pulpit was too high for him.[37] The resentment worked both ways, as when a parishioner told her rector that 'he were as good stand by the highe way side and take a purse as take his tithes wrongfully.'[38]

Most of the time, most people accepted the social hierarchies of early modern England. But the conflicts over status – whether seating in church or insults to social betters – remind us that the social hierarchy was constantly negotiated. Conflicts emerged for several reasons: because the boundaries were often uncertain, because different hierarchies might come into conflict, and because the social hierarchy was assumed to be a moral one as well. The process of negotiating place in the hierarchy was not always peaceful. While few people openly rejected the social hierarchy, they often jostled for a better position in it or tried to reduce the claims to respect of those above them.

The many changes of the Elizabethan period had a significant impact on its social hierarchies. On the one hand, a growing population created increased demand for food and goods, leading to inflation. Those who provided the food and goods for this growing population – largely yeoman farmers and gentry and urban merchants – grew in wealth and, in practice, social status. The social hierarchies of Elizabethan England were tested by these developments, as we have seen. The key to the success – and the survival – of the hierarchies was their very fuzziness. What was imagined as fixed was in reality fluid. As both Smith and Harrison were aware, there were opportunities for money to substitute for birth to allow for movement to a 'better' place in the social order. Equally, the role of local notables such as churchwardens in establishing the visual order of the community enabled them to respond to disjunctures between moral and social worth: as experienced in a local community, the social hierarchy responded as much to the real situations of people's lives as it did to social theory. So, while the place of individuals in the hierarchies might move, no one had to question the hierarchies themselves. The social hierarchy could adapt to the economic and social transformations taking place in Elizabethan England without too much struggle.

FURTHER READING

Amussen, Susan Dwyer, *An Ordered Society: Gender and Class in Early Modern England* (Oxford, 1988).

Campbell, Mildred, *The English Yeoman in the Tudor and Early Stuart Age* (1942).

Esser, Raingard, '"They Obey All Magistrates and All Good Lawes . . . and We Thinke Our Cittie Happie to Enjoye Them": Migrants and Urban Stability in Early Modern English Towns', *Urban History*, 34 (2007): 64–75.

Flather, Amanda, *The Politics of Place: A Study of Church Seating in Essex, c. 1580–1640* (Leicester, 1999).

French, Henry, *The Middle Sort of People in Provincial England, 1600–1750* (Oxford, 2007).

Heal, Felicity, *Hospitality in Early Modern England* (Oxford, 1990).

Heal, Felicity, and Holmes, Clive, *The Gentry in England and Wales, 1500–1700* (Palo Alto, Calif., 1994).

Hindle, Steve, 'Hierarchy and Community in the Elizabethan Parish: The Swallowfield Articles of 1596', *Historical Journal*, 42 (1999): 835–51.

—— 'Beating the Bounds of the Parish: Order, Memory, and Identity in the English Local Community, c. 1500–1700', in Michael Halvorson and Karen E. Spierling (eds.), *Defining Community in Early Modern Europe* (Aldershot and Burlington, Vt., 2008), pp. 205–28.

Jackson, Christine, 'A Town Governed by a Company of Geese in Furred Gowns: Political and Social Conflict in Reading *c.* 1620–40', *Southern History*, 29 (2007): 29–58.

Kent, Joan R., *The English Village Constable, 1580–1642: A Social and Administrative Study* (Oxford, 1986).

Laslett, Peter, *The World We Have Lost: England before the Industrial Age*, 2nd edn (New York, 1972).

Marsh, Christopher, 'Order and Place in England, 1580–1640: The View from the Pew', *Journal of British Studies*, 44 (1) (2005): 3–26.

Phythian-Adams, Charles, 'Ceremony and the Citizen: The Communal Year at Coventry, 1450–1550', in Peter Clark and Paul Slack (ed.), *Crisis and Order in English Towns, 1500–1700: Essays in Urban History* (1972), pp. 57–85.

Pollock, Linda A., 'Honor, Gender, and Reconciliation in Elite Culture, 1570–1700', *Journal of British Studies*, 46 (2007): 3–29.

Postles, David, *Social Proprieties: Social Relations in Early-Modern England (1500–1680)* (Washington, DC, 2006).

Shepard, Alexandra, 'Poverty, Labour and the Language of Social Description in Early Modern England', *Past & Present*, 201 (2008): 51–95.

Underdown, David, *Fire from Heaven: Life in an English Town in the Seventeenth Century* (London, 1992).

Withington, Phil, 'Company and Sociability in Early Modern England', *Social History [London]*, 32 (2007): 291–307.

Wood, Andy, '"Poore Men Woll Speke One Daye": Plebeian Languages of Deference and Defiance in England, *c.* 1520–1640', in Tim Harris (ed.), *The Politics of the Excluded, c. 1500–1850* (Basingstoke and New York, 2001), pp. 67–98.

Wrightson, Keith, *English Society, 1580–1680* (New Brunswick, 1982).

—— 'Sorts of People in Tudor and Stuart England', in Jonathan Barry and Christopher Wilson Brooks (eds.), *The Middling Sort of People: Culture, Society and Politics in England, 1550–1800* (Basingstoke and London, 1994), pp. 28–51.

—— 'Mutualities and Obligations: Changing Social Relationships in Early Modern England', *Proceedings of the British Academy*, 139 (2006): 157–94.

NOTES

1 'An Exhortation Concerning Good Order and Obedience to Rulers and Magistrates', in Thomas Cranmer, *Certaine Sermons Appointed by the Queenes Maiestie to Be Declared and Redde* . . . (London, 1574).

2 William Shakespeare, *Troilus and Cressida*, Act I, Scene 3, lines 85–6, 109–10.

3 Cranmer 'An Exhortation', p. 69.

4 John Fit John, *A Diamond Most Precious* . . . (London, 1577), fol. Biii.

5 Thomas Smith, *De republica anglorum: A Discourse on the Commonwealth of England*, ed. L. Alston (Cambridge, 1906), p. 31; William Harrison, *The Description of England*, ed. George Edelin (Ithaca, NY, 1968), p. 94.

6 Harrison, *Description of England*, p. 94

7 Harrison, *Description of England*, pp. 94–113.

8 Harrison, *Description of England*, p. 113; Smith, *De republica anglorum*, pp. 39–40.

9 Quoted in David Underdown, *Somerset in the Civil War and Interregnum* (Newton Abbott, 1973), p. 16.

10 Smith, *De republica anglorum*, p. 42.

11 Harrison, *Description of England*, p. 115.

12 Harrison, *Description of England*, pp. 117–18; Smith, *De republica anglorum*, p. 43.

13 Harrison, *Description of England*, pp. 118–19; Smith, *De republica anglorum*, p. 46.

14 William Gouge, *Of Domesticall Duties: Eight Treatises* (London, 1622), fol. 2v.

15 Thomas Platter, 'Travels in England in 1599', in Peter Razzell (ed.), *The Journals of Two Travellers in Elizabethan and Early Stuart England* (London, 1995), pp. 1–106; p. 59.

16 Quoted by Roy Strong, *The Cult of Elizabeth* (Berkeley, Calif., 1977), p. 31.

17 Quoted by Jennifer Harrison, 'Lord Mayor's Day in the 1590s', *History Today*, 42 (1) (1992): 37–43.

18 Quoted by Strong, *Cult of Elizabeth*, p. 120.

19 Quoted by Ronald Hutton, *The Rise and Fall of Merrie England: The Ritual Year, 1400–1700* (Oxford, 1994), p. 122.

20 Norfolk RO, FCB/1, fols. 2–2v.

21 Quoted by Christopher Marsh, 'Order and Place in England, 1580–1640: The View from the Pew', *Journal of British Studies*, 44 (1) (2005): 3–26; p. 9.

22 Quoted by Marsh, 'Order and Place', p. 13.

23 Oxfordshire RO, MS Arch., Papers Oxon., *c.* 118 (1617) John Neale con. Mrs Dawson, fol. 90; *Somerset and Dorset Notes and Queries*, 17 (1921–3), 'Tarrant Crawford Churchwarden's Accounts', pp. 162–3.

24 *The Statutes of the Realm*, vol. IV, p. 239 (1&2 Philip & Mary C. 2).

25 Platter, 'Travels in England', p. 45.

26 Oxfordshire RO, MS Arch., Papers Oxon., *c.* 118, John Neele con. Mrs Dawson, fols. 89v–93, 94v–105, 105v–107, 146v–160, 164v–170, 183v–4v, 187–7v, 197, 206–206v.

27 Norf. RO DEP/37, July 1618, William Balliston con. John Fayerman, fols. 377v–388, especially fols. 378, 380v.

28 Norf. RO DEP/28, William Ellyot, Cler, John Tooley ad Thomas Bygott con. Silvestre Oldman, Gent., fols. 444–5v.

29 Norf. RO DEP/35, July 1609, Skener con. Leman and Pescodd, fols. 202b, 248.

30 Norf. RO DEP/28, Thomas Spooner Gent. con. Thomas Copping, fols. 422, 525–6, 530.

31 Norf. RO ANF/1/2, 1590, Bireham Newton.

32 Norf. RO DEP/37, Huxley Cler. con. Humphrey Wilson, fols. 130r–v.

33 Norf. RO, Quarter Sessions, C/S3/20, 8 August 1615.
34 Norf. RO DEP/33, Oates Con Hunt, fols. 449v.
35 Norf RO DEP/36, Samuel Hooke, Cler., con. Thomas Chapman, fols. 241v–42v; DEP/37, Mr Nuttall Con Spinke, fols. 30–1, 116–17; DEP/26, Mr Robinson Cler., con. Burrell, fols. 275v–76, 277.
36 Norf. RO DEP/33, Ashe con. Ineson, fols. 187v–88, 284–6, 308.
37 Norf. RO DEP/38, Pigott, Gent., con. Hodgson, Cler., fols. 105–7v.
38 Norf. RO DEP/37, Payne, Cler., con. Elizabeth Stone, fols. 102–4v.

CHAPTER SEVENTEEN

NOBILITY AND GENTRY

Janet Dickinson

The nobility and the gentry were vital to the governance of England in the sixteenth century; the alliance between the Crown and the nobility was fundamental to the maintenance of order and the practice of government. For many years, the nobility and gentry were curiously neglected in the historiography of Elizabethan England, but recently this has changed, and historians are moving towards a more sensitive and more subtle appreciation of their role in Tudor society and government.

For all their significance, the nobility and gentry constituted only a small proportion of society. The titled nobility – dukes, marquesses, earls, viscounts and barons – amounted to a group of fifty-seven men at the start of Elizabeth's reign. Nobility could be either inherited through the male line or bestowed by the monarch, as in 1564 when Elizabeth raised Robert Dudley to the earldom of Leicester, and in 1571 when William Cecil was made Baron Burghley. Elizabeth was notoriously cautious about adding to the ranks of the nobility, with the result that numbers remained at a relatively low level throughout her reign. There was only one duke in England, Thomas Howard, 4th Duke of Norfolk, the Queen's cousin, who went to the scaffold in 1572. After that, the senior rank in England was that of marquess. Beneath them were the gentry, a term that encompassed a vast range of definitions, from the younger sons of the nobility to country squires, including many men who would have been defined as 'noble' in much of Continental Europe as well as men with only slim pretensions towards gentility.

Contemporaries paid great attention to the question of what marked out the 'gentleman' and the 'nobleman' from his neighbours. Courtesy books, manuals of gentility and educational guides, often translated from French or Italian, were published in increasing numbers, advising on the correct manners and behaviour of the elite. Theoretically, true nobility was something that could only be conferred by birth; in practice, matters were a great deal more fluid. Failed lines of inheritance and royal attainders meant that, of the sixty-two peers living in 1560, only twenty-five held titles that went back to before 1509. Indeed, of the seventy-four peerages that existed during Elizabeth's reign, twenty-five had died out by 1640.

Those raised up very quickly acquired their own noble lineage; following his ennoblement, Burghley commissioned a number of genealogies, tracing the (fictional) history of the Cecils back to noble origins. Similarly, by the end of the century, the Spencer family of Northamptonshire, descended from sheep farmers, had accumulated such wealth and social status that the College of Arms 'obligingly furnished the family . . . with a pedigree deriving their descent from the ancient house of Despenser, earls of Gloucester and Winchester'.[1] These kinds of claims to noble lineage were not always entirely convincing to contemporaries: the Queen's Secretary of State, Sir Thomas Smith, wrote disparagingly of those freshly ennobled men who would go the heralds, pay money and receive 'armes newly made and invented, the title whereof shall pretende to have beene found by the said Herauld in perusing and viewing of olde registers, where his auncestors in times past had bin recorded to beare the same'.[2] But they sufficed to gloss over the question of whether nobility was dependent on noble birth. However, when in 1590, Sir William Segar wrote that 'the true nobilitie of men, is *Vertue,* and that he is trulie noble that is vertuous, bee he borne of high or of lowe Parents', it was a sign that the definition of true nobility may have been expanding to acknowledge social reality.[3] It was not until the massive expansion in what eventually amounted to the sale of honours under James I that the value of noble titles really came into question.

The gentry were a great deal more difficult to define. The term itself contained three social gradations: knights, esquires and gentlemen. In its simplest form, the title of 'gentleman' simply denoted someone who his neighbours considered to be such, usually, though not always, through the ownership of land and the holding of local office. In essence, if a man lived as a gentleman, identified himself as a gentleman and was recognised as such by his peers, then he was a member of the gentry. That said, there were clear distinctions within the order. At the upper end were the younger sons of the nobility; at the lowest, the rising members of urban elites who could now afford to live a gentleman's lifestyle and to send their sons to be educated at the universities and the Inns of Court. Whereas in the medieval period the ownership of land had denoted gentility, the gentry now included educated professionals: doctors, teachers and academics, members of the clergy and crown servants. As Sir Thomas Smith put it in his *De republica anglorum:*

> as for gentlemen, they be made good cheape in England. For whosoever studieth the lawes of the realme, who studieth in the universities, who professed liberall sciences, and to be shorte, who can live idly and without manuall labour, and will beare the port, charge and countenaunce of a gentleman, he shall be called master, for that is the title which men give to esquires and other gentlemen, and shall be taken for a gentleman.[4]

The numbers of the gentry expanded rapidly during the sixteenth century, mirroring the expansion of government in the period following the redistribution of land after the dissolution of the monasteries. From 1524, where there were around 200 knightly families and 4,000–5,000 lesser esquires and gentlemen, numbers increased by 1600 to as many as 500 knights and 16,000 esquires and gentlemen. Even allowing for exaggeration, it is clear that the expansion of the gentry far exceeded levels of population growth, 'perhaps multiplying four times over while the population at large rather more than doubled'.[5]

That 'rise of the gentry', R. H. Tawney argued in a famous article in 1941, reflected a fundamental shift of power and wealth from the titled nobility to a rising class of gentry families, a process that led inexorably to the English Civil War, seen in this perspective as an epic struggle between a declining nobility and a rising gentry. The subsequent historiographical debate over the issue, the so-called 'storm over the gentry', produced a number of articles, energetically debating the 'rise of the gentry' thesis, culminating in Lawrence Stone's massive study, *The Crisis of the Aristocracy, 1558–1641*, in which Stone ultimately failed to convince that the nobility was in terminal decline but offered a vivid depiction of noble and gentry life. Drawing on Stone's thesis, Mervyn James's study of the mental worlds of the nobility and gentry reflected the prevailing historiography of the 1960s, offering a sophisticated account of a shift from a regionalised lineage culture founded in the noble household to a state-sponsored culture of service to the Tudor monarchy, which exerted a 'monopoly of honour and violence'.[6]

All of these studies were characterised by an effort to cast the relationship between the nobility and the gentry within a narrative schematic of the long-term causes of the Civil War, focusing on economic fluctuations, changing social relations and the exercise of authority. In reaction, in the 1970s, the emergence of 'revisionist' studies of the Civil War, paying greater attention to the specific circumstances of the outbreak of conflict and challenging the notion that it was the product of long-term shifts in society and culture, meant that the twin ideas of a long-term crisis of the aristocracy and rise of the gentry were themselves increasingly challenged. Sweeping surveys went out of fashion, replaced by detailed studies of the court and of the localities, of county communities. These studies paid much greater attention to the workings of local government and to the ways in which networks of kinship and patronage played out beyond the court. The revisionists' shift of attention away from the social and economic 'causes' of the Civil War resulted in a narrowing of attention on the early seventeenth-century court, and consequently closer attention was paid to the relationship of the nobility and gentry to the Crown and to the significance of their role in government.

In parallel to the increased attention being paid to the nobility in Stuart England, George Bernard's account of the role of the nobility in England drew attention to the community of interests between the Tudor monarchs and their nobility and to the continuing power and political significance of the nobility – at court and in the localities – arguing that they 'remained powerful, socially, economically, politically and ideologically'.[7] Barry Coward's study of the Stanley Earls of Derby and Susan Doran's examination of Thomas Radcliffe, Earl of Sussex, effectively disproved Stone's assertion that the Elizabethan nobility were suffering an economic crisis, resulting in a loss of power and influence. On the contrary, the Stanley family dominated their local society, also reaching out to other leading families and to the court; Sussex enjoyed a long career in royal service. More recent work on the importance of the nobility in the seventeenth century has confirmed this view. Increasingly, it has become clear that Stone's distinction between the nobility and the gentry is misleading, as is his focus on tensions and conflicts of interest. Instead, they should be understood as sharing largely the same interests and co-operating together with the monarchy.

GOVERNMENT

Members of the gentry undoubtedly performed a vital role in local government. As seen in earlier chapters, men from leading gentry families sought election as members of parliament (MPs) and served as justices of the peace (JPs) or deputy lieutenants, often performing multiple roles: it has been calculated that from the 1540s onwards, some 60–90 per cent of courtiers were also MPs or JPs. The direct benefits of holding such offices were not necessarily obvious as they carried no salary and involved an increasing amount of work, and even expenditure – yet men competed for these posts. The rapid expansion of the commissions of the peace, from about ten justices per shire at the beginning of the sixteenth century to forty or fifty in the middle of Elizabeth's reign and up to ninety by the end of the century, was matched by the clamour for appointment. There was also more business for the justices to deal with; of the 306 statutes of duties in place in 1599, seventy-five dated from the period 1558–97. In part, the desire for appointment is explained by the fact that high offices were a recognition of an individual's existing social standing, which itself brought potential rewards in terms of developing his further social status, forging alliances within the local community and providing opportunities to lobby at the court for more tangible rewards. But there was also a sense in which officeholders saw it as their public duty to serve the Queen and the commonwealth and sought office for these reasons. William Lambarde, a Kent JP and author of several manuals of instructions for local officials, instructed the county's quarter sessions in 1582 that they were there 'for the glory of God and the service of our prince, but also the common benefit of this our country [county] and the particular good of us all'.[8]

There is evidence that the government took an increasing interest in the fitness of those appointed to office, Burghley drawing up annotated lists of acceptable candidates to be appointed as JPs, but there were limits to the control that central government could exert. In Kent, Martin Barnham of Bilsington was removed from the commission of the peace '"three small times" but on every occasion he was quickly restored. His son ascribed these recalls to Barnham's personal merit yet an equally vital factor, no doubt, was the government's recognition that it could not do without the services of such an important county gentleman.'[9]

Barnham's case demonstrates the limitations that local interests and influences sometimes placed on the government's power and control of the localities. Diarmaid MacCulloch's study of Suffolk in the 1580s and 1590s has shown an increasing resistance on the part of local gentlemen to the demands of central government, even when the national military situation became critical. By contrast, in 1580, Sir John Thynne's notes for the Wiltshire quarter sessions 'dwelt heavily on how local authority must take care of national issues'.[10] Overall, the relationship between the centre and localities was one of mutual dependency and benefit. Networks of patronage and kinship linked the localities to the court, a reciprocal relationship in which the lesser gentry sought advancement and reward and political influence beyond their locality and those closer to the political centre were able to construct a power base to extend their influence and garner support throughout government. These networks also played an important role in connecting the localities to central government, enabling gentry leaders to represent local interests at court, as when in 1585 Sir James Hales wrote to Burghley 'on behalf of a friend and good neighbour of mine [William Lovelace junior] . . . that in a matter urged against him . . . it would please you to afford him your honourable favour'.[11]

At the centre, it was the nobility that dominated. Elizabeth's first Privy Council included the Earls of Derby, Shrewsbury and Arundel and the Lords Howard and Clinton, members of established magnate families, alongside the more recently ennobled Marquess of Northampton and the Earls of Pembroke and Bedford. Although membership of the Council remained fairly static, other noblemen were added during the next thirty years: the Duke of Norfolk, the Earls of Leicester, Sussex, Shrewsbury, Warwick and Derby, Lords Hunsdon, Howard of Effingham, Buckhurst and Cobham. It was only as this generation died out and Elizabeth failed to replace them that the role of the nobility in the council began to decline. During the 1590s, the only great noble to gain admittance was the Earl of Essex; after his revolt in 1601, the Earls of Shrewsbury and Worcester were added.

It is possible to say that by this point aristocratic birth and land ownership were no longer sufficient qualifications for entry into the governing elite. Yet how far this was a deliberate policy of exclusion and how far it was simply a reflection of the ageing Queen's refusal to fill vacancies and to rely on those beyond a trusted group of proven loyalty may be questioned. What it certainly did not reflect was any opening up of the council to those below the ranks of the nobility and upper gentry. Although some of the members of her first council were of relatively humble origins – Sir John Mason, Sir William Petre and Sir Nicholas Bacon – by the 1590s, it was dominated by members of a limited number of powerful families, tied to the Queen by blood and long service. The predominant family was the Cecils: Burghley and his son Robert descended from a minor gentry family that first rose to prominence in the service of Henry VII and achieved significant landowning status by the end of Henry VIII's reign.

Their dominance of Elizabeth's government reflected the extent to which the decision-making process remained in the hands of a small elite. It is striking how far members of that elite were dependent on royal favour for their continued hold on power. The most extreme example of this was the 2nd Earl of Essex, whose fall from favour in 1599 was swiftly followed by bankruptcy and desperation in 1601, but others who incurred Elizabeth's disfavour found this reflected in their exclusion from court or high office. Following the Queen's discovery of his illicit marriage to Elizabeth Throckmorton in 1591, Sir Walter Ralegh was banned from the court until 1597. Leicester's nephew and heir, Philip Sidney, widely admired by his contemporaries, never secured the Queen's full favour, and his career never achieved the expected heights.

In some instances, the removal of noble families from positions of power and influence under Elizabeth could be said to have been initiated by the actions of earlier Tudor governments. In the north, by the time of Elizabeth's accession, the power of the Percys, Nevilles, Cliffords and Dacres had been weakened by the appointment of southern nobles as well as local gentry of lesser status to the wardenships of the Northern Marches. Elizabeth continued the policy, appointing Lord Grey of Wilton as warden of the East and Middle Marches. Although the 4th Lord Dacre was appointed warden of the West March, following his death in 1563 the Queen reverted to policy, appointing men of proven loyalty such as William Grey, 13th Baron Grey de Wilton, the Earl of Bedford, Lord Willoughby, Lord Hunsdon and his sons, Sir John and Sir Robert Carey, as well as lesser local landowners such as Lord Scrope, Lord Eure and Sir John Forster. The exclusion of the Earls of Northumberland and Westmorland contributed to their rebellion in 1569, which itself hastened the decline of the great northern families. This did not necessarily result in more stable government in the region, but at the end of Elizabeth's reign it was Thomas, Lord Burghley, eldest son of William Cecil, who was sent to bring order to the region, not a more senior noble.

Yet the process by which government of the localities became concentrated in the hands of a chosen few selected by the Crown should not be overestimated. In the localities, it was only where the great noble families had died out or had been weakened (such as by the succession of minors) or otherwise removed from power that the gentry rose to take over the significant local offices.

In some counties, the removal of the leading noble family resulted in unrest and instability. A. Hassell Smith has shown how in Norfolk, following the fall of the 4th Duke in 1572, county government fell into factional in-fighting between the leading gentry families. Up to this point, Norfolk had exercised dominant control over government, holding the most important offices and, more crucially, operating a patronage network unrivalled by any other significant nobleman in the region. His conception of his own role in the county was little different from that of any late-medieval nobleman, as seen when he told William Cecil that 'I wold have bene sorye that my cuntrye mene schuld have hade cawse to have judged that enye matter concerning the Quenes Majestyes sarvys in Norfolke or Suffolke shulde rather thave bene committyd off first to others than to me.' After his removal, men scrambled to find new patrons and new ways of accessing the court. From 1572, county government was fought over by rival gentry groups, loosely focused on Sir Arthur Heveningham and Sir Nathaniel Bacon. Heveningham deliberately sought to assume the Duke's place; one of his rivals, Edward Flowerdew, commented that he 'hath ... challenged more superioritie, aucthoritie and jurisdiction over other men and their lyvings than the nobleman that hath lyved in that countrey hath done'.[12] Having won the patronage of Leicester, Flowerdew rose to become a successful and prominent lawyer, engaging in a series of private and public disputes with Heveningham that culminated in a violent encounter as Flowerdew rode to the 1582/3 Epiphany sessions at Norwich. Enraged by a recent exchange of letters in which Flowerdew had expatiated at some length on Heveningham's inability to control his temper, the latter rode out and challenged Flowerdew to a duel; when refused, 'he spurred his horse after him, threatened to kill him, and struck him on the head.' On other occasions, the tensions between the two men broke out in public accusations and insults at quarter sessions.

In Suffolk, where the Duke of Norfolk had been powerful but not all-dominant, the consequences of his removal were much less serious, as MacCulloch's study of the region has shown. There was already a group of powerful, Protestant gentry who possessed their own routes of access to the court and exerted their own patronage, centred on the families of Lord Wentworth and the Wingfields of Letheringham. There was also Sir Nicholas Bacon, appointed Lord Keeper of the

Great Seal at Elizabeth's accession, with whom Norfolk worked in relative amity. Tensions certainly existed between the group of predominantly Protestant gentry and Norfolk's more religiously conservative followers, but on the Duke's fall, his followers chose discretion over unrest. The major difference between the counties of Norfolk and Suffolk appears to have been a shared sense that private quarrels should not be allowed to interrupt the efficient running of local government, part of a strong sense of county community that was a considerable source of pride to its inhabitants. On a show of discontent by Nicholas Bacon (son of Lord Keeper Bacon) in 1588, on finding that he had twenty fewer men under his command than his fellow captain, the deputy lieutenants of the county urged him to be reasonable: 'our contry hath for many years caryed great credit for the good agrement emongest the gent., and lamentable yt were that so small a cause shuld be the begynnyng of any disagrement.'[13]

Elsewhere, local government usually ran much more smoothly where the great families retained their dominance of local society. The Stanley Earls of Derby retained their pre-eminence in north-west England, partly because of the extent of their dominance of patronage networks in the region, which enabled them to forge 'bonds of dependence' with other leading families. Though Barry Coward's study of the region has uncovered evidence of competition over land, office and the profits of justice, the rewards of loyalty and harmony outweighed these tensions. Those that were prepared to serve the Stanleys received favours of office and representation at court, amongst other benefits. Yet the relationship between the family and local gentry was not simply a question of economic benefit and reward; rather, it reflected a shared sense of the structure of local society. The funeral of the 3rd Earl of Derby in 1572, conducted on a grand scale, recreated the social hierarchy in its cortège. Led by eighty of the late Earl's gentlemen, fifty knights and esquires all on horseback, followed by leading household officials, the procession was completed by the gentlemen's servants and 500 yeomen. The hearse was accompanied by esquires drawn from leading gentry families, as was the new Earl, symbolising the bonds of loyalty and continuity. Ultimately it was the dominant social status of the Stanleys in local society that ensured that those linked to them through patronage and kinship bonds occupied the leading offices of Lancashire and Cheshire.

The one group of powerful landowners that lost power and influence during Elizabeth's reign was the Catholic nobility and gentry. In October 1564, the Council instructed the bishops to report on the gentry's and JPs' religion and to recommend who should be appointed and who should be removed: '431 JPs [were reported] as favourable to the Church settlement, 264 as neutral, and 157 as hinderers of the newly established Church.'[14] It was already clear that religious conformity was the most vital qualification for serving the Queen, but the lack of experienced Protestant gentry and nobility in some counties meant that Catholics could not immediately be excluded from government. In Sussex, the most powerful nobles were the Catholic peers, the Earl of Arundel and Lord Lumley. Arundel was appointed Lord Lieutenant in 1559, but in 1569, after he and Lumley got caught up in the thwarted plan to marry the Duke of Norfolk to Mary, Queen of Scots, they were excluded, and the office passed to the Protestant Lords Buckhurst and De La Warr. Even then, the religious complexion of the county meant that the demonstrably loyal Catholic Lord

Montague was appointed alongside them. After the Northern Rising, it was necessary and possible for the government to pay close attention to the religious allegiances of those that served in local government and to make it clear that religious conformity would be rewarded.

From the 1570s, the issue of Catholic loyalty became even more pressing, following the issuing of a papal bull deposing the Queen and absolving Catholics from loyalty to her government. Those who refused to attend Protestant services were subjected to heavier financial impositions, which, in the case of Sir Thomas Tresham, exacerbated an already difficult economic situation to leave him heavily in debt. Between 1581 and 1605 he paid recusancy fines of almost £8,000, the equivalent of two and a half years of income.

Catholics were also barred from the higher offices in government that might have helped to recompense them for their fines. General orders were issued removing recusants from the Commission of the Peace, and in 1579 the Oath of Supremacy was administered to all JPs, effectively removing those that refused to conform from significant offices. In Sussex, according to R. B. Manning, 'the proportion of Catholics among the heads of eighty-eight families who [held significant office during Elizabeth's reign] fell from one half in the 1560s to one-sixth in the 1590s.'[15] Lord Montague was not reappointed to the lieutenancy of the county in 1585, on the outbreak of war with Spain, and his activities with the local militia also ceased around this time.

This process forced loyal Catholics to find other ways of fulfilling their roles as the leaders of society. Military service offered one way of demonstrating their loyalty. In 1594, Tresham affirmed that his tenants were liable 'to furnish a man fit for service, either to himself or his son, if employed in Her Majesty's wars beyond seas'.[16] In 1588, after the Armada was sighted, the Crown summoned the nobility to London to defend the Queen. According to Burghley's account of the episode (which may or may not be reliable), Lord Montague was prominent amongst those that responded:

> The first that shewed his Bands to the Quéene, was that Noble, vertuous, honorable man, the *Viscount Mountague,* who, howsoeuer men do iudge of him for opinion in Religion, yet to tell you the truth, he is reported alwaes to haue professed, as now also at this time he did professe and protest solemnely, both to the Quéene, and to all her Court, in open Assemblies, that he now came, though he was very sickly, and in age, with a full resolution to liue and die in defence of the Quéene, and of his countrie, against all Inuaders, whether it were Pope, King or Potentate whatsoeuer, and in that quarell he would hazard his life, his children, his lands and goods.[17]

Accompanied by his son and grandson and by almost 200 mounted soldiers, the image of the aged Lord Montague prepared to fight and die for his Protestant queen was of obvious use to Burghley as a counter to the Catholic threat, but it also pointed to the extent to which Catholic nobles and gentry were compelled to choose between their faith and their responsibilities of loyalty and service to the Queen, vital aspects of gentle identity.

WARFARE

In the absence of a standing, professional army, it was the men raised and led by the nobility and leading gentry who maintained law and order at home and pursued the regime's interests abroad. Still primarily identified as a warrior elite, members of the nobility and gentry raised and led royal forces at home and abroad: for example, the Earl of Warwick led troops to France in 1562; the Earl of Leicester led forces to the Netherlands in 1585; the Earl of Sussex headed up Elizabeth's forces in Ireland during his appointment as Lord Lieutenant and later led the royal army that put down the rising of 1569; the Earl of Essex led the army raised to face Tyrone's rebellion in Ireland in 1598–9.

The nobility's role in raising and leading royal forces at home and abroad did undergo changes during the sixteenth century, not least in response to technical advancements in the development of artillery and gunpowder. The increasing costs of warfare meant that it was no longer possible for any but the wealthiest nobles to provide and equip a substantial number of men, and the limitations placed on the noble affinity meant that the numbers of liveried retainers were controlled. In this respect, there had been changes. Alongside this, the government developed other means of raising forces, notably through the shire levies. The development of the Elizabethan militia reduced the government's dependency on the forces raised through the noble affinity. In 1550–1, the Crown had extended the office of the lord lieutenancy to every county, and this office became permanent in 1585, but the significance of this development should not be overstated. In the early part of her reign, Elizabeth only appointed lord lieutenants in times of crisis – at her accession and in 1569, during the Northern Rising. Outside of these times, the office was discontinued. While the office eventually became permanent after the outbreak of war with Spain, it was only later that it became the basis for an independent royal army. There was no official salary attached to the position; George, 2nd Lord Hunsdon, seeking to succeed to his father's place as Lord Lieutenant of Norfolk and Suffolk, described the post as a 'matter of honor and pleasure not of profitt'.[18] Moreover, notwithstanding the rise of professional soldiers and the increasing need for the more specialised training they could provide, it was recognised that the role of raising and leading troops could only be performed by the gentry and nobility. John Peyton, appointed Muster-Master in Cornwall in 1595, wrote that 'the gentlemen of the counties are the only captains to draw the persons or the purses of the common people into martial actions'.[19]

Although the Northern Rising of 1569 was put down by forces raised through the shire levies, Leicester's army accompanying him to the Netherlands in 1585–6 was essentially a noble affinity. Simon Adams's examination of its composition has corroborated the Earl's own description of his forces as 'servants and friends'.[20] Although this expedition may retrospectively be understood as the last time such a substantial force was recruited through a noble's personal following, and in time it may be said that the establishment of the lords lieutenancies was part of the gradual process by which the waging of war and maintenance of order were taken over by the government and out of the control of the nobility, this did not happen during Elizabeth's reign.

CHIVALRIC CULTURE

The idea of service to the monarch, God and the commonweal was deeply embedded in noble and gentry culture. The government made efforts to reinforce the link. In a series of speeches to MPs and JPs from 1559 to 1576, Lord Keeper Bacon enjoined his gentry audience to ensure 'the good governance of the realm' and 'the preservacion of the common weale', reminding them that they 'owed a duty to God, to the Queen, to "your Contrie whose weale it concerneth universallye"'.[21] In part, Bacon's comments reflected the effects of the expansion of literacy and humanist models of education during the sixteenth century, but they also had earlier foundations. The idea of the nobility and gentry as an elite order set aside to take special care of the commonweal dated back to the origins of the settling of the knightly order in the twelfth century. Members of this order of society were identified as an elite, set apart by birth and by the possession and the practice of a set of special values – loyalty, fellowship, honour, faith and service of the common good/commonweal – all of which bound the Elizabethan gentry and nobility to the Queen and supported the roles they played in government and society.

It is clear that the Elizabethan nobility and gentry continued to see themselves first and foremost as a knightly order. The continuing popularity of tilts and tournaments reflected this, as did the literary tastes of the gentry and nobility. Chivalric romances, one of the key ways in which the values and ideals of chivalry were passed down to new generations, were widely read by members of the elite, for pleasure, for instruction, and as an exemplary guide to behaviour. The Queen's godson, Sir John Harington, carried out the first English translation of Ludovico Ariosto's epic romance *Orlando Furioso* in 1591, though it was widely read in its French and Italian editions before that date. In his *Defence of Poesie,* Philip Sidney described the educative function of the *Amadis:* 'Truely I have knowen men that ... with reading the *Amadis de Gaule* ... have found their harts mooved to the exercise of courtesie, liberalitie, and especially courage.'[22]

Sidney's *Arcadia* and Spenser's *The Faerie Queene* drew upon earlier romances, adapting the genre to fit their own purposes. It was often in the literature of the period that the values of the nobility and gentry were reflected and reaffirmed: the function of poetry, according to Sidney, was to 'teach and delight', to move its readers to 'well dooing' and to the attainment of virtue.[23]

This dual purpose, of entertainment and education, informed the Elizabethan project to 'fashion an ideal gentleman', set out by Spenser in *The Faerie Queene.* The ultimate example of the Elizabethan gentleman was Sidney himself, widely acknowledged by his contemporaries as the embodiment of the gentlemanly ideal. His lack of favour from the Queen did not prevent him from being widely admired by his contemporaries, and his death in September 1586 turned him into a Protestant hero. Fighting with the English army sent to assist the Dutch rebels in their struggle against Philip II, he suffered a serious wound to his thigh in a skirmish at Zutphen and died from gangrene on 17 October 1586. He was widely and extravagantly mourned, notably by Elizabeth herself, and a large number of literary memorials were published that cast considerable light on the values held by Elizabethan gentlemen. As John Phillips put it, in his account of the funeral, published in 1587:

> sweet *Sidney* . . . [was] the flower of curtesie, who in his life time gave a perfect light in his conversation to leade men to virtue . . . that by his example they might both learne to feare God, to glory in sincerity, to abound in loyalty, & to become carefull lovers of their native countrie.[24]

The manner of his heroic death perfectly encapsulated the values which united the Elizabethan nobility and gentry as a martial fellowship in the service of the Queen. Sidney embodied the key elements of the chivalric ethos – military prowess, concern for the common good, chivalric fellowship and duty and loyalty to the monarch – and it was these values that his Elizabethan biographers were most eager to inculcate in their readers.

LOYALTY AND REBELLION

Membership of the elite community of honour was a vital criterion of gentility. Those that broke their bonds of loyalty by committing treason against the monarch were forcibly excluded. Following his farcical entry into London in 1601, swiftly termed a 'rebellion' by the government, the Earl of Essex was visited in the Tower by the Usher of the Black Rod, who physically stripped him of his Order of the Garter, whilst at Windsor, home of the order, his hatchments were torn down and thrown out of the chapel. By Elizabeth's reign, noble and gentry rebellion against the monarchy was unusual, and usually limited in its aims, constrained at least in part by a complicated language of loyalty and obedience, which rebels almost invariably invoked to claim that their actions were not intended against the monarch but their evil counsellors, with their corrupt policies.

The 1569 Rising of the Northern Earls has been characterised as being more serious in intent, with its overtones of religious dissent and suspected aim of deposing Elizabeth in favour of Mary, Queen of Scots. Yet, in most respects, the rising can be seen to have conformed to the usual shape of a noble rebellion. Motivated by a confused mixture of religious conservatism and resentment at being excluded from the major northern offices that they considered to be theirs by right of birth and status, the earls were reluctant rebels at best. Surrounded by Catholic advisers, they were at first drawn into the plan to marry the Duke of Norfolk to Mary, Queen of Scots, then, following his imprisonment in the Tower, began to mobilise their retinues for their own protection, fearing a similar fate. They constantly protested their loyalty to the Crown; Westmorland, urged by his Catholic officers to rise for religion, replied 'No . . . those that seem to take that quarrel in other countries are accounted as rebels; and therefore I will never blot my house, which hath been this long preserved without staining.'[25] Elizabeth's insistence that they come to court, combined with continuing pressure from their advisers, backed the earls into a situation in which they found themselves in open revolt, claiming to march for true religion and for the deposition of false councillors. After some threatening times, when the earls headed south and outnumbered royal forces in the region, popular apathy and the earls' inability to pay their mercenaries combined to dispel the threat, and they soon retreated, pursued by royal forces under the command of the Earl of Sussex, Lord President of the Council of the North, who drove the rebels into Scotland and eventual arrest or flight abroad.

Although it was ultimately put down with relative ease, the rising demonstrates the significance of the support of the nobility and gentry to the survival of Elizabeth's rule. The extremely harsh punishment carried out against the rebels – about 450 were executed, comparing with 178 after the Pilgrimage of Grace, and ninety after Wyatt's rising – suggests the seriousness with which the regime took the rising and its possible consequences. By contrast, the smaller-scale Essex 'rebellion' in 1601, after which only five men were executed, may be seen as an attempt to force access to the Queen rather than a full-scale rebellion and attempt on the Crown.

THE QUEEN

Securing access to the Queen was a vital part of politics in Elizabethan England. As recent studies have shown, the Queen was at the heart of political life, not just as an object of aspiration and devotion but also as an active participant in the decision-making process. The royal court, and, by extension, London, was the centre of political activity during Elizabeth's reign. Beyond the court, there were fewer opportunities for the gentry to meet the Queen in person. However, the practical requirements of sanitation, coupled with outbreaks of endemic disease in London meant that the court still retained some of its itinerant character, undertaking a series of summer progresses. Elizabeth's progresses were important, as they took the Queen out of London and its environs and allowed for contact with a wider group of her subjects, albeit still rather limited in numbers. Most often, the Queen's visits revolved around the homes of her close friends and advisers, including most of the members of her Privy Council, thus enabling the business of government to continue away from London.

Royal visits offered an opportunity for the Elizabethan gentry and nobility to display their ability to offer appropriate hospitality to the Queen and her household, to reaffirm their power and authority by their capacity to do so. The political importance of the Queen's progresses contributed to the emergence of the prodigy-house to produce a range of magnificent country palaces such as Hardwick Hall and Longleat House. The Cecils led the way, William and Robert between them creating three grand prodigy-houses: Burghley House, Theobalds and, in James's reign, Hatfield House. Sir Christopher Hatton spent his fortune building Holdenby Hall in Northamptonshire explicitly to honour the Queen, vowing that he would not live in the house before she visited. She never did visit, and Hatton had few opportunities to visit his property before his death in 1591, heavily indebted to the Queen.

Admittance to the royal presence was also used as a reward for loyal service; the honour of hosting the Queen when on progress was, for much of her reign, welcomed as a significant sign of royal favour. Burghley's return to favour after the execution of Mary, Queen of Scots, was marked by Elizabeth's visit to his Hertfordshire estate, Theobalds. In his capacity as Lieutenant of the Royal Manor at Woodstock, Sir Henry Lee hosted the Queen in 1572, 1574 and 1575 and then received her at his own home at Ditchley in Oxfordshire in 1592, staging lavish entertainments to mark her visit, the apogee of his career. There is, however, some evidence that towards the end of her reign, Elizabeth's hosts were sometimes rather less welcoming, perhaps realising the limited nature of the rewards she was likely to bestow. Lee wrote to refuse the honour of another visit in June 1600, pleading poverty and citing the Queen's failure to reward him sufficiently after her previous visits. He would, he said, have 'entertained her "as often beforetime, if my fortune answered my desire, or part of her Highness' many promises performed"'.[26]

The choice of hosts on progress was also used as a way of communicating central government policies to the localities. In the progress of 1591, the first to be made after the Armada, Elizabeth visited 'five Catholic-affiliated homes in Sussex and Hampshire, the largest number in any such year'.[27] Lord Montague's loyalty was recognised by a six-day visit to his home at Cowdray, where he staged a series of entertainments dealing with the issue of loyalty. One of the staged speeches echoed Burghley's description of Montague's behaviour in 1588. Elizabeth was taken to an oak tree 'wheron her Majesties armes and all the armes of the noblemen and gentlemen of that shire, were hanged in escutchions most beutifull', and a 'wilde man' assured her that 'all these honourable lords, and gentlemen, whose shieldes your Majestie doeth here beholde . . . when your Majestie shall but stande in feare of any daunger, will bring their bodies, their purses, their soules, to your Highness, being their heart, their head, and their soveraigne'.[28]

In this way, the progresses could be used to reaffirm the ties of loyalty and service, even of personal friendship that bound the Queen to her Catholic nobility and gentry.

CONCLUSION

In many ways, the Elizabethan nobility and gentry constituted an exception in early modern Europe. The cultural homogeneity of the English gentry and nobility, and the extent to which their interests were identified with those of the monarch made for a stability and continuity that England's neighbours sometimes lacked. The personal relationships that Elizabeth built up with her nobility and gentry were lacking in much of Europe. In France, the combination of a number of powerful, politically ambitious noble families and religious conflict produced a situation in which, during the seventeenth century, the monarchy distanced itself from its most powerful subjects and the honours system became an overtly state-sponsored means of binding the aristocracy to the Crown.

Closer to home, Wales was more or less successfully integrated into Tudor government, though gentry culture retained its distinctiveness. By contrast, Ireland's greater nobility fits much more readily into the medieval and Continental model of 'over-mighty subjects' and had proved resistant to Tudor government throughout the sixteenth century. Successive English governors sought to find ways of working with the great Irish magnates. As Ciaran Brady's study has shown, Elizabeth sought not to destroy the four great earls of Kildare, Ormond, Clanricarde and Desmond; indeed, she needed to work with them to govern Ireland, but she also needed to find ways of restraining their power, just as that of the English nobility had been controlled after the Wars of the Roses. Yet, ultimately, as shown in Chapter 10, the effort failed as a fundamental conflict of interests, the effort to reform Irish local government along English patterns and the brutality of the methods employed by some of the Elizabethan governors resulted in the English Crown becoming alienated from the Old English as well as the Gaelic lords, culminating in Hugh O'Neill, Earl of Tyrone's rebellion of 1594, otherwise known as the Nine Years' War.

The failure of Elizabeth's government to co-operate with the Irish nobility highlights the extent to which co-operation rather than conflict characterised the English nobility's relationship with the Crown. And this was something that continued down the social scale into the ranks of the gentry. Though, as we have seen, county government did not always run smoothly and there were certainly rivalries and tensions, it was not the case that the gentry and nobility were engaged in a struggle for power. It has often been argued that, in France, the *noblesse d'épée* and greater nobles were deliberately excluded from the major offices of administration and local government, in favour of the *noblesse de robe,* a new order of men, rising from the merchant and professional classes, often through the purchase of office. Some effort has been made to apply this model to England, but the evidence for this is slim and ultimately unconvincing. Though the numbers of the gentry were steadily increasing throughout the sixteenth century, this was not at the expense of the nobility, and they were not replaced in local and central government, except in exceptional cases where factors such as religious conformity and the natural extinction of male lines intervened. The Elizabethan nobility and gentry were not only involved in the practice of government and of war but also in the making of decisions at court and in council. The Queen relied on them to lead her armies and to serve on her Privy Council, as well as governing the localities, where power devolved down through the lower ranks of the gentry, involving local elites in the practice of government at all levels. In turn, the nobility and gentry were bound to the Queen by ties of loyalty, duty and service, ensuring stability of government and of society that enabled the regime to survive war, economic crisis and internal rebellion.

FURTHER READING

Adams, Simon (ed.), *Leicester and the Court* (Manchester, 2002).

Asch, Ronald G., *Nobilities in Transition, 1550–1700: Courtiers and Rebels in Britain and Europe* (London, 2003).

Bernard, G. W., *Power and Politics in Tudor England* (Aldershot, 2000).

Braddick, Michael J., *State Formation in Early Modern England, c. 1550–1700* (Cambridge, 2000).

Brady, Ciaran, *The Chief Governors: The Rise and Fall of Reform Government in Tudor Ireland, 1536–1588* (Cambridge, 1994).

Clark, Peter, *English Provincial Society from the Reformation to the Revolution: Religion, Politics and Society in Kent, 1500–1640* (Hassocks, 1977).

Coward, Barry, *The Stanleys: Lords Stanley and Earls of Derby 1385–1672: The Origins, Wealth and Power of a Landowning Family* (Manchester, 1983).

Cust, Richard, 'Reading for Magistracy: The Mental World of Sir John Newdigate', in John F. McDiarmid (ed.), *The Monarchical Republic of Early Modern England* (Aldershot, 2007), pp. 181–99.

Doran, Susan, 'The Finances of an Elizabethan Nobleman and Royal Servant: A Case Study of Thomas Radcliffe, 3rd Earl of Sussex', *Bulletin of the Institute of Historical Research,* 61 (October) (1988): 286–300.

Hassell Smith, A., *County and Court: Government and Politics in Norfolk, 1558–1603* (Oxford, 1974).
Hexter, J. H., 'The Storm over the Gentry', in *Reappraisals in History* (London, 1961), pp. 117–41.
James, M. E., *Family, Lineage and Civil Society: A Study of Society, Politics and Mentality in the Durham Region, 1550–1640* (Oxford, 1974).
James, Mervyn, *Society, Politics and Culture: Studies in Early Modern England* (Cambridge, 1986).
Jones, Gwynfor, *Concepts of Order and Gentility in Wales, 1540–1640* (Dyfed, 1992).
Kaushik, S., 'Resistance, Loyalty and Recusant Politics: Sir Thomas Tresham and the Elizabethan State', *Midland History*, 21 (1996): 37–72.
MacCaffrey, W. T., 'Place and Patronage in Elizabethan Politics', in S. T. Bindoff, J. Hurstfield and C. H. Williams (eds.), *Elizabethan Government and Society: Essays Presented to Sir John Neale* (London, 1961), pp. 95–126.
MacCulloch, Diarmaid, *Suffolk and the Tudors: Politics and Religion in an English County, 1500–1600* (Oxford, 1986).
Manning, Roger B., *Religion and Society in Elizabethan Sussex: A Study of the Enforcement of the Religious Settlement, 1558–1603* (Leicester, 1969).
Mears, Natalie, *Queenship and Political Discourse in the Elizabethan Realms* (Cambridge, 2005).
Questier, Michael C., *Catholicism and Community in Early Modern England: Politics, Aristocratic Patronage and Religion, c. 1550–1640* (Cambridge, 2006).
Stone, Lawrence, *The Crisis of the Aristocracy, 1558–1641* (Oxford, 1965).
Tawney, R. H., 'The Rise of the Gentry, 1558–1640', *Economic History Review*, Old Ser., 11 (1941): 1–38.
Tighe, W. J., 'Courtiers and Politics in Elizabethan Herefordshire: Sir James Croft, His Friends and His Foes', *Historical Journal*, 32 (3) (1989): 257–79.
Wall, Alison, *Power and Protest in England, 1525–1640* (London, 2000).
Younger, Neil, 'Securing the Monarchical Republic: The Remaking of the Lord Lieutenancies, 1585', *Historical Research*, 83 (February) (2010): 69–82.

NOTES

1 Mary E. Finch, *The Wealth of Five Northamptonshire Families, 1540–1640* (Oxford, 1956), p. 38.
2 Sir Thomas Smith, *De republica anglorum* (London, 1583), p. 28.
3 William Segar, *The Book of Honor and Arms* (London, 1590), vol. I, p. 34.
4 Smith, *De republica anglorum*, p. 27.
5 Felicity Heal and Clive Holmes, *The Gentry in England and Wales, 1500–1700* (Palo Alto, Calif., 1994), pp. 11–12.
6 Mervyn James, 'English Politics and the Concept of Honour, 1485–1642', in *Society, Politics and Culture: Studies in Early Modern England* (Cambridge, 1986), pp. 308–415.
7 G. W. Bernard, 'Introduction', in *Power and Politics in Tudor England* (Aldershot, 2000), pp. 1–19; p. 1. Bernard's argument was developed through a series of works: *The Power of the Early Tudor Nobility: A Study of the Fourth and Fifth Earls of Shrewsbury* (Brighton, 1985); 'The Tudor Nobility in Perspective', in G. W. Bernard (ed.), *The Tudor Nobility* (Manchester, 1992); 'The Continuing Power of the Tudor Nobility', in *Power and Politics in Tudor England* (Aldershot, 2000), pp. 20–50.
8 Alison Wall, *Power and Protest in England, 1525–1640* (London, 2000), p. 104.
9 Peter Clark, *English Provincial Society from the Reformation to the Revolution: Religion, Politics and Society in Kent, 1500–1640* (Hassocks, 1977), pp. 127–8, 261.
10 Wall, *Power and Protest in England*, p. 100.

11 Clark, *English Provincial Society*, p. 124.
12 A. Hassell Smith, *County and Court: Government and Politics in Norfolk, 1558–1603* (Oxford, 1974), pp. 157–8.
13 Diarmaid MacCulloch, *Suffolk and the Tudors: Politics and Religion in an English County, 1500–1600* (Oxford, 1986), p. 116.
14 Wall, *Power and Protest in England*, p. 49.
15 Roger B. Manning, *Religion and Society in Elizabethan Sussex: A Study of the Enforcement of the Religious Settlement, 1558–1603* (Leicester, 1969), p. xv.
16 *Calendar of State Papers Domestic Series ... Edward VI, Mary I, Elizabeth, James I*, ed. by R. Lemon and M. A. E. Green (London, 1865–72; repr. Liechtenstein, 1967), 1591–4, p. 471.
17 William Cecil, *The Copie of a Letter Sent Out of England to Don Bernardin Mendoza Ambassador in France for the King of Spaine, Declaring the State of England, Contrary to the Opinion of* Don Bernardin, *and of All His Partizans Spaniardes and Others* (London, 1588).
18 Cited in Neil Younger, 'War and the Counties: The Elizabethan Lord Lieutenancy, 1585–1603' Ph.D. thesis, University of Birmingham, 2007, pp. 261–2. Hunsdon was unsuccessful in his appeal but was appointed as Joint Lieutenant of Hampshire with the Marquess of Winchester and Lord Mountjoy.
19 Penry Williams, *The Tudor Regime* (Oxford, 1979), p. 123.
20 Simon Adams, 'A Puritan Crusade? The Composition of the Earl of Leicester's Expedition to the Netherlands, 1585–86', *Leicester and the Court* (Manchester, 2002), pp. 176–95.
21 Heal and Holmes, *The Gentry in England and Wales*, p. 198.
22 *The Defence of Poesie* is also known as *An Apologie for Poetrie:* Sir Philip Sidney, *An Apologie for Poetrie* (London, 1595).
23 Sidney, *An Apologie for Poetrie.*
24 John Phillips, *The Life and Death of Sir Phillip Sidney, Late Lord Governour of Flushing His Funerals Solemnized in Paules Churche Where He Lyeth Interred; with the Whole Order of the Mournful Show, as They Marched through the City of London, on Thursday the 16 of February 1587* (London, 1587).
25 Cuthbert Sharp, *Memorials of the Rebellion of 1569* (London, 1840), p. 196.
26 Mary Hill Cole, *The Portable Queen: Elizabeth I and the Politics of Ceremony* (Amherst, Mass., 1999), pp. 90–1.
27 Cole, *The Portable Queen*, pp. 27–8.
28 Michael C. Questier, *Catholicism and Community in Early Modern England: Politics, Aristocratic Patronage and Religion, c. 1550–1640* (Cambridge, 2006), pp. 171–2.

CHAPTER EIGHTEEN

POVERTY AND THE POOR LAWS

Steve Hindle

It is a cliché, though one with deep roots in Judaeo-Christian culture, that the poor are always with us (Matthew 26:11). Elizabethan England, increasingly familiar as it was with this kind of scriptural idiom, was a society in which the poor were not only present but increasingly problematic. There were, as we shall see, more poor people in both absolute and relative terms in England in the 1590s than had been the case even half a century earlier. But late-sixteenth-century Englishmen and women were gradually forced to recognise that the problem of poverty was not simply a matter of increasing numbers but also of changing typology. The discovery of a large proportion of the population, especially in the towns, who were entirely willing to support themselves through their own labour but were unable to do so with any regularity, was a shock to an intellectual system long accustomed to an easy distinction between the able-bodied but wilfully idle on the one hand and the disabled impotent poor on the other. Elizabethan policy-makers accordingly designed a relief system which had to deal not only with the conventional problems of life-cycle poverty and congenital idleness but also now with the problems of under- and unemployment. This system, arguably one of the greatest and most enduring achievements of the Elizabethan age, had a profound effect not only upon the poor themselves, however they were defined, but also on the entire pattern of social and economic relations in urban and rural communities alike. The Elizabethans created, however incrementally (perhaps even haphazardly), nothing less than a bureaucratised welfare system which not only radically transformed the life chances of that small but significant minority who constituted the very poorest people in English society but also generated an archive which, if read against the grain, offers extraordinary insights into the life experiences of that larger constituency who, although rarely on regular relief and lacking a formal voice or authority in the commonwealth, made shift to survive as best they could.

PERCEPTIONS OF POVERTY

Elizabethan England was confronted with significant changes in both the nature and scale of poverty. Down to the middle years of the sixteenth century, the causes and characteristics of the long-standing problem of the poor had been understood in terms that would have been familiar throughout the medieval period. Indeed, the traditional binary classification of the poor into the *deserving* and *undeserving* had been a commonplace for many centuries and was underpinned by scripture, especially the key text in Saint Paul's letters to the Thessalonians in which the apostle emphasises the duty to labour: 'if a man shall not work, then neither shall he eat' (2 Thessalonians 3:10). This classical and oft-cited iteration of the imperative to work justified the refusal of charity and sustenance to those who, though able-bodied, were unwilling to support themselves through their labour. While the 'impotent' poor, so-called because of their powerlessness through old age, illness, disability or extreme youth to support themselves through their own efforts, were regarded as worthy 'objects of charity', those whose idleness was entirely voluntary were regarded as undeserving. 'Idleness', it should be emphasised, was not in this worldview simply the economic condition of unemployment but a moral failing that suggested that the claimant for relief was wilfully work-shy. Throughout the medieval period and into the early sixteenth century, these 'sturdy beggars' were treated as vagabonds or vagrants and were regarded with extraordinary hostility, their bodies being regarded as targets on which their status as a separate and dependent class could legitimately be marked. Scorched flesh, either in the shape of the letter 'V' for 'vagabond' or letter 'R' for 'rogue', was the painful symbol of a distinction between the worthy and unworthy poor that was the moral inheritance of Elizabethan householder, who might easily distinguish between the known, neighbourhood needy, familiar as lifelong residents of the parish who would be relieved with charity in cash and kind, and the shiftless migrant who sought to make a living through aggressive begging and casual theft.

Right down to the 1560s and 1570s, these stereotypes were easily recognised on the streets of the metropolis, of provincial towns and of rural villages. In the larger towns of southern and central England, however, civic elites were becoming increasingly conscious that the numbers of poor people, and the threat they posed to social and political order, were growing. As the number of beggars increased, towns such as Norwich, Salisbury and Warwick were becoming suffused with an atmosphere of dirt, pollution and peril, and the small knots of reliable men who ran these urban corporations accordingly began to take measures to ascertain the nature and scale of the problem. Their preferred method was to carry out urban censuses of the poor in which the number of relief claimants could be counted and the causes of their misery identified. Urban magistracies expected to find that the ranks of the deserving poor had been swollen by hordes of shiftless migrants who saw an opportunity to gull the wealthy householders of prosperous towns into relieving them. Indeed, the literary stereotype of the 'rogue', developed so effectively in Thomas Harman's *Caveat for Common Cursitors Vulgarly Called Vagabonds* (1566) and others who imitated it, taught the respectable town-dweller to distrust the deceits and disguises with which the vagrant underworld was riddled. Faked diseases and fraudulent testimonials of misfortune, the purveyors of the 'rogue literature' of the day insisted, concealed a quite ruthless determination to trick the unsuspecting into sympathy and charity. In fact, however, the surveys and listings of the poor of the 1570s and 1580s revealed that the very nature of the poverty problem had changed: the increasing numbers of poor were made up not of Harman's 'common cursitors' or 'runagate rakehells' but rather of under- and unemployed workers who were perfectly willing to labour to support themselves and their families if they could find work that was sufficiently regular or remunerated to enable them to do so. Structural changes in the English economy, especially the growth of population and its associated problems of price inflation and labour surplus, had been compounded by difficulties in the textile industry, caused partly by dislocations of foreign trade and partly by harvest failures which meant that the demand for consumer goods slumped as the price of food increased. Together, these trends radically transformed the nature of poverty in Elizabethan England.

The deserving poor had once been very easily identified. They were respectable individuals who had lived long lives of labour, taking extraordinary pains to maintain themselves and their families, until failing eyesight and arthritic limbs meant that they could no longer do so. Or they were newly married couples who had saved long and hard through years of apprenticeship or service to amass the necessary assets to get married and set up their own nuclear family households, only to find that the births of their children, usually in quick succession after the wedding, proved to be not only an emotional blessing but also a financial burden. Recently married couples 'over-burdened' with children not yet old enough to contribute to household income through their labour were, like the elderly and the very young, victims of the kind of 'life-cycle poverty' that afflicts all families in both historical and contemporary societies, especially those where nuclear family households (lacking the extra earning capacity and mutual aid which might be afforded by co-resident kin) were the norm. Where poverty is largely a function of one's position in the life cycle, the poor are difficult to identify as a class since virtually all members of a population are, at one or more points in their life course, vulnerable to the loss of their economic independence. But Elizabethan England witnessed the emergence, especially in those towns where the textile industry had once been dominant, of a new group of poor people who were not simply victims of the rhythms of the life cycle: the 'labouring poor', as they became known, were vulnerable because of irregular work and falling wages to poverty throughout their lives. Indeed, for the very first time in English history, the poor had themselves become a permanent and easily identified class, with many of them being born into poverty, leading their entire lives in poverty and dying in poverty. This was the point in English history at which 'life-cycle poverty' and 'inherited poverty' began to intersect, and the problems of endemic misery associated with long-term indigence became an enduring feature of the life experience of that very significant proportion of the population who supported themselves through meagre and insecure wages. A simple distinction between the deserving and the undeserving was therefore no longer adequate in the face of late-sixteenth-century social and economic change.

THE ELIZABETHAN POOR LAWS

Whereas early-sixteenth-century attempts to introduce the statutory relief of the poor had been predicated on the binary classification with which generations of householders had been familiar, the MPs who staffed the committees responsible for drafting poor-relief legislation in the 1560s, 1570s and 1590s now had to cater for the labouring poor as well as for the worthy 'shame-faced' poor and for sturdy beggars. Influenced partly by the experience of those civic elites who had experimented with systematic poor-relief schemes from the middle of the century, and partly by their own experience as magistrates confronted with growing problems of labour mobility, these MPs created a statutory code which has cumulatively come to be known to historians as the 'Elizabethan poor laws'. The term is conventionally applied to the two statutes of 1598 and 1601 but it more properly also includes the piecemeal development of formal poor relief in earlier statutes of 1563, 1572 and 1576. The earlier legislation had been consistent on the need to punish the vagrant poor with increasing severity, but the relief of the deserving was gradually devolved first in the statute of 1563 to magistrates who were required to draw up lists of the indigent in their own divisions or hundreds, and subsequently from 1572 to collectors of the poor who were responsible for distributing relief in cash and kind to the deserving poor in every parish. By 1598, the legislation had come to embody three principles, each of which provided the basis for the treatment of one of the three groups of poor people whose plight was now so familiar.

The impotent poor were to be relieved in their own homes in cash or kind by overseers of the poor, two of whom were appointed – as unpaid officers serving only for a year at a time – in each parish. These overseers were to assess all householders for their ability to contribute to a parish rate or levy, usually paid by all owners of property at a fixed sum per acre of land or per pound of rental value. These levies were usually collected once a year and kept in the parish chest from which they would be disbursed, sometimes monthly or more commonly every week, to those poor members of the community who were regarded as both indigent and deserving. The legislation emphasised, however, that the overseers should ensure that the recipient of relief was entirely unable to contribute to their maintenance through labour and that he or she had no lineal kin (children, grandparents or grandchildren) who were able to support them. In this respect, the parish 'collection' or 'pension' as it became known, was only ever intended as a last resort even for those who were regarded as deserving.

The vagrant poor, conversely, were the targets of corporal punishment and labour discipline. Vagrants were to be apprehended by parish constables, taken to the whipping post to be lashed until their backs were bloody and then conducted to the parish boundary where the constable of the adjacent community would conduct them across the parish, and so on across every parish, until the wanderer was returned to their last place of settlement. Uncertainty over what actually constituted a settlement (the parish of one's birth, the place where one had been apprenticed or employed, or the place where one had enjoyed a period of settled residence?) proved problematic and varied between the statutes, with the net effect that most constables were simply content to move vagrants on to the boundary and leave it at that. Recidivist vagrants, or 'incorrigible rogues' as they were known, could be sent to the county 'bridewells' or houses of correction where they were set on work, usually beating hemp for the making of thread, and disciplined to develop habits of industry. The vagrancy provisions of the Elizabethan statutes were therefore symbolised by the apparatus of social discipline – whip-stocks, pillories and manacles – with which the cities, towns and villages of England became littered.

By far the most problematic group was, of course, the labouring poor. The Elizabethan statutes insisted that overseers of the poor should provide them with the opportunity to work in their own homes by using parish funds to purchase hemp or wool which idle hands might beat or tease. The intention was that the goods, usually cloth or yarn, produced by paupers would be sold and the sums raised funnelled back into the purchase of further raw materials. Although it was anticipated that schemes of this kind might run at a loss, especially in their early stages, the institutionalisation of the work-ethic was regarded as exemplary to all the poor. There was an associated recognition that the households of the labouring poor were being pulled into immiseration, debt and destitution not so much by low income as by heavy expenditure. Policy-makers therefore sought ways of reducing the burden of children on poor parents, especially by the removal of children of serviceable age into apprenticeships in the households and workshops of their more prosperous neighbours. Thus, from 1598, children as young as seven could be forced into apprenticeship, which for boys might last until the age of twenty-four and for girls until the age of twenty-one (or before that age if they got married). The intention was to provide training in husbandry for boys and housewifery for girls in an institution which was idealised as a 'seminary of mercy', though it was envisaged that the masters of these children would doubtless see them more formally apprenticed into the seven-year service contracts stipulated by craft guilds by the time they reached their mid-teens.

THE ORIGINS OF ELIZABETHAN WELFARE PROVISION

This, then, was a system characterised by targeted transfer payments to the deserving, corporal punishment for the undeserving and labour discipline for the unemployed and their children. The statutes should be understood as reflecting the changing thinking of the times about the causes of poverty, about the charitable obligations of Christians and about the paternal responsibilities of the Elizabethan state. After all, this great statutory code was not created simply because there were more, or more threatening, poor people in England by the 1590s. The nature of the legislation also owes something to the wider characteristics of Elizabethan society and culture.

Some of these features were of very long standing. In the first place, the idiom in which the Elizabethan poor laws were drafted – a language of industry juxtaposed with idleness, of worthiness contrasted with unworthiness – reflects the highly moralised understanding of economic change in sixteenth-century society. This was a world in which the laws of supply and demand, let alone the modern social science of economics of which they form the centrepiece, had yet to be discovered. High prices were interpreted not as a consequence of burgeoning demand at a time of short and unsteady supply but as the result of human greed or (to use the contemporary scriptural idiom) 'covetousness'. Harvest failure was regarded less as the result of unreliable and inefficient agricultural techniques than as the providential judgement of a wrathful God punishing the sins of a disobedient people. The problem of poverty was similarly regarded as a consequence of idleness, a moral failing to be corrected through labour discipline rather than an economic condition to be remedied through fiscal stimulus. The 'moral economy' of poverty finds its most obvious expression in the distinction – an ethical rather than an economic distinction – between the deserving and the undeserving poor, but it also explains the emphasis on inculcating habits of industry in the young, in the idle and even (in so far as it was possible) in the disabled, all of whom, it was argued, should become accustomed to supporting themselves through their labour.

This moralised sense of economic behaviour was also fundamentally linked to developing Renaissance ideas of the 'commonwealth', and of the most appropriate relationship between governors and governed in sixteenth-century society. There were, of course, numerous metaphors used to describe the sixteenth-century social order, most famously the 'great chain of being' in which the estates, degrees and sorts of men were merely the earthly expression of a wider cosmic hierarchy. Perhaps the most significant image, however, was that of 'the body politic', a vision of an organically unified population in which all the members – head, belly, hands and feet – were mutually interdependent and in which the health of the whole depended on well-being among, and appropriate conduct by, each subject. The common good depended upon the maintenance of health and harmony, conditions which could be perpetuated only if there was consensus over whether diseased limbs of the body politic should be healed and restored or stigmatised and excised. From this perspective, vagrants were a cancer on the body politic which ought to be amputated in order to prevent the whole from destruction and dissolution. In turn, the deserving poor were victims of a disease which the governors of society had both power and responsibility to heal. As Christian humanist ideas spread into England, first through the works of Thomas More and subsequently of Thomas Elyot and Thomas Smith in the early and middle years of the sixteenth century, such thinking about the poor had become axiomatic, and by the 1570s it was obvious that the State must bear some responsibility for the creation and maintenance of 'the best state of a commonwealth', especially by securing the welfare of its most unfortunate citizens. By the 1590s, this view had received statutory expression in the creation of a nationally co-ordinated system of rate-based parish relief in which a compulsory tax on landed wealth was the central feature.

If Renaissance ideas about civic obligation set the political context for the legislation, then the Reformation provided the ideological impulse. It was incumbent on the newly Protestant governing class to provide a new institutional setting for poor relief in the wake of their destruction of those institutions – monasteries, hospitals and confraternities among them – which had performed such impressive charitable work before the Reformation. The officers of the civil parish to this extent filled the vacuum left by the attrition of guild wardens, hospital treasures and monastic almoners. But the Reformation was less a matter of institutional defoliation than of cultural revolution, marking a radical discontinuity in attitudes towards charity. Whereas the supernatural economy of traditional religion had involved the reciprocal exchange of alms for prayers and benefited the spiritual well-being of the benefactor as much as the bodily well-being of the pauper, the soteriology of Calvinist Protestantism saw charity not as a means to salvation but merely as an outward sign of election. The logocentric culture of Protestantism also ensured that charity became more heavily influenced by the kind of scriptural fundamentalism that casually (perhaps even callously) rendered the foundational text 2 Thessalonians 3:10 as a justification for letting the work-shy starve. Notions of discrimination between the deserving and the undeserving poor had always been latent in Catholic culture and had probably intensified in hard times when tougher decisions had to be made about the most appropriate allocation of charitable resources. But the Calvinist emphasis on the duty to labour provided a harder edge of scriptural justification for withholding alms from the idle. This was, furthermore, a worldview in which the inscrutable judgements of an omnipotent God divided humankind into a small number of the elect saved amid a sea of the reprobate, a theological distinction which seemed to mirror the economic reality of a tiny but prosperous elite being overwhelmed by the poor multitude. The doctrine of double and absolute predestination might have stipulated that the fate of one's soul was certain yet at the same time unknowable, but the proverbial wisdom that 'heaven helps those who help themselves' perfectly captured the moral economy of Protestantism. In the rigorous distinction between the deserving and the undeserving, in the brutal punishment of the wilfully idle, and in the emphasis on labour discipline, therefore, the Elizabethan poor laws, as befits legislation largely drafted by godly Protestant MPs such as Sir Edward Hext and Sir Robert Wroth, were distinctively Calvinist. This more discriminating 'Protestant' concept of charity was, then, perfectly suited to a world in which the labouring poor were being discovered and disciplined.

There was, finally, a broader legislative context for the Elizabethan poor laws which were only the central planks in a wider platform of social policy designed to regulate not only the condition but also the conduct of the poor. Elizabethan parliaments began a series of statutory innovations which were to be continued by their early Stuart successors. By the early years of the seventeenth century, it was a criminal offence not only to be a vagrant but also to be out of service; to give birth to an illegitimate child; to be drunk; to spend more than one hour in the alehouse; to swear profane oaths; or to commit those various misdemeanours – gleaning, hedge-breaking, pilfering among them – which were thought by MPs in 1601 to be generally characteristic of 'lewd and idle persons'. Little wonder that William Shakespeare could by 1608 envisage plebeians grumbling that the patricians were passing 'more piercing statutes daily to chain up and restrain the poor' (*Coriolanus,* Act I, Scene 1, ll. 82–4). Regulation and relief went hand in hand, as they do in all social-welfare policies, and it was symptomatic of the anxiety, the arrogance and the sheer ambition of the Elizabethan state that its social policy should set such a distinctive moral agenda in which industry, sobriety, civility and respect for private property should loom so large. In this sense, the legislation passed in Elizabethan parliaments put the poor firmly in their place.

So much for the *nature* of the statutes, what of their *timing?* While the Acts of 1563 and 1572 probably owed much to political context (the former representing the Elizabethan regime's first opportunity to offer a distinctively Protestant response to the problem of poor relief since the crisis of the 'commotion time' of 1549, the latter influenced by a moral panic about vagrancy in the aftermath of the Northern Rising of 1569), the codification of 1598 was probably provoked by economic distress and the perceived need to manage the notorious 'crisis of the 1590s'. The harvest had always been the heartbeat of the sixteenth-century economy, and with one in every four harvests likely to be seriously deficient, periods of food shortage and rapidly rising prices (known to contemporaries as dearths) were far from unknown. But dearth threatened to become famine in those periods when harvests failed consecutively as they did in 1586–7 and 1587–8 and in the four years after 1594. When the long-run deterioration in real wages was punctuated by intersecting crises of war, dearth and sedition in the 1590s, the Privy Council exercised its itchy trigger-finger, firing circulars all over the country requiring magistrates to enforce social policy to the letter, to execute criminal justice with all the logic of exemplary punishment and to persuade the gentry to remain on their estates in order that they might preside over rural society as paragons of vigilance and hospitality. The winter of 1596–7 was particularly difficult, with the government panicked by rumours of conspiracy among the dispossessed ageing but angry young men of Oxfordshire, a county in which the rural poor had been hedged out of the land market by depopulating enclosure and in which large flocks of sheep symbolised the greed of a landed class more interested in profit than paternalism. Although the projected Oxfordshire 'rising of the people' came to nothing, the government first punished its ringleaders with the full judicial penalties for treason in levying war against the Crown by attacking enclosures and subsequently restored the laws against conversion of tillage to pasture, the repeal of which in 1593 had given the landlords of the south Midlands licence to create extensive sheep-runs on estates which had once been golden with corn.

But distress during that winter was even more extensive than the hot talk, overheard in alehouses and market squares, of cutting the throats of the Midland gentry suggests. The threat of widespread starvation spread beyond the traditionally vulnerable corn-deficient regions of the far north and north-west (where there were crises of subsistence in which the poor of County Durham, of Cumberland and of Westmorland seem to have starved quietly to death in the late 1580s and mid-1590s) into the Midlands. The Elizabethan bishops responded by co-ordinating a campaign of fasting and almsgiving in which they enjoined the clergy to preach up the virtues of hospitality and to encourage even modest householders to sacrifice their own dietary needs for the sake of the poor. Evidence from Buckinghamshire suggests that the campaign was successful, at least in the short term. Meals were forgone on Wednesday and Friday evenings, and the food saved through this frugality was given to the known needy as they begged round the kitchen doors of their better-off neighbours at supper time. This was the last systematic and extensive campaign of indirect relief in kind attempted in English history, and although contemporary commentators were confident that it prevented large numbers of poor people from falling into the pit of destruction, the reliance on exhortation rather than compulsion rendered it vulnerable to compassion fatigue as a further harvest failure in 1597 stretched the resources of householders still further. By the time parliament reconvened in 1597, MPs had decided that the nettle of compulsion had to be grasped and that general, informal hospitality to feed the poor should be superseded by bureaucratised assessment and taxation to subsidise their incomes.

THE EFFECTIVENESS OF POLICY ENFORCEMENT

The effectiveness with which the policies of relief and regulation stipulated by the Elizabethan poor laws were enforced varied considerably, and it is arguable that each of the provisions enjoyed a distinctive fate as central government and provincial magistracies sought to roll them out across town and countryside. Even so, it is striking that in virtually every respect, the provisions of the Elizabethan poor laws, even those of 1563, were anticipated in local experiments aimed at caring for and controlling the poor, many of them originating in mid-sixteenth-century towns. Poor rates, for example, were being collected and distributed in a number of 'Godly cities' and 'great and good towns' from as early as the late 1540s: in Norwich and York by 1550; in Exeter, Colchester, Ipswich, King's Lynn and Worcester by 1560; in Chester and Salisbury by 1570; in Gloucester, Hull, Leicester and Oxford by 1580; in Lincoln by 1600; and in Bristol and Reading by 1610. Implementation in rural communities seems to have been much patchier. The task of mapping the spread of parish relief across the countryside of Elizabethan England is rendered particularly difficult because the fragmentary calculations carried out by collectors for the poor were usually scrawled haphazardly in the margins of lengthy lists of churchwardens' expenditure. It is further complicated by the ambiguous language deployed by churchwardens, collectors and overseers alike to describe the mechanics of fund-raising. Their preferred idiom was 'collection', the meaning of which migrated over the course of the early modern period. 'Collection' originally implied the giving of alms inspired by clerical exhortation and only gradually came to mean the paying of parish rates under the compulsion of law. By the second half of the seventeenth century, moreover, the term was commonly used to describe not only the collection of money for a charitable purpose but also the money so collected. 'To take collection' or 'to be in collection' was, by then, to be in receipt of parish relief, and it is arguable that the use of the idiom in this sense in parish accounts is as reliable an indicator as any of the spread of formal rating and distribution for the poor. In the late sixteenth century, however, the practices implied by 'collection' might be altogether less uniform.

It is, nonetheless, true that the few extant sixteenth-century accounts – surviving variously in books kept by churchwardens, vicars and rectors, as well as overseers and vestrymen – suggest that collection of some kind was being practised in Clare, Suffolk, from as early as 1552; in the three Essex parishes of Ingatestone, Stock and Buttsbury from 1555; in Hadleigh, Suffolk, from 1558; in Heydon, Essex, and Northill, Bedfordshire, from 1563; in Great Bentley, Essex, from 1572; in Wivenhoe, Essex, from 1576; in Great Easton, Essex, from 1577; in Boreham, Essex, from 1585; in Lacock, Wiltshire, from 1589; in Eaton Socon, Bedfordshire, from 1591; in Elmstead, Essex, and Shorne, Kent, from 1598; and in Cowden, Kent, from 1599. The parish officers who drew up these accounts, however, often made only the haziest of distinctions between payments disbursed by churchwardens on the basis of collections at communion and other times and those made by collectors for the poor out of funds raised by assessments. Indeed, churchwardens had since the mid-fifteenth century been required to keep a parish 'poor box', usually kept in the church, into which donations might be made and from which alms were distributed at their discretion, a policy which (briefly) received statutory backing in 1536. These arrangements prevailed in many parishes throughout the sixteenth century, even though the legislation of 1572 had first introduced the principle of compulsory poor rates assessed and distributed by 'collectors' in each parish. The Elizabethan accounts both disclose a wide variety of fund-raising mechanisms and remind welfare historians of the importance of extreme sensitivity to the terminology overseers employed to describe their revenue. To take only the Essex parishes, for instance, income was derived from 'semi-voluntary, semi-compulsory' contributions in Heydon; from weekly collections that corresponded directly with disbursements in Boreham; from weekly and quarterly assessments in Wivenhoe and Great Easton respectively; and from annual rates in Elmstead. Perhaps the best evidence for the precocious adoption of the principle of rate-based assessment and distribution in rural England comes from the parish accounts surviving in the papers of the Surrey magistrate Sir George More of Loseley, which include lists of contributors to and beneficiaries of poor relief for twenty-three small parishes in the deanery of Stoke in the Archdeaconry of Surrey for the years 1573 and 1574. Under the influence of magistrates such as More, and others including Nathaniel Bacon of Stiffkey, Norfolk, and Francis Barrington of Hatfield Broad Oak, Essex, the early history of parish relief could be a success story inscribed in audited accounts which have survived for posterity. Elsewhere, historians of the enforcement of poor-law policy tend to argue from silence, for only one in fourteen parishes has an extant overseers' account book surviving from the seventeenth, let alone the sixteenth, century. It nonetheless seems probable that regular rate-based relief spread slowly beyond the smaller parishes of the south and east in the Elizabethan period and only reached the Midlands and the north by the 1630s.

Historians are far less optimistic about the effectiveness of the other key provisions of the legislation. The apprehension, punishment and expulsion of vagrants were rendered highly problematic not only by the ambiguous definition of the parish of settlement to which the vagrant should be returned but also by the vague wording with respect to identifying vagrants themselves. After all, the 'wanderers' targeted by the statutes might include incorrigible rogues but they might also be migrant labourers genuinely seeking work at a time when labour mobility was at a premium. Indeed, it is not difficult to imagine that some migrants brought with them skills, especially in particular specialised crafts or trades, which might meet local needs and therefore result not in their expulsion but their accommodation. Overall, the rogue literature of the day notwithstanding, it proved extraordinarily difficult for parish officers and householders alike to distinguish between the wilful idlers identified in the statutes and the migrant labourers who were forced to beg and steal to survive as they tramped from town to town in search of work. In most cases, parish constables decided against punishing them for their mobility and only apprehended them if they were suspected of serious property crime which might require a magistrate to help the victim frame a bill of indictment for felony. While most vagrants, therefore, were simply given a crust or a coin with which to make their way beyond the parish boundary, a small minority, especially those who were convicted of crimes of profit (especially horse theft) rather than the crimes of desperation (especially the pilfering of grain or foodstuffs) upon which criminal trial juries might look more sympathetically, ended their desperate lives on the gallows. Even those who were formally treated as the statutes required, being conducted from constable to constable under passports sealed with the authority of magistrates and stipulating the route and the number of days they were allowed to take, quite possibly carried forged papers. There was a lively trade in counterfeit documents and no shortage of forgers with a keen eye, a steady hand and sufficient knowledge of both geography and magistrates' names (to say nothing of sheer brass neck) to produce plausible paperwork.

Even less successful was the creation of work for the labouring poor. Much the most effective means was the targeted provision of tools for individual paupers, especially the purchase by overseers of spinning wheels and distaffs for widows who might support their young families through domestic participation in the early stages of production in the textile industry in town and countryside alike. Where more general schemes were attempted, however, they usually resulted in financial failure caused not only by inefficient management and the risk of the embezzlement of finished goods and raw materials but also by the very poor quality of the cloth produced. In most cases, parish officers quickly recognised that the interests of ratepayers were far better served by providing even the labouring poor with pensions rather than with raw materials. A more concerted effort was, however, made with respect to the apprenticeship of the children of the labouring poor, with overseers deciding that the investment of a small cash premium to persuade a householder (especially a householder beyond the parish boundary) to take on the training and maintenance of a parish boy or girl might in the long run represent a considerable saving for the ratepayers. Most of those apprenticed in this way, it should be emphasised, were not orphans, and many were forced very young into leaving their homes against the wishes of their parents, who might be threatened with the withdrawal of their parish pensions if they refused to let their children go or enticed them back once they had left. It is also clear that the good intentions of the statutes notwithstanding, there was little in the way of human capital formation attempted here: most boys spent their years of parish apprenticeship picking stones, weeding crops and scaring birds, while their sisters endured regimes of domestic drudgery which probably fitted them more appropriately for a lifetime (during both marriage and widowhood) of more of the same. On the whole, then, the labouring poor were treated similarly to the deserving, with the added caveat that they were vulnerable to having their children apprenticed when parish officers judged that they could not rear them effectively. As such, Elizabethan society bequeathed a significant pool of badly managed labour to its early seventeenth-century successor.

THE IMPACT OF POOR RELIEF ON SOCIAL AND ECONOMIC RELATIONS

What difference did any of this make to the experience of poverty in Elizabethan England? In the first place, there is considerable evidence of economic amelioration, especially of the condition of the elderly who were the most visible victims of life-cycle poverty. Overseers' accounts of their disbursements are replete with payments of shillings and sixpences to widows, and these regular payments were very frequently supplemented with casual payments in kind at times of need: parish officers paid for food, for clothing, for shoes, for rent, for fuel, even for medical care and finally for funerals whenever they were necessary. This extraordinary sensitivity to individual need presupposed a network of surveillance and vigilance in which the parish officers would make regular visits to the households of the poor to see what was wanting. The system could be generous enough to prolong the lives of those who might otherwise have succumbed to hunger and to related illness. Indeed, it has been argued that the subsistence crisis that afflicted the Lake Counties in the 1590s proved so devastating precisely because institutional poor relief had yet to be enforced across the sprawling upland parishes of this dark corner of the land. It is probably not coincidental, therefore, that English society slipped from the shadow of famine in the mid-seventeenth century at around about the same time that rate-based parish relief was finally enforced across the whole of the country.

Even so, it would be a mistake to assume that the parish pension, typically sixpence a week in the early years of the system, constituted in and of itself a living for an elderly pauper, let alone for a young family overburdened with children. Collection was only ever intended as a supplement to the income that the poor might cobble together from paid work, from casual charity, from exploiting the natural resources of field, forest and fen in gleaning corn, pasturing animals and collecting fuel. To this extent, parish poor relief was only one component in an economy of makeshifts which also included the support of kin, the kindness of neighbours and the charity and hospitality of the rich. The low level of parish pensions explains why ancient habits of mutual aid and philanthropy proved so resilient well after the Elizabethan statutes were introduced: the casual doles, endowed bread charities and subsidised corn that poured forth from the purses of middling and gentry houses both during the lifetimes and after the deaths of benefactors were not simply throwbacks to an older tradition of almsgiving but a necessary supplement to a relief system which was at best only ever a safety net for a very small minority of those in need. For at the margins of the relief system were the 'casual' poor, forever teetering on the edge of indigence into which they might fall if common rights were extinguished, if work proved irregular, if prices rose beyond a certain threshold or if the obligations of gentry hospitality were abrogated. These people made shift to survive through a range of strategies and practices which were far more characteristic of the experience of poverty than the receipt of the parish pension.

For those lucky enough to be on relief, moreover, there was a social and moral price to be paid for their dependency. The very act of accepting a parish pension was a potent reminder of social distance and a powerful reinforcement of habits of deference and subordination. Whereas the poor of early sixteenth-century England had been encouraged to adopt postures of humility as they begged casual alms from their neighbours on street corners and in church porches, and the reciprocities of the gift exchange had accordingly been ubiquitous, late-sixteenth-century recipients of poor relief no longer had regular contact with their better-off neighbours, receiving their weekly pension at the hands of the parish overseers in the sequestered site of their own homes. Recipients of charity are, of course, always beholden to their benefactors in some degree, but the regular bureaucratised nature of parish relief institutionalised this sense of dependency. The poor of the parish were expected to be grateful for the gift of parish relief, and were not to expect it as a right. Those who proved clamorous might easily have their pensions abated or withheld if their conduct fell short of the standards felt appropriate by parish overseers. Indeed, the entire system of poor relief was shot through with discretion, the overseer enjoying extraordinary powers to exercise his own judgement in verifying claims of indigence and setting the criteria of deservingness. To this extent, the officers of the civil parish were empowered not only to improve the condition but also to regulate the conduct of the poor. As the system became institutionalised across the county, overseers employed the logic of exemplary punishment to withdraw the pensions of those idlers, drunkards, pilferers fornicators, bastard-bearers and Sabbath-breakers who, their manifest poverty notwithstanding, failed to conform to the canons of social respectability. To be sure, overseers could not let the poor starve, and could be prosecuted if they failed to enforce the terms of the statutes, but they might exercise very considerable influence over the ways in which the poor chose to live their lives.

CONCLUSION: THE PARADOX OF BUREAUCRATIC RELIEF

The Elizabethan poor laws constituted a tremendous political achievement and were revolutionary by European standards. No other European state had the political ambition, let alone the infrastructural reach, to co-ordinate a national system of parish-based taxation to fund transfer payments to its poorer subjects. One index of this achievement is the sheer longevity of the system Elizabethan MPs created, for the 'old poor law' (as it became known) remained essentially unamended until the principle of parish-funded outdoor relief was abrogated in 1834.

The system created in the 1560s, 1570s and 1590s spread slowly across the country, but where it was precociously enforced it had proved as early as the turn of the century that it could be extraordinarily benevolent and sympathetic to those in genuine need. The targeted payments of cash sums recorded in overseers' accounts, supplemented as they were by occasional gratuities of food, fuel and clothing, are entirely characteristic of a system which could be remarkably sensitive to local need, fine-tuning the allocation of resources to ensure that relief was provided where want was most obvious. But the system could also be grudging, never contributing enough to the household budgets of the poor to enable them to subsist entirely 'on the parish', and it could be mean, dictating appropriate postures and conduct among those it was designed to help and excluding altogether those whose behaviour was disdained by the overseers. The system was in this respect Janus-faced, smiling beneficently on the deserving and frowning severely on the undeserving. But there was no paradox in a relief which could simultaneously be so generous and so exclusive. Welfare systems invariably presuppose limits on eligibility and entitlement precisely because taxpayers' resources are not infinite and benefits have to be restricted accordingly. The Elizabethan poor laws, which provided the framework for a very early historical example of just such a system, were no exception.

In one key element, however, the Elizabethan relief system really was paradoxical. It might be thought at first sight that the institutionalisation of parish relief would extinguish older traditions of charity and mutual aid through which countless generations of poor people had long made shift to survive. But precisely because the parish pension was only ever designed as an income supplement, those older traditions proved remarkably enduring. Parish relief accordingly became entwined with, and had to be accommodated to, existing practices of charity and support.

It was, furthermore, a privilege only ever enjoyed by a tiny minority, for the poor on relief were a relatively small core of the indigent surrounded by a periphery of penumbral poor, who were still making shift even after the poor laws were being enforced.

To this extent, the experience of poverty among the overwhelming majority of the indigent in Elizabethan England is obscured, rather than revealed, by the lists of disbursements drawn up by overseers and audited by magistrates: irregular half-penny dribblings cumulatively building into weekly pensions which were, in turn, supplemented with increasing frequency by gratuities 'in want', by subsidies for fuel, and by payments for nursing and medical treatment, only to be terminated in terse reference to shrouds wound, coffins stuffed with wool and bells tolled. Only very occasionally, most often where a pauper made an appeal to a justice of the peace, do the lives that lie behind these calculations bleed through the overseer's scrawl. When given the opportunity, the stories prospective pensioners chose to tell about the strategies through which they had kept body and soul together were narratives of struggle and courage, and sometimes of defiance and resentment. They testified to the very wide range of resources on which the poor might draw in making shift: goods borrowed, rent forborne, faggots gathered, food cadged. Without the parish relief system that generated these archives, evidence of survival strategies of this kind simply would not survive. In explaining how they had struggled to remain independent for so long, these petitioners surely spoke, however subconsciously, not only for the much larger constituency of those who laboured for a living until age and incapacity drove them into dependency but also for countless generations of poor people who had lived and died before rates were ever assessed or pensions distributed. In administering parish relief, therefore, Elizabethan overseers and magistrates recorded for posterity the ancient traditions of mutual aid which that very system was designed first to supplement and ultimately to replace.

FURTHER READING

Beier, A. L., *Masterless Men: The Vagrancy Problem in England, 1560–1640* (London, 1985).

Ben-Amos, I. K., *The Culture of Giving: Informal Support and Gift-Exchange in Early Modern England* (Cambridge, 2008).

Botelho, Lynn, *Old Age and the English Poor Law, 1500–1700* (Woodbridge, 2004).

Carroll, William C., *Fat King, Lean Beggar: Representations of Poverty in the Age of Shakespeare* (Ithaca, NY, 1996).

Collinson, Patrick, 'Puritanism and the Poor', in Rosemary Horrox and Sarah Rees Jones (eds.), *Pragmatic Utopias: Ideals and Communities, 1200–1630* (Cambridge, 2001), pp. 242–58.

Dionne, Craig, and Mentz, Steve (eds.), *Rogues and Early Modern English Culture* (Ann Arbor, Mich., 2004).

Griffiths, Paul, *Lost Londons: Change, Crime and Control in the Capital City, 1550–1660* (Cambridge, 2008).

Heal, Felicity, *Hospitality in Early Modern England* (Oxford, 1990).

Hindle, Steve, 'Dearth, Fasting and Alms: The Campaign for General Hospitality in Late Elizabethan England', *Past and Present*, 172 (2001): 44–86.

—— *On the Parish? The Micro-Politics of Poor Relief in Rural England, c. 1550–1750* (Oxford, 2004).

—— 'Technologies of Identification under the Old Poor Law', *The Local Historian*, 36 (4) (2006): 220–36.

Kent, Joan R., 'Population Mobility and Alms: Poor Migrants in the Midlands during the Early Seventeenth Century', *Local Population Studies*, 27 (1981): 35–51.

Lawson, P. G., 'Property Crime and Hard Times in England, 1559–1624', *Law and History Review*, 4 (1986): 95–127.

McIntosh, Marjorie K., 'Local Responses to the Poor in Late Medieval and Tudor England', *Continuity and Change*, 3 (1988): 209–45.

Newman-Brown, W., 'The Receipt of Poor Relief and Family Situation: Aldenham, Hertfordshire, 1630–90', in R. M. Smith (ed.), *Land, Kinship and Life-Cycle* (Cambridge, 1984), pp. 405–22.

Pelling, Margaret, *The Common Lot: Sickness, Medical Occupations and the Urban Poor in Early Modern England* (London, 1998).

Rushton, Peter, 'The Poor Law, the Parish and the Community in North-East England, 1600–1800', *Northern History*, 25 (1989): 135–52.

Slack, Paul, *Poverty and Policy in Tudor and Stuart England* (London, 1988).

—— *From Reformation to Improvement: Public Welfare in Early Modern England* (Oxford, 1998).

—— 'Great and Good Towns, 1540–1700', in Peter Clark (ed.), *The Cambridge Urban History of Britain* (Cambridge, 2000), vol. II, pp. 347–76.

Wales, Tim, 'Poverty, Poor Relief and the Life-Cycle: Some Evidence from Seventeenth-Century Norfolk', in R. M. Smith (ed.), *Land, Kinship and Life-Cycle* (Cambridge, 1984), pp. 351–404.

Walter, John, 'A "Rising of the People"? The Oxfordshire Rising of 1596', *Past and Present*, 107 (1985): 90–143; reprinted in John Walter (ed.), *Crowds and Popular Politics in Early Modern England* (Manchester, 2006), pp. 73–123.

Walter, John, and Schofield, Roger (eds.), *Famine, Disease and the Social Order in Early Modern Society* (Cambridge, 1989).

Woodbridge, Linda, *Vagrancy, Homelessness and English Renaissance Literature* (Urbana, Ill., 2001).

Wrightson, Keith, and Levine, David, *Poverty and Piety in an English Village: Terling, 1525–1700*, 2nd edn (Oxford, 1995).

CHAPTER NINETEEN

TUDOR TROUBLES

Problems of youth in Elizabethan England

Paul Griffiths

'Was there ever seen less obedience in youth of all sorts', Philip Stubbes ranted and raved in 1583, none do as they are told, and they could not care less about 'superiors, parents, masters, and governors'.[1] Little was right in his topsy-turvy world, and Stubbes let people know this in words that soared to new peaks of hyperbole and hysteria. But he was on more solid ground this time. Not only was his one voice in a chorus that saw a misspent youth as a root of evil, but in his fairly short lifetime (*c.* 1555–*c.* 1610) new strictures and structures emerged to control this 'most dangerous age of all'.[2] In a nutshell, problems of youth were re-imagined in Elizabethan England, all the more poignant in a nation still young in its Protestant bearing. The Reformation was on the rollercoaster ride of troubled adolescence in 1560, the reign had teething troubles, the Queen was not a fully adult woman with marriage behind her, and empire was rocking in its cradle. This 'beleaguered isle' was first and foremost young with the raw imperfections pinned on youth: stormy, impulsive, in two minds and not yet steady on its feet.[3] Like youth, the nation was unsettled. The true Protestant anti-Catholic patriot still had growing up to do. And wistful Catholics did not rule out a return to the aged wrong-headed religion. England's new-found youth was at risk from all sides in an anxious age where many died short of adulthood. No one could remember a time when metaphors and meanings of youth were so contemporary and sensitive. Old folks are 'out of date', John Stockwood said in 1578.[4] There was more reason correspondingly to make the young toe the line, to keep the socialisation clock ticking over with no hitches, one generation replacing another without a glitch, this the first generation not to come of age in a Catholic land. The turning of generations was more acute if royal succession was a crunch issue. William Gouge later called 'continual and perpetual succession' of 'callings' the 'necessity of all necessities'.[5] So youth could not be imagined in terms of doom and gloom alone. Something brighter gave hope that a young Protestant nation and its first youth would reach level-headed maturity. In an apparent contradiction that was in fact a calculated juxtaposition, youth was called a hopeful age when good might grow from promising seed. Change was in the air after 1558, but traditional regulatory principles and practices could not cope with the realities and perceptions of the youth problem.

Youth was volatile like the wind or like kicking colts that, if left without reins, would run and run until finally exhausted. One uneasy moralist called youth a lusty 'leaping time', and in so doing drew attention to the often-troubled nature of socialisation in a society in which youth lasted for a long time. It began around the age of leaving home for the first time and the start of puberty (around age fourteen) and lasted until the moment when young people became fully fledged adults through marriage or setting up a household of their own. Another moralist thought of youth as a shipwrecked age and 'a seething pot of scum'. Heat, noise, excess, temperatures racing, senses boiled in young 'hot-spurs'. 'Their pots are boiling,' William Higford said simply. The elderly shepherd in *The Winter's Tale* wished that there was nothing between the ages of ten and twenty-three or that people would fall into deep sleep and wake up having magically stepped from childhood into adulthood.[6] Unarticulated puberty is a quandary behind this morality, biology and psychology. Middle-aged William Guild believed that youth plunged with 'headlong force unto vice, lust, and pleasures of the flesh'. Venus guides us through 'our blossoming lustfull age,' Henry Cuffe said, not cheerfully but jadedly.[7] But youth was also the 'chusing time' in which to pick between virtue and vice, or to choose right religion, to go back to the Elizabethan dilemma. It was vital, therefore, to count on 'aptness' in youth, which, however, was double-edged as it could have ended up in hope or despair.[8] But it did offer something. 'The ragged colt [his apprentice] might still prove a good horse,' Touchstone muses in *Eastward Ho* (1605) upon hearing that he was shortly to hang. He now felt sorry for his botched life.[9] But there was not a minute to lose, the clock was ticking, and before long young people would be bogged down in the world. A proverb urged Elizabethans to strike while the iron was hot. 'Bee new men now', one author almost pleaded, 'this day, this night, this hour in which thou art admonished.'[10]

'There is the place, in yougthe is the time,' Queen Elizabeth's teacher, Roger Ascham, told anyone wanting society to change for the better, mindful that the young were the lifeblood of religious reform.[11] And so attitudes towards youth were an apparent mishmash of contrary perceptions, coexisting in strategic counterpoint: a curse in one sentence and a last hope in the next. The space in between was made legible and positive by beliefs that youth was the best time to teach and train, when people were 'malleable', 'tractable' and 'flexible'. 'Best to bend while 'tis a twig' was a proverb that stuck in the mind. It is easy to 'bend' a 'young and tender plant' as well as youth, a moralist said with the future in mind, as 'now they will bend, now they be pliable, now they will work.'[12] Youth was as 'clammie' wax that might 'receive any impression', William Vaughan wrote in 1600, but once 'hardened it receiveth none'. Seize the day, he told masters and parents, 'imprint discipline' before it is too late.[13] His haste reflected the tempo of the times, but it was also rooted in thinking about the successes and failures of pedagogy. Youth, William Guild said, was 'the first age capable' of understanding religion. Teaching children is like teaching parrots, William Gouge said drily, they cannot 'conceive' what we say. Youth, on the other hand, was called the 'age of discretion', a time when people could fathom knowledge, size up situations and choose responsibly. The consensus was that people became blessed by this intelligence around the age of fourteen but that it soon faded if someone chose wrongly and sank into the wickedness of the world. Things were in the balance in the critical teens, unlike later life when, one moralist quipped, people 'never change colour'.[14] It was the road taken in early youth that mattered for the time to come, and there was no turning back once someone got sucked into the delights of the world.

One thing for certain is that it was getting harder to become a fully fledged adult with requisite worth. A man did not amount to much without a wife, house to head or decent job. 'An unmarried man is but halfe a man', Matthew Griffith said in all seriousness.[15] But there were more incomplete adulthoods in Elizabethan England, people who were stranded in limbo, not yet fixed firmly in the roles assigned to them by patriarchal codes, women as well as men. It is possible that more lives were turned upside down by the population boom than by religious change. The grim reality for anyone trying to scrape by was the debris left behind by sharp demographic and economic pressures: soaring prices, job losses, land shortages, dwindling resources and grinding poverty. These debilitating hardships, along with increasingly commercial, competitive and insecure economic environments that slammed into subsistence sectors with all the force of an oncoming train, had negative impacts on the life-course progress of young people from the middle and lower classes. Not everyone was cut to the bone, not even in England's pauper basement. But there were cracks in enough household economies to hinder the shift from youth to newly anointed adult for uncomfortably high numbers of people. All this in an institution – the household – that was already unsteady as birth, death and the comings and goings of apprentices/servants added or subtracted members at regular intervals. And if the family was strained in strapped times, so too were the institutions of apprenticeship and service, weighted with the extra millstone created by the Statute of Artificers of 1563, though it was only patchily put into effect. The situation of apprentices/servants has been called 'unsettled'.

A handbook for overseers of the poor warned that young people had 'wavering and wandering minds' and found it hard to stay somewhere for long.[16] People of all ages were moving in growing numbers, hunting high and low for jobs, mulling over moving to large towns where there was more to do, and voluntarily or involuntarily shifting from position to position with bouts of empty living with little to do. Some struck it lucky and settled in jobs and apprenticeships. Others struggled to stay above water. Work was not always hard to come by, but the downside was that it was insecure and intermittent. There were high turnover rates of servants and fluid lodging cultures. Young people slipped in and out of cities, staying for a while, heading home, coming back, like twelve-year-old William Miller from Seething, Norfolk, who was rounded up 'roginge and begginge' in Norwich in 1596, having been 'divers tymes heretofore' kicked out of the city.[17] There were real 'problems' of youth in Elizabethan England that could rock societies big and small, but adding to the sense of alarm were perceptions of this 'deadly age' and its dangerous independence and inevitable immorality. Real or imagined, the problems of youth became sharper in each new decade of the Elizabethan age.

Countless 'unproductive youngsters' criss-crossed the country or stayed at home, only to get in trouble for not having toeholds in service. More people grew up outside socialisation in service, often through circumstance not choice. With fewer jobs to go round, a labour glut and more household heads out of work, policies and prosecutions homed in on single women who risked falling into treble trouble for living alone, working at home or traipsing up and down selling in broad daylight.

It was harder now to square repressive patriarchal norms with the realities of scores of young urban women making livings from casual work or picking up skills informally at home from parents, siblings and relations. There was enough of this twilight work outside the regulatory reach of civic rulers for one historian to argue that an 'urban crisis of gender' taxed towns before 1600.[18] Civic authorities tried to limit women to 'honest' service and linked independent lifestyles with inevitable immorality. Steps to stop this non-compliance began around 1580. Liverpool women whose work caused 'great inconvenience' were singled out in 1577. On the other side of the country, in Norwich, magistrates called for stiffer implementation of the Statute of Artificers in the same year to make sure that 'no maydes [being able to serve] hyre[d] chambers' on their own. In Southampton, crackdowns began around the same time to curb 'churmaids', who, as a group, were imagined to live and work outside rules. Manchester's Court Leet took action in 1584 to rein in single women living 'at their own hands' whose baking and brewing took away work from hard-up breadwinners and who were caught 'abusinge themselves with younge men havinge not anny man to controle them'. Prosecutions of single women living 'at their own hand' or 'out of service' began in earnest towards 1600 and doubled, trebled and even quadrupled in later decades.[19]

With each year that passed by without marriage, single women had more autonomy but lingered in shaky limbo. As economic conditions slumped, young men too slid into halfway houses between youth and adulthood. Coming of age was just one measure of fully groomed adulthood. Economic independence and marriage were slipping beyond the reach of many men, who, as they drew near to their mid-twenties, saw a drab third-class future of dependent wage labour stretching ahead of them. Their own workshop was a daydream, and start-up costs in the region of £75 for tanners or shopkeepers, £50 for ironmongers and at least £100 to make a start in textiles were too steep for journeymen just out of apprenticeships and short of money. And land was also harder to get hold of. Numbers of journeymen wage workers – or 'day-labouring men' as Robert Greene christened them in 1592 – kept climbing. They were wedged in this 'intermediate status' for a decade or so in Chester's building trades, not really getting ahead, standing still on the life course. A Rye journeyman tallow chandler was still with his master in 1606 four decades after he got his first wage from him. He might have been at ease earning enough to get by without the added stress of running a shop. Perhaps he had never wanted to marry and never thought of himself as incomplete. Many other journeymen elsewhere were up in arms about their lot in life, however. Opportunities were shrinking, and a stream of petitions from journeymen complained that masters had taken on too many apprentices or foreigners, and they now feared falling below the poverty line and needing to beg, steal or sign up for degrading work to get from one day to the next. They were not master craftsmen or adult members of civic bodies, and not yet fully men but 'day-labouring men' left to float. Oxfordshire labourer Bartholomew Steer had had enough of this nothing status in 1596. There was no prospect of a farm of his own. Land was out of reach for him and for others, itching to climb life's ladder, who joined him to plot a rising to get better chances. Steer ended up on the gallows as he could no longer stand the cruel vicissitudes of the life course. Others did not go this far, but they simmered with frustration all the same. Their niggling limbo was a product of Elizabethan demographics and an economy gone haywire. Just being able to stand on their own two feet meant everything to them as they struggled to get out of Gloriana's deep underbelly.

It was not a paradox that youth posed both problems and solutions at the same time. This was consistent with the prevailing view that binary polarities made clear the nature of right and wrong in preaching, prose and plays. The moral narrative of the play is set in stone early on in *Eastward Ho* (1605) when Touchstone says he has two apprentices, 'one of a boundless prodigality, the other of a most hopeful industrie'. And, as with Hogarth's *Industry and Idleness* (1747), we follow bad apples to the gallows: 'You see the issue of your sloth,' Touchstone lectures his upstart apprentice who is shortly to hang at Tyburn, 'Of sloth cometh pleasure, of pleasure cometh riot, of riot comes whoring, of whoring comes spending, of spending comes want, of want comes theft, of theft comes hanging.' Servants who 'drop out' of service 'are many times eaten up by Tyborne,' Henry Crosse noted in Elizabeth's last year on the throne.[20] England would be better and safer if its youth were under the thumb of older householders – work would get done on time, crime would plummet, churches would be crowded on Sundays with no clowning around, households would be stable and there would be little need to be anxious about the future. Wishful thinking perhaps but, at the start and end of the Elizabethan world, landmark legislation set new horizons for socialisation, extending compulsory apprenticeship/service to all but the well-to-do.

Under the Statute of Artificers (1563), any unmarried woman older than eleven and younger than forty was to go into service; boys were to be groomed for adulthood in apprenticeships that could not end before age twenty-four. The Poor Law (1598), with its focus on work, shirkers and shady lifestyles, also made it clear that youth was to be spent in service or apprenticeship. Most damning of all was to lack an 'ordinary and daily trade of life' to get by. In effect, the life cycle was put in a new frame. Other legislation, this time from 1576, gave green lights to authorities to bind children until twenty-four for sons of the poor and eighteen for their sisters (raised later to twenty-one when parishes were also told to bind children from hard-up families with large litters). There had been local steps to stretch apprenticeship to age twenty-four before 1563, but in that year the course of growing up changed to help a shaky nation stand on its own feet. In between the legislative pillars of 1563 and 1598, this drive to tame and train youth became national in scope and scale and was hammered home in new forms of literature and instruction: in 'last dying' speeches by felons on gallows, the nationwide movement to catechise youth that was in the hands of a resolute reformed clergy and in what would become a flood of cheap print and conduct books whose aims included putting teenagers on the right road. This was urgent since the household was a make-or-break stumbling block for the new religion and political nation. Reformation, a later preacher said anxiously, 'sticks here' (meaning the household).[21] The links between the family, generational succession and political and religious security were as strong now in the universal concerns of the Elizabethan world as they had ever been.

The Statute of Artificers made it easier for magistrates to keep tabs on wages and labour supply. But in many minds it was linked to curbing the 'heat' of youth. A memorandum on its first decade said that if followed to the letter, it would 'reforme the unadvised rashness and licentiousness of youth', words that echo stock images in moral writing for and about youth. Preaching four decades later, William Guild warned that youth 'is carried with headlong force unto vice, lust, and vaine pleasures of the flesh', and 'hath need of straiter discipline' and 'harder brydling'.[22] Behind the 1563 Statute of Artificers was a moral climate in which clothes, witchcraft, forgery, prophecies, light-fingered servants, poisoners, perjurers, Gypsies, sodomy and socialisation were all put on the table for discussion in the same parliament. Indeed, there was a barrage of complaints when repeal of the Statute of Artificers was proposed in the free-market atmosphere around 1800, which was light years away from the interventionist creed prevalent in 1563. One concern was that quality of work would slump: more than 32,000 craftsmen begged Parliament not to lamely surrender England's 'first place in the world' which hinged on apprenticeship. Another was what would happen to youth if apprenticeship was no longer obligatory: one MP bleakly stated that repeal would be 'ruinous to the morals of youth'; someone else said that there would be nothing to stop young people from turning into 'vagabonds and blackguards'. In the event, repeal sailed through Parliament in 1814, and it is no accident that it is around then that historians argue that juvenile delinquency first became a widespread issue.

Clearly apprenticeship and service went hand in hand with controls on youth, but never more so than at the start of Elizabeth's reign when the population was uncommonly youthful. England was in the midst of a population boom: resources were thin on the ground, jobs dried up, and people took to the road to make ends meet. The country lurched from one year to the next as inflation soared sky high, wages hit rock bottom, harvest failures drained grain supplies, plague laid towns low, and war took a heavy toll in times of real or rumoured riots in which young people were often the leaders. Of all problems, the most pressing were poverty and increasing numbers of poor youth. A raft of regulations tried to stop the rot. The opening of houses of correction gathered steam in Elizabethan England, and young people soon filled their cells. Magistrates wanted more limits on youth through service. And ideas of reforming offenders leaned heavily towards youth, as it was felt that a criminal career could be stopped in its tracks if short, sharp, shocks were dished out to wayward youth. There was much at stake in 1558: a generation, a nation, a Reformation and developing demographics did not bode well for the future.

This shift from youth into adulthood was depicted as socialisation into office or a full-time job and household head (if male). Gerontocracy was solid as a rock in ruling ideologies, as Joan English of Great Mongham in Kent found to her cost after using 'hir tonge inordinatlie towards hir elders and betters'.[23] Youth's subordinate status was displayed in rituals that were both cautions and lessons: public punishments, various parades, designated clothing, or in churches with a custom-built 'boys gallery', 'maids pew', 'servants pew', 'young mens gallery' or 'mens daughters seats'.[24] The fifth commandment to honour parents was stretched to cover all situations where subordination was at stake in a society where rulers were said to be fathers from the king all the way down to the mayor of England's smallest town. The seventh commandment was extended to warn young people about masturbation, binging, sex, flashy clothes, sleepiness, 'a rolling eye', 'lascivious pictures', 'love-books', mixed dancing, 'wanton touches' and 'ridiculous motions'. Obedience, morality and piety were drummed into people by catechisers, preachers, teachers, parents, masters and anyone else who cared enough to give local black sheep warning words. This was patriarchy's grand plan at any rate, though things did not always go smoothly: you do 'nothing but prattle,' John Peacock of Essex told his minister in the middle of catechising; while another Essex youth was caught 'laughing in the tyme of the sermon because the minister did tell the dutie of servants'.[25] Juvenile delinquency in and out of the home, real or imagined, is the reason why conduct books are punctured all through by contradictions and a gap between the ideals and realities of growing up that was big enough for one scholar to call textbook socialisation a 'lost cause' (why else drone on about youthful slip-ups if they did not test patriarchies to their limits?).[26]

Socialisation was not a given; an honourable adulthood with standing in the world had to be earned. The worth of being a hard-working householder was a mark of distinction with ripe qualities, such as reason, even-headedness and quick-wittedness. This was why calling someone 'boy' could bring him down a peg or two. 'I will use you like a boy,' an Essex churchwarden jeered at William Gassock after grabbing a bell from his hands: 'boy on your face,' Gassock snapped back, 'I am as good a man as you.'[27] Paths to adulthood were known to all, even if they were not always realistic. From age twelve until marriage a girl's lot was to learn 'huswifery', one author said in conventional mode. Boys had career opportunities, and their main aim was to train in a 'calling'. Most began apprenticeship or service in the 'critical teens' (age fourteen to sixteen), though others from families too poor to cope began pauper service around six years earlier. Hard-up families got help from parishes to cover apprenticeship premiums which were on the low side on the whole. But they stretched from a few pounds in manual jobs to £200 in high-end mercantile and craft trades. Business contacts or relatives might put families in touch with a likely master. Sons also stepped into fathers' shoes, as in seafaring families along the south coast, for instance. The proportion of apprentices from well-off gentry and yeoman backgrounds was on the rise, doubling to one in five in Bristol (1530–1630), reaching 10 per cent in London, slightly more in Southampton and, unsurprisingly, the well-to-do were over-represented in high-end trades. Seven years was the minimum time-span for apprenticeships, though some terms dragged on for a dozen years or more. Servants served from year to year, but many stayed put for a while: stints of four to six years were not uncommon, and trusty long-stayers served deep into middle age. Apprentices were, for the most part, recruited locally. Twenty-five miles was on the long side for York, Worcester or Leicester, but not London, where people arrived from all over the land (eight in ten apprentices in Elizabethan London had been born elsewhere). Somewhere in the region of 4,000–5,000 apprentices began new terms in London each year in 1600; the figure was closer to 200 in Bristol, while Southampton added a dozen or so apprentices each year.

Apprentices were male in a society that gave next to no recognition to female careers. Not one girl appears among 8,000 or so apprentices beginning terms in fifteen London guilds in 1580–1640. Apprentices of countryside craftsmen were also male for the most part. A handful of women apprentices served in Bristol, Southampton and Salisbury at any one time. Blacksmiths, ironmongers, printers, goldsmiths and watchmakers took girls under their wing, mostly training them to become wives and mothers, taking care of households, buying and selling in markets, helping in shops. The balance between the sexes was greater in pauper and parish apprenticeships. In some places, roughly equal numbers of needy boys and girls were apprenticed, because of the high number of orphans. Most well-off middling householders had a handful of apprentices and servants under their roofs, although over half of Bristol's apprentices served alone (caps were often put on the number a master could take). Wealthy farmers hired four or more servants, more men than women. Poorer farmers often made do with a single maid who would be a Jill-of-all-trades, spinning, perhaps, taking care of livestock, dairying, cooking, doing housework, all things done on larger farms with more labourers. Expectations differed between apprentices and servants and boys and girls. For many, apprenticeship was a once-in-a-lifetime chance to move up social ladders and become a citizen and perhaps a civic bigwig. Rags-to-riches tales such as Dick Whittington's made people dream of what might be. Fourteen-year-old Martin Bowes headed south from a well-off York family. He became London's mayor in middle life and was knighted by the Queen. There was a job after apprenticeship if luck did not run out, and some not long free of apprenticeships got a head start by marrying wealthy widows. Servants also favoured settling into stable work. Some became career servants, shepherds, housekeepers and the like, including Richard Pennington whose 'above fortie yeares' spell was not atypical. Many in service, where wages and room and board were norms, put money away for a rainy day or marriage, though women's pay was lower, half that of men in some places. Apprentices could expect wages towards the end of their term when with skills to sell they were wage labourers in all but name. But many had stolen away by then, as we shall shortly see.[28]

Apprenticeship comes from the Latin *apprendere* (to learn), although it involved more than picking up the tools of a trade. It was also a moral relation signed and sealed in indentures which were the grounds for mutual obligations taken seriously enough to be enforceable by law. A Liverpool lad (William Bothill) joined a tailor's household in 1565, and, in his fairly typical indenture, he pledged that he would serve 'well, truelie, faythfullie and diligentlie as a true apprentice' for twelve years and shun 'cards, dice, bowls, hores, harlots, [sex and] alehowses'. Nor could he slip out of the house without his master's say-so. Trade guilds added rules to keep apprentices on the straight and narrow. Any caught having sex in Norwich could have been asked to 'duble their yeares', for instance. In 1603, Newcastle's Merchant Adventurers told masters not to let boys 'daunce, dice, carde, mum' or wear 'undecent apparrell' or 'haire longe, nor locks at their eares like ruffians'. It was also immoral to spread idle chit-chat about masters or reveal secrets. A London weaver's wife told his boy in 1577 that 'he must have his ears nailed if he betrayed his master's counsel except for felony, murder or treason.'[29] There were ideas of 'true' apprentices and how apprentices 'ought to be used', expectations that masters would care for them in sickness and health, put food on the table, replace tatty clothes and check that soap was available. Punishment and correction were officially authorised so long as they were 'moderate' and blame was beyond any doubt.

But there were risks involved when an apprentice moved in with a master. They might be meeting for the first time, if the new master lived some distance from their home. A teeming city might seem exhilarating with limitless possibilities, but it was also unfamiliar, with the risk of accidents, fire, plague, syphilis, smallpox, crime, overcrowding, third-rate sanitation, workplace trouble or trade slumps. Hurdles for would-be citizens included the demographic lottery of higher urban death rates. Away from home, people might give into unhappiness, loneliness or despair, hearing the footsteps of a harsh master or taunts from older hands. It's hardly surprising that scores of Richard Napier's mentally ill patients were servants or that bedwetting embarrassed many in strange households. And in spite of legal shields, young people were at first outsiders, raising plausible concerns that they might infect households with disease or bad behaviour. They hoped to get fair treatment, but there were inevitable vulnerabilities in their status. They might sleep in a 'maids chamber', 'apprentices chamber' or 'garret'. But many were squeezed together like sardines, and a Cambridgeshire couple did nothing exceptional in making 'men and maidservants [sleep] in one bedd'.[30] It is not hard to see the scope for unwelcome sex or how people living under the same roof could cover up sex (same-sex sex hardly ever shows up in sources). There was little breathing room in typical households. Defending herself from a charge of illegitimacy with her fellow Gavin Clark in 1603, Mary Field told London Bridewell 'that she could not goe into the garrett nor into any other place but [he] would follow her'. Maids in weak positions had to be on their guard. 'Thowe art my servant and I may doe with thee what I please,' Robert Parker reminded Alice Ashemore over the course of sexual abuse that lasted for a year. Whether cleaning the house, washing clothes, making beds or cooking, girls bumped into others in the unavoidable intimacy of confined spaces.[31] The cloak-and-dagger world of abusive households means that an unknowable but sizeable amount of exploitation remains a domestic secret. But the bulk of women brought to court for illegitimacy, infanticide or leaving children for someone else to care for were victims of honey-tongued or forceful masters or co-workers. Pregnant, kicked out of a house, alone with reputation at stake, many girls were in dire need: marry me or kill me, one begged her boyfriend on her knees after finding out she was pregnant. And some boys had to fend off mistresses who would not take no for an answer. John Orrede of London spoke of his trials and tribulations living with his mistress in 1575: she often stood beside his bed whispering 'provocations of incontynent lyfe', and one time, when he was sitting eating by the fire with his fellow, she 'lifted upp her clothes above the naville [showing] hirselfe naked' and 'clapped hirselfe on the bare buttocke saeinge look here are neither scabbes nor seales'.[32]

Other problems brought to court involved violence and neglect for the most part. Some masters were too poor or sick to give guidance and so their charges were turned over to someone else. Other young people were bruised and battered by 'unreasonable', 'extraordinary' or 'immoderate correction' with fists, arms, legs, teeth, staffs, bottles, pots, chains, keys, sticks, chairs, rope, rods or anything else close by. Stock images of exploited apprentices and servants were made familiar in cheap print and cases that sparked talk and prosecution. A pewterer was 'found faulty' for 'burnying [his apprentice's] face with a hot irone' in 1591. Sickly fourteen-year-old Ellen Bolintout from Norwich was beaten with a stick 'tyll she was black and blewe', her 'skynne' was slashed by a 'woolcarde', and to cap it all salt was rubbed into her wounds to her 'great grefe'. Harsh household heads were warned to be 'moderate' and 'gentle' in future. A London clothworker was told 'to use reasonable correction and not to be over furious for every little faulte'. The meaning of 'reasonable' is fuzzy, although another London clothworker was warned to give 'one blow' on the back with his staff 'and noe more', and Titus Oates of Norwich was told that 'eight stripes at any one time' was enough.[33] Servants complained to the courts about unpaid back pay, that they were left to languish in bad health or shabby conditions and that their masters were not doing their jobs. A young London fishmonger was found near death in 1603 with 'the fleshe of his legg rotted off'. While Thomas Gerrard of Norwich was found 'extremely eaten with lice', one of many servants in various times and places found 'runne full of vermen'.[34] Rogue masters let themselves down but also their trade or craft which depended for legitimacy on abiding ideas of brotherhood. Guilds preferred to settle disputes within their fold, so long as offences were not appalling. They also tried to patch up broken relations and keep households together, unless the latest cruelty was the final straw. Senses of blame and shame were public by implication and, if need be, were made more so by punishing heavy-handed masters through the streets of the city. Unlike these bad apples, an apprentice who told his master 'that he would not tarry with him for he kept a whore in his house' did his level best to stick to civic moralities. The fair treatment of apprentices and servants was a civic and social convention, binding and enforceable.

It is easy to write doom-and-gloom histories of domestic interfaces in an England beset by stormy households. Socialisation strings snapped, leaving life courses in the balance. There were many masters like London fishmonger Arthur Mouse who was taken to task in 1600 for 'tak[ing] many apprentizes and bring[ing] them upp very few or none to any purpose'.[35] It is tempting to see young people adrift in households with no one to turn to. But the cases that we now write about exist because someone outside a household stepped in after hearing word of abuse: worried neighbours in cultures that sanctioned snooping on others, anxious family, alert officers or guild members. Most apprentices and servants did not live far away from home, and we should see the two places as cooperating, not remote. There were support networks, even in London, where many migrant maids had family or kin nearby. News travelled fast. Parents, if alive, kept in touch with children they put in service: sending things, visiting, taking them home if they felt under the weather. This grapevine, an early warning system, triggered if matters threatened to get out of hand, intervening if they did. And time and again we find cases where magistrates took the side of apprentices and servants, following legal standards of proof and truth to look into abuse and coming down hard on guilty masters according to a form of moral patriarchy (the Statute of Artificers told servants to go to a justice if they had 'just cause to complaine'). Not all such disputes ended well for the servants, since the interests of guilds and governments were also taken into account. Besides, most did not get anywhere near courts, and many were settled by some form of out-of-court mediation. But the odds were not always stacked against the young, especially apprentices who had indentures and premiums to fall back on.

There is also a temptation to think that master–servant relations always suffered strain. But, like marriage, it might be better to think of give and take on both sides. Many masters got on well with apprentices and servants, although tranquillity and stability are harder to find in court books. Wills or first-person narratives are more promising: bequests and gifts speak of good relations that blossomed into friendships. Years later, former servants might go back to give a master or mistress helping hands if they fell sick. And it was fairly common for young people to get help to set up shop or settle down, generosity that helped life cycles to turn. Just seven apprentices were sacked in Elizabethan Rye, and only one case of abuse was recorded, prompting Graham Mayhew to note that masters and apprentices lived as 'normal' families in an envelope of 'security'. Rye's stories remind us of the potential for rosy relations, but we cannot gauge the nature of domestic relations from an absence of abuse on paper. What we miss are day-to-day tensions which are bound to happen in large households: hearsay, bickering, jealousies, unrequited love, favouritism, taking sides. There were also pecking orders leading inevitably to grudges. 'Everyone did triumph over me,' astrologer-physician Simon Forman remembered when he was 'the youngest apprentice of four' and got saddled with 'all the worst tasks'. Asked to brush his master's cloak one Sunday morning, a touchy London clothworker's apprentice snapped back 'that it was fyt for the maydeservant and the younger apprentice as fir himself to brush it [and] refused to do it'. It is easy to imagine how ill feeling might boil over in the sort of cramped proximity that made one Norwich apprentice push 'a hot iron upon one of his fellows willingly' in 1574.[36]

And sometimes things got so heated that compromise became a distant dream. One apprentice told friends that 'his master was his mortall enemie'. Others were 'mutinous' or 'rebellious', and masters at the end of their tethers admitted that their apprentices 'could [no longer] be ruled'. A weary London fishmonger acknowledged that his apprentice 'groweth worse to worse'. Other masters were punched, kicked, scratched, stabbed and left dazed after being bashed on the head with crockery, various items of furniture, sticks, stones and pricey ornaments. One apprentice swore he would 'run [his master] through with a knife' and 'marrie his mistris'.[37] 'Slanderous', 'unfitting', 'vile', 'lewde' and 'hard words' rained down on household heads, who were called liars, cowards, whoremongers, debtors, smutty or crippled by 'French poxe'. An apprentice with a chip on his shoulder told aldermen that his master was trying to kill him and that there was a freshly dug grave in the garden. Households leaked gossip and secrets like running water. A moralist called servants 'running vessels that can keepe nothing'. It was hard to keep something private in modest-sized porous rooms, with servants drifting in and out all the time. They knew that this gave them an upper hand to pressure masters and mistresses, to blackmail them and to settle old scores. Apprentices and servants are found on record giving evidence against masters and mistresses.[38] The final humiliation for a master was to see his apprentice ripping up indentures, a defiant act with symbolic touches leaving authority in tatters. 'Naughty' Walter Smith 'rent in peeces his indentures of prentishood' in 1560.[39] Running away was a more persistent problem. Some runaways took off 'often', 'comonly' or 'continualie'. John Baldwin of London did 'nothing but runn away', magistrates said. William Comber from the same city made off over 'xx tymes' and wasted 'xxx pounds [of his master's money] at dice'. Elizabeth Carter slipped away nine times in two months. James Bowyer vanished four times in a week. Many ran away only once after something unnerved them – a stringent ticking-off, 'over correccon', a maid was startled to find 'pictures of crucifixes and beades' in a cubby hole, and one apprentice said casually that there was 'no great cause' for his disappearance.[40]

Apprentices and servants also got get their own back by stealing something. Robert Coles stole from his master in 1573 'thinking by that meanes to make [him] banckroupte'.[41] Trust was essential in households, but boxes, cupboards, chests and shelves all contained temptations for people with little money. One moaned 'that it was a hard matter if an apprentice could not in the tyme of his yeares get some money', putting into words simmering frustrations that made some turn thief.[42] Light-fingered apprentices and servants helped themselves to cloth, clothes, clocks, plates, spoons, hats, herbs, fruit, meat, bottles, brass, candles, aprons, ropes, sheets, spices, stirrups, stockings, sugar and shoes, as well as money ranging from a few pennies to over £100 on red-letter days. Others cooked the books or traded goods on the sly. They were egged on by friends, fences and receivers, but more often by their own greed or need. Some apprentices needed a few shillings for sex in bawdy houses, including John Madammer who owned up to 'haunt[ing] harlots', and who, like Elizabeth Hall, who had sex with her boyfriend every time her master took his turn to watch ('everie tenth night', she said, around 150 times in all), query the idea that most young people were 'resolutely unerotic' or 'steadfastly celibate' 400 years ago.[43] Apprentices and servants also stole in order to have what we now call a social life, and in their countless thousands they show that despite the seemingly repressive lives drawn for them in indentures or conduct books, young people had freedom to meet, drink, play, party and, for many, to fall in love and pick the person they wanted to marry, especially in towns and cities.

London apprentices were rapped on the knuckles for hanging around in alehouses, 'daunsing scholes, dycing houses, tennys courtes, bowling allies, brothell houses' and playhouses. And while apprentice cultures were features of life there, youth cultures shaped identities for people all over the land.[44] There were sticklers who prudishly or puritanically held that anything with a whisper of immorality was out of bounds, but, on the whole, adults gave at least tacit tolerance towards young people. After all, they had once been young themselves, and there seemed to be little harm in play, high spirits and getting to know what it was like to fall in and out of love or to have a good time in alehouses. But there were protocols and points where someone went too far that differed by gender. Young men had time to sow their wild oats. Girls, too, should have been able within reason to mix with others in and out of the house. This was tolerable so long as work was not impaired, young people knew their place and they did not bring shame on themselves or a household. The household was a cornerstone of the unsteady Elizabethan nation-state, and magistrates gave short shrift to anyone breaking rules about work, time or play. But there were thorns in the side of domestic patriarchies: pests such as carpenter's apprentice John Moras who stayed out of his master's house 'when it pleased him'; a gang of apprentices who turned order on its head by saying they would play 'in despight of whosoever' told them not to; two 'frequenters of alehowses' who said they would 'kill them that call them into question for their lewd courses'; and a Wapping apprentice who landed in deep water for 'absenting himself from his master's service night by night'.[45] What was normally in question here was not the nature of patriarchy per se but the longing of young people to grow up in peer groups, to minimise adult interference and to create identities of their own.

Elizabethan youth valued independence of attitude, sexual expression, social life and appearance. Some chic apprentices hankered after clothes and stole to buy staples of the stylish man about town such as Spanish leather shoes, satin hose and doublet and silk stockings. By-laws raged about 'monstrousness in apparell' (three in one year in London in 1572). A merchant tailor's lad was caught strutting along a street in 'monstrous great hose' with glitzy 'stuffinge and lyning' and was made to kneel outside his master's house in plain doublet and hose, while the offending lining was ripped to shreds. 'Now-a-dayes' few 'know their place,' Arthur Dent said in 1601, 'all is out of joynt' in 'apparrel'.[46] Some youngsters stuck to their guns, however, no matter who said otherwise. Randolph Christopher, who was 'neither to God, the quene nor his father obediente', ended up in court in 1575 for wasting time and his father's money 'at dice'. Many adults gladly opened the doors of alehouses, bawdy houses or gaming houses when money crossed palms. A cook was punished in 1561 for hosting 'banquets' and selling apple pies and tarts 'to the distrucon of youth'.[47] Young people were leading lights in robust urban night cultures despite curfews and repeated warnings to stay indoors after dark. We see them slipping out of windows and scampering over walls and rooftops. A carpenter's apprentice downed tools to spend all day at plays, and, when he found himself locked out, he climbed walls and opened windows to get back in: 'theare is no body that can rule him,' his master said, at his wits' end. Fishmonger John Nash stayed out all night sixty times last year, his master told the company court.[48] It was hard to keep a lid on young people all the time, and some took advantage when sent on errands. 'Drunkard' Issac Allingworth's master moaned that 'he cannot send him abroad but he pilfer[s] his napkins' and 'runns to the alehouse.' Another apprentice was whipped for sneaking off to play dice when sent to fetch wood. While a Temple Bar woman ran out of patience in 1576 and took her maid to court saying she 'could not send her for a tub of water but she would be amongst' serving men. Walking through Moorgate in 1562, Allesandro Magno was struck by how often he saw young women 'play[ing] with young lads, even though they do not know them,' he added, disapprovingly.[49]

Domestic discipline broke down from time to time, but more troubling was the high drop-out rate of apprentices – 'not one in twenty' completes his term, Thomas Tryon said in 1695. He got his sums wrong, but a century earlier over half of London apprentices go missing from records, and the rate was sky-high elsewhere: three-quarters in Norwich (1500–1700), eight in ten in Bristol (1500–1600) and Salisbury (1610–20). Perhaps one in ten went to early graves. Others left after learning the basics of a trade and choosing to make a living at home rather than stick around in servitude. Some were poached or changed trades by choice, or ran away to war, perhaps roused by jingoistic apprentice literatures. Crime dragged others away. Towns had openings to make money on the side.[50] Whatever the driving force, coming of age was rarely a textbook progression. There was more to life than being a freeman at twenty-four or the drudgery of service. Whether dropping out, going back home or staying in service, many yearned for room and space to grow up in their own way. In *The Four Prentises of London* (*c.* 1594), a grocer's apprentice, Eustace, gripes, 'I cannot go to break-fast in the morning / with my kinde mates and fellow-prentices / but he [his master] cries Eustace'.[51] We must think of socialisation in terms of tensions and finding middle ground or accommodations with alternative expressions of manhood or what it meant to be a working woman. High jinks, heavy drinking, violence and sex offered counter-masculinities that shared common ground with patriarchies stressing male assertiveness. But many sought solace in conformity inside oppressive cultures, though it is impossible to know where the balance lies, except that most people lived hybrid youths blending conformity and autonomy. And we must not forget those who welcomed religious light, such as young William Gouge who, when his class got 'liberty for sports' on 'play days', stayed alone with books, delving deeper into the faith that meant life itself for him. It could be hard going to stay on the right side of holiness with the world dripping with temptations. Young Richard Baxter looking longingly out of his window as people danced on the green and aching to join them but never doing so sums up this dilemma in a single snapshot. So, too, do images of puritan Samuel Ward tossing and turning in his undergraduate bed in Cambridge, fretting about 'longing after damsons', gorging on plums and pears, 'overmuch myrth at bowling', 'goyng to the taverne', and 'my adulterous dreame'.[52]

There was inevitably variety in a society punctured by differences rooted in class, opportunity, gender, age and town and country. And because of this galaxy of difference it is no surprise that socialisation was one of life's most variable experiences. There was bright optimism in the air when the Queen was crowned, but in more darkly realistic and pensive moments people felt that there was trouble ahead. The nation-state was still rocky on its feet. But things worked out quite well in the end. The Queen had a long life although she herself was frozen on the life course. The Protestant nation grew up with her, relieved to make it to middle age, by which time a generation of staunchly evangelical ministers made sure that large swathes of the population felt themselves to be loyal Protestants. It had been useful to think of the nation-state as young, unsteady and needing protecting and nurturing. This appeal to youth and anxiety drew people towards the Crown and faith. But the political nation had come of age by 1600, although it was still somewhat 'out of joynt', not least because problems of youth had gone from bad to worse. The Elizabethan state grew up in one of the most difficult half-centuries in England's long history, reaching its fourth decade in the 1590s, the most testing decade of all in the sixteenth century, when concern about law and order had never been higher. There were more than a few rough legacies handed on by the Elizabethan world, and one of the more insurmountable appeared to be the slowing down of life-course progress.

Whether working for a wage, doing nothing to scratch a living or lacking the wherewithal to tie the knot, many Elizabethans floated in life-course limbo, some so long that they were adults in age alone. This increasing incompleteness was one outcome of the growing insecurities and complexities of the Elizabethan world as it tottered through tough times as population boomed and opportunities dwindled. Most societies, needless to say, are almost always convinced that its current generation of youth is the worst that there has ever been. Philip Stubbes was certain that this was the case in 1583. He looked around him and saw nothing but irreverence and immorality: 'smouching and slabbering', 'filthie groping and uncleane handling'.[53] We can feel his disgust like a shudder through time. His complaint was a timeless lament. But we must never forget that now and again real changes deep in society and culture alter or sharpen contexts, concepts, concerns and controls, not just for current generations but for others not yet born. The Elizabethan world was one such turning point. These problems deepened even more in later decades, but they were no less Elizabethan in origin for all that.

FURTHER READING

Adair, Richard, *Courtship, Illegitimacy, and Marriage in Early Modern England* (Manchester, 1996).

Beier, A. L., *Masterless Men: The Vagrancy Problem in England, 1560–1640* (1985).

Ben-Amos, Ilana Krausman, 'Women Apprentices in the Trades and Crafts of Early Modern Bristol', *Continuity and Change*, 6 (2) (1991): 227–52.

—— 'Failure to Become Freemen: Urban Apprentices in Early Modern England', *Social History*, 16 (2) (1991): 155–72.

—— *Adolescence and Youth in Early Modern England* (New Haven, Conn., 1994).

—— 'Reciprocal Bonding: Parents and Their Offspring in Early Modern England', *Journal of Family History*, 25 (3) (2000): 291–312.

—— *The Culture of Giving: Informal Support and Gift-Exchange in Early Modern England* (Cambridge, 2008).

Bindoff, S. T., 'The Making of the Statute of Artificers', in Joel Hurstfield Bindoff and C. H. Williams (eds.), *Elizabethan Government and Society: Essays Presented to Sir John Neale* (London, 1961), pp. 56–74.

Boulton, Jeremy, 'London 1540–1700', in Peter Clark (ed.), *The Cambridge Urban History of Britain: Volume II, 1540–1840* (Cambridge, 2000), pp. 315–46.

Braddick, Michael J., *State Formation in Early Modern England, c. 1550–1700* (Cambridge, 2000).

Brigden, Susan, 'Youth and the English Reformation', *Past and Present*, 95 (1982): 37–67.

Brodsky, Vivien, 'Widows in Late Elizabethan London: Remarriage, Economic Opportunity, and Family Reorientations', in Lloyd Bonfield, Richard M. Smith, and Keith Wrightson (eds.), *The World We Have Gained: Histories of Population and Social Structure* (Oxford, 1986), pp. 315–46.

Brooks, Christopher, 'Apprenticeship, Social Mobility and the Middling Sort, 1550–1800', in Jonathan Barry and Christopher Brooks (eds.), *The Middling Sort of People: Culture, Society and Politics in England, 1550–1800* (Basingstoke, 1994), pp. 52–83.

Burnett, M. T., 'Masters and Servants in Moral and Religious Treatises, *c.* 1580–*c.* 1642', in Arthur Marwick (ed.), *The Arts, Literature, and Society* (London and New York, 1990), pp. 48–75.

—— *Masters and Servants in English Renaissance Drama and Culture* (Basingstoke, 1997).

Capp, Bernard, *When Gossips Meet: Women, Family, and Neighbourhood in Early Modern England* (Oxford, 2003).

Challis, C. E., 'Apprentices, Goldsmiths, and the North in Sixteenth- and Seventeenth-Century England', *Northern History*, 37 (2000): 61–70.

Clark, Peter, 'Migrants in the City: The Process of Social Adaptation in English Towns, 1500–1800', in Peter Clark and David Souden (eds.), *Migration and Society in Early Modern England* (London, 1987), pp. 267–91.

Collinson, Patrick, *The Birthpangs of Protestant England: Religious and Cultural Change in the Sixteenth and Seventeenth Centuries* (Basingstoke, 1988).

Derry, T. K., 'The Repeal of the Apprenticeship Clauses of the Statute of Apprentices', *Economic History Review*, 3 (1931–2): 67–87.

Elliott, V. B., 'Single Women in the London Marriage Market: Age, Status, and Mobility, 1598–1619', in R. B. Outhwaite (ed.), *Marriage and Society: Studies in the Social History of Marriage* (London, 1981), pp. 81–100.

Elton, G. R., *The Parliament of England, 1559–1581* (Cambridge, 1986).

Estabrook, Carl B., *Urbane and Rustic England: Cultural Ties and Social Spheres in the Provinces, 1660–1780* (Palo Alto, Calif., 1998).

Fumerton, Patricia, *Unsettled: The Culture of Mobility and the Working Poor in Early Modern England* (Chicago, Ill., 2006).

Fury, Cheryl A., 'Training and Education in the Elizabethan Maritime Community, 1585–1603', *The Mariner's Mirror*, 85 (1999): 147–61.

Gowing, Laura, *Common Bodies: Women, Touch, and Power in Seventeenth-Century England* (New Haven, Conn., 2003).

Grassby, Richard, *The Business Community of Seventeenth-Century England* (Cambridge, 1995).

Green, Ian, '"For Children in Yeeres and Children in Understanding": The Emergence of the English Catechism under Elizabeth and the Early Stuarts', *Journal of Ecclesiastical History*, 37 (3) (1986): 397–425.

Griffiths, Paul, *Youth and Authority: Formative Experiences in England, 1560–1640* (Oxford, 1996).

—— 'Masterless Young People in Norwich, 1560–1645', in Paul Griffiths, Adam Fox and Steve Hindle (eds.), *The Experience of Authority in Early Modern England* (Basingstoke, 1996), pp. 146–86.

—— 'Juvenile Delinquency in Time', in Pamela Cox and Heather Shore (eds.), *Becoming Delinquent: British and European Youth, 1650–1950* (Aldershot, 2002), pp. 25–43.

Hindle, Steve, *On the Parish? The Micro-Politics of Poor Relief in Rural England, c. 1550–1750* (Oxford, 2004).

Howard, Sharon, 'Servants in Early Modern Wales: Co-operation, Conflict, and Survival', *Llafur*, 9 (2004): 33–43.

Ingram, Martin, *Church Courts, Sex, and Marriage in England, 1570–1640* (Cambridge, 1987).

—— 'Child Sexual Abuse in Early Modern England', in Michael J. Braddick and John Walter (eds.), *Negotiating Power in Early Modern Society: Order, Hierarchy, and Subordination in Britain and Ireland* (Cambridge, 2001), pp. 63–84.

Macdonald, Michael, *Mystical Bedlam: Madness, Anxiety, and Healing in Seventeenth-Century England* (Cambridge, 1981).

McIntosh, Marjorie Keniston, *Working Women in English Society, 1300–1620* (Cambridge, 2005).

Mayhew, G., 'Life-Cycle Service and the Family Unit in Early Modern Rye', *Continuity and Change*, 6 (3) (1991): 202–26.

Mendelson, Sara and Patricia Crawford, *Women in Early Modern England, 1550–1720* (Oxford, 1998).

O'Hara, Diana, *Courtship and Constraint: Rethinking the Making of Marriage in Tudor England* (Manchester, 2000).

Palliser, D. M., 'The Trade Gilds of Tudor York', in P. Clark and P. Slack (eds.), *Crisis and Order in English Towns, 500–1700: Essays in Urban History* (Toronto, 1972), pp. 86–116.

Patten, John, 'Patterns of Migration and Movement of Labour to Three Pre-Industrial East Anglian Towns', in Peter Clark and David Souden (eds.), *Migration and Society in Early Modern England* (London, 1987), pp. 77–106.

Pelling, Margaret, 'Apprenticeship, Health and Social Cohesion in Early Modern London', *History Workshop Journal*, 37 (1994): 33–56.

Rappaport, Steve, *Worlds Within Worlds: Structures of Life in Sixteenth-Century London* (Cambridge, 1989).

Robertson, James, 'The Adventures of Dick Whittington and the Social Construction of Elizabethan London', in Ian Anders Gadd and Patrick Wallis (eds.), *Guilds, Society, and Economy in London, 1450–1800* (London, 2002), pp. 51–66.

Rushton, Peter, 'The Matter in Variance: Adolescents and Domestic Conflict in the Pre-Industrial Economy of Northeast England, 1600–1800', *Journal of Social History,* 25 (1991): 89–107.

Seaver, Paul S., 'Work, Discipline, and the Apprentice in Early Modern London', in Penelope Gouk (ed.), *Wellsprings of Achievement: Cultural and Economic Dynamics in Early Modern England and Japan* (Aldershot, 1995), pp. 159–79.

Sharpe, Pamela, 'Poor Children as Apprentices in Colyton, 1598–1830', *Continuity and Change,* 6 (3) (1991): 253–70.

Shepard, Alexandra, *Meanings of Manhood in Early Modern England* (Oxford, 2003).

—— 'Poverty, Labour, and the Language of Social Description in Early Modern England', *Past and Present,* 201 (2008): 51–95.

Snell, K. D. M., 'The Apprenticeship System in British History: The Fragmentation of an Institution', *History of Education,* 25 (1996): 303–21.

Walter, John, 'A "Rising of the People"? The Oxfordshire Rising of 1596', *Past and Present,* 107 (1985): 90–143.

—— 'Faces in the Crowd: Gender and Age in the Early Modern English Crowd', in Helen Berry and Elizabeth Foyster (eds.), *The Family in Early Modern England* (Cambridge, 2007), pp. 96–125.

Whitney, C. '"Usually in the Werking Daies": Playgoing, Journeymen, Apprentices, and Servants in Guild Records, 1582–92', *Shakespeare Quarterly,* 50 (1999): 433–58.

Whittle, Jane, 'Housewives and Servants in Rural England, 1440–1650: Evidence of Women's Work from Probate Documents', *Transactions of the Royal Historical Society,* 15 (2005): 51–74.

—— 'Servants in Rural England, *c.* 1450–1650: Hired Work as a Means of Accumulating Wealth and Skills before Marriage', in Maria Agren and Amy Louise Erickson (eds.), *The Marital Economy in Scandinavia and Britain, 1400–1900* (Aldershot, 2005), pp. 89–110.

Woodward, Donald, 'The Background to the Statute of Artificers: The Genesis of Labour Policy, 1558–63', *Economic History Review,* 2nd Series, 33 (1) (1980): 32–44.

—— *Men at Work: Labourers and Building Craftsmen in the Towns of Northern England, 1450–1750* (Cambridge, 1995).

Wright, S., '"Churmaids, Huswyfes, and Hucksters": The Employment of Women in Tudor and Stuart Salisbury', in L. Charles and L. Duffin (eds.), *Women and Work in Pre-Industrial England* (London, 1985), pp. 100–21.

Wrightson, Keith, *English Society, 1580–1680* (London, 1982).

—— *Earthly Necessities: Economic Lives in Early Modern Britain* (New Haven, Conn., 2000).

—— 'Mutualities and Obligations: Changing Social Relationships in Early Modern England', *Proceedings of the British Academy,* 139 (2006): 157–94.

Weiner, C. Z., 'The Beleaguered Isle: A Study of Elizabethan and Early Jacobean Anti-Catholicism', *Past and Present,* 51 (1971): 27–62.

NOTES

1 Stubbes is quoted in David Underdown, *Revel, Riot, and Rebellion: Popular Politics and Culture in England, 1603–1660* (Oxford, 1985), p. 48.

2 Anon., *The Office of Christian Parents* (Cambridge, 1616), p. 159.

3 C. Z. Weiner, 'The Beleaguered Isle: A Study of Elizabethan and Early Jacobean Anti-Catholicism', *Past and Present,* 51 (1971): 27–62.

4 John Stockwood, *A Sermon Preached at St Paules Crosse on Saint Bartholomew's Day, 24 August 1578* (1578), p. 55.
5 William Gouge, *Of Domesticall Duties* (1622), p. 360.
6 William Shakespeare, *The Winter's Tale,* Act III, Scene 3, ll. 64–70.
7 William Guild, *The Young Man's Inquisition or Trial* (1608), pp. 20–1; Henry Cuffe, *The Difference of the Ages of a Man's Life* (1607), p. 121.
8 Paul Griffiths, *Youth and Authority: Formative Experiences in England, 1560–1640* (Oxford, 1996), p. 55; Henry Crosse, *Vertue's Common-Wealth* (1603), p. 44; Richard Greenham, *The Works of Richard Greenham* (Amsterdam and New York), p. 289.
9 George Chapman et al., *Eastward Ho* (1605) (New York, 1970), sig. H3.
10 W.P., *The Prentises's Practice in Godlinesse and His True Freedome* (1613), fol. 28v.
11 Roger Ascham, *The Scholemaster* (1570), in *English Works,* ed. W. A. Wright (Cambridge, 1970), p. 210. See Susan Brigden, 'Youth and the English Reformation', *Past and Present,* 95 (1982): 37–67.
12 Quoted in Griffiths, *Youth and Authority,* pp. 39, 51; Robert Shelford, *Lectures or Readings . . . Concerning the Vertuous Education of Youth* (1606), p. 126.
13 William Vaughan, *The Golden-Grove* (1600), Part 3, fol. V8.
14 Guild, *Young Man's Inquisition,* p. 22; Gouge, *Domesticall Duties,* pp. 545, 547.
15 Matthew Griffith, *Bethel; or, A Forme for Families* (1634), p. 19.
16 Patricia Fumerton, *Unsettled: The Culture of Mobility and the Working Poor in Early Modern England* (Chicago, Ill., 2006), Chapter 2; Anon., *An Ease for Overseers* (Cambridge, 1601), p. 27.
17 N[orwich and Norfolk] R[ecord] O[ffice] NMC 13, fol. 23.
18 Roberts, 'Women and Work', pp. 96, and 92–5.
19 NRO Assembly Minute Book 4, fol. 139; J. P. Earwaker (ed.), *The Court Leet Records of the Manor of Manchester from 1552 to 1686,* 6 vols. (Manchester, 1884–90), vol. I, p. 241; vol. II, pp. 37, 43.
20 Chapman et al., *Eastward Ho,* fols. A3, G3; Crosse, *Vertue's Common-Wealth.*
21 Daniel Cawdrey, *Family Reformation Promoted* (1656), p. 46.
22 Guild, *Young Man's Inquisition,* p. 20.
23 Canterbury Cathedral Library and Archives, X. 1. 7, fol. 174.
24 Guildhall Library (London) MSS 9235/2, fol. 208; 942/1, fols. 73v, 201v, 216; 559/1, fol. 19; 6836, fol. 54v; 2895/1, fols. 211v, 224v; 1002/1, fol. 449; 645/1, fol. 67v; 1046/1, fol. 2; 878/1, fol. 187.
25 Essex Record Office Colchester D/ACA 43, fols. 98, 107.
26 Mark Thornton Burnett, 'Masters and Servants in Moral and Religious Treatises, *c.* 1580–*c.* 1642', in Arthur Marwick (ed.), *The Arts, Literature, and Society* (London and New York, 1990), p. 53.
27 F. G. Emmison, *Elizabethan Life,* p. 137.
28 L[ondon] M[etropolitan] A[rchives] Repertories of the Court of Aldermen 45, fol. 445.
29 J. A. Twemlow (ed.), *Liverpool Town Books . . . 1550–1603,* 2 vols. (Liverpool, 1918, 1935), vol. I, pp. 526–7; NRO Norwich Mayor's Courtbooks (NMC) 7, fols. 592–3; J. R. Boyle and F. W. Dendy (eds.), *Extracts from the Records of the Merchant Adventurers of Newcastle-Upon-Tyne,* 2 vols. (Durham, 1895, 1899), vol. I, pp. 22–3; Bridewell Hospital Courtbooks (BHC) 3, fol. 268.
30 C[ambridge] U[university] L[ibrary] UL EDR B/2/14, fol. 138v.
31 BHC 4, fol. 354; 5, fol. 23v.
32 BHC 2, fols. 188v–9v.
33 GL MS 5770/3, fol. 28v; NRO NMC 10, fol. 177; 15, fol. 125v; C[lothworkers'] H[all] London NRO Minute Books, 1581–1605, fol. 81v; 1558–81, fol. 208.
34 GL MS 5770/1, fol. 346; NRO NMC 11, fol. 321; BHC 5, fol. 113.
35 GL MS 5770/1, fol. 255.
36 *The Autobiography and Personal Diary of Dr Simon Forman,* ed. J. O. Halliwell (1849), pp. 6 and 6–8; CH Minute Book, 1605–23, fol. 211; NRO NMC 9, fol. 469.
37 BHC 2, fol. 146; GL MS 5770/1, fols. 140–1; BHC 4, fol. 345v.
38 BHC 1, fols. 220v–1; Francis Dillingham, *Christian Oeconomy* (1609), fol. 49v.

39 BHC 1, fol. 76.
40 All quotes from Griffiths, *Youth and Authority*, pp. 327–9.
41 CH Minute Book, 1558–81, fol. 177.
42 GL MS 5770/1, fol. 274.
43 BHC 2, fol. 107v; 5, fol. 360v. Quoting Edward Shorter, *The Making of the Modern Family* (1976), pp. 98–9; and John R. Gillis, *For Better for Worse: British Marriages, 1600 to the Present* (Oxford, 1985), pp. 11, 15.
44 LMA Journals of Common Council 28, fols. 161–2v.
45 BHC 1, fol. 194v; GL MS 5770/1, fol. 280; BHC 5, fols. 433, 203v.
46 LMA Rep. 17, fols. 353–3v, 389, 454v, 78v; Arthur Dent, *The Plaine-Man's Pathway to Heaven* (1601) (Amsterdam, 1974), pp. 58–9.
47 BHC 2, fol. 113v; 1, fol. 125.
48 First case quoted in Charles Whitney, '"Usually in the Werking Daies": Playgoing Journeymen, Apprentices and Servants in Guild Records, 1582–92', *Shakespeare Quarterly*, 50 (1999), p. 446; GL MS 5770/2, fol. 99.
49 BHC 3, fols. 223v, 225v; 1, fol. 180v; 2, fol. 213; 'The London Journal of Allesandro Magno 1562', ed. Caroline Barron, Christopher Coleman and Claire Gobb, *London Journal*, 9 (1983), p. 144.
50 Tryon is quoted in Carl B. *Estabrook, Urbane and Rustic England: Cultural Ties and Social Spheres in the Provinces, 1660–1780* (Palo Alto, Calif., 1998), p. 28.
51 Quoted in Mark Thornton Burnett, *Masters and Servants in English Renaissance Drama: Authority and Obedience* (London and New York, 1997), p. 32.
52 T. Gouge, *A Narrative of the Life and Death of Dr Gouge* (1665), sig. A1; M. M. Knappen (ed.), *Two Elizabethan Puritan Diaries by Richard Greenham and Samuel Ward* (Chicago, Ill., 1933), pp. 103–15.
53 Philip Stubbes, *An Anatomie of Abuses* (1583), ed. A. Freeman (New York, 1973), sigs. M8–M8v.

CHAPTER TWENTY

WOMEN

Tim Stretton

Successive generations of scholars in the twentieth century made bold yet contradictory assertions about the lives of women during the reign of Elizabeth. Some assumed that the example of a female sovereign provided women with a living precedent for the potential of female power and autonomy. Others, by contrast, suggested that Elizabeth's manipulation of gender norms – playing up her bodily weakness, emphasising her masculine princely powers and refusing to compromise her authority by marrying – revealed the limits of female independence. Some historians alleged that the Protestant character of the Elizabethan settlement privileged companionship within marriage and helped set women on an eventual course to equality. Others disagreed, arguing that Protestantism entrenched the power and authority of husbands and fathers at the expense of wives and daughters. A number found in Shakespeare's plays evidence of strong female roles suggesting a new and heightened respect for women's worth. Others read the same plays yet concluded the opposite: Shakespeare gave his female characters limited roles that conformed to restrictive gender stereotypes and which were performed not by women but by young boys.

These disparate observations can leave a modern reader confused and bemused. The ability to reach such contradictory conclusions is a testament to the enigmatic nature of the surviving evidence about women, so much of which was produced, recorded, censored or otherwise influenced by male hands and male sensibilities. To an unquestioning eye, conduct books detailing ideal female behaviour might suggest that the majority of women were chaste, silent and obedient. Ecclesiastical court records, by contrast, can give the impression that most women were sexually threatening, outspoken and uncontrollable. Other disagreements stem from the nature of historians' interests and interpretations. Scholars in the 1970s focused on Elizabethan women's subordination and told a depressing tale of male power and of women's limited rights, economic impoverishment and prominent roles as victims of physical and sexual violence. More recently, historians interested in female agency have painted a more optimistic picture, demonstrating how individual women evaded patriarchal restrictions or developed strategies to survive them, how they negotiated some of the terms of their subordinate positions and exercised surprising degrees of independence.

A number of the apparent contradictions surrounding women's experiences under Elizabeth reflect the character of the age itself, which in various areas was in a state of flux and uncertainty, with new possibilities, cultural forms and social habits threatening to unsettle a deeply conservative social order. Changes in population levels, economic activity, religious ideas, litigation levels, architecture and consumer behaviour did not begin at Elizabeth's coronation, and most persisted after her death. However, while her reign does not represent a unique and sharply defined watershed in the history of gender relations, this rich mixture of change occurring against a backdrop of continuity influenced women in particular ways, benefiting some, hurting others and passing others by altogether.

A sense of the times and of the mix of constraints and opportunities women faced during Elizabeth's reign can be glimpsed in the life of one woman, Alice Barnham, who was born ten years before Elizabeth and outlived her by a year, dying in May 1604 at the age of eighty.[1] In common with most women in pre-modern England, Alice's social status was rooted in her family linkages. The daughter of William Bradbridge, a mercer who served as mayor of Chichester, and wife and then widow of Francis Barnham, a London draper whose father had been a yeoman, she inhabited the upper ranks of the middling sort. What sets her apart from her

Figure 20.1 Alice Barnham and her sons (long identified as *Lady Ingram and Her Two Sons Martin and Steven*) (*c.* 1557, artist unknown). Image courtesy Berger Collection at the Denver Art Museum.

contemporaries is that we know what she looked like, thanks to a portrait of her with two of her sons, Martin and Steven, painted in 1557 or 1558 (see Figure 20.1). Over the course of their marriage, Alice and her husband amassed considerable wealth. According to a family memoir they were worth £1,000 at their marriage but had incomes of over £1,000 a year when Francis died in 1576, rising to £3,000 a year later in Alice's widowhood. Francis had begun his career in Henry VIII's court, but according to his grandson he found his placement with the Lord Steward 'a slow way of preferment' and left after two years to begin an apprenticeship with a draper. He soon rose to some prominence in civic governance, becoming a churchwarden, serving on the board of governors of Bridewell and then Saint Thomas's Hospital, and then rising to be an alderman and finally sheriff of London. It seems that Alice worked as a silk woman, and she and her husband became rich through a combination of her importing and his exporting, land speculation and moneylending at high interest. Alice almost certainly played a key role in this last endeavour, where her stocks of imported silks and domestic wares appear to have featured in complicated transactions in goods designed to disguise loans of money and so evade prohibitions against usury. She also managed and expanded the family's assets while her husband was absent and during more than two decades of widowhood, taking on apprentices in her own name and playing an influential role in helping to establish her surviving sons as wealthy and successful country gentlemen.

Later in Elizabeth's reign, Alice came close to remarrying, agreeing terms for a marriage settlement with Sir Thomas Ramsay, a wealthy alderman and former lord mayor of London. After scrutinising the value of her existing jointure, Sir Thomas discovered that it included a lease to one of her sons for rent below market rates, and he asked Alice to call the lease in, suggesting that they could use the house each summer. Alice agreed and arranged a meeting at which her son returned the lease to her in the presence of Sir Thomas, who immediately 'named a speedy date' for the consummation of their marriage. According to family lore, Alice turned to her eager suitor and said:

> be not so hasty, except it be to appoint your wedding day with some other wife, for on me I assure you you must not reckon. For I shall never think myself happily bestowed upon a husband that setteth so small a value on me as you have done in making this little improvement of my jointure (for that I know was indeed your aim) a necessary condition of your match with me.

In dismissing Sir Thomas, Alice explained how this meeting had confirmed her opinion of his nature, 'which is surely so set upon covetousness as would have given me but small comfort in you' and demonstrated the loyalty and love of her son, to whom she immediately returned the lease.[2] Right to the last Alice exercised a striking degree of control over her life and would have counted herself a model Elizabethan woman: a good daughter, wife, mother and widow, and a successful silk woman, land speculator, matchmaker, mistress then household head and a devout servant of her God.

Alice's life was far from typical, but it provides an evocative illustration of how Elizabethans mixed and made sense of old values and new possibilities. On the one hand, Alice can be identified as one of the last silk women, a member of a female craft monopoly dating from medieval times that during her lifetime was overrun by male professionals. On the other hand, despite her position in a medieval profession, she and her husband were 'new' Tudors, taking advantage of new ways of spending money and asserting status that included obtaining coats of arms, building elaborate funerary monuments and commissioning family portraits. The painting of Alice and her sons ranks as one of the earliest private portraits in England of a woman outside of the ranks of the aristocracy. The inscription above her head in the painting reads 'I was born the 7 of September on a Sonday, 1523, tornid from that I was unto that ye see *Anno Domani* 1557.' This cryptic reference to a transformation 'from what I was into what you see' is deeply personal and suggests a novel focus on the individual and on family privacy.

THE GENDER ORDER AND ECONOMIC AND SOCIAL CHANGE

In almost every context in Elizabethan society women enjoyed less power and fewer privileges and options than men of an equivalent social level. Men's pre-eminence was virtually universal, but it was not monolithic. Rather than flowing from a single unified system of female subordination, Elizabethan attitudes to women were shaped by a multitude of ideas and assumptions drawn from the Bible, scientific ideas about nature, medical views of the body, laws and legal ideology, custom, convention, humour and proverbial wisdom. The weight of opinion from so many different sources gave assumptions about male superiority and female dependence a rare power, but the nature and variety of these sources also produced complexities, ambiguities and contradictions that allowed women self-esteem and gave them room to manoeuvre within a largely male-dominated world. Readings of Genesis, for example, confirmed that women were the spiritual equals of men yet inferior to them in the hierarchy of creation. How could they be both? The wedding service in the Book of Common Prayer explained that a wife was to obey and serve her husband and be in subjection to him in all things, just as Sarah had obeyed Abraham 'calling him Lord'. However, conduct books made clear that this subservience was to be accompanied by competence and the ability to wield authority, so that a woman such as Alice Barnham would not only manage the household and govern her children but also give orders to male servants and apprentices.

Patriarchal ideology privileged the rule of fathers, but it did not afford men a complete monopoly over power and property, with the result that daughters could inherit major estates and a woman could reign as queen (although parliament named Elizabeth supreme governor, not supreme head, of the English church). The focus of the elites was on hierarchy, rooted in the belief that order and control depended on everyone in society, from the lowliest labourer right up to the monarch, being subject to the rule of a higher authority, with the result that subordination was a watchword for men as well as for women. These complementary beliefs in patriarchy and hierarchy were so entrenched as to be almost beyond question. However, aspects of both beliefs came under strain in the wake of economic and social change, raising concerns among the elites whose interests they served.

As other essays in this volume make clear, decades of sustained population growth (either side of the influenza or other epidemics that swept the country around the time of Elizabeth's accession) increased demand for everything from land and foodstuffs to housing, books and luxury goods, inflating prices and steadily expanding the size and sophistication of local and national markets. In this changing economic climate merchants and yeomen prospered as never before, a new reality that Francis Barnham recognised when he turned his back on service within the royal household and chose the life of a merchant in London. The ability of Francis and Alice to make their fortunes in the city, in part by loaning money to cash-strapped aristocrats, and to transform their sons into gentlemen, represented a disruption to the neat and static divisions of the biblically inspired social order that assumed a place for everyone and everyone in their place. One response to this subtle but significant refiguring of the relative social importance of money and land was an increase in social commentary on the subject of status. Authors strived in vain to stem the tide of change and to map out the elusive qualities other than mere wealth that set the gentry and aristocracy apart from the rest of the population, while sumptuary legislation attempted to defy fashion and restrict the clothes, fabrics and furs men and women of different ranks could wear.

Allied to this unease about social climbing and falling was a more general concern about order, especially among gentry and elites already unsettled by the religious upheavals and attempted rebellions of previous decades. The Tudor expansion of the State's sphere of influence quickened its pace under Elizabeth, visible in rising numbers of proclamations, statutes, regulations and rules. Unease at the growing number of young people living and working away from the controlling influence of their parents, for example, helped prompt parliament to enact the 1563 Statute of Artificers, designed to ensure that all single males under twenty-five be apprenticed or in service. In 1570, in the wake of the Northern Rebellion, the Crown and church authorities appointed a new 'Homily against Disobedience and Willful Rebellion' to be read in parish churches, bolstering the existing 'Homily of Obedience'. These state-sanctioned calls for obedience were rarely as effective as their framers intended, judging by the riotous behaviour of urban bands of apprentices and the vocal and sometimes violent responses of men and women to food shortages and rising prices, but they indicate the depth of elite concern.

The sense that the social order was in disarray also stretched to the gender order. Ecclesiastical presentments of moral offences including illegitimacy, fornication and adultery increased significantly in the years following the 1570s, and women predominated in the lists of those accused. Ballads, pamphlets, sermons and plays presented positive and negative female stereotypes, railing against disorderly women and praising the chaste and the modest. Few of the sentiments expressed in print were new, but the volume of comment, spurred by concerns about disorder and facilitated by the growing availability of cheap print, increased the tempo of long-running debates. The flood of paper and parchment represented more than a simple capturing in print of the adages, jokes and norms of the existing oral culture, for the printing and circulation of ideas and woodcut images created its own cultural effects. Print had the potential to travel further and last longer than oral exchanges, whether kept in books or pasted up on alehouse walls, and was accessible to the illiterate as well as the literate in a culture where discussion and reading aloud in parlours, churches and alehouses was common. Amongst their many targets, ballad and broadsheet writers depicted a wild and scandalous cast of wilful wives, fornicating widows, unnatural mothers and female criminals, and the brunt of much of their jocular or heartfelt ire was not women themselves but the men who should be keeping them in check. The reputation of male householders depended on effectively managing their households, including governing their wives, and many jokes were made at the expense of the emasculated or cuckolded husband who failed to control his wife or to satisfy and so contain her rampant sexuality.

Some historians have detected in this outpouring of comment, and in the contemporary fixation on male and female honour and reputation, signs of a 'crisis' in gender relations that amounted to a crisis in patriarchal ideology itself.[3] Crisis seems too strong a word to describe what was clearly an ongoing struggle to define norms and to prescribe acceptable behaviour, but anxiety about female sexuality and independence does seem to have run higher under Elizabeth than in preceding reigns and expressed itself in regulations and laws as well as published works. Where the Statute of Artificers focused primarily on men under twenty-five, it specifically empowered local authorities to order into service any unmarried women between the ages of twelve and forty on pain of imprisonment. Members of parliament clearly expected women in their childbearing years to be under the control of a husband and felt it necessary to place single and widowed women under the control of a master to prevent them living 'at their own hand'. Calls for wifely obedience rang from pulpits, with the 1563 'Homily of Matrimony' reiterating the prescriptions of the prayer-book marriage service. Most of these supports of the gender hierarchy took aim at women from the lower orders – no one sought to force merchant wives or elite women into service – but concerns about women knew few class boundaries. The publication in 1558 of John Knox's, *The First Blast of the Trumpet against the Monstrous Regiment of Women,* for example, initiated a lively debate about the limits and legitimacy of female rule that would have been difficult to imagine a century before.[4]

Women actively participated in this consumption and circulation of ideas in print, as authors, translators, readers and listeners. As a literate woman, proudly displaying in her portrait her fluency with quill and ink, Alice Barnham was in a minority, but the numbers of women acquiring these skills was growing, especially in London and other urban centres. Women also attended plays in the new London playhouses and in the tavern courtyards and halls across the country where travelling players performed, witnessing forms of drama that explored an expansive range of subjects including the humorous or tragic consequences that could arise from gender roles and the expectations that surrounded them.

LAW, PROPERTY RIGHTS AND LITIGATION

Where literary sources can be equivocal, laws and legal conventions provide stark evidence of the nature and extent of patriarchal ideology in Elizabethan England. The common law, for example, regarded a wife who killed her husband in the same category as a servant who killed his or her master. Each was guilty not simply of murder but of petty treason, a crime against the State. The common law also favoured sons over daughters in inheritance, through the custom of primogeniture, and stripped away from married women control of any property they brought to marriage or acquired during marriage. In the Law French used by common lawyers, at marriage a *feme sole* became a *feme covert,* as a husband covered his wife's legal personality with his own, all but extinguishing her independent rights so that she could not bring lawsuits or enter into contracts without his permission.

Thanks to this 'coverture', a married woman's real property or land fell under her husband's control for the duration of marriage (and afterwards if he outlived her) while her monies, livestock, house-wares and other moveable property became his outright. A potent symbol of the power of coverture can be seen in the English naming practice that saw a married woman give up her surname and take the name of her husband. In the rest of Europe at this time, by contrast, wives shared in communal property with their husbands or maintained separate property during marriage, and they kept the names they had been born with. The channelling of property away from females and towards males at death and on marriage, and the difficulties wives faced in maintaining separate property, had far-reaching effects. Amy Erickson speculates that the poverty amongst widows that these measures helped to produce may help explain why England adopted formal systems of state-administered poor relief considerably earlier than its European neighbours.[5]

The common law restricted women's rights but it did not remove them altogether. In most matters of property single women and widows possessed the same rights (if not the same entitlements) as men, and a wife who outlived her husband had a right to claim dower, a life interest in the incomes of one-third of the lands her husband had held during marriage. Furthermore, while a married woman could not write a will or sue or be sued without her husband's consent, she could do so with his co-operation, with the result that during Elizabeth's reign a growing number of wives wrote wills, and more wives than either widows or single women put their names to lawsuits.

Other jurisdictions administering ecclesiastical law, equity and rural or urban custom operated alongside the common law, and each of these viewed women in slightly different ways and provided them with different rights. As a London silk woman, Alice Barnham benefited from a customary exception to coverture that permitted wives in the city engaged in certain trades to enjoy *feme sole* status as if they were not married. Equity courts such as Chancery offered additional support to women, recognising and enforcing uses and trusts that allowed married women to maintain control of some or all of their property during marriage by placing it in the hands of trustees. For well-placed women with sufficient resources and access to legal counsel this amounted to a significant improvement over existing common-law restrictions. For women without these advantages, however, these same equitable devices could prove disastrous, as fathers used them to disinherit their daughters and husbands used them to undermine their wives' entitlements to dower.

As in most societies, social practice in Elizabethan England regularly parted ways from legal theory. Under a strict reading of the rules of coverture it would have been impossible for Alice Barnham, despite her *feme sole* status as a silk woman, to buy and sell wares other than silks, provision her house, deal with tradesmen and women and direct her servants, but she did all of these things and more, thanks to the common-law presumption that she was acting as her husband's agent. Here we see the power and perhaps the patriarchal genius of English law. To most women it did not seem overly oppressive – an independent-minded woman such as Alice Barnham could work in tandem with her husband in the shared enterprise of bringing success to their household and family. Yet in instances where marital relations soured, English husbands enjoyed more legal authority at home than virtually any married men in Europe, including the ability to confine and to 'correct' their wives using force if necessary or to humiliate them by selling their clothes, jewellery and other personal possessions. Numerous forces acted to restrict husbands in the exercise of these powers, with sermons and advice manuals urging restraint and emphasising the obligations that came with authority, and neighbours and magistrates regularly intervening in cases of violence against married women. However, the authority itself was above question and provided patriarchal ideology with its defining force.

Despite these restrictions, English women possessed legal rights, and many exercised them. During Elizabeth's reign, almost every legal jurisdiction experienced an astonishing rise in business, with litigation levels doubling, tripling or quadrupling in just a few decades and rising to unprecedented levels. Women made up between 10 to 15 per cent of named litigants in the largest common-law and equity courts that sat in and around London's Westminster Hall, where on their own or with others they claimed dower, contested inheritance and fought or defended actions over debt, bonds, title to lands, trespass and a host of other matters. In the church courts, which did not recognise coverture, female participation rates were even higher, rising from a quarter of plaintiffs in 1570 to around a third in 1600 and approaching 50 per cent for defamation suits fought in London.[6]

Even relatively low percentages translate into very high numbers once the scale of the boom in litigation is appreciated. Accurate figures are difficult to compile, but a recent speculative estimate suggests that English litigants commenced over 1 million actions a year towards the end of Elizabeth's reign, at a time when the total population had not yet reached 4 million.[7] Given that each suit involved at least two parties, and that it was not unusual to see multiple plaintiffs or defendants and attending casts of witnesses, it appears that most of the population had experience of involvement in lawsuits, including many thousands of women.

Early modern litigants did not take lawsuits brought against them as personally as we might today, but such high levels of litigation still corroded visions of neighbourliness and supplied further evidence to Elizabethans that the world was out of joint. Justice in the sixteenth century was far from blind, but the majority of plaintiffs and complainants brought suit against their social equals or betters, so that it was common to see the middling sort suing the gentry, the gentry suing the aristocracy and women suing men. The sight and experience of thousands of women suing to protect their interests, travelling to meet lawyers or to appear in court, challenging men and winning victories over opponents of a higher social station confirmed the erosion of familiar certainties. The pace and scale of the expansion of litigation created its own confusion, allowing litigants sued in one jurisdiction to counter-sue or gain judgments in another. As in many periods of change in history, determined women found opportunities in this bustle and turmoil to sue and to appear and speak in courtrooms in person, and a number of wives found ways to slip the confining shackles of coverture. These instances of female independence became rarer in later periods as a growing concern with consistency aided by the publication of law reports discouraged exceptions to legal rules and courtrooms became more orderly, controlled and genteel spaces.

WOMEN AND EMPLOYMENT

The authors of Elizabethan advice literature advocated separate roles for men and women, suggesting that just as Adam delved while Eve span, God had made 'the man to travail abroad and the woman to keep home'.[8] Alice Barnham's active life as an independent silk woman makes a mockery of this strict demarcation of roles. However, while the idea that men went out into the world while women stayed at home remained a fantasy to anyone outside the ranks of the high gentry and aristocracy, it neatly encapsulates widely held perceptions that women's work was fundamentally different from men's work. Court records, for example, listed the trades or professions of men but identified women by their marital status, linking them – as daughter, wife or widow – to a named man. In an age when the production and harvesting of food still provided the lion's share of employment, women regularly did the same work as men, but despite the crucial contributions women made, they almost universally received less pay and less social recognition for their work than men.

Institutional rules and social pressures confined the majority of women to pursuing work that was an extension of their domestic responsibilities. Those who were not involved in agriculture worked in domestic service, in the food and drink trades, the cloth trades, as cooks, cleaners, nurses, wet nurses and pawnbrokers. They administered poor relief, made gloves or lace, knitted stockings, bought and sold second-hand clothes and goods, and provided board and lodging for other people's children, for orphans, pregnant women, the sick or the elderly. Others resorted to prostitution. Far fewer single women than men received formal training in skills and arts that took time to acquire, unless from their parents. This fact is reflected in the low numbers of female apprentices compared with male apprentices (excluding agricultural and domestic service), an imbalance that appears to have increased over the course of Elizabeth's reign. In addition, women faced restrictions on the places where it was acceptable for them to ply their trades. Urban authorities fretted over and sought to regulate street hawkers, laundresses and other women who worked unsupervised, suspecting them of being especially prone to gossiping, sexual immorality and other unsocial behaviour. Women's work was regularly sporadic and makeshift, and up and down the social scale women faced hostility if their employment was felt to threaten male household heads, male-dominated guilds and male competitors.

Just as in the realm of law, and in the face of popular opinion and prescriptive literature, many women displayed resilience and creativity in overcoming, evading or ignoring the barriers set up against them; and their contributions both as producers and consumers were essential to their households and to local, regional and national economies. The extent of female accomplishments can be observed in successful women's wills, in the scale of wealth individuals distributed to their heirs, kin and friends or devoted to charitable bequests and endowments. Family connections proved particularly helpful to women, allowing daughters to work in their father's enterprises and wives and widows to carry on crafts, such as printing, which were largely closed to single women.

The economic expansion under way during Elizabeth's reign increased opportunities for moneylending, benefiting those women who were deeply enmeshed in credit networks. However, it also encouraged increases in the scale of production of manufactured goods and put a premium on professional expertise and specialisation, all of which favoured men. Overall, the range and quality of economic opportunities open to women appears to have declined during this period, especially during the harsh years of the 1590s, leaving a greater proportion of female workers performing unskilled and poorly paid work. The silk trade provides an illustration of this shift in women's fortunes. Alice Barnham's pride in her craft can be sensed in the display of rich and exotic materials in her portrait: the shirt collars, ornamental ties on sleeves and the elaborate table covering on which she rests her paper. However, as rising demand pushed up the price of silk, and the call for ribbons, ornate laces and girdles expanded to include silk cloth woven on broad looms, male weavers and merchants began to encroach on this traditionally female occupation. Silk women could do little to resist these changes as they had never incorporated themselves into a formal guild, almost certainly as a result of the legal and economic effects of coverture. The silk trade went from being small scale and almost exclusively female to large scale and almost exclusively male, following a pattern that had already transformed the brewing trade and was in the early stages of transforming the medical field.

RELIGION

Religion presents historians investigating Elizabethan women with a curious paradox. For while the Christian faith supplied the central pillars of patriarchal ideology – the assumption of women's inferiority to men and repeated injunctions that they be chaste, silent and obedient – it also enriched women's lives in unparalleled ways and offered some the ability to transcend not just gender norms but also the restrictions imposed by class or status. The reform of religion altered certain constituents of this paradox but left the paradox itself intact. It is therefore all but impossible to draw overarching conclusions about the Reformation either improving or worsening women's lives. All historians can do is consider the effects of religious change on particular women or groups of women of the same social status and similar religious beliefs.

Religion held an important place for women throughout the early modern period. It offered spiritual fulfilment and ways of coping with suffering and loss, gave mothers authority over the spiritual upbringing of children and servants and provided a rare means for self-examination and self-expression. Piety was something women could excel at. Most Elizabethans accepted that women could display a stronger faith than men and perhaps more significantly that poor and illiterate women could be more pious than their elite neighbours, in some cases becoming exemplars of the spiritual life. The changes resulting from the reform of religion are well known: the closing of monasteries, the ending of clerical celibacy, the breaking of the priests' intercessory monopoly, the replacing of Latin with English, the emergence of a new emphasis on the written word, the growing preference for separate seating for men and women in church, the accommodation or transformation of traditional practices such as the 'churching' of women after childbirth. Yet historians still cannot agree on the extent to which crown and church authorities imposed reform from above or ordinary parishioners demanded and embraced it from below. Nevertheless, there seems to be a consensus that religious change alone did not fundamentally alter the lives or status of all women. For example, most historians accept that the reformed church increased the spiritual authority of heads of households, allowing fathers and husbands to assume some of the mantle of religious authority previously exclusive to priests, but in practice this new emphasis derived as much from state attempts to ensure conformity as from Protestant theology. It also needs to be considered in light of an accompanying stress on companionship in marriage and on the duties husbands owed wives in return for their obedience. Similarly, while the stress on close reading of the Scriptures transformed the religious experience of many women, its effects on women varied depending on their wealth, personal beliefs and whether or not they were literate.

What the reformation of religion did introduce was the prospect of choice. And with choice came new opportunities to defy conventional hierarchies of authority. John Foxe's *Acts and Monuments* first appeared in English in 1563 and quickly became one of the most popular texts in the country. Its detailed descriptions of the lives of the Marian martyrs showed poor women such as Alice Driver being eloquent and dignified in their defiance of Catholic authority. And despite Foxe's efforts to endorse the existing gender order, he described a number of married women, including Anne Askew, Alice Benden and 'a godly poor woman which suffered at Exeter', who openly defied their husbands to serve their God. In similar fashion, on the eve of Elizabeth's reign the same John Knox who was contemptuous of queenly rule successfully encouraged Anne Locke to travel to Geneva with her two children against her husband's wishes in search of 'the maist perfyt schoole of Chryst that ever was in the erth since the dayis of the Apostillis'.[9]

The ability for family members to make different choices – for a wife to be more or less devout than her husband, or for a Protestant husband or wife to have a Catholic spouse – not only created tensions within families but also created difficulties for crown and church authorities. A number of women took risks to support their particular visions of the Church. At one end of the religious spectrum, avid believers in reform took to the streets to protest against the wearing of vestments or to support nonconformist lecturers and ministers. At the other end, Catholic women protected priests and hid the vessels and linens required for the mass. A number of wives in wealthy Catholic families exploited their diminished legal status by attending celebrations of mass at home and staying away from divine service in defiance of the Act of Uniformity. Members of Parliament tied themselves in knots in their search for a solution to this problem of civic, religious and patriarchal disobedience by married women. The dilemma was this: collecting fines from wives was impossible when under coverture they owned no property, but to demand that husbands pay fines on their behalf would be to hold one person accountable for the crimes of another. Imprisonment was the usual penalty for failure to pay a fine, but could it be applied when payment was legally impossible? And was it fair to deprive a husband of his wife's company for something as personal as faith over which he could not be expected to have control? Some MPs argued that husbands should be held responsible for their wives' attendance at church. Others worried about the implications of such a move for other nonconformists. This indecision is reflected in the statutes: the 1581 Act to Retain the Queen's Majesty's Subjects in their Due Obedience provides imprisonment as the means of dealing with recalcitrant married women, but the 1593 Act against Popish Recusants exempts married women from fines or abjuration. The end result was that women continued to champion the Catholic faith throughout Elizabeth's reign and helped to ensure its survival.

The element of choice extended to how individual women manifested their beliefs. During Elizabeth's reign, 'godly' women gained a reputation for 'gadding' or travelling outside their home parishes to hear sermons from ministers whose views matched their own. The wealthy among them also sponsored particular ministers or left specific bequests to religious institutions or charitable causes that made clear their particular spiritual affiliations. Alice Barnham displayed her commitment to the reformed faith in her portrait through the careful choice of displayed texts. Her eldest son holds a copy of the *Proverbs of Solomon* open at the second chapter which reads 'My son receve ye these my wordes, the which shall be right wise', while she has just written the line 'That we alle may receve the same.' Her transformation 'from that I was unto that ye see' may also refer to a religious change, although not a simple conversion as she had been a believer in Protestant reform for some years before the portrait was painted. Religious faith is always deeply personal, but examples such as these suggest that women who exercised their religious autonomy in such individual ways were aware of, and some took comfort from, their difference from other believers. The contentious question for historians is what part beliefs about predestination played in this process, and whether or not it affected women as a group. Did a desire to distinguish between 'the elect' and 'the damned' help to inspire the clampdown on women guilty of moral offences noted earlier in this chapter? Or did population pressures, rising levels of poverty and vagrancy and more general concerns about social and patriarchal order spark these prosecutions?

POLITICS AND POWER

Laws, custom and social conventions ensured that women could not vote (except in the rarest circumstances), be elected as MPs or serve as judges, magistrates, aldermen, sheriffs or trial jurors. In this strict sense, every woman except the Queen was excluded from the public operation of power. However, historians have now expanded narrow definitions of high politics to include political culture, and it has become clear that Elizabethan women did participate in the political worlds of the nation, community and neighbourhood. Under Elizabeth, the previously all-male Privy Chamber now included well over a dozen salaried and unsalaried gentlewomen, with the bedchamber also staffed by paid female attendants, and the women who held these positions exercised considerable influence over those who sought to gain access to the Queen or to learn her mood.[10] The State Papers and the letter books of the aristocracy reveal how often elite women acted as the hub of their households, soliciting favours on behalf of family members, brokering marriages, offering advice and providing hospitality. Others wielded influence at court where their presence was crucial in elaborate social rituals and interactions involving dance, music and polite conversation which were the locations for forging, reshaping or exploiting relationships of clientage, patronage and political association.

Women of the gentry and merchant classes performed similar functions within their households and communities, and wives regularly stepped in when husbands were away on business, at sea, at war, attending parliament, at market or in prison. Acting as their husbands' agents, these women oversaw land transfers, invested or dispersed large amounts of money, directed lawsuits, advised estate stewards, journeymen or apprentices and made decisions of great import. Many continued this pattern as widows, accepting responsibilities and exercising considerable economic authority as executors or administrators of their late husbands' estates in such high numbers that they outnumbered men in the fulfilling of these roles. As the wife of a successful draper, 'worshipful mistress' Alice Barnham was a Company 'sister' with access to a room the Drapers' Company reserved for members' wives and took part in processions through London in the company of other elite draper wives. She could also use her privileged position to become a supplier to the company of silks, ribbons and decorations and other fineries connected with her activities as a silk woman. In common with widow executors and administrators, the extent of Alice's dependence on her husband for key aspects of her status and economic opportunities is undeniable evidence of women's subordinate position in Elizabethan society. Yet, by the same token, the extent of Alice's accomplishments are a mark of the success women could achieve, and the respect they could attract, when they fulfilled the roles entrusted to them.

Further down the social scale, women discussed political news and religion and participated in enclosure and food riots. They also played important roles in policing the morals of their communities. The outbursts of accusation and counter-accusation found in defamation cases reveal tense urban communities where women defended their family honour and made public the sexual indiscretions and unacceptable behaviour of others. When these exchanges made their way into the church courts, women continued the active process of marking out their position in local hierarchies and helping to define the words and actions that constituted honourable behaviour. Accusations of witchcraft, which were predominantly brought by and against women, served a similar purpose, as accusers shaped and reinforced community norms by supporting prosecutions of deviant behaviour. In a more positive vein, women from lower as well as higher social levels marshalled resources and influence and supported and advised other women through extensive networks of kin, neighbours and friends. Hierarchies of female friendship and authority can be detected in the choices expectant mothers made about which 'gossips' or 'god siblings' would support them through labour and childbirth, while midwives exercised more responsibilities than simply assisting with births: authorities called upon their expertise, either alone or as members of juries of matrons, to confirm claims of virginity or pregnancy and to help distinguish stillbirths from cases of infanticide. Despite the opposition of some Elizabethan reformers, they could also baptise infants 'in time of necessity' if they thought the child's life was in danger and often fulfilled important functions in the churching ceremony of thanksgiving that marked the return of new mothers to their congregations.

Women exerted influence or independence in all of these spheres, but it is important not to overstate the extent of their freedom and power. The move to a Privy Chamber dominated by women, for example, coincided with a decline in the importance of the Chamber, as other officers and departments took over many of this body's administrative functions. Married women who acted as their husband's agents were obviously restricted in their range of choices in ways that their husbands were not. And women who brought defamation suits, or made accusations of witchcraft or sexual immorality, against other women protected or cemented their positions in the community by acknowledging and supporting the patriarchal order that was responsible for limiting their choices in life. Women wielded power, but they rarely possessed it unconditionally, and their access to it was commonly temporary, usually delegated, and often accidental. Widows enjoyed the most freedom, but their access to power was also contingent, dependent on the vagaries of human mortality and often bound in by the competing desires of male (and female) heirs and by the expectation that they would honour their late husbands' legacies or expressed wishes.

CONCLUSION

Historians' forays into the rich archives of Elizabethan England continue to uncover unexpected amounts of information about women's lives, much of which confirms that while women were regularly subordinate, they were rarely submissive or passive. Again and again women can be found exerting their independence, challenging oppressive norms and fighting fire with fire in witty exchanges of banter with men and other women. This independence women displayed in their houses, on the streets, in the fields, at market, in church and in law courts produced varied reactions, impressing allies, infuriating rivals and causing anxiety among those in authority charged with maintaining the status quo. Nevertheless, in a fundamental sense, Elizabethans regarded every woman who exercised power as an exception. Elizabeth herself made it clear in public pronouncements that she was exceptional and did not consider herself a model for other women (although to some extent she became one in the seventeenth century). There is little evidence, therefore, that these examples of female independence produced any fundamental or lasting improvements to the gender hierarchy, and England in 1603 remained a patriarchal society that limited women's rights to property and restricted their access to power, just as it had been in 1558. The continuing challenge for historians is to explain this continuity by identifying the flexibility within patriarchal institutions and structures of thought that allowed them to persist or to be reinvented in the face of changes to the economic, social, religious and cultural fabric of society.

Changes to women's circumstances that did occur were smaller in scale and uneven in their effects, requiring historians to take a more focused view and to be alert to variations between individual experiences. As we have seen in the realm of property, for example, growing numbers of individuals used equitable instruments such as marriage settlements and trusts to protect married women's interests from the grasping hands of their husbands, in defiance of the rules of coverture. Yet others used them to restrict married women's access to property, or to disinherit daughters in favour of sons. Similarly, in the realm of employment, we have observed how changes in the economy reduced opportunities for women involved in the silk trade, but they increased possibilities for the many women involved in enterprises associated with providing hospitality, especially in growing urban centres. Women's experiences of religious change clearly depended on their personal beliefs and on the beliefs of their families and close kin.

Complexities such as these help to explain the differing historical interpretations highlighted at the beginning of this essay. They also show the difficulties – and some would say the foolhardiness – involved in attempts to average all women's status or experience. That does not mean, however, that generalisations cannot be made. For example, a number of changes underway during Elizabeth's reign benefited heads of households, bolstering their spiritual authority and increasing their control over the disposition of property at marriage and death. In the roughly 80 per cent of households headed by men these changes worked in men's favour, but in the remaining 20 per cent headed by women the opposite was the case. The slow but inexorable shift away from inheritance governed by custom towards individual control over property had other effects as well. During Elizabeth's reign many offices and privileges continued to be tied to inheritance and to control over particular lands, which meant that on occasion they fell into women's hands. Convention often intervened in these instances to limit or modify female involvement (ladies of the manor were expected to delegate the overseeing of their manor courts to estate stewards) but rarely to remove it altogether. Lady Dorothy Packington, for example, returned two MPs to the Parliament of 1572 because she was 'lord and owner of the town of Aylesbury'.[11] An unshakeable faith in the system of inheritance here outweighed concerns about women wielding authority, but in the centuries following Elizabeth's death exceptions of this kind became less common.

The recovery of the individual spirit of particular women, of the feistiness and dignity that Alice Barham exhibited when she told a former lord mayor of London to find another wife, is refreshing and surprising. It rescues Elizabethan women from the condescension of those who would paint them as passive and ignorant victims of a stifling and all-pervasive male power. However, a sustained focus on female autonomy and enterprise has the danger of diminishing the extent to which many women were victims, whether of sexual and physical violence, intimidation or belittlement. It is important to remember that for every Alice Barnham exercising her will and reaping the benefits of privilege there were hundreds of destitute widows scraping a makeshift existence and having to beg for bread or for poor relief. Historians continue to face the unenviable task of finding the correct balance between these two very different lines of inquiry. Taking a modern perspective is essential to identify discriminatory beliefs and uneven distributions of power, yet recovering the richness of women's individual experiences can require examining Elizabethan society and values on their own terms. The former approach carries with it the risk of anachronism, such as an undue focus on individual rights in a society that more often thought in terms of household strategies. The latter approach can be patronising, if it assumes that all Elizabethan women cheerfully accepted their lot in life. A combination of the two allows the gulf between restrictive laws and a harsh patriarchal ideology on the one hand and a more complicated reality of female agency on the other not simply to be recognised, but to be explored and explained.

FURTHER READING

Capp, Bernard, *When Gossips Meet: Women, Family and Neighbourhood in Early Modern England* (Oxford, 2003).

Cioni, Maria L., *Women and Law in Elizabethan England with Particular Reference to the Court of Chancery* (New York, 1985).

Crawford, Patricia, *Women and Religion in England 1500–1720* (London and New York, 1993).

Daybell, James (ed.), *Women and Politics in Early Modern England, 1450–1700* (Aldershot, 2004).

Erickson, Amy Louise, *Women and Property in Early Modern England* (London and New York, 1993).

Fletcher, Anthony, *Gender, Sex and Subordination in England, 1500–1800* (New Haven, Conn., 1995).

Foyster, Elizabeth A., *Manhood in Early Modern England: Honour, Sex, and Marriage* (London and New York, 1999).

Froide, Amy M., *Never Married: Single Women in Early Modern England* (Oxford, 2005).

Gowing, Laura, *Domestic Dangers: Women, Words, and Sex in Early Modern London* (Oxford, 1996).

Kermode, Jennifer and Walker, Garthine (eds.), *Women, Crime and the Courts in Early Modern England* (London, 2003).

McIntosh, Marjorie Keniston, *Working Women in English Society, 1300–1620* (Cambridge, 2005).

Mendelsohn, Sara, and Crawford, Patricia, *Women in Early Modern England, 1550–1720* (Oxford, 1999).

Orlin, Lena, Cowen, *Locating Privacy in Tudor London* (Oxford, 2007).

Pacheco, Anita (ed.), *A Companion to Early Modern Women's Writing* (Oxford, 2002).

Peters, Christine, *Patterns of Piety: Women, Gender, and Religion in Late Medieval and Reformation England* (Cambridge, 2003).

Prior, Mary (ed.), *Women in English Society, 1500–1800* (London and New York, 1985).

Richards, Judith M., '"To Promote a Woman to Beare Rule": Talking of Queens in Mid-Tudor England', *The Sixteenth Century Journal*, 28 (1) (1997): 101–21.

Shepard, Alexandra, *Meanings of Manhood in Early Modern England* (Oxford, 2003).

Shephard, Amanda, *Gender and Authority in Sixteenth-Century England: The Knox Debate* (Keele, 1994).

Stretton, Tim, *Women Waging Law in Elizabethan England* (Cambridge, 1998).

Walker, Garthine, *Crime, Gender and the Social Order in Early Modern England* (Cambridge, 2003).

NOTES

1 Information about Alice Barnham comes from Lena Cowen Orlin, *Locating Privacy in Tudor London* (Oxford, 2007). The author is extremely grateful to Lena Cowen Orlin for her kindness and scholarly generosity in providing chapters from this work prior to publication and to the Denver Art Museum for giving permission to reproduce Alice's portrait.

2 Lena Cowen Orlin (ed.), '"The Character of Sir Martin Barnham, Knight," by His Son Sir Francis Barnham', in James Dutcher and Anne Lake Prescott (eds.), *Renaissance Historicisms: Essays in Honor of Arthur F. Kinney* (Newark, Del., 2008), pp. 259–90, ll. 240–6. The memoir mistakenly refers to Sir John Ramsay, who was never Lord Mayor, instead of Sir Thomas; see p. 281, n. 27.

3 David Underdown, 'The Taming of the Scold: The Enforcement of Patriarchal Authority in Early Modern England', in Anthony Fletcher and John Stevenson (eds.), *Order and Disorder in Early Modern England* (Cambridge, 1985), pp. 116–136; and Susan D. Amussen, 'Gender, Family and the Social Order, 1560–1725', in Anthony Fletcher and John Stevenson (eds.), *Order and Disorder in Early Modern England* (Cambridge, 1985), pp. 196–217; Anthony Fletcher, *Gender, Sex and Subordination in England 1500–1800* (New Haven, Conn., 1995).

4 Amanda Shephard, *Gender and Authority in Sixteenth-Century England: The Knox Debate* (Keele, 1994).

5 Amy Louise Erickson, 'Coverture and Capitalism', *History Workshop Journal*, 59 (1) (2005): 1–16.

6 Laura Gowing, *Domestic Dangers: Women, Words, and Sex in Early Modern England* (Oxford, 1996), pp. 33–6.

7 Craig Muldrew, *The Economy of Obligation: The Culture of Credit and Social Relations in Early Modern England* (Basingstoke, 1998), p. 236.

8 Henry Smith, *A Preparative to Marriage* (London, 1591), as quoted in Shephard, *Gender and Authority*, p. 13.

9 As quoted in Patrick Collinson, 'The Role of Women in the English Reformation Illustrated by the Life and Friendships of Anne Locke', in *Godly People: Essays on English Protestantism and Puritanism* (London, 1983), pp. 273–87; p. 280.

10 Pamela Wright, 'A Change in Direction: The Ramifications of a Female Household, 1558–1603', in David Starkey (ed.), *The English Court: From the Wars of the Roses to the Civil War* (London and New York, 1987), pp. 147–72.

11 Bernard Capp, 'Separate Domains? Women and Authority in Early Modern England', in Paul Griffiths, Adam Fox and Steve Hindle (eds.), *The Experience of Authority in Early Modern England* (Basingstoke, 1996), pp. 117–45; p. 119.

CHAPTER TWENTY-ONE

FAMILY AND HOUSEHOLD

Alexandra Shepard

When Sir Thomas Smith wrote his account of the government of England whilst serving as Elizabeth I's ambassador in France, he included a description of 'an house or familie'. Smith defined his subject as 'the man, the woman, their children, their servauntes bonde and free, their cattell, their housholde stuffe, and all other things, which are reckoned in their possession, so long as all these remaine togeather in one'. The significance of this 'society' to Smith was as the first and 'most naturall' commonwealth that underpinned the wider political organisation of freemen.[1] It was a general assumption of his time that the household rather than the individual was the primary unit of society. As such the household was represented as a microcosm of good government and the fount of all order, organised along hierarchical principles that placed husbands above wives, parents over children and masters and mistresses in authority over servants. Smith's inclusion of cattle and other moveable goods, as well as his representation of the household as an 'oeconomy', requiring careful management as a producer and consumer of goods, also signalled its further primacy as an economic enterprise. The household's function as a unit of production and consumption shaped the nature and significance of 'familial' relations as much as the nurturing and socialising of children which we more readily associate with family life.

Smith's inclusion of a discussion of the household in his description of the workings of English government, as well as the complexity of his account, helps dispel at the outset certain myths about the Elizabethan family that often misinform assumptions about, and comparisons with, modern family life. First of all, the family was not considered a wholly private domain but was both analogous to the commonwealth and deemed critical to its smooth functioning. Second, large extended families were uncommon; it is not the case that the nuclear family was a recent invention. The household was ideally built around a married couple, their offspring and any servants, and so it rarely accommodated more than two generations. Although wider kinship ties could be important, it was first and foremost to these co-residents of a household that Elizabethans referred when they used the term 'family'. As a result of this inclusion of servants, familial ties involved more than marital alliances and biological bonds between parents and children. This was further complicated by the third key feature of sixteenth-century families and households: owing to high levels of mortality, households were made and remade with considerable frequency and did not always conform to the ideal. Remarriage was common, and much parenting was performed by single parents, step-parents and surrogates, creating shifting and complex webs of relationships which are often assumed to be unique to contemporary Western society as a result of high divorce rates.

It is partly because of these features that research into the character of family life in early modern England has generated such vigorous debate between historians. The principal subject of disagreement has been the emotional tenor of familial ties. According to a ground-breaking and highly influential study by Lawrence Stone, the Elizabethan family was governed by dynastic imperatives and was authoritarian in character. Amongst the propertied, marriage was approached in terms of transaction and alliance, and offspring remained emotionally peripheral even if strategically important. It was not until the eighteenth century, argued Stone, that the 'affective individualism' which we associate with companionate marriage and sentimentality towards children came to characterise a more enclosed nuclear family. This thesis prompted vigorous counter-claims that romantic love between spouses and deep-rooted parent–child bonds were in evidence both during and well before the Elizabethan period. The basis for such a wide spectrum of historical opinion is the difficulty of interpreting the evidence relating to people's *feelings* in the past. Instead of a quantitative change in levels of emotion over time, it is possible that Stone's evidence marked a qualitative shift in the terms of expression of familial love. Much of the source material documenting such relationships is restricted to elite social groups from which it would be unwise to generalise, and it is notoriously difficult to find and interpret direct evidence of children's experiences in the early modern past. It is also important to contextualise relationships within the customs and belief systems of the time rather than judging them anachronistically by today's standards or emphasising the timelessness of familial love.

A related subject of debate, growing out of more recent research into the history of women and gender relations, is the degree to which marriage constituted a battleground between the sexes. Was the founding bond of Elizabethan households one of oppressive subordination for women or did it entail a degree of parity or even rough and ready equality? Scholarship addressing this question has turned to a wider range of sources relating to a broader swathe of society (such as court records, wills, accounts and probate inventories) in order to recover the social practice of marriage and its basis as an economic partnership. This has avoided some of the pitfalls of approaching the history of the family principally in terms of emotional bonds, especially within an interpretative framework that assumes evolutionary progress towards modern sentiment, although it certainly has not generated consensus between historians about the levels of autonomy or constraint experienced by Elizabethan women within the context of marriage and the household.

Sir Thomas Smith's definition of family and household is a useful starting point for thinking about these issues since it is a reminder both that the relationships involved ranged beyond marital unions and parent–child ties, and that the household was much more than a site for the emotional enactment of these bonds. This chapter begins by exploring further the ways in which the Elizabethan household and the relationships it entailed were ideally represented and then investigates the ways in which its size and structure were shaped by the early modern demographic regime and the influence this had on the character of familial ties. The importance of the household as a unit of production will then be examined since imperatives for household management were inextricably bound up with its function as a self-sustaining economic enterprise.

A LITTLE COMMONWEALTH: THE IDEAL HOUSEHOLD

The family was idealised as the fount of stability and often imagined as a mini kingdom in its own right. As is the case today, it was the subject of a great deal of moralising, especially in religious discourse which promoted the good government of households as a key source and sign of godliness. It was a commonplace that order was principally invested in hierarchy in the Elizabethan world. According to the Homily on Obedience – one of the sermons which were preached regularly from parish pulpits by royal decree – the 'most excellent and perfect order' appointed by God rested in part on the hierarchies that placed husbands over wives, fathers over children and masters over servants. These relationships were analogous to the authority imbued in kings over their subjects, priests over the laity and rich over poor. The homily warned that chaos would ensue without due reverence to these hierarchies, in which

> no man shall ride or goe by the high way unrobbed, no man shall sleepe in his owne house or bedde unkilled, no man shall keepe his wife, children, and possession in quietnesse, all things shall bee common, and there must needes follow . . . [the] utter destruction both of soules, bodies, goodes, and common wealthes.[2]

The good government required to guard against such a nightmarish scenario, both within individual households and the wider polity, was 'patriarchal' in character. Literally meaning 'rule by fathers', patriarchy was the justification for the authority wielded both by kings over their subjects and by male household heads over their families. With divine roots in the power first conferred by God on Adam, the rights of fathers (and kings) to rule were deemed natural and therefore incontestable even if exercised unjustly. However, while privileging certain men on the grounds of gender, age and marital status, patriarchal theory did not advocate their unlimited authority over household subordinates. Alongside repeated injunctions against unruliness by wives, children and servants, advice on household government featured extensive warnings against tyrannical abuse in attempts to secure their obedience. This was a particular concern of Elizabethan marriage guidance, since the hierarchy separating husbands and wives was considered the narrowest of all household relations and therefore the hardest to gauge and the most easily overturned. The homily on matrimony, for example, exhorted wives to 'performe subjection' by obeying their husbands: the good wife was 'ready at hand at her husbands commandement, when she will apply her selfe to his will, when shee endevoureth her self to seeke his contentation, and to doe him pleasure'. The principal responsibility for marital harmony nonetheless rested with the husband who, while likened to a king in authority over a subordinate officer, was advised against dishonouring his status by denigrating his deputy. Husbands who believed it was 'a mans part to fume in anger, to fight with fist and staffe' would be rewarded with further discord; instead, the husband should aim to be 'the leader and authour of love, in cherishing and increasing concord' by exercising his authority in moderation.[3] According to Sir Thomas Smith, this resulted in an extremely delicate balance of power:

> God hath given to the man greater wit, bigger strength, and more courage to compell the woman to obey by reason or force, and to the woman bewtie, faire countenaunce, and sweete wordes to make the man to obey her againe for love. Thus ech obeyeth and commaundeth other, and they two togeather rule the house.[4]

Patriarchal privilege was also enshrined in the common-law doctrine of coverture, which merged the legal identity of married women with that of their husbands, endowing the latter with authority for both spouses and extensive property rights, although, as discussed by Tim Stretton above, there were various legal loopholes as well as everyday pragmatic concerns that limited the impact of coverture to a degree.

Even as ideally imagined, the patriarchal tenor of marital relations was further tempered by the acknowledgement that wives shared in the authority accorded to parents and to governors of servants. The fifth commandment, 'honour thy father and mother', was an oft-cited tenet that extended the imperative of a child's deference to both parents. Children were expected to comply with both parents' wishes and to express obedience with formal terms of address and subservient gestures such as serving food at the table and kneeling for a blessing. Parenthood was a source of pride and honour for mothers and fathers alike, albeit in different ways. Not least in the writings of men, motherhood was idealised as the epitome of womanhood, and selflessness in childbearing and child-rearing was eulogised as a primary source of female credit. And besides the more general associations between fatherhood and lineage, medical discourse linked paternity to male virility, especially when the offspring was male. According to domestic conduct writers (many of whom were clergy) fatherhood also imbued men with a pastoral authority and gave them responsibility for the spiritual instruction of their subordinates.

Although parenting involved a gendered division of labour, it was ideally imagined as a partnership between husband and wife. Primary responsibility for the care and socialisation of young children under the age of seven was considered the mother's domain, while arrangements for subsequent formal training or schooling were entrusted to fathers. The mother's experiences, dreams and imagination were deemed to have a powerfully formative effect on the developing foetus, and nurturing infants and children through their early years was not considered a trivial task. Husbands were expected to defer to the needs of their wives while pregnant and especially during the 'lying-in' period after childbirth. That this could place strain on the expected balance of power between spouses is suggested by humorous depictions of harassed husbands at the beck and call of confined wives and their female friends and neighbours or 'gossips' who tended them during and after the delivery of a baby. Elizabethan moralists acknowledged that wealthier women delegated the tasks of infant care to surrogates but were increasingly censorious of the custom of employing wet-nurses to feed their babies. Barthélemy Batt's *The Christian Mans Closet* urged mothers to nurse their own children because it was more 'natural' and better for the welfare of the child (fuelled by a mother's true love rather than a wet-nurse's greed for 'lucre'). The only exceptions were if the mother was diseased, weak or seeking to conceive another child.

Such advice is illustrative of the potential competition between conjugal duties and the demands of motherhood, since one of the reasons wealthier couples engaged wet-nurses was the expectation that breastfeeding mothers should abstain from sexual intercourse owing to the belief that semen spoiled their milk. It was also widely assumed that maternal authority was secondary to the ultimate sanction exercised by fathers on the grounds that men were deemed both more rational than women and less prone to cosset or over-indulge their offspring. Patriarchal privilege also conferred extensive legal rights to fathers which could work to disempower mothers in two ways. In cases of marital breakdown where child custody was in dispute, the patrilineal claims of fathers were privileged above the desires of mothers to remain with their children. When the paternity of a child carried by an unmarried women was in question, however, putative fathers had considerable latitude to disavow responsibility since the authorities were reluctant to proceed punitively on the basis of the mother's word alone. This is a reminder that the authority associated with parenthood for both men and women was very firmly tied to the marital bond as the primary link underpinning family life, household formation and patterns of inheritance. Offspring born out of wedlock were by contrast deemed a source of stigma for their parents, although the dishonour was likely to be more lasting in the mother's case than the father's.

Another aspect of household government shared by wives with their husbands was the management of servants and apprentices. Masters and mistresses were expected to act as surrogate parents to any young people in service roles that they admitted to their families for periods of time that could span anything from a few weeks to several years. As Paul Griffiths shows in a later chapter, the household was the primary training ground for children and youths in the principles of orderly behaviour and in the practical skills required to make a living. As such it was represented as critical to both the socialisation and containment of young people – much more so than formal schooling, which, although expanding during this period, was undertaken only by a minority. It was a widespread belief that children and youths were inherently sinful and needed careful 'bridling'. Puritan advice books in particular emphasised the vulnerability of the young to the orchestrations of the Devil. John Dod and Robert Cleaver's *A Godly Form of Household Government,* one of the most widely published domestic manuals of its time, warned that children were 'altogether inclind to evill'. The manual went on to caution household governors that unless a child was sufficiently disciplined, beginning with a process referred to as 'breaking its will' in its early years, it would become evermore 'proude, froward, wilfull, unrulie, and disobedient' until utterly overcome with vice.[5] Images of riotous youth were further reinforced by medical theories based on the four humours which constructed childhood and adolescence as phases of bodily chaos and imbalance. Young people's intemperance was attributed to a surfeit of heat and moisture in their physical make-up (outweighing the balancing influence of coldness and dryness) which rendered them unable to control their passions and unruly impulses. The solution, both to the temptations of the Devil and the physiological mayhem associated with youth, was the administration of strict discipline, exercised by force if necessary. A commonplace expression cautioned that to 'spare the rod' was to 'spoil the child', and this logic was extended to the discipline of servants and apprentices as well as their own children by household governors.

As idealised, therefore, the household represented the linchpin of an orderly society. The male household head was placed at the pinnacle of its hierarchical structure as principal ruler, estate manager, teacher and spiritual guide. While portrayed in a subordinate role, wives as deputies and partners to their husbands shared in some of the status and authority associated with domestic management in its widest sense as outlined by Sir Thomas Smith. Although disadvantaged by the gender hierarchy in relation to men and the constraints of coverture, wives were nonetheless privileged by their marital status which in many ways left them better placed than their unmarried or widowed counterparts. This was acknowledged in the importance attached to motherhood (within wedlock), the authority of mistresses over their servants and apprentices and the wider credit attributed to wives as 'honest matrons' and guardians of household and community morality. It also surfaced in the ambivalence expressed by conduct writers over the extent to which husbands should subject their wives to authoritarian rule. While physical discipline was advocated as a matter of course in the correction of unruly children and servants, wife-beating was often represented as defiling the conjugal bond and husbands were cautioned against inspiring hate rather than love and loyalty from their wives since the latter was deemed critical to the smooth functioning of the household. Although such sanctions were a long way from an ethos of companionate parity, they are a reminder of the ambiguities and tensions that arose from the commingling of authority and love in marital ideals, not least since husbands were also warned against falling victim to excessive passion for their wives which would, according to moralists, render them effeminate. The hierarchical structure expected to underpin household government was far from straightforward, involving interlocking and sometimes competing relations of power based on age and marital status as well as gender.

UNTIL DEATH DO US PART: HOUSEHOLD SIZE AND STRUCTURE

Households were not static entities. Their structure often departed from the ideal of a married couple ruling over their children and servants, across both the life cycle and the social spectrum. The persistent emphasis on the importance of well-ordered households was partly a response to their structural instability; by stressing the expected roles of different household members, moralists sidestepped the reality of a great deal of fluidity in family forms. Frequent divergence from the model was a product not only of social differences and life-cycle stages but also of a demographic regime that both limited opportunities for young people to form new households and regularly punctured their membership with high rates of mortality.

It was only with the advent of historical computing – enabling the systematic analysis of large amounts of data – that accurate assessments of the average size of households in the early modern past could be established by historians. A major finding of the 1970s was that the size of households remained remarkably constant from the Elizabethan period until the early twentieth century with a mean of between four and five members. This discovery was significant because it undermined the myth that the pre-industrial period in England was characterised by extended households, made up either of several generations of the same family or multiple households and characterised by their relatively large size. Instead, it was customary in Elizabethan times for a newly married couple to establish an independent household of their own. This had an enormous impact on the timing and negotiation of marriages, which was closely overseen not only by a couple's immediate family but also by the wider community. Critical to the decision-making process that preceded a betrothal was both the compatibility of the partners in the widest possible sense and their ability to support themselves and any offspring sufficiently and in keeping with their social station.

It might be assumed that by contrast to the dynastic constraints that dominated the matchmaking activities of landed families, people of more humble origins enjoyed greater freedom in their motives for marriage and choice of partner. However, this would oversimplify the many considerations that, to different degrees and in varying combinations, shaped courtship across the social spectrum. It is clear that political and financial concerns determined the marriage arrangements of the gentry, with large dowries sought for sons (especially the first-born) and landed prestige with favourable legal conditions desired for daughters to protect any assets they brought to the marriage. It was also generally conceded that, however great the potential alliance, young people should not be forced into a match that was abhorrent to them, just as they were not expected to contract themselves in marriage without parental consent. Compatibility of desire and temperament between partners was deemed as important as parity in status. So William Cecil's advice to his son warned not only against marrying a poor woman (however imbued with gentility) but also against any match that would inspire 'loathing' since a marriage choice was the basis of 'all thy furture good or ill'.[6]

Such concerns were not exclusive to the landed elite. Puritan advice books directed towards the middling ranks as well as the gentry, alongside popular ballads, cautioned against disparity between partners, whether of estate, affection, religious temperament, age or expectations, and emphasised the importance of companionship as the basis of a secure alliance. This was not at the expense of pragmatism, however. Marriage negotiations throughout the social scale involved close monitoring of the resources available to the couple to ensure that sufficient skill and property had been accumulated to support their independence. For the majority of the population this involved completing several years of training, either as servants in husbandry or apprentices in a craft or trade and gradually gathering at the very least enough moveable goods to establish an independent household. Owing to inflation in land prices and declining real wages, by the mid-sixteenth century those engaged in agricultural production (the vast majority) were dependent on some form of inheritance to secure the requisite land, livestock and household goods for self-sufficiency as smallholders if they were to avoid permanent dependence on wage labour. Given that the provision of such resources depended on the goodwill of parents, kin and often a wider network of 'friends' (in the sense of patrons such as godparents), marriage choices were subject to extensive scrutiny by interested parties who were concerned their investment was not squandered on an inappropriate match. In extreme cases, even the parish authorities could step in to prevent a marriage which was not deemed economically viable. While it is clear this could lead to conflict between individual desires and the perspective of family and friends, we should assume neither that such conflict was inevitable nor that financial security was an insignificant motive for parties seeking a spouse. In an unpredictable economic climate, with very little in the way of a safety net for struggling families with young mouths to feed, seeking a partner with the skills and resources to eke a sufficient living was as much an imperative for poorer couples as dynastic interests were to the rich. It should also be emphasised that this was of equal concern to men and women, since wives were expected to bring a 'portion' to marriage roughly comparable to that of their spouse in order to underpin the new household's material foundations. This established many marriages as economic partnerships from the outset, even if on wedlock the law of coverture transferred formal ownership of all moveable goods to the husband.

One of the principal consequences of the imperative of establishing an independent household on marriage was the delay of wedlock for the majority owing to the length of time it took for most couples to accrue the necessary resources. The mean age of first marriage in the later sixteenth century was roughly twenty-eight for men and twenty-six for women. Since marriage was in many ways the gateway to adulthood – as the precondition for managing a household, and so strongly associated with independence, self-sufficiency and the exercise of authority – the late age at which it was undertaken meant a prolonged period of youth that commonly extended well into the mid- to late twenties. Although there was some variation across the social scale in ages of first marriage – with earlier betrothals in particular for women from wealthier families – the overall effect of relatively late ages at marriage placed limits on reproductive capacity and average household size by reducing the number of women's childbearing years.

There was also a small but growing proportion of the population who never married, some because they were unable ever to gather sufficient resources and others because they did not find, or possibly wish for, a suitable spouse. Such lifelong singletons – especially those lacking in means – were actively discouraged from pursuing an independent living by expectations that they would be accommodated by relatives and by regulations that penalised single women below the age of forty and single men below the age of twenty-five for being 'at their own hand' rather than in service to an established household. Many endured a succession of service roles, while a few joined the marginal ranks of the vagrant population so feared by the Elizabethan authorities.

Further limits on marital fertility were imposed by a pattern of relatively long intervals between births. Given the absence of reliable contraception, it is likely that lengthy periods of breast-feeding restricted conception, both because of its role in suppressing ovulation and also because of the taboo proscribing sexual activity for breast-feeding women. It is also possible that couples took steps to limit their fertility once several children had survived well beyond infancy, if not before. Although evidence of Elizabethan reproductive practices is extremely scarce, it is likely that methods undertaken to limit the number of mouths to feed ranged from sexual abstinence and coitus interruptus to active attempts to terminate pregnancies during the early stages using herbal abortificants. Despite the existence of such strategies, married women might nonetheless expect to bear a child every two to three years during their fertile years.

Family size was also determined by the low life expectancy that was characteristic of the period. Life expectancy at birth barely exceeded forty in England during Elizabeth's reign. High levels of child mortality meant that around one in four children did not survive to the age of ten, with more than one in eight dying during their infancy. Debates between historians over levels of 'affect' in the early modern past have dwelt on the impact of such rates of child mortality on parental sentiment, with one line of argument suggesting that the high risk of infant death made parents resist close attachment. It might equally be argued that it stimulated greater love, given that the duration of the relationship could not be taken for granted. Although some parents gave the same name to subsequent siblings of a dead child – a practice that has been cited as evidence of a lack of concern for children as individuals – it is also clear from funerary monuments that deceased offspring were included in familial commemoration suggesting that their memory could remain significant for decades. The monument erected to commemorate the lawyer Robert Keilway (d. 1580), for example, featured an effigy of his grandson, who had died in 1570 aged 21 weeks, lying alongside Keilway. The monument was commissioned by his daughter Anne and her husband John Harrington, who are depicted along with their surviving daughter kneeling beside the effigies of Anne's father and their son (see Figures 21.1 and 21.2).

Such representations are reminders of the hardships associated with establishing the next generation as well as the difficulties of achieving an optimal family size, which, for many, had to be balanced against the insecurities stemming from economic uncertainty. It is probably pointless to treat the routine deaths of children as litmus tests for the presence or absence of parental feeling (which besides being very difficult to document also defies generalisation); what can be clearly observed, however, is the regularity with which family life was splintered by mortality, rendering a couple's childrearing years highly unpredictable as well as physically and emotionally demanding, besides limiting the number of children resident in the average household.

The mean household size of 4.75 members obscures the level of variation in both size and structure across the social spectrum, which was more marked than differences in age at first marriage and marital fertility. Extensive disparities in household size were often dictated by the number of servants rather than of the children contained within them. Aristocratic households employed tens, if not hundreds, of servants, set to a multitude of tasks, ranging from stable hands to estate managers. By contrast, membership of the poorest households could be limited to a mere two or three people, perhaps combining a parent and children or a widow and her lodger, but unlikely to include any servants at all. Such differences are clear

Figure 21.1 Monument to Robert Keilway and the Harrington family, Exton Parish Church, Leicestershire. © Courtauld Institute of Art.

Figure 21.2 Effigy of the infant Keilway Harrington, detail from Monument to Robert Keilway and the Harrington family, Exton Parish Church, Leicestershire. © Courtauld Institute of Art.

in a rare snapshot of the Middlesex village of Ealing captured in a census of its eighty-five households taken in 1599. The largest household (besides a school which boarded nineteen scholars) belonged to the gentleman Edward Vaughan and his wife Elizabeth and contained twenty-one members. Vaughan was a justice of the peace and an Exchequer official and by far the most influential Ealing resident. Besides his wife's 'waiting gentlewoman', their household included seven additional maidservants, one of whom was Elizabeth Vaughan's niece and another an eight-year-old orphan 'by them kept of charity'. They were supplemented by a butler, a cook, a coachman, a gardener, three servants in husbandry and four clerks. The Vaughans appear to have had no children of their own. At the other end of the social spectrum was the household of 'Collynns widow', aged forty-five, who lived on her own.[7] There were five other single-person households and an additional twelve households comprising just two members associated through a variety of relationships, ranging from a poor woman and her four-year-old child to an elderly husbandman and his adult son, and a widow and her maidservant.

All of these households represented a considerable departure from the ideal of a conjugal pair flanked by children and one or two servants. Of the entire village, not quite a fifth of Ealing families comprised all three elements. Only two-thirds of households were headed by a married couple, and roughly two-thirds included children. More than half of the households that were governed by only one adult were headed by women. Roughly one in every eight households in Ealing was presided over by a woman. Although the female-headed households tended to be smaller than average and therefore more marginal, some of the authority associated with household government accrued to these women alongside the responsibility for maintaining themselves and any dependants.

Just over a third of the households in Ealing included servants. In Elizabethan society, the majority of service roles were performed by young people as part of a life-cycle phase during which they lived in their employers' households and worked in return for bed, board, clothes and a small cash wage in order to acquire the requisite skills and some of the resources for their future independence. Depending on their age, and the size and scale of the household economy in which they were employed, servants could be expected to perform a wide range of menial tasks or might have undergone training in more specialised roles such as dairying in the case of girls or shepherding, hedging, ditching, furze-making or brick-burning in the case of boys. Lengthier and more formalised training was received by those young people serving apprenticeships which bound them to a master or mistress for a minimum of seven years and often a good deal longer. In most cases these positions came at a premium in return for food, lodging, clothes and, most importantly, instruction in a craft or trade that ultimately earned the apprentice the right to practise it in his or her own right and the capacity to make an independent living. The presence and number of servants or apprentices in a household was dictated not only by wealth and social status but also by the number and ages of resident children in relation to the nature and scale of the domestic economy. Wealthier households, such as those overseen by yeomen farmers with a sizeable acreage, could afford both to employ more servants than their poorer counterparts and, increasingly, to formally educate their own offspring, thereby removing them from the labour pool during their youth. At the other end of the social spectrum, children from poorer families were likely to be sent into service at far earlier ages as well as for longer stretches of their youth. Pauper apprentices – children removed from their families of origin and placed in other households by parish authorities – were often as young as six or seven.

The effect of all this was the regular traffic of children and young people between households, either through necessity or aspiration, for periods ranging from as little as a few weeks to the several years stretching between childhood and adulthood. Mary Rolfe, for example, when appearing as a witness before the church courts, declared that she had been a domestic servant to John Bowle of Warehorne in Kent for nine months since May 1597. Before that she had served with Mr Tanner of the same parish for a total of three and a quarter years, interspersed with a stretch of one year as a servant in the nearby parish of Newchurch. Prior to this she had lived in three other neighbouring parishes, including Woodchurch where she had been born. It is clear that she had been in service with at least three employers for a minimum of five years and possibly longer if her year in Saint Mary in the Marsh and another year preceding it in Warehorne were also spent in service, which, in that case, would have begun when she was aged fourteen. As in this case, the migration of young people between households, while frequent, involved relatively small distances. The exception to this rule was London, which drew teenagers from across the kingdom into domestic service to the extent that as many as one in eight Elizabethans who survived beyond childhood may have been temporarily absorbed into London households at some point in their lives.

Such comings and goings were often mediated by friends and kin, and it was not unusual for servants to be related in some way to their employers or at least well known to them. This could have assuaged some of the tensions that inevitably arose between household governors and their servants which received vivid elaboration in contemporary commentary. Servants were vilified in the rogue literature that flourished during the later sixteenth century which represented them as idle, pilfering, amorous, distrustful, disrespectful and disorderly. *The Fraternity of Vagabonds* included caricatures of twenty-five 'knaves', most of whom were servants, such as 'Chafe-Litter' who 'will pluck up the feather-bed or mattress, and piss in the bedstraw, and will never rise uncalled' and who cleans his shoes with his master's coverlet or curtains.[8] Domestic conduct books were also full of warnings to household heads about the potential threats posed by the servants they housed. The disciplinary records of towns and counties include plenty of real-life illustrations of these sorts of disorder. A London clothworker's apprentice, for example, was publicly whipped in 1580 for violence and slanderous words against his master and mistress, calling the latter a 'barren scolde whore', with 'divers other undecent and uncomelie speeches not to be suffred in any Apprentice or servaunte'.[9] Other common offences included theft, staying out of doors at night and running away. That servants ran away from their masters is also indicative of their vulnerability to abuse; the causes of friction in master–servant relations were far from one-sided. Servants and apprentices could be exposed to violent and sexual abuse from which they had very little protection. Household heads were expected to wield discipline over their subordinates, with only very extreme cases of abuse likely to provoke external intervention. Young women were additionally vulnerable to the sexual advances of masters, since they enjoyed little privacy or bodily autonomy in positions of service, often sleeping in the same room, if not the same bed, as their employers. In over two-fifths of cases of illegitimacy investigated by the London Bridewell and the Norwich mayoralty courts, the women involved accused their master or a close relative of his of paternity. While some of these unions may have been consensual, possibly fuelled by fantasies on the servant's part that she might one day supplant her mistress, it is clear that many had resulted from the unwelcome abuse of power. Alongside such cases, however, must be placed the many mundane examples of close bonds that could develop between servants and their employers (as well as between fellow servants) born of mutual respect and affection. These were evident in the bequests servants left to their master, mistress or their children and in the gifts of cash or clothing bestowed by employers who might also act on behalf of their servants to secure favourable marriage negotiations.

A key factor governing the timing of entry into service and its duration was the high level of mortality that, besides culling infants, functioned repeatedly to fracture the composition of households, often dramatically altering the prospects of the remaining members. Childbirth itself was a risky affair, with over 1 per cent of births resulting in maternal mortality. The death of one or both household governors had the severest consequences on the remaining dependants, especially their offspring. In the Sussex port of Rye between 1553 and 1604, barely one in four fathers survived to see any of their children reach adulthood, and nearly one in three died leaving all his children under the age of fourteen. The impact of a father's death on his surviving children could be enormous, and it often precipitated entry into care or service sometimes after an abrupt termination of schooling owing to the lack of funds. Entry into service and apprenticeship was often attendant upon the death of one or both parents rather than the coming of age. Thus, in 1611, Fraunces Goosey (aged ten) and Amy Goosey (aged four), daughters of the lately deceased Thomas Goosey, and 'havinge noe meanes or friends' to maintain them, were bound as apprentices to a victualler and a serge weaver respectively in Southampton.[10]

Low life expectancy during the Elizabethan period also resulted in high levels of remarriage. In Tudor Rye, the average first marriage lasted just over thirteen years before being cut short by the death of one spouse. Of all the weddings in the sixteenth century, roughly one-third involved remarriage for one or both partners. It appears that widowers remarried more quickly and readily than widows, which further illustrates the indispensability of wives to the successful management of households. Younger widows, possibly needing support for small children, were more likely to remarry than their older counterparts, whereas remarriage was one of the expedients favoured by elderly men seeking support in their dotage as well by as widowers with minors requiring care. Despite popular caricatures of the lusty widow, represented as an advantageous catch for young apprentices looking to establish themselves in a craft or trade by stepping into the shoes of their deceased master, women left alone were less hasty than men in considering matrimony for a second time possibly owing to desires to protect either their children's inheritance or their own independence from the restrictions of coverture. In addition to the flow of young people between families, therefore, households were frequently remade following the death of a spouse and remarriage of the surviving partner, creating multifarious relationships between parents, children, step-parents, stepchildren and half- and step-siblings.

The size and structure of Elizabethan households and the experiences of their members were shaped by the life course, the social status of their governors and the resources available to them and the ravages of death alongside regular cycles of birth and marriage. The relatively small average of between four and five people per unit obscures both the degree of variation in household forms and the fluidity of their membership. Each household was somewhat insecurely founded upon a constantly evolving web of relationships that extended well beyond a conjugal pair and their offspring. Servants came and went with the greatest regularity, often in conjunction with an annual hiring cycle, although this did not prevent some from forming long-term bonds with their employers. Apprentices were contracted to serve longer periods of time and, provided mortality did not intervene, spent a greater proportion of their childhood and youth with their master and mistress than with their parents and may have enjoyed closer proximity to their employer than some of his or her own children during this time. Although Elizabethan society was youth-heavy, the ranks of children were regularly depleted by mortality, making the establishment of the next generation within any household an unpredictable and demanding endeavour to be balanced against the resources available for its support. The fortunes of remaining children were heavily dependent on the survival of their parents, and in the event of the death of one or both parents became more precariously balanced in the hands of wider kin, friends, or (in the last resort) the parish authorities. Families were made and remade alongside marriages and re-marriages which, besides the traffic of young people between households, meant that a great deal of the authority associated with parenthood was distributed beyond those linked by direct biological bonds. This both mitigated the effects of the patriarchal character of family life, for example by conferring authority and independence on wives and widows, and contributed to the imperative to idealise the roles household governors were expected to undertake since the social and political stability associated with well-ordered households was not matched by stability in their personnel.

THE HOUSEHOLD ECONOMY

The Elizabethan household was, importantly, a unit of production and consumption besides being a site for the reproduction and socialisation of children and young people. Each household was an economic enterprise in which all of its members were expected to invest their labour to varying degrees according to age, gender and station. The scale of the enterprise, like household size, varied considerably according to wealth and social status and the types of production in which households were engaged. The principal goal of most households was self-sufficiency: an attribute that had moral overtones through its association with independence and 'honesty'. For the majority this was predicated on the quest for basic survival, while for the better placed it also involved the attainment of a standard of living appropriate to their status, as manifested by consumption patterns and the level of investment available for future generations. Household production was therefore directed more towards maintenance than profit in a society in which the majority were primarily focused on subsistence rather than commercial gain. 'Oeconomy' involved the close monitoring of the flow of resources in and out of the household, the careful organisation of labour and the protection of a household's 'credit' linked in the broadest possible terms to its reputation for honesty.

A key divide in early modern society existed between households which were in a position to produce a surplus for market and those vulnerable to market dependence for basic provisions, necessitating wage labour. In this primarily agricultural society, a household was ideally expected to be self-sustaining, producing enough to support its members, to pay any rent, dues and taxes, to reserve the following year's seed and raw materials and, whenever possible, to make provision for the future independence of children by way of indentures, schooling or early inheritance in the form of dowries or 'portions'. This required the careful balancing of resources and labour, juggling production for home consumption with production for exchange and, in some cases, work for wages. Women's work spinning yarn, for example, might be directed towards providing their families with basic clothing, by-passing the market for these goods, or it might be used to generate an income stream as piecework, depending on the balance of needs and market conditions. During a time of rapid inflation alongside several major harvest failures in the 1590s there was a great deal of pressure and unpredictability for households on the margins of subsistence which meant that increasing numbers were forced to turn to wage labour to supply their families' needs. Work for wages, unlike service, was often seasonal and therefore far from reliable as a source of income, poorly paid and undertaken as a last resort. (With longer-term contracts and at least part of their remuneration in kind in the way of bed, board and clothing servants were more cushioned than labourers against the impact of inflation.) As prices soared and cash wages declined in real terms, a far greater input was required to make good any shortfall in a household's subsistence which for growing numbers precipitated long-term dependence on wage labour alongside the gradual decimation of a small holding.

For the majority, provisioning the household was a collective task requiring the adaptability and resourcefulness of all its members with any productive capacity. Where both partners survived, household economy was very much a joint venture to which the contribution of each spouse was vital. While this involved the gendered division of labour between husband and wife, there was also considerable overlap in the tasks they performed and little room for hierarchical privilege. Besides the reproductive labour of regular pregnancies and the accompanying demands of childcare, married women provided for their families in myriad ways. In larger households, wives oversaw and undertook home-brewing and baking, and many women were responsible for the production of poultry and pigs and for dairying activities whether in relation to a large herd or a single cow. The labours of food storage and preparation fell to women, and the making and mending of clothes and linen (often with homespun yarn). In rural areas, the task of weeding crops was often undertaken by wives, as well as planting and growing herbs and vegetables. Their fuel gathering provided heat and light for their homes, and the corn that many of them gleaned after the harvest was an essential supplement to the stock required to see through the winter. In coastal areas they collected cockles, mussels and samphire to supplement the wildfowl and fish caught by their husbands. All of this limited recourse to the market for essentials, and in the cases when a surplus was available for sale, it was usually married women who took it to market.

Some wives also undertook wage labour, especially during the busiest periods of the agricultural year; some carded, spun and knit, while others performed service roles such as laundering or tending to the sick of their parish in return for small cash sums.

Agricultural work and wage labour tended to keep spouses apart for much of the working day, although husbands could occasionally be glimpsed offering temporary help with a range of domestic tasks. Households dependent on a craft or trade for the bulk of their maintenance often relied upon the greater proximity of husbands and wives, and it is likely there was more overlap in the tasks they performed given the propensity of many widows of craftsmen to take over their late husband's trade without having received any formal training. Husbands as well as wives performed multiple and varied tasks, often turning to a range of by-employments that could generate extra revenue and minimise the risk of depending too heavily on a single source of income.

Servants supplied the labour needs of a significant minority of households, with arduous hours and little formal regulation of their working conditions. Servants contributed between one-third and one-half of all hired agricultural labour and were ubiquitous in towns and cities. In the Essex town of Romford in the 1560s, for example, servants and apprentices made up around one-fifth of the population. Depending on their age and experience, and the size of the household in which they were employed, servants ranged from higher status specialists to menial drudges of all work solely at the beck and call of a master or mistress. Servants were critical to the productivity of their households, either through their direct industry or by taking on the burden of domestic tasks such as cooking, cleaning, washing and childcare, thereby enabling the productive capacity of others. In elite households, by contrast, servants performed such tasks principally to facilitate the leisure and display of their employers, contributing to the cultural capital of the gentry as well as the maintenance of their estates.

Children were also required to shoulder some of the burden of provisioning their households, although child labour was rarely intensive. A survey of late-medieval coroners' inquests detailing the circumstances of children's accidental death shows that until the age of seven or eight most could be glimpsed accompanying a parent at work rather than working themselves. After this age, however, they began to contribute to the household economy by helping with the harvest, gleaning, weeding, gathering fuel, fetching water, herding cattle and sheep, running errands and minding younger children. It was often at this stage that children were taken out of school; the cost of formal education after this point was twofold since in addition to tuition fees the household was denied a child's productive contribution. In poorer households children might have undertaken piecework such as spinning, weaving, knitting or making lace or buttons, and in extreme circumstances they generated the bulk of a household's income in this way. A census taken of the poor families of Norwich listed children as young as five undertaking such tasks. One William Harison, aged sixty and 'not hable to worke for that his rybes be broken', appeared to be solely supported by his eight-year-old daughter's industry spinning white warp.[11]

In most cases, the productive activities of all but the youngest members of each household, therefore, were critical to its maintenance. The economic security of a household was also more broadly bound up with its reputation for honesty, and the general conduct of its members was as important as their industry. Since the vast bulk of exchange was conducted on trust, the reputation of a household could affect its credit and the terms on which others might be willing to trade with it. This extended well beyond a household's reliability in paying outstanding debts and involved the general assessment of its members' moral probity and the degree to which the household was well governed. A householder's reputation for 'cosening' or cheating, hard dealing, or poor-quality produce would discourage others from exchange, while a reputation for indebtedness, spendthriftiness, drunkenness, idleness or an otherwise disordered household would deter others from extending credit. Household order was gauged with reference to sexual as well as economic reputations, with the unchastity of women deemed a particular symptom of disarray. As John Dod and Robert Cleaver emphasised in their guide to household government, 'as the provision of [the] houshould dependeth onely on the Husband: even so the honour of all dependeth onely on the woman.'[12] While this was a gross overstatement of the gendered division of labour both in provisioning the household and preserving its reputation, it helps to explain the dramatic rise in slander litigation initiated by married women against accusations of adultery and sexual incontinence at a time when households were becoming more mutually dependent on good credit relations. Not only was their own reputation at stake but so too was the economic well-being of their household. So Margaret Wilkinson, suing Agnes Shaw in 1599 for having called her a whore and a bawd, declared before the Vice-Chancellor's court in Cambridge that she would rather have lost £20 than suffered such a blow to her good name, while Thomas Reddit complained in the same court that his wife had lost a good deal of her laundering work as a result of rumours that he kept a bawdy house. A household's credit was nonetheless also vested in its ability to pay any outstanding debts, assessed in relation to its reputation for solvency, prompt payment and an appraisal of its stock of goods. Part of the social evaluation of households involved the calculation of their material worth on the basis of cattle, crops, tools, raw materials and the range of other moveable goods which were bracketed together as household 'stuff', including utensils, linens, beds and other furniture. The decision to extend credit to a household lacking such assets was an act of charity that was also often conditional on the behaviour of its members being judged honest.

Household 'oeconomy' was therefore inextricably bound up with household government and the good order derived from adherence to domestic duties by husbands and wives, servants and children. On the one hand, maintaining the family in most cases had to be a dual enterprise undertaken by both spouses if it was to be sufficiently accomplished, creating ties of mutual dependence that counteracted the hierarchical model of marriage. On the other hand, men tended to be credited with the task of provisioning their households while women's work often went unacknowledged, and, as the legal owners of all the goods jointly brought to a marriage (in the absence of a prenuptial settlement), husbands wielded ultimate authority over the distribution of household resources and the decision-making processes required to protect them. This could leave wives and any other dependants in a very vulnerable position, as frequently depicted by ballads and tracts bemoaning the excesses of tippling, gambling and tobacco smoking amongst householders who enjoyed the delights of the alehouse more than the labours of the field (see Figure

21.3). The economic well-being of many households also depended upon the labours of children and servants to varying degrees, founded upon the principles of deference and of life-cycle service that, especially in the latter case, provided for and contained young people in the lengthy wait before marriage. The honesty of all, in the broadest possible sense, was critical to the economic stability of households as well as the good order deemed necessary for a stable commonwealth.

Figure 21.3 Woodcut depicting a family alarmed by a pipe-smoking father, illustrating the ballad 'A Penny-worth of Good Counsell' which was directed to widows and maids as a warning to 'looke before they leape' into marriage. Image courtesy Mary Evans Picture Library.

FURTHER READING

Ågren, Maria and Amy Louise Erickson (eds.), *The Marital Economy in Scandinavia and Britain, 1400–1900* (Aldershot, 2005).

Amussen, Susan Dwyer, *An Ordered Society: Gender and Class in Early Modern England* (Oxford, 1988).

Anderson, Michael, *Approaches to the History of the Western Family, 1500–1914* (London, 1980).

Berry, Helen, and Foyster, Elizabeth (eds.), *The Family in Early Modern England* (Cambridge, 2007).

Capp, Bernard, *When Gossips Meet: Women, Family, and Neighbourhood in Early Modern England* (Oxford, 2003).

Coster, Will, *Family and Kinship in England 1450–1800* (Harlow, 2001).

Crawford, Patricia, *Blood, Bodies and Families in Early Modern England* (Harlow, 2004).

—— *Parents of Poor Children in England, 1580–1800* (Oxford 2010).

Cressy, David, *Birth, Marriage and Death: Ritual, Religion and the Life-Cycle in Tudor and Stuart England* (Oxford, 1997).

Cunningham, Hugh, *Children and Childhood in Western Society since 1500* (Harlow, 1995).

Erickson, Amy Louise, *Women and Property in Early Modern England* (London and New York, 1993).

Fildes, Valerie (ed.), *Women as Mothers in Pre-Industrial England: Essays in Memory of Dorothy McLaren* (London, 1990).

Flather, Amanda, *Gender and Space in Early Modern England* (Woodbridge, 2007).

Foyster, Elizabeth A., *Manhood in Early Modern England: Honour, Sex and Marriage* (Harlow, 1999).

Gowing, Laura, *Domestic Dangers: Women, Words, and Sex in Early Modern London* (Oxford, 1996).

Houlbrooke, Ralph A., *The English Family, 1450–1700* (London, 1984).

Ingram, Martin, *Church Courts, Sex and Marriage in England, 1570–1640* (Cambridge, 1987).

Kussmaul, Ann, *Servants in Husbandry in Early Modern England* (Cambridge, 1981).

Laslett, Peter, and Wall, Richard (eds.), *Household and Family in Past Time* (Cambridge, 1972).

MacFarlane, Alan, *Marriage and Love in England: Modes of Reproduction 1300–1840* (Oxford, 1986).

Mayhew, Graham, 'Life-Cycle Service and the Family Unit in Early Modern Rye', *Continuity and Change*, 6 (2) (1991): 201–26.

O'Hara, Diana, *Courtship and Constraint: Rethinking the Making of Marriage in Tudor England* (Manchester, 2000).

Outhwaite, R. B. (ed.), *Marriage and Society: Studies in the Social History of Marriage* (London, 1981).

Overton, Mark, Whittle, Jane, Dean, Darron and Hann, Andrew, *Production and Consumption in English Households, 1600–1750* (London and New York, 2004).

Pollock, Linda A., *Forgotten Children: Parent–Child Relations from 1500–1900* (Cambridge, 1983).

Shepard, Alexandra, *Meanings of Manhood in Early Modern England* (Oxford, 2003).

Stone, Lawrence, *The Family, Sex and Marriage in England, 1500–1800* (London, 1977).

Wrightson, Keith, 'The Family in Early Modern England: Continuity and Change', in Stephen Taylor, Richard Connors and Clyve Jones (eds.), *Hanoverian Britain and Empire: Essays in Memory of Philip Lawson* (Woodbridge, 1998), pp. 1–22.

Wrigley, E. A., and Schofield, R. S., *The Population History of England, 1541–1871: A Reconstruction* (Cambridge, 1981).

NOTES

1 Sir Thomas Smith, *De Republica Anglorum*, ed. Mary Dewar (Cambridge, 1982), pp. 58–9.

2 Thomas Cranmer, *Certain Sermones, or Homelies, Appoincted by the Kynges Maiestie, to Bee Declared and Read, by All Persones, Vicars, or Curates, Every Sondaie in Their Churches, Where Thei Have Cure* (London, 1551), sig. R. iiir–v.

3 *The Second Tome of Such Matters as Were Promised, and Entituled in the Former Part of Homilies. Set Out by the Authority of the Late Queenes Majestie: and to Be Read in Every Parish Church Agreeablie* (London, 1623), pp. 239–48.

4 Smith, *De Republica Anglorum*, p. 59.

5 John Dod and Robert Cleaver, *A Godlie Forme of Householde Government for the Ordering of Private Families, According to the Direction of Gods Word* (London, 1598), p. 294.

6 William Cecil, *The Counsell of a Father to His Sonne, in Ten Severall Precepts, Left as a Legacy at His Death* (London, 1617).
7 K. J. Allison, 'An Elizabethan Village "Census"', *Bulletin of the Institute of Historical Research*, 36 (93) (1963): 91–103.
8 Gāmini Salgādo, *Cony Catchers and Bawdy Baskets: An Anthology of Elizabethan Low Life* (Harmondsworth, 1972), p. 73.
9 Clothworkers' Hall, London, Court Orders 1558–81, fol. 245.
10 J. W. Horrocks (ed.), *The Assembly Books of Southampton*, 4 vols. (Southampton, 1924), vol. III, p. 10.
11 John F. Pound (ed.), *The Norwich Census of the Poor* (Norwich, 1971), p. 26.
12 Dod and Cleaver, *A Godlie Forme of Householde Government*, p. 171.

CHAPTER TWENTY-TWO

REBELLION AND DISORDER

K. J. Kesselring

Studies of rebellion, crime and disorder can expose the anxieties and actions of people at all levels of society. As such, these subjects have received attention from a wide range of social, political and legal historians. An early generation of social historians looked at the records of crime and the courts to examine the experiences of those men and women long left out of the historical record. These scholars valued riots and rebellions as moments when popular beliefs, norms and needs erupted from beneath the usual habits of deference. Their efforts reinvigorated and reshaped long established legal and political histories of the early modern period, for the records of riot, crime and disorder say much of the priorities of the politically powerful, too. Indeed, what counted as a crime or a riotous assembly in any given instance depended much on the definitions solidified in statute or constructed by the courts; what the authorities deemed 'disorder' might sometimes more objectively be seen as 'conflict'. Thus, much recent work on crime and rebellion has focused on the ways in which authority was constructed, experienced and challenged in interactions between governors and governed, on the nature of the relationships between rulers and ruled rather than the experiences of one group or the other.

Because of the nature of the questions that long underpinned studies of disorder, such histories are rarely segmented by reigns and are more often demarcated by dates of demographic or economic import. Yet, the Elizabethan period warrants a survey specific to itself, if for no other reason than to query its usual portrayal as a golden age of stability. In Queen Elizabeth's reign, rebellions of the medieval sort were left behind, and the disorders of the Continental wars of religion remained in the distance. The turmoils that plagued the earlier Tudors came to an end, while those of the Stuarts had yet to begin. By some measures, then, these were years of domestic peace. But these same years witnessed some of the highest murder and execution rates in recorded English history. A period of crisis in the criminal courts began in the 1580s which would stretch beyond Elizabeth's reign into the late 1620s. Historians today disagree about whether crime and rebellion should be seen as points linked on a continuum of social conflict, but many Elizabethans believed these links to be evident. For them, an evaluation of crime and rebellion as separate features of their world made little sense. And contemporaries were by no means so sanguine as historians in evaluating their world. Many an Elizabethan commoner located the golden age in the past, with longing or angry words of complaint. Their governors, in turn, feared the 'many-headed monster' of popular unrest and believed small crimes to be the seeds of serious tumults.

Elizabeth's Lord Keeper Nicholas Bacon regularly gathered justices before him in Star Chamber to exhort full implementation of the laws, even those against ostensibly petty offences. He warned that small sins left untreated inevitably ripened into greater crimes: 'from such roots, such plants, such plants, such fruits'. He urged that 'better it were for a man to be twice whipped than once hanged', appealing not for lighter penalties but for greater vigilance against the petty offender in order to prevent the slide to serious sins.[1] Conscientious justices of the peace (JPs) relayed this message to local juries. William Lambarde, for instance, repeatedly enjoined his presentment jurors to bring more offenders to the court's attention. Serious felonies represented only the top boughs of the 'tree of transgression': to kill the tree, the jurors had to 'hew in sunder the master roots and mores of idleness [and] unlawful games'.[2] Petty crimes and major conflicts thus existed on a continuum of disorder, the first leading inexorably to the second unless vigilantly policed.

Accordingly, vigilant policing along with violent repression became the order of the day. But repression alone did not suffice, and in early modern England, policing required broad participation. The expanding business of the criminal courts was a sign not just of heightened disorder but also of increased involvement in legal processes by the men of middling means who served as constables, jurors and agents of local government. The contrast between the abundance of criminal disorder and the scarcity of rebellion highlights important features of state formation in the Elizabethan period. Perceptions of a sufficiency of common interests and shared foes between the elites and enough of the people they governed helped Elizabeth's England navigate a period of economic and religious turmoil with little overt mass rebellion, leaving the desperate or disaffected with few options other than crime, complaint or compliance.

The contours of criminal and court activity are somewhat clearer in Elizabeth's reign than in those of her immediate predecessors, thanks to the survival of more records. The court of Queen's Bench, one of the three common-law courts at Westminster, was the superior court for criminal cases, but most trials for serious offences occurred in the counties under the justices of assize. With roots in the reign of Henry II, the assize system mandated six sets of two justices to travel on circuits about the country twice yearly, with special commissions that empowered them to hear and determine indictments brought before them and to clear the gaols of prisoners. Records of some such circuits survive sporadically from the Middle Ages, until about 1460. Only from 1559 onwards, and only from the five counties of the Home Circuit, do assize records from the Tudor period remain. A few pockets of quarter sessions records supplement these survivals. Quarter sessions, which had their beginnings in the fourteenth century, operated under the direction of local JPs and shared the trial of felonies with the assizes. Over the course of Elizabeth's reign, more and more of the business of trying serious felonies moved from the quarter sessions to the assizes, with violent and repeat offenders and legally complex cases more frequently heard at the latter. Whatever time local JPs might thereby have saved, however, was quickly consumed by the increasing number of minor offences coming before them. In some counties, justices held supplementary 'petty sessions' from the 1560s that became increasingly routine and occurred throughout the country by the 1630s; unfortunately, their records only survive in any significant number from about 1700. Boroughs and liberties had their own courts with criminal jurisdiction; while little work has yet been done with the borough courts' records, those from the palatine jurisdiction of Chester survive and have been used to supplement those of the Home Circuit assizes.

J. A. Sharpe and J. S. Cockburn have perhaps done the most to use these surviving records to chart broad patterns of continuity and change in the history of felony prosecution. Both are careful to stipulate what have now become standard warnings about the generation of statistics from past legal records; most particularly, they note that the 'dark figure' of unreported criminal behaviour means that quantification might well reflect changes in control more so than changes in levels of crime itself, a problem that may have been especially acute in a system largely dependent on unpaid amateur officials and the initiative of victims. Their studies and others have shown that despite earlier suppositions of a shift from offences against persons to offences against property (the supposed movement from *violence à vol* thought to mark the transition from medieval to modern), property offences predominated among prosecuted felonies at a rate of between two-thirds to three-quarters consistently throughout the early modern period. Next in order of frequency were homicides. Trials for rape, buggery, arson and even witchcraft were relatively rare. So too were prosecutions of female offenders; women accounted for only about 15 per cent of felony indictments in the Elizabethan years, and fewer of their number were convicted.

Such studies have also detected a dramatic rise in felony prosecutions dating from around 1580. In some areas and for some offences, prosecutions dipped slightly in the first years of the 1600s, only to climb again in the 1620s. Thereafter, felony prosecutions declined precipitously in the early 1640s with the onset of civil war but remained low even after the restoration of traditional court structures and personnel. While the beginning date of the upward movement in felony prosecutions remains imprecise because of the nature of the extant records, all studies show a significant increase from about 1580 to about 1630, at rates well above those explicable by increases in population, and at rates that would not be seen again. Executions followed a similar trajectory: an increase from the 1580s that spiked in the 1590s; a brief decline in the first years of the new century followed by a dramatic surge in the 1620s; a return to levels typical of the late sixteenth century over the 1630s; ending with a sharp decline to persistently lower numbers. As Sharpe notes by way of example, 'an average of twenty-six felons were executed each year by the Essex assizes between 1597 and 1603, a figure greater than the number executed on the whole of the Home Circuit in an average year in the mid-eighteenth century.'[3] The final years of Elizabeth's reign seem to have witnessed the highest numbers of hangings in any of the years for which we have records. Furthermore, the proportions of those tried for felony and subsequently executed increased in these years as well.

In discussing changing patterns of crime over time, scholars have paid particularly close attention to homicide rates. In part, the focus on homicide emerges from a belief that of all crimes it is the one most difficult to hide and most likely to be prosecuted consistently, thereby allowing a better sense of the crime itself rather than just patterns of control. The focus also comes from a sociological interest in homicide, and violence more generally, as a potential index of social stress or anomie. Lawrence Stone used previously published studies to suggest an overall downward trend in homicide from the fourteenth century, with one surge immediately before the Black Death and another in Elizabethan and Jacobean England, *c.* 1560–1620. Pointing to other indicators of social tension in these same years, such as higher rates of bastardy and denunciations for witchcraft, slander and sexual deviance, Stone saw these as:

> signs of a socio-cultural crisis in the village in the late sixteenth and early seventeenth centuries. This was probably brought on by a combination of socially unmanageable demographic growth, a collapse of cultural norms and controls in the wake of the Reformation, the spread of profit-oriented ideology, and a growing economic fissure between rich and poor.[4]

Stone's foray into criminal statistics earned reproofs from both Sharpe and Cockburn, the former pointing out that assessments of violence in a given society must consider how contemporaries perceived their situation and the latter refining Stone's numbers. Cockburn dismissed the medieval homicide ratios as fundamentally flawed because of insufficient knowledge of population numbers and focused his work on records from 1559 to 1971. He showed the real rise to be not from 1560, as Stone had said, but from the 1580s. In fact, that decade had the highest homicide rate of the entire 400-year period, at roughly six slayings per year per 100,000 people. The rate stayed above 5:100,000 for the remainder of Elizabeth's reign. Higher rates of felony prosecution (quite probably reflective of higher rates of criminal behaviour), higher proportions of guilty verdicts and executions, and the highest homicide rates in a 400-year period are hardly the stuff from which a reputation for an Elizabethan golden age can be built. Of course, much depends on one's vantage point. Homicide ratios of 6:100,000 look positively idyllic when compared to the rates for contemporary Italian and even French regions, which sometimes reached forty to sixty killings per 100,000 people. Furthermore, these same years of crisis, *c.* 1580–1630, also witnessed enough procedural, statutory and judicial innovation to prompt some legal historians to see these as years of laudable creativity. Under Elizabeth, the State grew ever more intrusive in its claims, regulating more and more actions under statute law and seeking ways to encourage prosecutions but also needing new means to deal with the increasing number of offences.

As Cockburn notes, the increase in the assizes' criminal business in Elizabeth's reign forced a number of changes to allow the ancient court to survive, most notably in respect to multiple arraignments and plea-bargaining. It had long been the custom that one jury heard several cases before offering its verdicts; Cockburn found that the number of prisoners tried before any given jury increased from 4.5 in the first years of Elizabeth's reign to a staggering 8.1 in the 1580s and would not fall below 6.6 for the remainder of the century. Such multiple arraignments undoubtedly helped the court speed its affairs along, but one wonders at what cost. Informal plea-bargaining also appeared, again in an attempt to expedite business in increasingly overburdened courts. Justices encouraged individuals to plead guilty to a lesser charge, exchanging charges of manslaughter for murder, or petty larceny for grand larceny, for example. Such plea-bargaining was almost unheard of before 1575, but thereafter increased steadily until it accounted for some 14 per cent of all pleas in the final years of the reign. Some 95 per cent of those who confessed to crimes post-1586 received punishments other than death in return for their compliance. Cockburn argues that such changes tipped the balance of power between judge and jury more firmly in favour of the former, resulting in a weakening of jury initiative that lasted until the 1650s. More importantly for present purposes, these changes also allowed the courts to hear more cases.

These years witnessed other changes, too, that built on previous Tudor initiatives but often in ways sufficiently distinctive to mark them as 'Elizabethan'. Benefit of clergy, the medieval privilege that allowed clerics to evade punishment from the royal courts, had become available to laymen who could feign clerical status by reading a passage of Scripture. Since the reign of Henry VII, it became increasingly secularised and limited to lesser felonies and to first-time offenders. In addition to tightening the restrictions, Elizabeth's parliaments severed the privilege's last ties to the ecclesiastical courts and allowed judges to order successful claimants to gaol for up to a year. Yet, even as parliament trimmed the list of offences to which benefit of clergy applied, justices encouraged its use by more and more convicts; whereas 9 per cent of Middlesex convicts used this means to evade the gallows in the 1550s, some 39 per cent did so in the 1590s. This extension helped authorities keep executions at broadly acceptable levels and helped encourage prosecutors who might not have thought a particular offender worthy of death.

So, too, did changes in pardoning practices. In what became known as 'circuit pardons', assize justices submitted lists of convicts they thought pardonable upon returning from the counties. In subsequent centuries, inclusion in a judge's list became the usual means of obtaining mercy; this practice had its tentative beginnings under Mary and became routine under Elizabeth. These circuit pardons allowed the Crown actively to seek out potential recipients for clemency in an attempt to control the number of executions, to ensure that poor and pitiable offenders did not figure too highly among the gallows fodder and to present the Crown as laudably merciful. In all, the patent rolls for Elizabeth's reign recorded some 1,730 individuals who escaped the noose thanks to a circuit pardon. Pardons conditional on transportation or military service, another staple of latter punitive options, also had their beginnings in Elizabethan initiatives. After several ad-hoc exchanges of mercy for service or exile, the Privy Council issued commissions in 1586 and 1602 to manage the process more effectively. Judicial opposition and an unwillingness to pay the attendant fees meant that conditional pardons did not become standard practice in the late sixteenth century, but their piecemeal implementation emerged from a sense that more flexible responses than death alone were necessary to encourage prosecutions and convictions. Plea-bargains, benefit of clergy and pardons – all ostensibly acts of mercy – allowed the courts to punish more people more effectively.

Perhaps the most frequently vilified agent of disorder and sign of troubled times, at least according to the well fed, was the vagrant. Earlier efforts to 'repress the sturdy beggar', to keep labourers in line and to feed the hungry enough to stave off desperation coalesced into two Elizabethan landmarks: the Statute of Artificers and the poor law. These were among the longest lived of Elizabethan statutes, shaping the experiences of much of the English population until the early 1800s. Both included penal sanctions to tame the disorderly. As Douglas Hay has noted, the law of master and servant encapsulated in the 1562 Statute of Artificers relied on a distinctive conjuncture of private contracts between employers and employees being enforced not by civil remedies but by magistrates' summary powers to impose fines, whipping and imprisonment. Justices' notebooks confirm the ready reliance upon such measures to compel labour and suppress wages. When such measures failed, the unemployed might find themselves subject to harsh vagrancy laws that stipulated yet more whippings and even death for repeat offences, or to the attentions of the poor-law officials. By the end of Elizabeth's reign, authorities recognised that not all the unemployed were unemployed by choice and that the stick of the vagrancy measures needed the carrot of relief for the humble poor.

Houses of correction supplemented these measures to deal with labour and relief. First seen with the Edwardian London Bridewell, such institutions appeared across the country in the last years of the century. Acts passed in 1576 and 1597 encouraged their foundation and use; by the turn of the century, at least a quarter of all counties had a minimum of one such reformatory. Intended to reform individuals through labour, these houses served as centres of both relief and punishment. They came to be used as dumping grounds for the idle, lewd and refractory, where 'vagabonds' and 'whores' were whipped and hopefully corrected. In the words of Paul Griffiths: 'petty crime was punished both quantitatively and qualitatively differently in the sixteenth century and after, and much of the energy and ingenuity in penal planning was at the point of first or minor offences, like vagrancy or small-scale theft.'[5] The bridewells, often seen as the precursors to modern penitentiaries, were focal points in this penal experimentation, a way to extend punitive measures to a broader range of offenders and increasingly important fixtures in the experiences of the early modern poor.

Contemporaries' discussions of these and other measures manifested concerns not just about petty pilfering but also about disorder becoming riotous or even rebellious. According to Bacon, the vagrant constituted not a minor annoyance but the 'seed of peril and tumult in a state'. While modern observers might see essential differences between crime and insurgency, Elizabethan authorities saw the difference as one merely of degree. Small sins soon became serious; once the shackles of subordination became loosened, they might easily be thrown off entirely. Sir John Smythe, for instance, warned Lord Burghley in 1590 that judges who failed to punish criminals risked rebellion on the order of the French jacquerie or Hungarian peasants' rebellion, for 'commonly the beginnings are very small and therefore lightly regarded, but once begun, they suddenly grow great, and then turn all to fire and blood'.[6] Some of the more distinctive developments of these years testify to this sense of encroaching danger and the perception of links between crimes that affected a few and those that threatened all. Despite self-satisfied statements by some that English law allowed no place for the Continental barbarism of torture, the Privy Council mandated its use to extract information from more and more people, most often the religiously disaffected but also humble rioters. Martial law was similarly extended to deal with the unruly poor; provost marshals routed vagrants from city streets to face summary execution. Star Chamber judges devised new definitions of sedition, and common-law justices constructed new treasons from the laws before them. Unhappily for not a few rioters, the career of that renowned jurist Sir Edward Coke was nearly coterminous with the crisis-ridden years from *c.* 1580–1630; first as Solicitor General and then as Attorney General, he proved his ability to convince justices to redefine once private wrongs as public crimes of the highest order.

But did the governors of Elizabethan England have objective justification for their fears that the 'many-headed monster' of popular rebellion was about to devour them? For much of the reign, the answer would have to be 'no'. Riotous assemblies were by no means uncommon, but most seem to have been fairly limited, even orderly affairs which could be construed as forms of negotiation. They resemble the eighteenth-century riots E. P. Thompson examined, with participants' actions rationally directed, shaped by customs of disobedience and done with the aim of protecting customary rights. Their 'disorders' had an order of their own. R. B. Manning's work on the riots of the Tudor period has emphasised protesters' use of custom to legitimise their actions and their efforts to hold their rulers up to their own rhetoric. In his search through the Elizabethan records of Star Chamber, Manning found 105 cases of riot tried in that court, but only seven of these included more than thirty people. Most of these represented attempts to assert a claim to use-rights on commons, wastes and woodlands. Furthermore, many participants tried working within or around legal definitions of riot. In common law, a riot consisted of any group of three or more persons assembled to an illegal end and was punished as a misdemeanour. Statute law passed under Queen Mary had declared twelve or more armed persons, or forty or more persons assembled for any purpose, who remained together for more than an hour after an order to disperse to be perpetrators of felony riot, punishable by death. Manning found rioters who broke into pairs to avoid charges of common-law riot and others who carefully left their endeavours just before the statutory one-hour limit. Most had a concrete objective to effect or point to make and planned no further action.

There were exceptions, however, and most dramatically so in the 1580s and 1590s. Dearth, harvest failures, unemployment in the clothing trades and the demands of conscription and taxation imposed by war fostered more volatile action from many people. The authorities responded not only with more ambitious regulation of grain markets, prosecution of landlords and masters who abandoned their dependants and improved poor relief, but also with heightened severity. These punishments in turn provoked responses. A number of London's apprentices riotously rescued their fellows from imprisonment on several occasions. Manning notes that between 1581 and 1602, London hosted no fewer than thirty-five significant riots, and many of these were protests against the harsh punishments imposed by city officials at the Crown's urging. Conflict was triggered not just by worsening conditions but also by heavy-handed royal intervention. After one episode in 1592, for instance, when the Knight Marshal of the Queen's household imprisoned a felt-maker, a group tried to break their colleague out of gaol. A fight ensued, in which some people died. The felt-makers captured the Knight Marshal's man who had killed one of their number and demanded that justice be done.

Subsequent examinations revealed that at least a few of these men had spoken of escalating their actions into full-scale rebellion against the Queen.

Tensions grew even worse in 1595. Manning deems the London riots of that summer – some twelve in the month of June – the 'most dangerous and prolonged urban uprising between the accession of the Tudor dynasty and the beginning of the Long Parliament'.[7] Riots over the price of fish and butter took place on 12 and 13 June. The butter rioters, roughly 300 apprentices, forcibly sold butter at 3d. a pound when the owners had demanded 5d. Some received whippings for their efforts, and the Privy Council imposed martial law on the city. Aggrieved by these punishments, a group of apprentices tore down the pillories in Cheapside and erected gallows outside the residence of Lord Mayor Sir Robert Spencer, who had too ardently embraced the Privy Council's punitive programme. On 29 June, some 1,000 apprentices gathered on Tower Hill. This event became farcical when the Lieutenant of the Tower, Sir Michael Blount, objected to the presence of the Lord Mayor and London sheriffs on his turf. Blount and the men of the Tower garrison forayed out to assault the Mayor's sword-bearer and rescued rioters who had been arrested. Some of the rioters were charged, not with misdemeanour or even felony but with treason on a tendentious reading of the 1571 treason statute. Blount's case was heard in Star Chamber; Coke's charge against the Lieutenant included a description of the London riot as he saw it. He suggested that the apprentices had intended to rob the wealthy and the well disposed and had sent 'libels, notes, writings, and messages passing to and fro between them and to win together with others'. He insisted that they had, furthermore, planned 'to take the sword of authority from the magistrates . . . to rule and command there as please themselves, as [proven] by the outrageous actions of some of them and by sundry speeches, letters, and writings cast forth by some of the said conspirators'.[8] Five of the rioters, charged in another court with levying war against the Crown, were sentenced to be hanged, drawn and quartered.

The mid-1590s were hard years, provoking serious riots outside of London, too. The years from 1595 to 1597 witnessed food riots in Essex, Kent, Somerset and elsewhere. While the usual characterisation of riot as a form of negotiation – as a way to remind magistrates of their paternalist duties – continued to apply, it became considerably strained. An Essex weaver told an assembled crowd, 'that it would never be better until men did rise & seek thereby an amendment and wished in his heart a hundred men would rise and he would be their captain to cut the throats of the rich Churls and the rich Cornmongers'.[9] A group in Somerset, forcibly imposing tolls on those who took grain from the market, reportedly declared 'that they were as good be slain in the market place as starve in their own houses'. In Oxfordshire, carpenter Bartholomew Steer and a few friends tried gathering men for a rebellion in November of 1596. Some in the area had already petitioned the Lord Lieutenant for relief after yet another disastrous harvest; while they adopted the usual forms of petitionary politics, their appeal carried more than the usual implicit threat and noted 'that if they could not have remedy, they would seek remedy themselves'. The local authorities apparently made one attempt to keep grain in the region, but the Privy Council, worried about more disturbances in London, stymied their effort. Bartholomew Steer, James Bradshaw and a few others discussed the failed petition and planned direct action. They travelled the area to recruit supporters, promising first that 'there would be a rising of the people to pull down the enclosures . . . and to lay the same open again'. In the short term, they would feed themselves with 'corn out of rich men's barns'. Their talk soon turned from attacking enclosures to attacking the gentlemen themselves, with plans for an armed march to London where they would join with the city's apprentices. A sentiment that more than food was at issue is perhaps seen in Steer's resolve that 'hap what would, for he could die but once and . . . he would not always live like a slave'. Yet, despite expressions of sympathy, Steer and three others waited in vain atop Enslow Hill on 21 November; none came to join them.

Such was the putative 'Oxfordshire Rebellion' of 1596. Not much of a rebellion in fact, it nonetheless became one in law. Sir Edward Coke headed up a special committee empowered to torture the men to learn the full details of their plans and pushed for them to be charged with high treason for compassing to levy war against the Queen. Steer and James Bradshaw disappear from the records, presumably having succumbed to either the torture or the imprisonment, but three others were indicted in February before a jury of Oxford gentlemen that included some of their intended victims. Coke's reading of the treason legislation proved sufficiently troublesome that the justices convened in April to discuss the matter. Three dissented, but the others agreed with Coke. Essentially, an action against a particular enclosure by the people immediately affected would continue to count as riot, but one against enclosures more generally thenceforth constituted high treason. Accordingly, Robert Burton and Richard Bradshaw were tried at Westminster and subsequently hanged, drawn and quartered on Enslow Hill. The decision in this case became an important precedent in the law of treason to be used against future troublemakers and serves as an index of the fears of the authorities in the perilous mid-1590s.

John Walter sees this failed rising as evidence that crisis and disorder cannot be neatly equated. The hardship in Oxfordshire, and elsewhere, was very real, and the planning quite competent, but yet no rising resulted. He suggests that more people might have joined had Steer and his fellows managed to achieve a critical mass of early supporters, 'but few were prepared to take the initial stride across the Rubicon of resentment to rebellion'.[10] And indeed, despite the many hardships of the Elizabethan years posed by demographic explosion, religious reformation and, in the later years, near constant warfare, rebellion was rare. There was an abundance of riot and much criminal disorder, but almost no mass revolts during Elizabeth's long reign. Certainly, a few people tried. Steer's attempt is reasonably well recorded, thanks to the legal innovations it inspired, but other efforts are often known only by passing references in the pardon rolls, assize files or state papers. Some carpenters, weavers and husbandmen did, like Steer, preach rebellion to market-day crowds or alehouse gatherings of people with deeply felt grievances, but, like Steer, few got very far. Despite the authorities' fears of vagrant armies overthrowing all order and of petty criminals banding together to destroy the State, no truly popular rebellions transpired.

Even elite conspirators, with better resources and more social capital at hand, rarely managed to move from conspiracy to effective action. The abortive coup led by the Earl of Essex in January 1601 is the best-known case in point. Essex had long been the Queen's well-rewarded favourite, using the gifts she bestowed to cultivate a sizeable clientele. His largesse and profligacy left him in hard financial straits when the royal bounty ended. With that, his thwarted ambition and injured pride motivating him, Essex gathered his aristocratic followers to seize the Queen. When bemused Londoners offered no help, the attempt collapsed, and Essex died a traitor's death. The scarcity of rebellion in this era stands in marked contrast to the many armed protests that bedevilled Elizabeth's predecessors and is often cited as further proof of Elizabeth's acumen and good governance. Yet, given that there were discontents – and discontented persons – aplenty, one must ask whether Elizabeth kept her subjects better contented or better controlled.

A brief examination of the one serious rebellion that did take place in Elizabethan England, the Northern Rising of 1569, might suggest answers. There had already been several serious riots that year. In Derbyshire, a group of men had armed themselves, camped on disputed land and associated with a man suspected to be peddling political prophecies, which were always feared by the authorities for their radicalising potential. In Cumberland, a group, variously estimated at 300 to 400 or 1,000 strong, destroyed the enclosures in a local forest and had as one of their leaders a man wanted for 'his notorious abusing of the Queen's Majesty's name and authority'; the authorities took their efforts seriously enough to try charging many of them with felony. In Suffolk, disruptions in the cloth trade prompted some to rise against foreign workers and, according to one alarmed local JP, 'to have spoiled all the gentlemen and worthy personages that they might overtake . . . and so marching towards London, to have provoked with this example the whole realm to the like uproar'.[11] The confession of one man confirmed the seriousness of the plotters' intent. James Fuller, a Suffolk sawyer, said that he and others had planned to rebel for lack of work or money. Once they had rung the bells to gather men, they planned to 'proceed and bring down [the] price of all things at our pleasure'. He had pledged his fellow plotters that this time, 'we will not be deceived as we were at the last rising, for then we were promised enough. But the more was a halter. But now we will appoint them that shall take the rich churls and set them on their horsebacks under a tree . . . and so let them hang.'[12] A group in Norfolk would later try to raise rebellion as well, but with no more luck than Fuller and his confederates. The only plan to get off the ground was the Northern Rising, a revolt led by two noblemen and directed not at economic grievances but at the restoration of Catholicism. But even this rebellion would be slow in beginning, quick in ending and ultimately an abject failure.

The Earls of Northumberland and Westmorland had, along with their close confederates, long complained about and conspired against Elizabeth's policies. They had suffered under the Tudor project of taming the north by the introduction of 'new men'; Northumberland, for instance, had lost the prestigious post of Border Warden to men of lesser status. So, too, had they suffered under the introduction of Protestantism. Northumberland had lost his position on the Commission of the Peace for his traditional religious views and believed the new faith responsible for the divisions and disorder in his world. Like many others, they also worried about an uncertain succession to an unmarried, childless queen. When Mary, Queen of Scots, arrived in England, the northern earls and their supporters saw her as the solution to their problems. But even with all their complaints and conspiring, they did not find it easy to make the move to actual rebellion. Only when they believed their arrest for their plotting was imminent did they take steps toward more open protest and then remained troubled by how to justify their actions to themselves and to others. They agonised over their options, consulting priests and writing to the Pope for guidance, believing that only if he excommunicated Elizabeth would armed opposition be justified and widely supported. The Earl of Sussex, president of the council in the north, advised Elizabeth to offer the Earls pardon; if given no reason to fear for their safety, they would not likely rebel. When she insisted upon their arrest, the Earls saw no choice but revolt.

Accordingly, on 13 November, they and some 300 of their men stormed into Durham Cathedral, overturned the communion table and celebrated a Catholic mass. Making the restoration of the old faith their central rallying cry, they declared themselves ready to remove those 'disordered and evil disposed persons' about the Queen who subverted the true Catholic faith, the ancient nobility and the rightful succession. Within days, thousands of armed men had joined them; precisely how many answered the Earls' call is unclear, for the Earls rejected those they deemed insufficiently armed and sent many back to their villages to await a subsequent call to action, but contemporaries estimated that some 5,500 to 6,000 marched or rode with the Earls at any given point. Despite older characterisations of this as a neo-feudal revolt, relatively few of the rebels had any tenurial ties to the leaders. Most joined not because of feudal loyalties but because of promises of pay, threats of coercion or agreement with the rebellion's aims. Whatever their disparate motives, their actions and self-depictions marked them as religious crusaders and defenders of the commonwealth. They bore time-hallowed banners bearing the Five Wounds of Christ and the motto 'God Speed the Plough', and they focused their violence on the symbols and instruments of the new faith. The rebels forcefully ejected married ministers, whose decisions to wed were taken as clear signs of Protestant commitment. The rebels and those who remained at home in the parishes set about dismantling the instruments of the new faith and restoring those of the old. They torched Protestant service books, restored altars and attended masses.

While the rebels' actions showed clear signs of Catholic conviction, they bore little evidence of strong planning or organisation. One group successfully besieged Barnard Castle, where many of the ostensible defenders leapt over the walls to join them, and another took the port of Hartlepool; but otherwise they marched aimlessly through the north. For some weeks, loyalist leaders barricaded themselves behind city and castle walls, knowing themselves outnumbered and fearing the wavering support of the men they had mustered. By mid-December, however, a massive southern army arrived in the north. The rebel leaders abandoned their men to flee across the border into Scotland. There, they linked up with Queen Mary's faction in the Scottish Civil War and hoped to revive their rebellion upon the arrival of better weather, foreign support and a papal excommunication. Other than a brief attempt at a rising led by their confederate Leonard Dacre in February of 1570, however, their hopes for resumed revolt bore no fruit. In the meantime, the bulk of the rebel army prepared to face the vengeance of an angry Elizabeth.

Elizabeth's response to this mass rebellion helps to explain why she was troubled by no subsequent events of its kind. She proved herself highly adept at both the material and ideological repression of the 'rebellious instinct'. Provost marshals hastily executed roughly 600 of the rebels, with some bodies purposefully left long on their gallows to 'continue hanging for terror'. While effecting perhaps the worst judicial death toll of any rebellion in Tudor England, these marshals carefully avoided executing anyone with land to their credit. William Cecil had expressly ordered that 'in every special place where the rebels did gather any people, and in every market town or great parish, there be execution by martial law, of some of the rebels that had no freehold, nor copyhold, nor any substance of lands.'[13] He wanted the others reserved for common-law trials, in order to ensure that the Queen obtained their land for herself. The disobedient would pay for their actions not just with their lives but also with their goods. By ancient custom and law, individuals guilty of treason forfeited their property to their prince, and Elizabeth would use this practice to unparalleled effect. Even before the rebels laid down their arms, Lord Hunsdon opined that 'if this rebellion be well used, it will be very beneficial to her Majesty'.[14] And such, in fact, was the case. The Queen acquired thousands of pounds' worth of land from those found guilty of treason and thousands in fines from those fortunate enough to receive pardons. The land had much political value, as a source of rewards for the faithful. Ultimately, the suppression of the rebellion offered more than just a tangible expression of royal power: it increased the capital at the disposal of the Elizabethan regime, and hence its ability to police and suppress disorder in the future.

The Crown also sought to contain and control this rebellion and to prevent future challenges by carefully constructing messages about the meanings of such protest. Much as Elizabeth was able to use the material repression of the revolt to her political advantage, so too would the cultural significance assigned to the rebellion promote a heightened loyalty. A new homily against rebellion joined the set texts to be preached regularly to churchgoers throughout the country. The *Homily against Disobedience and Wilful Rebellion,* nearly four times the length of the other homilies, had as its primary message the insistence that disobedience to one's prince equalled disobedience to God. It used history and Scripture to depict the moral and practical evils of disobedience and adduced the 1569 rebels themselves and their ties to the foreign pope as examples of the perfidy and perils of protest. In addition, an impressive stream of vituperative polemic poured off the presses. Dismayed southern Protestants printed ballads, sermon texts, pamphlets and lengthier tracts in condemnation of the rising, linking the rebels firmly with foreign and anti-religious enemies. They urged unmitigated severity against these offenders. According to one, 'no clemency, gentleness, . . . or loving dealing can win a papist while he continueth a papist, to love her Majesty.'[15] In a sermon preached at court then later published, Thomas Drant counselled that 'as it is true that two and two make four, that when the sun is in the midst of heaven it is noontime, . . . so it is infallibly true that no perfect papist can be to any Christian prince a good subject.' He urged that it 'is both good policy and good divinity to punish God's enemies and [the Queen's] enemies . . . let them in God's name feel the punishment of a club, an hatchet, or an halter, and in so doing, I dare say God shall be highly pleased'.[16] These polemicists sharpened a rhetoric that had its tentative beginnings in the denunciations of the earlier Pilgrims of Grace of 1536 and Prayer Book rebels of 1549. They used the terms 'papist' and 'traitor' as synonyms and deployed an anti-Catholic vocabulary that came to shape the events of subsequent decades.

A hint of the effectiveness of such denunciations of protest as inherently foreign might be seen in the dismissive response of one Oxfordshire landlord to a warning about Bartholomew Steer's intended rebellion in 1596: 'if there should be any such matters', he thought them likely to 'proceed by means of some papist or enemies to the state rather than of poor people'.[17] And Steer, as we have seen, found many sympathisers but few active supporters. So why did the Elizabethan years see so little rebellion, so few successful conversions of complaint into forceful action? In their survey of the Tudor rebellions, Anthony Fletcher and Diarmaid MacCulloch propose several answers. Part of the credit belonged to social changes that drew the yeomanry closer in material interest and intellectual inclination to their social superiors and away from the masses beneath them and part belonged to accidents of international politics that promoted a greater sense of national loyalty. Much of the credit was owed to Elizabeth herself. She refused to force a fundamental, much-needed reform of taxation, a decision that left many problems for her successors but that avoided confrontation in the short term. Finally, they emphasise that Elizabeth was simply better at the arts of governance than her predecessors had been: she more skilfully directed the public theatre of politics, constructed an imposing and yet sympathetic image of herself, played up the rhetoric of obedience and generally showed herself more responsive to the demands of her subjects. An examination of the 1569 rebellion shows all this to be true and adds a few nuances. Both elite and popular participation was necessary to launch a significant rebellion; whatever the depth of popular grievances, elite leadership provided much-needed resources and a sense of legitimacy to protest. Without that conjunction of interests, conspiracy rarely got far, as both Bartholomew Steer and the Earl of Essex would later find. As for the 'accidents' of international politics that fostered a greater sense of national loyalty, the most potent of these emerged from the rebellion itself: the papal excommunication and the ways it solidified emerging new identities and loyalties. It is perhaps significant that the next serious outbreak of rebellion occurred only after anti-Catholic, anti-foreign rhetoric had been turned against the Crown, when King Charles lost the secure status of the defender of English Protestantism. And, as the aftermath of the one serious Elizabethan revolt shows, the Queen was not just better than her predecessors at putting off problems and directing the public theatre of politics but she was also highly attentive to the physical and financial repression of 'the rebellious instinct'. The punishment of the rebels did much to limit the material ability of the former rebels to renew revolt and provided encouragement for future obedience. She was able to turn the rebellion to her financial and political advantage, to extract from it resources to cement or at least encourage the loyalty of others.

The Elizabethan period was clearly no golden age of tranquillity and order. In evaluating the degree of disorder in these years, the relative lack of mass rebellion must be weighed against climbing murder and execution rates. Many people responded to the hardships of the era with theft and violence, and some with organised (if limited) protest. If we were to look to Elizabeth's other kingdom, the record would look even worse: while Ireland would fall under English control by 1603, it had been even more violently disordered for much of her reign than under any of the previous Tudors. But in England enough people saw reasons for loyalty and compliance to ensure a modicum of stability, either refraining from rebellion or more actively aiding in the extension of state supervision and control. Fear kept many in line, whether fear of the gallows or fear of the vagrant and the 'foreign' papist. At times, royal actions aggravated disorder; at others, they provided incentives for obedience, even from the very fruits of disorder. Whether we see in the history of rebellion and crime signs of Elizabeth's success or failure depends very much on the perspective we chose to adopt, but a golden age of order it was not.

FURTHER READING

Archer, Ian, *The Pursuit of Stability: Social Relations in Elizabethan London* (Cambridge, 1991).

Cockburn, J. S. (ed.), *Crime in England, 1550–1800* (Princeton, NJ, 1977).

—— *Calendar of Assize Records, Home Circuit Indictments, Elizabeth I and James I: Introduction* (London, 1985).

Devereaux, Simon, and Griffiths, Paul (eds.), *Penal Practice and Culture, 1500–1900: Punishing the English* (New York, 2004).

Fletcher, Anthony, and MacCulloch, Diarmaid, *Tudor Rebellions*, 5th edn (London, 2004).

Fletcher, Anthony, and Stevenson, John (eds.), *Order and Disorder in Early Modern England* (Cambridge, 1985).

Hay, Douglas, and Craven, Paul (eds.), *Masters, Servants, and Magistrates in Britain and the Empire, 1562–1955* (Chapel Hill, NC, 2004).

Innes, Joanna, 'Prisons for the Poor: English Bridewells, 1555–1800', in F. Snyder and Douglas Hay (eds.), *Labour, Law, and Crime* (London, 1987).

James, Mervyn, *Society, Politics, and Culture: Studies in Early Modern England* (Cambridge, 1986).

Kesselring, K. J., *Mercy and Authority in the Tudor State* (Cambridge, 2003).

—— *The Northern Rebellion of 1569: Faith, Politics, and Protest in Elizabethan England* (Basingstoke, 2007).

Manning, Roger B., *Village Revolts: Social Protest and Popular Disturbances in England, 1509–1640* (Oxford, 1988).

Seaver, Paul S., 'Apprentice Riots in Early Modern London', in Joseph P. Ward (ed.), *Violence, Politics, and Gender in Early Modern England* (New York and Basingstoke, 2008), pp. 17–40.

Sharpe, J. A., *Crime in Early Modern England, 1550–1750*, 2nd edn (London, 1999).

Slack, Paul (ed.), *Rebellion, Popular Protest and the Social Order in Early Modern England* (Cambridge, 1984).

Thompson, E. P., 'The Moral Economy of the English Crowd in the Eighteenth Century', *Past and Present*, 50 (1971): 76–136.

Walker, Garthine, *Crime, Gender and Social Order in Early Modern England* (Cambridge, 2003).

Walker, Garthine and Kermode, Jenny (eds.), *Women, Crime and the Courts in Early Modern England* (Chapel Hill, NC, 1994).

Wall, Alison, *Power and Protest in England, 1525–1640* (London, 2000).

Walter, John, 'A "Rising of the People"? The Oxfordshire Rising of 1596', *Past and Present*, 107 (1985): 90–143.

Wood, Andy, *Riot, Rebellion and Popular Politics in Early Modern England* (New York, 2002).

NOTES

1 BL Additional MS 48065, fol. 6; TNA SP12/44/52.
2 *William Lambarde and Local Government: His 'Ephemeris' and Twenty-Nine Charges to Juries and Commissions*, ed. Conyers Read (New York, 1962), pp. 82, 85.
3 J. A. Sharpe, *Crime in Early Modern England, 1550–1750* (London, 1999), p. 92.
4 Lawrence Stone, 'Interpersonal Violence in English Society, 1300–1980', *Past and Present*, 101 (1983): 22–33; pp. 31–2.
5 Paul Griffiths, 'Bodies and Souls in Norwich: Punishing Petty Crime, 1540–1700', in Simon Devereaux and Paul Griffith (eds.), *Penal Practice and Culture, 1500–1900* (New York, 2004), p. 87.
6 Historical Manuscripts Commission, *Salisbury Manuscripts* (23 vols., London, 1883–1973), vol. IV, p. 5.
7 R. B. Manning, *Village Revolts: Social Protest and Popular Disturbances in England, 1509–1640* (Oxford, 1988), p. 208.
8 R. B. Manning, 'The Prosecution of Sir Michael Blount, Lieutenant of the Tower of London, 1595', *Bulletin of the Institute of Historical Research*, 62 (1984): 216–24, citing TNA STAC 5/A19/2.
9 The material in this paragraph and the one that follows is drawn from John Walter, 'A "Rising of the People"? The Oxfordshire Rising of 1596', *Past and Present*, 107 (1985): 90–143.
10 Walter, 'A "Rising of the People"?', p. 119.
11 John Strype, *Annals of the Reformation*, 4 vols. in 7 (New York, 1968), vol. I, Part 2, p. 346.
12 TNA C 66/1073, M. 31.
13 TNA SP 15/15, No. 139.
14 TNA SP 15/15, No. 95.
15 Thomas Norton, *A Warning Agaynst the Dangerous Practises of Papistes* (London, 1569), sigs. A4v, B4r.
16 Thomas Drant, *Two Sermons Preached* (London, 1570), sigs. K3r, K4r.
17 Quoted in Walter, 'A "Rising of the People"?', pp. 125–6.

PART IV

ECONOMY

CHAPTER TWENTY-THREE

COMMONWEALTH DISCOURSE AND ECONOMIC THOUGHT

The morality of exchange

David Harris Sacks

> There is a moral and religious, as well as a material, environment, which sets its stamp on the individual, even when he is least conscious of it.[1]

In *Religion and the Rise of Capitalism,* R. H. Tawney, the historian and Christian socialist, focused his readers' attention on what he called 'capitalist civilisation', a social system based on private property in which members of the labour force formally possess the legal freedom to contract for their work. English history, he argued, took a new turn during the early modern era, as Europe's political, economic and cultural centre shifted away from the Mediterranean basin toward the north-west and the Atlantic and European culture experienced the advent of significant changes in economic thought as well as religious thought.[2] While sixteenth-century commentators continued to display a profound scepticism derived from ancient and medieval moral philosophers and religious thinkers about the consequences of the profit economy for social relations, sixteenth-century social thought also reveals a keen understanding not only of how much economic change had affected the social and political environment of the era but also of how social welfare and the flourishing of the State depend on market exchange.

In Tawney's view, among the most momentous of intellectual and cultural changes witnessed during the early modern era was the emergence, as he claimed, of 'the doctrine that religion and economic interests form two separate and co-ordinated kingdoms, of which neither, without presumption, can encroach on the other'. This view, he argued, rested on a definition of the economy as an autonomous realm of social activity concerned with the acquisition, production and distribution of scarce resources, not, as it traditionally had been, as the art of household management, or as it was sometimes called, 'husbandry'. In earlier eras, 'the institution of property, the transactions of the market place, the whole fabric of society, and the whole range of its activities', stood 'by no absolute title', but 'rested on the assumption' that they must all 'justify themselves at the bar of religion'.[3] In what follows, we shall re-examine these issues to consider whether the sixteenth-century developments in economic thought and practice are best understood in Tawney's manner as dividing the secular from the sacred or as processes in which religious and economic thought change in tandem to create a new spiritual and moral paradigm.

In referring to earlier economic conceptions in which economic behaviour was subjected to trial before the court of religious doctrine, Tawney was thinking mainly of the 'theories of the Schoolmen' on such matters as usury, fair prices, and relations between landlords and their tenants.[4] But the Schoolmen themselves were largely relying for their economic ideas on the writings of ancient Greek and Latin ethical theorists for whom economic activities, in the words of the political economist Karl Polanyi, were 'submerged in . . . social relationships' in contrast to the world of modern capitalism which conceives of 'an economy' or 'the economy' as an autonomous and self-regulating mechanism for the production and distribution of goods and services, where 'social relations' can be said to be 'embedded in the economic system'.[5] However, this latter view can hardly be said to have existed in the sixteenth century. Instead, most commentaries at the time on economic matters concentrated on their country's condition, what in England, the Elizabethan and early Stuart writer Thomas Wilson called its 'state'.[6]

Although Wilson recognised that he lived in an era in which economic and social changes had occurred, for example in commodity prices and in the comparative prosperity of the different ranks and orders in English society, his view of English society and its economy was essentially static. Writing in anticipation of Queen Elizabeth I passing from the scene, his *The State of England, Anno Dom. 1600* treats its topics in analogy with a post-mortem inventory of the estate of a substantial head of household. Although the work is replete with statistical data – for example on the numbers and incomes of the members of the country's higher social ranks, on the ships of the royal fleet and their armaments and tonnages, on the numbers of men fit for military service, and on the revenues and expenditures of the Crown – it takes England's condition as if the facts of a single year represented what is true for the era as a whole.

Most other Elizabethan surveys describing the condition of English society, such as William Harrison's *Description of England* and Sir Thomas Smith's *De republica anglorum,* have characteristics similar to Wilson's account. These works provide significant details of the lives lived by English people of different ranks and callings and recognise that material well-being is a critical component of the common good, but they reveal little sense of economic processes or economic change. In this respect, they look back to an earlier vision of the social order of the kind captured, for example, in Edmund Dudley's *The Tree of Commonwealth,* written in 1509 or early 1510.

Dudley conceived of the English commonwealth as a great tree whose parts, each representing a particular political or socio-economic function, must work together in mutual support to maintain the welfare of the tree as a whole. Rooted in justice, truth, unity and, most of all, the love of God, the commonwealth, Dudley argues, would flourish under the good government of the monarch and the diligent performance of their godly and social duties by the clergy, the chivalrous classes and the commonalty, rural and urban, through their 'trew labor and lawfull busynes'.[7] Although, as Wrightson observes, Dudley 'placed economic prosperity and material well-being close to the heart of his definition of commonwealth', his ideal of society is that of 'the three estates', a hierarchical conception of social peace and religious and moral constancy dating from the beginning of the eleventh century.[8] As with Wilson and other Elizabethan commentators, who also stress the importance to the welfare of the English polity of what Dudley called 'Worldly prosperite', the focus is on the fruits of social co-operation, not the processes by which they were achieved.[9]

Indeed, well into the sixteenth century, economic understanding paid little attention to the means for improving material welfare and concentrated instead on the proportionate provision of things according to the role they played in upholding virtue and the commonweal. Although for convenience's sake most economic transactions were conducted in monetary terms, the model remained that of a system of barter in which buyers and sellers completed their exchanges according to a rule of equality conceived in strict arithmetical terms – so much of one thing being deemed the equal in social value of so much of another.

This understanding cast an uncertain ethical light on the uses of money and the operations of credit, two essentials for the conduct not just of large-scale, long-distance trade but also of nearly all economic exchange, save petty transactions in local markets. The provision of credit was especially problematic, since it raised questions about how to compensate lenders for the use of their funds without violating scriptural prohibitions against lending money at interest or the belief among medieval scholastics that making money from money was fraudulent. Lending certainly occurred, often employing cunning devices to avoid the prohibitions, but if the loan was made in a contract guaranteeing a fixed interest rate and therefore bearing no risk to the lender, it was deemed to be usurious. English law condemned such loans outright until in recognition that the 'damnable sin' could not be entirely eradicated from market exchange, statutes in 1545 (repealed in 1552) and in 1571 permitted interest of up to 10 per cent.[10] The compromise, therefore, preserved the view that taking interest was inherently sinful and left intact the moral and religious understanding of the economy derived from earlier theories, while seeking to constrain and regulate the evil.

These ideas are remote from the modern discipline of economics, which, as Lionel Robbins famously defined it, is 'the science which studies human behaviour as a relationship between ends and scarce means'. Its subject matter, then, is 'scarcity' itself, or in Robbins' terms, 'the disposal of scarce means' that have 'alternative uses'.[11] According to Polanyi, however, 'the problem of scarcity does not arise' in the economic thinking of the ancient moralists or the medieval and early modern ones following them. For these figures, Polanyi says, 'the economy . . . concerns . . . the relationship of the persons who make up the natural institution of the household' and the maintenance of their self-sufficiency, not its possessions, let alone the acquisition of wealth for its own sake.[12]

Nevertheless, as Aristotle reveals in an anecdote he tells in the *Politics,* a work the Elizabethan Gabriel Harvey said everyone in his day 'had by rote', the philosopher understood perfectly that making a profit in buying and selling depended on exploiting scarcities.[13] The story concerns Thales of Miletus, one of the Seven Sages of the archaic world, who is said to have created 'a monopoly' to gain a windfall profit from his correct prediction of future market conditions.[14] Taken literally, the word 'monopoly' means 'one seller'.

The details of this story are revealing in a number of respects. 'Reproached for his poverty', Aristotle says, Thales initiated his experiment to demonstrate the true nature of philosophy. Knowing by his skill in reading the stars 'that there would be a great harvest of olives in the coming year' but having only 'a little money, he gave deposits for the use of all the olive-presses in Chios and Miletus, which he hired at a low price because no one bid against him'. When the harvest proved him right, and the olive presses were in great demand, 'he let them out at any rate which he pleased, and made a great quantity of money. Thus he showed the world that philosophers can easily be rich if they like, but that their ambition is of another sort'. While Thales was thus 'supposed to have given striking proof of his wisdom', the passage concludes, 'his scheme for getting wealth is of universal application, and is nothing but the creation of a monopoly'. [15]

In this anecdote, Thales' main insight derives from his understanding of the ways in which organised human activities appropriate the resources of the natural world for gain and therefore in what modern scholarship has identified as the minimum requirements for the erection of a monopoly: 'a limited and concentrated supply, an imperative and inelastic demand, and a lack of adequate substitutes'.[16] The 'principle of universal application' of which Aristotle speaks, then, is the precept that profit arises from the allocation of relative scarcity.[17]

It was long understood, of course, that prices could be driven up artificially by restricting the supply of goods entering the market. In medieval England, for example, the practices known as engrossing, regrating and forestalling, by which traders held back goods from direct sale in the marketplace, were condemned by statute; they remained offences into the nineteenth century. For the medieval Schoolmen, these common mercantile practices were regarded as violating the principle of justice according to which the just price for a marketable item was either the one that public authorities had set in view of the public good or that was set by common estimation, namely by buyers and sellers freely bargaining for their sale. Profits won by manipulating the price through cunning were condemned 'as *turpe lucrum,* ill-gotten gains'.[18] But in its original Aristotelian form, the story of Thales of Miletus conveys a much deeper understanding of exchange, namely that scarcities are intrinsic to the production and distribution of goods and services and need not be artificially created for the purposes of private gain.

Since market trade exposes traders to the possibility of moral error and their communities to exploitation at their hands, Aristotelian ethical theory chose to distinguish forms of exchange morally appropriate for households from profit-seeking exchange. Aristotelians accept that exchange to obtain the things a household or a state needs for its welfare that it cannot produce by itself is a 'natural art', 'necessary and honourable' and consistent with the fundamentals of human happiness. Exchange for profit, however, 'is justly censured; for it is unnatural, and a mode by which men gain from one another'. It seeks 'riches of the spurious kind' and leads those engaged in it 'to believe that getting wealth is the object of household management, and the whole idea of their lives is that they ought either to increase their money without limit, or at any rate not lose it'; by these means it promotes personal greediness and corrodes a sense of community.[19]

Polanyi is correct, therefore, that Aristotelians from ancient times into the early modern era 'saw no room for the scarcity factor in the human economy'. For them, the proper, just or natural aim of trade is to balance supply and demand in a regime of equivalences and reciprocities, not to manipulate scarcity to promote private profit or gain as happens in retail or commercial trade. Hence, it was the wisdom of Thales to eschew avarice, abandon his monopoly and return to his philosophical studies once he had demonstrated their usefulness.[20]

The story of Thales, the monopolist, was widely familiar to the educated in the ancient, medieval and early modern periods. But it passed into the traditions of European ethical and political discourse in a somewhat different form than in Aristotle's original. Cicero, for example, gives a version of the tale where there is no mention of olive presses. In *De divinatione,* Cicero tells us that Thales, seeing the prospects of a bountiful olive harvest, used his philosophical foresight to buy 'up the entire olive crop in the district of Miletus before it had begun to bloom'.[21] Most medieval and Renaissance commentaries and editions or translations of Aristotle's *Politics,* from Saint Albertus Magnus and Saint Thomas Aquinas to Nicholas Oresme, Christine de Pizan, Leonardo Bruni, Louis Le Roy and John Case, carry the story in Cicero's form, with Thales buying up the abundant olives or the oil pressed from them, not contracting for the exclusive use of the olive press.

A moment's thought should make apparent the curious nature of this rendering, since under the conditions of abundance imagined in this story, there would have been no way for the sage to turn a profit though the acquisition of the olives themselves, or of olive oil pressed from them. Instead, the predicted abundance would have produced falling, not rising prices for the harvest and a devastating loss for the investor. From the perspective of people living in agrarian civilisations, however, the exact commercial details of Thales' enterprise were marginally relevant and difficult to comprehend. Since what was feared was shortage, the traditions of ethical and social thought focused on the provisionment and use of riches, not marketing. The idea that profits might come from the exploitation of scarcity was distant from their understanding of nature and its laws.

This feature of agrarian naturalism was captured in another widely known Aristotelian treatise, the *Oeconomics,* erroneously attributed to Aristotle himself. 'In regard to property', it says,

> the first care is that which comes naturally. Now in the course of nature the art of agriculture is prior . . . Agriculture ranks first because of its justice, for it does not take anything away from men, either with their consent, as do retail trading and mercenary arts, or against their will, as do the warlike arts. Further, agriculture is natural; for by nature all derive their sustenance from their mother, and so men derive it from the earth.[22]

Seen in this light, Thales' experiment, regardless of the version, involved exploitation for private purposes of the natural productivity of the land, which should have been used for the common good. It was immoral on its face, and Thales was saved only from outright condemnation by his worthy educational goal and the fact that his experiment was not repeated.

This privileging of land gave its possession and use paramount significance in ethical theory. All the recognised virtues – magnanimity, liberality, friendliness, justice, even courage – sprang from it, since land revenues provided the material resources needed for noble activities from the pursuit of honour and greatness, to the sharing of good will and fellowship, to the provision of charity, to the holding of office and making of judgements, to the bearing of arms. By removing the temptation for an individual to do things only 'for money', or 'to claim the things that bring repute, when he has not got them, or to claim more of them than he has', it also provided an underpinning for truthfulness.[23] In contrast, traders, it was believed, especially retail traders with their petty haggling, flourished through the misrepresentation of the quality of their goods and the condition of their credit. '[N]othing they profit, onlesse they lie apace,' said Cicero, here cited in an oft-reprinted sixteenth-century English translation. Wage labour also was regarded as based in this tradition, for, to quote Cicero again, 'in them the very hire is as it were the obligation of their bondage'.[24] In consequence, manual labour made one unfit for public service. In contrast, the mainstays of the commonwealth for Aristotelians and their Ciceronian allies were considered to be agrarian landlords, living on the labour of others, since the possession of land alone was thought to grant the security and independence necessary to live a virtuous life of voluntary activities grounded in reason.

By the early sixteenth century, this view of landownership as having an intrinsically moral dimension was a commonplace of social commentary. We find it, for example, not only in Edmund Dudley and in the writings of Thomas More and of the mid-sixteenth-century commonwealthmen, such as John Hales, Robert Crowley, Henry Brinkelow and the preacher Hugh Latimer, but also in populist literature reproaching mighty landlords for their greed and their unjust treatment of the poor commons. In this tradition, which can be traced in an unbroken chain from the ancient moral theorists and ethical admonitions of the Church Father into the early modern era, greedy interference with supply, especially of food and of vital raw materials, was judged the most serious of social crimes, while avarice, especially if associated with misappropriation of the natural produce of the land, was deemed among the gravest of moral breaches. It 'is the root of all evils,' said Saint Augustine, citing 1 Timothy 6:10.[25] In the words attributed to Saint Paul, it is a form of 'idolatry'.[26]

These ideas prevailed into the early modern era even in the most learned and sophisticated discussions of economic matters such as usury. In the hands of knowledgeable figures such as Sir Thomas More, whose service as a London lawyer and judge in one of the city's commercial courts gave him close-up experience of the moral dilemmas posed by economic exchange, they presented deeply grounded detailed understandings of market practices in regional, national and international trade as they had developed by the early sixteenth century.[27] However, sixteenth-century England was not yet a fully integrated market society, operating under the aegis of broad and impersonal market forces. Although large-scale manufacturing and commercial activities, particularly in the all-important wool and cloth trades, had long been conducted according to market principles, most other aspects of the economic order were locally based and lacked the abstract and impersonal character of this sort of market exchange. They arose, instead, in community settings where economic transactions were subject to important personal, social and moral considerations.

To put this point in general terms, sixteenth-century England possessed what is sometimes described as a dual economy. One segment, still small but growing, depended upon buying and selling for profit in large-scale markets, where issues of supply and demand largely determined what happened, while the other segment, affecting the majority of the population, operated outside those markets, relying upon exploitation of resources in the forests, commons and wastes; co-operation among neighbours or gift exchange; customary services owed to superiors; and engagement only in a very localised trade in a limited number of items among known traders and neighbours.

Under these conditions, the expansion of market-oriented and profit-driven aspects of economic life sometimes occurred at the expense of ingrained traditional practices closely associated with the most deeply felt moral beliefs and community feelings. While in the countryside whole villages sometimes found themselves pulled by market pressures away from their customary practices, in the towns, the story was bound to be somewhat different, since urban life centred on the exchange of goods and services in the marketplace. Nevertheless, medieval and early modern urban markets were not places of unencumbered free exchange but highly regulated by town governments as well as local guilds. As regional, national and international markets grew, however this old regulatory system was put under considerable strain, and the towns were subject to cross pressures similar to those affecting agrarian communities.

During the sixteenth century, therefore, customary practices and the communal traditions of exchange were continually being subverted by market-oriented activities in both countryside and town, without resulting in the replacement of previously accepted norms and values with new ones. In consequence, we continue to find most economic commentators in the sixteenth century adhering to received views of economic activity. Instead of thinking of commercial exchange mainly as the instrumental means for allocating scarce resources, it was treated as essentially moral – that is as a way to assure the general welfare of the community and its members, not just to provide for subsistence and survival. On this view, the social problems associated with market agriculture and profit-seeking bargaining in urban marketplaces were all understood to spring from the same human source: the sins of human covetousness and pride, and to result in the same evils: poverty and crime.

This focus on the morality of exchange fills the writings of the sixteenth-century economic commentators. We see this nowhere more impressively than in More's *Utopia,* first published in Latin in 1516 and, posthumously, in an English translation by Ralph Robynson in 1551. The Latin text, written as a work of philosophical inquiry and political satire for an educated humanist audience, was an international bestseller and had fifteen editions in total before 1700. The English translation, with a national audience of literate but not necessarily learned readers, appeared primarily as a commentary on current social, economic and political conditions, especially those associated with the agrarian problems of the age. It had seven editions in this same period, the first four of which – those of 1551, 1556, 1597 and 1624 – were published in times of economic misery and social unrest. Under these conditions, *Utopia,* well known to Elizabethan readers, came to be read as a work primarily concerned with the amelioration of economic distress and the improvement of welfare for the poor.

However, even when its readers focused on questions of social policy in the mid-Tudor and Elizabethan period, the mode of economic analysis represented in *Utopia* remained fixed on traditional ethical paradigms. We can see this clearly if we return again to the concept of monopoly, which More uses in the course of *Utopia*'s extensive commentary on the phenomenon of enclosure of arable land for pasture. There we read that 'sheep that were wont to be so meek and tame and so small eaters' now 'consume, destroy, and devour whole fields, houses, and cities':

> For one shepherd or herdsman is enough to eat up that ground with cattle, to the occupying whereof about husbandry many hands were requisite . . . And though the number of sheep increase never so fast, yet the price falleth not one mite, because there be so few sellers; for they be almost all [come] into a few men's hands, whom no need forceth to sell before they lust, and they lust not before they may sell as dear as they lust.

This criticism starts a review of the way the 'unreasonable covetousness of a few' had become the 'utter undoing' of England, not only in promoting 'wretched beggary and miserable poverty', but also in the 'great wantonness, importunate superfluity, and excessive riot' shown by members of its ruling elites. To cure these evils, the proposed remedy is that the English 'suffer not these rich men to buy up all to engross and forestall, and with their monopoly to keep the market alone as please them'.[28]

During the reign of Elizabeth I, the word 'monopoly' came to be applied specifically to royal grants or patents allowing individuals the exclusive right to manufacture and trade particular items. However, as used in *Utopia,* the concept of monopoly refers more generally to such practices as the cornering of the markets in certain commodities – particularly wool – in order to gain control over their sale or to the holding back of goods from trade in order to artificially drive up their price, ancient methods we have seen called in law regrating, engrossing and forestalling. Because of this association with the selfish exercise of power 'monopoly' became a synonym for 'greed' in the sixteenth century.

Nevertheless, Elizabethan readers of *Utopia* would not have found in it a work wishing to return England to a primitive economic state capable of producing goods only for bare subsistence. The island of Utopia, like the England on which it is modelled, is imagined as having a complex division of labour. The Utopians, men and women, not only farm but each also have some other useful occupation such as 'clothmaking in wool or flax . . . or the smith's craft'. Although luxuries are suppressed, the Utopians not only distribute commodities abundant in one part of their island to those places that lack sufficient supplies, they also trade the things they have in surplus 'into other countries' from which they bring in 'all such things as they lack at home'.[29] As in Aristotle's account of the 'natural art of wealth-getting', the emphasis is on the maintenance of self-sufficiency and therefore less on what is produced than on the spirit of service and co-operation in which production is conducted. No one is to 'sit idle'; everyone is to 'apply his own craft with earnest diligence' for the common good.[30]

Utopia, in effect, calls for production and consumption to follow the values of good neighbourhood that it was believed had once prevailed in communal life even in London and that in some ways was still manifested in cities, towns and villages where non-market forms of exchange continued to have influence. In these places, economic processes remained enmeshed within a framework of traditional social institutions and principles. Elizabethan readers of the book, therefore, would have found its view of the economy neither historical nor analytical but ethical, concerned primarily to judge and correct rather than to explain. This view, reinforced vigorously in the writings of the mid-sixteenth-century commonwealthmen, held that the proper cure for economic distress was the maintenance of a moral economy, grounded in the established, eternal values of charity and fellowship, which, it was believed, could alone preserve a community in wholeness and make possible a flourishing life within it.

With writings in this vein in mind, a number of historians have argued that modern notions about the economy emerged in England only during the 1600s, when, in the words of Joyce Oldham Appleby, 'men initially came to grips with the challenge of explaining the new market forces in their lives'. On this view, commentaries on economics and society in the sixteenth century remained constrained within ancient and medieval paradigms, while new thinking about commerce and industry came about only in response to the 'end of the old European order' in the seventeenth century when disruptions to the equilibrium between 'people and land, labour and repose, peasant and lord, king and kingdom, production and consumption, custom and circumstance . . . made even the turbulent late Middle Ages appear a part of a timeless order'.[31]

However, the inception of new and more sophisticated thinking about economics comes earlier – in the mid-Tudor and Elizabethan era – in response to the significant demographic growth, the rapid rise in prices and the agrarian and employment problems addressed by More and the commonwealthmen. These themes are well illustrated in the period by the discovery of the 'quantity theory of money' which shows a new understanding of the mechanisms of supply and demand in driving economic activity. Credit for this general explanation for the period's long-term price inflation of 250 to 300 per cent is usually given to Jean Bodin, the French jurist and political philosopher who first published his ideas in Paris in 1568. In the 1560s and 1570s, he attributed the rapid rise in prices in the sixteenth century largely to the 'abundance of gold and silver, which is greater . . . today than it had been during the past 400 years'.[32] In England, the figure who came closest to Bodin's thinking was Sir Thomas Smith, political and social theorist, sometime Regius Professor of Civil Law and Vice-Chancellor at Cambridge, Provost of Eton, one of the Secretaries of England's Privy Council in Edward VI's reign, Principal Secretary in Elizabeth I's, and twice England's ambassador to France in her reign, during which service he may well have become acquainted with Bodin.

Best characterised as a Renaissance polymath and statesman, Smith drew out the implications of his extensive humanist learning rather than breaking with the traditions of moral discourse inherited from the ancients. His writings, published and unpublished, as well as the various projects in which he engaged also reveal him to have had an astonishing range of interests, including astrology, alchemy, coinage and foreign exchange, colonial enterprise in Ireland, history and especially legal history, the proper pronunciation of ancient Greek and the proper, phonetic spelling of modern English – but most of all in political and ethical discourse, ancient and modern – with a special focus on what we might call the economic foundations of commonwealth.

In a work first drafted for private circulation in Edward VI's reign – a time of widespread social distress and agrarian risings – and published in 1581, Smith analysed the causes of inflation in his day in a distinctly anti-utopian manner that reflected his understanding of the role of economic motivations in human behaviour. Grounding his views was an understanding of the economy as a closed mechanistic system of discrete this-worldly causes and effects. '[A]s in a clock', he said, 'there be many wheels yet the first wheel being stirred it drives the next . . . and so forth until the last that moves the instrument strikes the clock', so he believed 'the rising of the prices of all victuals at the husbandman's hand is the cause of the raising of the rent or his lands', and ultimately 'is the great cause . . . that enclosures is the more used'.[33]

In Edward VI's reign, Smith had held that the chief cause of this inflation was the debasement of English coinage which induces 'strangers not only to buy our gold and silver for brass and to exhaust this realm of treasure but also to buy our chief commodities in manner for naught'. However, in revising the manuscript after Elizabeth I's 1559 recoinage, Smith acknowledged that although English coin had been 'restored to his former purity and perfection', prices had not fallen 'back to their old rate', but 'the dearth of things' had continued. Since he held that 'if the cause be removed the effect is also taken away', he knew his earlier explanation of the inflation has been faulty and looked again for what was driving it. In response, he now offered 'two special causes' for the price rise: the 'first and chiefest' preserved Smith's emphasis on the debasement of the coinage, which, he said, caused landlords to rack up their rents and their tenants in turn 'to sell . . . victuals dearer and to continue the dearth of them; and likewise other artificers' for their wares. However, the second, adapted from Bodin, saw the influx of 'gold and silver . . . from the Indies and other countries', which had created an unprecedented 'great store and plenty of treasure' in Europe, as sustaining the price revolution which Henry VIII had triggered with his debasements.[34]

However, Smith also understood not only that it would be 'very hard' to bring 'English wares' back to 'their old prices', but that attempting it also would impoverish 'the Commonweal in a very short time', since it would mean selling English commodities 'good cheap to strangers' while theirs would be 'dear unto us'.[35] Two interconnected causal principles, therefore, guided Smith's economic thought: first, his understanding that the economy operated as a self-adjusting mechanism and, second, his belief that in the activity of exchange 'men are more moved by peculiar gain: than of respect they have to common profit'.[36] Taken together, these two causes also implied that human beings, 'provoked with lucre', as he put it, could also be made to profit the commonwealth. 'Is it not an old saying in Latin *Honos alit artes?*', Smith asked, that is to say 'profit or advancement nourishes every faculty'.[37]

Smith's economic thinking was highly sophisticated and extremely well informed. Against the criticisms of the commonwealthmen, he saw no necessary evil in enclosure, so long as landlords not 'turn common arable fields into pastures', or violently enclose village commons without compensation to those with rights on them.[38] He also believed that with the correct application of reason and policy and a measure of economic protectionism, new industries could be encouraged, perhaps even through the issuance of patents for new inventions, so long as the State restrained the greed of commercial entrepreneurs.

But rather than abandoning ancient understandings of economic behaviour, he arrived at his views by adapting them, focusing especially on Aristotle in the *Politics,* a work Smith also relied heavily upon in his *De republica anglorum,* first written in 1565 and published posthumously in 1583. In the *Politics,* Aristotle had argued that the skill of profit-making exchange 'begins to be useful when the society increases'. 'When the family divided into parts', the philosopher says, 'the parts shared in many things, and different parts in different things, which they had to give in exchange for what they wanted'. 'For the art of exchange', he goes on, 'arises at first from what is natural, from the circumstance that some have too little, others too much'.[39] These conditions, then, create or reinforce mutual bonds of community between the parties.

Smith also believed trade to be the natural consequence of the uneven distribution of necessary and desirable commodities in the world. 'God', he said, had

> ordained that no country should have all the commodities but that that one lacks, another brings forth, and that that one country lacks, another has plenty thereof commonly in the same year, to the intent men may know that they have need of another's help and thereby love and society to grow amongst all men the more.[40]

By the time this passage appeared in print in 1581, the view it expressed, which was widely regarded as a universal truth, already had a long history traceable from Aristotle through ancient Stoics and early Christian writers to Erasmus in his *Querla pacis* (1517), which in 1521 was translated into English as *The Complaint of Peace.* Later it appears in Bodin's economic writings and in several works by Hugo Grotius. It also underpins the conception of the civilising benefits of international trade and colonial expansion put forth on behalf of England's leading wholesale merchants and the advocates of overseas exploration.

In this paradigm, market exchange not only represents one of the forces holding the social order in stability but also demonstrates the capacity of reason to overcome malice and discord. As such, it is one of the foundations of commonwealth, which Smith understood to be 'a society or doing of a multitude of free men collected together and united by common accord and covenants among themselves for the conservation of themselves as well in peace as in war'.[41] 'Every man', he said, 'is a member of the Commonweal, and that that is profitable to one may be profitable to another if he would exercise the same feat'. So long as what is 'profitable to each man by himself . . . be not prejudicial to any other that that is profitable to one and so to another may be profitable to all and so the whole Commonweal'. 'As a great mass of treasure consists of many pence', he argued, 'and one penny added to another . . . makes up the great sum so does each man added to another make up the whole body of a Commonweal'.[42] On this view, a commonwealth is a compound of the particular interests that composed it – neither more nor less than the sum of its parts.

These remarks may appear to uphold a view of society as composed of 'unmediated consenting individuals acting for their own interests', and that Smith, therefore, exhibited a form of 'individualism' of the same kind as seventeenth-century political economists are said to have held.[43] However, for Smith, and for most commentators of his day, the commonwealth does not begin with atomised individuals living in the state of nature but, as in Aristotle's *Politics,* with the formation of households initiated by the union of a husband and wife. As William Gouge put it in his early seventeenth-century treatise on domestic duties, each household was viewed as a 'little commonwealth' in its own right.[44] Similarly, to quote Thomas Wilson again, every English city also was understood to have 'a Common Wealth among themselves'.[45] Accordingly, the larger commonwealth of the nation or kingdom emerged from the beneficial exchange of goods and services among the multiplicity of little commonwealths of which it is composed.

For Smith, commonwealths are based more on what he called 'allurement and reward' than on the 'penalties of the law'. 'For what law', he asked,

> can compel men to be industrious in travail and labor of his body or studious to learn any science or knowledge of the mind? To these things men may be well provoked, encouraged, and allured as if they that be industrious and painful be rewarded well for their pains and be suffered to take gains and wealth as reward of their labors. And so likewise if they that be learned be advanced and honored according to their forwardness in learning, every man will then study either to be industrious in bodily labor or studious in things that pertain to knowledge.

At the time Smith wrote this passage, the word 'industry', referring to diligent, purposeful, intentional or goal-directed activity, especially in the pursuit of laborious and steady work, was relatively new to the English language, having appeared in common discourse only around 1500. Smith, in keeping with his Aristotelianism, understood it to depend upon the receipt of benefit, reward or profit. 'Take ... rewards from' human beings 'and go about to compel them by laws thereto', Smith asks, and 'what man will plough or dig the ground or exercise any manual art where is any pain? Or who will adventure overseas for any merchandise? Or use any faculty wherein peril of danger should be, seeing his reward shall be no more than this that sits still?'[46]

Richard Hakluyt, the well-connected Elizabethan geographer, Oxford Aristotelian and Church of England clergyman, writing in 1584 to promote Sir Walter Ralegh's English colonial settlement on Roanoke Island off the coast of what is now North Carolina, took a similar view of the goal-directed, advantage-driven motives underpinning human action and of the causal mechanisms that moved the economy. Colonies, he argued, would supply England with exotic commodities hitherto acquired at the second hand in European markets, would furnish raw materials for its finishing industries, would give employment to the hands of clothworkers and other artisans made idle by the dislocations of religious war, would raise customs revenues for the Crown and offer encouragement to mariners and shipwrights essential for the growth and maintenance of the navy; would become places to which criminals and the indigent could be sent to live productive lives; and by thus improving economic conditions, would furnish incentives for the growth of population, which Hakluyt saw as 'the honor and strength of a Prince'.[47]

Like Smith, Hakluyt conceived society to be a commonwealth of free persons who exchange their skills and the products of those skills for mutual benefit and the public good. His scripturally informed understanding of civilised life, stressed – as its starting place – the community's need for sufficient material resources if its members are to live well and do well. It also implied the human capacity to find the optimal means for producing the desired outcomes. To this end, Hakluyt promoted American colonial ventures for the affects they would have in promoting full employment in cloth manufacture and trade. Where England sent the bulk of its woollen fabrics to the Netherlands in only a partially wrought state, allowing its craftsmen to gain the profits of the finishing trades, cloths sent to the Americas, like those that were exported to England's new trades to Russia, Barbary, Turkey and Persia, would be 'full wrought by the poor natural subjects of this Realm'. If the Queen would now take 'these western discoveries in hands and plant there', he argues, 'it is like that in a short time we shall vent as great masse of clothe in those parts as ever we did in the Netherlands, and in time much more'.[48]

This prediction was widely off the mark, but it reveals that Hakluyt, like Smith, also understood economic exchange as a reciprocating feedback system in which particular actions produce predictable results. Take, for example, his arguments about poverty, which had become a deepening problem in the Elizabethan era. If England can send its wares to America and elsewhere in a finished state, he says, and bring back raw materials to be worked at home 'there need not [be] one poor creature to steal, to starve, or to beg as they do'.[49] The passage, which echoes Thomas More's analysis in *Utopia,* treats crime in some measure as a rational response to poverty and places the blame for it partly on failings in the structure of England's overseas trade. Hakluyt recognises that the poor, lacking work, seek their sustenance from theft, because the merchants, necessarily seeking their own advantage, choose to export unwrought and import wrought commodities because market conditions prevent them from profiting from the alternative. Change the state of the market, make it possible to export finished products and import unfinished ones at profitable prices, and the problem will correct itself.

'And if this come about that work may be had for the multitude', Hakluyt says, 'where the Realm hath now one thousand for the defence thereof, the same may have five thousand: For when people know how to live, and how to maintain and feed their wives and children, they will not abstain from marriage as they now do.' 'I dare truly affirm', he goes on, 'that if the number in this Realm were as great as all Spain and France . . . the people being industrious, industrious I say, there should be found victuals enough at the full in all bounty to suffice them all'.[50] This analysis attributes to the artisan and the husbandman, and to the wandering poor as well, the same rational capacities as shown by experienced merchants. What, then, gave Hakluyt his confidence in the industriousness of the people?

Part of the answer lies in an anti-Utopian Aristotelianism similar to Smith's. Like the latter, Hakluyt understood human nature to be intrinsically acquisitive as well as political and social. The flourishing life of civilisation required getting the things necessary to live and then using them purposefully and productively in social interchange. Industriousness, then, entailed the capacity to deliberate about and choose the best means to achieve these material ends and then to direct one's labour instrumentally to gain the wished-for benefits and effects.

Although Smith and Hakluyt, like the earlier commonwealthmen, believed society should be a harmony of persons each aiding the other in pursuit of the common good, as Aristotelians they resisted the theory that the social order should strive for the achievement of absolute unity. '[T]he nature of the state', according to Aristotle, is 'to be a plurality', and he is quite clear that there was 'a point at which a state may attain such a degree of unity as to be no longer a state', but something closer to an individual.[51] For Christian thinkers in this tradition it was necessary to leave ample room for individual consciences to meet their God-given duties.

This sense of society was already present in the political writings of the medieval schoolmen, such as Aquinas. It is captured especially well in a sermon by a preacher named Thomas Wimbledon which became one of the best-sellers of the English Reformation but was first given at Paul's Cross in the late 1380s. Having circulated widely in manuscript in the fourteenth and fifteenth centuries, it appeared in print in twenty-one editions between *c.* 1540 and 1635. It was also published in one version or another in every edition of John Foxe's *Acts and Monuments* from 1563, five of them in Elizabeth's reign, which also saw the publication of thirteen editions of the sermon itself in pamphlet form.

The most resonant element in Wimbledon's sermon is its emphasis on the moral autonomy of individuals in their collective pursuit of the common good. He begins with the parable of the vineyard in Saint Matthew's Gospel, where entrance into the kingdom of Heaven is compared to the actions of a householder who upon finding men standing idle sent them into his vineyard to work, paying every man a penny whether he had worked only a hour or the whole day. The Bible passage concludes: 'So the last shall be first and the first last: for many be called, but few chosen'.[52] However, rather than focusing on this element of exclusivity, Wimbledon emphasised the diversity of human callings and their interrelationships.

To explain, Wimbledon offers an analogy based, as in Dudley's *Tree of Commonwealth,* on the tradition of the three orders. But in contrast to Dudley, who emphasised social hierarchy, Wimbledon's treatment stresses the social interdependence of the different orders by drawing a comparison with the functions performed by different workmen in tending a vineyard. In a vineyard, Wimbledon says, 'dyuers labourers' trim the vines, raise them up, tend to the roots and so on. Their 'offices, all be so necessary to ye vyne that if any of them fayle . . . it shall . . . eyther let or vtterly destroye the growyng of the vyne'. '[N]one', he concludes, 'maye well be wythoute other'.[53] Here we have the image of a common enterprise to which each person voluntarily contributes his own skills, each equally important to the overall welfare of the community without becoming completely subordinated to it.

In framing this argument, the sermon placed special emphasis on the significance of labour for human life. 'The labourers', Wimbledon says, 'muste laboure bodyly, and wyth sore sweate, get out of ye erth, bodely sustenaunce bothe for them selfe and for other . . . [B]ut for labourers . . . prestes and knyghtes must become artifycers, plowme*n* and heardes[men]: or ellse muste for defaute of bodyly sustenaunce dye'. Humans, he argues, are unique in their sociability. According to him, 'euery vnreasonable beaste' is capable of living singly so long as it can find sustenance. 'But yf there were but one man in the world', although he had all the food necessary for survival, 'he shuld dye' or suffer deprivation in the absence of the shared efforts of fellow human beings. Wimbledon's reasoning turns explicitly on the human need to make the things necessary for survival. What beasts have for their sustenance 'without other preparynge or alterynge' is not accorded to mankind, he says. For

> if a man have corne, as it com*m*eth from the erth, yet it is no meate accordyng to hym, vntyll it be by mans crafte chaunged into bread. And thoughe he have fleshe or fyshe, yet whyle it is rawe, and not by mannes labour sodden [i.e. boiled], rosted, broyled, or baken, it accordeth not to mannes sustenaunce. Euen so, woll that ye shepe bereth must neades, by dyuers craftes be altered, & changed, [bef]or[e] it be able to clothe any man. And truly a ma*n* by hym self shulde neuer doo all those thynges.[54]

Wimbledon also stressed the role of exchange in the making of society. It is necessary, says the preacher, 'that some be husbandme*n*, some men of occupations, some marchauntes to fetch yt that one lande wanteth, from an other where . . . [there] is plentye'. This alone, he insists, 'shulde be a great cause, whye euery estate shoulde loue other . . . [f]or one of them is so nedeful to an other'. This principle extended to men in all social ranks, each of which is equally understood to be 'labourynge in thys worlde'. Anyone who 'lyued here, without labour or trauayl' is condemned to be denied 'the endlesse ioye of heauen'. The passage concludes with a citation from 1 Corinthians: 'Thus euery man laboure and trauayle after hys degre: For whe*n* the eueninge commeth (that is the ende of this world). Then shal euery ma*n* take rewarde good or bad: after as he hath laboured here'.[55]

The sixteenth-century commonwealthmen also placed great weight on the concept of a calling. Unlike Wimbledon, however, they stressed instead, as Thomas Becon had put it, that all who laboured should 'be quiet, & . . . meddle with their own business and . . . work with their own hands'.[56] These were simple precepts with ancient roots best summed up in the adage 'Let the cobbler stick to his last', a doctrine that underpinned the practices of craft guilds seeking to protect their members from competition. They stress the distinctiveness of the crafts, not their mutuality. However, with the onset of significant urban growth, especially of London, the simultaneous development of a more substantial and more integrated national and international trading economy, and the emergence in the writings of such figures as Smith and Hakluyt of a new understanding of market exchange as a reciprocating system of causes and effects, the doctrine of callings became a theory of the division of labour and, in this emerging new social and economic context, Wimbledon's emphasis on the mutually supportive activities of workmen in different crafts took on a transformed moral significance.

A further mark of this shift in economic understanding was the rediscovery of the 'universal' economic law of scarcity as revealed in Aristotle's original account of Thales' use of philosophical knowledge to gain a windfall profit. Writing in the 1580s, a well-informed writer retold the story by showing how 'Thales Milesius . . . proving by the knowledge [of Philosophie] that that yeare Olives would be scant, brought all into his owne handes, and showed by that Monopolie that Philosophie could also make money.' Although the author fails to see how unlikely it would have been for a poor man such as Thales to acquire all the olives, rather than the rights to the olive presses, in advance of the harvest, he is right on the mark in regard to the basic economic point: profit could come to Thales only if he assumed significant shortages in supply which would yield him substantially higher prices than would a normal harvest. In support of this view, the author offers a robust and unsentimental economic analysis of the mechanism – what Aristotle called the 'universal principle' – that made possible the extraction of profit from scarcity. It is 'the best policie', we read, 'so to governe our own comodities' that they remain in good 'estimacion and value' in foreign markets 'and not to be too deare at home', while foreign commodities are 'kept at lowe and base prices amonge us'. To secure this outcome, 'the thinges which we carrie out' must be of higher price than 'the things which we bringe in; else shall we sone make a poore land and a poore people'. So long as this is true, the author says, 'it semeth to me that it were muche better for the publique weale of vs all that the accesse of straungers into our Cuntrey were revived and allured againe' and they were allowed freedom to trade in England's markets.[57]

But if 'all forreine trafique' is 'brought into the handes of [a] fewe companies', then

> we most be driven not onely to buy the forreine wares at suche highe prices as the bringers of them do Sesse, but also sell our home comodities at such estimate as our marchantes liste to value them, being nowe lefte none with whome we buy or sell but they.

The author has in mind the privileges of the overseas trading companies such as the Merchant Adventurers, first founded in the early fifteenth century, and the newly formed Levant Company, founded in 1581, whose role in the economy became increasingly important in the later Elizabethan period and whose letters patent granted them and their members exclusive commercial privileges. The author's explanation for their commercial domination rests on his analysis of monopoly, which he defined in Aristotelian terms as 'an encrochement of . . . comodities into the handes of one or fewe, whereby the sole buyinge and sellinge of the same is brought into fewe handes, which ought to be free and comon to all the Citizens of the same Comonwealthe'. Monopolies, therefore, adversely affect markets, since it follows naturally that 'where there be many buyers and few sellers the thinge sould most nedes be dere'. Consequently, 'if the exercise of our trafique be equallie permitted to all, then shall the outlandishe [i.e. foreign] comodities be brought in with great plentie, and sould to the inhabitauntes of the Realme for little money'.[58]

Commercial as well as manufacturing monopolies were vocally denounced, especially but not exclusively by the artisans and tradesmen most directly affected by them. The opposition of the latter was grounded in the view that market exchange was a function of every occupation, not a craft or calling on its own as the members of the monopoly companies insisted, and that the companies' exclusive privileges violated the liberties of the subject protected by English law. But the most vigorously opposed monopolies in the period were industrial rather than commercial; they concerned the sole manufacturing, not only the sole trading, of particular commodities. Why?

The corruption of the patent system is one reason. By the 1580s, the original promoters of the monopolies – the projectors seeking exclusive rights for their schemes and inventions – typically enjoyed their patents only at second hand as the substitutes of the royal favourites who were the actual grantees. At the same time, the patents became subject to serious profiteering and abuse, and the prerogatives of the Crown were used to intercede on behalf of the patentees, coercing compliance and blocking litigation in the law courts. However, even before this 'scandalous phase', they were already a source of complaint, especially for damaging the livelihoods of craftsmen engaged in competing trades.[59]

In 1599, some of the basic legal issues involved in the monopolies had been aired in the case of *Davenant* v. *Hurdis* concerning certain by-laws of the Company of Merchant Tailors of London issued under its royal charter. In that case, the judges had found any economic regulation that deprived a man of the free exercise of his craft without his consent to be against common right and in violation of the liberties protected by the Magna Carta. Despite this decision, however, the Crown continued to issue or to renew its monopoly grants, and the matter became a major grievance in the Parliament of 1601. In consequence, the Crown quashed the most obnoxious of the patents and permitted the legality of the others to be tested before the courts in the case of *Darcy* v. *Allen* of 1602.

The main argument against the monopoly patents as articulated in Parliament in 1601 and by the lawyers and judges in *Darcy* v. *Allen* was that by granting exclusive manufacturing and trading rights to a few private individuals, monopolies deprived free men of their livelihoods, hence of their liberties as freeborn Englishmen. The central idea is that every free man had a godly obligation (not just a right) to earn his bread from his calling, a duty that could not be abridged without his consent. Therefore, a monopolist was said to be a *vir sanguinis,* a man of blood, who in preventing competitors from exercising their crafts not only threatened their existence as free men but their very survival.[60] Monopolists were 'Blood-suckers of the Common-wealth', said the MP Richard Martin. They sucked up 'the best and principallest Commodities, which the Earth . . . hath given Us . . . the Commodities of our own Labour, which with the Sweat of our Brows (even up to the Knees in Mire and Dirt) we have labour'd for'.[61] By thus depriving craftsmen of their ability to use their labour as they chose, they turned free subjects into bondmen.

Since human beings were understood not merely to be free to labour but called by God to do so, the opponents of the manufacturing monopolies believed that they interfered with men's voluntary performance of their spiritual as well as their worldly duties to God, their communities, their families and themselves. Although much else was said in condemnation of monopoly patents for manufactures – for example that they resulted in the production of poor-quality goods and that like the monopoly trading companies drove up prices – it was their threat to the vocations of craftsmen and shopkeepers that had the greatest ethical weight.

Wimbledon's frequently republished sermon spoke directly to this understanding in setting forth moral standards by which individuals could be praised or blamed for performing their social duties. However, his emphasis on the importance of labour to human virtue argued something quite foreign to Aristotle's own view as well as to later Roman, scholastic and Renaissance conceptions of society and of personal honour, glory and virtuous action. Aristotelian thinking treated 'practical wisdom' and 'doing' alone as belonging to the realm of moral virtue and relegated 'craft' and 'making' to a completely separate arena. 'Making', in Aristotle's terms, involves the pursuit of 'an end other than itself'.[62] Although what is made may contribute to living the good life, its creation cannot in itself be a final good since the action is not performed for its own sake. In Aristotelian terms, however, 'doing' involves actions, such as deliberation about the best means to achieve the desired ends, which are constitutive of human flourishing and ends in themselves.

On these grounds, the craftsman, in so far as he engages in labour, necessarily is devoid of virtue in Aristotelian ethics. Aristotle made the same point in sociological terms. Since, for him, the exercise of virtue entailed activities performed for the common good of a political community, it followed that only those liberated from the burdens of onerous labour could be virtuous. It was not just that citizens or governors needed to be free from dependency upon a master, they also required the leisure to engage in political deliberation and to serve the State. This meant that they would themselves be substantial property holders, relying on the labour of others to make possible their participation in the commonweal. The same goes for the performance of the virtues of liberality and magnificence, which depend upon the possession of ample wealth and the use of property. Neither is possible for the man who must labour daily for his bread.

Seen in this light, Wimbledon and the anti-monopolists of the Elizabethan era, despite their overt debt to Aristotelian doctrine, cast the moral obligations of human beings in a strikingly un-Aristotelian framework. For Wimbledon, and increasingly for mid-Tudor and Elizabethan commentators on economic matters, man's God-given nature rested squarely in the curse of Adam, and the human community depended for its well-being on the exchange of their labour and its fruits. All ranks and orders in society had a calling, from the king and his counsellors and magistrates, to the bishops and ministers of God's word, to the gentlemen and landlords, the merchants and lawyers, the husbandmen and craftsmen of the realm. Each depended on the others to properly perform his social functions, which it was his office, his God-given duty, to do. The test for virtue, as the test for sin, then shifted from weighing outward actions against abstract and fixed standards, to the manifestation of virtuous or sinful intentions or motivations in the inner arena of conscience. Hence, instead of 'religion and economic interests' coming to form two separate and co-ordinated kingdoms; in the early modern era, as Tawney had proposed, the two were transformed together in the new economic and religious environment of the era.[63] Out of the curse of Adam came the virtue of Adam, the virtue of hard work performed freely for the common good – the commonweal – in one's divinely ordained calling.

FURTHER READING

Appleby, Joyce Oldham, *Economic Thought and Ideology in Seventeenth-Century England* (Princeton, NJ, 1978).

Beier, A. L., *Masterless Men: The Vagrancy Problem in England, 1560–1640* (London, 1985).

Booth, William James, *Households: On the Moral Architecture of the Economy* (Ithaca, NY, 1993).

Clay, C. G. A., *Economic Expansion and Social Change: England, 1500–1700*, 2 vols. (Cambridge, 1984).

De Roover, Raymond, *Business, Banking, and Economic Thought in Late Medieval and Early Modern Europe: Selected Studies of Raymond De Roover*, ed. Julius Kirshner (Chicago, Ill., 1974).

Dewar, Mary, *Sir Thomas Smith: A Tudor Intellectual* (London, 1964).

Finkelstein, Andrea, *Harmony and Balance: An Intellectual History of Seventeenth-Century English Economic Thought* (Ann Arbor, Mich., 2000).

Fisher, F. J., *London and the English Economy, 1500–1700*, ed. P. J. Corfield and N. B. Harte (London, 1990).

Jones, Norman, *God and the Moneylenders: Usury and the Law in Early Modern England* (Oxford and Cambridge, Mass., 1989).

Jones, Whitney R. D., *The Tudor Commonwealth: A Study of the Impact of the Social and Economic Development of Mid-Tudor England upon Contemporary Concepts of the Nature and Duties of the Commonwealth* (London, 1970).

Langholm, Odd, *Price and Value in the Aristotelian Tradition: A Study in Scholastic Economic Sources* (Bergen, 1979).

—— *Wealth and Money in the Aristotelian Tradition: A Study in Scholastic Economic Sources* (Bergen, 1983).

—— *The Aristotelian Analysis of Usury* (Bergen, 1984).

McRae, Andrew, *Good Speed the Plough: The Representation of Agrarian England, 1500–1660* (Cambridge, 1996).

Meikle, Scott, *Aristotle's Economic Thought* (Oxford, 1995).

More, Sir Thomas, *Utopia*, trans. Ralph Robynson, ed. David Harris Sacks (Boston, Mass., and New York, 1999).

Muldrew, Craig, *The Economy of Obligation: The Culture of Credit and Social Relations in Early Modern England* (Basingstoke, 1998).

Newhauser, Richard W., *The Early History of Greed: The Sin of Avarice in Early Medieval Thought and Literature* (Cambridge, 2000).

Noonan, John T., *The Scholastic Theory of Usury* (Cambridge, Mass., 1957).

Polanyi, Karl, *The Great Transformation* (Boston, Mass., 1957).

—— 'Aristotle Discovers the Economy', in Karl Polanyi, Conrad M. Arensberg and Harry W. Pearson (eds.), *Trade and Market in the Early Empires: Economies in History and Theory* (Glencoe, Ill., 1957), pp. 64–94.

Sacks, David Harris, *The Widening Gate: Bristol and the Atlantic Economy, 1450–1700* (Berkeley, Calif., 1991).

—— 'The Countervailing of Benefits: Monopoly, Liberty and Benevolence in Elizabethan England', in Dale Hoak (ed.), *Tudor Political Culture* (Cambridge, 1995), pp. 272–91.

—— 'The Greed of Judas: Avarice, Monopoly, and the Moral Economy in England, ca. 1350–ca. 1660', *Journal of Medieval and Early Modern Studies*, 28 (2) (1998): 263–307.

—— 'The Prudence of Thrasymachus: Sir Thomas Smith and the Commonwealth of England', in Anthony T. Grafton and J. H. M. Salmon (eds.), *Historians and Ideologues: Essays in Honor of Donald R. Kelley* (Rochester, NY, 2001), pp. 89–122.

—— 'Discourses of Western Planting: Richard Hakluyt and the Making of the Atlantic World', in Peter C. Mancall (ed.), *The Atlantic World and Virginia, 1550–1624* (Chapel Hill, NC, 2007), pp. 410–53.

Smith, Sir Thomas, *A Discourse of the Commonweal of the Realm of England, Attributed to Sir Thomas Smith*, ed. Mary Dewar (Charlottesville, Va., 1969).

—— *De republica anglorum*, ed. Mary Dewar (Cambridge, 1982).

Slack, Paul, *Poverty and Policy in Tudor and Stuart England* (London, 1988).
Spiegel, Henry William, *The Growth of Economic Thought*, 3rd edn (Durham, NC, and London, 1991).
Tawney, R. H., *The Agrarian Problem in the Sixteenth Century* (New York, 1967).
—— *Religion and the Rise of Capitalism: A Historical Study* (Harmondsworth, 1984).
Thirsk, Joan (ed.), *The Agrarian History of England and Wales: Vol. IV: 1500–1640* (Cambridge, 1967).
—— *Economic Policy and Projects: The Development of Consumer Society in Early Modern England* (Oxford, 1978).
Viner, Jacob, *The Role of Providence in the Social Order: An Essay in Intellectual History* (Princeton, NJ, 1972).
—— *Religious Thought and Economic Society: Four Chapters of an Unfinished Work*, ed. Jacques Melitz and Donald Winch (Durham, NC, 1978).
White, Helen C., *Social Criticism in Popular Religious Literature of the Sixteenth Century* (New York, 1944).
Wilson, Thomas, *A Discourse upon Usury by Way of Dialogue and Orations for the Better Variety and More Delight of All Those that Shall Read This Treatise*, ed. R. H. Tawney (London, 1925).
Wood, Neal, 'Foundations of Political Economy: The New Moral Philosophy of Sir Thomas Smith', in Paul A. Fideler and T. F. Mayer (eds.), *Political Thought and the Tudor Commonwealth: Deep Structure, Discourse and Disguise* (London and New York: Routledge, 1992), pp. 140–68.
—— *Foundations of Political Economy: Some Early Tudor Views on State and Society* (Berkeley, Calif., 1994).
—— 'Avarice and Civil Unity: The Contribution of Sir Thomas Smith', *History of Political Thought*, 18 (1) (1997): 24–41.
Wrightson, Keith, *English Society, 1580–1680* (London, 1982).
—— *Earthly Necessities: Economic Lives in Early Modern Britain* (New Haven, Conn., 2000).

NOTES

1 R. H. Tawney, *Religion and the Rise of Capitalism: A Historical Study*, 3rd edn (Harmondsworth, 1984), p. 26.
2 Tawney, 'Preface to 1937 Edition', *Religion and the Rise of Capitalism*, pp. vii–ix. For the phrase 'capitalist civilisation', see R. H. Tawney, 'Foreword', in Max Weber, *The Protestant Ethic and the Spirit of Capitalism*, trans. Talcott Parson (London, 1930), p. 1(b).
3 Tawney, 'Preface', p. viii.
4 Tawney, 'Preface', p. viii.
5 Karl Polanyi, *The Great Transformation*, with a foreword by Robert M. MacIver (Boston, Mass., 1957), pp. 46, 57.
6 Thomas Wilson, *The State of England, Anno Dom. 1600*, ed. F. J. Fisher (London, 1936).
7 Edmund Dudley, *The Tree of Commonwealth: A Treatise Written by Edmund Dudley*, ed. D. M. Brodie (Cambridge, 1948), p. 67.
8 Keith Wrightson, *Earthly Necessities: Economic Lives in Early Modern Britain, 1470–1750* (New Haven, Conn., 2000), p. 28.
9 Dudley, *Tree of Commonwealth*, p. 54.
10 R. H. Tawney, 'The Damnable Sin of Usury', in Thomas Wilson, *A Discourse upon Usury by Way of Dialogue and Orations . . .* (1572), ed. R. H. Tawney (London, 1925), pp. 106–21.

11 Lionel Robbins, *An Essay on the Nature and Significance of Economic Science,* 2nd edn (London, 1935), p. 16.
12 Karl Polanyi, 'Aristotle Discovers the Economy', in Karl Polanyi, Conrad M. Arensberg, and Harry W. Pearson (eds.), *Trade and Market in the Early Empires: Economies in History and Theory* (Glencoe, Ill., 1957), p. 81.
13 Gabriel Harvey to Edmund Spenser (1579) in *Letter-Book of Gabriel Harvey, ad 1573–1580,* ed. Edward J. L. Scott (Westminster, 1884), p. 79.
14 The story appears at *Pol.* I, 11. 1259a7–23 in Aristotle, *The Politics,* trans. Benjamin Jowett, rev. Jonathan Barnes, in *The Complete Works of Aristotle: The Revised Oxford Translations,* ed. Jonathan Barnes, 2 vols. (Princeton, NJ, 1984), vol. II, pp. 1997–8.
15 *Pol.,* I.11.1259a9–22, in Aristotle, *Complete Works,* vol. II, p. 1998.
16 Lawrence Stone, *An Elizabethan: Sir Horatio Palavicino* (Oxford, 1956), p. 41.
17 *Pol.* I.11.1259a8, Aristotle, *Complete Works,* vol. II. p. 1998.
18 Raymond De Roover, 'Monopoly Theory Prior to Adam Smith: A Revision', *Quarterly Journal of Economics,* 65 (4) (1951), p. 498.
19 *Pol.* I.8.1256b37, I.8.1257b30–40, I.8.1158a36–B2 in Aristotle, *Complete Works,* vol. II. pp. 1994, 1995–6, 1997.
20 Polanyi, 'Aristotle Discovers the Economy', p. 82.
21 Marcu Tullius Cicero, *De divinitione,* I.49.111, in Marcus Tullius Cicero, *De senectute, de amicitia, divinitione,* trans. William Armistead Falconer (Cambridge, 1946), pp. 342–5; Note that Cicero has Thales acquire the oil pressed from the abundant olives.
22 *Ec.* 1.1343a25–B2, in Aristotle, *Economics,* trans. E. S. Forster with G. C. Armstrong, in Aristotle, *Complete Works,* vol. II, p. 2131.
23 *Nic. Eth.* IV.7.1127a21–22, 1127b12–14, in Aristotle, *Nicomachean Ethics,* trans. W. D. Ross, rev. J. O. Urmson, in Aristotle, *Complete Works,* vol. II, p. 1779.
24 Marcus Tullius Cicero, *Marcus Tullius Ciceroes Thre Bokes of Duties, to Marcys His Sonne, Turned Out of Latin into English by Nicolas Grimalde,* ed. Gerald O'Gorman (Washington, DC, 1960), p. 106.
25 Saint Augustine, *On Free Choice of the Will,* trans. Thomas Williams (Indianapolis, Ind., 1993), p. 104.
26 Colossians 3:5; see also Ephesians 5:5.
27 See, e.g., Thomas More, *Treatise on the Passion* (1534), in *The Complete Works of St. Thomas More,* vol. XIII, ed. Garry Haupt (New Haven, Conn., 1976), pp. 78–9.
28 Thomas More, *Utopia,* trans. Ralph Robynson, ed. David Harris Sacks (Boston, Mass., and New York, 1999), pp. 101, 102–3, 103–4.
29 More, *Utopia,* pp. 136, 148–9.
30 *Pol.* I.10.1257b19–21, in Aristotle, *Complete Works,* vol. II, p. 1995. More, *Utopia,* pp. 136–7.
31 Joyce Oldham Appleby, *Economic Thought and Ideology in Seventeenth-Century England* (Princeton, NJ, 1978), pp. ix, 3.
32 Jean Bodin, *Response to the Paradoxes of Malestroit,* trans. and ed. Henry Tudor and R. W. Dyson (Bristol, 1997), p. 59.
33 Sir Thomas Smith, *A Discourse of the Commonweal of This Realm of England, Attributed to Sir Thomas Smith,* ed. Mary Dewar (Charlottesville, Va., 1969), pp. 96, 98.
34 Smith, *Discourse of the Commonweal,* pp. 69, 143, 144–5.
35 Smith, *Discourse of the Commonweal,* p. 146.
36 Sir Thomas Smith and Thomas Smith, Esq., *A Letter Sent by I. B. Gentleman Vnto His Very Frende Maystet R. C. Esquire Wherin is Conteined a Large Discourse of the Peopling & Inhabiting the Cuntrie Called the Ardes and Other Adiacent in the North of Ireland, and Taken in Hand by Sir Thomas Smith One of the Queenes Maiesties Priuie Counsel, and Thomas Smith Esquire, His Sonne* (London, 1572), sig. D. Ir.
37 Smith, *Discourse of the Commonweal,* pp. 61, 58.
38 Smith, *Discourse of the Commonweal,* p. 50.
39 *Pol.* I.9.1257a15–17, I.9.1257a21–30, in Aristotle, *Complete Works,* vol. II, p. 1994.
40 Smith, *Discourse of the Commonweal,* p. 62.
41 Sir Thomas Smith, *De republica anglorum,* ed. Mary Dewar (Cambridge, 1982), p. 57.

42 Smith, *Discourse of the Commonweal,* pp. 51–2.
43 Neal Wood, *Foundations of Political Economy: Some Early Tudor Views on State and Society* (Berkeley, Calif., 1994), p. 201.
44 William Gouge, *Of Domesticall Duties, Eight Treatises* (London, 1622), p. 18.
45 Wilson, *State of England,* p. 20.
46 Smith, *Discourse of a Commonweal,* pp. 58–9.
47 Richard Hakluyt, *A Particular Discourse . . . Known as Discourse of Western Planting,* ed. David B. Quinn and Alison M. Quinn (London, 1993), pp. 32, 33.
48 Hakluyt, *Particular Discourse,* pp. 32, 33.
49 Hakluyt, *Particular Discourse,* pp. 32, 33.
50 Hakluyt, *Particular Discourse,* pp. 32, 33.
51 *Pol.* II.2.1261a18–22, II.5.1.1263b32–7, in Aristotle, *Complete Works,* vol. II, pp. 2001, 2005.
52 Matthew 20:16.
53 Thomas Wimbledon, *A Sermon No Lesse Fruteful Then Famous Made in the Yeare of Our Lorde God. M.CCC.lxxxvii . . .* (London), 1540?), sigs. A3v– A4[a]v.
54 Wimbledon, *Sermon,* sigs. A4[a]v; A4[b]r–v.
55 Wimbledon, *Sermon,* sigs. A4[b]v–A4[c]v; the Scriptural reference is to I Corinthians 7:20.
56 Thomas Becon, '[*The Flour of Godly Praiers*] *Most Worthy to Be Vsed in These Our Daies for the Saueguard, Health, and Comforte of All Degrees, and Estates* (London, *c.* 1550), fol. 32r.
57 Anon., 'A Discourse of Corporations', in R. H. Tawney and Eileen Power (eds.), *Tudor Economic Documents: Being Select Documents Illustrating the Economic and Social History of Tudor England,* 3 vols. (London, 1923), vol. III, pp. 266, 267–8.
58 Anon., 'Discourse of Corporations', vol. III, pp. 269, 266, 269.
59 Joan Thirsk, *Economic Policy and Projects: The Development of a Consumer Society* (Oxford, 1978), p. 51.
60 Sir Edward Coke, *The Third Part of the Institutes of the Lawes of England Concerning High Treason, and Other Pleas of the Crown, and Criminall Causes* (London, 1644), p. 181.
61 Heywood Townshend, *Historical Collections; or, An Exact Account of the Last Four Parliaments of Q. Elizabeth of Famous Memory* (London, 1680), pp. 233, 234.
62 *Nic. Eth.* VI.5.1140a25–9, 1140b6–7, in Aristotle, *Complete Works,* vol. II, p. 1800.
63 Tawney, 'Preface', p. viii.

CHAPTER TWENTY-FOUR

COMMERCE AND CONSUMPTION

Ian W. Archer

In 1580, Richard Hakluyt, a Middle Temple lawyer, enthusiast for overseas exploration and uncle to his more famous namesake, the author of *The Principall Navigations,* drew up instructions for Charles Jackman and Arthur Pet, who were preparing an expedition to find a route to China by way of the north-east passage. Among these was a list of 'things to be carried with you, whereof more or less is to be carried for a shew of our commodities to be made'. A huge range of the shop goods of London's drapers, haberdashers, glovers, cutlers, pewterers, locksmiths, cordwainers and glassmakers was to be assembled to impress the Chinese with the trading potential of their English visitors: cloths and linens of various kinds, haberdashery wares (including caps, combs, buttons, girdles and 'spectacles of the common sort; others of crystal trimmed with silver'), 'gloves of all sorts . . . points of all sorts', locks, keys and hinges 'whereof if vent may be hereafter we shall set our subjects in work' and 'a garnish of pewter for a shew of a vent of that English commodity'.[1]

At one level, Hakluyt's list testifies to the economic confidence of the Elizabethans. He appreciated that they were dealing with a civilised people, who would need convincing of the skill, wisdom and political sophistication of the newcomers: they were to take silver coins 'which is a thing that shall in silence speak to wise men more than you imagine'; the evidence that weights and measures were used would be 'a certain show of wisdom and of certain government settled here'. His list testifies to the variety of consumer goods available in Elizabeth's England and to the inventiveness of its artisans whose 'excellent workmanship' is to be commended. But beneath the text's surface lurk some of the preoccupations of the Elizabethan intelligentsia about the country's underlying economic weakness, beset by a growing problem of underemployed poor. Mariners' caps were to be taken,

> whereof if ample vent may be found it would turn to an infinite commodity of the common poor people by knitting . . . For in finding ample vent of anything that is to be wrought in this realm is more worth to our people, besides the gain of the merchant, than Christchurch, Bridewell, the Savoy and all the hospitals of England.

Moreover, many of the goods listed were probably not of English manufacture at all: the Spanish blankets, shoes of Spanish leather and Venice glasses are giveaways, and who in England would have been capable of making goggles ('glazen eyes to ride with against the dust')? The tensions within Hakluyt's text are echoed by differences of opinion among historians about the state of the Elizabethan economy: was this a period of growing impoverishment, culminating in the 'crisis of the 1590s', or was it a period of modest economic growth, fuelled by rising consumer demand among the middling groups?

Government pundits and intellectuals were among the pessimists. Hakluyt's list overlaps at several points with the lists of superfluous imports that they enumerated. Sir Thomas Smith, in *The Discourse of the Commonweal,* written in 1549 marvelled at the 'nombre . . . of trifles [that] commeth hether from beyonde the seas, that we might ether clene spare, or els make them with in oure owne Realme'.[2] William Cecil, Smith's friend and colleague, internalised the lessons about the outflow of bullion and the loss of employment opportunities for England's own poor. Among his papers are lists of imports in which the 'unnecessary wares' loom large. The list of 1559 valued imports of gloves at £2,636, knives at £1,558, hats at £7,915, looking glasses at £667, and drinking glasses at £663 10s. In 1564–5, 111,132 combs, 97,488 packs of playing cards, 19,620 inkhorns and 90 million pins were imported into London. In another list of 1565, linens accounted for £86,250 and worsteds for £18,374. The torrent of imported manufactured goods in the mid-century reflected their easy availability in Antwerp, on which England's overseas trade was dangerously dependent. Antwerp had become the entrepot of northern Europe, as a result of its favoured location at the intersection of trading routes (the east–west route from the Baltic to Biscay and the north–south routes through the Rhine Valley), its choice by the Portuguese as the staple town for the spices of the East and the proximity of well-developed industries such as cloth-finishing. By the beginning of Elizabeth's reign, London has been described as Antwerp's satellite, its merchants making easy profits by trading English broadcloth for the cornucopia of luxury goods and basic consumer items that so concerned the commentators. It was undoubtedly a beneficial arrangement for London and fuelled the early stages of the city's phenomenal growth in the sixteenth century, but with over 90 per cent of the country's cloth exports passing through the capital's port, the effect on provincial urban economies was stultifying. There was a real sense in which London's growth in this period was parasitic on the rest of the economy.

The dependence on imports reflects the relative technological backwardness of England at this date. Its printing industry, for example, was small by the standards of the other major European centres such as Antwerp, Paris and Venice; it never really developed the specialist trade in Latin books which were obtained through the Continental fairs, and the quality of its print meant that it was never a centre for luxury book products. The goldsmiths' shops of Cheapside were one of the city's top tourist attractions, but most of the more elaborate pieces came from overseas or were produced by aliens resident in England. Thirty-eight of the 127 items in the Earl of Pembroke's collection in 1561 were of foreign manufacture; that they were more highly valued is shown by the Earl's decision to exclude them from the sale of silver he made in that year. The lower standards of craft production by English goldsmiths are to be explained in part by the fact that they did not participate in the prolonged training and travel between different centres of production that characterised their Continental competitors. Although fledgling potteries were established in Elizabeth's reign, native pottery production was backward by Continental standards, and during the late sixteenth and early seventeenth centuries huge quantities of ceramics were imported into England from the Rhineland. Foreigners seem to have muscled in on even the production of the painted cloths which were common forms of interior decoration: in 1601 it was claimed that 'not a hundred yards of newe paynted cloth [is] made in a yeare here, by reason of soe muche paynted Flanders peeces brought from thence.'[3] Although England attracted a large number of religious refugees during the reign of Elizabeth, it was not the first choice for economic migrants. It has been noted that migrants to England in the 1560s tended to come not from the prosperous southern Netherlands but from the more depressed areas, while in the 1590s many migrants to London were drawn back to Amsterdam, a more attractive prospect than London.

The situation was, however, changing in Elizabeth's reign. The government fostered schemes for import substitution by issuing patents to protect those who brought in new techniques of production. In 1567, for example, a refugee from Antwerp named Jean Carre began manufacturing glass on the site of the former Crutched Friars in London; he later introduced nine Venetian glass workers, who under Jacomo Verzelini took over the business and obtained a patent in 1574. Although the English production was at first crude, by the 1620s the Venetian ambassador was complaining that English crystal glass rivalled that produced by his compatriots. In other sectors, industrial progress was due less to government initiative than to imitation of foreign techniques by Englishmen. Edmund Howes, writing in 1615, attributed the development of the worsted-stocking knitting industry to an English apprentice who in 1564 borrowed a pair from an Italian merchant and copied them, 'and so in short space they waxed common'.[4] It is a pretty tall story, but it might capture something of the processes of manufacturing adaptation. By 1595, stocking knitting had developed around Norwich, Doncaster and Richmond: the industry's relative dispersal suggests that it may have involved the commercialisation of embedded peasant techniques. Likewise, the development of the new draperies (lighter and more varied cloths suited to southern markets which gradually displaced the struggling broadcloths in England's export portfolio), particularly in East Anglia, was not simply the result of the injection of skill brought by waves of immigrants from the Low Countries to towns such as Colchester and Norwich but mobilised traditional peasant know-how.

The growing concern about the volume of manufactured imported goods and the gradual adaptation of English producers suggests that consumer demand may have been rising in Elizabeth's reign. Certainly, the most famous contemporary account of social change in the period, written by William Harrison and published in the 1577 edition of Holinshed's *Chronicles*, would seem to bear this out.

> The furniture of our houses also exceedeth and is grown in manner even to passing delicacy; and herein I do not speak of the nobility and gentry only but likewise of the lowest sort in most places of our South Country that have anything at all to take to. Certes in noblemen's houses it is not rare to see abundance of arras, rich hangings of tapestry, silver vessel, and so much other

plate as may furnish sundry cupboards, to the sum oftentimes of £1,000 or £2,000 at the least, whereby the value of this and the rest of their stuff doth grow to be almost inestimable. Likewise in the houses of knights, gentlemen, merchantmen, and some other wealthy citizens, it is not geason [uncommon] to behold generally their great provision of tapestry, Turkey work, pewter, brass, fine linen, and thereto costly cupboards of plate, worth £500 or £600 or £1,000, to be deemed by estimation. But as herein all these sorts do far exceed their elders and predecessors, and in neatness and curiosity the merchant all other, so in time past the costly furniture stayed there, whereas now it is descended yet lower, even unto the inferior artificers and many farmers, who, by virtue of their old and not of their new leases, have for the most part learned also to garnish their cupboards with plate, their joint beds with tapestry and silk hangings, and their tables with carpets and fine napery, whereby the wealth of our country. . . . doth infinitely appear.[5]

He goes on to describe three manifestations of rising living standards reported to him by the old men of his village. The first is 'the multitude of chimneys lately erected', reflecting improved heating and cooking facilities. The second is 'the great (although not general) amendment of lodging': whereas in the past people slept on straw pallets, nowadays feather-stuffed mattresses were more common. The third area of change is 'the exchange of vessel, as of treen [wooden] platters into pewter, and wooden spoons into silver or tin'.[6] Other social commentators bore out Harrison's judgement. Richard Carew, probably influenced by Harrison's passage, explained in his *Survey of Cornwall* (1602) that in the recent past Cornish dwellings had earth walls and lacked amenities such as window glass and chimneys; their beds were straw and blankets, while linen was uncommon. 'To conclude', he wrote, 'a mazer and a panne or two comprised all their substance: but now most of these fashions are banished, and the Cornish husbandman conformeth himselfe with a better universally supplied civilitie to the Easterne patterne.'[7]

Harrison is keen to emphasise the social depth of the changes he describes, as consumer goods are adopted by 'inferior artificers and many farmers', but there is reason to question their pervasiveness, not least because he inserts significant qualifiers, noting that change is more advanced in the southern parts, and that the improvements in lodging are 'not general'. Moreover, when he revised his account in 1587, he added a more pessimistic section on the 'losers', those who were the victims of rack-renting enclosing landlords and usurers. Historians have tended to square Harrison's circle by suggesting that what the period witnessed was a process of social polarisation, by which those with surpluses to sell on the market prospered from rising agricultural prices, while those who were dependent on the market for some or all of their foodstuffs (labourers, craftsmen and husbandmen) lost out particularly in years of dearth. Even the most optimistic measures of real wages suggest that they deteriorated by something of the order of 40 per cent. While we can accept this verdict in outline, there is still room for disagreement, however, about just how many people fell into the category of victims of economic change. The relevance of wage series to the real lives of craftsmen, many of whom were self-employed or who had buffers against the market in the form of small holdings, has been questioned, and we remain ignorant about the level of underemployment in the economy. While we know that the contribution of women and children to the family economy must be factored in, we have no satisfactory way of measuring family earnings. Poverty, although a serious problem for the Elizabethan authorities, was not as all-pervasive as some early social historians assumed. The notion that the tax-exempt should be counted as poor has been called into question. Most contemporary surveys suggest that around 5 per cent of households were in need of regular support, and another 15–20 per cent hovered on the margins of subsistence. An emphasis on social polarisation may have led us to underestimate the relative thickness of the middling groups. In an appendix to Stow's *Survey of London,* it was claimed that 'in number they of the middle place be first, and doe farre exceede both the rest: Hyrelings [by which he meant labourers] be next, and Marchantes bee the last.'[8]

We can go some way to quantifying the changes Harrison describes through the analysis of probate inventories, listings and valuations of the moveable goods of recently deceased persons taken by their neighbours. Craig Muldrew has adopted the simple expedient of counting the number of items separately listed in a sample of 330 probate inventories from a variety of locations to demonstrate the multiplication of consumer goods in this period. Between 1520 and 1600, the average number of goods per household increased by 68 per cent in Lincolnshire and 140 per cent in Chesterfield, with the rate of growth being fastest in the period 1550–80. While stressing that poorer households would have been unable to increase their consumption as significantly as the wealthy because of the need to spend a higher proportion of their income on basic foodstuffs, he suggests that rather than the poor owning fewer goods, social polarisation was reflected in the huge increase in goods among farmers and tradesmen compared with a largely static situation for the poor. Moreover, he notes that the poor were not altogether excluded from the culture of consumption because many owned a significant number of things. Take the example of the Chesterfield widow Isabell Johnson, who died in 1581. Her inventoried wealth totalled £7 1s. 9d., but among her possessions were two feather beds and two bolsters, a Flanders chests, eleven pewter dishes, three basins, two candlesticks, a brass mortar and pestle, four brass pots, two great spits, two silver spoons; her clothing consisted of a gown, a petticoat, a kirtle, a waistcoat and three handkerchiefs.

It would, however, be pushing the case too far to claim that the later sixteenth century witnessed a 'consumer revolution'. In the first place, even among the wealthier echelons, the range of goods on which surplus wealth might be spent was quite limited. Large amounts of wealth were still invested in displays of plate, ranging from around 26 per cent of inventoried wealth (Sir Henry Sharington of Lacock, 1575) to 60 per cent (the London alderman Sir Thomas Ramsey, 1590). Where furnishings were concerned, disproportionate amounts were spent on tapestries. The contents of the Earl of Leicester's castle at Kenilworth (excluding plate) were valued at £2,684 4s. 1d.; his tapestries accounted for nearly one-third of that (£837 4s. 3d.). Carpets used to cover tables were another £148 2s. 2d. Much was spent on beds and their accoutrements. At Kenilworth, the bedsteads with their apparel were valued at £571 11s. 8d., down beds and feather beds at £285 15s.; pillows at £13 12s., linen quilts at £11 10s., fustian blankets at £27 10s., counterpoints at £62 4s., sheets at £4 3s. 8d., and pillowcases at £39 4s., that is, about 39 per cent of the total inventoried value. By contrast, other rooms in the house were more sparsely furnished. Chairs, cushions and stools accounted for £92 2s., tables, forms and shelves for £25 2s. 10d., chests for £6 8s., and pictures and maps for £21 7s. 6d. The collection of table linen at Kenilworth was worth £42 4s., perhaps proportionately less than some others. Sir Thomas Ramsey's linen (including 312 damask napkins and 207 diaper napkins) was worth £151 16s. 6d.; the Earl of Bedford's in 1583 £82. It is clear that elite spending would have benefited a limited number of luxury tradesmen, also that a sizeable proportion of their expenditure was on goods imported from overseas. The correspondence of Sir Thomas Gresham, Elizabeth's financial agent in the Low Countries, is peppered with special commissions from leading courtiers and aristocrats. For William Cecil, Gresham provided items as varied as a clock, silk hose, silver candlesticks, tapestries, a wolf gown and even the stonework for the classical loggias at the minister's Theobalds residence near London.

The most comprehensive and sophisticated survey of inventories undertaken by Mark Overton and others unfortunately only begins in 1600, but its findings for the early seventeenth century are suggestive. Table 24.1 demonstrates the presence of certain types of good in Kent and Cornish inventories between 1600 and 1629. The data bears out some of Harrison's comments about the spread of feather beds, linen and pewter, but they were by no means universal, and some of the more novel items of furniture such as court cupboards and press cupboards, which provided opportunities for display, were much less common. It is also striking that the differences between Kent and Cornwall underline the scale of regional variation in the adoption of new consumer goods. It is also unsurprising that they were more widespread in urban areas, and it may well have been London merchants in contact with the arbiters of taste on the Continent who set the tone for new consumer goods among the social elites.

Table 24.1 Proportions on inventories recording certain types of household goods, 1603–29, percentages

	Cornwall	*Kent*
Court cupboards	1	12
Press cupboards	11	15
Tables (median number)	1	2
Carpets	21	18
Upholstered furniture	1	16
Feather beds	33	44
Cushions	12	37
Pewter	46	94
Cauldrons	24	22
Linen	59	92
Sheets	52	92
Tablecloths	32	69
Napkins	15	61

Although the scale of consumer demand should not be exaggerated, it is worth stressing that the sheer fact of population growth (from 2.4 million in 1540 to about 4.1 million in 1600) would have generated considerable extra spending. Take the often-neglected area of clothing, which, according to Gregory King, writing at the end of the seventeenth century, consumed about 25 per cent of the average family budget. It has been estimated that the cost of clothing a male child at the beginning of the seventeenth century was about 15s. 10d. and a female about 12s. 4d. The accounts for the maintenance of foundlings for a number of London parishes suggest that they might be spending as much as 20s. per annum on their clothing. We know rather less about the cost of adult clothing, but something might be gleaned from the assumptions made by charitable benefactors. Robert Dowe provided his almsmen with a gown of £2 3s. 4d. every three years, but they would have needed shirts and shoes more regularly. Robert Donkin left a bequest to provide frieze gowns, shirts and a pair of shoes for twelve men and gowns, smocks and shoes for twelve women. In the 1590s, the men's gowns (7 yards at 16d. per yard) cost 9s. 4d.; the women's (7.5 yards at 12d. per yard) cost 7s. 6d.; the men's shirts 2s., and the women's smocks 20d.; the shoes cost 12d. That represents a total expenditure of 12s. 4d. on the men's clothing and 10s. 2d on the women's. As the materials were more flimsy, Donkin's gowns were probably less hard-wearing than Dowe's and needed more regular replacement. Although the poor might have more recourse to the thriving second-hand market for clothing, it seems reasonable to assume expenditure of at least 15s. per head in the 1590s. If that is the case, then a population of 4.1 million would have been spending a minimum £3 million per annum on clothing. These are, of course, highly conservative estimates because they are based on spending by the poor. Others spent a lot more: the clothing for a soldier in the 1590s cost around £3; the London merchant Sir Thomas Ramsey's apparel was valued at £75 in 1590, while at the top of the scale Robert Dudley was spending as much as £1,200 per annum on clothing at the beginning of his political career in the 1560s. The true expenditure on clothing would have been very substantially more. So it is not surprising that shoemakers and tailors are normally among the top four occupations in urban economies. This exercise is sufficient to suggest a potentially much larger domestic market than we have previously realised. It is difficult to get meaningful comparators, but cloth exports in the 1560s have been valued at £1 million per annum.

More important than clothing in family budgets was food and drink. For the poor, the deterioration in real wages over the course of the sixteenth century meant that diets worsened as people switched from wheat to oats and barley and probably ate less meat. But it is not clear how malnourished the poor really were. Diet sheets drawn up for the institutionalised poor are apparently generous. That for the inmates of Bridewell Hospital drawn up in 1600 assumed that an able bodied male would be consuming 24 ounces of bread, and 4 pints of beer each day, with 6.5 ounces of beef on non-fast days and 4 ounces of cheese or 2 ounces of butter on fast days. A working woman would receive 16 ounces of bread and 2 pints of beer per day, with the same allowances for meat and dairy produce. It has been estimated that these diets would have provided a more than adequate 2,000–3,000 calories per day, and the presence of meat and dairy products suggests that there was a reasonable protein element. This is not to deny the reality of suffering in critical years of dearth such as the mid-1590s, and there is clear evidence of death by starvation in marginal pastoral districts, particularly in the north-west, but outside these areas there may well have been some room for manoeuvre in pauper budgets. Certainly for those above the ranks of the poor the evidence is for rising dietary standards in the later sixteenth century. Foreigners were impressed by the English diet. The Venetian Alessandro Magno visiting London in 1562 noted the abundance of beef and mutton ('it is almost impossible to believe that they could eat so much meat in one city alone') and the ready availability of dried cod, which he found 'tough and flavourless' and oysters, which were served roasted, stewed or fired with butter or, as most commonly, eaten raw with some barley bread.[9] Emmanuel van Meteren, an Antwerp merchant who had lived for a long time in London, noted that the English 'eat a great deal of meat: and as the Germans surpass the bounds of sobriety in drinking, these do the same in eating'.[10] Harrison likewise noted that the food of artificers 'consisteth principally in beef and such meat as the butcher selleth, that is to say, mutton, veal, lamb, pork, etc., whereof he findeth great store in the markets adjoining, beside souse, brawn, bacon, fruit, pies of fruit, fowls of sundry sorts, cheese, butter, eggs, etc'.[11] He claimed that the food provided at guild gatherings rivalled the tables of the nobility, while husbandmen out-vied each other in feasting at bride-ales and the churching of women. More elaborate diets are also suggested by the trade statistics. Imports of sugar quadrupled from 282,016 pounds in 1557 to over 1 million pounds by 1595. Currant imports to London from the Levant stood at over 1 million pounds a year in the 1590s; they were growing rapidly, and reached 3–5 million pounds in the 1620s. As Muldrew suggests, this represents about 1 pound per person. The imports of fruit, spices and groceries to East Anglia suggest consumption levels of 7–8.5 pounds per person each year in the 1590s.

Increasing consumption was not regarded as an unmitigated boon. To the extent that it encouraged ever more imports it generated intense concern about the balance of trade, but it also came into conflict with key elements of the prevailing ethical system. The Christian and classical traditions were hostile to accumulation for its own sake, both associating consumption with luxury, and luxury in turn with moral decadence and sexual concupiscence. The prevailing system of aristocratic ethics maintained that largesse (or 'conspicuous consumption' as we might call it) was an appropriate, indeed necessary, marker of the 'magnificence' that characterised the social elites, but that it was inappropriate for other social groups to imitate its forms. The social hierarchy was conceived of as a hierarchy of consumption, with particular forms of spending appropriate to each level. The most obvious example of this was the sumptuary legislation which carefully codified the types of clothing and fabric appropriate to each social group. It was also manifest in the hostility of Elizabeth's government to the consumption of venison (the food of the aristocracy) at guild feasts. These ethical assumptions were at odds with the habits of imitation and social emulation which were apparently common among the lower orders.

Excessive consumption was therefore associated by the moralists with economic and moral decay, social confusion, monstrosity and effeminacy. Philip Stubbes, anatomising the kingdom's abuses in a wonderfully splenetic tract, identified 'three cankers which in processe of time wil eat vp the whole common Welth, if speedy reformation be not had, namely, daintie Fare, gorgious Buildings, and sumptuous Apparel'.[12] The royal proclamation of 1574 associated the 'excess of apparel' with 'the superfluity of unnecessary foreign wares', which together threatened 'the manifest decay not only of a great part of the wealth of the whole realm . . . but also particularly the wasting and undoing of a great number of young gentlemen'.[13] Sir Thomas Smith, drawing on the lessons of his reading in classical history, had warned in the *Discourse,* that 'excesses [of clothing and food] were used in Rome a little before the decline of the Empire, as wise men have thought it the occasion of the decay therof . . . I pray God this realm may beware by that example, especially London, the head of this empire.'[14] Another insistent theme of government regulation was that failure to observe the laws has led to 'the confusion also of degrees in all places being great where the meanest are as richly appareled as their betters'. Philip Stubbes complained of 'such a confuse mingle mangle of apparell' that

> it is verie hard to knowe, who is noble, who is worshipfull, who is a gentleman, who is not: for you shall haue those, which are neither of the nobylitie gentilitie, nor yeomanry, no, nor yet anie Magistrat or Officer in the common welth, go daylie in silkes, veluets, satens, damasks, taffeties and such like, notwithstanding that they be both base by byrthe, meane be estate, & seruyle by calling. This is a great confusion & a general disorder.[15]

The gender order was likewise under threat from the effeminising effects of fashion: 'through our fond toyes and nice inuentions, we haue brought our selues into suche pusillanimitie, and effeminat condition, as we may seeme rather nice dames, and yonge gyrles, than puissante gents, or manlie men, as our forefathers haue bene'.[16] Female fashions threatened to make women indistinguishable from men: William Harrison's diatribe against the 'fantastical folly of fashion' attacks the women's

> doublets with pendant codpieces on the breast. . . . their galligaskins to bear out their bums. . . . their farthingales and diversely coloured netherstocks . . . , whereby their bodies are rather deformed than commended. I have met with some of these trulls in London so disguised that it hath passed my skill to discern whether they were men or women. Thus it is now come to pass that women are become men and men transformed into monsters.[17]

Fashion both destabilised gender identities and dehumanised.

Over the course of the next century, many of the assumptions which held back consumption were to be eroded, as the economic case for 'luxury' was developed. There were already counter-arguments being developed during Elizabeth's reign. The celebration of improved living standards that characterised authors such as Harrison (interestingly the attack on fashion is decoupled from the discussion of furnishings, which is much less moralised) and Carew fitted into a discourse of international competition establishing England's superiority over European rivals. When in 1615 Edmund Howes celebrated London's trade as 'the choicest store house of the world', he was plugging into a similar discourse of international comparison. Such arguments went with recognition of the positive role played by merchants in the commonwealth. For men such as the Hakluyts, 'commodity' and 'vent' were keywords; the development of overseas trade led to wealth and honour; and merchants therefore had a key role to play in the commonwealth. Within London, the excoriation of merchant usury and sharp practice in sermons was gradually displaced by other strands capable of recognising their potentially positive contribution. So, Robert Wilkinson, in a Paul's Cross sermon of 1607, celebrated the merchant as 'of al men the most adventurous in his labour, the most peacable upon the sea, the most profitable to the land, yea the merchant is the combination and union of lands and nations'.[18] The royal works official, local magistrate and MP, Edward Forset, writing in 1606, recognised that among the duties of the sovereign was 'to prouide for the nourishing and mainteining of the state with necessaries. . . . to cherish in the subiects an appetite of acquiring of commodities, to graunt to them places of Mart and Market for the digesting of the same vnto all parts of the Realme'.[19] That the sumptuary codes were so much at odds with consumer preferences explains the repeal of the existing apparel legislation in 1604 and the subsequent failure to replace it. Sumptuary distinctions between the classes still mattered, of course, but increasingly they were maintained by regular shifts in fashion, by which the elite kept one step ahead of their lower-class imitators.

Changing patterns of consumption were reflected in the changes in the retail environment. These were most marked in London. Retail outlets proliferated, increased in size and became more specialised, the first mall-like structures emerging in the Royal Exchange (1565) and Britain's Burse (1609). The sale of foodstuffs took place within a traditional structure of markets established in the thirteenth century: street markets for butchers were held in Eastcheap and the Newgate shambles; fish was obtainable from New Fish Street and Old Fish Street; the Stocks market had permanent stalls for both butchers and fishmongers; there were four grain markets (at Billingsgate and Queenhithe on the waterside and at Newgate Street and Gracechurch Street inland); there was a general street market for poultry, butter, cheese, fruits and flowers in Cheapside. There is some sign of pressure on these traditional market spaces in the sixteenth century. Billingsgate was expanded in 1523–5 and 1544; new market houses were built at Newgate in 1547 and Queenhithe in 1564–6, and both were enlarged in the 1590s; a new cornmeal market was established at Bishopsgate in 1599–1600. Market hours were extended both officially and unofficially. The meat markets were held six days per week; there were regular complaints of Sunday trading and trading by candlelight in Cheapside. Another indication that the markets could not cope with the pressure of rising demand was the proliferation of hucksters. The aldermen were particularly concerned to limit the activities of the fishwives who hawked fish in baskets about the city streets, but their licensing regime was overwhelmed by demand as the steadily increasing numbers of licences reveal: just fifty-two in 1561, 100 in 1570 and 160 in the 1590s.

For luxuries and household goods, shoppers would have recourse to more specialist retail outlets. Smith testifies to the proliferation and specialisation of retail facilities in sixteenth-century London.

> I have sene within these xxtie yeres, when there weare not of these haberdashers that sell French or millan cappes, glasses, daggers, swerdes, girdles and such thinges, not a dossen in all London. And now from the Towere to Westminster alonge, everie streat is full of them: and theire shoppes glisters and shine of

glasses, as well lookinge as drinckinge, yea all manor vesselles of the same stuffe; painted cruses, gaye daggers, knives, swordes, and girdles, that is able to make anie temporate man to gase on them and to bie sumwhat, thoughe it serve to no purpose necessarie.[20]

Increasing specialisation was apparent among shops: haberdashers, for example, divided between haberdashers of hats, haberdashers of small wares, paper dealers and specialists in toys and musical instruments. There was still a considerable degree of occupational zoning, most notably in Goldsmiths' Row in Cheapside. This 'beautiful frame of fair houses and shops' had been built by Thomas Wood, goldsmith in 1491 and bequeathed to his company in 1533. It was according to John Stow 'uniformly builded four storeys high, beautified towards the street with the goldsmiths' arms', and it was one of the celebrated tourist attractions of London.[21]

Over the course of the sixteenth century there was increasing demand for retail space. Derek Keene has demonstrated that by the end of Elizabeth's reign land values in the capital had recovered to the levels of the thirteenth century when the city's population had peaked before the Black Death. But the pattern of retailing was different between the two periods. Whereas in the thirteenth century minute shops and trading plots had proliferated, in the sixteenth century the retailing units were larger, and there were frequent amalgamations. Thus, in the early sixteenth century, a Cheapside location known as the Broad Seld comprised four shops and a number of small booths; when it was rebuilt in 1530, as 'The Key', it contained only one great shop measuring 60 feet by 21 feet. The most extraordinary shopping space of sixteenth-century London was the Royal Exchange, built by Sir Thomas Gresham in the 1560s as a meeting place for merchants modelled on the Antwerp bourse and incorporating shopping facilities. It had three galleries surrounding a classically inspired courtyard at that time very novel in London.

London loomed increasingly large in the shopping habits of the social elites. Although the housing developments which turned the West End into a fashionable gentry quarter were still some way off, the beginnings of the London 'season' can be dated to Elizabeth's reign. Increasing numbers of gentlemen stuffed into rather expensive lodgings visited the capital in pursuit of patronage, to deal with litigation and to enjoy the capital's expanding leisure facilities such as the theatre. While in London they would avail themselves of its shopping opportunities. If they did not visit London themselves, they often drew on the services of kin or other agents in the capital to furnish their needs, and gentry correspondence between the provinces and the capital is peppered with news about fashions and details of negotiations with tradesmen. The capital did not monopolise the shopping patterns of the elite, and it is worth emphasising that its impact was much lower in distant counties, but it was often the key source for luxuries and specialist goods. The Elizabethan Earls of Rutland, moving between their seat at Belvoir and the capital, drew on their estates for basic provisions, obtained fish from Stourbridge Fair and claret via Boston, but sack, muscadine and Rhenish wine, along with fruit and spices, came from London. Their accounts show that they had regular recourse to London suppliers for fashionable clothing and accessories, plate and jewels and cloth for liveries.

Although a little outside our period, the early seventeenth-century household accounts of the L'Estranges of Hunstanton in Norfolk are quite revealing of the pattern of gentry shopping. Norwich, King's Lynn and Walsingham were all important sources of consumer goods: attendance at the Norwich assizes was usually the excuse for shopping for groceries, books, clothing accessories and miscellaneous goods such as vial strings. Both Norwich and King's Lynn had specialist crafts such as bookbinders as well as medical practitioners. Craftsmen were available in the surrounding villages: there was a tailor at Ringstead and a saddler at Dereham. But for the more exotic goods, servants were sent to London two or three times a year. In 1612, for example, there were trips in June and December. In June, large quantities of expensive table linen with the story of Caleb and Joshua and a consignment of pewter were purchased. In December, the purchases included apparel for which the family's London tailor Mr Locke received £60, twelve red leather stools and four chairs of Russian leather, a Turkey carpet, a square cloth and cupboard cloth of turkey work, three feather beds and bolsters, a pair of down pillows, a pair of andirons (fire-dogs), a pewter cistern and a limbeck (a distilling vessel), and 50 pounds of sugar. The bills could be very expensive, as much as £185 8s. 8d. on a single trip in 1608, when the need to cut a figure was paramount because of Sir Hamon L'Estrange's service as sheriff. Getting these goods from London to Hunstanton could be a complex operation, sometimes combining land and water carriage. Freightage charges for goods sent by water were much lower, just 1s. per hundredweight as compared to 5s. per hundredweight by land.

The larger regional centres such as Norwich and Bristol boasted specialist shops similar to those found in the metropolis, though fewer in number. Smaller and struggling towns such as Coventry could not sustain a very high level of specialisation, and the norm was for more general shops in which mercery, haberdashery and sometimes grocery goods were combined. Other tradesmen kept a lock-up shop sometimes in more than one town but travelled around the countryside to sell goods directly to customers. Some quite small places, sometimes without market status, therefore boasted shops. Much to the annoyance of townsmen, but probably essential to the distribution of goods into the remoter rural areas, chapmen began to proliferate. To judge from the patterns of their indebtedness to Londoners, they were agents of economic integration between the capital and the provinces, chapmen in remote counties such as Shropshire, Cheshire and Northumberland buying their goods in London. For all that towns complained about competition from London and from itinerant traders, the Elizabethan period probably saw a modest recovery from their recent difficulties, as they were able to participate in the overall expansion of the market. The linkages between London and the provinces are clear from the sheer variety of consumer goods which could be found in pretty obscure places. The shop of James Backhouse (d. 1578) in Kirkby Lonsdale stocked a great variety of cloths in many different colours; he had a full range of groceries and a reasonable selection of books, not only primers, ABCs and catechisms but also classical texts including Virgil and Terence.

The economic development of the later sixteenth century meant that some progress was made towards import substitution; fledgling glass-making and pottery industries were established; there was a substantial expansion in output of the new draperies and knitted stockings. But opinion-formers were as anxious as ever about the dependence on imported goods. Thomas Milles, the customs official writing at the turn of the seventeenth century, chimed with Sir Thomas Smith's mid-sixteenth-century comments in his fulminations against 'forraine idle commodities'; 'our returnes (for the most part) being but toys and Tabacco, Bells or Bables, of things needlesse or bootlesse, doe shew how strangers for better wares can fat vs vp with pryde, or fodder vs with folly.'[22] There were new indulgences in the form of dangerous drugs such as tobacco, which would almost immediately generate a new moral panic, drawing on many of the conventional tropes of anti-consumerism. The commercial development of later Elizabethan and early Stuart England was indeed import-led, but historians have tended to evaluate this more positively, because many of the new commodities encouraged spin-off industries such as the Thames-side sugar-refining plants, while the expansion of trade in general fuelled ship-building, a key employer.

Moreover, over the course of Elizabeth's reign, England had begun, largely through force of circumstance, the long and painful process of diversifying its overseas trade, breaking its dependence on a single Continental entrepot. The Antwerp mart had been destabilised by the civil wars in the Low Countries in the 1560s and 1570s, and the London merchants had to seek out a new entrepot in Hamburg, and later at Middelburg and Stade, but it now proved much harder to secure access to the rich Italian textiles and the Oriental spices so much in demand among the Elizabethan elite. It was thus the rise in the price of imported goods that drove London's merchants into new areas. Taking advantage of the weakening of Venetian commerce during the 1570s, the Londoners established a presence in the western and central Mediterranean, from where they imported spices, pepper, dried fruit, wine and silks. The next step was the penetration of the Ottoman Empire to secure access to the silks and spices of the East which came by the overland routes, the Portuguese having failed to establish a full monopoly. In 1578–9, two London merchants, Richard Staper and Edward Osborne, sent William Harborne on a secret embassy to Sultan Murad III and secured commercial concessions. In 1581, the small group of merchants who traded there were incorporated as the Turkey Company, and in 1592 they merged with the Venice Company to form the Levant Company. But English trading strategies had come to depend on the overland routes to the East. The Muscovy Company sought trade routes eastwards through Persia; the Levant Company depended on the overland routes via the Persian Gulf to Syria. The flaws in this strategy became clear as the Dutch, taking advantage of Portuguese weakness in the East, began to penetrate there. It was also clear that individual enterprise was too high-risk in this sector, so when the East India Company was granted its charter in 1600 it was on the basis of the joint stock principle to spread risks.

There is something dangerously teleological in ending with these adumbrations of empire. English trade was still overwhelmingly concentrated on north-western Europe, the numbers of merchants involved in the Mediterranean trades were still very small, and the early East India voyages were very fragile affairs. But there was enormous public interest in the East India trade from the beginning, an indication of the degree to which commercial concerns were becoming more central to public political discourse. When, in 1609, Ben Jonson was commissioned to write an entertainment to celebrate the opening of the Earl of Salisbury's rival to the Royal

Exchange, Britain's Burse located in the Strand, it was the lure of the exotic commodities of the East to which he was drawn. As James, his wife and his heir approached, a shop boy addressed them:

> What doe you lacke? What is't you buy? Veary fine China stuffes, of all kindes and quallityes? China Chaynes, China Braceletts, China scarfes, China fannes, China girdles, China knives, China boxes, China Cabinetts, Casketts, Umbrellas, Sundyalls, Hower glasses, lookinge glasses, Burninge glasses, Concave glasses, Triangular glasses, Convexe glasses, Christall globes, Waxen pictures, Estrich Egges, Birds of paradise, Muskcads, Indian Mice, Indian ratts, China Dogges, and China cattes? Flowrs of silke, Mosaik fishes? Waxen fruict, and Purslane dishes? Very fine cages for Birds, Billyard Balls, Purses, Pipes, rattles, Basons, Ewers, Cups, Cans, Voyders, Toothpicks, Targets, falchions, Beards of all ages, Vizards, Spectacles? See what you lack.[23]

We began with a list of trade goods designed to impress the Chinese in 1580, but here is another list, a list of the imagined world of Oriental goods laid out before the English consumer. Once the prospect of direct contact with the East became proximate and real, there was no doubting the powerful pull exerted by their exotica over the imaginations and desires of the aristocratic consumers for whom Salisbury's new retail development was intended. The shop boy's list mingles commodities definitely from the East, such as porcelain, with what one suspects are English goods now transposed to an Oriental setting (the chains, bracelets and knives to be found in Cheapside) to add to their allure. England's 'glazen eyes to ride with against dust' had to give way before an altogether more tempting array of 'lookinge glasses, Burninge glasses, Concave glasses, Triangular glasses, Convexe glasses, Christall globes', and so forth. Here was a celebration of consumerism within the conventions of aristocratic and courtly entertainment, and from a poet who was generally at pains to avoid the smear of crass commercialism. There was no consumer revolution in Elizabethan England, but the world of consumer goods pressed ever more insistently on its imaginations and desires.

FURTHER READING

Alley, Hugh, *Hugh Alley's Caveat: The Markets of London in 1598: Folger MS V. A. 318*, ed. Ian Archer, Caroline Barron and Vanessa Harding (London, 1988).

Archer, Ian W., 'Material Londoners?' in Lena Cowen Orlin (ed.), *Material London, ca. 1600* (Pittsburgh, Pa., 2000), pp. 174–92.

—— 'Conspicuous Consumption Revisited: City and Court in the Reign of Elizabeth I', in Matthew P. Davies and Andrew Prescott (eds.), *London and the Kingdom: Essays in Honour of Caroline M. Barron* (Donington, 2008), pp. 38–57.

Bestall, J. M. and Fowkes, Dudley Vincent (eds.), *Chesterfield Wills and Inventories, 1521–1603* (Matlock, 1977).

Dietz, Brian, 'Overseas Trade and Metropolitan Growth' in A. L. Beier and R. A. P. Fairholt (eds.), *On an Inventory of the Household Goods of Sir Thomas Ramsey, Lord Mayor of London, 1577, Archaeologia*, 40 (1866): 311–42.

Beier, A. L. and Finlay, R. A. P. (eds.) *London, 1500–1700: The Making of the Metropolis* (London, 1986).

Fisher, F. J., 'The Development of London as a Centre of Conspicuous Consumption in the Sixteenth and Seventeenth Centuries', *Transactions of the Royal Historical Society,* 4th Ser., 30 (1948): 37–50.

Goldring, Elizabeth, 'The Earl of Leicester's Household Inventory of Kenilworth Castle, *c.* 1578', *English Heritage Historical Review,* 2 (2) (2007): 36–58.

Harris, Jonathan Gil, *Sick Economies: Drama, Mercantilism, and Disease in Shakespeare's England* (Philadelphia, Pa., 2004).

Keene, Derek, 'Ships and shipping in medieval London', in Lindy Grant (ed.), *Architecture and Archaeology in London* (British Archaeological Association, 1990).

—— 'Changes in London's Economic Hinterland as Indicated by Debt Cases in the Court of Common Pleas', in James A. Galloway (ed.), *Trade, Urban Hinterlands and Market Integration, c. 1300–1600* (London, 2000), pp. 59–81.

Luu, Lien Bich, *Immigrants and the Industries of London, 1500–1700* (Aldershot, 2005).

Mancall, Peter C., *Hakluyt's Promise: An Elizabethan's Obsession for an English America* (New Haven, Conn., 2007).

Muldrew, Craig, *The Economy of Obligation: The Culture of Credit and Social Relations in Early Modern England* (Basingstoke, 1998).

Overton, Mark, Whittle, Jane, Dean, Darron, and Hann, Andrew (eds.), *Production and Consumption in English Households, 1600–1750* (London, 2004).

Palliser, David Michael, *The Age of Elizabeth: England under the Later Tudors, 1547–1603,* 2nd edn (London, 1992).

Ramsay, George Daniel, *The City of London in International Politics at the Accession of Elizabeth Tudor* (Manchester, 1975).

Snodin, Michael, and Styles, John, *Design and the Decorative Arts: Britain 1500–1900* (London, 2001).

Spufford, Margaret, *The Great Reclothing of Rural England: Petty Chapmen and Their Wares in the Seventeenth Century* (London, 1985).

—— 'The Cost of Apparel in Seventeenth-Century England and the Accuracy of Gregory King', *Economic History Review,* 2nd Ser., 53 (4) (2000): 677–705.

Thirsk, Joan, *Economic Policy and Projects: The Development of a Consumer Society in Early Modern England* (Oxford, 1978).

Vernon, T. E., 'Inventory of Sir Henry Sharington: Contents of Lacock House, 1575', *Wiltshire Archaeological and Natural History Magazine,* 63 (1968): 72–82.

Willan, T. S., *The Inland Trade: Studies in English Internal Trade in the Sixteenth and Seventeenth Centuries* (Manchester, 1976).

Wrightson, Keith, *Earthly Necessities: Economic Lives in Early Modern Britain* (New Haven, Conn., 2000).

NOTES

1 R. H. Tawney and E. Power (eds.), *Tudor Economic Documents,* 3 vols. (London, 1924), vol. III, pp. 232–9.

2 *A Discourse of the Commonweal of This Realm of England,* ed. E. Lamond (Cambridge, 1895), p. 63.

3 T. E. Hartley (ed.), *Proceedings in the Parliaments of Elizabeth I,* 3 vols. (Leicester, 1981–95), vol. III, p. 470.

4 J. Stow, *The Annales; or, A Generall Chronicle of England, Begun First by Maister Iohn Stow, and After Him Continued and Augmented with Matters Forreyne, and Domestique, Auncient and Moderne, Vnto the Ende of This Present Yeere 1614. by Edmond Howes, Gentleman* (London, 1615), p. 866.

5 William Harrison, *The Description of England by William Harrison,* ed. G. Edelen (Washington DC, 1968), p. 200.

6 Harrison, *Description of England*, pp. 200–2.
7 R. Carew, *The Survey of Cornwall* (London, 1602), p. 66v.
8 J. Stow, *A Survey of London*, ed. C. L. Kingsford, 2 vols. (Oxford, 1908), vol. II, p. 208.
9 Alessandro Magno, 'The London Journal of Alessandro Magno 1562', ed. C. M. Barron, C. Coleman and C. Gobbi, *London Journal*, 9 (1983): 136–52; pp. 143, 147–8.
10 *England as Seen by Foreigners in the Days of Elizabeth and James the First*, ed. W. B. Rye (London, 1865), pp. 69–70.
11 Harrison, *Description of England*, p. 131.
12 P. Stubbes, *The Anatomie of Abuses . . .* (London, 1582), sig. J2v.
13 P. L. Hughes and J. F. Larkin (eds.), *Tudor Royal Proclamations*, 3 vols. (New Haven, Conn., 1964–9), vol. II, p. 381.
14 Smith, *Discourse*, p. 83.
15 Stubbes, *Anatomie of Abuses*, sig. C2v.
16 Stubbes, *Anatomie of Abuses*, sig. C1r–v.
17 Harrison, *Description of England*, pp. 145, 147.
18 R. Wilkinson, *The Merchant Royall a Sermon Preached at White-Hall before the Kings M.* (London, 1607), sig. D1.
19 E. Forsett, *A Comparative Discourse of the Bodies Natural and Politique* (London, 1606), pp. 13–14.
20 Smith, *Discourse*, p. 64.
21 Stow, *Survey of London*, vol. I, pp. 345–6.
22 T. Milles, *The Custumer's Replie or Second Apologie* (London, 1604), sig. D1v; *The Custumers's Alphabet and Primer* (London, 1608), sigs. D2–D2v.
23 J. Knowles, 'Jonson's Entertainment at Britain's Burse', in M. Butler (ed.), *Representing Ben Jonson* (Cambridge, 1999), p. 133.

CHAPTER TWENTY-FIVE

URBAN ECONOMIES

Muriel C. McClendon and Joseph P. Ward

Elizabethan England was a rural society in which most people lived and worked in small communities that were focused on agriculture. Towns served these communities as centres of distribution and trade, allowing rural villagers to acquire tools and other goods which they could not produce efficiently for themselves. Towns, in turn, were connected to one another, and to communities elsewhere in the wider world, through a network of exchange of goods and people. Historians do not always agree on the minimum size required of a community before it may be labelled 'urban', with some making the case that a population of 5,000 was required for a place to have all of the characteristics of an urban centre while others emphasise the ways in which relatively small settlements of no more than 400–500 people exhibited many distinctly urban characteristics. The discussion in the present essay is most influenced by this latter approach because it assumes that the primary function of an Elizabethan town was economic and that even relatively small communities played crucial roles in supplying commodities and immigrants to larger towns. Although many residents of a town could be employed in the agricultural sector, there would be a significant proportion of a town's inhabitants engaged in productive activity related only indirectly, if at all, to agriculture. Given that their primary reason for existence was economic, a survey of the economies of Elizabethan towns amounts to a survey of urban life generally.

Towns in Elizabethan England had sorted themselves into groupings associated with regional capitals such as York, Norwich and Bristol, with London sitting atop the hierarchy because of its unrivalled position of political and economic supremacy. As David Harris Sacks has put it, around the year 1600 London differed from other English towns because it 'was not just the dominant – the primate – in England's, and later Britain's developing urban system, but, since it drew its supplies, new inhabitants, and markets from the four corners of the land, it also had most of England, and later much of Britain, as its hinterland.'[1]

On the whole, English towns entered a period of relative economic vitality in the middle of the sixteenth century. Towns often fell prey to epidemics during the early modern period, so they needed to attract immigrants from their surrounding regions in order to maintain their populations. The population in the countryside regained levels seen previously only before the demographic collapse of the second half of the fourteenth century, after which more than half of the urban sites of 1350 being mere villages two centuries later. Still, the revival of urban life was only beginning during Elizabeth's reign, with only about 8 per cent of English people living in the twenty towns that had populations greater than 5,000 at the end of the sixteenth century. By contrast, at the end of the following century, thirty-two towns had more than 5,000 residents, and together they accounted for 17 per cent of the nation's total population.

The economic vitality of Elizabethan provincial towns is a subset of a larger issue related to the trends of growth and decline of pre-modern towns, which in turn is related to the general economic trends in the period. Towns were primarily centres of trade for their surrounding agrarian regions. While it is well known that England's urban communities were important centres of demand for agricultural products, it should also be remembered that towns were also sites of agricultural production. Many contained their own common lands, and it was not uncommon for urban dwellers to own livestock. Thus, urban and rural economies were inextricably linked in the early modern era. Activities which might be considered the exclusive province of rural areas, such as farming, were not unknown in English towns. In Worcester, for example, a number of residents kept and raised livestock, apparently to supplement the income they earned from their main occupations. In fact, pigs were sufficiently numerous there that the corporation was constantly concerned about the problems they caused as they roamed city streets. Some of York's residents also appear to have kept pigs, along with cattle, sheep and horses, which they grazed on lands between that city's walls and its boundaries. Not only did town-dwellers keep livestock, but some also grew agricultural products.

A more important distinction between urban and rural economies in the early modern period lies in the fact that most towns served as sites for the exchange of goods and services in a way that rural communities did not. As numerous scholars have pointed out, the most important towns were market centres, and market activities played a vital role in a town's and a region's economic health. It was not entirely unknown, though, for some villages to hold their own markets. Such villages have been labelled by some historians as 'market villages', rural settlements that took on the guise of urbanity on market days. However, these markets were of limited economic importance, as they tended to serve, at best, only their own populations and perhaps those of a few, nearby, similarly small settlements.

Recent research suggests that there were about 600 market towns across England in the sixteenth century. They ranged in size from settlements populated by 500 or 600 inhabitants to the largest provincial centres in the country, with populations in the thousands. The right to hold a market might be found in a town's charter and would specify the day or days on which a market could be held. Not all markets were formally chartered, however, but had arisen more or less spontaneously. Some of these had long lives before they received the formal recognition of a charter. Others, undoubtedly, rose and fell without leaving much, if any trace, in the written record. The existence of some others came to light only when they became subjects of controversy. Such was the case with wool market at Marshfield, whose status was challenged by the citizens of Elizabethan Bath. According to their complaint, the residents of nearby Marshfield and surrounding communities had customarily purchased wool at Bath. However, during an eruption of plague early in the Queen's reign, the authorities at Bath had barred outsiders entry into the town on market days in an effort to stem the spread of infection. Marshfield inhabitants had 'very uncharitably' responded by inviting customers of Bath's market to buy their yarn and woollen cloth, as well as other merchandise, at Marshfield.[2] While Bath's residents acknowledged Marshfield's right to hold a market, they rejected the inhabitants' attempt to hold a wool market.

While town marketplaces came in many shapes and sizes, they tended to conform to a few different configurations in the early modern era. Many, particularly those in smaller towns, consisted of a single street, while less commonly others might exist at the intersection of three different roads. Marketplaces in larger towns varied more widely in their arrangement, especially as they grew and spilled beyond their original boundaries. In such cases, marketing activity might be found in nearby streets, with particular streets devoted to the sale of particular products. The public buildings associated with urban markets stood close by, the most familiar being the market cross. Larger communities had several such crosses, each indicating the sale of a particular product, such as fish, meat or cheese. The very smallest towns had just a single market cross, with all their goods sold in one place. The market cross was not the only public structure associated with urban marketplaces. Most towns also had a market house, which was built in the market, and whose function varied by town. Some, for example, contained a court, a toll room and perhaps a jail cell.

Wherever market activity took place, even when disputed, it was subject to stringent regulation by local authorities. They attended to virtually every detail about the market. They decided on hours of operation, and who was permitted to trade. At Ipswich, for example, only freemen could set up stalls at the town's Cornhill, while at York non-freemen were licensed to sell their wares. Across England, local authorities enacted regulations concerning the trade in particular products and also considered the kinds and amounts of charges to be imposed on various carriers. In all of this, they were concerned both to maintain (and increase) the prosperity that the market brought to their communities as well as to ensure that local consumers were supplied with affordable food and drink. To that end, town markets were overseen by a wide variety of officers, whose numbers varied from four or five in smaller market towns to around fifty in larger ones. These officers, some of whom were elected to their posts and some of whom were appointed for a term of years, sought to ensure the quality and quantity of the goods that came into the market for sale. There were market officials, therefore, who supervised the sale of bread, testing its quality and fixing its price. Others inspected grain, fish and meat. The sale of beer was also subject to close inspection and supervision. Finished goods, such as cloth and leather, equally fell under the watch of various market officers, who carefully oversaw the weights and measures used in the marketplace as well. In some places, 'appraisers' settled disputes over price, maintaining peace and order.

An especially important and difficult duty that also fell to authorities regulating local markets involved tolls. The imposition of tolls was not uniform across England. The amounts levied varied, as did the particular transactions on which they could be collected. At some markets, no toll was collected on corn, for example, while others imposed a charge for each bushel sold. The levy and collection of tolls had to be recorded, as did any payments made from the funds collected. Not surprisingly, the payment of tolls was not popular among those who came to urban markets to buy and sell goods, and there were efforts at evasion. In the later sixteenth century, nearly two dozen communities around Worcester sought to challenge the tolls imposed on them there, claiming that they were part of the city's ancient demesne and therefore exempt.

That so many towns sought to escape tolls at Worcester, however annoying that effort must have been to local authorities, offers some indication of the popularity of the town's market. This would have been a source of pride to Worcester authorities, as urban prosperity was dependent, at least to some extent, on the vitality of the market. Tudor markets were chiefly sites of regional exchange and therefore depended on residents from the surrounding region to participate in them as both buyers and sellers. Alan Dyer has found that Worcester's market likely drew customers and suppliers from an area that stretched around twenty-five miles from east and between ten and twelve miles north to south. In northern England, many residents of the West Riding flocked to York to sample and sell wares. While regional trade was what chiefly sustained most town markets, longer-distance trading was not unknown. Such trade was more often in evidence in the great fairs which were held several times annually in some of the larger English towns. Here, buyers and sellers from greater distances gathered to conduct business.

In many of the larger towns, trades were regulated by guilds or companies which had authority to supervise apprentices and journeymen and to inspect the work of members. Throughout Elizabethan England, guilds tried to balance opportunities with resources, and their regulations tended to restrict the size of individual enterprises in order to prevent trade from being controlled by a small number of large firms. As Paul Griffiths shows in Chapter 19, apprenticeship was a common way for immigrants to enter a town, and ideally it was the pathway not only to the status of an independent householder but also to full citizenship rights in the community. Not all guilds were equally influential; in York, city alderman were drawn from only eighteen of more than ninety guilds, while London's aldermen were all members of one of the dozen wealthiest companies. The guilds encouraged a sense of solidarity among their members, in part to dampen competition among them, and they often provided valuable social services to members and their families, such as pensions for the widows, orphans and the elderly. In London, the livery companies were chartered by the Crown, and their rights to inspect products and craftsmanship extended outside the lord mayor's jurisdiction into the increasingly populous suburbs. The Elizabethan era may have been something of a high-water mark for England's guilds because most trade was local and conducted in family-centred shops and workshops.

Town governments secured their rights, including the ability to oversee markets, by royal charter, a process that typically involved the initiative of members of the local economic elite. They were the ones with the time and resources to pursue governmental work, and they also had the incentive to manage economic affairs. This leads historians typically to describe the nature of town governments as being 'oligarchic' in the sense of their being relatively closed and self-serving. Still, the life of a town was its economy, and contemporaries understood that only a few citizens had the ability to serve in important civic offices. As Robert Tittler has put it, 'the interests of most of the better sort who came to power in these years coincided in most respects with the interests of the towns themselves. They were compatible – and seen to be compatible – with what most contemporaries saw as the common good.' There certainly were times, and perhaps most importantly during the crisis years of the 1590s, when the privileges of the urban elite were challenged, but economic relations in Elizabethan towns rarely sparked class conflict because, ultimately, 'most contemporaries recognized at least in principle that only the wealthier and "better" sort could undertake the growing personal burdens of office, and that a number of factors worked to encourage oligarchic tendencies.'[3] The urban elite displayed, and perhaps tried to defend, their dominance in urban society by commissioning cultural works, such as town halls and portraits of mayors and other civic worthies. Such works had the cumulative effect of suggesting that a town was not only prosperous but also that it was of long-standing significance in its region, the very sort of place in which buyers and sellers could feel confident about doing business.

The economic elite in towns were expected to be charitable, and Elizabethan towns were centres of philanthropy. Writing at the end of the sixteenth century, John Stowe commented that: 'Wealth and riches . . . are increased chiefly in Townes and Citties both to the prince and people. The necessity of the poore and needy is in such places both sooner to be espied, and hath meanes to be more charitably relieved.'[4]

Prior to the Reformation, charitable practices were considered spiritually efficacious if they were intended as penance for sins. After the Reformation, new types of secular commemoration emerged in the aftermath of the dissolution of chantries, obits and other traditional ways to maintain a connection between the living and the dead by celebrating the memories of deceased benefactors. The interest of London livery companies in commemoration may have prompted members to entrust them with larger charitable benefactions. Before the Reformation, these included chantries and obits, but from Elizabeth's reign onward they generally involved the almshouses, pensions, lectureships and schools in London and the provinces that typified the well-known quest for godly reform. The companies developed new ways to honour the memories of deceased members who entrusted charitable endowments to their care, and these included constructing tables of company benefactors in their halls that were reminiscent of parish bede-rolls, commissioning paintings and statues of famous company members and displaying the arms of benefactors in stained glass in their hall.

Despite such efforts to encourage benefaction, urban charities could not always meet the demand. This was especially the case when crises such as poor harvests sent inhabitants of rural communities into towns in search of alms. During such periods, town governors would often respond to increased reports of theft, vagrancy and other aspects of social disorder associated with poverty. After undertaking a thorough review of both the need and the availability of charity in Elizabethan London, Ian Archer concluded that 'Poor relief, although limited in scope, might work to promote stability because of the way the exercise of philanthropy served to invest elite figures with reputations for charitable virtue', but Elizabethan poor relief was not always up to the challenge, and so it is 'quite clear that there was much unrelieved poverty in London, both because resources were maldistributed, and because the scale of the challenge, particularly in crisis years like the mid 1590s, ultimately proved too much for the authorities.'[5]

The prosperity of a town relied heavily on the prosperity of its surrounding region and the vitality of its trading partners. From the middle of the sixteenth century to the eve of the Civil War, agricultural marketing underwent a profound transformation marked by increasing regional specialisation in the face of a generally expanding population. As a result, communities large and small came to depend on regional and national markets supplying them with commodities. London was the engine for much of this development, but it could be seen to varying degrees throughout the nation. Wayfaring traders who specialised in particular aspects of the commodities trade gradually inserted themselves into the marketing of agricultural goods, undermining the traditional local markets. As they moved from town to town, these traders stimulated demand for warehouses and innkeepers. By the early seventeenth century, provincial towns such as Derby, Doncaster, Northampton, Salisbury and Shrewsbury developed reputations as centres for the trade in particular commodities, attracting buyers and sellers from across their region.

The economic history of provincial towns often reflected the health of key industries or products, especially in the clothing and textile trades. Towns that relieved heavily on one industry were vulnerable to fluctuations in that trade. Many towns suffered severely as a result in the slump in the export of cloth from the 1550s, and historians are familiar with the declarations of distress from urban authorities. The decline of Winchester, for example, can be explained, at least in part, by the loss of its cloth-producing industry. Better known is the case of Coventry, where decline in that city's cloth trade had been detected as early as the 1520s. While this distress was real, it was neither universal nor permanent. Cloth workers in Colchester and Norwich experienced difficulties in the earlier and middle decades of the sixteenth century, but the industries in both communities were reinvigorated in the later Elizabethan period with the introduction of the New Draperies. These were cloths which were lighter, more colourful, cheaper and ultimately more popular with consumers than the broadcloths that had been the traditional output of the English textile industry. Worcester's cloth industry was able to stave off rural competition by virtue of a 1534 statute that left it dominant through the end of the seventeenth century. In Gloucester, the robust medieval cloth trade was in decline by the late fifteenth century but was replaced in the earlier sixteenth by a successful trade in woollen caps, which provided considerable employment locally. However, Gloucester was not as fortunate as Worcester. By the middle decades of the sixteenth century, the once-thriving capping industry had fallen into decay, further underscoring the fluctuations in the economy to which urban communities were vulnerable.

The varying factors that influenced a town's economy are readily apparent in the experience of Elizabethan Chester. It was situated at a nodal point in the roadway system of northern Wales and Cheshire, a region whose administration it influenced as the seat of the Palatinate. Its port dominated the coastal trade along the eastern shore of the Irish Sea as well as the crossing to Dublin, and it controlled the customs from Harlech on the Welsh coast in the south to Carlisle in the north. Chester's importance grew when it became the base for the bishop of a new diocese created in 1540, and it was enhanced further when it became an administrative and supply base for the conquest of Ireland. This setting made Chester a regional centre for commerce and government similar to Bristol, Exeter, Norwich and York, though on a much smaller scale than these other regional centres.

Throughout the early modern period, Chester experienced several periods of sharp demographic decline followed by an increase in admissions to the freedom as a result of immigration from Chester's rural hinterland. This pattern was apparent during the second half of the sixteenth century in the wake of a major epidemic that hit Chester during the years 1557–62. Within a decade, its population had rebounded sharply, most likely as a result of greatly expanded trade with Ireland. During the period 1565–77, there were significant increases in the imports of skins, wool and yarn and dramatic increases in the exportation of soap, salt, hops and metalware. The regulation of admission to trades was sufficiently flexible to allow the numbers of freemen to grow along with Chester's economy; indeed, the proportion of household heads who were freemen expanded from 42 per cent in 1567–8 to 47 per cent five years later. Although Chester's population showed a consistent ability to recover from temporary setbacks throughout the period, each recovery seemed to stagnate when Chester could support about 1,800 households. This suggests that the there was a finite number of opportunities for newcomers to find a niche in Chester's economy or, at the least, that the additional cost of each successive opportunity after Chester's population had regained its pre-epidemic footing was greater than the cost of similar opportunities in other towns in the region.

Towns that relied heavily on one industry were quite vulnerable to fluctuations in that trade. Those in the west were susceptible to swings in the cloth industry; ports could fall victim to foreign policy by disrupting trade patterns, but military build-ups could help naval towns such as Portsmouth and Chatham. The adaptation of new techniques in the textile industry is a primary example of how the Elizabethan economy could evolve with changing circumstances. Towns in East Anglia, and especially Norwich, were in the vanguard of this movement. The native worsted industry was in steep decline during the middle years of the sixteenth century. Local merchants worked with the Duke of Norfolk to convince Queen Elizabeth to grant refuge to alien weavers, who brought their skills with them. The Strangers, as the alien weavers were called, brought new techniques and new products to the ailing cloth trade. By the early seventeenth century, East Anglian textile workers were producing a wide variety of cloths which were highly sought after in both domestic and overseas markets.

A key subset of Elizabethan towns were ports. During the later sixteenth century, several of these coastal towns – and a few that were inland, along major, navigable rivers – were centres of international trade. These leading ports ranked among the largest towns in England in 1600, with nine of the thirteen towns with populations greater than 5,000 serving as ports (London, Bristol, Newcastle, Exeter, Plymouth, King's Lynn, Gloucester, Chester and Hull). London served the south-east. Bristol and Chester were leading centres of trade with Ireland. York had long been a significant centre of domestic and international trade in the north, but increasingly Hull would serve its international markets. The economic life of ports serving international markets would be disrupted, however, by England's involvement in war, such as the extensive conflict with Spain during the final years of Elizabeth's reign. Many smaller, coastal towns served the domestic trade in commodities such as lumber and coal. During the later sixteenth century, towns throughout England became increasingly connected to London. The classic example of this process is the development of the Tyneside trade, which, by the 1590s, had made coal an essential fuel source for the metropolis. In their study of the coal industry in Whickham, David Levine and Keith Wrightson found that output 'rose modestly between the 1520s and the early 1570s, that it doubled between the latter date and 1595, and that thereafter it continued to expand rapidly'.[6]

The university towns of Oxford and Cambridge received an influx of students during the Elizabethan age, with three times as many students beginning their Oxford studies in the 1580s than was the case in the 1550s. This was spurred in part by the desire of the urban elites to prepare their sons for their future practical success. Growing interest in subjects based upon mathematics, such as cartography and geography, signalled the desire of the commercial elite for empire. As Lesley Cormack has argued, during the late sixteenth century demand increased for subjects which were viewed as potentially applicable to challenges a young man might face in his future career: 'Men with no interest in a clerical career began to see a few years at Oxford or Cambridge as a valuable part of their practical education, aiding them in future careers as merchants, politicians, courtiers, or even country gentlemen.'[7] Faculties in traditional subjects such as rhetoric, logic, mathematics and natural philosophy had to demonstrate the practical applicability of their fields in order to attract these new students. In this way, the commercial and administrative functions of the major towns in England, and especially of London, helped to shape the direction of university education and to stimulate the growth of the university towns.

By the time Elizabeth took the throne, the fortunes of provincial towns had been profoundly shaped by periodic demographic catastrophes. Even in the absence of evidence for a general decline among urban communities in the Tudor period, it is clear that towns faced some serious challenges, such as the ravages of disease. Plagues and other epidemics were unwelcome and destructive visitors to all of England in the later medieval period. Urban communities throughout the sixteenth and early seventeenth centuries could expect a serious outbreak of plague once every generation. Slack neatly summarises the influence of plagues on early modern urban society by stating: 'Plague appears less as an autonomous factor, a deus ex machina occasionally imposing its will on towns from outside, than as an integral and in the end familiar part of urban life.'[8] Such visitations could be demographically devastating. In 1579, for example, an outbreak of plague is estimated to have killed about one-third of Norwich's population.

Plagues often brought urban economic activity to a halt, as civic officials shut down markets and fairs in an effort to stem the spread of the disease. While some merchants protested against these measures for the detrimental effect that they had on business, consumers did not necessarily need official prohibitions to convince them to stay away from shops and alehouses when an epidemic threatened. These kinds of disruptions to economic life in the urban sector reverberated in the rural areas with which towns were so deeply enmeshed. Plagues that struck Newcastle resulted in disruptions in the coal and salt trades up and down England's east coast, and an outbreak in Bristol in 1603 damaged the economies of rural Herefordshire. As destructive as epidemics were, their negative effects on towns and their economies were usually not long-lasting. Immigration, particularly in larger towns, tended to erase declines in population that resulted from eruptions of sickness. It also appears that a number of the new migrants brought with them skills and resources that allowed them to replace those who had been lost to disease and thus to contribute to a recovery in the fortunes of urban industry; for example, the production of cloth among Dutch and Walloon weavers in Norwich peaked not long after the devastating plague of 1579. Some towns did not recover economically after epidemic assaults on their populations, but it seems that overall such revival was the hallmark of early modern urban economies rather than the exception.

One consequence of plague was a labour shortage in the countryside that persisted into the early sixteenth century and limited the ability of towns to maintain their populations. Rural populations rebounded from about 1540, eventually encouraging migration into towns. Alan Dyer has estimated that between '1525 and 1600 the total population of the leading 17 provincial towns rose from about 85,000 to about 130,000'. Population trends are not by themselves reliable indicators of the economic health of towns because their populations would ebb and flow with the vitality of their region. As Alan Dyer has put it, 'In the preindustrial economy, when towns attracted large numbers of very poor people, a reduced population was not necessarily a bad thing, for the slimmed town might well enjoy full employment and an enhanced per capita income.'[9]

Demographic growth was the most obvious aspect of change in metropolitan London. A consensus estimate among scholars of the metropolitan population trend during the sixteenth century suggests that there were about 50,000 people living in greater London in 1500; 75,000 in 1550; 200,000 in 1600. Frequent disasters, especially outbreaks of plague, are hidden in such round numbers, and London's population growth was possible only because of a steady stream of immigrants from both the English provinces and abroad. The Elizabethan government was concerned about what it perceived to be London's unnatural growth, and it took steps to limit new building, although this seems to have had little influence. In one of his first proclamations after entering England in 1603, King James reflected on 'the great confluence and accesse of excessive numbers of idle, indigent, dissolute and dangerous persons' in metropolitan London. James asserted that such crowded living conditions was one of the 'chiefest occasions of the great Plague and mortality' in the City of London and its suburbs, from which the disease 'most dangerously overspread, and infected many principall, and other parts of this Realme'. With the goal of promoting the health and safety of his subjects, James followed Elizabeth's example by forbidding the erection of new dwellings in greater London, and he had as little success as she did. In a subsequent proclamation in 1607, James fretted about the broader social and economic consequences of London's continued growth, noting the upward pressure London's increased population put on prices for basic goods as well as his view that 'the other good Townes and Borrowes of his kingdome by reason of so great receit for people in and about the said City, are much unpeopled, and in their trading, and otherwise decayed.'[10]

As it grew, London became an increasingly vibrant cultural centre. In the metropolis, though not exclusively there, English artists and patrons were able to participate in broader European trends in the visual and performing arts. It was the demand of consumers from among the Westminster elite, the denizens of the

Inns of Court and the City that provided demand for the products of London-based artists. It is particularly with the theatre, however, that London, especially during the Elizabethan period, made its greatest mark. Despite the constant complaints of the godly, Londoners provided the audiences for the first public theatres that took root just beyond the reach of the City magistrates. The theatres were a part of what might very loosely be described in modern terms as an emerging entertainment and hospitality industry, which was centred primarily on inns and taverns. Popular recreations, which included activities ranging from minstrel shows to bear-baiting, appealed to members of all social classes and contributed to the growth of consumer-based activities. London was also a centre for intellectual and scientific discoveries, in essence forming a third, though largely informal, university. Deborah Harkness has recovered in great depth and detail the assortment of naturalists centred in London's Lime Street and connected, through their shared interest in tulips, maps, spiders and natural curiosities of all types, to the pan-European network of like-minded individuals. They were 'a community of men in the heart of the City who worked tirelessly to increase natural knowledge'.[11] Although it is doubtful that any of these naturalists profited from such exchanges, their pursuit of their intellectual interests contributed to the general cultural energy of the metropolis, an energy which, in turn, had significant, if difficult to calculate, economic implications for both London and England. The economy of the Lime Street naturalists was based more on civility and collaboration than competition, which largely explains why the participants did not pursue individual publication and, therefore, have remained largely unknown to future generations.

In addition to the growth of London, the other obvious source of change for urban economies was the Reformation. Towns were an important focal point of religious life in early modern England. Before the Reformation, they housed the monasteries, convents, chantries, hospitals, parish churches and cathedrals to which members of both local and surrounding communities flocked for spiritual, material and cultural sustenance. Relics and shrines attracted pilgrims from outside city walls, as did the splendid religious processions which were a regular feature of the urban liturgical calendar. Monastic institutions were deeply enmeshed in their communities, dispensing charity to the needy, employing local inhabitants and sometimes offering education to urban and rural children, in addition to their regular rounds of prayers. Urban historians have long recognised the dramatic impact that the Reformation had on virtually every aspect of sixteenth-century urban life. Much of the attention that has been given to this issue has focused on the damage wrought by religious change: the architectural destruction that followed the dissolution of the monasteries, the loss of the livelihoods of those attached to monastic institutions, the disappearance of the plays and pageants that had honoured God and the saints, while drawing onlookers from surrounding areas inside city walls. Some towns irrevocably declined in the absence of ecclesiastical institutions that had done so much to sustain them politically, socially and economically, as well as religiously.

Recent scholarship has suggested, however, that the consequences of the Reformation were more nuanced than such depictions of loss and ruin seem to indicate. Some smaller towns may well have lost their status as urban communities as a result of monastic closings, but for some of the larger towns, the Reformation

– the dissolutions in particular – may, in the long run, have been a relatively positive economic development. Many of these communities entered the period from positions of greater economic range and strength and were thus better able to weather, and even take advantage of, the opportunities that at first appeared potentially devastating. The suppression of monastic institutions in the 1530s and of guild and chantry lands in the 1540s made considerable amounts of urban property available for sale. While town corporations did not, and sometimes were not able to, buy such lands as soon as they became available, it appears that a number did so later in the century, using their extensive knowledge of the area to their advantage. Bequests from individuals to town corporations also put more land at the disposal of urban governors. The Reformation thus put considerable resources into the hands of these townspeople, to which they never before had such access. This allowed these corporations to gain greater legal authority and to build stronger, stable local governments. While the Reformation spelled devastation for some smaller and less economically diverse communities, it was far from disastrous for all.

This overview of the Elizabethan urban economy has taken a holistic approach to the subject. Towns in the late sixteenth century were intimately connected to the broader social, cultural and political trends of the era. They were connected to their surrounding rural hinterlands and to other towns in England and abroad, through a network of exchange of goods and people. In their basic functions and status in realm, towns were, on the whole, fairly stable during Elizabeth's reign, but they were subject to challenges ranging from outbreaks of plague to religious change to agricultural crisis to the threat of foreign invasion. In this way, the economies of Elizabethan towns were like the rivers on which so many of them were situated, rarely changing yet never precisely the same from one moment to the next.

FURTHER READING

Borsay, Peter, and Proudfoot, Lindsay, 'The English and Irish Urban Experience, 1500–1800: Change, Convergence and Divergence', in P. Borsay and L. Proudfoot (eds.), *Provincial Towns in Early Modern England and Ireland: Change, Convergence and Divergence* (Oxford, 2002), pp. 1–27.

Clark, Peter (ed.), *The Cambridge Urban History of Britain, Vol. II, 1540–1840* (Cambridge, 2000).

Collinson, Patrick, and Craig, John (eds.), *The Reformation in English Towns, 1500–1640* (New York, 1998).

Gadd, Ian Anders, and Wallis, Patrick (eds.), *Guilds, Society, and Economy in London, 1450–1800* (London, 2002).

Galley, Chris, *The Demography of Early Modern Towns: York in the Sixteenth and Seventeenth Centuries* (Liverpool, 1998).

Goose, Nigel, and Luu, Lien (ed.), *Immigrants in Tudor and Early Stuart England* (Brighton, 2005).

Griffiths, Paul, and Jenner, Mark S. R. (eds.), *Londinopolis: Essays in the Cultural and Social History of Early Modern London* (Manchester, 2000).

Litzenberger, Caroline, The English Reformation and the Laity: Gloucestershire, 1540–1580 (Cambridge, 1997).

Manley, Lawrence, *Literature and Culture in Early Modern London* (Cambridge, 1995).

Martin, Luc, 'The Rise of the New Draperies in Norwich, 1550–1622' in N. Harte (ed.), *The New Draperies in the Low Countries and England* (Oxford, 1997), pp. 245–74.
McClendon, Muriel C., *The Quiet Reformation: Magistrates and the Emergence of Protestantism in Tudor Norwich* (Palo Alto, Calif., 1999).
Palliser, David M., *Tudor York* (Oxford, 1979).
Patterson, Catherine F., *Urban Patronage in Early Modern England: Corporate Boroughs, the Landed Elite, and the Crown, 1580–1640* (Palo Alto, Calif., 1999).
Reed, Michael (ed.), *English Towns in Decline, 1350–1800* (Leicester, 1986).
Sacks, David Harris, *The Widening Gate: Bristol and the Atlantic Economy, 1450–1700* (Berkeley, Calif., 1991).
Schen, Claire S., *Charity and Lay Piety in Reformation London, 1500–1620* (Aldershot, 2002).
Slack, Paul, *The Impact of Plague in Tudor and Stuart England* (London, 1985).
Tittler, Robert, *The Face of the City: Civic Portraiture and Civic Identity in Early Modern England* (Manchester, 2007).
Ward, Joseph P., *Metropolitan Communities: Trade Guilds, Identity, and Change in Early Modern London* (Palo Alto, Calif., 1997).
Wrightson, Keith, *Earthly Necessities: Economic Lives in Early Modern Britain* (New Haven, Conn., 2000).

NOTES

1 David Harris Sacks, 'London's Dominion: The Metropolis, the Market Economy, and the State', in Lena Cowen Orlin (ed.), *Material London c. 1600* (Philadelphia, Pa., 2000), p. 20.
2 Quoted in Alan Everitt, 'The Marketing of Agricultural Produce', in Joan Thirsk (ed.), *The Agrarian History of England and Wales* (Cambridge, 1967), vol. IV, p. 476.
3 Robert Tittler, *The Reformation and the Towns in England: Politics and Political Culture, c. 1540–1640* (Oxford, 1998), pp. 183–4.
4 John Stowe, *A Survey of London*, ed. C. L. Kingsford (Oxford, 1908), vol. II, p. 198.
5 Ian Archer, *The Pursuit of Stability: Social Relations in Elizabethan London* (Cambridge, 1991), p. 203.
6 David Levine and Keith Wrightson, *The Making of an Industrial Society: Whickham 1560–1765* (Oxford, 1991), p. 30.
7 Lesley B. Cormack, *Charting an Empire: Geography at the English Universities, 1580–1620* (Chicago, Ill., 1997), pp. 22–3.
8 P. Slack, *The Impact of Plague in Tudor and Stuart England* (London, 1985), pp. 111–12.
9 A. Dyer, *Decline and Growth in English Towns, 1400–1640* (Cambridge, 1991), pp. 2 and 47.
10 James F. Larkin and Paul L. Hughes (eds.), *Stuart Royal Proclamations*, 2 vols. (Oxford: 1973), vol. I, pp. 47–8 and 171–5. Additional Jacobean proclamations concerning building in London are at pp. 111–12, 267–9, 398–400, 428–31, 485–8 and 597–8.
11 Deborah E. Harkness, *The Jewel House: Elizabethan London and the Scientific Revolution* (New Haven, Conn., 2007), p. 55.

CHAPTER TWENTY-SIX

RURAL ECONOMIES UNDER STRESS

'A world so altered'

R. W. Hoyle

Let us start with some figures pregnant with implication. In 1524–5, the population of England was in the range of 2.2–2.4 million people. By the accession of Queen Elizabeth, it had reached about 3 million, and by the time of her death in 1603, around 4 million. It continued to rise until the late 1630s, when it plateaued at about 5 million people. Over this century, the population more than doubled, and over the Queen's reign it increased by a third. And yet we do not see this producing food shortages, malnutrition or distress. It is true that there were years of famine in north-western England in 1586–7, 1595–7 and later in 1622–3, the ripples of which were felt throughout England. These years arose not from year-on-year pressure on food supplies but from years of catastrophically poor weather in which the crops failed. Generally speaking, farmers seem to have met the demands of the enlarged population more than adequately. Indeed, the problem they faced may well have been one of overproduction of grain. In 1593, after a succession of good years and confident of future food supplies, parliament repealed the legislation forbidding depopulating enclosures (where arable was converted into pasture). The legislation was reimposed in 1597–8, a year of high prices, national distress and localised famine, but the parliamentary debates of both 1597–8 and 1601 show that overproduction had emerged as a problem.

Elizabethan farming ought to be considered to be a success story. Exactly how farmers came to produce so much more is something of a mystery. We do not know whether it was achieved by increasing the area under cultivation, or by increasing the productivity of each unit of land, or whether the same number of labourers worked harder, or a larger number of labourers worked in much the same fashion as before. Contemporaries were less sanguine. They consistently argued that there was something wrong with the countryside, with agriculture and landownership. In 1562, the cleric Augustine Bernher, then living at Southam in Warwickshire, complained of the secularisation of church property by gentlemen, the same gentlemen who 'intreat their poor tenants with raising of rents, taking of fines and other extreme dealings' so that 'they are compelled day and night to cry unto God for vengeance against them'.[1] In the following decade, Philip Stubbes, in his *Anatomy of Abuses,* which, in many respects, is a rant against the degeneracy of the society in which he lived, turned his pen on the landlords under the heading of 'Covetousness in England'. He did not mince his words.

> People leaving these godly means do all run headlong to covetousness and ambition, attempting always and assaying all means possible to heap up riches. So likewise, landlords make merchandise of their poor tenants, racking their rents, raising their fines and incomes and setting them so straight upon tenter hooks as no man can live on them. Besides that, as though this pillage and pollage were not rapacious enough, they take in and enclose commons, moors, heaths and other common pastures where out the poor commonalty were want to have all their provision and feeding for their cattle and (which is more) corn for themselves to live upon; all which are now in most places taken from them by those greedy puttocks to the great impoverishing and utter beggaring of many whole towns and parishes, whose tragical cries and incessant clamours have long since pierced the skies and presented themselves before the majesty of God, crying 'How long Lord, how long will you defer to revenge this villainy done to thy poor saints and silly members upon the earth?'[2]

One of Stubbes' contemporaries, the Essex clergyman William Harrison, offered a more balanced view in his *Description of England,* first published in 1577: 'There are old men yet dwelling in the village where I remain which have noted three things to be marvellously altered in England within their sound remembrance, and three other things too much increased.'[3] The first was the proliferation of chimneys, which, in turn, reflected the creation of heated rooms in place of a single open hall. The second was the 'great [although not general] amendment of lodging', the spread of sheets, pillows and feather mattresses in place of straw pallets. (A page or two before, he described the recent appearance of quality furnishings in farmers' houses.)[4] The third was the disappearance of wooden plates and the appearance in their place of pewter. It had been rare to find as many as four pieces of pewter in a farmer's house 'and yet for all this frugality . . . they were scarce able to live and pay their rents at their days without the selling of a cow or a horse or more, although they had but £4 at the uttermost by the year'. Farmers in those days had no money, but

> whereas in my time . . . £4 of old rent be improved to £40, £50 or £100, yet will the farmer . . . think his gains very small towards the end of his term [lease] if he have not six or seven years' rent lying by him, therewith to purchase a new lease, beside a fair garnish of pewter on his cupboard, with so much more in odd vessel going about the house, three or four feather beds, so many coverlets and carpets of tapestry, a silver salt, a bowl for wine (if not a whole nest) and a dozen of spoons to furnish up the suit [set].

But most of this money would be paid to a landlord for a new lease, and it had become the practice to buy a new lease well before the end of the old to prevent an interloper from securing a lease in succession to the sitting tenant. And the old men plainly had firm views about what had altered for the worse. Housekeeping or hospitality 'whereby the poor have been relieved' was much decayed. And they spoke 'also of three things that are grown to be very grievous unto them'. The first was the enhancing of rents which we have already mentioned, the second

> the daily oppression of copyholders, whose lords seek to bring their poor tenants almost into plain servitude and misery, daily devising new means and seeking up all the old how to cut them shorter and shorter, doubling, trebling and now and then seven times increasing their fines, driving them also for every trifle to lose and forfeit their tenures . . . to the end that they may fleece them yet more[.]

The third thing of which they complained was usury and the excessive rates of interest demanded. Harrison then went on to outline a fourth area of grievance, landlords who valued their leases at 'a secret estimation of the wealth and credit of the taker . . . so that of the lessee be thought to be worth £100, he shall pay no less for his term or else another to enter with hard and doubtful covenants'. Moreover, landlords were becoming 'graziers, butchers, tanners, sheepmasters and woodmen and *denique quid non* [finally what not?] thereby to enrich themselves and bring all of the wealth of the country into their own hands'. Elsewhere, he condemned landlords for forcing up the price of grain.

> For albeit there be much more ground eared [cultivated] now almost in every place than hath been of late years, yet such a price of corn continueth in each town and market without any just cause (except it be that landlords do get licences to carry corn out of the land only to keep prices up for their own private gain and ruin of the commonwealth) that the artificer and the poor labouring man is not able to reach unto it but is driven to content himself with horse corn, I mean beans, peason, oats, tares and lentils. . . .If the world last a while after this rate, wheat and rye will be no grain for poor men to feed on.[5]

From the end of the century, we have two very different accounts of conditions, one rooted in the tradition of anti-landlord invective, the other more economic and understanding in its approach. Here is William Vaughan, in *The Golden Grove* (1600).

> now a days yeomanry is decayed, hospitality gone to wrack and husbandry almost quite fallen. The reason is, because landlords, not contented with such revenues as their predecessors received, nor yet satisfied, that they live like swinish Epicures, quietly at their ease, doing no good to the commonwealth, do leave no ground for tillage, but do enclose for pasture may thousand acres of ground within one hedge. The husbandmen are thrust out of their own, or else by deceit, constrained to sell all that they have. So either by hook or by crook, they must needs depart away seely souls, men, women and children. And not this extremity only do our wicked Ahabs show, but also with the loss of Naboth's life do they do glut their overgreedy minds. This is the cause why corn in England is become dearer than it was wont to be, yet not withstanding

> all this, sheep and wool are nothing better cheap, but rather their price are much enhanced. Thus do our remorseless Puttocks lie lurking for the poor commons, to spoil them of their tenements, but they shall not long enjoy them. And why? Because they are oppressors of the poor and not helpers, their bellies are never filled, therefore shall they soon perish in their covetousness.[6]

Thomas Wilson, writing in 1600 a survey of England which remained unpublished until 1936, described a countryside in flux, but without resorting to the moral criticism that informed the others. In its place, he offered an economic understanding and an elementary categorisation of the inhabitants of the countryside into classes. The gentry

> which were wont to addict themselves to the wars, are now for the most part grown to become good husbands and know as well how to improve their lands to the uttermost as the farmer or countryman, so that they take their farms into their hands as the leases expire, and either till [them] themselves or let them out to those who will give most.

This had brought about the decay of the yeoman, some of whom had become servants to gentlemen, but 'I know many yeomen in divers provinces in England which are able to spend between £300 and £500 yearly by their lands and leases and some twice and some thrice as much.' But these men educated their sons in the law, and the gentry

> perceiving them unfit to do them that service that their fathers did, when their leases do expire turn them out of their lands which was never wont to be done . . . and let them to such as are not by their bad penniworths able to gentlemen it as others have done.

Then there were 'yeomen' of 'meaner ability called freeholders', able to keep good herds of milk kine and five or six horses to till their grounds besides young beasts and sheep. They were often worth between £300 and £500 in substance and stock. Finally there were copyholders, 'some of them men of as great ability as any of the rest, and some poor and live chiefly upon country labour, working by the day for meat and drink and small wages.'[7]

Finally, to stray slightly into the reign of James I, we might turn to an example of the kind of invective directed against enclosure, a matter touched on by Stubbes. It needs to be explained that what the commentators were against was not enclosure *per se* but one particular type of enclosure, depopulating enclosure, in which arable land was converted to pasture. Not only did this diminish the area sown, but contemporaries also believed that it brought about a strong out-migration from enclosed villages. The Lincolnshire clergyman Francis Trigge, writing in 1604, claimed to know of an example where enclosure had reduced 320 communicants to 'scant 160'. In his polemic, *The Humble Petition of Two Sisters, the Church and the Commonwealth, for the Restoring of Their Ancient Commons and Liberties, which Late Enclosure with Depopulation Uncharitably Hath Taken Away,* he quoted Proverbs 14:28 on his title page: 'In the multitude of the people is the honour of a king, and for the want of people, cometh the destruction of the prince.'[8] This was the case which Trigge and the other anti-enclosure polemicists wished to make: the organisation of the land was not merely a matter of preference or advantage to landlords, but was a matter of importance for the State. But Trigge's objections to enclosure were only partly made in economic terms. His first chapter explained how enclosure 'decayeth tillage', his second how 'it depeopleth towns', but thereafter he explained the evil of depopulating enclosure in moral and Christian terms, finally explaining how 'Inclosure with depopulation is a sin whereof God shall make special enquiry at the day of judgement.' His book ended with a call for the encloser to repent with speed, before it was too late for them.

These five authors offer us a range of views of what people thought was happening in the countryside. Some farmers were plainly doing very well and were able to invest their profits in better-quality housing, furnishings and education (Harrison and Wilson). But these same people were oppressed by landlords who raised their rents and demanded excessive cash balances for new leases (Bernher, Stubbes, Harrison and Vaughan). Landlords pressed ahead with enclosure for their own private benefit, forcing people off the land, and Harrison accused them of forcing up the price of foodstuffs by playing the market. Wilson simply holds that the gentry had become good managers of their lands, knowing how to secure the maximum income from them either by making leases at competitive rates or taking farms in hand: in a way, Wilson accepts the market in land and tenancies where the others find it immoral and corrosive of natural arrangements. Bernher, Stubbes, Harrison and Vaughan all identify landlords as the villains of the piece and suggest that relationships within the countryside were antagonistic, with the tenants crying to God to avenge them. So we have a paradox: the apparent of success of agriculture in meeting the demands of a growing population coupled with the economic and social complaints about the condition of the countryside. We need not take these criticisms and complaints at face value. As Yates has recently shown, much of the mid-century literature of complaint was stylised and conventional, and it is clear that a great deal of the Elizabethan literature which we have reviewed is moral rather than economic in its understanding. So, the question may be asked: what was the experience of the countryside in the later sixteenth century?

I

The key to the ailments of rural society lies in the population growth with which we began this essay. Late medieval population showed a progressive decline over 150 or more years. Although popularly attributed to the Black Death, decline was already under way before plague entered England in 1348. Continued decline may have been a reaction to adverse disease regimes, but this may not be a complete explanation of either why the population continued to shrink or why at some point at the end of the fifteenth century it started to grow again.

Landlords therefore suffered a protracted decline in the demand for land. Confronted by a tenants' market, they reacted in three ways. One reaction was to allow tenants to increase the size of their holdings, and this saw the emergence of a category of large tenants, the yeomen. A second was where tenant demand was weakest, arable was abandoned and put down to grass. Village desertion was a real if largely localised phenomenon. The third was that rents and fines inevitably fell.

The renewed population growth of the early sixteenth century overturned the assumptions of the fifteenth century, but in unpredictable ways. There was, first of all, no renewed subdivision of holdings to increase the number of livelihoods that could be obtained from the land. On the contrary, the number of farms probably continued to shrink as yeomen farmers bought out their neighbours and amalgamated holdings (engrossment) to make bigger farms. This was only possible because of the new commercial opportunities which a rising population allowed. It exacerbated a growing land shortage but also enhanced the wealth of the yeomanry as both Harrison and Wilson described. It was though at the cost of growing inequalities of wealth and an increase in the number of landless.

One aspect of the proliferation of poor, landless men and women was the appearance in villages – initially in the south-east – of by-laws against inmates or lodgers and forbidding the sub-division of houses. Other reports speak of the appearance of cottages by roadsides. As this population had no access to land, it was, in a sense, an urban population in the countryside, dependent on markets, itinerant badgers (pedlars) and alehouses for foodstuffs, and income from wage labour for its livelihood. The statute of 1589, which insisted that new cottages should have 4 acres of land, was an attempt to inject an element of self-sufficiency into the landless. The appearance of this sub-class was very much to the advantage of the yeomen. It gave them a (plentiful) supply of cheap labour and the possibility of dabbling in property rental, and it increased local markets for their produce. At the same time, yeomen might be engaged in a struggle to maintain discipline within their own villages, particularly when faced with what they read as the sexual incontinency of the young, a problem which became particularly acute as marriage became harder to achieve and parishes were forced to accept financial responsibility for the support of their poor.

Where landlords had converted arable to pasture, it was not returned to arable. In fact, the conversion of arable to pasture through enclosure continued throughout the sixteenth century – there are some particularly notorious examples from the very end of the century. This served to exacerbate the shortage of land, but pasture was also more valuable to the landlord than arable for it persistently commanded higher rents. As enclosure, and the conversion which followed, were blamed for high prices in famine years, depopulating landlords were open to public criticism which government was liable to echo.

The increased demand for land allowed landlords to raise rents, particularly the fines taken at the commencement of a tenancy. This was a matter of comment by the end of the 1540s. It also gave them the incentive to enclose waste for rent, a pattern which was under way in the north by the 1530s and seemingly drew peasant opposition.

So, as the demand for land increased, the market for tenancies shifted from being a tenants' market to being a landlords' market in which tenants – even in Pembrokeshire – might compete against each other for land:

> in times past ... few sought leases for most commonly the landlord rather made suit for a good tenant to take his land than the tenant to the landlord ... now ... the world is so altered with the poor tenants that he standeth in bodily fear of his greedy neighbour, that in two or three years eare [before] his lease end, he must bow to his lord for a new lease.[9]

Tenants appreciated this and whereever possible claimed an inheritable right in their lands.

In conditions of a new economic buoyancy, landlords competed with their tenants for the profits of farming, and by the end of Henry VIII's reign there was a recognition amongst peasant communities, especially in the east of England, that they were under pressure from a resurgent landlordism. The tensions within rural society were exacerbated further by the impact of Henry VIII's final French war, and in particular by his decision, maintained after his death by Protector Somerset, to finance the war in part by the debasement of the currency. This produced a roaring inflation as copper replaced silver in the coinage. The principles of bullionist inflation were not widely understood, but contemporaries were well aware of rising prices which they associated with failings in the supply of foodstuffs. Hence the connection was made between inflation, enclosure and conversion, and profiteering by farmers. Somerset established commissions in the summer of 1548 to investigate the scale of enclosure and launch prosecutions against enclosing landlords. In the summer of 1549, government control of the countryside of south-east England disintegrated. There was a rash of anti-enclosure rioting. Camps were established which petitioned the government for redress against landlords, including the return of rents to the level of 1509. The petition from the Mousehold Camp outside Norwich is, in effect, a critique of landlord behaviour. The government's response was to promise concessions to persuade the camps to disperse. When the Mousehold Camp attempted to negotiate further and refused to disband until it received the government's answer, attempts were made to drive the commons back home. On the second attempt this resulted in a pitched battle between the commons and the government's army in which several hundred Norfolk peasants were killed. None of the concessions made earlier in the summer by the government were ever honoured. But the grievances did not go away, and an unknown body of Norfolk tenants submitted an elaborate and articulate petition to Queen Mary at the beginning of her reign complaining of their treatment at the hands of their landlords.

This was a deeply cathartic episode, and the reaction of Elizabethan landlords to the multiple problems they faced cannot be understood without appreciating the impact of 1549 on their thinking. Their own tenants had shown a capacity to organise and mobilise. In some cases they had taken landlords prisoner. They had questioned the whole character of rural relationships. Faced with a determined agrarian movement, there was little that government could do to maintain order. A generation later, William Cecil, Lord Burghley, made a private note that having lived through 1549, the prospect of the Armada held no terror for him. The analysis that gained ground, and which was held by many of those who lived through the episode, was that landlords had brought the whole episode on themselves by their greed. William Harrison blamed the landlords for the rebellion, sympathising with people who thought that 'a short end in the wars to be better than a miserable life in peace'.[10] Anti-landlord rhetoric remained a constant refrain throughout Elizabeth's reign and has its origin in the events of these years. The tenants of Glossopdale, Derbyshire, did the reputation of the 6th Earl of Shrewsbury a great deal of damage at court when they complained to the Queen about his aggressive landlordism at the end of the 1570s. Conversely, landlords who allowed their tenants to continue to hold their land at moderate rents and fines, including Burghley himself, received praise for it. It is noticeable that the Crown's own estates were run on very traditional lines throughout Elizabeth's reign, with only modest fines being demanded.

The problem that landlords faced was that after the sharp episode of inflation, their real incomes had approximately halved over the space of a decade. That, of course, served to transfer the profits of farming back into the hands of the tenants and left the landlords with the problem of recapturing the share of farming profits which they achieved by 1540. Because of the public hostility towards landlordism, there are signs that they were inhibited from doing this in the first part of the reign. This appears in what landlords did not do. One of the effects of 1549 was to freeze peasant property rights in the state they had reached by that year. In much of the south-east, tenants had acquired customary estates of inheritance – copyhold of inheritance – in their lands. These were generally not challenged by landlords after 1549. Outside this area, peasant property rights were only part-formed, and, particularly in the west of England, copyhold meant an estate for named lives, and the right of inheritance was never achieved. Within south-eastern England, Elizabethan disputes over tenancy tended to focus on the rate of fines and the ownership of timber on the copyholders' lands and not the principle of copyhold itself. Landlords were therefore locked into tenurial arrangements which served them very badly in a rising market for land. And whilst parliament was willing and able to regulate the labour contract and laid down the terms on which Oxford and Cambridge colleges could lease their land, it never interfered in the relationship between landlord and tenant generally and so never gave the landlords the sort of advantage in tenurial arrangements that they might well have welcomed. Hence, it can be suggested that the generation who lived through 1549 always remained conscious of the dangers of oppressing tenants and feared that aggressive landlordism would inspire new acts of agrarian or political violence. The accounts of the witnesses we quoted earlier show that there remained a great deal of bitterness amongst tenants at their treatment by their landlords, perhaps a sign that the tenants had not yet fully accommodated the idea that they were contractually rather than socially tied to their landlords.

It was only after the middle of the Queen's reign that landlords seem to have made real inroads into recovering what they had lost. In doing so, they had three strategies to employ. The first two were to compete with their tenants for the profits of agriculture. In the first, landlords took to farming themselves, often taking land back from their tenants and cultivating it in hand. As early as 1537 we find one Norfolk peasant complaining to another that 'the gentlemen buy up all the grain, keep all the cattle in their hands and hold all the farms so that poor men can have no living'.[11] The idea that landlords should not be farmers appears in the Mousehold articles of 1549, and Harrison makes the same criticism of gentlemen a generation later. But the gentry needed to farm to live. Dr Thirsk has suggested that there was a revival of gentry demesne farming (although we differ in that she sees this as an intellectual interest where I would stress financial need). At Earls Colne in Essex, Roger Harlakenden, a lawyer who bought the manors in the village out of the wreckage of the earldom of Oxford in the 1580s, quickly established hop-growing on a large scale. It is clear that in north Oxfordshire, where the smaller gentry were committed to sheep grazing, they pursued strategies of adding their tenants' lands to their demesnes when they could. The second strategy landlords employed was to compete for profit by amending the terms of tenancy and raising rents and fines. The example which is often cited is that of the Earls of Pembroke on their Wiltshire estates, but substantial rises in fines were not just a southern phenomenon but can be found even in Cumberland and Westmorland. George Owen saw fines as a new innovation in Pembrokeshire. In this they were aided by a new technology which allowed them to understand what they owned and its potential value in a new way. This was the measured survey (which may or may not have come with a map), and which replaced surveys estimated by eye or which used customary units such as oxgangs and virgates. And the new technology gave the landlord an exact estimate of the value of a tenement, based on its acreage and a value per acre where before he had been forced to rely on the valuation placed on land by the tenant or his neighbours. There are reports of surveyors touting for business through handbills posted in London. Thereafter, the take-up of the measured survey seems to have been quite quick in southern England after the mid-1570s although somewhat delayed in the north, where the value of land probably made the investment in the surveyor's fee so much harder to justify. By the end of the century, one Essex landowner was employing a surveyor to value tenements as they became vacant so that the highest rent could be demanded of the incoming tenant. 'The common people are in great fear when [a] survey is to be made of their land,' wrote Edward Warsop in 1583. John Norden's *Surveyor's Dialogue* (1607) was an account of what the surveyor could do for the landlord but one which acknowledged just how unpopular the surveyor might be with the tenants.

The third approach was for lords to compete with their tenants for the control of the land through enclosure. Enclosure took several forms, not all of which drew criticism from contemporaries. But one form, the enclosure of arable land, which normally involved the conversion of arable to pasture, drew particularly strong condemnation. As we saw in the comments of Francis Twigge, it was seen to be depopulating the countryside, forcing the migration of the poor within the countryside or into towns in the search for work.

Enclosure involves the dividing of common land into several smaller plots of privately owned land. The common right which was abolished by enclosure might be a seasonal one over open field fallow, when the farmers of the village exercised the right to graze collectively, or it might be the right to graze open or waste ground, whether moorland, heathland or marshland. When open field land was enclosed, the rights of ownership were redistributed to form units within a ring fence.

The enclosure of open fields could produce efficiencies in output and might be justified for that reason. But open field enclosure was often an answer to the local uncompetitiveness of arable production. It took advantage of the greater profits which could be generated by switching into cattle or sheep production. Most notably it offered landlords a much greater rent income than arable could generate.

Enclosure was therefore an aspect of the commercialisation of agriculture within England, a reaction to opportunity. The smaller labour needs of pastoral economies produced out-migration, unemployment and eventual depopulation. Because of the social ills it created, depopulating enclosure was illegal throughout the sixteenth century except for a short interlude between the parliaments of 1593 and 1597. (Actually, what was illegal was the engrossment of tenements and the conversion of arable into pasture and not enclosure per se.)

In fact, for all the grip it had on the imagination of contemporaries, depopulating enclosure was quite localised in its incidence. It was most prevalent in the east Midland counties from north Oxfordshire, north Buckinghamshire and Bedfordshire through Northamptonshire and Leicestershire and into Lincolnshire. It continued northwards along the east coast and seems to have been particularly severe in Northumberland and County Durham. Within that area, depopulating enclosure reshaped not only the landscape but also the place of people within it. As John Walter showed in a justly famous account of the Oxfordshire 'revolt' of 1595, the landscape of the north of the county had been transformed, and the poor men who talked of rebellion (but who failed to rebel) knew only too well that their lives had been blighted by what they saw as the avarice of private landowners. Depopulating enclosure also bore on urban populations, if only because many town-dwellers had been displaced from the countryside. In years of high prices they blamed conversion for forcing up the price of foodstuffs. The enclosing Northamptonshire landlord, Sir Thomas Tresham, was warned not to proceed with the enclosure of Great Houghton in 1604: 'you could not remove all the tenants without much clamour, and especially when it is so near to Northampton, whose affections are well known to you.'[12] This was percipient: in the summer of 1607 new hedges on a number of newly enclosed and depopulated manors were overthrown by crowds, many drawn from the neighbouring towns. It would be wrong though to see the enclosure of open field as being invariably imposed by landlords on unwilling tenants. There is good evidence to show that individual farmers enclosed open field where they could, but the historian's attention has often been held by a small number of improving landlords – often recent purchasers of manors – who remodelled entire villages at a stroke.

The events of May and June 1607, and the reaction against enclosing and depopulation within government circles that followed (with commissions of enquiry sent into selected counties, and prosecutions in Star Chamber of enclosers), showed government policy coming full circle. Much of the anti-enclosure legislation had been repealed in 1593, although exactly why is a mystery. It is possible that the repeal was as much a cause as a symptom of a newly resurgent movement towards enclosure. In 1597, much of the legislation was re-enacted after a succession of hard years during which people's minds again turned to the evils of enclosure. The parliamentary debates in 1597, and again in 1601, when an attempt was made to repeal the new legislation, shows that by that time there were clear divisions between those who felt that social considerations should be pre-eminent, and so the bar on enclosure should remain, and those who took a more economically liberal viewpoint and saw the ability to use land for its greatest profit as being a right which ownership should confer on landowners. But there were no attempts to enforce the newly re-enacted statutes at the end of the 1590s, and it was only after the riots of 1607 confirmed the worst fears of those who placed the maintenance of order over economic progress that the government acted.

There was much less government concern about the enclosure of waste. In fact, wasteland enclosure could even be approved of as a modernising project. This is not to say that it came without social costs, but much less attention has been paid to these. As it failed to catch the attention of contemporaries, it is much more poorly documented and so harder to assess its scale and distribution. Where the enclosure of wasteland does find a place in the central archives is where it was contested and the injured party took a suit to the central courts, especially Star Chamber. Much of the litigation there actually concerns boundary disputes, where the enclosures made by one manorial lord spilled over onto land claimed by a neighbouring lord. These disputes often took the form of one village mobilising and pulling down hedges or walls erected by another. Disputes within villages, where tenants took legal action against a landlord, are far from unknown, but the reputational damage and delay that litigation could inflict on a lord and his enclosure project was an invitation to the lord to negotiate and secure his tenants' support. And here we perhaps see the crux of the matter. Tenant communities were not invariably opposed to the enclosure of wasteland. In fact, many could see advantage in it, and might embark on enclosure themselves with or without their lord's sanction. Enclosure might be forced on villages for commons, by their nature, were extensive open spaces, and the enclosure of one village's section of a common tended to force the enclosure of the others. Where lords were clever enough to make their tenants the beneficiaries of their enclosure project, then they might go along with it even if it meant that they came to pay for an asset which had previously been free: where the profit was intended to stick to the lord's hands alone, then they could well oppose.

This may be illustrated by two examples from northern England, both of which show how enclosure could form part of a larger seigniorial agenda to raise income from a manor. The Earl of Shrewsbury, who we met before as a modernising landlord at Glossopdale, was also a serial encloser. At Bolsover in Nottinghamshire he was enclosing on a large scale in the mid-1570s. Shrewsbury failed to secure the support of his tenants, and they petitioned the Queen with a whole series of grievances, not only about the Earl's enclosures but also his use of the commons for rabbit warrens, his overstocking of the commons with his own cattle, his refusal to allow them to dig coalmines in the manor or to take timber for repairs. The tenants' petition was referred to two judges who ruled in 1579 that the Earl should keep a recently made close of 240 acres in Shuttlewood but the tenants should have their own close of 120 acres made. Shrewsbury was then to make no further use of the remaining unenclosed wastes and was to remove his warrens. He was also allowed to make a partial enclosure of the open fields of the manor.

At the beginning of the new century, Lord Gerard enclosed the wastes of his manor of Nether Wyresdale in the Lancashire Pennines near Lancaster. Gerard had fought a hard campaign against his tenants in the 1590s to disprove their claim to hold their tenements by customary tenure. In 1602, he enclosed the wastes, striking an enclosure agreement with at least some of his tenants in early 1603. The newly enclosed land was offered to the sitting tenants at what Gerard, at least, considered to be favourable terms. Gerard wrapped his enclosure in the twin preoccupations of the times, justifying it in terms of both agricultural improvement and schemes to set the idle poor on work.

The enclosure of wastes could always be justified in terms of improvement but it came with a social cost. Unenclosed wastes drew the footloose to them for they offered the possibility of making a living by running livestock. It was this livelihood that enclosure removed. Even where small tenants were offered a close in return for their common rights, it was no substitute for open moorland. The voice of the small commoner was not often heard, but just over the hill from Wyresdale, at West Bradford, the commissioners enclosing the commons of the manor in 1589 went to the trouble of asking the tenants who opposed enclosure why they were against it. One reasonably large tenant, with 26 acres of land, four kine, three young beasts, two horses and twelve sheep, told them that the unenclosed waste provided 'the greater part of his living', and he was plainly apprehensive about what would follow enclosure. It was a common early-seventeenth-century practice to compensate the poor with a cow pasture that allowed a vestigial commoners' economy to remain in place if only to avoid allegations of contriving a depopulation.

Anyone whose life stretched from the mid-sixteenth to the mid-seventeenth century (the life span, say, of Shakespeare) would have seen the landscape transformed. What had been open field was divided by hedges and often turned over to grass. '[W]here many good husbandmen dwelt there is nothing left but a great house without a fire; the lord commonly sojurn at London; and the husbandman and ploughs, he only maintains a shepherd and his dog.'[13] Our observer would have seen open moorland or heath come to be divided by walls. He would have witnessed the proliferation of squatter cabins along the sides of commons and the verges of roads.

Enclosure was a dimension of the struggle for agricultural profit. It was by no means a simple struggle. In some places the competing parties were landlords and their tenants. In others it was rival villages who tried to maximise their use of what had been open assets. In many places one may suspect that enclosure served to shut the poorer inhabitants out of commons or at least limit their claims over them. Stubbes, Vaughan, Twigge and a whole host of other commentators, most of them clerical, were well aware of the casualties of this struggle. For a writer like Wilson, whose natural sympathies lay with landowners, enclosure was doubtless all part of the way in which the gentry had 'grown to become good husbands'.

II

If some landlords (not all) succeeded in clawing back some of the profits of a buoyant agricultural economy, it is clear from both Harrison and Wilson that the tenants themselves achieved a degree of prosperity based on either their ownership of the land, their ownership of a sound property right in the land (even if it was subject to the payment of rents of fines, sometimes at exorbitant rates) or the possession of a secure term in their property (twenty-one years or three lives being common).

We can gain insights into what was happening at the level of the individual farm in a number of ways. Probate inventories list the farmers' stock at the time of their death but whilst they survive in large numbers, they are not without problems. Of course, the level of a farmer's stock differs over the year, and whilst inventories list the corn in the garners and beasts in the fields, they never give us precise details of the area of a farm. But they do allow us to get a sense of the scale of a farming operation and the balance of a farm between arable and pasture. Where they have been looked at in large numbers and over a wide area, and especially by Mark Overton in Norfolk and Suffolk, they reveal that farms were carefully tailored to take advantage of their natural endowments. In short, farming was a capitalist enterprise. Individual farms were organised to turn a profit.

Contemporaries were aware of a fundamental distinction within the countryside, between areas of arable (which were characterised by villages and arable open fields) and areas predominantly of pasture, where farms were often dispersed and the landscape already enclosed. They were also keenly aware of the importance of location. Here it must be appreciated that the cost of transporting corn by road was very high compared to the cost of transporting it by sea or inland river. Areas without ready access to a town, or who could not trans-ship goods from road to water, were placed at a disadvantage against their better-located neighbours. The natural tendency of these disadvantaged farms was to turn to producing either dairy products, butter and cheese, which could stand the cost of carriage, live cattle, which could be driven to the place where they were to be slaughtered, or sheep. Specialisation of this sort was nothing new. Campbell has shown how this logic was clearly understood and acted on by the beginning of the fourteenth century by the owners of demesnes, and the sophistication of the systems of internal trade which served London even at that time. In the sixteenth century, depopulating enclosure must be seen as a severe example of the way in which farms were forced to specialise, in this case by the adoption of extensive sheep rearing.

It is in the nature of things that the carriage of goods by land is poorly documented, but the traffic in coastal waters is well described by the port books maintained by the customs officers. These show, for instance, the importance of a few north Kent ports for the supply of grain to London. King's Lynn 'regularly carried corn to every port between Berwick [upon Tweed] and Bristol and, on occasion, went as far west as Beaumaris and Dublin'. The most regular markets for Norfolk corn transhipped through that port were Newcastle, Yorkshire, London and the garrison town of Berwick-upon-Tweed. In effect, Norfolk allowed London to be heated by coal, for it was Norfolk grain that fed the Newcastle colliers and Norfolk boats that carried grain one way and coal the other. Large quantities of grain were also shipped from Lynn to Selby in Yorkshire, which may have acted as a regional entrepot for purchasers from the industrialising areas of the West Riding. In 1587, York was said to draw its barley from Lincolnshire and it is possible to find examples of York merchants active both there and nearer home in Holderness. The point is that whilst London drew its grain from within a fairly narrow area, there were long-distance trades in grain up and down the east coast and extending over scores of miles. There was also an export trade into the Low Countries. Norfolk grain and dairy produce were shipped from Lynn. Kentish grain and barrelled beer were also shipped to the Low Countries and ports such as Dunkirk, and there was a considerable export trade in East Anglian and Kentish grain to Spain, Portugal and even Italy. There were similar trades in grain to Spain through Bristol: but the West Country also looked to Ireland as an outlet for its produce.

The export trade was a licit trade in years when the price of grain was low: in other years, smuggled exports certainly continued, although it is hard to be sure on what scale. In years of high prices, government could suddenly become vigilant over the movement of foodstuffs and the corn factors, who were an absolutely necessary element in organising the trade, could suddenly be denounced as parasites and profiteers. In the hard conditions of 1595, corn-profiteering was denounced as a sin next only to usury in a sermon preached in York Minster. In these years, government and magistrates could suddenly become impractically sentimental over trade, seeing middlemen of all sorts as an evil, and magistrates attempted to impose the old ideal that farmers should bring their grain to market and expose it for sale to all comers when it was more usual for farmers to sell by sample and contract.

The sale of meat, and of butter and cheese, was far less controversial, but the supply chains could be equally long. Beeves would normally move several times in their lives, often being sold as two- or three-year-old beasts in northern or Welsh markets before being moved to Midland or East Anglian pastures and then sold on to be driven to London. They would then have a final gloss put on them, often grazing the marshes to the east of London before being slaughtered. For many 'arable' farmers in lowland England, the purchase of young beeves to be kept for a year or two before being sold on must have been an integral part of their farming. Specialist butter- and cheese-producing areas had emerged by the end of the century. Again, this implies long-distance trades. Much of the metropolis's butter and cheese came from Suffolk. For areas which were unable to compete on transport cost with Suffolk butter, there were again export opportunities. Some found its way to the Low Countries, whilst Welsh butter had a regular sale in La Rochelle and Bordeaux.

III

This, then, was a society in which the production of agricultural produce for sale was absolutely normal. Grain, butter and cheese, live cattle and wool were conveyed over long distances. Marketing arrangements were sophisticated, and there was an increasing tendency for goods to be sold by private contract. Private marketing created some discomfort, particularly in years of high prices when government and the magistracy attempted to assuage public fears by insisting that farmers brought corn to market. In these years, there occurred occasional instances of wagons and, in 1586, barks on the river Severn, being seized by hungry men and women, and the grain they were carrying taken and distributed amongst the crowd. Maintaining the food supply of London was of paramount concern to the Privy Council, who would trade the risk of disturbances and hunger in the grain-growing counties for the certainty that the capital was adequately fed.

The supply of foodstuffs was too important to be left to the market alone in years of distress. Given that exports were normally prohibited, it is impossible to claim that there was a free market in food in the sixteenth century. The same would be true of the market in agricultural labour. This was managed even more closely by the magistracy than food markets, with aims which altered over time as economic conditions changed. A statutory framework controlling labour had been in existence since after the population collapse of the Black Death. By the mid-sixteenth century, a large body of legislation had accumulated which was codified by the Statute of

Artificers of 1563. The timing of this legislative initiative is not without interest. There are signs that a bill was brought forward in 1559 and that in other circumstances some legislative initiative would have passed into law then. The renewed interest in employment at this time can be connected both to the monetary inflation of prices and wages in the 1540s and also to conditions after the influenza epidemic of 1557–8 (which in turn followed a severe famine). The scale of population loss in the 1550s has been the subject of some debate. Wrigley and Schofield's figures show a decline of 5.5 per cent between 1556 and 1561, and this may be taken as a minimum. The new legislation may therefore follow on a period of population decline which left a legacy of labour shortage and rising wages. It may also reflect another problem. There are hints of an outflow of labour into the burgeoning textile trades. Successive mid-century acts attempted to restrict recruitment, but they do not tell us whether the attraction of weaving was the higher wages or the possibility of early independence and marriage.

We can see that labour was also engaged in a struggle to secure its share of agricultural profits, but the statute was designed to contrive a labour market which advantaged the employer. Early modern agricultural labour tended to be employed in one or two ways, either by the day or as co-residential servants who had annual contracts. For day labourers, wages were paid with or without food and drink, and lower rates might be paid for shorter days in winter. The statute acknowledged both forms of labour and laid down regulations for their conduct, including penalties for servants who left their employer during their contracted term or employers who dismissed servants. But the statute also had a markedly coercive aspect, forcing people into work unless they could claim a specific exemption. Anyone aged between twelve and sixty who was neither in employment nor exempt (as, for instance, the heir to someone worth £10 per year in lands or £40 in goods) could be compelled to work as a servant in husbandry. Unmarried women between the ages of twelve and forty could also be compelled to work. Servants had to give notice of their intention to leave their employment; they were not allowed to leave their parish without a testimonial declaring that their departure had been lawful. In addition, constables were empowered to force all artificers and other persons capable of labouring to work in the harvest as required; and men who were normally accustomed to travel to seek harvest work elsewhere were only allowed to do so on securing a certificate from a magistrate. Servants were also to present themselves at hiring sessions where details of their contracts would be noted, or the fact of their unemployment advertised to prospective employers. The aspect of the statute which has attracted most attention though is the power placed on magistrates to determine maximum wage rates annually, taking into consideration 'the plenty or scarcity of the time'. The penalty for giving wages higher than those laid down was ten days' imprisonment and a fine of £5; for asking wages over the rate, twenty-one days' imprisonment.

The statute was conceived in conditions of labour shortage. Whilst some of its provisions, for instance the compulsory harvest service, seem to have quickly fallen into abeyance, the annual issue of wage rates county by county continued into the eighteenth century. Historians have perhaps been confused by the fact that rates were not issued annually by justices of the peace (JPs), but once settled they remained in place for a number of years, restated annually until a price shock forced revision.

The Kent wage rates compiled in 1563 were reissued without amendment until 1589. Moreover, evidence accumulates, so far mostly from the east of England, that the JPs enforced these rates and that labourers and servants who did not adhere to the Act were actively prosecuted. Jane Whittle has shown that the labour laws were enforced in Norfolk throughout the middle years of the century, with a large number of suits being brought for poaching servants. Labourers were also prosecuted for seeking wages in excess of the statutory maximums, and some men were ordered to accept placements as servants. Whittle also found the indictment of a labourer in 1558 for counselling his fellow labourers to demand excessive wages. The same determination to enforce the labour laws is found in Essex in the 1560s and early 1570s: but it seems that the urgency to prosecute men out of work then rather faded. Even before the records cease, there seems to be an acknowledgement that masterless men were genuinely unemployed and not shirking employment. A presentment from Coggeshall in 1582 reported seven weavers, fifteen fullers and two shoemakers out of contract and one imagines not willingly so.

This reflects a larger change taking place within rural society. It progressively altered over Elizabeth's reign from being a labour market where it was important to stop employees bargaining for the best price for their labour to one in which unemployment was rife. By 1624, the Somerset clergyman Richard Eburne, an unusually sympathetic witness to the state of the poor, admitted that some were poor because they were deliberately idle, but others would gladly work if only they could get it, and many would work more if only work were available. Hence wages fell to accommodate this reality. To a degree this was concealed by an increase in the face value of the labourer's wage. The median wage rate for an agricultural day wage without food and drink in southern England has been calculated to have been 4.33d. in the 1530s and 4.66d. in the 1540s, but then it increased rapidly in the light of inflation to 6.33d. in the 1550s and 7d. in the 1560s. It then came to rest for most of half a century at between 8d. and 9d. Contemporaries were aware of the creeping rise of wage rates. New rates were issued in Hertfordshire in 1592, and in 1599 the Essex grand jury sought a revision of the rates, acknowledging that as employers they were already paying over the rates, and suggesting 8d. a day as an appropriate winter wage rate without meat and drink and 10d. for a summer rate (3d. and 4d. if foodstuffs were provided). If, however, we look at the purchasing value of the wage, then it falls by a third over the second half of the century to about 60 per cent of its value in the 1530s.

This calculation may overstate the case and has been treated with scepticism, historians having pondered how labourers managed to live in such diminished circumstances. Part of the answer is that adult male wages were only one element in a household's income and there may have been more work available for women in spinning. Men and women may have worked more days in the year: they may also have been able to achieve a degree of self-sufficiency through having access to commons and land, although one suspects that this became rarer over time. But it seems certain that the standard of living fell over the century. Harrison, as we saw, certainly thought that the labourer's diet had declined over 'late years' as the price of corn rose and the labourer traded down to eat horse provender.

Many counties found a partial answer to the problem of a growing rural population in the expansion of cloth-making and its associated trades, often on a putting-out basis. The advantage of textile production was that it offered copious female employment in spinning. The disadvantage was that cloth-making was prone to slumps. The industry became notorious for the exploitation of its workforce. The conventional view was that the clothing trades maintained in work large numbers of poor who would otherwise have no living at all. The Vicar of Bildeston in the Suffolk clothing district turned this logic on its head in a withering sermon ('A Caveat for Clothiers') published in 1603. 'The poor must work for little rather than sit for nothing,' he said, and he drew a picture of the clothier making good profits on the back of exploitative wages.

By this time, the lack of prospects in the countryside were encouraging migration to towns in the search for work. This rural exodus certainly placed town economies under pressure, and from the 1570s onwards we find them trying to ascertain the scale of the problem by conducting censuses of the poor and unemployed. The attraction of town to the rural poor doubtless increased as some towns – Hadleigh in Suffolk, for instance, close to Bildeston – developed rudimentary systems of poor relief. But, as the cynical vicar of Layston, Hertfordshire, warned his parishioners in 1636, the better the provision for the poor, the more poor it attracted. The poor law of 1597–8, reinstated in 1601, may therefore be seen as an attempt to root the poor in their rural parishes. The statute changed the dynamics of enclosure: if landscape change deprived the poor of their livelihoods, the parish remained obliged to make provision for the welfare of the dispossessed, hence the appearance of cow pastures. The act required parishes to make good shortfalls in local employment by providing stocks of wool for spinning and weaving. They quickly found that parish stocks could not be made to pay.

As their numbers grew, the poor's claim on village society was often tenuous. They lacked both common rights and labour rights. Increasingly, the temper of the villages in which they lived grew hostile towards them, as may be seen by the withdrawal of hospitality (the feeding of the begging poor at the doors of richer inhabitants) and its replacement by a weekly payment. The proliferation of by-laws against inmates and the sub-division of houses attempted to make it hard for the transient poor to secure a toehold. Those who slipped into sexual incontinency or who took refuge in the alehouse for cooked food, shelter and warmth as well as ale could be prosecuted for their affront to decent behaviour. In 1624, Richard Eburne, in his *A Plain Pathway to Plantations*, could suggest that the rural poor were better off moving to America than lingering in England in a state of poverty.

IV

Our commentators recognised the scale of change in the later-sixteenth-century countryside but they concentrated on certain features of it, ignoring others. They recognised the resurgent landlordism of the second half of the century even if they failed to appreciate what was at stake for the gentry. They saw how the standard of living of the yeomen had changed. They said little or nothing about the immiseration of a large part of the rural population, the aspect of change which has tended to attract the attention of the most recent generation of historians.

Farmers, on the other hand, do indeed seem to have being doing very nicely over much of the reign. The literary evidence of their prosperity is impressive enough, but it is also supported by our knowledge of their material possessions. And yet, when contemporaries speak of the withdrawal of hospitality by these people, we recognise that prosperity was won at a price. Landowners too often seem to have regained ground from the destructive inflation of the mid-century. But the cost of doing so was to their reputations. The new model gentlemen shed many of the attributes that backward-looking contemporaries thought defined the gentleman. They abandoned hospitality. They had to raise rents (often in the form of entry fines) to recoup lost income. This often necessitated unpalatable disputes with their tenants. They had to extend their rent rolls through enclosure, which involved an element of dispossession. In many cases, they became farmers themselves and joined in a scramble for the use of commons and wastes. In order to survive, landowners had to learn to compete with their tenants for the profits of agriculture. And these, particularly the profits of arable agriculture, were not invariably as buoyant as might be thought. Where they failed to do this – either because they were not quick enough to grasp the changed temper of the times or because they found raising rents and quarrelling with tenants to be morally reprehensible – they found themselves living off capital. In this altered world, there was no longer room for landlords who valued good lordship and the command of men, and who placed generous hospitality above modernising their estates. All of this is well understood by historians, but in a society with little economic understanding, the landowner's alleged insatiable greed made him an easy target for polemicists. They should not be allowed the last word.

FURTHER READING

Harvey, P. D. A., 'Estate Surveyors and the Spread of the Scale-Map in England, 1550–80', *Landscape History*, 15 (1993): 37–49.

Hipkin, Stephen, 'The Structure, Development, and Politics of the Kent Grain Trade, 1552–1647', *Economic History Review*, 61, Suppl. 1 (2008): 99–139.

Hoyle, R. W., 'Agriculture and Rural Society', in Norman Jones and Robert Tittler (eds.), *The Blackwell Companion to Tudor Britain* (Oxford, 2004), pp. 311–29.

—— 'Estate Management, Tenurial Change and Capitalist Farming in Sixteenth-Century England', in S. Cavaciocchi (ed.), *Il Mercatao Della Terra Secc. XIII–XVIII* (Prato, 2004), pp. 353–82.

Kerridge, Eric, *Agrarian Problems in the Sixteenth Century and After* (London, 1969).

Manning, Roger B., *Village Revolts: Social Protest and Popular Protest in England, 1509–1640* (Oxford, 1988).

Minchinton, Walter E., *Wage Regulation in Pre-Industrial England* (Newton Abbot, 1972).

Outhwaite, R. B., 'Progress and Backwardness in English Agriculture, 1500–1650', *Economic History Review*, 2nd Ser., 39 (1986): 1–18.

—— *Dearth, Public Policy, and Social Disturbance in England, 1550–1800* (Cambridge, 1995).

Overton, Mark, *Agricultural Revolution in England: The Transformation of the Agrarian Economy, 1500–1850* (Cambridge, 1996).

Palliser, D. M., 'Tawney's Century: Brave New World or Malthusian Trap?', *Economic History Review*, 2nd Ser., 35 (1982): 339–53.

Parker, L. A., 'The Agrarian Revolution at Cotesbach, 1501–1612', *Transactions of the Leicestershire Archaeological Society*, 24 (1948): 41–75.

Thirsk, Joan (ed.), *The Agrarian History of England and Wales*, vol. IV: *1500–1640* (Cambridge, 1967).

Walter, John, 'A "Rising of the People"? The Oxfordshire Rising of 1596', *Past and Present*, 107 (1985): 90–143.

Whittle, Jane, *The Development of Agrarian Capitalism: Land and Labour in Norfolk, 1440–1580* (Oxford, 2000).

Wood, Andy, *The 1549 Rebellions and the Making of Early Modern England* (Cambridge, 2007).

Wrightson, Keith, 'Aspects of Social Differentiation in Rural England, c. 1580–1660', *Journal of Peasant Studies*, 5 (1977): 33–47.

—— *Earthly Necessities: Economic Lives in Early Modern Britain* (New Haven, Conn., 2000).

Wrightson, Keith and Levine, David, *Poverty and Piety in an English Village: Terling, 1525–1700* (Oxford, 1979).

Wrigley, E. A. and Schofield, R. S., *The Population History of England, 1541–1871: A Reconstruction* (Cambridge: Cambridge University Press, 1989).

Yates, Margaret, 'Between Fact and Fiction: Henry Brinklow's *Complaynt* against Rapacious Landlords', *Agricultural History Review*, 54 (2006): 24–44.

—— *Town and Countryside in Western Berkshire, c. 1327–c. 1600: Social and Economic Change* (Woodbridge, 2007).

NOTES

1 Cited in E. I. Fripp (ed.), *Minutes and Accounts of the Corporation of Stratford-upon-Avon, 1553–1620* (Dugdale Soc., 10, 1929), p. xv.

2 Philip Stubbes, *The Anatomie of Abuses*, ed. Margaret Jane Kidnie (Tempe, Ariz., 2002), p. 169.

3 William Harrison, *The Description of England: The Classic Contemporary Account of Tudor Social Life by William Harrison*, ed. Georges Edelen (New York, 1968), pp. 200–4.

4 Harrison, *Description of England*, p. 200.

5 Harrison, *Description of England*, p. 133.

6 William Vaughan, *The Golden Grove* (1600), Book 3, Chapter 22.

7 'The State of England (1600) by Sir Thomas Wilson', ed. F. J. Fisher, *Camden Miscellany* XVI (Camden third ser., 52, 1936), pp. 18–20.

8 Harrison did not write about enclosure except in the context of emparkment, perhaps because this was not an issue in Essex; but one of his side notes held that 'the decay of the people is the destruction of a kingdom', reflecting the same sentiments as Trigge. Harrison, *Description of England*, p. 256, n. 7.

9 *The Description of Pembrokeshire by George Owen of Henllys, Lord of Kemes*, ed. Henry Owen (2 vols. in 4, Cymmrodorian Rec. Ser, 1, 1892–1936), Pt. 1, p. 190, cited by F. J. Fisher, 'Tawney's Century', in F. J. Fisher (ed.), *Essays in the Economic and Social History of Tudor and Stuart England* (Cambridge, 1961), pp. 1–14; p. 9.

10 Harrison, *Description of England*, p. 257.

11 Cited by Andy Wood, *The 1549 Rebellions and the Making of Early Modern England* (Cambridge, 2007), p. 7.

12 M. E. Finch, *The Wealth of Five Northamptonshire Families, 1540–1640* (n.p., 1956), p. 89.

13 Anon., *The True Narration of the Entertainment of His Royal Majesty from the Time of His Departure from Edinburgh Till His Receiving at London ...* (1603); reprinted in C. H. Firth (ed.), *Stuart Tracts, 1603–93* (Westminster, 1903), p. 42.

PART V

CULTURE

CHAPTER TWENTY-SEVEN

WHO KILLED ROBIN HOOD?

Transformations in popular culture

Martin Ingram

'Popular culture' continues to be an elusive quarry. Though the term is widely current in cultural studies and literary criticism, and indeed also in common speech, it has had a chequered career among historians since Peter Burke's *Popular Culture in Early Modern Europe* (1978) made it for a time both fashionable and highly controversial. Between the fifteenth and the eighteenth centuries, Burke argued, many games, calendar rituals and other popular customs and beliefs were discountenanced by church and state authorities and measures taken to suppress or reform them. At the same time, there was a growing divergence between the outlook and values of elite groups (nobles, gentlemen and some middle-class elements in town and country) and those of the mass of the people. The former first distanced themselves from, then became increasingly hostile towards, elements of popular culture which they had formerly patronised. This notion of a 'reform of popular culture' was paralleled in the work of Keith Wrightson, who argued that whereas 'in the middle of the reign of Elizabeth, English villagers had largely shared a common fund of traditional beliefs, values and standards of behaviour', a century later 'that common heritage had become the property of those "rusticall", "rude," "silly ignorants" who remained wedded to their superstitions and their disorders'.[1] In a backhanded way, the idea of 'reform' also had resonance for historians such as Barry Reay, who were inclined to see popular culture in terms of resistance or opposition to hegemonic authority. The logic of Burke's argument was ultimately to stress the vulnerability of popular culture to attacks from above; but Burke saw the process of change as long and slow, and his interpretation was not inconsistent with the idea that elements of popular culture could be put to powerful use as 'weapons of the weak'.[2]

Yet these approaches gradually succumbed to criticism, much of which pivoted on basic assumptions about what was meant by popular culture. Burke concentrated on such phenomena as rituals, festivities, songs and stories, but potentially his definition of culture – 'a system of shared meanings, attitudes and values, and the symbolic forms (performances, artefacts) in which they are expressed or embodied' – was much broader, encompassing how people 'saw their world, how they lived, worked, worshipped, what they believed, their attitudes towards the law, politics, the church, the supernatural, their family, marriage, in short, . . . everything'.[3] This wider vision made the 'reform' argument more difficult to sustain in any straightforward way. More fundamental was the criticism that Burke's model, framed in terms of 'elite' and 'popular', made it hard to do justice not only to the middling ranks but also to diverse groups *within* the elites and *among* common people – not to mention the problems of capturing regional variations, metropolitan, urban and rural differences, the important issue of gender and a host of other subtleties. On the other hand, it tended to ignore areas of *shared* meanings or elements of common culture, while obscuring the fact that cultural artefacts cannot simply be assigned to particular social levels. Rather, what matters is how similar artefacts are understood, interpreted, exploited, consumed – in Chartier's terms 'appropriated' – by diverse individuals and social groups.[4] More basically, Burke's 'layer cake' model of culture, albeit one that recognised a degree of exchange between high and low, was too rigid – culture is better understood as fluid and protean, subject not only to complex exchanges but also to sudden transformations.[5]

It is now likewise a commonplace that there are no sources that provide an unrefracted view of popular culture; and yet, on the other hand, it is simplistic to think of the sources that do exist as 'contaminated' by agents of the 'learned' and 'the elite' or to imagine that there can ever have been a wholly autochthonous 'popular culture'. Elite and popular, literate and oral, learned and homespun interacted in ways that were both complex and creative. Broadside ballads offer a good example. They embody elements of orally transmitted song, but that tradition was, at least originally, as much the property of elite groups as of the common people. Moreover, far from being simple carriers of old verses, broadsides often announced themselves to be 'a new ballad' precisely because novelty was a selling point. It follows that many of these new productions were the work of professional writers in a complex relationship with 'popular culture' however defined; and the messages embodied in the ballads, far from being a simple reflection of the popular outlook, were actually designed to influence popular thinking – sometimes to the point of being heavily didactic. Yet, in so far as they did help to shape attitudes, they thereby became an element of an ever-changing popular culture. It should also be recalled that our knowledge of these ballads is heavily dependent on collections made by people of relatively high status. We cannot tell whether they were self-consciously slumming when they acquired them, simply enjoyed them for what they were, or had more complex motives for seeking them out.

This does not mean that historians should shy away from the term 'popular culture', which retains a genuine utility. It not only identifies a broad subject area and emphasises that the focus of inquiry is the experience of people outside the ranks of the aristocracy and gentry and of other social and intellectual elites; it also offers a point of contact with literary scholars working on the period, the more so since self-conscious *representations* of popular culture – whether hostile, nostalgic, or exploratory, and serving a variety of literary, dramatic and polemical purposes – featured increasingly in the work of contemporary writers. Amid the diversity of views on the meaning of the term, rigidly doctrinaire positions are best avoided. A creative alternative is to recognise that all the approaches already mentioned – a broad view of popular culture, a narrower view stressing games and festivities, the idea of 'reform' initiated by certain elite groups, the notion that some forms of popular culture could be vehicles for opposition or resistance, and an imagined entity discernible in the literature of the period – have at least something to offer in trying to capture 'popular culture' and its transformations in Elizabethan England. This essay will start by sketching some of the broad features of the culture of ordinary English people, both men and women, and how they were changing. It will then focus more sharply on phenomena that have sometimes been seen as the epitome of popular culture – the world of May games and other calendar festivities, and on related ritual happenings such as 'ridings' and 'rough music'.

A WORLD OF CHANGE

Elizabethan society and culture were in many respects highly repressive; they were also legalistic, to an extent scarcely imaginable today. A wide range of behaviour, from the practice of agriculture to personal morality, was subject to more or less intermittent legal regulation; it was not until 1604 that the sumptuary laws, which tried to enforce the wearing of apparel appropriate to one's station, finally lapsed. Some of the restrictive tendencies were driven by political uncertainties and religious change; but the tensions associated with what William Harrison described as 'the great increase of people in these daies' were also a powerful force.[6] Thus it was that in 1572 a wide range of migrant people became punishable as vagabonds, including all 'Fencers, Bearwardes, Comon Players in Enterludes & Mynstrels [and] Juglers', unless they were under the patronage of a great personage or licensed by the justices.[7] In the long run, this measure may have promoted the emergence of professional companies of players, but the immediate purpose was unquestionably repressive.

The Statute of Artificers (1563) was another measure symbolic of the restrictive tendencies in Elizabethan society. Originally passed at a time of labour shortage, its underlying principles proved applicable also to the conditions of rising population and worsening employment opportunities in the closing years of the reign. Its effect was to promote apprenticeship and to direct as many young people as possible into household or farm service, restricting the freedom of youth and helping to push up marriage ages. This was the demographic backdrop to the growing concern about dancing and festivities which is evident by the turn of the century. But while the tendency of the statute was to restrict the young, in terms of gender the effects were more varied. The emphasis on the authority of male householders as masters of servants and apprentices may also have benefited wives and widows, who exercised power as 'dames' within the household. On the other hand, it may have served to reinforce the strain of misogyny – humorously mild or destructively bitter according to circumstances and the vagaries of men's tempers – that was, and remained, a stock element of 'popular culture' in the more inclusive sense of a set of attitudes and assumptions which were common coin at all social levels. This was the period when witchcraft accusations became commonplace, when the scolding women who had long been stigmatised became, at least in some communities, subject to the harsher punishment of the ducking stool and when fairy lore and other folk beliefs came to be seen as old wives' tales. The underlying contempt for old women's notions is nicely caught in Thomas Nashe's reminiscences of his Suffolk boyhood:

> I haue heard aged mumping beldams as they sat warming their knees ouer a coale scratch ouer the argument verie curiously, and they would bid yong folks beware on what day they par'd their nayles, tell what luck euerie one should haue by the day of the weeke he was borne on; show how many yeares a man should liue by the number of wrinkles on his forhead . . . When I was a little childe, I was a great auditor of theirs, and had all their witchcrafts at my finger endes.[8]

Other cultural developments were more expansive. The fact that the growth of London was powered by heavy migration – out as well as in and extending into the far corners of the realm – facilitated the exchange of ideas and information and fostered cultural integration. Of course there remained a variety of marked regional accents, and not merely among the poor – it was said that Sir Walter Ralegh 'spake broade Devonshire to his dyeing day' – while dialect and other linguistic differences of region, community and occupation made for a richly variegated popular culture. Yet the idea that 'it is scarcely possible to speak of a national language' and the implication that people of different regions could barely comprehend each other are more questionable.[9] Court records in the form of witnesses' statements from all over the country, though peppered with occasional dialect words or other regional usages, are on the whole more striking for their essential similarity of language. It is unlikely that they were heavily reworked by the scribes who actually wrote them, because they had to be read back to the deponent before being authenticated with a signature or mark.

Cultural exchange and integration were to be promoted even more in the seventeenth century by the impact of print and the spread of literacy, but these developments were already getting a purchase on the world of popular culture in Elizabeth's reign. Perhaps half a million copies of broadside ballads were produced in the later sixteenth century, while almanacs, in which a core of calendrical and astrological information was supplemented by a huge range of useful or amusing material on a wide range of subjects, were likewise churned out in very large numbers. The ability to read 'print hand' – the capacity to digest handwriting was a higher-level skill, and the ability to write was greater yet – was not yet expected of ordinary people, perhaps not even those of substance and position. In Chester in 1585, Mayor Brerewood's address to the town watch had to be 'made' by someone else and learnt by heart by the Mayor himself, 'for although he could nether write nor read yet was of excelent memory & very brave and gentile partes otherways'.[10] But is there not a hint of apology in this account? Increasingly, it is plain, reading was recognised to be more than just a handy skill and was more and more taught in the petty schools that existed in numerous parishes, if not in the household by masters and mistresses. By the end of Elizabeth's reign a local officer who could not read might find himself the butt of ridicule.

Another stimulus to the spread of literacy was unquestionably the Protestant religion, with its emphasis on the Scriptures and its vernacular liturgy – especially as the religious motive applied to women as well as men. More generally, both the

Bible and the Book of Common Prayer were enormously powerful agents of change. They promoted cultural integration while at the same time feeding the imagination in ways that generated diversity, and their language seeped into, perhaps saturated, not only religious but also everyday mentalities. In other respects, the impact of religious change on popular culture can hardly be exaggerated. In the short term, as Eamon Duffy and others have argued, the effects were largely destructive, sweeping away a world of observances deeply rooted in popular piety; with them went numerous local institutions and associations and a host of images and other artefacts.

Music, perforce, was also moving with the times. Except in a few privileged places, notably the Chapel Royal, the elaborate polyphonic music that had been a feature of the pre-Reformation church could no longer be practised. As a result, the professional singers and musicians that even some quite small communities had aspired to employ were for the most part squeezed out. The 1559 royal injunctions were clearly suspicious of all forms of church music, but did allow that

> for the comforting of such that delight in music, it may be permitted, that in the beginning, or in the end of Common Prayers, either at morning or evening, there may be sung an hymn, or such like song, to the praise of Almighty God, in the best sort of melody and music that may be conveniently devised, having respect that the sentence of the hymn may be understanded and perceived.[11]

Congregations apparently seized on this concession and exceeded it, to the extent that the singing of metrical psalms became a common feature of church services – sustained by the numerous editions of John Day's *Whole Booke of Psalms* (1562). According to Bishop Jewel early in the reign, parishes in London and elsewhere began to vie with each other in congregational singing, so that 'You may now sometimes see at Paul's Cross, after the sermon, six thousand persons, old and young, of both sexes, all singing together, and praising God.'[12] Beat Kümin may be right to see the development, which must have affected secular music-making too, as one by which parishioners 'moved from being patrons and consumers to performers'.[13]

On this view it is wrong to see ordinary people simply as passive victims of cultural change. Things happened that they could not resist, but they were apt to seize the new opportunities presented by such changes; and some of the shifts of the period reveal a powerful synergy between official policies and the popular imagination. Among the circumstances that helped to promote a sense of Protestant identity fused with a sense of xenophobic Englishness were the long wars against Spain from 1585, and in particular the massive invasion scare of 1588. The papal bull of excommunication of 1570 – originally intended to coincide with the Northern Rising of the previous year – had probably begun the process earlier. Certainly the interrelated themes of anti-popery, patriotism and loyalty to the Queen were vigorously promoted in the spate of broadside ballads penned in the wake of these two events.

Culturally, the most interesting consequence was a new quasi-national calendar festival, of which the most marked and widespread feature was the ringing of church bells, to celebrate the Queen's accession on 17 November. The Protestant

Prayer Book had abolished numerous saints' days; this was an addition to the calendar, though not one entailing a holiday from work. The celebrations had begun as spontaneous expressions of loyalty in a few parishes in London and large provincial towns in southern England in the late 1560s, but they became much more widespread after 1569. The event was officially recognised in 1576, with the publication of an order of service for the day (enlarged 1578), and by the time Elizabeth died, Accession Day was being honoured in every shire in the realm, though not all communities participated or did so every year. There were elaborations. In 1587, the preacher Isaac Colfe envisioned 'the cheerfulness of our countenances, the decency of our garments, the songs of our lips, the clapping of our hands, our melody on instruments of music, the making of bonfires, the ringing of bells, the sounding of trumpets, the display of banners, the shooting of guns' and other 'testimonies of rejoicing' on this 'special day ordained of the Lord . . . for the happiness of England'.[14] So it was that the corporation of Oxford, for example, paid for a sermon in 1571, sponsored organ music in 1572, had a drummer in 1587 and celebrated with bonfires in 1590. But in many places activities were much sparser. In some parishes the Queen's birthday was also marked by bell-ringing, albeit on a smaller scale, especially in the 1590s – no doubt a tribute to Elizabeth's longevity. Perhaps surprisingly, the Armada victory failed to generate an annual celebration.

A related issue, important for our understanding of both national identity and popular culture, was Englishmen's sense of martial prowess. The great military successes of the fourteenth and fifteenth centuries, at Crécy, Poitiers and Agincourt, were associated with skill with the longbow. Successive kings and military commentators dreaded its disuse, and numerous proclamations and acts of parliament urged the need to uphold archery. Evidence from local records and coroners' inquisitions on fatal accidents has shown that until the mid-sixteenth century Englishmen did, on the whole, do their archery practice. Not everyone could or wanted to be a professional archer – easily recognisable by the overdevelopment of the right shoulder muscles as a result of constantly drawing the great war bow – but a reasonable level of skill was something that most men could aspire to and strive to pass on to their sons.[15]

It took longer than is sometimes imagined for the bow to fall into desuetude as a military weapon, but its use undoubtedly did go into terminal decline in Elizabeth's reign, and regular archery practice fell away too. What effect did this have on men's outlook and sense of self? Pride in naval success could have only limited purchase on the minds of those who dwelt in the inland counties, but there were other ways in which the martial spirit could find expression. There is evidence that musters were not, as is sometimes thought, sullen and reluctant gatherings, but were welcomed as opportunities for the display of masculinity with the up-to-date trappings of guns, pipes and drums. Thence there was a direct link with popular festivities. As is well known, some of the popular sports of the period, notably football (commonly pitting against each other large groups of men and youths from neighbouring communities), were close in nature to combat, and there was an agonistic element in other games and dances too. As will be seen in the next section, the trappings of muster organisation often featured in these activities.

PAGEANTS, PLAYS AND GAMES

The rich cycle of pageants, plays and games that punctuated the ritual calendar in late medieval and early Tudor times have been much researched of late. It is now understood that, far from being survivals from time immemorial, far less relics of an ancient pagan past, they were closely associated with religious and ecclesiastical developments and fashions; they had identifiable origins, often at some point in the fifteenth century; and they were subject to change. But the onset of religious Reformation entailed some particularly brutal ruptures, especially when the religious climate became stridently Protestant in the reign of Edward VI. Under Mary there was a vigorous revival, some of the energy of which persisted into the 1560s and 1570s. But the middle and later years of Elizabeth's reign were on the whole a period of decline, during which some features of the popular culture of ritual celebration were whittled away or disappeared for ever.

Some major provincial towns and cities, notably Coventry, Norwich, York and Chester, were famous for elaborate cycles of miracle and mystery plays, associated with the midsummer feast of Corpus Christi or with Whitsun. The Chester plays, according to a later account,

> weare the historie of the bible, composed . . . that the simple mighte understand the scripture . . . The actores or players, weare the companies or trades men of the Citti of Chester, who at theire owne costes and charges, sett forth and alsoe played the same playes . . . The places where they weare played were in every streete of the Cittie, that all people that would mighte behoulde the same: The manner of these playes was, every company made a pageant on which they played theire partes, which pagiant was a scaffolde, or a high foure square buildinge, with .2. rowmes a higher and a lower, the lower hanged aboute richly and closse, into which, none, but the actors came, on the higher they played their partes beinge all open to the behoulders, this was sett on .4. wheeles, and soe drawne from streete to street.[16]

It was possible for such dramatic spectacles to survive in a Protestant climate by the excision of religiously offensive elements, but they nonetheless tended to come under increasing pressure as Elizabeth's reign progressed. In Chester there were disputes over the plays already in the 1560s, some regarding them as superstitious. In 1572, the Archbishop of York forbade them, apparently at the instigation of dissentients in the city, but his inhibition arrived too late to stop the plays that year. In 1575, the council voted to stage the cycle again, but moved the performance to midsummer and confined it to one day instead of three, and to one place within the city instead of the usual four or five. Nonetheless, the mayor, John Savage, was pursued by the Archbishop of York and called before the Privy Council in London. The matter was smoothed over, and neither Savage nor other members of the city council were punished. But clearly the issue had become simply too contentious, and, apart from a partial performance before Lord Strange and other notables in 1578, the Chester plays were never staged again.

Even plays which were not explicitly religious in content were tainted by association. Coventry boasted a Hock Tuesday play, created in 1416, based on the widespread custom whereby on the second Tuesday after Easter, women would raise money for the parish church by capturing men and holding them to ransom. (On Hock Monday men captured women for the same purpose, but, whether because females tended to have less money about their persons or for other reasons, they were generally less successful in fund-raising.) The play celebrated a supposedly historical event, the defeat of Danish oppressors by the citizens of Coventry, and consisted of a simulated battle in which the Danes were at length 'beaten doun, overcom and many led captive for triumph by our English weémen'.[17]

Interestingly, what purports to be Robert Laneham's eyewitness account of a performance of this play before the Queen at Kenilworth, during her summer progress in 1575, includes a list of books supposedly known – perhaps even owned – by one of the participants, a mason going by the name of Captain Cox. Apart from almanacs, 'a bunch of ballets & songs all auncient . . . fair wrapt up in Parchment and bound with a whipcord', a miscellany of works such as 'The Ship of Foolz', 'the hundred Mery talez', 'Hikskorner', and 'Boords breviary of health', and a collection bearing on the nature of women such as 'The wife lapt in a Morels skin', 'the Seaven sororz of wemen' and 'the Nutbrooun maid', he had 'at his fingers endz' a host of chivalric romances and similar literature, such as 'king Arthurz book', 'Bevys of Hampton', 'Syr Gawyn' and 'Robinhood'. This list was no doubt intended to denote a mind full of old-fashioned stuff; and indeed the Coventry Hocktide play was itself an endangered species. The Coventry men had come before the Queen to

> petition that they moought renu noow their olld storial sheaw . . . for pastime woont too bee plaid in oour Citee yeérely: without ill exampl of mannerz, papistry, or ony superstition: . . . tyll noow of late laid dooun, they knu no cauz why, onless it wear by the zeal of certain theyr Preacherz: men very commendabl for their behaviour and learning, & sweét in their sermons, but sumwhat too sour in preaching awey theyr pastime.[18]

The show was reprieved and enacted sporadically thereafter; but its central place in city life had gone.

The martial spirit of Captain Cox – 'hardy az Gawin . . . a good Marshall at musters . . . floorishing with hiz tonswoord' – is as evident from his behaviour as from his library; and the Coventry play was not the only opportunity for the men of mid-sixteenth-century England to strut their stuff in armour and weapons in a holiday context.[19] Most substantial towns put on a 'marching watch' – a parade of armed men, led by the mayor or sheriffs and usually organised by craft guilds – at Christmas or midsummer; indeed, in June there were often two parades, on the eves of Saint Peter and Saint John. They had originated as a means of maintaining public order at times of the year when licence could be expected; but they themselves rapidly developed festive attributes. They marched in the night, illuminated by cresset lights and accompanied by banners; they were enlivened by music, drumming and gunfire; and in some places they generated spectacular pageants. At York, 'Yule and Yules wife' rode through the city on Saint Thomas's day (21 December), while in Coventry in 1533 the company of Cappers carried a giant with illuminated eyes.

The giant was an innovation copied from London, which indeed – since it did not have elaborate religious play cycles or citywide Corpus Christ processions – had developed its midsummer marching watches to an extraordinary peak of elaboration. Nostalgically evoked in a famous passage in Stow's *Survey,* in reality they were already a thing of the past at the beginning of Elizabeth's reign. Cancelled in 1539 at the behest of Henry VIII, who wished to pressure the citizens into providing a more purposefully military muster, they were briefly revived before finally succumbing in the late 1540s against the background of heavy war taxation, which left little money for more light-hearted pursuits. The Armourers' Company petitioned for a revival in the 1560s, but what they got – 'standing' watches rather than parades – were on a much reduced scale. It would seem that, apart from other considerations, the City fathers feared that these events threatened public order, a concern evident in other towns too – though some of these did maintain marching watches till later in the century. In London the pageantry shifted to what has become known as the Lord Mayor's Show, the celebration of his inauguration on 29 October, a more passive affair that gave the citizenry no opportunity to command the streets in martial array.

The demise of the Midsummer Watch may have provided the excuse for other shows in London – or perhaps they were organised as a deliberate act of compensation. The city chronicler Henry Machyn records how at Saint John Zachary's on 24 June 1559

> ther was a May-game . . . with a gyant, and drums and guns [and the] ix wordes [Worthies], with spechys, and a goodly pagant with a quen . . . and dyvers odur, with spechys; and then sant Gorge and the dragon, the mores dansse, and after Robyn Hode and lytyll John, and M[aid Marian] and frere Tuke, and thay had spechys rond a-bowt London.[20]

Since the next day they played before the Queen at Greenwich, these were evidently staged spectacles rather than events that the populace participated in en masse. They had affinities with the activities of the Lords of Misrule of aristocratic households, which Machyn also records; and the reference to the morris is telling, since in England this had originated as a spectacular, acrobatic dance, performed by professionals or at least highly trained players, patronised first in royal and noble households and later by town guilds or civic authorities. That the London authorities were, on the other hand, decidedly hostile to impromptu performances is shown by a 1575 Bridewell case, when an apprentice was sharply questioned about May games supposed to have been 'broughte into London'. He denied all knowledge of games in Eastcheap, outside Temple Bar, or elsewhere in the city, protesting further that he had never said that 'there shold be sene a Maye game, as the like was not sene this Cth yeres'. Another man had asked him 'whate sporte was about this towne in the hollie daies,' but he affirmed that 'he knewe of none, but two or three drome[s] & awnsientes & suche like shewes in Southwarke'.[21]

It was in the countryside and in the smaller towns, especially in the southern and western parts of England, that May games and summer lords were to be found in their natural habitat. They had flourished in the late fifteenth century and even more in the reign of Henry VIII, and underwent an impressive revival in many places under Mary and in the early years of Elizabeth's reign. The famous literary exploiter of puritan prejudices, Philip Stubbes, provides a vivid (if blatantly hostile) account of such May-time customs.

> First, all the wilde-heds of the Parish, conventing togither, chuse them a Graund-Captain (of all mischeefe) whome they innoble with the title of 'my Lord of Mis-rule', and him they crowne with great solemnitie, and adopt for their king. This king anointed chuseth forth twentie, fortie, threescore or a hundred lustie Guttes, like to him self, to waighte uppon his lordlie Maiestie, and to guarde his noble person. Then, everie one of these his men, he investeth with his liveries of green, yellow, or some other light wanton colour; And as though that were not (baudie) gaudie enough, I should say, they bedecke them selves with scarfs, ribbons & laces hanged all over with golde rings, precious stones, & other jewels: this doon, they tye about either leg xx. or xl. bels, with rich handkerchiefs in their hands . . . Thus al things set in order, then have they their Hobby-horses, dragons & other Antiques, together with their baudie Pipers and thundering Drummers to strike up the devils daunce withal; then, marche these heathen company towards the Church and Church-yard, their pipers pipeing, their drummers thundering, their stumps dauncing, their bels jyngling, their handkerchefs swinging about their heds like madmen, their hobbie horses and other monsters skirmishing amongst the route.

Stubbes likewise gives an account of the fetching in of summer boughs on May eve, the erection of the maypole, the building of 'sommer haules, bowers, and arbors', and the accompanying dancing; and the fund-raising events known as church ales with which these summer games were often associated:

> The Church-wardens . . . with the consent of the whole Parish provide half a score or twenty quarters of mault, wherof some they buy of the Church-stock, and some is given them of the Parishioners them selves, every one conferring somewhat, according to his abilitie; which mault, beeing made into very strong ale or beere, it is set to sale.[22]

Stubbes is less explicit about the other means used to raise funds for the church, though he mentions that summer lords and kings commonly sold mock livery badges made of paper. More strikingly, many parishes, particularly in the Thames valley region, had games featuring Robin Hood and his merry men, Maid Marian (usually a transvestite male), and other figures associated with the greenwood legend, such as the 'shrive' (sheriff). Sometimes these performances overlapped with morris dancing. The spectacular morris provided an effective focus for fund-raising; and who better to extort money for a good cause than Robin Hood? Parish players travelled far and wide to gather contributions, while churchwardens keen to make a large profit from their 'ale' exploited every means to encourage people not only from their own but neighbouring parishes to turn up, drink up and pay up.

A good example is provided by the Wiltshire village of Winterslow. In the 1540s its 'king ale' was small in scale and yielded only modest profits. But there was a substantial feast in 1553 and another in 1555, when the size of the payment to the 'mynstrell' (2s. 8d.) indicated a more ambitious effort than hitherto to provide musical entertainment. As a result, returns began to rise. By the early 1560s the churchwardens were laying out money at similar events in neighbouring parishes (including Titherley, across the border in Hampshire), while the inhabitants of those places came in turn to spend at Winterslow, with satisfactory financial results. In 1563 'morys-gere' was hired as an added attraction, while 1574 saw not only the outlay for minstrels and morris dancing but also payments to a drum player and to 'Spencer the taberer too dayes vis viii*d*'. The following year comestibles, and the means to prepare them, included wood, hedgewood for firing, malt, hops, wheat, a calf, two sheep, a quarter of mutton, pepper, saffron, oatmeal, salt, currants, raisins, cheese and butter – not a bad spread for a small village. Takings came not only from Winterslow itself but also from the neighbouring parishes of Winterbourne, Porton, Idmiston, Boscombe and Dean, and there were further receipts 'of Salsbery men' and 'of more straungers'. It is clear, moreover, that festivities were not confined to the occasion of the king ale itself, for there was a separate payment for minstrels on May Day as well as for performances at Whitsun and on Trinity Sunday.[23]

The holding of king ales at Winterslow continued throughout the century, still making good profits. However, they became more intermittent as time went on, and the last one recorded in the churchwardens' accounts was in 1602. In some places, ales and associated festivities had succumbed much earlier. Kingston upon Thames (Surrey) is a striking case. In the early sixteenth century there seems to have been a full week of festivities associated with the town's Whitsun fair, participants in the Robin Hood game being dressed gallantly in Kendal green with hats and gloves. Proceedings were so elaborate because the town had the royal palace of Richmond ever in its sights – indeed was it not called Kingston? – and it could utilise the river for access to nearby parishes. Yet these activities had virtually ceased by 1562. Similarly, the borough of Reading had been a major centre of festive games in the early sixteenth century but became one of the first places to stop them altogether in Elizabeth's reign; the demise of former 'colleccions or gatheringes' was formally noticed in the churchwardens' accounts of Saint Laurence parish in 1572–3.[24]

What had happened? The collapse of these popular customs cannot be ascribed to any one single factor. First it should be re-emphasised that events such as church ales and Robin Hood plays were not fixed traditions that had existed from time immemorial. They had been devised for specific ends and could be abandoned when they were no longer fit for purpose. They also had to appeal to current popular taste and could therefore be vulnerable to fashion – especially in social contexts that had pretensions to sophistication. In time, the appeal of Robin Hood wore thin. More basically, they required a great deal of hard work. Success might lead to success, but failure – resulting from incompetent organisation, embezzlement of funds, financial overstretch or just a run of wet weather – might lead to disillusionment.

Festivities were fragile, or at least highly sensitive, in other respects too. They were associated with the parish and hence with an ethos that prized unity and harmony. Indeed, it was a stock argument in favour of church ales that they were conducive to 'Christian love, conforming of mens behaviour to a civill conversation, compounding of controversies, appeasing of quarrels'.[25] If dissension and debate arose, the whole point was lost. It is plain that, irrespective of contentious religious issues, matters were not always completely harmonious. This is why in some places the election and order of succession of the summer lord and his leading subordinates were formally recorded by the churchwardens – either to avoid quarrels over precedence or to ensure that someone was available to act. At Wing (Buckinghamshire) in 1565, it was laid down that

> all suche yonge men as shall hereafter by order of the hole parryshe be chosen for to be lorde at Whytsontyde for the behafe of the churche, and refuse so to be, shall forfeyt and pay for the use of the churche iiis. iiiid. to be levyed uppon the sayde yonge men and theyr fathers and maysters wherere the just default can be founde; and every mayde refusyng to be lady for the sayd purpose to forfet unto the sayde use xxd. to be levyed in lyke order as is before expressed. And yt is provydyd that all suche howses out of the whiche the sayde lords or ladyes, or one of them, are chosen to stand fre from that purpose and charge for the space of vi yere then next ensuynge.[26]

At one level this is impressive testimony to the embedding of these festivities in the local social hierarchy and structures of parish administration. The subtext is that they were contested and had to be sustained by quasi-legal orders.

As has been seen, eating and drinking with people from neighbouring communities was also a major feature of these events and was commended by some contemporaries. From a more jaundiced viewpoint, the 'drinkings' that they expected can be seen as a kind of tribute, even blackmail, and lack of provision in good measure could lead to trouble. This was the more so since, paralleling these customs of hospitality between neighbouring communities, were other traditions of downright *hostility* – sometimes expressed in ferocious inter-village games of football or other sports, at other times taking the form of mass incursions, with drums and banners, as like as not led by men with bells on their legs in the manner of morris dancers. This raises the broader question of disorders associated with church ales, May games and other festivities throughout the year. Fuelled as they were with copious amounts of drink, fights, quarrels, or at least unseemly behaviour were hardly to be avoided. The 'very title of ale was somewhat nasty,' conceded Carew.[27] Sexual licence was also to be feared. Discounting the utter licentiousness imagined by hostile critics, there were inevitably cases such as that of an unmarried Leicester couple who admitted having sex 'that night that the mummers went abroade' in the Christmas holidays of 1596.[28] The general context, summed up in the phrase 'reformation of manners', was one in which public attitudes to bastard-bearing and other sexual transgressions were slowly hardening; and in which justices of the peace, backed up by the Privy Council and by statute, were gradually seeking to control the drink trade by a system of licensing and to crack down on drunkenness and associated disorder. In such circumstances, church ales and the games associated with them were bound to come under scrutiny.

Part of the stimulus to 'reformation of manners' was the steep rise in population that characterised the later decades of Elizabeth's reign, leading to growing problems of poverty and – especially in wartime conditions – fears of disorder. Population rise also had a more direct impact on parish festivities in that increasing numbers of households, particularly of poor inhabitants, made events more difficult to manage and no doubt made some more substantial inhabitants feel that they had more to lose than to gain. An associated development was a growing emphasis on the parish as a unit of local administration, especially for the relief of the poor, and hence the increasing bureaucratisation of parish finances. It is clear that in many places church ales were extinguished when their fund-raising function was replaced by rates. But even this development could be more halting than is sometimes supposed. To take an example, the churchwardens' accounts of the Wiltshire market town of Mere suggest that the most flourishing period of the parish ale was in the 1560s and 1570s. Ales continued into the 1580s and early 1590s but more intermittently; in 1592–3 and 1594–5 it was stated explicitly that no church ale was held. In 1583–4, a 'Booke of Rates' was mentioned, and such references soon became commonplace, while no ales were held at all in the closing years of the reign. Yet ales were to be revived under James I between 1605 and 1613, after which they disappeared for ever.[29]

Obviously religious changes – the impact of Protestantism, especially as certain elements of Protestant belief, outlook and practice mutated into puritanism – were another important dimension. It is hard to assess the real impact of printed diatribes such as that of Philip Stubbes or John Northbrooke. No doubt they were preaching largely to the converted, but even those who disagreed with their strictures could hardly ignore the current of disapproval. Probably of greater direct effect was preaching by hostile ministers and their local efforts to dissuade their parishioners from sponsoring or attending events of which they disapproved. 'Of late times', noted Carew, 'many Ministers have by their ernest invectives, both condemned these Saints feasts as superstitious, and suppressed the Church-ales as licencious'.[30] In 1581, Anthony Anderson, minister of Medbourne (Leicestershire), published a book lamenting that 'Idolatrous feastes are daylie kept, the Church Saint muste have hys wake daye, which is all spent (being the Lords Sabboth) in Bearebating, *Bacchus* cheere, and *Venus* fylthy sports.' From church court records we know something of the reaction in his parish: on the occasion of his 'preaching against bonefyres', a certain Mistress Marston 'sayd alowde in the church . . . it is not godes word that Mr Anderson preacheth'.[31]

The church authorities did not take an unequivocally hostile stance towards popular festivities. But they did prosecute churchwardens and others, including minstrels and morris dancers, who were responsible for keeping people away from church on Sundays or holidays or who habitually stayed away themselves. They also took action if ales and other festivities encroached on church or churchyard – post-Reformation bishops and archdeacons were more consistent than their predecessors in drawing a line between the sacred and the profane. They were likewise hostile to activities that savoured of 'popish superstition' or might even be thought of as pagan usages. These latter concerns were especially strong in the north, in areas where the advance of Protestantism was shaky and slow; especially as there were suspicions that recusants or crypto-Catholics sometimes used old customs, such as the 'dressing' of wells, both as a means to draw the people away from Protestant services and in order to disrupt the proceedings. Thus around 1596 it was claimed that a group of nine people 'and others' of Aldburgh, Yorkshire, havyng folowed theire vanitie althe night in sekynge there Mawmet commonly called the Floure of thwell would nedes bringe the same on a barrow into the churche in prayer times and althoughe they were admonished by one of the churche wardons . . . for to leave of theyre enterprise and not to trouble the congregation, yet they would not, but proceded forward with suche a noyse of pyping, blowyng of an horne, ringynge or strikinge of basons, and showtinge of people that the minister was constreyned to leave of readinge of prayer.[32]

Fears of a link between festivities and Catholicism explain why so august a body as the Northern High Commission concerned itself with the matter and why it was Edmund Grindal, as Archbishop of York, who in 1571 issued one of the earliest and most explicit prohibitions, ordering that

the minister and churchwardens shall not suffer any lords of misrule or summer lords or ladies, or any disguised persons or others in Christmas or at May games, or anye minstrels, morrice-dancers, or others, at rush bearings, or at any other times, to come unreverently into any church or chappel, or church-yard, and there dance or play any unseemly partes, with scoffs, jests, wanton gestures, or ribald talk.[33]

Thereafter, the visitation articles of a number of bishops in the southern province included similar prohibitions. But the most comprehensive orders against church ales were the work of the secular justices of the peace in Somerset and Devon, the latter citing 'many disorders, contemptes of Lawe, and other enormytyes . . . commytted to the great prophanasion of the Lordes Saboth, the dishoner of Almighty god, encrease of basterdy and dissolute liff, and of very many other mischeiffes and inconvenyences to the great hurt of the common wealth'.[34]

Strictures such as these, combined with local pressures and parochial conflicts, gradually eroded many popular customs. When they did not disappear altogether, they were pushed to the margins. Churchwardens and other local officers, if they did not turn outright hostile, ceased to patronise them; as a result, probably, they tended to slip down the social scale in terms of support and popularity. Yet the extent of the attrition before the end of Elizabeth's reign should not be exaggerated. In some communities, special circumstances upheld festive traditions. In the parish of Thame, Oxfordshire, there were two separate villages that held festivities away from the parish church and thus escaped the pressures of the ecclesiastical authorities. Throughout the reign, Oxford itself maintained festive activities in all its seven parishes, perhaps in part because of the presence of so many young people (though the same did not apply in Cambridge). On Ascension Day 1598 and the two Sundays preceding,

A greate nomber of the inhabitantes of Oxeforde, boyes, woemen and men, assembled themselves together early in the morninge of theis dayes with drome and shott, and other weapons, and men attyred in woemens apparrell and brought into the towne a woeman bedeckte with garlandes and flowers named by them the Queene of May. They also had morrish daunces and other disordered and unseemely sportes.[35]

An even more impressive May game was enacted at South Kyme, Lincolnshire, in 1601. The events culminated in late July when men of that village, including retainers of Sir Edward Dymoke, paraded on horseback with a drum and flag and 'reedes tyed together lyke speares, with a paynted paper of[f] the toppes of them', met up with men of the neighbouring township of Coningsby, likewise with drum and flag, and were said to have 'drunk the towne of Cunsbye . . . drye'. On this occasion, it was claimed, the unpopular Earl of Lincoln and his retinue were affronted and one of his men thrown from his horse. Subsequently, 'at the setting up of a Maypole in South Kyme', there was enacted a satirical play called *The Death of the Lord of Kyme*. It featured a devil, fool and vice, and among many elaborations was a 'Dirige' which 'expressed by name moste of the knowne lewde and licentious women in the Cities of London and Lincoln and towne of Boston, concludinge in their songes after everie of theire names, ora pro nobis'. The interlude was followed by a mock sermon, supposedly based on 'a text out of the book of Mabb', preached by a man in a black gown with a pot of ale instead of an hourglass in the 'pulpit', concluding with 'The Marcie of Musterd seed and the blessinge of Bullbeefe and the peace of Pottelucke be with you all. Amen.'[36]

RIDINGS, ROUGH MUSIC AND MOCKING RHYMES

The satirical element in the events at South Kyme overlapped with two very striking manifestations of popular culture: mocking rhymes and 'ridings', the latter usually accompanied by what a later period would call 'rough music'. Far from being in decline by the end of Elizabeth's reign, both were in many areas in the process of elaboration and development. This is especially true of 'railing rhymes'. They were penned by the learned elite as well as being composed by ordinary people, and the targets of satire included the very greatest – and the government policies associated with them – as well as more humble folk. Indeed it was a mocking rhyme, nailed to the maypole, that was used to drive home the criticism of the Earl of Lincoln at South Kyme. It has been thought that a trend-setting publication was Joseph Hall's *Virgidemiarum* or 'sheaf of rods' of 1597–8, which made satire or epigram based on classical models increasingly fashionable; while detailed studies of the phenomenon, at both high and low social levels, have concentrated mostly on the reign of James I, utilising as a major source the records of the Star Chamber, which treated such productions as libels. Certainly the development of mocking rhymes was closely associated with the increasing impact of print culture in the seventeenth century. Dividing a rhyme into a 'First' and 'Second Part' mimicked the format of broadside ballads, and it was often specified that the rhyme should be sung to a well-known ballad tune such as 'Bonny Nell'.

But already in the reign of Elizabeth satirical rhymes were a well-established feature of village, small town and even city life. The most basic version imaginable surfaced at Melton Mowbray, Leicestershire, around 1570: 'One, towe, three, fowre, Mawde Home is a hore.' That this memorable and familiar formula was not used more often was probably because it was considered too simple. Although in retrospect many of these rhymes read as crude doggerel, in their time the authors of malicious verses prided themselves on their wit and strove hard to find biting words, telling imagery and deliberately hilarious rhymes. More characteristic was an effort from Humberstone in the same county in 1573: running to eleven stanzas, it made out that the intended victim was a complaisant cuckold or 'wittol', driving the point home with the thumping refrain:

> Hei, ho Symkyn, shall John youre man
> Youre wifes bearde tryme?

More succinct, albeit fractured in rhythm, was a sly song from Islip, Oxfordshire, in 1584:

> Yf I had as faire a face
> As John Williams his daughter Elsabeth hass
> Then wold I were a taudrie lace
> As goodman Boltes daughter Marie dosse,
> And if I had as mutche money in my pursse
> As Cadmans daughter Margarett hasse
> Then wold I have a basterd lesse
> Then Butlers mayde Helen hasse.[37]

As these examples indicate, cuckoldry, adultery and other forms of sexual transgression were frequent objects of attack. Yet, while the rhymesters claimed the high moral ground, a real concern for morality was not necessarily their motive for action, and they could equally well lampoon personal misfortune such as physical deformity or express pure envy of better-off neighbours. The satirical genre could also be used to register disapproval of religious changes or of the 'godly', or to take the 'learned' down a peg or two; it could also be deployed against corrupt justices, rack-renters or enclosing landlords. The political sensitivity of such targets, together with the fact that even the greatest could find themselves the victims of lampoons, explains why the authorities often took a harsh view of these 'libels'. But, unless the victim was universally unpopular, they were often disapproved of likewise by many ordinary people, who regarded them as nasty, underhand and likely to stir up trouble in local society.

'Ridings', another means of evoking hostile derision, were rather different. They took the form of noisy parades, in which the victim, a substitute (customarily the 'next neighbour nearest the church'), or effigies representing the victim or victims was placed on a horse or, in a more basic version, astride a 'cowlstaff' or 'stang'. Often the rider was made to face backwards, perhaps holding the horse's tail. Armed men accompanied the procession, and raucous 'rough music' was provided by shrill cries, drums, gunfire, the ringing of bells and the clashing of pots and basins. Some features were similar to those associated with May games and perhaps represented a shift of the energies associated with such festivities – increasingly under attack as they were – into what could be represented as wholesome forms of community justice. For these forms also bore a strong resemblance to the official shame punishments meted out by city and borough courts and by the Star Chamber, which often featured the backward-facing ride and 'vile minstrelsy'. In popular usage they were used in quasi-penal fashion in only two main ways. The first was to punish people who refused to join in festivities or behaved in what were felt to be inappropriate ways on holidays. Thus, a man reported how on 30 December 1586 he was playing at 'tables' in the Swan at Chichester when one 'who then played the parte of a lorde of mysrule came in . . . and sayde that that game was no Cristmas game & so perforce toke . . . [him] from thence & made hym ryde on a staffe to the highe crosse.' The second was to shame a couple when a wife so far departed from the duty of obedience expected of her that she actually beat her husband – especially if the matter became public or the husband's response was particularly abject. Thus, in a Cambridge case in 1586, 'Johane Johnson did strike & beate . . . Cutbert hir husband, [who] . . . sayd unto his sayd wief Oh good wief (Johnson) doe not beate me noe more aboute the shins nor face'; whereupon a certain James Jurdeine did

> ryde aboute ye towne & streates . . . uppon a cowlstaffe uppon the backes of twoe men, and did by signes, woordes, tokens, behaviours & gestures . . . publishe that the sayd Johane had beaten the sayd Cutbert hir husband and that the sayd Cutbert had behaved him selfe evell & unsemely towards his sayd wief and the sayd Johane towards hir sayd husband.[38]

A quasi-penal intention – on this occasion singling out the wife for particular opprobrium – was even more clearly expressed in a Suffolk case of 1604, where in justification of what had been done it was claimed that 'not onely the woman which had offended might be shamed for her misdemenour towardes her husband but other women also by her shame might be admonished [not] to offend in like sort.'[39] Yet this was no grim-faced, sober-sided application of social sanctions. Ridings not only involved, as has been seen, a festive element and drew on the repertory of May games and similar customs; they also embodied a humorous reflection on the real-life complexities of husband–wife relations (which could never conform exactly to the strictures of patriarchal theory), and represented an explosion of energy triggered by the 'world turned upside down' spectacle of the wife who wore the breeches – the whole event fuelled, in all probability, by copious supplies of alcohol.

At the same time, they did violently reinscribe conventional gender roles and, interestingly, linked male dominance with martial prowess. One of the earliest accounts of these ridings, in the handwriting of John Stow, recorded that in London on 'ye xxx day of Aprill [1565] one mane rode on two staves borne on iiii mens showldars at St Katheryns for that his next neybor sofferyd his wyffe to beat hym; there went with hym nigh iiic [three hundred] men with handgunes and pikes, well armyd in cowrslytts.'[40]

The proceedings of the Court of Aldermen reveal the circumstances of this impressive manifestation. As noted earlier, the Armourers' Company had successfully petitioned the City to order a special civic watch of armed men to take place throughout the city on May Eve. Unlike the marching watches mounted in previous reigns, it was intended to be a restrained occasion, without 'any manner of cresset light, drumslade or other minstrelsy'; but evidently the inhabitants of Saint Katherine's viewed this martial event as the perfect opportunity to shame a beaten husband and his wife and hence enliven the proceedings.[41] At that stage, it would seem, the authorities were relatively complaisant, and there are other descriptions of similar events around that time. The paucity of metropolitan references later in the reign suggests that such boisterous manifestations of popular culture were squeezed off the streets of London – though they were to feature again in the late seventeenth and eighteenth centuries. They continued to flourish in the provinces, however. The fact that they were so closely associated with the defence of patriarchal values no doubt helped to protect them, despite their disorderly nature and elements that might otherwise have been construed as subversive parodies of judicial forms.

AFTER ELIZABETH

Cultures are defined by collision. By the end of Elizabeth's reign there were contacts and conflicts enough to ensure that people became more and more conscious of what, in retrospect, we may term 'popular culture', while the crossovers between professional (often metropolitan) productions and amateur efforts were becoming increasingly complex. In 1600, Will Kemp danced the morris from London to Norwich, supposedly in nine days. (With rest days in between, he was in fact on the road for nearly a month.) He was already the most famous stage clown of his day, and this remarkable publicity stunt and money-raising venture made him even more so. Along the way he engaged with the country people, some of whom (including women) danced with him. Within Kemp's lifetime, meanwhile, a growing band of professional playwrights were producing dramas of ever-increasing sophistication. There is a case for considering some of these plays as a form of popular culture in themselves, albeit one that involved relatively little direct participation and also affected attitudes to more traditional practices. While they played mainly to London audiences, they did tour the provinces intermittently, no doubt raising expectations of what drama should be and hence rendering amateur efforts vulnerable to criticism from those in the know. The professional playwrights themselves mercilessly satirised the work of 'rude mechanicals'. On the other hand, the fact that so many elements of traditional popular culture – hobgoblins and hobby horses, feasts and fairies, maypoles and morris dances – regularly featured in such plays, whether in faithful or fanciful representations, kept them constantly in the public mind and gave them, as it were, an extra dimension of imaginative existence. Such images, often in idealised or nostalgic form, increasingly featured in poetry too. In the real-life countryside and in provincial towns, recurrent conflicts between godly opponents of the 'devil's dance' and all those not averse to ales and sports and dances – including many young people of all classes, not to mention professional minstrels and the like whose livelihoods were at stake – kept the issue of the licitness or otherwise of these activities very much in the public eye, and no doubt made them more attractive to people who liked to provoke the precisians. In 1617–18, James I's 'Declaration of Sports' raised people's consciousness even more, while in the reign of Charles I, divergent attitudes to maypoles, cakes and ale came to stand proxy for much broader ecclesiological and political positions. The 'puritan revolution' and the celebrations that marked the Restoration were to carry even further this process of creeping politicisation. The practices that had become associated with popular culture in the reign of Elizabeth, and the tensions to which they had given rise, resonated long into the seventeenth century.

FURTHER READING

Burke, Peter, *Popular Culture in Early Modern Europe,* 3rd edn (Farnham, 2009).
Collinson, Patrick, 'Elizabethan and Jacobean Puritanism as Forms of Popular Religious Culture', in Christopher Durston and Jacqueline Eales (eds.), *The Culture of English Puritanism, 1560–1700* (Basingstoke, 1996).
Cressy, David, *Bonfires and Bells: National Memory and the Protestant Calendar in Elizabethan and Stuart England* (London, 1989).
Forrest, John, *The History of Morris Dancing, 1458–1750* (Toronto, 1999).
Fox, Adam, *Oral and Literate Culture in England, 1500–1700* (Oxford, 2000).
Goring, Jeremy, *Godly Exercises or the Devil's Dance? Puritanism and Popular Culture in Pre-Civil War England* (London, 1983).
Harris, Tim (ed.), *Popular Culture in England, c. 1500–1850* (Basingstoke, 1995).
Hutton, Ronald, *The Rise and Fall of Merry England: The Ritual Year, 1400–1700* (Oxford, 1994).
—— *The Stations of the Sun: A History of the Ritual Year in Britain* (Oxford, 1996).
Ingram, Martin, 'Ridings, Rough Music and the "Reform of Popular Culture" in Early Modern England', *Past and Present,* 105 (1984): 79–113.
Johnston, Alexandra F., 'The Robin Hood of the Records', in Lois Potter (ed.), *Playing Robin Hood: The Legend as Performance in Five Centuries* (Newark, Del., 1999), pp. 27–44.
Johnston, Alexandra F., and Maclean, Sally-Beth, 'Reformation and Resistance in Thames/Severn Parishes: The Dramatic Witness', in Katherine L. French, Gary G. Gibbs and Beat Kümin (eds.), *The Parish in English Life, 1400–1600* (Manchester and New York, 1997), pp. 178–200.
Kümin, Beat, 'Masses, Morris and Metrical Psalms: Music in the English Parish, *c.* 1400–1600', in Fiona Kisby (ed.), *Music and Musicians in Renaissance Cities and Towns* (Cambridge, 2001), pp. 70–81.
Lamb, Mary Ellen, *The Popular Culture of Shakespeare, Spenser, and Jonson* (London and New York, 2006).
Lancashire, Anne, *London Civic Theatre: City Drama and Pageantry from Roman Times to 1558* (Cambridge, 2002).
Phythian-Adams, Charles, 'Ceremony and the Citizen: The Communal Year at Coventry, 1450–1550', in Peter Clark and Paul Slack (eds.), *Crisis and Order in English Towns, 1500–1700: Essays in Urban History* (London, 1972), pp. 57–85.
Reay, Barry (ed.), *Popular Culture in Seventeenth-Century England* (London and Sydney, 1985).
—— *Popular Cultures in England, 1550–1750* (London and New York, 1998).
Thomas, Keith, *Religion and the Decline of Magic: Studies in Popular Beliefs in Sixteenth and Seventeenth Century England* (London, 1971).
Walsham, Alexandra, *Providence in Early Modern England* (Oxford, 1999).

NOTES

1 Keith Wrightson, *English Society, 1580–1680* (London, 1982), p. 220.
2 Barry Reay, 'Introduction: Popular Culture in Early Modern England', in Barry Reay (ed.), *Popular Culture in Seventeenth-Century England* (London, 1985), pp. 13–23. For the idea of 'weapons of the weak', see James C. Scott, *Weapons of the Weak: Everyday Forms of Peasant Resistance* (New Haven, Conn., 1985).
3 Peter Burke, *Popular Culture in Early Modern Europe* (London, 1978), p. xi; Tim Harris, 'Problematising Popular Culture', in Tim Harris (ed.), *Popular Culture in England, c. 1500–1850* (Basingstoke, 1995), pp. 1–27, 216–22; p. 10.

4 Roger Chartier, 'Culture as Appropriation: Popular Cultural Uses in Early Modern France', in Steven L. Kaplan (ed.), *Understanding Popular Culture: Europe from the Middle Ages to the Nineteenth Century* (Berlin, 1984), pp. 229–53.
5 See Peter Burke, *Popular Culture in Early Modern Europe*, 3rd edn (Farnham, 2009), especially pp. 1–19, for his responses to these and other criticisms.
6 *Harrison's Description of England in Shakspere's Youth*, ed. Frederick J. Furnivall, 2 vols. (London, 1877–8), vol. I, p. 215.
7 14 Eliz. *c.* 5.
8 Quoted in Adam Fox, *Oral and Literate Culture in England, 1500–1700* (Oxford, 2000), p. 182.
9 Fox, *Oral and Literate Culture*, pp. 51, 61.
10 *Records of Early English Drama: Chester*, ed. Lawrence M. Clopper (Manchester, 1972), p. 142.
11 *Visitation Articles and Injunctions of the Period of the Reformation*, ed. W. H. Frere and W. M. Kennedy, 3 vols. (London, 1910), vol. III, p. 23.
12 *The Works of John Jewel*, ed. J. Ayre, 4 vols. (Cambridge, 1845–50), vol. IV, p. 1231.
13 Beat Kümin, 'Masses, Morris and Metrical Psalms: Music in the English Parish, *c.* 1400–1600', in Fiona Kisby (ed.), *Music and Musicians in Renaissance Cities and Towns* (Cambridge, 2001), pp. 70–81; p. 81.
14 Quoted in David Cressy, *Bonfires and Bells: National Memory and the Protestant Calendar in Elizabethan and Stuart England* (London, 1989), p. 67.
15 Steven Gunn, 'Archery Practice in Early Tudor England', *Past and Present*, 209 (2010): 53–81.
16 *Records of Early English Drama: Chester*, pp. 324–5.
17 Robert Laneham, *A Letter* (1575) (Menston, 1968), p. 37.
18 Laneham, *A Letter*, pp. 32–3.
19 Laneham, *A Letter*, pp. 34, 36.
20 *The Diary of Henry Machyn*, ed. John Gough Nichols (London, 1848), p. 201.
21 GL, MS 33011/2 (microfilm), Bridewell Court Book, 1574–6, fols. 139v, 140r.
22 *Phillip Stubbes's Anatomy of the Abuses in England in Shakspere's Youth, ad 1583*, ed. Frederick J. Furnivall, 2 vols. (London, 1877–82), vol. I, pp. 147, 150.
23 Quotations from W. Symonds, 'Winterslow Church Reckonings', *Wiltshire Archaeological and Natural History Magazine*, 36 (1909–10): 27–49.
24 Cited in Alexandra F. Johnston and Sally-Beth Maclean, 'Reformation and Resistance in Thames/Severn Parishes: The Dramatic Witness', in Katherine L. French, Gary G. Gibbs and Beat Kümin (eds.), *The Parish in English Life, 1400–1600* (Manchester and New York, 1997), pp. 178–200; p. 178.
25 *The Survey of Cornwall by Richard Carew*, ed. John Chynoweth, Nicholas Orme and Alexandra Walsham (Exeter, 2004), fol. 69r.
26 Quoted in J. Charles Cox, *Churchwardens' Accounts from the Fourteenth Century to the Close of the Seventeenth Century* (London, 1913), p. 285.
27 Carew, *Survey of Cornwall*, fol. 69v.
28 Leicestershire Record Office, BR II/18/4, No. 208.
29 Thomas H. Baker, 'The Churchwardens' Accounts of Mere', *Wiltshire Archaeological and Natural History Magazine*, 35 (1907–8): 23–92, 210–82; p. 74 and *passim*.
30 Carew, *Survey of Cornwall*, fol. 69r.
31 Anthony Anderson, *The Shield of Our Safetie* (London, 1581), sig. T4v; Leicestershire RO, 1 D 41/13/9, fol. 21a.
32 J. S. Purvis, *Tudor Parish Documents of the Diocese of York* (Cambridge, 1948), p. 169.
33 *Visitation Articles and Injunctions*, vol. III, p. 291.
34 *Records of Early English Drama: Devon*, ed. John M. Wasson (Toronto, 1986), p. 294.
35 *Records of Early English Drama: Oxford*, ed. John R. Elliott, Jr., Alan H. Nelson, Alexander F. Johnston and Diana Wyatt, 2 vols. (Toronto, 2004), vol. I, p. 246.

36 Norreys Jephson O'Conor, *Godes Peace and the Queenes: Vicissitudes of a House, 1539–1615* (London, 1934), pp. 110, 111, 114, 115, 118, 120.

37 Leicestershire RO, 1 D 41/4/86r; 1 D 41/4/114b; *The Archdeacon's Court: Liber Actorum, 1584*, ed. E. R. Brinkworth, Oxfordshire Record Society, 23, 2 vols. (Oxford, 1942–6), vol. I, p. 12. 'Tawdry' derives from 'Saint Audrey', denoting a species of finery commonly worn in the period.

38 West Sussex RO, EpI/17/6, fol. 79v; CUL, University Archives, Commissary Court, I/2 fol. 93v.

39 TNA, STAC 8/249/19, m. 18.

40 *Three Fifteenth-Century Chronicles*, ed. J. Gairdner (London, 1880), p. 132.

41 Martin Ingram, 'Juridical Folklore in England Illustrated by Rough Music', in Christopher W. Brooks and Michael Lobban (eds.), *Communities and Courts in Britain, 1150–1900* (London and Rio Grande, 1997), pp. 61–82; p. 78.

CHAPTER TWENTY-EIGHT

WITCHCRAFT AND THE DEVIL

Darren Oldridge

In the celebrated opening of *The Discovery of Witchcraft* (1584), the Kentish gentleman Reginald Scot declared that 'fables of witchcraft' had taken 'fast hold and deepe root in the heart of man'. These fables and 'wonderfull tales' were a matter of national and international concern.[1] As the first English author of a major treatise on the subject, Scot was inspired by allegations of harmful magic in his locality in the early 1580s, but his intervention belonged to a much wider interest in witchcraft in the second half of the sixteenth century. The English Witchcraft Act of 1563 was paralleled by similar legislation in Scotland, the Spanish Netherlands and some German principalities in the first decade of Elizabeth's reign, and coincided with a new wave of major publications on the subject. It was against this background that Scot, a profoundly sceptical thinker, observed that 'the world is now so bewitched and over-run with this fond error'.[2]

The witch trials of Elizabethan England were a local manifestation of this international trend, and historians have increasingly viewed them in this light. The pioneering research of Alan Macfarlane and Keith Thomas in the 1970s focused attention on the role of interpersonal conflicts in English witchcraft and emphasised allegations of harmful sorcery above the religious aspects of the crime. Compared to the devil-ridden fantasies of Continental demonologists, English witchcraft seemed a tepid and practical affair. In the past two decades, however, many scholars have challenged the apparently distinctive qualities of English witch beliefs. In part, this reflects a renewed interest in the demonic elements that were often present in allegations of destructive sorcery: it was no accident that Agnes Waterhouse, the first woman hanged for the crime in England in 1566, confessed to keeping a familiar spirit named 'Satan'. Equally, it has become apparent that European witch persecutions were often driven by popular fears of harmful magic similar to those found in England. Thus it appears, in the words of James Sharpe, that Elizabethan witchcraft was 'a variation on a European theme'.[3]

This variation was relatively mild. Around 500 witches were hanged in England between the passage of the 1563 Act and the repeal of the witchcraft laws in 1736. This compares to over 1,000 in Scotland in the same period, despite its much smaller population. Elizabethan England escaped the mass trials that consumed parts of

Germany in the 1580s and 1590s, though major witch-hunts occurred in East Anglia and Newcastle following the Civil War. In England and elsewhere, such persecutions were made possible by the introduction of legal sanctions against activities that had vexed ordinary people long before the age of witch trials, and were now overlaid with concerns about the Devil's activity in the world. The experience of witchcraft in different regions was shaped by the configuration of these elements and their operation in specific social and legal contexts.

The most basic ingredient of witchcraft was the fear of destructive magic – or *maleficium* – which could be directed against individuals or property. There was no consensus on the symptoms of *maleficium* except that they ran counter to the normal course of nature: thus sudden and unexpected illnesses, exceptional weather or unpredictable calamities were all potentially acts of witchcraft. Allegations were by no means indiscriminate, however. The attribution of *maleficium* depended largely on the existence of a plausible witch figure – usually a woman with a reputation for harmful sorcery – and evidence of some ill feeling between the suspects and their supposed victim. Such allegations did not usually lead to formal legal proceedings. Both in England and mainland Europe, it appears that many years were required for a suspect to build a reputation for *maleficium,* and court records frequently indicate that acts of alleged witchcraft took place over long periods without reaching the attention of the law. Thus Agnes Brown, a witch executed at Northampton in 1612, was 'ever noted to be of an ill nature and wicked disposition, hateful and malicious, and many years before she died both hated and feared among her neighbours'.[4]

The second ingredient in witch beliefs was the Devil. The Devil's involvement in *maleficium* was emphasised most often by learned writers on the subject; but this did not mean that he was absent from popular ideas about the crime. Broadly speaking, the demonic component of witchcraft was of two main types. First, some people believed that witches employed demons to perform sorcery. This could involve a formal compact between the witch and the Devil, who subsequently provided the means to work magic. Second, some believed that witches belonged to a secret conspiracy of Satanists. The members of this sect not only renounced their baptism to enter a demonic pact, but also joined in nocturnal assemblies or 'sabbaths' to desecrate Christian rites and to worship the Devil. This last idea was a late addition to European demonology and left relatively few traces in the records of English trials. Nonetheless, it circulated in Elizabethan England through reports of Continental witchcraft and translations of French and German books. The anonymous author of a pamphlet on the trial of witches from the Essex village of Saint Osyth in 1582 quoted the French demonologist Jean Bodin, and declared that witches 'worshippe Satan, unto whome they have sworne allegiaunce'.[5]

The pattern of Elizabethan witchcraft emerged from the interaction of these elements. It was also influenced by a nexus of particular social, legal and religious circumstances. Since some beliefs were distributed unevenly in the population – the idea of the formal pact with Satan was more common among learned writers and their readers than ordinary people, for example – English witch persecutions also involved the interplay of different social groups. This was a two-way process. Ordinary people were not the passive recipients of demonological ideas imposed from above; on the contrary, widely held beliefs about good and bad magic and folkloric views of the witch's association with 'imps' played a major role in trials. Moreover, the identification of witchcraft with women – a particularly striking feature in English prosecutions – probably originated in popular beliefs rather than learned theory: villagers normally accused women rather than men of *maleficium* in the church courts of late medieval England, and later demonologists provided little intellectual basis for viewing witchcraft primarily as a female crime. Thus, in some respects, Elizabethan witchcraft illustrated the 'synergy between official policies and the popular imagination' that Martin Ingram describes in Chapter 27. The pages that follow sketch out the contours of witchcraft in sixteenth-century England and locate the phenomenon within the dynamics of the Elizabethan Reformation and English law.

THE DEVIL, MAGIC AND THE LAW

When Reginald Scot made the first English entry into the literature of witchcraft, he also presented an extreme version of the Protestant understanding of the Devil that had emerged within the Elizabethan Church. In the second part of his treatise, entitled *A Discourse upon Devils and Spirits,* he came close to defining all spirits, including the Devil and the Holy Ghost, as interior powers that compelled the human mind. 'In summe', he wrote, the word 'spirit'

> doth signifie a secret force and power, wherewith our minds are moved and directed; if unto holie things, then it is the motion of the holie spirit, of the spirit of Christ and of God; if unto evill things, then it is the suggestion of the wicked spirit, of the divell, and of Satan.

Viewed in this way, belief in witches was a manifestation of the wicked spirit: the unreasonable and non-scriptural basis of this belief was, Scot claimed, proof of its demonic nature. He also denied that Satan, as a disembodied spirit, could assume any kind of fleshly body: 'his forme is so proper and peculiar (in mine opinion) unto himselfe, as he cannot alter it, but needs be content therewith, as with that which God hath ordained for him.' This argument abolished the physical 'imps' or 'familiar spirits' that had featured prominently in recent witch trials in Essex. Scot dismissed the belief in such creatures as an ignorant fancy, presumably inspired by the Devil in his role as the father of misconceptions and lies.[6]

Scot's sceptical demonology occupied an extreme position in the spectrum of English (and European) Protestantism and exposed him to allegations of denying the existence of spirits altogether. Nonetheless, his thinking took a direction that was followed by many other Elizabethan reformers, and was distinguished mainly by his willingness to travel further than most towards some of its more radical conclusions. Three main tendencies characterised English Protestant thinking about the Devil. First, the sovereignty of God meant that Satan, despite his depravity and malice, acted always as a tool of divine justice. He was a kind of unwilling enforcer of God's law, and was permitted to do evil only for the higher purpose of good. This view followed from the doctrine of providence, whereby, as the Oxford theologian Edward Cradocke affirmed in 1572, God decreed that 'all thinges in heaven, and under heaven be continually governed and provided for'.[7] The logic of providentialism encouraged English Protestants to examine their own consciences in the face of misfortune: God sent calamities to punish misdeeds or to test the faithful, even when he used the Devil as his tool. The proper response was self-reflection and the renewal of faith, not the persecution of witches.

The second characteristic of the Protestant Devil was his favoured method of attack. He operated mainly and most powerfully as a tempter and purveyor of falsehood. While most English Protestants accepted Satan as an external force and acknowledged his capacity to intervene directly in the physical world, they nonetheless tended to emphasise his intellectual role as the author of 'crafty persuasions, deceitfull and false illusions'.[8] This was a corollary of the Protestant elevation of belief and faith above works: as religion became a matter of understanding God's word and receiving his grace, the Devil's attempts to pollute the mind became more important. An interior experience of God led to an interior experience of Satan. The authors of catechisms and books of religious instruction, and writers of 'spiritual autobiographies', engaged with the Devil mainly as a source of temptation. The struggle to overcome him involved vigilance and self-examination and could become – in its more intense manifestations – a kind of daily combat with indwelling evil. In *The Christian Manuell* (1576), the Exeter divine John Wootton called Christians to fight a 'grievous and dayly battell which is never ended before the daye of death, for . . . the devyll rusheth upon us with great vehemency and undermyneth us with a thousand temptations'.[9] Within the providential context of English Protestantism, such spiritual assaults were permitted by God to test the faithful: they called believers to examine their consciences and renew their faith, and by this process the Devil's advances could be repelled.

Satan's role as the 'father of lies' complemented the third tendency in English Protestant demonism.[10] This was the alliance between the Devil and Rome. For most Protestant thinkers in the second half of the sixteenth century, Catholicism was the Devil's masterpiece. This was true at the cosmic level of God's unfolding plan for the world, in which the Pope was the Antichrist described in the Book of Revelation, and his 'malignant church and congregation' was 'the misticall bodie of Antichriste'.[11] In the world of practical politics also, the Devil was naturally allied with the enemies of the Queen: indeed, Norman Jones has shown that fears of a Catholic conspiracy to destroy Elizabeth by necromancy encouraged the introduction of the Witchcraft Act in 1563. More subtly, the demonic nature of popery was evidenced in parish religion, as the attachment of many ordinary people to pre-Reformation beliefs and an essentially works-based Christianity indicated the extent of Satan's kingdom of falsehood. Thus, the official Catholic Church and her political allies were combined with the more insidious force of popular 'superstition' and indifference to Protestant teachings. The Devil's power to deceive was at work in both phenomena. While God's guiding hand ensured that his children would ultimately prevail, they seemed destined to inhabit a world in which the Devil's party outnumbered them. This perception was most intense among the more committed English Protestants – those derided as 'puritans' by their less rigorous neighbours; and for such people the experience of social hostility probably reinforced their conviction that Satan was 'the prince of this world'.[12]

Elizabethan Protestants, then, tended to view Satan as a powerful spiritual presence that operated within God's providential order. These attitudes coexisted alongside other ideas about witchcraft and 'unclean spirits' which predated the Reformation. The most basic of these was the belief in good and bad magic, which appears to have permeated all social levels. The Queen consulted the astrologer and alchemist John Dee regarding the date of her coronation in 1558. The copious records of the Buckinghamshire curate and astrological physician Richard Napier indicate the widespread acceptance of magic and fear of *maleficium* in the 1590s and the early decades of the seventeenth century, when his patients included the Earls of Sunderland and Sussex. At a village level, 'cunning' men and women made an income from selling charms, detecting witches and deflecting curses with counter-magical rituals. The operation of this magical economy was recorded in the numerous depositions of Elizabethan witch trials, including the earliest surviving testimony from the village of Waltham in Essex in 1563. Among the statements made against Elizabeth Lewis was a claim by one of her neighbours that her own husband had called her a witch. 'I may thank my wife for my lameness', he allegedly said, 'for she has bewitched me lame, and when I sent for the cunning man of Witham he told me that it was my wife's doing.'[13]

Towards the end of the period, an incident from the Norfolk village of Hockham illuminates more starkly the world of cunning folk, witches and their victims. In 1600, a maid named Joan Harvey accused one of her neighbours, the eighty-year-old Mother Francis, of afflicting her with an unnatural illness. The suspect was held in Norwich gaol until Harvey was examined by a physician, who determined that she was not bewitched. Upon her release, Mother Francis was visited by her victim and 'scratched'. This involved Harvey drawing blood from the old woman in order to relieve the symptoms of her *maleficium*. The alleged witch died some weeks later, prompting her relatives to accuse Harvey of causing her death. This provoked an anonymous author to write an account of Mother Francis's history. She was, the writer claimed, 'reputed to be a witch these 30 years, and by signs some cunning folks (as they are termed) have declared her to be a witch'. She had caused the death of cattle and visited sickness on her neighbours and their children. Two of her victims had died. The author displayed a confident acceptance of the supernatural signs of wicked magic, based largely on the invisible bonds that tied the witch to her victims. Thus he reported that Mother Francis had been 'much tormented' when people burned objects that she had cursed. Her victims had called out her name on their deathbeds, and their bodies bore the marks of unnatural disease. During Joan Harvey's sickness, the old woman's proximity to her victim provided further evidence of bewitchment:

> In all the maids fits almost, she would be either nigh the house where the maid was, or come stealing by it. . . . Also, when she was by force brought in (as was tried often), the maid was strangely frighted, and fearfully tormented, though well before; and when the witch began to come in the streets to her the maid in the house a good way off, began to be tormented; and the nigher the witch came, the more she was tormented; and half out of her wits she was, when the witch was there.

As this instance indicates, the wider community appears to have recognised the signs of *maleficium* and to have exploited these to identify the person responsible.

The whole bleak drama, culminating in Harvey's scratching of her supposed tormenter, testifies to a culture immersed in magical and counter-magical beliefs.[14]

Alongside the fear of destructive magic, it was widely believed that witches employed supernatural beings to torment their neighbours. Described variously as 'imps', 'bugs' or 'spirits', these small creatures were sent by their owners on malicious errands against those they wished to harm. It is likely that these creatures were involved more often in acts of witchcraft than surviving court records suggest, as they feature prominently in some pamphlets based on trials for which the spare legal documentation fails to mention any 'spirits'. The Essex minister George Gifford lends weight to this suspicion with his description of popular witch beliefs in 1587. If a sceptical man were to ask how 'poore old women' could perform feats of terrible magic, Gifford writes, he could expect this typical reply:

> O syr, they do it not by themselues. They have their spirites which they keepe at home in a corner, some of them twoo, some three, some five: these they send when they be displeased, and wil them for to plague a man in his body, or in his cattle. This matter hath bene tryed: for divers well disposed men, even for very pity to see what hurt witches do by sending their spirites, have seriously taken the matter in hande . . . They have found where shee kept them in wooll. What meate shee gave them, what likenes they had, what were their names, whether they were hees or shees, and how many men they had killed.[15]

These noxious creatures were involved in another unpleasant aspect of Elizabethan witchcraft. This was the belief, perhaps unique to England, that witches suckled their imps with blood from 'teats' concealed on their bodies, often located near to their genitals. This belief meant that the discovery of such teats on a suspect's body could count as an indication of guilt. Groups of women were sometimes appointed to search the accused for these incriminating excrescences, an activity first recorded in the leet court of Southampton in 1579.

The widespread fear of *maleficium* and recourse to counter-magic for its detection and relief, combined with belief in witches' association with spiteful imps, were central to popular attitudes about witchcraft. These ideas almost certainly predated the Reformation, and provided the cultural background in which Protestants developed their understanding of the crime. The character of English witchcraft was also shaped by its legal context. The Elizabethan statute of 1563 made it a capital offence to cause death by magic and established a series of lesser punishments for other magical activities. This meant that the most serious cases had to pass through a number of legal procedures. Allegations arising in village communities were first heard by justices of the peace, who were obliged to refer them to the assize court if they appeared sufficiently strong. Here the grand jury first assessed the validity of the charges, and could pass on what they deemed to be 'true bills' of indictment to a full jury trial under a crown-appointed judge. Finally, appeals could be made to commute the sentence of death if a guilty verdict was reached. This process moved the case away from the community in which it originally arose and imposed fairly strict legal safeguards on the treatment of suspects. The result was a relatively low level of executions: the surviving records of the assize courts for the south-east of England indicate that less than a quarter of accused witches were hanged. This compares to a much higher level of executions in Scotland, where trials were frequently conducted by local officers operating under warrants from the Privy Council. At the same time, the English system meant that allegations normally emerged within local communities without strong direction from above. This allowed traditional ideas about witchcraft to emerge in the trials, and these ideas to circulate widely in printed accounts of 'notorious' cases.

These, then, were the ingredients of Elizabethan witchcraft: the encounter between traditional beliefs about harmful magic and Protestant attitudes towards the Devil, mediated by the structure of English law. The interplay between these elements is considered below.

ELIZABETHAN WITCHCRAFT

English Protestant ideas about the Devil were not naturally conducive to witch-hunting. The strong emphasis on providence and a spiritualised Satan was expressed most forcefully in the scepticism of Reginald Scot; but it also led more moderate thinkers to discourage and dismiss allegations of witchcraft. George Gifford, the godly divine who led an energetic and influential ministry at Maldon in Essex throughout the 1580s and 1590s, provides one striking example. Unlike Scot, Gifford did not deny that the Devil could take bodily form; but he insisted that he exerted his influence overwhelmingly within the mind. Indeed, wicked spirits only assumed physical shapes to distract their victims from the true nature of their power: 'I doe not say that they be not mightie and terrible because they appeare in such shapes, but I affirm that their appearing so is to cover and hide their mightinesse and effectual working, which they exercise in the darke harts of men.' Moreover, Satan operated only with the permission of God. To attribute his activities to his association with witches was to ignore divine providence. Gifford made this point succinctly in 1593:

> The devill hath a kingdome, but it is in darkenesse and corruption of sinne. He hath no right nor power over Gods creatures, no not so much as to kill one flye, or to take one eare of corne out of anie mans barne, unlesse power be given him. . . . Then tell me, who giveth the devill this power then, when the witch sendeth him, to kill or to lame man or beast? Doth the witch give it him? Do you think he had power to doe harme, but no mind till she mooved him? Or doe you take it that her sending giveth him power, which he had not?[16]

It was not only foolish to misattribute the Devil's power in this way, but it also obscured the higher purposes of God. The Christian response to misfortune was to submit prayerfully to His will. By blaming witches for their troubles people failed to do this. Worse still, they often sought help from cunning folk whose superstitious practices God had expressly forbidden. At a more practical level, allegations of *maleficium* encouraged rancour and division within communities that Satan was happy to exploit. It was through such deception and misdirection that the Devil maintained his kingdom of sin.

Demonology of this kind probably helped to constrain the persecution of witches. Some aspects of Elizabethan Protestantism could lead in a different direction, however. For a start, the view of the Devil embraced by men like George Gifford did not exclude the possibility that some people could enter demonic pacts, even if such pacts were based on a false understanding of Satan's power. Equally, the idea that the Devil was involved in *all* superstitious beliefs could encourage a much harsher interpretation of witchcraft than one based on *maleficium* alone. If the whole economy of cunning folk and their clients served the 'father of lies', the reach of witchcraft was far greater than most ordinary people realised: indeed, the most dangerous witches were those who ostensibly sought to help rather than harm, since they enjoyed popular support. The Cambridge theologian William Perkins drove this idea to its brutal conclusion. Abandoning the focus on *maleficium* that characterised traditional witch beliefs, Perkins defined a witch as 'a magician who either by open or secret league, wittingly and willingly, consenteth to use the aide and assistance of the devil in the working of wonders'. This definition was not only consistent with Protestant providentialism, but also allowed Perkins to include those 'good' magicians 'who only heale and cure the hurts inflicted upon men and cattell by badde witches'.[17] This was Satan's master plan: to use *maleficium* to drive people into the hands of his most deadly associates. Perkins noted that healing magicians were guilty of witchcraft only if they knew that their practices contravened God's law; but if they did, this meant that they had entered an implicit or 'secret league' with Satan and should be punished by death.

Perkins' emphatically religious model of witchcraft might, in different circumstances, have linked the eradication of witches to the campaign to build a reformed Christian society in Elizabethan England. This was, in Brian Levack's view, one of the dynamics that contributed to the intense witch-hunts in contemporary Scotland. The English legal context precluded this possibility, however, by defining witchcraft as a crime against the person and by providing a relatively centralised and judicious system for dealing with the offence. The legal framework did not exist in Perkins' lifetime to turn his interpretation of witchcraft into a practical reality; nor, after the Jacobean statute of 1604 made trafficking with spirits a capital crime, was there much desire in local communities to accuse cunning men and women of witchcraft without suspicions of *maleficium*.

As this indicates, Protestant ideas about witchcraft often ran counter to traditional beliefs. This was as true for sceptics such as Scot and Gifford as it was for Perkins. But the application of these ideas was also tempered by practical circumstances. Timothy Scott McGinnis is probably correct that Scot and Perkins developed their austere demonologies in the spirit of pure theological speculation, while Gifford was more attuned to the pastoral needs of his congregation at Maldon. Similar concerns affected the approach of other Elizabethan churchmen, not all of whom maintained the Essex pastor's consistent providentialism. When parishioners made allegations of *maleficium* they offered clergy the chance to expose the perils of folk magic; such allegations could also highlight the dangers and demonic affiliations of popery, while linking these to long-standing popular concerns. English Protestants exploited the potential of witchcraft to teach anti-Catholic lessons from the beginning of the trials. In 1566 *The Examination of John Walsh*, a pamphlet recording the admissions of a cunning man before the church court at Exeter, contained a preface denouncing the witchcraft of Roman priests and warning readers 'to flee from them and these dyvelish practises as from devils incarnate'. The published confession of Agnes Waterhouse, who was hanged for witchcraft at Chelmsford assizes in the same year, described how she was forced by the Devil in the form of a familiar spirit to say prayers in Latin rather than English.[18] While such episodes provided a platform for condemning Catholic involvement in all magical arts – indeed, John Walsh was apparently guilty only of sorcery – this tactic inevitably focused attention on the traditional forms of witchcraft that were feared in local communities and punished by law.

The alignment of religious beliefs and folklore was illustrated in some contemporary accounts of Elizabethan witch trials. In 1593, John and Alice Samuel, and their daughter Agnes, were convicted at Huntington assizes for bewitching the children of the Throckmorton family of Warboys and causing the death of Lady Cromwell. The case was recorded in a detailed pamphlet entitled *The Most Strange and Admirable Discoverie of the Three Witches of Warboys* (1593), which provides a complex and partisan narrative of the events leading to the executions. In November 1589, the daughters of Robert Throckmorton succumbed to an apparently unnatural sickness and began to accuse one of their neighbours, the elderly Alice Samuel, of causing their distress. Their symptoms and allegations continued over the next two years, and attracted the attention of the Throckmortons' extended family and the rector of Warboys, Francis Dorrington. The observations of the various participants in the story were woven into the published account; and these contributions, as Marion Gibson has shown, reflected contrasting approaches to the problems posed by the girls' condition. One of their uncles, Gilbert Pickering, sought 'proofs' of witchcraft through the traditional methods of scratching the suspects and observing their victims' response to their physical proximity; Henry Pickering, another uncle and a student at Cambridge, appears to have introduced a theological perspective based on the suspects' supposed entanglement with the Devil. In the narrative of the events leading to Lady Cromwell's bewitchment and death, the role of folk beliefs about witchcraft was strongly evident. While visiting the Throckmortons' house, Lady Cromwell cut a lock of hair from Alice Samuel and instructed the mother of the afflicted children to burn it. That night the lady 'suffered many things in her dreame concerning Mother Samuel, and was very strangely tormented in her sleep by a cat (as she imagined) which Mother Samuel had sent unto her'.[19] This nocturnal attack marked the start of the bewitchment that took her life. In this crucial part of the text, the author acknowledged Lady Cromwell's advocacy of a counter-magical remedy for *maleficium* and linked her sickness to the witch's imp. The pamphlet blended elements of folklore and demonology in a narrative that supported the condemnation of the witches and elided any conflict between its various sources. That this was possible and desirable indicates the alliance that was forged between Protestantism and traditional witch beliefs.

This process was most pronounced in cases of demonic possession. These were linked to *maleficium* in Tudor England, as the victims of possession customarily accused witches of visiting them with evil spirits. Since Christ had commanded his disciples to cast out demons (Mark 3:15), the ability to cure the possessed was also a sign of the True Church. Indeed, Jesuit missionaries exploited this potential in the mid-1580s through a series of exorcisms in the Buckinghamshire home of Sir George Peckham. Their leader, William Weston, later wrote that 'there were many people who, given the opportunity of observing the majestic power of the Church over evil spirits and monsters, would see and acknowledge at once the difference between the two religions, and award the victory to the Catholic faith.'[20] A similar logic informed Protestant dispossessions. Elizabethan churchmen sought not only to relieve the suffering of possessed individuals but also to demonstrate the truth and power of the reformed faith. The martyrologist John Foxe was involved in two such incidents in London in 1574; and the godly divine John Darrell enlivened his ministry with several dramatic dispossessions in the 1580s and 1590s. In these cases the pastoral concerns of Protestant divines were broadly consistent with traditional witch beliefs, and a fusion of demonology and folklore appears to have occurred.

This process was exemplified by the case of Thomas Darling, a thirteen-year-old boy from Burton-on-Trent who was possessed by wicked spirits in 1596. Darling's story was presented as an exemplum of godly religion in a pamphlet published in the following year and probably composed by Jesse Bee, a godly 'man of trade' who attended the boy's dispossession and gathered information from others who took part. Bee was reluctant to endorse what he saw as 'superstition': he denounced the practice of 'scratching' witches to remove their *maleficium* as a form of witchcraft in itself, 'whereof there bee great store used in our land to the great dishonor of God'.[21] Nonetheless, his attempt to place Darling's story within the framework of Protestant theology was compromised by the folkloric elements on which it largely depended. Moreover, his repudiation of scratching implied that he tolerated the other traditional witch beliefs at the heart of his narrative that he described without comment.

Thomas Darling was a 'religious and godly' adolescent who aspired to become a preacher. In February 1596 he was afflicted with fainting fits and delirium, during which he was menaced by a creature like a green cat. A physician decided that his condition was natural; but as his fits became more distressing his family approached Jesse Bee for further advice. Bee sat with the boy and read the opening lines of Saint John's Gospel – a text traditionally used to repel evil spirits – and he was overwhelmed by convulsions as he heard the words. When the visitor 'either ceased to speake of anie comfortable matter, or to read the scriptures, the boy was quiet from his fits: but when he was so religiously occupied they came thicke upon him'. This led Bee to suggest that the boy was bewitched. Darling then described how he had been cursed by an old woman on the day that his suffering began. Suspicion fell on two women with reputations for *maleficium:* Elizabeth Wright and her daughter Alice Gooderidge. Both were tested for signs of witchcraft. When Alice was brought into the boy's chamber he suffered intense pain; later her mother was made to 'looke upon the boy: which as soone as ever shee did, he fell into a strange and cruell fit'. Asked to recite the Lord's Prayer, both women stumbled at the line 'Lead us not into temptation.' A search of Wright's body discovered 'a thing much like the udder of an ewe' behind her right shoulder; and on her daughter's stomach was found 'a hole of the bignesse of two pence, fresh and bloudy, as though some great wart had beene cut off the place'. Alice Gooderidge was subsequently committed to Derby gaol.[22]

Towards the end of May, the preacher John Darrell came to assist the afflicted boy. He decided that Darling was possessed and organised a regime of prayer and fasting among his family to aide his deliverance. There followed several days in which the demons inhabiting Darling's body expressed their hatred and dread of the Scriptures, and at one point threatened to quit the boy to enter those aiding his dispossession. As the spirits struggled against their pious tormenters, one was heard to say that 'we cannot prevaile: let us goe to our mistres and torment her, I have had a draught of her blood today.' After further batteries of prayer the spirits were ousted, and the last one made an abject departure:

> At last (being laid upon his bed) anon hee began to heave and lift vehemently at his stomacke, and getting up some flem and choller (poynting with his finger and following with his eyes) hee said: Looke, looke, see you not the mouse that is gone out of my mouth: and so poynted after it unto the furthest part of the parlor. Then hee fell into a quiet trance.

Darling's recovery followed soon afterwards, accompanied by a voice that said 'My son arise up and walke, the evill spirit is gone from thee.' The next day, the boy's uncle discovered that Alice Gooderidge, still confined to gaol, had suffered terrible pains in the hours after his deliverance. He concluded that 'the divell was as good as his word, when he said he would torment her.'[23]

Like the pamphlet account of the trial at Huntington three years earlier, this narrative allied Protestant thinking with traditional beliefs. As a participant and reporter of the events, Jesse Bee was keen to show how they affirmed the power of God's word and the faithfulness of Darrell's ministry: Satan was tormented by Scripture; his expulsion was achieved through the power of Christ alone, unembellished by the ritual and holy objects that accompanied Catholic exorcisms, and the pious victim of possession was fortified by his faith and the prayerful support of true Christians. It was not surprising that the incident was publicised for the edification of a godly audience. At the same time, however, the events described in the pamphlet were driven by assumptions that predated the Reformation. Bee expected a witch to be the source of the boy's afflictions, and this led to the naming of suspects with long-standing reputations for *maleficium*. While he condemned the practice of scratching, he apparently accepted other folkloric techniques that were used to test the suspects. Alongside the quasi-magical use of the Lord's Prayer, these included the belief that the witch's proximity to her victim would increase his distress through the magical bond between them. Most obviously, the demons that possessed Darling's body were the witch's imps: they suckled blood from her teats, and one of them scuttled from his mouth in the shape of a mouse. These discrepancies could, with ingenuity, be made consistent with a particularly inscrutable version of divine providence; but their presence in the story indicates how traditional ideas shaped the course of events.

Such episodes indicate the potential for English Protestants to lead witch persecutions fuelled by popular ideas of *maleficium*. This potential was realised only sporadically in Elizabeth's reign, however. Three broad factors explain this outcome. First, the English legal context was not conducive to witch hunts. Alice Gooderidge died in Derby gaol in 1596; but had she lived she would almost certainly have escaped execution. The definition of witchcraft as a secular crime discouraged the kind of religious campaign against witchcraft instigated by Jesse Bee and John Darrell in Burton, and the structure of the courts made it relatively hard to secure capital convictions for the offence. Second, the emphasis on providence and a spiritualised Satan in English demonology meant that it was often sceptical of witchcraft allegations. Even William Perkins, the fiercest Elizabethan writer on the subject, was more concerned with apparently harmless acts of magic than malefic witches such as Alice Gooderidge. Finally, those cases of demonic possession that were most likely to unite churchmen and ordinary people against *maleficium* were also highly controversial, and for precisely the reasons that they appealed to men such as John Darrell. In 1598 the church hierarchy sought to suppress dispossessions because of the publicity and prestige they conferred on 'puritan' clergy. Thomas Darling was summoned to London and bullied into confessing to fraud; John Darrell was tried and convicted of teaching Darling and other demoniacs to feign the symptoms of possession. By the end of Elizabeth's reign, such ruthless interventions made clergy reluctant to attempt dispossessions and contained the potential for witch hunts. If the radical scepticism of Reginald Scot never became orthodox, distrust of the 'fables of witchcraft' helped to prevent major persecutions in Elizabethan England.

FURTHER READING

Behringer, Wolfgang, *Witches and Witch-Hunts* (Cambridge, 2004).

Briggs, Robin, *Witches and Neighbours,* 2nd edn (Oxford, 1998).

Gibson, Marion, *Reading Witchcraft: Stories of Early English Witches* (London and New York, 1999).

Johnstone, Nathan, *The Devil and Demonism in Early Modern England* (Cambridge, 2006).

Jones, Norman, 'Defining Superstitions: Treasonous Catholics and the Act against Witchcraft of 1563', in Charles Carlton (ed.), *State, Sovereigns and Society in Early Modern England* (Stroud, 1998).

Levack, Brian P., *Witch-Hunting in Scotland: Law, Politics and Religion* (London and New York, 2008).

Macfarlane, Alan, *Witchcraft in Tudor and Stuart England,* 2nd edn (London, 1999).

McGinnis, Timothy Scott, 'Subtiltie Exposed: Pastoral Perspectives on Witch Belief in the Thought of George Gifford', *Sixteenth Century Journal,* 33 (3) (2002): 665–86.

Oldridge, Darren, *The Devil in Tudor and Stuart England* (Stroud, 2010).

Sharpe, James, *Instruments of Darkness: Witchcraft in England, 1550–1750* (London, 1996).

NOTES

1 Reginald Scot, *The Discoverie of Witchcraft* (London, 1584), pp. 1, 482.

2 Scot, *Discoverie of Witchcraft,* p. 4.

3 James Sharpe, *Instruments of Darkness: Witchcraft in England, 1550–1750* (London, 1996), p. 32.

4 C. L'Estrange Ewen, *Witchcraft and Demonism* (London, 1933), p. 206.

5 W. W., *A True and Just Recorde of the Information, Examination and Confession of All the Witches, Taken at S. Oses in the Countie of Essex* (London, 1582), Preface. See Marion Gibson's edition of this text for the influence of Jean Bodin: Marion Gibson (ed.), *Early Modern Witches: Witchcraft Cases in Contemporary Writing* (London, 2000), pp. 75–6.

6 Scot, *Discoverie of Witchcraft,* pp. 541, 542, 547.

7 Edward Cradock, *The Shippe of Assured Safetie* (London, 1572), p. 274.

8 John Olde, *A Short Description of Antichrist* (London, 1555), fol. 2v.

9 John Wotton, *The Christian Manuell; or, Of the Life and Maners of True Christians* (London, 1576), fol. 179v.

10 This title was taken from John 8:44: 'He was a murderer from the beginning, and abode not in the truth, because there is no truth in him. When he speaketh a lie, he speaketh of his own: for he is a liar, and the father of it.'

11 Olde, *Short Description*, fol. 7v.

12 The dynamics described here were not necessarily confined to English Protestantism: they might be expected to operate in other contexts in which religion was internalised, and believers assumed that the spirit of error directed the 'false church' of their enemies. In this context, a comparison between devout Protestant and Catholic ideas of the Devil in Elizabethan England would be revealing. The biblical quotation is from John 12:31.

13 The Waltham depositions are reproduced in Peter Haining (ed.), *The Witchcraft Papers* (London, 1974), pp. 24–6.

14 The document is reproduced in Ewen, *Witchcraft and Demonism*, pp. 191–3.

15 George Gifford, *A Discourse of the Subtill Practises of Deuilles by Witches and Sorcerers* (London, 1587), sig. G3.

16 George Gifford, *A Dialogue Concerning Witches and Witchcraftes* (London, 1593), sigs. C2, D1v.

17 William Perkins, *A Discourse on the Damned Art of Witchcraft* (Cambridge, 1608), pp. 167, 174.

18 Both pamphlets are included in Gibson, *Early Modern Witches*. For references, see pp. 24, 28.

19 *The Most Strange and Admirable Discoverie of the Three Witches of Warboys* (London, 1593), sigs. D4–D4v.

20 William Weston, *The Autobiography of an Elizabethan*, trans. Philip Caraman (London, 1955), p. 27.

21 *The Most Wonderfull and True Storie of a Certaine Witch Named Alse Gooderige of Stapen Hill* (London, 1597), p. 6.

22 *Alse Gooderige of Stapen Hill*, pp. 4–5, 7, 8–9.

23 *Alse Gooderige of Stapen Hill*, pp. 33, 35, 36, 37–8.

CHAPTER TWENTY-NINE

NEWS

Joad Raymond

> *Messires,* what newes from Fraunce, can you tell? Still warres, warres. A heavie hearing truly: yet if you be in good health, have many schollers, get good store of Crowns, and drinke good wine, I doubt not but you shall do well, & I desire the good God of heaven to continue it so still. Have they had a fruitful vintage in France this yere, or no? me thinks our Bourdeaux wines are very deare, and in good faith I am very sorie for it. But they will bee at a more reasonable reckoning, if these same loftie leaguers would once crouch & come to some good co*m*position.[1]

John Eliot's *Ortho-epia Gallica: Eliot's Fruits for the French: Interlaced with a Double New Invention, which Teacheth to Speak Truly, Speedily and Volubly the French-Tongue* (1593) is a work that demonstrates the sensitivity of the Elizabethan book trade to public demand. It is a French phrase book and phonetic pronunciation guide that responds both to the fashionable prose and cultural posturing of the Elizabethan prodigals and to the new and expanding appetite for news from France. The prefaces, to French tutors and gentlemen readers and students, are written in the hyperbolic style of Thomas Nashe and Robert Greene. The dialogues through which readers are instructed (much like a modern study guide) reflect perceptions of typical contemporary conversations in London and Paris. One located at 'La Bourse' begins with five ways of asking for news: 'What newes in Fraunce? . . . What bruit in the world? . . . Know you no newes? What say they from Barbarie, Italie, from Spaine, and Turkie? Is there no good newes?'[2] The dialogue set at a bookseller's shop also begins with advertising the latest news from France. This emphasis is to be expected from a French language guide, but it also indicates contemporary concerns, and, perhaps, the commercial justification for the book: English interest in news of the French Wars of Religion. The two-way exchange between oral communication and print – print idealises existing conversations in order to facilitate future ones – is also indicative of wider movements in Elizabethan culture between the spoken and inked word. These wider movements are fundamental to the transformation in the culture of news in early modern England and Wales.

'WHAT NEWS?' VOICE, MANUSCRIPT, PRINT

News needs to be defined in two ways or should be understood as having two, imperfectly discrete aspects. First it is an object: the news, rumours, fact, information and sometimes opinions on contemporary matters. It is the news of the conversion of Henry of Navarre, Henry IV of France, from Protestantism to Roman Catholicism in 1593, of Huguenot responses to this fact, and of English Protestant interpretations of the significance of this event for French politics. Second, it is a means of communication, one involving several media, all of which participate in some shared practical and conceptual elements. As a means of communication, news binds two or more parties together in an exchange of information and opinion: it comprehends, to name a few of the most significant forms, conversations in the street, written correspondence, private and professional, and paragraphs within letters, topical ballads, libels, printed pamphlets and newspapers, proclamations and the playing out of current affairs on the stage. It is a pattern of communication: a response to the question 'What news?'

To buy a printed item of news, or to pick it up from a bookseller's stall, is implicitly to ask this question, 'what news?', as much as to voice it to a passing acquaintance, or to urge a correspondent to write soon. In Elizabethan England and Wales (in common with much of late-sixteenth-century Europe), these forms of exchange modify each other, and with increasing intensity. Stories that begin with word of mouth appear in correspondence, or in written libels, and then find their way into print; and as printed stories they are used to confirm the spoken word. A ballad might be encountered sung by a voice, as a printed broadside, as a transcript of a performance or a printed text, as a commercial separate, as part of a miscellany, or in print or manuscript pasted on the wall of an alehouse or tavern (which practice widely disseminated texts, even among the impecunious). There is a dynamic exchange between these modes, and they cannot simply be considered as alternatives. But precisely because they are complementary they serve increasingly divergent purposes within society. The commercial manuscript newsletter, for example, which emerges in the Elizabethan period, is within half a century largely displaced by print. Those commercial newsletters that survive, therefore, adapt their purpose: either they comment on the news and supplement a printed item (often sent to accompany the newsletter) with additional and more recent news; or they present themselves as a more socially exclusive and therefore superior form for certain kinds of readers, largely irrespective of the content (and in this form they survive into the later seventeenth century). The advent of commercial printed news in Elizabethan England and Wales changed manuscript news, and the ways in which printed news developed were adapted to the existing channels of manuscript communication.

Studies of popular politics show that rumour, gossip and news played an important role in mobilising action; during the sixteenth century, print supplemented these communication networks. Evidence of conversations is limited and partial. Conversations about news survive in diaries and correspondence because they are unusual and memorable, and these sources understate the mundane, the role of everyday pleasantries. The Swallowfield articles, for example, a set of proposals about governance drafted by the 'chief Inhabitants' of an Elizabethan parish, are an end product that bear witness to conversations and reveal the intersections between local and national news and politics.[3] But sources such as this, or the diary of the Suffolk clergyman John Rous, inevitably emphasise conversations in which at least one party was literate. Court records focus on the libellous, and show the dynamism of oral exchange and the transitions between the spoken word, the anonymous manuscript publicly circulated, and the verbal examination of news and opinion in a legal framework; but they show little of the ordinary content of news, except perhaps where its limits lay. Libels, such as 'He that in Belgia fought for Englandes Queene', commemorating the military victories of the Earl of Essex in the 1580s and 1590s, and contrasting them with his ignominious end at the hands of the cunning politician 'Cankred Cecil', Lord Burghley, were copied down in personal manuscript miscellanies too, converting news into a matter of record.[4] Libels were intensively literary, observing conventions and poetic forms; they were nonetheless an influential news genre. The same can be said of ballads (ballads and blues songs functioned as media of news transmission in the early twentieth century in the deep South of the USA). Sermons also stray into news, such as those preached against Martin Marprelate in 1589, or those celebrating the defeat of the Armada in 1588. All, however, testify to the vibrancy of spoken communication of news from the perspective of the interface between the oral and manuscript or print.

Most oral news was local; this is not to say that news did not travel from further afield but that communities were defined primarily by local news and only secondarily by regional, national or international (which news was inflected through more local concerns). Letters were a means by which the gentry communicated news over greater distances, relying on carrier networks and acquaintance (a postal service was not introduced until 1635). Early printed news publications – such as *The Copy of a Letter Written by One in London to His Friend Concerning the Credit of the Late Published Detection of the Doings of the Lady Marie of Scotland* (1572) – echoed letters in their language and form, even if they did not initially derive from an actual letter. The letter was, as all news media, both a form of communication and an associated genre, with conventions and therefore expectations, which could be adapted to other forms of communication. The letter form, with its conventions of an authorial voice, an addressee, familiarity or an intimate exchange, was absorbed into other forms, such as the commercial newsletter or printed pamphlet, in which the author was a fictional identity, or the author and reader unknown to each other.

From informal and familiar news correspondence coalesced and solidified the production of commercial newsletters. Professional scribes began to produce subscription newsletters in England around 1580, lagging behind, as in many aspects of English news culture, the rest of Europe. In Venice scribes regularly produced *avisi* or *gazetti* from the 1530s onwards, which digested other letters, and included headings, as would later printed news, indicating date and place of origins. Printed news did not appear there until much later. Manuscript news entertained and informed Europe's elite, though it was doubtless subject to a 'trickle-down' effect. News was also essential, however, to merchants involved in any kind of international trade. The Fugger family, proprietors of an Augsburg financial house, produced from 1568 onwards regular newsletters, containing both economic and political news, that were distributed widely across Europe. These and other newsletters were transported, across land and sea, by merchants as well as by the various forms of postal and carrier services. News followed trade routes. England's place in Europe, and its perception of its place in Europe, were shaped by these networks of communication; it was because of them that London seemed further away from Scandinavia, for example, than did Edinburgh or Glasgow.

Commercial newsletters only became common in England after Elizabeth's reign. Unlike printed news they were not subject to pre-publication licensing or, ordinarily, to other forms of censorship (by which I mean the set of practices that constrained the free exercise of speech in print, at the centre of which was pre-publication licensing). Senders and recipients did risk interception, in which case they were subject to various forms of legal action for offences including scandal and libel. Interception and scrutiny of the post was, however, not a common occurrence, perhaps because the manuscript dissemination of news was not perceived by the government to be a significant danger. Newsletters were, nonetheless, much concerned with overseas news. This was not, or not only, because of concern over the dangers of reporting domestic political news, but because foreign news interested readers, because of its commercial ramifications, because of interest in wars, and, which is related, because of interest in the fate of Protestantism. These interests intensified during the Thirty Years War (1618–48), which resulted in the emergence of printed news periodicals across Europe; but they were current during Elizabeth's reign, not least because of the French Wars of Religion (1562–98). There is a sense in which news of Protestants in France was domestic news.

THE SOCIOLOGY OF NEWS

Newsletters therefore shaped communities and geography. Newsletters informed the values and religious identity of communities, participated in the imagining of what Benedict Anderson has called, for a later period, 'imagined communities'. Anderson describes, with this felicitous formulation, the formation of national consciousness by print culture and incipient capitalism, but this process of defining and locating a regional identity seems to me to be brought about by various modes of news-communication. Nor is it based only on the sharing of news of a community by that community. International news, news that crosses political, geographical and linguistic boundaries, is fundamental to the shaping of a community, much as the county shapes experience of the country, and as local politics is in a dialogue with national politics. Fellow feeling for Protestants crossed the Channel, as did rumours of Catholic invasion. But newsletters did so directly only for a small segment of the population, and indirectly for a much larger group.

Language was less unambiguously a boundary: the second language in England was Latin, and competence in French, Spanish, Italian and other European tongues was rare. While Latin correspondence could be freely understood, it was more difficult to import news in the vernacular, and hence news that originated overseas was more likely to have been mediated, politicised, filtered and interpreted before it travelled. It was perhaps in response to linguistic concerns, as well as through economic decisions concerning circulation, that the first printed news periodical in Europe was in Latin: *Mercurius gallobelgicus*, a semi-annual volume mainly concerned with military conflict, was published in Cologne and then Frankfurt between

1594 and 1635. This preceded by a decade news periodicals in the vernacular. However, it is remarkable how the stories told in popular cultural forms in one country resonate, or are retold in others: this phenomenon suggests that news does migrate between languages even for the non-elite, though it might do so slowly. Popular cultures, national cultures and language cultures have different parameters. Language boundaries are in some ways more profound than geopolitical ones, but they were permeated by news communication in ways that are not presently understood.

It is the interaction between the various forms of news communication that defines news culture; debates about the relative importance of any one, without significant qualification with regard to social status, geography, or content, is reductive. Literary texts were passed on in manuscript forms, copied discretely or into a miscellany. The dynamic culture of manuscript transmission has been studied by literary scholars, though these scholars have tended to focus on elite forms. Counting them does not demonstrate their popularity. Meanwhile historians have tended to focus on slander and libel, and outline the networks of communication, though the materials are by definition exceptional. Accounts of printed materials have tended to focus either on textual properties or on social existence. This has proved an obstacle to a fuller picture of the cultural life of news, which necessarily requires consideration from the perspectives of form, content and use, and consideration of multiple forms.

Recent anglophone scholarship on the history of print culture, much of it influenced by French *histoire du livre,* has established a process of acculturation, by which printed books became an integral part of everyday life in England and Wales. There has been much debate, however, over the chronology of this acculturation: while it is agreed that books became influential, and were recognised as a social force, at some point between the Reformation and the early eighteenth century, the contours of this shift are contested (by, for example, Alexandra Halasz, myself, Steve Pincus and Mark Knights). Such arguments are based on a quantitative analysis of book production, accounts of growing literacy rates in the period, and on a less quantifiable analysis of acts of reception, by individuals or institutions, plus some other contextual information, such as royal proclamations expressing concern over pamphlets. One quantitative picture of book production, based on a crude title count of extant titles, appears in Figure 29.1: it shows a gradual yet significant overall increase over Elizabeth's reign, with considerable fluctuation year by year. These figures ignore survival rates and publication format, and for these and other reasons must be regarded as only a fragment of a larger picture.

There has been much less scholarship on the sociology of reading and reception, in part because of a paucity of direct evidence (and, perhaps, a superfluity of indirect evidence). One example of an alternative approach, from a later period, is David Zaret's work on petitions in the 1640s. Zaret argues that the printed petition effected a profound transformation in the conduct of politics in public. While print only amplified existing tendencies, he argues, the profound quantitative increase in the circulation of news in the 1640s produced a qualitative revolution. Political conflict assumed a dialogic order, and central to its dialogues was the petition, a medium through which the governors and the governed exchanged messages. Hence popular print altered politics in a way that voice and manuscript could not. While Zaret's account may understate the significance of other print genres, it shows how a radical shift can take place through quantitative change (beyond suggestions of a tipping point), and it takes us beyond arguments about relative influence towards an understanding of the interaction of communicative networks and the complementary roles that various modes can adopt.

Attempts to describe the impact of news media on Elizabethan England and Wales in qualitative terms have focused on publicity, and the notion of a 'public sphere'. Contemporaries would have been more likely to understand this as 'popularity'. In the 1610s 'popularity' would become associated with opposition to the Crown, but the concept was formulated in the 1580s to designate the (implicitly dangerous) cultivation of support among the people without a necessarily factional dimension. John Whitgift, the Earl of Essex and Martin Marprelate all chased popularity. At the same time the idea of, and fear of, the 'multitude' was being developed and expressed. News media were an integral part of this development, as the news in its various forms was a means of communicating with the public and therefore of chasing popularity. The 1580s were also, as Alastair Bellany and others have shown, the beginning of the high period of the political libel. It was also the decade in which printed pamphlets of foreign news were first produced in considerable numbers; and it was a decade of pamphlet controversy. It opened with an exchange of polemical pamphlets around the English Jesuit Edmund Campion in 1581; it ended with the Marprelate tracts, anonymous pamphlets which used the form to combine polemic and news in an attack on the Established Church. The Marprelate controversy followed patterns established by earlier controversial pamphlet exchanges, but it caused the largest stir, rippling through other forms of communication, and was remembered through the next century. At this same time, numerous writers expressed anxiety about the unruliness of the press, and in 1586 the Star Chamber issued decrees, subjecting the press to ecclesiastical licensing, seeking to amend the 'greate enormities and abuses . . . commonly used and practised by dyvers contentyous and disorderlye persons professinge the arte or mysterye of Pryntinge or sellinge of bookes'.[5] There are grounds, then, for seeing the incipience of a new kind of publicity dynamic, perhaps even a 'public sphere' in the 1580s.

The phrase 'public sphere' belongs to Jürgen Habermas, who offered it as a way of describing a virtual community that develops within market capitalism, providing a space for criticism and political debate. Within the public sphere private individuals come together as a public, independently of institutions, such as parliament or court, in which the public is represented, and discuss news and opinion. This happens in real places that exist between the private and public domains, such as alehouses, taverns, and, later, coffee houses. In the public sphere everyone is notionally equal and has an equal right of access; debate is governed by reason (rather than violence); and debate is non-instrumental, steered neither by political or commercial forces. The power of the public sphere lies partly in its capacity to co-ordinate discrete discussions in various and geographically dispersed spaces. This debate is oral, but it is co-ordinated by print, because of its prolific and inexpensive reproduction (and greater legibility among the semi-educated). Habermas's account of the initial formation of the public sphere may exaggerate the importance of print

– though his analysis has the benefit of being specific about what the role of print is – but his contention is that a public sphere first emerges in England (before the rest of Europe) in 1694–5. Many scholars have tried to move this genesis back to earlier moments where there has been dynamic discussion and debate about religion and politics, such as the 1640s and the 1620s; and even more have used the quotable collocation 'public sphere', or fragments of Habermas's argument, without sensitivity to its whole, and its methodological nuances (notably his insistence that the public sphere is non-instrumental, and thus threatened by commercial interests). It might be preferable to construct a new model and devise a new vocabulary using contemporary terms and categories, one that adequately captures the intentions and motives of those participating in this play of popularity and persuasion.

Nonetheless, a cogent case has been made that there was something like a public sphere in Elizabethan England. This 'post-Reformation public sphere', as Peter Lake and Steve Pincus characterise it, did not have a continuous existence, or even a sustained development, but moments of openness and closure, governed by circumstances within the government, the book trade and popular conflict about both religious and non-religious topics. In this model, the 1580s and 1590s were one such moment, for the reasons outlined above. The argument emphatically places print on centre stage, while acknowledging the role of the use of multiple media to combat opponents' arguments. The government did not only seek to apprehend Campion and Marprelate; William Cecil actively commissioned responses to them, in press, pulpit and in the playhouses, hence engaging in a dynamic of publicity. *A Particular Declaration ... of the ... Traitorous Affection Borne against Her Majesty by Edmund Campion* (1582), reported: 'Some disloyal and unnatural Subjects ... have published divers slanderous Pamphlets and seditious Libels, as well in this Realm, as in Foreign Parts, in sundry strange languages, in excuse and justification of the said Traytors.'[6] Campion's polemical campaign, followed by another by the Jesuit Robert Persons, stung the Privy Council into verbal retaliation, though the commissioned authors stressed that they sought to quell rather than to feed rumour. The sphere closed down towards the end of the 1590s and was not again so open until the late 1610s and 1620s. This vision of a 'post-Reformation public sphere' is more sensitive to the particular circumstances of news communication and debate in Tudor England, recognising the limitations of a sociological model that seeks to describe an ideal in spite of the messy realities of history, though it retains the potential disadvantage of the term 'public sphere' and the, perhaps unintended, implication of Habermasian principles. It seems unlikely that the phrase will be dispensed with (like 'puritan', perhaps, long recognised as problematic among historians, but without an agreed-upon alternative), and, while the notion that critical debate was shaped by a shared principle of reason, equality of access and non-instrumentalism has been abandoned, the notion that a sphere of popular, public debate was established in Elizabethan England will inform future narratives of, and research on the period.

REPORTS, DISCOURSES, LETTERS

Manuscript newsletters were flexible: they could be duplicated verbatim, copied into notebooks, digested into other narratives, circulated via diverse social means.

Printed news differed significantly: it operated under more rigorous financial constraints, as a minimum number of copies of any pamphlet had to be printed and sold in order for the publisher to break even. Large editions were more profitable, but could also be sold at a lower unit price. Print, however, was subject to pre-publication licensing, whereas writers of manuscript news could operate with comparative impunity. Large editions were harder to conceal than individual, bespoke manuscripts, and they could be traced to printing houses. Perhaps the most significant characteristic of print, however, was not simply its prolific nature, but its low cost. Paper for printing was coarser and consequently less expensive than manuscript paper, so much so that a printed sheet of news retailed for a penny or two, significantly less than an equivalent quantity of blank writing paper. The fees professional newsletter writers charged (in the seventeenth century, at least) reflected the time spent in copying as well, perhaps, as the exclusive nature of the product and the elite status of the subscriber. Scribes were aware of the superior status of manuscript news, and while news in both manuscript and print was satirised for being unreliable, only the latter was satirised for being common or vulgar. This reflects the perceived social status of the audience, and it indicates that print was able to reach a socially broader readership.

Printed news came in various forms, each mediating a variety of kinds of news. Broadside ballads were a popular form, loosely mediating between oral and print culture and thus effectively reaching a broad audience, literate and illiterate. Some ballads reflected an official position and could perhaps be labelled 'propaganda'; others were produced for speculative, commercial reasons; news ballads straddled this divide. Providential signs were one topic of news ballads: monstrous births, which were numerous in the first decade of Elizabeth's reign, and prodigies. Such ballads, read in a providential context, carried social and political significance, but did so indirectly. The broadsheet by J.P. entitled *A Marvellous Strange Deformed Swine* (1570?), describes a pig with body parts resembling those of other animals, born in Denmark and brought to England. The author specifies that the pig is a warning against sins, and especially covetousness, to Protestant and Papist alike; but the allusion to recent treasons suggests that its main concern is with the recent Northern Rebellion, and the disorderly body of the pig represents the political and social inversion implicit in that event. Other ballads directly addressed political news of national significance, which was rare in Tudor print culture. William Elderton's *A Ballad Intituled Northumberland News* (1570) and *Prepare Ye to the Plough* (1570) reported the rebellion of the northern earls, for example, supplementing a series of propagandistic tracts that may have been intended for a narrower audience. Ballads offered a socially (and geographically) mobile mixture of news and entertainment – including visual entertainment, as they were, unlike most cheap print, illustrated – and this versatility was personified in the character of the ballad-monger Autolycus in Shakespeare's *The Winter's Tale* (1609–11). He explains himself:

> My traffic is sheets. When the kite builds, look to lesser linen. My father named me Autolycus, who being, as I am, littered under Mercury, was likewise a snapper-up of unconsidered trifles. With die and drab, I purchased this caparison, and my revenue is the silly cheat. Beating and hanging are terrors to me.[7]

Mercury is the patron of news, lies and theft, suggesting one assessment of the value of news ballads in this period.

Domestic political news was rare, for reasons that will appear below. When Henry Percy, 8th Earl of Northumberland (whose brother had been executed for his part in the 1569 Northern Rebellion) was imprisoned in the Tower for conspiring to place Mary, Queen of Scots, on the throne and committed suicide while awaiting trial, the government, to deflect rumours of assassination, apparently authorised publication of *A True and Summary Report of the Declaration of Some Part of the Earle of Northumberland's Treasons, Delivered Publicly in the Court at the Starchamber by the Lord Chancellor and Others of Her Majesties Most Honourable Privy Council, and Council Learned, by Her Majesty's Special Commandment, Together with the Examinations & Depositions of Sundry Persons* (1585). Though the pamphlet is anonymous, the author outlines the reliability of the notes he took during the trial and the circumstances in which he took them. The tone of the pamphlet's account of how the Earl killed himself with a triple-charged dagge (pistol) is firmly empirical. The examination of the body showed

> his heart pearced and torne in divers lobes of pieces, three of his ribbes broken, the Chine bone of his backe cut almost in sunder, and under the poynt of the shoulder blade on the right side within the skinne, three bullets were founde by the Lord *Hunsdon,* which he cause the Surgion in his presence to cut out, lying al three close together within the breadth and compasse of an ynche or there about.[8]

The message is Protestant, and though the pamphlet asks for the preservation of the Queen from her enemies, the providentialism is understated. This is not the case for most news pamphlets, however, which present news – of strange sights, crimes and apt punishments, strange births, pseudo-miracles and executions – as calls for repentance or signs of divine justice. Thomas Day's *Wonderful Strange Sights Seen in the Element, over the City of London and Other Places, on Monday Being the Second Day of September* (1583) combines a prose narrative of lights in the sky with a ballad calling England to repent. Day tells his readers that God sends 'creatures, and miraculous tokens, strange monsters, blazing commets, unwonted enundations of waters, straunge fishes, perrillous warres, earthquakings, and last of all, firye constellations'.[9] Like the report on Northumberland, *Wonderful Strange Sights* concludes with praise of the Queen, asking for a happy reign and the maintenance of the Gospel: this is common in printed pamphlets of news.

In Elizabethan England and Wales there was an increasing supply of pamphlets of news which originated from two main sources: manuscript newsletters and foreign news pamphlets. Printed newsletters did not conceal their origins: the genre typographically followed the scribal form and used the authority of the sender, either as an eyewitness or a socially elevated and therefore reliable relater, to testify to the veracity of the news. Those newsletters that were printed tended to be optimistic in tone and were frequently openly anti-papist. A.M.'s *The True Report of the Prosperous Success which God Have unto Our English Soldiers against the Foreign Bands of Our Roman Enemies, Lately Arrived (but Soon Enough to Their Cost) in Ireland,* licensed for publication on 20 December 1580, advertised that the news had been 'Gathered out of the Letters of moste credit and circumstance, that have beene sent over'. The editor justified himself:

> And having considered how that it is not onely usuall among the people, to be desirous to know newes, but also necessary that this happy newes should be knowen unto all (aswell to the true religious and obedient subject, for his comfort, as to the supersticious disloyall recusant, for his utter dismaying and confusion): I have thought it not amis to bestow some light paines of my little leisure, in gathering one sound discourse out of those sundry fragments which have come to my hands.

The actual news covered four of the eight pages.[10] Though the author's name was not stated, the dedication to George Gifford, the clergyman and author who would later attend the deathbed of the Protestant hero Sir Philip Sidney, borrowed his status to indicate the truth value of the publication.

Perhaps the most quantitatively significant form of printed news was also the most noteworthy development in Elizabethan news culture. Between 1589, when Henry of Navarre became King of France, and about 1593, when he reconverted to Catholicism, there appeared a spate of pamphlets, some in letter form, some as narratives, all translated from French *occasionnels*. There had been earlier publications of this sort (such as *The King's Edict, for the Reuniting of His Subjects*, 1585), but the temporary convergence of Anglo-French interests sparked one of the earliest fashion trends in the English book trade. These were anything but the 'steady-sellers' that Ian Green analyses, claiming that repeat editions are the test of popular print culture: most appeared in a single edition, but the test of their popularity was the ongoing demand. News changes, so repeat editions are rare: but the demand is continuous. The dozens of pamphlets in these years include such titles as *Directions from the King, to the Governors of the Provinces, Concerning the Death of the Duke of Guise* (1589); *A True Discourse of the Most Happy Victories Obtained by the French King* (1589); *A Recital of All That which Hath Happened in the Kings Army Since the Taking of the Suburbs of Paris* (1590); *News Sent to the Lady Princess of Orange* (1589); *A Letter Sent by the French King unto Monsieur De La Verune Lieutenant for His Majesty at Caen in Normandy, Concerning the Most Happy Victory* (1590); *A True Discourse of the Most Horrible and Barbarous Murders and Massacres Committed by the Troupes of the Duke of Savoy* (1590); *News from France . . . with Some Notes and News from Dervern in Holland* (1591); *News Out of France on the First of the Month of March* (1592); *A Journal, Wherein Is Truly Set Down from Day to Day, What Was Done, and Worthy of Noting in Both the Armies, from the Coming of the Duke of Parma into France, Until the Eighteenth of May 1592* (1592). All were between one and three sheets in length. The titles suggest the conceptual vocabulary deployed to present and define news: 'discourse', 'recital', 'news', 'notes', 'true'. The titles also show a concern with literary genre ('directions', 'letter', 'journal'), with place of origin and with time.

This plethora of printed news – all of the examples I have given above are representative of press output more generally – intensified the search for means of communicating news and exploring the way news informed readers. While these printed pamphlets began with the relatively stable epistolary genre, they soon supplemented, developed and transformed it. The letters of professional scribes were serial productions, but this did not immediately transfer to printed news. These letters of news from France were, like stories of crimes and monstrous births, occasional publications, released as and when news arrived. The pamphlet *Two Notorious Murders. One Committed by a Tanner on His Wives Son, Near Hornchurch in Essex. The Other on a Grazier Near Aylesbury in Buckinghamshire. With These Is Intermixed Another Murderous Intending Felony at Ruislip in Middlesex. All Done This Last Month* (1595) shows how occasional news items could be patched together to make up a saleable item. Yet the intensity of French news production in the early 1590s led to experiments with serial news. Before the appearance of weekly newspapers in Strasbourg and Antwerp in 1605, even before the advent of *Mercurius Gallobelgicus* in 1594, the London printer John Wolfe (who had a reputation for surreptitious printing before he was co-opted into the senior ranks of the Stationers' Company, the trade guild that from 1557 oversaw printing in England and Wales) explored ways of creating a serial news publication. In a series of French news pamphlets, including *News Out of France on the First of the Month of March* (1592), *The Chief Occurrences of Both the Armies* (1592) and *The Continual Following of the French King* (1592), he used similar typography to indicate continuity (though not the stability of the same title); he indicated sequential news and consecutive dates. His news pamphlets were taken from several sources and were therefore in a sense 'edited'. Though they were not strictly periodicals (the interval between publication varied) and did not bear issue numbers, these anticipated, in seriality, physical continuity and heterogeneity of news, the corantos of the 1620s and newsbooks of the 1640s. This is significant from two perspectives: in terms of the long-term development of news media, seriality is, along with periodicity, central to the definition of the newspaper, which would later become a formative element in European political institutions and processes. Second, serial publication asserts the expectation that more, associated news will be forthcoming and intimates the understanding that the flow of news is connected, that one set of events is a cause or consequence of another. It suggests that news and history are connected, that one is living in the tides of history, that time is passing and that the individual experience of time is associated with the time in which political events happen at home and overseas.

LIBERTY OF DISCOURSE

This brief abundance of French news broaches the distinction between domestic and foreign news. The historiography of news has emphasised the difference between news from home and abroad on a number of grounds. First, early commercial printed news of politics was exclusively foreign in focus. While news of providence, crimes and wonders could originate in Britain, parliamentary proceedings and speeches, and the actions of the Privy Council were not touched upon at all in printed pamphlets, except for those that originated within the government and were officially published. When the Spanish Armada was destroyed in 1588, ballads celebrated the fact: this patriotic, providential event was uncontroversial, and these publications may in any case have been officially allowed. Thomas Deloney's

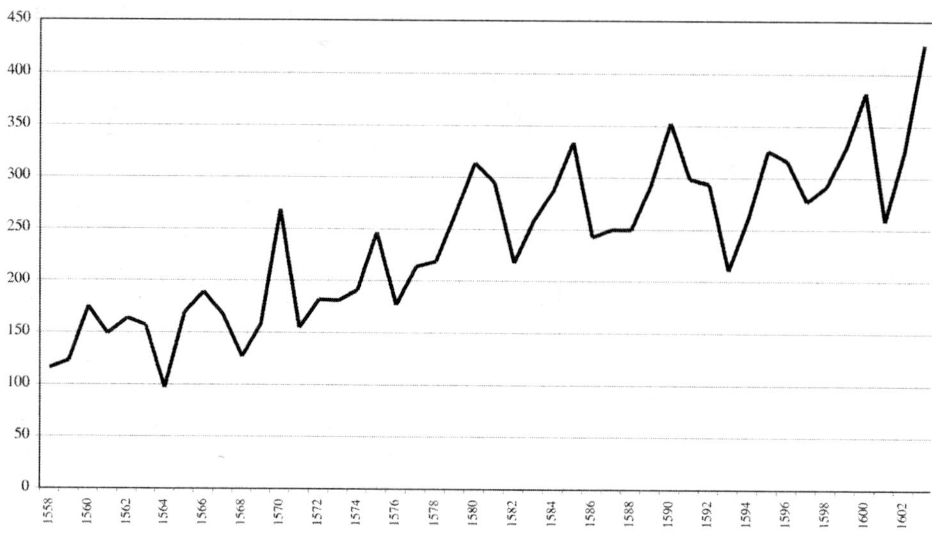

Figure 29.1 Number of titles published 1558–1603.

A New Ballet of the Strange and Most Cruel Whips which the Spaniards Had Prepared to Whip and Torment English Men and Women (1588) is incontrovertibly a domestic news publication, but it was consensual and risked no offence (except perhaps to English Catholics). Its patriotic vision, its restricted content and perhaps its poetic form limit its power as a news item. A prose pamphlet produced by John Wolfe, *A True Discourse of the Army which the King of Spain Caused to Bee Assembled in the Haven of Lisbon, in the Kingdom of Portugal, in the Year 1588. Against England the which Began to Go Out of the Said Haven, on the 29. and 30. of May . . . Whereunto Is Added the Verses that Were Printed in the First Page of the Dutch Copy Printed at Cologne, with Answers to Them, and to Don Bernardin De Mendozza* (1588) was, significantly, translated from the French, and, in any case, is presented as foreign news. It is conspicuous that such a momentous event did not result in an increase in titles published (see Figure 29.1); this would not have been the case by the mid-seventeenth century, when press output was sensitive to current affairs.

Three conclusions are possible: first, publishers and readers did not desire to read news in print; second, there were legal restrictions on the publication of domestic news; third, norms and conventions governing the printing of news placed pressure on reporting certain kinds of material, especially those relating to England and Wales, and especially those relating to political institutions and the nobility. These three are not, of course, exclusive. The role of the first has been understood: it is too easy to assume that men and women in Elizabethan England and Wales were driven by the same appetite for news that their descendants were. In fact, the production of foreign news reports throughout the early modern period suggests that, far from being a poor substitute for domestic news, it was the object of powerful demand. This was not least because of fellow feeling for Protestants on the Continent, and a concern about the future of Protestantism during these times of war and Catholic triumph. Foreign news was also harder to obtain by oral means among a non-elite audience. Manuscript newsletters, however, report more generously on domestic news, suggesting that there was demand for it. Historians of the book trade and of the news have instead emphasised the second, asserting that it was illegal to print domestic news. No such legislation is extant, however, and this ban seems to be a myth. However, there were indirect forms of legal constraint, the impact of which cannot be discounted. Repeated Elizabethan proclamations express concern about rumour and its relationship to sedition. Under the injunctions governing printing passed in 1559, and the Star Chamber decree of 1586, all publications were subject to pre-publication licensing (in practice not all publications followed this procedure, and most of those that did not passed without response), and so news publications were subject to ad-hoc censorship and prevention. Finally, some of the early records (the 'Red Book') of the Stationers' Company are missing, and it is possible that these restricted its liberty to print news. The minimalist accounts of censorship prevalent in recent revisionist historiography, which stresses the absence of systematic censorship laws and the laxity of the implementation of sanctions, overstate the case.

The third conclusion is probably the most significant, but it develops from these comments on the second. The pressures on printed news cannot be reduced to positive legislation and proclamation. Customs, expectations and propriety or norms of conduct also shaped the production of news. These were shaped by legislation, which undisputedly takes a dim view of discussions of news and matters of state. News-based conversation is assumed to be suspicious or morally doubtful in nature, and therefore the presupposition is that news is something that needs to be controlled and limited. The reliability of reports was, as Steven Shapin has demonstrated in relation to notions of truth more generally, proportionate to the social standing of the witness: only in the hands of the social elite could the news be trusted, whereas in the hands of the vulgar it was mere rumour and gossip. Publishers and printers were cautious of what materials they handed, and it did not take many exemplary cases, such as John Stubbs's *Discovery of a Gaping Gulf* (1579), the Marprelate tracts (1588–9) and the 1599 Bishops' ban, to remind stationers that there were limits to acceptable conduct and that they might be punished for transgressing them. The small number of publishing offences which met with punishment has been taken as evidence of the limitations of (even absence of) censorship: it could equally be taken to signify the success of self-regulation and the effectiveness of the cultural pressures against speech. The lack of domestic news in Elizabethan print culture, even as foreign news burgeoned, indicates that social restrictions were reliable.

Among the pressures limiting news circulation were commercial and social factors. The book trade in England and Wales was governed by the Stationers' Company, which operated a monopoly, granted by the government in return for ensuring that the book trade was orderly and well regulated. It had a monopoly over the importation of printing paper, which was not manufactured in Britain. Books were, moreover, luxury commodities, and therefore were ordinarily affordable only to a tiny percentage of the population. David Cressy estimates that in 1600 about 10 per cent of women and 30 per cent of men in England were literate, with literacy concentrated in London where the book trade was centred. Others have suggested that these figures should be regarded as a minimum and that forms of literacy were more diverse and more widespread. Print was, for example, not only cheaper than manuscript; it was easier to read. These and other factors limited the dissemination of written and printed news at least as effectively as the law.

THE CULTURE OF NEWS

Nevertheless, print was only one channel for news, and where that channel was blocked, other means could facilitate its flow. Literary representations of news exchange were primarily satirical but nonetheless offer an essential but neglected means of understanding the categories with which contemporaries understood their own actions and the world. Albeit from a later period, when print and manuscript news had been more thoroughly acculturated than in Elizabethan England and Wales, Ben Jonson's masque *Newes from the New World* (1620) explores the relation between the vocal, written and printed transmission of news. A scrivener, concerned only with profitability, pushes aside credibility and complains at the innovation of printed news: 'it is the Printing I am offended at, I would have no newes printed; for when they are printed they leave to bee newes; while they are written though they be false, they remaine newes still.' The printer counters that news is truly only true news, and for gullible customers only printed news is true: 'It is the Printing of 'hem makes 'hem newes to a great many, who will indeed believe nothing but what's in Print.' This suggests the development of a critical attitude to news, a sifting of rumour from supported fact. He too, however, is concerned only with profit: 'For those I doe keep my Presses, and so many Pens going to bring forth wholesome relations, which once in halfe a score yeares (as the age growes forgetfull) I Print over againe with a new date.'[11] News was very rarely recycled in this way, and Jonson's satire is focused on the profit motive and the repetitiousness of some kinds of news, though it does speak to the way much reporting of news followed identical patterns. Jonson's later play, *The Staple of Newes* (1626), shows customers without scepticism, driven only by unbounded appetite and the desire to share news sociably. While professional manuscript-newsletter writers were sometimes scornful of printed news items, they frequently enclosed them within newsletters, as examples of the 'common' news which they were supplementing with their more specialised service. Print was sometimes accepted as a means of confirming news which had first arrived by voice.

One news medium that sat on the boundary between the written and the vocal was the stage; players were the 'abstracts and brief chronicles of the time' (*Hamlet*, Act II Scene 2, line 504), alongside news publications. Christopher Marlowe's *The Massacre at Paris* was performed in 1592, in the midst of the vogue for French news, from which it drew some of its materials. Shakespeare wrote *Love's Labour's Lost*, set in Henry of Navarre's park, in 1594–5, taking his characters' names and contextual references from news pamphlets. Other plays, such as *Henry VI, Part 2*, written in 1591 and published in 1594 as *The First Part of the Contention betwixt the Two Famous Houses of Yorke and Lancaster*, a title that perhaps echoes a news pamphlet, show a concern not only with Anglo-French relations but also with the way news shapes the world and concerns of the characters. In the third act of *Henry V* (performed 1599), Catherine, daughter to Charles VI of France, takes a lesson in English that mirrors John Eliot's *Ortho-epia Gallica,* though full of bawdy bilingual puns. In the final scene Henry woos Catherine in eloquent English and broken French that he might have learned from Eliot. When Shakespeare's characters exchange news it is shaped by content, by the event or fact communicated, and by the medium of communication that establishes the selfhood of characters through verbal interaction. Shakespeare's characters ask time and again 'What news?', and his drama frequently turns on the arrival of news, and the *anagnorisis* of characters hearing news. There is sufficient ground for thinking that this derives in part from the culture of printed news in the 1590s.

Because of this dual aspect of news, the interdependence of medium and message, any brief account of the news can only offer a partial picture. In this essay I have looked at the existence of and interaction between various modes of news communication and outlined some of the ways they developed during the Elizabethan period (which necessarily emphasises print). Except in the case of French news pamphlets, where there was a direct association between form and content, only incidentally has this involved the matter of news, the everyday and quotidian material exchanged through these media. To the question 'What news?', almost any answer would do.

FURTHER READING

Anderson, Benedict, *Imagined Communities: Reflections on the Origin and Spread of Nationalism* (London, 1983).

Bellany, Alastair, *The Politics of Court Scandal in Early Modern England: News Culture and the Overbury Affair, 1603–1660* (Cambridge, 2002).

Clegg, Cyndia Susan, *Press Censorship in Elizabethan England* (Cambridge, 1997).

Cressy, D., *Literacy and the Social Order: Reading and Writing in Tudor and Stuart England* (Cambridge: Cambridge University Press, 1980).

Cust, Richard, 'News and Politics in Early Seventeenth-Century England', *Past and Present,* 112 (1986): 60–90.

Fox, Adam, *Oral and Literate Culture in England, 1500–1700* (Oxford, 2000).

Fox, Adam, and Woolf, Daniel (eds.), *The Spoken Word: Oral Culture in Britain, 1500–1850* (Manchester and New York, 2002).

Green, Ian, *Print and Protestantism in Early Modern England* (Oxford, 2000).

Habermas, Jürgen, *The Structural Transformation of the Public Sphere: An Inquiry into a Category of Bourgeois Society,* trans. Thomas Burger with the assistance of Frederick Lawrence (Cambridge, Mass., 1989).

Halasz, Alexandra, *The Marketplace of Print: Pamphlets and the Public Sphere in Early Modern England* (Cambridge, 1997).

Knights, Mark, *Representation and Misrepresentation in Later Stuart Britain: Partisanship and Political Culture* (Oxford, 2005).

Lake, Peter, and Pincus, Steve, 'Rethinking the Public Sphere in Early Modern England', *Journal of British Studies,* 45 (2006): 270–92.

—— (eds.), *The Politics of the Public Sphere in Early Modern England* (Manchester, 2008).

Lake, Peter, Cogswell, Thomas, and Cust, Richard (eds.), *Politics, Religion and Popularity: Early Stuart Essays in Honour of Conrad Russell* (Cambridge, 2002).

Lander, Jesse M., *Inventing Polemic: Religion, Print, and Literary Culture in Early Modern England* (Cambridge, 2006).

Love, Harold, *Scribal Publication in Seventeenth-Century England* (Oxford, 1993).

McKenzie, D. F. and Barnard, John (eds.), *The Cambridge History of the Book in Britain, Vol. IV: 1557–1695* (Cambridge, 2002).
Parmalee, Lisa Ferrarou, *Good Newes from Fraunce: French Anti-League Propaganda in Late Elizabethan England* (Rochester, NY, 1996).
Raymond, Joad, *Pamphlets and Pamphleteering in Early Modern Britain* (Cambridge, 2003).
—— (ed.), *News Networks in Seventeenth-Century Britain and Europe* (London, 2006).
—— *The Oxford History of Popular Print Culture*, vol. I (Oxford, forthcoming).
Shapin, S., *A Social History of Truth: Civility and Science in Seventeenth-Century England* (Chicago: University of Chicago Press, 1994).
Voss, Paul J., *Elizabethan News Pamphlets: Shakespeare, Spenser, Marlowe and the Birth of Journalism* (Pittsburgh, Pa., 2001).
Zaret, David, *Origins of Democratic Culture: Printing, Petitions, and the Public Sphere in Early Modern England* (Princeton, NJ, 2000).

NOTES

1 John Eliot, *Ortho-epia Gallica* (London, 1593), sig. A3r.
2 Eliot, *Ortho-epia Gallica*, pp. 26–7.
3 Steve Hindle, 'Hierarchy and Community in the Elizabethan Parish: The Swallowfield Articles of 1596', *Historical Journal*, 42 (3) (1999): 835–51.
4 CUL, Add. MS 4138, fol. 49r.
5 Edward Arber (ed.), *A Transcript of the Registers of the Company of Stationers*, 5 vols. (1875–94), vol. II, pp. 807–12.
6 Quoted by Matthias A. Shaaber, *Some Forerunners of the Newspaper in England, 1476–1622* (Philadelphia, Pa., 1929), p. 46.
7 William Shakespeare, *The Winters Tale*, Act IV, Scene 3, ll. 25–8; in *The Norton Shakespeare*, ed. Stephen Greenblatt (New York and London, 1997).
8 *A True and Summarie Reporte* (London, 1585), p. 19.
9 Thomas Day, *Wonderfvll Straunge Sightes* (London, 1583), sig. A2r.
10 A.M., *The True Reporte of the Prosperous Successe* (London, 1581), sig. Aiiv.
11 C. H. Herford, Percy Simpson and Evelyn Simpson (eds.), *Ben Jonson*, 11 vols. (Oxford, 1925–52), vol. VII, pp. 514–15.

CHAPTER THIRTY

INTELLECTUAL DEVELOPMENTS

Freyja Cox Jensen

The reign of Elizabeth I was a pivotal period in England's intellectual history. Reforms and innovations introduced during these years often proved the foundation of diverse kinds of modern intellectual culture. This was a time of obvious flowering in the fields of music and English literature, but the changes were broader than this: the Elizabethan years witnessed England's rehabilitation as an intellectual player on the European stage, the rise of a national consciousness that had implications for the development of history and science into the disciplines we recognise today, and saw an educational reform movement that surpassed anything that followed until the twentieth century. This was, in fact, the true arrival and expression of the English Renaissance in its many forms, and it was simultaneously the culmination of centuries of Latinate culture: both an ending and a new beginning. The following pages explore the various shifts in learning and thinking as expressed in formal and informal education, Latin writing, printing and the new forms of science that were appearing in England.

The age of Elizabeth has often been called an 'educational revolution'. Critics may debate the extent to which this is true, but it is beyond all doubt that significant attempts were made to reform education in Elizabethan England. Education was the foundation upon which society's intellectual culture was built, comprising both formal schooling and more unofficial methods. New theories about learning targeted a variety of levels of society: the nobility and gentry, the merchant classes and the lower orders. These theories focused on all kinds of environment, from the universities to private households, and while the success of the new educational strategies was sometimes dubious, it is clear that pedagogical theories were developing rapidly, as was the very concept of what constituted education.

Childhood education in a formal school setting was one area in which these new ideas found practical expression. Ultimately conservative in their aims of using schools to promote social unity and the official state religion, the reformers of the school system nevertheless made some significant changes to the role of schools within society, as humanist theories of active citizenship and good government promoted an expansion in the provision of education for boys and young men, and a rise in standards. An education was becoming increasingly important for advancement in many fields; the man aiming at a career in trade or one of the professions was expected to be educated to a reasonable level. For this reason, the Elizabethan period saw a vast extension of the grammar-school system across England; it was designed to cater for the needs of the laity, both the gentle classes and the newer, professional orders. These now included the married Protestant clergy, who expected their children to be educated, and the formidable and wealthy merchant classes. Men from all of the higher social ranks founded boys' schools – clerics, lawyers, tradesmen and merchants and courtiers – so that by the end of the sixteenth century, England had roughly 360 grammar schools, one for every 12,000 people living in the country, a far greater provision than existed even in Victorian times.

As the figures demonstrate, a grammar-school education was by no means available to every boy, neither did all but the most radical thinkers ever consider that this should be the case. Any girls who were educated outside the home usually only attended the elementary schools. On the rare occasions that they did matriculate at a grammar school, they were only permitted to stay for the first few years and were not taught Latin; the statutes of Banbury Grammar School in 1594, for example, allowed girls to study in the vernacular until the age of nine, when they were required to leave. Since women were not expected to engage actively in public life, a Latin education would be no use to them and might disrupt the social order. Grammar schools were envisaged as places for the inculcation of Christian virtues and the production of good servants of the commonwealth, of sufficient intellectual calibre and drawn from the right kind of social background, as the growing corpus of educational literature was quick to point out. Roger Ascham's *Schoolmaster* (1570), a manual for the private schooling of young noblemen that also discoursed on general educational concerns, stressed the importance of schools in forming a boy's character, so that he 'may most easily be brought well to serve God and country both by virtue and wisdom'.[1] The Church canons of 1571 encouraged schooling in order to provide candidates for the Church or for civil service, ordering schoolmasters to report annually to their bishop on the progress of boys 'which are of that apteness, & so forward in learnyng, that there may be good hope they will become fitte, either for the common wealth, or for the holy ministerie'.[2] Very occasionally, some more progressive thinkers on education believed that learning should be available to the most able, regardless of their social status; one such was Richard Barnes, Bishop of Durham, who issued a set of injunctions in 1577 for the reform of education in his diocese. He stipulated that any clergyman not licensed to preach should teach every child in his parish to read and write for free. Those boys who showed themselves 'apt to learn and of pregnant capacity, then they shall exhort their parents to set them to schools and learning of the good and liberal sciences', while those who showed little talent for letters, 'they shall move and require their parents to set to learn husbandry or other good crafts, that yet so they may grow to be good members to the country and commonweal'.[3] For the further education of girls, no provision was made.

The rearing of subjects who would serve queen and country was a goal common to all educational authors, but Bishop Barnes's preference for education according to ability irrespective of class was not popular. A developing genre of educational literature explained the purposes of education and the theoretical methods for achieving the best results: this literature exhibited a keen awareness of the tension between providing learning so that godly morals and good citizenship were encouraged and men could directly access Scripture, and notions of educating people beyond their station and thus disrupting civic harmony. Richard Mulcaster, Headmaster of Merchant Taylor's School between 1561 and 1586, and High Master at Saint Paul's from 1596 onwards, observed in his educational treatise of 1581 that boys, 'be set to schoole, to qualifie themselues, to learne how to be religious and louing, how to gouerne and obey, how to fore cast and preuent, how to defende and assaile, and in short, how to performe that excellently by labour, wherunto they are borne but rudely by nature'.[4]

Recognising, however, that the perceived advantages of attending grammar school might entice parents to send boys of unsuitable quality to be thus educated, Mulcaster goes on to stress that:

> Sure all children may not be set to schole, nay not though priuate circumstance say yea. And therefore scholes may not be set vp for all. . . . [I]t seemeth to me very plain that all children be not set to school, but only such as for natural wits and sufficient maintenance, either of their natural parents or civil patrons, shall be honestly and well supported in their study, till the commonwealth minding to use their service appoint their provision.[5]

With a learned and erudite queen on the throne, the question of education for women was a sensitive one, and Mulcaster does make some comment about providing basic schooling for girls of better birth; however, there is always the proviso that such training must not interfere in any way with the education of boys and young men.

The Crown was equally keen to regulate grammar-school education, recognising that the schools represented an opportunity for strengthening the Royal Supremacy and that anyone involved in shaping the minds of young men had the potential to do either great service or great harm to the State; as Ascham observed, 'the good or ill bringing up of children doth as much serve to the good or ill service of God, our prince and our whole countrie as any one thing doth beside.'[6] The royal injunctions of 1559 developed a national system for the licensing of schoolmasters and required 'that al teachers of chyldren shal stirre & move them to the love & due reverence of Gods true religion, nowe truely set forth by publyke aucthoritie'.[7] A series of Church canons and parliamentary Acts during Elizabeth's reign imposed further conditions upon the schools, prescribing standard textbooks and elaborating upon existing requirements for the licensing of schoolmasters, so that it became unlawful 'for any to teach the Latine tongue, or to instructe children, neyther openly in the scholes, neither privately in any mans house, but whome the Bishop of that diocesse hath allowed, & to whome he hath geven licence to teach under the seale of his office'.[8]

At the start of Elizabeth's reign, Latin was the main subject of study in the grammar schools, augmented occasionally with a little Greek in the upper forms and very rarely with Hebrew in the larger establishments. Days were long, and holidays were short; boys were expected to spend their time translating Latin into English, English into Latin, reading and analysing Latin texts and completing various exercises such as declarations and disputations. There was very little provision made for teaching boys who arrived at the grammar schools around the age of seven unable to read and write properly. It was expected that the first steps in a boy's education would be taken at home with his parents, with a local clergyman or perhaps in a small 'petty' or 'dame' school run for small boys and girls by an unlicensed person. This was an unreliable method of teaching reading and writing, and for a boy to enter grammar school without basic functional literacy was a common enough occurrence to generate many complaints. Francis Clement wrote about the inadequacies of the men and women who taught in these small, local establishments in *The Petty School* (1587), bemoaning how 'children, as we see, almost everywhere are first taught either in private by men or women altogether rude and utterly ignorant of the due composing and just spelling of words'.[9] The grammar schools adapted themselves in the latter half of the sixteenth century in order to address this problem, employing ushers or pupil-teachers to instruct the lowest forms in the correct use of letters. Additionally, educational reformers began to call for separate methods of teaching literacy outside the grammar-school system, so that boys who never intended to study Latin, and also girls, might learn to read and write in English, and so that some orthographical uniformity might be imposed upon the English language.

It was commonly thought by the educationalists that any literate person might teach others how to read, and over the course of the last four decades of the sixteenth century, manuals on the teaching of reading were produced in growing quantities for use in the home, the workshop or other similarly informal environments, where women could also participate. In 1570, John Hart published his *Method or Comfortable Beginning for All Unlearned, Whereby They Might Be Taught to Read English in a Very Short Time,* with the intention that:

> some one such in a house, as now can reade our present maner, may be able to teach it to all the rest of the house, even the whiles their handes may be otherwyse well occupied, in working for their living, or otherwise being idle or sitting by the fyre, without any further let or cost.[10]

Schoolmasters also promoted the good teaching of English and attempted to regulate spelling; Mulcaster issued *The First Part of the Elementarie which Entreateth Chiefly of the Right Writing of Our English Tongue* in 1582 in order to improve 'the right writing of our English tung, a verie necessarie point, and of force to be handled ... For can reading be right before writing be righted, seing we read nothing else, but what we se writen?'[11] *The English Schoolmaster* by Edmund Coote appeared in 1596, for use by those who had no access to a school education but who could work informally with someone who might help them to learn; the work was so popular that it became commonly used in the lower forms of formal schools and had entered its twenty-fifth edition by 1625. Although it is clear that the majority of the population never learned to write, new approaches and methods meant that literacy rates did increase dramatically over the Elizabethan years, and almost one quarter of adult males could sign their names by the start of the seventeenth century, suggesting that even more were able to read.

The reign of Elizabeth saw an expansion not only in the provision of teaching, but also in the conception of learning, and what constituted education. This manifested itself in sophisticated programmes for what would today be called 'adult and community education'. London was the centre of these developments, where business was expanding and the new trading companies flourished. The blossoming vitality of the City was in a large part due to its community of merchants and traders; as these men gained in wealth and standing, they sought to better themselves through forms of education relevant to their business concerns. Opportunities for intellectual advancement were provided for those men who cared to utilise them: one such was Gresham College, an institution administered by the Mercers' Company and the mayor and commonalty of London, endowed by Sir Thomas Gresham. It opened in 1596 at the Gresham home in Bishopsgate Street and provided lectures in the liberal sciences delivered in English for the benefit of merchants and other citizens who chose to attend. A practical application of learning was the central tenet of the college's philosophy; for example, the Professor of Astronomy, Edward Brerewood, was required to lecture on matters of geography and navigational techniques so that mariners might learn useful arts. Attendance was free, and lectures were given daily in term time except on Sundays, in Latin in the morning in order that visiting foreigners might understand, and in English in the afternoons. Other forms of vocational adult education were also devised: in 1582, the Royal College of Physicians set up the Lumleian lectures on medical matters, which commenced in 1584 and continued into the seventeenth century. A scientific lecture was given in Leadenhall Chapel, cosmography lectures could be heard at Blackfriars, while Deptford became a centre for the study of hydrography and navigation.

Ideas about the kind of education suitable for the nobility and gentry also changed in the years Elizabeth was on the throne. The humanists' insistence on practical ends found expression in plans for new establishments, never realised but much debated, such as Humphrey Gilbert's proposed academy in London. This was to be a place where future governors learned not only traditional school studies but also 'matters of action meet for present practice, both of peace and war', that they might better serve the commonwealth in later years.[12] Education was increasingly becoming essential to the self-image of the gentle classes: learning had always been connected with gentility in the humanist tradition, and it was gentlemen who were best suited to the possession of knowledge. Moreover, it was crucial that they be educated properly so that they might govern well and keep the country in sound moral and social order. The translation of Castiglione's *The Courtier* into English by Sir Thomas Hoby in 1561 only reinforced these ideals of civility, civic duty and active service; at the same time, prevailing opinion as to the nature of the education that might instil gentle virtues in well-born young men was also becoming more sophisticated and more wide-ranging. No longer was a traditional university education sufficient, but increasingly a gentleman must gain additional learning by foreign travel and further study at one of the Inns of Court. The Inns were enlarged under Elizabeth to provide for their growing clientele, and a stint at this centre of legal training became almost a prerequisite for a young man aiming for parliament. This latter was another suitable 'finishing' for a gentleman's education; the Commons provided a practical outlet for the rhetorical arts learned in the universities, and parliament was ever more popular a destination for the university graduate of gentle birth. Numerous other gentlemanly initiatives also flourished under Elizabeth, such as the Society of Antiquaries, which was founded in the mid-1580s by William Camden, amongst others, to provide a forum for the study of Britain's history and antiquarian artefacts. Nor were gentlewomen entirely neglected; it was increasingly common for girls to be educated to a modest standard in the homes of the wealthy gentry and nobility, even if very few families made provision for their daughters to learn any more than reading and writing in the vernacular, and the most basic Latin and Greek.

While these new forms of learning were springing up around England, the twin jewels in the crown of the Elizabethan education system were still the universities at Oxford and Cambridge. These remained emphatically closed to women, and in 1561 Elizabeth banned even the wives or female family members from coming within the college precincts in order to prevent them from 'distracting' the men engaged in academic study within their walls. The late sixteenth century saw subtle but critical adjustments to the universities' methods and functions, and the beginnings of a return to their former glory as internationally respected centres of learning. As other kinds of education expanded, so too did the universities, with admissions in the Elizabethan period nearly double those earlier in the sixteenth century. New colleges were founded: Emmanuel and Sidney Sussex at Cambridge in 1584 and 1596, and Jesus College at Oxford in 1571. University and college libraries swelled in size as the medieval practice of chaining books gave way to more modern methods of shelving, while developments in cataloguing led to the production of Thomas James's monumental *Ecloga Oxonio-Cantabrigiensis* (a collection of manuscripts catalogues in Oxford and Cambridge colleges) in 1600. Colleges such as Saint John's College and Christ Church, Oxford, followed the example of Magdalen, appointing librarians, and, between 1598 and 1602, Thomas Bodley restored the neglected library of Duke Humfrey. Keen interest from courtiers such as William Cecil, Robert Devereux, Robert Dudley and Christopher Hatton, all of whom served as chancellors at one of the universities, encouraged the transformation of the old intellectual centres. The Crown, too, was aware of the potential value of these tools of authority. The Queen and her Privy Council attempted to exercise a degree of control over the universities: in 1581, the new matriculation statutes at Oxford required all students to subscribe not only to the statutes of the University, but also to the Thirty-Nine Articles and the Royal Supremacy.

Nor did the syllabus remain unchanged, but mirrored the more tangible elements of the universities in adapting to the new requirements of the Elizabethan world. Teaching within colleges became firmly established, and although the statutes demonstrate little alteration in the chief subjects required of undergraduates, namely logic and rhetoric, the mediation of the syllabus to students by the colleges allowed for a remarkable degree of flexibility in the texts that were used. Superficially, the scholastic method remained enshrined in the statutes, focusing on a syllogistic and reductive study of primarily Aristotelian texts, but an increasingly humanist flavour pervaded the actual learning that went on within college walls. This was a state of affairs encouraged by the presence of growing numbers of young gentlemen who left without taking a degree and who attended because it was fashionable to do so; these made up roughly half of the undergraduate body. It may well be that there had long been these non-graduating, gentle fellow-commoners in the halls and colleges – the evidence is too sparse to be conclusive one way or another – but it is clear from writings surviving in the form of notebooks and diaries that growing pressure was placed upon individual tutors to tailor the curriculum to the more diverse and practical demands of these wealthy students.

The universities also played a major role in the perpetuation of a central feature of the age, one often neglected in modern scholarship: the Latin intellectual culture of Elizabethan England. Latinate learning was not a new development of the late Tudor years, for Latin had been the language of the intellectual elite for many centuries, but the Elizabethan years witnessed a flowering of English Latinity that marked the culmination of centuries of learned endeavour. Inspired by the humanist movement, England's Latin writers consciously emulated a fluid, classical style, moving away from the drier medieval Latin which had lingered until the mid-sixteenth century. These men produced a vigorous body of writings on every conceivable subject, stimulating and reflecting a vibrant Latinate culture among the intellectual elite which reached its zenith towards the end of Elizabeth's reign and was to disappear gradually over the course of the next hundred years.

This Elizabethan Latin culture was fostered by the grammar schools and thrived within the Church and at court. Its focal point, however, was in the universities, where scholarly and courtly learning interacted, and it flourished especially when publishing began again at Oxford and Cambridge after 1586. Latin provided a means of intellectual exchange with Continental scholars, and nearly all important debates among learned men even within England were conducted in Latin. Participation within this culture was necessarily limited to those who had a good command of the language: the educated elite, if not always the traditional nobility and gentry. Nonetheless, several important issues arising from learned Latinate culture percolated through society in the Elizabethan years, as disputes in the universities gave rise to new teaching methods and new materials for private and informal education.

The changing nature of the curricula of the schools and universities originated in part in the Latinate circles at the universities, as part of the international humanist reaction against scholasticism. Often referred to as an anti-Aristotelian movement, the widespread protests against the old style of learning were not a rejection of Aristotle himself, whose works continued to form the basis of undergraduate studies throughout the early modern period. There was, however, a strong move by some academics away from the traditional ways of teaching logic in the universities. The problems of medieval, scholastic Aristotelianism derived from a distortion of the original texts, where Aristotle's syllogistic method of presenting the fruits of knowledge had come to be seen as his method of obtaining knowledge; the result was a dry study of logic concerned more with itself than with any new discovery of learning. Opponents of this methodology included the Frenchman Petrus Ramus, who led a group of Continental thinkers seeking to reform and simplify the study of logic by reappropriating Aristotle's 'topics' and creating a system of classification by which a student could enter a common bank of wisdom in order to access an ordered, universal 'knowledge'. This challenge to tradition provoked strong reactions and left a lasting legacy in the wider system of formal education in England.

Ramism was always a controversial school of thought. It failed to replace the old system satisfactorily, and much of the traditional teaching of Aristotelian logic continued in the universities. But in the second half of Elizabeth's reign, Ramist ideas were actively discussed in intellectual circles, and Ramist influences can be detected in a wide variety of writings, most obviously in the pro-Ramist works of William Temple, *Admonitio de unica P Rami methodo* (1580), and *Pro mildapetti de unica methodo* (1581). Ramus's ideas gained in prominence after his death at the Saint Bartholomew's Day Massacre; his ideas were cannily linked with an ordered, Protestant way of thinking by the publisher of the 1574 English translation of his *Logic,* the title page of which advertised his martyrdom; anti-Catholic as well as anti-scholastic feeling was harnessed to the horse of Ramist rationalisation. Thus, Ramism took hold most firmly at the puritan centres in the universities, especially Magdalen College, Oxford, and Saint John's, Emmanuel, and Christ's Colleges, Cambridge, where it was embraced by men such as Lawrence Chaderton and Gabriel Harvey. The anti-hierarchical nature of Ramism, and its insistence on the availability and utility of knowledge, appealed to puritan idealists, who connected it with their professionalisation of the Protestant clergy. Notable preachers such as Thomas Cartwright and William Perkins were disciples of Ramus, and Ramist teaching in the Cambridge colleges was responsible for the dissemination of this new way of thinking throughout the land as young men graduated and went forth to preach. Translators of Ramus emphasised the potential for godly applications of his thought, using him as a model for sermons, and replacing ancient examples with biblical ones as Dudley Fenner did in his *Arts of Logic and Rhetoric* (1584). Graduates from the Ramist colleges also spread the new, simplified logic to the grammar schools. William Kempe of Trinity College, Cambridge, went on to become Master of Plymouth School and published a Ramist programme for the teaching of rhetoric and logic to boys, *The Education of Children in Learning* (1588); Charles Butler of Magdalen College, Oxford, went on to become Master of the Holy Ghost School in Basingstoke, and his *Rameae rhetoricae* (1597) was a highly popular Ramist school text, which ran into ten editions in the seventeenth century. Ramist diagrams were a popular way for students to organise their notes and can be seen even in university notebooks reflecting a very traditional course of study based on Aristotle. Even if Ramism failed to topple Aristotelian logic, elements of Ramus's thought certainly became prevalent in Elizabethan England and endured long afterward.

Another controversy within the Latin intellectual circles of the later sixteenth century was the oft-debated issue of Ciceronianism. The reign of Elizabeth dawned with a shifting appreciation of what elegant Latin writing should be, as medieval styles were shrugged off and Cicero's pure, golden-age Latin was increasingly adopted as the most desirable form of prose. Over the years, however, problems emerged with this 'Ciceronian' Latin, when writers attempted excessive emulation of Cicero, refusing to use words that had not existed in the first century BCE; theological writers ran into difficulties using the word *flamen,* meaning a priest who served in the temples of Ancient Rome, to describe a Protestant minister, and thus imparting a pagan flavour to their works entirely at odds with their sentiments. Complaints about excessively zealous Ciceronians abounded; Philip Sidney famously wrote to his younger brother Robert in 1580 that Ciceronianism was 'the chief abuse of Oxford'.[13] The anti-Ciceronians were not really opposed to Cicero being the chief model of Latin style any more than Ramists opposed the teaching of Aristotle; rather, it was the way in which Aristotle was taught, or Cicero copied, that was the problem, a dry insistence on particulars and rules which prevented any advances and which privileged style over content. Gabriel Harvey's *Ciceronianus* is the most comprehensive statement of the case. Published in 1577, the work explains that Cicero is indeed the best Latin writer, but the Ciceronians err in only ever following Cicero, to the neglect of all other authors. Shades of the humanist insistence on practical utility in learning can be discerned in Harvey's work, which emphasises the importance of correct meaning and good content in Latin writing, rather than an empty concentration on words; influenced by Ramus' *Ciceronianus,* Harvey insists that a good writer must study the other masters of the Latin language, such as Caesar, Livy, Sallust, Pliny, Virgil, as well as Cicero, and read the writings of modern scholars such as Ramus, Freigius and Erasmus. This more moderate attitude to modelling prose on Cicero found great favour in England, and during the Elizabethan period the Latin language developed accordingly until a fluid and graceful style was commonly preferred over strict Ciceronian phrasing.

That this was increasingly the case is demonstrated by the large number of guides on the writing of elegant Latin that were published under Elizabeth, both for schools and for private use. Castellio's *Dialogorum sacrorum libri quatuor* (1560) and Cordier's *Colloquiorum scholasticorum libri quatuour* (1584) were intended for use in schools and ran into many editions by the end of the century. Dictionaries and thesauruses poured from the presses, in English–Latin and Latin–English format; the standard text was Thomas Cooper's *Thesaurus linguae romanae et britannicae* (1565), which entered at least four more editions over the next three decades. As the standard of English Latin writing reached a comparable level with that on the Continent, so the number and variety of works written in Latin by Englishmen increased. Latin, with its greater vocabulary and more developed syntax, was the language of choice for serious, scholarly writings on any topic, and it provided a medium for participation in European intellectual culture. Books were published across borders: several hundred books by English writers were published in Latin in France, Germany and Italy in the second half of the sixteenth century, and the works of European Latin scholars were produced in England. Some of these works were theological, for Latin was the language English scholars had to use to engage in international religious debate and defend the Elizabethan settlement against Continental detractors. Latin writings on other subjects also increased in number, whether the writing was prose, poetry or drama; the years from 1570 onwards saw the great renaissance of literature in England, not only in English but also in Latin. One in every ten works printed in England during the reign of Elizabeth was a piece of Latin writing, and this proportion becomes even more significant when it is remembered that, unlike English printed material, very little of the Latin writing was ephemeral or trivial.

Care must be taken when generalising about the readership of intellectual writings: the demarcation between 'high' culture, as embodied by elite Latinate learning, and what is commonly called 'popular culture' is often too firmly drawn, and it is clear that many different relationships existed between various groups of readers in society and their Latin and English texts. As Latin literature flourished, it was accompanied by a new vitality in vernacular intellectual culture. Men and women who participated in England's classical, Latinate culture also took part in English intellectual activities, while it is by no means certain that even those further down the social scale were entirely excluded from an interaction with Latin texts. A strong second-hand book trade and a large import market make it hard to reconstruct the size of readerships accurately, but it is probable that by the end of the reign of Elizabeth there was a significant audience for all kinds of intellectual printed material a fair way down the social order. Growing out of the expanding provision of education and connected with the print trade in a symbiotic relationship, a rise in reading literacy encouraged the production of both scholarly and less learned works in the English language, while the increasing availability of vernacular reading materials stimulated interest in owning and reading such texts. Cheap print was available for just a few pence and could be passed around communities or transmitted orally through group readings in the home even where functional literacy was lacking. The print trade actively contributed to the dissemination of learning, producing a growing number of titles aimed at an increasingly broad market. Between 1558 and 1603, there were 7,430 new titles published in England, over 1,000 of which were original, English sermons. One in every ten titles was a book specifically designed for educational purposes, such as primers and grammars, while the proportion of titles that can be broadly defined as 'literature' rose over the period from thirteen to twenty-five percent of the market.

The large number of classical texts translated into English for the first time is perhaps the clearest demonstration of the increasing availability of intellectual reading matter in the vernacular. The Elizabethan age saw over 170 English translations of ancient Greek and Latin works, making the old learning accessible to those without the time, inclination or ability to read the classics in their original languages. Notoriously reluctant to print in Latin, the English press relied on the import of Latin and Greek works from Europe; in many cases, English translations were often produced in England long before English printers began producing the original language edition of a text. The work of the Roman historian Florus, for example, appeared in an English version by Philemon Holland in 1600, but no Latin editions were printed in England until well into the reign of Charles I. Translations were an important part of the Protestant, humanist ideology, functioning as a medium through which the governing classes might be efficiently educated, and through which important knowledge and values might be made available to a greater number of men and women. This was the great age of classical translation, led in the early years by men such as Arthur Golding, who translated Justinus' *Historia* (1564), Caesar's *Commentaries* and Ovid's *Metamorphoses* (1565), and the works of Seneca (1578); a second edition of his Caesar was issued in 1590. One of the most popular of all classical texts, Richard North's translation of Plutarch's *Lives,* was first published in 1579, appearing in further, augmented editions again in the same year, and in 1595 and 1603. William Barker produced a translation of Appian's *Roman History* (1578), and Christopher Marlowe's version of Lucan's *Pharsalia* appeared in 1600. The end of Elizabeth's reign also saw the start of Philemon Holland's long career as a provider of classical learning in the vernacular; as well as his translation of Florus, he produced an English version of Livy (1600), following it with translations of Pliny's *Natural History* (1601) and Plutarch's *Moralia* (1603). Numerous editions of the works of Cicero appeared in English throughout the period, supplementing the Latin copies that were used as school textbooks and for more advanced private study. Collections of excerpts from translations of classical works also gained in popularity, with books of epigrams and compendia of quotations becoming increasingly numerous; they were joined by printed commonplace books as aids to improvement and learning, providing distillations of knowledge suitable for quick reference and easy assimilation. Timothy Kendall's *Floweres of Epigrams* (1577) and the highly popular *Wit's Commonwealth* (1597) are but two examples of a large body of such works.

Indeed, so important was the translation of texts considered that it became a literary art in its own right, an enterprise that promoted the good of the commonwealth, and these altruistic aims were stated in textual introductions and prefaces to the readers. Often accused of cheapening learning by those who jealously guarded their privileged access to knowledge, the Elizabethan translators presented their activities as a duty and emphasised all mankind's right to experience the learning of the classical past, just as some groups of Protestants advocated a common right to the Scriptures. Abraham Flemming's translation of letters by Cicero, Pliny and Isocrates (1576) was subtitled, 'a looking glasse for the unlearned'; the epistle by the translator is addressed 'to the learned and unlearned Reader'. It states the intention of offering 'pleasure to the learned . . . and profite to the unlearned', since the contents of the work will 'arme and enable them against ignoraunce, the adversarie and sworne enimie of understanding'.[14] Philemon Holland explains to his readers that, in translating Livy, he has a desire 'to performe in some sort, that which is profitable to the most'. Therefore, he continues, 'according to this purpose & intent of mine I framed my pen, not to any affected phrase, but to a meane and popular stile'. His ultimate hope is that the learning contained within Livy would spread far and wide through his translation, 'not as a traveller to sojourn for a time, in the Court only or the Universities; but to remain here still both in city and country'.[15]

Important as the increases in availability of traditional forms of education and scholarship were, perhaps the greatest intellectual advances in Elizabethan England occurred in 'new' fields of learning. This was an era in which knowledge was rapidly expanding, along with notions of what knowledge could be, and the second half of the sixteenth century saw the laying of the foundations of the scientific revolution and the beginnings of a new philosophy of learning. Learning was not yet concerned with the search for absolute truth, since truth was the province of God; rather, artists and natural philosophers sought to create virtue through which they might attain knowledge, in order to glorify God and, increasingly, England, through their endeavours. This emphasis on activity and on attaining knowledge by means of practical creation reflects the contemporary ideals of virtuous action and civic duty, and was driven at least in part by the new opportunities arising from overseas exploration and commercial competition, which gave rise to many new manuals and innovative methods of self-education which formed a crucial part of intellectual culture in the Elizabethan years.

Commerce with Europe, intellectual as well as mercantile, was fostered by prominent Elizabethan traders and courtiers. London's Royal Exchange, founded by Sir Thomas Gresham in 1565 and officially opened by the Queen in 1571, provided a forum for the exchange of ideas across international boundaries, as the practitioners of the new scientific arts from several nations came together to discuss their ideas as they were applied in commercial activities. The public's interest in mechanical and scientific developments deepened as immigrants brought with them new and complex devices for telling the time, and the trade in mechanical instruments testifies to their increasing worth as 'cultural currency'.[16] A growing realisation that communication with foreigners was essential to England's commercial relations prompted an interest in the learning of vernacular European languages, and the influx of religious refugees from France especially improved the private learning of French in England. Two of the most famous manuals produced as aids to language learning were by the second-generation immigrant, Claude de Sainliens, popularly known as 'Holyband'. His book *The French Schoolemaster* was first published in 1573, while a simplified pocket version, *The French Littleton,* digested its contents for easy access. These works concentrated on the practical uses of language, and were designed to teach men how to speak French in order to communicate. Holyband also produced more theoretical texts for those seeking a deeper understanding of the French language, including several dictionaries and guides to the declension of verbs, but it was the practical guides that proved the most popular, entering numerous editions after their first publication.

Many of those who did not need to communicate directly with foreigners also felt an increased need to share in the learning produced in Europe. The classics remained important for a general education, but the new knowledge being 'produced' on the Continent was also translated into English in quantities never seen before, in order that England could compete on an international basis, as the translators often implied. When George Baker translated Gesner's *The New Jewel of Health* (1576), he observed how far the English fell behind their Continental counterparts, 'For what kinde of science or knowledge ever was invented by man, which is not nowe in the Italian or French?'[17] And in 1580, John Florio translated Jacques Cartier's *A Short and Brief Narration of the Two Navigations and Discoveries to the Northwest Parts Called New France* as an incitement to trade with the New World, intending 'to animate and encourage the English marchants' by demonstrating the gains 'which both the Spaniards, the Portugales, and the Venetians have severally gained by suche navigations and travailes'.[18]

The Elizabethan age also saw the rise of a new kind of historical consciousness and the development of a national identity legitimated by ancient precedents. As defenders of the English Church searched the past for historical justifications to be used in the debates accompanying the rise of Protestantism, an interest in a specifically English past was stimulated. History had long been held by the humanists to be a valuable subject of study, prized for its ability to instil good morals in readers, and, increasingly, under Elizabeth writers produced works focusing on England's past as well as that of the classical world. Chronicle histories in the medieval style were expanded: Richard Grafton's *An Abridgement of the Chronicles of England* (1562) developed material from John Hardyng's early-fifteenth-century work and appeared in five further editions over the following decade, each expanding its scope up to the year of publication. John Stow's rival *Summary of English Chronicles* (1565) charted English history from the arrival of the Trojan Brutus until the year of publication; it was issued again several times, notably in 1592 as *The Annals of England,* the title most commonly used today. In 1577, Raphael Holinshed's *Chronicle* was published, a huge tome of nearly 3,000 pages of British history, which entered another, augmented edition ten years later.

In addition to these larger, chronicle histories, an antiquarian interest in the precise details of England's past developed, characterised by a focus on original documents and material evidence such as coins and architectural ruins and a concern with the classification of evidence, marking the beginning of the development of the modern historical method. Antiquarianism moved away from the traditional humanist concept of history as a form of literature; new discoveries abroad emphasised the importance of accurate information in the form of charts and geographical descriptions, and the English response was a comparative cataloguing of England in a detailed and precise manner by the regional antiquarians known as chorographers. Again, the glorification of God and of England was a common aim among these chorographers, who claimed England as God's chosen country; as John Norden wrote in the introduction to his regional study of Middlesex, published in 1593, he had undertaken the work 'with a desire to take pains to profite my Countrey', that England which 'may be truely called Olbion a happie Countrie'.[19] Chorography included geography as well as history, along with elements of mathematics and cartography, as an area was described as exactly as possible with reference both to its past and present state. The tradition, with its origins in classical works by Ptolemy, Strabo and Pliny, developed in a peculiarly English fashion during Elizabeth's reign, with county studies being produced separately until William Camden's *Britannia,* first published in Latin in 1586, set a whole new standard for such works by presenting a survey of the whole of England. The work had reached its sixth edition by 1607, and its popularity shows the growing importance of national studies in an age where state identity was a matter of concern as the worldview expanded.

Scientific knowledge, too, began to evolve in Elizabethan England in ways that laid the foundations for the modernisation of method and practice over the following centuries. These changes in England's intellectual culture were substantially shaped by the effects of Europe's religious wars, by the influx of refugees seeking safety in Elizabeth's Protestant havens, their individual communities and the ways in which they became integrated into Elizabethan society, particularly in the capital. The results of the London census of 1571 show that one in twenty people living in the city was a non-native worker; these immigrants included not only refugees from the Netherlands but also French, Danish, Spanish, Italian and Portugese men and women, bringing with them 'Strange' attitudes and values.[20] The first decades of Elizabeth's reign saw the introduction of new ideas on mathematics and God by lay thinkers from the Netherlands and Italy, linking science and mysticism in order to arrive at new knowledge about the nature of creation, often underpinned by conciliatory impulses, while in the field of natural science the impact of foreign ideas can be clearly seen, with numerous immigrant surgeons, midwives, alchemists, instrument-makers and distillers working in Elizabethan England. Negotiation, competition and compromise between the newcomers and existing practitioners influenced the patterns of scientific advances, with collaborative projects and independent areas of research depending on the relationships between English and 'Strange' workers. A significant proportion of these practitioners of natural science were women, working not only in the more traditionally 'female' fields of midwifery and herbal remedies but also in other areas of empirical scientific study. Here, in London's cosmopolitan environment, the culture of the 'new' learning created spaces which women could fill, taking on roles which were denied them in most other spheres of life.

Experimentalism was a shared value among those working in the scientific arts, with an emphasis on practical observation rather than theory. Francis Bacon is often regarded as the first proponent of experimentalism. His natural philosophy is seen as the basis of the scientific revolution, calling for practical, empirical research in a clear application of the humanist ideal of the *vita activa*. The famous Baconian writings of the early seventeenth century were firmly rooted in his works of the 1590s, which stated the aridity of scholastic disputation which 'never brought to light one effect of nature before unknown' but only deconstructed itself.[21] In fact, much of what he suggested as necessary for the advancement of knowledge – a large body of experimentalists and observers working in non-traditional, practical ways – was at least partly an articulation of existing practices rather than a completely innovative ideology. Bacon's status and his position as one of the educated elite moving in courtly circles are one of the reasons his scientific thought is so much better known than the practices of his urban contemporaries, both male and female, of the middling sort.[22]

But not all forms of experimental research found favour in Elizabethan England, and Bacon was merely one of many critics of less skilled scientific practitioners, warning that the purity of natural philosophy was being tainted by 'quacks' and charlatans, and by dangerous ideas imported from the Continent. Nowhere was this complaint more strongly articulated than in the opposition to the alchemical arts. Alchemy has always had a murky reputation, fed by rumour and misconception; popular notions of alchemy in early modern England associated it with astrology and the occult, with cabbalistic beliefs and with the search for immortality or artificial gold. In fact, the alchemical sciences that developed in the Elizabethan period were a peculiarly English brand of compromise, drawing on the writings of the German philosopher Paracelsus (1493–1541) in a highly selective and moderate fashion. Far from being the gnostic heresies that his detractors would have had the public believe, Paracelsus' ideas were a synthesis of medicine, chemistry and cosmography, a natural magic that aimed at a deeper understanding of God through an analysis of the relationship between the macrocosm that was the universe and the microcosm that was man. Anti-Aristotelian in the same way that Ramists and Baconians would later become, Paracelsus himself saw his philosophy as based upon faith and prayer, more religious and pious than Aristotelian, pagan logic, which did not advance knowledge; moreover, it had practical uses, since through the study of nature, cures could be found for bodily ills. This aspect of Paracelsian philosophy was the one which found a lasting home in English scientific thought; in nearly all cases where alchemical ideas were expressed in England, the connection between medicine and chemistry was emphasised, and it is probably more helpful to speak of the English iatrochemists rather than 'alchemists' or 'Paracelsians'.

Paracelsian thought developed nearly half a century later in England than in the rest of Europe, and in different ways. As with much of the newer kind of learning, it was moderated in ways that would fit it for the Elizabethan context, with an emphasis on practical and commercial utility. The first real publicity the philosophy received was through Erastus' attack on Paracelsus, reproduced in a preface written by the surgeon George Baker in 1574; earlier accounts by William Turner and

William Bullein had made reference to Paracelsian ideas in works on the waters at Bath and on surgery, but these had had little real impact. Certain aspects of Paracelsianism, however, were more successfully imported and propagated. This is particularly the case for medicinal chemical thought ('iatrochemistry'), which had formed only a small part of Paracelsus' own writings but which was less religiously controversial and practically far more useful than many of his other ideas. Chemical medicine arrived in England through translations of Konrad Gesner's recipe books which gave instructions on preparations of chemical cures; these included *The Treasure of Euonymus* (1559), the second part of which was translated by Thomas Hill and published in 1576 as the very popular *New Jewel of Health*. The works of Gesner advocated iatrochemistry but the author was deeply suspicious of wider Paracelsian thought; they therefore contributed to the development of a very limited English Paracelsianism which bore little resemblance to German alchemical thought other than in a belief that chemical medicines could cure human ailments.

This selective, practical medicine based on chemistry was a significant development in Elizabethan scientific thought, adopted by individual natural philosophers and established institutions alike. Care was taken by exponents of this medical philosophy to stress its compatibility with Elizabethan society and religion, as may be clearly seen in *The Difference between the Ancient Physic . . . and the Latter Physic* (1585), an apology for Paracelsianism written by Richard Bostocke. Bostocke emphasised the aim of the 'chemical philosophers' as the search after the Holy Trinity in everything they did, the triune God in whom were mirrored the three key elements of salt, sulphur and mercury of which all things were made. For Bostocke, medicine was 'the searching out of the secretes of nature . . . the exercise whereof is Mechanicall, and to be accomplished with labor'; furthermore, it was an appropriate science for any true Protestant since iatrochemistry was a pure and ancient form art whose original practitioners were Adam, Moses and Abraham.[23] The traditional, Galenic medicine was a gross, heathen corruption of this original, God-given science, polluted by centuries of Catholic, Aristotelian scholastic study. That Bostocke's vindication of chemical medicine was generally accepted is demonstrated in the way in which iatrochemistry found favour even in the heart of the medical establishment. In 1589, the Royal College of Physicians in London included a section on chemical remedies in the plans for its pharmacopoeia of medicines; although the work was not completed at the time, the college's sympathy to the new science was reflected in its welcoming of physicians who used the chemical methods. Acceptance of medicinal chemistry was also evidenced in the books of chemical recipes published by John Hester, and texts on medicines such as the *Antidotarie* of the surgeon John Banister (1589) and William Clever's compendium *The Flower of Physic* (1590). Most famously, John Gerarde's *Herball* (1597) promoted iatrochemistry while dissociating it from Paracelsianism; an appended letter by Stephen Bredwell called for an end to Paracelsian thought in England while simultaneously crying for the establishment of a lectureship in chemistry at the Royal College of Physicians. By 1603, a typically English intellectual consensus had been reached, whereby chemical medicine was revered for its practical uses, while the Paracelsian theory from which it had been derived was widely discarded.

A similar Elizabethan modification occurred in the field of mathematics. Traditionally viewed with suspicion and, like alchemy, suffering from scholastic and occult taints, the mathematical arts were not highly regarded in the early years of Elizabeth's reign. Indeed, Roger Ascham's *Schoolmaster* specifically warned of the dangers of too much mathematical study, protesting that 'some wittes, moderate enough by nature, be many tymes marde by ouer moch studie and vse of some sciences, namelie, Musicke, Arithmetick, and Geometrie'.[24] In the 1560s, schools only used the most basic of mathematical textbooks, and accounts were still kept in Roman numerals; texts concerned with the education of a gentleman such as Elyot's *Book Named the Governor* often entirely ignored the subject. Yet mathematics did develop during the Elizabethan period, owing to the promotion of its practical uses by mathematicians and their patrons, who exploited utilitarian aspects of maths for the advancement of the English nation. Mathematics could serve the Elizabethan interests of 'serving God' and 'furdering the Weale, common or private', as John Dee explained in his *Mathematical Preface* to the first English translation of Euclid's *Element of Geometry* (1570); he pointed out the utility of branches of the mathematical arts such as astronomy, cosmography, statistics and geometry, also stating how important it was for the physician, the judge and the military commander to have a sound grasp of arithmetic.[25] Pure mathematics for its own sake remained of marginal interest, but the practical implications of mathematical learning were considerable, as intellectual society swiftly realised. Thus, when Thomas Hood, Fellow of Trinity College, Cambridge, was appointed as the first lecturer for the London mathematical lectureship contrived by Sir Thomas Smith in the wake of the Armada of 1588, he was detailed to provide mathematical learning in an appropriate form for the captains of London's trained bands, teaching the subject as it could be applied to fortification, surveying and gunnery, that they might be prepared to meet the threat of Spanish invasion.

Indeed, military and naval mathematics gained enormous popularity, and the advances that were made in practical, navigational techniques through new, mathematical methods resulted in a striking reform of maritime trade and exploration. At the beginning of the reign, experience had been the basis of navigational skill, with pilots plying the same trade routes they had always sailed and which they had learned as young apprentices. By the end of the century, voyages of exploration had ventured forth to seek a north-eastern and a north-western passage to Asia via the Arctic, and expeditions had sailed to found colonies in the New World. The initial disasters and losses lessened over the years as new technologies derived from mathematics and astronomy became more widespread and new instruments were introduced, allowing the navigation of unfamiliar waters. As in so many other areas of intellectual improvement, the impetus to innovate came largely from external sources: from the sense that England needed to keep up with rivals on the Continent, from the new discoveries made in far-flung corners of the world, and from the investors and merchants who employed the pilots in order to make their money. Traditional navigational methods used unreliable magnetic compasses and rutters, books of landmarks and clues, so that a pilot had to be familiar with his route if he was to arrive safely. But in order to expand their profits and recover investments, merchants needed to enter the Asian markets, trading in precious spices, and Asia was only accessible in the 1560s by the two southern passages, which were controlled by the Spanish and the Portuguese. New routes were needed, which could only be discovered by exploration of uncharted waters. A merchant investing in trade overseas also needed to know if his project was likely to be successful, for he could be ruined if it failed; mathematical, rather than experiential, navigation gave him an opportunity to understand the risks of a voyage, and make an informed judgement.

The new learning was often imported, most notably from the skilled navigators of the Netherlands and the Iberian peninsula. Spanish navigational knowledge was brought to England by Stephen Boroughs, who returned home in 1560 after spending time at the *Casa de Contratación* in Seville, and who clearly understood the need for England to catch up with Continental developments. He brought with him a Spanish manual, which was translated as *The Arte of Navigation* (1561), the first English-language navigation handbook. The book included sections on new instruments that should be used and stressed the importance of mathematical techniques for good navigation. Dutch influences also shaped the improvement of English mathematical navigation in the later Elizabethan period; in 1588, Anthony Ashley's *Mirror of the Sea* was published, a translation of a Dutch manual by Lucas Janszoon Wagenaer. Commissioned by the Privy Council at the instigation of the Lord High Admiral Howard of Effingham, it was issued as an explanation of the new, Dutch set of sea charts of Western Europe, the North Sea and the Baltic, which were the most accurate ever produced. Most significantly of all, there was a shift in the 1590s towards acceptance of Gerard Mercator's thirty-year-old method allowing for the curve of the seas, marking the beginning of the end of the old system of plain charts; Edward Wright's *Certain Errors in Navigation* and the 1599 edition of Hakluyt's *Principal Navigations* both publicised the flaws of the old charts and heralded a new age of charting the oceans. By the end of Elizabeth's reign, books and treatises on new navigational techniques were common, and the practices were broadly accepted; *The Seamans Secrets* (1595) by the Arctic explorer John Davis, treated practical navigation, while Thomas Blundeville's popular *Exercises* (1594) for young gentlemen stressed the importance of mathematical learning.[26] Mathematics, when practically applied, had become irrevocably useful to English development, and it was widely accepted, as it had never been before, that upon the mathematical arts could be built a flourishing commercial empire.

In 1603, England still had a long road to travel before arriving at the era of the scientific revolution and the dawning of the truly 'modern' age. Part of the significance of the Elizabethan intellectual context lies in England's medieval past: the late sixteenth century represents the pinnacle of classical culture, giving expression to the full realisation of centuries of Latin legacy in a newly revitalised way which would never again be repeated. However, in the fundamental shift in certain circles from an Aristotelian, logic-based learning to a broader experimental philosophy can be found the seeds of modern scientific thought, while the new forms of natural philosophy and the emphasis on schooling find echoes in today's educational methods. Above all, the expansion of learning and concepts of what learning could be, and the application of new skills and technologies in the service of commerce, have given us an Elizabethan intellectual inheritance from which our contemporary society derives much of its character.

FURTHER READING

Literacy

Stephens, W. B., 'Literacy in England, Scotland and Wales, 1500–1900', *History of Education Quarterly*, 30 (4) (1990): 545–71.

Wheale, Nigel, *Writing and Society: Literacy, Print and Politics in Britain 1590–1660* (London, 1999).

Schools

Baldwin, T. W., *William Shakespere's Small Latine & Lesse Greeke* (Urbana, Ill., 1944).

Jewell, Helen M., *Education in Early Modern England* (London, 1998).

O'Day, Rosemary, *Education and Society, 1500–1800* (London, 1982).

Simon, Joan, *Education and Society in Tudor England* (Cambridge, 1966).

Stone, Lawrence, 'The Educational Revolution in England, 1560–1640', *Past and Present,* 28 (1) (1964): 41–80.

Universities

Feingold, Mordecai, 'The Humanities', in Nicholas Tyacke (ed.), *The History of the University of Oxford, Vol. III: Seventeenth Century Oxford* (Oxford, 1997), pp. 211–357.

McConica, James (ed.), *The History of the University of Oxford, Vol. III: The Collegiate University* (Oxford, 1986).

Morgan, Victor (ed.), *A History of the University of Cambridge, Vol. II: 1546–1750* (Cambridge, 2004).

Todd, Margot, *Christian Humanism and the Puritan Social Order* (Cambridge, 1987).

Latin intellectual culture

Binns, J. W., *Intellectual Culture in Elizabethan and Jacobean England: The Latin Writings of the Age* (Leeds, 1990).

History and antiquarianism

Hadfield, Andrew, *Literature, Politics and National Identity: Reformation to Renaissance* (Cambridge, 1994).

Mendyk, Stan A. E., *'Speculum Britanniae': Regional Study, Antiquarianism, and Science in Britain to 1700* (Toronto, 1989).

Woolf, D. R., *The Social Circulation of the Past: English Historical Culture, 1500–1730* (Oxford, 2003).

Science, medicine and natural philosophy

Debus, A. G., *The English Paracelsians* (London, 1965).

Gaukroger, Stephen, *Francis Bacon and the Transformation of Early Modern Philosophy* (Cambridge, 2001).

Harkness, Deborah E., '"Strange" Ideas and "English" Knowledge: Natural Science Exchange in Elizabethan London', in Pamela H. Smith and Paula Finden (eds.), *Merchants and Marvels: Commerce, Science and Art in Early Modern Europe* (New York and London, 2002).

—— *The Jewel House: Elizabethan London and the Scientific Revolution* (New Haven, Conn., 2007).

Spiller, Elizabeth, *Science, Reading and Renaissance Literature: The Art of Making Knowledge, 1580–1670* (Cambridge, 2004).

Navigation and mathematics

Ash, Eric H., *Power, Knowledge and Expertise in Elizabethan England* (Baltimore, Md., 2004).

NOTES

1 Roger Ascham, *The Scholemaster . . .* (London, 1570), sig. 11r.
2 Church of England, *A Booke of Certaine Canons, Concernyng Some Parte of the Discipline of the Churche of England* (London, 1571), sig. Div.
3 Quoted in Kenneth Charlton, *Education in Renaissance England* (London, 1965), p. 95.
4 Richard Mulcaster, *Positions Vvherin Those Primitiue Circumstances Be Examined, which Are Necessarie for the Training Vp of Children, Either for Skill in Their Booke, or Health in Their Bodie. Vvritten by Richard Mulcaster, Master of the Schoole Erected in London Anno .1561. in the Parish of Sainct Laurence Povvntneie, by the Vvorshipfull Companie of the Merchaunt Tailers of the Said Citie* (London, 1581), sig. Riiir.
5 Mulcaster, *Positions*, sig. Sir, Siiv–Siiir.
6 Ascham, *Scholemaster*, sig. 4r.
7 *Iniunctions Geven by the Quenes Maiestie . . .* (London, 1559), sig. Ciiir (Injunction 41).
8 Church of England, *A Booke of Certaine Canons*, sig. Dir.
9 Francis Clement, *The Petie Schole . . .* (London, 1587), sig. Aiiv.
10 John Hart, *A Methode or Comfortable Beginning for All Vnlearned, Whereby They May Be Taught to Read English in a Very Short Time, Vvith Pleasure* (London, 1570), sig. *2r.
11 Richard Mulcaster, *The First Part of the Elementarie Vvhich Entreateth Chefelie of the Right Writing of Our English Tung* (London, 1582), sig. *Iiiiv.
12 Humphrey Gilbert, 'The Erection of an Achademy in London', fol. 6v; quoted in Eric H. Ash, *Power, Knowledge and Expertise in Elizabethan England* (Baltimore, Md., 2004), p. 1.
13 Quoted in Charlton, *Education in Renaissance England*, p. 153.
14 Abraham Flemming, *A Panoplie of Epistles; or, A Looking Glasse for the Vnlearned . . . Gathered and Translated Out of Latine into English, by Abraham Flemming* (London, 1576), sig. 5r.
15 Livy, *The Romane Historie Vvritten by T. Livius of Padua. Also, the Breviaries of L. Florus . . . Translated Out of Latine into English, by Philemon Holland, Doctor in Physicke* (London, 1600), 'To the Reader'.
16 Deborah E. Harkness, '"Strange" Ideas and "English" Knowledge: Natural Science Exchange in Elizabethan London', in Pamela H Smith and Paula Finden (eds.), *Merchants and Marvels: Commerce, Science and Art in Early Modern Europe* (New York and London, 2002), pp. 137–62; p. 147.
17 Konrad Gesner, *The Newe Iewell of Health* (London, 1576), sig. *3r.
18 Quoted in Louis B. Wright, *Middle-Class Culture in Elizabethan England* (Ithaca, NY, 1935), p. 526.
19 John Norden, *Speculum Britanniae* (London, 1593), sig. A3v, B4v.
20 Harkness, '"Strange"' Ideas', p. 138.
21 Francis Bacon, 'Mr Bacon in Praise of Learning' (composed 1592); quoted in Joan Simon, *Education and Society in Tudor England* (Cambridge, 1966), p. 393.
22 Bacon, 'Mr Bacon in Praise of Learning.'
23 Richard Bostocke, *The Difference betwene the Auncient Phisicke, First Taught by the Godly Forefathers . . . and the Latter Phisicke Proceeding from Idolaters, Ethnickes, and Heathen . . . and Wherein the Naturall Philosophie of Aristotle Doth Differ from the*

Trueth of Gods Worde, and Is Iniurious to Christianitie and Sounde Doctrine (London, 1585), sig. Bir.

24 Ascham, *Scholemaster*, sig. Div.

25 Euclid, *The Elements of Geometrie of the Most Auncient Philosopher Euclide of Megara. Faithfully (Now First) Translated into the Englishe Toung, by H. Billingsley, Citizen of London. Whereunto Are Annexed Certaine Scholies, Annotations, and Inuentions, of the Best Mathematiciens, Both of Time Past, and in This Our Age. With a Very Fruitfull Praeface Made by M. I. Dee* (London, 1570), sig. Aiiiir.

26 John Davis, *The Seamans Secrets Deuided into 2 Partes* ... (London, 1595); Thomas Blundeville, *M. Blundevile His Exercises Containing Sixe Treatises* (London, 1594).

CHAPTER THIRTY-ONE

THEATRE

Lawrence Manley

In *Palladis Tamia,* his 1598 survey of English cultural achievements, Francis Meres singles out Shakespeare for special distinction: 'As *Plautus and Seneca* are accounted the best for Comedy and Tragedy among the Latines: so Shakespeare among ye English is the most excellent in both kinds for the stage.' Meres goes on, however, to posit a series of parallels through which Englishmen rival all the achievements of the ancient world. Just as 'Tragicke Poets flourished in Greece ... and ... among the Latines', so 'our best for Tragedie' include 'the Lord *Buckhurst,* Doctor *Leg* of Cambridge, Doctor *Edes,* of Oxforde, master Edward Ferris, the Authour of *The Mirrour for Magistrates, Marlow, Peele, Watson, Kid, Shakespeare, Drayton, Chapman, Decker,* and *Benjamin Johnson.*' Against 'the best Poets for Comedy among the Greekes ... and Latines' Meres touts

> the best for Comedy amongst us ... *Edward* Earle of Oxforde, Doctor *Gager* of Oxforde, Maister Rowley once a rare Scholler of learned Pembrooke Hall in Cambridge, Maister Edwardes one of her Majesties Chappell, eloquent and wittie *John Lilly, Lodge, Gascoyne, Greene, Shakespeare, Thomas Nash, Thomas Heywood, Anthony Mundye* our best plotter, *Chapman, Porter, Wilson, Hathway,* and *Henry Chettle.*[1]

Meres's survey points, at the end of the age of Elizabeth I, to what is at once a cultural Renaissance, based on the humanist ideal of reviving antiquity, and a national self-realisation that has given Englishmen what the poet Edmund Spenser had called a 'kingdom of our own language'.[2]

Meres's catalogue assembles a remarkable social diversity within its precise hierarchical framework. Moving simultaneously downward through social ranks and chronologically forward from the first decade of Elizabeth's reign to the late Elizabethan popular stage, Meres names two peers of the realm (Buckhurst, Oxford), four members of the universities (Legge, Edes, Gager, Rowley), two court officials (Ferrers, Edwards), three MAs (Peele, Lyly, Greene), two BAs (Marlowe, Nashe), two college dropouts (Watson, Heywood), two members of the Inns of Court (Lodge, Gascoyne), the sons of a scrivener, a glover, a butcher, a yeoman copyholder, a dyer and a stationer (Kyd, Shakespeare, Drayton, Chapman, Chettle, Munday), two writers whose fathers are obscure (Dekker, Jonson) and three writers (Porter, Wilson, Hathaway) who, with Chettle, are known mainly for their collaboration in authoring ready-made plays for Philip Henslowe, owner of the Rose Theatre. The inclusiveness and diversity of Meres's list, which amounts to a microcosm of English society, reminds us that Elizabethan drama was created not just by authors but in and by a variety of social institutions, from the court to universities and schools, to civic entities, to the private and public commercial stage. With this institutional variety go the many influences and purposes that shaped Elizabethan theatre – the humanist revival of the classics, the academic cultivation of eloquence, the deliberation of political and religious agendas, the spectacular celebration of power, the commercialisation of popular culture. None of these developments are wholly separable from the others. Their reciprocal connections made Elizabethan theatre a medium of extraordinary cultural complexity and richness.

To see Elizabethan theatre in the light of overlapping institutions and spheres of interest, Paul Yachnin has explained, is to avoid the two extremes of narrow agent-centred explanation (the pursuit of fixed ideas and agendas by individual authors, actors, companies, and patrons) and totalising accounts of a disembodied hegemonic authority and its equally disembodied subverters. To understand how specific institutions and agendas could reciprocate, and why the result could be the cultural achievement Meres celebrates, it is worth noting at the outset, and at the risk of totalising, some of the common features of theatrical performance in the period. The most obvious of these is the communal nature of performance, its association with particular bodies: the school, the great house, the court, the parish, town, or civic guild, the theatrical partnership, the commercial theatre. Second, and following from this communal background, is the derivation of theatrical performance from, and in most cases its continuing association with, holiday festivities that marked crucial transitions in the ceremonial year. By tradition, theatrical performance was associated with the major religious feasts: the religious cycle plays of the urban guilds were linked to the feasts of Corpus Christi and, later, Whitsuntide, while performances at court, at the Inns of Court, and at schools and universities were principally associated with Christmas and the extended festive season from Advent through Shrovetide, when the court revels, the Boy Bishop or Lord of Misrule at the universities, and the Christmas Prince at the Inns of Court hosted festive proceedings that included plays and interludes. Like great-house performances, which stemmed from the medieval relation between lord and minstrel (the term 'interlude' designates a performance between courses of a festive meal), theatre in these other settings was governed, in the spirit of *communitas,* by a degree of licence that gave permission to air controversy within the limits of play and imaginative hypothesis. Like other rituals and ceremonies associated with holidays, theatrical performances were 'liminal' in nature, capable of accommodating contradictory states of affairs through the resources of mimicry and parodic inversion, and they assumed the licence to express and debate matters normally taken for granted. Where theatre is concerned, the most crucial licence was the permission to enact disturbing events and situations – tragic conflicts, failed transitions, political divisions, controversial ideas – too dangerous to contemplate in public view outside the framework of licensed hypothesis.

Scholars continue to debate the social effects of these ludic permissions associated with festivity and theatre. C. L. Barber, who pioneered the study of connections between Shakespearian comedy and the folk and festive motifs of holiday inversion, declared that the ludic pattern led 'through release to clarification', resulting in social consolidation and harmony.[3] The anthropologist Victor Turner more darkly declared that the *communitas* values associated with ceremony, festivity and theatre, expressing the solidarity of the collective group, were immediately 'put into the service of normativeness'. 'The experience of communitas', he explained, 'striving to replicate itself, develops a social structure, in which initially free and innovative relationships between individuals become converted into norm-governed relationships between social personae.'[4] The theory that festive licence was merely a 'safety valve' for the 'controlled escape of steam' has much in common with these views and with the view of literary new historicists that theatrical subversion was licensed only that it might be contained.[5] Certainly Elizabethan authorities feared that public performances in London and elsewhere were a potential source of public disorder, and on some occasions it seems they may have been so. But the overturning of existing social order is not the only measure of innovation or of Elizabethan theatre's capacity for accommodating different perspectives. Against theories that stress the conservative effects of performance we may set Turner's further observation that 'the key communitas values . . . put into abeyance by the politically successful' or dominant party to a ludic or ceremonial transaction could 'generate metaphors and symbols which later fractionate into sets and arrays of cultural values', thereby creating 'the latent system of political alternatives from which novelties . . . arise'.[6] Given the many institutional frameworks of Elizabethan performance, as well as their transactional nature, the underlying conditions of *communitas* and dramatic licence could, as Turner suggests, generate multiple understandings and varied interpretations of the same public event. So much is evident from the London coronation entry of Elizabeth I in 1559, where the customary hieratic symbolism of the royal advent, celebrating the monarch's quasi-divine status and miraculous powers, was balanced by pageants and performances conducted in the language of political covenant.

As in ceremony, so in theatre, the meanings of performance were framed in countless ways: by the complex patterns of hospitality and patronage that surrounded performance and by the different interests and purposes of the many parties to the theatrical event – the sponsors of the event, the patrons of the performers, the performers themselves, the authors, the sometimes many-layered audiences and later readers and revivers of the performance text. Differences in these framing conditions, varying with setting and changing over time, shaped the history of Elizabethan theatre and enabled it to function as a versatile medium of cultural expression and social innovation. The following capsule history, organised roughly around each of the four decades of the reign, examines some of the leading functions, kinds and achievements of Elizabethan theatre under the rubrics of counsel (theatre's deliberative intervention in questions of religion and politics), compliment (its service as an ornament of the Crown, nobility, and nation), commerce (its development as a medium of popular consumption) and conscience (its contribution to ethical innovation and early modern individualism). Though chronological in form, the narrative that follows is designed to show that reciprocal connections and evolving traditions linked the various functions, achievements and kinds of theatre throughout the period. Elizabethan theatre developed within and against the grain of many different institutions; it enriched and complicated every one of them.

COUNSEL

In the first months of the new queen's reign, it might have seemed as if the role of theatre would return to its polemical uses under Thomas Cromwell and during the reign of Edward VI, to whom Martin Bucer had explained that Protestant theatre might be used 'to renew all forms of piety and virtue among the people'.[7] Twelfth Night festivities in 1559 included a court masque 'of crows in the habits of Cardinals, of asses habited as Bishops, and of wolves representing Abbots'; at the same time there was 'a masquerade of friars in the streets of London'.[8] These raucous anti-Catholic performances may have helped to bring about the proclamation of May 1559 which set theatrical policy for the first dozen years of Elizabeth's reign: an inhibition that required local authorities to review in advance 'all maner Interludes to be played eyther openly or privately' and to

> permyt none to be played wherin either matters of religion or of the governaunce of the estate of the common weale shalbe handled or treated, beyng no meete matters to be wrytten or treated upon, but by menne of aucthoritie, learning and wisedom, nor to be handled before any audience, but of grave and discreete persons.[9]

The saving exceptions in this measure – allowing for the treatment of religion and government by 'menne of aucthoritie' and before audiences 'of grave and discreete persons' – provided a broad degree of licence and shaped the conditions of theatre for the 1560s and beyond.

One crucial site of permissible theatrical activity was the Inns of Court, where the members' pursuit of 'noble mennes pastimes' included Christmas revels in which 'some interlude or Tragedy' was 'devised' and 'played by the Gentlemen of the same house'.[10] In the tragedy of *Gorboduc,* which was mounted during the 1561/2 Twelfth Night revels over which Robert Dudley presided as Lord of Misrule and was then performed before the Queen at Whitehall two weeks later, the Inner Temple authors Thomas Norton and Thomas Sackville created a foundational model for theatrical counsel in the Elizabethan age. Dealing with the division of the kingdom by a monarch's capricious will and with the civil chaos that follows from a troubled succession, the play explored an astonishing array of contemporary perspectives on the urgent matters of the Queen's marriage and the future of the succession. In its unfavourable treatment of foreign claimants and its insistence that the realm should not be subjected to 'the heavy yoke of foreign governance' (Act V, Scene 2, l. 172), the play seems to rule out Mary Stuart as a future queen and thus to endorse support for the Suffolk succession of Lady Katherine Grey; but the airing of this position would also have been a reminder of the prominence of the opposite view among members of the Inns of Court audience. Two weeks later at Whitehall, when *Gorboduc* was performed before the Queen, the play was accompanied by masques celebrating Dudley as the Queen's defender and proposing that marriage to him was the proper solution to the succession problem represented in *Gorboduc*. By adopting from Senecan tragedy (and especially from the philosopher Seneca's confrontation with the tyrant Nero in the *Octavia*) its own exploration of the problem of counsel, *Gorboduc* glanced at the young queen's need for parliament and senior male counsellors. More importantly, it found in the example of Seneca's *Octavia* a model for theatrical counsel that would resonate through the rest of the reign.

Although *Gorboduc* was offering itself as a model for theatre *as* counsel, the play's actual treatment of the politics of English counsel invites debate, since it advances both the view that the succession should be decided by 'common counsel of you all / In parliament' (Act V, Scene 2, ll. 157–9) and the view that chaos would result unless the monarch first declares a succession for parliament to confirm. In conflict with each other, both of these positions are to some degree in conflict with the play's further suggestion that the key to a stable regime is to secure the succession through marriage of the Queen. Even the viewpoints of *Gorboduc*'s two authors diverge, as Norton's emphasis on the role of the gentry in council and parliament in the first three acts gives way, in the final two, to Sackville's celebration of the heroic role of the nobility in quelling popular rebellion. Under the protection of licensed *communitas*, and through the obvious consensus that a secure succession prevents division in the kingdom, *Gorboduc* generated a variety of meanings, and not just at Whitehall on 18 January 1562, but in the printed editions that subsequently appeared, under differing political conditions, in 1565, 1570 (when a passage asserting that 'no causes serves whereby the subject may / Call to account the doings of his prince' was omitted), and 1590 (when the same passage was restored and the text was paired with Lydgate's *Serpent of Division*). There were also subsequent stage revivals of the Gorboduc story in a popular public theatre play of the 1590s on the Seven Deadly Sins, in a new script written and licensed for the Lord Admiral's Men in 1600, and in plays by the Queen's Men and the later Chamberlain's/King's Men dealing with the closely analogous story of King Lear. This is what it is, in Turner's terms, for theatrical performance to 'generate metaphors and symbols which later fractionate into sets and arrays of cultural values' and thereby to create the basis for 'political alternatives'.

A much later example of performance as counsel at the Inns of Court was the complex depiction of the monarch's conscience in *The Misfortunes of Arthur* (1587/8), the last play staged for the Queen at the Inns. The play assumes as background both the recent execution of Mary Stuart and the impending war with Spain, but its focus, in probing King Arthur's response to Mordred's treachery, is a domestic concern of the 1580s, the Catholic threat within. The play ends with a militantly Protestant prophesy,

> That Rebelles, Traytors, and Conspirators,
> The semenarye of lewde *Catiline*,
> The Bastard Covie of Italian birdes,
> Shall feele the flames of euer flaming fire.

But in the dark Senecan world of this political tragedy, where counsel works 'sometimes lesse: and sometimes nought at al', the bellicose counsel of Arthur's advisers is pitted against the tender conscience of the king, who declares that 'now this age requires a sager course, / And will, advisde by harmes, to wisedome yeelds'.[11] In showing the cost of Arthur's victory over Mordred – the destruction of the kingdom – the play's overt political counsel on the policing of Catholic traitors is framed by a complexity of thought that is genuinely tragic.

Along with plays produced by the Inns, other plays at court and in the universities offered licensed counsel on controversial matters, and they, too, generated a variety of perspectives. On the occasion of the Queen's visit to Cambridge in August 1564, for example, an iconoclastic play from the Henrician era, Nicholas Udall's now-lost *Ezekias,* was revived at the King's College Chapel. The performance depicted not only Ezekias's destruction of the brazen serpent but also (in scenes that may have been added to the play for the occasion) the subsequent Assyrian threat that emerged from Israel's sin of backsliding into heathen worship – a clear reference to the dangers of Elizabeth's pursuit of moderate religious policy. Having endured *Ezekias,* the Queen declined to attend another play scheduled for the following night, but when she departed Cambridge, a group of players, 'anxious for her to hear' their unperformed play, followed her to her first stop at Hinchenbrooke House, where they presented a satire against transubstantiation in which 'the bishop of London' (i.e. the Catholic Edmund Bonner) was depicted 'carrying a lamb in his hand as if he were eating it' and was followed by 'the figure of a dog with the Host in his mouth'.[12] The Queen was counselled more decorously but no less earnestly at Oxford in 1566 when the audience applauded Richard Edwards's now-lost *Palamon and Arcite* at the moment when Venus declared it was the destiny of the heroine, Diana's chaste devotee Emilye, to marry. The Queen thanked Edwards, but her response to the play may be better measured by her equivocal remark when Edwards pointed out his former tutor in Corpus Christi: 'Certainly he did not give thee whipping enough.'[13]

The avowed aims of university drama – 'to recreate owre selves, . . . to practyse our owne style', and 'to embowlden our yuthe' – were in many respects inward-looking, but they had important outward-looking effects.[14] In scholars such as Peele, Lyly, Nashe, Greene and Marlowe, who witnessed and in some cases participated in college plays, the universities produced the key theatrical innovators whose classical training and rhetorical flair would shape the late Elizabethan popular stage. The Latin drama of Thomas Legge, Master of Gonville and Caius and later Vice-Chancellor of Cambridge, also provided models that influenced the treatment of history, politics and religion on the popular stage. Legge's *Ricardus Tertius* (1579), the first English history play based on chronicle sources, set the pattern for the large-scale popular theatre history plays of the 1580s and 1590s. The most politically daring of Legge's plays, however, may have been the unperformed *Solymitana Clades,* a 10,000-line rendering, from the pages of Josephus, of the destruction of the Temple of Jerusalem under Titus Vespasianus. The play was nearing completion around 1590 when, Thomas Fuller reports, 'some Plageary filched it from him just as it was to be acted.'[15] In its surviving manuscript, Legge's play is a hellacious Senecan brew – an unremitting bloodbath depicting the murderous and suicidal acts committed by the Zealot faction during Titus's reluctant siege of the city. Legge follows the tradition of medieval plays on the subject by representing the fall of Jerusalem as a just consequence of the Jews' crucifixion of

Christ. But as a northern Catholic whose dramatic activities and protection of recusant students earned him a dangerous denunciation from his puritan colleagues, Legge reserves his deepest venom for the mad atrocities of the Jewish Zealot faction. In Titus's contemplation of the burning Temple, Legge offers a sceptical and politique comment on the violence and persecution that result when religious zealotry combines with political power: 'What manner of nation is this, which attributes murderousness to religion or calls infanticide by the name of sacrifice? What kind of God makes such a demand? What kind of priest makes such offerings?'[16] In their treatment of religious faction, persecution and the conscience of the prince, both *The Misfortunes of Arthur* and *Solymitana Clades* (which may have become the 'titus & vespaccia' performed in 1592 at the Rose Theatre in London) demonstrate the complexities that could emerge from the traditions of licensed counsel at the Inns and universities, where 'menne of authoritie' treated 'matters of religion or . . . government' before audiences 'of grave and discrete persons'.

Counsel was an important subject and function of early Elizabethan court theatre as well. Richard Edwards's mildly satirical *Damon and Pithias* (1564, published 1571), set at the court of the Syracusan tyrant Dionysus, explored the way that honest counsel is threatened by the combination of abject flattery with tyrannical caprice. While celebrating, in amity and 'pleasant urbanitie', the courtly virtues that compromise between bluntness and sycophancy, Edward's play simultaneously registered a delicate protest against the 'trimmer kynde of myrth' that court performances required, and it placed before the court the darker Senecan truth that 'Who is in fauour now, to morrow is out agayne'.[17] If the *Horestes* (1567) of 'John Pikeryng' is the 'Orestes' played at court during the revels of 1567/8, there would similarly have been more than one way of seeing this play's ambivalent counsel and its subtle application of classical revenge to events in Scotland in early 1567. Through the counsel of revenge that is offered to the conscience-stricken prince Horestes, the play seems to proffer to Elizabeth, who was reluctant to support the deposing and punishment of Mary, the militant advice to 'be bold, & feare no fate . . . Her faute is great and punnyshment, it is worthy for to haue'.[18] But the play elsewhere cautiously advises that 'ouer rashe in doinge ought, doth often danger bringe' (l. 579), and many of its features seem to question the wisdom of violent political action. The marriage that concludes the play vindicates the avenging hero, but without extinguishing the quizzical spirit embodied in the play's ambiguous use of the gospel injunction: 'loke what measure ye meate, y^{t} same againe shalbe' (l. 1093). Both the gospel phrase and the example of Horestes' dilemma would prove crucial to the later moral complexities of Shakespeare's *Measure for Measure* and *Hamlet*.

The concluding prayer of *Horestes*, which indicates the play was not only performed at court but also on the public stage, is a reminder that many of the plays performed at court by professional troupes under noble patronage – as well as other plays belonging to these authorised companies or licensed for performance by local officials within the framework specified by the 1559 proclamation – could also be performed at touring venues throughout the country, or circulated in print, or subsequently adapted for later revivals. During the 1560s and 1570s, the printing or public performance of current court plays was supplemented by the printing or reprinting of other works, pre-Marian reformist plays by John Bale and others, for example, and more recent works of a similarly reformist bent – such as *New Custom* (1573) and *The Tide Tarrieth No Man* (1576) – in which authorised companies like Leicester's Men addressed religious controversies of the early Elizabethan years. Within the framework of licensed performance, early Elizabethan theatre thus encompassed a variety of interests, venues, institutions and kinds of counsel.

COMPLIMENT

The diversity and sometimes controversial nature of counsel in early Elizabethan theatre may have been one cause of tightened restrictions on theatrical licence in the early 1570s, beginning with the Acte for the Punishment of Vacabondes (29 June 1572). This measure threatened with the penalties for vagabondage 'all Comon Players in Enterludes & Minstrels, not belonging to any Baron of this Realme or towards any other honorable Personage of greater Degree'.[19] Other factors that may have led to tightened restrictions on playing include the key political developments that consolidated support for the regime and enhanced the Queen's authority – the settlement in religion, the receding urgency of the Queen's marriage, the successful suppression of the Northern Rebellion (1569), the galvanising papal bull that declared Elizabeth a heretic and deprived her of her title (1570). In the changed political situation of the 1570s, several new developments (the requirement that playing companies be patronised by noblemen, the suppression of the traditional religious cycle plays in the provinces, the invention of pageants and performances associated with the royal progress and the cultivation of panegyric wit in plays at court) combined to bring theatrical practices more closely into line with the interests of the Crown and court. Paradoxically, however, this movement towards tightened control and politically narrowed purposes actually established the conditions through which court-focused performance generated a field of expanding theatrical possibilities.

A key factor in the centralising of theatrical control was the decline of the urban mysteries, a development which came partly from active intervention by church authorities and local reformers and partly from the declining economic fortunes of provincial towns. The traditional Corpus Christi cycles at York and Coventry ended in 1569 and 1579; those in Newcastle and Lincoln in 1568–9. In some cases, the older performance traditions were altered to suit the needs of the Elizabethan regime. At Chester, for example, the processional route and subject matter of the traditional Whitsun plays were several times altered 'to reflect the greater glory of the Mayor and his brethren' before they were discontinued in 1575.[20] In Essex, town-sponsored drama had actually increased during the vestments controversy of the 1560s, when church vestments (which Bishop John Jewel had called 'theatrical habits') were transformed into players' garments for use in reformed sacred dramas that continued to be performed until the height of Protestant 'prophesyings' in 1574–6. Coventry's 'Hock Tuesday' play depicting the conquest of the Danes, disallowed in 1561, was presented as being 'without ill exampl of mannerz, papistry, or ony superstition' to Elizabeth at Kenilworth in 1575, and it was thereafter intermittently revived by town authorities. The town council of Coventry also allowed, from 1584, the performance of a *Destruction of Jerusalem* at Midsummer, and from 1591 a *King Edward IV*.[21]

The decline of religious cycle plays combined with expanded touring by leading professional companies to produce a stronger relationship between court-sponsored playing and local communities. In 1574, Leicester's Men became the first company to be licensed under the terms of the 1572 vagabondage act 'to use, exercise, and occupie the arte and facultye of playenge Comedies, Tragedies, Enterludes, and stage playes . . . thoroughout oure Realme of England'. The patent came with the additional restriction that the company's plays were to be 'before sene & allowed' 'by the Master of the Revels'.[22] This expansion in the duties of the Master of the Revels, who had previously been responsible for arranging court performances by 'calling together . . . sundry players and persuing, fitting and reforming theier matters otherwise not convenient to be showen before her Majestie', was another measure that extended government control over theatre outside the court.[23] Despite this new oversight, Leicester's commitments to Protestant reform and anti-Catholic interventions abroad, as well as his evident patronage of 'advanced Protestant preachers, pamphleteers and printers', suggest that the repertory of his troupe did not shy from matters of political and religious controversy. Support for this suggestion is found in the plays of Robert Wilson, who wrote and performed for Leicester's Men works such as *The Three Ladies of London* (1581), a reformist play that attacked simony and the ignorance of the clergy, and *The Cobbler's Prophecy,* whose militant anti-Spanish patriotism may have been the cause of the Queen's outburst against the Earl of Leicester at a court performance in 1587–8. Although Leicester's Men dominated court performances in the 1570s, the court's austerity in spending for festivities led it to rely increasingly for entertainment on several other professional companies as well – Warwick's, Clinton's/Howard's, Sussex's and Derby's. Through widespread touring in the provinces and regular playing in London, all of these adult companies extended the influence of their noble patrons and laid the groundwork for the development of a fully-fledged commercial theatre.

Also transforming theatrical life outside of London was the development of pageantry and panegyrical performance connected with the royal progresses of the Queen. As the medium through which 'the Queen and her hosts exchanged ceremonial messages that advanced their own agendas', progress entertainments drew on the idealisations of pastoral romance and classical mythology in order to enhance the power and image of the Queen.[24] Although the aims of such entertainments were panegyrical, they were also adapted to the various perspectives of their noble patrons, their presenters and their local audiences, and they often involved competing agendas and points of view. If the 1575 Kenilworth entertainment commended the pageant's patron Leicester as a descendant of King Arthur and an ideal spouse for Elizabeth, Leicester's agenda was undermined by a subsequent entertainment at Woodstock, sponsored by Sir Henry Lee, which counselled Leicester and all good subjects to submission and self-sacrificing service as the proper bearing toward the Queen. In civic entertainments offered at Norwich in 1578, local magistrates used the evolving image of the virgin queen to advance their own protestant agenda by praising her as a Deborah, a 'mighty hand' of the Lord against the Catholic enemies abroad. *The Four Foster Children of Desire,* a chivalric triumph at court in 1581, was probably commissioned by the Queen for the purposes of encouraging negotiation with the French, but it simultaneously lent support to policies recommended by Protestant courtiers such as Sir Philip Sidney, who participated in the event, and it undermined the influence of those other participants who, like the Earl of Arundel, held opposing views.

The panegyrical impulses developed in royal pageantry and progress entertainments also contributed to the transformation of traditional child performances at court. Combining classical myth and Platonism with the rituals of courtly love, the plays of university-educated authors such as George Peele and John Lyly defined a new mode of courtliness based on the ideals of eroticised devotion and sacrificial service to a gracious female sovereign. Lyly's plays glance, in a distant way, at weighty matters such as the succession, domestic unrest and conflicts abroad, but in their mixture of idealism and witty cynicism the plays are primarily concerned with a key feature of Elizabeth's court: the subordination of male courtiers to a female monarch within an elaborate system of courtly patronage and favour. Through parody, burlesque and witty repartee, however, the plays also offer an ongoing critique of the ideals of courtliness they seemingly advance.[25] By means of delicate fable and allegory, they hint at the darker realities of court life, exploring, but also exemplifying in their modus operandi, the ways that counsel confronts power and truthfulness contends with servility.

Many of these newly fashionable plays belonged jointly to the worlds of court ceremony and commercial entertainment. From at least 1575, when the London Court of Aldermen received complaints that Sebastian Westcote, Master of the Children of Paul's, was keeping 'playes and resorte of the people to great gaine', child actors were performing their court plays commercially in the cathedral precincts.[26] Within a year, a similar theatre had been established at Blackfriars for the Children of the Chapel Royal. From 1583, Lyly's plays, with the support of his patron the Earl of Oxford, were being mounted by various combinations of boy companies at the indoor theatres at Saint Paul's and Blackfriars. Thus, while they derived from the traditions of courtly compliment, Lyly's plays adapted well as commercial fare offered to the elite outside the court. The plays allowed a taste of court performance, but differences between actual court performance and a theatrical marketplace catering to an upwardly mobile elite probably heightened the ironic manner of the plays, thereby adding to the ambivalent and sceptical effects of their wit.

Meanwhile, a London market had also developed for performances by the adult companies on whom the court increasingly relied for its seasonal entertainment. A Privy Council minute of December 1578, for example, called upon the Lord Mayor

> to suffer the Children of Her Majesties Chappell, the servauntes of the Lord Chamberlaine, therle of Warwicke, the Erle of Leicester, the Earle of Essex and the Children of Powles . . . to exercise playing in the Cittie . . . by reason that the companies aforenamed are appointed to playe . . . before her Majestie.[27]

Just a few years earlier, in 1574, the London Common Council had responded to 'the inordinate hauntyinge of great multitudes of people . . . to playes, enterludes, and shewes' at inns around the city with measures that would have subjected such performances to municipal licensing and taxation. It may have been this proposed scheme for civic control that led, later in the decade, to the construction of permanent commercial theatres just outside the City's jurisdiction. Towards the end of the decade, the licensing of companies to perform at court had produced a situation in which Leicester's Men, Warwick's Men and several others were regularly performing at three new public theatres in the suburbs – the Theatre (1576) and Curtain (1577) in Shoreditch and a theatre (1576) at Newington Butts in Surrey – and at four or more inns within the City. By 1578, when John Stockwood delivered from the pulpit of Paul's Cross his fiery sermon against 'the gaine that is reaped of eighte ordinarie places in the Citie', a publicity war against the London theatres was under way.[28]

COMMERCE

Many reasons were given for suppressing the public stage. From the standpoint of the City of London, the theatres were seen as a potential source of epidemic disease, crime and public disorder, though another motive for the City's opposition was protection of closely guarded prerogatives in its dealings with the court and Privy Council. Religious objections lodged by clergymen and hired polemicists included the theatres' violation of the sabbath and their irreverent mingling of 'scurrility with divinity' in representing 'upon scaffolds God's divine mysteries'.[29] It has been argued by Patrick Collinson that this opposition to representing Scripture and religious subject matter reflects a division within later Elizabethan Protestantism, a disinvestment from the mid-Tudor pattern of exploiting the arts for their polemical potential and the development instead of an 'iconophobic' scripturalism that drove a wedge between puritans and the secular culture. The majority of anti-theatrical writers, however, were not puritans but conformist clergy and lay writers probably commissioned by the London citizenry, and their opposition to the London theatres was driven not so much by theology as by the fundamental discursive challenge that theatre posed to the traditional form of authority in London – an alliance of ministry and magistracy that maintained order through the power of the word and the sword. As a later writer explained,

> God only gave authority of public instruction and correction but to two sorts of men: to his ecclesiastical ministers and temporal magistrates. He never instituted a third authority of players, or ordained that they should serve in his ministry, and therefore are they to be rejected with their use and quality.[30]

From the theatre's creation of a new domain of public discourse there followed many of the arguments against its various mobilities – social, commercial and representational. The London theatres, it was claimed, brought the whole commonwealth into disorder by illicitly mixing vulgar and criminal elements with others out of their proper places: servants and apprentices drawn from work, parishioners seduced from worship, wives lured from domestic privacy, gentry from their rural duties by idle recreation. Instead of fulfilling their callings at work, theatregoers sought recreation in a world of illusion created by estate-less players who, 'under the title of their maisters or as reteiners, are privileged to roave abroad and publish their mametree'.[31] Performing not just on holidays but also on workdays (their work was playing), and juggling 'the monie out of other mens purses into their own hands' for a product without value, players thrived (in contravention of the Protestant ideal of inward sincerity) by the vices of pretence and dissimulation.[32]

When, additionally, the players attacked London's merchant class for usury and hard dealing and its clergy for corruption and incompetence – as they did in works such as *The Three Ladies of London* (1581) and *A Looking Glass for London* (1594) – they were guilty of the further crime of publicising 'the faults and scandals of great men, as magistrates, ministers, and such as hold public places'.[33]

Anxieties about theatre's discursive challenge to established authority and orthodox opinion were probably behind a 1581 expansion in the powers of the Master of the Revels, who was authorised

> to warne commaunde and appointe in all places within this our Realme of England . . . all and every plaier or plaiers witheir playmakers, belonginge to any noble man or otherwise, . . . to appeare before him . . . with all such plaies, Tragedies, Comedies or showes as they shall in readiness or meane to sett forth, and them to recite before our said Servant or his sufficient deputie, whom we ordeyne appointe and aucthorise . . . of all such showes, plaies, plaiers and playmakers, together with their playing places, to order and reforme, auctorise and put downe, as shalbe thought meete or unmeete unto himself.[34]

This expansion in the censorship powers of the Master of the Revels was followed, in March 1583, by a bold attempt to bring all of the most talented theatre professionals of the age into one company under the direct patronage of the Queen. The formation of the Queen's Men was meant to weaken the other leading companies from which the Queen's players were taken, to reduce rivalry among noble patrons for court performances by their companies, 'to increase the prestige of their patron throughout the land, to harness the theatre in the service of a moderate Protestant ideology', and to provide, through the company's wide travels, information useful to the government.[35] Together with the amalgamated boys' companies who were mounting Lyly's plays at court, the Queen's Men held exclusive sway over all performances at court between 1583 and 1585. Where Lyly's plays celebrated the virtues of the Queen and the ideals of her court, the Queen's Men turned to the English chronicles in order to dramatise the elements of Tudor political doctrine: patriotism and mystical kingship in *The Famous Victories of Henry V,* the evils of a divided kingdom in *King Leir,* the emergence of the Tudor dynasty in *The True Tragedy of Richard III* and opposition to papal interference in *The Troublesome Reign of King John,* a play that reminded audiences, 'If Englands Peeres and people joyne in one, / Nor Pope, nor Fraunce, nor Spaine can doo them wrong.'[36]

Ironically, the formation of the Queen's Men was another innovation that, while originating in an attempt to bring playing under official control, had the ultimate effect of expanding the activities of professional performers. Less than two years after the creation of the Queen's Men, the Privy Council passed along to the City of London the company's request to once again perform in London in preparation for the court season, but the City protested that 'last yere when such toleration was of the Quenes players only, all the places of playing were filled with men calling themselves the Quenes players.'[37] Rival companies, invoking the authorised mission of the Queen's Men, were asserting the privilege of playing as a service to the Crown in order to exploit commercial opportunities of 'rehearsing' their plays before the London public. By December 1586, Leicester's Men, who had lost several of their best actors to the Queen's Men in 1583, had been sufficiently reconstituted to resume performing at court and elsewhere. Meanwhile, companies sponsored by the Lord Chamberlain and the Lord Admiral had offered plays at court in 1585–6, and the latter company, graced by the rising star Edward Alleyn, probably began performing at yet another new London theatre, Philip Henslowe's Rose, not long after it was built in 1587. The Queen's Men had clearly set the pattern by which other large-scale companies would seek to dominate the popular stage. And in putting the English past and its political implications before the public, the company had pioneered a form that, in the hands of abler writers, would subject the national identity to thorough scrutiny. Thomas Heywood, writing in defence of theatre in 1612, could say that plays had 'instructed such as cannot reade in the discovery of all our English chronicles' and enabled ordinary Englishmen to 'discourse of any notable thing even from William the Conqueror, nay, from the landing of Brute, until this day'.[38]

Together with the Children of Paul's, the Queen's Men had also brought religious controversy onto the London stage. Contemporary allusions to 'hir Maiesties men', to Lyly and to plays at Saint Paul's suggest that these two 'court-sponsored' companies, boys and adults, were foremost among those commissioned in early 1589 (probably at Archbishop Whitgift's behest) to subject the pseudonymous 'Martin Marprelate' to theatrical ridicule. But references to the 'many thousand eie witnesses' who saw these anti-Martinist performances, as well as descriptions of the 'sundrie waies' that 'Martin' was 'very curstlie handled', lend credence to the sweeping claim that 'euerie Stage plaier made a jest of him.'[39] Martin was reportedly 'wormed and launced' at the Theatre in Shoreditch, portrayed as 'the Mayd Marian', 'attired like an Ape on the Stage' and dressed 'with a cocks combe, an apes face, a wolfs bellie, cats clawes &c'.[40] Sir Francis Bacon complained in the summer of 1589 of 'this immodest and deformed manner . . . whereby matters of religion are handled in the style of the stage', and by October the authorities grew sufficiently alarmed by the apparent popularity and proliferation of theatrical satire to bring the anti-Martinist performances to an end. Within months there followed a Privy Council proposal for a new censorship commission to deal with players who 'handle in their playes certen matters of Divinytie and State unfit to be suffred'.[41]

Perhaps partly as a result of their involvement in the Marprelate affair, the Queen's Men ceased to appear regularly at court after 1590–1 and, with reduced personnel, spent most of their time touring the provinces. 'The plays in Paul's were dissolved', according to Lyly, at about the same time.[42] Ironically, the two companies through which the court had sought to sponsor and control theatrical activity in the 1580s had – perhaps to their own cost – brought controversy to a new level on the public stage, and they left in their wake a theatre industry that, through difficult times, continued to grow and innovate.

CONSCIENCE

The nature and intellectual impact of professional playing in the last decade of Elizabeth's reign may be gauged from the diary of Philip Henslowe, owner of the Rose Theatre. The diary records daily receipts from the various companies playing at the Rose between 1592 and 1597. In the busy repertories of these companies, old and new plays rotated in performance six days of the week, with companies offering one to two dozen different plays per season or as many as thirty to thirty-five per year. Similar practices were probably observed by other companies at the Theatre and the Curtain in Shoreditch and later at the Swan (1596), the Globe (1599) and the Fortune (1600). The publication of playbooks offers another measure of the increasing commercial activity: in the history of printing up to 1589, slightly more than ninety plays, interludes and entertainments (including editions of classical and Continental authors) were issued from English presses; approximately the same number were issued in the thirteen years between 1590 and the end of the reign. For those same years, we know from the register of the Company of Stationers of another thirty plays now lost, and from records of performance like Henslowe's diary we may add a further 225 lost works; a further fifty plays performed in these years but only published after 1603 bring the total somewhere close to 400 plays and entertainments first performed or published in England from 1590 to 1603.

Originating under different auspices, many of these plays were printed for sale to readers, while others were performed in towns and great houses by companies on extensive provincial tours. In London itself, by 1595, an estimated 15,000 people per week were attending performances by the Lord Admiral's and Lord Chamberlain's Men. A precise profile of the London audience is hard to construct, but there is little question that it was remarkably diverse and reflective of the city itself, which was home to one in nine Englishmen at some point during their lives and a magnet to countless immigrants and visitors from Europe and beyond. In the course of its transactions with the London audience, the popular theatrical marketplace produced an extraordinary heterogeneity of matter – a body of plays dealing with current events and controversies, with the history of England and the ancient world, with lands and peoples across the globe, with domestic matters ranging from love, marriage, gender and sexuality to money, class and crime. This variety of matter was matched to a hybridity of form in which plots, genres, social decora and intellectual perspectives were mixed in every conceivable combination.

The artistic possibilities of the medium were expanded by a new generation of writers – Marlowe, Kyd and Shakespeare chief among them – whose multi-perspectival work demanded an unprecedented complexity of response. The plays of Marlowe, written to the formulas of the episodic heroic play (*Tamburlaine I & II*), the morality (*Doctor Faustus*), the admonitory fall of princes chronicle (*Edward II*) and revenge tragedy (*The Jew of Malta*), famously accommodate and solicit sharply conflicting views of their charismatic and terrifying villain-heroes. Sustained by Marlowe's powerfully engaging rhetoric, organised around provocative antitheses and ironic juxtapositions and creating irresolvable interpretive dilemmas, these open-ended plays encouraged spectators to interpret from a variety of viewpoints. Even in the maimed and truncated text that survives, for example, Marlowe's savagely ironic depiction of the Saint Bartholomew's Day massacre in *The Massacre at Paris* offers conflicting points of view on the relationship between religion and political violence. Henry III's dying call for a revenge that will 'fire Paris' and 'keenly slice the catholics' sounds like a rallying cry to Protestant interventionists; but Marlowe's treatment of the horrors of religious violence undermines such bloody instincts, as does his careful parallel between the Catholic atrocities of

1572 and Protestant treacheries extending from the Huguenot victory at Coutras to the assassination of Henry III.[43] While building upon anti-Catholic propaganda, the play uses mass violence to force the Protestant audience into contemplation of its own unexamined emotions, instincts and values.

Shakespeare, too, worked through the open-ended juxtaposition of opposing perspectives in history plays such as *Richard II* and *Henry V,* and no less so in his seemingly more consensual comic works, which include his provocative treatment of gender and marriage in *The Taming of the Shrew* and his exploration of race, religion and justice in *The Merchant of Venice.* But where Marlowe treats his audience in the manner of a religious mob or an army, sweeping them forward on a tide of emotion and rhetoric only to bring them up short by confronting them with the shocking consequences of their unexamined sympathies, Shakespeare treats the members of his audience more individually, as if they were fair-minded members of a jury or parliament; he carefully rehearses, in his own judicial, parliamentary, council and forum scenes, the conflicting claims of Lancaster and York, Richard II and Bolingbroke, Brutus and Caesar. On the eve of Agincourt, in the colloquy between the disguised Henry V and his common soldiers, Shakespeare airs the conflicting views that continue to this day to divide audiences and critics on the problematic representation of this hero-king. On the one hand, Stephen Greenblatt has seen in Henry V's complaint that kings are 'subject to the breath / Of every fool' (Act IV, Scene 1, ll. 232–3) the play's critique of popular judgement and its invalidation of 'the subversive doubts [it] continually awakens . . . in an effort to intensify the power of the king and his war.' On the other hand, Louis Adrian Montrose, citing the play's reminder to the audience that ''tis your thoughts that now must deck our kings' (Prologue, 28), sees in the doubts and criticism of Henry's soldiers not the common breath of fools but a validation of 'the imaginative authority of the common subject in constituting the political authority of the sovereign'.[44] The problematic dialogue between the King and his soldiers is followed, however, by the solitary prayer of the King – a prayer modelled on the gospel scene at Gethsemane, where Christ asked to be spared the events of the morrow. In this prayer, Shakespeare depicts the King's private moral agony over his questionable possession of the crown at the very moment this agony dissolves – with the admission that 'all that I can do' to appease God 'is nothing worth' – into a grimly heroic acceptance of the desanctified leadership to which he has been called. The effect of staging, within the mind of the King himself, the conflict between two equally compelling but conflicting moralities, one private, one public, is not to simplify the audience's judgment of the king and crown but to create a political tragedy of Machiavellian proportions.

As Henry V's prayer at Agincourt suggests, a corollary to the multi-perspectivism of the Elizabethan popular stage was the rendering of conflicting claims as they impinge on individual consciousness. Many factors have been cited as contributing to the turn toward inward experience both on and off the late Elizabethan stage – the development of Protestant spirituality, the necessity of outward dissimulation under authoritarian circumstances, the forensic parsing of private intentions through the construction of probable narratives, the solvent effects of social change on the traditional structure of social relations. To these causes may be added the mobilities of theatre itself, where the daily negotiation of norms, values and power relations, performed before a socially diverse audience, created opportunities for independent thinking and self-awareness. In Kyd's *The Spanish Tragedy,* a seminal influence in this regard, the rendering of 'conscience' – the Elizabethan term for thought and consciousness as well as for the faculty of moral deliberation – is effected through the terms of Senecan tradition. Reaching back, through early Elizabethan plays such as *Gorboduc* and *Horestes,* to the problem of counsel confronting power in Seneca's own *Octavia, The Spanish Tragedy* isolates the conscientious hero in a morally oblivious world he seems powerless to change. With Hieronymo's isolation go the conditions that make up the revenger's private dilemma: epistemological doubt as to truth and facts, moral uncertainty as to the justice of actions contemplated and his mad commitment to his private cause. Just as the inward turn of the wrath-filled Senecan hero – his adherence to a *privilegium,* an inner empire of 'radical, unpredicated independence' – has been linked to his outward political disempowerment, so the inward turn of the drama itself has been linked to the powerlessness of late Elizabethan commercial theatre, to its exchange of overt public counsel for the privileged indeterminacy of private awareness and expanded consciousness.[45] But such arguments distinguish too sharply between political purpose and theatrical polyvalence, and they underestimate the long-term continuities between the older traditions of theatrical counsel and the new self-awareness fostered by theatrical commerce. Conscience had often been personified in traditional homiletic drama before it found embodiment in Hieronymo or Hamlet, and conscientious moral complications, we have seen, were not unknown to the older traditions of theatrical counsel and courtly compliment: *Horestes* was a predecessor to *The Spanish Tragedy* and to *Hamlet* just as surely as *The Misfortunes of Arthur* was their contemporary.

If the Elizabethan theatre's expansion of possibilities for the mind was not an overt political innovation, it was certainly – as the theatre's opponents seem to have recognised in calling it 'a third authority' to the word and the sword – an artistic and ethical innovation with political implications. In *The Spanish Tragedy,* Hieronymo's private dilemma impacts the public life of two royal houses, Portugal and Spain. Hieronymo is a theatricalist whose awareness is both shaped and shared through ambiguous performances, from the opening masque, in which English knights unseat Spanish kings, to the closing multilingual masque, in which the hero takes action by giving theatrical embodiment to his moral perceptions and, incidentally, butchers the royal house of Spain. But the opacity of Hieronymo's final performance to its onstage audience – an opacity through which Kyd figures the indeterminacies of his own play – suggest that the theatre shapes reality by creating modes of awareness that outstrip in their complexity any univocal political interpretation.

This is why, in one of the last and greatest of Elizabethan plays, the magnificent self-awareness of the hero is represented through its opposite – a splendid objectivity that uses the metaphor of theatre to generate multiple perspectives on the hero's dilemma. *Hamlet* is in fact a compendium of the theatrical heritage of its time. Just as the play offers a variety of perspectives on a political situation – is Denmark a hereditary kingdom, a matriarchy, an elective principality? – so it illuminates the hero's mind and situation through his contemplation of a variety of dramatic forms, scenarios and performances. The play embodies an example of court performance in the Mousetrap, and it alludes to a university drama in which Polonius played

Julius Caesar and was slain by Brutus; it also includes a veteran company of adult professional actors forced into travelling by the recent popularity of their private theatre rivals in 'the city' (the boys' companies of London, discontinued in 1590–1, had been newly revived in 1600). If the Player's speech, featuring both the conscientious pause of the wrathful Pyrrhus and the grief of his bereaved victim Hecuba, takes in the many public consequences of private moral purpose, the play-within-the-play renders – through its anthologising of Elizabethan theatrical styles and genres – an ambiguous portrait of Hamlet as both a just prince and a savage regicide. The success of *Hamlet* as a culmination of all that Elizabethan theatre had achieved depends, in other words, on its being a conscious retrospect and reflection on that theatre's history. *Hamlet* is an imaginative counterpart to Francis Meres's summary of the various purposes and venues from which Elizabethan theatre had been formed; no less than the social heterogeneity of Meres's list, the palimpsest of Elizabethan theatre in *Hamlet* shows what it means for the communal nature of theatre to 'generate metaphors and symbols which later fractionate into sets and arrays of cultural values'.

FURTHER READING

Bevington, David, *Tudor Drama and Politics: A Critical Approach to Topical Meaning* (Cambridge, Mass., 1968).

Braden, Gordon, *Renaissance Tragedy and the Senecan Tradition: Anger's Privilege* (New Haven, Conn., 1985).

Cartwright, Kent, *Theatre and Humanism: English Drama in the Sixteenth Century* (Cambridge, 1999).

Coldeway, John C., 'The Last Rise and Final Demise of Essex Town Drama', *Modern Language Quarterly*, 36 (1975): 239–60.

Collinson, Patrick, *The Birthpangs of Protestant England* (London, 1988).

Cox, John D. and Kastan, David Scott (eds.), *A New History of Early English Drama* (New York, 1997).

Dawson, Anthony B. and Yachnin, Paul, *The Culture of Playgoing in Shakespeare's England: A Collaborative Debate* (Cambridge and New York, 2001).

Doran, Susan, 'Juno *Versus* Diana: The Treatment of Elizabeth I's Marriage in Plays and Entertainments, 1561–81', *The Historical Journal*, 32 (2) (1995): 271–4.

Dutton, Richard, *Mastering the Revels: The Regulation and Censorship of English Renaissance Drama* (Iowa City, Iowa, 1991).

Gardiner, Harold C., *Mysteries' End: An Investigation of the Last Days of the Medieval Religious Stage* (New Haven, Conn., 1946).

Griffin, Benjamin, 'The Breaking of the Giants: Historical Drama in London and Coventry', *English Literary Renaissance*, 29 (1999): 3–21.

Gurr, Andrew, *Playgoing in Shakespeare's London* (Cambridge, 1987).

—— *The Shakespearean Stage, 1572–1642*, 3rd edn (Cambridge, 1992).

Hunter, G. K., *John Lyly: The Humanist as Courtier* (London, 1962).

Hutson, Lorna, *The Invention of Suspicion: Law and Mimesis in Shakespeare and Renaissance Drama* (Oxford, 2007).

Ingram, William, *The Business of Playing: The Beginnings of Adult Professional Theatre in Elizabethan London* (Ithaca, NY, 1992).

James, Henry, and Walker, Greg, 'The Politics of *Gorboduc*', *English Historical Review*, 110 (1995): 109–21.

Jones, Norman, and White, Paul Whitfield, '*Gorboduc* and Royal Marriage Politics', *English Literary Renaissance,* 24 (1996): 1–13.

McMillin, Scott, and MacLean, Sally-Beth, *The Queen's Men and Their Plays* (Cambridge, 1998).

Manley, Lawrence, *Literature and Culture in Early Modern London* (Cambridge, 1995).

Maus, Katharine, *Inwardness and Theatre in the English Renaissance* (Chicago, Ill., 1995).

Mills, David, 'Chester Ceremonial: Re-Creation and Recreation in the English "Medieval" Town', *Urban History Yearbook,* 18 (1991): 1–19.

Phillips, James E., 'A Revaluation of *Horestes*', *Huntington Library Quarterly,* 18 (1955): 227–44.

Shapiro, Michael, *Children of the Revels: The Boy Companies of Shakespeare's Time and Their Plays* (New York, 1977).

White, Paul Whitfield, *Theatre and Reformation: Protestantism, Patronage, and Playing in Tudor England* (Cambridge, 1993).

—— 'The Bible as Play in Reformation England', in Jane Milling and Peter Thomson (eds.), *The Cambridge History of British Theatre: Vol. I: Origins to 1660* (Cambridge, 2004), pp. 87–115.

Womack, Peter, *English Renaissance Drama* (Oxford, 2006).

NOTES

1 *Francis Meres's Treatise 'Poetrie': A Critical Edition,* ed. Don Cameron Allen, *University of Illinois Studies in Language and Literature,* 16 (3–4) (1933): 76–9.

2 Edmund Spenser, *The Works of Edmund Spenser,* ed. Edwin Greenlaw et al., 11 vols. (Baltimore, Md., 1932–57), vol. X, p. 16.

3 C. L. Barber, *Shakespeare's Festive Comedy: A Study of Dramatic Form and Its Relation to Social Custom* (Princeton, NJ, 1959), p. 6.

4 Victor Turner, *From Ritual to Theater: The Human Seriousness of Play* (New York, 1982), p. 54.

5 Peter Burke, *Popular Culture in Early Modern Europe* (New York, 1979), p. 202.

6 Turner, *From Ritual to Theater,* p. 50.

7 *De honestis ludis* (1551), in Glynne Wickham, *Early English Stages, 1300–1660, Vol. II: 1576 to 1660, Part I* (London, 1963), pp. 329–31; p. 330.

8 E. K. Chambers, *The Elizabethan Stage,* 4 vols. (Oxford, 1923), vol. I, pp. 155–6.

9 Chambers, *Elizabethan Stage,* vol. IV, p. 263.

10 Sir John Fortescue and Nicholas Bacon, quoted in Marie Axton, *The Queen's Two Bodies: Drama and the Elizabethan Succession* (London, 1977), p. 6.

11 *'The Misfortunes of Arthur': A Critical Old-Spelling Edition,* ed. Brian Jay Corrigan (New York, 1992), Act V, Scene 2, ll. 13–16; Act IV, Scene 1, ll. 33; Act III, Scene 1, ll. 136–7.

12 CSP Span., 3 vols. (London, 1892), vol. II, p. 375.

13 For several versions of the anecdote, see *Records of Early English Drama: Oxford,* ed. John R. Elliott, 2 vols. (Toronto, 2004), vol. I, p. 133.

14 Karl Young, 'William Gager's Defence of the Stage', *Transactions of the Wisconsin Academy of Sciences, Arts, and Letters,* 18 (1916): 614, cited in J. W. Binns, *Intellectual Culture in Elizabethan and Jacobean England: The Latin Writings of the Age* (Leeds, 1990), p. 121.

15 Thomas Fuller, *The History of the Worthies of England* (London, 1662), p. 276.

16 *Solimytana Clades,* ll. 7501–4, in *Thomas Legge: the Complete Plays,* ed. and trans. Dana Sutton, 2 vols. (New York, 1993), vol. II, p. 454.

17 *Richard Edwards' 'Damon and Pithias': A Critical Old-Spelling Edition,* ed. D. Jerry White (New York, 1980), ll. 49, 60, 1220.

18 *A Newe Enterlude of Vice Conteyninge, the Historye of Horestes* (1567), ed. Daniel Selzer (Oxford, 1962), ll. 557, 629.
19 Chambers, *Elizabethan Stage*, vol. IV, p. 270.
20 Robert Tittler, *The Reformation and the Towns in England: Politics and Culture, c. 1540–1640* (Oxford, 1998), pp. 316–17.
21 Benjamin Griffin, 'The Breaking of the Giants: Historical Drama in London and Coventry', *English Literary Renaissance*, 29 (1) (1999): 3–21.
22 Chambers, *Elizabethan Stage*, vol. II, pp. 87–8.
23 Richard Dutton, *Mastering the Revels: The Regulation and Censorship of English Renaissance Drama* (Iowa City, Iowa, 1991), p. 34, citing Chambers, *Notes on the History of the Revels Office under the Tudors* (London, 1906), p. 54.
24 Mary Hill Cole, *The Portable Queen: Elizabeth I and the Politics of Ceremony* (Amherst, Mass., 1999), p. 4.
25 G. K. Hunter, *John Lyly: The Humanist as Courtier* (London, 1962), p. 136.
26 London Court of Common Council, *Repertories*, 19, fol. 18.
27 Chambers, *Elizabethan Stage*, vol. IV, p. 278.
28 Chambers, *Elizabethan Stage*, vol. IV, pp. 273, 200.
29 John Northbrooke, *A Treatise against Dicing, Dancing, Plays, and Interludes, with Other Idle Pastimes* (1577), in Tanya Pollard (ed.), *Shakespeare's Theatre: A Sourcebook* (Oxford, 2004), pp. 1–18; p. 7.
30 I.G. (John Greene), *A Refutation of the Apology for Actors* (1615), in Tanya Pollard (ed.), *Shakespeare's Theatre: A Sourcebook* (Oxford, 2004), pp. 255–73; p. 255.
31 Anthony Munday, *A Second and Third Blast of Retrait from Plaies and Theatres* (1580), in Chambers, *Elizabethan Stage*, vol. IV, pp. 208–12; p. 210.
32 Chambers, *Elizabethan Stage*, vol. IV, p. 214.
33 Henry Crosse, *Vertues Common-Wealth* (1603), in Pollard, *Shakespeare's Theatre: A Sourcebook*, pp. 188–97; p. 190.
34 Chambers, *Elizabethan Stage*, vol. IV, pp. 285–7.
35 Scott McMillin and Sally-Beth MacLean, *The Queen's Men and Their Plays* (Cambridge, 1998), p. 24.
36 *The Troublesome Raigne of King John of England* (1591), ed. J. W. Sider (New York, 1979), p. 182.
37 Chambers, *Elizabethan Stage*, vol. IV, p. 302.
38 *An Apology for Actors* (1612), sigs. F_3-F_3v.
39 *Martins Months Minde*, sigs. E4–F.
40 *The First Parte of Pasqvils Apologie* (1590) and *The Returne of . . . Pasqvill of England* (1589), in *The Works of Thomas Nashe*, ed. Ronald B. McKerrow, 5 vols. (Oxford, 1904–10), vol. I, pp. 105–36; p. 35; 83; *Pappe with an Hatchet* (1589), in *The Complete Works of John Lyly*, ed. R. Warwick Bond, 3 vols. (Oxford, 1902), vol. III, pp. 393–414; p. 408.
41 *An Advertisement Touching the Controversies of the Church of England*, in Brian Vickers (ed.), *Francis Bacon* (Oxford, 1996), pp. 1–19; p. 3; Chambers, *Elizabethan Stage*, vol. IV, p. 306.
42 'The Printer to the Reader', in *Endymion*, ed. David Bevington (Manchester, 1996), p. 74.
43 *The Massacre at Paris*, ed. H. J. Oliver (London, 1968), Scene 24, ll. 98–102, p. 162.
44 Stephen Greenblatt, *Shakespearean Negotiations: The Circulation of Social Energy in Renaissance England* (Berkeley, Calif., 1988), pp. 62–3; Louis Montrose, *The Purpose of Playing: Shakespeare and the Cultural Politics of the Elizabethan Theatre* (Chicago, Ill., 1996), p. 82.
45 Gordon Braden, *Renaissance Tragedy and the Senecan Tradition: Anger's Privilege* (New Haven, Conn., 1985), pp. 21–3, 66–7.

CHAPTER THIRTY-TWO

POETRY

Steven W. May

Verse permeated everyday life in Tudor England to a degree unknown in modern times. It was sung to music at church, in homes and on the streets by vendors and ballad-mongers. Many Elizabethans circulated poetry from hand to hand in manuscript. Verses also crop up in about one-third of all books and pamphlets issued from the press during Elizabeth's reign. Prose texts were regularly interrupted with poetic excerpts used to illustrate, validate or clarify the surrounding content. These snippets of verse were often translated from classical sources and introduced with the formulaic 'as the poet says', or 'in the words of the poet'. Verse titles and adages adorned paintings and were painted on the walls of taverns. At meals, verses were inscribed around the borders of trenchers on which food was served, while the handles of eating utensils were sometimes inscribed with such philosophical musings as 'Better it is a poor house to hold / than to lie in prison in fetters of gold'.[1] Elizabethans readily composed verses (if not poetry) as occasion served. When 'adventurers' in the lottery of 1567–8 were encouraged to individualise their entries with a 'devise, prose, or poesie', at least a third of them composed original verses to mark their lots.[2] The age's books are replete with ownership rhymes, one of the most popular formula being, 'Iste liber pertinet, bear it well in mind / Ad me Iohannem Dell, both courteous and kind.'[3]

In order to understand poetry as a cultural force in Elizabethan society we must consider not just its most literary, 'poetic' manifestations, but its pervasive presence in everyday life. In fact, most surviving verse of the Elizabethan age was practical, instructional or illustrative rather than explicitly literary. Verse was usually subordinate to some larger purpose. Devotional poetry, for example, was religious first but only secondarily 'poetic'; it was fashioned to enhance the worship experience, not to upstage it. In what follows, I concentrate on what was the most widely read Elizabethan poetry as measured by its survival in both printed and manuscript sources. This survey includes, of course, the age's 'best' poetry, for most of what we value today was also popular at the time. Simultaneously, however, a great deal of mediocre poetry (and some that was rather worse) was as popular or even more widely read than the finest poetry. In its full cultural context, Elizabethan poetic taste and the role of poetry in that culture differ significantly from accounts that focus only on poetry written and still recognised as literary art.

Elizabethans regularly encountered verse in their most prosaic and frequently reprinted books. Early in Elizabeth's reign, for example, someone noticed that prose instructions recording when the Exchequer opened for business would be more memorable if converted into verse:

> Eight days before any term be,
> The Exchequer openeth for certeintie.
> Excepte the terme of Trinitie,
> That openeth but four days before truly.[4]

By the end of the reign this rough quatrain had appeared in at least thirty-four editions of almanacs, in precedent books and even the Book of Common Prayer. Robert Record's *The Ground of Arts: Teaching the work and Practice of Arithmetic,* with thirteen editions between 1561 and 1600, included as many as a half-dozen poems, two of them designed to help readers remember mathematical rules.[5] It has seldom been recognised that the age's best known non-literary books are suffused with poetry. Both editions of Holinshed's *Chronicles,* for example, are anthologies of English and Latin verse, with 126 English poems in the 1587 edition. Hakluyt's 'Voyages' (*The Principal Navigations,* 1598–1600) also included dozens of poems. The most ambitious use of verse for instructive as opposed to literary purposes is Thomas Tusser's *A Hundreth Good Points of Husbandry.* First published in 1557, the book was expanded to *Five Hundreth Points* in 1573 and saw sixteen editions by 1599. Although Tusser's work is a verse anthology on such subjects as friendship and marriage, most of the book's 130-odd poems educate readers about all aspects of farm work and estate management. Tusser's best-seller illustrates the degree to which Elizabethans viewed poetry as merely a somewhat more elegant and memorable alternative to prose, not necessarily an art form created for strictly aesthetic effects.

Few examples of early Elizabethan verse suggest that English poetry hovered on the brink of a golden age. Their aesthetic value generally ranges from marginal to nil, and for specifiable reasons. Poets at mid-century faced three major deficiencies when they sat down to write: uncertainty about how to forge a rhythmic line of verse, a limited array of poetic forms to choose from and uncertainty about the style and level of language most suitable for poetry.[6] The quatrain concerning the Exchequer cited above illustrates the metrical problems characteristic of early Tudor verse. During the fifteenth century, English poets lost the ability to forge lines of accentual-syllabic verse that creates rhythm through a regular alternation of stressed and unstressed syllables. Scots never lost the secret of accentual-syllabic rhythm, but its rediscovery during the 1530s by such English poets as Sir Thomas Wyatt, Nicholas Grimald and Henry Howard, Earl of Surrey, owes nothing palpable to Scottish influences.

The second liability, a poverty of forms, left English poets of the first half of the sixteenth century to compose some 72 per cent of their extant verse in just four rhyme schemes, all of them invented or used by Chaucer: tetrameter and pentameter couplets, rhyme royal and 'Monk's Tale' stanza.[7] The third problem confronting early Tudor writers was to develop a level of diction and rhetoric appropriate to the tone and content of their verse. The extremes are represented by the 'aureate' style, featuring unusual words and newly coined Latin derivatives as popularised by the fifteenth-century poet monk John Lydgate, versus a racy, plain style sprinkled with slang and dialect words developed by the Henrician court poet John Skelton. Elizabethan poets were left to puzzle over the figures of speech and diction level appropriate for any given poem.

The rediscovery of accentual-syllabic metrics toward the end of Henry VIII's reign was disseminated in a number of printed books, among the most influential being the *Songs and Sonnets,* first published in 1557 by Richard Tottel and commonly referred to as Tottel's *Miscellany.* This anthology, with eight editions during Elizabeth's reign, provided not only a model for regular iambic scansion but also introduced dozens of new forms including sonnets in both the Petrarchan and Surreyean or English rhyme schemes (the latter devised, along with blank verse, by the Earl of Surrey), the 'sixain' stanza (rhyming ababcc), terza rima and ottava rima. The poems by Wyatt alone in this volume appear in twenty-nine different stanza forms. Tottel had prefaced his *Miscellany* with the patriotic assurance that 'our tong is able in that kynde [poetry] to do as praiseworthely as the rest'.[8] The most immediate influence of the *Songs and Sonnets,* accordingly, was to encourage a number of individuals to set forth books of verse as explicitly literary publications, not that this was an innovation. Skelton and Stephen Hawes had published one-poet editions earlier in the century, while the Middle English poetry of Chaucer, Lydgate and John Gower was frequently reprinted throughout the period.

The earliest professional Elizabethan poets – Barnaby Googe, George Turberville, Isabella Whitney and Thomas Howell foremost among them – excerpted from the poetry of Tottel's *Miscellany* and related works a uniform poetic style with a narrow range of forms and rhetorical devices. They largely ignored, for example, the Italian and English forms of the sonnet pioneered by Wyatt and Surrey, along with Surrey's blank verse and the new metres and stanzas that circulated in manuscript or were known from the *Songs and Sonnets.* The style they cultivated instead, termed 'drab' by C. S. Lewis, dominated English verse well into the 1580s. It prevailed in part because it responded head-on to the challenges faced by the emerging Tudor poetic. This response, however, proved transitional rather than permanent mostly because its emphasis on artifice over substance reduced poetry to a rhetorically ornamental art.

With regard to poetic form, Googe, Turberville, Whitney, Howell and their followers favoured long-line couplets in iambic heptameter (called 'fourteeners' because there were fourteen beats per couplet) or 'poulter's measure', a hexameter followed by a heptameter for a total of thirteen beats per couplet (by analogy with the practice of Elizabethan poulterers, who gave a thirteenth egg to customers who bought a dozen). The 'sixain' stanza was a third form that remained immensely popular for another century. With iambic tetrameter and pentameter couplets, these few stanzas dominated poetic output during the first three decades of Elizabeth's reign. In whatever metre, lines were overwhelmingly end stopped and terminated with masculine (one-syllable) rhymes, further to emphasise the beat. Contemporary poets seized on these long-line forms because the regular iambic feet amplified – relentlessly – their exaggerated rhythms.

The second distinctive characteristic of this mid-century style was its dependence on a limited range of rhetorical devices. Individual poets might vary the recipe with different tropes and schemes, yet the basic formula was to develop each theme in a poem with supporting examples set forth in alliterative phrases. Alliteration, with other repetitive schemes such as anaphora and isocolon, are the hallmarks of this style, schemes that also accentuate metrical regularity. Poetic language was laced with allusions from classical mythology and history but was seldom overly learned or aureate.

The collections of original literary verse published by these professional authors represented the cutting edge of English poetry as an art form, yet they attracted little popular attention. Only Howell's *Newe Sonets* saw more than a single edition. The mid-century style was disseminated more efficiently by Tottel's *Miscellany* and another very popular anthology the *Paradise of Dainty Devices,* which saw eight editions between 1576 and 1606. 'Drab' poetics not only held sway from mid-century through the 1580s, it persisted well into the seventeenth century, long after it had been entirely superseded by the superior techniques of later Elizabethan verse. After all, the plain style offered fledgling poets a sure guide to rhythmic verse, with models for the overall development of any poetic theme along with line-by-line formulae anchored in a limited range of easily manipulated rhetorical devices. The aesthetics of the mid-century style focused on appreciating the learning and creativity with which the poet used examples to illustrate a theme while conveying those examples in highly rhythmic lines of verse. Thus rhetorical virtuosity trumped emotional or dramatic effect as the chief pleasure of such poetry. The preferred subjects cultivated by these early Elizabethan poets included verse epitaphs, male friendship, practical and moral wisdom, exhortations to virtue and warnings against immoral behaviour, especially frivolous love.[9]

This aversion to love poems or, in fact, anything written for entertainment alone, was ultimately motivated by the age's steadfast religious convictions. Elizabethans' religious commitment, whether Protestant or Catholic, is difficult to exaggerate. In daily life, their zeal decreed that activities lacking moral (if not specifically religious) ends, hindered salvation and were ultimately indefensible. Nevertheless, only about 18 per cent of the poems printed or transcribed during the era is religious in nature, compared with some 75 per cent of extant medieval verse.[10] Yet these figures do not reflect any serious decline in religious fervour. Rather, the increase in poetic genres during the Renaissance meant that a fairly constant output of devotional verse was diluted in an ever-expanding pool of other subjects.

Poems in the service of religion were, in fact, among the best known of the entire era. The most potent non-literary influence on English verse throughout Elizabeth's reign, for example, was undoubtedly the 'Sternhold and Hopkins' metrical psalter. Begun by Thomas Sternhold and John Hopkins before Elizabeth came to the throne, the first edition to offer all 150 psalms in English metre, *The Whole Book of Psalms,* appeared in 1562. This was no two-man collaboration but an anthology of up to 180 devotional poems by at least ten poets, including William Whittingham, Thomas Norton, William Kethe and Bishop Richard Cox. Counting versions of the work appended to copies of the Scottish liturgy and the Book of Common Prayer, the complete psalter went through more than 160 Elizabethan editions, while many individual psalms were also set to music and published separately. Although more than a dozen poetic forms can be found in these volumes, they are dominated by the long-line couplets typical of the mid-century tradition. Their exaggerated rhythms, reinforced by musical settings, drove home the effect of regular iambic metres throughout Elizabeth's reign and for several centuries to come.

In addition to the *Whole Book of Psalms,* two poems in the preliminaries of many copies of both the Bishops' and Geneva bibles rank among the most widely distributed lyrics of the age.[11] Another devotional bestseller was William Hunnis's *Seven Sobs of a Sorrowful Soul for Sin,* with seven editions from 1583 to 1602. Hunnis's sing-song rhythms often detract from his penitential sincerity, yet one of his best poems here was more widely dispersed than any of the others. Hunnis had already published 'Alack when I look back' in the *Paradise of Dainty Devices,* where it appeared in another seven editions of that popular anthology. Its first stanza conveys sincere emotion despite its deployment in poulter's measure couplets:

Alack when I look back, upon my youth that's past,
And deeply ponder youth's offence, and youth's reward at last.
With sighs and tears I say, O God I not deny,
My youth with folly hath deserved, with folly for to die.
But yet if ever sinful man might mercy move to ruth,
Good Lord, with mercy do forgive the follies of my youth.[12]

During the 1570s, a second generation of publishing poets expanded the subjects treated by early Elizabethan verse, with an increasing emphasis on love lyrics. George Gascoigne was by far the most popular and talented of these plain style practitioners. His collected works, first published in 1573 as *A Hundreth Sundry Flowers,* saw three revised editions by 1587. Gascoigne's is arguably the best collection of lyric verse between Tottel and Spenser's *Shepheardes Calendar* (1579). He not only experimented with more forms than most of his contemporaries, he attempted a wide variety of genres, including verse letters, drama, a masque, autobiographical narrative and formal satire. Gascoigne also wrote one of the earliest guides to the writing of English poetry, his 'Certayne Notes of Instruction Concerning the Making of Verse or Ryme in English' (1575). Other competing one-poet anthologies include George Whetstone's *Rocke of Regard* (1576), Nicholas Breton's *A Floorish upon Fancie* and *The Workes of a Young Wyt* (both issued in 1577), J.C.'s *A Poore Knight his Pallace of Priuate Pleasures* (1579), and H.C.'s *Forrest of Fancy* (1579). Among these works, only Breton's *A Floorish,* with three editions by 1585, could claim any degree of popularity.

While Gascoigne perfected mid-century poetics, his work was not quite as popular as that of the exiled Catholic writer John Heywood. Heywood's non-dramatic verse, a carry-over from Henrician times, had appeared in print as early as 1546. In 1562, his 'Dialogue of Proverbs' was combined with a collection of 600 epigrams also based on adages and published as *John Heywoods Works.* The 'Dialogue' incorporates in 2,730 lines of verse several thousand conventional adages and sayings. Heywood was esteemed a great wit, yet his epigrams rarely transcend a grade-schooler's taste in wordplay and humour:

Beggars sing before thieves, but what of that?
When beggars sing so, thieves see nought to laugh at.[13]

Thou canst hold my nose to the grindstone:
So can not I thine, for thou hast none.[14]

Ill gotten, ill spent: be that tale true to tell,
Thou art never like to spend penny well.[15]

As these examples show, Heywood's verse was roughly accentual throughout, not accentual-syllabic, yet his *Works* saw five editions by 1598. Timothy Kendall's *Flowers of Epigrams* (1577) forms a puzzling contrast to Heywood's success. Kendall gathered more than 600 epigrams from classical and neo-Latin sources (lifting many of his translations, without acknowledgement, from George Turberville and other writers). The *Flowers* are set forth in regular metres, cover a broad array of topics and are on the whole more mature and polished than Heywood at his best, yet Kendall's book saw only this one edition.

Verse in the mid-century style, practical and literary, also circulated widely in manuscript. Throughout the Renaissance an ever-increasing volume of transcribed material, much of it in verse, passed from hand to hand. Single sheets, pamphlets and whole books of verse were compiled, exchanged, recopied and passed along to others. Given the loss rates among these manuscripts, it is likely that two or three extant copies of a poem represent very widespread contemporary circulation. Occasional lyrics were especially common in manuscript circulation, and despite the supposition that manuscript culture paid little attention to authorship, many of the most widely disseminated works were attributed (not always correctly) by a majority of the scribes who copied them. Foremost among these is the penitential hymn allegedly sung on his deathbed in 1576 by Walter, 1st Earl of Essex.[16] Although the poem was attributed that same year to Francis Kinwelmarsh in *The Paradise of Dainty Devices,* thirteen of its eighteen Elizabethan manuscript texts suggest that Essex wrote it. Queen Elizabeth's 'The doubt of future foes', her poetic musing in the aftermath of the Northern Rebellion of 1569–70, survives in eight contemporary manuscripts, each attributed to the Queen.[17] An obscure participant in the 1586 Babington assassination plot, Chidiock Tichburne, gained immortality as the author of a three-stanza lament for his premature death.[18] Six of its nine complete Elizabethan manuscript texts assign it to Tichburne.

The mid-century poetic logjam broke up very gradually during the 1580s as poets experimented with alternative rhythms modulated with substitute feet (for example, adding occasional trochaic or anapestic feet to impart variety to a predominately iambic poem). They also attempted new stanza forms and a broader range of rhetorical effects. George Chapman's translation of Homer reveals dramatically the technical superiority of the best late Elizabethan poets. Chapman's *Iliad* is written in fourteener couplets, albeit fourteeners fashioned with such subtle variety of sound and rhythm as to set the form light years apart from its mid-century norm. Above all, the 'golden' or 'new' poetry placed form and rhetoric in the service of meaning and effect, rather than as ends in themselves.

Edmund Spenser's *Shepherdes Calendar* (1579) is often cited as the first significant breakthrough in the movement toward the best Elizabethan poetry. Its twelve poems or eclogues, one for each month, covered a range of subjects from love lament to praise of the Queen to satire of both Catholicism and aspects of the state church. The *Calendar* was Spenser's one best-seller, with four Elizabethan editions, plus two more by 1617. However, its cultivation of a rustic, native English pastoral tradition found few imitators. Along with complicated stanzas and refrains (March, August), the *Calendar* included rough four-stress verse (February, May, September) and ample alliteration in the mid-century manner. Sir Philip Sidney explicitly disavowed Spenser's rustic diction and modelled his own pastoral verse on classical and Continental precedents.[19] His elegant, imported style became the dominant influence on the enthusiastic cultivation of pastoralism in verse and prose from the late 1580s onward.

Sidney was likewise the formative influence on the development of mature, 'golden' Elizabethan poetry. A version of his pastoral romance, the *Arcadia,* was published with thirty-six poems in 1590, a revised edition appeared in 1593 with seventy-four poems, and that of 1598 (with other works) set forth 231 poems. The first genuine English sonnet sequence, Sidney's *Astrophil and Stella,* appeared in a corrupt edition in 1591 and was twice reprinted before a corrected text appeared in the 1598 *Arcadia* volume. But Sidney's revolutionary advances in English poetry had begun to influence his contemporaries some years before 1590, since his poems were more widely circulated in manuscript during Elizabeth's reign than those of any other individual poet. Even before his death in 1586, the *Arcadia* was being widely copied, as were individual poems from this and his 'Certain Sonnets' collection.[20] Sidney's advances included the introduction of trochaic metre plus the cultivation of dozens of new or neglected stanza forms including the sestina, double sestina, ottava rima, and terza rima. Above all, Sidney aimed to subordinate rhetoric to the aesthetic effects of his poems. What he accomplished transcended the mid-century manner and ultimately replaced it. And while Sidney, like most courtier poets, specialised in the love lyric, his canon offered new and exciting models in many other genres: several types of verse narrative, including a moral parable and beast fable, traditional love laments, Anacreontic whimsey, rejections of love and the lover, blazons and a witty mock-blazon.[21] Sidney also wrote personal elegies, an epithalamion, dialogues, debates and a partial translation of the psalms.[22]

The publication of Sidney's *Astrophil and Stella* launched the 'sonnet craze' of the 1590s. What readers discovered in Sidney's work was the Petrarchan technique of using individual lyrics to create narrative effect, as if arranging a collection of photographs in chronological order so that a story can be pieced together from them. At least fifteen different sonnet sequences were published in the 1590s, but only Michael Drayton's *Idea,* Samuel Daniel's *Delia,* Henry Constable's *Diana* and Richard Barnefield's *Cynthia* ('With Certaine Sonnets' to Ganymede) shared with *Astrophil and Stella* the distinction of being reprinted. Even Spenser's sequence, the *Amoretti* (1595), saw only one edition despite its appended *Epithalamion,* an exquisite wedding poem. Shakespeare wrote many of his sonnets during Elizabeth's reign, although the entire collection did not see print until 1609 when, again, only one edition of the work was called for.

Sidney summed up the overall shift in aesthetic intent from mid-century to the 'golden' style when he asserted with regard to earlier love poetry that, 'truly many of such writings as come under the banner of unresistible love, if I were a mistress, would never persuade me they were in love'.[23] Instead of dazzling his mistress with rhetoric for its own sake, Sidney wrote love poetry designed to move the beloved with emotionally charged expression of love's passion. This he accomplished from both male and female perspectives, for 'poetry' to Sidney was what we term creative writing of all kinds, and some of his best Arcadian love poetry speaks from the woman's viewpoint. The initial stanza of the Tenth Song from *Astrophil and Stella* illustrates most of his innovations in style, metre, and form:

> O dear life, when shall it be,
> That mine eyes thine eyes may see?
> And in them thy mind discover,
> Whether absence have had force
> Thy remembrance to divorce,
> From the image of thy lover?[24]

As an address to the beloved in absence, these simple words express longing, doubt and commitment. The trochaic tetrameter rhythm gives an insistent urgency to the lover's questions, the stanza, rhyming aabccb is enjambed in lines 4–5 (the sense carries over without pause from one line to the next), while here the feminine rhymes of lines 3 and 6 enhance the personal, conversational tone of the passage. Comparable effects occur in the works of Wyatt and Surrey, but in few other English poets who wrote during the interim.

Sidney included eight quantitative poems in the *Arcadia,* poems whose rhythms were produced, as in Greek and Latin poetry, by differences in the time it takes to pronounce adjacent syllables. Sidney thus revived the ultimately futile experiment with English verse in classical metres. The Renaissance nurtured a profound sense of cultural inferiority, viewing the achievements of ancient Greece and Rome as much superior to almost everything that contemporary society had achieved. For Elizabethans, poetry was inextricably connected to rhyme, a rhetorical device that classical poets deplored. Roger Ascham had encouraged the writing of quantitative verse in English before Elizabeth came to the throne. Its peculiar effect can be heard in these 'English hexameters' from Eclogue 13 of the *Old Arcadia*:

> Now by thy words I begin, most famous Lady, to gather
> Comfort into my soule. I do finde, I do find what a blessing
> Is chauncéd to my life, that from such muddy abundance
> Of carking agonies (to estates which still be adherent)
> Desteny keepes me aloofe.[25]

Sidney's protégé Abraham Fraunce began publishing English quantitative verse in 1587, producing more than 7,000 lines of it in five printed works. Robert Greene, Thomas Bradshaw and John Dickenson included quantitative lyrics in works of prose fiction, and even Spenser experimented with unrhymed classical metres. Aesthetically, by far the most successful practitioner of English classical metres was the musician Thomas Campion. The quantitative gambit played itself out early in the seventeenth century, its most fitting epitaph, perhaps, being Ben Jonson's verdict that Abraham Fraunce 'in his English Hexameters was a foole'.[26]

The Elizabethans' reverence for the literary heritage of Greece and Rome also found outlet in verse renderings of classical texts, and these tended to be a good deal more popular than translations from the Continental vernaculars. George Turberville translated Ovid's *Heroides* as Ovid's *Heroycall Epistles* (seven editions, 1567–1600). Nearly as popular was Arthur Golding's translation of Ovid's *Metamorphoses* (six editions, 1565–1603). Thomas Phaer's translation of Virgil's *Aeneid* (completed by Thomas Twyne) saw five Elizabethan editions (1562–1600), while Richard Stanyhurst's version of the first four books in quantitative metres reached only two editions (1582–3). Seneca's tragedies appeared in a collected edition in 1581. Among Continental vernacular poets, Du Bartas was perhaps the most popular, with eight titles translated during Elizabeth's reign, three of which reached a second edition.

In addition to the circulation of Sidney's verse in manuscript and print, the 'golden' lyrics that began to appear in songbooks toward the end of the 1580s also helped to displace mid-century poetics. These songs typically were cast in short-line forms, with simple language and rhetoric. The musician William Byrd, who had access to courtier texts, set some of them to music in his *Psalms, Sonnets and Songs* (1588), followed by his *Songs of Sundry Natures* in 1589. Both appeared in multiple editions and included verse by such courtiers as Sidney, his friend Edward Dyer and Sir Walter Ralegh. Nicholas Yonge's *Musica transalpina,* with two editions in 1588, and Thomas Watson's *First Set of Italian Madrigals Englished* (1590) offered sprightly selections of Italian love lyrics skilfully translated into English. Watson's earlier collection of translated Italian verse, *Ekatompathia; or, Passionate Century of Love* (1582) had likewise replaced some plain style conventions with a greater array of rhetorical devices and emotional effects. The books of madrigals and airs appearing in the 1590s and beyond, especially those by such popular composers as John Dowland, Thomas Morley and Thomas Weelkes, conveyed high-quality verse, mostly amorous in nature, to a wide audience.

The new poetry also affected the composition of devotional verse. Henry Lok, Barnabe Barnes and William Alabaster, among others, wrote collections of religious sonnets. While Sidney's translation of Psalms 1–43 falls short of his best poetry, his sister, Mary Herbert, Countess of Pembroke, completed the series with distinction. The Sidney–Herbert psalter had just begun to circulate in manuscript towards the end of Elizabeth's reign. Its survival in seventeen manuscripts bears witness to scores if not hundreds of seventeenth-century copies.[27] In language, thought and technical proficiency, her work is the pre-eminent Elizabethan translation of the psalter. A second very popular and skilful devotional poet was Robert Southwell, SJ, executed in 1595 for promoting Catholicism in England. Between 1595 and 1602 at least thirteen editions of his poetry, already circulating in Catholic circles in manuscript, appeared in print. English publishers secured licenses for Southwell's verse by simply editing out its most blatant Catholic content. Overall, Southwell's metres and forms appear old-fashioned, as do some of his alliterative phrases and commonplace expression. These habits were reinforced as he transformed to religious purposes secular love poems such as Edward Dyer's 'He that his mirth hath lost', and Thomas Watson's 'I joy not peace'. But Southwell also tried his hand at trochaic metres and unusual rhyme schemes.[28] Among his lyrics are some of the most powerful devotional poems of the Reformation.

In addition, Southwell's most ambitious poem, *Saint Peter's Complaint,* inspired a well-defined and very popular sub-genre of religious penitential verse. The *Complaint* no doubt owes something to an equally lengthy work by his co-religionist Philip Howard, Earl of Arundel. Arundel's 'Of the Four Last Things' is a penitential lament in sixain stanzas.[29] It survives in nine contemporary manuscripts, testifying to a very wide readership. But whereas Arundel's anonymous narrator scolds the reader into penitence, Southwell's Saint Peter mourns his denial of Christ in abjectly personal, humble terms:

> And could I rate so high a life so base?
> Did feare with love cast so uneven accompt:
> That for this goale I should runne Judas race,
> And Caiphas rage in cruelty surmount?[30]

Imitators sprang up almost immediately; all employ the first-person confessional voice, sixain form and occasional feminine rhymes that marked Southwell's style. In addition to Saint Peter, copycat laments by Adam and Mary Magdalene also appeared. The most popular imitation, however, was no poetic fiction. Robert Devereux, Earl of Essex, composed it in the Tower of London in February 1601, a few days before being beheaded for treason. Essex confessed his guilt not only for his attempted *coup d'état* but for a whole lifetime of sin:

> The traitor Judas, heire borne to perdition,
> Who for a trifle did his Lord betray,
> In equall doome deserveth more remission,
> Then my defaults can challenge any way;
> He solde him once, that once for gaine was done;
> I oftentimes, yet lesse then nothing wonne.[31]

The work saw two anonymous Elizabethan editions, was reprinted in 1621 and survives in five manuscripts. Orlando Gibbons and John Dowland set to music several stanzas from the poem, while G. Ellis plagiarised most of it in his *Lamentation of the Lost Sheep* (1605).

As her subjects increasingly took pride in their country during Elizabeth's reign, their patriotism inspired a growing interest in the English past that found varied expressions in the arts. Ballads and patriotic jingles celebrated national triumphs, past and present, from Flodden Field to the defeat of the Northern Rebellion in 1570 and of the Spanish Armada in 1588. Gamesters learned about their country's history and geography from verses printed on the backs of their playing cards. Elizabethans invented the English history play and fully developed its theatrical potential. One of their sources for these plays, and one of the reign's most popular collections of narrative verse, was William Baldwin's *Mirror for Magistrates.* His plan called for the ghosts of English historical figures, from Richard II to the rebel Jack Cade, to lament before him their tragic downfalls:

> O ryghteous God thy judgementes are true,
> For looke what measure we other awarde,

The same for us agayne is preparde:
Take heed ye princes by examples past,
Blood wyll have blood, eyther fyrst or last.[32]

Seven editions appeared between 1559 and 1578. Following up on this success, John Higgins set forth *The First Part of the Mirror for Magistrates* in 1574, followed by Thomas Blennerhasset's *Second Part of the Mirror for Magistrates* (1578). The complaints by real and imaginary figures in these continuations extended from England's mythical origins to the time of William the Conqueror.

The influence of the various *Mirrors* was substantial and long-lasting, especially their most popular poem, Thomas Churchyard's 'Tragedy of Shore's Wife'.[33] This lament appeared in editions of Baldwin's *Mirror* after 1563. Churchyard reprinted it in 1593, while William Byrd set two of its stanzas to music. Churchyard's Jane Shore, the mistress of King Edward IV, emerges as a sympathetic character, although her persistent moralising and redundancy detract from her appeal. During the 1590s, with all the *Mirrors* out of print, Samuel Daniel and Michael Drayton culled the historical record for other royal concubines whose ghosts they could impersonate in verse. Daniel appended 'The Complaynt of Rosamond' to *Delia,* the sonnet sequence he published in 1592. The work was reprinted seven times before the end of the reign.[34] Drayton followed Daniel's lead with *The Legend of Matilda,* mistress of King John (three editions, 1594–6). His *Piers Gaveston,* which also saw three editions (*c.* 1594–6), varied the theme by presenting the ghost of King Edward II's homosexual favourite. Shakespeare's *Rape of Lucrece* (1594) owes much to this tradition, including its rhyme royal form, although his heroine is a Roman rather than English dame.

Both Daniel and Drayton also celebrated the national past with narratives centred on times of upheaval. Daniel's *Civil Wars,* first published in 1595, treats the Wars of the Roses and begins in Virgilian epic fashion: 'I sing the civil wars, tumultuous broils', but, as Ben Jonson observed, 'Daniel wrott Civill Warres, and yett hath not one batle in all his Book.'[35] As a narrator of heroic tales, Daniel has more in common with Henry James than Homer, yet his *Civil Wars* enjoyed five editions by 1602. Drayton returned to the troubled reign of Edward II with *Mortimeriados* (two editions, 1596), a chronicle in epic style of Edward's deposition. Drayton expanded this story in *The Barons' Wars* (1603). However, *England's Heroical Epistles,* first published in 1597, was his most original and popular contribution to poetry grounded in English history. An expanded version of the work was reprinted four more times during Elizabeth's reign. The *Heroical Epistles* also exemplifies the Renaissance concern to restore contemporary civilisation to the (supposed) superiority of Greek and Roman times. Drayton modelled his work on Ovid's *Heroides,* Latin verse letters by mythical figures only three of whom are men. Drayton's *Epistles,* however, are paired letters between famous royal and noble English couples such as Henry II and Rosamond, King John and Matilda.

The finest work of Elizabethan poetry inspired by patriotism (and moral didacticism) is Spenser's *Faerie Queene.* The first three books appeared in 1590, were then reprinted with Books 4–6 in 1596, but not again until 1609. Spenser composed, nevertheless, the most ambitious, ingeniously crafted poem of the sixteenth century, albeit he completed only half his plan for a national heroic narrative in twelve books. On its literal level, *The Faerie Queene* is an action-packed adventure story well suited for production as a Technicolor, animated cartoon. Its allegorical levels of meaning, however, simultaneously present, interpret and celebrate a great deal of English history, along with expositions of moral and psychological dilemmas in keeping with the work's purpose as set forth in Spenser's introductory 'Letter', to 'fashion a gentleman or noble person in vertuous and gentle discipline'.[36]

Years before Spenser and other 'golden' poets began treating the national past in poetry, the attorney William Warner had begun a comprehensive history of England in verse. The first four books of *Albion's England* appeared in 1586; by the edition of 1602, Warner had treated English history through most of Elizabeth's reign in thirteen books and more than 9,500 lines of verse.[37] He wrote throughout in fourteener couplets; here is an excerpt from his anti-Catholic treatment of the execution of Mary, Queen of Scots:

> So doth the Popes false Calendar of Saints of Sense bereave
> Our Traytors, who dye papists that therein it them receave.
> Was never yet Religion heard so pestilent as this,
> Their murdring us, for Lawfull, of their Creed a portion is:[38]

Yet with six editions by 1602 (plus a continuation in 1606, and a seventh edition in 1612), *Albion's England* was far more popular than *The Faerie Queene* and ranks among the most popular poems based on English history from the last two decades of Elizabeth's reign.

Along with historical narratives, narrative poems concerned with romantic love proliferated during Elizabeth's reign. Medieval survivals of the kind are found in the seven Elizabethan editions of Chaucer's works. Arthur Broke's *Tragical History of Romeus and Juliet,* the source for Shakespeare's play, saw three editions between 1562 and 1587.[39] George Gascoigne, Bernard Garter and Thomas Lodge also wrote amorous narratives that saw multiple editions, while many retellings of love stories from Ovid's *Metamorphoses* appeared as well, few of which saw more than a single edition.[40] During the 1590s, however, parodies of these tales emerged as another very popular narrative genre. Critics refer to these different genres unsystematically as 'Ovidian narrative', 'epyllion' and 'minor epic'. Among them was Shakespeare's *Venus and Adonis* (1593), his most popular work, with sixteen editions by 1636. Shakespeare altered Ovid's myth just enough to make the situation ridiculous, in that Venus woos a prepubescent Adonis who is biologically unable to respond to her attempted seduction. Nearly as popular was Christopher Marlowe's *Hero and Leander,* with ten editions from 1598 to 1637. Marlowe's Leander is described in terms of feminine beauty: 'For in his looks were all that men desire', while (aside from her white hands) Hero's beauty is strictly a function of her costume rather than her physique.[41] A further comic discrepancy concerns the narrator's attitude towards what he recounts versus the reality of the situation. Marlowe's narrator notes, for instance, that Hero's hand trembled when Leander touched it because 'Love deeply grounded, hardly is dissembled', yet the lovers first saw each other only moments before and have not yet spoken to one another.[42] Chaucer had used this same humorous technique in 'The Nun's Priest's Tale', as Pope would later in *The Rape of the Lock.* George Chapman composed a humourless conclusion to

Marlowe's poem which was published with all editions after the first, while Henry Petowe contrived an equally bland sequel, 'Hero and Leanders Further Fortunes' (1598).[43] Several contemporary poets got the joke, however; Shakespeare's and Marlowe's parodies were imitated during Elizabeth's reign by John Marston's *Metamorphosis of Pigmalion's Image* (1598), John Weever's *Faunus and Melliflora* (1600), and F.B.'s *Salmacis and Hermaphroditus* (1602). At the same time, other poets continued to produce straightforward, tragic love stories such as Thomas Edwards's 'Cephalus and Procris' (1595), and H.L.'s 'The Legend of Orpheus and Euridice' (1597).[44]

The satiric spirit governed much of the verse written during the last decade of Elizabeth's reign. Indeed, by 1599, so much acrimonious wrangling had reached print that government censors ordered the Stationers' Company to hand over for burning a considerable store of satiric books and pamphlets. Joseph Hall's *Virgidimiarum* (six editions, 1597–1602) was one of these books; in its 'Prologue' Hall boasted, 'I first adventure: follow me who list, / and be the second English Satyrist'.[45] But Hall was far from the first, for verse satire in many forms and fashions had a long pedigree by Elizabeth's reign and flourished throughout it in both manuscript and print. The age's most virulent libel and satire circulated primarily in manuscript. The 'Bashe Libel', for instance, a lively attack on Elizabeth's Victualler of the Navy, Edward Bashe, is found in three Elizabethan and four later manuscripts.[46] It circulated in manuscript as late as the 1620s. Ralegh's general satiric attack on the central government beginning 'Go soul, the body's guest' survives in six Elizabethan manuscripts and at least a score of later ones.[47] Verse replies that attacked Ralegh joined satires of government officials in defence of the Earl of Essex after his disgrace in 1599. A cluster of these satiric and libellous poems was copied and recopied for years after Essex's execution in 1601.[48]

Abundant if somewhat less inflammatory printed satire was also available. A number of satires from the reign of Henry VIII had been reprinted during the 1560s, among them two editions of Skelton's works, plus Andrew Barclay's translation of Sebastian Brant's *Ship of Fools* (1570), a broad social satire couched in more than 14,000 lines of verse. From 1560 to 1590 verse satire on religious grounds, Protestant and Catholic, was commonplace. Among the forty-odd poems in Elizabethan editions of Foxe's *Actes and Monuments* (the 'Book of Martyrs') are a half-dozen satires, including attacks on Bishop Edmund Bonner and Pope Julius II.[49] The Marprelate controversy (1589–90) was conducted primarily in prose but also generated several dozen poems attacking the state church, the reformers, or both. Published satires were relatively general but might still specify the failings of various trades and callings, foremost among them being lawyers, physicians and courtiers. Early Elizabethan satire was also set forth in a wide variety of poetic genres. Some writers returned to the tradition of medieval dream vision as exemplified in the fourteenth-century *Piers Plowman* (which reached a fourth printed edition in 1561). John Hall, for example, used two dream visions in his *Court of Virtue* (1565) to describe a wholly sinful society and to denounce astrology and witchcraft.[50] Robert Crowley satirised not only social conditions in general but also alehouses, gambling and bowling alleys in his *33 Epigrams* (1573). In the *First Part of the Eight Liberal Sciences* (1576–9), Ulpian Fulwell satirised oppressive landlords through a fictional 'Tom Tapster', who encourages his master to adopt unethical practices.[51] Edward

Hake set forth eight satiric verse dialogues to expose the corrupting power of money in *News Out of Paul's Churchyard* (1579).

Compared with this diversity of early satiric genres, late Elizabethan printed satires were relatively impoverished. They were largely restricted to scornful first-person tirades imitating the formal satires of Horace, Juvenal and Persius, or satiric epigrams modelled on Martial. Both types attributed vice and folly to victims disguised under pseudonyms: Matho, Ruffus, Titus, Cacus and the rest. These later satirists benefited from the superior poetic techniques that had emerged by the 1590s, yet their overall level of creativity fell short of their predecessors'. For the most part, the writers of both epigram and formal satire revisited the same targets singled out by earlier satirists. Joseph Hall, for example, attacked lawyers, doctors and astrologers.[52] Richard Barnfield's *Encomion of Lady Pecunia* (1598) and Breton's 'Mad-Caps Out upon Money' (1602) railed at the pervasive, sinful influence of wealth.[53] Marston's *Scourge of Villainy* (three editions, 1598–9), emphasised lechery. Two new targets did emerge in the 1590s, however, the first being tobacco (which was popularised in England during the 1580s) and the second literary satire. Hall's scornful criticism of various kinds of poetry and plays in the first instalment of *Virgidimiarum* was repeated in the formal satire and epigrams of other poets. Moreover, these attacks fed upon themselves. Marston made fun of Hall in his *Metamorphosis of Pigmalions Image* (1598), and Hall caused an epigram that insulted Marston to be pasted into every copy of the *Metamorphosis* sold in Cambridge. In *The Whipping of the Satire* (1601), John Weever attacked Marston, Everard Guilpin and Ben Jonson and was himself vilified for doing so (apparently by Guilpin) in *The Whipper of the Satyre* (1601). This satirists' free for all shows the extent to which poetry had risen to national prominence in the course of Elizabeth's reign.

No such debate about good or bad versifying could have found a popular audience much before the 1590s. When Elizabeth took the throne, vernacular poetry was generally considered a trivial if not pernicious pastime. Her first Lord Keeper, Sir Nicholas Bacon, was both an original poet and a translator, but he termed his collected verses 'The Recreacons of his Age'. Less charitable were the outright attacks on poetry by preachers and even the Queen's tutor, Roger Ascham.[54] Yet the Queen herself was known to write and translate poetry, while verse published during her reign by such prestigious figures as Sir Francis Drake, the Earl of Oxford, the Countess of Pembroke and King James of Scotland confirmed the respectability of poetry as an art form well before the end of the reign. Few economic benefits accompanied its rising status, however. Elizabeth recognised no poet laureate, nor did she fund a poet in residence at her court. A number of her courtiers wrote verse, but this was a wholly optional rather than obligatory attainment for successful courtiership.

For professional poets, rewards were normally intermittent and tied to specific events. A few hack writers, notably William Elderton and Thomas Deloney, eked out meagre livings writing ballads. Wealthy subjects who entertained the Queen on her progress visits routinely hired poets such as George Gascoigne, Thomas Churchyard and Sir John Davies, to compose works for her flattery and amusement. George Peele and Anthony Munday among others earned commissions for 'civic pageantry' such as the Lord Mayors' shows presented in London. The only other practical way to market one's writing was through the publication of books and pamphlets, but here too poetry seldom offered a steady source of income. Authors received, at most, two lump-sum rewards for publishing their writings. First, the publisher bought all rights to the work when it went to press. The author gained no royalties or further profit from the work no matter how often it was reprinted. Second, the author normally sent a copy of the book to its dedicatee in hope of some further reward. A few writers secured lasting patronage this way to judge from their multiple dedications of poetic works to a single patron. Abraham Fraunce's dedications to the Countess of Pembroke and her relatives, for example, argue that they consistently rewarded him for his efforts. Similarly, after dedicating *Venus and Adonis* to the Earl of Southampton, Shakespeare dedicated *The Rape of Lucrece* to him the next year, another indication of patronage. In practice, however, most poets dedicated their works to one prospective patron after another in a largely vain effort to find some continuing support.

During Elizabeth's reign, English poets revolutionised the national art form. They cultivated a range of genres far broader than anything attempted by earlier generations, including odes, epithalamia, the country-house poem, rondelays and sonnet sequences. They harnessed the rhetorical schemes and tropes into the service of aesthetics to enhance the meanings and effects of their poetry. Diction levels were calibrated to the same purpose. They bequeathed to their successors all the forms they would need for centuries to come, from heroic couplets and blank verse to the most intricate rhyming stanzas. Finally, they played out the quantitative gambit but left standing in perfected cadences the iambic, trochaic and anapestic metres that would dominate English verse until both rhyme and metre gradually disappeared from poetry during the twentieth century. Meanwhile, and throughout Elizabeth's reign, verse without literary pretensions was applied to a broad range of utilitarian purposes. And in both literary and non-literary contexts the rhetoric-centred, metrically rigid tradition of mid-century verse maintained its popularity with poets and consumers alike, in print and manuscript, for decades to come.

FURTHER READING

Attridge, Derek, *Well-Weighed Syllables: Elizabethan Verse in Classical Metres* (Cambridge, 1974).

Bell, Ilona, *Elizabethan Women and the Poetry of Courtship* (Cambridge, 1998).

Brink, Jean R., *Michael Drayton Revisited* (Boston, Mass., 1990).

Budra, Paul Vincent, *A Mirror for Magistrates and the* De Casibus *Tradition* (Toronto, 2000).

Hamilton, A. C., *Sir Philip Sidney: A Study of His Life and Works* (Cambridge, 1977).

Hankins, John Erskine, *Source and Meaning in Spenser's Allegory* (Oxford, 1971).

Jones, Malcolm, '"Such Pretty Things Would Soon Be Gone": The Neglected Genres of Popular Verse, 1480–1650', in Michael Hattaway (ed.), *A Companion to English Renaissance Literature and Culture* (Malden, Mass. and Oxford, 2000), pp. 442–63.

Lewis, C. S., *English Literature in the Sixteenth Century Excluding Drama* (Oxford, 1954).

Marotti, Arthur, *Manuscript, Print, and the English Renaissance Lyric* (Ithaca, NY, 1995).

May, Steven W., *The Elizabethan Courtier Poets* (Columbia, Miss., 1991).

Roche, Thomas P., Jr., *Petrarch and the English Sonnet Sequences* (New York, 1989).

Scott-Warren, Jason, *Early Modern English Literature* (Cambridge and Malden, Mass., 2005).

Smith, Hallett, *Elizabethan Poetry: A Study in Conventions, Meaning, and Expression* (Cambridge, Mass., 1952).

Zim, Rivkah, *English Metrical Psalms: Poetry as Praise and Prayer 1535–1601* (Cambridge, 1987).

NOTES

1 Peter Brown (ed.), *British Cutlery* (York, 2001), p. 72.

2 *A Very Rich Lotterie Generall Without Any Blanckes* (London, 1567), p. 2.

3 EV 12631, reference number (as in subsequent citations) to the complete poem record in Steven W. May and William A. Ringler, Jr., *Elizabethan Poetry: A Bibliography and First-Line Index of English Verse, 1559–1603* (London, 2004). Ralph Hanna III, *Papers of the Bibliographical Society of America*, 74 (1980), p. 247.

4 May and Ringler, *Elizabethan Poetry*, EV 5684.

5 May and Ringler, *Elizabethan Poetry*, EV 8085, 27820.

6 Sir Philip Sidney, *The Poems of Sir Philip Sidney*, ed. William A. Ringler, Jr. (Oxford, 1962), p. lii.

7 William A. Ringler, Jr., *Bibliography and Index of English Verse Printed 1476–1558* (London and New York, 1988), p. 6.

8 'The Printer to the Reader', *Songes and Sonettes* (London, 1557), sig. A1v.

9 Cathy Shrank, '"Matters of Love as of Discourse": The English Sonnet, 1560–80', *Studies in Philology*, 105 (2008): 30–49.

10 May and Ringler, *Elizabethan Poetry* p. xvi.

11 Paul J. Voss, '"Created Good and Faire": The Fictive Imagination and Sacred Texts in Elizabethan England', *Literature and Theology*, 14 (2000), pp. 125–44.

12 May and Ringler, *Elizabethan Poetry*, EV 1366.

13 May and Ringler, *Elizabethan Poetry*, EV 3545.

14 May and Ringler, *Elizabethan Poetry*, EV 25910.

15 May and Ringler, *Elizabethan Poetry*, EV 11658.

16 May and Ringler, *Elizabethan Poetry*, EV 17057.

17 May and Ringler, *Elizabethan Poetry*, EV 22262.

18 May and Ringler, *Elizabethan Poetry*, EV 15464.

19 Sir Philip Sidney, *Miscellaneous Prose of Sir Philip Sidney*, ed. Katherine Duncan-Jones and Jan Van Dorsten (Oxford, 1973), p. 112.

20 H. R. Woudhuysen, *Sir Philip Sidney and the Circulation of Manuscripts, 1558–1640* (Oxford, 1996), pp. 242–6.

21 May and Ringler, *Elizabethan Poetry*, EV 595, 2709, 17745, 192113, 25816, 29059, 28757.

22 May and Ringler, *Elizabethan Poetry*, EV 6264, 9123, 13418.

23 Sidney, *Miscellaneous Prose*, pp. 116–17.

24 May and Ringler, *Elizabethan Poetry*, EV 16753, ll. 1–6.

25 May and Ringler, *Elizabethan Poetry*, EV 13141, 11. 93–8.

26 R. F. Patterson (ed.), *Ben Jonson's Conversations with William Drummond of Hawthornden* (New York, 1974), p. 6.

27 Mary Sidney Herbert, *The Collected Works of Mary Sidney Herbert Countess of Pembroke*, eds Margaret P. Hannay, Noel J. Kinnamon and Michael G. Brennan, 2 vols. (Oxford, 1998), vol. II, p. 308.

28 May and Ringler, *Elizabethan Poetry*, EV 20080, 20230.

29 May and Ringler, *Elizabethan Poetry*, EV 17760.

30 Robert Southwell, *The Poems of Robert Southwell, S.J.*, ed. James H. McDonald and Nancy Pollard Brown (Oxford, 1967), ll. 97–100.

31 Steven W. May, 'The Poems of Edward DeVere, Seventeenth Earl of Oxford, and of Robert Devereux, Second Earl of Essex', *Studies in Philology*, Texts and Studies Issue (1980), p. 51, ll. 109–14.

32 'Thomas, Duke of Gloucester', *The Mirror for Magistrates*, ed. Lily B. Campbell (New York, 1970), ll. 199–203.
33 May and Ringler, *Elizabethan Poetry*, EV 1952.
34 May and Ringler, *Elizabethan Poetry*, EV 18664.
35 Patterson, *Ben Jonson's Conversations*, p. 20.
36 Christopher Marlowe, *The Collected Poems of Christopher Marlowe*, ed. Patrick Cheney and Brian J. Striar (New York and Oxford, 2006), p. 84.
37 May and Ringler, *Elizabethan Poetry*, EV 10339.
38 1602, sig. R5.
39 EV 25003.
40 EV 9818, 29906, 28090.
41 Marlowe, *Collected Poems*, l. 184.
42 Joseph Hall, *The Poems of Joseph Hall*, ed. Arnold Davenport (Liverpool, 1969), p. 11, ll. 3–4.
43 May and Ringler, *Elizabethan Poetry*, EV 30098.
44 May and Ringler, *Elizabethan Poetry*, EV 6038, 1087.
45 May and Ringler, *Elizabethan Poetry*, EV 1189, 4581, 12846; Walter Ralegh, *The Poems of Sir Walter Ralegh: A Historical Edition*, ed. Michael Rudick (Tempe, Ariz., 1999), pp. xlii–xlvii.
46 May and Ringler, *Elizabethan Poetry*, EV 9921.
47 May and Ringler, *Elizabethan Poetry*, EV 7534.
48 Edwin Haviland Miller, *The Professional Writer in Elizabethan England* (Cambridge, Mass., 1959), pp. 20–1.
49 May and Ringler, *Elizabethan Poetry*, EV 14973, 29600.
50 May and Ringler, *Elizabethan Poetry*, EV 29575, 7180.
51 May and Ringler, *Elizabethan Poetry*, EV 2585.
52 May and Ringler, *Elizabethan Poetry*, EV 30712, 31987, 12287.
53 May and Ringler, *Elizabethan Poetry*, EV 17395.

CHAPTER THIRTY-THREE

THE VISUAL ARTS

Richard L. Williams

The visual arts in Elizabethan England have until relatively recently been held in what can only be described as cultural disdain. The opening sentence of the 1964 volume *Sculpture in Britain, 1530–1830*, which was to remain the standard textbook on the subject for the next thirty years, declared that 'The history of English sculpture in the sixteenth century is a sorry tale.'[1] The equivalent standard history of painting dismissed Elizabethan portraiture as 'of an even mediocrity'.[2] A similar contempt was broadcast to a wider public by Kenneth Clark in his magisterial survey, *Civilisation* (1969), in which he considered it 'debatable how far Elizabethan England can be called civilised'.[3] His dilemma was only alleviated by recalling such names as Shakespeare, Spenser, Dowland and Byrd. Within this list of poets and musicians there was clearly no place for individuals associated with the visual arts. It would appear that Elizabethan England had singularly failed to produce its Michelangelo, its Titian or even its native successor to Holbein.

Although such attitudes still retain an influential force today, many art historians, particularly since the 1980s, have questioned and challenged the very assumptions on which these judgements have been made. This chapter will seek to set out some of the alternative perspectives from which the visual arts in Elizabethan England have been interpreted in more recent years. These approaches do not seek to rehabilitate the aesthetic reputation of Elizabethan art by asserting for it a position within the canon of 'high art', but rather to set aside the aesthetic concerns and judgements of the connoisseur, in order to examine Elizabethan imagery across a broader range of media and to situate it more specifically within its historical and cultural context.

THE NOTION OF 'ART' AND THE 'ARTIST'

Elizabethan culture has stubbornly refused to conform to the expectations placed upon it by traditional art history. For example, the art historian's search for 'great artists' within a given period formed part of a tradition dating back to Giorgio Vasari in the mid-sixteenth century. According to this tradition, historical periods that failed to produce individuals deemed worthy of inclusion within the canon of great artists, judged according to a restrictive and essentially Italianate aesthetic, would thereafter be dismissed as backward. Vasari's conception was to be developed further by the Romantic movement of the nineteenth century to create the characterisation of the artist, still potent today, as a creative genius who employs his (rarely 'her') art as a vehicle for creativity and self-expression. Yet, to apply these conceptions retrospectively to the radically different culture of sixteenth-century England seems anachronistic and destined to result in the disappointed assessments of the Elizabethan visual arts quoted earlier.

The word 'art' was not used in sixteenth-century England in the sense it was later to acquire. Rather, the arts were understood according to a much older classificatory system that had pervaded European culture since antiquity. This distinguished the more prestigious liberal arts from the lowly mechanical arts. The seven liberal arts, including mathematics and music, were characterised as intellectually demanding accomplishments expected of the highly educated gentleman. By contrast, the mechanical arts comprised menial skills, such as cooking or spinning, associated with manual labour. Painting and sculpture suffered a lowly reputation since they had traditionally been classed in the lower, menial category. Although attempts to raise their status to liberal arts had begun in Renaissance Italy, few beyond a tiny elite in sixteenth-century England seemed to have embraced this foreign notion. Thus, painters and sculptors were generally regarded as nothing more than lowly craftsmen, who had to work with their hands to earn a living.

The social position of Elizabethan painters is neatly encapsulated in the 1579 self-portrait by George Gower, who was later to become Serjeant Painter to the Queen (Figure 33.1). Very unusually for a professional painter, Gower had been born into a gentry family. In the verse inscription at the top right of the picture Gower mused on this dual identity, asking himself which he esteemed more: his skill as a painter or his status as a gentleman. The juxtaposition is also expressed visually in the portrait through symbolic imagery, in this case a pair of scales in which his family coat of arms on one side is literally weighed against a pair of dividers, representing his painter's craft, on the other. This combination of symbolic image with an inscription being used to convey a personal thought or message was termed an *impresa* or 'device' and was a highly fashionable convention of Elizabethan portraiture. Far less conventional, however, was Gower's verdict in which he esteemed his painter's skill more highly than his pedigree, thereby going very much against the grain of contemporary values. However, it is telling that Gower felt the need to go to such lengths to justify his choice of career and that the very terms of his argument acknowledged that to be a painter and to be a gentleman were considered binary oppositions in Elizabethan cultural discourse.

In place of the prestige of 'the artist', the esteem in which the visual arts were held in Elizabethan England was governed predominantly by their potential in the display of magnificence. The virtue of 'magnificence', from its initial formulation by Aristotle, had come to exert a governing influence on the patronage of the visual arts in medieval and early modern Europe. Individuals of high standing were expected to make an outward display commensurate with their social status. Elite members of society had traditionally achieved this by favouring objects fashioned from the most expensive materials. The corollary of this was that in Tudor England the visual arts were still largely valued according to their material cost, and thus a

Figure 33.1 Engraved print after the self-portrait by George Gower (private collection) (1579). Printed copy by James Basire in 1800, mistakenly labelled 'Thomas Gower'. © The Trustees of the British Museum.

painting, which was nothing more than a piece of wood or canvas covered in oil, could not compete in magnificence with artefacts renowned for being prohibitively expensive such as tapestry or goldsmiths' work.

In later centuries, European art theory established and entrenched a hierarchical relationship that privileged the so-called 'fine arts' over the 'decorative arts'. By the nineteenth century this difference had been institutionalised by founding national galleries solely for paintings and leaving museums of decorative arts to house what remained. It would, however, be a gross distortion to view Elizabethan culture according to these values since the hierarchical relationship which they embody was effectively reversed in sixteenth-century England. Painting for most English patrons at the time occupied an inferior position compared with such 'decorative arts' as jewellery or tapestry.

The inferiority of painting is apparent from those Elizabethan painted cloths and wall paintings which were deliberately intended to resemble tapestry. Paintings on cloth were often displayed like tapestries, without frames and suspended as wall hangings. Their painted borders might be closely modelled on the decorative borders found on tapestries, as in the case of four painted cloths surviving at Hardwick Hall in Derbyshire (Figure 33.2). The latter were painted at the end of the sixteenth century for the Countess of Shrewsbury, whose coat of arms and initials they bear. A similar effect was achieved at Hill Hall in Essex, in which wall paintings not

Figure 33.2 John Balechouse (?), close-up of painted cloth depicting the Conversion of Saul (National Trust, Hardwick Hall) (*c.* 1600–1). Photo ©NTPL/John Hammond. Source: The National Trust Photo Library.

only mimicked the fruit, flowers and other motifs of tapestry borders but even introduced a *trompe l'oeil* effect in which the corner of the fictive tapestry apparently curled away from the wall. Paintings could thus only give the illusion of magnificence, by pretending to be something that afforded the sort of prestige they failed to command themselves.

The prestige of certain materials enhanced the status of the producer as well as the consumer. Since long before the reign of Elizabeth I, goldsmiths had been widely considered a superior class of craftsmen on account of the precious materials with which they worked, and also because of their connection with the production, regulation and even lending of money. A 1563 royal proclamation concerning the pay and conditions deemed appropriate to various craftsmen recommended an annual remuneration for goldsmiths that was precisely double that for a painter. The two crafts came together in the production of portrait miniatures. It became highly fashionable to have portrait miniatures set by goldsmiths into elaborate jewelled lockets which could then be worn about the body. Unfortunately, very few of these original settings survive, but the Gresley Jewel (Figure 33.3) is a rare exception. Encasing portraits painted by Nicholas Hilliard, the locket illustrates contemporary skill in working with gold, enamels and semi-precious stones. Today it is Hilliard's portraits that are the focus of numerous scholarly books and exhibitions devoted to miniatures, whereas in the eyes of an Elizabethan observer, the intricate lockets of the goldsmith seem likely to have taken precedence over the paintings within. Referring to a portrait miniature, Shakespeare's Olivia commands the disguised Viola, 'Here; wear this jewel for me, 'tis my picture', suggesting that it was conceived primarily as a jewel containing a portrait rather than as a portrait in a jewelled frame.[4]

The taste for goldsmiths' work and indeed tapestry was not restricted to the court elite, however. These were the status symbols to which much of the rest of English society aspired. Such aspirations are evoked quite compellingly by a poster printed in 1567 to advertise the first English lottery (Figure 33.4). In order to tempt the eye of potential subscribers, the poster illustrated the prizes to be won. These included bags and chests of money but the most numerous prizes were cups, bowls, spoons and other ware of the goldsmith. The only prize on the poster not to be connected with goldsmiths' work was a tapestry. These then, were the goods calculated to be most desirable to the mass market of lottery-ticket buyers. It embodied a taste that the gentry, merchant classes and even the yeomanry were increasingly able to indulge as the sixteenth century progressed. Household inventories confirm that objects such as silver or pewter vessels, sets of silver spoons and the like were becoming more affordable to a wider section of society. The same was true of painted cloths which, by the reign of Elizabeth I, were to be found in the houses of bakers and grocers.

Figure 33.3 Nicholas Hilliard, *The Gresley Jewel* (*c.* 1580s). Image courtesy of Victoria & Albert Museum, London, UK/The Bridgeman Art Library.

Figure 33.4 *A Poster for the First English Lottery* (1567).
By permission of the Folger Shakespeare Library.

Wall paintings intended to mimic tapestry were to be found not only in the country houses of great courtiers but also in more modest manor houses.

Although certain parallels suggest themselves with the 'conspicuous consumption' associated with modern capitalist societies there were important differences. The preference for goods fashioned from costly materials had very practical advantages. In an age before bank deposit accounts the purchase of an item of goldsmiths' work was a convenient and socially advantageous form in which to store wealth. Should the need for ready cash arise, assets such as jewellery or gold plate could be realised immediately by having them melted down. Tapestries could easily be sold in a thriving market for second-hand goods that held none of the stigma that it often has for the modern consumer.

PORTRAITURE

The vast majority of paintings to have survived from the Elizabethan period are portraits. These were the sorts of painting most likely to be preserved by succeeding generations within a family or an institution, no matter how old-fashioned they might come to appear, on account of the importance of the persons depicted. By contrast, other sorts of painted work have mostly disappeared over the centuries through neglect or being deliberately discarded. These chances of survival have effectively distorted subsequent perceptions of Elizabethan painting, leaving the misleading impression that it was restricted in scope to portraiture alone (a point that will be addressed below).

Nevertheless, the demand for portraiture in Elizabethan England was undoubtedly increasing, and was doing so among a broader section of society. While most scholarly literature has been devoted to portraits of royalty and of courtiers, attention has recently been paid to the large numbers of paintings of successful merchants and other members of the 'middling sort'. Portraits of civic dignitaries were also commissioned in increasing numbers, although these have remained largely unstudied in provincial collections.

In spite of their relatively low status as mere paintings, formal portraits were valued for the various useful functions they could serve. Images of the Queen, whether commissioned by the monarch herself or by others, were always required to meet certain expectations and to fulfil particular political functions that render them a quite distinctive category. These are issues that are discussed separately in Susan Doran's chapter in this volume.

As for portraits of her subjects, these could vary widely in function, although many were generally commemorative in purpose. Appointment to an office – whether at court or in the regions – could be the occasion to commission a portrait. So too might participation in prestigious events, such as the tilting matches held to mark the Queen's accession day, after which young knights might pose for their likeness dressed in extravagant suits of armour. It was often in portraits of courtiers such as these that the allegorical language of the *impresa* was employed. Landmarks in one's personal life might also be celebrated in this way, be it a coming of age, betrothal, marriage or even on the eve of childbirth. What have been termed 'pregnancy portraits' seem to have been an innovation in Elizabethan England in which the heavily expectant mother was portrayed in celebration of the forthcoming birth or alternatively as a memorial should she not survive it. Portraits specifically painted as a memorial or those simply intended to serve a didactic purpose might include visual elements from the memento mori tradition, such as a skull, in order to chasten the viewer into leading a more morally responsible and godly life. These functions were often indicated through the inclusion of an explanatory text either within the picture itself or on the frame (that so few original frames survive is thus potentially a great loss). Inscriptions might include dates, the age of the sitter, a learned phrase or even lengthy poems, as in George Gower's self-portrait (Figure 33.1).

In contrast to these more formal and public projections of the individual associated with portraits painted in oils, the tradition of the portrait miniature cultivated a greater sense of intimacy. The earliest miniatures produced in England date from the time of Henry VIII but they achieved an unparalleled popularity among a more socially varied clientele in the reign of Elizabeth. The word 'miniature', however, was not adopted until the seventeenth century. In Tudor England, miniature painting was referred to as 'limning', from the same Latin root as 'illumination'. In fact, the technique of the miniaturist was fundamentally the same as that of the manuscript illuminator: painting on vellum using a water-based medium together with thicker paint bound in egg white or gum arabic. The miniaturist would, however, paste his vellum onto a stiffer surface for support, and, as surviving examples show, the reverse side of a playing card was found to be ideal for this. Freed from the confines of a book or manuscript a portrait miniature might be kept separately in a draw or cabinet, perhaps in an elaborate box, or else, as with the Gresley Jewel mentioned earlier (Figure 33.3), set into a locket to be worn about the body.

The great popularity of miniatures in Elizabeth's reign might in part have been encouraged by the example of the Queen, who gave portraits of herself in miniature as a token of her special favour. Living up to her parsimonious reputation it would appear that Elizabeth usually gave only the painted miniature as a gift, leaving it to the recipients to commission and pay for their own jewelled locket. As with large-scale oil paintings, miniatures of the Queen could serve as a public sign of her political endorsement of an individual or even of a particular faction at court, in addition to the more conventional functions of gift-giving that were an established part of international diplomacy.

However, beyond the protocol of political exchange, the portrait miniature was more commonly used as a love token. It is in this regard that the apparent intimacy of the miniature is most significant. Although large-scale oil portraits were sometimes kept behind a set of curtains which had to be drawn back to reveal the painting, the locket of a miniature not only had to be opened but its size required that it was held in the hand of one viewer at a time and brought up close to the eyes. A sense of closer proximity to the sitter might be further enhanced by adopting a bust-length, close-up format, as in the Gresley Jewel (Figure 33.3). The latter has the unusual feature of a second portrait in the lid, presumably of Gresley's wife, so that when the locket was closed the lips of the two figures would meet in a perpetual embrace.

The role of the miniature as a love token is repeatedly alluded to in Elizabethan drama and poetry. In turn, some miniatures borrowed from the Petrarchan tradition of love poetry, as in the portrait of an unknown man painted by either Hilliard or

Figure 33.5 Nicholas Hilliard or Isaac Oliver, *Unknown Man against a Background of Flames* (*c.* 1600). © Victoria and Albert Museum, London.

Isaac Oliver, in which the flames of his passion flare around him quite literally (Figure 33.5). The object of his desire is surely depicted within the closed locket he wears around his neck and which he might be about to hold to his heart. The lovesick melancholy that is tormenting him is also manifested in his dishevelled appearance, wearing only a shirt that is open to the navel. Such a lack of decorum in dress can appear quite startling compared with the stiff formality of most Elizabethan portraits. It appears to reveal deep emotion rather than just the sitter's social status, to move behind the public façade and enter the realm of experience.

However, the ideal of the portrait as an exposure of the private self or as a revealing index of individuality belongs to a later tradition. In contrast, portraits of the Renaissance period, especially of humanist scholars, would often include inscriptions stressing that, no matter how skilled the painter, an image could only reproduce the outward features of the sitter and no more. Thus, miniatures such as that of the unknown man (Figure 33.5) can only create an illusion of greater intimacy, as though the person has been observed in an unguarded moment. In reality they are no less artificial than the more formal portraits intended for public display; they simply conform to an alternative set of conventions. The role of the lovesick gallant was merely one of many stereotypes available for upper-class young men to imitate. The open shirt, flames and the like were standard signs to signify that chosen identity in a similar way that official robes, a chain of office and a coat of arms might serve to construct a sitter's identity as a mayor, for example.

If Elizabethan portraiture followed a different set of priorities compared with portraiture in later centuries, this might help to account for its highly distinctive

Figure 33.6 British School. A young lady aged twenty-one (1569).
Image © Tate, London 2010.

mode of representation. Many portraits, in oils and in miniature, often depict the sitter in an icon-like composition with the body flattened into a highly stylised, almost abstract shape on the surface of the picture. For example, the body of an unidentified young woman as depicted by an unknown painter in a portrait at Tate Britain dated 1569, gives little sense of three-dimensional form (Figure 33.6). The left arm appears almost flattened so as to display the pattern on the sleeve with the minimum disruption by modelling. The face is not painted to mimic the surface texture of skin or to suggest plasticity through subtle effects of light and shade but is mask-like and seemingly devoid of expression and individuality.

This style of portraiture did not conform to the later expectations of traditional art history. Following the model formulated by Vasari, art history had been written as an unfolding narrative of evolutionary progress in which the visual arts came to achieve a greater sense of naturalism. Painting in England failed to observe such an evolution; in fact, it seemed to be in regression. The illusionistic and 'life-like' portraits painted by Holbein at the court of Henry VIII had come to be replaced by highly 'unnatural', stylised icons in Elizabeth's reign. The principal reason given by many art historians in the twentieth century to account for what they considered a decline was that the visual arts in England were effectively isolated from the European mainstream following the Reformation.

It is certainly true that, since the break with Rome, foreign travel had become increasingly problematic (although still possible since Nicholas Hilliard travelled to France and fellow miniature painter Isaac Oliver is recorded in Venice in 1596). It is also true that Italian painters and sculptors who had worked in England early in the reign of Henry VIII were now inhibited from coming to a Protestant country, especially after Elizabeth was excommunicated by the Pope. However, the prevailing notion that England was culturally isolated has been largely determined by another bias, the discipline of art history inherited from Vasari, which privileges the Italian visual arts over those of northern Europe. Italian art asserted a canonical status against which other work was to be measured. The direct impact of Italian art on Elizabethan England was very limited, but to conclude that this amounts to cultural isolation requires the downplaying or disregarding of the continued flow of influences and craftsmen coming from France, parts of Germany and, above all, from the Netherlands.

England imported large numbers of printed pictures from the Netherlands, whether narrative, allegorical or ornamental, which were used as models by craftsmen working in virtually all media from metalwork to needlework. Netherlandish painters and sculptors came to England, many as refugees fleeing religious persecution, and established thriving workshops in Southwark. These immigrant craftsmen came from a tradition of portraiture famous for its astonishing effects of naturalism, both in paintings and in sculpted figures such as effigies on funerary monuments. In contrast, the highly stylised portraits attributed to native English painters, such as the Tate's *Young Woman* (Figure 33.6), might be assumed to be the product of the inadequate training available to painters in England, together with a sorry lack of talent. This assumption underlies the damning summation of the Elizabethan visual arts by Kenneth Clark and others quoted at the opening of this chapter.

However, it is possible to interpret the latter type of portrait as being painted, quite self-consciously, according to a highly distinctive aesthetic. For example, there are Elizabethan portraits in this style signed by Hans Eworth, an Antwerp-born painter whose earlier works exhibit full mastery of illusionistic painting. His adoption of the icon-like style suggests that, at least in some instances, this was a visual idiom demanded by the English patron. Why a sitter might choose to be depicted in this way is hinted at in anecdotal evidence such as Nicholas Hilliard's record of a conversation he had with the Queen when painting her in miniature. Elizabeth and her painter agreed that her face ought to be painted as though brightly illuminated and without shadow since the latter would only serve to obscure her features when painted at such a small scale. Additionally, Hilliard seems to have invested the issue with a moral dimension in believing that shadow corrupted the truth and clarity of line.

If the expressionless, mask-like representation of the face in these portraits deliberately followed a visual convention then the rationale underpinning this can be interpreted in several different ways. One suggestion is that these Elizabethan 'icons' consciously evoked earlier medieval depictions of monarchs and saints in order to invest contemporary sitters with a similar air of authority and of time-honoured lineage. Another suggestion views the stylised nature of Elizabethan portraiture as attractive to those Protestants seeking to mitigate the dangers of idolatry. The risk was considered especially virulent in effigies sculpted for funerary

Figure 33.7 Bartholomew Ayte and Isaac James, *Monument to Richard Kingsmill and Family* (Highclere, Hampshire, 1601). Image courtesy Conway Library, The Courtauld Institute of Art, London.

monuments since these were positioned in the numinous atmosphere of a church. Prior to the Reformation, such monuments often encouraged the viewer to experience an empathy with or compassion for the deceased in the hope that prayers might be offered to aid the soul in purgatory. In Protestant England such prayers for the dead were unlawful and so it is conceivable that a less 'life-like' representation would be preferred as being less likely to evoke such an emotional identification with the figure.

Post-Reformation funerary monuments served more as a record of the pedigree and achievements of the person commemorated, sometimes with a lengthy inscription reading like a curriculum vitae (Figure 33.7). Alongside coats of arms, a tomb chest might include subsidiary figures of the deceased's sons and daughters kneeling in profile where they decrease in scale according to their age. The faces in each group of siblings can often appear identical, the only means of differentiating the eldest son from his younger brothers being the order of precedence in which the figures appear and their size. These marginal figures perhaps indicate most clearly that the mode of representation of Elizabethan monuments as a whole is one which values the dynastic over the mimetic.

Painted portraits might be read in a similar way. It was not the primary function of a formal court portrait to capture the personality or even the individuality of the sitter. This was true in other European courts such as the court of Saxony, where portraits painted by Lucas Cranach the Elder and his workshop in the first half of the sixteenth century share many of the characteristics associated with the Elizabethan portraits in question. Unlike Cranach's earliest portraits, those painted at court, particularly of women, include whitened, featureless faces that can sometimes defy differentiation. As with funerary monuments, painted portraits such as these seem more concerned with marking social status.

Elizabethan painted portraits could make a prominent display of a coat of arms or include an inscription to create a formal record of the sitter's status but other visual signs could reinforce the message (Figure 33.6). Costume, jewellery and other accessories such as a feather fan denoted wealth and class. The contemporary preoccupation with fabrics, and even the different grades of silks, velvets and other materials would have made Elizabethan observers far more adept at reading the visual language of dress than a modern viewer. For such a discriminating audience, therefore, it is hardly surprising that the mimetic skills of Elizabethan painters were applied to reproducing with great fidelity every detail of the adornment the sitter wished to be seen wearing. Each stitch of golden embroidery, each rivet and joint in a suit of armour, and even the intricate pattern of a lace ruff was often recorded with extraordinary precision. Court portraits were formal representations of the public image of the sitter and so informal expressions or emotions would have offended against decorum which governed the codes of behaviour and display deemed appropriate to members of the highest social classes. As mentioned above, even apparently informal portraits such as the man among flames (Figure 33.5) can be seen to follow equally standard codes of display.

However, these visual codes of outward display were far from static, and there was not one uniform style of court portraiture. Particularly from the final decade of Elizabeth's reign, some courtiers favoured portraits which employed modelling, light and shade and other illusionistic effects. This growing fascination with lifelike representation was reflected in late Elizabethan poetry and drama where it was commonly termed 'curious painting'. Marcus Gheeraerts the Younger, brought from the Netherlands as a child, and Isaac Oliver, the son of a Huguenot, exemplify the fashion for 'curious painting' in oil portraiture and in miniatures respectively. This development suggests that the criteria employed to evaluate paintings could come to include a greater stress on the aesthetic qualities of the work, at least for a minority within the court elite.

THE IMPACT OF THE REFORMATION

The destruction of religious sculpture, paintings, embroidery, metalwork and imagery in other media in the churches and cathedrals of Elizabethan England would undoubtedly have acted as one of the most conspicuous manifestations of the reassertion of Protestant reform in Elizabethan England. Elizabeth's bishops resumed an official programme of iconoclasm that had begun to be implemented by the regime of Edward VI. Although Henry VIII had ransacked the monasteries and pilgrimage sites, his new laws and regulations governing images in parish churches and other places of worship had remained unclear. Church images had still been permitted provided that they were not 'abused'. The confusion lay in the failure to offer a precise legal definition of the word 'abused' in this context. After Henry's death in 1547 the ambiguous legal position of ecclesiastical imagery persisted in the first year of the reign of Edward VI until, finally in February 1548, the ruling Privy Council issued an order for the removal of 'all' images from the churches. It was this order, reflecting the lurch in religious policy to radical Protestantism that began the more systematic destruction of the rich collections of church art that had accumulated in England over many centuries. Although iconoclastic riots did break out in some hotbeds of Protestantism, these were rare occurrences. Rather than at the hands of violent mobs of religious zealots, images were more usually dismantled by carpenters or other craftsmen hired for the job, calmly following the directions of form-filling officials.

Following the short-lived attempt by Mary I to reinstate as much ecclesiastical imagery and other paraphernalia as was practicable, the government of Elizabeth declared a return to the legal position governing church images established by the Edwardian regime. What it failed to specify, however, was whether it intended to reinstate the Edwardian policy that was in force before or after February 1548 when the destruction of 'all' images had been ordered. What must have been intended as a deliberate fudge reflected and accommodated divisions at the heart of the Elizabethan regime. The Queen herself, together with some of her more moderate bishops, believed that religious images could still have a legitimate role in churches provided that 'idolatrous' practices associated with Catholic worship were avoided. The Chapel Royal thus retained a silver crucifix with the corpus of Christ and traditional flanking figures of the Virgin Mary and Saint John on top of the communion table, despite being attacked and damaged on three separate occasions. Elizabeth's more radical bishops feared that the Queen's example would set an unwelcome precedent, but, owing to the subtly ambiguous legal position, in their diocese they were able to enforce the post-1548 policy established in Edward's reign that had shifted to uncompromising destruction. Many of the church images that had escaped the Edwardian destruction were now removed and destroyed, together with any replacements that had recently been introduced in the reign of Mary. Walls were whitewashed once again, with religious paintings often substituted with text panels quoting passages from the Bible or with the royal coat of arms.

Divisions among Protestants on the image question inevitably turned on the interpretation of Scripture. All sides agreed that 'true religion' comprised only those practices and beliefs that were verifiable by reference to the Word of God in the Bible, and in the second of the Ten Commandments God had condemned graven images as idolatrous. However, moderate Protestants tended to emphasise the part of the commandment that forbade the worshipping of such images, believing legitimate uses of images to be an issue of individual conscience, whereas radical Protestants understood the commandment to require the destruction of all church images as a matter of theological imperative.

Some modern scholars have claimed that the radical interpretation of the commandment became increasingly extreme in Elizabeth's reign, so that not just religious images in churches were affected but all imagery came to be condemned. According to this interpretation, after 1580 English culture could be described as 'iconophobic', which is defined as the total repudiation of all images, irrespective of either subject matter or context. Furthermore, this sudden switch to such an extreme position was not restricted to a radical Protestant minority but supposedly swept across the nation as a whole. In other words, every form of pictorial representation found in private houses and every other location was entirely unacceptable in late Tudor England. The indiscriminate eradication of all imagery apparently resulted in a new generation starved of visual stimulation having virtually never seen a picture.

Although this interpretation has remained the standard model of later Elizabethan visual culture it seems increasingly difficult to sustain. It fails to recognise the fundamental distinction between images in churches and those in a secular setting that even the most radical Protestant theologians, from Calvin to Zwingli, freely acknowledged. Churches were places of worship and thus a special case. For example, English Protestant catechisms which explained the Second Commandment for the benefit of the young stressed that a comprehensive rejection of all imagery was not intended. The same image which in a church would be condemned as idolatrous might be perfectly legitimate within the secular setting of a private house.

Not only do the most important theological sources rule out the fundamentalist position demanded of 'iconophobia', there is a steadily increasing body of visual evidence that demonstrates the continued access to imagery by all levels of society. Framed paintings might have remained relatively uncommon, for the cultural reasons set out earlier, but visual imagery including narrative depictions of Bible stories continued to flourish in those other media that, until now, have been neglected or ignored by art historians. Gentlewomen continued to illustrate figurative scenes in their needlework, and the merchant classes often chose biblical subjects for the decorative schemes in wood and plaster for their private houses. Other figures might adorn drinking vessels, pottery and the like, whereas the ubiquitous painted cloths became a common sight in local taverns where even the poorest members of society might see depictions of the parable of the Prodigal Son or other popular subjects. Printed books did not cease to be illustrated. Their numbers certainly remained limited, but this is likely to have been owing to such factors as the prohibitive costs involved rather than a radical Protestant rejection of illustration per se. Two of the books dearest to the radical Protestant movement in Elizabethan England, John Foxe's *Actes and Monuments* and the Geneva Bible, not only continued to be illustrated in all their editions, but these pictures also expanded in both number and scale. Even at the bottom of the market cheap print allowed the most modest households to display broadside woodcut prints on their walls. Particularly popular were printed ballad sheets that typically used printed pictures to advertise their subject matter to potential consumers. In this way, printed pictures, such as of Christ raising his hands in benediction, were sold openly under government licence to the broad mass of England's Protestant population throughout the Elizabethan period (Figure 33.8).

There is still much research to be done in order to understand how different groups of Elizabethan Protestants selected the subject matter of the visual imagery they owned and how traditional religious subjects might have been modified to conform to reformed sensibilities. Yet an impression is already emerging that no longer caricatures the impact of the Reformation on the visual arts in England as wholly destructive but also acknowledges the ways in which Protestantism stimulated a more creative cultural adaptation and transformation.

Figure 33.8 English, *Christ in Glory Illustrating the Ballad 'The Sorrowful Lamentation of a Penitent Sinner'*. (Ballad Collection of Samuel Pepys, Magdalene College Cambridge, volume II, no. 13). Image courtesy The Pepys Library, Magdalene College, Cambridge.

FROM IMAGES TO 'ART'

The Reformation had raised fundamental questions concerning the function of visual images. If their former role as a stimulus to prayer and devotion was condemned as idolatrous what now was their purpose? The answers given to this question varied from a continuity of those traditional, pre-Reformation uses of images that remained legitimate to the adoption of new ideas that required a re-evaluation of the status of the image itself.

Traditional functions of images would include the painted portraits and carved funerary monuments, which, as discussed earlier, were adapted to the changing religious culture. The use of images as a didactic tool and as a means of remembrance had been the two other primary justifications of the value of images promoted by the medieval Church which, unlike the devotional function, remained relevant in Protestant England. In fact, the didactic power of the image could be exploited to further the Protestant cause, as in the famous case of John Foxe's *Actes and Monuments* mentioned earlier, in which woodcut illustrations captured in horrific detail the sufferings of those who died for their Protestant faith. This was, however, an exceptional and very expensive publication. Elizabethan Protestants did not employ the printed image as 'propaganda' in the modern sense of a calculated programme of mass communication. Prints were not distributed free of charge to the general population but had to be purchased by those sufficiently interested and with sufficient means. Preaching was the preferred and far more effective means of communication in the sixteenth century.

Nevertheless, the ability of the visual image to reinforce more general moral and religious messages continued to be recognised by many Protestant householders.

Broadsheet prints addressed to the 'godly householder' sought to inculcate Protestant family values through daily exposure to its message. The more prosperous might commission painted allegories in the *memento mori* tradition, in which illustrations based on the Seven Ages of Man or the Dance of Death would serve as a remembrance of mortality and a warning to follow the godly life.

The medieval and Renaissance tradition of the image as exemplar seems to have continued to inform the choices of imagery found in the houses of the wealthy. The biblical and historical figures that comprised the Nine Worthies were still to be found painted, sculpted and printed as moral and religious role models. It was presumably with a similar aim that the Countess of Shrewsbury displayed paintings, embroideries and carvings of virtuous women from the Bible and classical mythology at Hardwick Hall. Other virtuous individuals were commemorated in battle scenes or among the series of painted portraits found in the houses of aristocrats, gentry and even university academics. Next to contemporary figures might be 'portraits' of Plato and other notables of the ancient world such as Roman emperors. Conversely, those considered notorious or villainous people are also sometimes listed among the paintings in household inventories, including the 'Great Turk'. This accounts for the otherwise anomalous presence among the Protestant Earl of Leicester's portraits of the Pope and Mary, Queen of Scots.

Towards the end of the reign of Elizabeth, however, paintings are described in the collection of the Queen and some of her courtiers that do not appear to conform to the traditional uses of images. After a conducted tour of Whitehall Palace in 1599, Thomas Platter, a medical student from Switzerland, noted in his diary that 'A picture of a Dutch cook with fruit was also very life-like and artistically painted.'[5] Other still-life paintings answering a similar description are recorded in the possession of the Earl of Leicester, the Earl of Pembroke and Lord Lumley. Although Netherlandish paintings of this nature often included subsidiary scenes of biblical stories, the descriptions of these pictures in English houses and palaces make no mention of any didactic content but rather marvel at the skill of the painter. The fascination with life-like or 'curious painting', as mentioned above, was reflected in late Elizabethan drama and poetry and resulted in an alternative to the icon-like style of court portraiture. Although the idea of celebrating a painting primarily for its aesthetic worth rather than its subject matter was still largely a foreign concept in sixteenth-century England, there is evidence of change in this regard.

Attitudes to painting, sculptures and the like had been transformed at the great courts of Europe as a result of the fashion for collecting. From its earlier origins in Italy this fashion had rapidly spread throughout the rest of Europe as the sixteenth century progressed. Paintings and other visual arts did not, however, form the entirety of these collections but were characteristically aligned with a cabinet of curiosities, comprising rare and exotic objects from across the world. Such collections had become an immense source of prestige for their owners, a fact that the English court could hardly fail to note, prompting the more internationally aware and ambitious to emulate the trend.

Thomas Platter was told that Queen Elizabeth 'took pleasure in such strange and lovely curios' which included a stuffed bird of paradise, pictures fashioned from peacock feathers, an immense whale rib 'besides other curiosities'. The Earl of Leicester kept curiosities such as a 'Tuske of a Sea Beare' with his paintings, and Sir Francis Walsingham is known to have owned similar objects. The best documented of these collections was that of the courtier Sir Walter Cope, whose treasures from China, Africa, America and elsewhere became something of a tourist attraction for important visitors to London.

Inevitably, this small elite of collectors in England were either well travelled themselves or else had access to agents on the Continent. What is significant in the present context is that these foreign contacts were used to acquire paintings as well as curiosities, following the Continental models. The Earl of Leicester had sought the services of a painter in Florence, secured the visit of the painter Federico Zuccaro from Rome, possibly imported pictures from Venice and was reported to have sought out paintings by specific Flemish artists when leading the troops in the Netherlands. Lord Burghley used the diplomatic agent Andrea de Loo to acquire 'pinture d'histoire' at Antwerp in 1586, and ten years later his son, Robert Cecil, employed the English ambassador in Paris to arrange the purchase of a painting he was particularly keen to acquire. The painter John de Critz also operated in Paris in the 1580s but on behalf of Sir Francis Walsingham, sending a picture of Saint John and a story taken from Ovid before offering to extend his field trip to Italy. Queen Elizabeth herself is reported to have made a bid for the altarpiece of the *Lamentation* by the famous Flemish painter Quentin Metsys which came onto the international art market in 1577. Her interest in this picture might have been what prompted the burgers of Ghent the following year to suggest sending Van Eyck's celebrated *Ghent Altarpiece* to her as a gift. The names of other painters from the Netherlands and elsewhere (including Holbein) feature in the 1590 inventory of Lord Lumley's pictures, which is exceptional in including names at all.

Although the aesthetic skills of foreign painters might always have been appreciated in England, this collecting activity marks a significant cultural shift. For example, when John Norden described Whitehall Palace in 1593 as 'adorned with manie fair galleries, stately furnished with most artificial, and delectable pictures, tables, and such like princely ornaments', he was assessing this display within the tradition of 'princely magnificence' described earlier.[6] However, 'princely ornaments' were no longer restricted to objects of high material cost, they could now include 'delectable pictures'.

It had become possible, therefore, for certain paintings to claim a cultural value on account of the fame and the prestige of their painter. English books and plays of the late sixteenth century sometimes name famous artists, such as Sir John Harrington's *Orlando Furioso* of 1591 which lists Leonardo, Mantegna, Giovanni Bellini and others. Even more significantly, Lord Lumley's inventory includes a picture described as 'Of Raphael de Urbino, the great paynter'.[7] The significance of this reference is often not fully appreciated since it did not record a picture attributed to Raphael but a portrait of him. It seems remarkable in itself that an Elizabethan collector would consider the likeness of a mere painter to merit inclusion in his portrait collection of notable individuals, never mind to describe Raphael as 'the great paynter'.

The elevation of certain painters from lowly craftsmen to figures of cultural prestige presupposed the elevation of painting from a mechanical to a liberal art. This idea is known to have been familiar to a group of humanist scholars in the circle of the poet John Leland back in the reign of Henry VIII. However, it seems to have made very little impact on the wider English culture of the sixteenth century. It was implied in Italian books which defined the behaviour and accomplishments of the ideal courtier such as Castiglione's *Il libro del Cortegiano*. This text, translated into English in 1561, included a discriminating knowledge of painting among the marks of a cultivated gentleman. However, the first book in English to set out Italian art theory in this matter in a more formal and systematic fashion was Richard Haydock's translation of Lomazzo's *Trattato dell'arte de la pittura,* and this was not published until 1598.

Thus, there is only limited evidence that a small minority of well-travelled or well-connected members of the elite in Elizabethan England had begun to embrace this re-evaluation of the significance of painting. This was not quite the appreciation of paintings as 'works of art', which, as discussed earlier, was a term belonging to a later age and carrying associations derived from subsequent cultural developments. Yet it marks perhaps a new direction in English culture that ultimately led towards such notions. The culture of collecting provided a new answer to questions as to the purpose of images following the Reformation. It privileged chosen paintings and other objects by conferring upon them a prestige and significance that was extraneous to religious ideology.

However, these collections forming in the royal palaces and grand residences of the court elite were part of a remote and largely unknowable world to the majority of Elizabethans. For them, painting and other visual arts continued to be regarded in the lowly terms described earlier. Painters and other craftsmen in England did not see their status rise; in fact, the miniature painter Nicholas Hilliard in his treatise written in the late 1590s was still bemoaning the fate of painters who were born in Elizabethan England 'under a savage government wherin arts be not esteemed'.[8] In this respect, perhaps, Hilliard might have shared the disappointed assessment of Elizabethan culture expressed by Kenneth Clarke with which this chapter began.

FURTHER READING

Aston, Margaret, *England's Iconoclasts: Vol. I, Laws against Images* (Oxford, 1988).

Erikson, Peter and Clark Hulse (eds.), *Early Modern Visual Culture: Representation, Race and Empire in Renaissance England* (Philadelphia, Pa., 2000).

Duffy, Eamon, *The Stripping of the Altars: Traditional Religion in England, 1400–1580* (New Haven, Conn., 1992).

Foister, Susan, 'Paintings and Other Works of Art in Sixteenth-Century English Inventories', *The Burlington Magazine,* 123 (1) (1981): 273–82.

Gent, Lucy, *Picture and Poetry, 1560–1620: Relations between Literature and the Visual Arts in the English Renaissance* (Leamington Spa, 1981).

—— (ed.), *Albion's Classicism: The Visual Arts in Britain* (New Haven, Conn., 1995).

Gent, Lucy, and Llewellyn, Nigel (eds.), *Renaissance Bodies: The Human Figure in English Culture, c. 1540–1660* (London, 1990).

Hamling, Tara, and Williams, Richard (eds.), *Art Re-formed? Reassessing the Impact of the Reformation on the Visual Arts* (Newcastle, 2007).

Hearn, Karen (ed.), *Dynasties: Painting in Tudor and Jacobean England, 1530–1630* (London, 1995).

—— *Marcus Gheeraerts I: Elizabethan Artist* (London, 2002).

Howard, Maurice, *The Tudor Image* (London, 1995).
Leslie, Michael, 'The Dialogue between Bodies and Souls: Pictures and Poesy in the English Renaissance', *Word and Image*, 1 (1) (1985): 16–30.
Llewellyn, Nigel, *Funeral Monuments in Post-Reformation England* (Cambridge, 2000).
Reynolds, Graham, 'The Painter Plays the Spider', *Apollo*, 79 (1964): 279–84.
Strong, Roy, *The English Icon* (London and New York, 1969).
—— *Artists of the Tudor Court: The Portrait Miniature Rediscovered* (London, 1983).
Thornton, Robert, and Cain, Thomas (eds.), *A Treatise Concerning the Arte of Limning by Nicholas Hilliard* (Manchester, 1981).
Tittler, Robert, *The Face of the City: Civic Portraiture and Civic Identity in Early Modern England* (Manchester, 2007).
Watt, Tessa, *Cheap Print and Popular Piety, 1550–1640* (Cambridge, 1991).
Wells-Cole, Anthony, *Art and Decoration in Elizabethan and Jacobean England* (New Haven, Conn., 1997).
Williams, Richard, 'Collecting and Religion in Late Sixteenth-Century England', in E. Chaney (ed.), *The Evolution of English Collecting: Receptions of Italian Art in the Tudor and Stuart Periods* (New Haven, Conn., 2003), pp. 159–200.

NOTES

1 Margaret Whinney, *Sculpture in Britain, 1530–1830* (London, 1988), p. 27.
2 Ellis Waterhouse, *Painting in Britain, 1530 to 1790* (London, 1988), p. 33.
3 Kenneth Clarke, *Civilisation: A Personal View* (London, 1969), p. 163.
4 William Shakespeare, *Twelfth Night*, Act III, Scene 4.
5 Thomas Platter, *The Journals of Two Travellers in Elizabethan and Early Stuart England* (London, 1995), p. 26.
6 From Norden's 1593 survey of Middlesex; extract in W. B. Rye, *England as Seen by Foreigners* (London, 1865), p. 99.
7 Lionel Cust, 'The Lumley Inventories', *Walpole Society*, 6 (1917–18), p. 25.
8 R. Thornton and T. Cain (eds.), *A Treatise Concerning the Art of Limning by Nicholas Hilliard* (Manchester, 1981), p. 67.

CHAPTER THIRTY-FOUR

ARCHITECTURE

Tara Hamling

In an article published in 1953, W. G. Hoskins agued that from the Elizabethan period until the outbreak of the Civil War a 'Great Rebuilding' of rural England occurred that revolutionised the housing of a considerable part of the population.[1] It is undoubtedly true that Elizabeth's reign was a period of great building activity that affected much of society, a fact remarked upon by contemporaries. This activity included the construction of new buildings as well as the extension and modification of existing structures. A range of socio-economic factors stimulated this building boom: stable government, a flourishing economy, increased social mobility and a general rise in living standards. The form and appearance of buildings changed dramatically as a result of technical developments, improvements in native manufacture of construction materials and the influence of new styles from the Continent. The concept of architecture as a form of expression and the role of architect as creative force was emerging during this period, and patrons within the upper levels of society were able to recruit specialist surveyors and craftsmen to help design their new buildings with practical and aesthetic considerations in mind. The increased productivity of printing presses in England and the Netherlands meant that visual sources of style were readily available in published form. Among the most influential were John Shute's *First and Chief Grounds of Architecture* (1563), which introduced English readers to the classical orders, and a series of engraved volumes by Jan Vredeman de Vries, which spread a taste for Netherlandish Mannerist ornament throughout northern Europe.

Subsequent scholars have refined Hoskins's discussion of the 'Great Rebuilding' not only to include regional and dating qualifications but also to argue that the transformation of the built environment which began in Elizabeth's reign was not confined to domestic housing but affected a range of building types in town and country as well as the physical alteration of the landscape itself. Research in this field has benefited from a general broadening of academic concerns in the second half of the twentieth century. The traditional, art-historical study of the design, style and aesthetic quality of great houses has been supplemented by critical approaches concerned with the significance of a range of buildings and spaces within their historical context. The influence of cultural studies, in particular, with its interest in mass or popular culture, has encouraged a wider definition of architecture to encompass more ordinary 'vernacular' buildings. The subject of enquiry has also expanded to include civic buildings, interior decoration, gardens and the setting of buildings within the urban or rural environment. Archaeology has enabled the reconstruction of structures that no longer stand above ground. Meanwhile, new theoretical approaches have placed emphasis on the critical interpretation of buildings; architecture as symbolic of power structures and relations; the relationship between space and social behaviour; the experience of architecture as part of daily life. While it cannot attempt to offer a comprehensive account, this chapter touches on some of these themes, providing an overview of the form, appearance and use of country houses, smaller domestic buildings (in town and country) and public buildings.

THE GREAT HOUSE

During the Elizabethan period there was a significant shift in the nature of architectural patronage. In the late medieval and early Tudor period great building was the preserve of the Crown and the Church. The dissolution of the monasteries and the Reformation curtailed ostentatious church building, and Queen Elizabeth chose not to undertake any sizeable building project, and certainly no palaces. Instead, it fell to courtiers to create monumental buildings of great splendour fit to receive and entertain queen and court during the summer progresses. These private mansions and occasional palaces were icons of power, proclaiming the wealth and lofty status of the nobles of England in their own lands. At the same time, these buildings expressed the ultimate authority of the monarch. In her absence, the nobles were entitled to such magnificent habitations to symbolise their authority as agents of the state. If she chose to visit, the owner and his family relinquished the house to the Queen, thus acting out the social hierarchy.

As well as extensive state rooms, a vast quantity of accommodation was required to lodge and service the mobile royal court, consisting of as many as 150 people. This need explains why many of these so-called 'prodigy houses' utilised the established plan of late medieval and early Tudor palaces, such as Richmond and Hampton Court, with extended wings of lodgings arranged around a courtyard and a block of state rooms on the inner side, opposite the entrance. This tried-and-tested arrangement fulfilled the practical and symbolic aspects of courtly life; not only did it maximise the amount of accommodation available and provide security for the inner range of state rooms, it also allowed precedence to be demarcated in spatial terms through the allocation of apartments according to rank.

The most extreme examples of the courtyard prodigy house were built by the statesmen closest to Elizabeth. William Cecil began work on Burghley House near Stamford three years before Elizabeth came to the throne, but much of the work there dates from a second phase of construction between 1573 and 1580. The plan and decoration of Burghley represents a transitional phase from early Tudor to Elizabethan style. The entrance façade to the outer court has a traditional turreted gatehouse four storeys high and towers at each end. Yet much of the ornament responds to Renaissance classicism: the chimneys on the roof are in the form of classical ruins, and the three-storeyed tower in the courtyard is embellished with classical motifs such as engaged columns and obelisks.

One great house was insufficient for Elizabeth's chief minister, and in 1564 Cecil started work on another: Theobalds, in Hertfordshire, described by John Norden in 1598 as 'a Princeley Seate', was even greater than Burghley House in scale and architectural ostentation. In its first form it consisted of two large courtyards, the base and inner courts, but by its completion in the 1580s it comprised five great courts. The house was demolished in the seventeenth century, but we know from contemporary accounts that the main courtyards had low entranceways with classical arches entering into covered walkways (loggias), an innovation in English architecture based on Italian Renaissance examples. The Queen rewarded this venture with no fewer than thirteen visits. In contrast, Sir Christopher Hatton failed to attract a visit from his queen despite building two courtyard houses, Holdenby and Kirby, both in Northamptonshire and both on a grand scale. Hatton's great house at Holdenby (no longer extant) was a double-courtyard building – a clear advertisement for a royal visit that never came. Kirby Hall was begun in 1570 for Sir Humphrey Stafford, a minor courtier, who seems to have nurtured hopes of entertaining his queen by embarking on such an ambitious house. The building was acquired by Hatton in 1575 and now survives as a picturesque ruin. The interior of its single, elongated courtyard is decorated with massive, ornate pilasters.

Figure 34.1 Kirby Hall, Northamptonshire. The main range on the south side of the courtyard (1570–5) with the ornate entrance porch (centre) and gigantic pilasters between the windows. Photo © John Critchley. Source: English Heritage Photo Library.

Opposite the entrance wing, the state apartments are entered through a highly embellished three-storey porch where the use of superimposed classical orders capped by a curved gable represents a typical Elizabethan mix of Italian and Dutch motifs (Figure 34.1).

While the ground plan of these courtyard houses evolved naturally and conveniently from medieval palaces, a significant development had occurred in the appearance of the building. The late-medieval palace was still defensive in character with the base court protecting the inner court and the outer walls of the courtyard ranges serving to enclose and protect the inner lodgings. Even the early Tudor palace of Hampton Court can be described as an inward-looking building with an imposing gatehouse and a solid mass of brick on the entrance façade broken only by spare and small windows. By contrast, the great courtyard houses of Burghley and Kirby are outward-looking, with an abundance of windows puncturing the façade and articulating a new atmosphere of security and assurance. The multiplication and expansion of windows, a major feature of Elizabethan architecture, indicates lavish expense on the costly material of glass but also allows and communicates a new relationship between the building and its surrounding landscape. Elizabethans were delighted by 'prospects', or views, of the gardens or chases for hunting, to be enjoyed from particular vantage points within and beyond the main house.

If the sprawling courtyard plan responded to the practical demands of housing the royal court by extending across the landscape, another approach to grand building is represented by a group of houses associated with the master mason and surveyor Robert Smythson. These buildings are much more compact in footprint, offering generous accommodation and magnificent state rooms arranged vertically over several floors. While the exteriors share the outward-looking emphasis of the new courtyard houses articulated through over-provision of windows, the design accentuates a sense of height with towers at the corners and lively sculptural detail at the roofline to lead the eye upwards.

An inscription on Smythson's funeral monument describes him as 'architector and survayor unto the most worthy house of Wollaton, and diverse others of great account'.[2] Wollaton was built for Sir Francis Willoughby between 1580 and 1588, no doubt with an eye to a possible visit from the Queen. The house is a fantasy castle and reflects the Elizabethan court's idealistic reinterpretation of England's Gothic past. The exterior of the building stimulates the eye with a glittering profusion of glass, the alternating recession and projection of the façade and the lively, robust ornament derived from Mannerist prints imported from the Netherlands. The design, with its elevated central block containing the great hall and great chamber above, is unique in England.

Another house related to Wollaton in style and plan is probably the most celebrated example of Elizabethan architecture. Hardwick Hall in Derbyshire was built between 1590 and 1597 for Elizabeth, Countess of Shrewsbury (Bess of Hardwick). It is assumed that Smythson provided the design as Wollaton and Hardwick share many characteristics: both are self-assured buildings sited on a prominent, hilltop position; both have the appearance of great height achieved through the use of towers; and both share a sense of depth through symmetrical projecting bays and the lantern-like quality of excessive fenestration. In other respects, however, the two houses are dissimilar. Hardwick is far more restrained than Wollaton, reflecting the character of the patron. By the time Bess turned her attention to this new building she was an extremely wealthy and powerful widow of sixty-three. During the course of her four marriages Bess accumulated a great fortune along with a wealth of experience as a builder. To judge from her later achievement at Hardwick it seems likely that Bess was a major force in the building of new country houses for her second and fourth husbands: Chatsworth in Derbyshire and Worksop in Nottinghamshire (both now lost).

Between 1587 and 1591 Bess embarked on an ambitious redevelopment of the old manor house at Hardwick, but this was soon abandoned in favour of a brand-new mansion designed as a cohesive whole. The advantages of starting from scratch are evident from the exterior of the new Hardwick Hall; the architecture communicates information about the social identity of the owner while articulating the size and status of the grand reception spaces contained within. The two principal elevations have classical colonnades with open loggias at ground level, indicating Bess's learning and taste (Figure 34.2). Above these, the house rises through another two storeys with third-floor turret chambers in the towers. Each successive storey is marked by horizontal string courses (a continuous narrow moulding which projects slightly from the surface of the wall) and windows of increasing height as a deliberate expression of the ascending hierarchy of rooms within, so that the

Figure 34.2 Hardwick Hall, Derbyshire (1590–1601), the entrance front. Photo ©NTPL/Nick Meers. Source: The National Trust Photo Library.

Figure 34.3 Hardwick Hall, Derbyshire, the great chamber.
Photo ©NTPL/Andreas von Einsiedel. Source: English Heritage Photo Library.

splendid state apartments on the second floor have windows from floor to ceiling. Bess's ownership of the building is announced from the rooftop; the Hardwick family arms is positioned at the centre of the parapet on the entrance front while each tower is capped with Bess's initials under a countess's coronet. Inside, the magnificent great chamber on the second floor (Figure 34.3) is decorated with a deep frieze of hand-modelled, painted plasterwork depicting scenes of hunting and classical goddesses. The massive chimneypiece is of carved alabaster with the royal arms above, a gesture of loyalty to queen and state.

Another house associated with Smythson represents a third design type for the greater country house. Doddington Hall in Lincolnshire was built between 1593 and 1600 for Thomas Tailor, Registrar to the Bishop of Lincoln (Figure 34.4). It represents the E-plan, so called because the floor plan – with wings projecting from a main block and a central, emphasised porch – resembles the letter E. Doddington is built in brick but given visual interest through the use of stone detailing for quoins (corner blocks), string courses and window frames. A sense of height and drama is created by the three turrets which rise 20 feet above the parapet level. The approach to the house reflects a mix of old and new; a traditional outer court is enclosed, but only by low garden walls. The retention of a gatehouse is a reference to more traditional manorial architecture and thus cements Tailor's new standing in the community.

Doddington, like other large E-planned houses, actually forms a double E, placed back to back. This is also called the H-plan, with the sideways H formed by projecting wings at all four corners and a central horizontal block. It is often said that the E-plan was adopted in honour of Queen Elizabeth. While this is dubious, it is the case that an interest in architecture as an allegorical device was characteristic of the period. The surveyor John Thorpe, whose volume of architectural plans and drawings survives in Sir John Soane's Museum, created a design for his own house based on his initials. The drawing, which would have resulted in an original, if bizarre, floor plan is accompanied by an inscription:

> These 2 letters I and T
> Joined together as you see
> Is mete for a dwelling house for mee.
> John Thorpe.

While the E-plan might have appealed to the Elizabethan delight in 'curious' (cunning) emblems and devices, more importantly it responded to the demand for convenience. It represents an expanded and developed version of an established and successful arrangement of internal space common in medieval manor houses, based around a great hall in the centre of the building. The evolution of this plan is discussed later in the chapter. In terms of the exterior appearance of the building there was a strikingly new development: the imposition of symmetry achieved through the regular spacing of windows, bays, gables and projecting wings. This desire for order and balance was one of the aspects of Renaissance classicism to endure through the second half of the sixteenth century. Other classical motifs, including columns with their associated orders and grotesque decoration (a combination of scrolling plants, figures and fanciful creatures) were appropriated along with elements of Netherlandish

Figure 34.4 Doddington Hall, Lincolnshire, 1593–1600, aerial view of entrance front including the outer court and gatehouse. Photo © Claire Birch, Doddington Hall.

Mannerism, particularly strapwork (resembling strips of curling leather crafted into intricate shapes). These influences from imported style combined with traditional native forms including heraldry and, later in Elizabeth's reign, a revivalist reinterpretation of Gothic style. This eclectic mix of influences is encapsulated in another celebrated example of the E-plan great house, Montacute House in Somerset.

Montacute was begun at the very end of the sixteenth century and completed in 1601 for Sir Edward Phelips, a lawyer made wealthy and powerful through a career in politics and court appointments. The up-and-coming status of Phelips is reflected in the design of his house, which, despite being brand new, is reminiscent of traditional manorial architecture and thus pretends an ancient pedigree for a newly elevated family. At the same time, Phelips's connections at court are indicated by references to the latest fashions. The design incorporates elements of Italian and Netherlandish style represented by the ordered symmetry and regularity of the façade, the incorporation of classical motifs (such as columns, obelisks and shell-niches) and the Dutch curved gables. Despite these references, the overall effect is restrained and typically English, in keeping with Phelips's own background, education and status. The many windows are distributed evenly but are not expansive. A balustraded wall around an outer court recalls the fortified forecourts of medieval manors. The third storey, containing the great gallery, 172 feet long, is embellished on the principal façade with carved statues of the Nine Worthies. Although dressed in Roman costume, these sculptures are naive in execution and resemble the stone figures of warriors atop the battlements of medieval castles (as, for example, at Alnwick Castle in Northumberland). In this way, Montacute perfectly encapsulates the character and social pretensions of its builder.

THE GENTRY HOUSE

The great number of country houses built or improved during Elizabeth's reign reflects the dramatic swelling of the gentry class in the early modern period. Alongside the hereditary lords of manors, a new group of country-house builders emerged as individuals made wealthy through trade, industry and the law invested in land and an impressive country seat in order to consolidate and advance their status in the local community. The country houses of Elizabethan gentlemen varied greatly in size and architectural pretension, reflecting the various degrees of rank within this class. Some of the houses built by members of the landowning gentry approach the ambition and magnificence of the great courtier houses; Montacute and Doddington fall into this category. These were built by men from the upper levels of the gentry, the minor aristocracy and very wealthy new men with connections at court. In general, however, the form and appearance of gentry houses were restricted by several factors. Large-scale building was limited by social and economic constraints as well as the nature and extent of the owner's education and experience.

First, as with other forms of visual and material display, the social code of decorum dictated that the scale, form and ornamentation of houses must be appropriate to the social class of the builder. While this encouraged the building of new country houses to attest the status of important men, it also imposed limitations on the scale and grandeur of gentry houses. Sir William Wentworth's letter of advice to his son, written in 1604, warned:

> Take hede of superfluitye in Building, for that is a monument of a gentleman that wanted discrecion and judgement. Let your house be too little for a daie or twoe, rather then too greate for a yeare; and for the furniture of your house, lett it be decent, not costlie, as also your apparel which otherwise wise men will hould vanitye.[3]

Allied to this social constraint was the practical limitation of expense. Builders at all levels of society were encouraged to make use of existing structures and to recycle materials wherever possible. At its most extreme, this resulted in the appropriation of sacked religious buildings as fashionable homes. From 1539, Lacock Abbey in Wiltshire was converted into the country seat of Sir William Sharington. The refashioning of this nunnery retained the medieval cloisters but added modern architectural features, including a great octagonal tower. Other builders utilised the fabric of monastic dwellings to construct new houses; Fountains Hall in Yorkshire was built between 1598 and 1604 on dissolved monastic lands, partly with stone robbed from the abbey ruins.

For many of the builders at gentry level, the extension of an existing medieval dwelling offered clear economic advantages, although incorporating older structures and fabric limited the degree of innovation possible and prevented a cohesive overall design. With these buildings, improvements tended to be piecemeal or periodic.

Figure 34.5 Little Moreton Hall, Cheshire. View of the gatehouse and south wing (*c.* 1570–80). Photo: ©NTPL/Derek Croucher.

Figure 34.6 Chastleton House, Oxfordshire (1607–12), the south front. ©NTPL/Andy Williams.

Sir John Moreton embarked on a series of improvements to his fifteenth-century timber mansion at Little Moreton in Cheshire between 1559 and 1580. The nature of the alterations underlines the restrictions imposed by attempting to update an existing building. Lacking space in the main house to incorporate a fashionable long gallery, Moreton squeezed one into the top floor of a three-storey gatehouse wing. The result, from the outside at least, is of a precarious and top-heavy mass of glass and timber (Figure 34.5).

Economic constraints also caused gentry builders to rely on locally available materials in the building of new extensions and complete houses, resulting in great regional diversity. Where possible, builders at this level employed the more permanent materials of brick and stone, often replacing earlier timber-framed structures. The use of durable materials offered increased protection from weather and fire but perhaps also symbolised the intended permanence of the structure and the social status it represented.

Where funds allowed, the building of brand-new country houses enabled members of the gentry to incorporate the latest fashions. Though slightly later, an example is Chastleton House in Oxfordshire, constructed between 1607 and 1612 by Walter Jones, a lawyer who invested his wealth in acquiring the lordship of a manor. Chastleton is built of local Cotswold stone around a small central courtyard but achieves the appearance of the compact, outward-looking houses of apparent great height fashionable in courtly circles. Although the exterior elevations are quite plain, the design emulates late Elizabethan great houses through projecting and receding planes and, as at Hardwick, the number of window lights visible on the exterior expresses the status of rooms within (Figure 34.6). The interior has the luxury of two staircases contained in projecting towers and a long gallery along the width of the second floor. The only give-away that this is the house of a gentleman, not a courtier, is the restricted use of applied ornament on the façade.

Along with the social code of decorum to restrict the amount and character of surface decoration, the type of materials employed also dictated the degree of ornamentation on the façade of buildings. Brick and stone might be interrupted with alternate layers of another material (such as flint) to create visual interest and variety, but in general these materials were incompatible with lavish or elaborate carving. This would have resulted in relatively plain and imposing frontages were it not for the fashion for expansive fenestration. The solidity of brick and stone façades are often eased by decorative detailing at the roofline, curved gables or chimneys. Timber, on the other hand, could be exploited for carved decoration and patterning throughout the building. In the parts of England where timber remained the cost-effective material of choice, gentry houses are distinguished from lesser dwellings by an excess of ornamental braces to the frame (see Figure 34.5).

A third constraint on the form and appearance of country houses was the extent of education and experience possessed by the builder. Most members of the gentry were tied through education and experience to their own native traditions and local communities and usually lacked any experience of courtly taste or Continental travel. Lacking direct engagement with Continental models or knowledge of foreign-language architectural treatises, gentry builders adopted a free interpretation of classical orders and motifs. This combined with a native evolution of late Gothic forms and the application of strapwork and grotesque decoration, which pervaded all the visual arts during this period.

In general, therefore, the architectural forms favoured for the gentry house represent an essentially insular development. By and large gentry houses were built to express and assert the status and wealth of the owner in his community through the simple language of new or updated living accommodation incorporating all the latest indicators of social status, the use of permanent construction materials, large and glazed windows, multiple, emphasised chimneys, a suite of reception rooms (including a long gallery) on two or more floors connected by a joined staircase, and plasterwork, panelling and textiles to brighten and insulate the interiors.

GARDENS AND GARDEN BUILDINGS

The design and development of country-house architecture was not restricted to the main house but embraced a complex of ancillary buildings, walls, terraces, gardens, ornamental features (including fountains and sculpture) and parkland. As the defensive inward-looking character of medieval buildings gave way to outward display, Elizabethan architecture extended into the landscape rather than being contained within protective walls. Gardens and estate land were thus designed with the same degree of attention as the main building. Indeed, among the Smythson drawings held in the Royal Institute of British Architects are several extended plans for houses at the centre of a patchwork of walled enclosures, formal gardens, garden buildings, walks and orchards. Estate maps from the period also provide vivid evidence for the ongoing development of the landscape surrounding country houses. Ralph Treswell's two surveys of the Holdenby estate, Northamptonshire, for example show major development to the setting of the house over a period of just eight years between 1580 and 1587.[4]

Most Elizabethan country houses had a series of gardens. Many areas functioned as working gardens for the provision of food, with associated structures such as dairies, bakehouses, brewhouses, fishponds and dovecotes. By the 1570s, however, the pleasure garden had become an essential feature of any house of status. The development of the pleasure garden was stimulated and supported by published treatises on the subject in English. Thomas Hill's *The Profitable Art of Gardening* (1568) and *The Gardeners Labyrinth* (1577) provided illustrated designs for knots and mazes and advice on planting. Formal gardens laid out with knotwork and mazes were attached to the main house so that they could be viewed from the windows above. In the gardens, mounds of earth (mounts) were created to serve as vantage points to survey the effect of the geometric patterns. Elaborately contrived knots were considered original and intriguing and thus appealed to the Elizabethan love of curiosities and ingenious devices. In this way, pleasure gardens not only catered to visual experience but also were designed to stimulate the intellect as well as the other senses, which were satisfied using scented herbs and flowers and fruit trees.

The areas surrounding greater houses provided important supplementary spaces for various aspects of social life that might be difficult to accommodate, due to issues of decorum or practical considerations, within the main house itself. With its series of walled enclosures, garden buildings, ornamental features and walks, the extended garden offered spaces for solitude as well as for exercise and recreation. Pleasure gardens also provided the setting for small and large-scale social gatherings. In the Elizabethan period, extravagant and exotic structures were erected in the landscape to cater to the whimsical aspects of country-house social life. The extravagant entertainments provided for Elizabeth at Kenilworth (1575) and Elvetham (1591) focused on outdoor attractions with temporary buildings and landscaping, including the massive artificial lake complete with islands, castle and ships created in the grounds at Elvetham.

Garden buildings for the purposes of pleasure were not only indicators of surplus wealth; they also provided opportunities for relaxation and high-dining. Many garden buildings seem to have been constructed as banqueting houses. Banquets were a luxury sweet course of sugared delicacies and spiced wines usually enjoyed as the culmination of lavish entertainments; a small group of favoured guests were impressed not only by the extravagant expenditure but also by the spectacle of such sumptuous and often fantastical culinary creations. Holding these banquets in an exotic building in one of the turret chambers on the roofline of the main house, or in the grounds, enhanced the sense of novelty and frivolity. The upper chamber of Sir William Sharington's tower at Lacock Abbey in Wiltshire still contains its original octagonal table (*c.* 1550) for serving delicacies.

Gatehouses were no longer required to guard the entrance to the main house, but many newly built houses continued to incorporate gatehouses as part of an impressive approach. The gatehouse symbolised the traditional manorial system and thus allowed the newly gentrified to pretend an ancient pedigree. These entranceways also provided useful additional accommodation and were adapted to new functions. They could serve as stores, lodgings for upper servants or assume a grander role as prospect chambers, reception spaces or guest apartments. Tixhall gatehouse in Staffordshire, all that remains of a Tudor mansion, was built around 1580 by Sir Walter Aston, and with its three storeys, look-out turrets and large windows probably served as a light-filled prospect chamber.

Other kinds of garden building offered occasional shelters for taking rest and meals while hunting or surveying the estate. The distance from the main house and the lack of any need for day-to-day functionality meant that these 'lodges' offered the opportunity for architectural invention and individual expression. The symbolic Triangular Lodge at Rushton, Northamptonshire encapsulates both these characteristics (Figure 34.7). Built by Sir Thomas Tresham in 1593–5 as an expression of

Figure 34.7 The Triangular Lodge, Rushton, Northamptonshire (1593–7). © English Heritage Photo Library.

his Roman Catholic faith, it represents the Trinity: the three-storey structure has three sides, each side is 33⅓ feet wide. The exterior is decorated with religious symbols and Tresham's own three-themed device of the trefoil. Some lodges offered more extensive apartments and were designed to accommodate larger parties as part of lavish entertainments or as vantage points (stands) for watching the chase. The stand at Chatsworth, Derbyshire (*c.* 1570), is a folly on the Gothic theme; this mock castle is three storeys high and topped with cylindrical turrets that must have offered extensive views across the landscape.

The association of pleasure gardens with indulgent sensory experience and their practical use as semi-private spaces for romantic encounters attracted the attention of moralists. In the 1595 edition of his *Anatomy of Abuses* the puritan zealot Phillip Stubbes offers this prudish comment on the use of garden buildings:

> they have Gardens . . . walled round about very high, with their Harbers [arbours], and bowers fit for the purpose, And least they might be espied in these open places, they have their banqueting houses with Galleries, Turrets, [and] what not els therein sumptuously erected: wherin they may (and doubtlesse do) many of them play the filthy persons.[5]

THE FARMHOUSE

It is fair to say that the middling ranks of the social spectrum experienced the most profound improvement in housing conditions. The steep rise in food prices in the sixteenth century meant that the freeholders and tenant farmers of rural England were able to invest surplus income in remodelling their houses. This potential for investment in building occurred at the same time that technological developments facilitated a revolution in the arrangement of domestic space. Whether they built new houses or developed existing structures, this class of builder focused on two goals: to improve the quality of internal space and to create more of it. This was achieved thanks to the increased availability of two materials in particular: brick and glass. The most fundamental change was the creation of chimneystacks – often the only part of a farmhouse built in brick. An allied development was the increased size and number of glazed windows.

Throughout the medieval period the more humble rural dwellings consisted of one large room (the hall) open at the roof to allow ventilation of a central hearth. In extended structures, bays at each end of the central hall provided additional areas for services, storage and living accommodation, but the hall was the only heated room and therefore the functional focus of daily life. Even where the end bays comprised two storeys, the use of this space was restricted by limited access. The central position of the double-height hall prevented direct movement between these two areas and so ladders were needed at each end.

In the sixteenth century, the increased use of brick allowed the insertion of a chimneystack into existing buildings so that the central hearth was now moved to one side of the hall and the smoke vented through a flue. With the space of the hall freed from its traditional function, it could be floored over to create an upper storey with extra rooms. The creation of additional fireplaces with flues off the main chimneystack, or the addition of more stacks, increased the comfort of other rooms, which also benefited from the insertion or creation of larger, and glazed, windows. Now that the upstairs was brought into use as comfortable living accommodation, more permanent staircases were required to provide easy access. A sturdy wooden staircase incorporated within the building not only improved communication between the various upper and lower rooms but also eliminated the need for the hall to function as a thoroughfare.

This subdivision of internal space greatly improved standards of comfort and privacy. Liberated from smoke and gloom, the interiors of farmhouses were airier and brighter, and the creation of new and distinct internal spaces allowed rooms to develop specialised functions. The preparation and cooking of food could shift from the hall to rooms at one end of the house while at the other end the parlour was given over to social and living space. As the main reception space for the provision of hospitality, the parlour usually contained the best bed, but the upper floor was increasingly used for sleeping as well as storage.

The optimum development of the hall-house plan is illustrated in a book aimed at the aspiring yeomanry, Gervase Markham's *The English Husbandman* (1613). Markham provides a floor plan of what he calls 'the model of a plaine country mans house' (Figure 34.8). The plan is of a fully developed, H-plan house with a central hall, five service rooms in one projecting wing and three larger rooms for entertaining in the other. Markham's plan is a representation of the ideal and this number of rooms, the two staircases and three chimneys would have been beyond the means of most farmers. It does, however, reflect the type of home lived in by the lesser gentry and wealthier yeomanry.

At the level of the farmhouse, the scale, pattern and form of these changes varied enormously across the country. The number of surviving examples of farmhouses

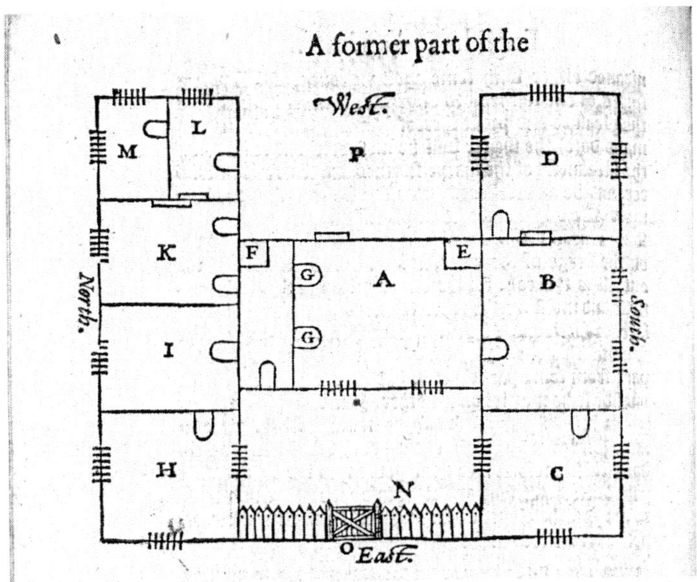

Figure 34.8 Gervase Markham's plan of 'a plaine country mans house' from *The English Husbandman* (1613). © The British Library Board. G.2383

built or significantly rebuilt during the sixteenth century reveals an uneven distribution. The abundance of examples in the south-eastern regions of the country reflects the prosperity of these areas in the Elizabethan period, while there are few in the far north of England. Builders at this level of society were completely dependent on local geology and knowledge so that different materials and plans were adopted in different regions, depending on local resources, techniques of construction and functional requirements. In general, timber and cob remained the most common building material for this class of building. Stone was utilised, especially in the limestone areas of England, but brick remained out of reach as the primary means of construction for those below the gentry, and was used only for chimneystacks. Nevertheless, the scale of farmhouses could vary according to the wealth and social ambitions of individual builders. If the larger houses built by prosperous yeomanry approach the scale and architectural sophistication of the houses of the lesser gentry, this reflects the new fluidity between these classes during Elizabeth's reign.

It is also evident that certain floor plans proved most convenient in adopting these new developments. Alongside the development of the formerly open-hall house, other plans evolved. Perhaps the most simple, yet sophisticated, response to the incorporation of chimneystacks was the lobby-entry house. This became increasingly common in the timber-framed areas of the country. An example is 'Pendean' farmhouse from Midhurst in Sussex, built *c.* 1609 as a small yeoman farmhouse; it is now re-erected in the grounds of the Weald and Downland Museum. The lobby-entry house centres around one large chimneystack, with an entrance at the front and a staircase at the rear (Figure 34.9). The chimneystack provides fireplace openings on both sides over two floors, an economical and effective use of just one chimney. This basic unit could be extended by the addition of bays at each end, although these required additional chimneystacks to heat the outer rooms.

Whatever the internal plan adopted or materials used in construction, the more pretentious examples of the various house types shared certain characteristics in their exterior appearance. The most significant innovation was the imposition of symmetry on the façade, which often masked an asymmetrical internal arrangement. The increased number and size of windows stood in contrast to the closed, blank faces of medieval dwellings. Perhaps the most significant change was the presence of large chimneystacks, which must have had a profound effect on the skyline. William Harrison's oft-quoted remark about the 'multitude of chimneys lately erected' in his *Description of England* (published in 1587) was a report of the gossip of old men living in Radwinter, Essex, in the 1570s. They remembered

> in their young days [i.e. *c.* 1510–20] there were not above two or three [chimneys], if so many, in most uplandish towns of the realm (the religious houses and manor places of their lords always excepted, and peradventure some great personages), but each one [man] made his fire against a reredos [wooden board] in the hall, where he dined and dressed his meat.[6]

Harrison's report offers a sense of how this dramatic transformation of the built environment was experienced by contemporaries.

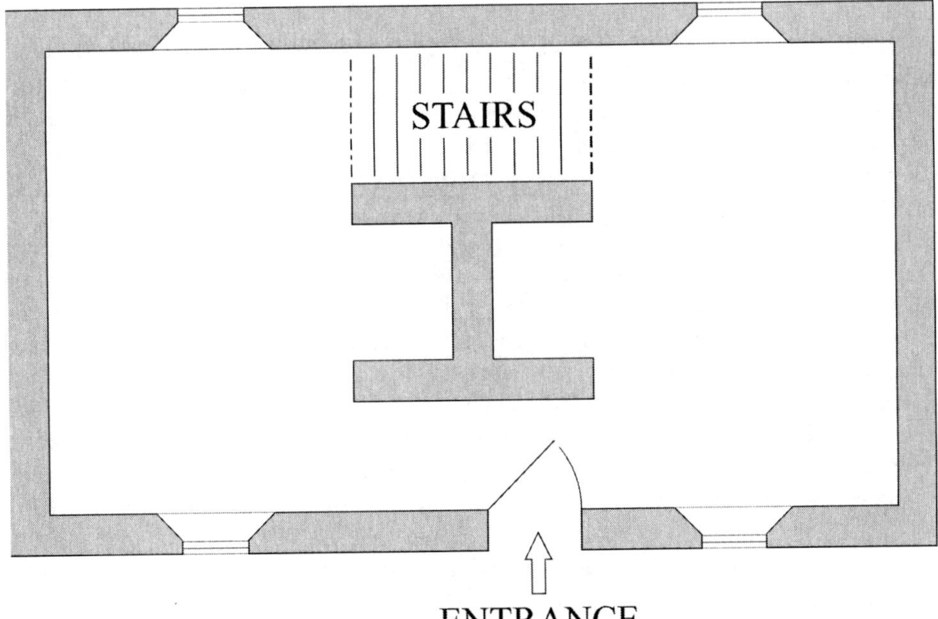

Figure 34.9 Simple plan of the lobby-entry house, with the chimney in the centre providing fireplaces to rooms on each side. Author's own diagram.

THE TOWN HOUSE

Building activity in towns boomed in the later sixteenth century as trade prospered and a significant increase in population put pressure on existing dwellings. More significantly, the rapid rise in the status of merchants led to higher expectations concerning living standards. New money desired convenient and comfortable housing but also wanted to stamp its mark on the urban community through the very visible display of a brand-new town house. The kinds of town houses built during Elizabeth's reign varied according to the locality and the requirements of individuals. The basic plans of the largest town houses conformed to two main types. First, the town mansions of the court elite, which generally followed the same courtyard plan as the greater country houses. These houses belonging to the courtier class were built mainly in London where none survive. They were essentially country mansions set down in the city making no concession to pressure on space through compactness of plan. An example of this kind of townhouse is Plas Mawr in Conway (North Wales), built between 1576 and 1585 for Robert Wynn, a Welsh merchant. Attached to the house is a walled courtyard entered through an imposing gatehouse ornamented with stepped gables.

The most common plan for domestic buildings in the cities and towns was what we might call the narrow, stacked house. This arrangement developed from a common medieval type and was ideally suited to the increasing demands on space in the prosperous towns of the Elizabethan period. Constructed of timber, the narrow stacked house maximised the space available on a limited footprint by ascending vertically over several storeys. The plan was particularly popular with wealthy merchants because even a massive house could occupy a prime position in the town centre, offering the potential to exploit commercial possibilities as well as the high-profile location. The ground floor usually consisted of a shop off the street with a kitchen or parlour (or both, in the larger houses) at the rear. The grandest reception room was elevated to the first floor, with bedrooms stacked in floors above, and possibly a garret in the attic. An example of the single-fronted town house is the Elizabethan House in Plymouth, now a museum. Built after 1584 as part of a new development to increase housing around the harbour area, the design manages to incorporate seven rooms ascending over three storeys thanks in part to a compact newel staircase (a spiral stair around a central pole).

Projecting upper storeys, jettied over the street or rear, is one of the characteristic features of this type of town house, as another means to maximise the available floor space inside. Bay windows on the street frontage also steal a few more feet of internal space while asserting the wealth and status of an owner who could afford excessive amounts of glazing. The grander houses were exercises in self-promotion, for the purposes of trade and social status, and the elaboration of features such as windows and corbels to support jettied upper storeys served to proclaim the status of the occupant. In addition to the pattern created by exaggerating the structural features of the visible wooden frame, the timber frontages of these houses were often adorned with decorative carving. An example is Harvard House in Stratford-upon-Avon, built in 1596 for Thomas Rogers, a butcher and cattle merchant. The elaborately carved façade (Figure 34.10) includes this date with Rogers's initials and those of his wife and son, a scrolling vine pattern, Tudor roses and a bull's head – presumably a reference to the owner's trade.

With a practical limit on the number of storeys that even the loftiest houses could support, the wealthiest citizens chose to multiply this plan sideways over additional plots to double, triple or even quadruple the accommodation. These mansions with their uniform appearance capped by rows of gables on the street frontage often resemble a row of separate houses despite being constructed as a single unit. A group of town houses built by clothiers in Shrewsbury represent these grander mansions. Sherar's mansion was built before 1573 as a triple-fronted, three-storey house. Another, known as Ireland's mansion, was constructed a few years later as a quadruple plan, while Owen's mansion dated 1592 is double-fronted.

Other builders chose to speculate with additional dwellings alongside their own plot to be sold once completed. The houses at 41 and 42 High Street in Exeter were built as a pair in 1564; each was one room wide and two rooms deep with a spiral (newel) stair at the centre of each building. At the rear was a detached kitchen block reached through a small courtyard. Inside, the houses were richly decorated. Painting directly onto the wall was a common form of interior decoration for houses of middling status. The remains of wall painting in the first floor room of No. 42, for example, depicts a band of text from Scripture in a decorative cartouche with blocks of red and blue-grey colouring below.

Figure 34.10 Harvard House, Stratford-upon-Avon, Warwickshire. A single-fronted town house with elaborate carving, dated 1596. Author's own photograph.

PUBLIC BUILDINGS

If a sharp increase in population acted as a fillip to the building of town houses for the wealthy, those at the bottom of the social spectrum also relied on urban elites to provide basic housing. Almshouses, as with other public buildings in towns, were often private benefactions built to establish and immortalise the status of wealthy individuals in their local communities. Such self-serving acts of generosity highlighted those aspects of the benefactor's own character considered desirable in the Elizabethan gentleman, such as charity and education.

Some of these establishments were very grand indeed, if conservative in plan and decoration. The almshouses and hospital erected in Croydon between 1596 and 1599 by John Whitgift, Archbishop of Canterbury, could accommodate up to forty people. Like the great mansions of the era, it consists of a quadrangle of lodgings around a courtyard. Unlike these courtyard mansions, however, it is lacking in ostentation. Built in brick with stone detailing, the entrance façade is plain and sober and the emphasis is on the inner courtyard. The design is inward-looking, as befits an establishment inhabited by humble people. Other almshouses were more modest in the scale of accommodation provided; the simple row of cottages in Mapledurham, Oxfordshire, founded in 1613 by John Lister offered lodgings for just six people.

Archbishop Whitgift's Croydon redevelopment included a schoolhouse and master's house. This type of establishment offered another opportunity for munificence combined with self-publicity. If almshouses proclaimed the patron's charity, the founding of schools proclaimed his learning. Many of the schools built in the later sixteenth century were simple rectangular buildings. Even the grander establishments built in stone lacked architectural invention and differed little from domestic dwellings in form and appearance. The grammar school founded by Lord Williams at Thame, Oxfordshire, in 1559 consists of a single large schoolroom with a dormitory above, but this is hidden behind the residential accommodation for the master, situated in the street range with its symmetrical façade and homely gable.

As well as a surge in the building of local schools, there was an expansion in the universities in the second half of the sixteenth century. Here again, there was little architectural innovation, and the Oxford and Cambridge colleges founded in the Elizabethan period were conventional in design and detailing. The inward-looking courtyard plan remained standard because it continued to cater to the function of these colleges as secluded seats of learning. This is exemplified by the conservatism of the second court of Saint John's College, Cambridge, added in 1598–1602. Nevertheless, the allegorical gates of Gonville and Caius College created by John Caius in the 1560s and 1570s offered an opportunity for architectural experimentation. A series of three gateways in classical style symbolised the path of academic life: the gates of Humility, Virtue and Honour. The latter, completed in 1575, is the most decorative, with its engaged columns, pediment and obelisks and is loosely based on designs by the Italian architect Sebastiano Serlio.

If the form and appearance of almshouses and schools tended towards the traditional and domestic, the town hall as the seat of civic government represents an alternative building type. A number of socio-economic factors placed a great deal of emphasis on this building. The State's increasing reliance on local government combined with the expansion of many market towns resulted in a desire for a suitable building to house the civic authority and to represent the prosperity of the town. Added to this was a desire on behalf of the local gentry and wealthy merchants who served as town officials to celebrate their elevated status in society.

Robert Tittler has identified an overall pattern of increase in the number of town halls that were erected or substantially rebuilt in the sixteenth century which reached a peak in the 1560s and 1570s. Usually sited in a prominent, isolated position in the middle of the marketplace these halls were both the symbolic heart of the town and its administrative centre. The standard type for the market hall consisted of a large upper chamber supported on pillars or arcades on at least three sides. The open ground floor served as shelter for market stalls while the upper-storey room served as a meeting hall for a range of administrative functions. Another common type occupied the same central position in the town but with a closed ground-floor and a street-side position.

Most of the newly constructed market or guild halls were vernacular in form and style, built from locally available materials (usually timber) to a traditional plan with English Gothic detailing. These were not adventurous buildings in architectural terms. The market hall from Titchfield in Hampshire, now rebuilt in the Weald and Downland Museum, is a simple and traditional two-storey structure constructed in timber. A similar market hall in Shrewsbury was built in 1567 but in 1596 it was replaced with a stone building. Despite the opportunity for architectural invention and embellishment, the result is a conservative and severe building with an open ground floor and arcades raised by solid columns, its status announced by an emphasised porch. In keeping with its function, the architecture expresses solemnity, strength and authority.

It is the case, however, that a handful of civic halls built during Elizabeth's reign display an unusual degree of architectural sophistication. These resulted from the intervention of powerful men who chose to sponsor such improvements in their local towns and thus stamp their mark on the urban environment as well as their country estate. Examples include Rothwell Market House, begun in *c.* 1578 under the direction of Sir Thomas Tresham who brought in the accomplished mason, William Grumbold, to work on the project. Rothwell's market-house façade to the street is simple in form, built in stone with an arcaded ground floor and fenestrated first floor but is rich in decoration, with classical pilasters supporting a frieze at each storey. The upper frieze is decorated with ninety shields with the arms of local dignitaries, showing Tresham's political alliances. A Latin inscription in the lower frieze runs around the middle of the building and proclaims the authorship of the building: 'This was the work of Thomas Tresham, Knight.'

Perhaps the most innovative project of this type was the renovation of the Exeter Guildhall in 1592–4 at an enormous cost of £800 over four years. Despite this expenditure, the building was only revamped, not rebuilt, with an Elizabethan frontage in classical style clamped to a much earlier building, most of which was retained within. The new façade communicates the power and strength of the civic authority through the fashionable language of classical architecture (Figure 34.11). The huge, solid pillars supporting the upper floors reflect the strength of the institution, while the more decorative pairs of columns at first-floor level indicate

Figure 34.11 Exeter Guildhall, Devon. Image courtesy of Exeter Museums.

the prestigious nature of the council rooms within. The first storey of the façade was originally surmounted by a second storey (dismantled in 1718); this was also adorned with paired columns, surmounted by obelisks, while in the centre was a gabled niche containing the royal arms, referring to the ultimate authority from which local government derived its privileges.

CONCLUSION

In conclusion, there are several aspects of Elizabethan housing that this chapter has not addressed. Although ordinary Elizabethans would have noticed transformations in the exteriors of buildings within the context of their public lives, it is unlikely that the bulk of society felt any direct benefit from this activity. The houses of the very poor – consisting of simple, single-room dwellings rebuilt every generation or so – do not survive, but it is unlikely that this class group experienced any of the improvements in living conditions that became the norm for their social superiors. Similarly the average citizen in towns (ordinary shopkeepers and tradesmen) would have occupied just one or two rooms (with one serving as a shop or workshop) in narrow urban tenements given over to multiple occupancy. Though such structures no longer survive in anything like their original form, the experience of such people can be reconstructed to some extent through archaeological investigation. Meanwhile, much more could be said about the decoration and furnishing of houses. The general improvement in housing conditions among the upper sections of society included the decoration and furnishing of interiors with fixtures and material goods; the 'great provision of tapestry, Turkey work, pewter, brass, fine linen, and thereto costly cupboards of plate' described by William Harrison in his *Description of England*.[7] A new interest in material-culture studies – concerned with the production, value and consumption of material goods within cultures – over the past two decades has refocused attention on the need to examine the relationship between investment in building and the acquisition and display of objects. These are just two areas where architectural history fruitfully intersects with other disciplines to continue producing insights into understudied aspects of Elizabethan life.

FURTHER READING

Airs, Malcolm, 'Architecture', in Boris Ford (ed.), *The Cambridge Guide to the Arts in Britain: Vol. III, Renaissance and Reformation* (Cambridge, 1989).

—— *The Tudor and Jacobean Country House: A Building History* (Sutton, 1998).

Ayres, James, *Domestic Interiors: The British Tradition, 1500–1850* (New Haven, Conn., 2003).

Cooper, Nicholas, *The Houses of the Gentry, 1480–1680* (New Haven, Conn., 1999).

Friedman, Alice T., *House and Household in Elizabethan England: Wollaton Hall and the Willoughby Family* (Chicago, Ill., 1989).

Girouard, Mark, *Life in the English Country House: A Social and Architectural History* (New Haven, Conn., 1978).

—— *Robert Smythson and the Elizabethan Country House* (New Haven, Conn., 1983).

—— *Elizabethan Architecture: Its Rise and Fall, 1540–1640* (New Haven, Conn., 2009).

Henderson, Paula, *The Tudor House and Garden: Architecture and Landscape in the Sixteenth and Early Seventeenth Centuries* (New Haven, Conn., 2005).

Howard, Maurice, *The Building of Elizabethan and Jacobean England* (New Haven, Conn., 2007).

Strong, Roy, *The Renaissance Garden in England* (London, 1979).

Summerson, John, *Architecture in Britain, 1530–1830*, 9th edn (New Haven, Conn., 1993).

Tittler, Robert, *Architecture and Power: The Town Hall and the English Urban Community c. 1500–1640* (Oxford, 1991).

Wells-Cole, Anthony, *Art and Decoration in Elizabethan and Jacobean England: The Influence of Continental Prints* (New Haven, Conn., 1997).

NOTES

1 W. G. Hoskins, 'The Rebuilding of Rural England, 1570–1640', *Past and Present*, 4 (1) (1953): 44–59.

2 Mark Girouard, 'Smythson, Robert (1534/5–1614)', in H. C. G. Matthew and Brian Harrison (eds.), *Oxford Dictionary of National Biography* (Oxford, 2004), available online at www.oxforddnb.com/view/article/37988 (accessed 20 March 2008).

3 *Wentworth Papers, 1597–1628*, ed. J. P. Cooper, Camden Fourth Series, vol. 12 (London, 1973), p. 14.

4 Paula Henderson, *The Tudor House and Garden* (New Haven, Conn., 2005) p. 88, Figures 108, 109.
5 Phillip Stubbes, *The Anatomie of Abuses* (London, 1595), p. 57.
6 William Harrison, *The Description of England* (1587), ed. Georges Edelen (New York, 1994), p. 201.
7 Harrison, *Description of England*, p. 200.

PART VI

THE OUTSIDE WORLD

CHAPTER THIRTY-FIVE

ENGLAND AND EUROPE, 1558–85

David Potter

In retrospect, the Elizabethan era was portrayed as a golden age, and successes, especially in defence against foreign invaders, were often taken for granted. R. B. Wernham suggested that the reign of Henry VIII saw the final phase of England as a Continental military power (the fall of Calais in 1558 symbolised this) and a shifting of emphasis to the oceanic and worldwide role of England in the reign of Elizabeth. At the time, though, the overwhelming impression would have been of danger and the looming fear of foreign conquest. In 1558–9, France seemed to pose the greatest threat, and, after the death of Henri II in July 1559, a Franco-Scottish dynastic link seemed about to sweep Elizabeth from her throne. Pessimism reigned, and in 1558 Armagil Waad famously observed 'warres with Fraunce and Scotland: the French King bestryding the Realm, having on foot in Callais and the other in Scotland: stedfast enmytye but no stedfast frendship abroade.'[1] Another observer compared England in 1559 to 'a bone thrown between two dogs'.[2] William Paget, in a note to the new queen's most trusted adviser, William Cecil, argued that the French were England's natural enemies, that their power was growing but that reliance on the Habsburgs was also dangerous: 'if we take part with nether of them, they will fasten theyr Fete both of them here, and make a Pyemont of us: If we take Part with one, we our selfs shalbe afterwards made a Preye of by the Victor.'[3] The comparison of England with lands in Italy, fought over by the great dynasties, was commonplace. The Count of Feria remarked in August 1559 that 'Englande wold be another Millanne to sett the princes together by the eares', while Chantonnay, Philip II's ambassador in France, thought that 'it wolde so cum to pass, as either we shulde be made a Piemont and be devided, or els a Milain, and so constrained to stand upon our gard untill we were weried.'[4] The deeply traditional Nicholas Wotton thought in January 1559 that, should France and Spain make peace, 'we wer not able long to resiste the French and the Scottes, and other whome the French wold sette in owr toppes; wherof might ensew, that the French shuld be Lords of England and Scotland to.'[5] The chronicler John Hayward summed up the heightened uncertainty:

> Every man's mynd was then travayled with a strange confusione of conceits, all things being immoderately eyther deaded or desired. Every report was

> greedily both inquired and received, all truthes suspected, diverse tales beleeved, many improbable conjectures hatched and nourished. Invasione of straungers, civill dissentione, the doubtefull dispositione of the succeeding Prince, were cast in every man's conceite as present perills; but noe man did buysy his witts in contriving remedyes.[6]

In the background there was a sense of defeat and strategic danger, brought about by the loss of Calais. This had confirmed anti-French instincts in England and came at the end of a decade of military and diplomatic reverses for England, first in the failure to maintain the military domination of the Lowlands of Scotland in 1548–9, then the agreed abandonment of Boulogne in 1550 and a peace with Scotland in 1551 which confirmed the effective French protectorate there. Ireland, too, became subject to much more foreign interference from the late 1540s. Though the view that mid-Tudor governments were basically dependent on either France or the Habsburgs has been exaggerated, these reverses shaped the fears and expectations of Elizabeth and of the men around her. In addition, the economic problems of the mid-Tudor years, harshest in the early 1550s but still evident on the eve of Elizabeth's accession, have encouraged one historian to view the problems of foreign relations as part of a 'mid-Tudor crisis'.[7] A council memorandum in 1557 underlined this pessimistic view:

> The warres the Queenes Majestie is utterly unable to maynteyn . . . the common people of this realme being presently many wayes greived and some pinced with famine and want of payment of money due to them, some miscontented for matters of Religion and generally all yet tasting of the smarte of the last warres it might be very daungerous to entangle them now with new warres.[8]

John Mason in November 1558 thought that 'our state can no longer bear these wars', and in December 1559, Nicholas Bacon summed up the odds: 'who is so ignorante, that knowes not that the kingdome and dominions that be under the governance of the crowne of Fraunce to be foure tymes as much as the realme of England.'[9] Such attitudes shaped the need to make peace at Cateau-Cambrésis in April 1559, with a face-saving formula over Calais.

The English experience of Philip II's role as king consort from 1554–8 had a lasting effect on public attitudes to Spaniards. The extent to which this modified traditional English francophobia, though, is more debatable. There seems little reason to doubt that the loss of Calais was blamed on Mary's entering the war with France under pressure from Philip. That the latter did little to salvage something for England at Cateau-Cambrésis scarcely helped. George Ferrers in 1568 thought that the loss of Calais had been 'such a buffet to England as had not happened in more than an hundred years before'.[10] In contrast, Philip's capture of Saint-Quentin had brought nothing to England. That Mary had died in shame at the loss of Calais was an article of faith to be established in the long run by Foxe. Hayward was unusual in observing that little could have been done:

> King Phillip held himselfe obliged in honor to procure a restitutione of that towne, which, under his government, and principally in his cause and quarrell,

> was lost [but] the French were unwilling to receive that people to any footing in France whoe had soe roughly overtrampled all ther country before.[11]

The relations between states continued to be conducted as relations between princes. The 'making of policy' under Elizabeth has been the object of much speculation in terms of the pressures and factions that surrounded her.[12] The Queen herself, like her predecessors, retained in theory ultimate control of decisions in an area which was quintessentially part of the royal prerogative. As Sir Thomas Smith was to put it: 'The Monarch of England, King or Queene, hath absolutelie in his power the authoritie of warre and peace, to defie what Prince it shall please him, and to bid him warre, and againe to reconcile him at his pleasure.'[13]

Some historians have discussed the 'making of policy' under Elizabeth, and many have assumed that there was a coherent 'foreign policy' in the period. If so, what personnel and institutions backed it up? Recent work on Tudor diplomacy has produced mixed responses to the question of whether there was, in effect, a professional Tudor diplomatic service. Even less certainty exists on the question of the expertise at the centre. Jeffrey Platt, for example, has argued strongly against Garrett Mattingly's view that there was, until the late seventeenth century, an inadequate diplomatic service in the key fields of a permanent staff, reliable archives, definite policies and the 'means of coordinating activities abroad'. Platt has instead maintained that 'a professional, efficient, de facto foreign office thrived in Elizabethan England.'[14]

In reality, while the capacity to make policy was inevitably limited by commercial and strategic interests, at times these were diverted by the Queen's personal needs and prejudices. This is why marriage negotiations played such a prominent role down to around 1580. The Queen's marriage was a major concern, not least because of the looming problem of the succession and the need for her to produce an heir. Quite apart from the role of the Earl of Leicester, a succession of foreign princes figured in these negotiations, from Philip II onwards. There were, of course, objections to all of them, in some cases because of their Catholicism, in others because their status was simply too feeble to match the Queen's. In fact, all Elizabeth's 'suitors' were fatally undermined either by the Queen's aversion, or the aversion of a section of the Privy Council. In the case of François d'Anjou, who came closest in 1579, it was Protestant public opinion that undermined the plan. Throughout, many diplomatic overtures were routinely accompanied by proposals of marriage; Elizabeth in that respect was no different from any other marriageable ruler. What ultimately marked her out was the combination of personal disinclination and political deadlock which meant that ultimately marriage was impossible. From the 1580s, the certainty that the Queen would have no heir dominated the succession and thus relations with Mary Stuart and James VI, bringing in foreign complications with Spain and France.

Despite the Queen's control of policy, the mid-Tudor period had seen the emergence of a significant public opinion on the making of policy – among the nobility, gentry and commercial interests – which became increasingly vocal as the reign went on. This opinion was often deeply marked by religious fears and inclinations. In addition, a privateering interest, groups of entrepreneurs who had come in the mid-Tudor period to view the worldwide possessions of Spain as ripe for plunder, immensely complicated any notion of making policy purely in dynastic terms. The Queen was bound to seek advice from her chosen councillors, a group who shared certain assumptions, though they differed in tactics. This may sometimes have had the effect of allowing her to play off her advisers against each other, but at times it limited her choices. The idea that the Elizabethan court was divided by two major factions, so much a part of traditional views, is now seriously questioned. Cecil, Leicester and Walsingham often worked together and shared many common assumptions; indeed, the regime could not have survived had this not been the case.

The fact that Elizabeth, within months of her accession, had made her inclinations towards a moderate Protestantism clear meant that to some extent her scope for decision-making was set. Those who advised her on foreign policy were, of course, a mixture whose differing views of the world and personal ambitions were a factor with which the Queen had to deal, but more united them than seriously divided them. The older statesmen, whose service went back to the later years of Henry VIII, were commonly deeply anti-French. William Paget in February 1559 wrote to Cecil of 'the Necessite of Friendship with the House of Burgundy . . . the naturall enmity betwene us and Fraunce'.[15] Nicholas Wotton, a diplomat both knowledgeable about France and experienced in its culture, wrote in January 1559 of 'the auncyent, immortall hatredde they beare unto us'.[16]

Hostility to France and the idea of using the alliance of Spain against her were commonplace in the first two years of the reign. Throckmorton could argue for seizing the opportunity of Henri II's death to recover Calais and for the opportunity 'to send now to the king of Spain as well to enter in amity and straight league with him and also be in hand with him for the recovery of Calais'.[17] In the 1560s, though, the experiences of English Protestants in the 1550s were amplified by a developing phobia about Spain. This began to displace the old hostility to a France, which, during its civil wars, could not pose a threat and which provided scope for alliance with co-religionists. Attitudes to France therefore became more ambivalent. As for Spain, hispanophobia was nourished by conflicts in the Atlantic from the 1540s and developed into a 'black legend' during the privateering voyages of the 1560s.[18] In the 1580s, Hakluyt, in his *Discourse of Western Planting*, originally a private paper drawn up for the political elite, reflected this influence when he claimed that 'the Spaniards have exercised moste outragious and more than Turkishe cruelties in all the west Indies' as did Walter Ralegh when he remarked that they had acted 'contrarie to all naturall humanitie'.[19] On the religious dimension, while James Wadsworth could write that the Spaniards made use of the Pope 'for their own particular ambitions and ends', Drake's chaplain claimed that they spread 'the poisonous infection of Popery wherever they went'.[20]

Elizabethan policy was from the start shaped by the fact that it had become impossible to ignore a prince's religion in the conventional calculations of power politics, no matter how cynical the ultimate objectives. Furthermore, the cause of international Protestantism was a major imperative in the thinking of political Protestantism represented by Leicester and Walsingham. We should, though, question whether religion played a uniformly dominant role in the formation of public opinion on foreign affairs. 'Public opinion' may have been easily persuaded of the perfidy or risibility of foreigners and their rulers. It was not so simple to convince people of the identification of dastardly foreigner and Catholic; this took some time. John Foxe's *Acts and Monuments,* for instance, was slow to gain an audience, having to wait until 1570 for a reprint (and revision) of its 1563 edition. Nor was it a simple matter to use printed propaganda, since the print runs were generally small.

A PERIOD OF ACTIVISM, 1559–63

Given the widespread defeatism at the time of Elizabeth's accession, it is remarkable that her first years were marked by unexpected successes in military interventionism. To some extent this was because, although the fears of foreign domination were great, after the Treaty of Cateau-Cambrésis (April 1559) it became more difficult for France and less necessary for Philip II to try to control England. The problems of military action in the early years are often held to explain the limits set by Elizabeth to a forward foreign policy after she had got her fingers burned at Le Havre in 1563. We need to ask whether this image of a cautious Elizabeth, often backed by Cecil, against a host of bellicose and activist advisers is correct, and, if so, when was the pattern established. Was it the case that, as one major historian of the period has argued, that 'the lessons learned at Newhaven (Le Havre) decisively shaped the strategies of English foreign policy for two decades to come'?[21]

The first major military operation came in Scotland in 1560 with the intervention, very much pushed by Cecil, against the faltering French-backed regime of the Regent Mary of Guise. Scotland had been one of the greatest preoccupations of English statesmen in the mid-Tudor years. Henry VIII decided to solve the problem of having his policy towards France impeded by the enemy in the north by decisive military action in 1541–2. This certainly smashed the Scottish army at Solway Moss but failed to control the country. The later part of his reign became bogged down in attempts to bribe, cajole and bully various factions within Scotland. Protector Somerset, between 1547 and 1549, was more systematic and drastic in his military action but was forced to concede defeat in the face of French military intervention on the part of the Scots. It has been argued that this was the period in which a serious ideological basis emerged for the first time for some kind of 'union' between the kingdoms. Roger Ascham, in a famous passage of his *Toxophilus* of 1545, wrote:

> yet one thynge would I wysshe for the Scottes, and that is this, that seinge one God, one faythe, one compasse of the see, one land and countrie, one tunge in speakynge, one maner in trade in lyuynge, lyke courage and stomake in war, lyje quicknesse of witte to learning, hath made Englande and Scotlande bothe one, they wolde suffre them no longer to be two: but cleane gyue over the Pope.[22]

William Thomas, in his encomium of Henry VIII in 1547, had thought the King's aim had been to unite the two realms in 'one self devyded nacion and realm, one self perpetuall united people, not for welth . . . but for the uniform quiet of their approved auncient contention'.[23] Cecil, who had had a hand in Somerset's propaganda offensive in Scotland in 1547–8, had developed both a geographical and ideological view that enabled him to conceive mentally and visually of Britain as one country. Early in 1560, he drew up a 'Memorial of certain points meet for restoring the Realme of Scotland to the ancient weal': 'the best worldly felicitie that Scotland can have is either to contynew in a perpetuall peace with the kingdom of Ingland or to be made one monarchie with England as they both make but one Ile divided from the rest of the world.' The French, he argued, would always seek 'to make Scotland an instrument to exercise therby theyr malice upon England to make a footestoole therof to looke over Ingland as they may'.[24] This idea of a dynastic union was also broached by Throckmorton in a letter to Robert Dudley in February 1560. For the Scottish opposition in 1560 this may have meant a marriage between Elizabeth and Arran, the next in line, though how practical this was is doubtful.

The opportunity in 1560 was a clear one: the Scottish regent's unpopular religious policy backed up by increasing numbers of French troops and officials had provoked a precarious opposition movement in the form of the Lords of the Congregation. If this were not supported, it was easy to see that the chance would not recur. Cecil's policy from the Treaty of Berwick with the Scottish lords in February 1560 to that of Edinburgh in July 1560 was shaped to this end and enabled him to conceive of using allies in Scotland also to help control Ireland. The treaty of Berwick provided for aid from Argyll 'to reduce the north partis of yrland to the perfyt obedience of England'.[25]

In March 1560, Cecil drew up a memorandum urging the Queen to action beginning: 'we doo all certenly thynk that the quene of Scotts and, for hir sake, her husband and the house of Guise, be in there harts mortall enemyes to your majesty's person.' By God's grace, though, recent events had provided an opportunity: 'First was the dethe of the French kyng, a man of grete activité and corradge: with hym fell the same and corrage of warr in France for a season: with hym decayed the wise counsellor the constable and such others as depended upon hym.'[26]

There seems little doubt that Cecil used the strident calls for action from agents abroad to press the case. Throughout 1559 and 1560, Throckmorton regularly reported to Elizabeth the insulting claims to legitimate succession made by Mary Stuart and François II, and it is from this period that the legend of the Guises as inveterate enemies of England begins to develop. In July 1559, he was reporting the dangers posed by France: 'we have great cause to suspect the French meaning towardes us; and the suspicion thereof on this side doth dayly rather increase then decrease.'[27] Just as Throckmorton had argued in July 1559 that 'now is a propice time' for the recovery of Calais, so the agents Killigrew and Jones argued at the end of that year that 'the French state at this time is so incumbred and in suche necessite, as it is thought, is ever there were a time of advantge over them, it is now. Wherefore, whatsoever is to be done against them it is to be done forthwith.'[28] Cecil's 'Brief Consideration of the Weighty Matter of Scotland' drawn up in August 1559 and revised in the spring of 1560 underlined the long-standing threat from France.[29]

There is evidence both that Cecil received backing from most of the Privy Council but also that it was fragile and that Elizabeth was very reluctant to act, especially after the initial reverse at Leith. The Queen throughout her reign was averse from grand strategies and was more at ease with short-term tactics. Cecil reported to Throckmorton in May 1560 that 'the Queen's Majestie never liketh this matter of Scotland . . . you knowe, what hangeth thereuppon; weak harted men, and flatterers will follow that waye . . . I have had such a torment herin with the Queen's Majestie, as an ague hath not in five fitts so much abated'.[30] In order to achieve his ends he had, as Jane Dawson has observed, to press and perhaps to exaggerate the threat from France in order to portray the action as one directed against France. Only in this way could he hope to establish a working alliance with the Scottish opposition that did not reawaken all the old fears about English domination. Although the failure of English forces at Leith may have confirmed Elizabeth's caution about such enterprises, the collapse of the French position as a result of their inability to reinforce the place and then the death of Mary of Guise paved the way for a diplomatic triumph personally masterminded by Cecil.

France itself was the second focus for military action, as that country began to descend into civil war. We can see the pressures for intervention at work from the beginning of the reign with the appointment, on Cecil's advice, of an ambassador in Nicholas Throckmorton who, while by no means a fanatic, used his extensive knowledge of France to build a case for action against what he saw as a dangerous threat to Elizabeth's throne. With the accession of Charles IX at the end of 1560 the theme of an embattled godly community of French Protestants in need of English help begins to emerge. Wallace MacCaffrey argues that, despite her inclination to a *cuius regio* principle, which would leave it up to each prince to decide the religion of his people, she could not in 1559–60 ignore the fate of Protestants in France. This left her unable to stand against the activist policies of her advisers.

Throckmorton had been pressing for some sort of action since 1560 and had been in contact with the Protestant leadership. MacCaffrey has argued that the most important internal consequence of the need to confront what was happening in France was the emergence of Robert Dudley as a major player in the making of foreign policy when he was ordered by Elizabeth to make a cautiously favourable reply to a letter from the Huguenot leader, the Prince of Condé. This, suggested MacCaffrey, lay at the start of their thirty-year rivalry over the making of policy, though it was not clear at the time. However, it needed the pushing of both Cecil and Dudley to get any action, and that Cecil had hoped to achieve something in France short of direct military intervention may have undermined this; the clarity of his thinking, apparent over Scotland, is certainly missing. Elizabeth had serious reservations about military intervention in the summer of 1562; as Cecil wrote to Throckmorton in August, she 'sticketh at the matter, one part desire to gain, on the other loth to adventure'.[31] She was perhaps prepared to listen to the activist case in 1562 as a result of the offers made by Condé and others in France for a foothold on the Norman coast which might conceivably give her the bargaining power to recover Calais. However, the printed declarations issued in September only hinted obliquely at this while emphasising the selfless goal of preserving the authority of the King of France in his childhood.

The English case for intervention was a curious one that did not involve outright war; England would occupy Le Havre on the basis that it was protecting it from the enemies of the French crown; hence the fact that the landing of troops in France did not lead immediately to formal war. The Treaty of Hampton Court on 20 September 1562 specified the troops and money to be sent to the French Protestants, and the vanguard landed on 4 October. When the army of intervention is looked at, the leadership of Warwick, Killigrew, Horsey and Leighton make clear its status as an enterprise led by Dudley's friends and allies. As Paul Hammer explains, the failure was the result both of bad luck, with the outbreak of disease in the English garrison, ineffective military organisation and the internal state of French politics.

The Treaty of Troyes with France (1564) effectively put an end to Elizabeth's immediate hopes of regaining Calais and, for the time being, to any ambitions for direct intervention on the European mainland. The Queen and many of her subjects, however, never abandoned the idea of regaining Calais. The desire to recover it, in fact, faded only imperceptibly through the Elizabethan period and was still there in the 1590s.

THE ECONOMIC DIMENSION: TRADE AND POLICY

Elizabeth could not exercise her prerogatives in foreign affairs without reference to the interests of her powerful and wealthy subjects. These, though, pulled in different directions. The years 1550–75 were generally adverse for the English economy, in part as a result of poor harvests but also because of the increasing instability of English export markets. After 1575, these conditions were reversed by a series of eleven good harvest and profits from exploitation of the Atlantic. Over-dependence on Antwerp, the struggle with the merchants of the Hanse and the emergence of new commercial techniques led to rapid change.

One of the pressures on English policy came from the 'privateers', who were profiting from the pillage of Atlantic shipping from the 1540s onwards. These periodically derailed attempts by statesmen and diplomats to achieve peace with Spain. Proclamations summoning private adventurers to fit out ships to attack enemies during the wars with France in 1544 and 1557 had severe and unexpected effects on relations with Spain, when Flemish goods carried in French ships could be seized. Complaint about these depredations by Spanish ambassadors became almost routine. The jurisdiction of the Admiralty made this worse from 1560 when it was proclaimed that, of goods seized from pirates, the Lord Admiral might keep one-third. The Spanish Empire of the Indies was ostensibly powerful but in reality difficult to defend against determined attack, a fact that the Plymouth seaman John Hawkins and his consortium exploited in the expeditions mounted between 1562 and 1568.

On the other hand, the mercantile interest, whose wealth depended until around 1570 on a stable relationship with the government of the Low Countries, posed a limitation on the Crown's freedom in dealing with Spain and pulled it towards compromise. William Camden was well aware of this economic imperative in his narrative of the shift of the Merchant Adventurers to Emden in 1564 and the embargo of 1569. Nor could the Crown safely ignore the Antwerp market, when – at least in the first years of the reign – it relied on it to raise loans through Sir Thomas Gresham. Ups and downs in the relations between Elizabeth and Philip II inevitably affected the availability of credit. London was, of course, by far the most important economic centre of England and was dominated politically and economically in the 1560s by its twelve traditional livery companies, by the members of the nationwide association of the Merchant Adventurers, a 'regulated company' whose headquarters was at Antwerp. The City paid a very significant proportion of taxes directly and through customs. Up to the early 1560s, the role of Antwerp as the 'vent' for English semi-finished cloth shipped by the Merchant Adventurers was central to the trade of London (raw wool exports shipped by the Staplers had declined in relative importance and, in any case, had never dominated London as did cloth). Around 1560, the value of English cloth exported every year to Antwerp was colossal and stood somewhere around £1 million. Trade was therefore a major consideration in the formation of policy, though this did not prevent interruptions of such trade for political reasons even before Elizabeth's accession. Towards the end of the sixteenth century, the Muscovy Company attributed its foundation to the fact that under Edward VI, the government:

> Findinge it inconvenient that the utterance of the commodities of England, especiallie clothe, shoulde so muche depend upon the Lowe Countries and Spaine and that it should be beneficiall to have a vent some other waies, did encourage his subjectes the merchauntes to adventure for disocoverie of the new trades northe warde.[32]

The crisis in outlets for English cloth had already led to attempts to find new northern routes under Mary. The Muscovy Company, a joint-stock company many of whose initial members were courtiers and nobles whose main participation was investment to discover a north-east passage to the Orient, had been founded in 1553 by 240 merchants. Many of these were Merchant Adventurers, and one-third of them had an interest in the cloth trade.[33]

One further determinant of English economic policy was set in May 1558 with the new 'Book of Rates', or customs regime, masterminded by Lord Treasurer Winchester, which effectively overhauled the financial base of the State by massively increasing tariffs (especially on cloth) and making evasion of customs much more difficult. One aspect of this was a significant increase in the tariff paid by foreign merchants exporting English cloth. The protests over this in the Low Countries were loud, especially as it appeared to abrogate part of the *Magnus Intercursus*. As G. D. Ramsay pointed out, the only way England might have avoided these provocative changes and maintained a free-trade relationship with Antwerp was to have reverted to a relationship much more characteristic of the fifteenth century and accepted a much less effective central government. As it was, the story of the 1560s and 1570s was that of the disengagement of English merchants from their traditional dependence on the Low Countries. Ramsay saw the underlying reasons for these changes as shaped by politics; yes, trade had its own dynamics but the conditions in which that trade was carried on had political connotations that were set by governments.

The complex interrelationship between the demands of trade, politics and religion are revealed by George Nedham's 1560 'Articles of Emden', almost certainly a presentation copy for the Queen. Nedham, a Merchant Adventurer with Europe-wide contacts, started from the experience of five trade embargoes suffered by English merchants at Antwerp since 1544. He had observed the commodity of the harbour of Emden in East Friesland, just beyond the jurisdiction of the Habsburg Low Countries, and had argued strongly in the reign of Mary for a transfer there of 'one parcel of your woollen commodity', at least part of the English cloth trade.

'Your Majesty thus having two strings to your bow may so use them as either of them [the foreign princes concerned] will seek the best they can to please you.'[34] These arguments came into their own in the winter of 1563–4, when the regent of the Low Countries used the outbreak of plague in London to put pressure on Elizabeth by banning the import of English cloth. Nedham and a minority of the Merchant Adventurers, mostly Protestant, led by their governor, John Marsh, were eager to press the case for a move to Emden, and, in fact, faced by financial disaster, the majority concurred. The cloth fleet sailed in May 1564, and, though the project was of mixed success, sufficient pressure was placed on Antwerp to force the regent to give way. It was in a state of discouragement that Nedham finished his *Letter to the Counts of East Friesland,* an argument for the diversification for English trade that was to come into its own again with the arrest by Alva in late December 1568 of all English merchants in the Low Countries. The ties between Nedham and Cecil now came into play. This time, the interruption was to last for five years, and the cloth fleet transferred to the safer port of Hamburg. That a merchant such as Nedham should have presumed to pronounce upon the formation of English policy might seem foolhardy, yet the previous reign had seen a great expansion of comment on foreign policy and Nedham's tract continues this. Ostensibly couched as a letter addressed to the princes who ruled in Emden, the tract gave a detailed account of the benefits in terms of employment and profit to the port receiving English cloth and raw wool. He estimated the total value of English cloth and wool exports at just over £1 million, the gain to workers processing them £306,666 and the profit to merchants £274,000 (art. 40–59). In politics, he denounced Philip II's policy in Germany (art. 26–39), shackled as it was to the designs of the pope (art. 60–9), and presented a gloomy history of the Anglo-Burgundian alliance, replete, as it could seem, with betrayals and half-hearted support (art. 70–86). Nedham's arguments on the diversification of English trade, though rooted in the events of 1564, proved increasingly relevant in subsequent decades, finding echoes not only in the government paper 'Reasons to Move the Forbearing of Traffic with Flanders' of 1572 but also in Hakluyt's *Discourse of Western Planting,* with its arguments for seeking a new market for English cloth in the colonisation of North America. When John Wheeler published his *Treatise of English Commerce* in 1601, he used much of Nedham's material, but the profile of English trade had by then been completely transformed, the role of Antwerp a distant memory and the Merchant Adventurers themselves under pressure from multiple competition.

The Spanish reoccupation of Antwerp in 1585, and the final extinction of its independence, simply confirmed the trend towards the diversification of English trade which had had many political and religious imperatives behind it. In reality, the trade with England had never fully recovered even after the 1574 Treaty of Bristol that restored the mart after the embargo. The Spanish Fury of 1576 (when Spanish troops ran amok in the city) had something to do with this as did the blockade of the Scheldt by the Dutch rebels. Merchant Adventurers continued to trade through Hamburg and then from 1580 through Emden again. In October 1582, the remaining English merchants at Antwerp agreed to move to Middelburg. After the capture of the city by Parma, the Antwerp merchants took their capital and expertise to the cities of Holland and Zeeland or even further afield.

The stimulus of the closure of the Scheldt in the 1570s meant that English merchants had to find markets directly for their cloths and sources for their imports in the Mediterranean, the Baltic and the Indies. Such routes had already been found in the north with the inception of the Muscovy Company. At first, it was the exploitation of the route through the Baltic to Narva from the mid-1560s that was most significant, but there were serious political problems stemming from the Livonian wars. The foundation of the Eastland Company in 1579 – like the Adventurers a 'regulated company' – was a response to the pressure for now outlets in the trade with Russia and also the result of the fragmentation of the Merchant Adventurers that itself followed from the diversification of English trade. The zone reserved for members of the company comprised Norway, Sweden and Poland plus all the southern Baltic lands east of the Oder (Narva was reserved for the Muscovy Company), and the ostensible objective was the more efficient conduct of trade and the defence of the interests of English merchants against local rulers. Most of the company's trade was, in fact, carried on with Poland and its dependencies and was heavily dominated by cloth exports and imports of raw materials, especially timber and other materials for naval construction.

FRANCE AND THE LOW COUNTRIES: CIVIL WAR AND THE QUESTION OF INTERVENTION

Despite the failure of 1563, England could not remain indifferent to the civil wars that broke out in France and the Low Countries in the 1560s and 1570s and were the main direct foreign problems that the Elizabethan government had to confront. Despite any qualms Elizabeth may have had about expenditure or about rebellion against lawful sovereigns, the growth of conflicts in France and the Low Countries that saw religion and politics intertwined meant that detachment was impossible. Thus, there was something of a turning point in English policy as revealed by William Cecil's policy paper of late 1569. In this, he argued that events had developed to such a point in the Low Countries and France that it was impossible to do nothing. In particular, the presence of the Army of Flanders, traditionally viewed as a counter-balance against the French, could only now be viewed as a direct threat. Besides measures for the refurbishment of English military potential, he now proposed a general Protestant alliance. It has sometimes been argued that Leicester and Walsingham were the consistent supporters of a 'Protestant cause' view of international relations, but this paper makes it clear that even the habitually cautious Cecil was prepared to view the world in terms of a battle with Catholic powers.

In France, while Elizabeth had some sympathy for the attempts of Catherine de Medici to maintain peace, the prospect of Guise domination that arose during the false peace of 1568 and again after the Saint Bartholomew's Day Massacre in 1572 presented severe dangers. The Queen's envoys to France actively fed such fears by stressing the Guise threat and urging English intervention. Henry Norris's despatches pushed a strong line in the war of 1568–9: the Cardinal of Lorraine, he told the Queen, was 'your cruel enemy'.[35] He repeatedly stressed the disarray of the royal government as well as the extent of the new wave of religious violence directed against the Protestants, 'so extreme as the very Papists, in whome remaineth any spark of piety, doth abhor to hear the same'.[36] His line was generally to talk up the prospects of the Huguenots despite their defeats and to underline the dangers of their overthrow. Norris was keen to seize the opportunity of the third civil war to gain control of La Rochelle. In September 1568 he wrote to Cecil of the chance to gain control of it 'now it hathe pleasid Gode agein to offer you a *tym* very *convenient* to *recompence* your sellfes of your *iniury* afor receyvid' and added 'whiche *omittid* I dowt the youngest in our countrey shall never see the like.'[37] The defeat of the Huguenots at the battle of Moncontour in 1569 was, he thought, 'of great consequence and long ago understanding the determination of the Catholic princes against the Protestants, if they can bring their designs to their desired effect, I shall not need to make any tedious rehearsal'.[38]

Practical help, however, remained limited. A report sent to the Huguenot leader, Admiral Coligny, from Paris in March 1569 claimed that Elizabeth had sent 20,000 écus to the Duke of Zweibrucken for the mercenaries he was leading to the help of Condé and Coligny, though whether this made much difference is arguable. In 1568, with the Huguenot cause under pressure, the Merchants Adventurers supplied munitions to La Rochelle in exchange for its produce, and in 1570 offers of money were again made to Coligny. The 1570 Peace of Saint-Germain, ostensibly advantageous to the Protestants, was seen by Norris as posing the danger of French action elsewhere, possibly in Scotland, but he finally concluded that the peace was fragile 'the very same causes yet remaining, we may presume of the like effects'.[39] Though E. I. Kouri has argued that underhand help to rebels in France and the Low Countries was normal realpolitik in the period and that Elizabeth 'wished to promote strife' though short of direct intervention, she showed her usual caution.[40] After 1570 she reverted to her instinct to try to build on the peace in France by bringing it into an alliance against Spain. Cecil argued the dangers of this in August 1571, but the Treaty of Blois was concluded in 1572, before the massacre. Again, in the fourth civil war that followed the massacre, supplies and money were secretly sent to La Rochelle.

In the Low Countries, Alva's arrival in August 1567 with 10,000 Spanish veterans gave Spain real military muscle. The dangers of a war with Spain prevented active English help to William of Orange, the leader of the Dutch rebels, in 1568, but the effective arrest at Plymouth and Southampton in December of the £80,000 loan from Genoese bankers being transported to Alva's army led to another trade embargo on both sides. The motives of the action remain shrouded in controversy, but there is no doubt that it made life more difficult for Alva while he was further outraged by the covert protection offered in England to the Dutch rebels and pirates known as the 'Sea Beggars'. Their expulsion from the south-east ports of England in March 1572, whatever its motives, had the effect of precipitating a new crisis in the Netherlands with their seizure of Brille.

Events in France and the Low Countries became closely interlinked, with plans by Coligny in France and Orange in Germany to carve up the Low Countries with English help. The Saint Bartholomew's Day Massacre put paid to this for a while but the idea was to resurface after 1579. In retrospect it looked to Camden that Elizabeth held a strong hand: 'Thus sate she as an heriocal princess and Umpire betwixt the *Spaniards*, the *French* and the Estates . . . And true it was that one hath written, that France and Spain are as it were the Scales in the Balance of Europe, and England the Tongue and Holder of the Balance.'[41]

Was Elizabeth really in a position to wield the balance of power in Europe, though? It is certainly the case that Elizabeth attempted to mediate between the Estates-General and Don John of Austria in 1578. Walsingham's agent, the soldier Thomas Churchyard, even published *A Lamentable and Pitifull Description of the Woefull Warres in Flaunders* as an attempt to justify this line (insisting disingenuously that English soldiers of fortune who had so far fought in the Low Countries were there on their own initiative) by playing down the heaviness of Spanish 'tyranny'. Wernham's view is that Elizabeth aimed essentially 'to get the Spanish army out of the Low Countries without letting the French in'.[42] Charles Wilson argued that Elizabeth's instinctive fear of rebellion led her to discount the Dutch rebels and that she had her own traditional reason for fearing French ambitions in the southern Low Countries. Wilson's analysis of what he saw as half-hearted and bungled intervention echoed Ralegh's remark that Elizabeth 'did everything by halves'. Wilson denies that English interests may have been best served by maintaining the Habsburg regime in the Low Countries in its traditional form as a bulwark against France. A traditionalist remote-control form of Spanish authority in the Low Countries was no longer on offer, and the logic of events had taken the rebellion too far. In Elizabeth's and Burghley's defence, it should be said that taking on a war with Spain was a massive and dangerous commitment, so it is hardly surprising that they sought to delay it as long as possible; Dutch interests were not necessarily identical with those of England, though the protagonists of the Protestant cause would have argued otherwise.

In any case, what this debate neglects is the fact that, though England did not intervene directly until 1585, its military potential was partly at the disposal of the rebels long before that. From the first major expedition to Zeeland in 1572, English volunteer troops under Thomas Morgan, author of *The Expeditions in Holland*, Edward Chester, Sir John Norris (who took 1,700 men to the Low Countries in 1578) and many others were crossing the sea quietly or with tacit government approval to fight in the cause of the rebels, recruited through personal connections and affinities of Protestant nobles and gentry, eventually paid for by the Estates-General. Participants in these 'voluntary wars', far from being the 'scum of the earth', were, as John Smythe asserted in *Certain Discourses Military*, for 'the greater part young gentlemen, and in a greater part of yeomen and yeomen's sons . . . desirous, of a gallantness of mind, to adventure themselves and see the wars. . . . being the very flower of England'.[43] When serious state-funded English military intervention began in 1585, then, the groundwork had already been laid by both military and naval developments and the transformation of English economic relations with the Low Countries.

CONCLUSION

Whatever the extent of the disagreements between Queen Elizabeth and her ministers and whatever motivations we might ascribe to them, what they could not avoid was that the international scene in which England was placed changed virtually out of all recognition between 1558 and 1603. At the start of that period, England was a small and weakened country prey to its neighbours' ambitions. It remained small in terms of population but the islands of Great Britain had become measurably closer to the prospect of a real union; France had collapsed (temporarily) as the major European power; Spain had supplanted her but was bogged down in military and financial problems. English economic and political horizons had expanded to the four corners of the globe and a new degree of self-confidence generated; England was undoubtedly now a formidable naval power in a era in which that would be increasingly significant and had acquired serious and up-to-date military clout. While participating fully in the European cultural scene, England as a Protestant nation increasingly saw itself as specially chosen by God and had taken decisive steps towards new identity. It was thus that it entered the new era of the Union of Crowns in 1603.

FURTHER READING

Adams, Simon, 'The Protestant Cause: Religious Alliance with the West European Calvinist Communities as a Political Issue in England, 1585–1630', D.Phil. thesis, Oxford University, 1973.

—— 'Eliza Enthroned? The Court and Politics', in C. Haigh (ed.), *The Reign of Elizabeth I*, pp. 55–78.

—— 'Favourites and Factions at the Elizabethan Court', in R. Asch and A. M. Birke (eds.), *Princes, Patronage and the Nobility* (Oxford, 1991).

Andrews, K. R., *Trade, Plunder and Settlement* (Cambridge, 1984).

Croly, Christopher P., *Religion and English Foreign Policy, 1558–64* (Cambridge, 2000).

Dawson, Jane E. A., 'Two Kingdoms or One? Ireland in Anglo-Scottish Relations in the Middle of the Sixteenth Century', in R. Mason (ed.), *Scotland and England* (Edinburgh, 1987), pp. 113–38.

—— 'William Cecil and the British Dimension of Early Elizabeth Foreign Policy', *History*, 74 (1989): 196–216.

Doran, Susan, *Monarchy and Matrimony: The Courtships of Elizabeth I* (London, 1996).

—— *Elizabeth I and Foreign Relations, 1558–1603* (Lancaster, 2000).

Doran, Susan, and Richardson, Glenn (eds.), *Tudor England and Its Neighbours* (Basingstoke, 2005).

Jones, Norman, 'Elizabeth's First Year', in C. Haigh (ed.), *The Reign of Elizabeth I* (London, 1984), pp. 27–53.

Kouri, E. I., *England and the Attempts to Form a Protestant Alliance in the Late 1560s* (Helsinki, 1981).

MacCaffrey, Wallace T., *The Shaping of the Elizabethan Regime* (London, 1969).

—— 'The Anjou Match and the Making of Elizabethan Foreign Policy', in Peter Clark et al. (eds.), *The English Commonwealth, 1547–1640* (Leicester, 1979).

—— 'The Newhaven Expedition, 1562–63', *Historical Journal*, 40 (1997): 1–21.

MacDermott, James, *England the Spanish Armada: The Necessary Quarrel* (New Haven, Conn., 2005).

Maltby, William S., *The Black Legend in England: The Development of Anti-Spanish Sentiment, 1558–1660* (Durham, NC, 1971).

Mattingly, Garrett, *Renaissance Diplomacy* (Oxford, 1955).

Mears, Natalie, 'Love-Making and Diplomacy: Elizabeth I and the Anjou Marriage Negotiations, *c.* 1578–82', *History*, 86 (2001): 442–66.

Merriman, Marcus, 'James Henrisoun and "Great Britain": British Union and the Scottish Commonwealth', in R. Mason (ed.), *Scotland and England* (Edinburgh, 1987), pp. 85–112.
Potter, David L., 'Mid-Tudor Foreign Policy and Diplomacy', in Susan Doran and Glenn Richardson (eds.), *Tudor England and Its Neighbours* (Basingstoke, 2005).
Ramsay, G. D., *English Overseas Trade during the Centuries of Emergence* (London, 1957).
—— *The City of London and International Politics at the Accession of Elizabeth Tudor* (Manchester, 1975).
—— (ed.), *The Politics of a Tudor Merchant Adventurer: A Letter to the Earls of East Friesland* (Manchester, 1979).
—— *The Queen's Merchants and the Revolt of the Netherlands* (Manchester, 1986).
Sutherland, Nicola, 'The Origins of Queen Elizabeth I's Relations with the Huguenots, 1558–1562', in *Princes, Politics and Religion, 1547–1589* (London, 1984), pp. 73–96.
Trim, David, 'The Foundation-Stone of the British Army? The Normandy Campaign of 1562', *Journal of the Society for Army Historical Research*, 77 (1999): 71–87.
Wernham, R. B., 'English Policy and the Revolt of the Netherlands', in J. S. Bromley and E. H. Kossmann (eds.), *Britain and the Netherlands* (London, 1960), pp. 30–2.
—— *The Making of Elizabethan Foreign Policy, 1558–1603* (Berkeley, Calif., 1963).
—— *Before the Armada: The Growth of English Foreign Policy, 1485–1588* (London, 1966).
—— *After the Armada: Elizabethan England and the Struggle for Western Europe, 1588–1595* (Oxford, 1984).
—— *The Return of the Armadas: The Last Years of the Elizabethan War against Spain, 1595–1603* (Oxford, 1994).
Webb, Henry J., *Elizabethan Military Science: The Books and the Practice* (Milwaukee, Wisc., 1965).
Willan, T. S., *The Early History of the Russia Company* (Manchester, 1956).
—— *The Muscovy Merchants of 1555* (Manchester, 1953).
Williamson, James A., *Hawkins* (London, 1949).
Wilson, Charles, *Queen Elizabeth and the Revolt of the Netherlands* (London, 1970).
Zins, Henryk, *England and the Baltic* (Manchester, 1972).

NOTES

1 TNA SP12/1, fol. 77.
2 *CSP For.*, II, No. 3, p. 3.
3 S. Haynes, *A Collection of State Papers . . . from the Year 1542 to 1570* (London, 1740), pp. 208–9. HMC, Calendar of the Manuscripts . . . Preserved at Hatfield House, vol. I, p. 151.
4 T. Wright, *Queen Elizabeth and Her Times*, 2 vols. (London, 1838), vol. I, p. 7; P. Forbes, *A Full View of the Public Transactions in the Reign of Queen Elizabeth*, 2 vols. (London, 1740–1), vol. I, pp. 237, 241.
5 Forbes, *Full View of the Public Transactions*, vol. I, p. 17.
6 John Hayward, *Annals of the First Four Years of the Reign of Queen Elizabeth*, (London, 1840), pp. 1–2.
7 W. R. D. Jones, *The Mid-Tudor Crisis, 1539–63* (London, 1973), p. 189.
8 BL Cotton MS, Titus C VII, fols. 198–9.
9 *CSP For.*, I, p. 6; BL Harleian MS 25 fol. 87v; *CSPF*, II, pp. 197–8.
10 A. F. Pollard, *Tudor Tracts, 1532–88* (London, 1903), p. 290.
11 Hayward, *Annals*, p. 34.
12 See R. B. Wernham, *The Making of Elizabeth Foreign Policy, 1558–1603* (Berkeley, Calif., 1963).
13 Sir Thomas Smith, *De republica anglorum* (1583), p. 85.

14 F. Jeffrey Platt, 'The Elizabethan "Foreign Office"', *The Historian*, 56 (1994). Garrett Mattingly, *Renaissance Diplomacy* (Oxford, 1955), p. 192.
15 Haynes, *State Papers*, pp. 208–9 (Cal. Hatfield I, 151).
16 9 January 1559, Forbes, *Transactions*, vol. I, pp. 18–19.
17 Forbes, *Transactions*, vol. I, p. 158.
18 James MacDermott, *England the Spanish Armada: The Necessary Quarrel* (New Haven, Conn., 2005), Chapters 1 and 2; Wallace T. MacCaffrey, *The Shaping of the Elizabethan Regime* (London, 1969), p. 191.
19 *Discourse of Western Planting* (1993), p. 52; *The Roanoke Voyages, 1584–1590*, Hakluyt Soc., 2nd Ser., 104–5 (Cambridge, 1955), vol. I, p. 490.
20 William S. Maltby, *The Black Legend in England: The Development of Anti-Spanish Sentiment, 1558–1660* (Durham, NC, 1971), p. 30.
21 Wallace T. MacCaffrey, 'The Newhaven Expedition, 1562–63', *Historical Journal*, 40 (1997): 1. David Trim, 'The Foundation-Stone of the British Army? The Normandy Campaign of 1562', *Journal of the Society for Army Historical Research*, 77 (1999): 71–87.
22 Roger Ascham, *English Works*, ed. W. A. Wright (Cambridge, 1904), p. 53.
23 William Thomas, *The Works of William Thomas*, ed. A. d'Aubant (London, 1774), p. 107.
24 BL Lansdowne MS 4, No. 9, fols. 26–7.
25 BL Cotton MS Caligula B 9, fols. 34 (not clearly summarised in *CSP For. 1559–60*, pp. 41–5 or in *CSP Scot.* I, pp. 323–4) Dawson, pp. 207–8 drew attention to this clause. See also Jane E. A. Dawson, 'Two Kingdoms or One? Ireland in Anglo-Scottish Relations in the Middle of the Sixteenth Century', in Roger Mason (ed.), *Scotland and England* (Edinburgh, 1987), pp. 113–38.
26 Forbes, *Transactions*, vol. I, pp. 391, 393.
27 4 July 1559, Forbes, *Transactions*, vol. I, p. 152.
28 Forbes, *Transactions*, vol. I, pp. 289–90.
29 Forbes, *Transactions*, vol. I, pp. 387–90.
30 Forbes, *Transactions*, vol. I, pp. 454–5.
31 TNA SP70/40/158.
32 Henryk Zins, *England and the Baltic* (Manchester, 1972), p. 37.
33 T. S. Willan, *The Early History of the Russia Company* (Manchester, 1956); Id., *The Muscovy Merchants of 1555* (Manchester, 1953).
34 BL Additional MS 35, 207, fol. 10.
35 Norris to the Queen, 11 August 1570, TNA SP70/113, fol. 115.
36 Norris to Cecil, 25 September, 29 October 1568, TNA SP70/102, fol. 67/103, fol. 92.
37 Norris to Cecil, 2 September 1568, TNA SP70/102, fol. 22, part in cipher.
38 Norris to the Queen, 5 October 1569, TNA SP70/108, fols. 135–6.
39 Norris to the Queen, 31 August 1570, TNA SP70/113, fol. 185.
40 E. I. Kouri, *England and the Attempts to Form a Protestant Alliance in the Late 1560s* (Helsinki, 1981), p. 43.
41 Camden, *Annals*, Ed. 1688, p. 223 (1577).
42 R. B. Wernham, 'English Policy and the Revolt of the Netherlands', in J. S. Bromley and E. H. Kossmann (eds.), *Britain and the Netherlands* (1960), pp. 30–2.
43 John Smythe, *Certain Discourses Military*, ed. J. R. Hale (Ithaca, NY, 1964), p. 26.

CHAPTER THIRTY-SIX

THE CATHOLIC THREAT AND THE MILITARY RESPONSE

Paul E. J. Hammer

When Elizabeth first succeeded to the throne in November 1558, the greatest threat posed by Catholicism concerned the legitimacy of her succession. As quite literally the embodiment of Henry VIII's break from the Church of Rome in 1533, Elizabeth's claim to the English throne seemed open to serious question in the eyes of many European Catholics. Henri II of France promptly asserted that the true sovereign of England should be his Franco-Scottish Catholic daughter-in-law, Mary, Queen of Scots. He lobbied the Pope to excommunicate Elizabeth and even urged Philip II to join him in a combined invasion of England. When Henri died in a jousting accident in July 1559, Mary's claim was sustained by her fifteen-year-old husband, who now became François II of France. This diplomatic aggression from France coincided with growing turmoil in Scotland, where Mary's mother, who governed there as regent with the support of a French army, faced rebellion from Scottish Protestants led by the Lords of the Congregation. As David Potter has shown in Chapter 35, the Scottish crisis proved a severe test for Elizabeth's new government to which she responded with military action.

The successful outcome of the Scottish campaign helped to encourage a broadly similar venture in support of French Protestants in 1562. This was the so-called Newhaven Expedition, when some 6,000 English troops were sent to Le Havre (which the Elizabethans called Newhaven) to reinforce the Huguenots in their struggle with Catholic forces in Normandy. Although they failed to prevent the fall of Rouen (despite the early dispatch of private 'volunteers' to assist in its defence), the English managed to stabilise the situation and helped the Huguenots to negotiate an acceptable peace treaty with the French Crown in the spring of 1563. However, Elizabeth's hope that the continued English occupation of Le Havre could be traded for the return of Calais – in marked contrast to the absence of serious concessions demanded of the Scots in 1560 – merely served to unite French Catholics and Protestants alike against the English. The English army consequently found itself besieged in a town whose main defences faced the sea rather than inland. After months of bombardment and an alarming number of deaths from disease, the English were forced to surrender on 28 July. Although the surviving English troops were allowed to head home with their weapons, Elizabeth's claim to Calais was effectively terminated and the returning soldiers brought back with them a plague that killed thousands of civilians, including 20,000 in London alone.

The humiliating defeat at Le Havre understandably made Elizabeth wary of relying too heavily upon the promises of foreigners in the future and, as we shall see, re-emphasised the military shortcomings of English armies. Both of these factors made Elizabeth determined thereafter to avoid open warfare against major European enemies. Yet the Huguenots – and later on the Protestant Dutch rebels – continued to call upon their co-religionist Elizabeth for military help against their Catholic foe. What was to be done?

In October 1572, Sir Arthur Champernowne, the vice-admiral for the county of Devon and one of the leading Protestants in the West Country, wrote to Elizabeth to plead for intervention in France in the wake of the recent massacres of French Protestants.[1] After the slaughter of thousands of Huguenots in Paris on Saint Bartholomew's Day (24 August) and in subsequent killings elsewhere in France, it seemed 'plaine' to Champernowne that but for the grace of God and the inability of Catholic powers to bring their 'barborous' plans to fruition, wholesale slaughter would also have been the fate of English Protestants: 'we see those same harts, which neyther heythen nor savage may matche, roving at us, those same bluddy handes pointing to us, the swerdes [i.e. swords], the fyres, whetting and kindled against us.' For Champernowne, as for many English Protestants of his time, the massacres in France seemed to be irrefutable proof that the forces of Catholicism sought the enforced conversion, or extermination, of all Protestants and were actively engaged in a vast international campaign to bring this about. As the leading Protestant monarchy of western Europe, England could not afford to believe that the fate of foreign Protestants was of no concern: 'we be embarked all in one ship ... if they the whiles make a wrack, may we be safe?' Champernowne proposed that English troops and supplies should be sent to assist the Huguenots, especially as their key coastal fortress of La Rochelle was about to be besieged. An enclosure with the letter suggested that a levy could be imposed on substantial land and property owners in England and Wales to fund the raising of 14,500 foot and 1,700 cavalry for this campaign at no cost to the Queen herself. By the standards of the day, this would have been a very large army, and Champernowne's assertions that such a force could have been sustained in this way were wildly optimistic.

Champernowne was well aware that this huge scheme had little real chance of being adopted. As a member of the delegation that had witnessed the ratification of England's new alliance with France (the Treaty of Blois) only a few months before, he realised that Elizabeth was unlikely to break diplomatic ties with France over events for which the French King denied all responsibility, however unconvincing those denials might seem. Champernowne therefore suggested that Elizabeth should provide assistance to the Huguenots by unofficial and deniable means, permitting 'some rashe willfull felo, lyke mysellf', to supply La Rochelle. Champernowne's willingness to play the role reflected both his eagerness for the international Protestant cause and the recent marriage of his son to the daughter of a Huguenot leader, the Comte de Montgomery. Although it had proved to be unhappy experience for both families, this marriage would enable Champernowne's intended intervention in France to be cast as a purely personal venture.

As long as he could be certain that Elizabeth privately supported his action, Champernowne would 'most willingly hazard lyfe, goods & [what] credyt I have in passing the enterpris'. The murderous treachery of the Catholics and the dubious denials of complicity in the killings by Charles IX of France would therefore be countered by equally disingenuous 'shewes of offens' by Elizabeth towards Champernowne for his efforts to assist the Huguenots. Under the cover of acting privately and in defiance of his sovereign's wishes, Champernowne expected to be able to raise large numbers of volunteers for this venture from his own county of Devon, where many of the Queen's subjects allegedly burned to avenge the killings in France. Ultimately, this was a claim that was only partially put to the test. Champernowne was not permitted to lead English volunteers to France himself in the spring of 1573 but had to be content with helping to organise a fleet that would sail for La Rochelle under the Comte de Montgomery. Significantly, however, this force included at least one of the Queen's own warships.

Although its final outcome caused its author considerable frustration, this letter captures some important features of English responses to the 'Catholic threat' during the middle years of Elizabeth's reign. Most obviously, it highlights the belief held by many of the Queen's more ardently Protestant subjects (and, crucially, by a substantial number of royal officials at every level of her government) that England was 'embarked all in one ship' with fellow Protestants overseas because they believed the Pope and the other Catholic princes of Europe were determined to obliterate Protestantism whenever and wherever they could. For many subscribers to this view, this imaginary international Catholic conspiracy had a distinctly apocalyptic quality, with the Pope being cast in the role of Antichrist and the Catholic princes as his supposedly enthusiastic henchmen in a conflict that held cosmic implications for Christendom. Supporting foreign Protestants in their stop-start civil wars against Catholic royal authority in France and the Low Countries was therefore not only a means of keeping Catholic enemies away from England itself but also a long-prophesied struggle in which some Englishmen felt called by God to participate.

This was not, however, an opinion which Elizabeth herself shared. From the start of her reign, a basic assumption of her foreign policy was that there was no monolithic 'Catholic threat' and that England's interests would best be protected by playing upon the inveterate rivalry between France and Spain, the two great Catholic monarchies of western Europe. Despite her genuine disgust at the Saint Bartholomew's Day Massacre and her grave concern at the role played in this affair by the French Crown, Elizabeth was determined to maintain her new alliance with France – if at all possible – in order to counter-balance the increasingly obvious threat to English interests now being posed by Philip II's Spanish empire. Although proposals for a marriage between Elizabeth and a brother of the French King had to be temporarily suspended, the hope of mobilising French support to counter the danger posed by Spain would remain at the heart of the Queen's diplomacy from 1572 until 1585.

Despite this overt policy, Champernowne's private urging of Elizabeth to permit deniable forms of intervention to aid the Huguenots suggests how the Queen's official diplomacy was sometimes accompanied – even contradicted – by unofficial actions during these years. Although Elizabeth made a show of formal friendship with France (and, indeed, with Spain), English authorities allowed French and Dutch

Protestant 'rebels' to shelter in England and repeatedly permitted 'private' volunteers from England and Wales to support their French or Dutch co-religionists with supplies and men in their wars. Despite her determination to maintain the viability of an alliance with France to deter aggression from Spain, just as she had previously looked to Spain as a counter-balance against hostility from France, Elizabeth was unwilling to see either French or Dutch Protestants crushed by force. The tension between these divergent objectives entailed a delicate balancing act. On the one hand, she sought to avoid giving France or Spain any overt cause for war. On the other hand, she needed to ensure that French and Dutch Protestants received sufficient aid to avoid defeat and to placate the vociferous demands for action on their behalf which emanated from her own subjects. As the presence of a royal warship in Montgommery's fleet in 1573 suggests, Elizabeth's willingness to support foreign Protestants often tested the limits of what might be termed unofficial or deniable actions. Indeed, the extent of such supposedly covert assistance in the 1560s and 1570s suggests that Elizabeth may perhaps have felt more protective towards foreign Protestant communities than much scholarship on the subject allows.

The nature of the Catholic threat was further complicated by the presence of Mary, Queen of Scots, in England after her forced abdication and flight from Scotland in 1568. Although detaining Mary in custody allowed a Protestant clique to rule Scotland in the name of her young son, James VI, it also made Mary a focus for scheming within England itself. As the failed Northern Rising of November and December 1569 showed, her arrival effectively opened up a new home front in England's confrontation with international Catholicism. Although the attempt by the Earls of Northumberland and Westmorland to rally support in the north under the Catholic banner quickly collapsed, their association with political manoeuvres involving Mary and their urgent (but unavailing) appeal for military assistance from the Spanish army in Flanders demonstrated how the various threats against Elizabeth might come together to challenge her. News of the Northern Rising also encouraged Pope Pius V to issue a bull of excommunication against Elizabeth (*Regnans in excelsis*) in the hope of forcing her deposition. In the event, the bull's main effect was to place English Catholics in a terrible divide between loyalty to their faith and loyalty to their sovereign, while providing ammunition for those English Protestants who equated Catholicism with sedition and treason. The dangers which now seemed to be crowding around the Elizabethan regime from Catholic enemies were further highlighted by the exposure in 1571 of the so-called Ridolfi Plot. This implicated Spain's ambassador to England in plotting with disaffected English aristocrats and revealed that Philip II was now willing to countenance an invasion of England to depose the 'tyrant' Elizabeth and replace her with Mary. The exposure of the plan cost the Duke of Norfolk his head and caused such uproar in the Parliament of 1572 that Elizabeth was barely able to resist pressure to move against Mary herself.

These alarming developments provoked a number of different responses from the Queen and her regime. The possibility that Mary, Queen of Scots, might succeed Elizabeth prompted many English Protestants to oppose Mary's claim. This created a long-running 'Elizabethan Exclusion Crisis' which would only be ended by Mary's execution in 1587. In the wake of the Ridolfi affair, detecting plots against the Queen became a major concern of Elizabeth's new Secretary of State, Sir Francis Walsingham, who had been England's ambassador in Paris during the Saint Bartholomew's Day Massacre. Although Walsingham (and other councillors) recruited spies at home and abroad for many purposes, one of the most enduring priorities was to obtain evidence that would compel Elizabeth to act against Mary by directly implicating her in a plot against Elizabeth's life. This effort would reach its climax in the 1580s and foster the growth of an informer culture in England which would persist beyond the end of the reign. The possibility of Mary's future succession, the papal bull of 1570 and the ominous events abroad also impacted upon domestic religious policy. Despite the increasingly bitter tone of clashes between the ecclesiastical authorities and their puritan critics, key members of the Privy Council were often prepared to shield puritan preachers from the bishops in the 1570s and 1580s because they seemed 'the most diligent barkers against the popish wolf'.[2] Diplomatically, Elizabeth's realisation that Philip II no longer felt constrained in his actions towards England by the concern that France would benefit if Mary gained the English throne encouraged her to make overtures to France for an alliance and to offer (barely) deniable support for French and Dutch Protestants.

Although there was a lull in the international tension during the mid-1570s, by the late 1570s there was a sense of crisis. The position of the Dutch rebels in their struggle against Philip II began to deteriorate rapidly after 1578 due to renewed Spanish pressure. Even the presence of several thousand English and Welsh volunteers (and many Scots) in the Dutch army failed to stem the Spanish advance under the Duke of Parma. The arrival of the Jesuits in England in 1580 reawakened fears of a Catholic fifth column at home, while the Throckmorton Plot (revealed in December 1583) exposed domestic intrigues involving the Spanish and French ambassadors for co-ordinating a Catholic rebellion in England with a seaborne invasion. The plot terminated formal Spanish diplomatic representation in England for the remainder of Elizabeth's reign (the last resident English ambassador had been forced to leave Spain in 1568). The enveloping sense of crisis became even more acute when the Dutch leader, William of Orange, was assassinated in July 1584. This not only weakened Dutch resistance to Parma but also raised the spectre that Elizabeth would become the next victim of a Catholic assassin and triggered the creation of the Bond of Association. Signed by the great and the good at public ceremonies across the realm, the bond effectively committed its signatories to slaughter Mary, Queen of Scots, and her Catholic supporters if Elizabeth were murdered. This would have been an English equivalent of the Saint Bartholomew's Day Massacre in France but with English Catholics as the putative victims.

During the later 1570s and early 1580s, the international Catholic threat seemed to be drawing closer to Elizabethan England in other ways too. In 1579, a small force of Italian and Spanish troops landed at Smerwick in southern Ireland and proclaimed a crusade against Elizabeth under the papal banner. Although this papal force was eventually besieged and slaughtered (after they had surrendered), the political implications were alarming, and Ireland, as David Edwards shows elsewhere in this volume, continued to be convulsed with rebellion until 1584.

The consequent fragility of Elizabeth's hold on Ireland created an acute strategic vulnerability which would weigh ever more heavily upon the minds of the Queen and her Council as her reign progressed: as the common saying ran, 'he who would

England win, must with Ireland begin.'[3] England's other 'postern gate', Scotland, also suddenly seemed to swing open to Catholic enemies in 1579. The arrival of James VI's French cousin, Esmé Stuart, and the eventual arrest and execution of the Earl of Morton, James's former regent, threatened the Protestant hold on power in Scotland and suggested a possible future return to Anglo-Scottish enmity. Ultimately, this danger was averted by promising James himself an annual pension in 1585, but for a few years it seemed that the fruits of the 1560 war (and further English intervention against supporters of Mary in Scotland during 1568–73) might be lost.

Faced with this combination of dangers, Elizabeth's response was to cling to her long-standing policy of looking to France for support against Philip II. However, the French king, Henri III, would not commit to a military alliance, leaving her uncertain about how to proceed. Meanwhile Philip seemed ever more dangerous, not least because of his acquisition of the Portuguese crown in 1580. Not only had he thereby gained access to the wealth of Portuguese outposts in Asia and the New World but he also gained a fleet of warships designed for the Atlantic – an ominous development from the English perspective. Alarmingly, Philip celebrated his triumph with the motto *Non sufficit orbis:* 'The world is not enough.'

The Privy Council debated the strategic situation in October 1584 and jointly agreed that England had no choice but to commit itself openly to war against Spain – in other words, the policy of the previous twenty years of limited, deniable aid to the Dutch needed to be abandoned, and quickly. The decisive argument for this momentous recommendation was not the imminent defeat of the Dutch but new intelligence which suggested that Philip was committed to an invasion of England as soon as the Low Countries were reconquered and which revealed various plans which had been suggested for this purpose during 1581–2. In this light, the Council believed England's choice lay between openly joining the Dutch now or facing alone an invasion by a victorious Spanish army borne in Dutch ships in a few years' time. Elizabeth herself continued to hope for the reassurance of French support until this option collapsed in March 1585. This finally cleared the way for direct negotiation with the Dutch on the specific terms for England's intervention in the Low Countries. These talks were progressing when news of the arrest of English ships in Spanish ports and of the besieging of Antwerp encouraged the making of three separate agreements in August 1585 (collectively known as the Treaty of Nonsuch) which later proved to be seriously flawed by their hasty drafting. In general, it was agreed that English troops would be permitted to garrison the Dutch ports of Flushing (Vlissinghen) and Brill (Den Brielle), which would effectively be mortgaged to the English Crown against the future repayment of Elizabeth's (imprecisely defined) war costs. In return for full control of these 'cautionary towns', Elizabeth ultimately agreed to send an army of 5,000 foot and 1,000 cavalry (plus another 1,400 men to garrison the cautionary towns). Despite the early despatch of an initial 2,000 men under John Norris, the English intervention came too late to save Antwerp.

The preparation and dispatch of Spain's invasion fleet between 1586 and 1588 unsurprisingly represented a period of marked ideological intensification in the struggle between the Elizabethan regime and its Catholic foes. In England, the revelation of the Babington Plot in 1586 represented the culmination of Sir Francis

Walsingham's long pursuit of evidence to implicate Mary, Queen of Scots, directly in a plot against Elizabeth, and news of this plot finally forced the Queen to move against Mary. Although she dragged her feet and tried to ensure that others would take the blame for Mary's fate, Elizabeth authorised her cousin's trial and signed the warrant for her execution in early 1587. The result was widespread revulsion on the Continent and in Scotland. As the prospect of a Spanish invasion increased, Catholic polemicists such as Cardinal William Allen confirmed the arguments of the Elizabethan regime by openly urging Catholics in England to support the invasion. Elizabeth's government responded by ramping up the execution of Catholic priests, although always emphasising that they died for treason not their religion (hence they suffered the common traitor's fate of being hanged, drawn and quartered). Nevertheless, the image of the 'Catholic threat' itself began to change in the late 1580s and early 1590s. Instead of being simply Catholic, the enemy increasingly began to be seen as explicitly Spanish Catholic. The ingrained belief that the papacy was orchestrating an international conspiracy against Protestants began to give way to claims that England was menaced by the 'malice' of Spain and that the Pope was merely 'hanging at his [Philip's] girdle'.[4] This greater emphasis upon Philip II and Spain as the chief driving force of the Catholic threat received added impetus from events in the months immediately preceding the arrival of the *Gran Armada* in the Channel. During the spring and early summer of 1588, Elizabeth's hope that some kind of peace could still be agreed encouraged her to pursue talks with representatives from the Duke of Parma in Flanders. It was only as the Armada was ready to sail from Spain and Parma's army prepared for the fleet's imminent arrival in northern waters that it emerged these representatives lacked the appropriate authority from Philip to make any kind of agreement. Elizabeth never trusted Philip again, and the memory of this duplicity would weigh heavily against subsequent consideration of peace with Spain.

ENGLAND'S MILITARY RESOURCES

In military terms, the Scottish campaign of 1560 confirmed both the efficacy of English sea power and the alarming weakness of its land forces. The English army at Leith had been hobbled by dissension among its commanders, a chronic shortage of money and supplies and the rawness of its troops. Faced with a more powerful French force, the outcome of the campaign might have been disastrous. Unlike the armies fielded by Henry VIII and Edward VI's government, Elizabeth's force was especially notable for failing to include a hard core of foreign mercenaries who could provide specialist skills and add stiffening to the English raw levies. Like the logistical problems (and especially the inadequate provision of siege guns), this decision was partly the result of trying to fight the campaign at the minimum possible cost – a result of the terrible state of the royal finances which Elizabeth had inherited. Unfortunately, the lack of foreign mercenaries was compounded by the recent loss of Calais to France in 1558, which had ended the tradition of the garrisons there providing a pool of experienced soldiers who were available for temporary deployment elsewhere.

Another influence upon Elizabethan England's semi-overt support for foreign Protestants in the 1570s was military. The experiences of war in Scotland and

Newhaven had proven that England was desperately short of experienced officers and soldiers. Too many of the recruits sent to war in 1560 and 1562–3 had also been armed with longbows and bills, instead of the guns and long pikes used by foreign armies. By allowing bands of volunteers to fight abroad with the Huguenots or Dutch for the sake of religion, Elizabeth's government was able to foster the acquisition of precious military skills and experience by at least some of the Queen's more 'forward' subjects. Members of the Privy Council therefore kept tabs on the gentlemen volunteers who served abroad, knowing that these men and the common soldiers who accompanied them would be critical to defending the realm if the Spanish threat ever became urgent. Broadly similar thinking was reflected in the continued departure of privateering ventures to the New World. Aggressive and opportunistic seamen such as John Hawkins and Francis Drake were permitted to conduct 'private' voyages in order to probe Spanish weaknesses and on condition that the Queen's coffers received a healthy share of any profit.

More systematic and expensive measures were also undertaken to modernise the realm's military institutions. Beginning in the early 1570s, substantial sums of money were spent each year on building new warships, or remodelling older ships, to make them more manoeuvrable and even more heavily armed. Although it was really an evolutionary process, this large naval modernisation programme has been described as 'the *Dreadnought* revolution of Tudor England' in honour of the *Dreadnought,* which was launched in 1573. A parallel effort was also launched to overhaul England's militia. This was an altogether larger and more difficult task because, unlike royal warships which the Queen herself owned, the militia was deeply embedded in English society and its costs were borne by private individuals and local communities. In theory, the militia of each county consisted of all its men aged between sixteen and sixty (excluding those who were exempt, such as clergymen), each of whom should be armed according to their relative wealth as laid out in a statute of 1558. Reforming the militia therefore involved all kinds of political difficulties and ultimately depended upon convincing local gentlemen to accept changes which had major implications for their relationships with their tenants and their gentry neighbours, as well as adding heavy new financial burdens upon the whole county community which ran far ahead of the now-outdated statutory requirements.

The primary thrust of the Council's reforms was to increase the proportion of English soldiers trained in the use of guns and pikes. These weapons added substantially to the costs of the county militias because gunpowder – unlike arrows – could not be reused and the pike required regular training as a unit that could only be conducted at musters, which entailed the payment of muster pay for all concerned. Learning to use these weapons efficiently instead of the traditional longbow and bill (a slashing weapon adapted from agricultural implements) also required expert trainers, whose salaries had to be met by the county even though these outsiders – mostly veterans of the religious wars on the Continent – were forced upon them by the Privy Council and their activities often upset established local hierarchies. For reasons of practicality and cost, the Council decreed that only a proportion of the militia should be equipped and trained with the new weapons. In effect, this concentrated all the resources on a subset of the old militia, creating 'trained bands' which supposedly included the men best suited to military service. Given the magnitude of the task and political sensitivities involved (for a start, the creation of the trained bands reduced the number of captaincies available to county gentlemen and raised the level of technical competence expected of them), it is not surprising that the Elizabethan reform of the militia had uneven results and that the trained bands commonly still included a substantial number of archers (and some bill-men) to complement the main body of pike and shot during the 1580s. Nevertheless, the establishment of the trained bands marked the Elizabethan regime's commitment to thorough-going military modernisation and would eventually lead to a new and more sophisticated approach to defending the realm from invasion.

Ironically, this strengthening of the realm's defences also exacerbated the military shortcomings of the forces sent overseas to Ireland or (later) to the Continent. One consequence of reserving most of the Queen's fittest subjects for service in the trained bands and retaining these precious troops strictly for defence of the realm was that forces raised for service overseas had to be recruited from other sources. In practice, this meant that these forces were largely constructed from poor quality conscripts drawn from the bottom end of society – those least able to complain about the very dubious legality of conscription for military service overseas. Local authorities sometimes even met their quotas by emptying town gaols. The poor quality of most of these recruits placed a heavier burden on officers and on the much smaller numbers of volunteers and men who were exempt from service in the militia by virtue of being servants and retainers of the aristocracy. Although most scholarship on Elizabethan England's wars has emphasised the problems associated with sending abroad armies largely composed of raw and often unwilling conscripts, very little attention has been given to the continued functioning – and importance – of recruiting through medieval-style aristocratic affinities which often gave these forces their best troops. These connections also provided many of the horsemen sent abroad. The result was that those Elizabethan expeditionary forces which featured a substantial aristocratic involvement (as many expeditions did) combined a mixture of men from the upper reaches of society – accompanied by troops recruited from their own servants and tenants – and very large numbers drawn from the opposite end of the social scale.

The peerage also played an important role in the defence of the realm. Peers and officers of the Queen's household (and at least some bishops) were expected to maintain small private militias which reflected the bond of personal service between them and their sovereign. Although fewer in number and more varied in their equipment than the trained bands, these troops could be mobilised in times of crisis without immediately burdening the Crown with the heavy bill for daily pay associated with calling out the trained bands. This important aristocratic dimension to Elizabethan military preparedness has received relatively little scholarly attention. In large measure, this reflects a strong – but erroneous – assumption on the part of many scholars that the military significance and enthusiasm of the nobility declined with the spread of gunpowder warfare. In fact, the Elizabethan peerage was extremely active in military affairs and this strong martial tradition persisted well into the next century.

England entered open war against Spain in 1585 with a strategy that sought both to minimise the vulnerability of its own land forces and to exploit what were believed to be Spanish vulnerabilities at sea. The main army which was sent to the Low Countries under the Earl of Leicester was given strict orders to adopt a defensive posture, much to the frustration of its officers. By contrast, a fleet was dispatched under Sir Francis Drake to sail along the Spanish coast before heading across the Atlantic in the hope of plundering Spain's settlements in the Caribbean. This aggressive naval strategy reflected ideas that had been developed in the privateering voyages of the 1560s and 1570s, and especially in Drake's circumnavigation of the globe between 1577 and 1580. The latter proved to be enormously lucrative and seemed to demonstrate that Philip's empire was vulnerable to attacks on its maritime lifelines. The plan was that, while Leicester's army prevented further Spanish advances in the Low Countries, Drake's expedition would capture enough booty to cover its own costs and at least partly subsidise Leicester's campaign. Elizabeth hoped that the resulting combination of military stalemate in the Low Countries and heavy losses to Drake – whose voyage would also demonstrate the vulnerability of Spain itself to future English expeditions – would convince Philip to negotiate some kind of compromise peace which would allow Dutch Protestants to retain their faith and liberties and remove the threat of a Spanish invasion of England. As in 1560, therefore, Elizabeth embraced open war in 1585 only with extreme reluctance and with the aim of removing an immediate strategic threat, not conquering any new territory. Indeed, rather than lock herself into a relationship with the Dutch which would prevent a negotiated peace with Philip, Elizabeth refused their offer of sovereignty over the Low Countries in July 1585 (as she had also previously refused a similar offer in 1576) and committed herself only to take the Dutch into her temporary 'protection'.

Inevitably, these optimistic calculations proved disastrously wrong. Leicester's campaign was soon soured by bitter rivalries among his officers (not least between Norris and Leicester himself), spiralling costs, and political tensions both with the Dutch leadership and between Leicester and Elizabeth. Drake's expedition only captured enough booty to cover part of its own costs but succeeded in conclusively proving to Philip that English naval expeditions – even those, like Drake's, which were really glorified privateering ventures – could not be permitted to continue. The twin goals of protecting his empire from further maritime incursions and removing the chief prop for the Dutch now both drove Philip to tackle these problems at their root, by initiating the 'enterprise of England'. Instead of forcing Philip into peace talks, England's entry into open war with Spain in 1585 provoked Spain into preparing the very invasion of England which the war had been intended to prevent.

Although Elizabeth continued to hope that she could make a peace with Philip, the Privy Council continued to push forward the transformation of England's military capacity as rapidly as possible. At the start of the war, the sustained involvement of substantial numbers of English 'volunteers' in the Continental wars of religion over the previous two decades had created a pool of experienced officers and soldiers, who had been in critically short supply in the 1560s. Once England began to maintain large numbers of troops in the Low Countries, military service there gradually began to produce a steady supply of 'old soldiers'. The result was a military system that finally replaced the loss of Calais in 1558: troops blooded in the Low Countries were repeatedly withdrawn to provide a veteran elite for

English forces being dispatched elsewhere, their places being taken by fresh recruits who would themselves eventually become 'old soldiers' (if they survived long enough). The first major test of this new system came in 1588, when 2,000 veterans were withdrawn from the Low Countries to stiffen the realm's defences against Spanish invasion. During the 1590s, this system became even more effective because of the new military techniques developed by the Dutch, which meant that England was able to call upon useful numbers of infantry trained in the latest military methods of the day and able to confront the much-vaunted Spanish army on even terms. For at least the next generation, fighting with the Dutch would also constitute the 'school of war' for young English officers. Although Elizabeth's armies continued to be based largely upon raw conscripts and suffered heavy attrition in the field (like all armies of this period), officers and soldiers trained and tested in the Low Countries began to give English forces a cutting edge which they had largely lacked since the 1540s.

Lessons learned fighting against Spain also encouraged a more sophisticated approach to national defence. Influenced by their experience in the Low Countries since the early 1570s (initially as volunteers serving the Dutch and latterly as soldiers of the Queen), leading officers convinced the Privy Council to abandon England's age-old strategy for repelling a foreign invader. Instead of a headlong rush to meet the enemy on the beaches, the trained bands of several counties would converge at an inland rendezvous while the Spanish were delayed by the pre-planned demolition of bridges, denied access to local food or horses, and found their advance impeded by a succession of newly built earthworks which were designed to bleed the invaders and exhaust their supplies by forcing them to make repeated costly assaults on these lightly held positions. The twofold aim was to avoid a demoralising early English defeat and to delay and weaken the invaders sufficiently for the trained bands to form into several separate armies which could launch co-ordinated operations against them. It is often assumed that Spain's famous *Gran Armada* of 1588 only had to land its troops in order to ensure a swift victory over Elizabeth's forces. In fact, the outcome of such a scenario is harder to predict. If the Spanish were unable to reinforce themselves by sea and the English held their nerve, this new strategy at least offered the possibility that a large-scale Spanish landing in 1588 might have proved much more costly than they expected and might even have resulted in the Spanish becoming surrounded and running short of supplies, forcing both sides into some kind of parley. Fortunately for England, the new anti-invasion strategy implemented in 1587–8 was never put to the test. However, the ability and willingness of Elizabeth's government to implement such a major change is itself significant. Not only did it reflect the fruits of sustained combat experience in the Low Countries and the new military possibilities opened up by the development of the trained bands, but it also underlined the excellence of the Privy Council's own contingency planning. From the very beginning of the reign, the Council had been conducting increasingly detailed surveys of the realm's maritime and military resources to ensure that planners had the best possible information. By the mid-1580s, these efforts gave Elizabeth's government a more detailed knowledge of her realm's military resources than its foreign contemporaries and the Council's information on shipping and seamen, in particular, was probably unmatched again in English history until the twentieth century.

THE WAR

In 1588, Philip II set his 'enterprise of England' into motion by despatching his *Gran Armada* to the English Channel. Famously, this resulted in 'the defeat of the Spanish Armada', the broad outlines of which – the Spanish fleet's inability to link up with Parma's army in Flanders, its loss of tactical cohesion after being attacked with fireships after mooring off Calais, its battering from the English fleet off Gravelines and its subsequent flight into the North Sea before straggling home to Spain with heavy losses by sailing around the north of Scotland and down the west coast of Ireland – are too well known to warrant detailed repetition here. However, this was not how the English had expected events to unfold. Rather than waiting for the Spanish to arrive in the Channel, as the old legend has it, most of the English fleet concentrated at Plymouth and three times tried to sail south to attack the *Gran Armada* while it gathered at Lisbon. This offensive strategy was another late change to previous defensive plans and reflected the urging of Sir Francis Drake at the end of March. Drake's successful attack on Spanish ships at Cadiz in the previous year ('the singeing of the king of Spain's beard') suggested that the Armada might be attacked in similar fashion if the English fleet were sufficiently large. Despite the mythology of small English warships bravely tackling huge Spanish ships, Elizabeth's naval leadership was confident that they out-gunned the enemy, which was less a fleet of warships than a huge and motley convoy of ships packed with soldiers. Confronting the Spanish fleet in its home waters also offered the prospect of a much shorter campaign which would minimise the difficulties of locating the enemy fleet and avoid the huge costs associated with the prolonged mobilisation of the trained bands. Unfortunately, contrary winds repeatedly blew the English fleet back home. The final storm also carried the Spanish north, leaving the English fleet pinned inside Plymouth Sound as the enemy fleet entered the Channel. Luckily for the English, Philip's inflexible instructions ensured that the Spanish commander Medina Sidonia was unable to take advantage of this situation.

The dramatic failure of the *Gran Armada* struck a severe blow to Philip's international prestige and offered a huge lift to Elizabeth and England. Along with Elizabeth's own 'miraculous' continued survival in the face of numerous Catholic 'plots', Spain's humiliation in 1588 became a staple of English propaganda. The events of 1588 also instilled an enduring sense of confidence about England's ability to contend with Spanish power, even if expressions of this confidence sometimes suggested it was rather fragile. When Elizabeth's fleet suffered its most spectacular defeat of the war with the loss of the *Revenge* off the Azores in 1591, Sir Walter Ralegh's pamphlet on the event instinctively turned back to 1588 to deflect attention away from the magnitude of this disaster, scornfully boasting that the Spanish 'did not in all their sailing rounde about England so much as sinke or take one ship, barke, pinnes, or cockbote of ours: or ever burnt so much as one sheepcote of this land'.[5]

English confidence ran high after the thwarting of the *Gran Armada* and prompted the launching of a counter-strike against Spain. By the time this expeditionary force sailed in the following spring, enthusiasm for the venture had swelled its size sufficiently to make it an English equivalent of the *Gran Armada* – supposedly 23,000 soldiers and sailors and some 180 vessels of all sizes. However, the cost of such a large force far exceeded what Elizabeth's empty treasury could support, which meant the expedition was heavily reliant upon funding from private sources, especially commercial interests in the City of London. The result was that its departure was delayed until April 1589, and its commanders, Sir Francis Drake and Sir John Norris, promised to accomplish multiple and incompatible objectives. While Elizabeth demanded that the force destroy the surviving ships from the *Gran Armada* which had found shelter in Spain's northern ports, most of those involved in the venture were chiefly focused upon sailing to Portugal and challenging Philip's hold over the Portuguese crown by stirring rebellion there. The result was that the fleet made no serious effort to destroy Spain's surviving warships (although it did spend two weeks pointlessly besieging Corunna), before heading to Portugal. After being landed by the fleet, the army made a six-day march inland through the summer heat to Lisbon. There was no local support for a rising against Spain, and the English lacked the numbers and heavy weaponry needed to besiege the city, even if they chose to risk a prolonged stay in enemy territory. There was no option but to retreat. Over the next few weeks, soldiers and seamen began to succumb to disease in large numbers. By early June, the expedition's third objective – to seize the Azores, the vital node for Spain's transatlantic shipping – was beyond the capacity of the weakened force and more and more ships started drifting home. Although Norris burned the Spanish town of Vigo and Drake unsuccessfully tried to sail for the Azores, the last survivors of the great expedition returned to England by early July. Between a third and a half of those who had set out in April failed to return and none of the expedition's objectives had been achieved.

The supremely disappointing – indeed, disastrous – outcome of the Portugal voyage typifies the problems associated with large-scale naval expeditions mounted by Elizabethan England. Although the exploits of Elizabethan sailors subsequently achieved near-mythical status in English history, the reality of these ventures was less satisfactory. This was partly because the Crown's financial weakness forced it to rely upon private commercial or aristocratic investors whose interest in securing a profit often conflicted with the military priorities set down by Elizabeth and the Council. The very boldness of the conception of these ventures also pushed contemporary sailing and food-preservation technologies to their very limits. Ideas which had been developed by naval commanders such as Drake or Hawkins when they operated as relatively small-scale privateers during the 1570s proved enormously difficult to execute with substantial fleets carrying large numbers of soldiers. One such strategy was the 'double blockade', which envisaged English ships hovering off the Iberian coast for months on end both to prevent Spanish ships leaving harbour and to intercept the annual treasure fleet returning to Spain from the New World via the Azores. This strategy repeatedly failed in the early 1590s, culminating in the loss of the *Revenge* in 1591. For the remainder of the decade, sustained operations off the Iberian coast were left to privateers and the Queen's warships largely remained in home waters to defend against Spain's growing new fleet. Another strategy was to block the silver shipments at their source by seizing a Spanish base in the New World. This idea encouraged the disastrous Panama expedition of 1595–6, in which both Drake and Hawkins died, and the Earl of Cumberland's brief occupation of San Juan de Puerto Rico in 1598. Perhaps the most spectacular English naval success in the 1590s was the capture of Cadiz, one of Spain's major ports. This humiliated Philip II and forced him into a painful rescheduling of his imperial finances, but, as with Cumberland in 1598, the English were unable to hold Cadiz. Moreover, like England's entry into open war against Spain in 1585, the shock of Cadiz's capture impelled Philip to reassert his honour by sending new armadas against Elizabeth's realms. Although they carried fewer troops and had much more limited objectives than the *Gran Armada* of 1588, the fleets which Spain sent north in the autumn of 1596 and again a year later managed to approach the English coast when its naval defences were in disarray. Luckily for England, autumn storms prevented the Spanish fleets from landing and caused them heavy losses.

Despite the later mythology associated with operations at sea, Elizabethan England's war with Spain was largely fought on land and (with the exception of Ireland) in concert with foreign allies. The nature of this war was transformed in 1589 by the failure of the Portugal expedition and by the succession of the Protestant Henri, Prince of Navarre as Henri IV of France. With the collapse of all the hopes invested in Dom Antonio, the Portuguese pretender, the failure to destroy Spain's fleet and the very heavy losses suffered on the voyage, the Portugal expedition ended England's one opportunity to strike a really damaging blow against Philip when Spain was vulnerable. After the disasters that had befallen their respective armadas in 1588–9, neither Spain nor England would be able to launch a similarly large expedition for several years. More important still was the accession of Henri IV, a Huguenot, to the French throne in 1589. This prompted large-scale civil war in France and encouraged Philip to intervene by diverting the Spanish Army of Flanders to assist the Catholic League there. This not only relieved the pressure on the Dutch but also necessitated the urgent dispatch of English troops to bolster Henri IV's faltering hold on his throne. The Dutch Revolt and Anglo-Spanish war consequently expanded into a more general war in north-western Europe. Between 1589 and 1595, substantial numbers of English troops fought in France, especially in Normandy and Brittany. Although a Triple Alliance with France and the Dutch was only formalised in October 1596 and some English troops were subsequently garrisoned in Picardy, the main English commitment in France ended when troops under Norris finally stormed a fort which the Spanish has established near the port of Brest in November 1594. By then, Elizabeth's growing mistrust of Henri IV (especially after he converted to Catholicism to win over his domestic opponents) and the heavy costs and casualties of these campaigns made the Queen anxious to limit her involvement on the Continent as much as possible. Although she ultimately declined to follow Henri IV in making peace with Spain in 1598 (the Treaty of Vervins), Elizabeth's determination to reduce the burden of war on the Continent resulted in a renegotiation of England's relationship with the Dutch that year and the wholesale transfer of English troops (other than those garrisoning the cautionary towns) into Dutch pay. It was as an elite unit of the Dutch army that English soldiers played a prominent role – and suffered heavy casualties – in the Dutch victories over the Spanish at Turnhout (1597) and Nieuwpoort (1600). The Dutch were also permitted to recruit fresh troops directly from England, and many ended up fighting in the terrible and ultimately unsuccessful struggle to defend Ostend (1601–4).

Elizabeth's determination to limit her military commitments on the Continent in the mid-1590s was also driven by the progressive collapse of her hold over Ireland. Beginning in 1594, more and more of the island became engulfed in what later became known as the Nine Years War (1594–1603) or Tyrone's Rebellion, after the chief Irish leader Hugh O'Neill, 2nd Earl of Tyrone. Tyrone proved to be a far more formidable enemy than Elizabeth and her government ever expected because he welded together a broad coalition of Irish leaders and guarded his own home territory in Ulster with a large army whose core was equipped and trained according to the best contemporary standards. The nadir for English interests came in the wake of a dramatic defeat of the main English army in Ireland at Yellow Ford in August 1598, which saw hundreds of men killed and wounded in the worst English defeat since the surrender at Newhaven in 1563. Some of the survivors of the disaster also deserted to the enemy (many of the 'English' troops were actually Irish) and large areas of Ireland now became indefensible. In response, Elizabeth's government embarked upon a truly massive build-up to confront Tyrone in the following spring, building an army of 16,000 foot (including 2,000 'old soldiers' withdrawn from the Low Countries) and 1,300 cavalry under the Earl of Essex, the hero of Cadiz. Essex succeeded in stabilising the situation and recovering control over much of the south and protecting the Pale around Dublin. However, Essex had promised to defeat Tyrone, and his failure to do more than conclude a truce with him by the end of the campaign season spelled the end of Essex's career. When he rushed home to explain himself to the Queen, he was promptly arrested. He was eventually stripped of all his offices and was executed as a traitor in February 1601 after publicly trying to rally support for himself in the streets of London. Nevertheless, Essex's semi-failure in 1599 pointed the way ahead for his successor in Ireland, his close friend Lord Mountjoy. Instead of a quick and dramatic victory, Essex showed that success in Ireland would have to be ground out slowly by occupying territory, systematically destroying local food production and picking apart Tyrone's Irish coalition. This brutal strategy of attrition required regular infusions of fresh troops and enormous quantities of food and supplies from England. Remarkably, the administrative and commercial infrastructure which had developed for war by the 1590s was able to meet these requirements. Contractors based in London produced literally millions of rations, while huge quantities of munitions and weapons were shipped across the Irish Sea. However, the human and financial cost was enormous. In addition to thousands of deaths (mainly through sickness), the Elizabethan campaigns in Ireland between 1599 and 1602 cost more than £1.1 million, and the total for the whole Nine Years War was almost £2 million. The latter figure was roughly one-third of Elizabeth's entire expenditure on war between 1585 and 1603.

In September 1601, a substantial Spanish army finally landed on British soil. About 3,400 veteran Spanish troops occupied the southern Irish port of Kinsale, with more expected to follow. Faced with the nightmare scenario of large-scale Spanish support for Tyrone, the Elizabethan government threw all available resources against Kinsale. Despite autumnal gales and bitter weather, English warships blockaded the port while thousands of troops began a siege on land. The losses were terrible, especially from sickness and exposure. However, Tyrone was compelled to leave Ulster and march south to relieve the Spanish. On Christmas Eve, Mountjoy's exhausted (and now outnumbered) besieging army finally confronted the advancing Irish force in open battle. Although their precious horses had begun to run short of feed, the English cavalry scattered their Irish counterparts (who rode on smaller mounts) and eventually broke the Irish infantry. Tyrone's army was routed with heavy losses. This victory proved decisive. With all hope of relief now apparently gone, the Spanish troops in Kinsale surrendered on 2 January 1602. Despite the excellent performance of its troops, Spain's invasion of Ireland had resulted in a humiliating defeat. Kinsale also demoralised the Irish. Although Tyrone would not agree to final terms of submission with Mountjoy for another year, the heart was ripped out of his expensive and carefully nurtured army at Kinsale and the Irish alliance began to splinter.

The generous terms which Tyrone received in the Treaty of Mellifont in the very last days of Elizabeth's reign finally opened the way for peace with Spain. Although this had been mooted when France had made a separate peace in 1598 and a series of unsatisfactory negotiations had been pursued with the Spanish administration in Flanders since 1599, the Privy Council had decided in May 1602 that peace with Spain would not be viable until England could deny Spain the opportunity to retaliate for continuing English support for the Dutch by stirring rebellion in Ireland. Ireland therefore had to be fully subdued in order to make possible a peace with Spain in which the English would not entirely abandon the Dutch. With this precondition finally met in March 1603, the way was opened for the government of Elizabeth's successor, James VI of Scotland, to negotiate an end to the Elizabethan war with Spain. Although neither England nor Spain had ever formally declared war upon each other, the open conflict between them had lasted almost twenty years. The Treaty of London which brought a formal end to hostilities in August 1604 represented a considerable diplomatic triumph for the English. Like Tyrone after Mellifont, however, the new Jacobean regime would learn that the peace could bring problems of its own.

FURTHER READING

Adams, Simon, 'Elizabeth I and the sovereignty of the Netherlands, 1576–1585', Transactions of the Royal Historical Society, 6th series, 14 (2004), 309–19.

Andrews, Kenneth R., *Elizabethan Privateering: English Privateering during the Spanish War, 1585–1603* (Cambridge, 1964).

Boynton, Lindsay, *The Elizabethan Militia, 1558–1638* (London, 1967).

Collinson, Patrick, 'The Elizabethan exclusion crisis and the Elizabethan polity', *Proceedings of the British Academy*, 84 (1994), 51–92.

Cruickshank, C. G., *Elizabeth's Army*, 2nd edn (Oxford, 1966).

Doran Susan and Richardson, Glenn (eds.), *Tudor England and Its Neighbours* (Basingstoke, 2005).

Earle, Peter, *The Last Fight of the Revenge* (London, 1992).

Falls, Cyril, *Elizabeth's Irish Wars* (London, 1950).

Fissel, Mark Charles, *English Warfare, 1511–1642* (London, 2001).

Hammer, Paul E. J., *Elizabeth's Wars: War, Government and Society in Tudor England, 1544–1604* (Basingstoke, 2003).

Martin, Colin, and Parker, Geoffrey, *The Spanish Armada,* 2nd edn (London, 1999).

Morgan, Hiram (ed.), *The Battle of Kinsale* (Bray, 2004).
Nolan, John S., 'The Militarization of Elizabethan England', *Journal of Military History*, 58 (3) (1994): 391–420.
—— *Sir John Norreys and the Elizabethan Military World* (Exeter, 1997).
Parker, Geoffrey, 'The *Dreadnought* Revolution of Tudor England', *The Mariner's Mirror*, 82 (1996): 269–300.
Rodger, N. A. M., *The Safeguard of the Sea: A Naval History of England, Vol. I: 1660–1649* (London, 1997).
Rodriguez-Salgado, M. J. and Adams, Simon (eds.), *England, Spain and the Gran Armada, 1585–1604* (Edinburgh, 1991).
Silke, John J., *Kinsale: The Spanish Intervention in Ireland at the End of the Elizabethan Wars* (Liverpool, 1970).
Trim, D. J. B., '"Fighting Jacob's wars": the employment of English and Welsh mercenaries in the European Wars of Religion: France and the Netherlands, 1562–1601', Ph.D. thesis, University of London, 2002.
Wernham, R. B., *After the Armada: Elizabethan England and the Struggle for Western Europe, 1588–1595* (Oxford, 1984).
—— *The Return of the Armadas: The Last Years of the Elizabethan War against Spain, 1595–1603* (Oxford, 1994).
Whitehead, Bertrand T., *Brags and Boasts: Propaganda in the Year of the Armada* (Stroud, 1994).
Younger, Neil, 'War and the Counties: The Elizabethan Lord Lieutenancy, 1585–1603', Ph.D. thesis, University of Birmingham, 2006.
—— 'If the Armada Had Landed: A Reappraisal of England's Defences in 1588', *History*, 93 (2008): 328–54.

NOTES

1 BL Lansdowne MS 15, fols. 198r–202r.
2 Quoted in Patrick Collinson, *The Elizabethan Puritan Movement* (Oxford, 1967), p. 247.
3 Quoted in Paul Hammer, *Elizabeth's Wars* (Houndsmill, 2003), p. 211.
4 Proclamation of 18 October 1591, 'Establishing Commissions against Seminary Priests and Jesuits'; reprinted in P. L. Hughes and J. F. Larkin (eds.), *Tudor Royal Proclamations, Vol. III: The Later Tudors (1588–1603)* (New Haven, Conn., 1969), p. 87.
5 (Sir Walter Ralegh), *A Report of the Truth of the Fight about Iles of the Acores This Last Sommer* (London, 1591), sig. A4r. For the *Revenge* and its loss, see Peter Earle, *The Last Fight of the Revenge* (London, 1992).

CHAPTER THIRTY-SEVEN

EXPLORATION, TRADE AND EMPIRE

Ken MacMillan

In the age of Elizabeth, the British Empire included just Ireland, Wales, Scotland and several surrounding islands. Calais, England's last vestige of its medieval empire on the Continent, was lost to France in 1558. By this time, the voyages of John Cabot and others to America in the early Tudor period were a distant memory. Thus, when Elizabeth came to the throne and throughout her reign, Britain was, in the words of the imperial proponent John Dee, an 'islandish monarchy'.[1] Yet it was during the Elizabethan age that many of England's best-known explorations took place. English knights such as Francis Drake, Martin Frobisher, Humphrey Gilbert, John Hawkins and Walter Ralegh travelled the oceans in search of new lands and trading opportunities. They circumnavigated the globe, explored the coasts of Africa, America, the Caribbean and Russia, engaged in trade, piracy and slavery, and attempted to establish English colonies in North America. Despite these efforts, by 1603, when Elizabeth died, England controlled no New World territory, had abandoned the slave trade and any interest in Africa and had established only a few risky and expensive trading networks in eastern Europe and Asia. For these reasons, many modern scholars dismiss Elizabethan exploration as a time of trial and failure, of plunder and piracy, and argue that the origins of the British Empire are to be found in later centuries. Even so, important lessons were learned during this period that facilitated the successful expansion of England in the seventeenth century and the remarkable success of the British Empire thereafter.

English interest in North America began in 1496, when Henry VII issued a charter to John Cabot and his sons to 'seeke out, discover, and find whatsoever isles, countreys, regions or provinces . . . whatsoever they be . . . which before this time have bene unknowen to all Christians'.[2] This charter mirrored the language of Pope Alexander VI's 1493 bull *Inter caetera,* which awarded the discoveries of Christopher Columbus to the rulers of Spain. In issuing a charter, Henry was both challenging the Pope's jurisdiction to dispose of non-Christian lands and implying that Columbus's discoveries were not as extensive as were sometimes assumed. Cabot sailed from Bristol in May 1497, travelled to Newfoundland in Canada, mapped a portion of the North American coastline and returned to England, initially believing that he had sailed to China. Several additional charters and some private investment followed between 1498 and 1536, which resulted in further voyages by Cabot (soon lost at sea), his son Sebastian and others from Bristol to Newfoundland and Labrador in the early sixteenth century. By this time, however, Portuguese and French fishermen were already a strong presence along the Grand Banks, and the English generally lacked the resources to compete among these wealthier European neighbours.

Under Queen Mary, explorers turned their attention to trade in the East. In 1553, Hugh Willoughby and Richard Chancellor consulted with the mathematicians John Dee and Thomas Digges before departing for the northern coast of Europe and Asia. While Willoughby and his crew froze to death after becoming trapped in ice, Chancellor found his way into the White Sea. Travelling by sled to Moscow, he presented royal letters of friendship to Tsar Ivan IV, whose positive reception resulted in Mary incorporating the Eastern adventurers as the Muscovy Company in 1555. Under its auspices, Chancellor (until his death the next year) and the pilot brothers Stephen and William Borough continued their search for the north-east passage via the Barents Sea. If it could be breached, English merchants could sail around the Tabin promontory (the east coast of Russia) and south to China, the world's most desirable region for trade in the early modern period. The Company abandoned the effort to find the passage in 1557, when it gained from the Tsar the exclusive right to trade in Russia and to travel through Russia into Persia (roughly modern-day Iran). The Company offered competition to Venetian and Ottoman traders, who sold Persians English goods they had purchased in Europe. Trading English kersey, a lightweight cloth, in exchange for raw silk and spices, Chancellor's successor, Anthony Jenkinson, maintained a sporadic trade until the early 1580s by keeping on generally friendly terms with the Tsar of Russia and the Shah of Persia. The death of Ivan in 1584 significantly damaged this trade. Meanwhile, the master pilots Arthur Pet and Charles Jackman renewed interest in the north-east passage in 1580. Although travelling further than the Boroughs, passing Novaya Zemyla and entering the Kara Sea, ice forced them to turn back, and only Pet managed to return to England. After Henry Hudson's failed north-east expedition in 1608, the English abandoned the attempt once and for all.

By 1581, the Russian–Persian trade route was eclipsed by the new English Turkey Company, a joint-stock company chartered by Elizabeth to trade within the Ottoman Empire. This empire, then the world's largest, included the former Byzantine Empire and parts of modern-day Egypt, Saudi Arabia, Iraq, Kuwait, the Balkans and Hungary. With the permission of Sultan Murad III, the English established several permanent factories on the eastern and southern coasts of the Mediterranean, including Smyrna, Istanbul and into the Holy Land. This water route was significantly more advantageous than the former route from Russia. The installation of an English ambassador to Constantinople from 1583, which enabled the efficient handling of diplomatic disputes, England's willingness to trade the raw materials necessary to produce weapons (in aid of Turkey's feuds with Spain and Persia) and rechartering the Company as the stronger Levant Company in 1592, all ensured that English trade with the Levant would continue beyond 1603.

However, trade in the East was both challenging and expensive. The Queen, English merchants and diplomats had to navigate a careful political and commercial policy, and Company factories and ships were constantly threatened by privateering (licensed piracy during wartime), piracy and plundering in the Mediterranean, internal warfare, temperamental rulers and trading competition with the better-established Dutch, French and Venetian traders. A captured ship or a rival offer for services could lead to financial ruin. In addition, although these trading opportunities could help to enrich England's economy, the countries in which they took place were all governed by recognised sovereign authorities. This meant that none of these activities could expand the English territorial empire in the same manner that Spain and Portugal were expanding. Thus, while the East had opened up many possibilities during the reign of Elizabeth, English explorers and merchants sought better opportunities for new commodities, cheaper and safer trade, and territorial expansion. It was widely believed that these could be found in the Atlantic world.

England's interest in the Atlantic was first piqued by trade and the possibility of expansion into the Portuguese-controlled region of West Africa. Of specific interest were the gold and pepper to be found in Guinea, a 2,000-mile coastal area also known as the Gold Coast (today, the coastal countries between Senegal and Nigeria). English voyages to this region began in 1553 and instantly involved clashes with Portuguese merchants. The Portuguese had been actively trading in the region since the mid-fifteenth century, had built several forts to express their sovereignty and asserted their rights to exclusivity on the basis of their 'discoveries' and 'possessions'. The situation became so tense in 1554 that the English agreed to turn a teenaged Martin Frobisher over to the Portuguese at their fort of São Jorge da Mina as a surety of good behaviour. Frobisher was allowed to return home in 1557, after Queen Mary, who was married to Philip of Spain and thus nominally supported the Iberian cause, officially forbade English activities in Guinea. Frobisher wanted to return to the Gold Coast in the first year of Elizabeth's reign to assault the castle in Mina, but these plans were halted by the imprisonment of his confederate in the project, a notorious pirate named Henry Strangways. Meanwhile, the English, particularly during the voyages of William Towerson, attracted further enmity by seizing Africans to bring back to England, plundering and burning the villages of those who refused to trade and, in 1560, seizing Portuguese ships carrying valuable cargos.

In 1561, the Portuguese ambassador in London formally protested against English activities in Africa. He complained of English seizure of ships and requested that the English be 'prohibited from trading to any of the regions conquered by the King of Portugal'.[3] Elizabeth curtly replied that evidenced piratical acts committed by the English would be punished, but that 'her meaning is . . . to restrain her subjects from haunting any new found [i.e. non-sovereign] land . . . wherein the King of Portugal had obedience, dominion, and tribute, and not from all places discovered, whereof he had no superiority at all.'[4] Articulating a position similar to that of Henry VII in the Cabot charter, Elizabeth emphasised that mere discovery was insufficient to establish a perpetual right to dominion. Instead, she demanded that the Portuguese restrict their pretensions to sovereignty – and, therefore, their ability to control trade – to those regions in which they had 'obedience, dominion, and tribute', or clear physical presence and the submission of the African people. She further suggested that if the King of Portugal had such authority, he would be able both to repel the English and to command the Africans not to trade with them. If the Africans continued to trade, they did not recognise Portuguese dominion and were, therefore, free to trade with whomever they pleased. Elizabeth had a vested interest in this issue. In June 1561, she authorised the use of four ships in the Guinea enterprise, presumably in hopes of dividends. This enterprise, though backed by royal support, amounted to little, and although the Queen never conceded Portuguese sovereignty in Guinea, trade had effectively ended by 1571, not to be resumed until the seventeenth century.

In the meantime, another trading activity involving Africa in the 1560s was England's first venture into the slave trade. Also backed in part by the Queen, the wealthy shipowner and merchant John Hawkins took part in four voyages between 1562 and 1568, with the intent to capture Africans from the west coast and sell them as slaves in the Spanish Caribbean, thereby mimicking Spanish slaving activities that had been ongoing since about 1520. Although Englishmen selling slaves in the Spanish New World was forbidden by a Spanish statute banning carrying unregistered goods to the Indies, success was anticipated because England and Spain were on generally good terms and because the Spanish colonists were seeking additional labour on their profitable Caribbean plantations. On his first voyage, Hawkins captured and plundered several Portuguese vessels in the region of Sierra Leone, gathered 300–400 African slaves, and arrived at the Indies in April 1563. Despite coming to the attention of the Spanish authorities and having much of his cargo confiscated, Hawkins returned to Plymouth that summer with substantial profits for his investors. Hoping for even greater returns, Elizabeth assigned Hawkins a large royal ship, *Jesus of Lubeck,* which flagged the fleet for a second, and extremely eventful, plundering voyage in 1564–5. Using his licence from Elizabeth as 'evidence' that he was not a pirate, Hawkins was again able to sell his cargo to Spanish colonials in the Indies and return to England with copious dividends. In 1566, Hawkins sent out his fleet for a third slaving voyage, but lacking the presence of the fast-talking Hawkins, the voyage was unsuccessful.

It is Hawkins's fourth and last voyage of 1567–9 for which he is most remembered. The largest of the slaving voyages, with six ships including two royal warships, this endeavour proceeded along the same lines as the first two. With more than 500 African slaves in his holds, Hawkins arrived in the Indies, touching upon many ports to dispose of his cargo before being forced by severe storms to San Juan de Ulúa, in Central America. There, Hawkins met considerable Spanish resistance when, coincidentally, a Spanish flotilla arrived. In the ensuing sea battle, Hawkins lost three-quarters of his men, was reduced to two ships and limped home to Plymouth after a financially disastrous expedition. By the time Hawkins returned, Anglo-Spanish relations were already becoming rocky because the English were supporting the rebellion in the Netherlands against their Spanish overlord. Within this new political climate, the Caribbean policy swiftly changed from one of tacitly accepted trade to unofficial plunder. Though officially disavowed by the Crown, the years between 1570 and 1577 saw at least a dozen plundering expeditions to the Caribbean, in which Francis Drake assaulted various Spanish colonies.

It was within this broader context of unofficial plunder that one of the best-known English explorations of the Elizabethan period occurred, Drake's circumnavigation of the world, 1577–80. As initially conceived, Drake would sail down the south coast of South America, through the Strait of Magellan, and north up the Pacific coast, seeking new trading and plundering opportunities in Chile and

Peru and returning along the same route. In order to allow for deniability, Elizabeth refused to commit royal ships to the enterprise, although she probably personally invested capital. Drake set sail with a modest fleet of barks and pinnaces, including his own small but well-equipped 150-ton man-of war, the *Pelican*, in November 1577. The fleet made its way down the West African coast plundering small Iberian vessels and picking up additional tonnage. By April 1578 Drake reached the coast of Brazil and tacked south, entering the Strait of Magellan in August. There, Drake renamed his flagship the *Golden Hind* (in honour of the arms of his patron, Sir Christopher Hatton), named several islands (such as those of Elizabeth and Saint George) and carried out a physical ceremony of possession to claim the Strait in Elizabeth's name. As planned, Drake tacked north along the west coast of South America, raiding a number of native coastal settlements, capturing a Spanish ship laden with some 80 pounds of gold and silver – a considerable fortune – and launching assaults on Spanish settlements in Central America. By June 1579, Drake landed in California or Oregon (the precise region is controversial) and claimed 'Nova Albion' for Elizabeth by erecting a post to which was attached a descriptive lead plate and an English sixpence. Departing the coast in midsummer, Drake proceeded, against his initial intentions, across the Pacific, arriving at Palau in early fall and continuing to the Moluccas (the Spice Islands) where he traded linens for cloves, ginger and pimento. The *Golden Hind* and the remainder of the fleet (some pinnaces having been lost) made their way around the Cape of Good Hope during the summer of 1580, arriving back in Plymouth in September.

Drake's return, though triumphant, was not without controversy. His plundering activities in the New World, plus claims to English sovereignty over the Strait of Magellan, were already known before he returned, to which were added his adventures in Nova Albion and the East Indies, respectively, if nominally, under Spanish and Portuguese control. Bernardino de Mendoza, the Spanish ambassador in London, had kept the King of Spain informed of Drake's actions since 1578 and officially sued for restitution on behalf of Spanish merchants. The State's official position was to surround the entire voyage with secrecy, including keeping closely guarded Drake's map and diary of the voyage, which are no longer extant. With Drake's activities now being mostly speculation and hearsay, Elizabeth informed de Mendoza that she found his claims of piracy exaggerated, allowing only a pittance of compensation. In reference to claims that Drake had intruded into and claimed for England portions of Spanish America, the Queen replied:

> The Spaniards have brought these evils on themselves by their injustice toward the English, whom, [against the law of nations], they have excluded from commerce with the West Indies. The Queen does not acknowledge that her subjects . . . may be excluded from the Indies on the claim that these have been donated to the king of Spain by the pope, whose authority to invest the Spanish king with the New World . . . she does not recognize. . . . The Spaniards have no claims to property there except that they have established a few settlements and named rivers and capes. This . . . imaginary right of property ought not to prevent other princes from carrying on commerce in those regions or establishing colonies there in places not inhabited by the Spaniards.[5]

Similar to Elizabeth's response to the Portuguese ambassador in 1562, the Queen challenged the jurisdiction of the Pope and the ability of Spain to claim title to the New World merely on the basis of 'discovery', when these were not followed up by taking physical possession of, and remaining in, the territory in question. Elizabeth's knighting of Drake in April 1581 reflects the State's support for his actions. Nor were Drake's Caribbean adventures at an end. With war on the immediate horizon by 1585, Drake was commissioned to return to the Caribbean for official privateering voyages that involved distressing the Queen's enemy. Drake and his fleet looted Santo Domingo, Cartagena, Cuba and Saint Augustine in Florida, before arriving at Walter Ralegh's new colony of Roanoke and bringing its demoralised colonists back to England in July 1586.

Ralegh's unsuccessful Roanoke colony was one of the last of a welter of North American projects that had their beginnings two decades earlier, when interest in the north-west passage emerged. In 1566, Humphrey Gilbert submitted to the Crown a proposal (published in 1576 as *A Discourse of a Discovery for a New Passage To Cataia;* see Figure 37.1) to discover the north-west passage under the auspices of the Muscovy Company. The Company, unwilling to allow Gilbert such a free hand, denied his proposal, and the project was shelved. Instead, Gilbert spent four years in Ireland commanding a brutal regime that would see him knighted in 1570, after which he served in the Netherlands. By 1574, Gilbert's plans for the north-west passage were taken up by Martin Frobisher, who had better relations with the Muscovy Company and received permission for the undertaking. Both Gilbert's and Frobisher's belief in the existence of the north-west passage was inspired by the world maps of Gerard Mercator and Abraham Ortelius, produced between 1564 and 1570. These maps speculated on the existence of an easily navigable passage across the northern coast of North America, egressing at the Strait of Anian, which separated North America from Asia. If these speculations were true – and so said the leading cartographers of the age – then English access to Asia was assured.

Further assurance on this matter came from John Dee, a respected mathematician who taught Frobisher the finer points of geometry and cosmography (celestial navigation) and would teach similar lessons to Pet and Jackman before their north-east attempt in 1580. Dee's more-than-mathematical interest in these enterprises became clear when, a few months after Frobisher departed, he wrote *The General and Rare Memorials Pertaining to the Perfect Art of Navigation.* Dee advocated the creation of a large trading corporation under state annexation, to be protected by a 'petty navy royal', which would be responsible for ensuring safe English travel in the northern seas and collecting taxes from foreigners who traded in English territories, thereby enriching royal coffers. Although good in theory, in practice Dee's plan was too expensive to implement, flew against the Crown's generally laissez-faire attitude toward foreign trade and would have been politically unwise at such a critical time in Anglo-Spanish relations. The Crown remained cautious about official state sanction and funding of risky and legally dubious overseas adventures. Before this treatise was published in September 1577, Dee had already written a substantially longer volume, never published, entitled 'Of Famous and Rich Discoveries'. In this volume, which might have been intended as promotional literature for Drake's, Frobisher's and Gilbert's forthcoming American activities (all

Figure 37.1 Humphrey Gilbert, *Discourse of a Discoverie*, 1576. Reproduced with permission of the Huntingdon Library, California.

linked by the patronage of Hatton, to whom *General and Rare Memorials* was dedicated), Dee recited a wealth of historical, geographical and hydrographical knowledge of the northern and eastern portions of the world in order to induce further searches for the northern passages. He argued that patriotic Englishmen should 'proceed upon the farther discovery of that part which yet is least known to Christian men', including the East Indies, the North Atlantic and North America. He also amplified an argument made in *General and Rare Memorials,* specifically 'that all the Northern Isles and regions septentrional [northern] do seem to be lawfully appropriate to the Crown of this Brytish Impire'.[6]

While bringing the term 'British Empire' into common usage, Dee conceived of this entity in deeply historical terms, basing his opinion on the claims of Geoffrey of Monmouth in *Historia Regum Brittaniae* (*c.* 1138), which upheld ancient 'British' claims to the 'Collateral Islands' (including Ireland, Iceland and Greenland, among others in the North Atlantic) based on the conquests of King Arthur. By the end of 1578, when Drake and Frobisher were still engaged in their explorations, Dee was relaying his arguments, especially via the unpublished treatise entitled 'Brytanici Imperii Limites' ('Limits of the British Empire'), directly to the Queen. Here, Dee drew upon extensive British activities in the North Atlantic, conducted by Arthur, the Welsh prince Madoc, John and Sebastian Cabot, Stephen Borough and others, and explicitly challenged the papal bull *Inter caetera,* all in order to prove to Elizabeth that she already had title to the Atlantic north of Florida. Dee argued that if colonisation projects were supported politically and financially by the Queen, 'your true and obedient subjectes will become marveilouslie emboldned and encouradged to spend their travailes, goodes, and lives (yf nede be) in the recovery, possession, and enjoying of such your Majesties imperiall territoris, duly recoverable and to be possessed.'[7] Though Dee's arguments did not engender much state support for exploration and colonisation, he was called to court in October 1580, when the Mendoza–Drake affair broke, to repeat his arguments, apparently with positive results.

While Dee was striving to broaden the Crown's interest in colonisation, Frobisher was exploring the North Atlantic (Figure 37.2). He departed England in three small ships in June 1576, passing the south coast of Greenland after about six weeks. Although one bark returned home, Frobisher continued west, arriving at Frobisher Bay (today it is Iqaluit in the Canadian territory of Nunavut) on Baffin Island, soon to be named Meta Incognita (literally, 'unknown place'). There, he came into contact with Inuk natives. During this ill-fated meeting, five of Frobisher's men were taken prisoner and were left behind, while Frobisher managed to capture one native, whom he brought back to England in October. Frobisher's most auspicious New World capture was a piece of black ore, which was quickly assayed and believed to be rich in gold. Consequently, Frobisher's second voyage, backed in part by Elizabeth, was a much larger undertaking flagged by a royal ship of 200 tons, *Ayde*, and expected to bring back a hold full of gold-rich ore. The fleet departed in May 1577 and arrived at Frobisher Bay by mid-July, where Frobisher took formal possession in Elizabeth's name. No efforts were made to penetrate further into the north-west passage. Instead, the expedition returned to England in September with a hold full of ore and three Inuk natives, who quickly died. A new voyage was authorised before the ore could be assayed, with the result that fifteen ships departed in May 1578. On this voyage, Frobisher was instructed to plant a colony of 100 men on the small island of Kodlunarn in Frobisher Bay and to fortify it as needed to hold the country. This represented the first planned English attempt at colonisation in North America. Although the colony was not planted, a house was built on Countess of Warwick Island, within the Bay, allegedly for the scientific purpose of seeing how the materials would stand up to an Arctic winter, in the event that a colony would be planted in the future. During this third voyage, Frobisher was also expected to continue searching for the north-west passage, which resulted in his entrance into the so-called Mistaken Strait (Hudson Strait) in July, 'mistaken' because of Frobisher's erroneous belief that it would lead to Asia.

Frobisher returned to England with more than 1,300 tons of ore, only to discover that his cargoes had finally been adjudged mere rock, to the financial and reputational ruin of Frobisher and his business partner Michael Lok. The Queen personally lost £4,000, a substantial sum even for a monarch, and was thereafter disinclined to invest in speculative exploratory ventures. Frobisher's reputation was only to be recovered when he was appointed Drake's vice-admiral on the 1585–6 West Indies raid. After a successful engagement with the Spanish Armada, he was knighted. A final Elizabethan attempt at the north-west passage was made by the sea captain John Davis in three voyages between 1585 and 1587. Davis rounded the northern tip of Baffin Island, travelled north-west to 73 degrees and continued westward, giving the names of his patrons to parts of northern Canada that remain

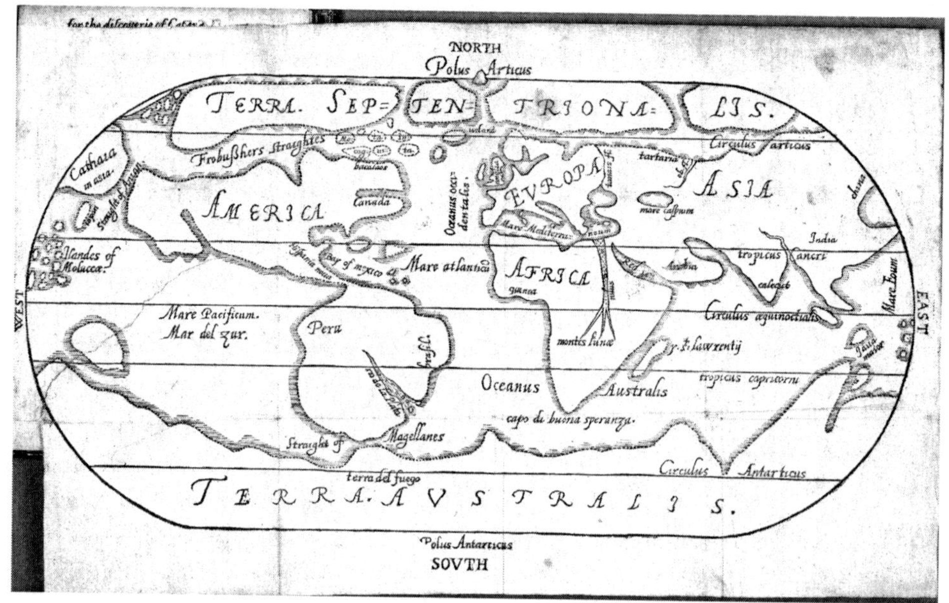

Figure 37.2 George Best, *True Discourse*, 1578.
Reproduced with permission of the Huntingdon Library, California.

to this day – Gilbert Sound, Cape Dyer, Cape Walsingham – before being repelled by ice. Although Davis, like Frobisher before him and Henry Hudson and others after him, did not discover the north-west passage, he had achieved much by helping to correct contemporary maps. Cartographers thereafter named the region of the North Atlantic between Greenland and Baffin Island Davis Strait.

As Frobisher's voyages were coming to an end, those of Humphrey Gilbert were being reinvented. Fresh from his activities in Ireland and the Netherlands, Gilbert submitted to the Queen in 1577 his 'Discourse How Her Majesty May Annoy the King of Spain'. Gilbert proposed distressing Spanish fishing in Newfoundland and shipping in the Caribbean by establishing a military base of operations at a strategic location in North America. Although he requested a charter of colonisation from the Queen, it is clear that Gilbert initially had little interest in planting a permanent colony. As intellectuals were warning at the time, true efforts at establishing colonies would be an expensive and unprofitable undertaking, and Gilbert was no philanthropic idealist. Instead, the charter of colonisation was to be a legitimising 'cloak' under which he could get his ships across the Atlantic in the guise of a coloniser rather than a pirate. Supported by English statesmen such as the principal secretary Sir Francis Walsingham, the poet Thomas Churchyard and John Dee, Gilbert received his colonial charter in June 1578.

This was an important charter, providing a blueprint for patents into the eighteenth century. Gilbert was authorised to 'discover searche finde out and viewe such remote heathen and barbarous landes countries and territories not actually possessed of any Christian prince'.[8] As had her grandfather before her, or perhaps even more so because she now headed a new church, the Queen was assuming the same or greater imperial status held by the Pope to bestow non-Christian lands, which Europeans generally believed existed outside of a state of sovereignty and were free for conquest. The fact that these lands were to be unpossessed by Christians implies that Gilbert was explicitly denied the right to distress Spanish territories. Intriguingly, given Gilbert's surreptitious purpose, the Queen also instructed him not to 'robbe or spoile by sea or by land or doe any acte of unjust and unlawfull hostilitie' to 'the subjectes of any . . . state being then in perfecte leage and amytie with us'. If such was done, Gilbert would be forced to 'make full restitution and satisfaction of all such injuries' or suffer dire consequences.[9] Thus, although the Queen knew perfectly well what Gilbert's intentions were, she officially disavowed any piratical activities committed against friendly nations, which at present still included Spain. Consistent with her official replies to the Portuguese and Spanish ambassadors, the Queen took measures to ensure that Gilbert maintain clear rights of sovereignty and possession of the territory. He was instructed to 'inhabite or remayne there to build and fortefie' and to 'encounter expulse repelle and resiste . . . all and every such person and persones' who 'shall attempte to inhabite within the said countries'.[10] This would help to ensure that English rights to the territory were not merely based on discovery but were also supported by physical possession and permanent English presence.

Without Crown financial or naval support – caused by a combination of royal disavowal and the recent sting of Frobisher's failures – Gilbert had difficulty raising funds for the voyage. He was eventually induced to grant substantial parcels of land in North America to Catholics headed by George Peckham and Thomas Gerard, who wished to escape England's harsh recusancy laws. Additional land was assigned to Dee and Philip Sidney, perhaps as rewards for appeals to the Queen on Gilbert's behalf or the result of financial assistance. Further funding came from a group of Southampton merchants, so that the enterprise took on a joint-stock dimension. In addition to funding, Gilbert also sought advice about where he should plant a colony. The lawyer and exploration enthusiast, the elder Richard Hakluyt, advised Gilbert to establish a secure, fortified 'seat' in a 'temperate climate' (presumably in the region of South Carolina), while the Bristol merchant Anthony Parkhurst recommended Newfoundland, perhaps because the prevailing winds and currents required Spanish fleets to pass close by on their return to Europe. Dee prepared a world map from a polar perspective for Gilbert in 1580, which showed a large river, beginning at the region of the Saint Lawrence, bisecting North America and egressing at the Pacific, which might have encouraged Gilbert – still an enthusiast of the north-west passage – to take Newfoundland colonisation more seriously. The younger Richard Hakluyt, cousin to the lawyer, also promoted Gilbert's attempt in a collection of documents entitled *Divers Voyages Concerning the Discovery of America* (1582; Figure 37.3).

In the course of the five intervening years, therefore, Gilbert's plans had matured. Steering away from his initial piratical intentions, his new scheme involved claiming a parcel of North America for the Queen and granting landed estates to his major investors. Thus, his intentions had essentially transmuted into conformity with the charter's language. This was, in part, because de Mendoza in England had long since informed Spanish authorities of Gilbert's plans, both removing the element of surprise and, because of the outcome of the Mendoza–Drake affair,

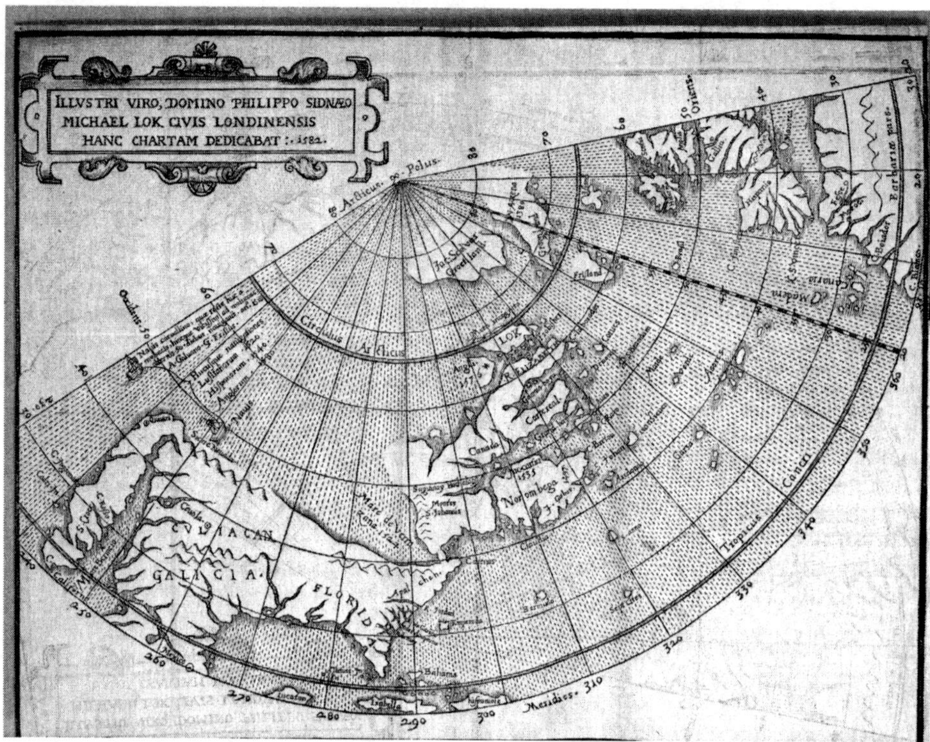

Figure 37.3 Michael Lok, from Richard Hakluyt, *Divers Voyages*, 1582. Reproduced with permission of the Huntingdon Library, California.

inducing the Spanish to improve the size and firepower of their Caribbean fleet. On 11 June 1583, five years to the day after he was issued his charter and precisely one year before it was due to expire, Gilbert finally left Plymouth. His fleet landed at Saint John's harbour on 5 August, where Gilbert, in the words of first-hand observer Edward Hayes:

> summoned the merchants, and masters, both English and strangers [European] to be present at his taking possession of those countries. Before whom openly was read and interpreted [translated] unto the strangers his Commission [charter] by virtue whereof he took possession of the same harbour of St. John's and 200 leagues every way, invested the Queen's majesty with the title and dignity thereof . . . and signified unto all men that from that time forward they should take the same land as a territory appertaining to the Queen of England, and himself authorised under her majesty to possess and enjoy it, and to ordain laws for the government thereof. . . . And afterward were erected not far from that place [in emulation of Drake's ceremony in Nova Albion] the arms of England engraven in lead.[11]

At least nominally, an English colony was thereby planted in North America. Gilbert's ceremonial act of possession would be used subsequently in diplomatic disputes to establish England legal rights to part of North America against the competing claims of France and Spain in the early seventeenth century.

Within two weeks of Gilbert's arrival sickness, apathy, desertion and the wreck of the flagship, *Delight,* in which eighty men drowned, reduced the fleet to two small ships. Under duress and coercion, Gilbert agreed by September to return to England, his colony never having been established. As reported by Hayes, Gilbert remained optimistic, intending to renew his charter and assemble another voyage, to be funded, he believed, by a £10,000 grant from the Queen. But on the return voyage, Gilbert met the harsh storms of the North Atlantic in the region of the Azores and, refusing to transfer to the larger bark from a small frigate, perished at sea. As legend has it, Gilbert went down clutching a copy of Thomas More's *Utopia* (1516), a humanist invention of the ideal commonwealth situated on a colonised newfound island. Gilbert's plans for colonisation were soon taken up by Peckham, who wrote *True Report of the Late Discoveries* (1583). In an effort to claim the millions of acres he was granted by Gilbert, Peckham praised Gilbert's scheme and reiterated the legal justifications already articulated by Dee and others for continuing with the English colonisation of the New World. These pleas amounted to nothing when soon afterwards Peckham was imprisoned for his recusancy.

The final major thrust toward North America in the Elizabethan age were the Roanoke voyages conducted under the patronage of Walter Ralegh, Gilbert's half-brother. As the inheritor of Gilbert's charter, Ralegh sought and received its renewal mere months before its expiry. The only modification in the charter was that Ralegh could not plant in Newfoundland, either because there were legal concerns over Gilbert's singular act of possession over a fishery that had been open to foreigners for nearly a century, because it was perceived that a more southerly plantation would better be able to distress Spanish shipping, or because such a colony would be safer from attack. Thus, Ralegh dispatched two men, Philip Amadas and Arthur Barlowe, on a reconnaissance mission to seek out a viable location in the American south, one far enough north to Spanish-occupied Florida. They ended up in the North Carolina Outer Banks, where they surveyed the landscape (including Roanoke Island) and made contact with the Carolina Algonquian natives. The only account of their voyage is that of Barlowe, which was carefully edited for publication by Ralegh to induce investment. This sanitised account said that the land could yield commodities consistent with a Mediterranean climate – including olives, grapes and sugar – which would thereby relieve England of its reliance on Spanish and French goods (oil and wine). The Outer Banks provided natural defensive capabilities that would protect the colonists while repelling foreigners. The native peoples, 'gentle, loving, and faithful, void of all guile and treason', were living in an innocent state of grace in an Edenic world that yielded its fruits without bodily labour.

Further inducement to settle in the region of 'Virginia' (the name authorised by Elizabeth for the new land) came from the younger Richard Hakluyt in a treatise now known as the 'Discourse of Western Planting' (1584). This treatise was commissioned by Ralegh in an effort to gain state funding for his enterprise. In twenty-one chapters, Hakluyt developed a comprehensive protocol for colonisation, beginning with the conversion of natives. Hakluyt, an Anglican priest, argued that it was a fundamental requirement of Christians to spread the gospel to 'idolaters', while Elizabeth, head of a new church, needed to challenge the perceived exclusive right of Catholics to undertake conversion. Hakluyt next expressed concerns about the 'beggarly' and 'dangerous' state of English trade in Africa, Europe and Asia, arguing that trade in the 'Mediterranean' climate of North America would yield the same commodities in a safer environment. He explained, as had Dee before him, that commodities could also bring money into the royal coffers by being subject to customs duties, which would help to enrich the nation and better maintain the royal navy. In addition, by the planting of a colony, the north-west passage to China 'may easely quickly and perfectly be searched oute'.[12] Several chapters were also devoted to concerns over Spanish power in the Indies. Establishing a successful colony would allow the English to distress Spanish trade, thereby making the King of Spain 'equal to the Princes his neighbours' in wealth and, thus, much less powerful. To prove England's right to settle, Hakluyt explained Elizabeth's historical rights over the North Atlantic and North America north of Florida. But the 'spedie planting' of North America 'by strong order of fortification' was necessary to prevent other European nations from establishing their own dominion. In the final chapter, Hakluyt listed everything necessary for the planting of a colony, including samples of flora and fauna, artisans, craftsmen, and 'men experte in the arte of fortification'.[13] Although articulated in a dynamic and compelling manner, few of Hakluyt's ideas were novel, and most had been argued earlier by Dee. Nonetheless, the treatise served its central purpose to a limited extent. The Queen knighted Ralegh, made a royal ship available, authorised him to impress men from port towns, released the soldier Ralph Lane from service in Ireland to head Ralegh's colony and encouraged powerful men such as Walsingham and Lord High Admiral Charles Howard to invest. However, these were not major concessions, and Ralegh, like Gilbert, had to amass considerable private funds.

The first voyage departed in April 1585 with seven ships and 600 men. The enterprise was under the command not of Ralegh, whose departure from England the Queen forbade and who never actually ventured to North America, but of his cousin, Richard Grenville, and his military expert Ralph Lane. Crossing the Atlantic in the direction of the West Indies, the royal *Tiger* was separated from the fleet and arrived in Puerto Rico, where Grenville replenished supplies and raided Spanish settlements before continuing to the Outer Banks and rejoining the fleet. Unfortunately, negotiating the Banks proved more difficult than expected, resulting in damage to the *Tiger* and the loss of stores. The plan to settle 600 men was quickly scuttled. Instead, Lane was to remain with just over 100 men and live off the land while Grenville returned to England in the *Tiger,* with the rest of the would-be colonisers, to resupply and return. Meanwhile, Lane supervised the building of a modest fort on Roanoke Island and set about exploring the region, discovering Chesapeake Bay, the future site of the Jamestown colony. Famine quickly became a critical issue. The optimism of Barlowe that the land would yield fruits without labour proved incorrect, and the colonists had arrived too late to sow crops. The natives also proved less gentle than Barlowe suggested and began organising an assault on the colony. Forewarned, Lane launched a pre-emptive strike with the result that the Algonquian chief Wingina was killed and the natives became increasingly hostile. Thus, when Drake showed up after his Caribbean campaign in 1586, Lane and his starving and fearful colonists gratefully accepted a lift to England.

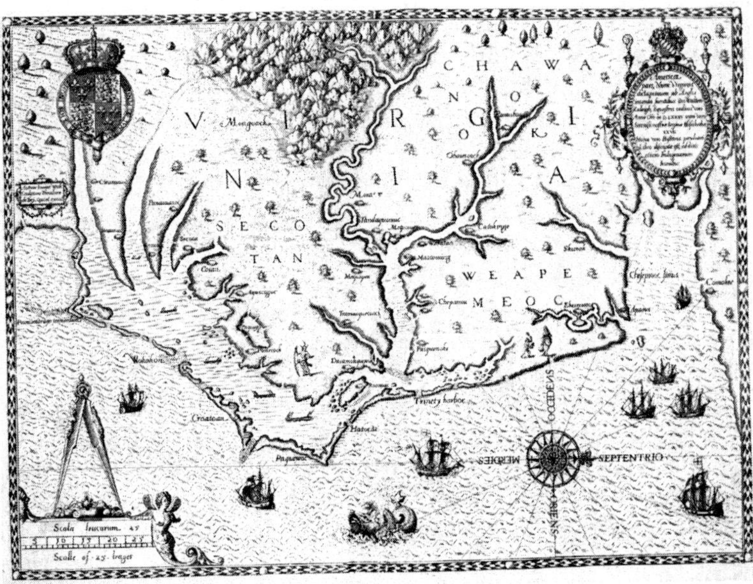

Figure 37.4 Theodore de Bry, from Thomas Hariot, *A Briefe and True Reporte* (1590). Reproduced with permission of the Huntingdon Library, California.

Ironically, the evacuation occurred mere weeks before Grenville returned with supplies. Finding Roanoke desolate, he made the peculiar decision to leave fifteen men behind with about a year's provisions, unaware that Chesapeake Bay had already been selected as a more appropriate site for any future colony. He was also unaware of the native enmity, ultimately leaving the fate of those left behind to the Algonquians. The most valuable fruits of this failed enterprise were the observations and images produced by Thomas Hariot and John White, respectively a scientist and artist, whose efforts were combined in *A Brief and True Report of the New Found Land of Virginia* (1588) and Theodore de Bry's *America* (1590; see Figure 37.4). Although these extremely popular treatises shared more in common with Barlowe's optimistic account than the more realistic view of Lane's returning colonists, they provided the best overall representation of American natives to exist for another half century. White was subsequently chosen to lead another colonising expedition, which departed in May 1587. Stopping to retrieve Grenville's now-lost refugees, White was caught up in a series of near-mutinies and was forced to rebuild at Roanoke rather than proceeding to Chesapeake Bay. By August he was on his way back to England to resupply, leaving behind 115 people, including his daughter and son-in-law and their daughter, Virginia Dare, the first English child born in America. He was never to see them again. By 1587, the Anglo-Spanish War, threatened for more than a decade, was in full operation, and the Queen, with the Armada on the horizon, ordered the stay of all English ships. By the time White could head up a recovery expedition in 1590, the rescuers found the colony abandoned, the word 'CROATOAN' written on a nearby tree. This indicated that the colonists had relocated to the nearby island of Croatoan, but weather prevented White from following up this clue. With the exception of a small expedition to New England by Charles Leigh in 1602, the Elizabethan North American experiment had come to an ignominious end.

As a result of the war with Spain, concluded by treaty only in 1604, English Atlantic activity for the remainder of the Elizabethan period principally involved licensed privateering in the Caribbean, in which many familiar personages – Drake, Frobisher, Grenville and Hawkins – were involved. The most significant exception to this privateering activity was Ralegh's voyage to South America, which departed in February 1595. Ralegh's motives were a mixture of a desire to raid Spanish settlements in Guiana, to gain the tribute of Caribbean natives against Spain in exchange for Elizabeth's protection and to find the mythical land of gold headed by El Dorado, from which Ralegh desired personal wealth and the Queen's favour. After landing in Trinidad, rousting a Spanish encampment and gaining native tribute on his way to the mainland, Ralegh travelled up the Orinoco river, collected some ore samples he believed to be gold-rich and returned to England. His *Discovery of the Large, Rich, and Beautiful Empire of Guiana* (1596) and an unprinted manuscript, 'Of the Voyage for Guiana', served as a record of his travels and a plea that Elizabeth provide him with the resources necessary to found a colony. Ralegh also took this opportunity to challenge the rapacious methods of Spanish conquistadors in America, instead advocating a gentle, virtuous and civil approach to imperial expansion that reflected a 'gentlemanly conquest'. Ralegh's ore sample turned out to be about as valuable as Frobisher's, and the Queen was unwilling to divert English resources to Guiana during a time of such heightened belligerency in the European theatre. Despondent but undeterred, Ralegh sent Lawrence Keymis on another Guiana voyage in 1596 and managed to keep English interest in the region alive well into the seventeenth century.

As the Elizabethan age reached its sunset, the East India Company would see its sunrise. Attempts at breaking into the Moluccan trade following Drake's visit there had been largely unsuccessful, excepting the voyage of Thomas Cavendish in 1586, which retraced Drake's route, and that of James Lancaster in 1591–4, during which most of the crew was lost. By end-century, however, English merchants who had profited from the Persia and Levant trade, recognising the declining power of Portugal in India and Indonesia, decided to pursue the trade more aggressively. They petitioned Elizabeth for a joint-stock charter, which was granted in 1600 and awarded the East India Company a monopoly of English trade to countries east of the Cape of Good Hope and west of Magellan Strait for fifteen years, excluding trade with countries actually possessed by another Christian prince. To command and navigate the first voyage, the Company hired, respectively, Lancaster and John Davis. To provide other forms of assistance, the younger Hakluyt was consulted. By this time, Hakluyt was renowned as the foremost expert in English travel after the 1589 publication, and 1598–1600 expanded republication, of his oft-printed collection *Principal Navigations, Traffiques, and Discoveries of the English Nation*.

By the time James Lancaster arrived back in England in September 1603, Elizabeth had been dead six months. No overseas empire had been established during her reign. On these grounds, it is tempting to dismiss Elizabethan exploration as a time of fruitless experimentation, only rarely punctuated by success. Yet this viewpoint misunderstands the educational value of these activities. Elizabeth and her explorers served the cause of expansion and empire well, in spite of the failure, errors and tragedy that surrounded many of these adventures, by teaching future colonisers and traders many essential lessons. Elizabethans realised that trade in East Europe and West Africa was fraught with difficulties, contributed to navigational knowledge that corrected contemporary maps, had found through trial and error parts of North America that were more likely to result in successful colonies and made several claims to sovereignty in the New World, all of which would facilitate early Stuart successes. Elizabeth's handling of diplomatic disputes as occasions arose, plus the writings of men such as Dee and Hakluyt, provided England with a sound legal, historical and intellectual foundation from which to establish permanent settlements. An enduring aspect of English overseas claims would be their preference for physical possession of territory, gaining the tribute of natives without aggressive conquest and the ability to hold land in defence of potential invasion, rather than mental claims to discovery and papal donation. By 1603, Elizabethans had taught their successors the importance of royal assistance and oversight, humanist and imperial rather than profit-driven motivations for colonisation, joint-stock companies that could provide capital and governance without impoverishing the State and establishing colonies that reflected the laws, customs and structure of England. All of these enduring characteristics of empire, though still needing refinement, would be strongly emphasised in the Stuart age.

FURTHER READING

Andrews, Kenneth R., *Elizabethan Privateering: English Privateering during the Spanish War, 1585–1603* (Cambridge, 1964).

—— *Trade, Plunder, and Settlement: Maritime Enterprise and the Genesis of the British Empire, 1480–1630* (Cambridge, 1984).

Andrews, K. R., Canny, N. P., and Hair, P. E. H. (eds.),*The Westward Enterprise: English Activities in Ireland, the Atlantic, and America, 1480–1650* (Liverpool, 1978).

Armitage, David, *The Ideological Origins of the British Empire* (Cambridge, 2000).

—— 'The Elizabethan Idea of Empire', *Transactions of the Royal Historical Society*, 14 (2004): 269–77.

Canny, Nicholas (ed.), *The Origins of Empire: British Overseas Enterprise to the Close of the Seventeenth Century* (Oxford, 1998).

Fitzmaurice, Andrew, *Humanism and America: An Intellectual History of English Colonisation, 1500–1625* (Cambridge and New York, 2003).

Kelsey, Harry, *Sir Francis Drake: The Queen's Pirate* (New Haven, Conn., 1998).

—— *Sir John Hawkins: Queen Elizabeth's Slave Trader* (New Haven, Conn., 2003).

Kuehn, Julia, and Smethurst, Paul (eds.), *Travel Writing, Form, and Empire: The Poetics and Politics of Mobility* (New York, 2009).

Kupperman, Karen Ordahl, *Indians and English: Facing Off in Early America* (Ithaca, NY, 2000).

—— *The Jamestown Project* (Cambridge, Mass., and London, 2007).

—— *Roanoke: The Abandoned Colony*, 2nd edn (Lanham, Md., 2007).

Macmillan, Ken, 'Discourse on History, Geography, and Law: John Dee and the Limits of the British Empire, 1576–80', *Canadian Journal of History*, 36 (1) (2001): 1–25.

—— *Sovereignty and Possession in the English New World: The Legal Foundations of Empire, 1576–1640* (Cambridge and New York, 2006).

McDermott, James, *Martin Frobisher: Elizabethan Privateer* (New Haven, Conn., 2001).

Mancall, Peter C. (ed.), *The Atlantic World and Virginia, 1550–1624* (Williamsburg, Va., 2007).

—— *Hakluyt's Promise: An Elizabethan's Obsession for an English America* (New Haven, Conn., 2007).

Quinn, David B. (ed.), *The Voyages and Colonising Enterprises of Sir Humphrey Gilbert*, 2 vols. (London, 1940).

—— (ed.) *The Roanoke Voyages, 1584–90*, 2 vols. (London, 1955).

—— *Explorers and Colonies: America, 1500–1625* (London, 1990).

NOTES

1 John Dee, *General and Rare Memorials Pertayning to the Perfect Arte of Navigation* (London, 1577), sig. Iiii.

2 'Letters Patent to John Cabot', in Henry Steele Commager and Milton Cantor (eds.), *Documents of American History* (Englewood Cliffs, NJ, 1988), vol. I, pp. 5–6; p. 5.

3 *CSP For., 1561*, ed. Joseph Stevenson (London, 1867), p. 54.

4 *CSP, For., 1562*, p. 95.

5 Quoted in Edward P. Cheyney, 'International Law under Queen Elizabeth', *English Historical Review*, 20 (79) (1905): 659–72; p. 660.

6 John Dee, 'Of Famous and Rich Discoveries', BL Cotton MS Vitellius, CVII, fols. 69v, 266v.

7 John Dee, *The Limits of the British Empire*, ed. Ken Macmillan with Jennifer Abeles (Westport, Conn., 2004), p. 91.

8 'Letters Patent to Sir Humphrey Gilbert', in David B. Quinn (ed.), *The Voyages and Colonising Enterprises of Sir Humphrey Gilbert*, 2 vols. (London, 1940), vol. I, pp. 188–94; p. 188.

9 'Letters Patent to Sir Humphrey Gilbert', p. 193.

10 'Letters Patent to Sir Humphrey Gilbert', pp. 189–90.

11 Richard Hakluyt, *Principal Navigations, Traffiques, and Discoveries of the English Nation* (London, 1589), p. 687.

12 Richard Hakluyt, 'Discourse of Western Planting, 1584', in *The Original Writings and Correspondence of the Two Richard Hakluyts*, ed. E. G. R. Taylor, 2 vols. (London, 1935), vol. II, pp. 211–326; p. 213.

13 Hakluyt, 'Discourse of Western Planting', vol. II, p. 322.

CHAPTER THIRTY-EIGHT

AWARENESS AND EXPERIENCES OF THE OUTSIDE WORLD

Matthew Dimmock

Where did the outside world begin for the inhabitants of Elizabethan England? At their doorsteps? At the limits of their towns or parishes? Many have argued for England's boundaries, others for the edges of Christendom, beyond which lay pagans, infidels and unknown marvels. For men and women of Elizabethan England, conceptions of the outside world were not stable but varied widely according to literacy, wealth and geographical location. There were extraordinarily well-travelled Elizabethans, whose beliefs, ambition or desire for wealth spread them across the known world. They were not the majority, however, whose insularity is well attested by contemporary sources. The Venetian Horatio Busino warned potential visitors to London that they should take care to 'avoid any strangeness of dress in the City'. The clerks and apprentices there were 'not well disposed to strangers, and were apt to ill-treat and rob them'. A tendency to look inward is further revealed in the common use of the term 'foreigner' for an unfamiliar Englishman – someone from another county – while an arrival from another country was a 'stranger' or 'alien'.[1]

For rural Elizabethans, the wider world was communicated through Bible and pulpit, through touring dramatic spectacles and proverbial folk and travellers' tales, creating a range of associations fuelled by fantasies of fabulous riches, danger and desire. This world was unconfined by the new technology of maps, which remained primarily the province of the wealthy, or by printed text and illustration, which were concentrated in urban centres. Consequently, the popular imagining of the inhabitants and geography of the wider world might be both visual and non-visual, based upon familiar biblical imagery, oral transmission and imaginary construction. The world beyond England's coasts was far more prominent for those Elizabethans involved in campaigning overseas, in trade, or living in ports and cities. These people ensured that this world never remained simply outside: as Ian Archer discusses, the further reaches of the globe were brought into the country and into the household in the form of commodities – carpets, porcelain, precious stones, fabrics, foodstuffs, spices – and this world also supplied vital markets for English goods. English men and women enthusiastically consumed and fervently desired goods with which the outside world was identified, and the products of their toil were, in turn, consumed elsewhere. Yet this world of opportunity could also be dangerous, threatening conquest, infection and the erasure of English identity. Despite such variation in attitudes, Elizabethan men and women recognised themselves to be Christians, and this meant some areas of the world were considerably more familiar than others. Since Henry VIII's break with Rome in 1534 (with the exception of England's brief return to the Roman Catholic fold under Mary I), Protestant England had established a close relationship with her co-religionists in the Netherlands, France and Germany – the origin of the overwhelming majority of immigrants into Elizabethan England, fleeing religious persecution.

Beyond this, however, centuries of English adherence to the universal Christian Church before the Reformation meant that certain crucial connections remained within a wider Christendom, and as a 'Christian prince' Elizabeth strove to maintain those connections. The basic contours of Christendom – its interconnections, its geography, history and peoples – were therefore widely known, with information concerning Christian kingdoms from Spain and Italy to Poland and Hungary, as well as detailed accounts of the Holy Land, available to English Protestants. But there was a world beyond Christendom, a world less easily defined, of different religions, ethnicities and cultures. It is this aspect of the 'Elizabethan world' with which this chapter is primarily concerned.

FROM THE PERIPHERY

In his 1585 text *The Valiant Acts and Victorious Battles of the English Nation,* Christopher Ocland described how, under their 'mayden' queen, 'Renowned England through the world, is bright blazed to be seen'.[2] Ocland was drawing upon a common formulation. 'It is not unknown to the world', wrote George Best in a 1578 account of Martin Frobisher's search for a north-west passage, 'that this our native country of England, in all ages hath bred up (and specially at this present aboundeth with) many forward and valiant minds, fit to take in hand any notable enterprise.'[3] England was the 'new Israel', inheritor of classical civilisation through Elizabeth, the legitimate ancestor of the Trojan Brutus. She was imagined as England's Queen of Sheba, to whom the world came to give tribute.

This was an elaborate fantasy. Elizabeth had indeed received emissaries and ambassadors from a range of Christian courts and from the Muslim powers of Morocco and the Ottoman Empire. Yet to most Christian monarchs – certainly after her excommunication by Pope Pius V in 1570 – she was a heretic queen heading a pariah state. Her association with Morocco and the Ottomans was a political and economic necessity generated out of England's increasing isolation in opposition to Catholic Spain and was vigorously denied by the Queen in response to chastisement by other Christian powers. Furthermore, in order to establish a trading relationship with the Ottomans (which began in 1580), Elizabeth had become tributary to Sultan Murad III, reflected in the constant demand for gifts from her ambassadors in Constantinople. Celebrating Protestant England's 'renown' throughout the world disguised a precarious position and forged a national myth.

The truth was quite different. England had historically occupied a position on the periphery 'of global systems dominated by Chinese, Indian, Persian, and Ottoman Empires'.[4] The Afro-Eurasian sphere into which English trade began to expand under Elizabeth was dominated by the conflict between Ottoman and Spanish forces, represented by many observers as apocalyptic in scale. The schism within Christendom following the initiation of Reformation in the early sixteenth century further isolated England – the religious orders and their houses dissolved by Henry VIII had linked the English into scholarly, financial and political networks that stretched across Christendom, and political and dynastic connections had been broken. England also had a long and prestigious history of pilgrimage and crusading, through which individual English Christians were devotionally connected to the rest of the Christian world and to Jerusalem. That had largely ended. Yet this peripheral status had its advantages: England found itself at the centre of a Protestant world, and the severing of allegiance to the papacy, as well as the rivalry with Spain, opened up new mercantile opportunities and contributed to the creation of a specifically English and Protestant national and imperial identity. The Anglo-Ottoman capitulations of 1580, English colonial efforts at Roanoke in the New World and the victory over the crusading Spanish Armada in 1588 (noted with approval in the Muslim courts of Rabat and Constantinople) were crucial stages in this process.

Textually, England was also on the periphery of things. While English print culture had developed considerably since William Caxton's first presses, notions of the world beyond Christendom were informed primarily by texts translated from French, Italian, Spanish and Latin. By the beginning of Elizabeth's reign in 1558, few English men or women had travelled beyond Christian realms, and still fewer had recorded their travels in print. Those that did included tales of pilgrimage and crusade, and the two combined in the famous *Travels* of Sir John Mandeville, perhaps the most popular secular text in circulation in the fifteenth and sixteenth centuries, first printed in English in 1496 and reprinted numerous times. Such texts coexisted with – and were informed by – a rich romance tradition, supplemented by translations of Italian *novelle,* which regularly featured crusading, exotica, distant realms, chivalric Muslim opponents and their desirable daughters.

Yet these belonged to a pre-Reformation pan-Christian culture. During Elizabeth's reign, growing numbers of English travellers published accounts of their experiences specifically for a Protestant English audience, including narratives of mercantile exploration, cartography and cosmography, colonial endeavour, captivity and diplomacy, often with a startling amount of detail. Richard Hakluyt collected both pre-Elizabethan voyages and contemporary sources to textually create an outward-looking, imperial England in his monumental *Principal Navigations, Voyages, Traffiques and Discoveries of the English Nation* of 1589. But in these texts and the culture in which they circulated there is no clearly defined notion of the world beyond Christendom – it was simultaneously observable and imaginary, a place of monsters, myths, riches, deviance and danger. It was also a protean place where the English became alien and English identity could be lost. Above all it was a place in which the English were commercially, religiously, scientifically and politically interested.

WORLDVIEWS

So how did Elizabethans imagine this wider world? Again, this depended upon wealth, location and status. The mapping of the world in medieval England was regularly based upon a TO map scheme, in which the three continents of the known world – Europe, Africa and Asia – were divided by the Mediterranean and the Nile (making a T shape) and circled by ocean. Asia was conventionally twice the size of both Europe and Africa and was placed in the upper portion of such maps – east, often signalled by the Garden of Eden, was at the top, with England on the western periphery, towards the bottom left. Jerusalem, the Holy City, occupied the very centre. Such maps could attain a remarkable level of sophistication and are based upon a conceptual and symbolic sense of the world with religion a governing cartographic principle.

While these maps were not widely seen, the worldview they embody is a profoundly important one and remained valid well into the Elizabethan period and beyond, long after the rediscovery of Ptolemy's *Geographia* (first printed in 1475), coexisting with and influencing new cartographies and popular conceptions of the wider world. Even those maps based firmly upon new cartographic principles retained a symbolic dimension and were used for symbolic purposes: this was especially true of the globe, incorporated by Elizabeth I into her own iconography (see the 'Armada Portrait' of 1588), but also of those maps brought onstage in plays such as *1 Henry IV* and *Tamburlaine Part II*. The latter's reference to 'those blind geographers / That make a triple region in the world' (*Tamburlaine Part I*, Act IV, Scene 4, ll. 78–9) might suggest that the triple division (Europe, Africa and Asia) that characterised the TO map had been rendered obsolete, yet their clear religious symbolism, which stemmed directly from the biblical narrative, was crucial even for later explorers and geographers. The three continents represented on such maps were often labelled after the three sons of Noah, who were considered to be the progenitors of the entire human race after the Flood. Asia was the inheritance of the descendants of Shem, Europe the descendants of Japheth and Africa the descendants of Cham. This became the basis for a range of ethno-religious theories current in Elizabethan England. Elaborate religious genealogies were established to explain the interrelation of the peoples and religions of the known world: Muslims, for instance, were widely thought to have been descended directly from Ishmael and Christians from Isaac, the two sons of Abraham. Complex hypotheses were also propounded to explain the existence of peoples in the New World, with the migration of the descendants of one brother or another important arguments for or against Christian European possession.

Religious genealogies also had a part to play in understanding ethno-religious differences. George Best gave lengthy consideration to the issue of skin colour, observing that since he had seen 'an Ethiopian as black as coal brought into England, who taking a fair English woman to Wife, begot a Son in all respects as black as the Father' then 'this blackness proceedeth rather of some natural infection' rather than climate darkening the skin (another popular theory). He then turned to Noah, remembering that after the Flood 'all the land that until this day hath been inhabited by sundry descents, must needs come of the offspring either of Shem, Cham, or Japheth.' Yet all three and their wives were white and thus can only 'have begotten and brought forth white children'. Blackness, argued Best, thus came into the world through the covetous sin of Cham (the progenitor of all Africans). While in the Ark, Noah had forbidden his sons from 'carnal copulation'. Expecting that the first-born child after the flood would inherit the earth, Cham had sex with his wife, and for this sin against his brothers, father and God, Cham was punished. The resulting child, Chus, was made 'so black and loathsome, that it might remain a spectacle of disobedience to all the world'. Thus you see, argued Best, 'the cause of the Ethiopians' blackness, is the curse and infection of blood, and not the distemperance of climate.'[5]

Best's theories were not considered outlandish. He had accompanied Martin Frobisher on two of his northward voyages, first as lieutenant, then as captain. His detailed account (later reproduced in Hakluyt's collection) reveals him to have been a skilled and intelligent observer, at the forefront of Elizabethan navigational, meteorological and cartographical developments. Rather than unusual, the intermingling of religion, science and geography in the man and his ideas was typical. Best was also, as his account abundantly reveals, interested in cosmography. He writes that well before travelling north with Frobisher he took great care to study 'the science of cosmography & the secrets of Navigation'.[6]

Popular and influential throughout Renaissance Europe, cosmography is the science of mapping the general features of the universe through description and often illustration. One early English example that utilised the format of the cosmography, while injecting it with humour and anecdote, is the physician and traveller Andrew Boorde's *The Fyrst Boke of the Introduction of Knowledge,* written in 1542 (and probably reprinted around 1550 and 1562). Rather than attempting to cover the whole world, Boorde's text extends from England through various Christian regions including France, Catalonia and Spain, with its final four entries – Barbary, Turkey, Egypt and 'Jury' (the land of the Jews) – in different ways beyond the bounds of Christendom. In his *Fyrst Boke* Boorde primarily organises his text according to peoples rather than carefully defined geographical units – he is interested in what defines an Englishman, since this, in turn, defines England. In attempting to map the world on cosmographical lines, Boorde, Sebastian Münster and others did so by establishing human typologies – a set of 'innate' characteristics, constituted and confirmed by religion, language, costume and habits (and, to some extent, geography). Illustration further aided definition and recognition. It was the unique combination of these factors that defined peoples, in the case of the 'Turk' just as with the Scot, and established an influential paradigm through which to understand the newly discovered peoples of the 'New World'.

Boorde's depiction of the 'Turk' is a useful example of the ways in which peoples beyond Christendom were repeatedly defined. It begins in verse:

> I am a turk and mahomet's law do keep
> I do prowl for my prey when others be asleep
> My law willeth me no swine's flesh to eat
> It shall not greatly force for I have other meat
> In using my raiment I am not variable
> For of promise I am not mutable.[7]

Immediately the 'Turk' is defined as a non-Christian – he is an adherent of 'Mahomet's' (Muhammad's) law. Similarly, in the section concerning Barbary, Boorde describes how there are 'white mores and black mores, they be Infidels and unchristened', and when concerned with Jews he writes, 'some call me a Jew / To

Jesu Christ I was never true.'[8] These other faiths are defined primarily through their *divergence* from Christianity. Boorde's own willingness to amplify the alien nature of such figures leads him to incorporate legends and polemic, hence his assertion that, like the Muslim bugbear of the popular imagination, this 'Turk' prowls through the night looking for his prey. Similarly, Boorde's Jew is represented as a lazy 'dawe' or simpleton. Noting that Islam forbids the eating of 'swine's flesh' and that the 'Turk' has a recognisable and set costume ('raiment'), Boorde then turns to another widespread notion of the 'Turk' that is less derogatory: that they keep their word ('of promise I am not mutable'). Following this opening verse, which combines the mythical with the apparently factual in a typical Christian formulation, Boorde further follows convention and turns again to Islam. He writes,

> The Turkes hath a law called Mahomet's law. And the book that their law is written in is called the Alkaron. Mahomet a false fellow made it, he seduced the people under this manner, he did bring up a dove and would put 2 or 3 peasen [peas] in his eare, and she would every day come to his ear and eat the peasen, and then the people would think the holy ghost, or an Angel did come and teach him what the people should do.[9]

As so often in such accounts, the figure of 'Mahomet' is highly prominent, signalling his presumed position as an (in)version of Christ (in some cases an antichrist), with the Qur'ān a heretical bible. Also crucial is the pronounced emphasis on the falsity of Islam – not only is the Prophet a 'false fellow', but this apparent miracle is revealed to be an elaborately staged stunt designed to seduce the people. This Christian mythology of Muhammad, widely circulated in Elizabethan England, is another example of writers looking back to earlier models to explain the wider world. It was created and elaborated over many years but was largely complete by the early fourteenth century, and the portrait of Muhammad in the popular *Travels* of Sir John Mandeville, or in Ranulph Higden's influential *Polychronicon,* was based upon anti-Muslim material that was already 200 or 300 years old in the fifteenth century. Although the study of Hebrew and Judaism was central to sixteenth-century biblical scholarship and the Reformation, popular conceptions of Judaism in Elizabethan England similarly owed a great deal to medieval polemic.

Having personally encountered the peoples he describes, Boorde's reliance on medieval stereotype might seem surprising, were it not typical of early modern travel texts. Like Best, Boorde was a product of his age, and in his travels seems to have sought to confirm what he had already learnt about these peoples from acknowledged authorities. Yet accounts such as these were not simply polemical, they were also commercially orientated, and Boorde reveals a keen eye for mercantile detail. Not only does he discuss the currency of each location he covers – the 'money the which is in Turkey is Gold and Silver and Brass' – but also the rudiments of language (particularly counting) and potential trading goods. The combination of a contemporary cosmographical template, underpinned by a medieval system of categorisation, with an obsessive interest in commercial possibilities, all qualified by an English Protestant sensibility, formed the dominant approach to both new and old worlds by Elizabethan writers. This conceptual apparatus was equally applicable to those concerned with describing the world as a whole and those who brought the descriptive empiricism of cosmography to bear on specific locations.

Both Walter Ralegh in his *Disoverie of the Large, Rich and Beautiful Empire of Guiana* (1595) and Thomas Hariot in his *A Brief and True Report of the New Found Land of Virginia* (1588) utilise this formula. Although describing different locations, each writer is keen to emphasise the value of these 'new world' territories to an English audience, focusing primarily upon 'marchantable commodities' (the title of Hariot's opening chapter) and upon mineral and vegetable resources in particular. Between them, these two authors also give a sense of the strategies available for the representation of natives. Hariot considers the Algonquians that he encounters to be 'simple' pagan idolaters. They believe 'that there are many Gods' and they 'think that all the gods are of human shape, & therefore they represent them by images in the forms of men, which they call *Kawasowok*'.[10] For Hariot this is an advantage: not only are the natives apparently pliant, but their belief in any religion at all is important, since 'although it be far from the truth, yet being as it is, there is hope that it may be the easier and sooner reformed.' The English have a duty to bring such peoples to 'civility' through the 'embracing of true religion'.[11]

Alternatively, Ralegh's conception of Guiana is of an empty, Edenic land that 'hath yet her maidenhead', that is waiting for English mastery.[12] Natives, when referenced, often fit the category of cannibal, a term that features prominently in Elizabethan imaginings of the wider world to the south, east and west – although interestingly Ralegh and his companions are themselves mistaken for cannibals by one group of Arwacas. It was a relatively recent coinage, probably originating in Columbus's adaptation of New World terms such as 'carib' (Shakespeare's Caliban is a further derivation). But it also corresponds to the well-known classical figure of the anthropophagus, the eater of human flesh described by Herodotus. While 'cannibal' was initially designated solely for those who were thought to eat their fellow humans, it quickly became a term used to signal any fearsome native or 'savage' (although it always retains associations with flesh-eating) and could be used to justify Christian European appropriation and colonisation. The opposition of native savagery and barbarism to Christian civility (particularly of an English Protestant kind) again draws upon a classical division and was widespread enough to be questioned by some, most prominently Michel de Montaigne in his celebrated essay 'On Cannibals'.

Strategies for understanding and representing the inhabitants of both 'new' and 'old' worlds were essentially similar, with travellers and writers both drawing upon received knowledge and already established models to explain the religion, behaviour, customs and appearance of these people. Some writers turned to myth, arguing that 'there are some that thinke' that this 'new worlde' was 'described long since by *Plato*, vnder the name and Title of *Atlantica*' or had been predicted by '*Seneca*' in 'a Poeticall spirite of Prophesie'.[13] What was strange became more familiar and encounters (at least textual encounters) were conducted on Christian European terms. Texts such as those produced by Ralegh and Hariot also contained vivid illustrations that were intended to validate the truth of the descriptions, and artists were often key participants in voyages of 'discovery'. Perhaps most famous was John White, prominent in the establishment of the English colony at Roanoke in 1587, who produced iconic images of the Algonquians (and flora and fauna) for Hariot's text. Yet just as Hariot's eyewitness account had an agenda – he sought to persuade colonists to settle in Virginia – White's images were subtly altered for publication: the natives in particular were 'Europeanised' for Christian consumption. Furthermore, while they began as studies of a specific people, White's images quickly became stock images of all New World natives, an ethnographic type to be placed alongside the other peoples of the known world.[14]

As the outside world was being organised and reorganised according to theories of climatological or ethno-religious difference, the position the English self-consciously occupied within it is revealing. As Boorde explains:

> I am an Englishman, and naked I stand here
> Musing in my mind, what raiment I shall wear
> Now I will wear I cannot tell what
> All new fashions, be pleasant to me.[15]

Accompanying these verses is an image of a bearded man in nothing but a loincloth and a hat, carrying a roll of fabric over one arm and holding a large pair of scissors in the other – the tools of a tailor. Unlike the 'Turk', whom Boorde describes as 'not mutable' in his dress, the Englishman is variable, a slave to fashions and consequently lacking in any firm character of his own. This notion was tremendously influential since, as Mary Floyd-Wilson has recognised, '[t]hroughout the sixteenth and seventeenth centuries, English writers come back again and again to Boorde's portrait' and this 'English' image would appear in costume books, representing all the 'nations' of the world, which circulated throughout Europe in this period.[16] Indeed, in an interesting twist it came to represent Europe as a whole on the title page of Hans Wiegel's *Habitus praecipuorum* (1577), indicating the degree to which all of Europe was bewitched by goods, costumes and stories from the world beyond its bounds.[17]

In the English case, many argued that this 'inconstancie' was the consequence of a changeable climate, while others asserted that it was interaction with other cultures that itself robbed a nation of its identity. This was not simply polemic – William Harrison, in his 1587 *Description of England,* lambasted the 'fantastical folly of our nation, even from the courtier to the carter'. He can think of no better way to 'inveigh against this enormity' than to describe English attire:

> such is our mutability that today there is none to the Spanish guise, tomorrow the French toys are most fine and delectable, ere long no such apparel as that which is after the High Almain [German] fashion, by and by the Turkish manner is generally best thought of, otherwise the Morisco [Moorish] gowns, the Barbarian sleeves . . . make such a comely vesture that, except it were a dog in a doublet, you shall not see any so disguised as are my countrymen of England.[18]

Luxuriating in goods brought from overseas, unnaturally disguising themselves in the national costumes of others, Harrison's countrymen foolishly ape the outside world to the point that they are defined simply by their capacity to do so. This is the world of the cosmographers, a place of fixed costumes, nations and identities – the Spanish, the French, the High Almain, the Turkish, the Morisco – and English readers are lambasted for self-indulgently drowning in a world of goods. In this way, moralists like Harrison recognised that the outside world threatened to transform, if not overwhelm, the hitherto stable world of home.

A WORLD OF GOODS

Not everyone subscribed to William Harrison's vision of a national identity eroded into 'inconstancie' by a predilection for alien fripperies. Despite this apparent love of all things new and strange, Englishmen erupted with violence towards strangers (under Elizabeth alone attacks upon immigrants are recorded in 1573, 1575, 1581, 1583, 1586, 1587, 1593 and 1595). Their primary grievances were not about specific goods but rather about 'alien' mercantile communities taking jobs, driving up rents, undercutting native businesses and generally driving the English into penury. The allegiance of such merchants – even those with denizen status – was considered intrinsically suspect, hence they were often polemically characterised as Jews.

There were thus clear fault lines in England's relationship with the outside world, and, although late-sixteenth-century England was exposed to 'exotic' goods of a range and in quantities never seen before, there were those in print and on the public stage that portrayed this influx as trash traded for true English wares of superior value. Robert Wilson's play *Three Ladies of London* (*c.* 1581) features a despicable alien merchant named Mercadorus who sells English goods 'beyond the sea' including wheat, peas, barley, oats, leather, tallow, beef and bacon. In return he brings nothing but 'trifles' and 'trinkets' for the 'Gentlewoman of England', goods such as 'coloured bones, glass, beads . . . Amber, Jet, Coral, Christall and every such bauble'. Strangers outside the realm 'laugh' at the English, who are being blatantly fooled.[19] There was clearly a great deal of popular anxiety about the outside world infiltrating and overwhelming England. Yet such virulent opposition in some quarters to the trade in 'trifles' should not obscure the fact that simultaneously wealthy English men and women were increasingly having their portraits painted littered with luxury goods that advertised their taste, wealth, contacts and power.

The influx of goods from beyond the bounds of Christendom did not begin in Elizabeth's reign. Spices and silks, as well as luxury goods, had reached the British Isles from the East through trade routes established for centuries, although they were rare and expensive. Returning crusaders and pilgrims brought such goods with them directly from the Holy Land, and monarchs would receive them through the exchange of embassies and the elaborate giving of gifts that accompanied them. English merchants plied their trade predominantly across northern European coasts before 1500, with only intermittent voyages recorded to North Africa and the east ern Mediterranean. There was undoubtedly a considerable desire for such goods in England, and fantasies of Asia as a place of infinite riches and magic indicate the potency of such associations. Marlowe's Barabas, from *The Jew of Malta* (1590), is a classic mercantile intermediary and opens the play with a vision of the overwhelming Eastern wealth he commands: his 'argosy' loaded with 'spice and silks', his 'Bags of fiery opals, sapphires, amethysts, / Jacinths, hard topaz, green-grass emeralds, / Beauteous rubies, sparkling diamonds, / And seld-seen costly stones' (Act I, Scene 1, ll. 25–8). Alternatively, casual references to luxury items such as 'Turkey cushions bossed with pearl' (*The Taming of the Shrew,* Act II, Scene 1, l. 345) and 'Turkish tapestry' (*The Comedy of Errors,* Act IV, Scene 1, l. 104) indicate the familiar and domestic nature of goods from the outside world. But here, as with much textual material, English men and women experienced the outside world at a remove: spices from the Moluccas, for instance, travelled the Silk Routes, through the Ottoman Empire and then often through Venice before their dissemination in the north. Many hands meant prohibitive expense, and Elizabeth's reign saw repeated efforts by Englishmen to establish a north-east and north-west passage by sea or by land to make direct contact with Asian markets.

Trade was also changing English tastes. The Portuguese establishment of a sea route around Africa to India and the Spice Islands brought a considerable increase in the one central element of this eastbound trade: pepper. Consumption of pepper increased significantly in northern Europe in the late sixteenth century as prices fell. The importation of sugar, both from Asia and North Africa (it would later be transplanted to the Americas) followed a similar pattern. For many in England, either pepper or sugar would have been a first taste of the world beyond Christendom. Other sought-after goods were similar: nutmeg, cloves, mace, indigo, ginger and cinnamon, but also soda ash for soap and medicinal gums and drugs. Tea and coffee would, from the mid-seventeenth century, prove phenomenally popular (and the latter would, like sugar, be colonially transplanted to the Americas). The fears voiced by Boorde, Harrison and others about English 'inconstancie' in donning the fashions of other nations was about more than just clothes. Many feared that the popularity of exotic foodstuffs and trinkets would have the same effect – and this was exemplified in the popularity of the 'alien herb', tobacco, an import from the Americas prominent in the westward trade of the seventeenth century.

English attempts to tap directly into these distant trade routes had some success and were galvanised by the establishment of joint-stock trading companies – the Muscovy Company in 1555, the Levant Company in 1581, the Barbary Company in 1585, the Virginia Company in 1606 and the organisation that would later dwarf them all, the East India Company, in 1600. Of these, it was the Levant Company that proved commercially and politically the more important during Elizabeth's reign. The commodities that reached England from beyond Christendom tended to arrive via well-known centres such as Venice, Lisbon and Antwerp, and three dominant empires – Spain and the Habsburgs, the Ottomans and the Portuguese – controlled European supply. One prominent consequence of the Reformation was the conspicuous isolation of Elizabethan England, particularly after the papal excommunication of Elizabeth in 1570, the Spanish sack of Antwerp in 1576 and the Spanish annexation of Portugal in 1580. Trade lay largely in the hands of Catholic adversaries. One avenue remained open, however, and, defying papal prohibitions to which they no longer owed allegiance, the English court sent an ambassador to the Ottoman 'Porte' in Constantinople in 1578. An experienced merchant, William Harborne agitated against the 'idolatrous' Spanish (opposed to the Ottomans) and in 1580 was granted a series of 'capitulations' which allowed the English trading privileges in Ottoman domains, much to the dismay of the Spanish.

This relationship was to be a fruitful one and would complicate oppositional notions of Islam and the 'Turk' that had hitherto dominated Christian culture. It was codified in a series of documents published by Hakluyt in his *Principal Navigations* along with an extensive correspondence between Elizabeth I and the Ottoman ruler Murad III. These letters strove to establish an identification between Protestantism and Islam on the basis of a shared abhorrence of idolatry. In her first letter, Elizabeth was styled as 'the most invincible and most mighty defender of the Christian faith against all kind of idolatries, of all that live amongst the Christians, and falsely profess the name of Christ'.[20] Not only would this relationship prompt a considerable increase in the flow of goods from England into the Mediterranean and from Ottoman domains directly to England, but it would provoke an avalanche of printed and dramatic texts describing the 'Turk' and Islam for an English audience.

SPECTACLES OF DIFFERENCE

Elizabethan England is often identified as a culture of ceremony and display. Just as power was established and maintained through the acting out of public ritual – royal and civic processions and pageants for instance – the outside world was defined and understood through spectacle. From medieval civic drama an elaborate system of signs had constructed and often exaggerated key characteristics that confirmed a character's difference and conversely affirmed a stable and 'natural' Christian identity. The 'type' of the Jew, the Saracen, or Turk, and the Moor (as discussed above) were perhaps the most striking, the Jew defined by a cloak of gabardine and distorted facial features; the Turk by a turban, a moustache, a scimitar and luxurious robes. The blackness of the 'sooty' Moor (particularly the 'blackamoor') was proverbial – to attempt to 'wash the Ethiop white' was to attempt the impossible – and carried a series of religious connotations, as in George Best's discussion of the curse of Cham. The Jew, Turk and Moor could also be variously interchangeable. In medieval drama, evil characters – such as King Herod – regularly reveal their devotion to 'Mahomet', as do numerous Jews.[21] Similarly, distinctions between the North African Moor and the Turk were never entirely clear and are blurred in a play such as George Peele's *Battle of Alcazar* (*c.* 1589). These three key 'old world' figures were further augmented by a galaxy of different alien 'types' – Tartars, Persians, Spaniards, Poles, Italians, Germans, French, Irish, Welsh, Scots – with whom 'Jewish', 'Turkish' or 'Moorish' characteristics might be associated.

These were costumes and tricks, however, and while they served their purpose on the English stage, their very theatricality seems to have provoked certain anxieties. If an actor can simply become a Turk or Jew – or indeed a king – by just taking on their external signs, then how might one identify a 'real' Turk or Jew? Such fears came to the fore in the trial of Roderigo Lopez, the 'Jewish' physician executed for attempting to poison the Queen. On a broader scale, at a time when infiltration by Catholics, visually no different from the English, was a constant fear, peoples of the outside world needed to be unequivocally and indelibly defined. 'True' blackness could not be washed away, and Catholic devotion to the mass and 'papist' ritual were grasped as markers of absolute difference. For Jews and Turks English writers and dramatists became obsessed with the permanent mark of faith represented by circumcision. English sailors returning from trading voyages to the Mediterranean were reportedly stripped and inspected to be sure they had not 'turned Turk' while away, as so many of their compatriots had done: circumcision offered a permanent marker of divergence from (and a rejection of) Christianity and thus was associated with villainy.

In Christopher Marlowe's *The Jew of Malta* Barabas spectacularly affirms this after purchasing a Turkish slave, Ithamore, at the Maltese slave market. After an enthusiastic litany of crimes, including the poisoning of wells, betrayal, usury and 'extorting, cozening, forfeiting, / And tricks belonging to the brokery' (Act II, Scene 3, ll. 192–3), and a corresponding response from Ithamore focusing upon violence against Christian pilgrims, Barabas joyously exclaims: 'Why this is something. Make account of me / As of thy fellow; we are villains both. / Both circumcisèd, we hate Christians both' (Act II, Scene 3, ll. 214–16). Circumcision is here an indication of solidarity in opposition to Christendom and an indelible mark upon the malevolent alien. Shakespeare exploits these associations to powerful effect in *Othello* (1603), a play set against the backdrop of Christian–Muslim conflict and which largely takes place on an island – Cyprus – claimed by both sides (it had been taken by the Ottomans in 1570). Having killed Desdemona and been discovered, in his final speech Othello enacts the collapse of his Moorish-Venetian identity:

> Set you down this;
> And say besides that in Aleppo once,
> Where a malignant and a turbaned Turk
> Beat a Venetian and traduced the state,
> I took by th'throat the circumcisèd dog
> And smote him – thus.
> *He stabs himself.*
> (Act V, Scene 2, ll. 350–5)

Here Othello recalls an episode in which he acted as a faithful servant of Venice – in Aleppo (a key trading centre within the Ottoman Empire) he caught and killed a Turk, 'malignant and Turbaned', who had beaten a Venetian and disparaged Venice. Yet Othello has himself now killed a Venetian and undermined Venice, so in this story identifies himself with the 'circumcisèd' Turk and stabs himself as he recalls killing that Turk. The two coalesce in one moment of brutal physicality. Othello cannot be both a faithful servant of Venice and simultaneously its enemy, nor, it seems, can he be both Venetian *and* Moor. His inability to permanently reconcile two apparently contradictory identities, epitomised in continual references to blackness, is the product of a conception of identity that valued purity and constancy above all things. This same conception informed English rioters against 'alien' communities in London – if the refugees were French, then their hearts would 'continue naturally French' and thus they could not be 'trustie to our Cuntrye'.[22]

There were, however, certain legitimate circumstances in which religious identity (with its inevitable ethnic and national associations) might be fundamentally changed. Conversion had been a significant part of Christian approaches to non-

Christian peoples for centuries and was enshrined in Christian narratives of revelation. In Protestant England, the inevitability of 'alien' conversion – whether from Catholicism, Judaism, Islam or paganism – was crucial to a sense of England's destiny and the status of the English as God's chosen people. This is clearly signalled in two conversion ceremonies that took place in London, recorded in John Foxe's *A Sermon Preached at the Christening of a Certaine Iew, at London* (1578) and Meredith Hanmer's *The Baptizing of a Turke* (1586). Between them, these texts rail against the 'blinde arrogancie of the Iewish Nation' and the blindness 'of all Infidels, *Iewes, Turkes,* and *Saracens*' while using the plight of these individual converts as proof positive that all their 'Nations' will inevitably convert to 'true' Christianity in the end.[23] As the use of the word 'true' suggests, these accounts are also used to lambast Catholicism, conspicuously rejected by both converts for its 'grosse monuments of manifest idolatrie, those fantasticall deuises and friuolous forgeries of signes and Images'.[24]

Whether these 'circumcisèd' converts found assimilation easy is unknown – they disappear from the historical record – but conversion to Christianity and consequent assimilation does exist on the stage and often depends upon gender. Both Barabas in *The Jew of Malta* and Shylock in *The Merchant of Venice* appear inassimilable – both in religion and trade they are defined, and define themselves, apart. Neither have wives, and both have young marriageable daughters, Abigail and Jessica, who prove irresistible to the Christian men they encounter. There are conspicuously no sons. While both Jews are positioned to pose questions about Christian assumptions and Christian justice, this arrangement of elderly father and young daughter is a formula for the ejection of Judaism through assimilation. Once outmanoeuvred, the Jew is either broken or dead and is in no position to father any further children. The daughters both convert, and although Abigail dies – a consequence of her earlier deceptions – Jessica is married to a Christian husband. The threat of the Jew that both plays dramatise is thus contained and neutralised.

Conversion from Christianity occurs in very different circumstances on the stage, and it is revealing that while there are many references to the 'renegado', a Christian convert to Islam, there are no instances of Christian conversion to Judaism in these plays. This is in part a topical reflection of the thousands of Christians who were converting to Islam in this period but is also the product of a conception of Judaism that completely elides religious and ethno-national identities. Jews are always Jews on the early modern stage, even when they are Muslims. Christian conversions to Islam in the drama, however, are often tragic-comic, undertaken by fools and offstage. Basilisco in *Soliman and Perseda* (*c.* 1592) reports his conversion, and attendant circumcision, in uncomprehendingly comic terms: 'Amidst their Church they bound me to a piller, and to make triall of my valiancie, they lopt a collop of my tendrest member . . . That done they set me on a milk white Asse, compassing me with goodly ceremonies' (Act IV, Scene 2, ll. 17–19). Alternatively, the conversion scene at the heart of Robert Daborne's *A Christian Turn'd Turk* (1612) features an elaborately constructed and fantastical dumb show in which the English pirate Ward is inducted into Islam through the ritual use of a turban, a sword and an oath taken on a 'Mahomet's head'. The Chorus solemnly warns the audience that Ward dares to strike against the 'face of heaven' (Act VIII, Scene 6) and affirms that 'black deeds will have black ends' (Act VIII, Scene 28). Stage conversions to an 'alien' religion required a total rejection of belief, kin, nation, queen and even name – it was a guarantee of damnation and thus an abandonment of the 'truth', the total opposite to the affirmation of Protestant 'truth' in Foxe and Hanmer's conversion sermons.

In dramatising such episodes and characters the Elizabethan public stage repeatedly probed the nature of England's (and Christendom's) position in the wider world, constructing and revealing that world to an English gaze and asserting the veracity of the Protestant faith. Another way of affirming faith through the spectacle of difference was in the performance or display of monstrosity. Monsters of all kinds abound in the English popular imagination, whether as hybrid figures, as cannibals, amazons, witches or demons. The monster – like the figure of the 'alien' – allowed a sustained reflection upon the nature of deviance and thus what it meant to be English and Protestant. Alexander Ross would later write that a 'Monster brought out of *Africa*' was 'for people to gaze, not to dote upon'. Furthermore, the 'sight of a Monster or mishapen creature should induce the beholder to praise God, who hath not made him such'.[25] The dividing line between monster and 'alien' was therefore far from distinct, and the display of monsters on Elizabethan England's stages and in travelling fairs might involve deformed bodies, malformed animals and other 'prodigies of nature' alongside indigenous peoples from Africa and the Americas. Trinculo's first reaction upon encountering Caliban in Shakespeare's *The Tempest* is confusion as to whether he is 'a man, or a fish?' (Act II, Scene 2, l. 23). But then his thoughts turn to profit:

> Were I in England now – as once I was – and had but this fish painted, not a holiday-fool there but would give a piece of silver. There would this monster make a man; any strange beast there makes a man. When they will not give a doit to relieve a lame beggar, they will lay out ten to see a dead Indian.
>
> (Act II, Scene 2, ll. 25–30)

The English, Trinculo suggests, are so dazzled by monsters from the outside world that they will pay any amount of money to view them, and thus owning a monster will 'make a man' – make his fortune. Stephano, when he comes across Caliban and Trinculo sheltering under a cloak, assumes they are one four-legged 'monster of the isle' (Act II, Scene 2, l. 59) and hopes to 'recover him, and keep him tame, and get to Naples with him' to make him 'a present for any emperor' (Act II, Scene 2, ll. 62–3). Again the outside world – here embodied in the unfamiliar 'moon calf' Caliban – is associated with profit thanks to the endless appetite of the English for such novelties. Set on an 'enchanted isle' in the Mediterranean near to the coast of North Africa, but drawing upon narratives of new world natives and Bermudan shipwrecks, *The Tempest* draws out the complexities of England's attitudes to the wider world while displaying a version of that world to its audience. As in many of the plays I have mentioned, this world is a composite creation, layering old and new worlds upon each other, exploring strategies of domination and the nature of 'foreignness' in a world in which all the characters speak English. It again indicates that dramatic spectacles in Elizabethan England were expected to make the unfamiliar familiar and the familiar unfamiliar.

LOCATING THE GLOBE IN ENGLAND, AND ENGLAND ON THE GLOBE

In 1592, Emery Molyneux's terrestrial globe – the first to be made in England – was completed and presented to Queen Elizabeth. Immediately celebrated for its 'superior size, lightness, detail and accuracy' it incorporated recent cartographical advances alongside renditions of sailing ships and sea monsters.[26] Yet Molyneux's globe was also a powerful political statement. Prominent across its surface was marked a series of renowned English voyages, including those undertaken for Elizabeth by Drake and Cavendish and the settlement of Virginia. Even more emphatic was the stamp of the Queen's coat of arms across the North American continent. England was no longer on the periphery of an outside world experienced and created elsewhere: instead, her sailors, soldiers, merchants and cartographers were creating the world anew.

Similarly, England's writers and dramatists were developing the idea of the *theatrum mundi,* the theatre of the world, to create the spectacle of an English world in print and on the stage. Just as Molyneux's globe was displaying English claims upon the outside world, the stage at the Globe Theatre was displaying the outside world to the English, and for the English. As Elizabeth had come to the throne in 1558, England's position in this world was precarious and difficult, with no clear sense of the future. At her death in 1603, England's place had been transformed. English men and women were conscious of the wider world and their place within it as never before, and a combination of trade, exploration, seamanship and political skill – as well as literature – would place England at the forefront of global developments in succeeding centuries.

FURTHER READING

Brotton, Jerry, *The Renaissance Bazaar: From the Silk Road to Michelangelo* (Oxford, 2002).

Burton, Jonathan, *Traffic and Turning: Islam and English Drama, 1579–1624* (Newark, Del., 2005).

Burton, Jonathan, and Loomba, Ania, *Race in Early Modern England: A Documentary Companion* (Basingstoke, 2007).

Dimmock, Matthew, *New Turkes: Dramatizing Islam and the Ottomans in Early Modern England* (Aldershot, 2005).

Dimmock, Matthew, and Hadfield, Andrew (eds.), *The Religions of the Book: Christian Perceptions, 1400–1660* (Basingstoke, 2008).

Floyd-Wilson, Mary, *English Ethnicity and Race in Early Modern Drama* (Cambridge, 2003).

Fuchs, Barbara, *Mimesis and Empire: The New World, Islam, and European Identities* (Cambridge, 2001).

Goose, Nigel, and Luu, Lien (eds.), *Immigrants in Tudor and Early Stuart England* (Eastbourne, 2005).

Habib, Imtiaz, *Black Lives in the English Archives, 1500–1677: Imprints of the Invisible* (Aldershot, 2007).

Hadfield, Andrew, *Literature, Travel and Colonial Writing in the English Renaissance* (Oxford, 2007).

Iyengar, Sujata, *Shades of Difference: Mythologies of Skin Colour in Early Modern England* (Philadephia, Pa., 2005).

Jowitt, Claire, *Voyage Drama and Gender Politics, 1589–1642: Real and Imagined Worlds* (Manchester 2003).
Kidd, Colin, *British Identities before Nationalism: Ethnicity and Nationhood in the Atlantic World, 1600–1800* (Cambridge, 1999).
Maclean, Gerald (ed.), *Reorienting the Renaissance: Cultural Exchanges with the East* (Basingstoke, 2005).
—— *Looking East: English Writing and the Ottoman Empire before 1800* (Basingstoke, 2007).
MacCulloch, Diarmaid, *Reformation: Europe's House Divided, 1490–1700* (London, 2003).
Mancke, Elizabeth, and Shammas, Carole (eds.), *The Creation of the British Atlantic World* (Baltimore, Md., 2005).
Matar, Nabil, *Islam in Britain, 1558–1685* (Cambridge, 1998).
—— *Britain and Barbary, 1589–1689* (Gainesville, Fla., 2005).
Mignolo, Walter, *The Darker Side of the Renaissance: Literacy, Territoriality, and Colonization* (Ann Arbor, Mich., 2003).
Sell, Jonathan P., *Rhetoric and Wonder in English Travel Writing, 1560–1613* (Aldershot, 2006).
Sloan, Kim, *A New World: England's First View of America* (London, 2007).
Thirsk, Joan, *Economic Policy and Projects: The Development of Consumer Society in Early Modern England* (Oxford, 1978).
Tyerman, Christopher, *England and the Crusades, 1095–1588* (Chicago, Ill., 1988).
Vitkus, Daniel J., *Turning Turk: English Theater and the Multicultural Mediterranean, 1570–1630* (Basingstoke, 2003).
Willan, Thomas Stuart, *Studies in Elizabethan Foreign Trade* (Manchester, 1959).

NOTES

1 Quoted in Laura Hunt Yungblut, *Strangers Settled Here Amongst Us: Policies, Perceptions and the Presence of Aliens in Elizabethan England* (London and New York, 1996), p. 47.
2 Christopher Ocland, *The Valiant Actes and Victorious Battailes of the English Nation* ... (London, 1585), p. 1b.
3 George Best, *A True Discourse of the Late Voyages of Discovery, for Finding of a Passage to Cathaya* ... (London, 1578). Dedication, sig. B1r.
4 Jonathan Burton, *Traffic and Turning: Islam and English Drama, 1579–1624* (Newark, Del., 2005), p. 38.
5 Best, *A True Discourse*, pp. 29–32.
6 Best, *A True Discourse*, Dedication sig. A3v.
7 Andrew Boorde, *The First Boke of the Introduction of Knowledge* (London, 1555), sig. M4r.
8 Boorde, *The First Boke*, sig. N2r.
9 Boorde, *The First Boke*, sig. N1v.
10 Thomas Hariot, *A Briefe and True Report of the New Found Land of Virginia* (1590), ed. Paul Hulton (New York, 1972), pp. 25–6.
11 Hariot, *A Briefe and True Report*, p. 25.
12 Walter Ralegh, *The Discoverie of the Large, Rich and Bewtiful Empyre of Guiana* (1596), ed. Neil L. Whitehead (Manchester, 1997), pp. 98–101; and in the text pp. 22, 29, 33, 37, 43, 47, 51, 71, 90–1.
13 Stephen Bateman, *Batman Vpon Bartholome, His Booke De Proprietatibus Rerum* (London, 1542), p. 250.
14 Kim Sloane (ed.), *A New World: England's First View of America* (London, 2007), pp. 86–9.
15 Boorde, *The First Boke*, sig. A3r.

16 Mary Floyd-Wilson, *English Ethnicity and Race in Early Modern Drama* (Cambridge, 2003), p. 55.
17 Hans Weigel, *Habitus praecipuorum populorum* (Nuremberg, 1577). See also Sloane, *A New World*, pp. 147–8.
18 William Harrison, *The Description of England* (1587), ed. Georges Edelen, 2nd edn (New York, 1994), pp. 145–6.
19 Robert Wilson, *A Right Excellent and Famous Comoedy Called the Three Ladies of London*, ed. John S. Farmer (London, 1911); quoted and analysed in Matthew Dimmock, *New Turkes: Dramatizing Islam and the Ottomans in Early Modern England* (Aldershot, 2005), pp. 95–7.
20 Richard Hakluyt, *The Principall Navigations, Voiages and Discoveries of the English Nation* (London, 1589), p. 168.
21 Michael R. Paull, 'The Figure of Mahomet in Middle English Literature', unpublished doctoral thesis, University of North Carolina, 1969, pp. 196–252.
22 Sir Nicholas Bacon, quoted in Yungblut, *Strangers Settled Here Amongst Us*, p. 36.
23 John Foxe, *A Sermon Preached at the Christening of a Certain Iew at London* (London, 1578), sig. C2r and Meredith Hanmer, *The Baptizing of a Turke* (London, 1586), sig. F3v.
24 Foxe, *A Sermon*, sig. N1v.
25 Alexander Ross, 'A Needful Caveat, or Admonition, for Them Who Desire to Know What Use May Be Made of, or If There Be Danger in Reading the *Alcoran*' (unpaginated: p. 6), preface to the anonymous translation, *The Alcoran of Mahomet, Translated Out of Arabick into French, by the Sieur du Ryer* (London, 1649), pp. 1–2.
26 R. M. Fisher, 'William Crashawe and the Middle Temple Globes, 1605–15', *The Geographical Journal*, 140 (1) (1974): 105–22; p. 107.

INDEX

Note: page references in *italics* indicate illustrations